A COMMENTARY ON

THE BOOK OF PSALMS

SAINT ROBERT BELLARMINE

TRANSLATED BY FR. JOHN O'SULLIVAN

Caritas Publishing

Printed with
Ecclesiastical Approval

✠ David Moriarty
Bishop of Kerry

First printing 1866.

CC∅
With the Evangelists and Saints throughout history,
you are *encouraged* to freely copy and share this material
for the glory of God and the salvation of souls!

Paperback ISBN: 1945275715
Hardback ISBN: 1945275723

CONTENTS

LIFE OF BELLARMINE i

Ecclesiastical Approval iii

Translator's Preface iv

PSALM 1
The happiness of the just: and the evil state of the wicked. 1

PSALM 2
The vain efforts of persecutors against Christ and his Church. 4

PSALM 3
The psalm of David when he fled from the face of his son Absalom. 8

PSALM 4
The prophet teaches us to fly to God in tribulation, with confidence in him. 9

PSALM 5
A prayer to God against the iniquities of men. 13

PSALM 6
A prayer of a penitent sinner, under the scourge of God. The first penitential psalm. 16

PSALM 7
David, trusting in the justice of his cause, prayeth for God's help against his enemies. 20

PSALM 8
God is wonderful in his works; especially in mankind, singularly exalted by the incarnation of Christ. 25

PSALM 9
The Church praiseth God for his protection against her enemies. 29

PSALM 10
The just man's confidence in God, in the midst of persecutions. 39

PSALM 11
The prophet calls for God's help against the wicked. 42

PSALM 12
A prayer in tribulation. 44

PSALM 13
The general corruption of man before our redemption by Christ. 46

PSALM 14
What kind of men shall dwell in the heavenly Sion. 49

PSALM 15
Christ's future victory and triumph over the world, and death. 51

PSALM 16
A just man's prayer in tribulation against the malice of his enemies. 55

PSALM 17
David's thanks to God for his delivery from all his enemies. 59

PSALM 18
The works of God show forth his glory: his law is greatly to be esteemed and loved. 71

PSALM 19
A prayer for the king. 76

PSALM 20
Praise to God for Christ's exaltation after his Passion. 80

PSALM 21
Christ's Passion: and the conversion of the gentiles. 83

PSALM 22
God's spiritual benefits to faithful souls. 92

PSALM 23
Who are they that shall ascend to heaven; Christ's triumphant Ascension thither. 95

PSALM 24
A prayer for grace, mercy, and protection against our enemies. 98

PSALM 25
David's prayer to God in his distress, to be delivered, that he may come to worship him in his tabernacle. 106

PSALM 26
David's faith and hope in God. 110

PSALM 27
David's prayer that his enemies may not prevail over him. 115

PSALM 28
An invitation to glorify God, with a commemoration of his mighty works. . . . 118

PSALM 29
David praiseth God for his deliverance, and his merciful dealings with him. 124

PSALM 30
A prayer of a just man under affliction. 129

PSALM 31
The second penitential psalm. 136

PSALM 32
An exhortation to praise God, and to trust in him. 145

PSALM 33
An exhortation to the praise and service of God. 154

PSALM 34
David, in the person of Christ, prayeth against his persecutors; prophetically foreshowing the punishments that shall fall upon them. 163

PSALM 35
The malice of sinners, and the goodness of God. 172

PSALM 36
An exhortation to despise this world, and the short prosperity of the wicked; and to trust in Providence. 178

PSALM 37
A prayer of a penitent for the remission of his sins. The third penitential psalm. . . . 189

PSALM 38
A just man's peace and patience in his sufferings: considering the vanity of the world, and the providence of God. 197

PSALM 39
Christ's coming, and redeeming mankind. 203

PSALM 40
The happiness of him that shall believe in Christ, notwithstanding the humility and poverty in which he shall come: the malice of his enemies, especially of the traitor Judas. 210

PSALM 41
The fervent desire of the just after God: hope in afflictions. 215

PSALM 42
The prophet aspireth after the temple and altar of God. *221*

PSALM 43
The Church commemorates former favors, and present afflictions: under which she prays for succor. *222*

PSALM 44
The excellence of Christ's kingdom and the endowments of his Church. *230*

PSALM 45
The Church, in persecution, trusteth in the protection of God. *242*

PSALM 46
The gentiles are invited to praise God for the establishment of the kingdom of Christ. *247*

PSALM 47
God is greatly to be praised for the establishment of his Church.. . . . . *249*

PSALM 48
The folly of worldlings who live on in sin, without thinking of death or hell. . . . *254*

PSALM 49
The coming of Christ: who prefers virtue and inward purity before the blood victims. *261*

PSALM 50
The repentance and confession of David after his sin. The fourth penitential psalm. . *268*

PSALM 51
David condemns the wickedness of Doeg, and foretells his destruction. *277*

PSALM 52
The general corruption of man before the coming of Christ.. . . . . *280*

PSALM 53
A prayer for help in distress. *281*

PSALM 54
A prayer of a just man under persecution from the wicked. It agrees to Christ persecuted by the Jews, and betrayed by Judas. *283*

PSALM 55
A prayer of David in danger and distress. *290*

PSALM 56
The prophet prays in his affliction, and praises God for his delivery. *293*

PSALM 57
David reproves the wicked, and foretells their punishment. *295*

PSALM 58
A prayer to be delivered from the wicked, with confidence in God's help and protection. It agrees to Christ and his enemies the Jews. *299*

PSALM 59
After many afflictions, the Church of Christ shall prevail. *304*

PSALM 60
A prayer for the coming of the kingdom of Christ, which shall have no end. . . . *308*

PSALM 61
The prophet encourages himself and all others to trust in God, and serve him. . . *311*

PSALM 62
The prophet aspireth after God. . . . *314*

PSALM 63
A prayer in affliction, with confidence in God that he will bring to naught the machinations of persecutors.. . . . . *319*

PSALM 64
God is to be praised in his Church, to which all nations shall be called.. . . . . . . *323*

PSALM 65
An invitation to praise God. *328*

PSALM 66
A prayer for the propagation of the Church. 334

PSALM 67
The glorious establishment of the Church of the New Testament, prefigured by the benefits bestowed on the people of Israel.. . 336

PSALM 68
Christ in his Passion declareth the greatness of his sufferings, and the malice of his persecutors the Jews; and foretelleth their reprobation. 347

PSALM 69
A prayer in persecution. 362

PSALM 70
A prayer for perseverance. 362

PSALM 71
A prophecy of the coming of Christ, and of his kingdom: prefigured by Solomon and his happy reign. 368

PSALM 72
The temptation of the weak, upon seeing the prosperity of the wicked, is overcome by the consideration of the justice of God, who will quickly render to every one according to his works. 376

PSALM 73
A prayer of the Church under grievous persecutions.. 383

PSALM 74
There is a just judgment to come: therefore let the wicked take care.. 389

PSALM 75
God is known in his Church: and exerts his power in protecting it. It alludes to the slaughter of the Assyrians, in the days of King Ezechias. 392

PSALM 76
The faithful have recourse to God in trouble of mind, with confidence in his mercy and power. 395

PSALM 77
God's great benefits to the people of Israel, notwithstanding their ingratitude. . . 401

PSALM 78
The Church in time of persecution prayeth for relief. It seems to belong to the time of the Machabees.. 414

PSALM 79
A prayer for the Church in tribulation, commemorating God's former favors.. . . 418

PSALM 80
An invitation to a solemn praising of God. 423

PSALM 81
An exhortation to judges and men in power. 427

PSALM 82
A prayer against the enemies of God's Church. 431

PSALM 83
The soul aspireth after heaven; rejoicing in the meantime, in being in the communion of God's Church upon earth. 435

PSALM 84
The coming of Christ to bring peace and salvation to man. 440

PSALM 85
A prayer for God's grace to assist us to the end. 445

PSALM 86
The glory of the Church of Christ. . . 452

PSALM 87
A prayer of one under grievous affliction: it agrees to Christ in his Passion, and alludes to his death and burial.. 456

PSALM 88
The perpetuity of the Church of Christ, in consequence of the promises of God: which, notwithstanding, God permits her to suffer sometimes most grievous afflictions.. . 462

PSALM 89
A prayer for the mercy of God: recounting the shortness and miseries of the days of man. 478

PSALM 90
The just is secure under the protection of God. 484

PSALM 91
God is to be praised for his wondrous works. 499

PSALM 92
The glory and stability of the kingdom, that is of the Church of Christ. 504

PSALM 93
God shall judge and punish the oppressors of his people. 507

PSALM 94
An invitation to adore and serve God, and to hear his voice. 514

PSALM 95
An exhortation to praise God for the coming of Christ and his kingdom. 518

PSALM 96
All are invited to rejoice at the glorious coming and reign of Christ. 523

PSALM 97
All are again invited to praise the Lord, for the victories of Christ. 528

PSALM 98
The reign of the Lord in Sion; that is, of Christ in his Church. 533

PSALM 99
All are invited to rejoice in God the creator of all. 536

PSALM 100
The prophet exhorteth all by his example, to follow mercy and justice. 539

PSALM 101
A prayer for one in affliction: the fifth penitential psalm.. 542

PSALM 102
Thanksgiving to God for his mercies. . . 552

PSALM 103
God is to be praised for his mighty works; and wonderful providence. 559

PSALM 104
A thanksgiving to God for his benefits to his people of Israel.. 568

PSALM 105
A confession of the manifold sins and ingratitudes of the Israelites. 578

PSALM 106
All are invited to give thanks to God for his perpetual providence over men.. 586

PSALM 107
The prophet praiseth God for benefits received. 597

PSALM 108
David, in the person of Christ, prayeth against his persecutors; more especially the traitor Judas: foretelling and approving his just punishment for his obstinacy in sin, and final impenitence.. 597

PSALM 109
Christ's exaltation, and everlasting priesthood.. 607

PSALM 110
God is to be praised for his graces and benefits to his Church.. 613

PSALM 111
The good man is happy. 617

PSALM 112
God is to be praised, for his regard to the poor and humble.. 621

PSALM 113
God hath shown his power in delivering his people; idols are vain. The Hebrews divide this into two psalms. 623

PSALM 114
The prayer of a just man in affliction, with a lively confidence in God. 628

PSALM 115
This in the Hebrew is joined with the foregoing psalm, and continues to express the faith and gratitude of the psalmist.. 632

PSALM 116
All nations are called upon to praise God for his mercy and truth. 635

PSALM 117
The psalmist praises God for his delivery from evils; puts his whole trust in him, and foretells the coming of Christ.. 635

PSALM 118
Of the excellence of virtue consisting in the love and observance of the commandments of God.. 642
ALEPH 642
BETH 642
IMEL 642
DALETH 643
HE 643
VAU 643
ZAIN 643
HETH 644
TETH 644
JOD 644
CAPH 645
LAMED 645
MEM 645
NUN 646
SAMECH 646
AIN 646
PHE 646
SADE 647
COPH 647
RES 647
SIN 648
TAU 648

PSALM 119
A prayer in tribulation.. 682

PSALM 120
God is the keeper of his servants. . . . 684

PSALM 121
The desire and hope of the just for the coming of the kingdom of God, and the peace of his Church. 686

PSALM 122
A prayer in affliction, with confidence in God. 691

PSALM 123
The Church giveth glory to God for her deliverance from the hands of her enemies.. 694

PSALM 124
The just are always under God's protection. 696

PSALM 125
The people of God rejoice at their delivery from captivity. 698

PSALM 126
Nothing can be done without God's grace and blessing. 702

PSALM 127
The fear of God is the way to happiness. 706

PSALM 128
The Church of God is invincible; her persecutors come to nothing. 710

PSALM 129
A prayer of a sinner, trusting in the mercies of God. The sixth penitential psalm. . . . 712

PSALM 130
The prophet's humility. 717

PSALM 131
A prayer for the fulfilling of the promise made to David. 718

PSALM 132
The happiness of brotherly love and concord. 727

PSALM 133
An exhortation to praise God continually. 729

PSALM 134
An exhortation to praise God: the vanity of idols. 730

PSALM 135
God is to be praised for his wonderful works. 736

PSALM 136
The lamentation of the people of God in their captivity in Babylon. 739

PSALM 137
Thanksgiving to God for his benefits. . 744

PSALM 138
God's special providence over his servants. 747

PSALM 139
A prayer to be delivered from the wicked. 754

PSALM 140
A prayer against sinful words and deceitful flatterers. 759

PSALM 141
A prayer of David in extremity of danger. 763

PSALM 142
The psalmist in tribulation calleth upon God for his delivery. The seventh penitential psalm. 767

PSALM 143
The prophet praiseth God, and prayeth to be delivered from his enemies. No worldly happiness is to be compared with that of serving God. 773

PSALM 144
A psalm of praise, to the infinite majesty of God. 778

PSALM 145
We are not to trust in men, but in God alone. 787

PSALM 146
An exhortation to praise God for his benefits. 790

PSALM 147
The Church is called upon to praise God for his peculiar graces and favors to his people. In the Hebrew this psalm is joined to the foregoing. 794

PSALM 148
All creatures are invited to praise their creator. 798

PSALM 149
The Church is particularly bound to praise God. 802

PSALM 150
An exhortation to praise God with all sorts of instruments. 805

ABOUT THE TRANSLATOR. . 807

LIFE OF BELLARMINE

ROBERT BELLARMINE, the great champion of the prerogatives of the See of Rome, an Italian Jesuit, and one of the most celebrated controversial writers of his time, was born at Monte Pulciano, in Tuscany, in 1542. His mother, Cynthia Cervin, was sister to Pope Marcellus II. At eighteen years of age he entered into the Society of Jesus, and discovered such precocity of genius that he was employed in preaching before he was ordained Priest, which did not take place till 1569, when he was ordained Priest by Cornelius Jansenius, Bishop of Ghent, and was placed in the theological chair of the University of Louvain. His success in teaching and preaching was so great that he is said to have for his auditors persons of the Protestant persuasion, both from Holland and England. After a residence of seven years at Louvain he returned to Italy, when Gregory XIII chose him to give controversial lectures in the College which he had just founded, which he did with so much applause that Sixtus V sent him into France, as a person who might be of great service in case any dispute in religion should arise, as theologian to the Legate, Cardinal Gaetano. He returned to Rome in about ten months, where he had several offices conferred on him by his own Society, as well as by the Pope. Clement VIII, nine years afterwards, raised him to the Cardinalate with this eulogium, "We choose him, because the Church of God does not possess his equal in learning." In 1601, he was advanced to the Archbishopric of Capua, and displayed in his diocese a zeal equal to his learning. He devoted the third part of his revenue to the relief of the poor, visited the sick in the hospitals, and the prisoners in the dungeons, and, concealing the donor, secretly conveyed them money. After exercising his archiepiscopal functions, with singular attention for about four years, he was recalled to Rome by Paul V, who was anxious to have him about his person, on which occasion he resigned his Archbishopric, without receiving any pension from it. He continued to attend to ecclesiastical affairs till the year 1621, when, finding himself declining in health, he left the Vatican, and retired to a house of his Order, where he died, on the 17th of September, in the same year, at the age of 79. At his death, he bequeathed one half of his soul to the Virgin Mary, and the other half to Jesus Christ; and, after his decease, he was regarded as a saint. The Swiss guard belonging to the Pope were placed round his coffin, in order to keep off the crowd, which pressed to touch and kiss the body, and everything he had made use of was, carried away as a venerable and valuable relic.

Bellarmine, as a theological writer, was one of the most distinguished members of his Order, and no man ever defended the cause of the true Church, or of its visible Head, the supreme Vicar of Christ, with more success. The eminent writers of the Protestant sect, who dogmatised in his time, paid him a high compliment, as, during the space of forty or fifty years, there was scarcely one who did not make him a target for the artillery of error. Their attacks were vain; for, although he stated their objections with a force and clearness themselves might be happy to rival, he confuted them in such a manner as to leave no room for a reply. His chief work is his Controversies, 4 vols. Folio. His opinions of the power of the sovereign Pontiff over temporal princes did not give satisfaction to his patron, Sixtus V, as he rejected that power in a direct sense. He was, however, so strenuous an advocate of the indirect power that he seemed to consider the contrary opinion as bordering on heresy. Besides his Commentary on the Psalms, and other works, he has left to the Church a collection of Sermons, a Hebrew Grammar, and two Ascetical Treatises, entitled "The Sighs of the Doves," and "The Elevation of the Mind to God." These last productions of his pen breathe a solid and enlightened piety. The reader cannot fail to be struck with the piety, humility, and simplicity of his dedication of the present work to the Holy Father, which we here subjoin.

"Robert, Cardinal Bellarmine, of the Holy Roman Church, to our Most Holy Father and Lord, Paul the Fifth, Supreme Pontiff.

"The moment I was called from a religious Order to the dignity of the Cardinal by the command of the Supreme Pontiff, Clement VIII., I began to consider that the study and contemplation of sacred matter should not be easily abandoned by reason of the increase of public duties. And when I was in doubt as to what part of the sacred Scriptures I should select for meditation and for explanation, the Psalms that are daily read by all ecclesiastics, and understood by very few, at once occurred to me. Nor was I deterred by the number of those who had already taken great trouble in explaining the Psalms; for such is their obscurity that no amount of labour in explaining them would seem to be superfluous. I, therefore, spent any time I could spare from public duties, especially in the quiet of the night, in meditating on the Psalms of David, and not without pleasure and advantage to myself. And though I was engaged for the whole three years that I was Archbishop at Capua, and, after that, at Rome, in publishing various little treatises, during which time I had to suspend for several months the work I had thus begun, at length, however, through God's assistance, I have been enabled, within this year, to complete the Explanation of Psalms. I never intended to enter into, much less to adopt, the explanations offered by other commentators. My object was to try to be brief and clear, to defend the Vulgate as far as I was able, and to provide for the spiritual refection and devotion of the reader. Hence, if I am not mistaken, all the Psalms have been explained with sufficient clearness, though not at equal length; and, no doubt, complaints will be made of my having been too sparing in my notes on some of the Psalms, especially on some of the first, fair enough withal, and perhaps too diffuse, with some; but one's devotion is not equally ardent at all times, nor is his mind equally active, and I have composed this treatment of the Psalms more by my own meditation than by much reading of books. Be that as it may, I thought it but right, Most Holy Father, to present it to your Holiness, for the purpose of giving an account to you, my Father and my Lord, of the manner in which not only my public and official duties were discharged, but also how my time was occupied in private; as, also, that you, who, as judge, rule over the whole Church, as Vicar of Christ, may kindly correct any error that may have crept into this, as I expect, my last, publication. Meantime, I will pray God to grant your Holiness a long and happy life in this world, and a life of everlasting happiness in the next."

Ecclesiastical Approval

"As the Psalms of David form the principal part of the authorized prayers of the Church, it is most desirable that all the faithful should know their literal and mystic meaning. The Clergy and Religious, who are bound to recite the Divine Office, must daily read many of the Psalms. If, in addition to the meaning of the words, they know the historic sense of the Psalm, and its spiritual application to Christ and to his kingdom, they will, according to the counsel of St. Paul, pray with the spirit, and they will also pray with the understanding. (1 Cor. 15:15)

"In the early ages of the Church, the Psalms were so familiar to the laity, that it was found impossible to adopt the better version, made by St. Jerome from the Hebrew, for all had the older version by heart. In these days the Psalms are little used in the private devotions of lay Catholics; and forms of prayer, which have no authoritative sanction and which are often little recommendable either for sentiment or expression, are used instead of those which have been dictated by the Holy Ghost. The reason of this notable change in the practice of the faithful must be that they do not understand the Psalms. Any attempt to render them more intelligible, and thus to restore their use, is most praiseworthy. The Commentary of the venerable Cardinal Bellarmine is remarkable for clearness of exposition, and for suggesting the spiritual meanings best calculated to awaken and cherish devotion. Archdeacon O'Sullivan, P.P. of Kenmare, and V.G. of the Diocese of Kerry, has undertaken to translate this Commentary, omitting those portions which are purely philosophical, or which relate to the discrepancy and reconciliation of the texts and versions. We have seen a portion of the manuscript, and we believe that the translation is faithful. It will supply a most easy and ready means of understanding the Psalms, of appreciating their beauty, and of entering into the spirit of the inspired song.

✛ "David Moriarty,
"Bishop of Kerry."

Translator's Preface

The Cardinal's dedication to the Holy Father, and the approval of the Bishop of the Diocese of undertaking a translation of the Commentary, would form a sufficient, and perhaps the best, preface to the present translation of it. I would call special attention to the observation of the Bishop, "In these days the Psalms are little used in the private devotions of lay Catholics; and forms of prayer, which have no authoritative sanction, and which are often little recommendable, either for sentiment or expression, are used, instead of those which have been dictated by the Holy Ghost. The reason of this notable change in the practice of the faithful must be that they do not understand the Psalms."

It is for the use of the laity, principally, that I have undertaken this translation, at the same time that I cannot help thinking that it will prove a useful Book to the clergy also; as it will prove much more readable, and the explanation more unbroken than in the original which is encumbered with endless disquisitions on Hebrew roots, and different versions and readings, as well as the defense of the Vulgate, which the Cardinal avows was one of his principal objects in undertaking the Commentary. Divested of such discussions, the clergy, I am sure, will find greater pleasure in recurring to the pure, unbroken Commentary, from which the quantity of Greek and Hebrew lore in the original was sufficient to deter most of them.

I have also to observe that the Cardinal's prefaces to the several Psalms, interesting as they are to the scholar, seemed to me to be quite the reverse to the ordinary class of the laity, before whom it was my principal object to bring the study and the use of the Psalms, as a form of prayer. I have therefore, substituted the simple, substantial headings in the Douay, for the elaborate and learned disquisitions of the Cardinal, in the hope of making the book more readable and more attractive to the laity. My Rev. Brethren in the Ministry will, no doubt, detect many faults and errors in the translation, but when they understand that the time occupied in it was merely snatched from the duties of a parish in the mountains, consisting of 55,000 acres, they will, I am sure, make due allowance for them.

THE BOOK OF THE PSALMS

PSALM 1

The happiness of the just: and the evil state of the wicked.

1 Blessed is the man who hath not walked in the counsel of the ungodly, nor stood in the way of sinners, nor sat in the chair of pestilence.
2 But his will is in the law of the Lord, and on his law he shall meditate day and night.
3 And he shall be like a tree which is planted near the running waters, which shall bring forth its fruit, in due season. And his leaf shall not fall off: and all whatsoever he shall do shall prosper.
4 Not so the wicked, not so: but like the dust, which the wind driveth from the face of the earth.
5 Therefore the wicked shall not rise again in judgment: nor sinners in the council of the just.
6 For the Lord knoweth the way of the just: and the way of the wicked shall perish.

EXPLANATION OF THE PSALM

1. In the first and second verses the prophet teaches that happiness, as far as it is attainable in this world, is only to be had in conjunction with true justice. As the apostle teaches (Rom. 14) *"For the kingdom of God is not meat and drink; but justice and peace and joy in the Holy Ghost."* For the truly just are alone the friends of God, nay more, his children, and thus heirs of the kingdom, happy in the hope that belongs to the most perfect happiness, meanwhile, here below enjoying that solid joy and peace *"that surpasseth all understanding."* In this first verse he gives a negative description of the just man; in the second an affirmative, briefly stating here that he is just and thence happy who declines from evil and doeth good. Observe attentively and remember that David, as well as the other prophets, is very fond of repetitions, making the second part of a verse either a repetition or an explanation of the first. For instance, Ex. 15, *"He is my God and I will glorify him; the God of my father, and I will exalt him;"* Deut. 32, *"Let my doctrine gather as the rain, let my speech distill as the dew;"* Ps. 33, *"I will bless the Lord at all times, his praise shall be always in my mouth."* These ornamental repetitions are of frequent occurrence among the prophets. The first part of the verse, then, conveys to us the happiness of the man who breaks not the law of God; but David making use of a metaphor, conveys the idea in a poetic manner. "Happy," says he, *"is the man who hath not walked,"* etc.; that is to say, happy is he who is really just: and he is just who hath not gone in the counsel of the ungodly; that is to say, who has not followed the counsel, laws, or opinion of the wicked, which are altogether at variance with the way, that is, the law of God. The second part of the same verse expresses the same in similar words. For, when he says, *"Nor stood in the way of sinners,"* he does not mean standing but walking. Standing here does not mean simply to stand, but to walk, and to continue walking. *"Who hath not walked in the counsel of the ungodly, nor stood in the way of sinners,"* are here synonymous, for both convey that he is just who retires from the way, that is, from the law and counsel of sinners. And as the law of God is broken not only by the evil doer but also by the evil teacher, according to Mt. 5, *"Whosoever, therefore, shall break one of those least commandments, and shall teach men so, he shall be called the least in the kingdom of heaven;"* the prophet, therefore, adds: *"nor sat in the chair of pestilence;"* as much as to say, Blessed is he who neither in word nor deed broke through the law of God. *"To sit in the chair of pestilence"* means, to be among, to keep company with wicked men, with them to despise the law of God, as in nowise pertaining to a happy life, but, on the contrary, looking upon it as more advantageous to indulge in all the passions and desires of the flesh. The words, *"sitting in the chair of pestilence,"* are well expressed by Malach. 3, *"You have said: He laboreth in vain that serveth God, and what profit is it that we have kept his ordinances?"*

2. In this second verse the just man is affirmatively described; and here also we have two sentences, one of which is nearly a repetition of the other. He is truly said to be just or happy, who wishes to do the will of the Lord; because to be just in this life we are not required to be free from all manner of offense, for, St. James says, chap. 3, *"We all offend in many things;"* but it suffices for us to be so disposed towards the law of God, that we desire, above all things, to carry it out; and if we happen to fall into any sin, as undoubtedly we often do, that it is against our will we so fall, that is to say, against the love we entertain towards God and his law, thus making the matter a sin, not a crime, a venial one instead of a deadly one. The same is differently expressed in another psalm: *"The law of his God is in his heart."* For the will or the heart of a just man is in the law of God, and the law of God is in the will or the heart of the just. The law is in the heart, as it were, on its throne; and the heart is in the law, as it would be in anything ardently loved, constantly thought of and desired; which is further expressed in the next sentence:

"And on his law he shall meditate day and night;" that means to have the law so in his will, and his will in the law, by constantly exercising his mind in reflecting on and loving it, so that all his actions may be in accordance with it. The words, *"day and night,"* do not imply that the just man must at every moment be absorbed in the contemplation of the divine law; it means that he should most frequently reflect on it, and be mindful of it when he may have anything to think of, to say, or to do, in which he may apprehend a danger of its violation.

3. After declaring who should really be called just, the prophet now declares such just person to be happy, in his hope here, in the reality hereafter. He compares him to a tree growing by the riverside, having all the necessaries towards its perfect growth. For some trees produce leaves only, nor do they retain them long; other trees have the leaves, and keep them always, but the fruit thereon ripens either too soon or too late; others bring out the fruit, and always keep their leaves, but they do not bring all the fruit to maturity: the trees, therefore, which produce the leaves and the fruit, and though they keep the leaves still ripen all the fruit, alone deserve the name of being the most perfect, such are the pine, the palm, and the olive, to which the Scripture usually compares the just; and it is to such trees, the prophet compares them here. For the just, as the apostle has it, *"founded and rooted in charity,"* as being friends, are close to the living fountain, whence they always draw a flow of grace, and produce good works in the fitting time; everything *"cooperating with them to good,"* they are always blooming in glory and honor. For, though they may sometimes be despised by the carnal, they are held in honor by the wise, and, which is of more consequence, by the Angels, and even by God himself. This applies only to the present life, but with that, they produce their fruit in season, because they work out true salvation, to be had in the fitting time, namely, after their death; whereas the wicked look for it before their time, namely, in this world, and thus lose it here and there. And they always retain their leaves, because, according to St. Peter, they shall receive *"A neverfading crown of glory;"* and, according to Ps. 111, *"The just shall be in everlasting remembrance."* And, finally, *"Whatever they do shall prosper,"* because whatever they may do, even to the giving of the cup of cold water, shall receive a full and perfect reward.

4. Another argument in favor of the happiness of the just, drawn by the prophet from a contrast with the misery of the wicked. For, lest any one may suppose that the just enjoy the aforesaid favors in common with others, from natural causes, and not from the special providence of God, he adds, *"not so the wicked;"* that is to say, instead of such favor it will be quite the other way with them. In most beautiful language he contrasts the misery of the wicked with the happiness of the just. The just, by reason of the

abundance of divine grace, are verdant, and produce the fruit, and never lose their bloom or fail in repaying the labor expended on them. On the other hand, the wicked, wanting the divine grace, dry and barren, like the finest dust scattered by the wind, leave no trace of themselves, and not only lose glory, wealth, and pleasure—but even themselves, in the bargain, for all eternity.

5. A beautiful connection of the last verses of the psalm with the first. He started by saying that the just did not sit in council nor consort with the wicked; and now he says that the wicked will not rise in the company of the just, in other words, that a very different sentence is in store for each.

6. A reason for God's decision, viz., his knowledge of good and bad.

PSALM 2

The vain efforts of persecutors against Christ and his Church.

1 Why have the Gentiles raged, and the people devised vain things?
2 The kings of the earth stood up, and the princes met together, against the Lord and against his Christ.
3 Let us break their bonds asunder: and let us cast away their yoke from us.
4 He that dwelleth in heaven shall laugh at them: and the Lord shall deride them.
5 Then shall he speak to them in his anger, and trouble them in his rage.
6 But I am appointed king by him over Sion his holy mountain, preaching his commandment.
7 The Lord hath said to me: Thou art my son, this day have I begotten thee.
8 Ask of me, and I will give thee the Gentiles for thy inheritance, and the utmost parts of the earth for thy possession.
9 Thou shalt rule them with a rod of iron, and shalt break them in pieces like a potter's vessel.
10 And now, O ye kings, understand: receive instruction, you that judge the earth.
11 Serve ye the Lord with fear: and rejoice unto him with trembling.
12 Embrace discipline, lest at any time the Lord be angry, and you perish from the just way.
13 When his wrath shall be kindled in a short time, blessed are all they that trust in him.

Explanation of the psalm

1. David, recognizing in spirit the coming Messias, the many persecutions he was to undergo, to end in his most successful reign, commences by taunting his persecutors. *"And the people devised vain things,"* foreshadowing the folly of the Jews, *"when they took counsel to destroy Jesus."*

2. After saying in general, that both gentiles and people rose up against Christ, he now descends to particulars, and attributes the excitement not

so much to the people as to those placed over them. The first of whom was Herod. Next the princes and the people, as the gospel has it, *"All Jerusalem was troubled with him."* Then Pontius Pilate and the princes of that day. Then, after the passion and resurrection of our Lord, all the persecutions of the Roman emperors. So clearly foreshadowed is the Messias in this verse that the apostles, in the fourth chapter of the Acts, not only literally applied it to our Savior, but even the old Jewish Rabbis hold it to apply to the Savior the infatuated Jews are still foolishly looking out for! Observe the propriety of the words used here. The gentiles are said *"to rage,"* as if they were animals void of reason; while the Jewish people are made *"to meditate vain things,"* having taken counsel to destroy Jesus.

3. The prophet assigns a reason for such rage and conspiracy; it was for fear they may be subjected to the law of Christ, so opposed to their carnal desires, and the wisdom of the world. These words are then, as it were, spoken by the kings and princes. The law here gets the name of bonds and yoke, because such it is, in point of fact, to the wicked; whereas, to the just, it is *"sweeter than honey, and more desirable than gold and precious stones,"* as we read in Ps. 18.

4. Here the prophet shows again how vain was the labor of the kings and princes in assailing the Christian religion. For the religion of Christ is of divine origin, and nobody can offer resistance to God. *"He that dwelleth in heaven"* is very appropriate, inasmuch as it shows that God sees all, is above all, and without any trouble can baffle all their counsels, and demolish all their plans. *"Shall laugh at and deride them,"* means that God in his wisdom, by means of signs and wonders, through the patience of the martyrs, through the conversion of nations and peoples, and through other means known to himself alone, will so confound them that they shall be an object of laughter and ridicule to every one. That we see fulfilled. The pagan and the Jewish priesthood are now ridiculed by all. They have neither temples nor sacrifice; and all the persecutors of the Church have met a miserable end.

5. He explains the manner in which God has held the enemies of Christ up to ridicule, not in language, but in the most grievous punishments and afflictions; for instance, Herod, stricken by the Angel; Maximinus, eaten up by vermin, and others. Strictly speaking, God is not subject to anger or fury; his judgments are always tranquil; but he is metaphorically said to rage and to be angry, when he punishes with severity, especially when the correction does not conduce to the salvation of the culprit. Such anger and fury belong to those who do not, like physicians, hurt to heal, but hurt to kill. Thus, when David says, *"Lord, reprove me not in thy fury, nor correct me*

in thy anger," he prays for the reproof and correction of a father, not of an enemy; and that it may tend to his salvation, and not to his detriment.

6. Having spoken of the rebellious sentiments and expressions of Christ's enemies, he introduces the Redeemer now, as if answering them. I am appointed king, not by man, but by God, and therefore, man's threats I regard not. I am ordained king on Sion, his holy mountain; that is, on his Church, the city built on a mountain, of which Jerusalem was the type; the principal part of which, and most beloved and sanctified by God, was Sion, as he says in Ps. 86, *"The Lord loveth the gates of Sion beyond all the tabernacles of Jacob."*

7. Here is the beginning and the foundation of God's decree. For to Christ, as being the true and natural Son of God, is due all power in heaven and on earth. Three generations are here alluded to. The first, when in the day of eternity, I God begot you God. The second, when, on the day of your birth, I begot thee according to the flesh, made you God Man, without the seed of man, your mother remaining inviolate, without the stain of sin. Thirdly, I begot you today, that is, on the day of your resurrection, when, by my divine power, I restored you to life, and that a glorious and immortal one.

8. As if God the Father were to say: You my natural Son, the incarnation of my power raised from the dead, have just right to ask me for power over all nations as your inheritance, and the whole world, even to its remotest boundaries, as your possession of right.

We have to observe here, that the word inheritance is frequently applied in the Scripture to one's property, even though it may not have come to them by inheritance, and thus the people of God are called his inheritance, and he theirs. And as property was frequently divided among brothers by lot, and then measured by chains, the words inheritance, part, lot, chain, possession, became synonymous; two of them even are sometimes united, as, *"The Lord is the part of my inheritance,"* that is, the part that came to me by inheritance; and in another place, Deut. 32, *"Jacob, the lot of his inheritance,"* meaning that the people of Israel were the Lord's inheritance, which he selected for himself, measured with chains, and separated from the inheritance of others. Thus all nations are here said to be the inheritance of Christ, as the words, *"The utmost parts of the earth for thy possession,"* evidently convey. We are to observe, secondly, that by the kingdom of Christ is meant his spiritual kingdom, that is, his Church, which was to be spread over the whole world. The meaning of the verse then is, that Christ was placed king over Sion, that is, over God's people; but that his kingdom was not, like that of David or Solomon, confined to the kingdoms of Judea or Palestine, but was to extend over all nations, and to include all the kingdoms of the world, according to Daniel's prophecy, chap. 2, infidels even included, for *"All power on earth and in heaven is granted unto me,"* and he is *"appointed judge of the living and of the dead,"* Acts 10.

9. The extreme and most just power of Christ over his Church, and over all mankind, through which he can as easily reward the good and punish the wicked, as a potter can make and break the vessels of clay, is here indicated. In the first part, the iron rod expresses the most just, inflexible, and irresistible power of Christ; in the second, the vessels of clay expose the frailty of the human race. The word *"Break them in pieces"* does not imply that Christ will actually do so, but that he can do so if he wills; breaking their sins and infidelities in pieces, through his mercy, and from vessels of reproach forming them into vessels of honor; or breaking them in pieces in everlasting fire, in all justice, they having richly deserved it.

10. The prophet now exhorts the kings of this world on whom the people depend as their resistance to Christ has been in vain, to freely subject themselves to him, the true and supreme king of all kings; and as, generally speaking, from wrong judgment proceed wrong affections, he first exhorts them to correct their judgment, to understand the truth and be rightly informed. Then he exhorts them to correct their evil affections, and, instead of hating Christ, to begin to serve, to love, and to revere him. Hence he adds:

11. A wonderful admixture of love and fear, as if he were to say, blend love with your fear, and fear with your love. The Hebrew for *"fear"* signifies filial not slavish fear, and thus the meaning of the first part of the sentence is, serve the Lord as a son would his father; but also, when you exult as a child before him, forget not to fear him, as is beautifully conveyed in the second part of this verse.

12. The meaning of these words is, that the kings should not only correct their judgment and affections, and that they should be instructed and obedient but that they should do so with great fervor; because the Hebrew word implies that they should not only do the thing, but do it with all their might, their strength, and their desire, assigning a very cogent reason for it, *"lest at any time the Lord be angry, "and you perish from the just way."* The most grievous punishment inflicted on princes is when God, on account of their sins, gives them up to the *"reprobate sense,"* Rom. 1, permits them to be deceived by wicked counselors, and do much evil, for which they are lost to this world and the next; such were Pharaoh, Roboam, Achab, and others, in whom the most grievous sins became the punishment of other sins, such being not a small slip from the straight road, but an entire loss and extermination of the path of justice.

13. The conclusion of the Psalm, in which the holy prophet pronounces how it may be inferred from the preceding, how good and useful it is to love God and serve him with one's whole heart, for, in the day of judgment, which cannot be far distant, such people alone can have any confidence. He says, *"in a short time,"* to signify that the terrible day is shortly to come; for a thousand years are like yesterday that passed; nor can that be called long that has an end. *"His wrath shall be kindled,"* to give us to understand that the day of judgment will be exclusively a day of justice and revenge, leaving no place for mercy. *"Blessed are all they that trust in him;"* not that confidence will suffice—it will only when it is based on true friendship.

PSALM 3

The psalm of David when he fled from the face of his son Absalom.

1 Why, O Lord, are they multiplied that afflict me? many are they who rise up against me.
2 Many say to my soul: There is no salvation for him in his God.
3 But thou, O Lord art my protector, my glory, and the lifter up of my head.
4 I have cried to the Lord with my voice: and he hath heard me from his holy hill.
5 I have slept and taken my rest: and I have risen up, because the Lord hath protected me.
6 I will not fear thousands of the people, surrounding me: arise, O Lord; save me, O my God.
7 For thou hast struck all them who are my adversaries without cause: thou hast broken the teeth of sinners.
8 Salvation is of the Lord: and thy blessing is upon thy people.

Explanation of the Psalm

1. David, addressing himself in prayer to God, complains of and wonders at the number of his enemies, for, as we read in 2 Kings 15, *"All Israel was then most cordially following Absalom."* Such was the case with Christ, especially in his passion, for then his son, that is, his people, rebelled against him, crying out: *"we have no king but Caesar;"* and he, like a sick man and a fugitive, was obliged to fly from them through his death; but speedily returned through his resurrection. Absalom signifies the peace of the father, because, in fact, it was the son only that stirred up the war; but the father was always at peace, both as regards David, who wept at the death of his son, and as regards Christ, who prayed for his persecutors; and as Achitophel, the intimate friend and counselor of David, was the person to betray him in the rebellion of his son, and afterwards hanged himself, similar was the end of Judas, one of Christ's most familiar friends, who also hanged himself.

2. This would appear to apply to the inward temptations of the devil, seeking to make him despair, as if his confidence in God had been to no purpose. To it also may be referred what the people were then naturally saying, namely, that notwithstanding David's great confidence in God, he was then apparently entirely abandoned by him; a thing quite common for the ignorant to take up, when they see pious people in trouble. Thus, Job's wife reproaches him, *"Do you still remain in your simplicity?"* So with Tobias's wife, when she said, *"Your hope is now evidently come to nothing, and your alms now appear."* And so they said of Christ: *"He has confided in God, let him free him now if he will."*

3. What one in trouble, a just man such as David, and especially what Christ, the head of all the just, would say. The meaning is, many tell me I put my hope in God to no purpose; but they are quite mistaken, for you, Lord, never desert those that confide in thee; therefore you are *"my protector,"* to ward off the weapons of my enemies, not content with which you become *"my glory,"* that is to say, the cause of my glory. Hence it arises that you come to be *"the lifter up of my head;"* that is to say, you make me, who a while ago hung my head in grief and sorrow, hold it up now in joy and exultation.

4. A proof of David's confidence. He appealed to the Almighty, and, at once, he was heard. Observe the expression, *"I have cried with my voice;"* as much as to say, not silently, indifferently, or passively, but loudly, emphatically. *"From his holy hill,"* means either Sion, or, more probably, the kingdom of heaven.

5. In the persecution of Absalom David made no resistance, but lay down as one would to sleep, but soon after awoke, strengthened by the Lord to recover his kingdom, *"because the Lord hath protected"* him.

6. Clearly applicable to David, who, on recovering courage, rose up and got ready to meet his enemies; and, therefore, now exclaims he has no fear of the countless enemy, confiding, as he does, not in his own power, or the arms of his allies, but in God; and he therefore supplicates him to rise and save him from the hands of the enemy. Observe the connection between the word *"arise,"* in this verse, and *"I have risen,"* in the preceding, as much as to say, I have on your inspiration arisen, and do you now at my request arise in my defense.

7. An acknowledgment of the divine protection, and his deliverance from his enemies, whose teeth were so broken that, though they may bark, they could not possibly injure or bite.

8. An invocation of the divine blessing, and thanksgiving for the benefits conferred by him.

PSALM 4

The prophet teaches us to fly to God in tribulation, with confidence in him.

1 When I called upon him, the God of my justice heard me: when I was in distress, thou hast enlarged me. Have mercy on me: and hear my prayer.

2 ye sons of men, how long will you be dull of heart? why do you love vanity, and

seek after lying?
3 Know ye also that the Lord hath made his holy one wonderful: the Lord will hear me when I shall cry unto him.
4 Be angry, and sin not: the things you say in your hearts, be sorry for them upon your beds.
5 Offer up the sacrifice of justice, and trust in the Lord: many say, Who sheweth us good things?
6 The light of thy countenance O Lord, is signed upon us: thou hast given gladness in my heart.
7 By the fruit of their corn, their wine and oil, they are multiplied.
8 In peace in the selfsame I will sleep, and I will rest:
9 For thou, O Lord, singularly hast settled me in hope

Explanation of the psalm

1. David, in the person of the Church, or any faithful soul advising sinners to follow its example, exhorts them to be converted, to put their confidence in God, to abandon evil, and do good, giving himself as an example—for when he was in trouble, he invoked the Almighty, and was heard. "*The God of my justice heard me,*" that is to say, the God from whom all my justice proceeds, whose grace makes me just. He then tells how he was heard, "*When I was in distress thou hast enlarged me.*" God sometimes hears us by removing the tribulation; sometimes by giving patience to bear it, which is a greater favor; sometimes by not only giving the patience to bear it, but even to be glad of it, which is the greatest favor of all, and it is that of which the prophet speaks here. Tribulation hems us in; joy enlarges our hearts; but when one glories in tribulation, his sadness is changed into joy, and tribulations bring to such persons not hemming in, but enlargement. "*Have mercy on me; and hear my prayer.*" He asks for continuation of the grace, as if he said, Hear me always, pity me always, as you have done hitherto. The holy prophet knew that while here below we are always exposed to danger, if his mercy do not only go before, but also accompany and follow us.

2. That is to say, how long will you have a heart of stone, a hard one, inclined to the earth, thinking of nothing but the goods of this world? For, according to the Lord, "*The hearts are weighed down by excess, drunkenness, and the cares of this world;*" and because hardened hearts are not susceptible of celestial thoughts, but only of terrestrial and transitory, they only love what is terrestrial and transitory; and as we take trouble only in seeking for the things we ardently love, the prophet adds, "*Why do you love vanity, and seek after lying?*" The goods of this world are called vain and fallacious, because they are neither stable nor solid, though they may seem to be so; and are therefore, with justice, designated as false and fallacious, especially when compared to those of eternity.

3. This is the strongest reason that can be advanced for man holding himself disengaged from temporal things. Because the Holy One of God, meaning the Son of God, the only one among men free from sin, came from heaven to us. Hence the demon, in Mark 4, exclaimed: *"I know you are the Holy One of God."* And this Holy One went his way, doing good, suffering persecutions, despising the things of this world, holding up those of the other, and by such a new route arrived at eternal happiness, corporally reigning in heaven, and spiritually happy forever. And as he is our guide, and went before us to prepare a place for us; undoubtedly, if we walk in his footsteps, we will come to true and everlasting happiness. And as he is not only our Leader, but also our Advocate and Mediator, David therefore adds: *"The Lord will hear me when I shall cry unto him;"* that is to say, I am now quite sure of being heard when I know there is on the right hand of God an intercessor on my behalf.

4. The Holy Ghost having severely reproved and admonished mankind, and advised them to repent, tells them now what they ought to do, and instructs them to have a holy horror of sin, to resist their evil desires, and, by such means, to avoid sin; and, should they happen to fall, at once to be sorry and contrite; and not to stop at the doing no harm, but to go further, by offering the sacrifice of justice in doing good. *"Be angry, and sin not;"* that is to say, when your wicked and rebellious temper, the top and bottom of all our sins, stirs us up, let your anger vent itself on your own poor corrupt self; contend with it, so that you shall not fall into sin. St. Basil tells us that anger was implanted in us by God, to be a source of merit. *"The things you say in your hearts, be sorry for them upon your beds;"* that is to say, in the dead hour of night, when you shall be alone in your bedchamber, free from all cares; then turn over all your shortcomings, and in God's presence be sorry for them, imitating the example of David himself, who in Psalm 6 says, *"Every night I will wash my bed; I will water my couch with my tears,"* thus carrying out the advice he gave to others.

5. The second part of sanctity is here portrayed, namely, the going farther than doing no evil, but producing good. Good works are here called the sacrifice of justice, by reason of their being highly agreeable to God, and their contributing to his glory. *"Let them see your good works, that they may glorify your Father who is in heaven,"* saith our Lord. St. Paul on alms says: *"I have received your offerings in the odor of sweetness;"* on fasting, and other corporal works he has, Romans 12, *"I beseech you, therefore, that you present your bodies a living sacrifice, holy, pleasing to God;"* observe, though, how he adds: *"and trust in the Lord,"* for fear of presumption, which is always lying

in wait on our good works. We must work well, but in such manner as not to be proudly confident in our works, like the Pharisee, *"Who gave thanks to God, that he was not like other men,"* etc. Let us rather hope in the Lord, who will enable us to avoid sin, to produce good works, and arrive at the harbor of eternal salvation. For, as presumption is like a poison destroying the merit of our good works, so humble diffidence in our own strength, and a reliance on God, is like salt, seasoning and preserving all our good actions. *"Many say, Who showeth us good things?"* A common objection of the carnal, who are numerous, hence *"many."* When we preach to them the contempt of things here below, and exhort them to innocence and justice, many reply, Who will show us what is good, if the things we see and handle be not good? Who has come up from hell? Who has gone up to heaven?

6. The prophet replies by saying that the path of justice has been pointed out to us by God; that we have a master within us, the light of natural reason, to point out the real truth, for *"this light is signed upon us"* indelibly, that is, on our superior part; for we consist of two parts, the soul, the superior, and the body, the inferior. In the superior part is the light that puts us above the brutes, a light derived from the countenance of God, and wherein we are the image and likeness of God. By means of this light we can, in the first place, understand the road that leads to happiness; for the natural law, so written on our hearts, that even iniquity itself cannot blot it out, teaches that we should not do to another what we would not have done to ourselves, and therefore, that we must not steal, commit adultery, etc. Through the grace of God we can also understand that real happiness consists in making ourselves as like as possible to God, for the perfection of an image is to be as like as possible to the original. Such considerations produce great joy, hope, and love of God in the mind, for what is more pleasing than the reflection of one's being the living image of a thing of infinite beauty, and that he is dearly beloved by that same omnipotent original? However, as all have not such emotions, David concludes the verse by saying, thou hast *"given gladness,"* not in their hearts, but *"in mine,"* which all just and pious people equally experience.

7. Another argument from which men may understand that God is the author of all good, for it is he who, in the fitting time, multiplies the grain and produces the fruit, as St. Paul has it, Acts 14, *"Nevertheless he left not himself without testimony, doing good from heaven, giving rains and fruitful seasons, filling our hearts with food and gladness."*

8. David's conclusion then is, whatever the conduct of those whom I have been exhorting may be, my desire is to confide entirely in God, and rest altogether in him. *"In peace,"* that is, in the most perfect tranquillity; *"in the self same"* that is, in union, along with. *"I will sleep and rest,"* that is, I will

securely lie down, and profoundly sleep. Observe the word *"self same,"* a word of frequent use in the Psalms, and signifies with, or in union with.

9. A reason for his casting all his solicitude on God, and for his saying that he would sleep and rest in peace in the other world, because God, by his most true and faithful promises, made him to settle himself in hope alone. Thus the just man, the friend of God, dwells in divine hope alone, as he would in a fortified house, doing what in him lies for this world as well as for the next, not confiding in his own strength nor in anything created, but in God alone, and, therefore, is not confounded, but securely sleeps, and will sleep with equal security in the world to come.

PSALM 5

A prayer to God against the iniquities of men.

1 Give ear, O Lord, to my words, understand my cry.
2 Hearken to the voice of my prayer, O my King and my God.
3 For to thee will I pray: O Lord, in the morning thou shalt hear my voice.
4 In the morning I will stand before thee, and will see: because thou art not a God that willest iniquity.
5 Neither shall the wicked dwell near thee: nor shall the unjust abide before thy eyes.
6 Thou hatest all the workers of iniquity: Thou wilt destroy all that speak a lie. The bloody and the deceitful man the Lord will abhor.
7 But as for me in the multitude of thy mercy, I will come into thy house; I will worship towards thy holy temple, in thy fear.
8 Conduct me, O Lord, in thy justice: because of my enemies, direct my way in thy sight.
9 For there is no truth in their mouth; their heart is vain.
10 Their throat is an open sepulchre: they dealt deceitfully with their tongues: judge them, O God. Let them fall from their devices: according to the multitude of their wickedness cast them out: for they have provoked thee, O Lord.
11 But let all them be glad that hope in thee: they shall rejoice for ever, and thou shalt dwell in them. And all they that love thy name shall glory in thee:
12 For thou wilt bless the just. O Lord, thou hast crowned us, as with a shield of thy good will.

Explanation of the psalm

1-2. In three ways one is not heard by another; either because the words are not heard; or because the words are not understood; or because the person to whom they are addressed is otherwise engaged. God sees everything, understands everything, and looks after everything; but he is said, sometimes, to see not, to understand not, to abandon everything, because he so despises the intercessor; as if he did not see, understand, or care about his prayers. Therefore, the holy prophet, when about to pray, commences by asking that God may see, understand, and attend to him. Now God despises the suppliant as if he did not see him or hear him, when the one who puts up the prayer, puts it up in so distracted a way that he does not actually feel what he is saying, or prays so coldly that his prayer cannot possibly ascend. In such cases God holds himself as if he did not know what was wanted, when the petitioner himself did not seem to know, in his asking for things of no possible use to him, however urgent and ardent he may have been in asking for them. Then finally, God is like one paying no attention to the suppliant, when the suppliant is unworthy of being heard, by reason of his want of humility, confidence, or other requisites; or by reason of the sinful state in which he is still, and his having no idea of penance. The prophet then, inspired by the Holy Ghost, with consummate skill asks God for the gift of perfect prayer; that is to say, that when he shall pray, his prayers may not be repulsed, but that they may be heard, understood, and attended to adding, *"My King,"* for a king is supposed to hear his people; and *"My God,"* raising up an additional claim as a creature, and therefore depending on his Creator for everything.

3-4. I will not only pray, but I will stand up in contemplation; in the morning, before the cares of the world obtrude; and the principal subject of my meditation shall be your hatred of sin; your great regard for innocence and justice; and therefore, you being justice and the light, if I wish to please you, I must aim at justice and innocence, and hate iniquity.

5. God not only hates sin, but sinners too; and therefore, the wicked shall receive no hospitality from him: *"Nor shall the unjust abide before thy eyes;"* that is, you will not look long upon them with an eye of clemency. He may look upon them for a while with an eye of clemency and give them much of the goods of this world; but such will not be of long continuance, for in a short time he will fling them from his face unto eternal perdition.

6. God's hatred of evil, or evil doers, is not only negative, but he positively hates, seeks to destroy them, and, actually, will do so: and as sin is committed by act, word, thought, or desire, each is here enumerated; first, the *"Workers of iniquity;"* secondly, they that *"Speak a lie;"* thirdly, *"The bloody and the deceitful."*

7. After saying, that in the morning he would meditate on the hatred God bears to sin and to sinners, he now tells us the fruit of such meditation, saying, *"But as for me, in the multitude of thy mercy,"* as much as to say, relying on thy great mercy, and not on my own strength, to avoid sin, *"I will come into thy house,"* the house of prayer. *"I will worship towards thy holy temple,"* that

is to say, I will throw myself prostrate in presence of thy tabernacle, *"in thy fear,"* for in fear and trembling will I implore your assistance.

8. From God's house he now puts up the prayer that God may lead him in his justice; that is, through the paths of justice, by causing him to keep all his commandments, and thus to avoid all sin; which is the same as *"Direct my way in thy sight;"* in other words, make me walk the straight road, having God always before me. And he makes therein special mention of his enemies; for divine grace is needed against them, to direct, to protect, to anticipate, and to follow up the number of enemies who lie in wait for us, and seek to lead us to sin, be they demons or mortals, making use of threats or allurements. He includes in the word enemies all those who, however friendly they may appear to be, come in the way of our salvation. For, *"Man's domestics are his enemies."* The meaning, then, is, make me walk the straight road before thee. We should always ask the grace of God to walk in the way of his commandments.

9-10. He assigns a reason for his praying for help against his insidious enemies, namely, their purpose of injuring him, and the difficulty of avoiding their stratagems. *"There is no truth in their mouth,"* he says, because, when they want to deceive, they terrify, seeking to make one avoid some trifling evil, that thereby they may be led into a greater one; when they want to deceive us in another shape, they allure by persuading us to go after some good of no value, and thereby lose one of great value. *"Their heart is vain"* within, and they are perverse without. They relish nothing, desire nothing, and can, therefore, speak of nothing but what is vain. And he repeats the same in the following verse, but inverting the order of it. *"Their heart is an open sepulchre,"* being a repetition of, *"their heart is vain;"* and *"they dealt deceitfully with their tongues,"* being a repetition of, *"there is no truth in their mouth."* In making use then, of the words, *"throat," "open sepulchre,"* he implies that the mouth, throat, and tongue, being the members wherewith speech is pronounced or issued, are, as it were, the mouth of the sepulchre; and that the soul or heart, the seat of the bad, foul, horrid thoughts and desires, like fetid and putrid corpses, and exhaling the foul odors of sinful language form the interior of the sepulchre. And he therefore adds, *"They dealt deceitfully with their tongues;"* that is, my enemies, having no truth in their hearts, not only say what is false, but also what is deceitful, because they would, under the show of rectitude, persuade me to what is bad. *"Judge them, O Lord,"* etc. This must be taken more as a prophecy than an imprecation. It means that the enemies of the just will not only be excluded from the inheritance, but they will be condemned to eternal punishment, and will accomplish none of the objects they seek for. *"Judge them"* is more significant in the Hebrew, which makes it, *"condemn them." "Let them fall from their devices,"* that is, let them be disappointed in the hope they had of perverting the elect. *"According to the multitude of their wickedness cast them out,"* that is, their sins will drive them from the inheritance into everlasting darkness: *"for they have provoked thee, O Lord,"* that is to say, because when they thought themselves they were injuring others, it was in reality God they injured, as we have in 1 Kings 8, *"They have not cast you, but me out;"* and in Acts 5, *"You have not lied to men, but to God."*

11-12. The happy inheritance of the just, as promised in the Psalm, is here predicted. *"Let them all be glad that hope in thee,"* that is to say, though the just are now engaged in a laborious contest, let them rejoice in hope; not putting their hope in the vanities of this world, but in the true God, through whom, in the proper time, they will exult forever in his praise. *"And thou shalt dwell in them,"* making them, as it were, your habitation; they will, therefore, be in God, as he is in them; and he will be all unto all in them. And this external praise and exultation will arise from the immense internal joy and glory which will be their lot. *"For all they that love thy name shall glory in thee:"* namely, all the truly just, love making them the just, the friends, the sons of God. Their glory will arise from *"your blessing the just,"* that is, from your blessing every just man; and with the blessing, conferring favors on them, by giving them the crown of glory they deserve. And as the benevolence of God, who elected us before the foundation of the world, is the root of all good, inasmuch as from it proceed vocation, justification, merit, and glory itself, he thus concludes, *"O Lord, thou hast crowned us as with a shield of thy good will."* I acknowledge, O Lord, that all our happiness comes from thy grace and goodness, which, like the shield of the soldier, surrounds and protects us. The same idea is expressed in Psalm 102, *"Who crowneth thee in mercy and compassion."*

PSALM 6

A prayer of a penitent sinner, under the scourge of God. The first penitential psalm.

1 O Lord, rebuke me not in thy indignation, nor chastise me in thy wrath.
2 Have mercy on me, O Lord, for I am weak: heal me, O Lord, for my bones are troubled.
3 And my soul is troubled exceedingly: but thou, O Lord, how long?
4 Turn to me, O Lord, and deliver my soul: O save me for thy mercy's sake.
5 For there is no one in death, that is mindful of thee: and who shall confess to thee in hell?
6 I have laboured in my groanings, every night I will wash my bed: I will water my couch with my tears.
7 My eye is troubled through indignation: I have grown old amongst all my

enemies.

8 *Depart from me, all ye workers of iniquity: for the Lord hath heard the voice of my weeping.*

9 *The Lord hath heard my supplication: the Lord hath received my prayer.*

10 *Let all my enemies be ashamed, and be very much troubled: let them be turned back, and be ashamed very speedily.*

Explanation of the psalm

1. The prayer of one truly penitent and contrite, and hating sin supremely. For God then chastises the sinner in anger and rage, when the chastisement does not proceed from the fatherly love he bears us, with a view to our correction, but to annihilate the sinner, and to satisfy his own justice. This happens in this world, when the sinner is struck with blindness and obstinacy, so that sin becomes the punishment of sin; and in the other world, when the soul is consigned to hell's flames; stricken with such horror, and fearing the abyss of the judgments of God, he does not say against the scourge of punishment which, instead of separating from, rather brings us nearer to God; but he dreads the supreme evil and misfortune of being abandoned to the desires of his heart, to his ignominious passions, to obduracy, and blindness, and finally to eternal separation from God. Anger and fury are here synonymous, so are reprove and rebuke; for the prophets not infrequently use such repetitions, by way of emphasis or explanation.

2. The penitent uses some arguments to move God not to rebuke him in his fury, the first drawn from his own weakness, as if he said, Lord, do not look upon my sins as offenses against yourself; but as my own wretchedness and infirmity; and, therefore, punish me not as a judge, but as a physician heal me. Burn me, cut me, if you will; but with a view to heal me in your mercy, and not to destroy me in your justice. For our sins are real miseries, and the more malice we have in committing them, the greater do they become; while the less knowledge and fear we have of them, the greater is the misery it entails on us. Therefore, says he, *"Have mercy on me, for I am weak;"* that is to say, look with mercy on my sins, however great and numerous, in the light of so many diseases and infirmities, that make me weak and feeble. *"Heal me O Lord, for my bones are troubled."* The same idea in different language; for when God does have mercy, he removes the misery, and consequently, heals the sore; and thus, *"having mercy"* is synonymous with *"healing."* The same applies to *"because I am infirm,"* and *"my bones are troubled;"* for bones denote health and strength, and one's bones are said to be troubled when one's health fails, or his strength is impaired or debilitated.

3. A second argument from the consciousness of his sin, as he has it in Psalm 1, *"For I know my iniquity."* In other words, I am not only wretched, but I acknowledge it; and therefore, my soul, looking in upon its wretchedness and deformity, is so horrified, confused, and filled with wholesome fear, that it becomes impatient and clamorous; *"but thou, O Lord, how long?"* Why not pity me; why not heal me? The word *"how long,"* without any other word, is very significant, for it indicates the expression of a troubled soul unable to utter a full sentence.

4. The third argument, drawn from God's mercy; *"Turn to me;"* that is, look on me; for God's look is the source of all our good. *"Turn thy face, and we will be saved;"* and in another, Psalm 29, he says, *"You turned away your face, and I became confused;"* and when the *"Lord looked on Peter, he began to weep bitterly;"* and St. James, chap. 1, calls *"God the Father of lights;"* for as the sun by its light enlightens, warms, and enlivens our bodies, so God, looking upon us with an eye of affection, illuminates, inflames, and warms our souls. *"And deliver my soul;"* rescue it from the pit into which it has fallen; from the noose of the hunter, in which it is held bound and captive; deliver it from the hands of its enemies, into which sin has consigned it. *"Save me;"* that is, deliver me from the imminent damnation of hell; for, properly speaking, to save one, means to save them from the imminent danger of death. Observe the order followed here. First, God turns to us, and looks upon us with his grace. Secondly, we turn to him, and thus the soul is rescued from sin. Thirdly, so saved from sin, we are saved from the danger of imminent damnation. And all these stages in the process of justification, turn up, not from any previous merits of ours, (for what does a sinner merit but punishment?) but through the mercy of God; and he therefore adds, *"for thy mercy's sake,"* as if he said, I dare to ask so great a favor, having no reliance whatever on my own merits, but on your mercy.

5. A fourth argument, deduced from the glory of God. I ask, he says, not *"to be rebuked in thy fury,"* because in such case I should undoubtedly be consigned to eternal death; and thus both your praise and your memory would be partly lost, for the damned have no recollection of God, so as to praise him; nor is there any one in hell to confess to God, that is, to praise him by confessing his prodigies and his goodness. Some will have the death spoken of here, to the death of the body only; and by hell, they mean the grave; and make the sense to be, that the dead lying in their graves do not praise God, and are not mindful of him, as they have no feeling, and they quote the words of Ezechias, chap. 38, *"For hell will not confess to thee, nor will death praise thee,"* while it is pretty clear that Ezechias only asked to be delivered from the danger of corporal death. But I consider that the passage should be understood to mean everlasting death and the hell of the damned. For, though Ezechias feared the death of the body, he feared also the death of the soul, and, therefore, in his thanksgiving to God, he sang the canticle,

because he felt that the restoration of his bodily health was a sort of intimation to him, that God in his goodness had remitted his sins, and delivered him from the danger of hell, and therefore, he says: *"But you have rescued my soul that it may not be lost: you have cast all my sins behind your back, because hell will not confess to thee, nor death praise thee; they who descend into the lake will not expect thy truth."* All these arguments would be of no weight, were the death of the body alone in question here. For though the dead in the body and lying in their graves, are incapable of praising God, yet their souls live and praise him, and even their very bodies in the grave expect God's truth, that is, his faithful promise of resuscitating them. They alone who descend into the lake of eternal damnation neither expect God's truth, nor remember his benefices, nor give him present or future praise. So said passage of Ezechias has been understood by St. Jerome and the other fathers.

6. The fifth argument, drawn from fruits worthy of penance. For, as the apostle has it, 1 Cor. 11, *"If we would judge ourselves, we would not be judged;"* that is to say, if we would condemn and punish ourselves, God would not condemn nor punish us. For he spares those who do not spare themselves. He, therefore says, that he not only understands and detests his guilt, but that he will also, as far forth as he can, punish himself, both now and for the future. *"I have labored in my groanings,"* which means, I have deplored my sins with such a flood of tears, that I am thoroughly tired, though I do not still cease to shed them; for, *"I will wash my bed every night,"* means that every night, instead of enjoying sleep or rest, I will copiously deplore my sins, and water my couch with my tears. Here we must notice the profusion of tears and the long duration of them. For the Hebrew for washing conveys the idea, that the quantity of tears shed was so great that one might swim in them, and even the word watering implies a large quantity, when the whole bed was washed with them. *"I will water"* also is very significant, for it implies the quantity of tears shed to be so great that they ran like a stream. The words *"every night"* are ambiguous in the Hebrew, for they may signify the whole night, in which sense St. Jerome has taken it, or every night, as it is understood by the Septuagint. In either sense, wonderful to be told, and, perhaps, true in both senses, namely, that every night a long time was spent by him in shedding tears. A serious consideration for those who, after the commission of many and grievous sins, can scarce bring themselves to shed a single tear when they come to ask pardon for them.

7. The effect of such a profuse effusion of tears. The Hebrew, instead of the word *"trouble,"* has *"worn out"* or *"grown dark,"* to show how great was his anger and indignation with himself for the hideousness of his sins; and so profuse his tears in consequence, that his eyes grew dim and melted. *"I have grown old amongst my enemies;"* that means, I cannot but be highly indignant

with myself for never having perfectly conquered any vice, never subdued any of my spiritual enemies, but have grown old among them all. By enemies, he means all who provoke one to sin, be they demons or men, or vice itself, and evil habits.

8. Having taken to heart so much his having grown old amid his enemies, he exclaims, *"Depart from me;"* that is to say, relying on the divine assistance, I will consort no more with you, I will not yield to your temptations. *"For the Lord hath heard the voice of my weeping;"* that is to say, the Lord, moved to mercy by my tears, has not only forgiven them, but has given me greater grace to resist you.

9. An explanation of the former verse, and repeated two or three times, to show the certainty of his having been heard; and that thereby he may gather fresh courage to resist temptation.

10. A final prayer for a total end to his spiritual difficulties. *"Let them be ashamed and very much troubled"* for having effected nothing, but, on the contrary, having labored in vain. *"Let them be turned back"* to their own place from whence they came, *"And be ashamed very speedily;"* that is, let them be off as quickly as possible, and in confusion at my determination not to defer my conversion; but on the contrary, from this hour, this moment, I enter on the straight and perfect way of the Lord.

This conclusion may also be looked upon as a prayer for the conversion of those who, by their persecutions or their temptations, had been the cause of his sins. He prays that they too, by coming to know the truth, and to hate sin, *"May be ashamed, and very much troubled,"* and thus the more quickly converted to God. Finally, these words may be taken in the nature of an imprecation, to take effect on the day of judgment; for on that day all the wicked, whether men or demons, who attempted to stir up the just to impatience or to any other sin, *"Will be ashamed, and very much troubled,"* and will *"Be turned back"* to see the truth, but without benefiting themselves thereby. Then shall they say, as it is in Wisd. 5, *"We therefore have strayed, from the way of truth."* That will come about very quickly, because *"The day of the Lord tarrieth not,"* though we may think otherwise. But when it shall come, and come all of a sudden, then will be seen how quickly it came.

PSALM 7

David, trusting in the justice of his cause, prayeth for God's help against his enemies.

1 Lord my God, in thee have I put my trust: save me from all them that persecute me, and deliver me.

2 Lest at any time he seize upon my soul like a lion, while there is no one to redeem me, nor to save.

3 Lord my God, if I have done this thing, if there be iniquity in my hands:
4 If I have rendered to them that repaid me evils, let me deservedly fall empty before my enemies.
5 Let the enemy pursue my soul, and take it, and tread down my life on the earth, and bring down my glory to the dust.
6 Rise up, O Lord, in thy anger: and be thou exalted in the borders of my enemies. And arise, O Lord my God, in the precept which thou hast commanded:
7 And a congregation of people shall surround thee. And for their sakes return thou on high.
8 The Lord judgeth the people. Judge me, O Lord, according to my justice, and according to my innocence in me.
9 The wickedness of sinners shall be brought to nought: and thou shalt direct the just: the searcher of hearts and reins is God.
10 Just is my help from the Lord: who saveth the upright of heart.
11 God is a just judge, strong and patient: is he angry every day?
12 Except you will be converted, he will brandish his sword: he hath bent his bow and made it ready.
13 And in it he hath prepared the instruments of death, he hath made ready his arrows for them that burn.
14 Behold he hath been in labour with injustice; he hath conceived sorrow, and brought forth iniquity.
15 He hath opened a pit and dug it; and he is fallen into the hole he made.
16 His sorrow shall be turned on his own head: and his iniquity shall comedown upon his crown.
17 I will give glory to the Lord according to his justice: and will sing to the name of the Lord the most high.

EXPLANATION OF THE PSALM

1. **"In thee have I put my trust,"** because nearly all have deserted me, so that my very son Absalom, and my father in law Saul, seek to put me to death. I have no one to trust in but you, my God. *"Save me from all them that persecute me."* Numerous were his persecutors—some by their advice, some by their maledictions, some by war and arms.

2. Meaning the leader of the persecution; for fear, says he, Saul or Absalom *"seize upon my soul,"* that is, take my life without any mercy, just as the lion seizes on other animals, *"while there is no one to redeem me, nor to save,"* that is, if you do not redeem and save me; for David knew that all human industry, without God, was of no avail. The word *"redeem"* is used in the Scripture for any sort of deliverance, though, properly speaking, it supposes something to be paid on redemption. For, as God is said to sell those he alienates from his mercy, and delivers to the ministers of his justice for punishment;

so he is said to redeem those whom, in his mercy, he liberates, after rescuing them from the same ministers.

3-4. A reason assigned for asking deliverance of God, namely, on account of God's knowledge of his innocence, thereby refuting Saul and Semei's calumny of his plotting against Saul, and his invasion of the kingdom: for he asserts that he not only did not return evil for good, nor even evil for evil, but, on the contrary, that he returned good for evil. He first asserts that he did not return evil for good. *"If I have done this,"* that is, if I have conspired against the king, or invaded the kingdom by any fraud or force; *"if there be iniquity in my hands,"* that is, if I have done evil, returning it for good, I who was treated with such honor by Saul, adopted as his son in law, placed over a thousand soldiers—if I have been, as he asserts, the person to conspire against him, *"If I have rendered to them that repaid me evils;"* that means, when Saul and Semei, for all the favors I conferred on them, would only give evil in return, even to seek my death, I did not seek theirs, though I might easily, and could with impunity have done so. *"Let me deservedly fall empty before my enemies,"* which means, if such calumnies of theirs be not false, I don't murmur at, nor refuse to fall *"empty"* in battle, that is, without any military glory, having inflicted no injury on the enemy, and after having suffered a great deal.

5. The evils he imprecates on himself, if the calumnies of Saul or Semei be true. See how they rise. First, *"Let the enemy pursue my soul,"* that is, endeavor to kill me. Second, *"And take it,"* in such way that I cannot possibly escape when he takes me to kill me. Third, *"And tread down my life on the earth;"* put me to an ignominious death, such as the death of those who are trampled under foot, and bruised to atoms. Fourth, *"And bring down my glory to the dust;"* that my memory, instead of being exalted and revered, may be forever infamous and opprobrious.

6. Having asserted his innocence, he justly asks of God to defend him. And as God is metaphorically said to sleep when he does not help; and to rise from sleep when he begins to help, as in Psalm 53, *"Rise, why sleepest thou, O Lord?"* he now says, *"Rise in thy anger;"* that is, be angry with my enemies; repel and terrify them, lest they hurt me. *"And be exalted in the borders of my enemies,"* means much the same, for the meaning is, appear aloft in the borders of my enemies, that all may see you, and be sensible of your presence. *"And arise, O Lord my God, in the precept which thou hast commanded."*

Hitherto he had simply asked of God help against his enemies; he now assigns a reason for God's granting it; and that is, because God had ordered the judges of the land to free the innocent from their oppressors; whence it follows that God, who is the supreme Judge over all judges, ought to do so too. *"Rise in the precept thou hast commanded;"* that is, agreeably to the order you gave.

7. Your interference in reducing my enemies and defending me, will bring many to know you, to confess to you, to praise you, and to surround you with a congregation; for wherever any are congregated in thy name, there art thou in the midst of them. Having asserted that *"A congregation of people would surround him,"* he now adds, *"and for their sakes return on high."* As you have exalted yourself in the territory of my enemies, terrifying them from the throne of your justice, on my account, do the same when necessary—return on high again, for the sake of the congregation that praise thee.

8. A reason assigned for standing by and supporting the congregation of people that adhered to him; he, being the supreme Judge and Sovereign, to whom it properly appertained to protect and govern those under his charge. *"Judge me, O Lord, according to my justice, and according to my innocence in me."* The conclusion of the whole imprecation. Conscious of the falsehood of the calumny of Saul and Semei, and having God witness thereto, he asks him, as the supreme Judge, to judge his cause according to its justice and his innocence, and to give to every one their desert.

9. This may be called the second part of the Psalm, in which the prophet teaches evil doers that they harm themselves; and exhorts all to be converted from iniquity to justice. *"The wickedness of sinners shall be brought to naught;"* that is, let them do all in them lies—use all their efforts to injure the just—it will be all in vain, to no purpose; because *"You direct the just;"* by your providence you guide him, so that he shall neither turn to the right nor to the left. You alone can do so, for to you alone are the truly just known, inasmuch as it is you that search their hearts; that is, know their thoughts and their loins, that is, their desires.

10. From a universal opinion he infers, in particular, that it is right for him to expect help from the Lord; for it is just that God should help the just, for it belongs to him, as searcher of hearts, to save those that are upright of heart, that is, those who are truly just before God.

11. God is a just judge, both strong and patient; but not at all times angry or threatening, only when he is driven thereto by the evil doings of those who know how severely he prohibits certain actions to sinners; and yet they hesitate not in doing them.

12. To prove that God is not always angry or threatening, but that he only sometimes gives way to his wrath, and carries out the threats he menaced, he adds, *"Except you will be converted, he will brandish his sword,"* that is, he will so wield it in destruction, that it will appear to emit light; and he will use the bow as well as the sword, for, *"he hath bent his bow, and made it ready."* The sword and the bow are introduced to show that God strikes from near and from afar. When the sin committed is proximate and patent, then God strikes at once, and openly, as if with a sword. When the sin is remote, or occult, then he seems to strike from a distance, as if with an arrow.

13. For fear we should suppose that the divine weapons could be easily repelled or avoided, he says those weapons are *"instruments of death,"* that the arrows are made of inflammable matter, so as to become weapons of fire, penetrating and consuming, with the greatest rapidity, everything they strike. The literal translation would be, *"Vessels of death;"* but vessels are most frequently used in the Scriptures to signify arms or instruments; thus, in Psalm 70, *"Vessels of psalms;"* Is. 22, *"Vessels of music;"* Jeremias 50, *"Vessels of anger;"* chap. 51, *"Vessels of war."*

14. In the three following verses the prophet shows that such weapons, being really fiery weapons, are sent with the greatest force, and sure to be unerring. For God's providence so arranges that the very evil the sinners prepare for the just should prove fatal to themselves; for such is the wonderful hatred of God for sinners as to cause all their machinations to retort upon themselves. The sinner, says he, *"hath conceived sorrow and brought forth iniquity; and dug a pit,"* and dug it deeply, that he might take away the life of the just man, either publicly or privately; but, through God's intervention, the sinner fell into his own pit, and *"the sorrow he conceived,"* and the *"iniquity he brought forth,"* have redounded on his own head. To explain in detail, *"He hath been in labor with injustice."* That is to say, the sinner has been guilty of some act of violence or injustice to the just man. The word, *"He has been in labor"* is not to be looked upon here as different from the word *"brought forth,"* in the end of the verse; they both mean the same, as he presently explains more clearly what seed it is that he has been in *"labor with,"* or *"brought forth."* *"He hath conceived sorrow, and brought forth iniquity."* The seed as well as the fetus is conceived. *"Conception of sorrow,"* means conception of hatred, or envy of the neighbor, which are the seed of all evil; and hatred and envy are most properly designated by conception of sorrow, for hatred and envy distort and destroy the mind of the person possessed by them. From the bad seed thus conceived spring the bad actions, such as murder, rapine, detraction, false testimony, and the like; and though some may consider the three expressions, *"He hath been in labor with injustice;"* *"He hath conceived sorrow,"* and *"Brought forth iniquity,"* to refer to three different things, and parturition would seem to be midway between conception and birth; but, in reality, two things only, as I said before, are implied, because two only apply to the verse 2; next, *"His sorrow shall be turned on his own head, and his iniquity shall come down upon his crown;"* again, if *"the conceiving of sorrow"* be distinct from the *"being in labor with injustice,"* it ought to precede, not to follow. By the words then, *"he hath been in labor with injustice,"* is meant a summary of the entire, of which conception and bringing forth is an explanation.

15. After saying that the sinner had brought forth iniquity against the just, he adds, that *"he opened a pit"* giving us to understand by such similes, that the wicked plot against the just sometimes privately, sometimes openly; and as parturition and delving are sometimes troublesome and laborious enough, so are the evil doings of the sinner—hence the exclamation of the damned, Wisd. 5, *"We have walked the difficult ways." "And he is fallen into the hole he made."* The prophet now begins to show that the evil doings of the sinner hurt themselves alone, and that they are the sword and the arrows of God; and having finished with the latter, he takes it up again, saying: *"He hath opened a pit,"* in the hope that the just man, ignorant of its existence, may fall into it, but instead thereof himself fell in.

16. Not only occult sins, such as the opening of the pit, but even public, such as hatred or envy externally manifested, and the sins springing from hatred and envy, such as bloodshed and rapine and the like, will, by the divine dispensation, recoil on the evil doer; we have examples in Saul and David; the Jews and Christ; the persecutors and the martyrs.

17. The Psalm concludes in praise to God. Literally it is, *"I will confess,"* which expression in the Scriptures is constantly used for praise, for he who praises him confesses he is worthy of such praise *"according to his justice."* I will give him not more praise than he merits who so wonderfully delivers the just and punishes the sinner. *"And I will sing to the name of the Lord the Most High;"* the same idea in different language, viz., I will sing a hymn to the highest God, to the supreme Judge, who sits on a most lofty throne above all other judges.

PSALM 8

God is wonderful in his works; especially in mankind, singularly exalted by the incarnation of Christ.

1 Lord, our Lord, how admirable is thy name in the whole earth! for thy magnificence is elevated above the heavens.
2 Out of the mouth of infants and of sucklings thou hast perfected praise, because of thy enemies, that thou mayest destroy the enemy and the avenger.
3 For I will behold thy heavens, the works of thy fingers: the moon and the stars which thou hast founded.
4 What is man that thou art mindful of him? or the son of man that thou visitest him?
5 Thou hast made him a little less than the Angels, thou hast crowned him with glory and honour:
6 And hast set him over the works of thy hands.

7 *Thou hast subjected all things under his foot, all sheep and oxen: moreover the beasts also of the fields.*
8 *The birds of the air, and the fishes of the sea, that pass through the paths of the sea.*
9 *Lord our Lord, how admirable is thy name in all the earth!*

Explanation of the psalm

1. Reflecting on God's greatness, the prophet is wrapped in admiration at the idea of a God, so great in himself, condescending to look upon or to heap such and so many favors on man, a thing of dust and ashes. *"O Lord,"* says he, who art the source of all being, whence all created things are derived; and, therefore, *"Our Lord,"* that is to say, thou art Lord of all, *"how admirable is thy name in the whole earth!"* how wonderful is thy glory, or the good fame of thy name diffused through the whole world, to the great admiration of all who care to reflect on it. Isaias, chap. 6, says the same in other language: *"The whole earth is full of his glory."* He calls the name of God admirable, because though the admirers may be few, when few reflect on God's works; however, the name is most worthy of admiration when all creatures constantly praise the Creator in the sense that all beautiful productions are said to praise the producer, and in such wise the whole earth is full of the glory of God; for whatever is on earth, even to the minutest particle, declares the infinite power and wisdom of the Creator. *"For thy magnificence is elevated above the heavens."* A reason why God's name should be so admirable on earth, inasmuch as his magnificence is elevated above the heavens, that is, cannot be contained by them; it is such that the whole world cannot contain it. *"His glory covered the heavens, and the earth is full of his praise,"* Habacuc chap. 3. The magnificence of great princes is estimated from their expensive manner of living, their building great cities or palaces, their keeping up great retinues or armies, or their distribution of great presents. God created the universe for a palace, having the earth for its pavement, the heavens for its roof. He feeds all living things, who are beyond counting. He has already bestowed on the angels and saints, who are the most numerous, and will hereafter on the just, a most ample kingdom, not temporal but eternal. Truly great, then, is his magnificence.

2. An answer to an objection likely to be raised. If the glory of God so fill the earth and his magnificence be elevated above the heavens, how comes it that all do not know and praise him? The answer is, that God does not condescend to be known or praised by the proud, who presume on their own strength, but by the humble and the little ones, according to Mt. 11, *"I confess to thee, Father, because thou hast hidden these things from the wise and the prudent, and hast revealed them to the little ones."* Hence, God's glory and greatness are greatly increased, when he is known only by those he wishes should know him. This verse may have a double meaning. First, to understand infants and sucklings as meaning mankind, who really are such, when compared to the Angels, when there is question of understanding divine matters; and the sense would be from the mouth of mortals you have perfected praise, revealing your glory to them, *"because of thy enemies;"* that is, to confound the rebellious angels. *"That thou mayest destroy the enemy and the avenger;"* that is, that you may outwit the wisdom of your primary enemy, the devil, and his defenders, or avengers, the host of his followers, the reprobate angels. Secondly, by *"infants and sucklings,"* may be understood humble people, little ones in their own eyes, and not versed in the science of the world; like many of the prophets and apostles, and a great number of monks and holy virgins, and mere children too, who, in early years, have so perfectly understood the glory of God, that they had no hesitation in spilling their blood for it. In such sense did our Savior quote this very Psalm, Mt. 21, *"Have you never read that from the mouth of infants and sucklings he hath perfected praise?"* By enemies are meant the wise ones of this world, and their apologists, who, with all their knowledge of God, have not glorified him as such, and, therefore, *"became vain in their thoughts,"* as St. Paul expresses it.

3. Holy David ranks himself here among the infants and sucklings praising God; as if he were to say, here is one, a humble shepherd, to chant your praise. *"For I will behold the heavens;"* that is, I will attentively consider that wonderful work of yours, and praise you the Creator of such a work. He makes use of the phrase, *"the works of thy fingers;"* as much as to say, formed by your fingers, not by your arms, to show with what facility they were created by God; and furthermore, that valuable and precious works, not requiring labor but skill, are generally the work of the fingers and not of the arms. Mention is not made of the sun here, for it was mostly at night that David would so turn to contemplation; that being the time most meet for it. *"At midnight I rose to confess to thee,"* Ps. 118; and in Ps. 62, *"I will meditate on thee in the morning;"* and Isaias, chap. 62. *"My soul hath longed for thee in the night."* It is at night that the heavens are seen embellished with the moon and stars, *"Which thou hast founded;"* all created from nothing, raised by you from the foundation without having had any previous existence.

4. The greatness of God, in himself, having been established, he now proceeds to extol his greatness towards man. *"What is man,"* that you, the Creator of heaven and earth, deign to remember him? as if he said the greatest favor possible to be conferred on man, who is mere dust and ashes, is the bare remembrance of him by God; and as such remembrance is not a naked one, but with a view to confer favors on man, he adds, by way of

explanation, *"or the son of man that thou visitest him?"* Man, and the son of man, mean the same, unless one would raise an uncalled for distinction, by saying that the words, *"son of man,"* are used to show the divine favors were not conferred on the first man to the exclusion of his posterity. The word *"visitest him,"* implies the special providence God has for all men, especially that which he displayed, by coming into the world, assuming human flesh, *"being seen on earth, and conversing among men,"* Baruch 3. Such is, properly speaking, the visitation alluded to in Lk. 1. *"Blessed is the Lord God of Israel, who has visited and redeemed his people;"* and subsequently, same chapter, *"The orient from on high hath visited us."* Such visitation could not but elicit, *"What is man that thou art mindful of him? Or the son of man that thou visitest him?"*

5. This verse has a double meaning, a literal and an allegorical. In the literal sense, three favors of God to the human race are enumerated. First, being created by God of so noble a nature as to be very little less than that of the Angels. Secondly, to be so distinguished in honor and glory beyond all other creatures, inasmuch as he has been made to the image and likeness of God, and endowed with reason and free will. Thirdly, from the power and dominion over all things, especially animals, that have been conferred by God upon him; and, therefore, he adds:

6-8. By sheep and oxen are meant all domestic animals: by the beasts of the field are meant wild animals. The birds of the air, and the fish of the sea, are easily understood, including the monsters as well as the fish of the sea. To come now to the allegorical sense of the preceding verses, which is quite certain, and intended by God, if we believe St. Paul, in Heb. 2, and 1 Cor. 15, the meaning is, that Christ, man, by that most remarkable visitation of God; that is to say, by the incarnation of the Word, was made less than the Angels in some degree, by his passion, as would appear from the Angels coming to comfort him in his passion, whereas Angels are immortal, and exempt from all suffering; and, however, Christ suffered and died then and there. Absolutely speaking, however, Christ was always superior to the Angels, and superior in every respect. That was shown clearly, when he *"was crowned with honor and glory;"* that is to say, when in his resurrection in a glorious and immortal body, and by his wonderful ascension, he was exalted above all God's works, to the right hand of his Father. All things are subject to him, without exception, *"except him"* as the apostle, 1 Cor. 13, says, *"Who has subjected everything to him."* His principal subjects are, first, human beings, believers, included in *"sheep and oxen,"* subjects and prelates; and unbelievers, under the head of *"The beasts of the field."* "Then Angels, superior to mankind, come under the head of the birds of the air, that rise aloft, and constantly chant the praises of God. Finally, the fishes of the sea represent the evil spirits, who, from the lowest abyss are insensible to God's praise, and revel in the meanest and lowest dissipation.

9. A repetition of the first verse, as if he said, how justly I set out with the exclamation, *"O Lord our Lord, how admirable is thy name in all the earth."*

PSALM 9

The Church praiseth God for his protection against her enemies.

1 I will give praise to thee, O Lord, with my whole heart: I will relate all thy wonders.
2 I will be glad and rejoice in thee: I will sing to thy name, O thou most high.
3 When my enemy shall be turned back: they shall be weakened and perish before thy face.
4 For thou hast maintained my judgment and my cause: thou hast sat on the throne, who judgest justice.
5 Thou hast rebuked the Gentiles, and the wicked one hath perished: thou hast blotted out their name for ever and ever.
6 The swords of the enemy have failed unto the end: and their cities thou hast destroyed. Their memory hath perished with a noise.
7 But the Lord remaineth for ever. He hath prepared his throne in judgment:
8 And he shall judge the world in equity, he shall judge the people in justice.
9 And the Lord is become a refuge for the poor: a helper in due time in tribulation.
10 And let them trust in thee who know thy name: for thou hast not forsaken them that seek thee, O Lord.
11 Sing ye to the Lord, who dwelleth in Sion: declare his ways among the Gentiles:
12 For requiring their blood he hath remembered the: he hath not forgotten the cry of the poor.
13 Have mercy on me, O Lord: see my humiliation which I suffer from my enemies.
14 Thou that liftest me up from the gates of death, that I may declare all thy praises in the gates of the daughter of Sion.
15 I will rejoice in thy salvation: the Gentiles have stuck fast in the destruction which they have prepared. Their foot hath been taken in the very snare which they hid.
16 The Lord shall be known when he executeth judgments: the sinner hath been caught in the works of his own hands.
17 The wicked shall be turned into hell, all the nations that forget God.
18 For the poor man shall not be forgotten to the end: the patience of the poor shall not perish for ever.
19 Arise, O Lord, let not man be strengthened: let the Gentiles be judged in thy sight.
20 Appoint, O Lord, a lawgiver over them: that the Gentiles may know themselves

to be but men.

21 Why, O Lord, hast thou retired afar off? why dost thou slight us in our wants, in the time of trouble?

22 Whilst the wicked man is proud, the poor is set on fire: they are caught in the counsels which they devise.

23 For the sinner is praised in the desires of his soul: and the unjust man is blessed.

24 The sinner hath provoked the Lord according to the multitude of his wrath he will not seek him:

25 God is not before his eyes: his ways are filthy at all times. Thy judgments are removed from his sight: he shall rule over all his enemies.

26 For he hath said in his heart: I shall not be moved from generation to generation, and shall be without evil.

27 His mouth is full of cursing, and of bitterness, and of deceit: under his tongue are labour and sorrow.

28 He sitteth in ambush with the rich in private places, that he may kill the innocent.

29 His eyes are upon the poor man: He lieth in wait in secret like a lion in his den. He lieth in ambush that he may catch the poor man: to catch the poor, whilst he draweth him to him.

30 In his net he will bring him down, he will crouch and fall, when he shall have power over the poor.

31 For he hath said in his heart: God hath forgotten, he hath turned away his face not to see to the end.

32 Arise, O Lord God, let thy hand be exalted: forget not the poor.

33 Wherefore hath the wicked provoked God? for he hath said in his heart: He will not require it.

34 Thou seest it, for thou considerest labour and sorrow: that thou mayst deliver them into thy hands. To thee is the poor man left: thou wilt be a helper to the orphan.

35 Break thou the arm of the sinner and of the malignant: his sin shall be sought, and shall not be found.

36 The Lord shall reign to eternity, yea, for ever and ever: ye Gentiles shall perish from his land.

37 The Lord hath heard the desire of the poor: thy ear hath heard the preparation of their heart.

38 To judge for the fatherless and for the humble, that man may no more presume to magnify himself upon earth.

EXPLANATION OF THE PSALM

1. The matter of the Psalm is here proposed, viz., the praise of God for his wonderful works. The words, *"With my whole heart,"* signify the subject to

be praised is one of the highest importance, and, therefore, to be done with all his might and affections. The words, *"All thy wonders"* imply that the subject of his praise is so expansive as to comprehend in one view all the wonderful works of God. Such, in reality, was the redemption of man; a work of infinite mercy, in which are comprehended all the beneficent acts of God, as the apostle has it, Ephesians 1, *"To establish all things in Christ;"* that is, to comprehend, to reduce everything into one sum through him.

2. The same sentiment, in different language, or, perhaps, rather an explanation; as if he said, with exultation and joy will I confess to thee, with joy in my heart and exultation in my exterior, thus confessing with all my affections. Playing on the harp before thee, O Most High, will I relate all thy wonders, chanting them to thy glory.

3. He begins to narrate the victory of Christ over the devil and his satellites, and speaks in the person of the entire Church. *"When my enemy shall be turned back,"* that means, when my enemy, the devil, flying from your face, shall begin to turn back, then all his soldiers *"Shall be weakened, and perish;"* that is to say, the moment they see their leader to fly, they will become unnerved, will fly, scatter as if they had been actually destroyed. Of such flight the Lord himself speaks in the gospel, Jn. 12, *"Now is the judgment of the world, now shall the prince of this world be cast out."*

4. A reason assigned for the devil's flight and the scattering of his forces; for you, my Lord, the Son of God, *"hast maintained my judgment and my cause;"* that is, you have put an end to the litigation, the struggle, and the contest between mankind, or the Church and the devil. For the devil maintained that mankind was justly held in bondage by him, and therefore harassed it in a most tyrannical manner, until Christ, by his sufferings on the cross, thereby atoning for man, put an end to the struggle; hence the expression, *"Thou hast sat on the throne, who judgest justice,"* meaning the cross, as St. Leo has it, in his eighth Sermon on the Passion of our Lord: *"O unspeakable glory of the passion, in which are united the judgment seat of God, the judgment of the world, and the power of the crucified;"* and these are in reality the occult things of the Son, which by some are prefixed as a title to this Psalm. For he who, to all appearance, seemed to be guilty and was suffering punishment in the greatest ignominy, at that very moment was sitting on his throne, *"judged justice,"* that is, judged most justly, inasmuch as now that the price had been paid, man was delivered, and the devil despoiled of his dominion over him, and actually, as the apostle has it, Col. 2, *"Blotting out the handwriting of the decree which was against us, which was contrary to us, and the same he took out of the way, fastening it to the cross."*

5. The devil having been subdued through the cross, Christ our Lord, through his apostles, *"rebuked the gentiles,"* *"convicting the world of sin, of*

justice, and of judgment," as the Lord himself foretold: and in such manner *"The wicked one hath perished;"* that is the wickedness of idolatry perished, and man from impiety was brought to love God. Which was effected not only among the impious of that time, but Christ so entirely destroyed idolatry and the religion of the gentiles forever, that it can never appear again, having been plucked out from the roots. A thing we see already fulfilled, the Jews themselves, who were most prone to idolatry, having never attempted to return to it. *"Forever and ever,"* to signify true, real eternity, having no end, for fear any one should suppose that a very long time, but still a definite one, was intended.

6. A reason assigned for idolatry not being likely to return, inasmuch as the power of the devil and his strongholds had disappeared, and he has no means of carrying on an offensive or a defensive warfare, *"His swords having failed"*—*"unto the end;"* that is, thoroughly, without a single exception—not one remaining. By *"the swords of the enemy"* we may also understand the temptations, or suggestions, which may be looked upon as the words of the devil, in the same sense that the apostle calls the word of God, *"The sword of the Spirit."* The same apostle calls the temptations of the devil, *"weapons of fire;"* and such weapons are said *"to have failed,"* because they cannot injure those armed in the faith of Jesus Christ. In which sense, St. Anthony, in his life of St. Athanasius, quoted this very passage, proving therefrom that the temptations of the devil are most easily repulsed by the sign of the cross. By *"their cities"* may be understood all infidels, in whom the devil dwells without disturbance; these were destroyed by Christ when he put down idolatry. Our Lord himself seems to have this in view when he says, in Lk. 11, *"When a strong man armed keepeth his court, those things which he possessed are in peace. But if a stronger than he come upon him, and overcome him, he will take away all his armor, wherein he trusted, and will distribute his spoils."* When the devil held possession, everything he possessed was in peace; because, while man is in a state of infidelity, he is always in the power of the devil, however morally good his life may have been, as has been the case with many pagan philosophers. But Christ, having got possession, by the extirpation of infidelity and the introduction of the knowledge of the true God, the devil lost his all. *"Their memory has perished with a noise;"* that is to say, the memory of idolatry, idolaters, and of the whole kingdom of Satan has perished amidst much noise and confusion. For the whole world resisted Christ; the most powerful kings and emperors sought to stand up for and defend their idols; but the more the world raged, the more idolatry tottered, and the remembrance of it was being blotted out; and, finally, the cessation of persecution was succeeded by a total destruction of idolatry.

7. Christ's memory, on the contrary, will never fade after his death and resurrection. *"All power in heaven and on earth was given to him,"* which David alludes to here; as if he said, after such contest with the devil, the Lord *"Hath prepared,"* or, as the Hebrew has it, established *"His throne in judgment;"* that is, for the purpose of judging; and he, the Prince of the kings of the earth, *"Shall judge the world;"* meaning the people of the whole world, *"In equity and justice,"* two words used synonymously. Christ is said to sit in judgment on the world, though there may be many wicked and infidel princes in the world in rebellion against him, but who can, however, devise nothing—do nothing against his will and permission.

EXPLAINED ABOVE.

8-9. From the fact of Christ's being the future ruler, to govern with supreme justice, he infers the poor, who are usually oppressed by the great, will have great consolation. Let the poor fear no longer, for the Lord, sitting in heaven, *"Is become a refuge"* to them; and, furthermore, *"A helper in due time in tribulation;"* that is, when necessity may require it. For the divine help never comes so opportunely, as when we are overwhelmed in trouble, with no human being to console us; and this promise will be most surely fulfilled to all who truly seek and fear God; and therefore, he adds:

10. The prophet speaks now in the third, instead of the first person, a thing he often does, from some new inspiration. With great justice can all *"Who know your name;"* that is to say, not only by the sound of it, but in reality; and fully understand the significance of it, and thence know the power and the mercy of God, put their confidence in you in all their difficulties. Much more so can your friends, *"Since thou hast not forsaken;"* that is, you never have forsaken *"Those that seek thee."* By those *"That seek him"* he means those that covet his grace, and with all their heart seek to please him.

11. After a fervent appeal to God, he makes one to man in the same spirit; exhorting them too, to praise God, and to bring others to do so. The Lord is said *"To dwell in Sion,"* for there was the *"Ark of the testament,"* and *"The place of prayer;"* and this is put in here by way of apposition, that the true God may be distinguished from the false, who dwell in caves and the shrines of the gentiles. The word *"ways"* comprehends the thoughts, counsels, plans, inventions, the wonderful works of God, that are so resplendent in the redemption of man. Thus the meaning of the whole verse is: Sing to God a hymn of praise; announce to the gentiles his wonderful designs, his wonderful wisdom; and, in consequence, his wonderful works, that all nations, when they hear them, may unite in his praise.

12. The prophet returns to what he previously asserted: namely, that the Lord was a *"Just Judge,"* the *"Refuge of the poor in tribulation;"* and takes up an objection that may be possibly raised, to wit, the fact of our seeing the poor, however pious, persecuted by the wealthy, sometimes even unto death. The answer is, *"Praise God,"* says he, *"for though he sometimes seems to forget his poor,"* such is not the case. *"For requiring;"* that is to say, inquiring into their daily actions, and examining them severally. *"Their blood he hath remembered, he hath not forgotten the cry of the poor,"* who, in their persecutions, had appealed to him; which recollection of their sufferings will appear in its own time, when the punishment of the oppressors and the glory of the oppressed shall be declared.

13. Having thanked God for past favors, he now asks his assistance, in present and future difficulties. The prayer of the Church against her visible and invisible enemies. *"Have mercy on me, O Lord, see my humiliation,"* that is, my total prostration, caused by my enemies.

14. The first part of this verse has a connection with the verse preceding. The meaning is, *"Have mercy on me, O Lord, see my humiliation;"* you, O Lord, *"That liftest me up from the gates of death,"* meaning you that keep me far removed from the gates of death. Those gates are supposed to be very deep; for the prophet does not allude to the death of the body, but to the death of the soul by sin, or everlasting death; and, therefore, he makes use of the word *"Exalt,"* to be far removed from the said gates. By the *"Gates of death,"* or of hell, the multitude of our infernal enemies would seem to be implied. The great body of the Jewish people were wont to assemble at the gates, whether for matters of justice or any other public business, and thus the word *"Gates"* got to signify a large assemblage of the people. Hence, we have in Matthew, *"The gates of hell shall not prevail against her;"* and in the last chapter of Ecclesiasticus, *"From the gates of tribulation that have encompassed me."* And here we may note the beauty of the contrast between the gates of death, and the gates of the daughter of Sion or Jerusalem; the former are in the lowest bottom; the latter, on a high mountain: in the former are assembled the evil spirits; in the latter the people of God: from the gates of the former come forth nothing but temptations and war, that lead to death; the gates of the latter *"Are built on peace;"* for Jerusalem *"Has put peace as its boundary;"* and it is named as *"The vision of peace."* The Church, then, *"Is lifted up from the gates of death,"* to announce God's praise, *"In the gates of the daughter of Sion;"* which means being delivered from all temptations that may lead her to eternal death; to acknowledge the great grace conferred on her by her liberator, and to praise him with the Angels of God, who are in the gates of the heavenly Jerusalem.

15. Having been liberated from the *"gates of death,"* *"I will rejoice in thy salvation;"* that is, in the salvation you bestowed on me; since *"the gentiles who laid a snare for me"* have been caught in the very snare they laid, as they would in the deepest mud, from whence they cannot extricate themselves; in other words, their persecution did much harm to them, none to me; and the same may be said not only of their open and avowed persecution, but also of their private persecution, which, *"like a snare, they laid for me."* May be too, that the avowed persecutions of Diocletian and others of the Roman emperors, and the disguised persecutions of Julian the Apostate, and other heretical emperors, are here intended.

16. From this wonderful dispensation of Providence, who turns the arms and the wiles of the wicked on themselves, David gathers that God will come to be known. *"The Lord shall be known when he executeth judgment;"* that is, his judgments will be so admired that he will be known to be the true and supreme God; and mainly, through his providence in causing the sinner *"to be caught in the works of his own hands:"* namely, when he falls into *"the destruction he had prepared for others,"* and *"the snare which he had hid for them."*

17. To be taken as a prophecy, not as an imprecation. *"Shall be turned,"* means in the Hebrew, *"shall return;"* which is applied to sinners, inasmuch as the devil, when he seduced them, made them his slaves; and, therefore, they will return to him. For God created man in innocence: the devil made him a sinner. As our Savior, in Jn. 8, says, *"You are from your father, the devil."* The latter part of the verse, *"all the nations that forget God,"* declares who the sinners are that *"will return to hell:"* namely, all those *"who forget God."* For the forgetting of God is the root of all sin; for he who sins turns away from God unto the creature.

18. Sinners, therefore, who are in the habit of oppressing the poor will be cast into hell; for God, sooner or later, will avenge their wrongs; for, though he may seem to forget them for a time, *"he does not forget them to the end,"* but will one time remember them; and, therefore, *"the patience of the poor shall not perish forever."* When the patience of the poor is said not to perish, it does not mean that their patience in itself will be everlasting; but that it will in its effects, inasmuch as its reward will be everlasting.

19. Having predicted the final ruin of the wicked, he now asks for their coercion. *"Arise, O Lord, let not man be strengthened;"* that is, let not man, a handful of dust, prevail against God, his Creator. *"Let the gentiles be judged in thy sight;"* meaning, let judgment issue against them, as we have in another Psalm, *"Judge them, O God."*

20. The judgment that issued against the gentiles, who persecuted the Church, was quite manifest when they became subject to a Christian prince. They then plainly saw they were weak mortals, and could not prevail against Christ. That the prophet predicts, but in the shape of a prayer. The word *"lawgiver,"* in the Hebrew, means a teacher, or a terrible character. And as the prophet spoke of a terrible teacher, who was to teach and to command with authority, the Septuagint, most properly, used the word legislator. By the legislator, many have said Christ is meant; many more say, Antichrist is alluded to. Let every one have their own opinion. Mine is, that he alludes to Jovinianus, Valentinian, Theodosius, and such characters.

21. This verse, according to the Hebrew version, is the first of Psalm 10, but not recognized as such by the Septuagint; and it is most likely that such division of the Psalm was made in later times, by those who considered that the matter of the latter part of the Psalm was quite different from the first part; because, in the first part, hitherto the Church was exulting in the victory of God over his and her own enemies; and in the succeeding part she mourns over the success of the same enemies over the Church. The whole difference, though, consists, not in the matter, but in the times of which David prophesies. In the beginning of the Psalm, David exulted in spirit on account of the secret mysteries of the Son of God, who by his death subdued the evil spirits and paganism, and destroyed their idols; and then in the end of the said part, and the beginning of this part, foretells the persecutions that will be raised by the gentiles, and by the evil minded persons, assuming betimes such a magnitude that it would appear God had entirely forgotten the people he had delivered with such glory to himself; and as he said previously, *"The Lord is become a refuge for the poor; a helper in due time in tribulation:"* having before him another time, namely, that in which God permitted the poor to be oppressed by the more powerful, he says, *"Why, O Lord, hast thou retired afar off?"* that is to say, permitted such a raid of the unjust on the just, as if you were not present, and had *"retired afar off. Why dost thou slight us in our wants, in the time of trouble?"* Why not help us when we need help; and that is most in the time of trouble?

22. Rather a difficult verse, but the sense would seem to be, *"Whilst the wicked man is proud,"* that is, while in his prosperity he appears full of vain boasting, *"the poor is set on fire;"* that means, is scandalized, and lights internally with anger: *"They are caught in the counsels which they devise;"* that is, both one and the other are caught; the impious man, by attributing all his happiness to himself, and thus deceiving himself; and the just man, seeing such prosperity, and not understanding it, equally deceives and involves himself. The expression, *"The counsels which they devise,"* is a Graecism, and has been translated literally, and merely signifies their thoughts. This verse would seem to supply a reason for the preceding one, showing that the prophet had implored of God *"not to slight their wants in the time of trouble,"* because the prosperity of the wicked is equally hurtful to the sinner and to the just, contributing, as it does, to the pride of the former, and the scandal of the latter.

23. The reason assigned why prosperity makes *"the wicked man proud,"* and *"the poor is set on fire;"* because, when the sinner doeth evil, and by reason of his being in power, and having riches, he is praised by many, as if he were doing right; and his desires, however sinful and unjust, are applauded; and hence it comes that *"The unjust man is blessed,"* when he rather deserved to be cursed and reviled.

24. He goes on to explain the malice of the proud sinner: *"He hath provoked the Lord,"* at a time that he should have, with all his might, sought for a reconciliation with him; but, *"According to the multitude of his wrath he will not seek him;"* that is, his extravagant anger towards the afflicted poor will not let him seek God to be reconciled to him. For his mind has been so blinded by arrogance, that he never reflects how great an evil it is to provoke Almighty God.

25. The blind sinner thinks not of God. The Hebrew puts it more expressively, *"God is not in all his thoughts,"* meaning in none of his thoughts, however numerous they may be, he never turns on God. *"His ways are filthy at all times,"* a consequence of the preceding; for, when he never thinks of God, never directs his steps to God, or to ought but gratifying his carnal desires, all his ways, therefore, that is, all his actions are filthy with the mire of concupiscence. *"Thy judgments are removed from his sight."* The only thing that could turn him from his evil ways, the dreadful reflection on thy judgments, is far from his heart; and he, therefore, fearless of God, *"Rules over all his enemies;"* that is, tyrannically oppresses all he considers as such.

26. The vain confidence of the wicked man! who thinks that nothing can harm him. *"He hath said in his heart, I shall not be moved;"* nobody can disturb me, or bring me down from my station, forever and ever; I shall meet no evil.

27. Having described the heart of the wicked man that never thinks on God, or his judgments, nor fears anything from them, he now describes his mouth, and afterwards his actions. Under the head of malediction, *"or cursing,"* may be classed blasphemies against God, and railing against men; under *"bitterness"* come detraction, contention, murmuring, and such like, indicative of hatred and rancor; finally, *"to deceit"* belong calumnious lies, and perjuries. The expression, *"under his tongue are labor and sorrow,"* explains the effect of the evils so enumerated; for the effect of all the evil words of the impious *"is labor and sorrow, under his tongue;"* that is, the labor and sorrow of wretched mortals, and the matter on which his tongue is constantly exercised.

28. He comes now to describe the evil works, the oppression of the poor, making use of a metaphorical expression, taken from those who, when they meditate assassination, conceal themselves in a house for the purpose of observing the ingress and egress of those whose lives they are bent upon; and the meaning is, that those wicked and powerful people enter into a conspiracy with other rich and powerful people, to circumvent the poor by various arts and stratagems, and so destroy them entirely.

29-30. The metaphor used in the twenty-eighth verse is here explained by different metaphors. In that verse he compared the oppressor of the poor, to one man lying in ambush for another. In verse twenty-nine he compares him to a lion, lying in wait for the weaker beasts; and finally, to a man laying snares for wild beasts, and catching them. *"He lieth in wait to catch the poor,"* which he does by enticing him, when off his guard, and draws him to himself. *"In his net he will bring him down;"* that is, will oppress and trample on him; will fall down, and rush upon him. *"When he shall have power over the poor;"* when he shall have made himself entirely their master. These verses contain a beautiful allusion to the wicked man's intention, who then dreadfully comes into the slavery of the devil, when he seems to have made poor people slaves to himself.

31. The cause of all the impiety being the wicked man's thinking within himself, that God was, and ever would be, indifferent to human affairs.

32. A prayer to God to curb the wicked. *"Arise,"* as if from sleep, *"and let thy hand be exalted,"* to strike; for the hands of a passive man, or of one asleep, are either hanging down, or folded.

33. He again repeats the cause of the wicked man's offending God: namely, thinking that God will not punish him.

34. He contradicts the above by saying: you *"do see it,"* and you *"will require it,"* O God, because, *"Thou considered the labor and sorrow"* of the poor, and in due time you will *"deliver into thy hands"* the wicked to be punished; and justly, because to you, the Father of all, belongs the special care *"of the poor man and the orphan."*

35. *"Break thou the arm;"* that is, the power and strength of the sinner, that so humbled, he may repent and sin no more; so that afterwards *"his sin shall be sought, and shall not be found:"* as Isaias has it, 28, *"Vexation alone shall make you understand what you hear;"* and in Ps. 82, *"Fill their faces with shame, and they will seek thy name."*

36. He predicts the fulfillment of his prayer. *"The Lord shall reign;"* that is, always will reign in spite of his enemies; nay, his enemies even shall *"Perish from his land;"* that is, shall be exterminated from this world, for the world is God's land, as we read in Ps. 23, *"The earth is the Lord's, and the fullness thereof."*

37. He uses the past for the future tense, on account of the certainty of the thing being done; and the word *"Desire,"* instead of prayer, to show how sure and quickly they would be heard; as if he said, God, the searcher of hearts, will not wait for their prayers, but will even hear their desires, that usually precede prayer. *"Desire"* and *"Preparation of their heart"* are the same, desire being a preliminary to prayer.

38. *"The Lord hath heard the desire of the poor,"*—*"to judge for the fatherless and for the humble;"* that is, to protect the fatherless and the humble against their oppressors, in order that man, who is upon earth, a creature, should not *"Presume to magnify himself"* against God, who is in heaven, and man's Creator. All these denunciations of the oppressors of the poor are considered, by a figure, to apply to Antichrist. So St. Jerome and St. Augustine say: but if they are applied, as I consider they ought, in the literal sense, to the oppressors of the poor in general, they prove how great is the sin of such oppression, when the Holy Spirit denounces it at such length, and in such expressive language.

PSALM 10

The just man's confidence in God, in the midst of persecutions.

1 In the Lord I put my trust: how then do you say to my soul: Get thee away from hence to the mountain like a sparrow?
2 For, lo, the wicked have bent their bow; they have prepared their arrows in the quiver; to shoot in the dark the upright of heart.
3 For they have destroyed the things which thou hast made: but what has the just man done?
4 The Lord is in his holy temple, the Lord's throne is in heaven. His eyes look on the poor man: his eyelids examine the sons of men.
5 The Lord trieth the just and the wicked: but he that loveth iniquity hateth his own soul.
6 He shall rain snares upon sinners: fire and brimstone and storms of winds shall be the portion of their cup.
7 For the Lord is just, and hath loved justice: his countenance hath beheld righteousness.

Explanation of the psalm

1. The cry of the just man, who, under the weight of calumny is nigh tempted to despair and to desert his calling. *"In the Lord I put any trust."* He is everywhere, and all powerful. *"How then do you say to my soul,"* that is to me—the phrase being much in use among the Hebrews—that is, why seek to persuade me? He addresses either the demons tempting him, or his own internal concupiscence stirred up by the devil. *"Get thee away hence to the mountain like a sparrow;"* that means, give up your calling, and man's society, and go where there are no temptations, no dangers; for sparrows, when they dread the birds of prey, fly to the tops of mountains, where such birds cannot follow them. In regard of temptations, such mountains offer no protection, save in man's imagination; who, when subject to grievous temptations, imagine change of place will save them from such trouble; and who, in a fit of desperation, will put an end to their existence, as if it were the mountain to save them; while the just man is patient, and stands his ground—knowing these temptations to exist in all places—with God's help there to meet them.

2. A reason for flying to the mountains for deserting one's vocation from an excess of fear, suggested by temptations: namely, the just being daily persecuted by the wicked, whether by calumny or in any other shape. Calumny is compared *"to the arrows that shoot in the dark;"* to give us to understand that they not only inflict a grievous wound, but that it is nigh impossible to guard against them. The two verses taken together may be thus interpreted. One cannot now be upright of heart, seeing the number of snares daily laid for them on all sides; they must therefore fly away to an inaccessible mountain, shun the company of man altogether, a thing impossible: or succumb to custom, by deserting the paths of justice. The just man thus replies to the temptation, *"I will confide in the Lord,"* and will, therefore, neither fly to an inhabitable mountain, nor will desert the path of justice.

3. By an appeal to Heaven, he confirms the truth of the just being persecuted by the wicked; for the wicked *"have destroyed the things which thou hast made;"* that is, your most perfect laws, counsels, and the commands you gave your people: and, instead of doing good for evil, as you wish, they do evil for good, calumniating and persecuting the just without any pretence or reason. *"But what has the just man done?"* Nothing whatever; he has given them no provocation, *"But they hated without cause."*

4. He begins to assign a reason for confiding in God, and disregarding the threats of men, inasmuch as he is a judge sitting in heaven, whence he can see all things and has all men under control. *"The Lord is in his holy temple;"* by his holy temple he means the highest heavens, the temple not made by human hands; which he expresses more clearly when he adds, *"The Lord's throne is in heaven; His eyes look upon the poor."* From that highest throne, from which nothing can be hid, God beholds the poor; and, therefore, they cannot be harmed without God's knowledge or permission, a matter of the greatest consolation to them. What follows is more declaratory of the providence of God. For God not only sees men, but by a glance discerns and distinguishes the good from the bad, and all their works. The expression, *"His eyelids examine,"* means nothing more than he sees distinctly; such figurative expressions occur very often in the Psalms. The eyelids then here mean the eyes; the eyes, the mind: to interrogate means to know with as much

exactness as if he previously interrogated and examined with the greatest minuteness.

5. God not only knows exactly the just and the sinner, but he also rewards or punishes them according to their merit. Therefore, *"He that loveth iniquity hateth his own soul;"* that is to say, himself; for he will be most grievously punished for his iniquity, a beautiful and most elegant sentence. For he who loves iniquity, in seeming to love his soul, that is, himself, by gratifying himself, commits sin; and thereby, in reality hates his soul, and destroys it, as our Savior, John 12, has it, *"Who loves his soul shall lose it;"* in other words, who wrongfully loves himself truly hates himself.

6. A proof of the wicked *"having hated their own souls,"* because God will rain upon them in this life snares in the greatest abundance, as numerous as drops of rain; that is to say, will permit them daily to fall into fresh and greater sins, striking them with blindness, and *"giving them up to a reprobate sense,"* one of the most dreadful and severe punishments. And as to the next life, *"Fire and brimstone, and storms of winds;"* that is, the most burning and scorching blasts in hell, *"will be the part of their chalice;"* meaning their portion and inheritance. We have to observe that the word *"chalice"* signifies inheritance, a usual meaning for it in the Scripture, as, *"The Lord is the part of my inheritance, and of my chalice;"* when the two expressions mean the one thing, viz., his inheritance as he immediately explains by adding, *"You will restore my inheritance unto me."* Inheritance is called a cup, because as the cup at a feast, at least at the paschal feast, was divided among the guests, whence the expression of Lk. 22, *"Take and divide it between you;"* so an inheritance is divided between the sons of the same father. The same word inheritance is sometimes called, part or portion, as, *"The Lord is my part;"* in another place, *"The Lord is my portion;"* sometimes, *"The part of my inheritance;"* which does not mean that the Lord is a part of his inheritance, but that the Lord is the part that came to him by inheritance; so that inheritance and part of the inheritance mean the same: so, with regard to chalice and part of the chalice, which means the portion of the chalice that came to one upon a division. In very nice language he gives the children of the devil, to whom the Lord, in Jn. 8, said, *"You are from your father the devil,"* the inheritance belonging to him, namely, the horrible punishment designated by *"Fire, brimstone, and the spirit of winds."*

7. God, being strictly just in himself, must, of necessity, punish the wicked with great severity. *"For God is light, and there is no darkness in him; And hath loved justice,"* that is, good works in all those he created to his likeness, he repeats the same when he says, *"His countenance hath beheld righteousness;"* by righteousness is meant a declaration of justice. For the justice alluded to here is not the virtue that regulates the mutual dealings or intercourse of

man and man; but a universal justice, that embraces all virtues, the summary of which is the love of God and of the neighbor. *"For the end of the commandment is love."* 1 Tim. 1; and, *"Who loveth hath fulfilled the law."* Rom. 13. The expression, *"his countenance hath beheld righteousness,"* implies more than simply seeing; it means to see with a look of approbation, as the words in Ps. 1. *"The Lord knoweth the way of the just."* Thou hast loved justice and seen righteousness, mean the same thing.

PSALM 11

The prophet calls for God's help against the wicked.

1 Save me, O Lord, for there is now no saint: truths are decayed from among the children of men.
2 They have spoken vain things every one to his neighbour: with deceitful lips, and with a double heart have they spoken.
3 May the Lord destroy all deceitful lips, and the tongue that speaketh proud things.
4 Who have said: We will magnify our tongue; our lips are our own; who is Lord over us?
5 By reason of the misery of the needy, and the groans of the poor, now will I arise, saith the Lord. I will set him in safety; I will deal confidently in his regard.
6 The words of the Lord are pure words: as silver tried by the fire, purged from the earth refined seven times.
7 Thou, O Lord, wilt preserve us: and keep us from this generation for ever.
8 The wicked walk round about: according to thy highness, thou hast multiplied the children of men.

Explanation of the psalm

1. Save me, O Lord, from all dangers, for there is nobody else in whom I can confide; *"For there is now no saint;"* for there is scarce in the world to be found any one truly *"Pious and merciful,"* (for such is the real meaning of the Hebrew word,) and not merciful only, but truthful. For *"truths are decayed among the children of men;"* that is, scarce one can be found to speak the simple truth.

2. He proves that *"there is now no saint;"* that is, *"No pious and merciful man;"* since men in general, instead of speaking in a good and useful manner to their neighbor, *"Speak vain things"* only; things that cannot rescue them from dangers, whence they speak in vain.

He also proves that truth has failed since *"deceitful lips,"* that is, the lips of man, *"Have spoken with a double heart,"* saying one thing, and doing another; and thus seeking to deceive.

3. An imprecation, but in the spirit of prophecy. By way of imprecation, he predicts that it will come to pass, that all who seek to deceive, will be deceived themselves; and while they imagine they are profiting much by their dishonesty, will lose everything, and themselves along with it, for all eternity. *"The tongue that speaketh proud things;"* he that boasts of his frauds and deceits, as appears from the following verse.

4. He explains the connection, *"The tongue that speaketh proud things,"* and *"the deceitful lips:"* inasmuch as all deceitful people confide mostly in their tongue, so as to imagine they want nothing else, nor should they be subject in any way to the Lord. *"We will magnify our tongue;"* when we make it boast of all its frauds in procuring for us the happiness we enjoy: *"Our lips are our own,"* a very ambiguous phrase in the Latin text, but very clear in the Hebrew and Greek; and the meaning is, our lips are with us; that is, prove for us, stand up for us. The prophet proceeds to explain the confidence the wicked place in their lips, as if they were the most powerful weapon they could use against others; and, therefore, he makes them add, *"Who is Lord over us?"* As if they said, we acknowledge no superior, when through our tongue we hold all in subjection.

5. Having taught that confidence was not to be put in man, he now teaches that confidence is to be placed in God, whose promises are most faithful; by a figure of speech, making God himself speak and promise his assistance to the humble, and to the afflicted. *"By reason of the misery of the needy,"* who groan under the deceits and the oppressions of the wicked, I will not defer helping them, but *"now will I arise,"* as if from sleep, and will stand by them. *"I will set him in safety: I will deal confidently in his regard."* He explains what he will do upon rising: *"I will set him in safety;"* I will place them in safety, I will so establish them in safety, that they must forever be safe. *"I will deal confidently in his regard,"* that is, no one shall prevent, I will act boldly and freely in the matter. The Greek word implies confidence, freedom, and boldness.

6. The prophet now teaches that the foregoing promises are not like the promises of deceitful man, but most certain and true. *"The words of the Lord are pure words;"* that is, pure, chaste, and, as the Hebrew implies, not dyed, or counterfeit, but sincere and trustworthy, as *"Silver tried by the fire;"* that is, like the purest silver in sound, weight, and color, such as *"Silver tried in the fire,"* and not only in the fire, *"But purged from the earth;"* that is, approved of by the most versed in the trade of gold and silver; and finally, not once, *"But seven times refined."* In the Hebrew, the expression, *"Purged from the earth,"* is very obscure.

7. He infers from the preceding, that God will fulfill his promises. You, our Redeemer and Lord, will guard us, for the Greek, as well as the Hebrew word, implies, not only salvation, but, furthermore, an extension of it in guarding and preserving.

8. As if one asked, what will become of the wicked, while you protect us? He replies, *"The wicked will walk round about,"* (while we are quietly reposing under your wings,) constantly running after the things of this world, yet never coming at the enjoyment of their desires; and they will be forever thus *"Walking round about,"* while the world lasts, because, *"According to thy highness, thou hast multiplied the children of men,"* and *"the number of fools is infinite,"* and in such a multitude there must be forever an immense number of those *"Walking round about,"* straying from God.

PSALM 12

A prayer in tribulation.

1 How long, O Lord, wilt thou forget me unto the end? how long dost thou turn away thy face from me?
2 How long shall I take counsels in my soul, sorrow in my heart all the day?
3 How long shall my enemy be exalted over me?
4 Consider, and hear me, O Lord my God. Enlighten my eyes that I never sleep in death:
5 Lest at any time my enemy say: I have prevailed against him. They that trouble me will rejoice when I am moved:
6 But I have trusted in thy mercy. My heart shall rejoice in thy salvation: I will sing to the Lord, who giveth me good things: yea I will sing to the name of the Lord the most high.

Explanation of the psalm

1. When the sinful desires are very powerful, God seems to forget and to desert the soul; when the understanding is obscured by darkness, he seems to turn from the soul. He, being the light, illuminates, when he shows his face, and leaves all in darkness when he turns it away. The man under temptation then exclaims, in reference to the first, *"how long, O Lord, wilt thou forget me unto the end?"* And in reference to the second, *"How long dost thou turn away thy face from me?"*

2. Inverting the order, he complains, first, of the darkness he is wrapt in; secondly, of the sinful desires he is unwillingly subject to. In consequence of the obscurity of my understanding, *"How long shall I take counsels in my soul?"* That is to say, devise various plans to deliver myself from the evil; and, again, looking at these wicked desires that infest my heart, *"How long shall I have sorrow in my heart all the day?"* How long shall I have sorrow and grieve, for fear I may have offended God; and do so daily, that is, the whole day, without intermission.

3. Both evils are here comprehended. For the *"Enemy is then exalted"* over man, when he oppresses him, both by the suggestion of sinful thoughts, which he cannot banish; and by involving him in darkness he cannot dissipate; and thus, as if he were suffering grievously, he cries to God, *"How long shall my enemy be exalted over me?"*

4. He next invokes the divine assistance against both evils. *"Consider,"* that is, turn your face, *"and hear me,"* that is, don't forget, don't desert, help me; I entreat you, *"Enlighten my eyes."* The same prayer more clearly expressed and repeated, *"Enlighten:"* banish the darkness of my mind, by turning to, and regarding me, *"That I may never sleep in death:"* that by consenting to my evil desires, my soul may not be lost. The death of the soul or body is not uncommonly called sleep in the Scriptures, because God can as easily wake one from either, as we can wake the sleeping. The words that *"I may never sleep,"* signify that man, when he yields to temptation, sleeps as it were, and feels no further torment from the temptation: but as rest of that sort, so far from being wholesome, is fatal, the words *"In death"* are appended. Man, then, may be freed from temptation in two ways, either by banishing the tempter, through the grace of God; or by indulging his passions, by consenting to the sin: he prays here to be freed in the first manner, for fear, to his serious cost, he may be freed in the second manner; that is, by sleeping in the consent to sin, and he gives a reason for desiring to be freed from temptation in the next verse.

5. The devil certainly would exult on having conquered a servant of God, a thing that would tend to lessen God's glory. A reason assigned for his praying, *"Lest at any time my enemy say: I have prevailed against him."* For *"They that trouble me will rejoice when I am moved;"* that is, they will do so, not only on my entire prostration, but even on my appearing to be slightly shaken; for, as *"there is joy in heaven, for one sinner that does penance, more than for ninety nine just that do not need penance;"* so the evil spirits more exult in even the approach to sin of one perfect man, than they would in the reveling of confirmed sinners in the most grievous sins. Hence it would appear that David, in writing this Psalm, had merely in view the delivery of the just man from the temptation of the devil; and not, as some would have it, his own delivery from Saul's persecution. During that persecution, he was daily obliged to move about, in which case the words, *"They will rejoice when I am moved,"* as if he considered it of great importance not to move, would be quite inapplicable.

6. Another reason why the just man should be helped by God, because, *"trusting in his mercy,"* and not relying on his own strength, he resisted the tempter. The last reason he assigns for moving God to help him, is a promise that when freed from the temptation, he will not prove ungrateful to his liberator, but will thank God for the benefit, in heart, words, and deeds. *"My heart shall rejoice in thy salvation."* My heart shall bound with joy, on attaining salvation, attributing the whole to you, and praising you for it. The mouth will do its duty, for, *"I will sing to the Lord, who giveth me good things."* Deeds are comprehended in the expression, *"I will sing;"* for the word sing properly means in the Hebrew, to strike the harp. Hence the Scripture says, *"David sang with his hands,"* 1 Kings 18, and in Psalm 144:9, *"With a psaltry of ten strings will I sing unto thee."* He therefore promises, that he will exult in his heart, will sing with his mouth and strike the harp with his hands, that his entire body and soul may be engaged in celebrating God's praises. *"I will sing to the name"* means, to chant the praises of God.

PSALM 13

The general corruption of man before our redemption by Christ.

1 The fool hath said in his heart: There is no God, They are corrupt, and are become abominable in their ways: there is none that doth good, no not one.

2 The Lord hath looked down from heaven upon the children of men, to see if there be any that understand and seek God.

3 They are all gone aside, they are become unprofitable together: there is none that doth good, no not one. Their throat is an open sepulchre: with their tongues they acted deceitfully; the poison of asps is under their lips. Their mouth is full of cursing and bitterness; their feet are swift to shed blood. Destruction and unhappiness in their ways: and the way of peace they have not known: there is no fear of God before their eyes.

4 Shall not all they know that work iniquity, who devour my people as they eat bread?

5 They have not called upon the Lord: there have they trembled for fear, where there was no fear.

6 For the Lord is in the just generation: you have confounded the counsel of the poor man, but the Lord is his hope.

7 Who shall give out of Sion the salvation of Israel? when the Lord shall have turned away the captivity of his people, Jacob shall rejoice and Israel shall be glad.

EXPLANATION OF THE PSALM

1. To such a pitch of folly has human nature, corrupted in our first parent, arrived, that one can be found, without daring to express it, yet to *"say in his heart there is no God."* David does not convey here, that one particular person said so, but that men in general, through the corruption of their intellect, had come to such a pitch of blindness, as to become entirely regardless of their last end, and to think there was no God who regarded mankind, or to whom they would be accountable. *"The fool,"* that is, the man bereft of all sense, *"said in his heart, There is no God;"* that is, began to think God had no existence, and not only was the mind become corrupt and foolish, but also, so was the will; so that men, in general, leaned to sin, never to good; for the avoiding of sin, and the doing good, are very different things, when we speak of an act absolutely and perfectly good. For men without faith or grace, acting on the strength of corrupt nature alone, generally fall into sin; yet sometimes produce certain moral good works, which cannot be called sin; yet are not perfectly and absolutely good, when they do not bring man to the chief good. David, therefore, says, *"They are corrupt and become abominable in their ways;"* that is, in their desires or affections: hence themselves are corrupted and abominable. *"There is none that doeth good; no not one."* Mankind is so corrupted in desire and in iniquity, but still not so generally that all their desires and actions should be considered corrupt and unjust. For surely when an infidel, moved by compassion, has mercy on the poor or cares their children, he doeth no evil. But nobody depending on the strength of corrupt nature alone, can perfectly and absolutely produce a good action. Hence, we see, that this passage, when properly understood, proves nothing for the heretics who abuse it, to prove that all the acts of a sinner, or of a nonregenerated, are sins.

2-3. Having said that human nature was corrupt in mind and in will, he shows now whence he had such knowledge: namely, from revelation. For God, who knows everything, saw it, and revealed it to his prophets. He describes God looking down from heaven, as if he were a mortal from his lofty look out, to see *"If there be any that understood;"* that is, not corrupted in his mind; *"Or seeking God;"* that is, not corrupted in his will, who could understand and love, and thus seek God, who is the supreme good. What God knew, that is, made us know, he explains in those words: *"They are all gone aside;"* that is, he saw they had all become useless to God, inasmuch as they neither serve, worship, nor render him any tribute of praise; and, finally, that he saw none to do a work perfectly and absolutely good. *"Their throat is an open sepulchre."* The remainder of this verse is not in the Hebrew, nor in the Septuagint, nor in the Latin edition of Psalm 52, where the same passage occurs; but, whereas St. Paul, in Romans 3, quotes all these expressions consecutively, as if they belonged to one Psalm, we may consider they did originally belong to it, and were accidentally lost or omitted from it. These verses give us an idea of the malice of the wicked, who by word and deed do harm to their neighbor. *"Their throat is an open sepulchre."* For, as the stench of the putrid corpse exhales from an opened tomb, so from their mouth issues filthy language, the exhalation of their corrupted heart. *"With their tongues they acted deceitfully:"* that is, by making use, not only of filthy but deceitful language. *"The poison of asps is under their lips;"* which words are not only filthy and deceitful, but, furthermore, poisonous, and deadly, and leading to sin. *"Their mouth is full of cursing and bitterness; their feet are swift to shed blood."* Those abandoned characters not only rail and fiercely contend in language; but are involved in evil action, and injure every one. For they whose mouths are full of maledictions and railing, are always ready to run swiftly to slaughter and bloodshed. *"Destruction and unhappiness in their ways and the way of peace they have not known:"* that is, all their thoughts turn upon destruction, devastation, and affliction, of the neighbor, because *"The way of peace they have not known;"* that is, what belongs to peace. *"There is no fear of God before their eyes."* The root of all the aforesaid evils; because they clearly cast overboard all fear of God, saying in their hearts, *"There is no God."*

4. Here we can justly infer, that this universal corruption of human nature is to be understood of human nature in itself and depending on its own natural strength alone. For, through the grace of God, men become truly just and pious, and they are designated here as *"My people"* who are despised and persecuted by the wicked. *"Shall all they know that work iniquity;"* addressed to the wicked, by way of reproof, as if he said, will they be always insensible, will they ever open their eyes, will they ever begin to learn? *"Who devour my people as they eat bread;"* which means, that the wicked may, from such evils, be warned of their iniquity. For as bread, though eaten daily, is always relished; so the wicked take pleasure in daily harassing the poor, and never tire of it.

5. A reason assigned for such wickedness, namely: *"They have not called upon the Lord:"* they put their trust not in God, but in things created; and, therefore, *"There have they trembled for fear, where there was no fear;"* and, therefore, not knowing in whom to hope, or whom to fear, they trembled at encountering adversity, or going back in their prosperity; things of small moment, and transitory, which should have been above their consideration: whereas, had they put their trust in God, *"And sought the kingdom of God and his justice, all these things shall be added unto you."*

6. Another reason for the wicked being seized with fear, when there is no ground for fear, *"For the Lord is in the just generation;"* which means, as the wicked neither invoked nor trusted in God, he deserts them, and takes up with *"The just generation:"* and once deserted by God, the true light, truth itself they walk in darkness, and therefore fear when they have no cause for fear. He then appeals to the wicked themselves. *"You have confounded the counsel of the poor man, but the Lord is his hope."* Are you so blind as not only to abandon God yourselves, but even to mock those who have not? For you *"Have confounded;"* that is, derided, made the poor man blush, for

doing what you call a foolish thing, the putting his hope in God, whereas he entirely depends on him. For to the worldly it seems a foolish thing to put our trust in God whom we don't see; and not to trust in the riches of this world and other things we do see.

7. This last verse is a prayer to God for the speedy coming of the Savior, to deliver mankind from that captivity of the devil, in which all the wicked and perverse, whose sins and enormities he had just described, were bound. *"Who shall give out of Sion the salvation of Israel?"* That is, would that salvation to Israel should quickly come from Sion; *"For salvation is from the Jews;"* as the Lord said to the Samaritan woman, John 4; and not only from the Jews, that is, from the tribe of Juda, but from the family of David, whose city was named Sion. Salvation, therefore, or the promised Savior, was promised and expected from Sion, the city of David; that is, from the stock of David, who was to save Israel; that is, his people. Christ is called *"Savior of Israel his people;"* because, though in reality he came to save the whole world, he did not actually save beyond a certain number, who are called the people of God and spiritual Israel. *"When the Lord shall have turned away the captivity of his people, Jacob shall rejoice, and Israel shall be glad."* As much as to say, I beseech and pray for *"salvation from Sion;"* and, therefore, for the Savior *"to free us from captivity;"* because, when that shall be effected, then truly and perfectly, *"Jacob shall rejoice, and Israel shall be glad;"* that is, the people of God, who are spiritually called Jacob and Israel, for both names belong to one person. And that such promises, and similar ones, belong not exclusively to the carnal Jews, but to God's people, composed of Jews and gentiles, is clearly established by St. Paul, in his Epistle to the Romans.

PSALM 14

What kind of men shall dwell in the heavenly Sion.

1 Lord, who shall dwell in thy tabernacle? or who shall rest in thy holy hill?
2 He that walketh without blemish, and worketh justice:
3 He that speaketh truth in his heart, who hath not used deceit in his tongue: Nor hath done evil to his neighbour: nor taken up a reproach against his neighbours.
4 In his sight the malignant is brought to nothing: but he glorifieth them that fear the Lord. He that sweareth to his neighbour, and deceiveth not;
5 He that hath not put out his money to usury, nor taken bribes against the innocent: He that doth these things shall not be moved for ever.

Explanation of the psalm

1. The prophet, in alluding to Mount Sion and the tabernacle of God thereon, means the *"heavenly Jerusalem,"* and the tabernacle not made by human hands; for the prophets foretold the kingdom of heaven through such figures: St. Paul makes frequent mention of the *"celestial tabernacle,"* Hebrew 8 and 9; and in chap. 12, Mount Sion is called *"The city of the living God;"* and St. John, in the Apocalypse, makes mention of *"the celestial Sion;"* and, in chap. 21, he says, *"Behold the tabernacle of God with man, and he will dwell with them."* The prophet then asks, *"Who is to dwell?"* That means, to have a fixed, certain residence, on the top of that lofty mount, from which, by reason of its out topping all others, there is no further ascent; for here on earth there can be no permanent residence nor real rest.

2. A most summary and comprehensive answer; as if he said, *"Who declineth from evil and doeth good?"* who does not offend God by the commission of a sin, or the omission of a duty? He who lives without committing a mortal sin *"walketh without blemish;"* and he who discharges all his obligations, not through fear of punishment, but from a sense of duty, is one *"that worketh justice."*

3. Coming now to particulars, he says, *"The man to dwell in the house of the Lord"* is he who doeth no evil in heart, mouth or action, *"Who speaketh truth in his heart."* For all who set more value than they ought on the things of this world, do not speak truth in their heart; and whoever consent to sin speak not truth in their heart, because they consider a matter will profit them, which rather injures. Thus, all the sins of the heart may be reduced to false judgment as their main root. Speaking of sins by the mouth, he says, *"Who hath not used deceit in his tongue;"* for detractions and flattery, and such sins, may be aptly styled *"deceits."* Such man not only did no evil himself, but did all in his way to prevent it in others, and thus committed no sin in his actions, *"nor taken up a reproach against his neighbor."* He has not listened to vituperation, detraction, stories or calumnies against his neighbor; and, instead of giving ear to the ill-disposed, has rather despised them; while, on the contrary, he has glorified, honored, and helped the good who fear God. Great praise is due to him who hates sin, not only in himself, but in others.

4. All this is explained above.

5. Having explained the virtues of a good man, in general, he now touches on one vice in particular, from which any one aspiring to be heir to the kingdom of heaven should be specially exempt, namely, avarice. His reason for touching on this vice in particular, is either because, according to Tim 1:6, *"It is the root of all evils,"* or because this vice always was and is still, peculiar to the Jews. Now, avarice turns up in contracts otherwise lawful, or in unlawful contracts, or in bribes. The first class come under *"He that sweareth to his neighbor, and deceiveth not."* The second class are designated by the expression, *"He that hath not put out his money to usury."* The third class, the worst of all, are they *"Who take bribes against the innocent."* *"He that doeth those things shall not be moved forever."* The question put in the first

verse is here answered. He says, that they who live according to what was just laid down will have an everlasting habitation in the kingdom of heaven. *"He that doeth,"* etc., will securely dwell in God's tabernacle, will rest in his holy mountain, without the slightest fear of ever being disturbed therein.

PSALM 15

Christ's future victory and triumph over the world, and death.

1 Preserve me, O Lord, for I have put trust in thee.
2 I have said to the Lord, thou art my God, for thou hast no need of my goods.
3 To the saints, who are in his land, he hath made wonderful all my desires in them.
4 Their infirmities were multiplied: afterwards they made haste. I will not gather together their meetings for blood offerings: nor will I be mindful of their names by my lips.
5 The Lord is the portion of my inheritance and of my cup: it is thou that wilt restore my inheritance to me.
6 The lines are fallen unto me in goodly places: for my inheritance is goodly to me.
7 I will bless the Lord, who hath given me understanding: moreover my reins also have corrected me even till night.
8 I set the Lord always in my sight: for he is at my right hand, that I be not moved.
9 Therefore my heart hath been glad, and my tongue hath rejoiced: moreover my flesh also shall rest in hope.
10 Because thou wilt not leave my soul in hell; nor wilt then give thy holy one to see corruption.
11 Thou hast made known to me the ways of life, thou shalt fill me with joy with thy countenance: at thy right hand are delights even to the end.

EXPLANATION OF THE PSALM

1. Which may be supposed to be said by Christ or by any sincere Christian; that is, guard, protect me from the impending trouble, for in thee alone, and in no created being, have I put my trust, which is evident from what follows: for,

2. I have confessed to the Lord, and said from my heart: *"Thou art my God,"* varying the expression from Lord, *"for thou hast no need of my goods,"* but I rather have need of thine; you, in nowise, depend on me, I entirely depend on you; you are, therefore, my only true and supreme Lord, and, therefore, in thee alone I hope and confide. These expressions proceed from the prophet in the person of Christ; at the time he was not only man, but liable to suffering and death.

3. *"As God has no need of my goods,"* I will seek to confer them on his elect, and of which friendly intentions God is witness, for *"He has made wonderful*

all my desires in them;" that is, all my benevolence and good will towards his saints and his elect. God is said to have made the benevolence of Christ to the elect wonderful, by declaring it both through the prophets, through the various figures of the Old Testament, as well as by the miracles of Christ and his apostles; and wonderful was Christ's love for his elect, when he laid down his life for them.

4. The effect of the benevolence of Christ towards his elect; they who, by reason of the grievous wounds of sin, so as to be unable to walk, when healed by the grace of God now began to run in the way of the commandments. *"Their infirmities are multiplied;"* that is, their spiritual infirmities and diseases; hence the apostle to the Romans, chap. 5, *"When we were as yet infirm, Christ suffered for us;"* and, in a few verses after, in explanation of the passage, he says: *"When we were sinners."* The Hebrew for *"infirmity"* is made by many translators to stand for *"idols;"* such is not its signification; it properly means infirmity accompanied with pain, and may be figuratively applied to idols; because idols are infirm and powerless, or because they make sinners of men, and thus infirm. *"Afterwards they made haste,"* which means the very weakest among them, made so by the multiplicity of their sins, but afterwards, restored by grace, became so strong *"as to exult in running their way."* Such was the case in the infancy of the Church, when the converts so hastened to the scaffold. *"I will not gather together their meetings for blood offerings;"* I do not approve of their *"meetings for blood offerings;"* and, therefore, I will not call them together, *"nor will I be mindful of their names by my lips;"* I will not only refuse to call such meetings together, but I will not even speak or make mention of such meetings. The connection between this latter part and the beginning of the verse now appears, for he assigns a reason why the elect, after having fallen into a number of sins, and especially idolatry, made such haste *"in running in the way of the Lord;"* because, in consequence of their having the most thorough abhorrence of idols and of their worship, so much so, as not to allow their name even to be mentioned; he therefore cleansed the elect in Christ from the sin of idolatry, and thus made them saints, *"To run in the way of his commandments."*

5. Having declared his detestation of idols and of sin, he adds his reason for so doing: because he places all his happiness in God alone. An expression most becoming the Redeemer who, entirely *"separated from sinners,"* and in thorough union with God the Father, places all his happiness in him. A thing we, too, as far as we are able, are bound to. *"The Lord is the portion of my inheritance;"* that is, the portion which came to me by inheritance, my whole, my all, my everything; *"and of my cup;"* a repetition of the idea, for the word *"cup,"* from being divided among the guests, is often made to signify the inheritance which is divided among the children. If you will,

"inheritance" may signify substantial wealth, or valuables, and *"cup,"* delicacies; when the meaning would be, that all my substantial and refined pleasures are fixed in God alone; *"it is thou that wilt restore my inheritance to me."* These words are supposed to have been used by Christ, while yet a mortal, before he had got full possession of his inheritance. When we use them, we hold all happiness in God in desire, but not yet in actual possession. That possession is in God's keeping, and he will hand it over to us on the last day, as he did to Christ on the day of his resurrection. St. Paul alludes to this when he says, *"For I know whom I have believed; and I am certain that he is able to keep that which I have committed to him, against that day."*

6. By a simile drawn from an inheritance in this world, he declares the superiority of that in eternity, for those who seek God and his glory. When an inheritance was divided among a family, the fields were measured with lines, and divided, and lots were cast for the several divisions; and the lines were said to fall in goodly places, when the best part of the land was had by lot. The meaning then is, I have obtained the best part of the inheritance by a most fortunate cast or lot, *"for my inheritance is goodly to me;"* a mere repetition of the same. He alludes to the division by lot; that he may remind us that the principle of the inheritance comes from predestination, and predestination in our regard is a sort of lot; whence St. Paul, Ephes. 1:11, says, *"In whom we are also called by lot;"* and Coloss. 1:12, *"To be partakers of the lot of the saints."*

7. Thanks to God for having inspired him with the thought, and inflamed him with the desire of choosing so valuable an inheritance. *"I will bless the Lord."* I will praise him, the author of such a blessing, *"who hath given me understanding,"* who makes me know, and prudently choose the inheritance; *"moreover my reins also have corrected me even till night."* Reins or loins, in the Scriptures signify affections, or desires; whence the expression, *"Searching the heart and reins;"* and, *"prove my heart and my reins;"* the heart signifying the thoughts; the reins, the affections: *"night"* means the time of tribulation; and day, that of prosperity: the expression *"correct me,"* would be more properly translated by the word *"instructed."* Thus the sense will be: not only in prosperity, but in adversity, my whole affections, inflamed to love God, instructed me in a most urgent manner to bear my sufferings patiently, hoping for the best always from Almighty God.

8. From the intelligent and affectionate manner in which he praised God, in the preceding verse, it is quite clear God must have been always before his eyes, for the soul is more where it loves, than where it animates. *"For he is at my right hand, that I be not moved;"* nor was I deceived in having God always before my eyes; that is, the eyes of my heart; for he is really always on my right hand, as if he were protecting my side, and preceding me, like

a brave auxiliary; that I may not be disturbed from my path, but persist and persevere to the very end.

9. He now tells what that *"great inheritance"* is that God is *"to restore"* to him and to others, who have chosen God. *"Therefore,"* because the *"Lord is on my right hand,"* a most faithful helper and protector, *"my heart hath been glad,"* with that true and solid joy of which our Lord speaks in the gospel, when he says, *"Your heart shall rejoice, and nobody shall take your joy from you." "And my tongue hath rejoiced,"* because eternal joy is wont to show itself externally; moreover my flesh also shall rest in hope;" that is, my soul shall rejoice, and my flesh shall sleep in secure and placid death, being in certain expectation of a very speedy resurrection.

10. This is explained by the apostles Peter and Paul, Acts 2 and 13; and though, strictly speaking; it applies to Christ alone, whose soul was not left in hell, meaning the limbo of the holy fathers; nor did his body in the sepulchre undergo any putrefaction, yet we can all apply it to ourselves, inasmuch as we are members of Christ, and through him, as the apostle has it, *"God has raised us up together,"* 2 Ephes.; and because our souls will not be left in hell, meaning purgatory, nor will our flesh see corruption.

11. The complete promise of the inheritance is here explained. *"Thou hast made known to me the ways of life;"* you have *"taught me the way"* of returning to life from death. A most beautiful metaphor, by which the mode of resurrection is called a way unknown up to that time, because nobody to that time, with the exception of Christ, had truly risen. And he adds, you have not only taught me the way of rising from the dead, but *"Thou wilt fill me with joy with thy countenance;"* making me glorious, immortal, and happy, by showing me your countenance; because, from the beatific vision, in which consists essential happiness, glory even redounds on the body, which glory was the only one that Christ had not always; for his soul had such glory from the time of his conception, *"at thy right hand are delights even to the end."* Not content with conferring glory on me, you will place me on your right hand in heaven, where the glory will be everlasting. All which apply to the elect too, in a certain sense; to whom God shows the road to life when he teaches them that the observance of his law is the way to the kingdom of heaven. *"He fills the elect too, with joy,"* when he shows himself to them, *"face to face;"* when, *with his right hand he offers them* "delights even unto the end;" when he places them on his right hand, and with his right hand fills them, as if from an inexhaustible fountain, with delights interminable. We may here note the incredible rashness of Theodore Bera, *"You will not leave my soul in hell;" "You will not leave my body in the grave."* If this be not a corruption of the sacred text, we have none. I have demonstrated most clearly in the *"Controversies,"* that the words in this passage and in Acts 2, signify, both in the Hebrew and in the Greek, not *"corpse"* and *"grave,"* but *"soul"* and *"hell,"* and can signify nothing else.

PSALM 16

A just man's prayer in tribulation against the malice of his enemies.

1 Hear, O Lord, my justice: attend to my supplication. Give ear unto my prayer, which proceedeth not from deceitful lips.
2 Let my judgment come forth from thy countenance: let thy eyes behold the things that are equitable.
3 Thou hast proved my heart, and visited it by night, thou hast tried me by fire: and iniquity hath not been found in me.
4 That my mouth may not speak the works of men: for the sake of the words of thy lips, I have kept hard ways.
5 Perfect thou my goings in thy paths: that my footsteps be not moved.
6 I have cried to thee, for thou, O God, hast heard me: O incline thy ear unto me, and hear my words.
7 Show forth thy wonderful mercies; thou who savest them that trust in thee.
8 From them that resist thy right hand keep me, as the apple of thy eye. Protect me under the shadow of thy wings.
9 From the face of the wicked who have afflicted me. My enemies have surrounded my soul:
10 They have shut up their fat: their mouth hath spoken proudly.
11 They have cast me forth and now they have surrounded me: they have set their eyes bowing down to the earth.
12 They have taken me, as a lion prepared for the prey; and as a young lion dwelling in secret places.
13 Arise, O Lord, disappoint him and supplant him; deliver my soul from the wicked one: thy sword
14 From the enemies of thy hand. O Lord, divide them from the few of the earth in their life: their belly is filled from thy hidden stores. They are full of children: and they have left to their little ones the rest of their substance.
15 But as for me, I will appear before thy sight in justice: I shall be satisfied when thy glory shall appear.

Explanation of the psalm

1. He first prays that his just cause may be heard, for with a just judge, the cause is more regarded than the person; he asks then that his prayer may be attended to; for God not only loves justice, but also the just; and, as St. James has it, *"The prayer of the just availeth much."* He finally unites both justice and prayer, when he says, *"Give ear unto my prayer which proceedeth not from deceitful lips;"* that is, my prayer that does not proceed from deceitful lips, but is based on justice. The meaning then is, Lord, may justice move thee; may prayer, the prayer of the just, move thee.

2. Another argument from the justice of God, as if he said: To you, O God, I appeal; by you, as being the most just of judges, I wished to be judged. *"From thy countenance;"* that is, from thy mouth let judgment proceed—my sentence be pronounced. *"Let thy eyes behold the things that are equitable."* Close not thy eyes, and cloak not the calumnies of the wicked, but open them and see what justice demands.

3. A reason assigned for wishing to be judged by God, for he alone searches the hearts, and thoroughly knows the innocence of his servants. *"Thou hast proved my heart;"* you have tried me where no one else can, interiorly; you have proved my sincerity, and he tells how *"Thou hast visited it by night."* On two occasions one's interior may be seen; when an opportunity offers for sinning in private, and in the time of tribulation: for there are many wicked persons, to all appearance with a fair exterior, when they have an opportunity of committing sin in private, without any fear of detection, then only show what they are made of. So in the time of prosperity, the bad cannot be distinguished from the good, but apply the fire of persecution, and the gold shines out, the stubble burns. The first is expressed by the words, *"Visited it by night;"* that is, in secret, when an opportunity for committing sin presented itself; the second comes under the words, *"Thou hast tried me by fire;"* that is, with grievous tribulations; and yet thou hast found no iniquity in me.

4. He shows how it happened that *"There was no iniquity found in him,"* from the fact of his having kept to *"The hard ways"* of justice; not for any earthly hope or reason, but because such was agreeable to God's commands. For those who observe God's commandments from human motives do so exteriorly, when they are likely to be observed, and thus the latent iniquity is detected in them; but they who observe the commandments, in order to please God, keep them externally and internally, and thus no iniquity is detected in such persons. He therefore says: *"I have kept hard ways;"* that is, I have kept to the road of justice, however rough and rugged, nor has tribulation of any sort caused me to go out of it. *"For the sake of the words of thy lips,"* influenced thereto by your commandments, your threats, and your promises, *"That my mouth may not speak the works of men:"* that I may not be obliged to ask the help of man; that I may not put my hope in man; *"Nor speak* (meaning praise) *the works of men."*

5. Acknowledging that it was not by his own strength, but by the grace of God, that he remained in the narrow path of justice, he asks God to confirm the favor. *"Perfect thou my goings in thy paths: that my footsteps be not*

moved:" strengthen and make sure my footsteps in this your path, for fear, if deprived of thy help, I may stray from it.

6. Having explained the arguments derived from his own innocence, and from the justice of God, he again repeats the prayer in the beginning of the Psalm. Lord, to thee *"I have cried, for thou hast heard me."* I have cried with confidence to thee, for on all occasions you have heard me, and now too, with your usual benignity, *"Incline your ear to me, and hear my words."*

7. A third argument derived from God's mercy. I have proved my innocence; have appealed to your justice. I now invoke your mercy, for, however innocent I may consider myself of the crimes for which I am suffering, I may have many other sins for which I may be justly punished. *"Show forth thy wonderful mercies"* then. Astonish every one at the extent of them in delivering me, for to you it belongs to deliver all who put their trust in thee.

8. Protect me, as you would *"The apple of your eye,"* with the greatest care, from those *"that resist thy right hand:"* in injuring those whom you protect, or who refuse to walk where you lead. This does not contradict the passage in the book of Esther, *"There is no one who can resist thy will."* For the will spoken of there, is the will of his good pleasure which is always carried out; but here is meant the will of his expression, which is not always carried out, for God permits the wicked to do many things opposed to his expressed will; that is, against his law, and afterwards punishes them according to their merits. *"The apple of your eye,"* a most delicate, though valuable article, requiring the greatest care, and, therefore, provided by nature with various coverings, as well as with brows and eye lashes; such are we, frail and delicate, and such is the care we stand in need of. *"Protect me under the shadow of thy wings."* The same petition, under another figure. As the chickens are covered by the wings of the hen, are hidden, and lie securely under them, so that the birds of prey cannot hurt them; the just man prays to be so protected from his persecutors.

9. *"The face of the wicked,"* signifies the sight of the wicked; as the wings of the hen cover the chickens, and prevent their being seen by the birds of prey; or it may mean the bite or the anger of the wicked, for their teeth, as well as their anger, are displayed in the faces. *"Who have afflicted me,"* means that the just man, having been so often and so severely bitten by the wicked, appeals to God's protection, for fear of being entirely destroyed under the repeated biting. Such similes are of frequent occurrence in the Holy Scripture. *"I will rejoice under the cover of thy wings,"* Psalm 62; *"He will overshadow thee with his shoulders: and under his wings thou shalt trust,"* Psalm 90; and the Lord himself, in Mt. 23, *"How often would I have gathered together thy children, as the hen gathereth her chickens under her wings, and thou would not."* *"My enemies have surrounded my soul."* The last argument drawn from

the malice of his enemies. They have surrounded, pressed in upon me on every side.

10. That is, they have no mercy, though they see me reduced to the last extremities. *"Shut up their fat"* is synonymous with, *"Closing his bowels;"* that is, having no mercy, according to 1 Jn. 3, *"He that hath the substance of this world, and shall see his brother in need, and shall shut up his bowels from him: how doth the charity of God abide in him?"* As fat increases, the bowels generally close; and the prophet chose the former expression, that he may not only declare the fact, but the cause of the bowels being closed, namely, the increase of the fat, which means, the wealth of this world, which causes man to be proud, to despise his neighbor, and thus spiritually *"Shut up his bowels."*

11. In order to show the malice of his enemies, he goes on to show how they assail him, now in one way, presently in quite a different manner, yet always in a destructive manner. One time *"They cast me forth;"* Now *"they surround me:"* those who just banished me from sharing or enjoying anything with them now seek me, surround me that they may overwhelm me with injuries; and the reason is, because *"they have set their eyes bowing down to the earth;"* meaning they have firmly resolved not to look up to God, who is in heaven, nor to fear him; but to look down on the earth alone and seek for the things that belong to it.

12. They have not only surrounded me, but treated me with the greatest cruelty; with the same cruelty and avidity that a lion pounces on its prey, *"and as a young lion dwelling in secret places;"* the same idea repeated.

13. Having explained the malice of his enemies, he asks of God, who alone can do it, to come and free him. *"Arise, O Lord;"* do not defer your help any longer, *"disappoint him;"* that wicked man, who like a lion laid hold on me to devour me, disappoint his teeth, that he may not fasten them in me and kill me. And, in fact, it is God alone that can *"disappoint"* the action of any one or thing, however violent; as he disappointed the teeth of the lions from hurting; Daniel, and the fury of the fire from consuming the three thrown into the furnace; a source of consolation to the just, who know God's power to be equal to protect them from either the teeth of the lion or the flames of the furnace. *"Supplant him."* Deceive him; make him, by thy wonderful providence, suppose that when he is fastening his teeth in his own flesh, he is fastening them in the flesh of the just. *"Deliver my soul from the wicked."* Do not allow me to be killed by the wicked, raging like a roaring lion; but save me, protect me. *"Thy sword;"* some connect it with the preceding; others make it the beginning of the next sentence. If we adopt the reading of the Vulgate, the meaning is, deliver my soul from the wicked; to do which you must take *"thy sword"* from your enemies; meaning their power of harm.

14. A prophetic imprecation, in which is predicted separation of the wicked from the just, the former obtaining the goods of this world, the latter those of the world to come. *"Divide them from the few;"* separate the crowd of the wicked from *"your little flock," "in their life,"* not only in the world to come, which is sure to them, but even in the present, which may be properly called *"their life,"* which alone they love and seek, separating themselves from the just, who are dead to the world. The separation consists herein, that *"their belly is filled from thy hidden stores;"* that is, they fill their belly with the fruits and good things of the earth, supplied by God's bounty, from his hidden treasures every succeeding year, and say it is their own portion. *"They are full of children: and they have left to their little ones the rest of their substance."* They abound in children, to whom they leave the residue of what themselves cannot consume, for the children of this world look upon it as supreme happiness to abound in riches, and to be blessed with heirs to enjoy them.

15. The difference herein consists, they covet an abundance of the good things of this world. *"But I,"* as well as the rest of the just, will *"hunger after justice"* here, to have satiety of glory and happiness hereafter; and, as I study to live in justice, in thy sight here, your glory will appear to me hereafter; and then will I be truly satisfied, having no more to seek or to desire.

PSALM 17

David's thanks to God for his delivery from all his enemies.

1 I will love thee, O Lord, my strength:
2 The Lord is my firmament, my refuge, and my deliverer. My God is my helper, and in him will I put my trust. My protector and the horn of my salvation, and my support.
3 Praising I will call upon the Lord: and I shall be saved from my enemies.
4 The sorrows of death surrounded me: and the torrents of iniquity troubled me.
5 The sorrows of hell encompassed me: and the snares of death prevented me.
6 In my affliction I called upon the Lord, and I cried to my God: And he heard my voice from his holy temple: and my cry before him came into his ears.
7 The earth shook and trembled: the foundations of the mountains were troubled and were moved, because he was angry with them.
8 There went up a smoke in his wrath: and a fire flamed from his face: coals were kindled by it.
9 He bowed the heavens, and came down: and darkness was under his feet.
10 And he ascended upon the cherubim, and he flew; he flew upon the wings of the winds.
11 And he made darkness his covert, his pavilion round about him: dark waters in the clouds of the air.

12 At the brightness that was before him the clouds passed, hail and coals of fire.
13 And the Lord thundered from heaven, and the highest gave his voice: hail and coals of fire.
14 And he sent forth his arrows, and he scattered them: he multiplied lightnings, and troubled them.
15 Then the fountains of waters appeared, and the foundations of the world were discovered: At thy rebuke, O Lord, at the blast of the spirit of thy wrath.
16 He sent from on high, and took me: and received me out of many waters.
17 He delivered me from my strongest enemies, and from them that hated me: for they were too strong for me.
18 They prevented me in the day of my affliction: and the Lord became my protector.
19 And he brought me forth into a large place: he saved me, because he was well pleased with me.
20 And the Lord will reward me according to my justice; and will repay me according to the cleanness of my hands:
21 Because I have kept the ways of the Lord; and have not done wickedly against my God.
22 For till his judgments are in my sight: and his justices I have not put away from me.
23 And I shall be spotless with him: and shall keep myself from my iniquity.
24 And the Lord will reward me according to my justice; and according to the cleanness of my hands before his eyes.
25 With the holy, thou wilt be holy; and with the innocent man thou wilt be innocent.
26 And with the elect thou wilt be elect: and with the perverse thou wilt be perverted.
27 For thou wilt save the humble people; but wilt bring down the eyes of the proud.
28 For thou lightest my lamp, O Lord: O my God enlighten my darkness.
29 For by thee I shall be delivered from temptation; and through my God I shall go over a wall.
30 As for my God, his way is undefiled: the words of the Lord are fire tried: he is the protector of all that trust in him.
31 For who is God but the Lord? or who is God but our God?
32 God who hath girt me with strength; and made my way blameless.
33 Who hath made my feet like the feet of harts: and who setteth me upon high places.
34 Who teacheth my hands to war: and thou hast made my arms like a brazen bow.
35 And thou hast given me the protection of thy salvation: and thy right hand

hath held me up: And thy discipline hath corrected me unto the end: and thy discipline, the same shall teach me.

36 *Thou hast enlarged my steps under me; and my feet are not weakened.*

37 *I will pursue after my enemies, and overtake them: and I will not turn again till they are consumed.*

38 *I will break them, and they shall not be able to stand: they shall fall under my feet.*

39 *And thou hast girded me with strength unto battle; and hast subdued under me them that rose up against me.*

40 *And thou hast made my enemies turn their back upon me, and hast destroyed them that hated me.*

41 *They cried, but there was none to save them, to the Lord: but he heard them not.*

42 *And I shall beat them as small as the dust before the wind; I shall bring them to nought, like the dirt in the streets.*

43 *Thou wilt deliver me from the contradictions of the people: thou wilt make me head of the Gentiles.*

44 *A people, which I knew not, hath served me: at the hearing of the ear they have obeyed me.*

45 *The children that are strangers have lied to me, strange children have faded away, and have halted from their paths.*

46 *The Lord liveth, and blessed be my God, and let the God of my salvation be exalted:*

47 *God, who avengest me, and subduest the people under me, my deliverer from my enemies.*

48 *And thou wilt lift me up above them that rise up against me: from the unjust man thou wilt deliver me.*

49 *Therefore will I give glory to thee, O Lord, among the nations, and I will sing a psalm to thy name.*

50 *Giving great deliverance to his king, and shewing mercy to David his anointed: and to his seed for ever.*

EXPLANATION OF THE PSALM

1-2. What he expressed in one word, *"my strength,"* he now explains by several words, *"my firmament, my refuge, my deliverer:"* as if he said, I may justly call him my strength, when he is all the above names to me. When I lie down, he is my firmament; when I am in danger, he is my refuge; should I fall into the hands of the enemy, he will deliver me; and thus, in every respect, he is my strength and my courage. *"My God is my helper, and in him will I put my trust: my protector and the horn of my salvation;"* In the height of his affection to God, he repeats the epithets he used in the preceding verse, *"my helper, my protector, and the horn of my salvation;"* which correspond to *"my firmament, my refuge, and my deliverer."* His *"helper,"* because he keeps him upright, prevents him from falling, (rock being the derivation of the word in Hebrew,) according to Psalm 39, *"He has put my feet on a rock;"* and he therefore most properly adds, *"in him will I put my trust"* as being the surest of all foundations. *"My protector,"* in the Hebrew, *"my shield,"* to protect him from his enemies: *"the horn of my salvation:"* a most familiar expression in the Scriptures, to signify the power or means of salvation; being a metaphor, taken from horned animals, who use their horns for protection; thus, in Psalm 131, *"I will bring forth a horn to David."* I will make David all powerful to conquer his enemies; like a rampant bull, with his horns full grown, and not like a sluggish calf, that has not yet got them. Ezech. 39. *"In that day a horn shall bud forth to the house of Israel."* Micheas 1:4, *"I will make thy horn iron."* Lk. 1, *"He hath raised up a horn of salvation to us."* God, then, is called a *"horn of safety"* to David, and to all the just, because through him they are powerfully armed against their enemies, by putting their strength not in themselves, but in the Divine help and assistance; in the spirit of the apostle, *"I can do all things in him who strengtheneth me."* The expression, *"horn of safety,"* corresponds with, *"and any deliverer,"* for God delivers us through the *"horn of safety:"* that is, through his own saving power. Finally, the word, *"my support,"* comprises all the rest, and corresponds to *"my strength:"* for whosoever God supports, he frees, protects, and confirms.

3. A conclusion from the preceding. I will, therefore, constantly praise God for so many benefits received; and in my difficulties, with unbounded confidence, will I apply to him, certain of being delivered from all manner of enemies.

4-5. He now enters, in detail, on God's favors to him. He was in manifest danger of death, when Saul was lying in wait for him, to kill him, which danger he describes in various metaphors. *"The sorrows of death surrounded me."* I was surrounded by so many dangers, that I despaired of my corporal safety; and, therefore, depressed with the grief and trouble of mind, incident to those whose death is at hand; *"and the torrents of iniquity troubled me:"* The grief and trouble above named, from the number, that like a torrent invaded and *"troubled me,"* after the manner of those who are hurried down, and whirled about by a roaring torrent. *"The sorrows of hell encompassed me,"* a repetition of the first part of the preceding verse, with the substitution of *"hell"* for *"death."* They are, however, synonymous, for before the death of Christ, all went to hell, though not the same part of it; and, therefore, death and hell meant the same; the sorrows of hell, then, mean such sorrow as those usually suffer who are about to depart from this world to the next; *"and the snares of death prevented me:"* a repetition of *"the torrents of iniquity troubled me."* For, as David was troubled with the *"sorrows of death,"* by reason of the multitude of wicked ones rising up against him, so *"the snares of death"* that *"prevented"* [encompassed] him, was the cause of the pains of hell to him. By the *"snares of death,"* he means the conspiracies of the wicked against him; and thus the meaning of the two verses is, that David, reflecting on his imminent danger of death, from the open invasion of his enemies rushing on him, like a roaring torrent, carrying everything before it—as well as from the conspiracies of the same enemies, in lurk for him, with snares, as for the unwary—was in great trouble.

6. Having told the extent of his danger, he now says that he had recourse to God through prayer, and that he was heard. *"In my affliction."* In the height of my troubles from Saul's persecution, and in many similar troubles, *"I called upon the Lord,"* in whom I am wont to put my entire confidence; *"and I cried to my God."* A repetition in much use with David. *"And he heard my voice from his holy temple."* My prayer reached the very summit of heaven, which is the temple of God; not made by human hands; truly holy, and can neither be violated nor polluted; *"and my cry before him came into his ears."* A repetition, and to some extent an explanation, of the preceding verse; as much as to say, my importunity bursting forth with great affection, poured forth in his sight; that is, poured forth by me, with God before my eyes, has been heard.

7. The effect of having been heard by God, for he received such help from him against his enemies as enabled him to master and destroy them, and get possession again of his kingdom. The anger of God towards his enemies is most poetically described, for as the entire kingdom is in confusion when the king is angry, and makes preparation for war; so, when the King of the whole world is angry, the whole world is confused; and especially the three visible elements, earth, air, and water. He does not mean to imply that these three elements were actually confused, though the words seem to mean so much; but he means to tell us that such is God's anger, that it can rock the earth to its very foundations; that it can cause in the air constant storms, dark clouds, thunder and lightning; and lastly, that it can so dry up the fountains, and the rivers, and the sea itself, so as to expose the caverns and the sources of the fountains. Beginning with the earth. *"The earth shook and trembled; the foundations were troubled, and were moved, because he was angry with them."* When God is angry with the earth, every bit of it shakes and trembles, not only on its surface, but to its very center. And such concussion ensues not only when God is angry, but also when he makes known his presence on earth, for the earth is then in fearful reverence, acknowledging the majesty of the Creator. Thus, on the resurrection of Christ, there was a great motion of the earth; the same happened at his death; and in another

Psalm we read, *"At the presence of the Lord the earth was moved." "Because he was angry with them;"* not with the earth and the mountains, but with the people living thereon, and that by reason of their sins.

8. A further explanation of God's action on the earth, when he chooses to show his presence thereon, making the earth not only to tremble, but even to smoke and to burn, which, Exod. 20 and Hebrews 12, tell us happened when he gave the law on Mount Sinai, *"There went up a smoke in his wrath;"* that is, in his anger he kindled such a fire on earth that created an immense smoke, *"and a fire flamed from his face;"* heat and smoke were accompanied by a destructive fire; *"coals were kindled by it;"* the anger of God made it burn so as to turn the whole earth into live coals, as he says in another place, Psalm 103, *"Who looketh on the earth, and makes it tremble: who touches the mountains, and they smoke."*

9. Passing from the earth to the air, he shows what happens there when God wishes to manifest his presence or his anger. God is said to bow the heavens when he lets down a cloud in which he appears. The clouds ordinarily appear as a part of the heavens, and it is in a cloud God was wont to show himself, as appears from Num. 9, 1 Kings 3:8, Mt. 17, and in other places. *"He bowed the heavens, and came down;"* this means he let down a cloud, and showed himself in or through it; *"And darkness was under his feet."* God dwelt in the cloud, as if he had darkness under his feet; all metaphorical expressions, to give us to understand that God may be present without one seeing him.

10. He goes on describing God's action on the air, when he means to display his anger to man. He brings before us God in the shape of a man in arms, on a chariot, moving with the greatest velocity, and discharging his weapons against his enemies. The clouds are his chariot, according to Psalm 103: *"Thou makest the clouds thy chariot, who walkest upon the wings of the winds."* The swiftest winds are his horses, who carry the clouds hither and thither. His weapons are the lightning that he shoots from the clouds. A truly wonderful description! No chariot lighter than the clouds, no horse fleeter than the wind, no weapons compared to the thunder of heaven. The chariots, too, fight from a vantage ground, whence they can harm without being harmed. *"He ascended upon the Cherubim;"* that is, God uses not only the clouds as a house or tent, but he uses them as a chariot, with the Cherubim as charioteers, and the winds as his horses. He is said *"to ascend upon the Cherubim,"* and *"to fly on the wings of the winds:"* that we may understand that he is not governed by, but that he governs the charioteers; and that he is the principal mover and guide both of the chariot and its driver. These expressions hold too, because God uses the services of the Angels in moving the clouds, which are a sort of aerial and most rapid chariots, as being drawn by the winds, a sort of winged quadrupeds, and, therefore, instead of walking, fly, and that fleeter than any bird.

11. Lest it may be supposed that God appeared visibly in the clouds, as he would in a chariot, he says he was invisibly present, and for that purpose made use of dark clouds, as a symbol of his being invisible. There is in these words a most elegant and poetic metaphor. *"He made darkness his covert."* God so wrapped himself up in the dark clouds, that he lay as if in a hiding place, the dark clouds acting the part of a screen to him. *"His pavilion round about him,"* the same clouds being like a tent round about him, covering him on all sides. *"Dark waters in the clouds of the air,"* the tent above named being a dark cloud, as dark as those fully charged with rain, and when so dense and aqueous, may not improperly be called *"dark waters in the clouds of the air."*

12. A description of the celestial warfare from the clouds, as if they were the armed chariots of the Deity. At the word of God the cloud opens, hail and lightning, like red hot coals, are at once projected. *"At the brightness that was before him, the clouds passed."* Beautiful! The clouds burst by reason of the brightness of the latent Deity, as if they could not stand such brightness, and therefore burst and dissolve in his presence, vanish and pass away. *"Hail and coals of fire"* issue forth in abundance from the rupture. It happened in Pharaoh's time, Exod, chap. 9, *"And the hail and fire mixed with it drove on together."* The same happened in Josue's wars against the five kings, Jos. 10, and on various other occasions.

13. A repetition of the above in different language. The cloud bursts, the dreadful crash called thunder is heard, generally followed by the thunderbolt. It is elegantly styled *"His voice,"* not only because God alone can produce or emit it, but because the sound is so great and so terrific, that to God alone it should be attributed as his own voice. Hence, God himself says to Job, 40, *"If you have an arm like God, and if you thunder with like voice."* *"And the highest gave his voice,"* from which proceeded hail and lightning like red hot coals.

14. An explanation of the preceding verses, particularly of the words, *"coals of fire."* These coals of fire were sent out on the bursting of the clouds, because God *"Sent forth his arrows,"* meaning his lightning. *"And multiplied"* them, and in such manner *"Scattered and confused his enemies."*

15. God's wonderful action on the waters next. They were suddenly and miraculously dried up. It happened in the Red Sea, and in the Jordan, as we read in Exod. 14, and Josue 4, on which occasions the bottom of the sea and of the river was exposed; which bottom is called here *"The foundations of the world,"* because they are so much lower than the surface of the land. *"The fountains of waters appeared."* At God's bidding, the waters were dried

up, and then appeared the bottom of the fountains, and of the rivers, and of the sea; and thus *"The foundations,"* or the lowest parts of the earth, *"Were discovered." "At thy rebuke, O Lord."* What dried them? God's rebuke—his order. How did he rebuke them? *"At the blast of the spirit of thy wrath."* A metaphorical and poetical appellation of the wind, through whose agency, God in his anger, and for the purpose of rebuke, dried up the waters; for the Scripture tells us, Exod. 14, that it was by a scorching wind that the waters of the Red Sea were dried up. Thus, what he might have simply expressed as follows, You, Lord, by a most powerful wind, dried up the waters of the sea; he expresses in a more elegant and figurative manner, when he says, You rebuked the waters for hindering the passage of your people; you blew on them in the spirit of your wrath, and at once they fled; as he expresses it in Psalm 113, *"What ailed thee, O sea, that thou didst flee?"*

16. He now returns to relate God's kindness to him in delivering him from his enemies. From the seventh verse to the present, he dwelt entirely on the power of God; and as he commenced by saying, *"The torrents of iniquity troubled me,"* and spoke in the foregoing verse of God's spirit drying up the waters, so as to expose the bottom of the sea, and of the rivers, following up the same metaphor, he says now, *"He sent from on high and took me."* He reached out his hand from on high to the very depth of the torrent, and *"Took me,"* and thus brought me out from *"Many waters;"* that is to say, rescued me, drowned and overwhelmed in a multiplicity of troubles.

17. What he said in a metaphorical sense in the last verse, he now explains in ordinary language; the words, *"they were too strong for me,"* must be taken in an imperfect sense, according to St. Jerome; for he assigns a reason why he had more need of the assistance of God, as his enemies were stronger than himself.

18. God's goodness acknowledged again. My enemies, without any provocation, were the first to injure me; attacked me off my guard, *"prevented,"* (that is, surrounded,) me without my knowing it; but the Lord was watching for me, and rendered all their machinations harmless.

19. Again and again he brings up his delivery. To show how deeply God's goodness was fixed in his mind. *"He brought me into a large place."* When I was angustiated in a place where I may be easily overcome he brought me into *"a large place,"* where I may roam about at pleasure, having my enemies at a distance. *"He saved me because he was well pleased with me."* My salvation from so many imminent dangers was all owing to his immense mercy in so loving me. For though David presently will put his own merits forward, he well knew that these very merits are God's gratuitous gifts.

20-24. Having praised God for having delivered him from his enemies, he now adds that his delivery will be always sure to him, not only through mercy, but even through justice, because he not only hitherto did, but for the future will, lead the life of the just. For God, just in himself, loves, helps, and protects the just, *"will reward me according to my justice."* Having done so heretofore, he will continue to reward me according to my merit, *"Any according to the cleanness of my hands."* As I feel my justice not only in my heart but in my hands; that is, to just within and without, just in my heart, just in my actions, so God will reward me before himself and before men, and will guard me within and without. Is not this presumption? Why trumpet so his own merits? There is no presumption when the thing is done with sincerity, and God acknowledged to be the author of all our merit. Nehemias did so, so did Esdras, Ezechias, Isaias, and Esther. But how could David make such assertions? He who had been guilty of murder and adultery! He who exclaimed, Psalm 18, *"Who can understand sins? From my secret ones cleanse me, O Lord;"* and, in Psalm 113, *"For in thy sight no man living shall be justified."* This objection leads some to think that David does not speak absolutely of his own justice, but of the justice of his cause, as compared with that of his enemies; others will have it that he limits his justice to his having remained in the true faith which his enemies did not, but the expressions, *"Because I have kept the ways of the Lord;" "All his judgments are in nay sight;" "I shall be spotless with him,"* are adverse to these opinions. We must only say, then, that David upholds his justice, inasmuch as he always had a sincere desire of serving God, and a firm purpose of never violating his law, and should he chance to slip, that he at once repented, and sincerely returned to God. The expression, *"Who can understand sins?"* may be understood of venial sins that are not inconsistent with justice; and the words, *"For in thy sight no man living shall be justified,"* may be understood of that justice which man may have independent of grace. For in such manner can no man be justified, for the just are only so through God's sanctifying grace.

25-26. A reason for his having said he would get according to his justice from God, because God gives to every one according to his works. He speaks to God here, *"With the holy thou wilt be holy;"* with the pious and the merciful thou wilt deal kindly and mercifully. To the man who is innocent, that is, who doeth no injury, thou wilt do no injury, nor permit others to do it. *"With the elect thou wilt be elect;"* with the sincere and pure minded, (for such is the meaning of the Hebrew,) you will deal sincerely and candidly; *"And with the perverse thou wilt be perverted:"* he who showeth not mercy shall not meet with mercy from you; who harms shall be harmed by you; who acts not honestly, but roguishly, him will you similarly deal with.

27. He explains the two last verses, as if he said: *"With the holy, thou wilt be holy; and with the innocent thou wilt be innocent:"* because *"Thou wilt save the humble people;"* that is, because humility, the guardian of all virtues, is most

pleasing to you, and to all humble souls you give your grace; but, *"with the perverse thou wilt be perverted;"* because you *"will bring down the eyes of the proud;"* that is, because pride, the queen of vices, is highly displeasing to thee, and, therefore, you always raise up the humble, and level all the proud. He makes special mention of the eyes here, because it is in them and the eyebrows that pride mostly shows itself.

28. Having spoken highly of his own justice and purity, he now points out their sources; and, therefore, praises God, especially as it was from him he had light, strength, and every other virtue. *"For thou lightest my lamp, O Lord:"* from thee I have the beginning of all good, which is light to distinguish true happiness from false, and true evils from false ones; for the first wound inflicted on human nature by original sin, was ignorance of the real good; and, therefore, the first cure begins by Divine light; *"Thou lightest my lamp:"* you alone light up the interior eye of my heart. *"O my God, enlighten my darkness."* Father of lights, the true light, in whom there is no darkness, as you have hitherto lighted up the inward eyes of my heart, proceed now to enlighten my darkness by banishing it completely. For without the grace of God to enlighten us, all is pure darkness in our hearts, so far as supernatural mysteries are concerned.

29. The particle *"for"* is frequently redundant in the Psalms, so is the particle *"and,"* which requires to be noted, that a connection with something foregoing may not be looked for. The prophet having said that he had got from God that light, that is, the beginning of good works and true justice, now adds, that he got also courage and strength to do or to avoid those things such light prompted him to. *"By thee I shall be delivered from temptation."* Relying on thy assistance to strengthen me, I will overcome all temptation, and conquer all evil; *"Through my God I shall go over a wall."* Depending on the same divine assistance, and strengthened from the same source, I will accomplish everything, however difficult, were it even the surmounting of a lofty wall.

30. The reason why he has received so much light and strength from God, and why he so confides in him, is because God is true, good, and the protector of all that confide in him; and because he is the only true God, true Lord, from whom such things can be expected. *"His way is undefiled;"* that God of mine, whose way is undefiled, who is most holy, and acts most justly. *"The words of the Lord are fire tried."* As gold is tried and proved in the fire, so the promises of the Lord are most certain and proved.

31. Another reason for confiding in him, for expecting light and strength from him, he alone being our true God. Whence we learn that our God alone is the true God, and as such that he is the true, firm, and solid rock

in which we may safely confide and rest; and all who confide in any other thing must of necessity be deceived and confounded.

32. He now comes to mention in particular the gifts he got from God, by means of which he got freed from his enemies, and got possession again of his kingdom. He places strength and innocence first, two virtues rarely united, for the strong are always too ready to injure the weak. David, however, was truly strong, yet truly innocent, so much so, that even though it was in his power, he would not slay his enemy Saul.

33-34. He gives the particulars of the expression, *"Girt me with strength,"* by telling us how God bestowed on him wonderful agility in his feet, dexterity in his hands, and strength in his arms. The feet of the stag were not more nimble in topping the highest mountains, as he expresses it, *"In setting himself upon high places;"* as he proved, when in his flight from Saul, he was obliged to shelter in the highest and most inaccessible tops of the mountains. He adds, that his hands were trained to battle; and that he had arms of brass, to signify his strength and skill in military matters, of which there can be no doubt, if we only read the First and Second Books of Kings. The stone from his sling, fixed in the very head of Goliath, bears testimony to his dexterity, as do the bears and the lions killed by the mere strength of his arms.

35. He declares now his innocence, of which he had already spoken, when he said, ver. 32, *"Thou hast made my way blameless;"* for, as God was pleased to give him the grace of living blameless, he, therefore, constantly protected him; *"Thou hast given me the protection of thy salvation;"* for the celerity of foot, the dexterity of hand, and strength of arm against the king and his whole army would have been of little value, had he not had *"The protection of salvation"* too, that is, the divine protection to save him, and *"the right hand (of God) to hold him up,"* and support him. *"And thy discipline hath corrected me to the end, and thy discipline the same shall teach me."* This, too, goes to show the innocence or *"the blameless way"* of David. I not only had the benefit of your protection, but your discipline; that is, your knowledge, which is had from the study of your law, so directed me, that I could not go astray; and when there was fear I might stray, by studying and inspecting it diligently *"I got corrected,"* set right, and so persevered to the end. *"And thy discipline the same shall teach me."* By such discipline we may also understand the correction of a father, in which spirit God sometimes chastised David by temporary calamities, when, through human frailty, he would fall into some defects.

36. He proceeds to relate his victories, attributing them all to God; you have made me advance at a rapid pace in enlarging my kingdom, and I am not yet tired.

37-38. These expressions, spoken in the future time, do not belong to it, but to the past tense, as will appear from the following verse.

39. Hence it appears the prophet in the two preceding verses spoke of the past. As I said, *"I will pursue after my enemies and overtake them:"* God helped me to do it, for *"He girded me with strength"* to fight, and *"subdued under me;"* that is, made those fall, *"that rose up against me."* *"Girding with strength"* is a common expression in the Scripture; thus, in Psalm 64, *"Being girded with power who troublest the depths of the sea;"* and, in Psalm 92, *"The Lord is clothed with strength, and hath girded himself;"* and, Isaias 51, *"Put on strength, O thou arm of the Lord;"* and, finally, in Lk. 24, *"But stay you in the city till you be endowed with power from on high."* He gives him to understand that, as strength and courage are of more value in a battle than the sword and helmet, the praise of the victory should be given more to the giver of the former than of the latter.

40. He returns to the same thing over and over, attributing the flight of his enemies to God's interference entirely.

41. Another cause of the victory assigned, for God not only heard his prayers, but he refused to listen to those of his adversaries, though they put them up to him.

42. He speaks now of the remnant of his enemies. I have conquered them; but if any handful remain, I will crush them into the smallest pieces, and scatter them as dust is carried before the wind; and sweep them from the earth, as the mud of the streets is hurried along by a vehement wind.

43. That had been done already; for, before he wrote this Psalm, he had been delivered from the *"contradictions"* and rebellion *"of the people;"* and *"was made head of the gentiles;"* that is, became master of the kingdom. We are, therefore, to suppose him using the future tense for the past, a thing usual in the Hebrew, or he insinuates a continuation of past favors of that sort.

44-45. He had just reason for asking *"to be delivered from the contradictions of his people,"* having met with more fidelity and allegiance from some of the gentiles, than from the children of the people of Israel. A prophecy manifestly applying to Christ, rejected by the Jews, acknowledged by the gentiles. *"The people which I knew not:"* the Gabaonites, the Gethei, and others whom I knew not as brothers, *"served me:"* *"at the hearing of the ear they have obeyed me,"* at once, most promptly, the moment they heard the command. *"The children that are strangers;"* that is, the degenerate in their morals, *"lied to me;"* that is, deceived me, gave me sham obedience. *"They have faded away;"* fallen from me like dried leaves; that is, they have not behaved properly and fairly by me; alluding to the rebellion of Absalom, under the son of Bochrus, and others, *"and have halted from their paths."* The children of adultery, who give sham service, *"halt from their paths;"* that is, turn from the straight path, in which they should have walked.

46. A conclusion of praise. Now, it appears that the Lord does live, and as he lives, so may he always live; and *"let the God of my salvation be exalted."*

47. May that God who avenged the injuries offered me, and subdued the people who rebelled against me, and delivered me from the plots and attacks of my raging enemies, Saul and Absalom, be exalted.

48. A prayer for the continuation of the divine favors; namely, that he may be so *"lifted up above them that rise up against him,"* that they may struggle in vain when they cannot possibly reach so high, and thus, that he may be delivered *"from the unjust man."*

49. Therefore, for this reason, *"I will give glory;"* that is, with praise will I acknowledge thy favors, not privately, but openly, before the whole body of the people, that all may learn to put their trust in the Lord.

50. May God increase and multiply safety of body, soul, and all other things beside, to the king he hath chosen; and may he deal everlasting mercy to David who has been ordered by him to be anointed as king, and to all his successors forever. Which prayer was fulfilled in Christ Jesus our Lord, who reigneth, and will reign for all eternity. Amen.

PSALM 18

The works of God show forth his glory: his law is greatly to be esteemed and loved.

1 The heavens shew forth the glory of God, and the firmament declareth the work of his hands.

2 Day to day uttereth speech, and night to night sheweth knowledge.

3 There are no speeches nor languages, where their voices are not heard.

4 Their sound hath gone forth into all the earth: and their words unto the ends of the world.

5 He hath set his tabernacle in the sun: and he, as a bridegroom coming out of his bride chamber, Hath rejoiced as a giant to run the way:

6 His going out is from the end of heaven, And his circuit even to the end thereof: and there is no one that can hide himself from his heat.

7 The law of the Lord is unspotted, converting souls: the testimony of the Lord is faithful, giving wisdom to little ones.

8 The justices of the Lord are right, rejoicing hearts: the commandment of the Lord is lightsome, enlightening the eyes.

9 The fear of the Lord is holy, enduring for ever and ever: the judgments of the Lord are true, justified in themselves.

10 More to be desired than gold and many precious stones: and sweeter than honey and the honeycomb.

11 For thy servant keepeth them, and in keeping them there is a great reward.
12 Who can understand sins? from my secret ones cleanse me, O Lord:
13 And from those of others spare thy servant. If they shall have no dominion over me, then shall I be without spot: and I shall be cleansed from the greatest sin.
14 And the words of my mouth shall be such as may please: and the meditation of my heart always in thy sight. O Lord, my helper, and my redeemer

Explanation of the psalm

1. Being about to institute a comparison between the law of God and his heavens, and thence to extol his law, he sets out by saying, that such are the grandeur of the heavens, that they at once proclaim the grandeur of their Maker. The heavens show forth the glory of God;" that is to say, the heavens preeminently, beyond all the other works of God, by their grandeur and beauty make his glory known to us; *"and the firmament declareth the work of his hands."* The same repeated, for heavens and firmament signify the same thing, namely, the whole celestial display, consisting of son, moon, stars, etc., for we read in Genesis, that *"God called the firmament heaven,"* and in it placed the sun, moon, and stars. The word *"heaven,"* and *"heavens,"* are used indiscriminately in the Psalms, and governed by verbs in the plural, as well as the singular number, as are all nouns of multitude. The firmament, comprising all the heavenly bodies, announces and declares to men the work of the hands of God; that is his principal and most beautiful work, from which we may form some idea of his greatness and his glory.

2. What a beautiful announcement is that of God's glory by the heavens. For three reasons. First because they announce it incessantly. Second, because they do it in the language of all nations. Third, because they announce it to the whole world. How do they do it incessantly? This verse shows us how, for the heavens announce his glory day and night by the beauty of the sun in the day, and that of the stars by night; but as the days and nights pass away, and are succeeded by others, the Psalmist most beautifully and poetically imagines one day having performed his course, and spent it in announcing the glory of God, and then hands over the duty to the following day to do likewise; and so with the night, having done her part, gives in charge to the following night to do the same; and thus, *"Day to day uttereth speech:"* when its course has run, it warns the following to be ready, *"And night to night indicates knowledge."* When the night too has finished her task of praising God, she warns the following to be ready for the duty; and thus, without intermission, without interruption, day and night fall in, and lead the choir in chanting the praises of their Creator.

3. He now proves that the preaching of the heavens is delivered in all languages, that is to say, can be understood by all nations, as if the heavens

spoke in the language of every one of them: because all nations, when they behold the beauty and the excellence of the heavens, cannot but understand the excellence and the superiority of him who made them.

4. The third source of praise of the eloquence of the heavens is, that they announce God's glory, not only without intermission, and in all languages, but they do it, furthermore, all over the world. By sound is not meant noise, but the announcement of that glory that arises from beholding the beauty of the heavenly bodies. *"Into all the earth,"* and *"Into the ends of the world,"* mean the same, and is only a repetition of frequent use in the Psalms. St. Paul quotes this passage in proof of the preaching of Christ having reached all nations; from which we are to understand, that the apostles are allegorically meant here by the heavens. And in truth, the holy apostles and other holy preachers of the word, may deservedly be so compared to the heavens. For, by contemplation they are raised above the earth, ample through their charity, splendid through their wisdom, always serene through their peace of mind, through their intelligence quickly moved by obedience, thundering in their reproofs, flashing by their miracles, profuse in their gifts to others; and, in the spirit of true liberality, seeking nothing from them; free from the slightest speck, as regards sanctity of life; and, finally, the resting place of the supreme king, by reason of their perfect sanctity. *"For the soul of the just is the seat of wisdom."*

5. Though the whole heavens declare the glory of God, the most splendid object in them, the sun, does so especially. The sun, then, being the most excellent object in the entire world, there God *"Set his tabernacle."* He calls it a tabernacle, not a house, because he dwells there only for a while, during this short time of our peregrination, when we see him *"Through a glass,"* the glass of creatures, of which the sun is the principal. But when we shall come to our country, we shall see God, not *"In his tabernacle in the sun,"* but in his own home, the home of eternity. The prophet proves that God *"Set his tabernacle in the sun,"* by three arguments: the first, derived from its beauty, the second, from its strength, the third, from its beneficence. *"And he as a bridegroom coming out of his bride chamber."* Here is the argument from his beauty. He rises, beautiful, bright, ornamented as a bridegroom in his wedding garments; and what can be grander, more beautiful, or more striking than the rising sun?

6. A second argument front the sun's power and strength, which performs an immeasurable journey daily at such speed, without the smallest fatigue. *"He rejoiced as a giant,"* or as a stout, robust person, full of alacrity, (for such is the force of the Hebrew,) such as is peculiar to those who enter on anything with pleasure. *"His going out is from the end of heaven, and his circuit even to the end thereof."* By the end of heaven is meant the east, for there

he rises, and never stops till he comes there again; and thus, *"His circuit is even to the end thereof: and there is no one that can hide himself from his heat."* The last argument, taken from the service rendered unto all created things by the sun. For the sun, by his enlivening heat, so fosters and nourishes all things, that he may be called the common parent of all things, on land and in the sea. Hence, the sun so assiduously and carefully traverses the entire globe, visits all creation, *"That nothing can hide itself;"* that is, lose a share of his wonderful favors.

7. The comparison is now applied. Beautiful are the heavens, more beautiful is the sun, but far and away more beautiful is the law of the Lord. Bright are the heavens, more bright is the sun, but much more bright is the law of the Lord. Useful are the heavens to man, more useful is the sun, but more useful than any is the law of the Lord. He then enumerates six encomiums of the divine law. First, *"The law of the Lord is unspotted, converting souls."* Most beautiful is the law of the Lord, without spot, without stain tolerating nothing sinful, as the laws of man do; and thus, when properly studied and considered, brings the soul to love it, and consequently to love God, its author. The second encomium is in the words, *"The testimony of the Lord is faithful, giving wisdom to little ones."* By *"testimony"* we are to understand the same law, because, in the Scriptures, and especially in the Psalms, God's law is not only called the law, the precept, the commandment, and the like, which other writers also apply to it; but is further styled the testimony, the justice, the justification, the judgment, as any one can see, especially in Psalm 118. It is called the *"testimony,"* because it bears testimony to men, what the will of God is, what he requires of us, what punishments he has in store for the wicked, what rewards for the just. He says then, *"The testimony of the Lord is faithful;"* that is, God's law, that will most assuredly reward the good and punish the wicked. *"Giving wisdom to little ones;"* that means, giving to the poor in understanding the light of prudence to direct them in doing good, and avoiding evil. By *"little ones"* he means those who do not abound in the wisdom of the world; and by *"wisdom"* he means that spiritual prudence that helps us to reform our habits, and mould them to the shape of the law of God.

8. The third encomium on the divine law is, that once we begin to love it, of which the first encomium treats, and to observe it, as treated of in the second, it diffuses a most extraordinary joy in the person, for nothing can be pleasanter than a good conscience. *"The justices of the Lord;"* that is, his law, his commandments, being most just, and making the observer of them just, *"are right"* and gladful; that is, *"rejoicing the hearts;"* for upright hearts harmonize with *"right"* precepts; and they, therefore, are glad, and rejoice when an occasion offers for the observance of the commandments. The

fourth encomium is, *"The commandment of the Lord is lightsome, enlightening the eyes."* The law of the Lord, through the bright light of divine wisdom, illuminates our intellectual vision, because it makes us understand God's will, and what is really good and really bad. God's law illuminates also in a preparatory manner, for wisdom will not approach the malevolent soul; and nothing proves such an obstacle to our knowing God, which is the essence of wisdom, as impurity of heart. *"Blessed are the clean of heart, for they shall see God."*

9. The fifth encomium is, that the law of the Lord causes the above named goods to be not only temporal but eternal; for the fear of the Lord, that makes one tremble at the idea of offending God, *"endures forever and ever:"* as to its reward, the rewards to be had from the observance of the law do not terminate with death, but hold forever, as he says in Psalm 9, *"The patience of the poor shall not perish forever."* Both Greek and Hebrew imply, that the fear spoken of here is not that of a slave, but that of a child, without any admixture of servility; that of which Psalm 111 speaks, *"Blessed is the man that feareth the Lord; he shall delight exceedingly in his commandments."* For he who works from servile fear does not observe the commandments freely, but unwillingly; but he who is influenced by filial fear *"Delights exceedingly in his commandments;"* that is, is most anxious and desirous to observe them. The last encomium is, that the law of the Lord, being true and just in itself, needs no justification from any other quarter. *"The judgments of the Lord are true, justified in themselves."* *"The judgments of the Lord"*—meaning his commandments, because through them God judges man, and they are the standard and the rule whereby to distinguish virtue from vice, and good works from bad—*"are justified in themselves;"* they require no one to prove they are just, the pure fact of their being God's commands being quite sufficient for it. Along with that, the ten commandments, that are mainly alluded to here being nothing more than the principles of the natural law, so abound in justice, that they hold in all times, places, and circumstances, so as to admit of no dispensation; whereas other laws are obliged to yield betimes to circumstances.

10. The conclusion from the foregoing. Since God's law is so good, so much preferable to all the riches and delicacies of this world, for they are *"More to be desired than gold and many precious stones: and sweeter than honey and the honey comb;"* that is, not only sweeter than honey itself, but sweeter than it is in its purest state, when it is overflowing the honeycomb. The word honey comb is introduced to correspond with the words, *"many precious stones,"* in the first part of the verse. How far removed is this truth from the ideas of the carnal! What a number of such people to be found who, for a small lucre, or a trifling gratification, are ready to despise God's commandments!

And yet, nothing can be more true than that the observance of God's law is of more service, and confers greater happiness than any amount of wealth or worldly pleasure.

11. He proves by an example, or rather by his own experience, the truth of what he asserted. For, says he, your servant knows it by his own experience, having received innumerable favors from you, so long as he observed your commandments.

12. Having stated that he observed the commandments of God, he now corrects himself, and excepts sins of ignorance, which can hardly be guarded against, such as arise from human frailty.

13. The meaning of *"From those of others spare thy servant,"* is not to ask of God to forgive us the sins of others, in which sense this passage is commonly quoted but we ask God to protect us from the company of the wicked. For men of good will, such as David was, should especially guard against being ignorant of their own offenses, and especially against being seduced by the wicked; and the meaning of the prayer is, from those of others, that is, from men of other habits, *"Spare thy servant;"* that is, by sparing him, keep those ill disposed people from the friendship of thy servant. He next assigns a reason for his fear of keeping up any familiarity with the wicked, for if those bad men *"shall have no dominion over me,"* that is to say, by their familiarity get no hold of and master me, and thus bring me to act with them, *"then shall I be without spot,"* and *"cleansed from the greatest sin;"* namely, mortal sin; for every mortal sin may be called *"the greatest crime,"* because it turns us away from our good and great God; and directly leads us to the fearful punishment of hell.

14. Then shall I not only *"be without spot,"* but even the words of my mouth will be agreeable; and the hymns I chant to your praise, both with heart and voice, will be always pleasing to thee, coming as they will from a clear heart and simple mouth. May my canticles find favor with thee, through your own grace, and not through my merits; for, if I am *"without spot,"* *"cleansed from the greatest sin,"* and if my words are *"such as may please,"* the whole is thy gift, thy work, thy action, thou who art *"my helper, my Redeemer:"* my helper in prosperity, my Redeemer in adversity.

PSALM 19

A prayer for the king.

1 May the Lord hear thee in the day of tribulation: may the name of the God of Jacob protect thee.
2 May he send thee help from the sanctuary: and defend thee out of Sion.
3 May he be mindful of all thy sacrifices: and may thy whole burnt offering be made fat.

*4 May he give thee according to thy own heart; and confirm all thy counsels.
5 We will rejoice in thy salvation; and in the name of our God we shall be exalted.
6 The Lord fulfill all thy petitions: now have I known that the Lord hath saved his anointed. He will hear him from his holy heaven: the salvation of his right hand is in powers.
7 Some trust in chariots, and some in horses: but we will call upon the name of the Lord our God.
8 They are bound, and have fallen; but we are risen, and are set upright. O Lord, save the king: and hear us in the day that we shall call upon thee*

EXPLANATION OF THE PSALM

1. Whereas David does not mention any one's name, there is no doubt, but he addresses himself to him on whom all the longings of the just and the predictions of the prophets were centered. And, as if he were beholding Christ on the approach of his passion, arming himself with prayer, on coming forward to fight with the devil, he exclaims, *"May the Lord hear thee in the day of tribulation:"* that is, in your passion, when, as the apostle has it, Heb. 5, *"Who offering up prayers and supplications, with a strong cry and tears, to him that was able to save him from death, was heard for his reverence."* He was heard, however, not by escaping death, but by dying that he may destroy death; and by rising, restore life; and so that shame may be turned into glory, and mortality into immortality, as he says himself, Jn. 17, *"Father, the hour is come, glorify thy Son;"* and this is the hearing of which the prophet speaks, on which the following bears, *"May the name of the God of Jacob protect thee."* By the word *"name,"* we are to understand the invocation, as we have in the last chapter of Mk. *"In my name they will cast out devils."* It may also signify power or authority, as Jn. 5, *"I have come in the name of my Father."* Or it may simply mean, God himself; for in the Scriptures the word *"name"* is used for the person to whom it belongs, as when St. Peter, Acts 4, says, *"For there is no other name under heaven, given to men, whereby we must be saved."* He adds, *"the name of the God of Jacob,"* to signify the people of God, of whom Christ is the head; as if he said, May the God of his people protect thee; for if the head be protected, the whole body of the people will be consequently saved. We seek protection from the enemies' weapons, for fear we may be hurt by them; and then, indeed, they would have been truly hurtful, could they have obstructed Christ's resurrection, his name, or his religion, or the extension or propagation of his Church.

2. The sanctuary means Sion, as will presently appear, and was called holy by reason of the Ark of the Testament being placed on it. But another Sion, the heavenly one, would seem to be intended here, that of which the apostle speaks, Heb. 12, *"But you are come to mount Sion, and to the city of the living God, that heavenly Jerusalem."* Sion is introduced here to show that God beholds everything, as if from some elevated look out, (for such is the meaning of the word Sion,) whence he can easily behold Christ in his struggles, and supply him with reinforcements; and a place so high, from whence everything can be so easily seen, is not the mountain bearing that name, but the celestial Sion and thus, *"May he send thee help from the sanctuary,"* means from the highest heavens whence he beholds all things; *"And defend thee out of Sion,"* that is, from his lofty watch tower, from which he observes you.

3. Since our Lord, when about to combat the enemy of the human race, had recourse not only to prayer, but also to sacrifice; that is, not only prayed in words, but sacrificed in reality, and, as he had alluded to his prayer by the expression, *"May the Lord hear thee;"* he now touches on the sacrifice by saying, *"May he be mindful of all thy sacrifices."* May he not despise them, but may he remember and regard them; *"and may thy whole burnt offering be made fat."* May it be acceptable, as acceptable as the holocaust of fatted animals, for the fatter the better; and the more perfect an animal is, the more valuable is the holocaust. Hence, Daniel, chap. 3, *"And as in thousands of fat lambs, so let our sacrifice be made in thy sight this day that it may please thee."* Now, Christ offered many sacrifices, and at last a holocaust, and therefore the prophet says, *"May he be mindful of all thy sacrifices."* The many sacrifices are his numerous sufferings for the glory of God, whilst among us; the holocaust is that in which he ultimately offered himself up entirely, by dying on the cross; and thus, the meaning is, may the Lord always remember the passion and death of Christ. This would appear to be rather a prophecy than a prayer; in God's sight, the passion of Christ, even from the beginning of the world, was always before him; is now, and ever will be before him; and is the source of infinite blessings to us.

4. The object of both prayer and sacrifice declared, that is, may God hear thee, and accept of thy sacrifice; that you may come at the end you seek, and accomplish what you desire, and that there may be no one to mar you therein. *"May he give thee according to thy own heart."* Give you your wish, your heart's desire, *"And confirm all thy counsels:"* carry out all your plans, further all your wishes, confirm all your desires; thus the meaning will be, may God hear thee, and receive thy sacrifice; that you may upset the machinations of the devil, redeem man from bondage, and give eternal life to those that believe in thee; for that such was the desire of Christ's heart, on such did his whole wisdom and deliberations turn, is evident from the gospel, Jn. 1:3, *"For this purpose the Son of God appeared, that he might destroy the works of the devil:"* and St. Paul, 1 Tim. 1, *"Christ came into this world to save sinners:"* and the Lord himself says, Lk. 12, *"The Son of Man came to seek and save what was lost."*

5. When our prayer shall have been granted, when you shall have conquered the enemy, *"We will rejoice"* interiorly as well as exteriorly, *"In thy salvation;"* that is, for your safe return from the war, in which safety we also share. *"And in the name of our Lord,"* who granted such a victory, *"We shall be exalted,"* we shall consider and look upon ourselves as great and wonderful, not by reason of our own merit, but by reason of the great God to whom we belong.

6. Another repetition of his good wishes. *"May the Lord,"* therefore, *"fulfill all thy petitions,"* from which so many blessings are to follow. *"Now have I known that the Lord hath saved his anointed. He will hear him from his holy heaven; the salvation of his right hand is in powers."* I am, therefore, emboldened in asking again, that the Lord may hear thee, may grant all your petitions; because, by a divine revelation, I now know that they will all be granted. *"For I have known that the Lord hath saved,"* that he certainly will save his Christ, and by predestination has already saved him, raised him from the dead, placed him in heaven, and stretched his enemies under his feet *"He will hear him from his holy heaven."* Having stated that he saved him, he now explains, that he meant by salvation, a previous degree, not yet put into execution, but one that will certainly be carried out; *"for he will hear him from his holy heaven,"* and thus *"The Lord will save his Christ."* *"The salvation of his right hand is in powers."* This may be explained in two senses. The word *"powers"* may mean power and strength, (and the Hebrew favors such meaning,) and then it will read, Christ, *"The salvation of his right hand,"* will appear in great power; or the word powers may mean, princes and kings (and the Greek and Latin favor such meaning,) and then the meaning would be, *"He will hear him from his holy heaven, and in his powers;"* because, in appointing princes and rulers, or protecting them afterwards, *"The salvation of his right hand"* is peculiarly necessary. For though princes may seem to have many safeguards, such as horses, chariots, arms and soldiers, fortresses and munitions, all these are nothing, if *"The salvation of the right hand"* of God be not there too with them: and he, therefore, with great propriety, adds in the next verse,

7. He goes on with the account of Christ's victory, as he had foreseen, saying: *"Some trust in chariots and some in horses."* Some of the enemy trusted in armed chariots, some in ferocious horses, by which he comprehends all the instruments or weapons that were formerly used in war or for fight. *"But we,"* with Christ for our head and king, do not confide so much in horses or in chariots, as we do *"In the name of the Lord our God."*

8. He shows how much more profitable it is to put one's trust in God, than in horses and chariots. They who did, *"Are bound, and have fallen; we who trusted in God are risen, and set upright."* See the wonderful change! Before the victory of Christ, the enemy of the human race bore himself aloft, as if

in chariots and horses, and trampled on man, prostrate through original sin; in like manner, the princes of the Jews, Herod and Pilate, and other visible enemies of Christ, in their insolence, insulted the suffering Christ and his humble disciples, but soon after, *"The former were bound, and have fallen;"* while the latter *"have risen, and set upright,"* and will remain forever. *"O Lord, save the king, and hear us in the day, that we shall call upon thee."* He concludes, by uniting the first and last verses. Having commenced with *"May the Lord hear thee in the day of tribulation,"* he confirms it, by directing his prayer to God. *"O Lord, save the king"* from his tribulation; and us too, *"In the day we shall call upon thee;"* that is, in our tribulation, when we shall invoke none but thee.

PSALM 20

Praise to God for Christ's exaltation after his Passion.

1 In thy strength, O Lord, the king shall joy; and in thy salvation he shall rejoice exceedingly.
2 Thou hast given him his heart's desire: and hast not withholden from him the will of his lips.
3 For thou hast prevented him with blessings of sweetness: thou hast set on his head a crown of precious stones.
4 He asked life of thee: and thou hast given him length of days for ever and ever.
5 His glory is great in thy salvation: glory and great beauty shalt thou lay upon him.
6 For thou shalt give him to be a blessing for ever and ever: thou shalt make him joyful in gladness with thy countenance.
7 For the king hopeth in the Lord: and through the mercy of the most High he shall not be moved.
8 Let thy hand be found by all thy enemies: let thy right hand find out all them that hate thee.
9 Thou shalt make them as an oven of fire, in the time of thy anger: the Lord shall trouble them in his wrath, and fire shall devour them.
10 Their fruit shalt thou destroy from the earth: and their seed from among the children of men.
11 For they have intended evils against thee: they have devised counsels which they have not been able to establish.
12 For thou shalt make them turn their back: in thy remnants thou shalt prepare their face.
13 Be thou exalted, O Lord, in thy own strength: we will sing and praise thy power

EXPLANATION OF THE PSALM

1. Having obtained a victory, *"The King,"* Christ, *"Shall joy in thy strength,"* for the strength and power he got from you to triumph so successfully over his enemies; *"And in thy salvation,"* the salvation you gave him, *"shall rejoice,"* nay, even *"rejoice exceedingly."* One part of the verse thus explains the other.

2. Words corresponding to *"May he give thee according to thy own heart,"* in the last Psalm, a Hebrew idiom, by which granting a petition means, giving the thing asked for, as we read in 1 Kings 1:18. The priest Heli says to Anna, *"The God of Israel grant thee thy petition which thou hast asked of him;"* thus, *"Thou hast given him his heart's desire"* means, thou hast given him what he desired; *"And hast not withheld from him the will of his lips;"* you have not refused him what he, by the expression of his lips, showed he wished for and desired. In one word that Christ got all he wished for in his heart and expressed with his lips.

3. How justly Christ must have rejoiced to find he not only got what he asked, but that God even anticipated his wishes, bestowed the greatest favors on him, without his even asking them. *"Thou hast prevented him (anticipated) with blessings of sweetness;"* and the meaning is, that Christ, without his asking them, was liberally endowed with God's gifts, such as being conceived by the Holy Ghost, the being united in person with the Word, the infusion of all knowledge and virtue, and the beatific vision, all of which he got at the very instant of his conception, and was therefore *"prevented (anticipated) with the blessings of sweetness."*

"Thou hast set on his head a crown of precious stones," would seem to refer to his royalty and his priesthood, which, too, he had from his conception, and hence the name Christ; for a crown of gold marks the king as well as the priest.

4. He got the above named gifts by anticipation, without asking them; but corporeal glory and immortality and other gifts, he afterwards asked and got. *"He asked life,"* which he did on the eve of his passion. *"He offered up prayers and supplications to him that was able to save him from death,"* Heb. 5, *"but God gave him length of days, forever and ever,"* meaning life everlasting, that, *"rising again from the dead, he may die no more, death shall have no more dominion over him,"* Rom. 6. Jansenius would have David alluded to here; Euthymius and Theodoret, before him, say Ezechias was meant; but this verse disproves both, for neither David nor Ezechias got that length of days here mentioned.

5. God not only gave him life *"forever and ever,"* but he also *"exalted him, and gave him a name which is above every name,"* Phil. 2; for that was truly *"the great glory he had in thy salvation,"* the salvation through which God saved him; and hence, *"thou wilt lay upon him glory and great beauty,"* in lieu of the ignominious crown of thorns his enemies put upon him, rendering him, as Isaias, chap. 3, has it, *"without beauty or comeliness."*

6. Having been *"exalted to the right hand of the Father,"* with *"a name above every name,"* a universal benediction of those *"that are in heaven, on earth, and in hell,"* will follow. *"Thou shalt give him to be a blessing;"* you will set him up as a common, a universal subject for thanksgiving, that all may bless him. *"Thou shalt make him joyful in gladness with thy countenance;"* signifying the joy consequent on the enjoyment of all those blessings; *"With thy countenance"* means, in thy presence, or before thee.

7. The aforesaid blessings will be fixed and firm for eternity, *"For the king hopeth in the Lord;"* in the infinite power of God, and not in the strength of man; *"And through the mercy of the Most High,"* through the infinite goodness of him who is above all, and to whom all are subject; *"He,"* therefore, *"shall not be moved;"* he will not waver, but remain secure for eternity.

8. Proving that neither Christ nor his kingdom will be disturbed, because all his enemies will be destroyed. *"Let thy hand be found by all thy enemies, to punish them, which he repeats in the second part of the verse. He would seem now to address Christ rather than the Fathers because Christ was the special object of the hatred of the Jews, and of his other persecutors; and it is of him Psalm 109 speaks, "Sit on my right hand, until I make thy enemies thy footstool."*

9. The punishment of his enemies described, *"Thou shalt make them,"* namely, his enemies, *"as an oven of fire,"* to burn on all sides, like *"a lighted oven," "in the time of thy anger;"* in the day of thy wrath, viz., the day of judgment. For Christ our Lord *"Shall trouble them in his wrath,"* and then, at his command, everlasting fire will devour them, and make them *"like an oven of fire."*

10. For fear any one may object that the posterity of Christ's enemies would, one time or another, stand up for their fathers, and offer violence to Christ, the prophet now adds, that not only will his enemies be destroyed, but the same destruction will extend to their children, and to all their posterity.

11. Most justly shall they be punished, because they unjustly sought to injure you. With great propriety and accuracy David says, *"They have intended evils against thee."* they could only intend them, for Christ, *"in whom there was no sin,"* could not be directly subject to punishment; but these wicked men *"intended,"* and, as it were, distorted such evils against him, such as contumelies, wounds, stripes, death itself, seeking to turn the innocent Christ from his path. *"They have devised counsels which they have not been able to establish."* They had the evil intention of destroying Christ, and of obstructing his kingdom; a thing they could not accomplish, because God converted all these persecutions to the good of Christ himself, and of his faithful servants.

12. The great misfortune of the wicked is here described; scourging alone is to be their lot; and, to add to their misfortune, they will have a view of God's elect, in the highest glory and happiness. *"Thou shalt make them turn their back."* Nothing but their back shall be seen; they shall be all back, to be scourged all over. *"In thy remnants thou shalt prepare their face;"* the word *"prepare"* signifies *"to direct,"* in the Hebrew; and then the meaning is, you will direct their countenance, that is, of the wicked, to look *"at thy remnants;"* that is, the elect, whom you have left to yourself, and of whom it is written, Rom. 9, *"The remnants will be saved."* This is a very difficult passage. Theodoret and Euthymius explain it thus: *"Thou shalt make them turn their back:"* rout them, make then fly, turn their back. *"In thy remnants:"* that is, in those that remain after them, their children. *"Thou shalt prepare their face:"* thou shalt satisfy thy anger. Let the reader choose between the two interpretations.

13. The Psalm concludes with a pious effusion of praise to Christ our King, with a prediction of what is to happen after the final destruction of all the wicked. *"Be thou exalted, O Lord, in thy own strength."* You that once appeared so humble, so infirm even, as to suffer crucifixion, now, in your strength and power, after subduing your enemies, and shoving them into Gehenna, *"be exalted"* to the very highest heavens; meanwhile, *"we,"* thy elect, *"will sing,"* with our voice, and with all manner of musical instruments will celebrate thy power and glory, in the hope of one day coming to thy kingdom, there to praise thee forever and ever.

PSALM 21

Christ's Passion: and the conversion of the gentiles.

1 God my God, look upon me: why hast thou forsaken me? Far from my salvation are the words of my sins.

2 my God, I shall cry by day, and thou wilt not hear: and by night, and it shall not be reputed as folly in me.

3 But thou dwellest in the holy place, the praise of Israel.

4 In thee have our fathers hoped: they have hoped, and thou hast delivered them.

5 They cried to thee, and they were saved: they trusted in thee, and were not confounded.

6 But I am a worm, and no man: the reproach of men, and the outcast of the people.

7 All they that saw me have laughed me to scorn: they have spoken with the lips, and wagged the head.

8 He hoped in the Lord, let him deliver him: let him save him, seeing he delighteth in him.

9 For thou art he that hast drawn me out of the womb: my hope from the breasts

of my mother.
10 I was cast upon thee from the womb. From my mother's womb thou art my God,
11 Depart not from me. For tribulation is very near: for there is none to help me.
12 Many calves have surrounded me: fat bulls have besieged me.
13 They have opened their mouths against me, as a lion ravening and roaring.
14 I am poured out like water; and all my bones are scattered. My heart is become like wax melting in the midst of my bowels.
15 My strength is dried up like a potsherd, and my tongue hath cleaved to my jaws: and thou hast brought me down into the dust of death.
16 For many dogs have encompassed me: the council of the malignant hath besieged me. They have dug my hands and feet.
17 They have numbered all my bones. And they have looked and stared upon me.
18 They parted my garments amongst them; and upon my vesture they cast lots.
19 But thou, O Lord, remove not thy help to a distance from me; look towards my defence.
20 Deliver, O God, my soul from the sword: my only one from the hand of the dog.
21 Save me from the lion's mouth; and my lowness from the horns of the unicorns.
22 I will declare thy name to my brethren: in the midst of the church will I praise thee.
23 Ye that fear the Lord, praise him: all ye the seed of Jacob, glorify him.
24 Let all the seed of Israel fear him: because he hath not slighted nor despised the supplication of the poor man. Neither hath he turned away his face from me: and when I cried to him he heard me.
25 With thee is my praise in a great church: I will pay my vows in the sight of them that fear him.
26 The poor shall eat and shall be filled: and they shall praise the Lord that seek him: their hearts shall live for ever and ever.
27 All the ends of the earth shall remember, and shall be converted to the Lord: And all the kindreds of the Gentiles shall adore in his sight.
28 For the kingdom is the Lord's; and he shall have dominion over the nations.
29 All the fat ones of the earth have eaten and have adored: all they that go down to the earth shall fall before him.
30 And to him my soul shall live: and my seed shall serve him.
31 There shall be declared to the Lord a generation to come: and the heavens shall shew forth his justice to a people that shall be born, which the Lord hath made

EXPLANATION OF THE PSALM

1. David speaks here in the person of Christ hanging on the cross, in the height of his suffering, as appears from Mt. 27, in which we read that the Redeemer, just before he expired, exclaimed: *"O God, my God, why hast thou forsaken me?"* The words, *"Look upon me,"* are not in the Hebrew; they were added by the Septuagint, for explanation sake. When Christ complains of having been forsaken by God, we are not to understand that he was forsaken by the Second Person, or that there was a dissolution of the hypostatic union, or that he lost the favor and friendship of the Father; but he signifies to us that God permitted his human nature to undergo those dreadful torments, and to suffer an ignominious death, from which he could, if he chose, most easily deliver him. Nor did such complaints proceed either from impatience or ignorance, as if Christ were ignorant of the cause of his suffering, or was not most willing to bear such abandonment in his suffering; such complaints were only a declaration of his most bitter sufferings. And whereas, through the whole course of his passion, with such patience did our Lord suffer, as not to let a single groan or sigh escape from him, so now, lest the bystanders may readily believe that he was rendered impassible by some superior power; therefore, when his last moments were nigh, he protests that he is true man, truly passible; forsaken by his Father in his sufferings, the bitterness and acuteness of which he then intimately felt. *"O God, my God;"* looking upon himself as a mere servant, he addresses the Father as his God, because, at that very moment, he was worshipping him as the true God, offering to him the most perfect sacrifice that ever had been offered, the sacrifice of his body. *"Look upon me;"* he asks him to behold how he suffers for his honor, to acknowledge, therefore, the obedience of his Son, and to accept the sacrifice so offered for the human race. *"Why hast thou forsaken me?"* As if he were surprised! Is it possible you could allow your beloved and only begotten Son to be overwhelmed in such an abyss of pain and sorrow? Similar expressions are met in Jn. 3, *"God so loved the world, that he gave his only begotten Son;"* and, Rom. 8, *"He did not spare his own Son, but delivered him up for us all."* *"Far from my salvation are the words of my sins."* Many, afraid of imputing sin to Christ, give a very forced explanation of these words. Some read them by way of interrogation, without any authority whatever. Others explain thus, *"My sins,"* having none, *"are far from my salvation;"* that is, are no obstacle to it. Without entering into other interpretations, mere gratuitous ones, inconsistent with the punctuation, the meaning simply is: with justice I said I was forsaken in my sufferings, because my exemption from them would be incompatible with my satisfying for the sins of the human race, which I have taken upon me, and which I mean to wipe away. And that Christ could take the sins of the human race upon himself, as if they were his own, is plainly shown in the

Scripture, 1 Peter 2, *"Who his own self bore our sins in his body upon the tree:"* Isaias 53, *"And the Lord hath laid on him the iniquity of us all:"* and, 2 Cor. 5, *"Him who knew no sin he hath made sin for us;"* that is, a victim for sin. As a victim for sin, then, must be immolated, in order to cleanse from the sin, so Christ, having undertaken to become the victim for the sins of the world, with much propriety says, *"Far from my salvation are the words of my sins;"* that is, I cannot avoid death, since the sins of the whole world are upon me to satisfy for them. *"The words of my sins"* is a Hebraism, meaning the sins themselves. *"Are far from my salvation,"* are inconsistent with my salvation, and I must, therefore, needs suffer.

2. He assigns another proof of his being forsaken by God, and without any hope of temporal salvation. Though I may cry out day and night to be delivered from this death of the body, you will not hear me. He alludes to his two prayers, one at night in the garden, the other by day on the cross. *"And it shall not be reputed as folly in me."* Though I may cry, and though I know you will not hear me, so far as my escaping temporal punishment or suffering is concerned; still, it will *"not be folly in me,"* because my principal object, the redemption of the human race, will be effected, and I will not be kept in death, but will rise to life everlasting.

3. He proves that it was not folly in him to cry out at night, even though he was not heard by day, and that for four reasons. First, because God is holy and merciful. Secondly, because he is wont kindly to hear those that call upon him. Thirdly, because he is in the greatest straits. Fourthly, because, from his nativity, he has confided in God, and in him alone. The present verse contains the first reason. You, O Lord, will certainly hear me, for you *"dwell in the holy place;"* you are all sanctity and piety; malice or cruelty cannot come near you, and, therefore, you are *"the praise"* of thy people *"Israel;"* both because the people of Israel praise thee, and they are praised on your account. For the greatest praise thy people can have is their having a God so holy in every respect.

4-5. Reason the second, from the instances of his kindness, numbers of which are to be found in Judges. As often as the children of Israel appealed to him, so often did he send them one of the judges to deliver them, such as Gedeon, Samson, Samuel etc.

6-8. The third reason, derived from the straits in which Christ is placed. *"But I am a worm, and no man:"* I am just now in that position that I am not only *"made less than the Angels,"* but even made less than man. *"Despised and the most abject of men,"* Isaias 53, nay, even beneath them, when even Barabbas and the robbers were preferred to me, and thus, I am now become so wretched, more *"a worm than a man;"* *"the reproach of men;"* at whom men blush, as they would at some opprobrious character; as did Peter, when he swore a solemn oath, *"he knew not the man;"* and *"the outcast of the people;"* one so rejected by the very scum of the people, that they called out, *"Not this man but Barabbas." "All they that saw me have laughed me to scorn:"* When they saw me in that state they all mocked me, all manner of persons, high and low, priests and laics, Jews and gentiles; which was fulfilled when, as St. Luke 23, writes, *"And the people stood beholding, and the rulers with them derided. And the soldiers also mocked him." "They have spoken with the lips, and wagged the head."* This, too, was accomplished, as St. Matthew writes, chap. 27, *"They blasphemed him, wagging their heads, and saying, Vah, thou who destroyest the temple of God." "He hoped in the Lord, let him deliver him: let him save him, seeing he delighteth in him."* St. Matthew testifies in the same place that the Jews made use of the very words, saying, *"He trusted in God, let him deliver him now, if he will."* Wonderful prophecy, predicting not only the facts, but the very words that would be used on the occasion.

9-10. The fourth reason, drawn from the eternal innocence of Christ. The word *"For"* does not imply a consequence; it is very often used in the Scriptures as a mere copulative; sometimes it is quite redundant. *"You art he that hast drawn me out of the womb."* I am thine from my birth; specially so, because I have not been born like others; but, through thy singular favor, have been both conceived and born, my mother's virginity remaining intact. *"My hope from the breasts of my mother."* Not content with having *"drawn me out of the womb,"* it is you who principally nourished me; for, though apparently on the breast of any mother, I know milk from heaven was supplied by you; and, therefore, from her very breasts, I learned to hope and confide in thee. *"I was cast upon thee from the womb;"* The moment I left my mother's womb, I fell into thy bosom, where I was cared with such singular love and affection. *"From my mother's womb thou art my God."* As well as you, from the moment of my birth, so providentially protected me, so I, from the earliest dawn of my life, began to serve and to love you as my God.

11. *"Depart not from me,"* according to some, is a part of the preceding verse, a matter of no great moment; it means, since *"I was cast upon thee from the womb,"* since *"thou art my God,"* I may with justice ask you to *"depart not from me,"* especially when my most grievous and my last *"tribulation is very near;"* that is, my death. *"For tribulation is very near."* This verse may, perhaps, apply to his agony in the garden, when he was so overwhelmed with fear at the idea of his approaching passion; but, I am more inclined to think it should be understood of his actual passion at hand, both because he uses the perfect tense, when he says, *"They have dug my hands and feet." "They parted my garments amongst them;"* and because he, before that, quoted the language of the Jews, boasting of their having nailed him to the cross; and, finally, because the very first verse of this Psalm was quoted by our Savior,

when hanging on his cross. According, then, to his expression in the 2nd verse, *"it shall not be reputed as folly in me."* I will not cry to thee to deliver me from death, but not to detain me therein.

12. An account of the cruelty of his enemies, whom he compares to bulls, lions, and dogs. He alludes to the High Priests and Pharisees, who insult him like bulls, goring him, as it were, with their horns, saying *"Vah, thou that destroyest the temple of God;"* or, like lions with their mouths open, hungering for him; thirsting for his blood, and bellowing, *"Away with him, away with him, crucify him;"* or like dogs gnawing and biting him when they belied him, saying, *"We have found this man perverting our nation;"* and again, *"If he were not a malefactor we would not have delivered him up to thee:"* which calumnies and detractions were the cause of our Lord's immediate crucifixion; and, therefore, he says presently, *"They have dug my hands and feet."* To come now to particulars. *"Many calves have surrounded me."* We are not to understand young weak calves, but grown, with horns, almost bulls; for the following, *"fat bulls have besieged me,"* is only a repetition. The High Priests and Pharisees are called *"strong"* and *"fat,"* because they were powerful and rich. Some will have it that by the *"calves"* he meant the populace; by the *"bulls,"* the Pharisees; not at all improbable; but I prefer the first explanation.

13. The High Priests and Pharisees panting for his death.

14-15. He tells in these verses how he dealt with the cruelty of his enemies. He offered no opposition to their violence, but always exhibited the humility, patience, and mildness, spoken of in Isaias, chap. 1, *"I have not turned away my face from them that rebuke me and spit upon me;"* and by 1 St. Peter, 2, *"Who when he was reviled, did not revile; when he suffered he threatened not, but delivered himself to him that judged him unjustly."* He, therefore, says, *"I am poured out like water;"* I made no resistance, allowed myself to be turned, driven in all directions, as one would turn a stream of water. *"And all my bones are scattered;"* I have lost all my strength, not in reality, but I do not wish to exercise it. I let my enemies use theirs, according to St. Luke 22, *"This is your hour and the power of darkness."* I have, therefore, shown myself weak and feeble in my resistance, as if I were flesh entirely; *"And all my bones are scattered;"* and thus incapable of resistance. *"My heart is become like wax melting in the midst of my bowels;"* I have patiently borne, and meekly borne, all those injuries before man, but I have been also interiorly *"humble of heart;"* which heart has not been swollen with anger, nor hardened with rage, in a spirit of vengeance, but has been on the contrary, like *"melted wax,"* in the spirit of affection and love to them, in the spirit of mercy for their blindness, by virtue of which I prayed of you, *"Father, forgive them, for they know not what they do." "In the midst of my bowels;"* a usual phrase in the Scripture, to express our internal feelings; thus, John 7, *"Out of his belly shall flow rivers of living water:"* and, Cant. 5, *"My bowels were moved at his touch:"* *"My strength is dried up like a potsherd."* My whole strength has dwindled away, dried up like a brickbat, when I allowed myself to be tied and beaten as if I were incapable of resisting them. *"And my tongue adhered to my jaws:"* I did not choose to say an offensive word to my enemies, or to complain of their wrongs. *"And thou hast brought me down into the jaws of death."* In consequence of their persecutions, and my non resistance, you have, my God, without whose permission nothing can happen, brought me to my death and burial.

16-17. He tells us how he was *"brought to the dust of death:"* *"For many dogs encompassed me;"* meaning many detractors, namely, the High Priests and Pharisees, who, by accusing me falsely of seducing the people, of refusing to pay tribute, of aiming at the sovereignty, and similar charges, forced Pilate to give me up to the soldiers for crucifixion. *"The council of the malignant hath besieged me;"* an explanation merely of the last passage; for *"the many dogs"* are no other than the council; that is, the assembly *"of the malignant."* The same malignant set, though they did not so with their own hands, did it through others. *"They have dug my hands and feet."* They drove the nails through. *"They have numbered all my bones,"* a thing they could easily do, when his blessed hands were stretched out, and the strain on his whole body rendered his ribs and other bones so visible and so easy of counting. *"And they have looked and stared upon me."* To add to the punishment of the cross, there was the ignominy of his nakedness. They inspected my whole person with the greatest curiosity, there being nothing to cover it.

18. All which was fulfilled to the letter, as may be read in St. John, chap. 19.

19. He returns to the prayer with which he commenced the Psalm, and to which he recurred again in verses 10 and 11, and now resumes it here. Having gone through the details of his passion, he now prays to God for a speedy resurrection, as it is it that will deliver him perfectly from the persecution of his enemies. *"But thou, O Lord, remove not thy help to a distance from me."* My enemies have arrived at the height of their malice, have put out all their strength against me; it is, therefore, your part to look to me now, to defer your help no longer, but kindly to defend me against their machinations.

20-21. He tells the sort of assistance he requires. *"Deliver my soul from the sword."* Deliver me from the instrument of death, making use of the word sword for any instrument, a thing common in the Scriptures, 2 Kings 12, *"The sword shall not depart from thy house;"* Ezechiel 33, *"And see the sword coming upon the land;"* Rom. 8, *"Who, then, shall separate us from the love of Christ? Shall tribulation? or distress? or famine? or nakedness? or persecution? or the sword?"* In like manner, the word soul is used here for life, a thing not uncommon in the Scriptures. *"My only one from the hand of the dog;"* by *"the dog,"* he means those dogs he had already spoken of; but he makes use here of the singular number by a figure, to show that the malice of them all appeared to be now concentrated in one, and, therefore, so much the more violent and malignant. *"My only one;"* he means his own life, which he loved in a singular manner, as being that of the incarnate Word. *"Save me from the lion's mouth;"* that lion of which ver. 13. says, *"They have opened their mouths against me, as a lion ravening and roaring;" "and my lowness from the horns of the unicorn."* He said before, *"Fat bulls have besieged me."* Unicorns are now substituted for bulls, being much more fierce and wild, to show that the cruelty and ferocity of his enemies, so far from being softened by his many sufferings, was only excited and increased. Now, in all these petitions the Lord does not ask to have his temporal life spared; but, as we have repeatedly explained before, he asks that his life may be repaired quickly, and so repaired that he shall be no longer exposed or subject to the bite of the dog, the claws of the lion, or the horn of the bull or the unicorn.

22. He now begins to tell the fruit of his resurrection, the conversion of the world to God. *"I will declare thy name to my brethren. When I shall have risen, I will send my apostles through the entire world, and through them, "I will declare my name;"* that is, I will impart the knowledge of thy name and of thy Godhead to all men through them; all being my brothers, by reason of the flesh I assumed; and thus, *"in the midst of the church will I praise thee;"* no longer in a corner of Judea, but in the midst of the immense church, composed of Jews and gentiles, through the mouths of my ministers will I praise thee. St. Paul, writing to the Hebrews, quotes this passage, chap. 2, *"For which cause he is not ashamed to call them brethren, saying: I will declare thy name to my brethren: in the midst of the church I will praise thee."*

23-24. Having said that he would *"praise God in the midst of the church,"* which was to be effected by getting his faithful to do so, he now exhorts the faithful to praise God, *"Ye that fear the Lord;"* ye who know and worship him; for fearing God, in the Scriptures, is synonymous with worshipping him; thus, Jonas, when questioned about his people, says, *"I am a Hebrew, and I fear the God who made the heavens and the earth;"* and Daniel says, *"Let all fear the God of Daniel;"* and it is said of Judith, *"that she feared God exceedingly."* The meaning, then, is, you who know and worship the true God, praise him; and, lest we should imagine this exhortation was addressed to a few, the Jews, for instance, he adds, *"All ye seed of Jacob, glorify him. Let all the seed of Israel fear him;"* that means, glorify, praise, and fear God, all ye children of Israel, and not only ye who are children in the flesh, but ye who are children according to the promise, namely, all the gentiles converted to Christianity; *"Because he hath not slighted nor despised the supplication of the poor man."* He assigns a reason for wishing God to be praised by all, namely, because he heard the prayer he put up to him for his resurrection and glory, for his victory over the devil, and for the redemption of the human race. He calls himself *"a poor man,"* as, in truth, he was, when, in his agony, hanging on the cross, he hung naked, deserted, and suffering from hunger and thirst. *"Neither hath he turned away his face from me, and when I cried to him he heard me."* A repetition of the preceding sentences.

25. Having encouraged his faithful to praise God, he now predicts the certainty of it. The praise I will chant to thee through my faithful will not be from a corner, nor from a handful of the Jews, but from the church of all nations. *"I will pay my vows in the sight of them that fear him."* Vows here signify sacrifices and oblations, as Isaias 9 has it, *"They shall worship him in victims and offerings, and they shall make vows to the Lord, and perform them;"* for when Christ saw how agreeable was the holocaust of his death to the Almighty, he promises now that, through his ministers, he will, in the best manner he can, most frequently renew the same holocaust, which he says, in the words, *"I will pay my vows in the sight of them that fear him;"* through my ministers, the priests of the New Testament, I will most constantly immolate that most agreeable of all sacrifices to God; *"in the sight of them that fear him;"* of those that acknowledge, worship him, for the sacrifice may not be performed before infidels.

26. Of this sacrifice *"the poor shall eat,"* when they acknowledge their spiritual neediness and poverty; *"and shall be filled, because they will taste of the good, exceeding all good; "and they shall praise the Lord,"* thanking him for such an immense favor: *"that seek him;"* those that hunger for and eagerly seek him; *"their hearts shall live forever."* Such will be the fruit of this reflection, that the hearts nourished by such excellent and noble food will lead a spiritual life—a life of grace here, and of glory forever; for so the Truth speaketh, in John 6, *"Whosoever eateth of this bread shall live forever."* For, as perishable food supports the body for a time, so the imperishable food confers life everlasting.

27. He shows how it will happen that he shall have to praise God *"in a great church,"* because all nations will be converted to God through the merits of the sacrifice on the cross. *"They shall remember"* their first origin, how they were formed in their first parent, a thing they had quite forgotten, through original sin; and, therefore, they said to the wood and the stones, *"Thou art my father,"* Jerem. 3 *"They shall remember"* their first creation, *"and all the ends of the earth shall be converted to the Lord;"* that is, all the nations on the face of the globe, even to its remotest ends; that is to say, some from every nation. *"And all the kindred of the gentiles shall adore in his sight."* An explanation of the preceding verse; because, *"adoring"* the Lord, and being

converted to the Lord, imply the same thing; namely, the abandonment of idolatry by the whole human race all over the world.

28. They will deservedly be converted to and adore the Lord, because he, not the infernal spirits, being the true and natural king of all, will justly *"have dominion over the nations."*

29. Having stated that *"The poor shall eat and shall be filled, and shall praise the Lord;"* and that *"All the kindred of the gentiles shall adore in his sight,"* for fear any one may suppose it was only the poor and the hungry would be called and converted, he now introduces the rich and the powerful. *"All the fat ones have eaten, and have adored."* The very *"fat ones"* of this world, who abound in its blessings, such as princes, emperors, kings, they, too, shall eat of the Lord's table, and will adore and praise the common Lord, whose sway is over all nations. In the style of the prophets, the perfect tense is used here for the future. Finally the words *"that go down to the earth,"* mean all mortals who to earth must return. *"Shall fall before him;"* shall bend their knees, and adore; and thus the conversion of the gentiles, the fruit of our Lord's passion and resurrection, will be truly general.

30. He concludes by saying, that he and his posterity would thence forward live for God's glory alone, and for his faithful service; the soul is put here for the entire man, which is often done in the Scripture.

31. An explanation of the expression, *"My seed shall serve him,"* for *"the generation to come;"* meaning the people, under the new dispensation, will get good news concerning the Lord and his justice, the justice of Faith. *"Then shall be declared to the Lord a generation to come;"* that means, the generation to come shall get the news; it shall be announced to them, for it is a Greek phrase, like the expression, *"The poor have the gospel preached to them;"* whereas, literally translated, it would mean, the poor preached the gospel: the meaning, then, is, not that the Lord will be declared to the generation to come, but the generation to come will be declared, as enlisted to the Lord; this is plain from the following, where he says, *"The heavens shall show forth his justice to a people that shall be born;"* now, *"that shall be born,"* and *"the generation to come,"* are one and the same. The Lord, then, will be declared to the coming generation, for the heavens, that holy people, will do it. The justice of faith is called the justice of God, which makes men truly just, and which God gratuitously gives to those who believe in Christ. For the gospel strongly inculcates that we are all sinners, that we cannot be justified of ourselves, but that through faith in Christ we are to expect justice from God alone.

PSALM 22

God's spiritual benefits to faithful souls.

PSALM 22

1 The Lord ruleth me: and I shall want nothing.
2 He hath set me in a place of pasture. He hath brought me up, on the water of refreshment:
3 He hath converted my soul. He hath led me on the paths of justice, for his own name's sake.
4 For though I should walk in the midst of the shadow of death, I will fear no evils, for thou art with me. Thy rod and thy staff, they have comforted me.
5 Thou hast prepared a table before me against them that afflict me. Thou hast anointed my head with oil; and my chalice which inebriateth me, how goodly is it!
6 And thy mercy will follow me all the days of my life. And that I may dwell in the house of the Lord unto length of days.

EXPLANATION OF THE PSALM

1. The happiness of the elect, under the figure of sheep in charge of some excellent shepherd, is described in this Psalm. David, one of such sheep, exclaims, *"The Lord ruleth me, and I shall want nothing;"* I am one of God's sheep, and he being a most wise, powerful, and good shepherd, I may confidently assert, *"I shall want nothing."* This is the language of one of the happy, *"on the road,"* and *"in hope."* For the happy, actually so, and *"at home,"* do not use the future tense, but the present, because they are done with labor and grief, and have already *"entered into the joy of their Lord."* But the blessed on the road, and in hope, cannot say, I want nothing, being subject to many passions; but they can justly say, *"I will want nothing;"* because, when they will want they will get; when they shall be hungry, they will not fail to be supplied with food; when they shall be sick, they will be sure of a physician. The words, *"I shall want nothing,"* come to be explained by him after. Sheep require, first, rich pasture; secondly, pure water; thirdly, one to bring them back when they stray; fourthly, to be brought through easy passages; fifthly, to be protected from wolves and wild beasts; sixthly, to be supported when tired and weary; seventhly, if cut or maimed by passing through cliffs or rocks, to be cured; and, lastly, at the close of day, at the end of their journey, to have a home wherein they may securely rest. All these matters God gives in abundance to his elect, and they can, therefore, justly say, *"I shall want nothing."* David takes up the first in these words, *"He hath set me in a place of pasture;"* not in a barren or desert spot, but in prairie land, where an abundance of the choicest and most wholesome grass is to be had; where the sheep have food in abundance; the food, in a spiritual sense, being the knowledge of God, his sacraments, especially the Eucharist, Truth himself, for these are what support, nourish, and increase the spiritual life within us.

2. The second necessary for the sheep, viz., to have not only plenty of wholesome pasture, but to have plenty of pure water at hand, to be cooled in the heat and the thirst. The spiritual water that extinguishes the thirst of us sheep, is the grace of God, of which Christ himself speaks in the Gospel, Jn. 4, *"Whosoever shall drink of the water I will give him, shall not thirst forever."* Nothing is so effectual in curbing our carnal desires, as a taste of the love of God; to the soul who once tastes of it, everything else seems insipid.

3. The third want of the sheep, the being brought back when they stray; for man, though he may by his own strength turn from God, cannot by his own strength return to him. He says then: The good shepherd sought me out when I strayed, brought me back, and, more than that, never allowed me to stray again—a peculiar privilege to the elect. *"He hath led me on the paths of justice."* The fourth duty of the shepherd, made me walk in the narrow path of his commandments; and, thereby, lead the life of the just. That he effected by taking from the power and strength of the tempter, by an increase of charity, by additional sweetness, by illuminating with his justice, by enticements, by excitement, by endearment, by terror, and other innumerable ways, on which, if we would only reflect for a moment, we would never cease, during our whole lifetime, to return thanks to so sweet a Pastor; the more so, when all this has been done, not by reason of our previous merits, but *"on account of his own name, that he may make known the riches of his mercy to the praise of the glory of his grace."*

4. The fifth service rendered the sheep, is their protection from wolves and other wild beasts. *"For though I should walk in the midst of the shadow of death;"* through dark, dreary places, exposed to all manner of dangers from wild beasts, robbers, precipices, *"I will fear no evils, for thou art with me."* And, in truth, no one can well imagine the security a faithful soul feels when they bring to mind that God, who cannot be resisted, accompanies them. *"The shadow of death"* is of frequent recurrence in the Scripture; the proper meaning of which is that dense darkness, which shuts out all light, and is caused by death. The blind are said to be in darkness, because they see nothing; and with much more reason are the dead said to be so, because they feel nothing. Hence, the poets make the dead to dwell in shady places, wrapped up in darkness; and hence, the Scripture promiscuously uses darkness for the shadow of death, to explain one through the other, as in Job 3, *"Let darkness and the shadow of death cover it;"* and Job 10, *"To a land that is dark, and covered with the mist of death;"* Isaias 9, *"The people that walked in darkness have seen a great light; to them that dwelt in the region of the shadow of death, light is risen;"* in each of which passages *"dwelling in darkness,"* and *"dwelling in the region of the shadow of death,"* are used to signify the same thing. And as dark places are exposed to a great many dangers, and we

generally go through them with no small amount of fear, David, therefore, says, *"Though I should walk in the midst of the shadow of death:"* in dense darkness, surrounded by danger, *"I will fear no evils, for thou art with me. Thy rod and thy staff, they have comforted me."* The sixth benefit conferred on the sheep, their being supported when weary. He now drops the simile of the sheep, and takes up the shepherd, for sheep are not supported, when weary, by a staff, but are carried on the shoulders of the shepherd; which God is always ready to offer his faithful souls when weary.

5. The seventh favor, namely, the wonderful consolation extended by God to his elect, in the troubles incidental to them in this world. The meaning of this verse is, not that God has prepared a table, wine and oil, against his enemies, as if they were the weapons wherewith to fight; but the meaning is, that God provides great consolations to meet great tribulations; and, as the enemy seeks to do us much injury, so God pours upon us many consolations, which are pictured as if we were enjoying a feast, where the table was overspread with the choicest meats, with the rarest wines, and the most precious perfumed ointments, such as we read of Mary Magdalen having poured on the head of our Savior. *"Against them that afflict me."* This is clearer in the Greek, and the meaning of it is, that out of the persecution and trouble prepared for me by my enemies, you have extracted great consolation—a well furnished table for me. *"thou hast anointed my head with oil."* Thou hast poured precious ointment on my head, and thus *"made my face cheerful with oil:"* nor was there wanting the cup of wine, inebriating me with thy grace, so *"goodly,"* and so *"gladdening to the heart."* Such another passage occurs in Psalm 93, *"According to the multitude of my sorrows in my heart, thy comforts have given joy to my soul."* And in 2 Cor. 7, *"I am filled with comfort: I exceedingly abound with joy in all our tribulation."*

6. This is the last good, that brings to the supreme good. *"Thy mercy will follow me,"* not for a time, but forever, which is the peculiar privilege of the elect. *"And that I may dwell;"* that is, it will follow me for that purpose, *"to dwell in the house of the Lord, unto length of days;"* that is, forever.

PSALM 23

Who are they that shall ascend to heaven; Christ's triumphant Ascension thither.

1 The earth is the Lord's and the fulness thereof: the world, and all they that dwell therein.
2 For he hath founded it upon the seas; and hath prepared it upon the rivers.
3 Who shall ascend into the mountain of the Lord: or who shall stand in his holy place?
4 The innocent in hands, and clean of heart, who hath not taken his soul in vain,

nor sworn deceitfully to his neighbour.
5 He shall receive a blessing from the Lord, and mercy from God his Saviour.
6 This is the generation of them that seek him, of them that seek the face of the God of Jacob.
7 Lift up your gates, O ye princes, and be ye lifted up, O eternal gates: and the King of Glory shall enter in.
8 Who is this King of Glory? the Lord who is strong and mighty: the Lord mighty in battle.
9 Lift up your gates, O ye princes, and be ye lifted up, O eternal gates: and the King of Glory shall enter in.
10 Who is this King of Glory? the Lord of hosts, he is the King of Glory.

EXPLANATION OF THE PSALM

1. David proposes proving that of the immense family of the human race, Christ alone, and a few, very few others, as compared with the crowd, will enter God's most holy and happy house; and for fear people may think they were not God's creatures, but belonged to some other creator, as the Marcionists and Manicheans afterwards thought, he premises those two verses, in which he lays down that God is the Creator and Lord of the entire world, and of everything in it. *"The earth is the Lord's, and the fullness thereof;"* that is, everything that is on or in it, and fills it. The second part of the verse explains the first, in which he states that it is principally to man he alludes, for to man alone the words, *"that dwell therein,"* can be applied.

2. He proves God to be Lord of the earth, and of all that dwell thereon, because it was he created the earth, and made it out top the waters so as to be habitable; for had he not made it higher than the sea and the rivers, they would have rushed in upon and overwhelmed it. God, then, having made the earth habitable, it follows that he is the Lord of all, both because man was made from the earth, and to the earth will return; and because man holds the earth here not as its Lord and master, but as a husbandman placed there by God to till and cultivate it.

3. Whereas all men are servants and husbandmen of God, and all equally till the land which is God's. *"Who shall ascend into the mountains of the Lord:"* Will there be any one, and who will he be, worthy of ascending to the place where God is said peculiarly to dwell?

4. There will; they will ascend into the mountain of the Lord who have the four conditions here specified: First, they must be *"Innocent in hands;"* must have committed no sin. Second, must be *"Clean of heart,"* free from sinful thoughts or desires. Third, *"Who hath not taken his soul in vain;"* who not only has neither done nor thought any evil, but has done and thought everything that God could require of him, in order to obtain the end for which he was created. Fourth, *"Nor sworn deceitfully to his neighbor;"* easily understood. And thus the man who seeks to be worthy of *"ascending into the mountain of the Lord,"* must be perfect in every respect in his heart, in his language, in his actions, in the perfect discharge of all the duties that appertain to his station in life. Such conditions are to be found in Christ alone. He is the only one of whom it can be said, *"Who did no sin, neither was guile found in his mouth;"* and as David says, in Psalm 13, *"There is none that doeth good, no not one;"* and Isaias, *"We have all strayed like sheep;"* and St. Paul, Rom. 3, *"All have sinned and need the glory of God;"* and, therefore, the Lord himself justly says, John 3, *"And no man hath ascended into heaven, but he that descended from heaven, the Son of Man, who is in heaven."* All others are terrestrials, sprung from the earth. He alone is celestial, come from heaven; holy, innocent, unpolluted, set aside from sinners, and by his ascension, higher than the heavens. And it was not Christ alone that was to ascend to the mountain of the Lord, but his body too, the Church, which he *"Cleansed with his blood, that he might present it to himself, a glorious church; not having spot nor wrinkle, nor any such thing, but that it should be holy and without blemish,"* Ephes. 5; and, therefore, in the next verse, he says:

5. *"He,"* that is, Christ, *"shall receive a blessing from the Lord,"* favors in abundance, *"and mercy from God his Savior,"* for his body, the Church, in whose regard he is the Savior, because life everlasting in the kingdom of heaven, though justice to Christ, is mercy to the faithful; for, though the just deserve eternal life, by reason of God's goodness, their own merits have the effect, through God's mercy only, and thus are truly called the gifts of God. Hence, in Psalm 102, we have, *"Who crowneth thee in mercy and compassion;"* and in Rom. 6, *"For the wages of sin is death: but the grace of God, everlasting life."*

6. The prophet now declares that the one he spoke of, *"The innocent in hands,"* the *"clean of heart, who shall ascend into the mountain of the Lord,"* and *"shall receive a blessing,"* and *"mercy from God"* is Christ, the head, and not only the head, but the head with the body of the Church. *"This is the generation of them that seek him;"* that means, he that ascends to heaven, is the generator of those that are regenerated in Christ, whose principal study is to seek God, to thirst for a sight of his face, and to make for his holy mountain, with all their strength. And, in fact, a unique and perhaps characteristic sign of the elect of God, is to have a longing desire for their home, their country—heaven. The generation of the children of this world seek everything in preference to God, dread nothing more than death; and, if they got their choice, would prefer living always in this world, to *"being dissolved and being with Christ."*

7. The holy prophet, having foreseen that one would be found worthy of *"going up into the mountain of the Lord,"* namely, Christ, declares that he will go up at once, and that the eternal gates of heaven will be opened to him. And in a poetic strain he at once addresses now the *"Princes"* of heaven, the Angels; then the *"gates"* themselves; orders the Angels to open, and the gates to be opened, nay, even spontaneously to admit the approaching King of Glory. He makes use of the words, *"Lift up,"* and *"be ye lifted,"* to show these are not ordinary gates, hanged to a wall or a post, but to the roof or ceiling, to show they should be raised up for admission.

8. He introduces him to the Princes of the heavenly Jerusalem as King, *"Who is this king of glory?"* not that the Angels, on the day of his ascension, were ignorant of Christ's being the King of Glory, but to express their admiration at the novelty of human flesh ascending to the highest heavens, not as a guest or a stranger, but as the Lord of a glorious and everlasting community. The prophet answers, that Christ is the King of Glory, the Lord most valiant and powerful, who showed his power in battle against the prince of darkness, whom he conquered, despoiled, and left in chains.

9-10. The prophet imagines some hesitation on the part of the Angels in opening the gates, and he, therefore, second time thunders. *"Lift up your gates, O ye princes, and be ye lifted up, O eternal gates,"* thereby giving us to understand the great novelty of the matter, to find a terrestrial rising above celestial bodies—human flesh soaring above the angelic spirits themselves, to the amazement, wonder, and admiration of all nature. The Angels ask again, Who is this King of Glory? *"The Lord of Hosts is the King of Glory,"* is the reply. At the sound of that most familiar name, they at once open, and with joy receive the King of Glory. *"Lord of hosts"* is the peculiar title of the Creator, and never applied to any one in the Scriptures, but to God exclusively. The Hebrew word has been sometimes translated God of armies, as God really is, presiding over his armies of Angels, that are innumerable and most powerful; and besides, having all created beings serving under him, as we read in Psalm 148, *"Fire, hail, snow, ice, stormy winds which fulfill his word."* Pharaoh had a fair experience of his being the God of armies, when not only the Angels were brought to war upon him, but even the minutest animals, such as frogs, flies, and gnats, and along with them things inanimate, such as hail, fire, darkness, pestilence, and the like. Some have translated *"Lord of Hosts," "Lord of virtues;"* but those who do, take *"virtues"* in the same sense as *"Hosts,"* and not in the sense of what is generally understood by virtues, namely, good moral actions or qualities.

PSALM 24

A prayer for grace, mercy, and protection against our enemies.

1 To thee, O Lord, have I lifted up my soul.
2 In thee, O my God, I put my trust; let me not be ashamed.
3 Neither let my enemies laugh at me: for none of them that wait on thee shall be confounded.
4 Let all them be confounded that act unjust things without cause. shew, O Lord, thy ways to me, and teach me thy paths.
5 Direct me in thy truth, and teach me; for thou art God my Saviour; and on thee have I waited all the day long.
6 Remember, O Lord, thy bowels of compassion; and thy mercies that are from the beginning of the world.
7 The sins of my youth and my ignorances do not remember. According to thy mercy remember thou me: for thy goodness' sake, O Lord.
8 The Lord is sweet and righteous: therefore he will give a law to sinners in the way.
9 He will guide the mild in judgment: he will teach the meek his ways.
10 All the ways of the Lord are mercy and truth, to them that seek after his covenant and his testimonies.
11 For thy name's sake, O Lord, thou wilt pardon my sin: for it is great.
12 Who is the man that feareth the Lord? He hath appointed him a law in the way he hath chosen.
13 His soul shall dwell in good things: and his seed shall inherit the land.
14 The Lord is a firmament to them that fear him: and his covenant shall be made manifest to them.
15 My eyes are ever towards the Lord: for he shall pluck my feet out of the snare.
16 Look thou upon me, and have mercy on me; for I am alone and poor.
17 The troubles of my heart are multiplied: deliver me from my necessities.
18 See my abjection and my labour; and forgive me all my sins.
19 Consider my enemies for they are multiplied, and have hated me with an unjust hatred.
20 Keep thou my soul, and deliver me: I shall not be ashamed, for I have hoped in thee.
21 The innocent and the upright have adhered to me: because I have waited on thee.
22 Deliver Israel, O God, from all his tribulations.

EXPLANATION OF THE PSALM

1. Having found no rest in creatures, but on the contrary, *"briers and thorns"* everywhere; disgusted with my former mode of life, and having torn my soul from the affections that tied it down to the earth, *"I lifted it up"* to thee. Through constant reflection, and love inspired by you, to you I began to cling, hoping for help from you in my temptations; and since *"I put my trust in you, let me not be ashamed;"* that is, I will not go from you in confusion, without having obtained the help I need, and thus be made *"to blush"* before my enemies.

2–3. An explanation of the words, *"To blush before my enemies,"* in the preceding verse, for he should blush if his *"enemies were to laugh at him"* for having vainly trusted in God. By *"my enemies,"* may be understood, both the wicked in this world, and the evil spirits, whose rejoicing and scoffing would produce intolerable confusion, were we seriously to reflect on it. He then gives a reason for his hope *"of not being confounded,"* because *"none of them that wait on thee shall be confounded;"* that means, because we have learned by long experience, from the examples of our ancestors, and from your own promises, that those who put their trust in you, and patiently expect your help, were never disappointed in their *"waiting on you."* To *"wait on the Lord"* is a very common expression in the Scriptures, and means to expect him in the certain hope of assistance.

4. This verse may be interpreted in two ways; first, to signify that those who sin without cause, meaning those who sin through malice, and not through infirmity or ignorance, *"would be confounded."* Such persons think neither of doing penance, nor of abandoning sin, and if they hope for anything from God, their hope is presumption. Another more literal meaning may be offered, viz., that both the visible and invisible enemies of the just would be confounded, for their persecutions of the just will be all in vain, because they will not accomplish the end they propose to themselves, the ruin of the just, and the bringing them to hell; whereas, on the contrary, such persecution becomes only an occasion to the just of exercising their virtue, and a source of everlasting merit. The prophet then throws back the confusion on his enemies, saying, Lord, do not allow me to be confounded, as I will, if my enemies laugh at me, and exult in my ruin; but, on the contrary, let them be confounded, when they see they have been persecuting me, and provoking me to impatience, without effecting their object, and in vain.

"Show, O Lord, thy ways to me, and teach me thy paths." By *"thy ways,"* we understand his law, which is really the way to God. *"If thou wilt enter into life, keep the commandments;"* and the prophet having asked the Lord's help against temptations, explains what help he specially wishes for, and says, *"Show, O Lord, thy ways to me,"* make me tread in the way of your commandments—*"and teach me thy paths;"* that is, show me that most narrow road of thy most just law, for thus will I escape the mocking of all my enemies, and instead of being confounded, all they who, by their temptations, sought to harass me, will be confounded. He asks to be taught the paths of the Lord, not speculatively, but practically; that is to say, he asks for such grace as may move his will to observe the commandments cheerfully.

5. A repetition of the foregoing, and a reason assigned for it. *"Direct me in thy truth."* If left to myself, I will at once turn aside to the right or to the left, deserting the path of your commandments, on account of the prosperity or the adversity of this world: do you, therefore, take me by the hand, and direct me by the help of thy grace in the right path, *"in thy truth;"* namely, in thy law, which is the truest of all paths. *"For all thy commands are truth,"* Psalm 118—*"For thou art God my Savior;"* of thee I ask this help, because you alone, being God, can save my soul; for there is no other physician that understands the diseases of the soul; and, therefore, there is no one able to cure them but God alone, much less is there one able to restore them to perfect health; and I specially ask this favor, which I hope, too, to obtain, because *"On thee have I waited all the day long;"* that is, with perseverance and patience I have waited for thy medicine, and look for relief from nobody else. It is a source of great merit with God never to give up the hope of his help in temptations, or to look to human consolation.

6. When God allows the soul to be harassed by temptation, or to wallow in sin, he seems to have forgotten his mercy; and thus the just man, after a long struggle with temptation, and seeing that, however he may desire it, he cannot guard against relapsing into sin, cries out to God to remember his former compassion and mercies. Between compassion and mercy there is this difference only, that the former seems to be the actual exercise or practice of mercy, the latter the habit of the virtue in the mind; and the same difference is observable in the Hebrew, though the words are much more dissimilar. The meaning then is—Remember, O Lord, that you were compassionate *"from eternity,"* and not only compassionate, but in the habit of showing mercy, and the most paternal tenderness to thy children; and, therefore, mercy is thy distinguishing, as well as thy natural, tendency.

7. He places forgetfulness in beautiful opposition to remembrance. Remember thy mercy, but forget my sins; for one is the cause of the other, for God then remembers his mercy when he does not wish to remember our sins any longer, but so remits and blots them out, as if they were consigned to eternal oblivion. He remembers, however, the sins and ignorance of youth; that is, the sins committed through human infirmity and ignorance, because to those more than any others does his mercy lend itself, according to the apostle, 1 Tim. 1, *"But I obtained the mercy of God, because I did it ignorantly;"* and, perhaps, David had no other sins to account for; and this certainly is the prayer of a just man, who seems to have had to contend with such sins only; and with that, sins committed through malice are not forgiven through prayer alone, but need *"Fruits worthy of penance."* *"According to thy mercy, remember thou me."* He declares what he said in the

words, Remember thy bowels of compassion;" and forget my sins; for all this takes place when *"God remembers the sinner according to his mercy."*

8. He assures himself of the certainty of obtaining the object of his hope, by reason of God's goodness and justice; and thus, that he is wont to correct delinquents freely, because thereby he exercises his mercy towards man, and his justice towards sin; and the meaning is, *"The Lord is sweet and righteous;"* and, therefore, loves man, and hates sin; and, therefore, *"gives a law;"* that is, declares and points it out *"to sinners in the way,"* to persuade them to abandon the old path, and, from being bad and wicked, to become good and just.

9. A qualification of the expression in the last verse, *"He will give a law to sinners;"* which he says here does not apply to all sinners, but only to the mild and the meek, who do not resist God's teachings, but rather covet instruction. *"We will guide the mild in judgment;"* that means, he will lead the humble and the mild through the straight path of his law, (for law and judgment appear to be synonymous, as we explained in Psalm 18,) which he then explains in other words, *"He will teach the meek his ways,"* that is, to the meek he will give the grace of knowing and loving, and thus fulfilling his law. Observe that the proud are not altogether excluded from the grace of God, but have their place assigned them. The proud, to be sure, are incapable of perfection, of which this Psalm principally treats, until, from the influence of fear, they do penance, and then, having shaken off the fear, become mild and humble. The grace of God, then, first softens and subdues the proud and the obstinate, and when thus humbled and contrite, *"It guides them in judgment,"* and *"teaches them his ways."*

10. Having stated that not only were the meek guided by God, but that all God's dealings with such souls were acts of mercy and justice, justice meaning the honor and truth that oblige men to perform their promises. *"The ways of the Lord,"* mean here his works, they being, in some respect, the *"way"* in which he comes to us; unless we prefer to understand the expression as meaning the Lord's rules or customs, and, as it were, the law he uses. Thus, the *"Ways of the Lord;"* the law he gives us, by means of which, as by a straight road, we ascend direct to God, is sometimes intended by the expression; at other times, it signifies the law he uses himself, when, through his works, he descends to us. And as David had previously spoken at great length on the former, he now speaks of the latter, that is, of the law he made for himself, and which he observes towards us; and he, therefore, lays down, *"All the ways of the Lord are mercy and truth;"* that is, his law, his custom, his mode of dealing with us, are all in mercy and truth; so that whatever he promises in his mercy, he invariably carries out in his truth. Who doth God so deal with? *"With those that seek after his covenant and his*

testimonies." He gives the name of testament, or *"covenant,"* to that bargain he made with man, when he gave him the law, that they should be his people, and he should be their God; which bargain is called a testament in the Scripture, because it contains a promise of inheritance, and require to be confirmed by the death of the testator, as it really was by the death of Christ, as a sign of which Moses sprinkled the whole people with blood, saying, *"This is the blood of the covenant which the Lord hath made with you,"* Exod. 24, and Heb. 9. He calls the law that God gave us *"His testimonies,"* because, as we have already stated, through the law God testifies his will to us. With those, then, who seek for the compact entered into by God with man to observe it, and, in like manner, seek for the law of God to carry it out, that is, with men of good will, fearing and loving God, he deals with such in the law of mercy and truth.

11. From the general law in which God deals with those that fear him, the prophet infers that he has a fair hope of his sins being forgiven. *"For thy name's sake, O Lord,"* to make known thy mercy and thy truth, *"Thou wilt pardon my sin, for it is great."* The word great may signify numerous, as a great people, in which sense St. James uses it, when he says, *"We all offend in many things:"* or, on account of the magnitude and the grievousness of the sins, for holy souls look upon trifles as grievous, which trifles are really grievous, if we consider the greatness of the person offended.

12. The prophet is now like one in love, now sighing for what he loves, now praising it, again sighing and longing for it. The just man was in love with the grace of God, ardently longed for the forgiveness of his sins, for the grace of living well, and pleasing God, and, therefore, now asks God's grace thereto; at one time he praises the grace, and declares the happiness of those that fear God, that is, of those who have got such a grace; and again he returns to desire and to ask for it. Thus, in this verse and the two following, he declares the advantages those who fear God enjoy. *"Who is the man that feareth the Lord?"* Let such a man come forward and learn from me what a fortunate man he is. The next sentence, *"He hath appointed him a law in the way he hath chosen."* Many think this a part of the happiness hereinbefore alluded to; that is to say, that man, fearing the Lord, will, in the first place, have the privilege of being instructed by God *"in the way he hath chosen;"* that is, in the state of life he may select. Not a bad interpretation, but I prefer another. The prophets are very much in the habit of repeating the same idea twice in the same verse, sometimes for explanation; and I imagine the meaning of the passage, *"Who is the man that feareth the Lord?"* to be, who, I say, is the man that God has instructed in his law, in the way that man has selected; that is, in the direct path of living a holy life, and moving to God, which he has already chosen of his free will. One part of the verse thus explains the

other, for that is he who fears God, who, by his grace, chooses the road to him, which road is none other than the observance of the commandments.
13. The happiness of the man fearing God consists in this, that *"his soul,"* the man fearing the Lord, *"shall dwell in good things,"* shall enjoy those good things, not for a while, or in a transitory way, but forever, permanently. Nothing can be more true, for *"To them that love God, all things work together unto good,"* as the apostle, in his Epistle to the Romans, has it. Therefore, he that fears God must be always happy. In prosperity he will know how to enjoy it; in adversity, patience and the hope of a great reward in the kingdom of heaven will come to his help. Thus, he will always be glad, and rejoice. And himself will not only dwell in good things, but even his children; *"His seed shall inherit the land;"* inheritance and possession signifying the same thing, as we have already explained in Psalm 15. The children of those who fear God will possess the land, because they will live in peace therein, without any one to injure them, in the sense we have alluded to; because to the good *"All things work together unto good;"* and their very tribulations become a source of joy and merit.
14. The reason why those who fear God shall always *"Dwell in good things,"* is, because they do not depend on perishable and transitory things, but God himself is *"their firmament;"* that is, their hope is based on the friendship and help of God. Firmament means foundation, on which they rest, that foundation being God himself; and their reason for depending on him is, because *"his covenant"* makes it *"manifest to them."* They who fear God know right well, and often call to mind, the treaty he entered into with man, to be their God, and to be a most loving parent to them, on the condition of their observing his laws; and they can, therefore, understand how, by reason of this compact, they can depend upon God, as upon a most solid foundation.
15. Having enlarged for a while on the happiness of those that fear the Lord, he now returns to wish and to pray for it: *"My eyes are ever towards the Lord."* My mind's eye has God ever before it, as being entirely dependent on him. The most effectual mode of prayer is, for one to place themselves in a most abject position, before the one from whom help is expected, and to propitiate the benignity of the great, rather by modestly, silently, and quietly pointing to our poverty, than by stunning them with our clamor. As we have in Psalm 122, *"As the eyes of the handmaid are on the hands of her mistress; so are our eyes unto the Lord our God until he have mercy on us." "For he shall pluck thy feet out of the snare."* I have my eyes so intently fixed on God, because he will, as I trust, deliver me from all danger of temptations, which, like snares, beset us on all sides while here below. The expression may also mean, that I always keep up the intention of pleasing God, and of doing nothing opposed to his will. It may also mean the contemplation of the divine beauty,

which is always before the mind's eye of those that seriously love God; but, I consider the first explanation the most literal.

16. As he is always looking to God, he justly asks to be looked upon by him. Such was his silent prayer when he had his *"eyes ever toward the Lord,"* hoping he may regard with mercy his loneliness and his poverty. He says he is *"alone,"* lonely and desolate, or (which is better) because he had in spirit detached himself from the whole world, and attached himself to God alone. He calls himself *"poor,"* because in his humility he looked upon himself as destitute of all virtues and merits.

17. I am more inclined to think the temptations of sin are referred to here, rather than temporal troubles. David was one of those who, with the apostle, Rom. 7, groaned and said, *"But I see another law in my members, fighting against the law of my mind, and captivating me in the law of sin, that is in my members. Unhappy man that I am, who shall deliver me from the body of this death."* "The necessities," from which he seeks to be delivered, seem to be those most troublesome motions of concupiscence, which, in spite of us, will sometimes torment us, and even lead us to sin.

18. He follows up the prayer, and asks forgiveness for the sins into which he may have fallen by the force of temptation. For, though a soul fearing God may be grievously afflicted, and take great pains in resisting concupiscence, still the just man falls seven times; and yet, from his fall, he may be proved to be just; because, at once, by his tears, his prayers, and his contrition, he quickly wipes away the filth and dirt into which he had incautiously fallen. By *"abjection,"* we are not to understand the virtue of humility; but his abjection, properly speaking, his meanness. For the just man, when he means to become quite perfect, looks down thoroughly on himself, and still does not escape sin. Instead of *"Forgive me my sins,"* the Hebrew has *"bear my sins,"* expressive of the trouble of the true child of God, for fear God may be displeased by the great number of them; and he, therefore, exclaims, *"bear them."* Do not be fatigued in carrying them, and supporting my weakness.

19. He argues now from the number and the cruelty of his enemies. Lord, says he, you have seen *"My abjection and my labor;"* behold, now, the multitude, the cruelty, and the iniquity of my spiritual enemies. The enemies who seek to draw us to sin, and incessantly inflame our concupiscence with red hot weapons, are the demons whom St. Paul calls *"The spirits of wickedness;"* that they are innumerable is well known; and that they burn with the worst sort of hatred, with *"An unjust hatred"* against us, is equally well known. Hatred is said to be unjust, or most unjust, when one hates another without cause, without any provocation. The hatred may also be said to be unjust, when one seeks to harm another; not for any lucre or benefit, to be derived therefrom, but, from the mere spirit of mischief. Such is the hatred of the devil towards the human race, especially towards the elect; for mankind never did any harm to the devil, but he, blinded by envy, was the ruin of man. *"By the envy of the devil, death came into the world,"* Wisd. 2. The same evil one now harasses the faithful by temptations, not for the purpose of deriving any benefit therefrom, but to gratify his delight in the ruin of the just.

20. Surrounded as I am by so many enemies, especially invisible ones, to resist whom I feel my own strength unequal, I have, therefore, recourse to you *"to keep my soul,"* and by your care of it, to free and deliver me from them. For freeing and delivering from the enemy does not suppose that a capture has been made, it equally applies when a capture is prevented. *"Thou hast delivered my soul out of the lower hell,"* Psalm 85, which means, as it does here, you have prevented my falling into it. The meaning may be also, Keep my soul in the prison of this body, in which I am detained a captive, *"For the law of my members holds me a captive in the law of sin,"* and afterwards, in the fitting time, deliver me.

21. Having said, in the preceding verse, that *"I shall not be ashamed, for I have hoped in thee,"* he gives a reason why he would fear to be ashamed at being deserted by God, and the reason is, that *"many innocent and upright,"* through the force of his example, especially from seeing him hope in God alone, *"adhered to thee,"* who certainly would cause him to blush and to be confounded were they to see him disappointed. *"I shall not be ashamed,"* then, has quite a different meaning in the end of the Psalm from what it had in the beginning of it. In the beginning the meaning was, *"I will not be ashamed"* before my enemies in their insolence; here it is, *"I will not be ashamed"* before my friends in their kind condolence.

22. David, being not only one of God's people, but also the prince and head of others, having prayed at sufficient length for himself, he now adds a prayer for his people; a general one, as being unable to enter into the peculiar wants and difficulties of each individual.

PSALM 25

David's prayer to God in his distress, to be delivered, that he may come to worship him in his tabernacle.

1 Judge me, O Lord, for I have walked in my innocence: and I have put my trust in the Lord, and shall not be weakened.
2 Prove me, O Lord, and try me; burn my reins and my heart.
3 For thy mercy is before my eyes; and I am well pleased with thy truth.
4 I have not sat with the council of vanity: neither will I go in with the doers of unjust things.
5 I have hated the assembly of the malignant; and with the wicked I will not sit.

*6 I will wash my hands among the innocent; and will compass thy altar, O Lord:
7 That I may hear the voice of thy praise: and tell of all thy wondrous works.
8 I have loved, O Lord, the beauty of thy house; and the place where thy glory dwelleth.
9 Take not away my soul, O God, with the wicked: nor my life with bloody men:
10 In whose hands are iniquities: their right hand is filled with gifts.
11 But as for me, I have walked in my innocence: redeem me, and have mercy on me.
12 My foot hath stood in the direct way: in the churches I will bless thee, O Lord.*

Explanation of the Psalm

1. David, having a misunderstanding with the king, appeals to the King of kings, there being none other to whom he could appeal. *"Judge me, O Lord."* Be you, O Lord, my judge; let not Saul take it on him, but do it yourself. *"For I have walked in my innocence,"* with confidence I challenge God's judgment, because my conscience which God alone beholds, does not reprove me, *"For I have walked in my innocence."* I have led an innocent life. *"I have put my trust in the Lord, and shall not be weakened."* Trusting in God's justice, I will not fail, but will conquer.

2. Having stated that he led an innocent life, he proves it by the testimony of God himself, who neither can deceive nor be deceived; for he does not tell God to *"prove and try him,"* in order to come at truth of which he was ignorant, but that he may make known to others what he in secret sees. David then, on the strength of a good conscience, and in the sincerity of his heart, speaks to the Lord, saying. *"Prove me and try me;"* search with the greatest diligence, examine the inmost and deepest recesses of my heart; nay more, *"burn my reins and my heart,"* examine my thoughts and desires as carefully as gold, when tested by the fire. I do not think David asks here to be proved and tried by adversity, or that *"his reins and heart"* should be scorched by the fire of tribulation, when he seems to be asking for the very contrary; but he asks, as I stated before, to be *"proved and tried"* by a most minute examination and inspection; and God having the most minute and exact knowledge of everything, that he may declare to the world the innocence of his servant, and thus silence the calumny of his enemies.

3. He assigns a reason for wishing to be *"proved and tried,"* inasmuch as his conscience encouraged him therein, as if he said, I beg of you to prove me, for I have trod thy paths, for *"all thy ways are mercy and truth,"* Psalm 24; and *"thy mercy is before my eyes,"* which I always look upon and consider, in the hope of being able to imitate it, and to act by my neighbors in conformity with it; *"And I am well pleased with thy truth."* It has pleased me, and I have therefore lived according to it.

4-5. Theodoret, in my opinion, most properly says, that these words apply to the idolatrous assemblies of the gentiles in their temples, of which David had the greatest abhorrence, and which he witnessed while in exile with the king of the Philistines. Everything, he says, here appears to be put in opposition to what he says in other parts of the Psalm, for instance, *"I have loved, O Lord, the beauty of thy house;"* and a little before that, *"I will compass thy altar, O Lord;"* and herein after, *"In the churches will I bless thee, O Lord."* He calls the assembly of the idolaters the *"council of vanity,"* for what can be more vain? What, more vain than idols, false images? As the apostle says, *"We know that an idol is nothing in the world,"* 1 Cor. 7. Throughout the Scriptures idols are called vain, or vanities, Deut. 32, *"They have provoked me with that which was no God and have angered me with their vanities;"* and 1 Kings 12, *"And turned not aside after vain things, which shall never profit you, nor deliver you, because they are vain."* See also 3 Kings 16; Jeremias 2, and various other passages. The same idolaters are styled, *"Doers of unjust things,"* because the height of injustice is to give to creatures the worship due to God alone. *"The council of vanity,"* in one verse is called the *"Assembly of the malignant"* in the next; *"Doers of unjust things"* in the same verse are called the *"Wicked,"* a name peculiarly appropriate to idolaters, in the following verse.

6. Having expressed his hatred of the conventicles of the idolatrous infidels, among whom he was then living, he adds, that he has, on the contrary, the most intense love for the tabernacle of the Lord and the assembly of the saints; and briefly states what he means to do when, through God's assistance, he shall have been called from exile to his own country. *"I will wash my hands among the innocent; and will compass thy altar, O Lord."* Before I go into thy temple, I will do what all pious people are wont to do: *"I will wash my hands,"* and go about your altar joining those in the act of it, in hymns of praise. For the meaning. Some will have it, that David alludes to the washing of hands, as a proof or sign of one's innocence, as Pilate washed his hands before the Jews, saying, *"I am innocent of the blood of this just man;"* as if he said, See, I have washed my hands, do not pollute them with the blood of this just man; and I, therefore, dare not condemn him. We often use a similar expression when we wish to get out of a thing. We say, *"I wash my hands out of it."* I consider, however, the sense more likely to be, and more in keeping with the rest of the chapter, to consider David alluding to a custom of the Jews, who, previous to their entering into the tabernacle, purified both themselves and the victims they offered, which purifications or lotions, are called by the apostle Heb. 9, *"Divers washings and justifications of the flesh;"* and, as those external lotions ought to be the sign of internal purity, David, therefore, says, *"I will wash my hands among the innocent,"* as a sign of my real internal purity, as an innocent person would wash them;

and not with the hypocrites, who do so with clean hands and unclean heart. The expression, *"I will compass thy altar,"* some understand of the number of victims; but I rather think it refers to those who in hymns of praise will go about the altar, as the following Psalm has it, *"I have gone round, and have offered up a sacrifice of jubilation;"* and in the very next verse to this we have, *"That I may hear the voice of thy praise; and tell of all thy wondrous works."*

7. An explanation of the expression, *"I will compass thy altar, O Lord,"* that with the choir of worshipers I may hear, and join in singing the praises of the Lord. St. Augustine, arguing against the Pelagians, proves, with great accuracy and piety, from this passage, that they only hear the voice of God's praise who refer all their actions, and all they possess, to God's free gift. For the hearts of the just, *"who have ears to hear,"* are always devoted to God's praise, thanking him for all their own merits and virtues; whereas, on the contrary, those who presume on their own justice, and are swollen with the idea of their own perfections, as if they had them by their own exertions, and not from God, do not hear *"the voice of thy praise,"* but the voice of their own praise.

8. Nothing gave him more trouble in his exile than the being unable to see the tabernacle of the Lord. His mind, deeply inflamed with the love of God, looked upon no spot on the earth more beautiful than that where God was wont to show himself visibly. The tabernacle that contained the ark of the covenant was called, *"The house of God," "the place of the habitation of his glory,"* because a bright cloud would frequently descend thereon, to signify God's presence there; the God *"who inhabiteth light inaccessible,"* Jam. 1:6, and because there, too, was the oracle from which God gave his responses.

9. Having appealed to God, at first, as a judge, and having exposed his innocence, of which God was witness, he concludes by a prayer, that judgment may be delivered in his favor, *"Take not away my soul, O God, with the wicked."* Do not condemn me as you do the wicked; *"My soul"* means me, as it does frequently through the Scriptures; and by *"Bloody men,"* he means those who, like so many homicides, were persecuting him.

10. He tells us who are the wicked and the bloody men of whom he spoke in the foregoing verse; they are those who receive bribes for unfair judgments, glancing at the sins of those in power, the judges. With much point he says, *"In whose hands are iniquities;"* attributing the iniquity to that part of the body that touches the bribe, to show the bribe was the cause of the iniquity.

11. He repeats his reason for not being condemned with the wicked, namely, because *"He walked in his innocence;"* that is, led an innocent life. *"Redeem me, and have mercy on me."* Deliver me from my present troubles, and then have mercy on me, that I may not fall into them again. The words *"redeem"* and *"deliver,"* most frequently have the same meaning in the Scriptures,

unless, perhaps, the Holy Ghost may insinuate that any deliverance of the elect from tribulation may be called redemption, inasmuch as such is effected through the blood of Christ our Redeemer.

12. These words have reference to the concluding expression in the last verse, *"have mercy on me."* I have asked to be delivered from my present trouble by reason of the rectitude of my life; I ask for future mercy, because *"My foot hath stood;"* that is to say, is firmly fixed and planted in the direct, honest road, and, therefore, I cannot easily leave the straight path of thy law; and, in thanksgiving for it, *"I will bless thee"* and praise thee *"in the churches,"* the assemblies of the pious.

PSALM 26

David's faith and hope in God.

1 The Lord is my light and my salvation, whom shall I fear? The Lord is the protector of my life: of whom shall I be afraid?
2 Whilst the wicked draw near against me, to eat my flesh. My enemies that trouble me, have themselves been weakened, and have fallen.
3 If armies in camp should stand together against me, my heart shall not fear. If a battle should rise up against me, in this will I be confident.
4 One thing I have asked of the Lord, this will I seek after; that I may dwell in the house of the Lord all the days of my life. That I may see the delight of the Lord, and may visit his temple.
5 For he hath hidden me in his tabernacle; in the day of evils, he hath protected me in the secret place of his tabernacle.
6 He hath exalted me upon a rock: and now he hath lifted up my head above my enemies. I have gone round, and have offered up in his tabernacle a sacrifice of jubilation: I will sing, and recite a psalm to the Lord.
7 Hear, O Lord, my voice, with which I have cried to thee: have mercy on me and hear me.
8 My heart hath said to thee: My face hath sought thee: thy face, O Lord, will I still seek.
9 Turn not away thy face from me; decline not in thy wrath from thy servant. Be thou my helper, forsake me not; do not thou despise me, O God my Saviour.
10 For my father and my mother have left me: but the Lord hath taken me up.
11 Set me, O Lord, a law in thy way, and guide me in the right path, because of my enemies.
12 Deliver me not over to the will of them that trouble me; for unjust witnesses have risen up against me; and iniquity hath lied to itself.
13 I believe to see the good things of the Lord in the land of the living.
14 Expect the Lord, do manfully, and let thy heart take courage, and wait thou for the Lord.

Explanation of the psalm

1. Tribulation brings on darkness, prosperity brings light and serenity; for tribulation confuses and confounds the soul, so that it cannot easily see how it ought to act, and thence is provoked to impatience, or to some other sin. But should God, by his divine light, dispel the darkness, the soul at once sees that the tribulation, which in the darkness of the night brought such horrors with it, was temporary and trifling; and sees, at the same time, that tribulation, when God protects us, can not only do us no harm, but even tends marvelously to our good. David, having learned this by experience, exclaims, therefore, for himself, and in the person of all the elect, *"The Lord is my light and my salvation, whom shall I fear?"* In other words, ignorance and infirmity made me timid in my tribulation, but once the Lord *"enlightened"* my mind, he made me clearly see that no temporal calamity can be grievous or continuous, and healed my soul with the ointment of divine love. *"I fear no one,"* for truth expels darkness, and *"perfect charity casteth out fear,"* 1 John 4. *"The Lord is the protector of my life, of whom shall I be afraid?"* another reason why he should no longer fear. The Lord not only is *"my light and my salvation,"* he will not desert me when enlightened and saved, but will constantly protect me with the shield of his providence and benevolence. *"Of whom shall I be afraid,"* then? *"If God be for us, who is against us?"* If a king, with a powerful armed escort, has no reason to fear, why should a servant of God, protected by his powerful and immortal master, have any fear about him? *"Protected by the sign of the cross, instead of shield and helmet, I will securely penetrate the ranks of the enemy,"* says St. Martin; for he was one of those who could confidently say, *"The Lord is the protector of my life, of whom shall I be afraid?"*

2. He describes the effects of God's protection, and, as is usual with the prophets, makes use of the past for the future tense, to show the certainty of the matter. The meaning is, God will so protect me, that when they who wish me harm, *"shall draw near against me,"* like dogs or lions, *"seeking to eat my flesh,"* *"these enemies that so trouble me"* will become *"so weak"* and *"so fallen"* by their efforts, that, instead of harming me, they will only damage themselves. That such is the case is clear from the example, not only of David himself, but of Christ, and the martyrs, and of all the saints.

3. To show what unbounded confidence he has in God, he now says that he not only despises his enemies individually, but that he even fears not *"armies in camp"* of his enemies, and not only so encamped but even in actual battle.

4. This *"one thing,"* so asked, is thought by some to mean the house where the ark of the covenant lay; who will have it that he asks to return from exile, that he may be near the ark. I prefer the opinion of St. Augustine, who understands it of heaven, which seems to be not only the true, but even the literal meaning. For David does not ask to dwell near *"the house of the Lord,"* but *"in the house of the Lord;"* and it is well known that David never lived in the house of the Lord, but in his own palace, which was a good distance from the tabernacle, more so before the tabernacle was brought to Mount Sion; and he could, had he so chosen it, when he was king, have lived as near as he pleased to the tabernacle. Along with that, this verse is a counterpart of one in Psalm 83, *"Blessed are they that dwell in thy house, O Lord; they shall praise thee forever and ever;"* a phrase that can only be applied to those that dwell in God's house in heaven. Finally, David, holy and perfect as he was, would never have so ardently desired or asked for any temporal favor in such terms as, *"one thing I have asked of the Lord,"* as if nothing else was to be asked. The prophet then, in this passage, tells us what is the real foundation of his confidence in God, and why he fears no temporal calamity. The foundation is a fervent love of God, for he that fervently loves the supreme and everlasting good, sets no value whatever on the things of this world. *"One thing I have asked of the Lord; this I will seek after."* I ask for nothing temporal; I care not for the loss of the whole world, provided I be found worthy of possessing one thing; for that one thing alone do I care; that one thing alone have I asked; that one thing alone will I ask; namely, *"to dwell in the house of the Lord;"* not for a while, but, *"For all the days of my life;"* that is, during the life of the saints with God, which will certainly have no termination. Observe the point in the words, *"That I may dwell in the house of the Lord;"* for while here on earth we are the children, as well as the friends of God; however, we do not dwell with, but rather walk with God; nor do we rest in his house, but in his tent. *"That I may see the delight of the Lord, and may visit his temple."* He tells us why he longs to dwell in the house of the Lord, because there perfect happiness reigns. For there is to be seen the beauty of God's house and of the heavenly host; where nothing profane can enter, but where there is a daily sacrifice of jubilation and praise.

5. He assigns a reason for having so boldly asked for a place in the house of the Lord, and a sight of his beauty; because he had already got a taste of his sweetness, and a pledge of his love: as if he briefly said, Having received the grace, I dare to ask for the glory. The whole is metaphorical; for, correctly speaking, David was not *"hid in the tabernacle"* of the Lord, when Saul was in pursuit of him; but the whole passage means, in the evil days of the present time, God has defended and protected me as effectually as if he had placed and hidden me in the inmost recesses of his tabernacle, and from such condescension on God's part, I confidently hope that I will one day arrive at his house, *"The one thing I have asked;"* the one thing *"I will seek after."* The second part of the verse is, in other words, a repetition of the first.

6. By another metaphor he conveys the same idea; namely, that he was so defended and protected by God's providence as if he were in a lofty and well fortified tower. Isaias uses the same metaphor when he says, 33:16, *"He shall dwell on high; the fortifications of rocks shall be his highness."* The meaning then is, *"He hath exalted me upon a rock;"* placed me in an elevated, fortified position, and hence, *"My head is lifted up above my enemies;"* I have subdued and vanquished them all. Thus is described not only the protection and defense of the just, who cannot possibly be injured by any machinations of the enemy, according to 1 Peter 3, *"And who is he that can hurt you, if you be zealous of good?"* but even we are told how the just arrived at such security; namely, by elevating the mind in contemplation to God and to eternity. For he that seriously meditates on eternity, and has an ardent love for God, is placed on a very lofty and well fortified tower, so that nothing can harm him, all earthly things having now become so vile in his sight. *"I have gone round."* The prophet having spoken of contemplation, is himself now wrapped in it; is raised up above everything earthly, and breaks out in admiration of God's works, and of the Almighty producer of them. *"I have gone round."* I have taken a mental survey of God's works in heaven and on earth; *"And have offered up in his tabernacle a sacrifice of jubilation;"* in this great tabernacle of God, the heavens, which I have ascended in spirit; in a loud voice, proceeding from intense admiration, I have offered my tribute of praise to God, the most agreeable sacrifice I could possibly offer him, as we read in another Psalm, *"Offer to God the sacrifice of praise;"* and, in the same Psalm, *"The sacrifice of praise shall glorify me,"* a thing I have not only already done, but will do daily, for *"I will sing and recite a psalm to the Lord."*

7. He reverts to *"One thing I have asked of the Lord,"* which one petition he asks may be granted, burning as he is with a vehement desire of beholding his beloved. *"Hear, O Lord, my voice with which I have cried to thee;"* namely, when I asked for the *"One thing."* *"Have mercy on me,"* suffering as I am in my exile, *"and hear me."*

8-9. These verses require more to be reflected on and put into practice than to be explained. *"My heart hath said to thee."* My desires have spoken to thee. *"My face hath sought thee."* My interior eyes, fixed in the face of my soul, look for thy beauty—despise everything else. *"Thy face, O Lord, will I still seek."* It shall be always my study to look for a sight of thee, in the hope not only of seeing thee face to face in the world to come; but that also, in this world, too, I may study one thing only, to catch your looks, and through them to be enlightened and inflamed. *"Turn not away thy face from me."* Keep your eyes constantly on me, for fear my light may grow dark, and my charity grow cold. *"Decline not in thy wrath from thy servant."* Allow me not to fall into sin, for fear you may desert me in your anger. St. Augustine justly observes that the fear alluded to here is not servile, but holy fear. Servile fear wishes for the master's absence, to be able to offend with impunity, and, therefore, would not make use of the expression, *"Decline not,"* but would rather say, Go away, and decline; but holy fear, that truly loves the beloved, fears nothing more than his departure. *"Be thou my helper."* Having asked God *"not to decline in his wrath from his servant,"* and that, from a consideration of the impossibility of his avoiding, by his own strength, the sins that provoke the anger of God, he cries out to him to continue helping him. The just man, then, asks God's help to avoid sin; but should he unfortunately fall, he begs he may not be discarded entirely, but that he may, in mercy, be pardoned and cured; and he, therefore, adds, *"O God, any Savior;"* for a Savior's duty is to heal and to cure, instead of rejecting and despising the unfortunate.

10. A very urgent reason assigned for God's assisting him, there being none that loves us so ardently. Observe the third person used for the second in the end of the verse; instead of saying, Thou hast taken me up, he says, *"The Lord hath taken me up,"* and that through reverence for God. A similar change of person occurs in Genesis, where Rachel says to her father, *"Let not my Lord be angry at my not being able to rise before you;"* and, in Kings, Nathan says to David, *"Has this word gone out from my Lord the king?"* The expression, then, *"The Lord hath taken me up,"* is the same as, You, O Lord, have taken me up. These words beautifully express the goodness of God, for David was then no child, to feel the want of parents; nor could it have been any great loss to him to be without his parents, who then would rather have been a burden than a loss to him; the meaning then is, I am like a new born babe, deserted, abandoned by its natural parents, and thus exposed to all manner of danger; but when so cast away and deserted, you, O Lord, have, in the excess of your goodness, taken me up, fostered, nourished, and cherished me. And, in fact, any one that will only reflect on the frailty of human nature, the power of our invisible enemies, and how much we need the grace of God in all our actions, will not deny that we are, with the greatest justice, compared to infants exposed and abandoned by their parents. So convinced was Ezechias, the prophet, of his infirmity in this respect, that it was not to an exposed infant, but to a swallow's young, unfledged, that he compared himself, Isaias 58, *"Like the young of a swallow, so will I cry."*

11. Having compared himself to an exposed, deserted infant, adopted by God, he anon fairly asks to be shown how to walk. He asks the grace of being able to observe all his holy commandments, which he never loses sight of through the whole one hundred and fifty Psalms. What else could he do? when it was the only path to that heavenly house of God, which he had just declared to be the only wish and desire of his heart. *"And guide me in the right path, because of my enemies;"* that is, direct me in the way of your

commandments, which is truly *"the right path;"* the most just, however narrow it may be. Others will have it that, *"Teach me thy way"* is a request for internal inspiration; and *"Direct me in the right path,"* means a petition for a loving desire of observing the commandments. The Words, *"Because of my enemies,"* imply the necessity of the grace of God in this pilgrimage here below, to protect us from our visible, as well as from our invisible enemies, who are in daily ambush, watching us, seeking to divert us from the straight road of virtue to the rugged and difficult passes of vice.

12. The same petition continued. He asks to be saved from being delivered up to *"the will"* of his enemies, especially his invisible ones. A similar expression occurs in Luke 23, *"He gave Jesus up to their will."* *"For unjust witnesses have risen up,"* is by many referred to the false witnesses that so calumniated David; not an improbable explanation; but I consider that the sentence will be more in accordance with what preceded, as well as with what follows, and also with the subject of the whole Psalm, if we interpret these words as applying to the temptations, whether of demons or of men, who, by false promises, or by threats, seek to bring the just to impatience, or to any other sin, as we have in Psalm 118, *"The wicked have told me fables, but not as thy law."*

13. He tells us why *"iniquity hath lied to itself."* For I, in spite of all my enemies, *"believe,"* have the strongest confidence, that *"I will see the good things of the Lord;"* that is, those good things which, before God, are good; which make man happy, which alone are really good; and that, *"in the land of the living,"* in that land where death hath no place, no dominion.

14. He concludes by an apostrophe to himself, to have patience and confidence in God, saying, My soul, as you desire to dwell in the house of God, as you have so many pledges of his love, as you *"believe to see the good things of the Lord in the land of the living,"* do not be disheartened in your trouble, do not look for any earthly consolation, but *"wait patiently,"* take courage in the Lord, act the part of a man, until the evil days shall have passed away, and the good ones shall have arrived.

PSALM 27

David's prayer that his enemies may not prevail over him.

1 Unto thee will I cry, O Lord: O my God, be not thou silent to me: lest thou be silent to me, I become like them that go down into the pit.

2 Hear, O Lord, the voice of my supplication, when I pray to thee; when I lift up my hands to thy holy temple.

3 Draw me not away together with the wicked; and with the workers of iniquity destroy me not: Who speak peace with their neighbour, but evils are in their hearts.

*4 Give them according to their works, and according to the wickedness of their inventions. According to the works of their hands give thou to them: render to them their reward.
5 Because they have not understood the works of the Lord, and the operations of his hands: thou shalt destroy them, and shalt not build them up.
6 Blessed be the Lord, for he hath heard the voice of my supplication.
7 The Lord is my helper and my protector: in him hath my heart confided, and I have been helped. And my flesh hath flourished again, and with my will I will give praise to him.
8 The Lord is the strength of his people, and the protector of the salvation of his anointed.
9 Save, O Lord, thy people, and bless thy inheritance: and rule them and exalt them for ever.*

Explanation of the Psalm

1. Words spoken by Christ as he hung on the cross, asking for a speedy resurrection. *"Be not thou silent;"* do not turn from me, as if you were deaf, and did not hear me. He asks in a few words, that he may be heard, and get an answer from God that his prayer would be heard. *"Lest if thou be silent to me, I become like them that go down into the pit;"* he wishes for an answer, because if God will not hear him, and give him a favorable answer, he will be like all other mortals who die and go to the lower regions, never to return therefrom. *"Lest if thou be silent to me;"* for fear you may not hear me, and I may, in consequence, become like those *"that go down into the pit,"* never to come out of it but on the day of judgment. Another explanation may be offered, viz., If you do not hear me, I will be like the dead; for, as the dead can do nothing whatever, so man, without God's assistance, can do nothing.

2. The expression, *"Be not silent,"* is more clearly expressed, for now he says, *"Hear, O Lord, the voice of my supplication,"* for he wished for an answer from God, to show he had been heard. *"When I pray to thee;"* the Hebrew implies, that when he did pray, he had his hands stretched out, for both Hebrews and gentiles were wont so to extend their hands in prayer; and, in using this expression, the prophet had before him the hands of our Lord extended on the cross and raised to heaven; for then, with the greatest truth, could he say, *"When I pray to thee, when I lift up my hands;"* when he prayed from the cross.

3. Christ alone could say truly what this verse contains, because he was the only one, in every respect, *"separated from sinners."* And, being the only person in whom sin could find no place, he, with the greatest justice, asks that he may not be judged; that he may not perish with sinners, but that he should rather slay death itself; and, by rising from the dead, bear away

a most triumphant victory from the prince of death, and from death itself. The meaning then, is, Do not drag me to death with others who are sinners, for I am no sinner. *"Who speak peace with their neighbor, but evils are in their hearts."* He describes sinners in general from the sin most common and most universal among them, as he says in Psalm 115, *"Every man is a liar;"* and in Palm 42, *"Deliver me from the unjust and deceitful man;"* and, speaking of Christ, 1 St. Peter 2, says, *"Who did no sin, neither was guile found in his mouth;"* as if sin and guile in his mouth were nearly synonymous terms. And there are very many who wish to appear friends, to be full of good will to their neighbor; and are so blinded by self love, that they have malice in their heart, and are entirely absorbed in hatred or envy towards the same neighbor.

4. This is not an imprecation, but a prophecy, as we before observed. The meaning is, that the wicked will have a wretched end of it, unless, from being wicked, they become good; and the meaning is, you will give them the punishment their works deserve; *"And according to the wickedness of their inventions;"* which means, that as they, in their malice, invented and devised various modes of harassing the just, so you, in your wisdom, will find various ways of tormenting the sinner. *"Render to them their reward."* As they give the just evil for good, retort such conduct on them, by bringing down the evil they intended for the just, on their own heads.

5. From this verse it is clear that the preceding verse was a prophecy, and not an imprecation; for, he does not say destroy them, but thou shalt destroy them, in the future tense. Here the root of all evil is declared, that root being an unwillingness to understand the works of the Lord, the non appliance of one's mind to learn, know, and reflect upon the wonderful things God was pleased to do in the creation, redemption, and government of the human race; for any one reflecting on them could not fail to be wonderfully inflamed with the love of God. Hence, St. Paul, 1 Cor. 2, says, *"For if they had known it, they never would have crucified the Lord of glory."* And the Lord himself says, Luke 19, *"If thou also hadst known, and that in this thy day, the things that are for thy peace. They shall not leave in thee a stone upon a stone; because thou hast not known the time of thy visitation."* *"Because they have not understood the works of the Lord, and the operations of his hands;"* the latter words would seem to imply that in speaking of God's works he means those that were directly done through himself, and not through secondary causes, such as the creation, the Incarnation, the miracles, Resurrection, and Ascension of our Lord, and the like; and he says, as sinners did not understand the works of the Lord, and particularly those produced by his own hands, namely, what he directly produced; therefore you, O Lord, *"will destroy them;"* and when you will destroy them, you will not regret

having done so; and thus you will never *"build them up."* The prophet takes up the words, *"the operations of his hands,"* as if it were a building God had in hands, and he says, As they did not understand the building of God, he will destroy them, and never again build them up; a thing that directly applies to the city, the temple, and the very kingdom of the Jews, which God, on account of their infidelity, destroyed, and which he will never build up again. It applies also to every sinner who does not bear in mind that he is an edifice raised by God, made to his own image, redeemed by his own blood, enriched with innumerable favors of nature and grace; but, nevertheless, will be so destroyed that they will never be rebuilt, and not more than a ruin of the edifice will be left, so that their punishment may be eternal.

6. He now passes to foretell the glory of the Lord's resurrection, and in the person of Christ he thanks God in this verse.

7. He explains in what respect his prayer was heard, and says, *"The Lord is my helper,"* as he is wont to be. Therefore, *"In him hath my heart confided;"* which means, relying on the help and protection of God, I have not refused to engage in combat with the devil, and with death itself; nor have I been disappointed in my hope, for God's help was such, that I had a very easy victory, *"And my flesh hath flourished again."* He describes the effect of God's help and protection, namely, his glorious resurrection, for which he praises God with his whole heart. My flesh, that had withered up in death, is not only restored to life, but to the bloom of youth, health, joy, and beauty. Therefore, *"With my will, I will give praise to him"* in praise and thanksgiving.

8. Such is to be the matter, the subject of the praise of which he spoke in the preceding verse, namely, *"The Lord is the strength of his people,"* a thing he proved when he so effectually protected the *"salvation of the anointed,"* (Christ,) who is the head of the whole people, and on whom the strength and safety of the whole people depend.

9. Christ, the head of the Church, having been glorified, it remains that his body, the people of God, who are his peculiar inheritance, he having acquired it with his blood, should be equally glorified. Christ then says to his Father, or the prophet says to Christ, *"Save thy people,"* and, in order to save them, *"Bless them,"* by justifying them *"Rule them,"* by shielding, by protecting them on the road; *"Exalt"* them, by glorifying them by glorifying them to eternity.

PSALM 28

An invitation to glorify God, with a commemoration of his mighty works.

1 Bring to the Lord, O ye children of God: bring to the Lord the offspring of rams.
2 Bring to the Lord glory and honour: bring to the Lord glory to his name: adore ye the Lord in his holy court.

*3 The voice of the Lord is upon the waters; the God of majesty hath thundered, The Lord is upon many waters.
4 The voice of the Lord is in power; the voice of the Lord in magnificence.
5 The voice of the Lord breaketh the cedars: yea, the Lord shall break the cedars of Libanus.
6 And shall reduce them to pieces, as a calf of Libanus, and as the beloved son of unicorns.
7 The voice of the Lord divideth the flame of fire:
8 The voice of the Lord shaketh the desert: and the Lord shall shake the desert of Cades.
9 The voice of the Lord prepareth the stags: and he will discover the thick woods: and in his temple all shall speak his glory.
10 The Lord maketh the flood to dwell: and the Lord shall sit king for ever. The Lord will give strength to his people: the Lord will bless his people with peace*

EXPLANATION OF THE PSALM

1. The prophet, being about to chant the praises of the divine power, stirs up God's peculiar people, to whom he was known, for *"God is known in Judea, in Israel great is his name,"* Psalm 73, to honor that power with the victims of the season, the hymns of their voice, and the prostration of their bodies. Taking the summons to refer to a later period, the explanation would be, that when about to chant the praises of the divinity, the perfecter of the tabernacle, that is, of the Church, who is the mother of all God's children, he invites those children, so called by the inspiration of heaven, to offer to God sacrifice of praise. *"Bring to the Lord, O ye children of God, the offspring of rams;"* you that have been made children of God by the blood of the immaculate Lamb, bring your own lambs, bring the sacrifice of praise and thanksgiving, as he further explains in the following verse.

2. The prophet tells us what sort of sacrifice we should offer to God, namely, *"Glory and honor;"* that is, in your words and your works glorify the Lord; and not only in your words and works, but even in the carriage of your person, which should be so reverential as to make it appear to all that you acknowledge him as your supreme Master, and that you adore him as such. *"Bring to the Lord glory to his name."*

Bring glory to the Lord, that is, to his name, by celebrating the name, fame, and knowledge of the Lord. *"Adore ye the Lord in his holy court."* The holy court may mean either the vestibule of the Jewish tabernacle, to which all could resort, while the priests alone were permitted to enter the tabernacle; or the Catholic Church, which is like the porch or vestibule of the heavenly tabernacle. All, good and bad, are promiscuously permitted to enter the Church, but they alone will enter the heavenly tabernacle who can say to Christ, *"Thou hast made us a kingdom and priests to our God."*

3. He now explains why he invited us to celebrate and praise the power of God, and the reason is, because the *"voice of the Lord"* has a wonderful influence on the elements of nature, as well as on the spiritual fabric of the Church. He then describes God's action on the waters, on the air, on the fire, and, finally, on the earth; these four elements being the principal ones of this world here below, as known to us. God's action on the water is described in the first chapter of Genesis, where it is said that *"The spirit of the Lord moved over the waters;" "And God said, Let there be a firmament made amidst the waters, and let it divide the waters from the waters." "God also said, Let the waters that are under the heavens be gathered together in one place, and let the dry land appear."* Then was *"the voice of the Lord upon the waters,"* when God commanded a division in them, and, on their division, their retirement into one place, to the caverns of the earth, so that the earth may be habitable. That voice or command of God is called thunder; for, as thunder prostrates and makes us submit and obey, so, at the command of God, the waters retired, and betook themselves into lower places. This voice and thunder of God *"was upon the waters,"* because at that time water covered the whole surface of the earth, and there was, therefore, an immense abyss of water on the earth. This is more clearly described in Psalm 103, where he says, *"The deep, like a garment, is its clothing; above the mountains shall the waters stand;"* that is, the earth was covered all over by an immense body of water, so as even to cover the mountains. *"At thy rebuke they shall flee; at the voice of thy thunder they shall fear. The mountains ascend, and the plains descend into the place which thou hast founded for them;"* that is, at God's command the waters retired as they would from a thunderbolt; and then there appeared the mountains raised up and the plains depressed. *"Thou hast set bounds to them which they shall not pass over; neither shall they return to cover the earth."* At the voice of the Lord, not only have the waters retired and left the earth dry and habitable, but by reason of the same voice, a limit has been put to them which they will never dare to transgress. Another interpretation refers this passage to the beginning of the preaching of the gospel, which had its first rise when God, on the baptism of Christ in the Jordan, announced to the whole world that Jesus Christ was his Son, which is, as it were, the compendium of the Gospel. *"The voice of the Lord on the waters"* would then mean that magnificent declaration of God, on the baptism of Christ, *"This is my beloved Son in whom I am well pleased."* And then *"The God of majesty thundered, and thundered upon many waters,"* because then was instituted baptism, and all the waters of the world got the power of regenerating the children of God.

4. The praise here attributed to God's voice can be well applied to either interpretation. For the voice of the Lord, in the first stages of creation, ordering the waters to divide, to betake themselves to the lower caverns of the earth, never to return, was not an empty or idle command, or without producing its effect; as thunder, that, generally speaking, does no more than make a great noise, but was full of nerve, efficacious and glorious, and produced the effect required. So also the voice of the Gospel, intoned by God himself, taken up by Christ and his apostles, was not an empty parade of words, like that of many philosophers and orators, but was most effective, being confirmed by signs and miracles. The efficacy of the preaching is conveyed in the words, *"in power;"* the splendor and glory of the miracles, in the word, *"magnificence,"* as St. Paul has it, 1 Cor. 2, *"My preaching was not in the persuasive words of human wisdom, but in the showing of the spirit and power;"* and, 1 Thess. chap. 1, *"For our gospel hath not been to you in word only, but in power also, and in the Holy Ghost."*

5. According to the first interpretation, the prophet passes now from the action of God upon the waters to his action on the air; and he tells us that *"the voice of the Lord,"* namely, his orders, raise the winds and the storms, which, in Psalm 118, he calls, *"Stormy winds which fulfill his word."* How wonderful is God's power! that can give such force and strength to a thing apparently so weak and feeble, that will, in one moment, tear up and lay prostrate the largest trees, that many men could not accomplish in many days. He quotes *"cedars,"* and the *"cedars of Libanus,"* they being the largest, deepest rooted, and longest lived trees in the world. According to the second explanation, the cedars of Libanus are those high people who, by reason of their power, their wisdom, or their eloquence, are so very high in their own estimation; or, in reference to the fragrance of the cedar, those people who are entirely devoted to pleasure and gluttony; or, in reference to density of foliage and endurance, those who are perverse and obstinate in error. All such cedars will be broken to pieces by the preaching of the Gospel, and brought down to Christian mildness and humility, and to the bringing forth fruits worthy of penance. History abounds in such examples.

6. According to the first explanation, the meaning of this passage is very easy and very beautiful, when explained through the Hebrew, and it means, The voice of the Lord will not only break the cedars of Libanus, but will even tear up entire cedars from the roots, and make them bound like so many calves. And not only the calves, but even the mountains themselves, will be made to bound like a young unicorn. Similar to it is the expression in Psalm 113, *"The mountains skipped like rams, and the hills like the lambs of sheep."* According to the second interpretation, the meaning would be, The sound of the Gospel will not only break the cedars of Libanus, that is, men, however proud and high they may be, and bring them down to the humility of the Christian religion; but will even tear up the same cedars from the roots, and make them bound to another place; that is, will entirely detach them from all earthly affections, and bring them to nearly an angelic life; a thing clearly carried out in the apostles, who became so religious and so perfect upon earth, as to appear more like Angels than like men. And it is not one isolated cedar, but a whole forest of them, that the preaching of the gospel causes to bound and leap; that means, that it is not an individual or two that will be brought to faith, religion, and perfection, but whole masses and congregations. *"And as the beloved sons of unicorns,"* a most graceful animal in its movements, light and agile; such will be the avidity of all tribes and nations to obey the Gospel. According to the second interpretation, the meaning would be, The preaching of the Gospel will not only humble the powerful and the wise, but it will break them into pieces, and make them as small as a calf on Libanus. By the calf we properly understand Christ, who was not only humble and mild as a suckling calf, but was also offered up in sacrifice to God. *"And as the beloved sons of unicorns;"* that means, when those proud cedars of Libanus shall have been destroyed, the beloved Christ, the most beloved of his father, the desired of all nations, will appear, no longer the helpless calf, but the son of a most valiant unicorn. The majesty of God and the omnipotence of Christ then began for the first time to show itself, when, through the preaching of the fishermen, the orators, the philosophers, nay, the very kings of the world, began to believe in Christ. On the strength of the unicorn, see Job 36:7.

7. The prophet now passes from the action of God on the air to his action on the fire, and says, *"His voice,"* that is, his power and authority, *"divideth the flames of fire,"* which he does when, at his command, the thunderbolts of heaven, the most destructive and dreadful weapons that can be used against man, issue, as it were, from the forges of heaven, and are *"divided,"* to intimate how sharp and acute they are, as Moses expresses, when he makes the Lord say, *"If I shall whet my sword as lightning."* According to the second interpretation, the voice of the Lord is the preaching of the Gospel, which divides the flames of fire, because the Holy Ghost sends various shafts in various ways through the hearts of men; and it was in such *"cloven tongues, as it were of fire,"* that the Holy Ghost settled on the apostles on the day of Pentecost.

8. His action on the earth is now the subject. The Hebrew for shaking implies more than mere shaking; it implies a shaking, previous to parturition, or the production of something. Thus, God's wonderful power is brought out when he appears to be able not only to lay waste and denude the forests of Libanus, and make it a desert; but when he can from the very desert call

up trees and animals, making it thus to shake with parturition. We have something like this idea in Psalm 106, *"He hath turned rivers into a wilderness: a fruitful land into barrenness. He hath turned a wilderness into pools of water. And hath placed there the hungry: and they made a city for their habitation. And they sowed fields, and planted vineyards."* According to the second interpretation, the meaning would be, The barbarians who were, up to that time, so backward in the cultivation of their souls, and in the grace of God, so that, compared to other nations, they might have been called deserted, would also be brought to the light of the Gospel.

9. According to the first interpretation, the prophet, having praised God's power in all the elements, water, air, fire, and earth, turns now to animals and plants, and afterwards to man. *"The voice of the Lord prepareth the stags."* See God's dealing with them! Job, chap. 39, tells us they bring forth their young with the greatest difficulty, and the reason seems to be that they bring them forth in a most perfect state, so that the moment they leave the mother's womb they go to pasture, and never more trouble the mother, as we read in the same passage. *"Preparing the stags,"* then, means helping them in their difficult parturition, through which they could never pass, had not Providence mercifully helped them through it. *"And he will discover the thick woods."* In the Hebrew it is, *"Will open the woods,"* and the meaning is, that nothing can be concealed or hidden from God, for he penetrates everything, acts upon everything, not only on animals, but on plants and trees, and men, too; and, therefore, he follows up by, *"And in his temple all shall speak his glory."* All creatures in the universe, for the universe is God's temple, will praise and glorify him.

According to the second interpretation, it would be thus, *"The voice of the Lord prepareth the stags."* The preaching of the Gospel prepares devoted souls, aiming at perfection, and blasting with their spirit the poisoned serpents, to produce wonderful things; for what can be more wonderful, or more surprising, than for a weak, infirm man to do any thing deserving of life everlasting. And since the voice of the Lord causes such wonderful works, it will, therefore, *"Discover the thick woods;"* that is, on the day of judgment, *"It will bring to light the hidden things of darkness, and will make manifest the counsels of the heart,"* 1 Cor. 4; and then will God's justice appear in that great theatre or temple, and will be recognized by the wicked, as well as by the just; for then will *"Every knee be bent to Christ;"* and all, whether with or against their will, shall exclaim, *"Thou art just, O Lord, and right is thy judgment;"* and thus, *"All in his temple shall speak his glory."*

10. According to the first interpretation, the meaning is, that a reason is assigned here for all things giving glory to God, for *"He maketh the flood to dwell;"* he pours out his wholesome rain in such abundance on the earth, as

to supply all the vegetable world with nutrition, which, in their turn, give support to animal life; and *"the Lord shall sit king forever;"* for it is he that guides, governs, and directs all these matters.

According to the second interpretation, when the Lord, on the day of judgment, shall have *"discovered the thick woods,"* and his justice shall have been praised by all, then he will *"make a flood to dwell,"* inundating the wicked with all manner of evils; and thus, all resistance being broken down, the whole power of demons, bad men, and all power in general being swept away, *"the Lord shall sit King forever."* Some will have the flood here spoken of to refer to the deluge, others to baptism; and those who so explain it being of great weight and high position, I will not contradict them. *"The Lord will give strength to his people: the Lord will bless his people with peace."*

The conclusion of the Psalm, in which, according to the first interpretation, having praised God for his dealings with all the inferior things and creatures of the world, he now praises him for *"giving strength to his people;"* nerve and strength to subdue all their enemies, and then to rest in profound and undisturbed peace. According to the second interpretation, herein is a promise of *"strength"* to resist temptation in this our pilgrimage, and a *"Blessing;"* namely, everlasting life in the world to come. Some pious people have remarked the significance of the words, the *"Voice of the Lord,"* being repeated exactly seven times in this chapter, and that this has reference to the seven Sacraments. Thus, the voice of the Lord *"On the waters"* alludes to Baptism; *"In power,"* confirmation, *"In magnificence,"* the Eucharist; *"Breaking the cedars"*, Penance; *"Shaking the desert,"* Orders; *"Dividing the flame of fire;"* Matrimony; *"Prepareth the stags,"* Extreme Unction.

PSALM 29

David praiseth God for his deliverance, and his merciful dealings with him.

1 I will extol thee, O Lord, for thou hast upheld me: and hast not made my enemies to rejoice over me.
2 O Lord my God, I have cried to thee, and then hast healed me.
3 Thou hast brought forth, O Lord, my soul from hell: thou hast saved me from them that go down into the pit.
4 Sing to the Lord, O ye his saints: and give praise to the memory of his holiness.
5 For wrath is in his indignation; and life in his good will. In the evening weeping shall have place, and in the morning gladness.
6 And in my abundance I said: I shall never be moved.
7 O Lord, in thy favour, thou gavest strength to my beauty. Thou turnedst away thy face from me, and I became troubled.
8 To thee, O Lord, will I cry: and I will make supplication to my God.

9 What profit is there in my blood, whilst I go down to corruption? Shall dust confess to thee, or declare thy truth?
10 The Lord hath heard, and hath had mercy on me: the Lord became my helper.
11 Thou hast turned for me my mourning into joy: thou hast cut my sackcloth, and hast compassed me with gladness:
12 To the end that my glory may sing to thee, and I may not regret: O Lord my God, I will give praise to thee for ever.

EXPLANATION OF THE PSALM

1. David, now established on his throne, after fortifying the citadel of Sion, and the city having been called after his name, finally, having built a most magnificent palace, and acknowledging God to be the author of so many favors, offers him the tribute of praise, saying, *"I will extol thee, O Lord."* Exalted as thou art incapable of being more exalted; yet, to those who are not so fully cognizant of thy greatness, I will, as far as in me lies, by my preaching, *"extol thee,"* so that all may acknowledge thee to be the supreme Lord of all. *"For thou hast upheld me,"* raised me from nothing, from the lowest depths, even to the throne of thy kingdom. You have extolled me and I will therefore extol you; attributing my exaltation, not to my own merits, but to your greatness; you have exalted me, and I will humble myself in order to exalt you. *"And hast not made my enemies to rejoice over me."* The consequence of such exaltation was, that his enemies, who were most numerous, and were for a long time seeking for his death, got no reason to be glad of his death, which they most eagerly looked for; but, on the contrary, had much source of grief at his exaltation, which with all their might they sought to obstruct.

In a prophetic sense, David speaks in the person of Christ; and of all the elect in general, as well as in particular, who, he foresaw, would be exalted in the kingdom of heaven, himself included. *"I will extol thee, O Lord, for thou hast upheld me;"* that means, how truly, O Lord, internally and externally will I extol thee, for my exaltation has led me to some idea of your immense sublimity; for, from the lowest earth, from the depth of misery, from mortality itself, thou hast raised me up and upheld me to the glory of resurrection and immortality, and thus to a heavenly and everlasting kingdom. *"And hast not made my enemies to rejoice over me;"* you have not indulged them in their impious desires of effecting my eternal destruction, a thing ardently sought for by the evil spirits in this and in the other world. The Jews, it is true, rejoiced when they extorted the sentence of death against Christ from Pilate; and the wicked not infrequently rejoice when they can deprive their neighbors of their properties, their riches, or even their lives; but their joy is short lived, followed by interminable punishment, so that it may rather be called the dream of joy than the reality of it.

2-3. The prophet brings to his memory how he was angustiated, previous to his getting possession of the kingdom, to show how true was his statement, that *"His enemies were not made to rejoice over him."* *"O Lord my God, I have cried to thee;"* when I was in frequent danger of death, and sick at heart in consequence, you, O my God, have healed me, and so delivered me from impending death, as if you had taken me out of hell itself. *"Thou hast saved me from them that go down into the pit;"* means the very same, but that it is a little more obscure. The meaning is, You have raised me from the dead, which may with propriety be applied to David, who had suffered such persecution, and was driven to death's door thereby. In a prophetic sense, it applies literally to Christ. *"Thou hast healed me"* of the wounds I suffered on the cross. *"Brought my soul from hell,"* from Limbo, and *"saved me"* by my resurrection. All the saints can equally exclaim on the last day, *"Thou hast healed me,"* most completely, in soul and body; *"And brought my soul from hell,"* for you have not let me into the hell of the damned. *"And saved me from them that go down into the pit,"* inasmuch as you have given me salvation, and life everlasting. The same idea turns up in Psalm 102, *"Who healeth all thy diseases, who redeemeth thy life from destruction."*

4. Looking at the innumerable temporal blessings David had received from God, and the everlasting blessings his saints had received, he thinks it unbecoming in himself alone to thank God, and therefore invites all who had received similar favors to join him in praise. *"Give praise to the memory of his holiness"* means, praise his holy memory; just as *"in his holy mountain"* means the mountain of his holiness, by a Hebraism that uses the genitive for the ablative case; and the meaning is, praise him, praise his holy memory, because his remembrance of you was a holy one, a pious one, a paternal one, bent on rewarding you instead of punishing you. And, in truth, it is owing to God's great goodness alone, which we should ever gratefully bear in mind, that while we, who always need his help, so often forget him, he, who wants nothing from us, should constantly bear us in mind; which he did in a most singular manner, when he sent his only Son to become our Savior; and, therefore, no wonder David should exclaim, in Psalm 8, *"What is man that thou art mindful of him?"*

5. He assigns a reason for having said that the holy recollection of God ought to be praised, because when God punishes us, he does so by reason of the *"indignation"* one's sins provoke, that is, through a strict sense of justice; but in other respects, in his will and election it is to us life, not punishment. By anger then, we understand punishment and chastisement, called anger from its proceeding from anger. By indignation, is to be understood, according to St. Basil, the just judgment of God, *"In the evening, weeping shall have place, and in the morning, gladness."* He proves that God's anger towards the elect is only temporary, because to the lamentation produced by castigation and penance, joy will immediately succeed; and praise and thanksgiving is always connected with forgiveness and reconciliation, for between the evening and morning, that is, between day and night, nothing intervenes. Observe the propriety of attributing grief to the night, joy to the day, because, when we fall into sin, the light of divine grace abandons us; when we get to be reconciled, it comes back to us. Again, our passage through this world, in which we are mourning for our sins, groaning and sighing for our true country, heaven, is our night, in which we have no glimpse of God, the sun of justice; but the life to come, which 1 St. Peter, chap. 1, describes as one in which we shall *"Rejoice with an unspeakable and glorified joy,"* will be our day, because we shall see God face to face. This was fulfilled to the letter in Christ, who in the evening died in pain and suffering, in the morning rose in triumph and joy.

6. The alternations of anger and of life, of weeping and of gladness, alluded to in general by the prophet in the preceding verses, are now explained in detail; the prophet speaking sometimes in his own person, sometimes in that of the elect. First, speaking of himself, he says, that previous to his being put over the kingdom, such was his wealth, and in such peace did he possess it, that he thought his happiness should be everlasting. He would appear to allude to the time when, after having slain Goliath, he was in the highest favor with the king, the king's son, and the whole mass of the people, to such an extent, that he was elected to be a tribune, and got the king's daughter in marriage; and of that time he says, *"In my abundance I said:"* when I was so fortunate, and had such an abundance of everything, *"I shall never be moved."* My happiness seems so firmly established that it must be everlasting.

7. He assigns a reason for his having said, *"I shall never be moved;"* because you, O my God, givest *"strength,"* nerve, and power, *"to my beauty,"* to my happiness; *"in thy favor,"* because such was your will, wish, and decree. *"Thou turned away thy face from me, and I became troubled."* Now come the reverses. In the midst of all the aforesaid happiness, *"thou turned away thy face from me;"* you allowed me to incur the king's displeasure, *"and I became troubled,"* suffered banishment, had to fly, ran several risks of death, and many other misfortunes. All these risks and dangers are more applicable, however, to the elect, in their troubles and peregrinations here below. Any one of the elect can justly say: In my abundance, that is, while God favored me with much grace, and his spiritual favors, I said I will never be moved. So said Peter, one of his principal elect, when he said, *"Even though*

I should die with thee, I will not deny thee." "O Lord, in thy favor thou gavest strength to my beauty;" that is, my strength was not my own but yours; for the whole beauty of my soul had its rise from the light of your justice and wisdom, and was kept up and maintained by your assistance. *"You turned your face away from me."* To punish my presumption, you abandoned me, left me to myself; and, at once, I collapsed, fell, and *"became troubled."* As regards Christ, these verses will apply to him, speaking in the person of his Church, his members, or even as speaking in his own person. For, as he said on the cross, *"My God, why hast thou forsaken me?"* so he could say, *"Thou turned thy face away from me,"* not because he was an enemy, but because he seemed to desert him in his passion; and then the meaning would be, *"And in my abundance I said:"* My human nature, having been endowed with the choicest graces, far and away beyond any other mortal, inasmuch as it was hypostatically united to God, the fountain of all grace, said, *"I shall never be moved:"* nothing can harm, hurt, or disturb me. *"O Lord, in thy favor:"* that means, to my beauty and my excellence, already superior to that of all men and Angels, you have added strength and power; that is, the indissoluble tie of the hypostatic union, and that *"in thy favor,"* which no one can resist. *"Thou turned away thy face from me."* Notwithstanding that indissoluble tie of the hypostatic union, and without injuring *"the strength of my beauty,"* you *"turned away your face from me:"* from defending me, but it was for the salvation of mankind; and you wished the cup of my most bitter passion not to pass from me, that I may free mankind; therefore, *"I became troubled:"* began to fear, to grow weary, and to be sad, and I exclaimed, *"My soul is sorrowful unto death."* We are not to infer from this that Christ had to suffer anything he did not expect, or of which he had no previous knowledge, for nothing could have injured or have harmed him against his own will; but he suffered the persecutions freely, and thus *"troubled"* himself. And, as Christ said to his Father, *"Thou turned away thy face from me,"* so he could say to himself, I have turned away the face of my divinity from helping my humanity, and thus willingly and knowingly I have been troubled.

8-9. These expressions are to be taken in the past, and not in the future tense; a thing not uncommon among the Hebrews. David then, in a historic sense, states that, in the time of his tribulation and danger, he cried out to the Lord, and, among other things, threw out to him, that his death would be of no use to the Lord, for, once dead, he could praise him no more. *"To thee, O Lord, will I cry."* When I became troubled, by the aversion of your face from me, I did not despair of your mercy, but *"I cried out to thee;"* and in terms of deprecation said, *"What profit is there in my blood?"* That is, what will the spilling of my blood profit you, when my enemies shall have put me to death, and I shall have come to rottenness in the grave? Dust can offer you no tribute of praise. According to a prophetic and higher interpretation it means, that Christ, in his passion, cried out and prayed to the Lord, which was fulfilled at the time he, according to the apostle, Hebrews 5, *"With a strong cry and tears, offered up prayers and supplications to him that was able to save him from death."* It was at that time he said, *"What profit is there in my blood whilst I go down to corruption?"* That is, how will my spilling my blood on the cross conduce to the glory of God or the salvation of mankind, if my body like that of all other mortals, is to rot and perish in the grave? For, as the apostle says, 1 Cor. 15, *"If Christ be not risen again your faith is vain;"* and Christ himself could not have returned to announce God's truth to his apostles; nor could poor mortals, who are but dust and ashes, become spiritual, become children of God; to confess to him, and announce his truth to others, that is, the justice and the fidelity of God.

These words may be applied to each of the elect, who, touched with sorrow for having fallen into sin, cried out to God for pardon, that they may be able to confess to him, and announce to other sinners how true he is to his promises.

10. This verse clearly shows that the preceding verses should have been understood in the past instead of the future tense. The prophet asserts here, both in his own person, that of Christ, and that of the elect, that his cry was heard by God.

11. Here is the effect of his having been heard. David, from a wretched exile, becomes a powerful king. Christ rises from the dead, thus gaining a victory over death itself. Every one of the elect, on arriving at their heavenly kingdom from this valley of tears, can most justly exclaim, *"Thou hast turned for me my mourning into joy, thou hast cut my sack cloth, and hast compassed me with gladness."* You have changed my garb of mourning into that of joy, and you have not taken it simply off, but *"hast cut"* it, entirely destroyed it, as a sign that I am not to put it on again. The *"sack cloth"* means that wretched garb of mortality and misery that has been entirely destroyed, of no longer use to the saints, much less to Christ, who, *"Rising from the dead, dies no more."*

12. The final end of the glory of Christ and his saints is the praise of God: *"Blessed are those who dwell in thy house, forever and ever they will praise thee."* Let my glory, then, not my groans, for fear of death or of sin, sing to thee.

PSALM 30

A prayer of a just man under affliction.

1 In thee, O Lord, have I hoped, let me never be confounded: deliver me in thy justice.

2 Bow down thy ear to me: make haste to deliver me. Be thou unto me a God, a

protector, and a house of refuge, to save me.
3 For thou art my strength and my refuge; and for thy name's sake thou wilt lead me, and nourish me.
4 Thou wilt bring me out of this snare, which they have hidden for me: for thou art my protector.
5 Into thy hands I commend my spirit: thou hast redeemed me, O Lord, the God of truth.
6 Thou hast hated them that regard vanities, to no purpose. But I have hoped in the Lord:
7 I will be glad and rejoice in thy mercy. For thou hast regarded my humility, thou hast saved my soul out of distresses.
8 And thou hast not shut me up in the hands of the enemy: thou hast set my feet in a spacious place.
9 Have mercy on me, O Lord, for I am afflicted: my eye is troubled with wrath, my soul, and my belly:
10 For my life is wasted with grief: and my years in sighs. My strength is weakened through poverty and my bones are disturbed.
11 I am become a reproach among all my enemies, and very much to my neighbours; and a fear to my acquaintance. They that saw me without fled from me.
12 I am forgotten as one dead from the heart. I am become as a vessel that is destroyed.
13 For I have heard the blame of many that dwell round about. While they assembled together against me, they consulted to take away my life.
14 But I have put my trust in thee, O Lord: I said: Thou art my God.
15 My lots are in thy hands. Deliver me out of the hands of my enemies; and from them that persecute me.
16 Make thy face to shine upon thy servant; save me in thy mercy.
17 Let me not be confounded, O Lord, for I have called upon thee. Let the wicked be ashamed, and be brought down to hell.
18 Let deceitful lips be made dumb. Which speak iniquity against the just, with pride and abuse.
19 how great is the multitude of thy sweetness, O Lord, which thou hast hidden for them that fear thee! Which thou hast wrought for them that hope in thee, in the sight of the sons of men.
20 Thou shalt hide them in the secret of thy face, from the disturbance of men. Thou shalt protect them in thy tabernacle from the contradiction of tongues.
21 Blessed be the Lord, for he hath shewn his wonderful mercy to me in a fortified city.
22 But I said in the excess of my mind: I am cast away from before thy eyes. Therefore thou hast heard the voice of my prayer, when I cried to thee.

23 love the Lord, all ye his saints: for the Lord will require truth, and will repay them abundantly that act proudly.
24 Do ye manfully, and let your heart be strengthened, all ye that hope in the Lord.

EXPLANATION OF THE PSALM

1. King David, in his flight from Absalom, destitute of all earthly assistance, appeals to God, and says, *"In thee have I hoped,"* and I am therefore confident, as you are all powerful, and most true to me, that you will not disappoint me in my hope. Agreeable to such hope, therefore, *"Deliver me in thy justice;"* that justice that prompts you to punish the wicked and free the just.
2. The persecution was pressing on him; his friends had sent him word to rest in no one place, to continue his flight, unless he chose to be destroyed; and therefore he prays to be heard at once, and to be delivered from the impending danger. *"Be thou unto me a God, a protector, and a house of refuge, to save me."* Be like a well protected strong house to me; for there is no fortified place in this champaign country to which I can fly.
3. You are my stronghold to which I will fly for refuge. *"And for thy name's sake thou wilt lead me, and nourish me,"* corresponds exactly with David's history. His flight was so sudden, that he knew not whither to betake himself, nor whence to obtain the necessaries of life, until Providence directed Siba to him, with two hundred loaves of bread, a hundred bunches of raisins, a hundred cakes of figs, and a vessel of wine; and he therefore says, *"For thy name's sake,"* for the glory of your name, you will lead me to a safe place, and there supply me with provisions.
4. You will not only bring me to a safe place, and there provide for me, but you will also deliver me from the conspiracy, which, like a hidden snare, they have laid for me; alluding, to the conspiracy got up in Hebron against him by Absalom, when he neither dreaded nor even thought of the like.
5. Though full of hope, when he said, *"Thou wilt bring me out of this snare,"* being not yet quite secure of his life, he adds, *"Into thy hands I commend my spirit,"* to your care I entrust my life. And, as you have at other times frequently *"redeemed me,"* saved me from death, you who are a most true and most faithful God. These expressions lead many to think that the whole Psalm has reference to Christ, by reason of his having, while hanging on the cross, exclaimed, *"Father, into thy hands I commend my spirit."* But though the Psalm, to the letter, may not be applicable to Christ, the Lord might have taken these words from the Psalm, when he wished to commend his spirit to his Father, just as St. Nicholas, in his last moments, repeated this with the preceding verses; and we, not infrequently, ourselves use them. The words, *"Thou hast redeemed me, O Lord, the God of truth,"* appear to

be against the application of the verse to Christ, for, instead of being the redeemed, he is the Redeemer. St. Augustine, attributes the first part of the verse to Christ, the latter to his people; for he is of opinion that the prophet is fond of speaking in the person of different characters—sometimes of Christ, sometimes in that of the people. All right and pious enough, when one is looking for a mystic sense or explanation; but when we look for the literal sense, it does not appear why different persons should be introduced, when there is nothing in the context or the punctuation to call for such change.

6. He assigns another reason for having *"commended"* his life to the hands of God, because God is wont to hate them who, instead of trusting in him, trust in *"vanities,"* that can afford them no possible help. *"Thou hast hated them that regard vanities to no purpose;"* those who regard dreams or omens, or the responses of demons, as Saul did, when he consulted the pythoness. Under the word *"vanities,"* may also be included those who, relying on human industry, craft, cunning, human aid or help to the exclusion of the divine help and counsel; all of which are vain and useless; and he, therefore, adds the words *"to no purpose,"* for all such exertions are, in reality, *"to no purpose." "But I have hoped in the Lord:"* not so with me, I hoped in none, in nothing but God.

7-8. As *"I hoped in the Lord,"* I will *"be glad and rejoice in thy mercy,"* for the Divine mercy never deserts those who hope in him. *"For thou hast regarded."* He brings up past favors, in the hope that, by his acknowledgment of them, he may obtain fresh ones. *"I will be glad and rejoice in thy mercy,"* for I have a pledge of it in my deliverance from Saul; for then you *"regarded my humility,"* my abjection, and affliction; and then you *"saved my soul"* from the troubles that surrounded me, and from which I could not extricate myself. *"And thou hast not shut me up in the hands of the enemy;"* you did not allow Saul, who sought my death, to accomplish his purpose; but *"thou hast set my feet in a spacious place;"* you freed me from the troubles that encompassed me, and placed me, free and disembarrassed, as it were, on an open plain; at liberty to go about at pleasure.

9. Bearing past favors in mind, he prays for future ones, and relates his misfortunes. *"Have mercy on me, O Lord."* As you have had mercy on me in former tribulations, have mercy now, too; for tribulation has again set in on me; and here they are, *"My eye is troubled with wrath."* Whose wrath? God's or his own? I rather think, with St. Augustine, God's; for, it is clear, from the First and Second Book of Kings, that David, in all his persecutions, never burst into wrath, but was always most mild and most patient; and I, therefore, take the meaning to be, *"in thy wrath,"* in which you punish me for my sins, *"my eye is troubled;"* my corporeal eye has grown dim with my tears; or,

the eye of my soul has grown dark: *"my soul,"* too, is confused, for it has been fearfully frightened; so also has been *"my belly,"* the very interior of my soul; that is, my memory; the receptacle of my thoughts. Thus the prophet makes brief allusion to the functions of the soul eye representing the intellect; the soul, the will; and the belly, the memory.

10. David, being now an old man, could justly say, *"For my life is wasted with grief:"* was spent in constant trouble and *"sighs."* In the first thirty years of his life his troubles were innumerable. On being made king, for seven years he had to wage war against the descendants of Saul; he then had various wars with neighboring kingdoms; then with his own son. Then, the very care of a kingdom, to one who wishes to govern it conscientiously, is enough to *"waste"* one, and make them *"sigh." "My strength is weakened through poverty."* In addition to all his other afflictions, he has lost his strength. The first and last members of this sentence are synonymous; they mean the same thing: *"my strength is weakened,"* is the same as *"my bones are disturbed;"* for bones stand for health, power, strength. That was literally the case with David. He had to fly, without any provision whatever, to the most desert places; not only on foot, but even barefooted; and there to remain until relieved by his friends.

11. Another misfortune, consequent on his notorious persecution, the neighboring people, *"enemies"* of his, having heard of his base flight, began to despise him. His *"acquaintances,"* too began to fear that Absalom, should he succeed, may wreak his vengeance on them for having proved friendly to David. *"They that saw me without;"* an explanation of a fear to my acquaintance. Many of my acquaintance, when they saw me an outcast and afflicted, *"Fled from me,"* ran, fearing for their lives, should they be found to have come near me; and thus,

12. Their heart neither remembers me nor thinks of me, no more than if I were dead and buried, for they consider I am just as if such had been the case with me. *"I am become as a vessel that is destroyed."* My friends and acquaintances have not only abandoned and forgotten me; but even the people around me despise and look down upon me, as they would upon a broken vessel, of no use or value, which is evident from the abuse they heap upon me. He evidently alludes here to Semei's abuse, who, not content with abusing him, sought to stone him; looking upon him as an outcast and an exile, and as a broken vessel, that should be thrown into the sewer. And though the Scripture makes mention of Semei alone abusing him, it is probable that others did the same, and that they are here alluded to, when he says, *"I have heard the blame of many."*

13. After the abuse of Semei, a conspiracy was entered into, in the presence of Absalom, to take David's life, which is here alluded to. I am abused to my

face; behind my back a conspiracy is entered into at Jerusalem to have my life.

14. The holy soul, in all his troubles, shows he did not despond, because he did not put his trust in the fallacious help of man, but in the all powerful God, whom no one can resist. *"But I have put my trust in thee, O Lord."* Why? Because *"I said"* in my heart, *"Thou art my God."* I have a great protector, without whose consent no one can take my life, because,

15. My life does not depend on lot or chance, but depends on your will and power. *"Deliver me out of the hands of my enemies."* The meaning is quite plain, and needs no explanation.

16-17. The same petition renewed, but with additional arguments, calculated to move God to mercy. *"Make thy face to shine upon thy servant;"* that means, show me your face, or look on me, which is the same. For as God, when he is angry with us by reason of our sins, is said to turn away his face, or to put a cloud between him and us, and not to look on us; so, on the contrary, when he is reconciled, he is said to turn his face to us to regard us, and make *"it shine upon us, so as to make us, too, a mass of light. He, therefore, first asks to be reconciled to God, in case he should have been angry with him; and assigns as a reason, his being a servant most ready at all times to do God's behest and commands.* He then adds, *"Save me,"* which is only the consequence of reconciliation; and to move him thereto, he adds, *"In thy mercy,"* not through my merits, but through your own pure mercy; and he adds a third argument, *"Let me not be confounded, for I have called upon thee."* For it is the duty of a good and faithful master, who has promised to help those that confide in him, not to suffer one who so unceasingly and so confidently invoked him to be confounded. *"Let the wicked be ashamed, and be brought down to hell."*

A prophetic imprecation, and one fulfilled immediately after; for Achitophel, the principal minister of Absalom, who had advised the most impious proceeding against David, was so confused, on his plans being defeated by divine Providence, and being unable to bear up against the confusion consequent thereon, hanged himself; and thus, *"The wicked became ashamed, and was brought down to hell."*

18. Achitophel's lips are called deceitful, because for a long time he pretended to be the fast friend of David; but the moment he got the opportunity, he betrayed his perfidy. *"Which speak against the just;"* against David, who had offered no injury to either Achitophel or to Absalom; and they spoke *"Iniquity;"* gave advice full of injustice, *"With pride and abuse;"* that is, with the greatest contempt and arrogance.

19. The holy prophet, feeling that he had been heard, and having felt a gleam of heavenly consolation, exclaims in admiration, as above. The verse may be thus explained. In the time of tribulation, God conceals the *"Multitude of his sweetness;"* that is, the unbounded rewards he has in store for the just, in order to prove them; but in a little time after he displays those very prizes and rewards, *"In the sight of the sons of men,"* that his servants may learn from thence to have greater hope in him. Thus, for a time he concealed his sweetness from David, while he was flying from his son's persecution; but soon after he displayed the extent of his goodness to him, when he restored his kingdom to him in the greatest triumph. The very same thing happens to all the just, whose reward is now hid, but will appear to all on the day of judgment. It may be interpreted differently; thus, Truly manifold are the consolations, O Lord, that you pour into the inmost recesses of the hearts of those that fear you—that fear you with a filial, fond, and loving, not a servile, fear. For this is *"The hidden manna which no man knoweth but he that receiveth it."* Such as was felt by David, when, in Psalm 93, he said, *"According to the multitude of my sorrows in my heart, thy comforts have given joy to my soul."* And, as St. Paul, 2 Cor. 7, says, *"I am filled with comfort, I exceedingly abound with joy in all our tribulation."* And if, in time of tribulation, such be the *"Multitude of the sweetness"* in the heart of the exile, who can conceive the amount of the joy in his heart when his triumph shall have been accomplished! *"Which thou hast wrought for them that hope in thee, in the sight of the sons of men."* The sweetness *"Thou hast wrought"* for those who refuse all consolation but yours is perfect, most copious, most abundant; and all this *"In the sight of the sons of men;"* that is, in spite of them all, before their face; because the more pain they inflict externally, the more consolations you multiply internally. This sweetness is infused into the hearts of the just, *"In the sight of the sons of men,"* in another way, when the sons of men, who persecute the children of God, see what and how they suffer; for, carnal as they are, with the palate of their soul infected by sin, they cannot feel, nor even have an idea of the sweetness, though they see its effects in the meekness, patience, nay, even hilarity and peace of the just; and thus, their sweetness is, to a certain extent, hidden in the sight of the sons of men, though its effects are apparent.

20. He gives a description of the manner in which the just feel the sweetness of God in the day of tribulation; for, by love and contemplation, they are carried up to God; and in him find a house of refuge, as he says in this very Psalm, *"Be thou unto me a God, a protector, and a house of refuge;"* for those who know how to take refuge in God, think as little of all manner of tribulation as if it did not at all belong to them. *"Thou shalt hide them,"* those that fear thee, *"In the secret of thy face;"* in that hidden place, that is, in thy face; for the soul wrapt up in contemplation, feeling that God is attentively looking on it, observant of God's slightest expression, burning with love

at the idea of God's beauty that is lodged, in dwelling, proof against *"The disturbance of men;"* that is, from all manner of evil that usually disturbs man. *"Thou shalt protect them in thy tabernacle;"* the same just will be protected in the very house in which yourself is lodged, for God has no house capable of containing him, he is his own house; and those who, in love and contemplation, dwell in God, *"Make the Most High their refuge. No evil shall come to them, nor shall the scourge come near their dwelling,"* as it is beautifully expressed in Psalm 90. In this tabernacle they are protected, not only from evil doers, as was explained in the preceding verse, but also from evil speakers, for such is the meaning of *"The contradiction of tongues,"* for they who can call upon God as a witness, care little for what man can say. And if the face of the Lord be such a retreat and a refuge to the elect, in the time when he is seen only *"Through a glass in an obscure manner,"* how will matters be when we shall see him as he really is? Then truly will our dwelling be in Jerusalem, the vision of peace, of which is written, in Psalm 147, *"Who hath placed peace in thy borders."*

21. He now applies to himself, as being one of the just, what he had said in general, touching the consolation they feel in their troubles, and thanks God for it. *"Blessed be the Lord, for his wonderful mercy to me in a fortified city,"* because he *"So hid me in the secret of his face,"* which is like *"a fortified city,"* that my enemies could do me no harm.

22. He accuses himself of the despondence he was in when his persecution commenced. When I was almost idiotic through fear, I said to myself, *"I am cast away from before thy eyes;"* that is, you wish me no longer to govern; or no longer to live, as appears from your withholding that look of benignity and kindness, and that help with which you were wont to countenance me. As we read, in 2 Kings 15, of David, *"If I shall find grace in the sight of the Lord, he will bring me again. If he shall say to me, Thou pleasest me not, I am ready, let him do that which is good before him."*

23-24. He now encourages all pious people, similarly suffering, not to cease loving God, and putting their trust in him; for, though the wicked may seem to persecute them with impunity for a while, they will ultimately suffer the bitterest punishment for it.

PSALM 31

The second penitential psalm.

1 Blessed are they whose iniquities are forgiven, and whose sins are covered.
2 Blessed is the man to whom the Lord hath not imputed sin, and in whose spirit there is no guile.
3 Because I was silent my bones grew old; whilst I cried out all the day long.
4 For day and night thy hand was heavy upon me: I am turned in my anguish,

whilst the thorn is fastened.
5 I have acknowledged my sin to thee, and my injustice I have not concealed. I said I will confess against myself my injustice to the Lord: and thou hast forgiven the wickedness of my sin.
6 For this shall every one that is holy pray to thee in a seasonable time. And yet in a flood of many waters, they shall not come nigh unto him.
7 Thou art my refuge from the trouble which hath encompassed me: my joy, deliver me from them that surround me.
8 I will give thee understanding, and I will instruct thee in this way, in which thou shalt go: I will fix my eyes upon thee.
9 Do not become like the horse and the mule, who have no understanding. With bit and bridle bind fast their jaws, who come not near unto thee.
10 Many are the scourges of the sinner, but mercy shall encompass him that hopeth in the Lord.
11 Be glad in the Lord, and rejoice, ye just, and glory, all ye right of heart.

EXPLANATION OF THE PSALM

1-2. No one can fairly appreciate the value of health until they have had to deplore the loss of it. It was only when David tasted of the bitterness of sin that he first began to feel the sweetness of innocence. Hence, this Penitential Psalm starts in the praise of pardon and innocence; for they heal the soul, and are opposed to that sickness that is brought on by sin. He begins with pardon, as well for the sake of advancing from the inferior to the superior, as also, because it was only very lately his health had been restored. *"Blessed are they whose iniquities are forgiven."* How happy are they, who, notwithstanding their fall, are, still, not despised by God; but, roused by his grace, are converted to penance, and thus obtain pardon. *"And whose sins are covered;"* the same idea in different language; for sins, when forgiven, are covered and hidden, so as to appear no more; on which we shall presently have more to say. *"Blessed is the man to whom the Lord hath not imputed sin."* A transition from pardon, which applies to the many, to innocence, which belongs to the few, exclaiming, O truly happy and lucky he; who has done nothing that can be counted sin; and to whom, therefore, the Lord, who is most just in his judgments, *"hath not imputed sin."* And not only has been free from actual sin, but even *"in whose spirit there is no guile;"* never committed sin in thought or word; for the word *"Spirit"* embraces both; that is, thought and words, in the former sense, being called the heart or the mind; and, in the latter sense, the spirit of the mouth or lips. Of the former, the apostle speaks, 1 Cor 2, *"For what man knoweth the things of a man, but the spirit of a man, that is in him?"* Of the latter, 1 Cor. 14, *"I will pray in the spirit, I will pray also with the understanding: I will sing with the spirit, I will also sing with the understanding."* By innocence, we are to understand here, not the natural innocence, without the intervention of divine grace, which is of no effect; but, that innocence which God, by a gift of singular grace, has given to a few; through which the sin committed by others, namely, original sin, is so condoned, as not to suffer them, voluntarily, to commit any mortal sin; and this is the highest order of forgiveness. All manner of innocence, then, has a certain amount of remission of sin in connection with it; and of all, with the exception of Christ, it may be said, *"They all sinned, and need the grace of God."* St. Paul, therefore, quotes this passage to prove that nobody could be justified by any works, but those springing from grace; and says, Rom. 4, *"But to him that worketh not, yet believeth in him who justifieth the impious, his faith is reputed to justice, according to the purpose of the grace of God."* As David also termeth the blessedness of a man, to whom God reputeth justice without works; *"Blessed are they whose iniquities are forgiven, and whose sins are covered. Blessed is the man to whom the Lord hath not imputed sin."* From which it would appear that the Apostle understands the prophet to say, that they are not blessed who, by their own strength, work out justice; but they, who, through God's grace, have been pardoned; and thus acquired justice. The prophet seems to have particular individuals in view here. Job, for instance, who says, in chap. 27, *"Till I die I will not depart from my innocence. My justifications which I have begun to hold, I will not forsake: for my heart doth not reprehend me in all my life."* Abel, Henoch, Noe, Abraham, Isaac, and Jacob, who are said in the Scriptures to have been free from sin, come under this head; and, perhaps, in spirit, he foresaw Jeremias. Both John the Baptist, sanctified in the womb, and the Virgin Mother, by a higher privilege, preserved not only from actual, but even from original sin. Heretics of the present day seek to prove three false dogmas from these verses. The Psalm has the title of understanding; the Holy Ghost, perhaps, having foreseen it would be so misunderstood. They assert that justification consists solely in the remission of sin, and not in the infusion of justice; from David having absolutely said, *"Blessed are they whose sins are forgiven."* They say also, that this remission of sins is not a real, but an apparent remission, which does not actually remove the sins, but covers them, hides them, and renders them not imputable. They furthermore assert, from this passage, that once the sin is forgiven, no satisfaction need follow; for, if God exact even temporal punishment of the person justified, how can he be said not to impute sin? How can he be said not to impute while he punishes?

The holy prophet, however, who chose for a title to the Psalm that of understanding, clearly understood that God remitted no sin whatever without an infusion of his justice, and understood that thereby men from being wicked became, not only not wicked, but truly just; for, as the sun cannot expel the darkness without pouring in his light, so the sun of justice, and the Father of Men does not forgive sin but through the grace or justice which he pours into them; and therefore St. Paul, quoting this very passage, says, *"As David also termeth the blessedness of a man to whom God reputeth justice without works,"* from which words of the Apostle may be clearly inferred, that justice is really and truly included in the remission or nonimputation of sin. Both errors are easily refuted by an explanation of the words, *"covered,"* and *"not imputed."* Sins are said here to be *"covered,"* not that they exist though covered and hidden from us, but because they are entirely destroyed, and grace has taken their place, and thus they are truly covered, so that even God, from whom nothing can be hidden, cannot see them; and thus the prophet uses various metaphors, to signify the remission of sins, so that the deficiency of explanation in one, may be supplied by another. The most remarkable occurs in Psalm 50, where he says, *"Thou shalt sprinkle me with hyssop, and I shall be cleansed: thou shalt wash me, and I shall be made whiter than snow."* Here the forgiveness of sins is said not merely to cover the stain and to hide it, but really to wash it, and to wash it in such a way as even to make it white even whiter than snow. What means, then, the removal of a stain, and the increasing its whiteness, but the removal of sin, and the infusion of grace? What means the substitution of light for darkness, but the removal of sin, and substitution of justice? We have the same in Isaias, chap. 1, *"If your sins be as scarlet, they shall be made white as snow; and if they be as red as crimson, they shall be white as wool."* All the holy fathers so understand this passage, for they say the sins are covered, not that they remain, though they don't appear; but that they are entirely removed, and do not appear, because they are not there; just as a plaster not only hides the wound but even removes it. As to the word *"imputed,"* our adversaries are quite mistaken. In the Scripture, it means, that we will not be held accountable, as we read in Wisdom 12, *"Or who shall accuse thee, (impute to thee.) if the nations perish which thou hast made;"* that is, who can bring you to an account, if all mankind be lost? who will bring you in guilty? In Ezechiel, chap. 33, God says of the penitent sinner, *"None of his sins which he had committed, shall be imputed to him,"* that he shall not be brought to an account for them; and in 2 Paralip. 30, *"The Lord, who is good, will show mercy to all them who with their whole heart seek the Lord God of their fathers, and will not impute it to them that they are not sanctified;"* meaning that he will easily pardon, will not be over strict in settling with them, by reason of their being more or less unprepared. Job 42 has *"That folly may not be imputed to you;"* and in 2 Tim. 4, *"But all forsook me; may it not be laid to their charge;"* that is, imputed to them; and in his Epistle to Philemon, *"And if he hath wronged thee in anything or is in thy debt, put it to my account, (impute it to me,) I will repay it;"*

that is, charge me with it, I wish to be your debtor thereon. Now, sin can be said to be not imputed in two ways. First, when one has committed no sin, in reality owes nothing, and in such sense we understand that passage of the Book of Wisdom, already quoted, *"Who shall impute it to thee if the nations perish which thou hast made."* For though all mankind were to perish, God would not have been the cause, and therefore it could not be imputed to him. In a similar sense we have explained this expression of David, *"Blessed is the man to whom the Lord hath not imputed sin;"* that is, who has willfully done no evil to make him a debtor and a culprit before God. Secondly, if the sins have been condoned and forgiven, so that there now remains nothing to be imputed, in which sense many interpret this passage, as if the prophet were to say, Blessed is the man whom God will not call to account for his sins, because they have been already condoned and forgiven; which exposition we do not reject, though we prefer the first, because it agrees better with the following words, *"And in whose spirit there is no guile."* The third mode of imputation devised by the heretics is, that though the sin remains in the soul of the sinner, still it is not considered or looked upon as sin by God, a notion having nothing in Scripture to support it, but even totally disproved by the Scripture; for when it says in various places, especially in Psalm 5, *"Thou hatest all the workers of iniquity, thou wilt destroy all that speak a lie;"* and if he hears and wishes to destroy all the wicked, he certainly must impute sin to them, so long as they remain in that state. Who can imagine that God, the just judge, who has no regard of persons, will not impute sin but justice, at the very time the unfortunate is wallowing in the mire of sin; so that whatever he may do, according to the Lutherans, is a sin. St. Justin, Martyr, in his dialogue with Tripto, in refuting an error, similar to that of the Lutherans, says, *"Blessed is the man to whom the Lord hath not imputed sin;"* that is, to the penitent, whose sins God hath forgiven; and not in the sense that you erroneously preach up, that is, that the mere knowledge of God will get forgiveness for you, however numerous your sins may be. What we have stated of the nonimputation of sin, may be applied also to the imputation of justice. For, in the Scripture, the imputation of justice does not mean the reputing one to be just, when he really is not just, but it means the being reputed just by God, who is infallible. That expression in Genesis, *"Abraham believed in God, and it was reputed to him unto justice,"* quoted by St. Paul, Rom. 4, and St. James, chap. 2, signifies nothing more than the act of faith by Abraham was a just work, and considered as such by God. That passage in Psalm 105, *"Then Phinees stood up and pacified him, and the slaughter ceased. And it was reputed to him unto justice to generation and generation for evermore."* What does it mean, but that the zeal of Phinees, in destroying certain sinners, was a most meritorious act, was considered as such by God, so much so, that the priesthood was secured to him, to his sons, and posterity for a number of years after in consequence. Of the same import is that expression in Rom. 4, *"Now, to him that worketh, the reward is not reckoned according to grace, but according to debt."* What does that mean, but that the reward is justly due to him that does a work worthy of reward. And what the Apostle frequently repeats in the same chapter, that *"faith was reputed unto justice,"* does not mean that faith was not actually, but was merely reputed justice; but it means, that faith working by charity was the very purest justice; not acquired by works previous to grace, but the gift and the infusion of God, and therefore reputed and accepted by God as true justice. The nonimputation of sin, then, does not mean that sin remains though not punished, but it signifies that there is nothing in the justified that can be accounted sin. Hence it can be seen how easily solved are the objections of the Lutherans on satisfaction; for if sin be not imputed by reason of the innocence of one's life, no wonder that no satisfaction should be required of him that has done nothing to deserve it: but if the sin be not imputed by reason of pardon through grace, then the eternal punishment will not follow, but the temporal will, as we see happened David, to whom the prophet said, *"The Lord also hath taken away thy sin; thou shalt not die: nevertheless, because thou hast given occasion to the enemies of the Lord to blaspheme, for this thing, the child that is born to thee shall surely die."* Here we see that the sin was not imputed to his own death, but to the death of his son; that David was justified, and yet he had to suffer much in the death of his son, as a punishment for the sin he had committed.

3. Having thus put the happiness of the just before us, he deplores his own wretchedness thus, Happy they, but wretched me, who have not only lost my innocence, but put off, for an indefinite time, the asking pardon of my sins, and when I did at length avow them, began to cry out so constantly, that my bones were ground and weakened, my whole strength consumed and wasted. *"Because I was silent;"* and a long time he was silent; for he not only did not avow his crime of adultery, but he sought by all means to stifle all knowledge of it. He first used all endeavors to induce Urias to cohabit with his wife, that the child begot by himself may be looked upon as the child of Urias; failing in that, he committed murder, in the hope that by marrying Urias's widow at once, any issue there might be should be considered as begotten after, and not previous to, the death of Urias. And, even after his marriage, he did not repent of his sin he waited for the birth of the child; and even then showed no symptoms of repentance until the prophet Nathan aroused him. Thus, for nearly a year, or longer, did he wallow in the mire of sin, and put off his conversion. He, therefore, says, *"Because I was silent."* Did not confess my sin at once, sought to hide and conceal it;

therefore, *"My bones grew old whilst I cried out all the day long."* When I did avow my sin, I cried out so long and so bitterly, that my very bones got weak and old.

4. David suffered many misfortunes in punishment of his sins. The child born in adultery died an infant: his daughter Thamar was deflowered by her own brother, Amon: the same Amon was slain by his brother Absalom; and Absalom himself, in rebellion against his father, was slain, all matters of deep sorrow and grief to David; and it is to those scourges he alludes, when he says, *"For day and night thy hand was heavy on me:"* constantly, without ceasing, you laid on me. *"I am turned in my anguish, whilst the thorn is fastened."* The scourge has been so severe, the thorn of tribulation has stuck so deep in me, that I have been brought to reflect on the enormity of my sins.

5. His conversion brought him to a true knowledge of his sins, which he seeks no longer to conceal, but to proclaim before God and man. *"I have acknowledged,"* does not imply that God did not know them previously. The judge, who has seen the accused committing the crime, knows he did the act, still he does not know it judicially until the culprit shall have pleaded guilty, or it shall have been proved by evidence. Thus, God saw David, saw him sinning, but wanting him to plead guilty, he applied the scourge, and then David did plead guilty, and said, not only, *"I have sinned before the Lord,"* which, previous to those scourges, he said to Nathan in private; but now, in public, he makes it known to the whole world, through this Psalm; and, therefore, most justly adds, *"And my injustice I have not concealed. I said I will confess against myself my injustice to the Lord, and thou hast forgiven the wickedness of my sin."* To the comfort and consolation of all penitents, he enters into the unspeakable dealings of God in his mercy with himself. For, though God, *"Who is light, and in whom there is no darkness,"* has the most intense horror of the darkness of sinners, and is ready to cast the sinner into *"external darkness"* and everlasting punishment if he do not repent, is yet so ready to forgive when the penitent is sincere, that by his mercy and his clemency, he goes before or anticipates the confession or acknowledgment of our sins. He appears to refer to the time when Nathan, with God's authority, upbraided him with his sins, and he at once, in a spirit of compunction, replied, *"I have sinned;"* and Nathan said, *"The Lord also hath taken away thy sin, thou shalt not die."* Seeing the pardon so quickly granted, he considered, as was the fact, that the sin must have been forgiven before he confessed at all, but not before he had become internally contrite, which contrition embraced hatred of sin, love of God, and a desire of confessing, and making satisfaction. *"I said I will confess."* In the bitterness of my heart I said, I will at once confess *"against myself my injustice;"* declare myself a culprit and a criminal, which you hardly waited for, as at once, with the clemency and the

kindness of a father, *"Thou hast forgiven the wickedness of my sin;"* as Nathan announced when he said, *"The Lord also hath taken away thy sin."*

6. The prophet now asserts that many will follow his example, and from it learn to have recourse to God, to ask pardon for their sins, and thus to be delivered from the great evils consequent on sin. The meaning is, As you so mercifully pardon those who do penance, *"every one that is holy,"* every pious person that is truly holy, truly penitent, and, having begun to hate sin, seeks to enter into the love of you, *"shall pray to thee,"* and will have confidence in their prayers, and that *"in a seasonable time,"* before the time of mercy shall have passed away; while we are here below, while God invites us to penance. *"Seek the Lord while he can be found; invoke him while he is near,"* says Isaias. The second part of the verse has a double meaning; one is, Every one that is holy shall pray to thee in a seasonable time, that *"in the flood of many waters, they shall not come nigh unto him;"* that is, that on the day of judgment, when all manner of punishments shall pour down upon the wicked like a deluge, and the opportune season of prayer and penance shall have passed, that then they may be saved from such punishments. This appears very clear in the Hebrew. The second meaning is, *"Every one that is holy shall pray to thee in a seasonable time,"* and will act well and wisely in doing so; because, *"in the flood of many waters,"* when the wicked shall be inundated with calamities, as the earth was with water in the time of Noe, then the wicked *"shall not come nigh unto him;"* that is, to God, having let their opportunity pass.

7. Having obtained remission of the sin, he now asks for remission of the punishment due to it; namely, his deliverance from the tribulation brought on him by the sin. He seems to allude to the persecution he was suffering from his son Absalom, of which he had said so much in the previous Psalm. Alludes also, perhaps, to the temptations of the evil spirits, that perpetually surround and harass us. *"Thou art my refuge from the trouble which hath encompassed me."* My friends have deserted me, my enemies hem me in and surround me on all sides, and I, therefore, have no certain refuge but in thy mercy, O God; you alone, then, are *"my joy,"* the cause of it, and deliver me, therefore, from them.

8. The Lord answers his prayer, and promises him the help he sought. He promises him three things. First, interior prudence, to enable him to guard against the snares of his enemies, and to distinguish them from his friends; that is conveyed in the words, *"I will give thee understanding;"* I will make thee intelligent and prudent. Secondly, the outward assistance of the singular providence of God, without which even the most prudent get into the greatest difficulties, and that is conveyed in the words, *"I will instruct thee in this way in which thou shalt go."* Thirdly, perseverance in grace, which is the

greatest favor of all, and peculiarly belongs to the elect. *"I will fix my eyes upon thee;"* I will not take them off you, but I will steadily and constantly look upon you with an eye of benignity, so that you shall never need the internal aid of prudence, or the external protection of providence.

9. The prophet now exhorts all, both good and bad, to learn from his example the evils consequent on sin, and the blessings to be derived from penance and virtue, he having tasted of both. Turning to the wicked first, he says, *"Do not become like the horse and the mule, who have no understanding."* Endowed with reason, but not guided by your animal propensities; be not like the horse and the mule in your licentious desires, as I was; be not like the horse and the mule, in tearing and lashing at your fellow creatures, as I have been in regard of Urias. *"With bit and bridle bind fast their jaws, who come not near unto thee."* He foretells the calamities in store for those who will act the part of the horse and the mule towards their neighbor. They will be forced by tribulations either to return to God, or will be prevented from injuring their neighbors to the extent they intended; but, as usual, this prophetic warning is expressed as if it were an imprecation. You will force those wicked men to obey you, as you would subdue a horse or a mule, with a bit and bridle, and make them obedient to you. The words bit and bridle are used in a metaphorical sense to signify the crosses and trials that God has sometimes recourse to, as he explains in the following verse.

10. An explanation of the bit and bridle. The impenitent sinner, still attached to sin, will be flayed with many a lash, both in this world and in the next. For, though sinners sometimes prosper, their sinful state is, in reality, a most grievous punishment, bringing with it punishments innumerable, solicitudes, anxieties, fears, dangers, remorse of conscience, and the like; nay, more; God, being a just judge, adds many other scourges; and, unless the sinner repent, and pray to God in the fitting season, he will undoubtedly come under the lash of the scourge that is everlasting. On the other hand the just man, who confides in the Lord, and not in human vanity, is so surrounded on all sides by the divine mercy, that the scourge cannot touch him on any side. Now, the divine mercy is the fountain of all good, and, therefore, when he says, *"Mercy shall encompass him that hopeth in the Lord,"* he means to give us some idea of the immense amount of blessings that those who attach themselves to God alone shall abundantly enjoy.

11. Having pronounced the just to be happy, in the beginning of the Psalm, he now in the end of it exhorts them to be glad, being a sort of indirect exhortation to persevere in justice, that their joy may be continuous also. *"Be glad in the Lord, and rejoice, ye just, and glory all ye right of heart."* You just have great reason for rejoicing and gladness; but let it be *"in the Lord,"* who is the source of all the blessings you enjoy. Be not dejected by the losses or the rubs of this world, because in the world to come you will be amply repaid for them, in *"a good measure, and pressed down, and shaken together, and running over;"* while, in the meantime, you will not be left without spiritual consolation here below. *"And glory all ye right of heart,"* is a repetition of the same, for *"glory"* does not mean to be proud or puffed up, but to celebrate and sing God's glory with joy; and the word is very generally used in the Scripture in such sense, as when the Apostle says, *"We glory in tribulations."* The word glory, meaning pride and vanity, is to be found in Psalm 51, where he says, *"Why do you glory in wickedness?"* Here it has quite a different meaning, that of joy and gladness. By the *"right of heart,"* we understand the just; because, from righteousness of heart comes righteousness in word and in deed; and they are the just, whose hearts, words, and actions are conformable to that most righteous rule, the law of God, from which righteousness it comes that God becomes pleasing to man, and man to God; and whatever happens man, through God's will or permission, is cheerfully received; and thus the heart becomes filled, not only with justice, but even *"with peace and joy in the Holy Ghost,"* which means the kingdom of God, as St. Paul, Rom. 14, explains it. With the greatest justice, then, David, having commenced with the expression, *"Blessed are they whose iniquities are forgiven,"* now concludes with, *"be glad in the Lord, and rejoice, ye just;"* for the just alone are happy, and are in possession of true and solid joy.

PSALM 32

An exhortation to praise God, and to trust in him.

1 Rejoice in the Lord, O ye just: praise becometh the upright.
2 Give praise to the Lord on the harp; sing to him with the psaltery, the instrument of ten strings.
3 Sing to him a new canticle, sing well unto him with a loud noise.
4 For the word of the Lord is right, and all his works are done with faithfulness.
5 He loveth mercy and judgment; the earth is full of the mercy of the Lord.
6 By the word of the Lord the heavens were established; and all the power of them by the spirit of his mouth:
7 Gathering together the waters of the sea, as in a vessel; laying up the depths in storehouses.
8 Let all the earth fear the Lord, and let all the inhabitants of the world be in awe of him.
9 For he spoke and they were made: he commanded and they were created.
10 The Lord bringeth to naught the counsels of nations; and he rejecteth the devices of people, and casteth away the counsels of princes.
11 But the counsel of the Lord standeth for ever: the thoughts of his heart to all generations.

12 Blessed is the nation whose God is the Lord: the people whom he hath chosen for his inheritance.
13 The Lord hath looked from heaven: he hath beheld all the sons of men.
14 From his habitation which he hath prepared, he hath looked upon all that dwell on the earth.
15 He who hath made the hearts of every one of them: who understandeth all their works.
16 The king is not saved by a great army: nor shall the giant be saved by his own great strength.
17 Vain is the horse for safety: neither shall he be saved by the abundance of his strength.
18 Behold the eyes of the Lord are on them that fear him: and on them that hope in his mercy.
19 To deliver their souls from death; and feed them in famine.
20 Our soul waiteth for the Lord: for he is our helper and protector.
21 For in him our heart shall rejoice: and in his holy name we have trusted.
22 Let thy mercy, O Lord, be upon us, as we have hoped in thee.

EXPLANATION OF THE PSALM

1. The rejoicing asked for here, includes the praising of God in joy; that is, praise him in rejoicing, not against your will, or in a sad or negligent manner, but with great affection, rejoicing and exulting in your hearts; and praise him not only internally but externally; because, *"praise becometh the upright;"* in other words, I specially invite you, ye just, to praise God, because it is the special duty of the just, who are called here the upright, as naturally they are; and with whom God, as being all righteousness, is always pleased. God is never pleased with the crooked or distorted; because his judgments and his actions are always straight and direct, and by no means square with the crookedness of the wicked; and hence, instead of freely praising God, they rather offend and blaspheme him.

2. He again exhorts the just to give God his tribute of praise, not only with their voice, but also with the musical instruments then used by the Jews; in which there is a mystical meaning, that we should praise God, not only by our words, but by our conduct; and, especially by the strict observance of the decalogue, signified by the instrument of ten strings; *"That men, seeing our good works, may glorify our father who is in heaven."* Mt. 6.

3. By way of epilogue he joins the substance of the two preceding verses in this one. He had said that we should praise him with our voice, and sing to him with our instruments, and reminded us that we should do everything accurately and carefully. *"Sing to him a new canticle;"* that is a repetition of *"rejoice in the Lord, O ye just;"* and we are ordered to sing to him, not in one of the old chants, but in *"a new canticle;"* composed expressly for the occasion. *"Sing well unto him with a loud noise,"* is a repetition of *"Give praise to the Lord on the harp;"* and he orders it to be done, not in the ordinary way, not carelessly, or coldly, but with great music and effect, to show the importance of the occasion; thus, the word, loud voice, does not refer to the human voice, but to the noise of the instrument. The holy fathers justly direct our attention to the difference between the old and the new chant of praise. The old canticle was the one sung by the old man, *"who born of the flesh, is flesh,"* has a taste for things of the world, and is delighted with them; he praises God when fortune smiles on him; but the new man, who, renewed in the spirit of his mind, longs after the things of the other world, and takes pleasure in those things alone that appertain to heaven; he, too, praises God, praises him always, even in his persecutions, knowing as he does that they tend to his good. We are also warned by the words, *"Sing well to him with a loud voice,"* that when we do sing to him, we must do it with great care, attentively, devoutly, and with great affection, and interior joy. St. Benedict, in his Rule, lays down that Psalmody is a divine work, and should be preferred to any other work. St. Bernard has:—"My dearly beloved, I advise you to assist at the Divine Office, with a pure intention and an active mind; I say active, because I wish you to be active, as well as reverent; neither lazy, nor drowsy, nor nodding; nor sparing your voice, or clipping the words, not skipping sentences, nor in a weak and tremulous voice, full of sloth and effeminacy, but in an open and manly tone, vigorous, as well as affectionate, give out the language of the Holy Spirit.

4. He now assigns the reasons why God should be praised with so much affection, taken from his goodness, his power, and his wisdom. Of his goodness he says, *"For the word of the Lord is right;"* that is, both words and acts of the Lord are most just, most faithful, and most holy, as he expresses in different language, in Psalm 144, *"The Lord is faithful in all his words; and holy in all his works."* By the *"word of the Lord,"* is meant what he commands, prohibits, promises, or threatens; and all these are most *"right and done with faithfulness."* For, he commands nothing but what is good, prohibits nothing but what is bad; and, whatever he promises or threatens, he will most faithfully carry out. Therefore, *"The word of the Lord is right,"* and he is *"faithful in all his words."* And his acts agree with his words; and, therefore, are said to be done in faithfulness; that is, they are faithful, just, and holy; and God is said to be holy in all his works.

5. The sanctity of the Lord in respect of words and actions, arises from his sanctity of will or of purpose, for *"He loveth mercy and judgment;* that means, he wishes first to give us the gifts of his grace, and then, according to the use we have made of them, to reward, or to punish us; and thus, all the ways of the Lord

are mercy and truth. In the first part of this verse we are informed of the goodness of God, arising from his mercy and justice; in the second, we are told that his mercy exceeds his justice, and is, as we have it in Psalm 118, "above all his works;" for to his mercy belongs the removal of every defeat and misery; and, as there are no created things that do not suffer some defect, there is nothing that does not need the mercy of God. Corruptible things of this world, however, suffer more and greater defects than the incorruptible things, that do not belong to this world; so that, when compared to them, they seem to have no defects; therefore, the prophet says, *"The earth is full of the mercy of the Lord;"* for by the earth he means, all corruptible things, for the earth is the dwelling place, not only of all mankind, all animals and plants, but also of birds and fishes; for though the former fly through the air, and the latter *"perambulate the paths of the sea,"* yet, both one and the other, rest on the earth. Now all corruptible things need the manifold mercy of God, to create, uphold, move, nourish, and repair them; but man, in addition, needs his mercy to go before him, to accompany him, to follow him, to forgive his sins, to arm, direct, and protect him, against the devil; and, therefore, he most justly says, *"The earth is full of the mercy of the Lord."* We are to consider here also, that the perfect mercy that can remove all defects, belongs to God alone, for no one, having any defect whatever, can remove those of others, and thus, God is a pure, everlasting, all powerful, impersonation of infinite perfection; with justice, then, doth the Church sing, *"O God whose province it is to have mercy."*

6. From praising his goodness, he comes now to praise his power, the principal and most conspicuous effect of which is the creation of heaven; the magnitude of which is increased by the reflection of its having been made by God without labor; in no time, without men or machinery, by his single word, and forever. He evidently alludes to the creation of the world, in Genesis 1, where *"God said: let the firmament, be, and the firmament was made, and He called the firmament heaven."* The second part of the verse, *"and all the power of them by the spirit of his mouth,"* would seem to be a mere repetition of the first part. For *"the word,"* and *"the spirit of his mouth,"* would seem to be much the same. By *"The power of them,"* is meant the stars, which, like a heavenly host, or celestial army, ornament the heavens to a wonderful degree, and shed their influence on things below. And though, by the *"Word of the Lord,"* and *"the spirit of his mouth,"* God's orders are clearly understood, such is the meaning of both; there is no doubt but the Holy Ghost meant to glance at the mystery of the Holy Trinity to be revealed in the New Testament. We are not to notice the objection, that the prophet attributes the creation of heaven to the Word, and the creation of the stars to the Holy Ghost, as if God the Father made the heavens through the Son, and

the stars through the Holy Ghost; because the acts of the Trinity cannot be separated, by reason of the unity of essence, which is the working power: and, therefore, when God the Father is said to have made the heavens through the Son, the Holy Ghost is not excluded; and when the power, or the celestial host, is said to have proceeded from the spirit of the mouth of the Lord, they are understood also to have proceeded from the Word, who proceeded from the mouth of the same Father, and from which Word the Spirit himself proceeded.

7. He goes on explaining God's power, who not only created the heavens and the stars by one word, but collected all the waters that, at the creation, covered the whole globe, and shut them up in the deepest caverns and recesses of the earth; just as easy as one would fill a vessel with water, or shut up his money in a chest. *"Laying up the depths in storehouses."* Shutting up the immense depths of waters that were on the earth and reached to the very heavens, with as much ease as one would shut up a sum of money in a safe. That the *"depths"* mean the mass of water that covered the earth is clear from Genesis 1, where it is said, *"Darkness was over the depths."* By *"treasures"* is sometimes meant an abundance of gold, silver, or precious stones, as, *"The kingdom of heaven is like a treasure hidden in a field."* Sometimes it means the place in which such things are kept, as, *"Every learned scribe produces from his treasure the new and the old;"* and we read of the Magi, that *"They opened their treasures, and offered unto him gold, frankincense, and myrrh,"* in which latter sense the word *"treasure"* is to be understood here.

8. From what he has said of God's power, he takes the occasion of exhorting all men to fear him, and have a horror of breaking his commandments.

9. The very best reason that could be offered for fearing God alone; because anything but God cannot harm us without God's permission; and, on the other hand, there is nothing outside God that can defend us from his anger; because all things depend upon him for existence, God made everything by one word; for this reason, that his word is all powerful, full of authority, and cannot be resisted; and he, therefore, adds, *"He commanded, and they were created."*

10. The prophet now comes to wisdom, to show that God deserves our praise in every respect. *"He brings to naught the counsels of nations."* The wisdom of God is so far beyond and above, the wisdom of mankind that God, in one moment, blasts, blights, renders null and void all the plans and plots of men, however wisely and deliberately they may seem to have been laid. He repeats that in the words, *"He rejecteth the devices of people;"* he rejects all their devices as if they were so many fools, and deals in like manner with their princes, whose counsels, however wise they may seem to be, and framed by counselors abounding in wisdom and learning, are still

"cast away" as of no value or importance. Truly wonderful is the wisdom of God, that catches the wise in their own cunning, and by some inexplicable dealing, so infatuates them, that what they judge will be of the highest importance and value to them, turns out to be the readiest road to their injury and destruction.

11. By an inscrutable wisdom, God mars the counsels of man, and does not allow them to accomplish what they purpose. Whereas, on the contrary, the wisdom of man is quite powerless against that of God; for, once he has decreed anything it is fixed to eternity. *"Every counsel of mine will stand, and every will of mine shall be done, saith the Lord,"* Isaias 43. Now, by *"counsel,"* as regards God, we are not to understand a consultation previous to election, for God has not to think a matter over, but, by one most simple act of his will, he decreed from eternity all he should ever do or carry out. The Scripture merely accommodates itself to our weakness and our usual manner of speaking, when it says, *"The counsel of the Lord standeth forever;"* that means, that what God in his wisdom has once decreed, cannot be disturbed nor be prevented being put into execution. He repeats that, when he says, *"The thoughts of his heart to all generations;"* that means, that whatever God once thought of doing can never be prevented, but will certainly be carried out, and in the way he intended. The Scripture, however, does not go so far in accommodating itself to our weakness as to exclude truth altogether, for, though there is no counsel with God previous to election, there is in his counsel what is most perfect, that is, the knowledge of all the means necessary to accomplish the most useful end; and though there may be in God one only, and that a most simple thought, that one, however, is equivalent to numberless ones.

12. From what he had said of the power, wisdom, and goodness of God, the prophet concludes that blessed must the people be, whose God is not an empty idol, but a Lord, most powerful, most wise, and most benevolent, on whose praises he had just been descanting; and then are we truly and perfectly happy, and blessed, when we have that great Lord for our God, and he has us for His peculiar people; the prophet then unites both when he says, *"Blessed is the nation whose God is the Lord;"* that is, blessed are they who acknowledge no God but the one Lord, *"by whose word the heavens were established;"* and in like manner, *"blessed are the people whom he hath chosen for his inheritance;"* that means, blessed are they whom the same great Lord hath chosen to be his own peculiar people, and as it were his own property and inheritance. These two things are so united that they cannot be separated, for they alone have the true God for their God, who worship him through faith, hope, and charity; and they only, whom he has chosen for his inheritance, whom he has preordained by his grace, called, and justified, and who worship him through faith, hope, and charity, and his people: a thing we should never lose sight of, for, whatever man may have, even though he may gain the entire world, he is still poor and wretched if he want God, who alone can fill up the bosom of his soul; and, on the other hand, he who possesses God, however poor he may be, is still happy and rich because, with God he has everything. Besides, man is God's image; now, the beauty and great perfection of an image is to be like the original as possible; and then he will be really like to God, and therefore most happy, *"when we shall see him as he is,"* Jn. 3; for God's happiness consists in seeing himself as he is; and thus, those who will never see him will be always most unlike him, and, therefore, truly miserable. Finally, anything beneath God is either meaner than man, as all corporal things, or equal to man, as the Angels are, for in the resurrection we will be equal to them. Now, nothing can make us more perfect, blessed, or happy, but something better and more perfect than ourselves; they, then, alone who cling to God, who become one spirit with him, are the only really happy; that is, they who love God, and are loved by him; who are happy here in hope, and are, in point of fact, happy when they cling to God by so happy a tie that can never be broken.

13-14. He proves what he said, namely, that, blessed is that people that have for their God the Lord, who made the heavens; because when God, looking down from heaven, as he would from an observatory, and seeing man, and knowing that no man, however brave or powerful he may appear to be, could be saved by his own merits; he looks upon his own people with the eye of a father, helps him and saves him, so that the just were deservedly called upon in the beginning of the Psalm to *"Rejoice in the Lord, O ye just."* He, therefore, says, *"The Lord hath looked down from heaven; he hath beheld all the sons of men;"* that means, the Lord in heaven, from whom nothing can be concealed, sees not only his own people, but all mankind, and their various capabilities. The following verse has the same meaning.

15. He tells us now, that when God saw the *"sons of men"* from heaven, it was not in the dim, confused, and uncertain way that we see objects placed at a great distance, but that he saw most distinctly and minutely all their actions; that is, what they were doing, or might do, in mind or body; and thus, he saw all the thoughts, desires, words, acts, past, present, and future, of all men in general, and of each in particular; and he proves God's power to see them thus, because *"he made the heart of every one of them;"* that is, he created their souls, and, therefore, their hearts; that is, their minds and will, from which all human actions spring; for he that could make the heart, could certainly search it. *"Of every one of them;"* that is, of every one of them separately, and, therefore he ought to understand all their works.

16. He explains what the all seeing eye really saw, and that was, that no one, by his own merits or exertions, could be delivered from the evils that surround us on all sides; and that we all need the mercy of God. He gives as an instance, that of the one most likely to boast of and confide in his own strength, the king. God saw that *"the king is not saved by a great army;"* great power, a great army, a great deal of money will not save or protect the king. *"Nor shall the giant be saved by his own great strength;"* his own strength will be as unserviceable to the strong, brave man, as is the great army to the king.

17. There are three things to rescue one from imminent danger; the strength of others, such as guards of soldiers; one's own strength; a swift horse; the two former to meet the danger, the latter to fly from it. The psalmist had already said that the two former were insufficient, he says now that the third is equally so; and we have examples of all in the Book of Kings. An immense military force was unable to protect Saul; Goliath, the great giant, was slain by the youth David; Joram, the son of Achab, flying away in a swift chariot, was killed by a swifter arrow. *"Vain is the horse for safety."* The man who depends on the velocity of his horses is greatly deceived; because such velocity may he impeded or overcome in a variety of ways, and is, therefore, very deceitful. *"Neither shall he be saved by the abundance of His strength."* The horse, whose power is principally in his swiftness, will not save himself and his rider by means of it.

18-19. The conclusion of the argument, whereby the prophet undertook to prove the happiness of the nation who had God for their Lord. For God sees all men, and sees what little they can do of themselves, without his assistance. He has, however, peculiar regard to the just, to help them, to deliver them from the danger of death, and to find fair support for them in this world. *"Behold, the eyes of the Lord are on them that fear him."* The truly just and the friends of God are beautifully described, as those who fear him and trust in him. For fear, without hope, is servile fear; hope, without fear, is presumption. Fear, combined with hope, is the mark of real love; that is, the generous love whereby God is loved, as a friend, a father, a spouse; such love, while it greatly fears doing anything that may possibly offend the beloved, still securely hopes and trusts that the mercy of the beloved will never be wanting. *"To deliver their souls from death, and feed them in famine."* God's reason for regarding with the eye of a father those who so fear him, while they trust in him, is to confer those two blessings on them, viz., to free them from the fear of death, and to support them while they live. As the just are afraid to offend God, he delivers them from the fear of being offended, that is, of their lives being endangered, which is a great blessing. To those who trust in his mercy, he shows perpetual mercy, *"while he feeds them in famine;"* and those two blessings can be understood of our corporal and temporal salvation, as well as of our spiritual and everlasting happiness. *"He delivers their souls from death."* Our corporal salvation is looked after, since God, by a singular providence, delivers us from the various dangers of death, we could never escape of ourselves, or through any human agency. And after thus delivering us, he provides us with all the necessaries of life, especially in time of famine, when so many others are in extremes. In a spiritual sense, he *"delivers their souls from death,"* when he either prevents their falling into sin, which is a spiritual death, or, if they have sinned, brings them back by wholesome penance to grace, which is the spiritual life of the soul; and thus, in both ways, he delivers their souls from everlasting death. And those who are living to God, by means of the Holy Spirit dwelling in them, *"he feeds in famine;"* while, in this desert, *"a desert barren and without water,"* on our journey to the land of promise, he feeds us with manna raining from heaven, and with water bursting from the rock; that is, while he supports and refreshes us by his heavenly consolations, he feeds, without satiating; he cools, without quenching our thirst; because the one and the other are reserved for the day when the glory of the Lord shall appear, when *"we shall be inebriated with the plenty of thy house; and thou shalt make them drink of the torrent of thy pleasure."*

20. Hitherto he had addressed the just, the servants of God, exhorting them to *"exult in the Lord,"* and to praise God as a most indulgent and most merciful father. He now gives the reply of the just, who say, *"Our soul waiteth for the Lord."* The just understand what the Holy Spirit wants when he invites them to exult and praise; that he wants them to do so, that they may thereby be encouraged to persevere in justice; to cling to God Almighty, not to turn from him through any amount of persecution; and, finally, to praise God more through their actions, than with their lips; and they reply that, marked as they have been by so many of God's signal favors, they will most steadily remain in his fear and his love. *"Our soul (say they) waiteth for the Lord."* Whatever may happen, it will not separate us from the love of God, nor will we look for any other to console us; but will patiently expect consolation from heaven, knowing it has been written, Habac. 2, *"If it make any delay, wait for it: for it shall surely come, and it shall not be slack."* The soul is said to wait, by a Hebraism, by which the soul is used for the entire man, especially in spiritual matters. Thus, in Isaias 26, *"Thy name and thy remembrance are the desire of the soul. My soul hath desired thee in the night;"* and, Lamentation 3, *"The Lord is good to them that hope in him, to the soul that seeketh him;"* and the most Blessed Virgin says, *"My soul doth magnify the Lord."* The just herein assign a reason for their having determined to wait for the Lord so long; because they know, from experience, that he always helped them in

their prosperity, and protected them most faithfully and effectually in their adversity.

21. The just having responded to the first desire of the Holy Spirit, they now respond to the second, viz., that they should *"rejoice in the Lord,"* as has been explained in the first verse of the Psalm. They say they will do so most willingly. *"In him our heart shall rejoice;"* having hoped in the Lord, they have been assisted and protected by him, and, therefore, having learned from experience, how good and how powerful he is, they *"rejoice in him,"* and *"trusting his name."*

22. The Psalm, as is frequently the case, concludes with a prayer, one quite apposite to the last verses, and to the entire Psalm, because it having been repeated that God has mercy on those that confide in him, and the just assert they did confide in him, and by reason of continuous danger, always need continuous mercy, they therefore conclude by, *"Let thy mercy, O Lord, be upon us;"* let it not cease, but continue; nay, even let new mercies be poured upon us, *"as we have hoped in thee,"* as your goodness led us to expect, and we promised to ourselves.

PSALM 33

An exhortation to the praise and service of God.

1 I will bless the Lord at all times, his praise shall be always in my mouth.
2 In the Lord shall my soul be praised: let the meek hear and rejoice.
3 magnify the Lord with me; and let us extol his name together.
4 I sought the Lord, and he heard me; and he delivered me from all my troubles.
5 Come ye to him and be enlightened: and your faces shall not be confounded.
6 This poor man cried, and the Lord heard him: and saved him out of all his troubles.
7 The angel of the Lord shall encamp round about them that fear him: and shall deliver them.
8 taste, and see that the Lord is sweet: blessed is the man that hopeth in him.
9 Fear the Lord, all ye his saints: for there is no want to them that fear him.
10 The rich have wanted, and have suffered hunger: but they that seek the Lord shall not be deprived of any good.
11 Come, children, hearken to me: I will teach you the fear of the Lord.
12 Who is the man that desireth life: who loveth to see good days?
13 Keep thy tongue from evil, and thy lips from speaking guile.
14 Turn away from evil and do good: seek after peace and pursue it.
15 The eyes of the Lord are upon the just: and his ears unto their prayers.
16 But the countenance of the Lord is against them that do evil things: to cut off the remembrance of them from the earth.
17 The just cried, and the Lord heard them: and delivered them out of all their

troubles.

18 The Lord is nigh unto them that are of a contrite heart: and he will save the humble of spirit.

19 Many are the afflictions of the just; but out of them all will the Lord deliver them.

20 The Lord keepeth all their bones, not one of them shall be broken.

21 The death of the wicked is very evil: and they that hate the just shall be guilty.

22 The Lord will redeem the souls of his servants: and none of them that trust in him shall offend.

Explanation of the psalm

1. This is called an alphabetical Psalm, by reason of the first verse beginning with the first letter of the alphabet, the second, with the second letter, and so on—done, possibly, that it may be easier committed to memory, and be often chanted by the faithful. He commences by returning thanks with great affection. I will never forget God's daily kindness, I will, rather *"bless him at all times,"* as long as I live, and he repeats it, saying, *"his praise shall be always in my mouth."* The word always does not mean every moment, every day, every night, as if one had nothing else to do; but it means that he will do so in the proper time and place, to the end of his life, nay, more, as those Psalms will be sung to the end of time, David will thus, through others, *"bless the Lord at all times."* This passage may be taken also in a spiritual sense, inasmuch as the just always praise God, when they are in the receipt of his favors as well as when they are afflicted by his trials, as Job did, when he said, *"The Lord hath given, and the Lord hath taken away, blessed be the name of the Lord."*

2. I will not be alone in blessing God for his kindness to me at all times, but others too will bless him; for, whosoever shall hear of it will praise me for having baffled that wicked king; and will, at the same time, praise and bless God, who enabled me by such cleverness to save myself from him. *"In the Lord shall my soul be praised;"* I will be praised by all who shall hear of it; but *"in the Lord,"* for he, who by his signal providence, inspired me with the true counsels, and helped me to carry them out, so as to produce the desired effect, deserves the principal praise. The Hebrew implies, that the soul, that is, the entire person, is to be praised by itself; and the meaning then is, I will glory to a great extent for this fact, not in myself, but in the Lord, through whose protection and assistance I have escaped the danger. We learn from this passage that it is not always a sin to glory, or to speak in terms of praise of our own actions, and that it is then only sinful when we praise what deserves no praise, or when we do not acknowledge God to be the primary source of all good. *"But he that glorieth, let him glory in the Lord;*

for not he that commendeth himself is approved, but he whom God commendeth." The next sentence, *"Let the meek hear and rejoice,"* implies, that the announcement of such joy is specially made to those to whom such dangers are familiar; such as the patient and the meek, such as are often oppressed by those in power, and find a most willing helper in God. *"Let the meek,"* the humble, the servants of God, like me, hear what happened to me, *"and rejoice,"* bless God for it.

3. He directs his discourse to the meek he had just told to hear and to rejoice, and he exhorts them not only to praise God individually, but to join and unite with him in praising God. *"O magnify the Lord with me."* Let us acknowledge the Lord, who alone is truly great to be really so, and he who alone is supreme, let us with our voices proclaim to be supreme, *"and extol his name;"* speak loudly of his knowledge and fame, of his power and majesty. God is much pleased that the faithful, not only in private, but also in public prayer in our churches, should praise and glorify him, *"that with one mouth you may unanimously glorify God,"* Rom. 15.

4. He now assigns a reason for wishing to bless God at all times, and that is, because he found him the best and most powerful of liberators. *"I sought the Lord"* when I was grievously harassed, I fled to the Lord, implored his assistance, approached him with confidence, *"and he heard me"* with his usual kindness and mercy; and the consequence was, that *"he delivered me from all my troubles."* Saul, the king, with his own hand, and through his satellites, sought to kill me, but through God's protection I escaped; in the hurry of my flight I could bring neither arms nor provisions with me, yet the mercy of God at once raised up Achimelech the priest, to supply me with both; soon after, by my own imprudence, I fell into the hands of Achis, king of the Philistines, but through the inspiration, help, and protection of the same God, by wonderful and unheard of stratagems, I escaped the danger. Thus God, my most kind Lord and loving Father, *"has delivered me from all the troubles"* that have hitherto befallen me.

5. He now commences a most beautiful and effective exhortation to love and fear God, and to cast all our solicitude on him. *"Come ye to him,"* or as it is in the Hebrew, *"look on him."* Behold, the light of consolation and gladness, when you remove the cloud of sadness that was darkening you up; for light signifies gladness, according to Psalm 96, *"Light is risen to the just, and joy to the right of heart."* The passage may also be explained in a higher and a mystical sense; *"come ye to him,"* through conversion, *"and be enlightened,"* by the grace of justification; for divine enlightenment confers spiritual life; hence, the apostle, Ephes. 5, says, *"Rise thou that sleepest, and arise from the dead, and Christ will enlighten thee;"* and Christ himself says, *"He that followeth me, walketh not in darkness, but shall have the light of life;"* and in Psalm

35, *"For with thee is the fountain of life, and in thy light we shall see light;"* where life and light are used synonymously. Besides, Baptism was formerly called, *"illumination;"* because, through it, men dead in sin, were regenerated, and from the darkness of sin, come to the light of life; *"come,"* therefore, *"to him,"* by conversion and penance, and he will be converted to you; and by the brightness of his countenance, that imparts so much vitality, coming as it does, from the increate Son and source of life, he will *"enlighten"* and vivify you. *"And your faces shall not be confounded;"* come with confidence, fear no repulse, he will hear you, receive you, and will not cause the slightest blush on your countenance. The face is said to be *"confounded,"* when the petitioner is refused, and goes away with a blush. Thus, Bethsabee said to king Solomon, *"I desire one small petition of thee, do not put me to confusion."*

6. He proves the necessity of having recourse to God when in trouble, by his own example. *"This poor man,"* himself, in so destitute a state, that he had to beg some food of a priest, *"cried,"* in faith and confidence, knocked by ardent prayer at the gate of divine mercy, and *"the Lord"* at once *"heard him, and saved him out of all his troubles."*

7. He already proved by example, he now proves by reason, that we should approach God in all confidence; because the Angel of the Lord, to whom [Psalm 90] he has given the just in charge, the moment he sees the soul in danger, is at once on the spot, and, as if with an encampment, so surrounds and protects it, that it can suffer no harm. Wonderful power of the Angels! One of them, equal to an army, whence it follows that those who fear God and have such a guard in waiting on them, should feel the greatest internal peace and security.

8. He goes on with his exhortation. Having said, *"Come ye to him,"* and having proved by his own experience, as well as by reason, that we should come to him in time of trouble, he now exhorts us to make a trial, and to prove by experience, that the fact is so. *"O taste and see that the Lord is sweet."* Try it, look at it, judge for yourselves, and see; begin to reject all other consolations, and put all your trust in God alone; and *"see,"* that is, know, learn, *"that the Lord is sweet"* to those that depend on him. And, in fact, what sweeter can be imagined than a soul full of love, with a good conscience, a pure heart, and a candid faith, reposing in the bosom of the Supreme Good. Truly *"blessed is the man that hopeth in him;"* that is, in peace with God, and, in a certain hope, reposes in him. We stated that in the expression, *"Come to him, and be enlightened,"* another meaning may be found, referring to those who are enlightened by justification; and, in like manner, the expression, *"O taste and see,"* may be taken as referring to those who are more advanced; who, after being spiritually regenerated, begin to grow, and to require nourishment; according to 1 St. Peter, 2, *"As new born infants desire*

the rational milk, without guile; that thereby you may grow unto salvation. If yet you have tasted that the Lord is sweet," where St. Peter quotes this passage of the Psalm in the same sense that we have explained it. Even St. Paul, Heb. 6, identifies enlightening with tasting, *"For it is impossible for those, who were once enlightened, have tasted also the heavenly gift, and were made partakers of the Holy Ghost."*

9. After exhorting them to try how sweet is the Lord, he now encourages them to fear him, that is, to observe his commandments; or, which amounts to the same, to persevere in the justice and love of God, that being the foundation of the confidence by which we approach to God, and taste of the sweetness of his benefits. This verse is most properly connected with the preceding, even in the more elevated sense, because, as it is by approaching we begin, and by tasting we advance, so it is by fear we are made perfect, not by servile fear, but by the pure and filial fear that is the characteristic of the saints and of the perfect. *"Fear the Lord all ye his saints,"* for that fear supposes perfect love, for the perfect lover fears vehemently lest he may offend his beloved in any way; and he, therefore, most diligently conforms himself to the will of God, and observes his word in every thing; and he that thus keeps his word, *"in this is the perfect love of God,"* as 1 St. John 2. has it. Speaking of this fear, Job 28, says, *"Behold, the fear of the Lord is wisdom itself,"* Eccli. 1, *"The fullness of wisdom is to fear God,"* and chap. 23, *"There is nothing better than the fear of God;"* and Isaias 2, speaking of Christ, says, *"The spirit of the fear of the Lord will fill him,"* and finally, Ecclesiastes, in the last chapter, says, *"Fear God and keep his commandments, for this is all man,"* as if he said: The whole perfection of man, and all the good he may have in life consists in this, through fear of God to observe all his commandments, and the following words, *"for there is no want to them that fear him,"* convey the same in the higher meaning, for the essence of perfection is to feel no want. And, what want can the friend of God, who owns everything, feel, when the property of friends is common; and if the just appear sometimes to be in want, they really are not so, because they get patience, better than any riches, to bear it; nor can they be said to want riches, who do not desire or covet them, for the soul, and not the money box, ought to abound in riches. Still the same prophet, or rather the same Holy Spirit, who by his words instructs the learned by the very same words, but understood in an humbler sense, instructs the ignorant also, and exhorts them to fear God, *"for there is no want to them that fear God;"* that is, that God will supply his servants with the temporal things of the world, and will not desert them in time of necessity. And we have, both in the Scriptures, and in the lives of the saints, numberless examples of the wonderful providence of God in supplying his servants with the necessaries of life.

10. He proves the preceding by instituting a comparison between the wicked with those that fear the Lord. The latter will not only feel no want, but the former will, however rich they may have previously been, and by the repeated scourges of God will be reduced to extreme poverty. *"The rich have wanted, and have suffered hunger;"* that is, those who had been rich began to hunger and to need, because riches are fallacious and uncertain, and exposed to many and various dangers; *"but they that seek the Lord shall not be deprived of any good;"* they who put their hope, not in riches, but in God, as those do who fear God, they, however poor they may be, *"shall not be deprived of any good;"* that is, shall want no good. These words have a higher meaning also, namely, that those who are attached to the temporalities of this world always hunger and need, for they are always covetous and desirous of having more; but *"they that seek the Lord,"* as they seek a thing of infinite value, a thing greater than their desires, for, according to St. John, *"God is greater than our heart,"* they *"shall not be deprived of any good,"* because, as they cling to the Supreme Good, they possess all that is good.

11. The prophet having exhorted all to fear God, shows now the advantage of this fear, and in what it consists. *"Come to me,"* to the school of the Holy Spirit, the best school you can frequent; *"hearken to me,"* or rather to the Spirit of the Lord speaking through me, for so David himself says, in 2 Kings 23, *"The Spirit of the Lord hath spoken by me, and his word by my tongue,"* and when you do, *"I will teach you to fear the Lord;"* that is, in what it consists, and how useful is the fear of the Lord, to which I have so often and so earnestly invited you, as being the essence and the acme of all good and of all perfection.

12. He now explains the advantages and the end of the fear of the Lord, for it brings us long life and *"good days;"* that is, that life of bliss of which the just have a foretaste in this world, while they have in their hearts the *"kingdom of God, which is justice, peace, and joy in the Holy Ghost;"* and will have complete possession of it in the world to come, *"when death shall be absorbed in victory." "Who is the man that desireth life?"* I promised to teach you the fear of the Lord, and I now fulfil my promise, and I tell you, that the end of the fear of the Lord is, what all covet, but few secure, that is, a true and a happy life. Now, those who wish to secure it must adopt the means I am going to point out; they, then, who say they wish for a happy life, and will not take the road that leads to it, they seem to be anything but serious in what they say, when they pursue the shadow and the image, instead of the reality. I therefore ask, who is he that really and truly wishes for true life, that truly loves to see good days, happy, blessed days?

13-14. The holy prophet now teaches how the fear of the Lord leads men to life, *"and to see good days;"* and lays down that the perfect observance of the commandments of God, or, in other words, the abstaining from all sins, of thought, word, or deed, is the true path to life, according to the words of our Savior, *"If thou wilt enter into life, keep the commandments;"* now, such observance of the law, and such abandonment of sin, springs from the fear of the Lord, and, therefore, it is the fear of the Lord that, through the observance of his law, makes us come to true life and *"good days."* *"Keep thy tongue from evil."* Beware of offending God through your tongue, by lies, by perjury, by detraction, by opprobrious language, etc. He commences with the tongue, because the sins committed by it are of more frequent occurrence, and guarded against with more difficulty, for which reason St. James says, chap. 3, *"If a man offend not in word, the same is a perfect man."* *"And thy lips from speaking guile."* Having prohibited in general all manner of sins of the tongue, he makes special mention of the sin of lying, as being much more grievous itself, and productive of various other sins. *"Turn away from evil."* From sins of word, he passes to sins of deed, and first admonishes us to avoid sins of commission, such as murder, adultery, etc.; and then he adds, *"and do good;"* to beware of sins of omission, such as neglecting to honor our parents; giving due worship to God at the proper time; neglect of prayer, alms, fasting, etc., and similar good works. *"Seek after peace, and pursue it."* He finally warns us to avoid sins of thought, such as anger, hatred, envy, and other minor affections of the soul; that thus we may have and retain true peace and tranquillity in everything we are concerned with. With great propriety, the prophet says, *"seek after peace;"* because the duty of a good man is not so much to be actually at peace with all, as to wish for it, and to be anxious for it; because, very often, others will not suffer us to be at peace with them; and, therefore, the apostle, Rom. 12, says, *"If it be possible, as much as is in you, have peace with all men;"* and David himself, in Psalm 119, says, *"With them that hated peace I was peaceable;"* which peace we are unable to maintain, not only with others, but even with ourselves; for we cannot maintain perfect peace whilst we are in this vale of misery. Hence the apostle says, Rom. 7, *"But I see another law in my members, fighting against the law of my mind."* However, though perfect peace with ourselves is impossible, we must seek for it, we must try to acquire it, by subduing the members, by fasts; by subjecting the flesh to the spirit, that it may learn not to rebel at all, or, at least, to rebel less than it does against the sway of the mind. Finally, we must, with all the powers of our soul, seek for the peace that awaits us in the heavenly Jerusalem; for they who long as they ought for that peace, readily despise all temporal good and evil; and thus, even in this world, possess that peace with God, the one thing principally established by filial fear.

15. He proves the assertion he made, viz., that they who avoid sin, and observe the commandments of God, have *"life and good days;"* and the reason is, because God constantly regards the just, and always hears their prayers; and how can they avoid having: *"good days,"* who spend their lives under an all powerful guardian? For if the just have any intimation of evils impending on them, and they cry to God, they find his ears open and attentive to them; if they do not know or expect the said evils, God watches for them, and saves them from many dangers themselves neither saw nor understood; for it is for such purpose *"the eyes of the Lord are upon the just,"* to guard them from the evils not reached by their own eyes. Wonderful goodness of God; Who should not be delighted at loving so good a God with his whole heart, and fearing him with the affection of a child? Who, on reflecting on these things, would not exclaim with the prophet, *"Pierce thou my flesh with thy fear?"* and, in another Psalm, 85, *"Let my heart rejoice, that it may fear thy name."* But the just are not always heard by God—yes, they are heard; and if God does not do for them what they ask, it is because it would not be expedient for themselves to have it done. He is like the physician, who hears the request of the patient praying to escape the bitter dose, and still does not hear him, in order that he may cure him.

16. By contrasting God's dealings with the wicked, the prophet greatly enhances his dealings with the just; for, *"as the eyes of the Lord are upon the just,"* to protect them, so he watches over *"those that do evil things;"* that is, over the wicked, not to protect them, but *"to cut off the remembrance of them from the earth;"* that is, that they may be utterly ruined and perish, and, not only themselves, but their children and all their posterity, until their memory be completely abolished. This does not always happen, either because the wicked themselves repent before the day of vengeance, or because their children and posterity do not follow their example, or because God's vengeance is stayed by some otherwise and sufficient reason; and the psalmist states here only what generally takes place, and which is laid down in the very beginning of the Decalogue, *"I am the Lord thy God, mighty, jealous, visiting the iniquity of the fathers unto the third and fourth generation of them that hate me."*

17. He proves the assertion, that *"the eyes of the Lord are upon the just,"* by the examples of the fathers in sacred history, such as Abraham, Isaac, Jacob, Joseph, Moses, Josue, Gideon, and others; and, perhaps, in spirit, foresaw and proclaimed the delivery of Daniel from the den of the lions; of the three children from the fiery furnace; of Susanna, condemned to death through false witnesses. Perhaps, too, he had before him the example of the Machabees, who did not escape death and torments; as well as the apostles and martyrs, and Christ himself, who most unjustly suffered the most grievous torments at the hands of their enemies and persecutors. For they, in the truest sense, are delivered from all tribulation, who, as the Church celebrates them, *"by a brief and holy death, possess a happy life."* They can most truly be said to have been heard when they cried, because they got what was so much superior to delivery from a temporal calamity. He gave them the precious gift of patience, and in reward of such patience a crown of everlasting glory.

18. He explains how God delivers the just from tribulation, and seems to enlarge on what he briefly threw out in Psalm 90, *"I am with him in tribulation; I will deliver him, and I will glorify him;"* that is, through patience I am with him in this life. *"I will deliver him,"* by the sleep of death; *"and glorify him,"* by a glorious resurrection. So he now says: *"The Lord is nigh unto them that are of a contrite heart;"* that is, God never deserts the just when they are afflicted and troubled in heart by injuries and persecutions, but is always at hand, ministering patience, mingling with it his heavenly consolations, to enable them to bear up against their trials, which will not be of long duration, for, presently, he will *"save the humble of spirit;"* those identical humble and afflicted in heart and spirit, and rescue them from all their troubles.

19. This verse properly belongs to the last part of the preceding verse: *"He will save the humble of spirit."* He will save them, however numerous their troubles may be, and will save them from all their troubles. For *"God will wipe away all tears from their eyes."* Here we are reminded that the faithful in this life are not promised an exemption from want, disease, ignominy, persecution, calumny, oppression, but are only promised spiritual consolation here, and full and perfect delivery hereafter.

20. This seems to apply to the glory of their resurrection, to which, undoubtedly, the expression of our Savior, *"A hair from your head shall not be lost,"* also applies. For that cannot be called broken, which, at once, becomes stronger and more beautiful than it was before it was broken. And, therefore, though the bones and all the members of the just may be scattered, or devoured by wild beasts, or cast into the sea, or consumed in the fire, God, however, preserves them all in the bosom of his providence; not one of them will be lost, but will all be renewed entire and glorified, at the resurrection.

21. For fear the wicked may suppose their pain and torments would be ended by death, as the atheists, or those who disbelieve the providence of God or the immortality of the soul, falsely persuade themselves of, the prophet adds, *"The death of the wicked is very evil,"* because it is the beginning of eternal torments; just as *"the death of the saints is precious,"* because it is the beginning of eternal rest and glory. *"And they that hate the just shall be guilty;"* that means, they who harass and hate the just, who persecute them, who look upon themselves as having accomplished a good work, and as conquerors, when they depress, despoil, and destroy the just, in the long run, *"they shall be guilty;"* that is, will stray from the paths of true happiness, and will speak in the language of Wisdom 5, *"Therefore we have erred from the way of truth; and the light of justice hath not shined unto us; and the sun of understanding hath not risen upon us. We wearied ourselves in the way of iniquity and destruction, and have walked through hard ways: but the way of the Lord we have not known. What hath pride profited us; or what advantage hath the boasting of riches brought us? All those things are passed away like a shadow."*

22. The Psalm concludes by predicting a lot to the just very different from that predicted for the wicked, *"The Lord will redeem"* from all slavery, consequently from all evil, *"the souls of his servants,"* so soon as he shall have brought them out of the prison of the body and thus the death of the just will be the best, as Balaam rightly said, *"May my soul die the death of the just, and may my last moments be like unto theirs,"* Num. 23. *"And none of them that trust in him shall offend,"* will not miss their aim, fail in their course, but will arrive at the goal of eternal happiness; *"all those"* who confide not in their own strength, but in God.

We have here to remark, that hope of any sort, no more than faith of any sort, or faith that is dead, will not suffice to obtain eternal life; but here it is said, that hope will procure eternal life, because he supposes it to be the hope of the just, of those who fear and love God, which the Apostle Peter calls *"lively (or living) hope."* Such hope and confidence as springs from patience, good works, and the testimony of a good conscience, according to St. Paul, Rom. 5., *"Patience worketh trial, and trial hope;"* and again, 1 Timothy 3, *"For they that have ministered well, shall purchase to themselves a good degree, and much confidence in the faith which is in Christ Jesus;"* and again, 1 John 3, *"If our heart do not reprehend us we have confidence towards God."* This living and perfect hope brings us at once to what we want, to everlasting glory, so that we ultimately got possession of the object of our hope.

PSALM 34

David, in the person of Christ, prayeth against his persecutors; prophetically foreshowing the punishments that shall fall upon them.

1 Judge thou, O Lord, them that wrong me: overthrow them that fight against me.
2 Take hold of arms and shield: and rise up to help me.
3 Bring out the sword, and shut up the way against them that persecute me: say to my soul: I am thy salvation.
4 Let them be confounded and ashamed that seek after my soul. Let them be turned back and be confounded that devise against me.
5 Let them become as dust before the wind: and let the angel of the Lord straiten

them.

6 Let their way become dark and slippery; and let the angel of the Lord pursue them.

7 For without cause they have hidden their net for me unto destruction: without cause they have upbraided my soul.

8 Let the snare which he knoweth not come upon him: and let the net which he hath hidden catch him: and let the net which he hath hidden catch him: and into that very snare let them fall.

9 But my soul shall rejoice in the Lord; and shall be delighted in his salvation.

10 All my bones shall say: Lord, who is like to thee? Who deliverest the poor from the hand of them that are stronger than he; the needy and the poor from them that strip him.

11 Unjust witnesses rising up have asked me things I knew not.

12 They repaid me evil for good: to the depriving me of my soul.

13 But as for me, when they were troublesome to me, I was clothed with haircloth. I humbled my soul with fasting; and my prayer shall be turned into my bosom.

14 As a neighbour and as an own brother, so did I please: as one mourning and sorrowful so was I humbled.

15 But they rejoiced against me, and came together: scourges were gathered together upon me, and I knew not.

16 They were separated, and repented not: they tempted me, they scoffed at me with scorn: they gnashed upon me with their teeth.

17 Lord, when wilt thou look upon me? rescue thou soul from their malice: my only one from the lions.

18 I will give thanks to thee in a great church; I will praise thee in a strong people.

19 Let not them that are my enemies wrongfully rejoice over me: who have hated me without cause, and wink with the eyes.

20 For they spoke indeed peaceably to me; and speaking in the anger of the earth they devised guile.

21 And they opened their mouth wide against me; they said: Well done, well done, our eyes have seen it.

22 Thou hast seen, O Lord, be not thou silent: O Lord, depart not from me.

23 Arise, and be attentive to my judgment: to my cause, my God, and my Lord.

24 Judge me, O Lord my God according to thy justice, and let them not rejoice over me.

25 Let them not say in their hearts: It is well, it is well, to our mind: neither let them say: We have swallowed him up.

26 Let them blush: and be ashamed together, who rejoice at my evils. Let them be clothed with confusion and shame, who speak great things against me.

27 Let them rejoice and be glad, who are well pleased with my justice, and let them say always: The Lord be magnified, who delights in the peace of his servant.

28 And my tongue shall meditate thy justice, thy praise all the day long.

EXPLANATION OF THE PSALM

1. A petition for help against persecutors in general. To understand this verse properly we should understand Hebrew, from which it clearly appears that the verse means; *"Judge them that judge me."* By a just judgment condemn them that unjustly condemned me, such as the chiefs of the Jews, Annas and Caiphas, and the chiefs of the gentiles, Pilate and Herod, who judged Christ most unjustly; and many kings and princes who, by most unjust judgments, condemned so many holy martyrs. And because the enemies of Christ and of his Church would have it appear that in their persecutions they were influenced only by a desire of upholding the law, and of acting agreeably to it; while they were, at the very time, acting as professed enemies, instead of impartial judges; and, with an assumption of piety, were only standing by their false superstitions, the Psalm adds: *"Overthrow them that fight against me;"* take up my cause, fight my battle; that when my enemies *"are overthrown"* by you, I may escape them, and depart the conqueror.

2. An explanation of the words, *"Overthrow them that fight against me;"* and as a warrior ought to be well armed with weapons defensive and offensive, he mentions the former in this verse, and the latter in the next; in the Hebrew the expression is, the shield and buckler; and to avoid a repetition of what appears to be much the same weapon, the Greeks and Latins translate it arms and the shield, that is, arms of protection and defense. The shield and buckler of God signify his good will, according to Psalm 5, *"O Lord, thou hast crowned us as with a shield of thy good will."* They likewise signify justice and equity, as in Wisdom 5, *"He will take equity for an invincible shield;"* and, indeed, the benevolence with which God protects us is a real shield, for, any one loved by God is perfectly secure; and of him can be said, *"Thou hast crowned him with a shield of thy good will."* The justice of God, called *"equity"* in the Scriptures, is the shield wherewith he protects from the judgments and the calumnies of the wicked; for, however severely and bitterly God may punish the wicked, he does so in justice, and, therefore, he regards not, and fears not, the sharpness or the bitterness of their tongues, or of their opinions, according to Psalm 50, *"That thou mayest be justified in thy words, and mayest overcome when thou art judged;"* and of it is said, *"He will take equity for an invincible shield;"* that is, when he shall come to the last judgment, and take up his arms to avenge himself on his enemies. There was, therefore, much significance in the repetition of the shield and buckler, since God takes up both, to protect us in his mercy and defend himself in his justice.

3. He now speaks of offensive arms, and says, unsheath your sword, and draw it against my persecutors. The word *"bring out,"* in the Hebrew, signifies a prompt and ready pull, the sword being sharp and in good order, and, therefore, easily drawn, as having no rust on it; *"and shut up the way against them that persecute me;"* put so many obstacles before them, that they will not be able to come near. The sword signifies the vindictive justice of God, that prompts him to punish the wicked, as we read in Deut. 32, *"If I shall whet my sword as the lightning, and my hand take hold on judgment; I will render vengeance to my enemies, and repay them that hate me;"* and in Wisdom 5, *"He will sharpen his severe wrath for a spear;"* for the sword and the spear are arms of offense. Wonderful reflection for a faithful soul, to feel that God stands there armed with sword, shield, and lance, for its protection and hears him speaking to the heart *"I am thy salvation."* For, though the assurance of the apostle, *"If God be for us, who is against us,"* ought to give us the greatest security, however, the Holy Ghost, to provide more effectually for our weakness, describes God in arms for us; and, in all description of arms, fighting against both the visible and invisible enemies, not only of the Church in general, but of each of the faithful in particular. *"Say to my soul: I am thy salvation."* God's defense of us; and, therefore, Christ asks for his Church and his faithful, that they may be apprised of such defense; and thereby have the more confidence. And though the term physician may seem to be more applicable to God here than *"salvation,"* still it is, in reality, more appropriate, because physicians and medicine do not always cure, and do not penetrate the substance of what they mean to cure; but God always does; he enters into the very recesses of our souls; and as a man in perfect health cannot but feel so, however destitute he may be in other respects, so it is impossible for the soul, when God is present by his grace, and wishes to heal it, not to be healed, however destitute it may be otherwise.

4. He tells us what is to happen to those against whom God takes up arms, saying, *"Let them be confounded and ashamed."* Let those who thought to slay me be ashamed of losing the victory; for the two words, confounded and ashamed, have the same meaning, as here there is not question of reverential shame, but of the shame suffered by one that has been beaten; *"that seek after my soul"* is an ambiguous expression, sometimes taken in a good sense. *"Flight hath failed me, and there is no one that hath regard to my soul,"* Psalm 141; that is, I have no refuge; there is no one to know me, to *"seek after"* me, to defend me. Sometimes it is taken in a bad sense, as in this passage, and in various others, and means, to endeavor to take away one's soul, that is, his life. *"Let them be turned back, and be confounded."* Let them be not only confounded and overwhelmed with shame, but *"let them be turned*

back;" retire in confusion, and conquered, *"that desire evil against me;"* they who planned my destruction.

5. He asks, in the third place, that they should not only be covered with confusion, and retire in confusion, but that the thing may be done quickly, and that they may be scattered in various places. Dust is carried by the wind with great force and with great speed to various places; and both force and speed are increased here by the terms used to designate them. For the term used for dust signifies the minutest, finest, lightest dust; and, therefore, the easier impelled; and it is not an ordinary wind that is to drive it, but *"the Angel of the Lord, straitening them."*

6. He ultimately asks that they should not only be scattered and compelled to fly but that they should be irremediably hurried on to destruction. Fugitives are favored by a knowledge of the way, by a safe and firm road; or, if the way be slippery, by moving slowly on it. He prays they may have no one of those things in their favor, but, on the contrary, that they may be obliged to fly in *"the dark,"* and on a *"slippery"* road, when both eyes and feet will be powerless; with the Angel of the Lord pressing on them so urgently that they must, of necessity, be utterly ruined. This has been all fulfilled in regard of the Jews and the other persecutors of Christ and of his Church, who, by the just judgment of God, are enveloped in the darkness of ignorance, and in the slippery ways of concupiscence; and by the *"pursuing"* anger of God are daily falling into greater sins, and thus hasten in full speed to everlasting misery. This will be more fully developed on the day of judgment, for then the wicked will be confounded and made ashamed in so unspeakable a manner, that they will rush headlong into the infernal pit, under pressure of God's vengeance; and forever, and as irremediably as the man who, in the dark, is hurled down a slippery precipice, from which he can never recover.

7-8. In the first six verses the prophet spoke in the person of Christ and of all the just, on persecutions in general; he now details three sorts of persecutions, generally inflicted on the just by sinners. First, they harass them by frauds and conspiracies. Secondly, by false witnesses. Thirdly, by open force, and that not confined to mere words. Of the first he says, *"For without cause they have hidden their net for me, to destruction."* As, without any provocation on my part, they have been incessantly laying snares for me, I pray God that he may, in his providence, turn those snares to their own destruction. Which imprecation, as we before remarked, is not to be looked upon as an imprecation, but rather a prophecy. God's providence often brings about such conspiracies to be of more harm to the conspirators themselves, sometimes to harm themselves, alone; like a torch which, set to burn a house, is burned itself before the house; sometimes is burned itself without burning the house at all; thus, the malice of the conspirators at once harms themselves; others, perhaps, not at all; certainly, less than it does the plotters; because injuries suffered are not at all as grievous as the injuries devised. *"They have hidden their net for me, to destruction."* They determined to hang me, to destroy me; they set a net to catch me for the purpose; *"without cause,"* when I did them no harm whatever; *"they have upbraided,"* offended, abused me; laying snares for me, as if I were a wild beast. *"Let the snare which he knoweth not come upon him."* May some unknown, unforeseen calamity, come on himself; may he fall into the same calamity he intended for me.

9-10. In these two verses the prophet describes the unspeakable joy of the just man when he finds himself delivered from those that lay in wait for him. The language is most poetic, metaphorical, and beautiful. The meaning is, When I shall have obtained my prayer, *"my soul,"* through which I live and move, through joy, *"shall rejoice in the Lord,"* in praise and thanksgiving, and will also *"be delighted in his salvation,"* which it sees now secure; or rather, will be delighted in God's salvation, or its Savior; and not only my soul, but my body and all its members, even the lowest and most abject, such as the bones; and not only my bones, but *"all my bones"* even the very smallest of them will rejoice, and, if they could speak, would exclaim, Lord, who is like to thee? for there is nothing on earth or in heaven more powerful, more kind, more wise, or more amiable than you, who so powerfully and so mercifully rescue the poor from the grip of a much more powerful enemy, who sought, by violence, to take away not only his property, but his life. *"All my bones shall say"* is similar to the expression in Psalm 102, *"Bless the Lord, O my soul: and let all that is within me bless his holy name;"* signifying the perfect joy that fills up the entire man. For sometimes the soul is in joy while the body is in pain, and then the joy is not complete and perfect; but when *"God shall heal all our languor,"* and *"fill up all our desires in good things,"* then, at length, shall the entire man, inspired by an unspeakable pleasure, diffused through all his members, even through his insensible bones, say to the Lord, *"Who is like thee?"* As insensible things are said to thirst when they need their necessary support, according to Psalm 62, *"For thee my soul hath thirst, for thee my flesh, O how many ways;"* thus, the same insensible things, when their wants are supplied, may be said to rejoice and be glad. *"Who is like to thee?"* who is equally disposed or powerful to *"deliver the poor from the hand of them that are stronger?"*

11-12. The prophet now comes to the second sort of persecutions, through which the wicked, by means of false witnesses, not privately, but openly persecute the just, and gives a highly wrought account of the wickedness of such witnesses. He says, *"they rose up."* They did not wait to be summoned, they volunteered, accusing me of things *"I knew not;"* things I not only did not do, but even did not think of. For, we are said to *"know not"* what we do not approve, nor never did, as if we did not know how to do them. Thus, the Apostle says of Christ, 2 Cor. 3, *"Him who knew no sin, he hath made sin for us."* Then he says, *"They have asked me,"* to show the forwardness and impudence of the said witnesses, who, not content with falsely accusing him before the judge, had the impudence to stand up and cross examine the accused themselves. Again, he says, *"They repaid me evil for good."* These false witnesses, so far from having been injured by me, had been heaped with favors, and from pure malice thus calumniated me. He finally adds, *"to the depriving me of my soul;"* to show that it was no trifling injury they sought to inflict on him, but the greatest of all injuries. *"The depriving him of his soul,"* may have two meanings; first, by taking it as a general destruction and devastation, such as befell Job, who, in one day, lost his wealth, his children, his health; and even applies to the very destruction of his memory and of his name. It, secondly, may be taken as applying to one's character, which, by the devil's agency, or by that of his ministers, gets so damaged, that the just man is all but deprived of his soul.

13. Before he begins to speak of the third class of persecutions, he tells us how he dealt with the second, and says that he neither did evil for evil, nor thought of revenge, but betook himself in great humility to pray to God. *"When they were troublesome to me."* I have not proudly insulted them, but, clothed in sackcloth, I began to fast, to make my prayers more acceptable to God. Sackcloth and fasting are the wings of prayer. The king of the Ninivites, when he turned to prayer in fasting and sackcloth, was heard, Jonas 3. We read the same of King Achab, where the wise man says, *"The prayer of him that humbled himself shall penetrate the clouds."* And he adds, *"And my prayer shall be turned into my bosom;"* to show he had no doubt of his prayers producing the desired effect. Prayers put up in such humility, will not come to me back in vain, but will fill my bosom with heavenly consolation.

14. This verse is much more clearly expressed in the Hebrew, and the meaning of it is, in my affliction I not only abstained from doing evil for evil, but I even did good for evil, for I felt towards my enemies, as a friend would for his friend, as a brother for a brother, or rather as a mother for her ailing and languishing child. For, as a mother, when she sees her child ailing, in sorrow and sadness bends over it to raise it up, so did I in regard of my enemies. He could not give a more eloquent or a more touching account of his feelings to them. David actually carried out what he expresses here in the person of Christ, in his own person, and in that of all the perfect. He loved Saul as a brother, while he lived, and deplored him as a child when he died. Christ did the same in a higher degree, for, when he saw the city, he wept over it,

and he compares his affection to that of the hen seeking to gather her little ones under her wings.

15. He tells us now how his persecutors did evil for good, and at the same time passes on to the third sort of persecutions; for the wicked, not content with harassing the just, by frauds and calumnies, seek also to injure them by doing them personal harm. *"But they rejoiced against me."* I was grieving for their troubles, they were rejoicing at mine; and, not content with such impiety, they *"came together,"* armed with scourges, to destroy me if they could; *"and I knew not,"* was quite ignorant of their designs; so that I could not take any means to protect myself; or I bore them with such patience as to make one think I was quite ignorant of what they were intending.

16. He goes on to relate the malice of his enemies, and says they were not able to accomplish their designs, divine providence having undertaken the protection of his own to save them from harm. That still did not quiet them. What they could not effect by the infliction of personal injury, they sought to effect by foul language, derision, and insults. *"They were separated."* The conventicle of those who came together to injure, to scourge me, *"was separated,"* scattered by the breath of God's will, but still *"they repented not,"* as they should have done; on the contrary, *"they tempted me, they scoffed at me with scorn, they gnashed upon me with their teeth."*

17. Having thus exposed all his persecutors, he now, in the person of all the just who suffer persecution, returns to prayer, and thereby connects the end with the beginning of the Psalm. And as God, when he neglects to punish the wicked, would seem to overlook them entirely, he says, *"Lord, when wilt thou look upon me?"* when will you prove to us that you see their wickedness, by punishing it? *"Rescue thou my soul from their malice."* Take my life out of the danger it is in, while I am in their power, and make me as secure as I was before; which he repeats and expresses more clearly, when he says, *"my only one from the lions."* I have one life only, and, therefore, very dear to me; save that by taking it out of the power of my enemies, who, like so many lions, seek to devour me, *"gnashing upon me with their teeth."* St. Augustine would apply the expression, *"my only one,"* to the Church which Christ prays may be delivered from its persecutors. That is true enough, but I think the word should be taken literally here, and that it means his soul, or his life, in the same sense in which we read it in Psalm 21, *"Deliver, O God, my soul from the sword, my only one from the hand of the dog."* The soul is very properly called the *"only one,"* as if it were the only object of our love. This temporal life is the foundation of all temporal good, while life everlasting is that of all good, and, therefore, the Lord says in the gospel, *"What doth it profit a man, if he gain the whole world, and lose his own soul, or what will a man give in exchange*

for his soul?" and yet, such is the folly of many, that for a nothing they freely lose that soul that should have been the only object of their love.

18. Should he be delivered from his enemies, he promises he will not be ungrateful. *"I will give thanks to thee in a great church."* I will not be silent as to your favors, but in public, before the whole congregation, I will proclaim them, which he repeats when he says, *"I will praise thee in a strong people;"* for giving thanks and praising are synonymous terms, so are the expressions, *"great church"* and *"strong people."* The Church is called great by reason of its numbers, so are the people called strong by reason of their number; for a people may be called strong when its numbers are such that they need have no fear of the enemy. The prophet would seem to have the Christian Church in view, in which God is daily praised for the delivery of the faithful. The Church of Christ is truly great, spread as it is all over the world, and truly strong, since *"the gates of hell shall not prevail against it."* The Church triumphant also will be a great Church, consisting, as it will, *"of a great crowd, which nobody could count,"* and of a strong people; for the same passage tells us they will all *"have palms in their hands."*

19. Returning to the prayer he had commenced, he begs to be delivered from his persecutors, especially from the hypocrites, who pretended to be his friends, while they were quite the reverse. *"Let not them that are my enemies wrongfully,"* they who, under the garb of friendship, still persecute me; which is the height of malice, to pretend to be one's friend while they are plotting for his ruin. *"Rejoice over me;"* let them not glory in my downfall. *"Who have hated me without cause, and wink with the eyes;"* who hate me without any reason, when I did them no harm, yet pretend to be my friends, saluting me, nodding at me, winking in approbation of everything I say. St. Augustine asks, What is the meaning of *"winking with the eyes?"* Expressing, through their eyes, something very different from what they have in their heart.

20. He now explains the term *"winking with the eyes."* They addressed me in terms of friendship, while they were bursting with anger within, and *"devised guile"* to destroy me.

21. The prophet now shows how faithfully he described his enemies, and their fictitious friendship, when the very set who, a little before, were caressing, and winking with their eyes on him, the moment they found he had fallen into the trap they had laid for him, at once *"they opened their mouth,"* and began openly to insult him, and to congratulate each other, *"Well done, well done, our eyes have seen it;"* his downfall we were so long and so anxiously looking for. This was all fulfilled in Christ; sometimes his enemies addressed him in the most flattering manner, *"We know that thou art truthful, and that thou teachest the way of God in truth;"* at the very time they were planning to take a hold of his language; and when they saw him nailed to the cross, *"they opened their mouths wide,"* insulting him, and exclaiming, *"Vah, you that destroy the temple of God, and in three days dost rebuild it; save thy own self."*

22-24. The prophet resumes his prayer, repeating it over and over, with a view to move God's affections. *"Thou hast seen, O Lord,"* the extent of the oppression suffered by your poor servant; *"be not thou silent,"* as if you either did not see, or were not able, or were not willing, to defend those that hope in thee. *"Depart not from me."* Do not desert me in my troubles; nay more, *"arise,"* and like a just and powerful judge, *"be attentive to my judgment,"* to the quarrel between me and my persecutors, and *"Judge me, O Lord, according to my justice;"* that is, if thy justice, which is supreme and infallible, decide that I am unjustly oppressed by my enemies, deliver me from their hands, that they may no longer *"rejoice over me."*

25-26. He here explains the meaning of a former expression, *"Let not my enemies wrongfully rejoice over me;"* for here he asks that they may not be able to *"say in their hearts;"* that is, to exult over me as if I were extinguished. Nor *"let them say: we have swallowed him up;"* as if I had been devoured by lions; but, on the contrary, having lost all hope of victory, *"Let them blush and be ashamed,"* every one of them, and that in no slight degree; but, *"let them be clothed with confusion and shame;"* these people who *"speak great things against me;"* who boasted of the power they had over me.

27-28. As well as the prophet prayed for the confusion of the wicked, he now prays that the just, the men of good will, who wish to keep their innocence, and desire their justice should appear openly, should exult and rejoice. He also exhorts those who are desirous of their own peace, such as will follow from their being delivered from their evils, to praise God. He finishes the Psalm in thanksgiving to God for all his favors. *"My tongue shall meditate thy justice;"* will be employed in declaring it; which he again repeats, by saying he will spend the *"whole day"* in doing so; that means frequently, repeatedly. St. Augustine remarks on this passage, that he is always praising God, who is always doing what is right.

PSALM 35

The malice of sinners, and the goodness of God.

1 The unjust hath said within himself, that he would sin: there is no fear of God before his eyes.
2 For in his sight he hath done deceitfully, that his iniquity may be found unto hatred.
3 The words of his mouth are iniquity and guile: he would not understand that he might do well.

4 He hath devised iniquity on his bed, he hath set himself on every way that is not good: but evil he hath not hated.
5 Lord, thy mercy is in heaven, and thy truth reacheth, even to the clouds.
6 Thy justice is as the mountains of God, thy judgments are a great deep. Men and beasts thou wilt preserve, O Lord:
7 how hast thou multiplied thy mercy, O God! But the children of men shall put their trust under the covert of thy wings.
8 They shall be inebriated with the plenty of thy house; and thou shalt make them drink of the torrent of thy pleasure.
9 For with thee is the fountain of life; and in thy light we shall see light.
10 Extend thy mercy to them that know thee, and thy justice to them that are right in heart.
11 Let not the foot of pride come to me, and let not the hand of the sinner move me.
12 There the workers of iniquity are fallen, they are cast out, and could not stand.

EXPLANATION OF THE PSALM

1. The prophet tells us the two primary roots of sin, one of which is in the will, whereby we determine on committing sin; the other is in the understanding, that does not consider the fear of the Lord forbidding sin. *"The unjust hath said within himself,"* that is, with himself, in his heart he determined to sin; that is, consented in his heart to sin. *"The fear of God is not before his eyes."* He so consented, because in his heart he did not think of the fear of the Lord, who sees everything. Fear is used here for the object of it; that is, he did not think that God was just, powerful, and all seeing; for if he did he would be more afraid of one so powerful. When we fear any one, we are afraid to do anything bad in his presence; and thus, he who fears God, dares not to sin interiorly, for God searches even our hearts.

2. In this verse he proves his assertion, that the unjust man does not possess the fear of the Lord. For in his sight he hath done deceitfully with God himself, and with all men, *"so that his iniquity may be found unto hatred,"* and not for pardon, a thing he certainly would not have done had he feared God. For who would dare to transgress in the presence of a judge for whom he entertained the slightest fear?

3. He said the wicked man acted deceitfully; he now says he speaks deceitfully, and will presently add that he even thinks deceitfully, to show how remarkable is the perversity of him that feareth not God. The words of his mouth are in accordance with his acts; unjust, nay even so unjust that they are nothing but *"iniquity and guile;"* whatever he says tends to open injury or to deceit. *"He would not understand that he might do well."* He cannot offer ignorance as an excuse, because it was voluntary; for he took no trouble to ascertain the law of justice, by self investigation, or by inquiring of others; having determined to lead a bad life, he despised the science of living well, that he may live badly.

4. In a retrograde order, he describes unjust acts, then sinful words, and now evil thoughts and affections; for though it is from the heart, as we read in the Gospel, that bad words and actions spring, still it is from the bad acts and words that we see and hear that we know the bad thoughts and desires that we can neither see nor hear. *"He hath devised iniquity in his bed;"* the bad actions and words were not produced or given utterance to suddenly, without premeditation, but devised long before in the privacy of his chamber. *"He hath set himself on every way that is not good, but evil he hath not hated."* While he was thinking in his heart, and devising various plans of operation, he approved of every bad counsel, and thus began to set himself, to enter on *"every way that is not good;"* and, his will being corrupted, instead of hating malice, he rather loved it, not because of its badness, but because of its utility. *"Every way that is not good,"* means every way that is bad; as if he said, No good counsel pleased him; on the contrary, he chose to follow every bad counsel; and thus stood in every way not good; that is, in every bad way.

5-6. He now passes to another part of the Psalm, and shows that, however great the malice of some, still the goodness of God, which consists of his justice and his mercy, is greater. Of his mercy he says, *"Thy mercy is in heaven."* So great is it that it reaches from the earth to the heavens, and fills all things, as is more clearly set forth in Psalm 107, *"For thy mercy is great, above the heavens."* To mercy he unites truth; that is, faithfulness, by virtue of which he carries out whatsoever he promises in his mercy, and of which be says, in Psalm 144, *"The Lord is faithful in all his words"*—*"and thy truth even to the clouds."* Mercy reaches even to the heavens with its attendant truth, which, too, reacheth to the clouds, that is, to heaven, where the clouds are. Nor is his justice, by virtue of which he gives to every one according to his works, less in God. For *"thy justice is as the mountains of God;"* great, like lofty mountains that sometimes out top the very clouds. Great things are often called *"things of God;"* as, *"like the cedars of God."* To his justice he unites his judgments, being acts of justice, and says, *"thy judgments are a great deep;"* profound and inscrutable, like the deepest gulf, that is called an abyss, impenetrable to human eye. By all these similes of the height and the depth of the divine mercy and justice, as well as of his truth and judgments, we are given to understand that, as our corporeal eyes cannot scan those things above the clouds or below the earth, no more can we understand the greatness of the justice and of the mercy of God. *"Men and beasts thou wilt preserve, O Lord."* The prophet now shows how boundless is God's mercy, extending as it does to man and beasts; preserving, nourishing, filling with the gifts of this world, not only men, rational beings, but even beasts; that is, men who, like beasts, are led by their appetites and sensuality only—whose malice he had already explained. Truly infinite and stupendous is the mercy and goodness of God, who, when he could, with the greatest justice, destroy and reduce to nothing the wicked and the blasphemer; yet, at the very time that they are blaspheming, railing at, and breaking through all his commandments, is actually supporting, nourishing, feeding them, filling them with his delights, making his sun to shine on them, and watering their fields and their gardens with his rain from heaven.

7. The first part of the verse is a burst of admiration. Having spoken of God's mercy to the wicked and the carnal, whom he designates as beasts, he now speaks of his mercy towards the pious and the spiritual, called by him *"the children of men,"* which may be called justice, in regard of the wicked too, who, he justly decreed, should have no share in such blessings. *"The children of men shall put their trust under the cover of thy wings."* The beasts ought to be contented with the safety of their bodies; it was the only thing they knew, sought, or cared for. But the children of men will be, like the chickens under the wings of the hen, O most loving God, gathered together in quiet, expecting all happiness from you alone. Such words tend to give us some idea of the special providence, and the singular benevolence of God towards the pious; and, on the other hand, of the perfect and unbounded confidence they have in God, like the solicitude of the hen in regard of her chickens, and their confidence when under her wings. Nothing can be more to the purpose than the same simile, and it is frequently used by the Psalmist, as in Psalm 90, *"In the cover of thy wings will I hope, my soul adhered to thee;"* and in Psalm 90, *"He will overshadow thee with his shoulders, and under his wings shalt thou trust."* How delightful is it not, and how preferable to all earthly delights, to be fostered under God's wings; to experience the love that exceeds that of a father or a mother, is a thing that no one knows, until they shall have experienced it.

8. Protection under the wings of God is had in this world, when there is danger from birds or beasts of prey; but he now speaks of the future rewards, and gives the best description he can of those unspeakable rewards, by similes drawn from corporeal objects; the first is taken from the recipient, the second from the thing received. The recipient of anything is then content when he is so full and laden, that he can desire no more. That plenty, satisfying the entire appetite, is most happily described here as inebriation. He that is fond of drink is never fully satisfied until he shall have got inebriated, for, instead of coveting more drink, he then falls asleep. So it is with us; we are never satisfied in this life, we never rest, no matter what the amount of our prosperity may be; then only do we become full, saturated, content,

and therefore happy, when we *"get inebriated with the plenty of God's house;"* for then, our appetite being thoroughly satisfied, we sink into the sleep of eternal rest. Observe, he says, shall *"be inebriated by the plenty,"* not by the wine, to give us to understand that the word is not to be taken in its literal sense or meaning. The next simile is drawn from the thing received: *"Thou shalt make them drink of the torrent of thy pleasure."* Three things are to be observed in a torrent. A great body of water rolling down from the mountains; a sudden inundation, a great river, all of a sudden, appears where a drop of water was not to be seen a few moments before; the force of the rolling water, carrying everything before it. Such will be the happiness of heaven! A great body of wisdom and knowledge will come down from the mountain, of which Ecclesiasticus writes, *"The word of God is high in the fountain of wisdom;"* that means, in the high mountain of the Deity is the word of God, the fountain of wisdom, from which mountain and fountain the blessed are suddenly inundated; for we who, through great labor, find after a long time in this world, imbibed wisdom in the minutest drops, will then, on a sudden, all at once, in one moment, after a clear vision of God, so abound in all knowledge, not only of things created, but of the very attributes of the Creator, that by the abundance of such wisdom and knowledge the soul will be hurried on to the love and the enjoyment of the supreme good. For in our heavenly home, we will not be free to love, or not to love, to enjoy, or not to enjoy, a blessing so great, but, through a most felicitous necessity, we will be driven to adhere to our supreme good, and, by a most intimate attachment, to revel in its sweetness.

9. He assigns a reason for the great inundation of wisdom and knowledge that will pour in upon the blessed from the vision of the Deity. Simply because *"he is the fountain of life,"* which is the same as the fountain of wisdom. God then, from the fact of his being the fountain of wisdom, is the fountain of life, for wisdom is life to the wise; and being the fountain of life he is the fountain of existence, because, life is existence to those that do exist. God, then, is called the fountain of wisdom, of life, of existence, because he derives his wisdom, his life, his essence, from no one, but is himself wisdom, life, existence; and all other things, whatever wisdom, life, existence they have, derive it from him. David uses the word fountain here to keep up the metaphor, as if he said, *"Thou shalt make them drink of the torrent of thy pleasure, for with thee is the fountain,"* from which it rises. He calls it *"the fountain of life,"* when one would think he should have called it the fountain of wisdom, because he wanted to show that the eternal life promised to the just, and desired by all as the supreme good, consisted entirely in this supreme wisdom, according to the Lord himself, Jn. 17, *"This is life everlasting, that they may know thee the only true God, and Jesus Christ whom thou hast*

sent." He then adds, *"and in thy light we shall see light,"* to explain, in plainer language, what he had metaphorically expressed; for it means, through you, who are the light and the source of light, we shall see you the inaccessible and never failing light. We see God now, but reflected through his creatures; we see him in our mind, but by reasoning, by inference from his works; finally, we see him in faith, but not in form; but then we will see God in himself, and, as the Apostle has it, face to face, or as St. John has it, *"we will see him as he is,"* and not in a picture. And, as the same St. John has it, *"God is light, there is no darkness in him."* He therefore most properly says here, *"in thy light,"* that is, in thy divinity, which is light, and not in types and figures, *"shall we see light,"* that is, yourself who art the true light that *"enlighteneth every man coming into the world."* From this passage theologians properly infer, that there is a light of glory necessary to see God. For, though God is light, according to St. Paul, he is an *"inaccessible light;"* and, therefore, unless the mind get a certain elevation, and be strengthened by a certain gift of God, called the light of glory, it cannot fix its gaze on that uncreated light. We shall, therefore, see the light which is God, but it will be *"in his light;"* that is, assisted by the light of his glory which he bestows on those he condescends to admit to the beatific vision. The first explanation, however, is more literal.

10. He now tells us that these great favors, of which he had been speaking, belong to the just alone, designated by him as the *"children of men,"* to distinguish them from the wicked, whom he called *"beasts."* He uses the imperative for the indicative mood, a thing not infrequent with the prophets. *"Extend thy mercy to them that know thee;"* that is, those alone who are familiarly and intimately acquainted with you, who live with you, who invoke you, who fear you in your commandments, and whom you hear in their prayers, in which style of language we have in the gospel, *"Amen, I say unto you, I know you not"*—*"and thy justice to them that are right in heart,"* and hold out or extend the same mercy which is also a crown of justice *"to them that are right in heart,"* to the just and the pious, whose heart is right and agreeable to thy righteousness and are, therefore, delighted with thy commandments and thy judgments; for the prophets as usual, put up the same prayer in different terms.

11. Solicitous for himself, fearful of missing such blessings, he now prays for the gift of perseverance, especially against a vice to which persons of his rank are very much exposed. *"Let not the foot of pride come to me."* Do not, pray thee, let the proud come near me, for fear they may, by words, or by example, or through any other channel, draw me from the state of grace into the mire of sin. By the proud and the sinner, whose hand and foot, that is, whose approach and power he fears, is meant, principally, the devil;

who is the king of all the children of pride; and after him, his servants and ministers. St. Augustine's explanation also will suit; which is: *"Let not the foot of pride come to me."* Let me not have the gait, the affectation of pride; *"and let not the hand of the sinner move me;"* let not the sinner have any influence over me that may bring me to sin; and thus, through my own fault, or through the temptation of others, be brought down from my position, and miserably fall.

12. He assigns a reason for his fear of pride; because, as Tobias says, chap. 4, *"From pride all perdition took its beginning;"* for the Angels and our first parents fell through pride, and through them sin entered into the world; and, after having so fallen from justice to iniquity, were banished from eternal happiness, and consigned to everlasting misery; for, *"God resists the proud, and to the humble he gives his Grace." "And could not stand,"* in that place of happiness where they had been put by God, with a view of promoting them to better, should they persevere in virtue.

PSALM 36

An exhortation to despise this world, and the short prosperity of the wicked; and to trust in Providence.

1 Be not emulous of evildoers; nor envy them that work iniquity.
2 For they shall shortly wither away as grass, and as the green herbs shall quickly fall.
3 Trust in the Lord, and do good, and dwell in the land, and thou shalt be fed with its riches.
4 Delight in the Lord, and he will give thee the requests of thy heart.
5 Commit thy way to the Lord, and trust in him, and he will do it.
6 And he will bring forth thy justice as the light, and thy judgment as the noonday.
7 Be subject to the Lord and pray to him Envy not the man who prospereth in his way; the man who doth unjust things.
8 Cease from anger, and leave rage; have no emulation to do evil.
9 For the evildoers shall be cut off: but they that wait upon the Lord shall inherit the land.
10 For yet a little while, and the wicked shall not be: and thou shalt seek his place, and shalt not find it.
11 But the meek shall inherit the land, and shall delight in abundance of peace.
12 The sinner shall watch the just man: and shall gnash upon him with his teeth.
13 But the Lord shall laugh at him: for he foreseeth that his day shall come.
14 The wicked have drawn out the sword: they have bent their bow. To cast down the poor and needy, to kill the upright of heart.
15 Let their sword enter into their own hearts, and let their bow be broken.
16 Better is a little to the just, than the great riches of the wicked.

17 For the arms of the wicked shall be broken in pieces; but the Lord strengtheneth the just.
18 The Lord knoweth the days of undefiled; and their inheritance shall be for ever.
19 They shall not be confounded in the evil time; and in the days of famine they shall be filled:
20 Because the wicked shall perish. And the enemies of the Lord, presently after they shall be honoured and exalted, shall come to nothing and vanish like smoke.
21 The sinner shall borrow, and not pay again; but the just sheweth mercy and shall give.
22 For such as bless him shall inherit the land: but such as curse him shall perish.
23 With the Lord shall the steps of a man be directed, and he shall like well his way.
24 When he shall fall he shall not be bruised, for the Lord putteth his hand under him.
25 I have been young, and now am old; and I have not seen the just forsaken, nor his seed seeking bread.
26 He sheweth mercy, and lendeth all the day long; and his seed shall be in blessing.
27 Decline from evil and do good, and dwell for ever and ever.
28 For the Lord loveth judgment, and will not forsake his saints: they shall be preserved for ever. The unjust shall be punished, and the seed of the wicked shall perish.
29 But the just shall inherit the land, and shall dwell therein for evermore.
30 The mouth of the just shall meditate wisdom: and his tongue shall speak judgment.
31 The law of his God is in his heart, and his steps shall not be supplanted.
32 The wicked watcheth the just man, and seeketh to put him to death,
33 But the Lord will not leave in his hands; nor condemn him when he shall be judged.
34 Expect the Lord and keep his way: and he will exalt thee to inherit the land: when the sinners shall perish thou shalt see.
35 I have seen the wicked highly exalted, and lifted up like the cedars of Libanus.
36 And I passed by, and lo, he was not: and I sought him and his place was not found.
37 Keep innocence, and behold justice: for there are remnants for the peaceable man.
38 But the unjust shall be destroyed together: the remnants of the wicked shall perish.
39 But the salvation of the just is from the Lord, and he is their protector in the time of trouble.

40 And the Lord will help them and deliver them: and he will rescue them from the wicked, and save them, because they have hoped in him.

Explanation of the psalm

1-2. The prophet, in the character of a spiritual physician, admonishes the faithful, when they see the wicked prospering, not to be tempted to imitate them, or to be indignant or angry with God, as if he were treating them unjustly; because the prosperity of the evil doer will not be of long duration; nay, it will even have but a very brief existence; and then will God's justice and providence, in not allowing them to exult and rejoice for any length of time, be made manifest to all. *"Be not emulous of evil doers."* Do not imitate them; do not seek to do as they do. If they do wrong, do not the same. *"Nor envy them that work iniquity."* When you see the wicked prosper, be not troubled, nor be angry with God for allowing them so to thrive in the world, as it is more clearly expressed in Psalm 72, *"How good is God to Israel, to them that are of a right heart! But my feet were almost moved; my steps had well nigh slipt, because I had a zeal on occasion of the wicked seeing the prosperity of sinners;"* that means, God seems good to those who know and love him; but, poor creature as I am, I fell into doubt and misgiving, burning with zeal, as I thought, for justice sake, and with anger at seeing the prosperity of the wicked, who, while more deserving of torments and punishment, abound in all the temporal blessings of this world. *"For they shall shortly wither away as grass."* A most appropriate idea for showing how short will be their prosperity. Grass and green herbs do not send their roots very deep into the earth, like the cedar and the palm tree, to which the just are usually compared. *"The just shall flourish like the palm tree; he shall grow up like the cedar of Libanus."* Hence, the grass and green herbs wither and rot in a short time; the cedar and the palm tree come to an immense age. And the prophet does not confine himself to their prosperity, which, he says, will be very brief in this world; but, he goes further, and says, themselves will be very quickly destroyed; and when they are gone, their happiness and prosperity is gone with them. And though they may enjoy many and prosperous years here, they are nothing compared to the lengthened, the everlasting happiness of the just. For *"the just shall live forever,"* Wisdom 5; and *"the just shall be in everlasting remembrance."* Any one that wishes to see the brevity and the velocity of all things temporal, painted to the life, let him refer to Wisdom, chap. 5, *"All those things are passed away like a shadow, and like a post that runneth on, and as a ship that passeth through the waves; whereof when it is gone by, the trace cannot be found, nor the path of its keel in the waters: or as when a bird flieth through the air; of the passage of which no mark can be found, but only the sound of the wings beating the light air, and parting it by the force of her flight; she moved her wings, and hath flown through; and there is no mark found afterwards of her way: or as when an arrow is shot at a mark, the divided air presently cometh together again, so that the passage thereof is not known: so we also being born, forthwith ceased to be; and have been able to show no mark of virtue; but are consumed in our wickedness."*

3-4. After seeking to frighten us out of our evil ways, David now tries to encourage us to do good. If you wish to be happy and blessed, understand who is the author of all happiness, look to him for it, and to no one else. *"Trust in the Lord,"* he, being master of all things, can alone give us what we want; but that our hope may be certain, and that we may not be confounded, *"do good;"* do what God's commandments direct you; for he cannot put his trust in him he knows to be incensed against him; and then in perfect security you will *"dwell in the land,"* for who can turn you out when you are known to be the friend of him to whom the earth, and *"the fullness thereof"* belongs? nay, more, *"you will be fed with its riches,"* for it will throw up its fruits in abundance to feed you. But to work, to be in God's peace, so that one may securely confide in him, they must have love; and, therefore, he says, *"Delight in the Lord;"* love God from your heart, let him be your delight, and then you will be safe, because, *"he will give thee the requests of thy heart,"* whatever your heart shall desire. An objection—we know many who *"trusted in the Lord,"* who *"did good,"* and who *"delighted in the Lord,"* and still were not allowed *"to dwell in the land,"* nor *"to be fed with its riches,"* nor to get *"the requests of their heart:"* to say nothing of the countless multitudes of holy souls who are in extreme want. Certainly St. Paul *"trusted in the Lord,"* and *"did good;"* and yet, according to himself, 1 Cor. 4, *"He was hungry and thirsty, and was naked, and was cast out as the refuse and the off scouring of this world:"* and though *"he delighted in the Lord,"* the Lord did not grant him *"the request of his heart;"* for, though he asked three times to *"be delivered from the sting of his flesh,"* yet he was not heard. The answer is: the greater part of those who are in extreme want do not *"trust in the Lord"* as they ought, do not observe his commandments as he requires, much less are they *"delighted in the Lord;"* for, to say nothing of the promises contained in this Psalm, Christ himself most clearly says to us, *"Behold the fowls of the air, for they sow not, neither do they reap nor gather into barns, yet your heavenly Father feedeth them. Are not you of much more value than they? Seek ye, therefore, first the kingdom of God and his justice, and all those things shall be added unto you."* There can be no doubt, then, but that God will provide all necessaries for his own, if they really put their trust in him, and keep his commandments. If the contrary sometimes happens, as was the case with St. Paul, the reason is, because God chose to give them something better, with which they are more contented, and that is the great merit of patience; for the very same Paul, who so described his want and his other tribulations, wrote in another place, *"I am filled with comfort, I exceedingly abound with joy in all our tribulation;"* and thus, though God did not grant *"the requests of his heart,"* by removing *"the sting of his flesh,"* he gave him an abundance of grace to convert that sting into a powerful source of triumph. He, therefore, withheld a thing of trifling value, that he may confer one of immense value, which he knew was the real *"request of his heart."*

5-6. The prophet, in the capacity of a skilful physician, had prescribed a remedy for the internal disease of hunger, thirst, and the like; he now prescribes for the external disease of persecutions and calumnies. When such things happen, we are not forbidden to defend ourselves, and to repel the calumnies; but prayer to God, confidence in God, should be our principal resource and remedy, as was the case with Susanna, who, when condemned to death, through swearing of false witnesses, with tears in her eyes looked up to heaven, *"for her heart had confidence in the Lord." "Commit thy way to the Lord, and trust in him, and he will do it."* In prayer before God disclose all your actions to him, confide in him, commit your whole case to him, *"and he will do it."* He will do justice to you. He will find out a means of detecting the falsehood of the witnesses who swore against you, so as to establish your innocence. That is more clearly expressed in the following, *"and he will bring forth thy justice as a light."* God, in his wonderful providence, will cause your justice that was, as it were, buried in darkness, by the calumnies of your persecutors, to emerge and be refulgent in great brightness, as light is seen when enkindled, or brought out from a closed and darkened lantern. He repeats it, saying, *"and thy judgment as the noon day."* He will establish your innocence as clearly, and make it to be seen as conspicuously as the sun is seen at noon. A thing literally carried out in the case of Susanna. At first her justice and her innocence were in darkness, she was convicted on the testimony not only of two witnesses, but even of two who professed to be together when they saw the thing, and whose character put them beyond suspicion; however, God at once raised up the spirit of Daniel, who, from the very lips of the same witnesses, so clearly establishes their own infamy, and the innocence of Susanna, that she was at once set at liberty, and they were consigned to an ignominious death.

7. The meaning of this passage, which may be considered as the fourth general spiritual rule, is, take care, and be always obedient to God; pray to him constantly, for fear the idea of seeing an unjust man successful in the world may tempt you and lead you to injustice. In fact, the success of the bad is a great temptation; but easily overcome by having God constantly before us, and clinging to him through prayer and obedience. Whoever will so unite himself to God stands, as it were, on an eminence; and, seeing the

happiness of the sinner to be transient and temporary, has no difficulty in spurning and despising it. He therefore, says, *"Be subject to the Lord, and pray to him."* Be obedient to God in all simplicity and honesty, and through prayer frequently converse and commune with him. *"Envy not the man who prospereth in his way."* Do not seek to rival the man who is prosperous in life; that is, the man who is dishonestly so.

8-9. This verse is a repetition and explanation of the first verse. Throughout the whole Psalm the same idea is frequently repeated and inculcated, to explain it more clearly, and thereby to fix it more firmly on the memory. In the first verse he said, *"Be not emulous of evil doers."* He now repeats, in clearer language, *"cease from anger, and leave rage;"* that is, when you see a bad man thriving, don't get vexed or angry, don't say, Why does this villain so prosper? Where is God's justice? Where his providence? In the eighth verse he said, *"have no emulation to do evil."* Do not seek to rival the wicked in their evil ways; do not imitate the enormities of those whose happiness you so envy, and adds, *"for the evil doers shall be cut off,"* to confirm what he had said before, *"for they shall wither away as grass."* He then adds, *"but they that wait upon the Lord shall inherit the land,"* to repeat and confirm what he had said before, *"trust in the Lord, and dwell in the land."* They wait on the Lord who patiently expect his promises, and expect them confidently, knowing the Lord, who made the promise, being both able and sure to carry it out; and thus, there is no doubt that the evil doers, though they may seem to flourish for a while, will not long flourish, but will be *"cut off"* from the land, and shoved into hell for eternal punishment; while those who keep themselves from sin, and expect their reward from God, *"they shall inhabit the land,"* for they shall get permanent hold of the land, of which they will never be deprived. In truth, when holy souls go to God, instead of losing possession of the land, they acquire both it and heaven along with it, when it is said of them, *"that he will put them over all his property."*

10-11. Having said, that *"the evil doers shall be cut off,"* he now adds, that it will soon happen. *"For yet a little while"* and that *"wicked"* man, who seemed so happy, *"shall not be,"* cannot be found; *"and thou shall seek his place and shalt not find it."* There will be no trace of him, like a barren tree torn up from the roots. *"But the meek,"* they who are neither indignant nor angry with God when they see the wicked prosper; but, on the contrary, patiently bear and take from God's hand what it may please him to send, they will *"inherit the land,"* not only this land of exile, but that land that only deserves the name, that fixed and firm land, of which the Lord speaks in Mat. 5, *"Blessed are the meek, for they shall possess the land;"* and as that land is called the Jerusalem, which means, the vision of peace, and whereas all its enemies are far removed from it, therefore *"they shall delight in the multitude of peace;"* they shall have great peace, because the number of inhabitants will be great to enjoy it; and the peace will be of long duration, or rather forever; and thus they shall enjoy the pleasure that peace always brings with it.

12-13. The just man is here advised to be in no great fear of the wicked, as God is guarding him. *"The sinner shall watch the just man;"* shall attentively look after everything he does, to see could he find any opening for destroying him; *"and shall gnash upon them with his teeth;"* like a dog, shall howl for his destruction, and through anger and fury expose his teeth, like a dog. *"But the Lord shall laugh at him."* God, who beholds everything, in whose hand are all things, so that even a leaf does not fall to the ground without his order or permission, *"shall laugh at him, for he foreseeth that his day shall come;"* he will laugh at him, because he sees the end of the wicked man is just at hand; and that he will be taken off before he can put any of his designs against the just man into execution. Though God may sometimes allow the wicked to slay the just, the wicked, however, kills himself first, for he kills his own soul; and since the death of the just is precious in the sight of the Lord, his death, instead of being a loss, is to him a gain; on the other hand, the death of the sinner is the very reverse—is the commencement of his eternal punishment; and thus the sinner is always hurried off before he can injure the just. He is, therefore, justly *"to be laughed at,"* who, while he lies in wait for another, sees not his own impending destruction.

14-15. The prophet explains here, what he had more obscurely expressed in the twelfth verse. He said there, *"The sinner shall watch the just man,"* which he explains here, by saying, *"The wicked have drawn out the sword, they have bent their bow."* The wicked stand with drawn swords, and bended bow, biding their time to shoot with the arrow, and slay with the sword the just man, *"who is poor and needy,"* but *"upright of heart."* But God, who from on high beholds everything, causes their *"swords to enter into their own hearts,"* and *"their bows to be broken,"* and to injure themselves alone; and thus, *"he will laugh at them."* What is said here of the real sword and quiver, may be also applied to the sword and quiver of the tongue, that sinners, perhaps oftener, make use of against the just. The just man is here designated as *"the upright of heart,"* because his heart is most conformable to the law of God, which is most upright; and as that law is the right way in which we must needs walk, the *"upright of heart"* is said to be right in his way, because he never departs from the right path, which is the law of the Lord. Observe also that the just man is called *"the poor and needful,"* because all the just are poor in spirit, and though they sometimes possess the riches of this world, they understand them not to be their own, since they have to render an account of them to God; or certainly David does not speak of all the just, but only of the poor and the needy, who are oppressed by the rich. Between the *"poor"* and *"needy,"* there is this difference, that the former signifies the humbler, the afflicted, the meek; while *"needy"* signifies, properly speaking, the one in want, who wishes for everything, because he is thoroughly destitute. Finally, the expression, *"Let their sword enter into their own hearts, and let their bow be broken,"* is more a prophecy than an imprecation. The sword of the sinner, drawn against the just, then enters into his own heart; when, while seeking to destroy the just, he really destroys himself. While he despoils the just man perhaps of his clothes, he robs himself of faith and charity; and while he deprives the just of his life, he deprives himself of the grace of God, which is the life of the soul; and while, by calumny, he shuts the just man up in prison, he precipitates himself into hell.

16-17. For fear the just should envy the rich wicked, and should, therefore, forsake justice to do evil, David encourages them in these two verses. *"Better is a little to the just, than the great riches of the wicked;"* that means, a trifling income will be of more value to the just man than an immense fortune to the sinner; and, therefore, the just man, with small means, is much happier than the sinner with a large revenue; and, therefore, justice, with little wealth, is more to be sought after than much wealth with justice. The reason is, because the just man, being guided by God, knows how to turn his riches to proper account: he is not avaricious, nor is he prodigal, and he is, therefore, neither needy, nor is he in want; he is not in debt, neither is he burdened with useless riches, to stimulate his pride or excite his passions. On the other hand, the sinner is both proud and prodigal, and knows not the use of money; hence he is always in want, always in debt, and cannot hold his position long, as appears from what follows, *"For the arms of the wicked shall be broken into pieces; but the Lord strengtheneth the just;"* that means, the power and strength of the sinner will easily fail, because he depends on the arm of the flesh, and his riches can afford him no help; but the strength and power of the just cannot fail, because he depends on the arm of God, who, being the friend of the just, confirms and supports him. Finally, the sinner, in spite of all his riches, will not escape everlasting death; because, when he shall die, he will carry nothing with him, nor will his glory descend with him, while the just man, who, instead of trusting in the riches of this world, trusted in God, shall live forever.

18-19. The prophet now confirms what he said a while ago, as to the happiness of the just, however scanty their fortune may be. *"The Lord knoweth the days of the undefiled."* God approves of their life, favors and blesses them; and, therefore, their days will be prolonged, and their inheritance shall be protected for a long time. *"They shall not be confounded in the evil time."* In the time of want and penury they will not be in confusion, because they will not be forced to beg; *"and in the days of famine they shall be filled."* So far from there being any fear of their dying of hunger in time of famine, they will be so supplied that they may eat to satiety; things that often happen in this life, but most certainly will in the next. For, after this life, a most unheard of season of sterility will set in, when no one can either sow or reap; and the rich man in hell will thirst for one drop of water even, without getting it. Then, indeed, the immaculate, who stored nothing on earth, but put up everything in heaven, shall find their everlasting inheritance, and will not be confounded with the begging of the foolish virgins, *"give us of your oil,"* but will be fully satiated when the glory of the Lord shall have appeared.

20. A reason why *"the inheritance of the just should be forever;"* and why *"they shall be filled in the days of famine."* That will be the case, *"because the wicked,"* who were wont to harass them, and deprive them of their property, *"shall perish."* The remainder of the verse corresponds with the two last verses, and the meaning is, Holy souls, as being friends of God, shall have the *"eternal inheritance,"* and in the *"evil day will not be confounded;"* but the enemies of the Lord, as all sinners are, on the contrary, shall enjoy a very brief felicity; for, so soon as ever they come to be exalted, they will vanish like smoke, which the more it is exalted, the more it is scattered, leaving not even a track of itself behind.

21-22. He confirms what he had stated in verse 16, viz., *"Better is a little to the just than the great riches of the wicked."* It frequently happens that the sinner, however rich, may borrow money without returning it, because they want to live, to be dressed, or to have finer houses than they can afford; hence, they are always in debt; while the just man, however limited in his fortune, knows how to make use of that little; and hence, can afford to *"have mercy on the poor,"* and *"shall give without expecting to get it back." "For such as bless him,"* that is God, *"shall inherit the land;"* and thus will always have something to give—*"but such as curse him;"* the ungrateful, the blasphemer, *"shall perish,"* so that even if they wished to give, they won't be able to do so.

23-24. He now begins to relate God's singular providence in regard of the just, in order to confirm them, for fear the prosperity of the wicked may induce them to commit sin. He states, then, that the life of the just is guided and guarded by God. *"With the Lord shall the steps of a man be directed."* The Lord, who made the just man, will direct his words and actions. *"And he shall like well his way;"* that is, either the just man shall like well and follow God's way, or God shall like his, that is, the path he is pursuing. *"When he shall fall, he shall not be bruised."* This may be referred to the disasters of the body as well as of the soul. For, should the just man meet any corporeal affliction or trouble, such as the falling down a precipice or into a pit, *"he shall not be bruised;"* he will not be entirely destroyed; for the *"Lord putteth his hand under him,"* assists him through his providence. Should he fall into the temptation of sin, *"he shall not be bruised;"* that is, he will not give full consent to mortal sin, nor will he lose his patience, his faith, or any other virtue, because God, by the assistance of his grace, will *"put his hand under him."*

25-26. He proves, from his own experience, that the just *"shall not be confounded in the evil time;"* and also, that *"in the days of famine they shall be filled."* I have been young, and now am old;" and in all that space of time *"have not seen the just forsaken;"* so as to be pinched by want; nor have I seen *"his seed seeking bread;"* that is, his children begging or seeking bread. On the contrary, I have seen the just man *"showing mercy and lending;"* so abounding in the riches of the world as to be able either to bestow altogether, or certainly to lend to his neighbors in their necessities; and, therefore, *"his seed,"* his descendants, not only shall feel no want, but they *"shall be in blessing;"* that is, blessed by God, they will abound in the goods of this world, or they will be blessed by all, as the children of the best of parents. Observe that the mendicant religions do not come under the sentence so pronounced here, because their mendicancy is voluntary, done through a love of poverty; nor can they be said to be forsaken by God, when he supports them by a wonderful providence. Other mendicants, generally speaking, are not the children of those who were wont *"to show mercy and to lend;"* to whom the promise was specially made. Very often they are neither just themselves nor the children of the just. Lastly, as we have already said, the truly just, and they who trust in God, though they may seem to be deserted by God, seeking a morsel of bread, like Lazarus, they have got something better than the goods of this world; nor would they give the virtue of patience they have got in exchange for all the riches of this world.

27-28. From what he had said of his experience from his youth to his old age, he concludes by an exhortation to *"decline from evil and do good,"* which are the two primary precepts of justice—*"and dwell forever and ever;"* be just, and you will, in security, *"dwell in the land"* forever. He assigns a reason why. Because *"the Lord loveth judgment;"* his just and holy servants; and I, therefore, assert that *"they shall be reserved forever."* This promise, to a certain extent, applies to this world, where the just, through various successions, are wont to *"dwell in the land"* for a long time; but, properly and absolutely speaking, it applies to the future life, which, in the land of the living, will be everlasting.

29. This verse, as well as the latter part of the preceding verse, are so clear as to need no explanation.

30-31. Having previously said that divine Providence was on the watch to see that the just should not be oppressed by the wicked, he now adds, that the just themselves, by their own wisdom, which, too, is a gift of God, would enable them to save themselves from *"their steps being supplanted"* by the wicked. *"The mouth of the just shall meditate wisdom."* The just man will speak with so much wisdom, that he will not be caught in his language. To *"meditate wisdom"* means to be discreet in our conversation, as we have explained before; which he repeats when he adds, *"and his tongue shall speak judgment;"* that is, the tongue of the just man will not scatter words at random, but will speak what is right, and at the right time, which is the essence of speaking with wisdom; and he assigns a reason for it, saying, *"the law of God is in his heart."*

The just man's conversation is naturally seasoned with wisdom, because he has *"the law of God in his heart;"* and, therefore, while he is speaking he has the commandments of God before him, that he may not offend by his tongue; and, besides, *"the law is a light,"* Prov. 6; and, as the same David says, Psalm 18, *"The law of the Lord enlighteneth the heart, giving wisdom to little ones;"* and it is, therefore, no wonder if the just man, who has it in his heart, who loves to think on it should speak with wisdom—*"and his steps shalt not be supplanted."* To supplant means to tumble another by tripping him, and that more by cunning and dexterity than by strength; but, as the just man always thinks wisely and acts wisely, he is always on his guard, and, therefore, his *"steps shall not be supplanted."*

32-33. These two verses are an explanation of the two preceding. *"The wicked watcheth the just man, and seeketh to put him to death,"* carefully observes what he says and what he does, in order *"to supplant him,"* *"and seeketh to put him to death;"* first to trip him up, then to kill him, a thing that very often happens in unjust prosecutions, when the judge or a false accuser seeks first to entrap an innocent person, and then to put him to death. *"But the Lord will not leave him in his hands."* The Lord will not allow the sinner so to keep the just man in his power, but will inspire him with wisdom, to detect the machinations of his enemies, and to speak with such wisdom as will enable him to elude them; *"nor condemn him when he shall be judged."* The judge will not condemn the just man, when he shall come before him, for God will not permit justice to be so perverted.

34. An exhortation to the just to hope in God, and persevere in justice. *"Expect the Lord."* Hope in God, even though he may seem to be tardy in his promise; *"and keep his way,"* observe his law, and turn not from the path of holiness and justice in which you have set out; *"and he will exalt thee to inherit the land,"* when his promises shall be fulfilled, that you may obtain the land of the living as your inheritance of right; *"when the sinners shall perish, thou shalt see."* When all sinners, condemned by the judgment of God, shall have perished you will see what you now hope for.

35-36. Having said that, *"when the sinners shall perish, thou shalt see;"* the just man may naturally ask, when that will happen? and he therefore now says it will be immediately, for *"I have seen the wicked highly exalted, and lifted up like the cedars of Libanus,"* and placed in the highest degree of dignity and power, so abounding in wealth, subjects, friends, and the like, that one would say his happiness must needs be everlasting; nevertheless, scarcely *"I passed by, and lo, he was not;"* that is, in my way, I saw that man raised and rooted like the cedars of Libanus; I had scarcely passed him, when I looked back, and he had disappeared. *"I sought him,"* asked where he was, looked for some traces of his greatness, *"and his place was not found,"* as if he had never been there. These things are now of daily experience. To say nothing of petty kings and princes, where are those most powerful monarchs of the Assyrians, Persians, Greeks, and Romans? Had history not recorded them, we would be in ignorance of their very existence. Thus, while the merest traces of such powers have disappeared, yet such is human pride, and so does it blind men up, that they cannot see what they actually touch; and will not acknowledge what they must, in spite of them, feel and experience.

37-38. A continuation of the exhortation. *"Keep innocence,"* by keeping yourself so, and *"behold justice,"* judge what is right towards your neighbor; *"for there are remnants for the peaceable man,"* because God will reward him, so that he will leave children after him. Or, in a higher meaning, because many good things are in store for the just after death, *"For their good works follow those who die in the Lord,"* Apoc. 14; on the contrary, *"the unjust shall be destroyed together,"* without any exception, and *"the remnants of the wicked shall perish;"* they will neither leave any property nor children to enjoy it, when they shall have consumed everything in their crimes and concupiscence.

39-40. A recapitulation of the whole Psalm sufficiently clear and perspicuous.

PSALM 37

A prayer of a penitent for the remission of his sins. The third penitential psalm.

1 Rebuke me not, O Lord, in thy indignation; nor chastise me in thy wrath.
2 For thy arrows are fastened in me: and thy hand hath been strong upon me.
3 There is no health in my flesh, because of thy wrath: there is no peace for my bones, because of my sins.
4 For my iniquities are gone over my head: and as a heavy burden are become heavy upon me.
5 My sores are putrified and corrupted, because of my foolishness.
6 I am become miserable, and am bowed down even to the end: I walked sorrowful all the day long.
7 For my loins are filled with illusions; and there is no health in my flesh.
8 I am afflicted and humbled exceedingly: I roared with the groaning of my heart.
9 Lord, all my desire is before thee, and my groaning is not hidden from thee.

10 My heart is troubled, my strength hath left me, and the light of my eyes itself is not with me.
11 My friends and my neighbours have drawn near, and stood against me. And they that were near me stood afar off:
12 And they that sought my soul used violence. And they that sought evils to me spoke vain things, and studied deceits all the day long.
13 But I, as a deaf man, heard not: and as a dumb man not opening his mouth.
14 And I became as a man that heareth not: and that hath no reproofs in his mouth.
15 For in thee, O Lord, have I hoped: thou wilt hear me, O Lord my God.
16 For I said: Lest at any time my enemies rejoice over me: and whilst my feet are moved, they speak great things against me.
17 For I am ready for scourges: and my sorrow is continually before me.
18 For I will declare my iniquity: and I will think for my sin.
19 But my enemies live, and are stronger that I: and they hate me wrongfully are multiplied.
20 They that render evil for good, have detracted me, because I followed goodness.
21 Forsake me not, O Lord my God: do not thou depart from me.
22 Attend unto my help, O Lord, the God of my salvation.

EXPLANATION OF THE PSALM

1. The penitent David prays to God not to punish him in his anger and his wrath, as the judge deals with the culprit; but in his mercy, as the physician does with the patient. See the beginning of Psalm 6, on the difference between indignation and wrath, where we make them to be synonymous; but we will make a difference, we would say with St. Augustine, that they who are condemned to hell *"are rebuked in indignation;"* and *"are chastised in wrath:"* but David prays to God to punish him for his sins neither in hell nor in purgatory, but here in this world. St. Augustine warns us not to make little of the fire of purgatory, as the fire there is more severe than anything one can suffer in this world. Another observation is, that though God's justice is taken here in the retributive sense, as well as in Psalm 2, verse 3, and Psalm 6, verse 1, still, in other places, it is used to signify the zeal of a father angry with his children, not with a view to destroy, but to protect them.

2. Knowing that nothing is of greater use in obtaining pardon of sin than a full knowledge of the evil of it, and the deploring our misfortune before God; in this and the few following verses he mourns over the unhappiness that mortal sin brings with it. He says, then, *"Rebuke me not in thy indignation;"* for I know, from experience, how severe it is; for *"thy arrows are fastened in me."* I have been scourged with many calamities by you for my sins; *"and thy hand hath been strong upon me;"* yes, *"your arrows are fastened in me;"* and not lightly, for *"your hand hath been strong upon me,"* to send them home, to drive them in deeper. By such punishments and troubles, he seems to allude to the death of his son by Bethsabee, the dishonor of his daughter, the murder of his son, his expulsion from his kingdom, and other troubles, which God, in his vengeance, poured upon him. Perhaps, by those *"arrows"* he also had in view those fearful rebukes he got from the prophet Nathan, 2 Kings 12, *"Thus saith the Lord God of Israel, I anointed thee king over Israel, and I delivered thee from the hand of Saul, and gave thee thy master's house, and thy master's wife into thy bosom, and gave thee the house of Israel and Juda. Why, therefore, hast thou despised the word of the Lord, to do evil in my sight? Thou hast killed Urias the Hethite with the sword, and hast taken his wife to be thy wife. Therefore the sword shall never depart from thy house."* Such a reproof for benefits conferred, and such threats, must have deeply affected David, and overwhelmed him with shame, fear, and sorrow.

3. He describes the effect of God's arrows, and says he is terribly confused, and cannot rest, while he brings to mind God's anger, and his own sins that provoked it. *"There is no health in my flesh, because of thy wrath,"* your angry looks, that are always present to my mind, make my flesh to grieve and pine away; for interior trouble has its effect on the body, makes it to waste, languish, and decay. *"There is no peace for my bones, because of my sins;"* the deformity and hideousness of my sin so confuse me, that I cannot rest, my very bones tremble.

4. He gives a reason for being so dreadfully confused when he reflects upon his sins, and says it is because they are so numerous and so great. As to their number, he states, *"for they have gone over my head."* Have grown into such a heap, that they all but crush me, as one who goes into a deep river, so as to allow the water to rise over his head, is overwhelmed by them. In regard of their magnitude, *"and as a heavy burden are become heavy upon me;"* my sins, like an insupportable burden, weigh down the powers of my soul, it being beyond my strength to satisfy so great a debt. David's sin was that of adultery, coupled with murder; and now, truly penitent, he sees the many aggravations of both. He had injured a faithful servant, in depriving him of his wife, as well as of his life; he had offended Bethsabee, whom he solicited to sin, and thus spiritually killed her; he had offended his own wives, by not remaining faithful to them; he had offended the whole kingdom, nay, even the very infidels, by his bad example, for which Nathan said to him, *"Thou hast caused the enemy to blaspheme the name of the Lord;"* he had, lastly, offended God himself, whose laws he had openly transgressed. Counting up, therefore, the number of crimes and offenses he had committed, and the number of persons he had injured by his sins, he could justly exclaim, *"My iniquities have gone over my head."* The grievousness of the sin

can be estimated from the circumstances. David put Urias to death; first, an innocent man; secondly, a most faithful man; thirdly, one actually in arms for him; fourthly, after committing adultery with his wife, he seeks to add to the disgrace; fifthly, because he sought to make the man his own executioner; sixthly, when he wrote to Joab to procure Urias's death, he gave him to understand that Urias was guilty of some grievous crime, and thus he injured the man's character. His ingratitude to God, however, was the blackest feature in the whole transaction. God had bestowed on him all manner of temporal and spiritual favors in the greatest abundance, made him a great king, an accomplished prophet, a brave general, endowed him with prudence, strength, beauty, riches, everything that the heart of man could desire; all of which contributed to aggravate the heinousness of his sins, and which he must have acutely felt when he exclaimed, *"My iniquities, as a heavy burden, are become heavy on me;"* and the reason why so few conceive the sorrow they ought for their sins is, that few look back upon them, and weigh them with the reflection that David did.

5. This applies to the time between the commission of the sin of adultery and the admonition of Nathan the prophet, more than nine months. It was after the birth of the child that Nathan reproved David, and, therefore, during the nine months, David put off healing the wound through penance. Meanwhile, a sort of veil of forgetfulness had been drawn over the wound, which prevented its being seen while it never healed it; the wounds, however, remained, began to *"putrefy and corrupt,"* and to become more incurable, which he now deplores, saying, *"My sores,"* not by the fault of the physician, but through carelessness and forgetfulness, *"are putrefied and corrupted, because of my foolishness."* My folly was the cause of not perceiving them, and the same folly caused me to allow them to putrefy, and thus spread the foul stench of the scandal in all quarters.

6. From the corruption and putrefaction of his sores he became *"miserable and bowed down,"* which can be understood in two senses, as regards the sin, or as regards the punishment. For he who sins grievously, especially against the sixth commandment, by the very fact becomes miserable, because he thereby abandons God, our supreme good; *"bows himself down"* to the earth, becomes like the beasts, and, therefore, miserable, very miserable, which is conveyed in the phrase, *"even to the end;"* namely, he is so miserable that he could not possibly be more so, or more *"bowed down;"* having given up the delights of the angels for the sensuality of the beasts. The expression, *"to the end,"* does not mean the end of life, or the world, or forever; but it means that he was so bowed down, that he could not be bowed down farther, as appears from the Hebrew. As regards the punishment, the passage may apply to that also; for the man guilty of sins of this class becomes

"miserable, and is bowed down" very much, by remorse of conscience, by fear of God's anger, and by the shame that so humbles and confounds him, that he has not the courage to raise his eyes to heaven. Both constructions of it can be united in this way. I am become miserable by reason of my sin, and the punishment consequent on it, and very much bowed down, because I have turned to carnal and groveling pleasure the face of that soul I should have fixed upon God; through shame, I dare not look up to heaven, and, thus humble and abject, I am forced to look upon the ground, and for all these reasons *"I walked sorrowful all the day long,"* my conscience always reproving and accusing one; for what pleasure can the wretch feel once he becomes cognizant of his own wretchedness.

7-8. He passes now from his own sins to the general corruption consequent on the sin of our first parents, which was the original source of his sin in particular; and from such corruption he says that he is afflicted and humbled, is continually roaring and groaning. *"For my loins,"* the seat of sensuality, having shaken off the yoke of original justice, are constantly bringing forth sinful and dangerous desires, and are thus *"filled with illusions"* of the evil spirits, *"and there is no health in my flesh,"* because nothing good is to be found therein," but, on the contrary, a nest of evil passions that weaken it; therefore, *"I am afflicted and humbled exceedingly,"* because I am ashamed to have to say that I, a rational being, should not keep myself beyond the reach of such low concupiscence; and, therefore, *"I roared,"* through grief, *"with the groaning of my heart,"* which provoked me so to cry out and bemoan.

9. Having said that the groanings of his heart caused him to roar; he now tells us to whom those groans were directed, viz., to him who *"searcheth the heart,"* and knows *"what the spirit desireth." "Lord, all my desire is before thee;"* you, O Lord alone, see the whole extent of my desires, which turn entirely on the being delivered from my evil concupiscence, that I may, at length, arrive at the sabbath of perfect rest; and, on this subject *"my groaning is not hidden from thee,"* similar to what the Apostle writes, Rom. 8, *"Even we ourselves groan within ourselves, waiting for the adoption of the sons of God, the redemption of our body."*

10. He goes on describing the corruption of human nature, and says, *"My heart is troubled,"* meaning, the intestinal war between his inferior and superior parts; and adds, *"my strength hath left me;"* for such is the weakness caused by the rebellion, that man must, whether he will or not, be subject to evil desires, and exclaim with the Apostle, Rom. 7, *"For, to will good is present with me, but to accomplish that which is good I find not."* Finally, he adds, *"and the light of my eyes itself is not with me."* The same rebellion has not only caused infirmity of purpose, but also blindness of intellect. We often judge of things not as they are, but as they appear to us; however badly disposed

we may be, as those laboring under fever think what is sweet is bitter, and what is bitter is sweet; and, therefore, he does not say, the light of my eyes is extinct, but, *"is not with me; for the light of prayer and of understanding is in the soul, but being oppressed by our corruptible body and our carnal desires, we cannot make use of it; and, therefore he says, the "light of my eyes,"* meaning interior light, *"is not with me,"* to guide me though it is really within me. It is there in reality, but not practically.

11. Having described the internal war, that is constantly going on within man, he now speaks of the external war, the persecutions and sufferings that are consequent on sin. He first complains of his friends and neighbors rising up against him; particularly in Absalom's rebellion; in which he was joined by a great number of David's friends and neighbors. *"And they that were near me stood afar off,"* while some of his friends, such as Absalom and his companions, pressed in upon him to put him to death; his own servants and soldiers *"who were near him,"* stood aloof and did not protect him.

12-14. All these are true to the letter, as may be seen in the Second Book of Kings, where, when Semei railed at David, called him the son of Belial, the invader of the kingdom, he bore it with the most incredible patience, and would not allow one of his followers to harm or even reprove him; and thus, it was literally true of him that *"he became as a deaf man, that heareth not; and as a dumb man, that hath no reproofs in his mouth."*

15. He assigns three reasons for having been so deaf and so silent; the first is, because he considered it would be of more service to him to put his trust in God, than in any defense he could set up for himself. I was silent, *"for in thee, O Lord, have I hoped."* I paid no attention to all the false and idle abuse so heaped upon me; because I was conscious that you, who are the just judge, giving to everyone according to their works, and in whom I have always hoped, was looking at, and hearing everything; and as I did put my trust in thee, *"thou wilt hear me, O Lord, my God,"* and deliver me from their *"unjust lips, and deceitful tongue."*

16. Another reason why he chose to be silent and deaf. It is better for me to have patience, and trust in God's assistance, for fear, by getting into impatience, and returning malediction for malediction, God may desert me, and thus, *"my enemies may rejoice over me;"* may glory in my fall: *"and whilst my feet are moved, they speak great things against me;"* that is, I have much reason to fear my enemies would greatly rejoice at my downfall; for, *"whilst my feet are moved,"* when they begin to totter, and I appear inclined to fall, (as was the case in his son's rebellion,) my *"enemies spoke great things against me,"* threatening me, and predicting the speedy loss of my kingdom.

17. A third reason for being silent and deaf before his enemies. My sins make me *"ready for scourges,"* not only of the tongue, but also of the lash;

because *"my sorrow,"* which I richly deserved, *"is continually before me."* Or, if you will, because *"my sorrow,"* that is, my sin, which is the cause of continual sorrow to me, never left my heart.

18. He assigns a reason for being prepared for the scourge, because I acknowledge and confess that I sinned, and thereby deserved it; *"and I will think for my sin,"* how I may make sufficient atonement for it. A salutary lesson to the sinner to use all efforts to make satisfaction, and gladly to seize on every opportunity of exercising their patience, when God is good enough to give them the opportunity.

19. Having explained the reasons why he thought proper to remain silent and deaf before his enemies, that by his patience he may propitiate the Almighty, he contrasts that patience with the malice of his enemies. He did not return evil for evil; they, on the contrary, returned evil for good; and yet they enjoyed life, they exulted and were strengthened, which are noted here by David, with a view of moving God to deal more mercifully with himself. *"My enemies live, and are stronger than me;"* I am humbled and afflicted, and yet bear everything as patiently as if I were deaf and dumb; in the meantime, *"my enemies live;"* are quite alive, and active, and exulting, *"and are stronger than me;"* have grown stronger and braver, and *"are multiplied;"* have increased in number *"who hate me wrongfully,"* without any just cause or provocation. He, probably, refers to Absalom's conspiracy, who falsely persuaded the people that the king would appoint no judges but unjust ones, which he would remedy were he appointed king. Hence the people rebelled, and *"with their whole heart followed Absalom."*

20. He proves his assertion as to his enemies hating him without any just cause, *"They that render evil for good have detracted me without cause, because I followed goodness."* Most truly have my enemies hated me without cause, for the very people that most detracted me were those that *"returned evil for good;"* for instance, his son Absalom, and his minister Achitophel. Absalom had received many favors from his father. A short time before, his life, which he had forfeited by the murder of his brother, had been spared; and still he denounced his father as unjust and careless, telling those who came to the king for justice, *"Your case seems to be fair and just, but the king will appoint no one to hear you."* 2 Kings 15. Achitophel, also, who was raised to the greatest honors by David, to be even his prime minister, forgot all and revolted to Absalom, and gave him most pernicious advice against his father. *"And they that render evil for good have detracted me;"* but they did so, *"because I followed goodness;"* because I acted sincerely and honestly in everything, in striking contrast to their unjust and impious thoughts and desires.

21-22. From what he said he infers that God will protect him, and prays he may, and nearly repeats the first verses of the Psalm. God punishes, in his indignation and in his wrath, when he deprives man of his grace, departs from him as from an enemy, and leaves him among his enemies, without giving him the slightest assistance. Having said in the beginning of the Psalm, *"Rebuke me not, O Lord, in thy indignation,"* so he now says again in the end, *"forsake me not, O Lord my God."* Let not your grace desert me, for you are the Lord that made me, and the God that created me for yourself, the supreme happiness. *"Do not depart from me,"* as from an enemy; but rather, as a father, *"attend unto my help;"* look with care to my assistance; you, *"O Lord, the God of my salvation,"* you who are the source of my salvation, from whom alone I expect it, and in whom alone I trust. Such seems to be the literal meaning of this Psalm. However, as many of the holy fathers apply the Psalm to Christ, and it is possible that the whole Psalm was intended for Christ, we now give an explanation of it in that sense.

Another explanation of the psalm 37

1. Christ speaks for his body, the Church, and prays it may be freed.
2. He says, he asks in justice for it, because he had taken upon himself the arrows of God's anger that were upon it.
3. He describes his passion generally, by reason of which, *"from the sole of his foot to the top of his head there was no health in him;"* and when he says, *"Because of my sins,"* we are not to understand his own sins, but those he made his own, that he might atone for them.
4. He says, the reason there was no health in him, from the sole of his foot to the top of his head, was, that the sins he undertook to atone for were so numerous and so grievous, that they rose over his head, and weighed him down.
5-7. He says those things for his body, deploring the corruption of the human race, as if one would say: I am sick in my feet, my hands, and my stomach; the heart is speaking meanwhile, but does not speak of the pain itself suffers, but of what the members suffer.
8. He now begins to enter into the details of his passion, alluding here to the prayer in the garden.
9-10. The prayer in the garden, still alluded to, in which he asked *"to have the chalice pass from him;"* and he began to *"be confused, to fear, to despond, and to be sad,"* and to feel the full force of his approaching passion; he would not have the strength and light of the divine consolation, so that an Angel from heaven had to come and strengthen him.
11. Fulfilled to the letter in Judas his friend, and the Jews his neighbors, when they laid hands on him. The latter was fulfilled in Peter, who followed him at a distance, and the Apostles who fled altogether.

12. Alluding to the council of the chief priests, anxiously seeking false witnesses to destroy him.

13-14. Literally applying to Christ, who first before Caiphas, then before Pilate and Herod, set up no defense, but *"like a lamb in the hands of the shearer, was silent,"* Isaias 53.

15. An allusion to the same silence. He was silent before man, because he would not be silent before God, from whom he expected his reward, the salvation of his people.

16. Christ displayed the most unconquerable patience, for fear his enemies should rejoice at his want of it. *"While his feet were moved;"* while he appeared for a while to be weak and infirm, *"they spoke great things against him, saying, "If he were not an evil doer, we would not have delivered him up to you." "We found this man perverting our nation."*

17. And so he was scourged, slapped on the face, and crowned with thorns.

18. He will declare a sin he did not commit, but which he assumed to atone for; and *"he will think,"* yes, and anxiously, how to destroy it thoroughly, which he did, *"when he bore our sins in his body upon the tree."* 1 Peter 2.

19. Accomplished when the chief priests, thinking they had succeeded, exulted, and insulted him as he hung upon the cross.

20. Namely, when they said to him on the cross, *"Vah, thou that destroyest the temple of God;"* and also, *"let him now come down from the cross."*

21. The very words our Savior made use of when he said, *"My God, my God, why hast thou forsaken me?"*

22. *"Because thou wilt not leave my soul in hell, nor wilt thou give thy Holy One to see corruption; but help me, show me the ways of life, and fill me with joy with thy countenance,"* Psalm 15.

PSALM 38

A just man's peace and patience in his sufferings: considering the vanity of the world, and the providence of God.

1 I said: I will take heed to my ways: that I sin not with my tongue. I have set guard to my mouth, when the sinner stood against me.

2 I was dumb, and was humbled, and kept silence from good things: and my sorrow was renewed.

3 My heart grew hot within me: and in my meditation a fire shall flame out.

4 I spoke with my tongue: O Lord, make me know my end. And what is the number of my days: that I may know what is wanting to me.

5 Behold thou hast made my days measurable: and my substance is as nothing before thee. And indeed all things are vanity: every man living.

6 Surely man passeth as an image: yea, and he is disquieted in vain. He storeth up: and he knoweth not for whom he shall gather these things.

7 And now what is my hope? is it not the Lord? and my substance is with thee.
8 Deliver thou me from all my iniquities: thou hast made me a reproach to the fool.
9 I was dumb, and I opened not my mouth, because thou hast done it.
10 Remove thy scourges from me. The strength of thy hand hath made me faint in rebukes:
11 Thou hast corrected man for iniquity. And thou hast made his soul to waste away like a spider: surely in vain is any man disquieted.
12 Hear my prayer, O Lord, and my supplication: give ear to my tears. Be not silent: for I am a stranger with thee, and a sojourner as all my fathers were.
13 forgive me, that I may be refreshed, before I go hence, and be no more.

Explanation of the psalm

1. David, in his solicitude not to lose true happiness, deliberated and firmly resolved to use great circumspection in all his acts, so that, if possible, he should not sin, even by word, as if he heard the Apostle saying, *"Walk with caution;"* or another Apostle, *"He that does not offend in word, he is a perfect man."* He commences, then, *"I said."* I resolved with myself, made it a law, determined *"I will take heed to my ways;"* that I will most cautiously walk in the way that leads to life, that I will take great care where I put my steps, for fear of falling into a pit, or knocking against a stone, or choosing the slobbery instead of the clean path, or the crooked instead of the straight road; in one word, I resolved and determined to consider and reflect upon all my actions. And, as nothing is easier or more dangerous than to fall into sin through our tongue; for; from the inconsiderate use of it, arise *"strife, contentions, quarrels,"* and other evils, so numerous, that St. James said, *"The tongue is a world of iniquity;"* the prophet, therefore, emphatically says, *"That I sin not with my tongue;"* that is to say, in this respect especially, *"I will take heed to my ways,"* *"that I may not sin with my tongue,"* for thus I will escape incalculable evils. *"I have set a guard to my mouth, when the sinner stood against me."* There is no time we are in greater danger of transgressing through our tongue than when we are provoked by detraction or by insult; and, therefore, the prophet says, *"I have set a guard to my mouth, when the sinner stood against me;"* that means, when any ill conditioned person should irritate me by detraction, reproaches, or injurious language of any sort, then, especially, *"I set a guard on my mouth,"* for fear of giving expression to anything I may afterwards regret.

2. He tells us what guard he put on his mouth. *"I was dumb,"* I was as silent as if I had been dumb, *"and was humbled;"* kept my patience in the greatest humility, *"and kept silence from good things,"* forbore even my just defense, and equally just reproof of those who offended me; *"and my sorrow was renewed,"* because I did not defend myself. Such is the explanation of St. Augustine.

3. He tells us the effect of the sorrow so renewed. *"My heart grew hot within me;"* from the sorrow so conceived, my heart began to warm into love; and then I began to meditate on the misery of man, the mercy of God, man's ingratitude, and the overflowing love of God towards all classes, even towards the ungrateful and the wicked. *"And in my meditation a fire shall flame out,"* such a fire as that of which the two disciples said, *"Was not our heart burning within us whilst he was speaking in the way, and opened to us the Scriptures?"* Careful and attentive meditation on spiritual matters is the ordinary way to light up within us the fire of the love of God.

4. In consequence of that internal heat, *"I spoke with my tongue,"* not with the tongue, as we understand it, but in the tongue known to myself. *"O Lord, make me know my end, and what is the number of my days;"* we are not to imagine, for a moment, that he asked to know how long he had to live; that would have been a sinful and an idle curiosity; and, therefore, he prefaced it by saying, *"I spoke with my tongue,"* in language of my own, with a meaning of my own. He meant then to convey that the life of man is extremely short, and next to nothing. But as very few seem to know such truth, however clear and confirmed by experience, he prays to God not to let him fall into the error so many have fallen into, of looking upon that to be lasting that was so very transitory. For why are the greater part of mankind so intent on amassing riches? Why do they fight and contend for them so fiercely? Why do they neglect and despise the future so entirely, but because they either do not think, or do not believe that the present life will fly away like a shadow? He says, therefore, *"O Lord, make me know my ends."* By thy grace enlighten me, that I may know the end of my life cannot be far away; *"and what is the number of my days,"* that by deep reflection I may see how few they are, and how short is my term here below. The following verses will prove this to be the true explanation. For though he was heard by the Lord, he does not say how long he had got to live; but he endeavors to prove, in various ways, that the term of human life is very short, especially when compared to eternity.

5. Having got the knowledge he asked from God, he states *"his days are measurable,"* so short that they can be easily measured; and, not satisfied with telling that so plainly, he adds, *"and my substance is as nothing before thee."* What signifies the shortness of my days, when *"my substance,"* my very essence, my existence, is nothing in thy presence. It may be something in the sight of man, who sees the present only, but *"before thee,"* who beholdest the future, who seest eternity that hath no bounds, it is absolutely nothing. For, what are a few years, that glide away so quickly, compared to boundless

eternity? *"And, indeed, all things are vanity."* He explains more fully, and endeavors to persuade us of the truth he saw himself so clearly, not only is our life extremely short, but even *"every man living,"* be he king or monarch, whom all admire, and to whom all look up, he too, is all vanity, for, whatever health, strengths, beauty, riches, dignity, or power he may be possessed of, is all frail, fragile, and passing.

6. The prophet, seeing mankind buried in such a profound sleep, in spite of the forcible language he had hitherto used, has now recourse to more forcible language, in the hope of rousing them. As it may be objected to him that man's life, after all, cannot be said to be nothing, when we see so many abounding in wealth, honors, health, strength, and the like; the prophet now asserts that such things are not real blessings, but the image and the shadow of true blessings; and, therefore, that men are fools in being troubled at not having them, or in losing them when they have them; just as a king who would fret and grieve for the loss of a toy kingdom, while he had his real kingdom. *"Surely man passeth as an image."* Man walks and passes through life in the image, not in the reality of things, having before him on his journey, not the realities, but the images and the shadows. This life is but an image of the happy life that alone is the true one; the health of this life is only an image of the immortality that alone deserves the name of health; the beauty of this world is only the shadow of the beauty with which we will be clothed when *"the just shall shine like the sun in the kingdom of their father."* The riches of this world are no riches, they are merely the image of the riches we shall have when we shall need nothing; for then God will be all unto all. The same may be said of wisdom, glory, grandeur, and everything else we call blessings. *"And he is disquieted in vain."* Man, in his anxiety for keeping what he has, or for acquiring more, is troubled. In vain does he rejoice when he gains, and deplore when he loses, as if all those things were valuable, solid, and permanent; while they are but imaginary, frail, and perishable. *"He storeth up, and he knoweth not for whom he shall gather those things."* By one argument, he proves how idle men are in laboring to acquire, increase, and protect the wealth of this world. People think they are storing up for their children and grandchildren, who will greatly revere the memory of their parents; while it not infrequently happens that those children die in early life, and the inheritance passes to a stranger or to an enemy. Often these very heirs, in a few years, squander and dissipate the savings and gatherings of the long life of the parents. Often an ungrateful heir comes in, who, instead of revering the memory of his parents, never ceases to damage and vilify it; and had all those things been foreseen, the owners would have sought to lodge their treasures in heaven, and certainly would have had a happier life of it here. See Ecclesiasticus, chap. 2, 4, 5 and 6.

7. Looking at the shortness and the vanity of this life, so clearly demonstrated, the prophet determines on putting his hope in God alone. *"And now,"* in this state of things, *"what is my hope?"* what do I hope for, ask for, wish for? *"is it not the Lord?"* is he not my hope, my desire. Turning to the Lord, then, he says, *"and my substance is with thee."* My life, my riches, are with you; I hold all things created as nothing, I desire you alone beyond everything, because in you alone is everything.

8. As he said he despised all things earthly, looked to God alone, and *"put all his hope in him;"* he, in consequence, adds, that his only trouble is for his sins, and not for the reproaches of men, *"Deliver thou me from all my iniquities."* They are the only things that can come in the way, and keep me from you; and, therefore, I earnestly pray you deliver me from them, from all of them; the past as well as the future, by blotting out the one, and preventing the other. Here we must remark, that the most perfect, though they despise the world, and seek God with their whole heart, have always something to ask forgiveness for; and, therefore, that they should be always sure to pray to God daily for pardon of their daily sins. *"Thou hast made me a reproach to the fool."* This part of the verse has reference to the following verse, and is thus connected with it. Thou hast made me a reproach to the fool, and I was dumb, and opened not my mouth. He means to convey, that by reason of his having said that all things earthly were vain and despicable, and that we should put our hope in God alone, he was derided by the fools, who did not understand the things that pertain to God. As the Gospel says of Christ our Lord, *"The Pharisees, who were all avaricious, heard those things, and scoffed at him."*

9. When I heard the fool reproach me, I neither answered nor defended myself; *"I was dumb;"* as if I had lost the use of my speech, nay, more, *"I opened not my mouth."* I behaved as if l were deaf, and heard none of their reproaches, for those who are dumb, without being deaf, open their mouth, and attempt an answer; but those who are deaf and dumb, neither speak nor make at attempt at it; and he assigns the reason why he did so, *"because thou hast done it;"* it was you caused those reproaches to be cast upon me; it was you held me up for derision. He assigns the very same reason for bearing the railing of Semei with so much patience, 2 Kings 15.; *"Let him alone, and let him curse; for the Lord hath bid him curse David: and who is he that shall dare say, why hath he done so?"* It must, however, be noted that God did not command Semei to rail at David, so as to make his obedience therein a meritorious act; for we know that Semei grievously sinned by so persecuting David, and that he was severely punished by Solomon for it afterwards; but God is said to have commanded Semei therein, because he saw his bad and evil dispositions, and made use of them to punish and correct David.

10-11. "Remove thy scourges from me." I willingly submit to the scoffs and reproaches of the fool, knowing them to proceed from your fatherly correction, for my humiliation; but I cannot stand your scourges, and I beseech of you dispense with them. By his *"scourges"* he means the racks and torments which God, in his anger, has recourse to; not as a father or a physician, but as a judge, in the spirit in which David already said, *"Lord, rebuke me not in thy anger."* Such scourges are blindness of intellect, hardness of heart, a reprobate sense, and damnation itself, to everlasting fire. *"The strength of thy hand hath made me faint with rebukes."* The reason he is so extremely anxious to escape the scourges of God is, because he has had experience, both in himself and in others, of their severity. As to himself—I have felt the force and *"the strength of thy hand,"* blighting and withering me, so *"that I fainted"* in thy rebukes, when you cruelly and fearfully *"rebuked me in your anger."* That he did when he suffered him, for his sin of adultery, to fall into the greater sin of murder; and into such blindness, that he did not come to himself for many months; nor know his state, that is, the loss of his soul: for no punishment is more grievous than when one sin is punished by the commission of another. The Apostle, Rom. 1., teaches us that sin is sometimes the punishment of sin; and a dreadful punishment; more to be feared than any other known punishment. *"Because that when they had known God, they have not glorified him as God. Wherefore God gave them up to the desires of their heart, to uncleanness, to dishonor their own bodies;"* and again, *"for this cause God delivered them up to shameful affections;"* and again, *"and as they liked not to have God in their knowledge, God delivered them up to a reprobate sense, to do those things which are not convenient."* The prophet then says, that in addition to such cruel punishment, *"thou hast corrected man for iniquity; and thou hast made his soul to waste away like a spider."* For the sins just named you have corrected the sinner in your wrath, and wasted away his soul like a spider, whose whole time is taken up in weaving webs to catch flies, and is, in the meantime, itself dried up and perishes. Thus the souls of the carnal, by the just judgment of God, are perpetually laboring in acquiring the things of this world, and in such labor waste all their understanding and intellect, whence the soul becomes so dried up and exhausted of the moisture of divine grace, as never to think of its salvation, or to be moved by the slightest desire of eternal happiness; as an antidote against which aridity the prophet asks, in Psalm 62., *"Let my soul be filled as with marrow and fatness."* He concludes by saying, surely in vain is any man disquieted. Any man whose soul wastes away like a spider, is disgusted without cause, labors in vain, is needlessly troubled, for *"what doth it profit a man if he gain the whole world, and lose his soul?"*

12. He concludes the Psalm by praying to God with great affection. The matter of his prayer will be explained presently; but we have to remark here, that by the word *"prayer"* is meant the simple petition; and by *"supplication,"* earnest, vehement, loud petition; by *"tears"* are meant the affections, that have more effect with God than any words. *"Be not silent."* He again demands to be heard, without telling what he wants; but he speaks to him who knows what the spirit desires. *"Be not silent."* Answer your petitioner, despise not his entreaties; for he who is silent on hearing a petition, is supposed thereby to refuse to grant it. He assigns a reason why he should be heard, *"for I am a stranger with thee and a sojourner, as all my fathers were."* For you know that I do not belong to this world, that I am *"a stranger and a sojourner"* in it, and, therefore, a citizen of Jerusalem, the city above, though I may wander here for a while. You have, then, a right to hear one of your own citizens, in his exile, crying to you from his wanderings. St. John Chrysostom remarks how great and spiritual a man David must have been, when, at the head of a kingdom, and abounding in riches, he so truly avows he is nothing more than a stranger and an exile.

13. He now explains what his prayer is, that of which he says in Psalm 31, *"For this shall every one that is holy pray to thee in a seasonable time."* He asks, then, *"with a strong cry and tears,"* for pardon of his sins, that, his conscience being at ease, he may return in joy from his wanderings to his country; and, in fine, he asks for grace and glory; a petition put up to God, by those alone who seek him with all their heart, and despise the world and its vanities. *"O forgive me;"* be not a harsh creditor; press me not for payment of the debt; seek not to recover what I have foolishly squandered; *"that I may be refreshed before I go hence;"* before I leave the world; for, if you do not forgive me here, I will not go to rest, but to prison; therefore, *"say to my soul, I am thy salvation,"* before you order it to leave my body, *"and be no more" "a stranger or a foreigner,"* but *"fellow citizen with the saints, and the domestic of God."*

PSALM 39

Christ's coming, and redeeming mankind.

1 With expectation I have waited for the Lord, and he was attentive to me.
2 And he heard my prayers, and brought me out of the pit of misery and the mire of dregs. And he set my feet upon a rock, and directed my steps.
3 And he put a new canticle into my mouth, a song to our God. Many shall see, and shall fear: and they shall hope in the Lord.
4 Blessed is the man whose trust is in the name of the Lord; and who hath not had regard to vanities, and lying follies.
5 Thou hast multiplied thy wonderful works, O Lord my God: and in thy

thoughts there is no one like to thee. I have declared and I have spoken they are multiplied above number.
6 Sacrifice and oblation thou didst not desire; but thou hast pierced ears for me. Burnt offering and sin offering thou didst not require:
7 Then said I, Behold I come. In the head of the book it is written of me
8 That I should do thy will: O my God, I have desired it, and thy law in the midst of my heart.
9 I have declared thy justice in a great church, lo, I will not restrain my lips: O Lord, thou knowest it.
10 I have not hid thy justice within my heart: I have declared thy truth and thy salvation. I have not concealed thy mercy and thy truth from a great council.
11 Withhold not thou, O Lord, thy tender mercies from me: thy mercy and thy truth have always upheld me.
12 For evils without number have surrounded me; my iniquities have overtaken me, and I was not able to see. They are multiplied above the hairs of my head: and my heart hath forsaken me.
13 Be pleased, O Lord, to deliver me, look down, O Lord, to help me.
14 Let them be confounded and ashamed together, that seek after my soul to take it away. Let them be turned backward and be ashamed that desire evils to me.
15 Let them immediately bear their confusion, that say to me: 'T is well, 't is well.
16 Let all that seek thee rejoice and be glad in thee: and let such as love thy salvation say always: The Lord be magnified.
17 But I am a beggar and poor: the Lord is careful for me. Thou art my helper and my protector: O my God, be not slack.

Explanation of the psalm

1. Christ, in the person of his people, declares how long the redemption was expected. It was looked for during four thousand years; while, in the meantime, mankind was promised deliverance from the miseries into which they had fallen by the sin of our first parents, sometimes through the prophets and patriarchs, sometimes through figures and oracles. "*With expectation I have waited for the Lord,*" for a long time, without any intermission. I have been expecting the Lord to have mercy, to visit and to free his people, "*and he was attentive to me.*" I have not been disappointed, for he has heard me.

2. He now explains the expression in the last verse, "*he was attentive to me,*" for "*he heard my prayers;*" and the consequence was, that "*he brought me out of the pit of misery and the mire of dregs.*" The Hebrew for "*pit of misery*" conveys the idea of a deep dark place, full of the "*mire of dregs,*" into which many have fallen, from whose groans and lamentations the greatest disorder and confusion ensue. Such is the state of the wicked, who have not known God and his commandments; and are stuck in the mud of their carnal desires,

that renders them not only incapable of arriving at eternal happiness, but causes them to quarrel and wrangle perpetually with each other. The grace of the Redeemer brings us out of this pit, so soon as we begin, through faith, to know the true God, the real and eternal happiness; and, liberated through hope and charity from our carnal desires, we have peace with God and with ourselves. *"And he set my feet upon a rock, and directed my steps."* He that had fallen into the *"pit of misery,"* fell from the path in which God had originally placed him, and made it a safe and easy path to the kingdom of heaven; and, therefore, he who afterwards rescued him *"from the pit of misery and the mire of dregs,"* put him back on a path solid and firm, and quite as straight and level; which is the meaning of, *"he set my feet upon a rock,"* the feet he rescued from a deep and miry pit he has put upon a high and firm rock, *"and the rock was Christ;"* for he says of himself, *"I am the way, the truth, and the life."* He, therefore, put the feet of the just on the faith, the doctrine, and the example of Christ, that they may follow his footsteps; *"and directed my steps."* He not only put me on the solid, but also on the straight road, and thus *"directed my steps in the way of peace."*

3. The moment God put me on the straight and firm road I began to *"sing a new canticle."* Theretofore, while I was the *"old man,"* I sung nothing but what turned upon the world and its pleasures; but once I became *"renewed in the spirit of my mind,"* I began to sing *"a new canticle"* on the love of God, one that God himself *"put into my mouth,"* which, therefore, is one most agreeable to him. *"Many shall see and shall fear, and they shall hope in the Lord."* God's people now delivered from the pit of misery, or Christ himself, in the person of his people, so delivered, foretells that many will be likewise delivered. *"Many shall see"* the pit of misery, and those that have been saved from it, *"and will fear and will hope in the Lord;"* will fear the pit, and put their trust in the deliverer, for the first step to salvation is, when God, by his grace, begins to open the eyes of the sinner, to see his miserable state, and to feel through whom he can be delivered, and thence begins *"to fear and to hope in the Lord."*

4. He invites, exhorts, and encourages all to imitate those who have been delivered. *"Blessed is the man whose trust is in the name of the Lord."* Truly happy is he who has really placed all his hope in the Lord, who alone is all powerful and merciful; and, therefore, is both willing and able to deliver from every trouble, all those that put their trust in him. To make the matter clearer, he adds, *"and who hath not regard to vanities, and lying follies;"* who looked for help from no one, especially from vain, empty things, that can save no one; *"and lying follies."* Such fallacious helps as have just been alluded to, including astrology, incantations, witchcraft, etc., in which many believe and confide, but which may be justly designated as *"lying follies."*

5. He now proceeds to explain that most profound mystery of man's redemption, through which many have been, and many more will be, brought out of *"the pit of misery and the mire of dregs;"* and he first states, in general, that the works of God are wonderful. *"Thou hast multiplied thy wonderful works, O Lord my God, and in thy thoughts there is no one like to thee."* There is no one like thee in thy thoughts, or the forecasting of thy wisdom, not one to be compared to thee. *"I have declared, and I have spoken; they are multiplied above number."* A reason assigned, why no one can be compared to God in regard of his wonderful works and profound thoughts; and he says, *"I have declared, and I have spoken;"* I have made known some of his wonderful works, through the prophets, through the wise, through the very elements of the world; for, *"the heavens show forth the glory of God, and the firmament declareth the works of his hands." "They are multiplied above number;"* they are so numerous that they are past counting, and, therefore, cannot be properly announced or explained.

6. Truly *"wonderful are all God's works;"* in all of them *"the depth of his thoughts"* most splendidly appear, but far and away, and beyond, and above all, in his work of the redemption: what can be imagined more marvelous than for God to stoop to the form of a servant, to become a beggar and a pauper, to rescue man from the *"pit of misery,"* and raise him to the enjoyment of heaven? To have the same God, in the form of a servant, scourged with rods, and crucified between robbers, that he may place his servants in the choir of Angels? and to carry out all these things with the greatest wisdom, the greatest justice, without offering the slightest injury to the Divinity, nay, even thereby augmenting his glory?! Christ himself, using the pen and the language of David, explains this mystery in the following verses. *"Sacrifice and oblation thou didst not desire;"* you would not be appeased by the sacrifice of cattle, nor by the oblation of bread and incense, but by a victim of infinite price; you, therefore, wished me to assume a mortal body, that by my *"obedience even unto death,"* I may atone for the disobedience of the first man; and since you refused *"sacrifice"* of cattle and *"oblation"* for sin, *"then said I: Behold, I come,"* that I may be the priest and the sacrifice; and thus satisfy for the human race, and *"bring them out of the pit of misery and the mire of dregs."* Observe here, that by *"sacrifice and oblations"* we are rather to understand the victim or matter offered, than the rite or ceremony. Observe also, that though the prophet says, *"sacrifice and oblations thou didst not desire,"* we are not thence to infer the sacrifices of the old law were of no value; what he conveys is, that they were of no value in regard of making satisfaction for sin, as the Apostle says to the Hebrews, *"For it is impossible that with the blood of oxen and goats, sins should be taken away." "But thou hast pierced ears for me."* There are a variety of versions of this

sentence, some conveying the idea of Christ having his ears ready for his father's command to save man; the present reading conveying the idea, that he was in the hands of his father, like a slave who had his ears pierced, ready, at a moment's notice, to do his master's bidding.

7-8. He said, *"Behold, I come;"* he now tells us why, *"that I should do thy will;"* and the will of God was, that he should sanctify us by the oblation of his body, by his passion and death; so the Apostle explains this passage in Hebrews 10, where he quotes it, and adds, *"by the which will we are sanctified by the oblation of the body of Jesus Christ once." "In the head of the book it is written of me."* What book? Some will have it, Genesis; some, the First Psalm; some, the Prophets; others, the Gospel of St. John; others, the Book of Life; all defensible; but I look upon the most simple and most literal interpretation to be, the summary, or the whole of the Holy Scriptures. The Hebrew favors this interpretation; instead of *"the head of the book,"* it is in the Hebrew, *"in the volume of the book,"* that is to say, in the whole volume, because the whole Scripture has reference to Christ. Hence, the Lord himself says, *"what is written in the law of Moses, and the Prophets and the Psalms must be fulfilled;"* and in the same gospel we read, *"He interpreted to the two disciples; all that was written of him in the Scriptures, beginning with Moses and all the Prophets."* And our Lord, speaking of the Scriptures in general, said, *"Search the Scriptures, for they bear testimony of me;" "In the head of the book,"* then, does not mean the first chapter or title page of the book; but the substance and the true meaning is, All the Scriptures testify that I came into the world *"that I should do thy will,"* by obedience to you in the most trifling matters. Turning, then, to the Father, he adds, *"O my God, I have desired it,"* I have most cheerfully accepted your decree; *"and thy law in the midst of my heart;"* I have put thy law in the midst of my heart; there is nothing I have been more desirous, more anxious for, than to obey your law. Speaking of the just, David says, *"God's law is in his heart;"* but; speaking of Christ, the head of the just, he says, *"his law is in the midst of his heart,"* and those who belong to Christ should have his Spirit, so that they may prefer his law to everything, so as to have it constantly before their memory, their will, and their understanding.

9. Though God's principal object in the death of Christ was, that he should atone for mankind, he willed also that Christ should previously announce the Gospel; that his preaching may be the path to his passion; and that he may be not only a Redeemer, but also a teacher and a preacher to man; and he, therefore, says now, *"I have declared thy justice;"* I have announced thy most just law, and the works it requires, and that publicly, before countless crowds of people, of which yourself are witness. And, in fact, Christ never ceased preaching. From his infancy he preached, by example, contempt

of the things of this world, modesty, temperance, humility. From his baptism, from the time that the Father said, *"Hear ye him,"* he began to preach, and never ceased to the day of his death, which he continued through his Apostles, and will continue, through their successors, to the end of the world.

10. Many preach while they expect any benefit thereby, or fear no injury in consequence; but when they cease to hope, or fear presses, they keep their preaching to themselves, and will not let it out. Not so with Christ; and, by his example, he tells us what to do thereon, and he, therefore says, *"I have declared thy justice,"* and *"have not hidden it in my heart,"* through negligence, fear, or any unworthy motive. His remarks on the justice that God requires from us, that is, that he announced it, and did not *"hide it,"* are now applied, in like manner, to God's justice and mercy, for he calls justice truth; that is, the fidelity with which he gives to every one according to his works; and he calls mercy salvation, which he mercifully holds out to those who hope in him. He says, then, *"I have declared thy truth and thy salvation;"* that is to say, I have announced *"the truth"* that is in you, declaring to all how faithfully and how inexplicably you reward the good, and terribly punish the wicked; and I have, at the same time, announced *"thy salvation;"* that is, with what mercy you save all those that trust in thee. *"I have not concealed thy mercy and thy truth from a great council."* What he called *"salvation,"* in the preceding sentence, he now expressly calls *"mercy,"* and connects it with truth, meaning justice. *"I have not concealed,"* through any fear whatever, *"from a great council,"* from any number however great, *"thy mercy and thy truth,"* but have publicly and boldly announced them. A fact easily proved from the Gospels.

11. He (Christ) passes now from his preaching to his passion; and, as well as he made known the justice and the mercy of the Father to mankind, he now prays to the Father not to defer the same mercy and justice towards himself, but by a speedy resurrection to deliver him from his death and passion. *"Withhold not thou, O Lord, thy tender mercies from me."* Father, you see how bitter are my sufferings for having made known your justice and mercy to man; do you, therefore, *"withhold not your mercies from me,"* by immediately raising me up, as hitherto *"thy mercy and thy truth have always upheld me."*

12. A reason for having said, *"withhold not, O Lord, thy tender mercies from me,"* because *"evils without number have surrounded me."* Christ's sufferings were truly without number, and seemed to crowd in upon him designedly. And they were thus innumerable, because our sins, for which he undertook to make satisfaction, were so. *"My iniquities,"* the iniquities of mankind, *"which the Father placed upon him,"* Isaias 53, and which he, therefore, looked upon as mine, *"that I may bear them in my body upon the tree;"* all those evils *"have overtaken me, and I was not able to see."* They were so numerous that they blinded me up. For *"they are multiplied above the hairs of my head;"* exceed my hairs in number; and thus, overwhelmed by their number, I fainted, *"and my heart hath forsaken me;"* my strength, my very life, forsook me. This expression of Christ's, *"I was unable to see,"* is not to be taken literally, as if the Lord could not see the number of the sins, by reason of their being so extremely numerous; for he certainly had a most accurate knowledge of all the sins, past, present, and future; but he uses the expressions in ordinary use, to signify how numerous were the sins he undertook to satisfy for. We have a similar expression in St. Mark 6, *"And he could not do any mighty work there, and he wondered because of their unbelief."* He could have done any works he pleased there, but he is said not to have been able to do them, to give us an idea of the incredulity of the people that prevented him from doing them.

13. He now returns to the prayer he commenced in verse 11, and prays to be delivered, by a speedy resurrection, from such evils. *"Be pleased, O Lord,"* Father, whom I must, by reason of the form of a servant I have assumed, call Lord, be pleased *"to deliver me"* from the many troubles that have surrounded me. *"look down, O Lord, to help me;"* you seem as if you had for some time abandoned me, *"and turned your face away from me,"* leaving me to go through the sufferings of the cross without the slightest consolation; but now *"look down to help me,"* that you may at once replenish me in the joy of a glorious resurrection.

14. Christ's enemies, who thought him entirely destroyed, were terribly confused at his resurrection. That he now prophesies in the form of an imprecation, a thing usual with the prophets. *"Let them be confounded and ashamed together."* Let them be overwhelmed with confusion *"that seek after my soul to take it away;"* who seek to take away my life by putting me to death, and totally extinguishing me. Such was the intention of the Jews, a thing they thought they had accomplished when they nailed him to the cross. But immediately after, when they heard of his resurrection, saw it confirmed by signs and wonders, and believed by the mass of the people, *"they were confounded and ashamed;"* and will be infinitely more so on the last day, then they shall see him whom they impiously presumed to judge, and against whom they suborned false witnesses, judging the whole world with the greatest justice. *"Let them be turned backward and be ashamed that desire evils to me."* A repetition of the preceding sentence, as if to strengthen it. *"Let them be turned back,"* retire in confusion, *"and be ashamed,"* blush with shame, "that desire evils to me; not only those who seek to kill me, but all who seek for my disgrace or confusion.

15. He repeats the same thing a third time, saying, *"Let them immediately bear their confusion that say to me: It is well, it is well."* Let not their confusion be deferred, but after three short days let them be confounded, as they were, *"who say to me, It is well, it is well;"* that is, those who gloried in having triumphed over me, and congratulated each other thereon.

16. As he prophesied confusion to his persecutors in the form of an imprecation, so he now predicts joy to his subjects in the same form. *"Let all that seek thee rejoice and be glad in thee."* All those who seek the glory of God, who love him and put their trust in him, *"will rejoice and be glad"* in God; that is, with divine and unspeakable joy, *"and say always, the Lord be magnified."* Let them not attribute any good they may have to themselves, but say, May *"the Lord be magnified"* by all *"who love thy salvation;"* who love the Savior you sent them, Christ Jesus; or who love and desire the true and everlasting salvation that you alone can confer.

17. He now returns to the state he was in at the time of his passion, (Christ,) and says, *"but I am a beggar and poor;"* needy and destitute of all human help. In the Hebrew, the first conveys the idea of poverty; the second of affliction; quite applicable to Christ, especially when he hung naked on the cross; but, however poor and afflicted he may have appeared to man, he was rich in the protection of his Father; and, therefore, he adds, *"the Lord is careful for me."* The Lord is concerned for me. He calls his Father *"the Lord,"* because he speaks in the person of a servant; that is, as the Son of Man, in which nature he hung upon the cross. *"Thou art my helper and my protector: O my God, be not slack."* What he had briefly expressed when he said, *"the Lord is careful for me,"* he now explains at greater length, saying, *"Thou art my helper and my protector."* For God the Father was *"careful"* for his Son, by helping and protecting him, helping him in overcoming past dangers, protecting him by removing future ones. *"O my God, be not slack;"* namely, to deliver me from all trouble by a speedy resurrection.

PSALM 40

The happiness of him that shall believe in Christ, notwithstanding the humility and poverty in which he shall come: the malice of his enemies, especially of the traitor Judas.

1 Blessed is he that understandeth concerning the needy and the poor: the Lord will deliver him in the evil day.

2 The Lord preserve him and give him life, and make him blessed upon the earth: and deliver him not up to the will of his enemies.

3 The Lord help him on his bed of sorrow: thou hast turned all his couch in his sickness.

4 I said: O Lord, be thou merciful to me: heal my soul, for I have sinned against

thee.

5 *My enemies have spoken evils against me: when shall he die and his name perish?*

6 *And if he came in to see me, he spoke vain things: his heart gathered together iniquity to itself. He went out and spoke to the same purpose.*

7 *All my enemies whispered together against me: they devised evils to me.*

8 *They determined against me an unjust word: shall he that sleepeth rise again no more?*

9 *For even the man of peace, in whom I trusted, who ate my bread, hath greatly supplanted me.*

10 *But thou, O Lord, have mercy on me, and raise me up again: and I will requite them.*

11 *By this I know, that thou hast had a good will for me: because my enemy shall not rejoice over me.*

12 *But thou hast upheld me by reason of my innocence: and hast established me in thy sight for ever.*

13 *Blessed bey the Lord the God of Israel from eternity to eternity. So be it. So be it.*

Explanation of the psalm

1. That is to say, Blessed is he who reflects with care on Christ in his poverty, he will find him to have been poor from choice, not from necessity, and chose it to enrich us through the same poverty. He will find him also, while poor to all appearance, internally rich; for in him *"are hidden all the treasures of wisdom and knowledge"* of God, Coloss. 2. He will also find him to have been poor in the flesh, while rich in his kingdom; for, while he was the *"heir of the universe,"* King of kings, and Lord of Lords, he was so poor as sometimes not to have *"a place whereon to lay his head."* Furthermore, *"blessed is he that understandeth"* Christ, the poor man, naked, hanging on his cross; that is, blessed is he who deeply meditates on his passion; for Jeremias had already said, *"Attend and see if there be sorrow like my sorrow;"* and the Apostle repeats the same, Heb. 12, *"For think diligently upon him who endureth such opposition from sinners against himself."* For they who understand, and seriously meditate on the passion of Christ, have an unspeakable treasure prepared for them. Finally, *"Blessed is he that understandeth concerning the needy and the poor;"* that is, Christ in his members, of whom he says, *"Amen I say to you, as long as you did it to one of these, my least brethren, you did it to me."* Observe, however, the Psalm does not say, Blessed is he that gives alms to the poor; but, *"blessed is he that understandeth concerning the needy and the poor;"* that is to give us to understand that he only is *"blessed"* who prudently considers the necessities of the poor, and gives to the proper person at the proper time, and the proper amount of relief; and that not from vain glory, or in the hope of any temporal reward, but from the pure love of God. *"The Lord will deliver him in the evil day."* The reason why *"he that understandeth concerning the needy and the poor is blessed,"* is because he will be saved from poverty himself; for *"the evil day"* signifies the day of want and need. By the *"evil day,"* however, in this passage, is meant the day of judgment, which will be a day of justice alone, and on which there will be extreme want of mercy and grace. On that day the lovers of the cross of Christ, and who, for his sake, had been generous to the poor, will be quite secure; for to them will be said, *"Come, ye blessed of my Father, possess the kingdom prepared for you from the foundation of the world. For I was hungry, and you gave me to eat: I was thirsty, and you gave me to drink: I was a stranger, and you took me in; naked, and you clothed me; sick, and you visited me: I was in prison, and you came to me."* Not only that, but even in this world will God deliver the merciful in *"the evil day,"* as we saw in Psalm 36, *"they shall not be confounded in the evil time, and in the days of famine they shall be filled."* God is delighted beyond measure when he sees his children, in imitation of their Father, freely sharing with others what they have freely received; and, therefore, returns with interest what is given to the poor, according to Prov. 19, *"he that hath mercy on the poor, lendeth to the Lord."*

2. He now explains the expression, *"the Lord will deliver him in the evil day;"* and, in the form of a prayer, predicts the blessings that will follow him *"that understandeth concerning the needy and the poor."* The Lord *"will preserve him,"* watch him while he lives, *"and give him life;"* on his death will bring him to life again, by causing him to rise with the just; *"and make him blessed upon the earth,"* make him truly, perfectly, and completely happy in the land of the living, *"and deliver him not up to the will of his enemies;"* will neither in this world, nor in the next, subject him to the will or power of his enemies, be they men or demons.

3. As he promised so many blessings to the merciful, to those who *"understand concerning the needy and the poor,"* from which one may suppose that pious souls of that sort would have no troubles to encounter in this world, he now prepares them for many tribulations and temptations in this their exile, but not without an assurance of divine help and consolation. *"The Lord help him on his bed of sorrow."* Should such a holy soul be struck down by any corporal or spiritual disease, *"the Lord will help him;"* will so console him to bear it with patience, and to feel it as a probation, from which probation such hope will arise, that he will be highly rejoiced, so as to glory in his troubles, saying, with the Apostle, *"I am filled with comfort, I exceedingly abound with joy in all our tribulation."* To prove that this would happen, he then brings an example from the past, saying, *"thou hast turned all his couch*

in his sickness." Such, my sweet and merciful God, has been your treatment of all your faithful; for when you saw any poor soul weighed down by temptations or afflictions, you tended and consoled him with all the care that a nurse turns and makes up the bed of a patient, seeking thereby to refresh and to relieve him.

4. Christ now begins to declare himself the *"needy and the poor man." "I said: O Lord, be thou merciful to me;"* have mercy on my mystic body, my weak members; *"heal my soul, for I have sinned against thee;"* I implore thy mercy, to heal the wounds of my faithful, whose sins I charge myself with, as if I had actually committed them. Another explanation of this verse may be to make Christ speak of his passion; thus, *"be thou merciful to me"* in my trouble, and quickly raise me, and thus free me from suffering; *"heal my soul"* which is *"sorrowful even unto death,"* and thus is sad, dejected languishing, fearing, grieving; *"for l have sinned against thee,"* for I have taken the sins of the whole world upon myself. That Christ does not speak of sins committed by himself is quite clear from verse 12, where he says, *"But thou hast upheld me by reason of my innocence;"* and, therefore, the person speaking here is not David, nor any one else, but he who alone was innocent, as far as his own acts were in question, while he bore the sins of others.

5. Evidently intended for the Pharisees and priests of the Jews, who thirsted intensely for the death of Christ, and had frequent conferences on the subject of it.

6. From the Jews he passes to Judas, *"and if he came in to see me,"* to see if the time had come for betraying me, *"he spoke vain things;"* invented some falsehood, for fear his purpose may be detected. This may refer also to others who came to Christ, *"tempting him, to ensnare him in his speech."* That person, however, *"spoke vain things"* to Christ, while, in the meantime, *"his heart gathered together iniquity to itself;"* that means, his heart was full of deceit, and he, therefore, multiplied and *"gathered together iniquity"* to himself, to his everlasting ruin. Such is the just reward of the liars and the deceivers. While they seek to deceive others, they are themselves deceived by Satan; and while they are plotting the destruction of others, are, in reality, planning their own ruin. *"He went out and spoke to the same purpose."* Judas, having assumed to be the friend of Christ, went out to his enemies, and assumed to be their friend.

7. Having got the proposal of the traitor Judas, his enemies began to whisper in conference with each other, fearing, if they spoke out, they may be heard, and they discussed the amount of the reward for betraying the Savior. *"They devised evils to me;"* took measures for my capture and subsequent death.

8. The consequence of the whispering among the Jews was, a fixed resolution to put Christ to death, because, *"they determined against me an unjust*

word." They passed a most unjust sentence and decree, that they would put me, no matter how innocent, to death. But he says immediately, *"shall he that sleepeth rise again no more?"* Which means, however unjust their decree may be, can they deprive me of the power of rising again? He calls his death sleep, because he can as easily rise from the dead as one can rouse his neighbor from sleep; a thing he foretold long before when he said, John 10, *"No man taketh my life away from me; but I lay it down of myself, and I have power to lay it down; and I have power to take it up again."*

9. He assigns now a reason for his enemies having *"determined an unjust word against him,"* and puts the blame on Judas. *"For even the man of my peace,"* with whom I was on the terms a master would be with his servant, or a teacher with his disciple, that man, *"in whom I trusted,"* in whom I could confide as a friend and an associate. *"Who ate my bread;"* who sat at my table as a child or a domestic; *"hath greatly supplanted me;"* in so insidiously betraying me to my enemies. Our Lord quotes this passage in John 13, *"I speak not of you all. I know whom I have chosen; but that the Scripture may be fulfilled: He that eateth bread with me, shall lift up his heel against me."* Observe here, with St. Augustine, that Judas is called *"the man of peace,"* because the prophet foresaw that Christ would be betrayed by a kiss, the sign of peace; which even our Savior alludes to, when he said, *"Friend, to what art thou come?"* and, *"Judas, dost thou betray the son of man with a kiss?"* In like manner the prophet says, *"who ate my bread;"* who sat at my table. We may also notice the expression, *"in whom I trusted;"* alluding to Christ's confidence in Judas, so that he made him his treasurer. Observe again, the prophet's sense of the aggravations; for he calls Judas *"the man of my peace;"* to show there was no quarrel, no cause of anger or enmity, between Christ and Judas; quite the reverse, for he adds, *"in whom I trusted,"* and made him treasurer of all I possessed in consequence.

Finally, he adds, that Judas was not only not his enemy, but was his friend; nay, more than his friend, on most intimate terms with him, loaded with favors by him. For, on the very night that he betrayed Christ, he not only partook of his ordinary meal with him, but even received the bread of Angels from him; had his feet washed by him; and, thus, had got the most convincing proofs of his extreme humility and love for him.

10. He now prays to his Father, and in the form of a prayer prophesies what was to happen; and, in fact, after his resurrection, he punished the Jews as they deserved. *"But thou, O Lord, have mercy on me, and raise me up again, and I will requite them,"* that means, they surely did *"determine against me an unjust word"* and by the treachery of my own disciple, *"who supplanted me,"* they will have my life; *"but thou, O Lord, have mercy on me,"* while dying on the cross, and immediately after *"raise me up again,"* and then, *"I will requite*

them," punish them as they deserve. And so he did punish them, and well. They have been dispersed and scattered all over the world, without a king, without a priest, without God, as Christ himself predicted, *"the kingdom of God shall be taken from you, and shall be given to a nation bringing forth the fruits thereof;"* again, *"your house shall be left to you desolate;"* and in another place, *"and they shall not leave in thee a stone upon a stone."*

11. He states his prayer was heard, and could be known to have been heard, because *"his enemy shall not rejoice over him."* Literally fulfilled in Judas, who hung himself before the death of Christ, and before he could make any use of his ill got bribe. This may also be applied to all his enemies, whose triumph was so short that it could hardly be called a triumph.

12. He informs his enemies that their joy on his death will be very brief, because he has been *"upheld and exalted by God by reason of his innocence."*

13. The conclusion, which may be either that of Christ or the prophet, conveys no more than all honor and glory being due to Christ by reason of his exaltation and the confusion of his enemies forever and ever. So be it, so be it, are merely expressions in confirmation and acclamation.

PSALM 41

The fervent desire of the just after God: hope in afflictions.

1 As the hart panteth after the fountains of water; so my soul panteth after thee, O God.

2 My soul hath thirsted after the strong living God; when shall I come and appear before the face of God?

3 My tears have been my bread day and night, whilst it is said to me daily: Where is thy God?

4 These things I remembered, and poured out my soul in me: for I shall go over into the place of the wonderful tabernacle, even to the house of God: With the voice of joy and praise; the noise of one feasting.

5 Why art thou sad, O my soul? and why dost thou trouble me? Hope in God, for I will still give praise to him: the salvation of my countenance,

6 And my God. My soul is troubled within myself: therefore will I remember thee from the land of Jordan and Hermoniim, from the little hill.

7 Deep calleth on deep, at the noise of thy flood-gates. All thy heights and thy billows have passed over me.

8 In the daytime the Lord hath commanded his mercy; and a canticle to him in the night. With me is prayer to the God of my life.

9 I will say to God: Thou art my support. Why hast thou forgotten me? and why go I mourning, whilst my enemy afflicteth me?

10 Whilst my bones are broken, my enemies who trouble me have reproached me; Whilst they say to me day be day: Where is thy God?

11 Why art thou cast down, O my soul? and why dost thou disquiet me? Hope thou in God, for I will still give praise to him: the salvation of my countenance, and my God.

Explanation of the psalm

1. Love is a fiery affection, and, therefore, cannot be restrained, but breaks forth in words and sighs. To express his love somehow, David compares himself to a thirsty stag, saying, *"As the hart panteth after the fountains of waters;"* a most happy and expressive simile. The stag is noted for four peculiarities. It is a deadly enemy to serpents, and constantly at war with them. When it is pursued by the hunters, it betakes itself to the highest mountains as quickly as possible. By some natural instinct, they singularly carry out the advice of the Apostle, *"Bear ye each other's burdens;"* for, according to St. Augustine, when they move in a body, or swim across a lake, the weaker ones rest their heads on the stronger, and are thus helped along. Finally, when they are tired after a combat with serpents, or a flight to the mountain, or from helping each other along, they seek to refresh themselves by copious droughts of water, from which they cannot be tempted or deterred. Such is a most perfect idea of the true lover of God. He has to wage a continued war against the serpents of his evil desires. When he is nigh overcome by temptation, or by persecutions, he flies away to the mount of contemplation, bears his neighbor's infirmities with the greatest patience, and, above all, thirsts ardently for God, from whom he will not be held back by any earthly happiness or trouble. Such was David, though a soldier; so was Paul, Peter, and the other Apostles and martyrs; such were all who felt they were, while here below, in exile, and, through good and evil days, never lost sight of that country, the supreme object of their wishes.

2. He explains the meaning of *"panting after God,"* and why he should be so sought after. St. Chrysostom observes, that three things usually excite our love, and through it our thirst and desires; and these are the beauty of the object, favors conferred on us, and love itself, for beautiful objects almost compel one to love them; favors conferred, lead us to love the giver; and love on their part provokes mutual love. Should these three things be united in one person, that is, could there be found or imagined any one of surpassing beauty, conferring boundless favors daily on another, for whom they feel the most intense and ardent love, how could the latter possibly stand by not ardently loving the former in return? David shows here that these three things are united in God, in regard of himself; and, therefore, states that *"he thirsts after him;"* that is, he is inflamed by love and desire towards him. *"My soul hath thirsted after the strong living God,"* as the most beautiful, most noble, most excellent of all things; comprising all good, *"strong,"* not transitory or perishable, but permanent, everlasting. *"Living,"* active, intelligent, loving, pouring down continual favors on us, having great regard for us, boundless love for us. Such thirst after what is so good, so kind, so loving of me, forces me, from my whole heart, to exclaim, *"When shall I come and appear before the face of the Lord?"* When will there be an end to my pilgrimage, when the commencement of any joys?

3. He that will reflect attentively on the three points already alluded to, namely, the incomprehensible beauty of God, the multitude of his favors, and the extent of his love that caused him to deliver up his only begotten Son for us, cannot but burst into tears in his desire for getting the full possession of so great a good. David seriously reflected on these points, and, he, therefore, adds, *"My tears have been my bread day and night."* My tears were my only food, I lived on them day and night; that is, during the whole term of my pilgrimage, whether in the days of prosperity, or the nights of adversity, my soul not only refused to be gladdened by any earthly consolation, or to be saddened by any temporal mishap; but, at all times, my tears have been my meat and my drink. *"Whilst it is said to me daily,"* by the wicked and the incredulous, *"Where is thy God?"* that means, while I wander about daily, *"seeking whom my soul loveth,"* my thoughts and my spirit said to me, *"Where is thy God?"* all those things you have seen in your search for him are beautiful, to be sure, but not like thy God. Where, then, is your God? Where will you look for him? When will you come and see the face of your God?

4. He goes on with the expression of his desires, *"he poured out his soul,"* which may be interpreted in three ways.

First, when about to enter the wonderful tabernacle, the very house of God. I cleared, banished all earthly delights out of my soul, that I may fill it with the delights of my Lord. Second, I extended, expanded my soul to be able to contain the immense good to be had in that wonderful tabernacle; where there is the *"never failing plenty of the house of the Lord."* Third, *"I poured out my soul:"* rose above it in contemplation, as it is expressed in Lam. 3, *"He shall sit solitary, and hold his peace; because he hath taken it upon himself."* And, in fact, in this our exile there is no more ready way of getting up to the *"wonderful tabernacle,"* and the actual house of God, than through our own soul, which is the image of God. It is more sublime than the heavens, and deeper than the abyss; and he who can steady his own soul and rise above it, will rise to him whose image it is, and he *"will go over to the place of the wonderful tabernacle and the house of God."* To touch briefly on this ascent, let us consider: the soul is a spirit, and, therefore, far exceeds all things corporeal; and thus, God being a spirit, and the Creator, not only of bodies but of spirits, therefore, far exceeds not only bodies, but even spirits. Again, the soul, however simple and indivisible, is yet entire in the body and in all its parts; filling all the members, yet occupying none exclusively; thus, God, while he is one, and indivisible, still fills the whole world and all created things, everywhere entire, present everywhere, confined nowhere. Thirdly, the soul does not move about in the body, still carries it, guides it, governs it, quickens and enlivens it, as we see from the death of any one; for, the moment the soul departs, the body falls down at once, and in one moment loses all power of motion, sense, beauty, everything. Now, what the soul is to the body, God is to the universe; not that God is the soul of the universe, as some philosophers vainly imagined; but, because he seems to have a certain resemblance to the soul in these respects; for, while he remains fixed and unmoved in himself, *"upholding all things by the word of his power,"* and, *"in him we live, move, and have our being."* Fourthly, the soul is intelligent, and our intellect has cognizance of all the senses, and knows many things beside, which no corporal sense can comprehend. So God is all intellect preeminently, replete with the knowledge of all men and Angels, and of infinitely more matters, far beyond our understanding. Fifthly, the soul knows many things not only in theory but even practically; hence, the endless productions of human ingenuity, in the various arts, trades, and manufactures; so exquisitely wrought as nearly to vie with nature; so also with the understanding of God, both in theory and practice, who without tools, without trouble, in a moment, by his sole word, from nothing made the universe. Sixthly, the soul is endowed with free will, and, therefore, moves the members of the body at its pleasure. Thus God, at his pleasure, governs all created things; and, therefore, David, in Psalm 118 says, *"for all things serve thee."* And, not only is the soul, in its essence, the image of God, but in a remote sense it is the image of the Trinity; for there is in the soul intelligence representing the Father; knowledge derived therefrom, representing the Word of the Father; and love, springing from such intelligence, and knowledge, representing the Holy Ghost. There is also in the soul memory, intellect, and will, which, to some extent, represent the three divine Persons. *"The soul then is poured in itself,"* and rises over itself in contemplation, that it may be enabled to pass over to the *"wonderful tabernacle;"* and, therefore, the prophet adds, *"for I shall go over to the place of the wonderful tabernacle, even to the house of God."* By the place of the wonderful tabernacle is meant, the heavenly Jerusalem, the tabernacle in heaven not made by human hands, where the house of God is, of which he said in Psalm 26. *"One thing I have asked of the Lord, this will I seek after; that I may dwell in the house of the Lord, all the days of my life."*—*"With the voice of joy and praise, the noise of one feasting."* He tells us now, that in that ecstasy in which *"he poured out his soul,"* and in contemplation arrived at the site of *"the wonderful tabernacle, even to the house of God,"* that he did not do so in silence, but in loud acclamations, in admiration, and praise, in such joy and jubilee, as those enjoying a banquet cheerful and glad, such as is meet for the soul wrapt up in contemplation of the joys of the heavenly Jerusalem.

5. With such spirits and mental consolation he seeks to dry up his tears, saying, *"Why art thou sad, O my soul?"* Why should tears be your bread day and night? Why will you by such incessant tears so *"trouble me?"* *"Hope in God,"* though you don't see him, you so ardently long for, yet hope in him, *"for I will still give praise to him;"* that means, though the time has not yet come, it will come when before his face I will praise God, and declare his mercies, and say to him, *"the salvation of my countenance;"* that is, you are my salvation, for you brighten up my countenance by your light, and my face to behold yours, *"and I will know as I am known;"* and from a clear knowledge I will say, *"thou art my God."*

6. He now tells the alternations of sadness and consolation that were wont to seize him; sadness, in fear of the dangers of this life; consolation, from the hope and promise of the future. *"My soul is troubled within myself."* Though I told my soul *"to hope in God,"* yet, when I looked in upon my weakness, and the little light and strength I possess, I was seized with great fear, and *"my soul was troubled;"* to cure which fear and terror I said, *"I will remember thee from the land of Jordan and Hermoniim, from the little hill."* I will take my eyes off myself, and fix them on you, instead of fixing my eyes on the Jordan before me; I will think of the river *"that gladdens your city, and the torrent of thy pleasure,"* enjoyed by those who are there with you; and from this little hill Hermoniim, before me, I will remember your holy mountain, in which you dwell with your holy Angels; and with such recollections I will console my soul and my desires. Whether Hermoniim be a different mountain from Mount Hermon is not very clear; most probably it is, for Hermoniim is here spoken of as a small, whereas Hermon was a very large mountain.

7. He goes on with an account of the dangers and temptations of this life, comparing them to an inundation, alluding to that of Noe. *"Deep calleth on deep."* An immense mass of water came rolling over me, and the moment it passed, another came in succession, as if called by the first. And those vast inundations poured in *"at the noise of thy flood gates;"* with such a noise and such a clamor, as if the flood gates of heaven were opened. *"All thy heights,"* all the lofty breakers, *"and thy billows have passed over me;"* the whole inundation, the universal deluge, passed over me. He alludes, as we said before, to the general deluge, when *"the cataracts of heaven were opened;"* that is, the quantity of rain that fell was such that would lead one to think some cataracts in heaven were opened, and that all the water burst forth with an unheard of force and violence, from which foundation arose the great abyss,

an immense depth and quantity of water. This metaphor is used here to give an idea of the great dangers and temptations to which God will sometimes expose his elect. Men such as David, truly spiritual, alone are aware of the extent and magnitude of these temptations; for it is such people only know the boundless machinations of the enemy, and how grievous a matter it is to fall away from the grace of God.

8. After having described the extraordinary amount of temptation endured by him, he now tells us how he was in turn relieved by the consolations he got. *"In the day time the Lord hath commanded his mercy,"* which means, after those inundations of waters, and those dreadful abysses had cleared away; *"in the day time"* of prosperity, *"the Lord hath commanded his mercy"* to visit and console me; *"and a canticle to him in the night,"* in the night of tribulation and temptation; even *"his canticle"* will not cease, for I will, even in the night, sing his praises, thank and glorify him. *"With me is prayer to the God of my life."* My song at night shall be in the secret of my heart, speaking with it rather than with my lips, looking upon him as the source of my salvation and my life, I will say to him,

9. He now admires the vicissitudes of the divine providence in governing us. If, O God, thou art really *"my support, why hast thou forgotten me?"* How does it come to pass that I should be overwhelmed by so many temptations and tribulations, that so pour down upon me, that, though you are my hope and my strength, you seem to have forsaken me? How does it happen again, that *"I go mourning whilst my enemy afflicteth me?"* while you are my helper and my protector.

10-11. Not only has my enemy *"afflicted me"* before your face, you who are *"my support,"* but even *"whilst my bones are broken,"* come to such a pitch of debility and infirmity, that I can scarce resist temptation. *"My enemies who trouble me have reproached me,"* asking me incessantly, *"Where is thy God?"* The very enemies who persecute and harass me, reproach me with the confidence I have in you, as if the confidence were of no avail, for they constantly ask, *"Where is thy God?"* who you boasted was *"your helper and protector."* So Tobias was reproached, *"where is thy hope for which thou gavest alms and buried the dead?"* and again, *"It is evident thy hope is come to nothing, and thy alms now appear."* So the Jews upbraided Christ on the cross, *"He trusted in God; let him deliver him now if he will."* Thus also, his incredulous enemies insulted David in his troubles, but though he was for the moment *"saddened and disquieted,"* he only reproved himself, saying, *"Why art thou cast down, O my soul? and why dost thou disquiet me? Hope thou in God, for I will still give praise to him;"* words we have already explained in verses 5 and 6 of this Psalm.

PSALM 42

The prophet aspireth after the temple and altar of God.

1 Judge me, O God, and distinguish my cause from the nation that is not holy: deliver me from the unjust and deceitful man.

2 For thou art God my strength: why hast thou cast me off? and why do I go sorrowful whilst the enemy afflicteth me?

3 Send forth thy light and thy truth: they have conducted me, and brought me unto thy holy hill, and into thy tabernacles.

4 And I will go in to the altar of God: to God who giveth joy to my youth.

5 To thee, O God my God, I will give praise upon the harp: why art thou sad, O my soul? and why dost thou disquiet me?

6 Hope in God, for I will still give praise to him: the salvation of my countenance, and my God.

Explanation of the Psalm

1. David, severely pressed by Saul, or tempted by demons, and having no human succor to fall back upon, appeals to God as a judge: *"Judge me, O God,"* for I have no one else to seek justice of but of you; *"and distinguish my cause from the nation that is not holy;"* and take cognizance of the charge brought against me by an unholy people. The Hebrew and the Greek imply, that he asks God not only to judge him, but to pronounce in his favor; and he further asks, *"Deliver me from the unjust and deceitful man;"* so judge my cause, that you will thereby deliver me from such men.

2. This verse is almost the same as the ninth verse of the last chapter. The meaning is, as you, *"O my God, art my strength,"* and in you alone I trust, why do you seem *"to have cast me off;"* and I, thus cast off, *"go sorrowful," "whilst the enemy afflicteth me?"* a friendly mode of expostulation, arising from his thorough confidence in God, in which he complains of God's allowing him to be so punished as if he had *"cast him off"* entirely.

3. This verse proves what a spiritual man was David, and that he was more concerned for his delivery from mortal sin and the loss of eternal life, than from any temporal troubles. For he says, *"Send forth thy light and thy truth;"* grant me the light of thy grace and thy mercy, thy truth, and thy faithfulness, *"for they will conduct me"* in my perilous pilgrimage, and *"bring me unto thy holy hill,"* the heavenly Jerusalem, *"and into thy tabernacles,"* into thine own house, where there are *"many mansions"* and many tabernacles for thy elect.

4. He tells us what he will do when he gets to the *"holy hill,"* just what all the others in possession of God's house are doing, offering God their sacrifice of praise, as David says in Psalm 83, *"Blessed are they that dwell in thy house, O Lord, they will praise thee forever and ever." "I will go in to the altar of God"* to offer up the sacrifice of praise; for the moment any one enters that house he becomes a priest, as we can infer from Apoc. 5, *"Thou has made us to our God a kingdom and priests."* And I will not only go to thy altar, but I will go in to *"God himself;"* I will appear before him as if I were brought into his most private apartment; *"to God who giveth joy to my youth,"* to the youth just acquired by me. For in heaven *"our youth, like that of the eagle, shall be renewed;"* and the Apostle says, Ephes. 4, *"Till we all meet unto a perfect man unto the measure of the age of the fullness of Christ."*

5-6. He tells more clearly what sacrifice he means to offer at the altar of God, when he shall have come into the tabernacle not made by hands, the eternal one in heaven. *"I will give praise to thee on the harp;"* I will praise thee by acknowledging thy mercies, thy justice, and all thy wonderful works, which praise shall not be confined to my lips, for my harp shall join them. The harp is figuratively introduced as an instrument in recording God's praises, as in Apoc. 5, *"Having each of them harps in their hands,"* and in chap. 14, *"And the voice I heard was that of harpers playing on their harps."* The remaining part of these has been explained in the latter end of the previous Psalm.

PSALM 43

The Church commemorates former favors, and present afflictions: under which she prays for succor.

1 We have heard, O God, with our ears: our fathers have declared to us, The work, thou hast wrought in their days, and in the days of old.
2 Thy hand destroyed the Gentiles, and thou plantedst them: thou didst afflict the people and cast them out.
3 For they got not the possession of the land by their own sword: neither did their own arm save them. But thy right hand and thy arm, and the light of thy countenance: because thou wast pleased with them.
4 Thou art thyself my king and my God, who commandest the saving of Jacob.
5 Through thee we will push down our enemies with the horn: and through thy name we will despise them that rise up against us.
6 For I will not trust in my bow: neither shall my sword save me.
7 But thou hast saved us from them that afflict us: and hast put them to shame that hate us.
8 In God shall we glory all the day long: and in thy name we will give praise for ever.
9 But now thou hast cast us off, and put us to shame: and thou, O God, wilt not go out with our armies.
10 Thou hast made us turn our back to our enemies: and they that hated us plundered for themselves.
11 Thou hast given us up like sheep to be eaten: thou hast scattered us among the nations.

12 Thou hast sold thy people for no price: and there was no reckoning in the exchange of them.
13 Thou hast made us a reproach to our neighbours, a scoff and derision to them that are round about us.
14 Thou hast made us a byword among the Gentiles: a shaking of the head among the people.
15 All the day long my shame is before me: and the confusion of my face hath covered me,
16 At the voice of him that reproacheth and detracteth me: at the face of the enemy and persecutor.
17 All these things have come upon us, yet we have not forgotten thee: and we have not done wickedly in they covenant.
18 And our heart hath not turned back: neither hast thou turned aside our steps from thy way.
19 For thou hast humbled us in the place of affliction: and the shadow of death hath covered us.
20 If we have forgotten the name of our God, and if we have spread forth our hands to a strange god:
21 Shall not God search out these things: for he knoweth the secrets of the heart. Because for thy sake we are killed all the day long: we are counted as sheep for the slaughter.
22 Arise, why sleepest thou, O Lord? arise, and cast us not off to the end.
23 Why turnest thou face away? and forgettest our want and our trouble?
24 For our soul is humbled down to the dust: our belly cleaveth to the earth.
25 Arise, O Lord, help us and redeem us for thy name's sake.

Explanation of the psalm

1. God's people under persecution, and groaning in affliction, brings to his recollection the wonderful things God was wont to do for the defense of his faithful, and wonders how he now seems to have deserted them, thereby hoping to move him to mercy. *"O God,"* says the prophet, speaking in the person of the Church, or the martyrs of both Testaments, *"we have heard with our ears,"* he might have said *"we have heard,"* simply, but he adds, *"with our ears,"* to express the greater certainty. St. John, in the beginning of his first epistle, uses the same language, *"What we have seen with our eyes, and our hands have handled,"* when he might have said, *"we have seen and handled;"* but such phrases, somehow, strengthen the assertions. They say, then, when they heard it, *"Our fathers have declared to us."* It was not by vague rumor, or from people we did not know, that we heard it, but from our fathers; men worthy of belief, who never could have deceived us, *"they declared to us."* What did they hear or learn from them? *"The work thou hast wrought in their days, and in the days of old."* Our fathers told us not only of the wonderful works you did in their own times, but in the times of their fathers before them.

2. Descending to particulars, he instances one of the wonderful works God did for his faithful in the days of their fathers, *"Thy hand destroyed the Gentiles;"* you scattered, and destroyed, and expelled from the land of promise the Chananeans and Jebuseans that dwelt therein, *"and thou planted them;"* you established our fathers in their place; *"Thou didst afflict the people and cast them out;"* you harassed them in various grievous battles, until you finally rooted and *"cast them out"* of the land of promise. From this passage we can infer that what he said in the first verse, *"Our fathers have declared to us the work thou hast wrought in their days,"* does not refer to one particular date or epoch, but to a succession of events. Because the things recorded here happened in the time of Moses and Josue, who could not possibly have stated these matters to the Machabees, nor to the Apostles, nor even to David himself, but that those facts were handed down from one generation to another. *"Thou planted them,"* a highly figurative expression, implying that the Hebrews were as firmly fixed and rooted in the land of promise as if they had grown there, and that it would be as difficult to expel them as it would be to tear up a tree from its roots. Trees, also, once planted, not only grow and get firmly fixed in the earth, but they also increase and multiply, as David himself, in a beautiful metaphor, expresses it in Psalm 79, *"Thou planted the roots thereof and it filled the land, the shadow of it covered the hills, and the branches thereof the cedars of God."*

3. He proves what he stated in the previous verse. *"For they got not the possession of the land by their own sword;"* that is to say, our fathers, it is true, in the days of Moses and Josue, fought with the Chananeans, but, had you not been their *"helper and protector,"* they would not only have failed in getting possession of the country, but they would not have been able to escape with their lives from the enemy, by reason of their being fewer in number, less skilled in war, and having fortified cities to oppose them. It was not, then, by their swords, or by their arms, that they got hold of the land of promise, *"but thy right hand, and thy arm, and the light of thy countenance,"* put them in possession, and preserved them in their battles with the Chananeans, from death or captivity; and all this, *"because thou wast pleased with them;"* all this was the consequence, not of their virtues or merits, but of your having freely chosen them to be your people. The truth of all this is evident from Josue 6, where we read that at the mere shout of the children of Israel, the walls of Jericho tumbled teetotally to the ground; and in chap. 10, where we read that while Josue was fighting, that God discharged a shower of hailstones

on the enemy; and the Scripture says, *"that many more were killed with the hailstones, than were slain by the swords of the children of Israel."*
4. God's people now expresses its admiration, saying, *"Thou art thyself my king and my God;"* you that assisted and protected our fathers by reason of being their king and their God, you are our God and our king too; the very same *"who commandest the saving of Jacob;"* you who were wont to save your people, called after Jacob. *"Who commandest;"* who savest your people, not by fighting for them, or helping them, as one king would another; but by a simple word, by a simple command.
5. He now shows that not only is God the same that he was in the days of their fathers, but that the people too are the same; and that they have the hope in God that their fathers had; and is, therefore, astonished how the same God can deal so differently with the same people; how he could bring them off conquerors on every occasion, and now permit them to be subdued and conquered. *"Through thee we will push down our enemies with the horn;"* we, too, if you help and protect us, will equally subdue our enemies; *"and through thy name we will despise them that rise up against us;"* once we invoke your name we will have no fear of the enemy, and will make little of any attempt of theirs upon us. *"We will push down our enemies with the horn,"* is a metaphor, taken from the bull, who uses his horns to strike down everything in his way; so we, relying on thy power, will break down every obstacle, and demolish all our enemies with the same ease and facility that the bull beats down everything before him.
6. He goes on with the resemblance between the past and present people of God. As they got not possession of the land by the sword, so I and my people *"will not trust in my bow;"* will not rely on our arms or our strength; *"neither shall my sword save me;"* I know and feel, that if we conquer, it will not be by our swords, but through your help.
7. He now explains the expression, *"my sword shall not save me,"* by saying, *"but thou hast saved us from those that afflict us;"* that is, I acknowledge my safety is not owing to my own strength, because, as often as I have been rescued from any danger, you *"have saved us from those that afflict us;"* and *"put to shame;"* so protecting us as to frustrate their designs, and cause them to retire in confusion *"that hate us;"* our enemies who sought to destroy us.
8. He infers from the foregoing, that God's people, whenever they shall be delivered from any tribulation, will thank God for it, and give him the whole glory thereof. *"In God shall we glory in him all the day long."* We won't glory in ourselves, but we will always glory in God who delivered us; *"and in thy name,"* and in the name of the Lord we will praise and glorify him forever.
9. The stricken people now begin to complain; they are astonished! *"But now!"* you, who so favored and cherished us, *"hast cast us off, and put us to*

shame." In the days of Antiochus, to be called a Jew was a disgrace; under the Roman emperors, the name of a Christian was stamped with infamy, and the faithful seemed to have been abandoned by God. *"And thou, O God, wilt not go out with our armies."* If we want to repel the incursions of our enemies, you, who always led us to the fight, will not now accompany us, to fight for your people.

10. The persecution continued. *"Thou hast made us turn our back to our enemies."* We that were in the van, have been thrown back into the rear; obliged to follow our enemies as so many captives. And our enemies *"that hated us,"* used their own discretion, and *"plundered for themselves,"* converted everything to their own use.

11. A beautiful description of the sufferings of the martyrs. You let us be slaughtered as if we were so many sheep, who are daily killed in great numbers, without being able to offer the slightest resistance. *"Thou hast scattered us amongst the nations,"* those who were not slaughtered, were dispersed all over the world; as has been the case with many of the saints.

12. He alludes to another description of punishment to which the martyrs were subjected, as if they were the vilest of slaves; they were employed in cutting marble, or attending cattle, or obliged to combat with wild beasts in the theatres, for the amusement of the people. *"Thou hast sold thy people for no price;"* you have handed them over to their enemies, and got nothing in return, *"and there was no reckoning in the exchange of them."* What you got in return for them was so small that it was not worth counting.

13. In addition to the corporal punishments, they were scoffed at and derided. God having suffered them to be visited by so many temporal calamities, all the neighbors around them began to scoff at and deride them.

14. When the gentiles wished to express anything very odious or baleful, they would compare it to us; and the people not only spoke in such terms of us, but they shook their heads at us, in hatred and derision.

15-16. He now describes the effect of his being so derided and jeered at; it quite confused and confounded him. During the whole of my persecution *"my shame was before me;"* it was always staring me in the face, and encompassing me all round like a veil and all this confusion was caused by *"the voice of him that reproacheth and detracteth me;"* by those who called me a fool for worshipping one that had been crucified; and an impious person for not worshipping the gods; falsely reproaching me with infanticide, incest, and similar crimes; and he explains who these were that so charged him when he adds, *"at the face of the enemy and the persecutor,"* all done by his enemies. Such confusion and shame, however, would not appear to apply to the holy martyrs, when it is written, *"he that shall be ashamed of me, the Son of man will be ashamed of him when he shall come in his majesty and that of* his Father," Luke 9; and again, *"He that shall acknowledge me before men, the Son of man will acknowledge him when he shall come with his holy Angels in the glory of his father."* The Lord does not prohibit shame and confusion when it does not prevent the acknowledgment of, or adherence to the truth. He censures those only who are so overcome by shame as not only not to acknowledge Christ, but even to deny him; and the following verse proves that it is not of such persons he speaks here.

17. Having related the favors of the Almighty to the fathers of old, and his desertion and abandonment of them in latter times, the prophet, speaking in their person, asserts that their sins cannot be alleged as a cause for treatment so different, and says, *"All these things have come upon us,"* we have suffered all these persecutions and troubles; and, however, *"we have not forgotten thee,"* we have not forsaken you to worship other gods. The term, *"forgetting God,"* is not infrequently applied to idolatry in the Scripture, as in Psalm 105, *"They changed their glory into the likeness of a calf that eateth grass. They forgot God who saved them, who had done great things in Egypt;"* and in Deuteronomy 32," They sacrificed to devils and not to God. Thou hast forsaken the God that begot thee, and hast forgotten, the Lord that created thee;" and in this very Psalm, *"if we have forgotten the name of our God, and if we have spread forth our hands to a strange god."* They then insist that they did not worship any other god; and, therefore, they say, *"We have not forgotten thee, and we have not done wickedly in thy Covenant;"* that is to say, we have not only not acknowledged other gods in forgetfulness of you, but we have not even *"done wickedly in thy covenant,"* the covenant you struck with us for our observance on Mount Sinai. And thus they protest that they neither deserted God, nor transgressed his law.

18. They repeat the same, in different terms, to establish their innocence more fully; for they say, when we did go with you we did so cordially, we neither turned back nor deserted you.

19. The latter part of this verse should be read first, thus, *"The shadow of death hath covered us, for thou hast humbled us in the place of affliction,"* which means that we have been immersed in the depth of miseries.

20-21. They now prove, by the testimony of God himself, that they did not forget him, as they already stated; for they say, *"If we have forgotten the name of our God, and if we have spread forth our hands to a strange god,"* that is, to pray to him, *"shall not God search out these things?"* Most certainly he will, and find out all, *"for he knoweth the secrets of the heart."* He will certainly find out that we did not forget his name, *"because for thy sake we are killed all the day long."* They conclude by asking God to put an end to the persecution, because they are daily put to death and tormented by reason of their adherence to him; *"We are counted as sheep for the slaughter,"* butchered every day like so many sheep, who are incapable of offering any resistance.

22. While your business is thus being done, and your servants are suffering so much in doing it, why are you silent, as if you were asleep, and were not cognizant of it? *"Arise from sleep;"* act as they do who rise from their sleep, and begin to see what they did not see before; *"arise"* to help us, *"and cast us not off"* from your favor *"to the end,"* to the consummation, until, through your assistance, there shall be an end to the persecution. St. Paul alludes to this passage in Rom. 8, where he says, *"Who then shall separate us from the love of Christ? shall tribulation? or distress? or famine? or nakedness? or danger? or persecutions? or the sword? As it is written: For thy sake we are put to death; we are accounted as sheep for the slaughter."*

23. He goes on with the same prayer, using two other metaphors. He drew one from sheep in the preceding verse, and now he takes one from the aversion of God's face; and the other from his forgetfulness; neither of which can, properly, be applied to God. God, however, is said to turn away his face, as if he did not see our wretchedness, when he does not help us; and he is also said to forget when he does not succor the needy and the troubled, as if he altogether forgot them.

24. Continuing the same prayer, and knowing that the prayer of the humble is most grateful to God, he now says, that he has humbled himself to such a degree, that he can humble himself no more. He who prays while he stands, can humble himself by kneeling; and he who prays in that position, can humble himself still more by prostration; but when once so humbled, he can go no further. Now, one can be humbled in mind and body even to the earth: in mind, if he truly reflect, and understand, and acknowledge that he is mere dust, in the language of Abraham, who said, *"I will speak to my Lord, I, who am but dust and ashes:"* in his body, if he prays prostrate on the earth, as Matthew and Mark relate of our Lord. If Luke says he prayed on that occasion, on his knees, it only shows that he began the prayer on his knees, and concluded it in a prostrate position. The petitioners here pray in both positions, for they say, *"For our soul is humbled down to the dust; our belly cleaveth to the earth."* Acknowledging ourselves to be dust, our bellies in prostration have adhered to the earth, while he prayed in that position.

25. He now adds the last and most efficacious reason for moving God to deal mercifully with his people; and that is, to save his name from further blasphemy. *"Arise, and help, us,"* in this our trouble; *"and redeem us;"* that is, deliver us, *"for thy name's sake;"* that it may no longer be blasphemed, but glorified; and, as *"thou hast sold thy people for no price,"* redeem them now without any price; not for our deserts, but *"for thy name's sake;"* through your mercy and kindness. For the better understanding of this, we will now

discuss a few points that naturally present themselves to the reader. The first is, how it happens that the speakers in this Psalm complain of being punished, without having in anywise offended; while other saints generally attribute their persecutions to their own sins. Daniel, for instance, speaking of the captivity in Babylon, says: *"We have sinned, we have committed iniquity, we have done wickedly, and have revolted; and we have gone aside from thy commandments and thy judgments."* And the three holy children thrown into the fiery furnace, from which they were miraculously delivered by God, confess to him as follows: *"For thou hast executed true judgments in all the things that thou hast brought upon us and upon Jerusalem the holy city; for we have sinned, and committed iniquity, departing from thee; and we have trespassed in all things."* Such also is the language of the Machabees: *"For we suffer thus for our sins."* The answer is, that God suffers his people to be persecuted by reason of their sins; but the inspired writers and speakers use different language, and different forms of speech. Sometimes they assume the person of the more infirm members, (*"for we are one body, and members one of another,"*) and charge themselves with the sins of their brethren, just as the tongue would charge itself for sins committed by the other members. Sometimes they speak in the person of the saints and of the perfect, who suffer grievously in the common persecution caused by the sins of others. Thus the Scriptures do not contradict each other, for Daniel and the Machabees spoke in the person of the infirm members; the persons speaking in this Psalm do it in their own proper, holy, and sanctified persons. The second question. When God persecutes the wicked, why does he punish the innocent along with them? The answer is: when the innocent so suffer, they are not persecuted, but tried; and God wishes, by a severe trial, as if by *"the fire of the fining pot,"* or *"the fan of the floor,"* so to purge his Church, and to make it appear who are the true, who are the false believers, who the gold, who the brass, who the grain, who the chaff; as the Apostle says, Rom. 5, *"Patience worketh trial;"* and in Wisdom 3, we read, *"God hath tried them, and found them worthy of himself; as gold in the furnace he hath proved them."* Question the third. Why, then, do the saints complain of persecution, and pray for a speedy termination of it? We are ordered to endure tribulation, not to love it; and nobody loves what he is merely bound to tolerate, though he may love the act of toleration; for though he may rejoice in the toleration of any thing, he would prefer not being called upon to tolerate it. With that, persecutions and temptations are dangerous, and the victory over them being uncertain, the saints must not be too confident, or rely too much on their own strength. A fourth question. Why does God sometimes pour down so many favors on his people, and enable them to master their enemies; and at other times deprive them of all such favors, and allow them to be subdued and conquered by their enemies? To let all see that the gifts of Providence come from himself alone, and not from the evil spirits, or by chance. He, then, gives these gifts to his friends when he deems it expedient; but, for fear they may cling to or adhere to them, and take up with a stable for a house, with an exile for their country, he often takes them from them, as we have explained at length in the beginning of Psalm 41.

PSALM 44

The excellence of Christ's kingdom and the endowments of his Church.

1 My heart hath uttered a good word I speak my works to the king; My tongue is the pen of a scrivener that writeth swiftly.
2 Thou art beautiful above the sons of men: grace is poured abroad in thy lips; therefore hath God blessed thee for ever.
3 Gird thy sword upon thy thigh, O thou most mighty.
4 With thy comeliness and thy beauty set out, proceed prosperously, and reign. Because of truth and meekness and justice: and thy right hand shall conduct thee wonderfully.
5 Thy arrows are sharp: under thee shall people fall, into the hearts of the king's enemies.
6 Thy throne, O God, is for ever and ever: the sceptre of thy kingdom is a sceptre of uprightness.
7 Thou hast loved justice, and hated iniquity: therefore God, thy God, hath anointed thee with the oil of gladness above thy fellows.
8 Myrrh and stacte and cassia perfume thy garments, from the ivory houses: out of which
9 The daughters of kings have delighted thee in thy glory. The queen stood on thy right hand, in gilded clothing; surrounded with variety.
10 Hearken, O daughter, and see, and incline thy ear: and forget thy people and thy father's house.
11 And the king shall greatly desire thy beauty; for he is the Lord thy God, and him they shall adore.
12 And the daughters of Tyre with gifts, yea, all the rich among the people, shall entreat thy countenance.
13 All the glory of the king's daughter is within in golden borders,
14 Clothed round about with varieties. After her shall virgins be brought to the king: her neighbours shall be brought to thee.
15 They shall be brought with gladness and rejoicing: they shall be brought into the temple of the king.
16 Instead of thy fathers, sons are born to thee: thou shalt make them princes over all the earth.
17 They shall remember thy name throughout all generations. Therefore shall

people praise thee for ever; yea, for ever and ever

EXPLANATION OF THE THE PSALM

1. This verse forms a preface to the rest of the Psalm. In it the prophet tells us that the whole proceeded from the mere inspiration of the Holy Ghost, without any cooperation on his part. For, though the whole of the holy Scripture is the word of God, and dictated by the Holy Spirit, there is, however, a great difference between the prophecies therein and the historical part, or the epistles. In the prophecies, the holy writers exercised neither their reflection, nor their memory, nor their reasoning powers; but they, simply, either wrote or spoke what God dictated to them, as Baruch testifies of Jeremias, when he said, *"With his mouth he pronounced all these words, as if he were reading to me."* But when the sacred writers undertook a history, or an epistle, God inspired them with the desire to write, and so directed them, that they should write correctly, and without any errors, but yet in such manner as to oblige them, at the same time, to exercise their own memory and genius, in recording such transactions, and in digesting the order and the manner of so writing, as the author of the Machabees testifies in chap. 2. of the Second Book, worth reading, but too long to quote here. David, then, when he chanted God's praises in the Psalms, or deplored his own calamities, or that of his people, drew upon his memory and his talents, and did not compose without some trouble; but when he comes to prophesy, as he does in this Psalm, he claims no part whatever therein beyond the mere service of his pen or of his tongue. Such is the essence of this preface, which was more clearly put by him in 2 Kings 23, where he says, *"The Spirit of the Lord hath spoken by me, and his word by my tongue."* He, therefore, says, *"my heart hath uttered a good word;"* that is, my mind, from the fullness and abundance of the divine light and heavenly revelations, has given to men this Psalm, containing *"a good word;"* that is, a most grateful and saving word to all mankind. To understand the passage fully, we must go into details. First, observe the word the prophet uses, *"hath uttered,"* which, if translated literally, would have been, *"belched up,"* to show that this Psalm was not composed by him, nor left to his discretion; but, like wind that is involuntarily cast off the stomach, that he was obliged to give it out whether he would or not. Secondly, the prophet wished to express that he was not giving out all that God had revealed to him, but only a part; for, though belching is a sign of repletion, it is small in itself; for the prophets see many things, *"of which it is not lawful for man to speak;"* and, therefore, Isaias said, *"My secret to myself;"* and those who have had revelations from God, confess that they could not find words to express what they saw; and hence, perhaps, the prophet says, *"my heart hath uttered a good word;"*

not good words, in the plural number. Thirdly, the Psalm is called a *"good word,"* because it does not predict any misfortune, such as the sacking of the city, or the captivity of the people, as the other prophecies do; but, on the contrary, all that is favorable and pleasant, and likely to bring great joy and gladness. Fourthly, in describing the emanation of this *"good word"* from the heart of David, he has regard to the production of the word eternal, and seeks to take us by the hand to lead us to understand the generation of the divine word, produced, not as sons are ordinarily produced, by generation, nor by election, nor chosen from a number of sons; but born of his father, the word of his mind, his only word, and, therefore, supremely excellent and good; so that the expression, *"good word,"* may be peculiarly applied to him. *"I speak my works to the king."* Some will have these words to mean, I confess my sins to God; or, I speak those verses of the king; or, I dedicate my work to the king; or, I address the king; which explanations I won't condemn; but the one I offer will agree better, I think, with what went before and what follows; for, in my opinion, this second sentence of the verse is only an explanation of the first part, and assigns a reason for his having said, *"My heart hath uttered a good word;"* just as if he said, I simply attribute all my acts to my king, who is God, and claim nothing for myself; therefore, I have not said, I have written this Psalm; but, *"my heart hath uttered a good word;"* because the thing did not proceed from me, but from the fullness of my illumination; which he explains more clearly in the next sentence, where he says, *"My tongue is the pen of a scrivener that writeth swiftly;"* that means, my tongue has certainly produced this Psalm, but not as my tongue, nor as a member of my body that is moved at my pleasure; but as the pen of the Holy Ghost, as if of a *"scrivener that writeth swiftly."* He says, (observe) that his tongue is the pen of a scrivener that writeth swiftly, and not the tongue of a spirit that speaketh swiftly; because he means to show that his tongue was like a pen, a mere instrument in announcing the prophecy, and not part of a whole, like the members of the body; *"that writeth swiftly,"* to give us to understand that the Holy Ghost needs no time to consider what, how, and when matters are to be written; for they only write slowly who require to consider what they are to write, and how they will give expression to their ideas.

2. He now commences the praises of Christ, praising him, first, for his beauty; secondly, for his eloquence; as well as for his strength and vigor; thirdly, for the qualities of his mind; lastly, for his royal dignity and power, to which he adds his external beauties, such as the grandeur of his palaces and robes. He begins with beauty, for he is describing a spouse; and, as regards a spouse, eloquence takes precedence of beauty, strength of eloquence, virtue of strength, and divinity of virtues; and, therefore, he says, *"Thou art*

beautiful above the sons of men." The sentence, though, seems abrupt and obscure, when he does not say who is that beautiful person; but, as we remarked before, his reason for beginning with, *"my heart hath uttered a good word,"* to let us see that he only uttered some of what he saw, and not the entire; and thus the meaning is, No wonder, Christ, thou shouldst be called beloved, for *"thou art beautiful above the sons of men."* Observe, he says, *"above the sons of men;"* not above the Angels, because God the Son did not become an Angel, but man; as if he said, You, my beloved, art man, but *"beautiful above the sons of men;"* and so he was; for, as regards his divinity, his beauty was boundless; as regards the qualities of his soul, he was more beautiful than any created spirit; and as regards the beauty of his glorified body, *"it is more beautiful than the sun;"* and *"the sun and moon admire his beauty."* Next comes, *"grace is poured abroad in thy lips,"* an encomium derived from the graces of his language, thereby adding to that derived from his beauty; and he says, *"it is poured abroad in thy lips,"* to show that the beauty of Christ's language was natural and permanent, and not acquired by study or practice; for we read in the Gospel, Luke 4, *"And they wondered at the words of grace that proceeded from his mouth;"* and, in John 7, *"never did man speak like this man."* Saints Peter, Andrew, James, John, Philip, and especially Saint Matthew, felt the force of his words, the secret power in them that caused them, by a simple call, to abandon their all, and follow him. What is more wonderful! the sea, the winds, fevers and diseases, nay, even the very dead, felt the power of his voice; which, after all, must appear no great wonder, when we consider that it was the divine and substantial word that spoke in his sweetest and most effective accents, in the flesh he had assumed; *"therefore hath God blessed thee forever."* No wonder you should *"be beautiful,"* and that *"grace should be on thy lips,"* because *"God hath blessed thee forever."*

3. From the praise of his beauty and his eloquence, he now comes to extol his bravery; and, by a figure of speech, instead of telling us in what his bravery consists, he calls upon him to *"Gird thy sword upon thy thigh, O thou most mighty;"* as much as to say, Come, beloved of God, who art not only most beautiful and graceful, but also most valiant and brave; come, put on thy armor; come, and deliver your people; and he tells us in the following verse what sort of armor he means, saying:

4. The words, *"With thy comeliness and thy beauty,"* may be connected with the preceding verse, and the reading would be, *"Gird thy sword upon thy thigh, in thy comeliness and thy beauty;"* or they can be connected with what follows; thus, *"With thy comeliness and thy beauty set out, proceed prosperously, and reign;"* but, in either reading, the meaning is the same; namely, that Christ has no other arms but *"his beauty and his comeliness."* To understand

which we must remember, that true and perfect beauty, as St. Augustine says, is the beauty of the soul that never stales, and pleases the eyes not only of men, but even of Angels, aye, even of God, who cannot be deceived. For, as ordinary beauty depends on a certain proportion of limb, and softness of complexion; thus the beauty of the soul is made up of justice, which is tantamount to the proportion of limb; and wisdom, which represents beauty of complexion; for it shines like light, or rather, as we read in Wisdom 7, *"being compared with the light she is found before it."* The soul, then, that is guided in its will by justice, and in its understanding by wisdom, is truly beautiful. For these two qualifications make it so, and through them most dear to God; and are, at the same time, the most powerful weapons that Christ used in conquering the devil. For Christ contended with the devil, not through his omnipotence, as he might have done, but through his wisdom and his justice; subduing his craft by the one, and his malice by the other. The devil, by his craft, prompted the first man to anger God by his disobedience; and thereby to deprive God of the honor due to him, and all mankind of eternal life; uniting malice with his craftiness, and prompted thereto, moreover, by envy, seeing the place from which he had fallen was destined for man; but the wisdom of Christ was more than a match for such craft, because, by the obedience he, as man, tendered to God, he gave much greater honor to him than he had lost by the disobedience of Adam; and by the same obedience secured a much greater share of glory for the human race than they would have enjoyed, had Adam not fallen. With that, Christ, by his love, (which is the essence of true and perfect justice,) conquered the envy and malice of the devil, for he loved even his enemies, prayed on the very cross for his persecutors, chose to suffer and to die, in order to reconcile his enemies to God, and to make them from being enemies, his friends, brethren, and coheirs; and all that is conveyed in the expression, *"in thy comeliness and thy beauty;"* that is to say, in the comeliness of thy wisdom, and the beauty of thy justice, guided and armed with the sword, and the bow set out, proceed prosperously and reign; which means, advance in battle against the devil, prosper in the fight, and after having conquered and subdued the prince of this world, take possession of your kingdom, that you may forever after rule in the heart of man, through faith and love. *"Because of truth and meekness and justice, and thy right hand shall conduct thee wonderfully."* He tells us why Christ should reign, and that is because he has the qualities that belong to a king, truth, meekness, and justice, from which we learn, that a king should be truthful and faithful to what he says, and just in what he does; which attributes are applied to God himself, in Psalm 144, *"The Lord is faithful in all his words, and holy in all his works;"* but, as there is a certain roughness or severity consequent on all justice, and is like a blemish on it, with Christ's justice, which is most perfect, he couples meekness. For Christ is meekly just, judging, to be sure, with the strictest justice, but without harshness, or moroseness, conciliating instead of repelling those whom he judges. *"And thy right hand shall conduct thee wonderfully."* By governing in such temper you will see your kingdom increase to a wonderful extent, and you will need no external aids, for your own *"right hand,"* your own strength and bravery will suffice *"to thee wonderfully,"* and so extend your kingdom until you shall have *"put all your enemies under your footstool."*

5. He tells us how the right hand of Christ will conduct him so wonderfully in extending his kingdom, because *"the arrows"* that you will let fly at them *"are sharp,"* and will, therefore, penetrate *"into the hearts of the king's enemies;"* your enemies will fall before you, and will be subdued by you. The arrows here signify the word of God, or the preaching of his word, for such are the instruments Christ generally uses in extending his kingdom; hence, he says in Psalm 2, *"But I am appointed king by him over Sion his holy mountain, preaching his commandment"* The word of God is called a sword, an arrow, a mallet, and various other instruments, for it has some similarity to them all. It is called a sharp arrow, for it wonderfully sinks into the heart of man, much deeper than the words of the most eloquent orator, as the Apostle, Heb. 4, says, *"for the word of God is living and effectual; and more penetrating than any two edged sword."* The words, *"under thee shall people fall,"* should be read as if in a parenthesis; and they will only fall, and not be killed; they will only die to sin that they may live to justice; that they may be subject to Christ, to be subject to whom is to reign.

6. He now comes to the supreme dignity of the Messiah, openly calls him God, and declares his throne will be everlasting. This passage is quoted by St. Paul to the Hebrews, to prove that Christ is as much above the Angels, as is a master over his servant; or the Creator above the creature. He then, says, *"Thy throne, O (Christ) God,"* will not be a transient one, as was that of David, or Solomon, but will flourish *"forever and ever."*

7. This verse may be interpreted in two ways, according to the force we put upon the word *"therefore"* in it. It may signify the effect produced, and the meaning would be, As you have loved justice and hated iniquity, by being *"obedient unto death, even to the death of the cross,"* therefore God anointed thee with the oil of gladness, that glorified thee, *"and gave thee a name that is above every name, that at thy name every knee should bend, of those that are in heaven, on earth, and in hell."* Such glorification is properly styled *"the unction of gladness;"* because it puts an end to all pain and sorrow; *"above thy fellows,"* has its own signification; for, though the Angels have been, and men will be, glorified, nobody ever was, or will be, exalted to the right hand of the Father; and nobody ever got, or will get, a name above every name,

with the exception of Christ, who is the head of men and Angels, and is at the same time God and man. In the second exposition, the word *"therefore"* is taken to signify the cause, and the meaning would be: you loved justice and hated iniquity, because God anointed you with the oil of spiritual grace in a much more copious manner than he gave it to any one else; and hence it arose that your graces were boundless, while all others got it in a limited manner, and only through you. Such is the explanation of St. Augustine, who calls our attention to the repetition of the word of God in this verse, and says, the first is the vocative, the second the nominative case, making the meaning to be, O Christ God! God your Father has anointed thee with the oil of gladness. The anointing, of course, applies only to his human nature.

8-9. A very difficult and obscure passage. The words need first to be explained. Myrrh is a well known bitter aromatic perfume. Stacte is a genuine term for a drop of anything, but seems to represent aloes here, which is also a bitter, but odoriferous gum, but different from myrrh; for we read in the Gospel, of Nicodemus having bought a hundred pounds of myrrh and aloes for the embalmment of Christ. Cassia is the bark of a tree, highly aromatic also. By houses of ivory are meant sumptuous palaces, whose walls are inlaid or covered with ivory; just as Nero's house was called golden, and the gates of Constantinople the golden gates, not because they were solid gold, but from the profusion of gilding on them; and thus is interpreted the expression in 3 Kings 22, *"The ivory house built by Achab;"* and, in Amos 3, *"The ivory houses will be ruined."* The expression *"daughters of kings,"* means the multitudes of various kingdoms; for the holy Scriptures most commonly use the expression, daughter of Jerusalem, daughter of Babylon, daughter of the Assyrians, of Tyre, to designate the people of those places; or the words may be taken literally to mean daughters of princes; that is, holy, exalted souls, for the whole sentence is figurative. To come now to the meaning. These aromatic substances represent the gifts of the Holy Ghost, who diffuses a wonderful odor of sanctity; and the prophet having in the previous verse spoken of the unction of Christ, when he said, *"therefore God, thy God, hath anointed thee,"* he now very properly introduces the myrrh, aloes, and cassia, in explanation of the beautiful odors consequent on such anointing, of which St. Paul speaks, 2 Cor. 2, when he says, *"For we are unto God the good odor of Christ."* And as Christ, in his passion, especially exhaled the strongest odors of virtue, of resolute patience, of humble obedience, and ardent love, he, therefore, brings in myrrh, bitter, but odoriferous, to represent patience; aloes, also bitter, though aromatic, to represent humility and obedience: of which St. Paul says,"He humbled himself, becoming obedient even unto death;" and, finally, cassia, warm and odoriferous, to represent that most ardent love that caused him to pray even for his persecutors, while they were nailing him to the cross. All these aromas flowed *"from the garments and the ivory houses"* of Christ. The *"garments"* mean Christ's humanity, that covered his divinity, as it were, with a garment or a veil; and the *"ivory houses"* represent the same humanity, which, like a fair temple of ivory, afforded a residence to the divinity. It is not unusual in the Scriptures to call our human nature by the name of garment and house; thus, in 2 Cor. 5, he unites them when he says, *"For we know if our earthly house of this habitation be dissolved, that we have a building of God, a house not made with hands, eternal in heaven. For in this also we groan, desiring to be clothed over with our habitation, which is from heaven, yet so that we may be found clothed, not naked. For we also who are in this tabernacle do groan, being burdened: because we would not be unclothed, but clothed over; that what is mortal may be swallowed up by life."* Here we have this mortal body of ours called a house and a tabernacle, as also a garment, with which *"we would not be unclothed, but clothed;"* and the heavenly house, in turn, a garment and a habitation. So with the human nature of Christ, that diffused such sweet odors of the virtues, it may be called a garment, and a house of ivory at the same time; unless one may wish to refer the garment to his soul, and the house of ivory to his body, which Christ himself seems to have had in view when he said to the Jews, *"Destroy this temple, and in three days I will build it up again."* The word *"ivory houses,"* being in the plural number, is an objection of no great value, for the prophet calls it a noun of multitude; just as we call a large establishment the buildings, though there, in reality, is only one object before our mind. *"Out of which the daughters of kings have delighted thee in thy glory;"* that is, from which perfumes, exhaling from the vestments and ivory houses of thy humanity; *"the daughters of kings;"* whether it means the royal and exalted souls, or multitudes of people from various kingdoms; *"have delighted thee,"* as they *"ran after thee to the odor of thy ointments."* For Christ is greatly delighted when he sees multitudes of the saints, attracted by his odors, running after them; and, in fact, any one, once they get but the slightest scent of such odors as flow from the patience, humility, and love of Christ, cannot be prevented from running after them, and will endure any amount of torments sooner than suffer themselves to be separated from him, exclaiming, with the Apostle, *"Who shall separate us from the love of Christ?"* And in this respect do the daughters of kings, when they run after the odor of his ointments, especially delight our Lord, because they do it to honor him, with a pure intention of glorifying him. The martyrs glorified God wonderfully when, by their sufferings, they ran after their master, to which himself alluded when he predicted Peter's suffering, on which the Gospel remarks, *"Signifying by what death he should glorify God."* *"The queen stood on thy right hand in gilded clothing, surrounded with variety."* The prophecies hitherto regarded the bridegroom; he now turns to the bride, by which bride, as all commentators allow, is meant the Church; for St. Paul to the Ephesians 5, lays down directly that the Church is the bride of Christ. The principal meaning of the passage, then, is to take the bride as designating the Church. Any faithful, holy soul even, may be intended by it; particularly the Blessed Virgin, who, together with being his mother according to the flesh, is his spouse according to the spirit, and holds the first place among the members of the Church. It is, then, most appropriately used in the festivals of the Blessed Virgin, and of other virgins, to whom, with great propriety, the Church says, *"Come, spouse of Christ."* David, then, addressing Christ, says, *"The queen stood on thy right hand."* Thy spouse, who, from the fact of her being so, is a queen, stood by thee, *"on thy right hand,"* quite close to thee, in the place of honor, on thy right hand, *"in gilded clothing,"* in precious garments, such as become a queen. Take up now the several words. The word *"stood,"* in the perfect, instead of the future tense, is used here, a practice much in use with the prophets, who see the future as if it had actually passed; and, as St. Chrysostom remarks, she stood, instead of being seated, as queens usually are, to imply her inferiority to God, for it is only an equal, such as the Son, that can sit with him; and, therefore, the Church, as well as all the heavenly powers, are always said to stand before God. The word, in Hebrew, implies standing firmly, as if to convey that the bride was so sure, safe, and firm in her position that there could be no possible danger of her being rejected or repudiated.

10. He now addresses the Church herself; in terms of the most pious and friendly admonition. He calls her *"daughter,"* either because he speaks in the person of God the Father, or as one of the fathers of the Church. If applied to the Blessed Virgin, it requires no straining of expression, she being truly the daughter of David. *"Hearken, O daughter,"* hear the voice of your spouse, *"and see,"* attentively consider what you hear, *"and incline thy ear;"* humbly obey his commands, *"and forget thy people and thy father's house,"* that you may the more freely serve your spouse, and forget the world and the things that belong to it, for the Church has been chosen from the world, and has come out from it; and though it is still in the world, it ought no more belong to it than does its spouse. By the world, is very properly understood the people who love the things of the world, which same world is the mansion of our old father Adam, who was driven into it from paradise. The word *"forget"* has much point in it, for it implies that we must cease to love the world so entirely and so completely, as if we had totally forgotten that we were ever in it, or that it had any existence.

11. He assigns a reason why the bride should leave her people, and her father's house, and be entirely devoted to the love of her heavenly spouse, and to his service, for thus *"the king shall greatly desire thy beauty,"* and wish to have thee above him. And since the principal beauty of the bride is interior, as will be explained in a few verses after this one, consisting in virtue, especially in obedience to the commandments, or in love of which all the commandments turn; he therefore adds, *"for he is the Lord thy God;"* that is to say, the principal reason for his so loving your beauty, which is based, mainly on your obedience, is, because *"he is the Lord thy God."* Nothing is more imperatively required by the Lord from his servants, or by God from his creatures, than obedience. And for fear there should be any mistake about his being the absolute Lord and true God, he adds, *"and him they shall adore;"* that is to say, your betrothed is one with whom you cannot claim equality, he is only so by grace, remaining still your Lord, and the Lord of all creatures, who are bound to adore him.

12. Having stated that the bridegroom would be adored, he now adds, that the bride too would get her share, would be honored as a queen, by presents and supplications. *"And the daughters of Tyre with gifts, yea, all the rich among the people, shall entreat thy countenance;"* the daughters of the gentiles, heretofore enemies to your Lord, will be brought under subjection to him, and will come to you, *"and entreat your countenance,"* will by your intercession, moving you not only by words and entreaties, but by gifts and presents: *"all the rich among the people,"* because, if the rich take up anything, consent or agree to it, the whole body generally follow them. *"The daughters of Tyre,"* the women of the city, meaning the whole city, but the women are specially named as generally having more immediate access to the queen, and more so than men have to the king; and as the bride here does not represent a single individual, but the Church, which is composed of men and women, so by the daughters of Tyre we understand, all the gentiles, be they men or women. Tyre was a great city of the gentiles, bounding the land of promise, and renowned for its greatness and riches, and is therefore made here to represent all the gentiles. *"With gifts,"* the offerings which the converted gentiles offered to build or to ornament churches, or to feed the poor, or for other pious purposes. *"Shall entreat thy countenance;"* some will have it, that thy countenance means the countenance of Christ, but the more simple explanation is, to refer to the Church. The expression is a Hebrew one, which signifies, to intercede for, or to deprecate one's anger: thus Saul says, in 1 Kings 8, *"And I have not appeased the face of the Lord;"* and in Psalm 94, *"Let us preoccupy his face in thanksgiving;"* and in Psalm 118, *"I entreated thy face with all my heart."* Entreating the face is an expression taken from the fact of our looking intently on the face of the person we seek to move, and judging from its expression, whether we are likely to succeed or to be refused.

13-14. Having spoken at such length of the beauty of the bride, for fear any one may suppose those beauties were beauties of the person, he now states that all those beauties were interior, regarding the mind alone. *"All her glory,"* whether as regards her person or her costly dress, are all spiritual, internal, and to be looked for in the heart alone. Hence St. Peter admonishes the women of his time to take the bride here described, as a model in the decoration of their interior. *"Whose adorning let it not be the outward plaiting of the hair, or the wearing of gold, or the putting on of apparel, but the hidden man of the heart, in the incorruptibility of a quiet and meek spirit, which is rich in the sight of God."* We are not, however, hence justified in censuring the external decorations of the Church, and the altars, on the occasion of administering the sacraments, and on great festivals, for question is here, not of material edifices, but of men, who are the people of God, and members of Christ, whose principal ornament and decorations should consist in their virtues; from which virtues, however, good works ought to spring, *"that those who see them, may glorify our Father who is in heaven,"* as our Savior says. The *"golden borders"* most appositely represent charity, which is compared to gold, as being the most precious and valuable of all the virtues. We have already explained the variegated vestment, for which vestment the Apostle seems to speak, when he says, *"Put ye on the bowels of mercy, benignity, humility, modesty, patience. After her shall virgins be brought to the king."* Though there is only one spouse of Christ, one only beloved by him, the universal Church, there are a certain portion specially beloved by him, enjoy certain prerogatives; and they are those who have dedicated their virginity to God, in the hope of being better able to please him; of whom the Apostle says, *"He that is without a wife, is solicitous for the things that belong to the Lord, how he may please God. But he that is with a wife, is solicitous for the things of the world, how he may please his wife: and he is divided. And the unmarried woman and the virgin thinketh on the things of the Lord, that she may be holy both in body and spirit. But she that is married thinketh on the things of the world, how she may please her husband."* Of such the prophet now speaks, and in these verses extols that virginity so precious in the sight of Christ, the virgin *"who feedeth among the lilies."* After her shall virgins be brought to the king. *"Next to his principal bride, the Church, shall rank all those celestial brides who have consecrated their virginity to God."* Her neighbors shall be brought to thee; that is, the only virgins that shall be introduced will be those that were neighbors to thee, by reason of acknowledging thy true Church.

15. He informs us of the joy consequent on such a number of nuptial feasts. The virgins will be *"brought with gladness and rejoicing,"* introduced to the nuptial feast, amidst the great joy and applause of the whole heavenly Jerusalem. He, perhaps, here alludes to the canticle which virgins alone were entitled to sing there. *"And they sung as it were a new canticle before the throne, and before the four living creatures and the ancients; and no man could say the canticle, but those hundred forty-four thousand who were purchased from the earth. These are they who were not defiled with women, for they are virgins. These follow the lamb, whithersoever he goeth."* Happy souls that follow the lamb in his virginal path, and in joy and gladness chant that new canticle, unknown to the fathers of old, and which can be chanted by none other than themselves, and in such jubilation will be introduced to the celestial tabernacle, which may be called a palace from its magnificence, and a temple from its holiness.

16. Having hitherto dilated on the dignity and the ornamentation of the bridegroom and the bride, he now comes to the fruit of the marriage; saying, that a most prosperous issue will come from it, that will govern the entire world. It is doubtful, though, whether he here addresses the bridegroom or the bride, but most probably the latter; because, he had advised her to forget her people and her father's house; and now, by way of consoling her for having left them, he promises her an abundance of children, and predicts that the fruit of the union between the Church and her heavenly spouse will be most prosperous and happy. *"Instead of thy fathers sons are born to thee."* Instead of your fathers, who are now dead, that is, instead of the patriarchs and prophets, and fathers, you have left behind, and you have been ordered to forget; *"sons are born to thee;"* that is, Apostles and Disciples of Christ, able to teach, and make laws for the entire world; therefore, *"thou shalt make them princes over all the earth."* And, in fact, the Apostles, the first children of the Church, made laws for the whole world, a thing never accomplished by any one temporal monarch. For, as St. John Chrysostom remarks, The Romans could not impose laws on the Persians, nor the Persians on the Romans; while the Apostles imposed laws upon both, and upon all other nations. And, as in the first age of the Church, the patriarch fathers had the Apostles as sons; thus, in the following age the Apostles as fathers had the Bishops as sons; who, though they may not be severally so, are, as a body, princes over the whole world; and, thus, by means of the succession of Bishops, the Church always has sons born to her for the fathers, for her to place in their position and dignities.

17. He concludes the Psalm by saying that those spiritual nuptials he had so lauded, and the fruit of the nuptials, would tend to the glory of God. For, says he, the sons who will supply the place of their fathers will become fathers in turn, and *"will remember thy name;"* will celebrate your grace and power, *"throughout all generations."* St. John Chrysostom remarks that this prophecy applies to David's own Psalms, that we now see celebrated and chanted all over the world. *"Therefore shall people praise thee forever; yea, for ever and ever."* From the fact of the Apostles and their successors, the Bishops, being always sure to *"remember his name,"* to chant and proclaim his praise, the prophet justly infers that the people entrusted to their care will do so too, and that *"for ever, yea, for ever and ever;"* that is, both here and hereafter.

PSALM 45

The Church, in persecution, trusteth in the protection of God.

1 Our God is our refuge and strength: a helper in troubles, which have found us exceedingly.
2 Therefore we will not fear, when the earth shall be troubled; and the mountains shall be removed into the heart of the sea.
3 Their waters roared and were troubled: the mountains were troubled with his strength.
4 The stream of the river maketh the city of God joyful: the most High hath sanctified his own tabernacle.
5 God is in the midst thereof, it shall not be moved: God will help it in the morning early.
6 Nations were troubled, and kingdoms were bowed down: he uttered his voice, the earth trembled.
7 The Lord of armies is with us: the God of Jacob is our protector.
8 Come and behold ye the works of the Lord: what wonders he hath done upon earth,
9 Making wars to cease even to the end of the earth. He shall destroy the bow, and break the weapons: and the shield he shall burn in the fire.
10 Be still and see that I am God; I will be exalted among the nations, and I will be exalted in the earth. The Lord of armies is with us: the God of Jacob is our protector.

Explanation of the psalm

1. The soldiers of Christ overcome temptation as often by flight as by patience. When they must fly, God is their safest *"refuge;"* when they have to suffer; God is their *"strength"* and support; in both cases he is *"their helper in troubles,"* by affording a refuge when they fly, and enabling them to conquer when they stand. The expression, *"which have found us exceedingly,"* gives us to understand that the persecutions suffered by the Church, in her infancy, were both grievous and severe, and the more so, because sudden and unexpected; for, as we read in the Acts of the Apostles, after the ascension of our Lord, and the descent of the Holy Ghost, the Church was progressing and increasing in Jerusalem in great peace and tranquillity; *"continuing daily with one accord in the temple, and breaking bread from house to house; they took their meat with gladness and simplicity of heart; praising God together, and having favor with all the people. And the Lord added daily to their society such as should be saved."* In a short time, however, a most violent persecution arose, the Apostles were scourged, Stephen was stoned, and all the Disciples, with the exception of the Apostles, were scattered.

2-3. Two most obscure verses; but we have only to follow St. Basil and St. Chrysostom. Having declared *"God their refuge and strength,"* he thinks he would remain unmoved, even though the sea and the land were to be turned upside down, and change places in fearful confusion. *"Therefore,"* say the people of God, *"we will not fear when the earth shall be troubled;"* whatever commotion may arise in it; *"and the mountains shall be removed into the heart of the sea;"* even though the very mountains, firmly fixed and planted by God himself, in such a way as to be looked upon as immovable, even though they may be tossed and rocked, and even cast into the deep; even in such case *"we will not fear,"* because God Almighty is *"our refuge and our strength."* *"Their waters roared and were troubled;"* that, too, however great the roaring and confusion, did not make us fear. *"The mountains were troubled with his strength."* Even though the very mountains, shaken from their foundations by the divine strength and power, should be hurled into the sea. For it is God alone who can so confuse the earth, hurl the mountains into the sea, and make it and the mountains along with it to tremble; according to Psalm 76, *"The waters saw thee, O God, and they were afraid; and the depths were troubled;"* and again, Psalm 103, *"He looketh upon the earth, and maketh it tremble;"* and, Isaias 51, *"But I am the Lord thy God, who trouble the sea, and the waves thereof swell."* Thus, in these verses, God's people declare how great is their confidence in him, when they would not entertain the slightest fear; even in the event of the whole world tumbling to atoms; from which also we may form some idea of the immense power of God, who can so shake and confuse all nature, as he really will previous to the last judgments, as we read in Luke 12, *"When there shall be great earthquakes in various places, and by reason of the confusion of the sea and the roaring of the waves, men shall be withering away from fear."* Then will God's people not only suffer no fear, but they will even look up, *"and lift up their heads,"* as it is expressed in the Gospel; for *"their redemption is at hand."* All this may have a figurative meaning; taking the earth to represent men of earthly views, and the mountains to represent men not only of earthly views, but also proud, insolent characters, such as the kings of old, so hostile to the Church of God; and the sea to represent that abyss of trouble and confusion, in which all such characters will be hustled on the day of judgment. Thus, *"The earth shall be troubled,"* when the impious lovers of it *"shall be troubled with terrible fear,"* Wisdom 5; and *"The mountains shall be removed into the heart of the sea;"* that is, when the mighty kings, who formerly persecuted the Church, shall be overwhelmed in the deep abyss; and then *"The waters roared, and were troubled;"* when the last scourge shall so confound and confuse the wicked and their rulers, when God's strength shall be brought to bear on them in his anger.

4–5. He now shows how it will happen that God's people shall entertain no fear, even when *"the earth shall be troubled, and the mountains removed into the heart of the sea;"* because, instead of the immense confusion with which the wicked will be overwhelmed, an abundance of pleasure to gladden the Church, will be poured in upon it; and, instead of the unsteadiness of the mountains, that will be cast into the heart of the sea, the Church will enjoy an everlasting stability, because God will be in the midst of it. *"The stream of the river maketh the city of God joyful."* That is to say, God's people will have no fear, *"when the earth shall be troubled;"* because, instead of the fierce waves of the rude sea dashing against his Church, the sweet, somniferous, plentiful, bright, and pleasant waters of the purling river will, in great abundance, wash it, and glide by it in pleasant streams. *"The Most High hath sanctified his own tabernacle."* No wonder the city of God should be joyful, when God saluted it, sanctified it, made it his own dwelling place, as we read in the Apocalypse, 21, *"Behold, the tabernacle of God with men, and he will dwell with them, and they shall be his people."* God is in the midst thereof, it shall not be moved. *"A contrast to the instability of the earth and the mountains; they will be moved and shaken, but the city of God need have no fear thereon, for"* God is in the midst thereof; *"that is, he never leaves it, is always present there,"* in the midst of it,"in its inmost recesses, in its heart; and, therefore, instead of being moved or shaken, it will remain fixed and firm forever. He concludes by showing how all this is to be effected, and when; by adding, *"God will help it in the morning early;"* the city of God must have all joy and gladness, and that forever, because God will help it early in the beginning of the day, in the opening day of everlasting happiness. The Scripture calls the time of infidelity the darkness of the night, and the time of faith the morning, as St. Paul, Rom. 13, says, *"The night hath passed, and the day appeareth;"* and 2 St. Peter, chap. 1, *"And we have the word of prophecy more firm; to which you do well to attend, as to a light shining in a dark place until the day dawn, and the morning star rise in your hearts;"* and the spouse in the Canticles, chap. 2, calls the beloved, *"Till the day break, and the shadows retire;"* and the prophet Malachias, chap. 4, says, *"But unto you that fear my name the sun of justice shall arise."*

6. He now expresses in plain language what he had hitherto expressed in figurative, namely, the ruin of the enemies of the Church, and the universal and lasting peace consequent thereon. He used the words earth and mountains before; he now speaks more clearly of nations and kingdoms. *"Nations were troubled,"* because their dissolution was approaching, *"and kingdoms were bowed down,"* tumbled from their glory, laid prostrate; *"he uttered his voice;"* God thundered from heaven, *"and the earth trembled."* This destruction of the kingdoms of the world was more clearly predicted by Daniel, chap. 2, where he says that the kingdom of Christ *"shall consume all these kingdoms, and itself shall stand forever,"* which has been explained by the Apostle, 1 Cor 15, when he says, *"Afterwards the end, when he shall have delivered up the kingdom to God and the Father, when he shall have abolished all principality, and authority, and power."*

7. In the midst of all this destruction of nations and kingdoms, God's people will have no fear whatever, because they can always say, *"The Lord of armies is with us." "The God of Jacob is our protector, he has undertaken it. He is called the Lord of armies,"* because his Angels who are most numerous and most powerful, obey his commands as we have in Psalm 102, *"Mighty in strength, and executing his word;"* and not only has he the Angels to carry out his orders, but, as we have it in Psalm 118, *"Fire, hail, snow, ice, strong winds, which fulfil his word,"* are also at his command, as we read in Psalm 118, *"All things obey him."* Thus this verse advances two arguments to prove clearly that God's people should entertain no fear; the first, from the fact of their being under the protection of God, who is all powerful to help them. The second, from the fact of his being most ready and willing to help them, as is clear from his styling himself the God of Jacob, the holy patriarch, and friend of God, from whose family he chose his only Son to assume human flesh.

8. He now exhorts all nations to reflect on God's wonderful doings, and especially on the fact that will turn up at last; namely, that when all the enemies of Christ shall be removed, or rather, *"laid under his footstool,"* there will be an end to all war; and God alone will reign supreme, with no one to resist or gainsay him. That is the kingdom we expect and pray for, when we say daily, *"Thy kingdom come." "Come, and behold ye,"* with the eye of faith and contemplation, and reflect on *"the works of the Lord what wonder he hath done upon earth;"* reflect upon God's works, (using the past for the future, in prophetic style,) in this world, so wonderful and stupendous as to deserve the name of prodigies. And these prodigies will include his *"making wars to cease even to the end of the earth,"* a really wonderful thing to say he could so put an end to all war, as to preclude the possibility of its being ever renewed.

9. He explains how he will *"make the wars to cease,"* for the Lord will destroy all their offensive arms, such as the bow and the lance and the arms of defense, viz., the shield; and without arms, war cannot be waged. Some will have these verses apply to the temporary peace the Church enjoyed, under Augustus or Constantine; but they are much more applicable to the everlasting peace in store for the Church, when she shall cease to be militant, and become triumphant, having conquered and subdued all her enemies.

10. Having just invited all to *"come, and behold the works of the Lord,"* he now tells them how they are to come, if they wish really to understand them; and to impress the necessity of it, as well as to induce them to come, he speaks in the person of the Lord himself, saying *"Be still, and see that I am God."* For to contemplate things divine, the mind must needs be disengaged from all worldly care, and avarice is at the bottom of all care; because it is from the lust of riches, dainties, honors, pleasure, and the like, that all troublesome thoughts are engendered, and never leave any one troubled with them at ease. Hence Jeremias says of the contemplative, Lam. 3, *"He shall sit solitary, and hold his peace; because he hath taken it upon himself,"* and the Lord commands us, Mat. 6, *"But thou when thou shalt pray, enter into thy chamber, and having shut the door, pray to thy father in secret."* And he explains by his practice what be meant by *"shutting the door,"* for, generally speaking, when he wanted to pray, he went up on a mountain, and went alone, to shut himself out from all the cares, noise, and concerns of this world. But, as we said, the principal stillness we require is, abstraction from the desire of anything earthly; for when any one will not wrap himself up in, or covet what he sees, however occupied he may be in helping his neighbor, he will easily collect himself when he chooses, and when necessary, and he will *"be still and see,"* that the Lord only *"is God."* He is the beginning and the end; he is the entire hope of the faithful on earth, and their true happiness in heaven. David was constantly occupied in governing his kingdom; St. Gregory, as well as many other holy popes, in discharging the duties of the pontificate, and yet they could enter into the most sublime contemplation, because they kept the wings of their souls unfettered and unsullied by the mire of concupiscence. The great Apostle himself, burdened as he was by the *"solicitude of all the Churches,"* obliged to seek a living by the *"labor of his hands,"* still being untrammeled, free from worldly desires, he, too, could *"be still," "and see,"* and was carried up to the third heaven, and *"heard the secret words which it is not granted to man to utter."* On the other hand, there are many idle persons, as far as the business of this world is concerned, but from their carnal desires and pursuits know not how to *"be still." "Be still,"* look out for holy retirement, bring to it a pure and tranquil mind, *"and see,"* on deep reflection, *"that I am God,"* that I alone am God; that no created

thing, however great or sublime, is God; I alone am him; that is, I alone am he, *"from whom, through whom, and in whom are all things,"* Rom. 2. I alone, am he, without whom you can do nothing, and are nothing; but in whom, and through whom, you can do everything. *"I will be exalted among the nations, and I will be exalted in the earth;"* that is to say, when I shall have done the wonderful things just enumerated, I will appear exalted before all nations, before the whole world, so *"that every knee shall bend, of those that are in heaven, on earth, and in hell."* In the end of the world, nobody will be found hardy enough to despise God, for all, with or against their will, will acknowledge his supreme dominion, and will be subject to him.

He concludes the Psalm by a repetition of verse 7, to show that the divine exhortation had the effect of stirring up and renewing the pious affections of the faithful.

PSALM 46

The gentiles are invited to praise God for the establishment of the kingdom of Christ.

1 clap your hands, all ye nations: shout unto God with the voice of Joy,

2 For the Lord is high, terrible: a great king over all the earth.

3 He hath subdued the people under us; and the nations under our feet.

4 He hath chosen for us his inheritance the beauty of Jacob which he hath loved.

5 God is ascended with jubilee, and the Lord with the sound of trumpet.

6 Sing praises to our God, sing ye: sing praises to our king, sing ye.

7 For God is the king of all the earth: sing ye wisely.

8 God shall reign over the nations: God sitteth on his holy throne.

9 The princes of the people are gathered together, with the God of Abraham: for the strong gods of the earth are exceedingly exalted.

EXPLANATION OF THE PSALM

1. The holy prophet invites all nations to express the gladness of their heart by their language and their gesture. He includes all, for the glory of the head is in common with that of the body, and the body comprises not only the Jews, but all nations; for the Church, which is Christ's body, is spread over all the world. From his invitation to clap hands, we are not to infer we are called upon to do so in the literal sense of the expression; but we are called upon to be as internally glad and joyful as those who give expression to their joy by clapping their hands, by dancing, and such gestures. Such is evidently his meaning; because, in Psalm 95, the same prophet calls not only on men to exult and applaud, but also on the heavens and earth, rivers, mountains, and trees, which are all metaphorical expressions, and signify nothing more than the abundance of joy in the mind of man, that would, if possible, bring all nature to share it with them.

2. He assigns a reason for having invited all nations to rejoice and exult, the first being derived from the greatness of Christ, who he declares to be *"high,"* by reason of his divinity, *"terrible,"* by reason of his power, and *"a great king,"* by reason of his providence and government. *"For the Lord is high."* Sing to him with applause and exultation, all ye nations, because Christ our Lord and God is high, cannot be higher, as regards his divine nature, in which he excels all created beings. Do so, because he is *"terrible,"* as regards his power, which nothing can resist. Do so, finally, because *"he is a great king over all the earth,"* being supreme, absolute, and universal rector of the whole world.

3. A second argument, drawn from the favors God originally conferred on his Church, when he brought it out of the land of Egypt; for then God brought his people into the land of promise, and subjected the nations and people in possession of it to his own people, and made them trample on the necks of the kings of those nations, as we read in Josue, chap. 1.

4. A third argument, drawn from another favor, by which the same Christ God, having ejected the Chananeans, and having introduced his people into their land, chose from the believing Jews, from his Apostles and the other Disciples, the primitive Church as his own and his peculiar inheritance. *"He hath chosen for us;"* that means, in us, or from us; *"his inheritance,"* his own peculiar people; *"the beauty of Jacob which he loved;"* that is, he selected the flower of the Jewish people, called after Jacob, for which he had a special love, and formed his Church from it, as his peculiar inheritance. We have here to remark that, though most of the Jews were stiff necked, and prone to idolatry, and, consequently, reprobate, there were, however, very many holy patriarchs among them, whose spirituality and innocence was most pleasing to God. Hence the Apostle, Rom. 11, says, *"The Jews were most dear to God, for the sake of the fathers;"* and that their church was the good olive tree, *"some of whose branches were broken, because of unbelief;"* and that the converted gentiles, whom he calls the wild olives, were grafted in their place; and to the same converted gentiles he thus addresses himself: *"And if some of the branches be broken, and thou, being a wild olive tree, art ingrafted in them, and art made partaker of the root and of the fatness of the olive tree. Boast not against the branches, but if thou boast, thou bearest not the root, but the root thee."* This, then, is *"the beauty of Jacob,"* that caused him *"to choose an inheritance"* from the Jewish people, which he afterwards caused to increase and multiply.

5. The fourth reason for joy and gladness; because, after the Lord *"chose his inheritance"* from the Jewish people, that is to say, selected his Apostles and

Disciples from among them, he ascended into heaven, and raised our nature, indissolubly united to his own, above all the heavens, above all the Angels, and above all created beings. For though this passage does not say to what place he ascended, it is clearly expressed in Psalm 67, *"He ascended on high, and led captivity captive;"* and, in the same Psalm, *"Who mounteth above the heaven of heavens to the east."* The meaning, then, is, *"God hath ascended,"* Christ has ascended, but by virtue of his own power, inasmuch as he is God. *"With jubilee and the sound of trumpet,"* which is to be understood of the spiritual rejoicing, and the chanting of the Angels; for, as far as the ascension of Christ before his Apostles was concerned, it occurred in silence, and they probably neither heard nor saw the chanting, nor the persons of the Angels, lest their attention may be diverted from the great mystery that was then in process; namely, the extraordinary elevation of that nature, to which was said, *"Thou art dust, and to dust thou shalt return,"* in its ascent in great glory and immortality above the highest heavens.

6-7. Before offering a fifth reason for praising God, he excites all to break out in repeated expressions of admiration at his having ascended so gloriously. *"Sing praises to him,"* by reason of his being our God; *"sing praises to him,"* by reason of his being King; and, thirdly, *"sing praises to him,"* because he is *"King of all the earth;"* and do so, not only repeatedly, but *"wisely,"* with care and attention, making no mistakes therein, for any duty rendered to a great king must be gone through in such manner.

8. A fifth reason for singing and chanting to God, *"with the voice of joy,"* derived from Christ, after his ascension to heaven, having sent his Apostles to preach the Gospel, and to gather the gentiles to his fold. *"God shall reign over the nations."* Christ, not content with the inheritance he got in the Jewish people, shall also reign over the gentiles; because, by the preaching of the Apostles, he will bring them all to the true faith. But, in the meantime, *"God sitteth on his holy throne,"* he sits at the right hand of his Father, the most holy, most just position he can occupy, and which *"no iniquity can touch."*

9. He explains the sentence, *"God shall reign over the nations,"* because the preaching of the Apostles would bring the *"princes of the people"* to the true faith, oblige them to abandon their idols, and turn to the God of Abraham, who is the only true God, that thus he may be their God, and they his people. *"For the strong gods of the earth are exceedingly exalted;"* the great men amongst the gentiles, who had been slaves of sin, and servants of their idols, are now, by their conversion, children of God, and heirs of the kingdom of heaven.

PSALM 47

God is greatly to be praised for the establishment of his Church.

1 Great is the Lord, and exceedingly to be praised in the city of our God, in his holy mountain.
2 With the joy of the whole earth is mount Sion founded, on the sides of the north, the city of the great king.
3 In her houses shall God be known, when he shall protect her.
4 For behold the kings of the earth assembled themselves: they gathered together.
5 So they saw, and they wondered, they were troubled, they were moved:
6 Trembling took hold of them. There were pains as of a woman in labour.
7 With a vehement wind thou shalt break in pieces the ships of Tharsis.
8 As we have heard, so have we seen, in the city of the Lord of hosts, in the city of our God: God hath founded it for ever.
9 We have received thy mercy, O God, in the midst of thy temple.
10 According to thy name, O God, so also is thy praise unto the ends of the earth: thy right hand is full of justice.
11 Let mount Sion rejoice, and the daughters of Juda be glad; because of thy judgments, O Lord.
12 Surround Sion, and encompass her: tell ye in her towers.
13 Set your hearts on her strength; and distribute her houses, that ye may relate it in another generation.
14 For this is God, our God unto eternity, and for ever and ever: he shall rule us for evermore.

Explanation of the Psalm

1. The prophet, being about to praise a certain edifice, commences by praising the architect, and says that in the holy city the wonderful skill and wisdom of God, who built it, is truly displayed. *"Great is the Lord, and exceedingly to be praised;"* and so he is, whether we look at his essence, his power, his wisdom, his justice, or his mercy, for all are infinite, everlasting, and incomprehensible; and thus, so much is God *"exceedingly to be praised,"* that all the Angels, all men, even all his own works would not suffice thereto; but of all things we have revealed, there is no one thing that can give us a greater idea of his greatness, or for which we should praise and thank him more, than the establishment of his Church; and, therefore, the prophet adds, *"in the city of our God, in his holy mountain;"* that is to say, the greatness of God, and for which he deserves so much praise, is conspicuous in the foundation and construction of his Church, which is *"the city of our God, in his holy mountain;"* that is, made as perfect as possible. For, it is said in Isaias 2, *"The mountain of the house of the Lord shall be prepared on top of mountains."* And the Lord himself calls his Church *"a city placed on a mountain."* To touch briefly on the remarkable points of this edifice, just consider, first, the incredible variety of nations, differing in language, manners, customs, and

laws, so uniting in the profession of one faith, and the use of the same sacraments, as to form one people, nay, even one family. Consider, secondly, the same Church, founded on Peter, a poor, ignorant, rude fisherman; and yet founded so firmly, that the gates of hell cannot prevail against it; for, in spite of that world in which Christ's Church is spending its exile, in spite of all the powers of darkness, in spite of all the persecutions of the wicked, she will ultimately arrive in safety at the land of promise; and, placed, at length, above the highest heavens, will reign undisturbed in everlasting happiness. Such things, certainly, could not be accomplished, but by the great God; that is, by a most powerful and skilful architect who, therefore, *"is exceedingly to be praised,"* or, rather, is beyond all praise.

2. The prophet assigns a reason why God should be so *"exceedingly praised"* in his Church, typified by Mount Sion and the city of Jerusalem, and assigns as a reason, God's having *"founded it with the joy of the whole earth,"* using the word *"founded"* in the present, not in the past tense; for the establishment of the Church is always going on, and never a thing of the past. Various churches are daily springing up where one never existed before. For the Church is not like a small house, that takes little time to build, but is rather a great city, spread over the world; built in various ages, by spiritual architects, successors of the Apostles, who, by their preaching, lay Christ as the corner stone, and erect a spiritual edifice thereon. That foundation is laid *"with the joy of the whole earth,"* because, throughout the world, the Church is established by the preaching of the Gospel, which never fails to bring the most unbounded spiritual joy and gladness to those who receive it. It is, therefore, that such knowledge is compared by the Lord to a *"treasure hidden in a field, which when a man hath found he hideth, and for joy thereof, goeth and selleth all he hath, and buyeth that field;"* and, in the Acts of the Apostles, when the Church was being founded in Jerusalem, it is said, *"They took their meat with gladness;"* and, in chap. 8, speaking of the preaching of Philip, and his establishment of the Church in Samaria, it says, *"And there was great joy in that city;"* and the eunuch of Queen Candace, when he heard the faith from the same Philip, and was baptized, *"went his way rejoicing;"* and, in chap. 13, we read that when St. Paul began to preach to the gentiles, and lay the foundation of the Church, *"The gentiles hearing this were glad, and glorified the word of the Lord."* When he talks of the foundation of Mount Sion, we are not to understand him as speaking of the mountain of that name; for that was in existence from the beginning of the world; but of the spiritual mountain, of which it was the type. Mount Sion means, then, the Church of Christ, so called by reason of the eminence of doctrine, and the perfection of life, to be found in the Church. The same Church is also styled *"The side of the north,"* because, as Mount Sion, lying on the north side of the land of

promise, protects it from the withering, bitter blasts of the north wind, so the Church of Christ is like a wall, warding off the spiritual north blast; that is, the blast of the unclean spirits; for those who nestle in the bosom of the Church, that is to say, who receive her doctrine and obey her laws, are not easily injured by the north blast, spreading its pernicious dogmas by example. Finally, the same Church is called *"The city of the great king,"* which tends much to ennoble it, by reason of the Church of Christ having him for its king, who is Prince of the kings of the earth, and King of kings, and Lord of Lords. All other authorities in the Church are but servants, servants, of Christ, as the Apostle says, *"Let a man so look upon us as the ministers of Christ and the dispensers of the mysteries of God."* Even the very supreme head of the Church calls himself the vicar of Christ, and not only acknowledges himself to be the servant of God, but even the servant of his servants.

3. He now assigns a second reason for the Lord being *"great and exceedingly to be praised"* in his city of Jerusalem, because he not only founded it well, but constantly protects and exalts it. God, who founded his Church like a royal city, will then especially *"be known in her houses;"* that is, by all her inhabitants, when, in time of persecution, *"he shall protect her."*

5-7. The Latin fathers, Ambrose, Jerome, and Augustine, explain these verses in a different way from the Greek fathers, Chrysostom, Theodoret, and Euthymius; the former apply it to the gentiles embracing the faith; the latter, to those resisting it. According to the Latins, the meaning is, The gentiles will cause God to be known in the Church. *"For behold, the kings of the earth,"* and their subjects, converted by the preaching and the miracles of the Apostles, assembled themselves, gathered together; that is to say, came into the one faith, out of various sects and superstitions, and became one people; so much so, *"that they had but one heart and one soul,"* as we read of the first Christians in the Acts, and their conversion was effected, for *"they saw"* the wonders and prodigies, *"and they wondered;"* and having come to a knowledge of the greatness of their error and their sin, in worshipping idols, instead of the true God, *"they were troubled, they were moved,"* by true penance; whence, also, *"trembling took hold of them;"* looking at the frightful risk they had so long run of eternal damnation. *"There were pains,"* no small or trifling ones, but smart, severe ones, like *"the pains of a woman in labor;"* which, however, ended in great joy. *"But when she hath brought forth the child, she remembereth no more the anguish, for joy that a man is born into the world."* Thus the sorrow of the penitent terminates in the most inexplicable joy, when the grace of adoption, the seed and the pledge of eternal salvation, is poured into his heart, and then is accomplished, *"With a vehement wind thou shalt break in pieces the ships of Tharsis,"* for the Holy Ghost, inhabiting the soul in process of justification, and inflaming it with the vehement warmth of his charity, *"breaks in pieces the ships of Tharsis;"* the vehicles of pride, luxury, and avarice; for we read in Kings and Paralipomenon, of the ships that hastened to Tharsis with flowing sails, bringing gold and silver from it; the swollen sails are the type of pride; the tossing of the ship, of luxury, and the gold and silver, of avarice.

8. These are the expressions of the children of the Church in rejoicing to know, by experience, what they had heard was promised, the stability of Christ's Church. We have more reason to rejoice thereon, for we have heard Christ say, *"On this rock I will build my Church, and the gates of hell shall not prevail against it;"* and now, after sixteen hundred years, after so many and so grievous persecutions, by pagans and heretics, we see it was impossible for the Church to have failed. The prophet then, speaking in the person of the faithful, says, *"As we have heard"* it foretold by the prophets and by the Apostles, *"so have we seen"* it accomplished in the Church, which is *"the city of the Lord of Hosts,"* whom all created things serve, and is, therefore, *"the Lord of Hosts;"* that is, of armies, *"who is our God."* But what we have seen and heard is, that *"God had founded it for ever,"* so that there is no danger of its ever being destroyed.

9. An admission on the part of God's people, that the great things God did, and still does for his Church, are not to be attributed to their own works or merits, but entirely to his mercy. The stability of thy Church and the other innumerable favors which we heard were promised, and we now see realized, have all come from your hands, and not from ours. We therefore acknowledge it *"in the midst of thy temple;"* publicly before all, that *"we have received your mercy;"* to it we attribute all our happiness.

10. He goes on, in the person of the same people, in praising God for the favors received from him, and as he commenced with, *"Great is the Lord, and exceedingly to be praised,"* he now says, *"According to thy name, so is also thy praise unto the ends of the earth;"* that is to say, the measure of your praise must be coordinate with the greatness of your name. For, as the name of God was made known all over the world, by the great and wonderful things done by God, in the establishment and propagation of his Church; so also is Christ praised through the whole world, even to its very extremities: and he tells us why God will be praised for his justice, *"Thy right hand is full of justice;"* for God's justice in rewarding the good, and punishing the wicked, is justly extolled all over the world. God's hand is said to be *"full of justice,"* not that there is no mercy in his hand, but that there is no place or room for injustice. *"For the Lord is just in all his works,"* Psalm 144.

11. As *"God's right hand is full of justice,"* the prophet exhorts his people to rejoice, knowing as they do, from experience, better than others, how just the Lord is. *"Let mount Sion rejoice;"* that is, his people signified by Mount Sion;

"and the daughters of Juda be glad;" let the women unite therein with them. *"Because of thy judgments;"* looking at the justice with which you protected your friends, and chastised your enemies.

12-13. He now, in the end of the Psalm, exhorts them to build up and fortify the holy city of which he spoke in the second verse. Such a city is not like an ordinary material city, which is at once founded and built: the founding and building of the city intended here, will be going on to the end of the world, and must be built and renewed with living stones, that will need daily to be put in, until the perfect city shall be dedicated on the day of judgment. So the Apostle says, Ephes. 2, *"In whom you are also built together into a habitation of God in the Spirit;"* and in chap. 4, he says, *"And some indeed he gave to be apostles, and some prophets, and others evangelists, and others pastors and teachers; for the perfection of the saints, for the work of the ministry, unto the edification of the body of Christ."* And 1 St. Peter, chap. 2, *"To whom approaching the spiritual stone, rejected indeed by men, but chosen and honored of God; be you also as living stones, built up, a spiritual house."* He, therefore, says, *"Surround Sion, and encompass her."* Surround the holy city with walls, where they are needed. Holy souls are called the walls of a city, for they protect the rest of the people from their enemies; *"Tell ye in his towers;"* announce it publicly from some elevated place, (as we have already said,) the preaching of the Gospel is the instrument to found and build the city. *"Set your hearts on her strength."* Think seriously on the defense of the city, that she may be in no wise exposed to the enemy; *"And distribute her houses;"* after the walls shall have been founded and built, set about the houses; and as a great many must needs be built, *"distribute"* their parts to the various workmen, that the houses may be the more quickly built, and the city be filled and increase; and thus it will come to pass *"that ye may relate it in another generation;"* that is, that by your having so multiplied God's people, posterity may have the knowledge of God himself.

14. This is what is to be told to posterity, that God, who did so many wonders in his holy city Jerusalem, *"He is our God unto eternity."* We will never desert him, nor will he desert us. We will be his people for ever, and *"he shall rule us for evermore."*

PSALM 48

The folly of worldlings who live on in sin, without thinking of death or hell.

1 Hear these things, all ye nations: give ear, all ye inhabitants of the world.
2 All you that are earthborn, and you sons of men: both rich and poor together.
3 My mouth shall speak wisdom: and the meditation of my heart understanding.
4 I will incline my ear to a parable; I will open my proposition on the psaltery.
5 Why shall I fear in the evil day? the iniquity of my heel shall encompass me.

6 They that trust in their own strength, and glory in the multitude of their riches,
7 No brother can redeem, nor shall man redeem: he shall not give to God his ransom,
8 Nor the price of the redemption of his soul: and shall labour for ever,
9 And shall still live unto the end.
10 He shall not see destruction, when he shall see the wise dying: the senseless and the fool shall perish together: And they shall leave their riches to strangers:
11 And their sepulchres shall be their houses for ever. Their dwelling places to all generations: they have called their lands by their names.
12 And man when he was in honour did not understand; he is compared to senseless beasts, and is become like to them.
13 This way of theirs is a stumblingblock to them: and afterwards they shall delight in their mouth.
14 They are laid in hell like sheep: death shall feed upon them. And the just shall have dominion over them in the morning; and their help shall decay in hell from their glory.
15 But God will redeem my soul from the hand of hell, when he shall receive me.
16 Be not thou afraid, when a man shall be made rich, and when the glory of his house shall be increased.
17 For when he shall die he shall take nothing away; nor shall his glory descend with him.
18 For in his lifetime his soul will be blessed: and he will praise thee when thou shalt do well to him.
19 He shall go in to the generations of his fathers: and he shall never see light.
20 Man when he was in honour did not understand: he hath been compared to senseless beasts, and made like to them.

EXPLANATION OF THE PSALM

1-2. This preface to the Psalm is written with a view to arrest the attention of the reader, by informing him that the matter to be treated of concerns all mankind, both present and future. The whole human race is, therefore, summoned to hear it; and as no known place could contain such a multitude, nor could the voice of any speaker reach them, we must only take it for granted that the prophet foresaw that his Psalms would be spread over the world, and to the end of time; and, therefore, that he was warranted in summoning all nations and people to hear him. *"Hear these things, all ye nations,"* because what I have to say concerns you all; *"Give ear, all ye inhabitants of the world,"* an explanation of the preceding sentence, as if he said, Don't hear in a cursory way, in an ordinary way, but take it in carefully, keep it there for future reflection. *"Ye inhabitants of the world"* is an explanation of *"all ye nations,"* which latter expression may lead one to think he referred only to the gentiles, to guard against which he adds, *"All ye inhabitants of the world,"* to show that he addressed Jews as well as gentiles, whether assembled in cities or scattered on hill side and in valleys. Furthermore, to embrace future as well as the present generations, he speaks more generally, saying, *"All you that are earth born and sons of men,"* hear ye all, all you sprung from the earth; for all past, present, and future men have one common mother, earth, one common father, Adam; *"Both rich and poor together,"* to show that what he has to say applies to all, rich and poor, for there shall be no more regard of persons in the assembly now about to be addressed, than there will be on the last day, when we will be all called up for judgment.

3-4. The second part of the preface, in which he seeks to arrest the attention of his audience from two sources, from the dignity of the matter, and the dignity of the teacher. The dignity of the matter arises from its consisting of wisdom and prudence, and the language being plain and simple, but metaphorical and abstruse, such as becomes important subjects, in order that it may not be despised, and that it may not be understood save by the attentive and the intelligent. *"My mouth shall speak wisdom,"* will teach what it is that makes a man wise; *"and the meditation of my heart, understanding;"* what I think of in my heart, when given expression to, will teach what is calculated to make men understand; this being an explanation of the first part of the verse, for, having said at first, *"My mouth shall speak,"* for fear we should suppose his mouth would speak at random, he adds, *"and the meditation of my heart;"* that is to say, my mouth shall utter what my heart shall have seriously reflected on. Having said that he would *"speak wisdom,"* for fear any one may suppose he intended the wisdom of the world, he adds, *"understanding,"* or prudence. He, therefore, gives us to understand that his discourse is about to be on matters full of wisdom and prudence; the former contributing to make man wise in the contemplation of first causes, and the latter prudent in the direction of his path through life. He now comes to the dignity of the teacher, saying, *"I will incline my ear to a parable,"* I will listen to the Spirit speaking to me, and implicitly obey him; and then, *"I will open my proposition on the psaltery,"* the proposition revealed to me and inspired by God. By parable is meant something obscure, that requires attention and study to understand it; such is the force of the word in Hebrew, and the word is applied, in Judges 14, to the riddle proposed by Samson, *"Out of the eater came forth meat, and out of the strong came forth sweetness:"* *"on the psaltery;"* to prepare his audience, he will unite music with his discourse, in order to soothe their minds, that they may apply, with the greater attention, to his most important communications.

5. Now comes the parable, introduced by so elaborate a preface, proposed by the prophet to the whole human race, and explained also by him. The

explanation, one would think, is as mysterious as is the parable, especially to worldlings, but not so to the true servants of God; *"Why shall I fear in the evil day?"* as if he said, what can frighten me on the day of judgment, which is called in Sophonias 1, *"A day of wrath, a day of tribulation and distress, a day of calamity and misery, a day of darkness and obscurity, a day of clouds and whirlwinds, a day of the trumpet and alarm."* In other words, what will make me secure on that dreadful day of judgment, when my final lot, for good or for evil, will be cast? A great question certainly, and intimately affecting all. He explains his own parable, however, by adding at once, *"The iniquity of my heel shall encompass me."* What will terrify me on that day will not be my poverty, for the Judge is incorruptible; will not be my lowness of birth, for he has no regard of persons; the malice of my advocate or witnesses will not harm, because all is known to the Judge; nor will the rank or power of my accusers, because the Judge has no fear of any one; no sort of iniquity will harm me, save and except the *"iniquity of my heel;"* that is, the iniquities of my old age, the iniquity persevered in to the end of my life, which, if found in me on that awful day, *"will encompass me,"* like a mound or a wall, leaving me no possible open for escape, for then there will be no room for penance or for pardon. On the other hand, what will render me secure and fearless on the same evil day, will not be riches, or nobility, the talent of my advocates or the power of my friends, but justice alone; and not every sort of justice, but the justice *"of my heel;"* that is, of the end of any life, whether I may have kept it from my youth, or obtained it by real and sincere penance.

6. The prophet having laid down, that for one to be secure in the evil day he had nothing but sin to fear, now adds, that many who do not understand the matter confide in their own strength, and thus glory in the riches they have acquired with great trouble, thinking there could be no fear of them in the evil day; and he proves that they are utterly mistaken, and that his parable and its explanation is most true. *"They that trust in their own strength,"* they who, relying on their own strength and power, as many of the children of the present day do, and fear not the evil day, consequently *"glory in the multitude of their riches,"* thinking that all things can be overcome and conquered by them. In fact, this world attaches great importance to wealth and riches, so that the wise man truly said, *"All things obey money."* But in the evil day there will be no such thing as money, nor, if there were, would it be of any help or value; and therefore, the prophet adds,

7. He shows how idle is any trust or confidence in money, for *"no brother can redeem,"* however great his riches may be, nobody will be able to redeem his brother by riches on the evil day; and if one's brother cannot do it, can any one else do it? *"He shall not give to God his ransom;"* however rich or opulent he may be, and though he may offer them all in mitigation of God's anger

on the evil day, they will neither avail for himself nor for any one else. For, as the Lord asks in the gospel, *"What will a man give in exchange for his soul?"* for the value of a human soul is beyond all the wealth of the world; and thus the blood of the only begotten of God, as being of infinite value, could alone purchase it; and thus he who, in contempt of this great favor, chooses to remain captive to the evil one, will come to the evil day and *"will not give to God his ransom."*

8-9. *"The price of the redemption of his soul"* is an explanation of the last expression, *"he shall not give to God his ransom,"* a price the Son of God alone could pay; and the meaning of the passage, according to St. Augustine is, he that *"trusted in the multitude of his riches"* will *"labor forever,"* because his labor will be endless; and his life will be short, because it will be to the end, and no longer. Thus they who trust in their riches will not only neglect paying the price of their redemption, but they will labor for all eternity with the rich man in his torments; and they will lead a life of voluptuousness, which alone seems life to them, *"unto the end"* appointed and ordained by God.

10. Having said that the wicked man would so live on to the end of his natural life, he adds, in continuation of it, *"He shall not see destruction when he shall see the wise dying."* He will continue the same career to his very old age, even though he may see the just and the wise cut off, and hurried away prematurely. For it often happens, that God gives length of days to those who are not to enjoy eternal life; as we see in the case of Lazarus, who died before the rich glutton. But, however prolonged the life of the wicked may be, it will ultimately have an end; and then is realized, *"The senseless and the fool shall perish together;"* and, thus, the meaning of the verse is, *"He shall not see destruction;"* though the fool, who trusts in his riches, may see many dying before him, he, too will ultimately come to the end of his natural life. St. Basil says the difference between the senseless and the fool is, that the former lacks sense to go through the ordinary business of life; while the latter, by no means lacks such worldly sense, but is sadly deficient as regards spirituals. *"And they shall leave their riches to strangers."* He called those who trust in their riches *"senseless and fools,"* as did our Lord in the Gospel, when he said to a certain rich man, *"Thou fool, this night do they require thy soul of thee, whose shall those things be, which thou hast provided?"* He, therefore, proves them to be real fools, because they know not how to make use of their riches, and they leave them to people of whom they have no knowledge whatever. *"The senseless and the fool shall perish,"* and, to heighten their folly, their riches will pass to strangers. St. Augustine justly observes, that even though the riches may pass to children or to nephews, they too, may be often called strangers, for they readily forget those gone before them; and even though they should chance not to forget them, they cannot help or assist them; like the rich man in hell, who had five brothers on earth, and could get no help from either of them, and thus, may be looked upon as quite strangers to him; the only one that could have helped was a stranger, Lazarus, who might have been a real friend and neighbor to him, had he been shown any mercy at the hands of the glutton.

11. They left their riches to others, keeping nothing for themselves but the narrow grave in which they are to lie forever. This will be *"their dwelling place to all generations;"* to the end of the world. *"They have called their lands by their names."* No trace of them but the name; foolish mortals endeavor to perpetuate their memory, by calling their estates, or their houses, or books written by them, or by compelling others to keep up their name; thus, hoping to enroll their names in the records of this world, as they cannot expect it in the next.

12. Digressing from the senseless and from those who put their trust in riches, the prophet reproves the whole human race, saying, *"And man when he was in honor did not understand;"* man, in preference to all other animals, honored by God with intelligence, reason, and free will, stamped with his own image, gifted with an immortal soul, and dominion over all things on earth; did not understand the value of all this, but *"is compared to senseless beasts,"* without understanding; *"and is become like to them;"* like cattle, is solely bent on the present, regardless of the future; a slave to the beastly passions, whose master he should be; regardless of solid and everlasting happiness; seeking for empty and transient pleasures, which he should have thoroughly despised, in the hope of thereby securing everlasting happiness.

13. He goes on in explaining, or rather deploring the misery of mankind. *"This way of theirs is a stumbling block to them."* The brutish life they lead, their habits, manners, and customs, are a *"stumbling block"* to them, it trips them up, utterly ruins them; and, to cap the climax of their misery, *"they shall delight in their mouth;"* they praise and applaud themselves and each other, for the crimes they commit, than which no folly can be greater.

14. Having said that men become like senseless beasts, by reason of their sins, he now states that theirs would be similar to such beasts, indicating the number, as well as the helplessness of those, who, after death, will be consigned to hell. Sheep are driven in flocks into the fold, and are brought to the slaughter house, without being capable of offering any resistance. Thus, God has less trouble in consigning the wicked, however rich and powerful they may have been, to everlasting punishment in hell, than would a shepherd to shut in his sheep, or hand them over to the butcher. *"Death shall feed upon them;"* death, like a wolf, will seize upon the wicked and consume them, as the wolf would so many sheep. *"And the just shall have no dominion over them in the morning."* He continues a relation of the misery of

the wicked consigned to hell, and says, that *"in the morning,"* that is, in the beginning of the new world, that will date from the general resurrection, the wicked will be entirely subject to the just, for the just will then sit in judgment on them, will lord it over them forever, and the wicked will have nothing whatever on that day to support them against the just, for all *"their help,"* which lay in their strength and power, *"shall decay,"* be of no avail in hell, *"from their glory,"* after all the glory they had in this world, while they dwelt in its noble palaces.

15. He now tells us what is to become of the just, among whom he numbers himself. Such, he says, will be the lot of the wicked, but the reverse will be the case with me, and with all like me, for *"God will redeem my soul from the hand of hell,"* will save me from hell, when he shall come and receive me. He seems here to allude to the redemption through Christ, and his descent into hell, for it was then truly, when he paid the price of the redemption of the just with his blood, and released them from the hand of hell, that he may be said to have taken those souls to himself.

16-17. He concludes, by exhorting the just, however poor, and those oppressed by the rich, not to fear them, as their term of this life will be very brief. *"Be thou not afraid when a man shall be made rich;"* do not dread his power, or let it make you forget the everlasting power of your omnipotent Creator; and do not fear when you see your enemy, not only grown into riches, but even *"the glory of his house increased"* by a numerous family, and wealthy relatives. *"For when he shall die,"* as die he must, be he rich or be he poor, *"he shall take nothing away,"* he will carry with him none of the goods of this world, *"nor shall his glory descend with him;"* neither his friends nor relations, nor his servants, much less his honors and dignities, will accompany him in his journey down. Thus, riches and the glory of the wicked are transient, their poverty and confusion are everlasting.

18. He assigns a reason why the wicked will not have the glory in hell that they had here. As they were wont to praise God only when he showered his favors on them, so God confines such favors to this world. *"For in his lifetime his soul will be blessed."* The blessing conferred on the wicked man will be confined to the term of this life, for it is only during this life that God will confer temporal favors on him, or that man will praise, or rather flatter him. *"And he will praise thee;"* on the other hand, the wicked man will praise and extol God: *"When thou shalt do well to him;"* when the world shall thrive and prosper with him; but if any reverse should take place, he will blaspheme God, not like the just man, saying, *"I will bless the Lord at all times, his praise shall be for ever in my mouth;"* or like Job, saying, *"The Lord hath given, and the Lord hath taken away, blessed be the name of the Lord."*

19. The wicked man is often favored by God with innumerable blessings in this world, either to reward him for some good that is in him, or to soften his heart, and bring him to repentance; but, failing in that, *"he shall go into the generations of his fathers,"* that as well as he shared in their crimes, he too may share in their punishment; *"and he shall never see light:"* having taken too much pleasure in the light of honors, and the glories of this world, and neglected looking for the light of the glories of heaven, by a just judgment he shall be consigned to eternal darkness.

20. A repetition of verse 12, to show that want of sense is the principal cause of man's misery, and that the majority of mankind would be shut out from eternal light, and consigned to darkness, for not having followed the light of reason; as also to account for so few comprehending the parable contained in this Psalm, such ignorance arising from the fact, sin caused *"man to be compared to senseless beasts, and made like to them."*

PSALM 49

The coming of Christ: who prefers virtue and inward purity before the blood victims.

1 The God of gods, the Lord hath spoken: and he hath called the earth. From the rising of the sun, to the going down thereof:
2 Out of Sion the loveliness of his beauty.
3 God shall come manifestly: our God shall come, and shall not keep silence. A fire shall burn before him: and a mighty tempest shall be round about him.
4 He shall call heaven from above, and the earth, to judge his people.
5 Gather ye together his saints to him: who set his covenant before sacrifices.
6 And the heavens shall declare his justice: for God is judge.
7 Hear, O my people, and I will speak: O Israel, and I will testify to thee: I am God, thy God.
8 I will not reprove thee for thy sacrifices: and thy burnt offerings are always in my sight.
9 I will not take calves out of thy house: nor he goats out of thy flocks.
10 For all the beasts of the woods are mine: the cattle on the hills, and the oxen.
11 I know all the fowls of the air: and with me is the beauty of the field.
12 If I should be hungry, I would not tell thee: for the world is mine, and the fulness thereof.
13 Shall I eat the flesh of bullocks? or shall I drink the blood of goats?
14 Offer to God the sacrifice of praise: and pay thy vows to the most High.
15 And call upon me in the day of trouble: I will deliver thee, and thou shalt glorify me.
16 But to the sinner God hath said: Why dost thou declare my justices, and take my covenant in thy mouth?

17 Seeing thou hast hated discipline: and hast cast my words behind thee.
18 If thou didst see a thief thou didst run with him: and with adulterers thou hast been a partaker.
19 Thy mouth hath abounded with evil, and thy tongue framed deceits.
20 Sitting thou didst speak against thy brother, and didst lay a scandal against thy mother's son:
21 These things hast thou done, and I was silent. Thou thoughtest unjustly that I should be like to thee: but I will reprove thee, and set before thy face.
22 Understand these things, you that forget God; lest he snatch you away, and there be none to deliver you.
23 The sacrifice of praise shall glorify me: and there is the way by which I will shew him the salvation of God.

EXPLANATION OF THE PSALM

1. Beginning with the first coming of the Messiah, he says that God, who was wont to speak through the prophets, speaks now himself, and addresses not only the Jews, but the *"whole earth,"* meaning its inhabitants, as he really did through his Apostles; for *"Their sound hath gone forth into all the earth."* He is called here *"Lord of Lords,"* to give us to understand that Christ is truly God, the Son of the true God, and enjoying the same divinity as his Father. There can be only one true God in reality, though many get the title, for instance, the gods of the gentiles, who are no more than demons; Angels and sanctified persons, by reason of their adoption, sometimes get the title; and the judges and rulers of the world, by way of comparison, sometimes are so called; but all these are subject to the one true and only God, who, therefore, is here styled *"God of gods."* He, therefore, says, Our Lord Christ, who is *"the God of gods"* on his arrival in this world, *"hath spoken"* the words of his Gospel; *"and he hath called the earth,"* in inviting all to hear him, as he did when he said, *"Come to me, all you who labor and are heavily laden, and I will refresh you." "From the rising of the sun to the going down thereof."* To give us to understand that by the word *"earth"* he did not mean Palestine, or any part of it, but the whole world.

2. He tells us in what place God began to speak. In Sion, as it was foretold by Isaias 2, *"For the law shall come forth from Sion, and the word of the law from Jerusalem;"* and, in the last chapter of Luke, *"It behooved Christ to suffer, and to rise again from the dead on the third day. And that penance and the remission of sins should be preached in his name among all nations, beginning at Jerusalem." "From the rising of the sun to the going down thereof, he hath called the earth;"* all created beings endowed with reason that inhabit the globe, *"Out of Sion, the loveliness of his beauty."* When the Lord spoke, he spoke from Sion, a city of rare and surpassing beauty, and so it was; it is styled in the Lamentations as being *"of perfect beauty,"* a most noble, ancient, and populous city, the seat of government, and of the high priest, having in it the tabernacle, the ark of the covenant, and many other accessories worthy of the capital of the kingdom and of religion; whence it was always considered the type of the divine and heavenly city.

3. He now foretells the second coming of Christ. The God of gods came and called the earth; but he came incognito, in the form of a servant, in human shape, in all his meekness, to redeem us by his death and passion; but he will secondly, *"Come manifestly,"* in all his pomp and power; not in an obscure manger, but in the clouds of heaven; not nailed to a cross between thieves, but on the judgment seat amidst his Angels. And he will not only *"come manifestly,"* but when he comes, *"he will not keep silence,"* as he did in his first coming, when, *"like a lamb led to the slaughter, he did not open his mouth,"* which silence he still observes, however cognizant he is of our sins; but he will come with a trumpet and with a dreadful noise, as we read in Matthew, *"He will send his Angels with the trumpet and a loud voice, and they will gather together his elect from the four winds;"* and, in 1 Thess 4, *"For the Lord himself shall come down from heaven with commandment, and with the voice of the Archangel, and with the trumpet of God;"* and, in 1 Cor 15, *"At the last trumpet, for the trumpet shall sound."* A fire shall burn before him: and a mighty tempest shall be round about him. *"Alluding to the general conflagration of the world; that is, of everything in it, such as cities, gardens, vineyards, palaces, all animals and perishable things; of which St. Peter says, in his Epistle,"* But the day of the Lord shall come as a thief, in which the heavens shall pass away with great violence, and the elements shall be dissolved with heat, and the earth and the works that are in it shall be burnt up. The meaning, then, is, *"A fire shall burn before him,"* to destroy everything on the face of the earth, and a *"mighty tempest shall be round about him;"* the whole world in confusion, land, sea, the air, the heavens, *"men withering away for fear and expectation of what shall come upon the whole world."*

4. There will be an immense crowd present, such will be the spectacle to witness. *"He shall call heaven from above;"* all the Angels will be summoned, as we read in Matthew, *"When the Son of man shall come in his majesty, and all his Angels with him."* He will summon the earth too: all from Adam down will appear there; and this great assembly will be called *"to judge his people;"* to sit in judgment on them, and to separate the good from the bad; as we read in Matthew, *"So shall it be at the end of the world, the Angels shall go out and shall separate the wicked from among the just;"* and again, *"He will separate the sheep from the goats;"* that is to say, the celestial Judge will have as little trouble on that day, in selecting the just from out of the wicked, as would the shepherd, in distinguishing the sheep from the goats in his flock.

5. Though all men will be brought up for judgment, it concerns the faithful especially, *"For they who do not believe are already judged,"* John 3; hence, in Matthew, the faithful are specially introduced for judgment; and question is made, not on their faith, but on their works. By *"the saints,"* then, we are to understand the faithful members of God's Church whether enrolled therein by circumcision or by baptism. Thus David says, in Psalm 85. *"Preserve my soul for I am holy;"* and the Apostle, in his Epistles, calls all Christians *"holy."* He then addresses the Angels, and says, *"Gather ye together his saints to him."* Bring up for judgment his own people who have been sanctified by him through the sacraments, and that such will be done through the Angels is clear from the passage in Matthew, *"The Angels shall go out, and shall separate the wicked from among the just;"* and further on, *"He shall send his Angels with a trumpet, and they shall gather together his elect."* *"Who set his covenant before sacrifices,"* explains who the saints are, they being those *"who set his covenant before sacrifices;"* which is expressed more clearly in the Hebrew, and means, they who have engaged themselves as God's people, which engagement has been ratified by sacrificing to him, in which, principally, his worship consists. The meaning of the passage, then, is, that God's saints would be summoned to judgment; that is, those who enter into an engagement with God to honor and serve him, and thus merit his blessing and protection.

6. When all shall have been assembled for judgment, then at length *"The heavens shall declare his justice."* Sentence will be passed from heaven on the good and on the bad, from which all will see how great is the justice of God, a thing we don't often see when he permits the just to be oppressed by the wicked; and all heaven and all its celestial spirits will confirm his justice, exclaiming, *"Thou art just, O Lord, and righteous is thy judgment."* Nor can the celestials be deceived, *"For God is judge,"* in whom injustice can have no place.

7. The prophet now turns to the instruction of the people, and tells on what subject they are to be judged, of what they are to account for in judgment, so that every one may prepare himself. To give greater weight to his admonitions he introduces God himself, speaking in a most paternal and friendly manner. *"Hear, O my people, and I will speak."* If you don't hear me, I will not speak to you, but I will speak to others who have ears to hear. For the Lord, most justly, in Matthew 11, and other places, often says, *"He that hath ears to hear, let him hear;"* for, as the ears of a deaf person are purely ornamental, and not useful; so those endowed with reason, and who will not apply it to understand anything concerning God, have the ears of their minds as if they had no such things at all. We must, then, when we wish God to speak to us, attentively reflect and consider on what he is saying. This he explains more clearly by adding, *"O Israel! and I will testify to thee."* Hear, Israel, my

people, and I will clearly show you what most concerns you. By Israel we are not to understand that people exclusively; the whole Christian world, who imitate the faith of Israel, are here comprehended; nay more, they are, perhaps, more specially alluded to; as the Apostle, Rom. 9, says, *"For all are not Israelites that are of Israel; neither are all they who are the seed of Abraham, children; but they that are the children of the promise, are counted for the seed."* *"I am God, thy God;"* a reason why we should hear him who speaks, he being no less than God, and peculiarly our God; from which we have the strongest assurance that he knows how, and wishes, to give us the most useful instruction. If he be God, he knows every thing; if he be our God, he loves us; and, therefore, wishes to teach us what is most useful.

8. God does not look for sacrifices, as if he wanted them, or by reason of their being very agreeable to him; he rather looks for interior virtue, consisting in faith, hope, love, and obedience; with such adjuncts sacrifices are acceptable; without them, quite odious and hateful. So Samuel, 1 Kings 15, says, *"Doth the Lord desire holocausts and victims, and not rather that the voice of the Lord should be obeyed?"* and Isaias, chap. 1, *"To what purpose do you offer me the multitude of your victims, saith the Lord?"* So our Lord himself speaks, Mat 23, *"Woe to you, Scribes and Pharisees, hypocrites: who pay title of mint, and anise, and cummin; and have let alone the weightier things of the law: judgment, and mercy, and faith."* And finally, David's own language, in Psalm 1, where he says *"For if thou hadst desired sacrifice I would indeed have given it; with burnt offerings thou wilt not be delighted. A sacrifice to God is an afflicted spirit, a contrite and humble heart, O God thou wilt not despise."* The meaning, then, is, *"I will not reprove thee for thy sacrifices."* I will not accuse you nor condemn you for the fewness of them, for they are sufficiently numerous, as *"thy burnt offerings are always in my sight,"* always to be found on my altar.

9-11. The second reason why God does not require sacrifice from us is, that he is himself Lord of everything, and if he wants sheep, or cattle, or birds, or any thing else, he can easily have them, without any trouble, having an intimate knowledge of them all, being their sovereign Master. *"I will not take calves out of thy house,"* because I have all such things of my own: beasts, birds, oxen; and not only beasts, birds, etc., but the *"beauty of the field;"* everything that grows; the fruits of the earth, that render the field beautiful, are mine.

12-13. A third reason assigned for God's requiring nothing from us, either for his necessities or his convenience, and that is, because he neither hungers nor thirsts; he is, consequently, subject to neither heat nor cold, nor does he need anything; and were he to need anything, his wants would be at once supplied, he being the Lord of all things. *"If I should hunger, I would not tell thee,"* to provide food for me, *"for the world is mine, and the fullness thereof.*" Being a spiritual and immortal substance, I require no solid food, and, therefore, I need no *"flesh of bullocks, or blood of goats."*

14-15. Having established the insufficiency of sacrifice, unaccompanied by interior submission and love, he now teaches us, that it is by such interior acts of virtue that God is most pleased, and that it is through such acts we can be saved in the last judgment. We have here to notice the difference between the praise of God, and the *"sacrifice of praise;"* we may praise God with our lips alone, but the *"sacrifice of praise"* can only be offered by those, who, on the altar of their hearts, light up the fire of charity, on which to pour the incense of praise to God; that is to say, by those who believe, and understand, to a certain extent, that God is supremely good, and after knowing and believing so much of him, love him with their whole heart, admire and praise him, as being most beautiful, most perfect, and most wise. The sacrifice of praise, then, is the mark and the consequence of our knowledge and love, and as the blessed in heaven always see and love God, of them is said, in Psalm 83, *"Blessed are they that dwell in thy house, O Lord; they shall praise thee for ever and ever."* He, therefore, says, *"Offer to God the sacrifice of praise,"* not with your bare lips, it must proceed from a thorough knowledge and love of God, *"and pay thy vows to the Most High."* When you shall have praised God, as God, look upon him in the light of being the source and spring of every blessing you enjoy; look upon your own nothingness, thank him, and pay him that tribute of obedience, the principal one among *"the vows"* due to him, that you promised, when you became one of his people and family; and that is more pleasing to him than any sacrifice whatever, *"For obedience is better than sacrifice,"* 1 Kings 15 *"And call upon me in the day of trouble;"* as you were wont, in your prosperity, to acknowledge me as the source of every blessing, so in your troubles you should fly to me, and put your whole hope and trust in me, because *"I will deliver thee"* from every trouble; and you, in return, *"shall glorify me"* by the sacrifice of praise and thanksgiving.

16. Having instructed the just, he now proceeds to take the wicked to task. *"To the sinner, God hath said:"* caused me to admonish him thus. *"Why dost thou declare my justices, and take my covenant in thy mouth?"* Why do you profess to know my law, to recount its precepts, to profess to belong to my family, to be a child of Abraham, when you neither observe my law, nor keep my compact, nor tread in Abraham's footsteps?

17. He first alludes to their secret sins, then to their public sins. *"Thou hast hated discipline,"* set your mind entirely against the spirit of the law of God, *"and cast my words behind thee;"* forgot and despised them as completely as if you had thrown them over your shoulder.

18. Hatred and forgetfulness of the law of God lead at once to sins of deed, such as theft and adultery; and as these two sins, springing from avarice and luxury, are most common, the prophet makes special mention of them. *"If thou didst see a thief, thou didst run with him;"* and observe, he does not say, you too stole, or you too committed adultery, but not content with transgressing, you did it openly, ran with the thief, and was a partaker with the other, thereby boasting and glorying in your wickedness.

19. He now passes to sins by word, saying, from your mouth, as if from a spring, was poured forth all manner of foul language, lies, falsehoods, and deceits.

20. To aggravate those sins by word, they were spoken, not against a stranger, but against his own brethren, and it was done, not from a sudden impulse of anger, but deliberately. *"Sitting,"* charges were invented, and calumnies spread abroad against the brother born of the same womb.

21. God was looking on all the while, bearing with him, unwilling to chastise him, in the hope of his conversion. Thus, God sees and is silent, as if he did not see at all; but soon will come the day of judgment, when, as it is expressed in the third verse of this Psalm, *"God will come manifestly, and shall not keep silence,"* as he here declares, for he says, *"Thou thought unjustly, that I shall be like to thee, but I will reprove thee, and set before thy face."* Unfortunate sinners, who have no fear of God, think their sins are not displeasing to him, but on the day of judgment they will understand what is said here, *"Thou thought unjustly, that I shall be like to thee;"* that I was wicked myself, and a friend of the wicked; but such is not the case, because *"I will reprove thee"* on the day of judgment, *"and set before thy face;"* make you to see the number and enormity of your sins, so that you cannot possibly gainsay the justice of your punishment.

22. An exhortation, on the part of the prophet, to those sinners who forget that God is a just and Almighty Judge, to reflect seriously on what has been just said, *"Lest he snatch you away,"* when they are thinking least of it, hurry them to judgment, and damn them as they deserve, *"And there be none to deliver you."*

23. God now concludes, by laying down, that the way of salvation lies entirely in the one sacrifice of praise, so that those who daily offer it will be saved on the day of judgment, and those who neglect it will be condemned amongst the reprobate. *"The sacrifice of praise shall glorify me;"* whosoever will offer me such sacrifice will be acceptable in my sight, I will feel myself honored by him; *"and there,"* in that sacrifice, *"is the way"* to salvation, for by that route you will arrive at the place where *"I will show him the salvation of God,"* divine, full, and perfect salvation. How does it happen, though, that the essence of salvation is made to depend on the *"Sacrifice of praise?"* St.

Augustine answers, because nobody truly praises God, unless he be really pious. The impious may praise him with their lips, but not by their lives; and thus their praise is idle, while their lives are in opposition to it. The *"Sacrifice of praise,"* too, as we have already observed, does not mean, simply, praise, but such praise as proceeds from the altar of our hearts, on which is burning the fire of love. The *"Sacrifice of praise,"* then, of necessity includes love; and it is, therefore, no wonder that it should be the sum of our salvation.

PSALM 50

The repentance and confession of David after his sin. The fourth penitential psalm.

1 Have mercy on me, O God, according to thy great mercy. And according to the multitude of thy tender mercies blot out my iniquity.
2 Wash me yet more from my iniquity, and cleanse me from my sin.
3 For I know my iniquity, and my sin is always before me.
4 To thee only have I sinned, and have done evil before thee: that thou mayst be justified in thy words and mayst overcome when thou art judged.
5 For behold I was conceived in iniquities; and in sins did my mother conceive me.
6 For behold thou hast loved truth: the uncertain and hidden things of thy wisdom thou hast made manifest to me.
7 Thou shalt sprinkle me with hyssop, and I shall be cleansed: thou shalt wash me, and I shall be made whiter than snow.
8 To my hearing thou shalt give joy and gladness: and the bones that have been humbled shall rejoice.
9 Turn away thy face from my sins, and blot out all my iniquities.
10 Create a clean heart in me, O God: and renew a right spirit within my bowels.
11 Cast me not away from thy face; and take not thy holy spirit from me.
12 Restore unto me the joy of thy salvation, and strengthen me with a perfect spirit.
13 I will teach the unjust thy ways: and the wicked shall be converted to thee.
14 Deliver me from blood, O God, thou God of my salvation: and my tongue shall extol thy justice.
15 Lord, thou wilt open my lips: and my mouth shall declare thy praise.
16 For if thou hadst desired sacrifice, I would indeed have given it: with burnt offerings thou wilt not be delighted.
17 A sacrifice to God is an afflicted spirit: a contrite and humbled heart, O God, thou wilt not despise.
18 Deal favourably, O Lord, in thy good will with Sion; that the walls of Jerusalem may be built up.
19 Then shalt thou accept the sacrifice of justice, oblations and whole burnt

offerings: then shall they lay calves upon thy altar.

EXPLANATION OF THE PSALM

1. The prophet begins with a prayer, asking forgiveness of his sins assigns his first reason for asking forgiveness, thinks he can move God to forgive; and afterwards assigns other reasons. *"Have mercy on me, O Lord."* In Psalms 111 and 123, David acknowledges and declares himself miserable, on account of the sin he committed, notwithstanding the abundance of the gifts of nature he was then enjoying; as, on the contrary, he declares those only happy *"who fear the Lord,"* and not those who abound in honors and riches; from which we may learn how erroneously the children of this world judge of misery and happiness. *"According to thy great mercy."* I dare to ask your mercy because I am a wretch, for mercy looks upon misery to remove it. He calls it *"great mercy,"* because sin is a great misfortune; and because the mercy, through which God gives us temporal blessings, is but a trifling mercy compared to the forgiveness of sin; for God often confers temporal favors on his enemies, even on those he will condemn on the last day; but the grace of the remission of sin he only gives to those whom he intends to adopt as his children, and the heirs of his kingdom. David, then, not content with the small amount of mercy, through which he had got a noble kingdom, immense wealth, a large family, and dominion over his enemies, and the like, asks for the *"great mercy,"* which he knew consisted in the forgiveness of his sins, and the restoration of grace. *"And, according to the multitude of thy tender mercies, blot out my iniquity."* He repeats and explains the same expression; *"Blot out my iniquity"* being a mere repetition of *"Have mercy on me, O God;"* and, *"According to the multitude of thy tender mercies"* being a repetition of *"According to thy great mercy;"* inverting the order of the expressions, and thereby giving a certain elegance to the verse. Those words, then, *"According to the multitude of thy tender mercies,"* give us to understand how unbounded is the mercy shown by God to his beloved children; for the Hebrew word, strictly speaking, signifies the tender love of a father, which the Scripture is wont to express by, *"The bowels of mercy;"* and the Church, in the Collect of the eleventh Sunday after Pentecost, thus expresses, *"O God, who, through the excess of your love, go farther than even the merits and even the prayers of your supplicants."* For, in fact, so great is the love of God for us, that he not only grants much more than we deserve, but even more than we dare to hope for. He shows that in the parable of the prodigal son. The father not only forgives the penitent but he runs to meet him, embraces him, kisses him, orders the most valuable clothes, and a precious ring for him, kills the fatted calf in compliment to him; and, finally, shows more marks of favor and love to him, after squandering all his property, than if he had returned after having achieved a signal victory over his enemies. *"Blot out my iniquity,"* refers to the sin and the stain left after it. David knew that he had not only incurred the punishment of everlasting death by his sin, but that it also left a stain on his soul that rendered it dark, deformed, and hateful to God; and the expression, *"Blot out,"* refers to both. When a debt is forgiven, the deeds are said to be cancelled, or blotted out; and stains are said to be blotted, when the thing stained is washed and purified. David, then, begs of God not to deal with him in the rigor of his justice, but with the mercy of a father, to forgive the sin, and wash away the stain left by it, by restoring the brightness of his grace.

2. Though the sin may be forgiven, and grace restored, there still remain in man the bad habits of vice, and the very concupiscence of the flesh, that make a man infirm and weak, just as he would be after having recovered from a heavy fit of sickness. The bad habits are gradually corrected by the practice of acts of virtue; but concupiscence, though it can be lessened, ordinarily speaking, is totally eradicated by death alone. And though our own earnest desires and endeavors go a great way to root out our vices, and to diminish our concupiscence, the grace of God, without which we can do nothing, with which we can do everything, is the principal agent therein. David was fully aware of all this, having written in Psalm 102, *"Bless the Lord, O my soul, and never forget all he hath done for thee, who forgiveth all thy iniquities, who healeth all thy diseases."* And, in this passage, after he had asked for the forgiveness of his sins, and, through Nathan the prophet, got this answer, *"The Lord also hath taken away thy sin, thou shalt not die,"* again begs to be washed and cleansed, to be more and more justified by additional graces; that, by the victory over his bad habits, and the repression of his concupiscence, his soul may become more fair and beautiful, and better able to resist temptation. He, therefore, says, *"Wash me yet more from my iniquity, and cleanse me from my sin;"* that is to say I confidently hope my sins are blotted out through your grace, and that my soul is washed and cleansed from the filth and stains left upon it by the action of sin; but I ask, beg, and desire to be washed again and again by a fresh infusion of grace, that my soul may thereby be both purified and strengthened. A simpler explanation would be, to make this second petition turn on the magnitude of his sins; as if he said, Had my sin been an ordinary one, a simple ablution would suffice; but being a great, grievous, enormous one, I need additional ablutions to wash away every vestige of my sins.

3. The second reason assigned by him for obtaining forgiveness is, that he admits it, confesses it, and punishes himself by keeping it constantly before him. Pardon me, *"For I know my iniquity;"* I neither excuse nor deny it, I freely acknowledge it, and I am constantly grieved in thinking of it; for it

"is always before me," staring me in the face, and piercing me like a javelin. An example for us in the recitation of the penitential Psalms. We should be able truly to say, *"My sin is always before me."* This we can do by keeping up a recollection of the sins that, through God's goodness, have been forgiven, for thus we will be constantly reminded of our great ingratitude to so great a benefactor.

4. The third reason for his asking pardon of God is, that he has no other judge to fear. *"To thee,"* not against thee, he says, *"have I sinned."* He had sinned against Urias, whose death he caused. He had sinned against Bethsabee, with whom he had committed adultery, and against the people, whom he scandalized; yet he says, *"To thee only have I sinned;"* as being the only judge before whom he could be convicted. There was no one else to sit in judgment on him, and if there were even, he could not be convicted, for want of evidence; for, though common report condemned him, there was no judicial proof of his guilt; still, he stood convicted before God, for his own conscience bore testimony against him before that God who searches the reins and heart; and he, therefore, candidly avows, *"And I have done evil before thee;"* for, though he did the evil in private, in the darkness of a closed chamber, he could not evade the all seeing eye of his Maker. *"That thou mayest be justified in thy words."* I confess myself a sinner, thereby acknowledging the justice of the words you pronounced upon me by Nathan the prophet, when he accused me of murder and adultery. *"And mayest overcome when thou art judged,"* a repetition of the same idea; as if he said, There is no use in denying my crimes, for, if put upon my trial, I must acknowledge them; you will gain the cause, I will be cast therein.

5. The fourth reason is derived from our first origin, and the transmission of original sin, making us infirm and prone to sin; and, thereby, the more worthy of mercy and pity. The iniquities and the sins alluded to could not have been the sins of David's parents, for his parents were pious and devout people; he alludes to the sins of our first parents, as is evident from the Hebrew.

6. The fifth reason, derived from the truth and simplicity of heart for which David was remarkable; God, being truth himself, has a special regard for men of truth, and, by reason of it, revealed many of the future mysteries to David, for there is scarcely a mystery appertaining to Christ or the Church, that he did not foresee and foretell in the Psalms. He, therefore, draws upon his own truthfulness now, to which he still adheres in confessing his sins, and by reason of such adherence to it he asks God to forgive him. *"Behold, thou hast loved truth;"* you have loved truth and sincerity of heart, as well as you hate duplicity and wickedness. *"The uncertain and hidden things of thy wisdom thou hast made known to me"* Loving truth as you do, and having formed me most truthful, you have rewarded me by revealing to me the

most secret, profound mysteries, proofs of your infinite wisdom. The word *"uncertain"* does not imply any of the divine mysteries to be uncertain, in the sense that there is a probability of their not coming to pass; but they are *"uncertain"* to us, in regard of the time of their fulfillment; thus, we say the day of judgments or of our death, is uncertain, though nobody questions the certainty of both one and the other.

7. He now discloses one of the: *"Uncertain and hidden things of his wisdom,"* namely, that in the new dispensation men would be sprinkled with water in baptism, and thereby perfectly justified, alluding to the ceremony described in Numbers 19, where three things are said to be necessary to expiate uncleanness: the ashes of a red heifer, burnt as a holocaust; water mixed with the ashes; and hyssop to sprinkle it. The ashes signified the death of Christ; the water, baptism; and hyssop, faith; for hyssop is a stunted plant, generally growing on a rock. In the typical expiation, the water purified, but by virtue of the ashes of the slain heifer, and the aspersion with the hyssop; thus, the baptismal water purifies, by the application of the death and merits of Christ, through faith. It is, then, to the real, as well as the figurative expiation, that David refers when he says, *"Thou shalt sprinkle me with hyssop, and I shall be cleansed;"* for he asks for the cleansing which he knew was only emblematic, that by hyssop, which, however, he knew would be converted into the reality of the institution of baptism. To show God was the primary author of such purification, he does not say, let the priest sprinkle me, but, sprinkle me yourself; to show the perfection of the thorough cleansing to be had in baptism, destroying sin most effectually, and giving additional grace.

8. The effect and sign of perfect justification is, when *"The Spirit himself giveth testimony to our spirit, that we are the sons of God."* The prophet having known this by experience, asks for it again, saying, *"To my hearing thou shalt give joy and gladness."* When you shall have perfectly cleansed me, you will, moreover, light up my interior with that spiritual joy and gladness that will make me feel my sins have been forgiven, and that I have been restored to your favor, and then *"The bones that have been humbled shall rejoice;"* *"the bones"* mean the powers of his mind, not the limbs of his body; for he says, immediately after, *"A contrite and humbled heart, O Lord, thou wilt not despise;"* and the meaning is, my mind, now dejected and weighed down, will then recover its strength, and rejoice when we learn that the fear that saddens and humbles us comes from God, and that it disposes the soul to the spirit of love that justifieth.

9. He now prays for the immediate accomplishment of what he predicted. He said previously, *"Thou shalt sprinkle me with hyssop, and I shall be cleansed;"* and also, *"To my hearing thou shalt give joy and gladness;"* and he

now asks for them at once; first, for the remission of his sins; *"Turn away thy face from my sins."* Do not look on my sins with a view to punish me, as Tobias said, *"Lord, do not remember my sins."* Such expressions are purely figurative, for God, from whom nothing can be hidden, can neither turn away his face from, nor forget, our sins; but he is said *"to turn away his face"* or to forget, when he acts as those do, who do not reflect or remember, and such people do not punish; *"And blot out all my iniquities;"* to make the pardon a lasting, permanent one, for he that turns his face away from a piece of writing, may look on it again and consider the matter of it, but when the writing is destroyed, *"blotted out,"* it can no longer be read, a proof that when sin is forgiven it is thoroughly forgiven.

10. This verse corresponds with, *"Thou shalt wash me and I shall be made whiter than snow;"* for he asks not only for a remission of his sins, but for such an infusion of grace as may renew his soul, and make it bright and beautiful, a petition, telling against those who make justification to consist solely in the remission of sin. We are not to take it that a new heart is asked for, when he says, *"Create;"* the expression merely expresses a wish that his heart may be thoroughly cleansed and purified, and made, as it were, a new heart. The meaning, then, is, create cleanness in my heart; and there is a certain point in the word *"Create,"* to imply that God finds nothing in the heart of a sinner, whence to form cleanness in it; but that entirely, through his own great mercy, without any merit on their part, it is, that he justifies men; for, even though sinners are disposed to justification by faith and penance, still, faith, penance, and all such things are purely the gift of God. *"And renew a right spirit within my bowels,"* an explanation of the preceding sentence, for, to let us see that the meaning of *"Creating a new heart,"* is nothing more than creating cleanness in the heart, he now adds, *"And renew a right spirit in my bowels,"* instead of renew my bowels. The bowels mean, the interior affections of the soul; that is, the will, which was just now called the heart; a *"right spirit"* means, a right affection, in other words, charity; for by avarice or cupidity the affections of the heart become distorted, turn to creatures, especially to self, while charity or love directs them to the things above, especially to God. *"A right spirit,"* then, *"is renewed in the bowels;"* when the heart having been cleansed by grace, an ardent love of God, that had been displaced by sin, is renewed in the soul.

11. He now, mindful of his frailty, asks for the grace of perseverance; lest, being too much raised up by grace, he may happen to fall again. The expression, *"Cast me not away from thy face,"* is used in the Scripture to designate those who are cast off by God, without any hope or chance of reconciliation. Thus, in 1 Kings 15, the Lord said to Samuel, *"How long wilt thou mourn over Saul whom I have rejected?"* and 2 Kings 7, *"But my mercy I will not take*

away from him as I took it from Saul, whom I removed from before my face;" and in 4 Kings 24, *"For the Lord was angry against Jerusalem, and against Juda, till he cast them out from his face."* He, therefore, says, *"Cast me not away from thy face."* Allow me not to lapse again into sin, for fear you should deprive me of your grace forever. My having been washed, and made white as snow, and having had a right spirit renewed within me, would be of little value, if I were ultimately to be *"cast away from your face,"* with the reprobate. That such may not be the case, that it may not come to pass, *"Take not thy Holy Spirit from me,"* give me the grace of perseverance, causing, through your grace, to make the Holy Spirit constantly abide in me, and thus preserve a *"right spirit in my bowels."* Hence we learn, that God deserts nobody, until himself is first deserted; and that he does not withdraw his Holy Spirit from the just, until they extinguish it in themselves by sin; still, man must get the gift of perseverance, to enable him to avoid sin, and extinguish thereby the Holy Spirit, as the Apostle says, *"Pray that you may do no evil;"* and it is to such gift this passage of the Psalm refers, for when David says, *"Take not thy Holy Spirit from me;"* he does not mean, don't take it if I shall fall into sin; but, don't take it, that I may not fall into sin.

12. This verse corresponds with the words, *"To my hearing thou shalt give joy and gladness;"* for, as he had predicted that an interior joy, borne testimony to by the Spirit speaking within him, would be the consequence of true and perfect justification, he now, after having asked for remission of his sins, and the infusion of grace with the gift of perseverance, asks for the sign and effect of such justification, saying, *"Restore unto me the joy of thy salvation."* Through sin I have lost grace, and the joy consequent on it; and as I asked for the restoration of grace, I now, consequently, ask for the *"joy of thy salvation;"* the joy that arises from the salvation you bestow on me; and for fear he should be over joyful, and thereby lulled into a dangerous security, he adds, *"And strengthen me with a perfect spirit."* I ask you to strengthen and confirm me in my good purposes by an inspiration of your perfect Spirit.

13. The fruit of his justification, tending to the glory of God and the benefit of many. Having been taken into favor after so many grievous offenses, *"I will teach,"* by word and example, *"thy ways,"* mercy, and justice; *"For all the ways of the Lord are mercy and truth;"* and the consequence will be, that the wicked, following my example, will be converted to thee. David was a signal example to all posterity of God's justice and mercy; of his mercy, because, notwithstanding his grievous crimes, the moment he exclaimed, *"I have sinned before the Lord,"* they were all forgiven; and of his justice, for the Lord inflicted most grievous temporal punishments on him, not only in the death of the son born in adultery, but soon after, in his expulsion from the kingdom, the public violation of his wives by his own son, and the

slaughter of his sons Amon and Absalom. His example was useful, not only to the people of his own time, but to all unto the end of the world; for this Psalm, composed by him, is in use, and will be in use: so long as the Church militant shall be in existence. David, then, carried out what he promised in this Psalm, for he taught the wicked the ways of the Lord, thereby bringing many sinners to God, and will, doubtless, bring many more. It is also most likely that David, upon his repentance, did preach up the mercy of God to many, and that, through his exhortations, many sinners were converted to God.

14. Having prayed shortly before for his sins to be washed away, and having promised that he would teach sinners the ways of the Lord, he now prays to be freed from the punishment which Urias's blood, unjustly spilt, called for, and promises to praise God's justice. *"Deliver me;"* save me from the voice of Urias's blood, which, unjustly spilled by me, cries out to thee and calls for vengeance; *"Deliver me,"* for he fancied he saw the blood, like a soldier in arms, staring him in the face; and, therefore, with great propriety, he adds, *"O God, the God of my salvation;"* for to deliver from imminent danger is the province of a Savior; and this, too, is a reason for his adding, *"and my tongue shall extol thy justice;"* for true deliverance and salvation was then had through the merits of Christ in prospective, as the same is had now through the same merits as of the past. The merits of Christ have in them the very essence of justice, and deserve the most unbounded praises both of lips and of heart on our part.

15. The consequence of the perfect justification and salvation of the sinner is, that his lips, which were wont to praise God, but were closed by sin, through his pardon should be opened again to praise and thank his Redeemer. He, therefore, says, *"O Lord, thou wilt open any lips,"* by forgiving and pardoning my sins, and restoring my joy and confidence; you will open my lips, and then *"my mouth shall declare thy praise,"* by proclaiming your mercy and justice, not only to the present but to all future ages.

16. He assigns a reason for offering the sacrifice of praise, because sacrifices of cattle are not pleasing to God; as if he said, *"My mouth shall announce thy praise,"* because I know you to prefer such sacrifice to that of brute animals; and if such sacrifices were pleasing to you, I would not hesitate in offering them. It is not to be inferred from this, that sacrifices of brute animals were in no respect pleasing to God, when it is clear, from the book of Leviticus, that they were instituted and ordered to be offered by him; but they are said to be of no value essentially, as if the slaughter of cattle were, in itself, a thing agreeable, or useful, or necessary to God. They are also said to be of no value in comparison with the sacrifice of the Eucharist, as appears from Malachias 1, where the old sacrifices, it is said, will cease, when *"The clean oblation will be offered in all nations."* Sacrifices are also said to be of no value when they are offered by sinners, as we have in Isaias 1, *"Obedience being more pleasing to God than the offering of victims."* Finally, sacrifices are said to be of no value as regards the expiation of sin; for, as the Apostle says, *"It is impossible that sins could be taken away by the blood of bulls and goats;"* and it is in such sense that David says here, *"If thou hadst desired sacrifice,"* for the remission of my sins, *"I would indeed have given it;"* but because *"with burnt offerings thou wilt not be delighted,"* so as to forgive me my sins through them, therefore *"My mouth shall declare thy praise;"* for, as we said in the explanation of the last Psalm, such sacrifice is the one most acceptable to God, being lighted on the altar of the heart with the fire of charity.

17. He explains more fully how acceptable to God is the sacrifice of praise; that sacrifice that springs from a contrite and humbled heart, when man, acknowledging his own misery and God's mercy, humbles himself before his power, attributing all honor and glory to him, and confusion and disgrace to himself, as we read in Daniel 9, *"Justice to thee, O Lord, but to us confusion of face;"* and a little further on, *"To us, O Lord, confusion of face, to our kings, our princes, and our fathers who have sinned, but to you, our Lord God, mercy and propitiation."* The expressions, *"afflicted spirit"* and *"contrite heart,"* are the same, and the one Hebrew expression is only given for both, but the interpreter chose to vary the words, and the meaning is the same. The spirit is said to be afflicted when the soul is affected with grief, and thus placed in trouble, by reason of the sin committed against God; so also, the heart is said to be contrite when the soul, full of grief for the sin committed, is, as it were, torn asunder, and reduced into powder, from its strong hardness and insensibility. Such contrition is the sacrifice most acceptable to God, for as well as he is offended by our sins, he is appeased by our repentance; and very properly is now added, *"A contrite and humbled heart, O Lord, thou wilt not despise;"* for God despises the proud, and resists them; but to the humble (who willingly submit to him) he always gives his grace, James 4.

18. The last reason assigned by David to appease God, to obtain perfect justice, and to make reparation after so grievous a fall; for he says, that as well as his fall proved an injury to the whole people, his recovery will be now a source of edification to them; and he, therefore, begs this favor for himself and for the whole city of Sion. *"Deal favorably, O Lord, in thy good will with Sion."* If I am not worthy of being heard, have regard to the city of which I am the head, and confer a favor on it by healing its head, *"in thy good will;"* in the good will, in which you were pleased to select this city as your own peculiar city. *"That the walls of Jerusalem may be built up,"* meaning himself, who, like a wall, guarded and defended the entire people.

19. The works of justice that please God as true spiritual sacrifices are the effect of justification, according to the Apostle, Heb. 13, *"And do not forget to do good, and to impart, for by such sacrifices God's favor is obtained;"* and 1 Pet. 2, *"Offer up spiritual sacrifices acceptable to God by Jesus Christ."*—*"Then,"* when I shall have been thoroughly renewed and justified, *"shalt thou accept the sacrifice of justice;"* all the good works of mine and my people, *"oblations and whole burnt offerings."* All which good works will be so many spiritual oblations, so many spiritual holocausts. Spiritual oblations are the offering of one's substance or property in alms for the love of God; and spiritual holocausts is the dedication of one's self entirely to do God's will and commands, according to Rom. 11, *"I beseech you therefore brethren, by the mercy of God, that you present your bodies a living sacrifice, holy, pleasing to God, your reasonable service."*—*"Then shall they lay calves upon thy altar."* When it shall be seen that such sacrifices of justice are the most acceptable to you, people will vie with each other in loading your altar, not with the ordinary sacrifices, but with the most precious; for that of the calf was considered the sacrifice most valuable; and thus the *"laying calves upon the altar"* means the offering of works of the most perfect justice to the Lord God.

PSALM 51

David condemns the wickedness of Doeg, and foretells his destruction.

1 Why dost thou glory in malice, thou that art mighty in iniquity?
2 All the day long thy tongue hath devised injustice: as a sharp razor, thou hast wrought deceit.
3 Thou hast loved malice more than goodness: and iniquity rather than to speak righteousness.
4 Thou hast loved all the words of ruin, O deceitful tongue.
5 Therefore will God destroy thee for ever: he will pluck thee out, and remove thee from thy dwelling place: and thy root out of the land of the living.
6 The just shall see and fear, and shall laugh at him, and say:
7 Behold the man that made not God his helper: But trusted in the abundance of his riches: and prevailed in his vanity.
8 But I, as a fruitful olive tree in the house of God, have hoped in the mercy of God for ever, yea for ever and ever.
9 I will praise thee for ever, because thou hast done it: and I will wait on thy name, for it is good in the sight of thy saints.

EXPLANATION OF THE PSALM

1. Cicero, in his oration against Catiline, thus commences, *"How long, Catiline, will you trifle with our patience?"* and in the same style David commences with a similar interrogation, for the purpose of sharpening his rebuke. *"Why dost thou glory in malice, thou that art mighty in iniquity?"* Doeg, the Idumean, boasted that by his accusations he had ruined a priest of the Lord, and his entire family; for when Saul heard from Doeg that David had been hospitably received by Achimelech the priest, he burst into such a rage, that he not only ordered Doeg to put Achimelech to death, but also eighty-five other priests that were along with him; he then sacked their city, slaying men and women, babes and sucklings, nay, even the sheep, cows, and asses. See what a torrent of evil flowed from the calumny; so that he justly deserved to be styled *"Mighty in iniquity."*

2. He draws a highly wrought picture of Doeg's false information, first saying that it was not a sudden, but a long premeditated information. *"All the day long thy tongue hath devised injustice."* You were constantly turning in your mind how to frame the false accusation, and, at length, when the opportunity offered, your tongue brought forth what it had been hatching for such a length of time; for, though thoughts are produced by the mind, David poetically attributes them to the tongue, as if the tongue was so radically bad in itself, that, though apparently silent, it was, in thought, speaking to itself. He then adds that the thing was put into execution with as much speed as a sharp razor would cut; elegantly contrasting the delay in forming the resolution with the celerity of putting it into execution; and, in fact, he lost very little time, when he got the opportunity, of carrying out what he had so long been hatching; for, in a very few words, he persuaded Saul that Achimelech the priest had entered into a conspiracy with David, which was a grievous deceit and imposition; and he, therefore, says, *"As a sharp razor, thou hast wrought deceit;"* that is, you deceived Saul, just as easily as a sharp razor cuts through the hair.

3. He tells us the source of that calumnious accusation, and says that it did not proceed from ignorance or accident, but from the perversity of the man; who always preferred evil to good, and lies to truth. *"Thou hast loved malice more than goodness;"* you were always more pleased to injure than to serve your neighbor; *"and iniquity rather than to speak righteously,"* to tell lies rather than truth. Observe, that instead of opposing falsehood to *"speaking righteously,"* he opposes *"iniquity"* to it, insinuating thereby, that Doeg's falsehood was not one simply so, or a mere lie; it was more, because it caused the death of Achimelech, and was thus an *"iniquity."*

4. He assigns further reason for calling Doeg's conduct a lie and an iniquity, and says it was a truly fatal, pernicious falsehood, causing, as it did, the ruin of so many innocent people. *"Thou hast loved all the words of ruin;"* all the language by which you could hurry innocent people headlong to their ruin and perdition; and it appears from the first book of Kings, that Doeg's lies caused the destruction of an entire City. *"O deceitful tongue"*—of Doeg.

5. He predicts that Doeg's sin will not go unpunished, but that everlasting ruin is in store for him, in return for the temporal ruin of the priests, of which he was the cause. *"Therefore will God destroy thee forever."* For this your sin God will utterly destroy you, not only in this world, but in the next; so that you shall be ruined for eternity, left absolutely desolate in this world, and damned forever in the world to come; such being the just retribution of the wicked, who, in seeking to injure others, injure themselves forever. He then explains in particular what he had laid down in general, saying, *"He will pluck thee out."* The first stage of your punishment will be your banishment, the loss of your home, property, and country, sending you abroad an exile and a wanderer; *"And thy root out of the land of the living,"* will eradicate you and all your posterity from the earth; for children are like roots, shot out by the parents, which afterwards support and nourish him in turn.

6–7. Many will profit and be instructed by the punishment of the wicked informer. *"The just shall see and fear;"* just and holy people will consider his case, and be horrified; *"And shall laugh at him, and say: Behold the man who made not God his helper, but trusted in the abundance of his riches;"* will laugh at him for having acted most foolishly, for not putting his trust in God, who is all powerful, instead of the frail riches of this world, which are so easily lost. *"And prevailed in his vanity;"* will jeer him for having endeavored to advance by fraud and lies, instead of true and solid virtue. The expression *"prevailed,"* does not imply that he really did prevail, but that he thought he might prevail; and, though he may seem to do so for a time, the end will prove that he had to yield, instead of prevailing; *"When the just shall stand in great constancy against those who hemmed them in,"* Wisdom 5.

8. He concludes the Psalm by showing that he has taken quite a different path; for I will not be plucked up, nor rooted out as a withered tree, like Doeg; but I will send down my roots deeper and deeper, like *"A fruitful olive tree,"* always in bloom, always bearing fruit; and, being such, I have, consequently, *"hoped in the mercy of God forever;"* hoped that God would assist me forever, and to eternity. Observe the contrast he draws between himself and Doeg, the Idumean, comparing him to a dry log, and himself to a fruitful olive tree; he predicts that Doeg will be rooted out of the land, while himself will be rooted in the house of God. Doeg put his trust in his own riches; David in God's mercy.

9. He returns thanks for a thing to happen, as if it had actually been done; for the future, as regards God and the prophets, is a matter of certainty, of the past. *"I will praise thee forever;"* I will always praise thee, *"because thou hast done it;"* have come to the determination of confounding him that trusteth in his riches, and consoling and comforting him that hopeth in thee. *"And I will wait on thy name;"* I will always hope in thee; such is the meaning of

"Wait on thee;" and the name of God is used here for God himself. *"For it is good in the sight of thy saints."* I will justly hope in your name, for your name is most sweet to the saints who have tasted of his sweetness.

PSALM 52

The general corruption of man before the coming of Christ.

1 The fool said in his heart: There is no God.
2 They are corrupted, and become abominable in iniquities: there is none that doth good.
3 God looked down from heaven on the children of men: to see if there were any that did understand, or did seek God.
4 All have gone aside, they are become unprofitable together, there is none that doth good, no not one.
5 Shall not all the workers of iniquity know, who eat up my people as they eat bread?
6 They have not called upon God: there have they trembled for fear, where there was no fear. For God hath scattered the bones of them that please men: they have been confounded, because God hath despised them.
7 Who will give out of Sion the salvation of Israel? when God shall bring back the captivity of his people, Jacob shall rejoice, and Israel shall be glad.

Explanation of the psalm

This Psalm is very nearly the same as Psalm 13, to which we refer our reader; the only difference of any consequence is in the 6th verse of Psalm 13, which has it thus, *"For the Lord is in the just generation, you have confounded the counsel of the poor man, but the Lord is his hope;"* whereas in the latter part of the 6th verse in this Psalm, the reading is, *"For God hath scattered the bones of them that please men, they have been confounded, because God hath despised them."* This, then, is the only verse that requires explanation here. It assigns a reason for the wicked trembling with fear, when they have no reason to fear, and the reason he assigns is, *"For God hath scattered their bones;"* has so enervated them, that they fear the merest trifles, a thing he brings about in his wonderful providence, rendering them foolish in their counsels, by impeding their efforts, and confounding their machinations. Bones are generally used as an expression in the Scripture to designate strength. *"Of them that please men,"* such people are always full of the fear of the world, of human respect, and their whole study is to please man; whereas, on the contrary, the Apostle teaches, *"If I did yet please men, I should not be the servant of Christ."* The prophet adds, *"They have been confounded, because God hath despised them,"* which seem to allude to the passage in Psalm 13, *"You have confounded the counsel of the poor man, but the Lord is his hope;"* you wicked have confounded the counsel of the poor man who put his trust in God, God will confound you, and make you blush, seeing all your counsels are vain, because you did not put your trust in God; and, therefore, he despised you and withheld his assistance from you. This may also have reference to the last judgment, when all the wicked will be confounded, for the universal Judge will then despise them, saying, *"I do not know you, depart into everlasting fire."* The last verse is altogether similar to the last verse of Psalm 13, but that here, instead of *"The Lord shall have turned away,"* we have, *"The Lord shall bring back."* But though turning away and bringing back seem to be very different expressions, in this place they bring out the same meaning, for God is said to turn away the captivity, when he destroys it, which he does, when he frees the captives, and he is said to bring back the captivity when he recalls the captives, and brings them back to their own country.

PSALM 53

A prayer for help in distress.

1 Save me, O God, by thy name, and judge me in thy strength.
2 God, hear my prayer: give ear to the words of my mouth.
3 For strangers have risen up against me; and the mighty have sought after my soul: and they have not set God before their eyes.
4 For behold God is my helper: and the Lord is the protector of my soul.
5 Turn back the evils upon my enemies; and cut them off in thy truth.
6 I will freely sacrifice to thee, and will give praise, O God, to thy name: because it is good:
7 For thou hast delivered me out of all trouble: and my eye hath looked down upon my enemies.

Explanation of the psalm

1. In defect of all human help, he prays to God for his help. *"Save me, O God, by thy name,"* in thy power, to which all things succumb; and he afterwards adds, *"in thy strength,"* expressing the same in different language. *"Judge me;"* that is, be my judge, defend me as I deserve, and avenge me of my enemy, for David had then none to appeal to but God alone to protect him from the king. This should serve as an example to us, never to despair of God's help, even though death should appear to be at our doors, for God is everywhere, has everything in his power, and never despises his clients when they may have recourse to him.

2. Having acknowledged the power of the Lord, he now begs of him to apply his power to himself. *"O God, hear my prayer;"* I know you can do anything but I pray that you may wish to do it. I, therefore, ask that you may hear the prayer I put up to you, to exercise your power in saving me. He repeats it,

"Give ear to the words of my mouth;" that is, turn not away your ears, and do not despise my prayer.

3. He explains the dangers from which he desires to be delivered, saying, *"For strangers have risen up against me;"* that is, the Zipheans, who, though seemingly neighbors, had their hearts far from me; rose up against me, urging Saul to persecute me; *"And the mighty have sought after my soul."* Saul, with a force in arms, sought to have my life. Saul's persecution was entirely grounded on his fears that David would, at one time come to the throne; and, therefore, sought to have his life at any risk; for though he knew him to be innocent, yet, so blinded was he by the desire of keeping the sovereignty in his own family, that he looked upon as fair and honorable, what, in reality, was the height of injustice; *"And they have not set God before their eyes;"* neither the Zipheans nor Saul and his satellites had the fear of God before them; the former preferring the king's favor to God's law; and the latter choosing to indulge in their ambition and lust for power, in preference to a love of justice, which God commands us to observe at all times. In fact the diverting one's mind from God and the natural law known to all, is the beginning of all evil.

4. They *"had not God before their eyes,"* but God had them before his eyes; saw their evil designs, and did not suffer them to carry them into effect. The word *"behold"* implies a sudden light from God of his assurance that he would not be wanting in the time of need; and he speaks in the present tense, to show his being as certain of it, as if the thing had been actually accomplished. And, in fact, God's interference was most sudden and unexpected; for, when Saul had so surrounded David with his army, that his escape seemed impossible, a messenger suddenly came to Saul, bringing news of the Philistines having come in a great body to ravage his kingdom; on hearing which he was obliged to give up the pursuit of David; who, in spirit, foresaw all this, and was, possibly, at the very moment pronouncing the words, *"For behold, God is my helper; and the Lord is the protector of my soul."*

5. Such imprecations, as we have more than once remarked, are to be read as predictions; and so this reads in the Hebrew; and, in fact, it then and there turned up; for Saul, who was pursuing David, was now pursued by the Philistines; and thus, the *"evils"* that hung a short time before over David, were now pouring in upon Saul. The second part of the verse, *"And cut them off in thy truth,"* was also carried out soon after, for Saul and his army, among whom, no doubt, were many of David's persecutors, perished in the mountains of Gelboe; *"In thy truth,"* means according to your promise, or your justice, by virtue of which you give unto every one according to their works.

6. Whether it was that the prophet foresaw his immediate escape from Saul, or that Saul, by reason of the Philistines' incursion, departed while David was actually praying; he returns thanks to God, and says, *"I will freely sacrifice to thee;"* with all my heart I will give the sacrifice of praise; and he repeats it in other words; *"And I will give praise to thy name;"* which means, to thyself; *"because it is good;"* for God's name, which means God himself, is the best of all; so that Christ said, *"One is good, God."* St. Augustine, taking up the word *"freely,"* properly observes, that God should be loved purely on his own account; not with a view to any reward, but for his supreme and unspeakable goodness; and he who so loves him, does so in adversity as well as in prosperity; for God is just as good when he chastises, as when he nourishes and refreshes.

7. He proves God's goodness from what happened, in having so speedily heard his servant; *"For thou hast delivered me out of all trouble."* In revealing my certain deliverance to me, you have, already in hope, *"delivered me from all trouble." "And my eye hath looked down upon my enemies;"* by virtue of the same revelation I have looked upon my enemies as already destroyed and prostrate; or, perhaps, they were actually so when the prophet was thus praying. This Psalm is daily recited in the canonical hour of Prime, in order that, in imitation of David, we may learn to strengthen ourselves with the arm of prayer against all our persecutors, at the beginning of each day, recollecting, *"That all who wish to live piously in Jesus Christ shall suffer persecution."*

PSALM 54

A prayer of a just man under persecution from the wicked. It agrees to Christ persecuted by the Jews, and betrayed by Judas.

1 Hear, O God, my prayer, and despise not my supplication:
2 Be attentive to me and hear me. I am grieved in my exercise; and am troubled,
3 At the voice of the enemy, and at the tribulation of the sinner. For they have cast iniquities upon me: and in wrath they were troublesome to me.
4 My heart is troubled within me: and the fear of death is fallen upon me.
5 Fear and trembling are come upon me: and darkness hath covered me.
6 And I said: Who will give me wings like a dove, and I will fly and be at rest?
7 Lo, I have gone far off flying away; and I abode in the wilderness.
8 I waited for him that hath saved me from pusillanimity of spirit, and a storm.
9 Cast down, O Lord, and divide their tongues; for I have seen iniquity and contradiction in the city.
10 Day and night shall iniquity surround it upon its walls: and in the midst thereof are labour,
11 And injustice. And usury and deceit have not departed from its streets.

12 For if my enemy had reviled me, I would verily have borne with it. And if he that hated me had spoken great things against me, I would perhaps have hidden myself from him.
13 But thou a man of one mind, my guide, and my familiar,
14 Who didst take sweetmeats together with me: in the house of God we walked with consent.
15 Let death come upon them, and let them go down alive into hell. For there is wickedness in their dwellings: in the midst of them.
16 But I have cried to God: and the Lord will save me.
17 Evening and morning, and at noon I will speak and declare: and he shall hear my voice.
18 He shall redeem my soul in peace from them that draw near to me: for among many they were with me.
19 God shall hear, and the Eternal shall humble them. For there is no change with them, and they have not feared God:
20 He hath stretched forth his hand to repay. They have defiled his covenant,
21 They are divided by the wrath Of his countenance, and his heart hath drawn near. His words are smoother than oil, and the same are darts.
22 Cast thy care upon the Lord, and he shall sustain thee: he shall not suffer the just to waver for ever.
23 But thou, O God, shalt bring them down into the pit of destruction. Bloody and deceitful men shall not live out half their days; but I will trust in thee, O Lord.

EXPLANATION OF THE PSALM

1. David begins with a preface to arrest the benevolence of the Judge, and asks for a kind and patient hearing, saying, *"Hear, O God, my prayer;"* and for fear the prayer, or the person offering it, may not be agreeable, he recommends both, and first the prayer, saying, *"And despise not my supplication;"* that is, my humble and suppliant prayer, for such is the force of the word in Hebrew.

2. He now refers to the person praying, *"Be attentive to me, and hear me."* Look on me in your mercy, listen to me patiently. It is possible that he repeats the same prayer three times, in reference to the Trinity; directing his *"prayer,"* to the Father; his *"supplication"* to the Son; and the person praying, to the Holy Ghost. The same prayer is repeated three times, to show his earnestness, as Christ did when he prayed in the garden, and as the Apostle Paul thrice asked of the Lord. *"I am grieved in my exercise, and am troubled."* He now tells us why he prays. He was persecuted fiercely by his enemies, which saddened and dejected him; and he longed to be freed from such persecution, and therefore, in exercising, or turning the thing in his mind, he was *"troubled"* and confounded, not only for the present, but for the future, because,

3. *"The voice of the enemy"* threatening, vowing vengeance, and *"the tribulation of the sinner,"* the troubles they vowed to inflict on me, also grieved and troubled me. *"The voice of the enemy"* may refer to Saul or Absalom, as regards David; Caiphas and Annas, as regards Christ; or any persecutor, in regard of the just. *"For they have cast iniquities upon me."* To show his fears were not groundless, *"they,"* his enemies, *"cast iniquities"* upon me; falsely accused me, reproached, abused me, *"and in wrath they were troublesome to me,"* such was the anger they got into against me, that they did not confine themselves to abusive language, but even sought to inflict personal injury.

4. Having said in the second verse that he was *"troubled,"* he now explains how he was troubled; it was in his heart, in the inmost recesses of it; and assigns a reason for it, saying, *"The fear of death is fallen upon me;"* nothing enters into the heart of man so deep, or upsets him so much, as the fear of death at the door; as was the case with David, when, with lamentations, he fled from Absalom; and with Christ, when he trembled in the garden, and fell into the bloody sweat, recorded in Mat. 26.

5. A repetition of the same idea, and a sort of summary of the whole thing. Fear got a hold of his soul, tremor of his body, and the gloom of grief enveloped the entire man; for, as joy exhilarates and expands the heart, so also sorrow contracts and confines it, and thus darkens it up; for which reason persons in grief fly to a dark chamber, hide themselves therein and close the windows.

6. Such are the expressions of the just, sighing for their heavenly country, where alone true rest is to be had; as if he said, Oh! that I could fly to the highest mountains of the heavenly Jerusalem, in imitation of the dove who escapes the bird of prey by soaring above him. The just man is, with great propriety, compared to a dove, harmless, prolific, innocent, conquering by flight instead of by resistance; and so with the just man, who flies from temptation, instead of wrestling with it.

7. Words most applicable to David, who, in his flight from Saul, and afterwards from Absalom, betook himself to the desert; as if he said, As I cannot, like a dove, ascend to a place of real rest, I did my utmost, for *"I have gone afar off, flying away;"* which is applicable to every just man in trouble, who, when he cannot get back to his own country, removes himself internally as far as he can from the tumult of the world, betakes himself to the solitude of his heart and conscience, where, alone, in conference with God, he finds rest to some extent.

8. In that solitude *"I waited for him,"* that is, for his help, *"that hath saved me"* as he often did before, *"from pusillanimity of spirit and a storm;"* that is, from

great temptation, with little strength to go through it. Two things are united to show the more than ordinary necessity for the help of God. If we have small temptations to encounter, with little strength of mind, or great temptations, with much strength of mind, the contest will not be so unequal; but if one with little strength of mind has to encounter great temptations, they cannot possibly bear up against them. Such, he says, is his case now; and he prays to God to increase his strength, or else to lessen the temptation, or, which is preferable, to do both.

9. Having hoped for salvation through the Lord, he now prays to him to baffle the designs of his enemies. *"Cast down."* Hurl my enemies into the abyss; for such is the force of the word in Hebrew; and he says how he wishes that to be done, by *"dividing their tongues;"* by causing such dissension among them, that they shall have no unity of purpose, and thus embarrass each other, as really happened to his enemies; for, after the taking of the city, when various plans for capturing David were suggested to Absalom, he was so infatuated by God as not to adopt the advice of Achitophel, but preferred another; and the consequence was that the expedition failed, and most of them miserably perished; and thus, by division of tongues, they were ruined. *"For I have seen iniquity and contradiction in the city."* Words quite applicable to David, who had witnessed a most villainous conspiracy against his person, and most palpable rebellion (called contradiction here, because they contradicted David when they chose Absalom as king,) in the city. These words are applicable, to Christ, as well as to every innocent person who suffers unjust persecution and contradiction from the citizens of Babylon; that is, from the votaries of pleasure, who always persecute and hate those who are not of the world; but live in it as if they were foreigners and strangers.

10-11. He proceeds in describing the wickedness of the city, from which he had suffered so much persecution, and most expressively says, that iniquity, like an armed soldiery, had so got possession of its walls, that it was impossible for justice to enter. *"Day and night,"* that is, at all hours, *"shall iniquity surround it upon its walls."* Vice, like a guard of soldiers on its walls will surround it; *"And in the midst thereof are labor and injustice;"* inside the city the poor were oppressed with *"labor"* by the *"injustice"* of the rich, who ground them down, and lorded it over them with impunity. *"And usury and deceit have not departed from its streets."* The oppression was partly open, for they required enormous usury in the streets; and partly private, for they harassed and circumvented the poor by various *"deceits."* Such was the state of things in David's time, at Jerusalem; infinitely worse in the days of our Savior; and are quite applicable nowadays to Babylon; that is, to the lovers of this world, in whom the concupiscence of the flesh, the concupiscence of the eyes, and the pride of life absolutely rule.

12-14. Having complained of the whole city and people in general, he now complains of one traitor in particular, who seems to be Achitophel, if we apply the Psalm to David; Judas, if to Christ; and any false friend, if we apply it to man in general. *"For if my enemy,"* any avowed one, *"had reviled me, I would verily have borne with it;"* it would be only what I should expect. *"And if he that hated;"* if such avowed enemy were to abuse, calumniate, and reproach me, *"I would perhaps, have hidden myself from him,"* to see would his anger cool in my absence, and to remove the occasion of his abuse. But I could not hide myself from you, nor could I dream of your betraying me, for you seemed to be *"a man of one mind"* with me, my most intimate friend, having only one heart, one soul with me; you were also *"my guide,"* my principal counselor, whose advice I always followed; for such was Achitophel, of whom we read in 2 Kings 16, *"That the counsel he gave in those days, was as if a man should consult God."* As regards Judas, he is called a *"guide,"* having been appointed by Christ, with the other Apostles, over the people, according to Psalm 44, *"Thou shalt make them princes over all the earth."* He was also *"his familiar,"* and *"took sweet meats with him,"* as is well known; and the meats are called sweet, because agreeable company makes them so. *"By sweet meats,"* St. Augustine says, the blessed Eucharist is meant, the sweetest of all meats, and possessing the flavor and virtue of all. Finally, he was not only of one mind, and his guide and familiar, but of the same opinion in regard of the sacred ceremonies; for *"In the house of God we walked with consent."* There was no dissension between us in regard of anything connected with the worship of God.

15. An imprecation, or rather a prophecy, in the shape of an imprecation, of the punishment that was justly inflicted on Dathan and Abiron, who, for their sedition and rebellion, were swallowed up alive, they went *"down alive into hell,"* and so did many of those who followed Absalom in his rebellion against David, when, as we read in 2 Kings 16, *"There were many more of the people whom the forest consumed, than whom the sword devoured that day."* The same came to pass in the siege of Jerusalem, when they dropped with hunger in the streets, or flung themselves from the walls; and the same happens to many sinners, who either close their eyes against the truth, or if they see it, still prefer remaining in a state in which they cannot possibly be saved. *"For there is wickedness in their dwellings, in the midst of them."* A reason assigned for so severe an imprecation. Those who prefer so wicked a life, will be justly swallowed up alive, and will undergo everlasting punishment, *"For there is wickedness in their dwellings,"* and dwellings that are not empty, but *"in the midst of them;"* that is, at the very time they were fully inhabited.

16-17. He foretells the death of his enemies, and his own safety, *"But I have cried to God"* with an earnest prayer, *"and he will save me"* in the danger with which I am beset; and, thenceforward I will cry to him, not once, but twice, thrice; I will cry to him at evenings morning, and noon," in telling and announcing my own misfortunes, and the mercies of the Lord, and *"he shall hear my voice."* The practice of praying three times in the day was an usual one, as we read in Daniel 6, perhaps in honor of the Most Holy Trinity, a mystery not unknown to the prophets. He says, *"Evening, morning, and noon,"* rather than, morning, noon, and evening, because their festivals began in the evening, and were celebrated, according to Leviticus 23, from evening to evening, and, therefore, evening was the first, a practice still observed by the Church that begins the office with the first vespers.

18. He tells us in what respect he will be heard by God. *"He shall redeem my soul in peace."* He will restore peace to it in spite of those *"that draw near to me,"* coming to close quarters to fight with me. *"for among many they were with me;"* my aggressors were most numerous, and I was singlehanded. This I consider the best interpretation of this most difficult passage.

19. I that am most unjustly oppressed, will be heard by him, *"who is eternal,"* and he will humble them. For there is no change with them, they have become hardened, and quite impenitent of their crimes. *"They have not feared God;"* they rather feared men, and, therefore,

20. To give them their deserts: and justly, *"For they have defiled his covenant"* by their scandalous lives, by not living up to the covenant God gave them, and therefore,

21. They are scattered and dispersed in God's anger, *"And his heart hath drawn near"* to punish and chastise them. *"his words are smoother than oil, and the same are darts."* He now reverts to the malice of the principal traitor, Achitophel, in regard of David; and Judas in respect to Christ. *"His words are smoother than oil;"* apparently soft, kind, smooth, and yet his language does not consist of words, but of darts; delighting the ear, but wounding the heart; such are all detractions, indelicate language, and all false presence of the betrayer.

22. In the end of the Psalm the prophet consoles himself and all in similar circumstances, and exhorts them to put their whole confidence in God, who is most undoubtedly solicitous for his servants and friends, as St. Peter reminds us in his 1 Epistle 5, *"Casting all your solicitude upon him, for he hath care of you,"* and is copiously explained by Christ himself, in the 6th chapter of Matthew, and in various other places; which passages are not to be understood as an encouragement to lead a life of idleness, and take no trouble about the world, but that we should not be over solicitous about the world, or depend more on our own strength and industry than on the providence and mercy of God. *"Cast thy care,"* you that fear God, *"upon the Lord;"* leave to divine providence what you need for your support, *"and he shall sustain thee."* He will provide you with all necessaries, blessing your labors and prospering your work; and will not only *"sustain"* and support you, but will defend you from your enemies. And, though he may sometimes *"suffer the just to waver,"* whether by want of the necessaries of life, or by the persecution of the wicked, it will not be *"forever."* These trials will not be of long duration, because God will not suffer the just to be always buffeted by the waves of affliction; for everlasting affliction belongs to the wicked alone, as the following verse expresses.

23. You, O Lord, in your capacity of Judge, will consign them to the pit of death, from which they will never rise. It is called the pit of destruction, for those who fall therein are perpetually dying; for they live always in punishment, that they may be always dying, and never find that death they so ardently long for. *"Bloody and deceitful men shall not live out half their days."* Not only will those men of blood be cast into *"the pit of destruction"* hereafter, but even in this life will their days be shortened, for it is only just that those who take away a life should lose their own. So God says, Gen. 9, *"Whosoever shall shed man's blood, his blood shall be shed;"* and the Lord himself said, *"For all that take the sword shall perish with the sword."* Now, all these testimonies in this Psalm, as well as those in Genesis and the Gospel, do not go to prove that all manner of persons who take life away shall lose their own; but those only who take it away unjustly, and especially, those who lie in ambush to do so, for such are, properly speaking, the *"bloody and deceitful men."* Again, he does not imply that all who waylay and kill will perish by the sword; but that, generally speaking, they will be judicially put to death, or killed in battle, or by themselves, or by some chance, which is no chance in the sight of God, but a disposition of his providence. Finally, the expression, *"shall not live out half their days,"* is not to be taken in the strict sense of the words, it being only a figure of speech, to express the shortness of their lives. An objection to this passage is raised, from an expression in Psalm 72, where the Psalmist complains of sinners, *"That full days shall be found in them,"* to which may be stated, in reply, that the passage quoted refers to sinners not guilty of shedding blood; or to a few who are an exception to the rule that shortens the days of sinners. The prophet concludes with that most usual expression of his, *"But I will trust in thee, O Lord,"* which seems to have reference to the aforesaid; thus, that I may escape from my secret enemies, as well as my avowed ones; that I may not incur the punishment of the wicked,

and fall into the pit of destruction; and that my days may not be cut short, *"I will put my trust in thee, O Lord,"* and not in my own strength.

PSALM 55

A prayer of David in danger and distress.

1 Have mercy on me, O God, for man hath trodden me under foot; all the day long he hath afflicted me fighting against me.
2 My enemies have trodden on me all the day long; for they are many that make war against me.
3 From the height of the day I shall fear: but I will trust in thee.
4 In God I will praise my words, in God I have put my trust: I will not fear what flesh can do against me.
5 All the day long they detested my words: all their thoughts were against me unto evil.
6 They will dwell and hide themselves: they will watch my heel. As they have waited for my soul,
7 For nothing shalt thou save them: in thy anger thou shalt break the people in pieces, O God,
8 I have declared to thee my life: thou hast set my tears in thy sight, As also in thy promise.
9 Then shall my enemies be turned back. In what day soever I shall call upon thee, behold I know thou art my God.
10 In God will I praise the word, in the Lord will I praise his speech. In God have I hoped, I will not fear what man can do to me.
11 In me, O God, are vows to thee, which I will pay, praises to thee:
12 Because thou hast delivered my soul from death, my feet from falling: that I may please in the sight of God, in the light of the living.

EXPLANATION OF THE PSALM

1. He commences with a prayer for mercy, by reason of his avowal of his misery. He was suffering a most undeserved persecution from Saul, and in seeking to avoid it, he fell into a more grievous one from the Philistines; and, during a short respite from both he was obliged to lie concealed in a cave, an exile, and a destitute. *"Have mercy on me, O Lord,"* you, the only refuge of the wretched, *"for man hath trodden me under foot,"* meaning Saul, whom he designates man, rather than Saul, to contrast him with God; as if he said, Have mercy on me, O Lord, for it is my fellowman that afflicts me; when the earth despises me, I look up to the heavens; when my fellow servant persecutes me, I fly to my master. *"All the day long he hath afflicted me,"* his injuries were not passing, or momentary, but they continued to be heaped on me, he never let me rest. The truth of all this is apparent from 1

Kings. Nor is there any difficulty in applying this to Christ, who became man for our sake, and yet was always oppressed by man, and was afflicted from the day of his birth, to that of his burial; and after him it may refer to his Church, which is doomed to encounter persecution and trouble, even to the day of judgment. By the word *"man,"* is meant, either the devil, who is called in the Gospel, *"The enemy,"* or mankind wanting the Spirit of God, and, therefore, purely man, as the Apostle, 1 Cor. 3, says, *"For, whereas there is amongst you envying and contention, are you not carnal, and walk according to man?"* and immediately after, *"Are you not men?"* Whence the Lord himself, Mat. 16, says, *"Whom do men say that the Son of Man is?" "But whom do you say that I am?"*

2. David was persecuted, and his death sought for, not only by Saul, but by all his retainers; and the devil is helped by all his fallen angels, in his assaults on the Church.

3. However numerous my enemies may be, I will not fear them, but *"from the height of the day I shall fear;"* that is, I will fear God's judgments, proceeding as they do from the most intense light, such as we have at midday, a light penetrating everything, even the inmost recesses of the heart; which fear shall be united with hope: for though I fear the brightness of your light, I will, at the same time, *"trust"* in your mercy and goodness.

4. He enters at greater length into the confidence he has in God, and his reasons for it. God had long since, through Samuel, promised him the kingdom, as we read in 1 Kings 13, where Samuel says of David, *"The Lord hath sought him a man according to his own heart; and him hath the Lord commanded to be prince over his people;"* and in 1 Kings 16, *"He anointed him in the midst of his brethren."* Such was the promise that inspired him with so much confidence, and to it he alludes, when he says, *"In God I will praise my words;"* that is, relying on God's assistance, I will ultimately praise the promises he made me, as most faithful, when they shall have been accomplished; and, therefore, *"I will not fear what flesh can do against me."* I will not fear the threats and persecutions of my enemies, who, being flesh, are weak and feeble, when compared with God, who has assured me of the kingdom. This verse can be easily referred to Christ, for the Angel, when speaking to the Virgin, said, *"The Lord will give him the throne of David his father;"* and Christ could say with the greatest truth, I will not fear what flesh can do against me.

5. He returns to an account of the malice of his enemies, and says, that all the time he was among them, they never ceased impugning all his words and actions, and seeking his death; which is just as applicable to the Scribes and Pharisees, calumniating and plotting against our Savior, as it is to David's enemies.

6. He now relates another malicious trait in his enemies. *"They will dwell and hide themselves,"* while they are apparently on the best of terms with me, living as friends and companions in one house with me, they will, meanwhile, hide themselves, plotting and conspiring against me: *"They will watch my heel,"* to trip me up, if possible, and destroy me. Such was the behavior of Saul's dependents towards David, and of the Jews towards Christ. Though he speaks in the future tense, he intends the past, the Hebrew idiom allowing, in many cases, the future to be used for the past.

7. He now predicts the ruin of his enemies, God, in his justice, awarding to them what they intended for their neighbor. *"As they have waited for my soul,"* as they privately lay in wait for me to have my life, so you, O God, *"for nothing shalt thou save them,"* nothing will induce you to save them; but, *"in thy anger thou shalt break the people in pieces,"* and pursue them to destruction. And so he did; for Saul and his troops perished in the mountains of Gelboe. The Jews had their city sacked by the Romans, and the survivors of the siege were scattered over all the world, and they will be signally punished on the day of judgment.

8. Having discussed the punishment of his enemies, he now returns to pray for himself, saying, *"O God, I have declared to thee my life;"* I have put before you in my prayers, all my journeys, casualties, and labors, (for the Hebrew word for life comprehends so much;) and *"Thou hast set my tears in thy sight;"* you, most merciful and kind Father, have not turned your face away, but you have looked upon my face with pity *"As also in thy promise;"* a thing you could not well avoid, having promised me faithfully that you would protect me.

9. He concludes by thanking and praising God. Behold, he says, I have known by experience that, *"in what day soever I shall call upon thee, behold, I know thou art my God;"* that is, by listening to my prayer, you will prove that you are my God.

10. This verse has been already explained, it being nearly identical with verse 4, the difference being hardly worth explanation.

11. For all the favors conferred on him, he promises that he will discharge all the vows of praise he made while in tribulation. *"In me, O God, are vows to thee,"* I have a lively recollection of them all, *"which I will pay, praises to thee;"* these vows being promises of constant hymns of praise and thanksgiving to thee for all the favors conferred on me.

12. We have now a summary of all God's favors. *"Because thou hast delivered my soul from death;"* you have saved me from Saul, or Achis, the king of the Philistines, who were bent on my ruin; *"My feet from falling;"* preserved me from falling into sin, notwithstanding the numerous temptations by which I was urged to destroy Saul, or to curse him; and saved me from the death

of the body, as well as of the soul. *"That I may please in the sight of God, in the light of the living;"* in the light of this life, which those who are dead enjoy not; and in the light of grace, which infidels and sinners have not; that I may, at length, come to the light of eternal glory enjoyed by those who alone, and properly speaking, can be classed among the living. These words are applicable to Christ, who, by his resurrection, was delivered from the death of the body, without any possibility of his ever again being subject to it, or to any suffering, and lives and reigns on the right hand of the Father, *"in the light of the living."* Amen.

PSALM 56

The prophet prays in his affliction, and praises God for his delivery.

1 Have mercy on me, O God, have mercy on me: for my soul trusteth in thee. And in the shadow of thy wings will I hope, until iniquity pass away.

2 I will cry to God the most High; to God who hath done good to me.

3 He hath sent from heaven and delivered me: he hath made them a reproach that trod upon me. God hath sent his mercy and his truth,

4 And he hath delivered my soul from the midst of the young lions. I slept troubled. The sons of men, whose teeth are weapons and arrows, and their tongue a sharp sword.

5 Be thou exalted, O God, above the heavens, and thy glory above all the earth.

6 They prepared a snare for my feet; and they bowed down my soul. They dug a pit before my face, and they are fallen into it.

7 My heart is ready, O God, my heart is ready: I will Sing, and rehearse a psalm.

8 Arise, O my glory, arise psaltery and harp: I will arise early.

9 I will give praise to thee, O Lord, among the people: I will sing a psalm to thee among the nations.

10 For thy mercy is magnified even to the heavens: and thy truth unto the clouds.

11 Be thou exalted, O God, above the heavens: and thy glory above all the earth.

EXPLANATION OF THE PSALM

1. David hiding in a cave, prays to God to be delivered from Saul's persecution; a type of Christ, who, too, concealed in a cave, as he was, while in the form of a servant, prays for the delivery of his body, the Church, from the persecution of Satan and his ministers. *"Have mercy on me, O God."* God of mercy, take me out of the misery I am suffering, while my life is in danger, through the persecution of Saul. *"For my soul trusteth in thee."* Whereas God promises his assistance to those that trust in him, confidence in God is the surest way to have his mercy extended to us. *"And in the shadow of thy wings will I hope."* I have not only hitherto trusted in thee, but I will persevere and continue to trust in thee as long as may be necessary, which will be *"until iniquity pass away;"* until our pilgrimage here shall have an end; for so long will iniquity be found in this world. The metaphor of *"The shadow of thy wings"* is of frequent use in the Scriptures; in Psalm 16, we have, *"Protect me under the shadow of thy wings;"* in Psalm 62, *"And I will rejoice under the covert of thy wings;"* in Psalm 90, *"Under his wings thou shalt trust;"* and our Lord himself, in Mat. 23, says, *"How often would I have gathered together thy children, as the hen gathereth her chickens under her wings, and thou wouldst not."* The meaning is, I will have as much confidence in your protection as the chickens have in that of their mother, when they gather under her wings for protection from the birds of prey; thereby conveying to us the signal love of God for his elect, and his special protection of them.

2. The confidence he has in God's protection will make him *"cry to God the Most High,"* as being supreme judge, far and away above all other judges; and his reason for doing so is, because he knows, from experience, the advantage of thus appealing to God; *"to God who hath done good to me;"* who enabled me to avenge myself of my enemies, (such is the force of the Hebrew.) Saul had so surrounded a mountain to which David had fled, that his escape seemed absolutely impossible, when God so ordered that news came to Saul of an incursion of the Philistines into his kingdom, that compelled him to withdraw his troops from the pursuit of David, to his own great disgrace and sorrow, to which he briefly alludes in the following verse.

3-4. *"He hath sent from heaven"* help and assistance, *"and delivered me,"* when I was surrounded by the enemy's legions, and all but killed or captured. *"He hath made them a reproach that trod upon me."* He disgraced Saul and his soldiers, who were about to trample me to the dust, when they were unable to effect their purpose, by reason of their having to retire to meet the Philistines. *"God hath sent his mercy and his truth;"* his two hands, as it were, *"his mercy,"* to deliver me; *"his truth,"* that is, his justice, to shame and confound my enemies. *"And he hath delivered my soul,"* meaning my life, *"from the midst of the young lions;"* from Saul and his soldiers, fierce and ferocious as any lions. Notwithstanding this delivery, however, *"I slept troubled;"* for I feared the detractions and the calumnies of my enemies, *"whose teeth are weapons, and their tongue a sharp sword;"* that is to say, though the impending danger from the young lions was removed, I knew I was not safe from the tongues of the detractors and calumniators, who, from a distance, could still shoot their darts at me; and, therefore, *"I slept troubled."*

5. Having related the extent of his fear, he prays to God to manifest his glory by inflicting punishment on his impious enemies. *"Be thou exalted, O God, above the heavens."* Sit on thy highest throne for judgment. *"And thy glory above all the earth."* Let your glory be made known to all on earth, that all may understand and praise your justice.

6. He assigns a reason for calling down God's vengeance on his enemies. For, along with many other persecutions, *"They prepared a snare for my feet,"* to trap me like a wild beast. *"And they bowed down my soul."* Their persecutions and plots were so numerous, that, from constant care and trouble, I got bent and bowed down. He then repeats the same in another metaphor. *"They dug a pit before my face;"* right in my path, in the hope of my falling into it; *"And they are fallen into it;"* caught in the trap themselves, as actually happened to Saul, who went into the cave of Engaddi, to answer a call of nature, in which cave David and his friends had taken refuge. They urged David that now was the time to have Saul's life, helpless and unsuspicious of danger as he was. David declined, but Saul fell into the pit.

7. He now, in the end of the Psalm, raises his soul to God, exclaiming, *"My heat is ready, O God, my heart is ready;"* ready to live, ready to die, ready to rule, ready to be trampled on, ready to take anything cheerfully from your hand. *"I will sing and rehearse a psalm;"* I will praise your justice, praise your mercy in song and music.

8. Having said he would *"sing and rehearse a psalm,"* that he may do it properly, he now invokes, not the muses, in the style of profane writers, but the Spirit of prophecy. *"Arise my glory;"* that is, that divine Spirit, through whose inspiration I have sung of the divine mysteries; *"Arise psaltery and harp;"* that is, my soul and my tongue; the psaltery, which yields the higher notes, representing the spirit; and the harp, which yields the lower notes, representing the tongue. *"I will arise early;"* the fittest time for contemplation, and for chanting God's praises.

9. When David did rise in the morning to sing God's praises, he says, *"I will give praise to thee, O Lord, among the people;"* that is, among the Jewish people; and, knowing that his Psalms would be chanted all over the world by the gentiles, as well as the Jews, he adds, *"I will sing a psalm to thee among the nations."*

10. The subject of his praise to all nations will be his mercy, which has become so great that it has risen up to the heavens; not that his mercy, absolutely speaking, has so risen, for being infinite, it admits of no increase but in his works; and, in like manner, *"thy truth,"* which also has risen to the heavens; *"clouds"* being used here to signify them, an expression used by Christ himself; who says, *"You shall see the Son of Man sitting on the right hand of God, and coming in the clouds of heaven."*

11. As God's mercy and truth reach the heavens, it is only meet that his praise and glory should fill the heavens and the earth.

PSALM 57

David reproves the wicked, and foretells their punishment.

1 If in very deed you speak justice: judge right things, ye sons of men.
2 For in your heart you work iniquity: your hands forge injustice in the earth.
3 The wicked are alienated from the womb; they have gone astray from the womb: they have spoken false things.
4 Their madness is according to the likeness of a serpent: like the deaf asp that stoppeth her ears:
5 Which will not hear the voice of the charmers; nor of the wizard that charmeth wisely.
6 God shall break in pieces their teeth in their mouth: the Lord shall break the grinders of the lions.
7 They shall come to nothing, like water running down; he hath bent his bow till they be weakened.
8 Like wax that melteth they shall be taken away: fire hath fallen on them, and they shall not see the sun.
9 Before your thorns could know the brier; he swalloweth them up, as alive, in his wrath.
10 The just shall rejoice when he shall see the revenge: he shall wash his hands in the blood of the sinner.
11 And man shall say: If indeed there be fruit to the just: there is indeed a God that judgeth them on the earth.

Explanation of the psalm

1. When men are asked whether it is right to steal, commit adultery, cheat, and the like, they, very properly, answer that it is not right; because the law written in their hearts teaches them so, and no one wishes to be robbed, abused, etc.; and thus, all evil doers stand convicted of deceit when they say so, and still rob, steal, commit adultery, etc.; things they would not do unless they believed a certain amount of good or advantage was in them. Not only that, but they stand convicted of falsehood while they cry up justice, and descant on the sin of theft, adultery, etc.; but they also prove themselves to be laboring under a deplorable blindness, loud in their denunciations of theft, etc., and, at the same time, devoted themselves to those vices, and dealing with others as they would not be dealt with themselves. For, if theft be good in itself, why are they unwilling to be plundered? If it be not good in itself, why plunder another? The Holy Spirit exclaims against such voluntary and inexcusable blindness, saying, *"If, in very deed, you speak justice,"* when you condemn theft, anger, etc.; *"judge right things, ye sons of men;"* consider in your hearts that you should not do them, and do not what you have acknowledged to be bad.

2. He shows he had reason for the admonition he gave them, to judge justly if they would speak justly; for, it appears, they did the very contrary; and thus spoke with the semblance of justice, while they were full of malice and deceit. *"For in your heart you work iniquity;"* you think of nothing but what is bad, and you do not stop there; for *"your hands forge injustice in the earth;"* your hands put into execution what your heart conceived.

3. Another misfortune of sinners is, that they fall, not after a lapse of years, but at once, almost from the cradle. *"The wicked are alienated from the womb."* Scarcely out of the womb when they leave the straight path, the path of life, of happiness. *"They have spoken false things;"* lies and falsehood being usually the first sin committed by children; in lies and falsehood our corrupt nature first shows itself.

4-5. Having told us that sin, as a disease, attacks us in our very infancy, he now adds that the disease is of long duration, but that it is also a most grievous disease; sinners being sometimes so overpowered by it, and hurried on to ruin others by it, that they may be compared to serpents of a certain kind, that will yield to no incantations whatever. *"Their madness,"* the madness of those grievous sinners, such as Saul, *"is according to the likeness of a serpent,"* that no art will tame; nay, even like a *"deaf asp,"* that stops her ears with her tail, for fear she should *"hear the voice of the charmers, nor of the wizard, that charmeth wisely;"* that is, of one well skilled in charming. Whether such be true of the asp or not is no matter, for David speaks according to general opinion on the subject. St. Augustine observes that this passage no more approves of the arts and practices of wizards and charmers, than do the parables of our Lord regarding the unjust steward, and the man who found the treasure in the farm, of their honesty in such cases.

6. Having painted the enormity of the sins of certain persons, Saul being the principal person in view, he now describes the punishments in store for such sinners, by most appropriate similes. The first is in this verse, the gist of which is, that however great and formidable the power of the sinner may appear to be, still that he would be deprived of it. No animal more terrible, more formidable than a lion, and his teeth are the weapons he makes most use of, and the most destructive to his enemies. *"God will break in pieces their teeth,"* the teeth of the sinners, who, like lions, tear and plunder the unoffending. However powerful and strong like lions they may appear to be; *"in their mouth,"* while they are alive, and not after death—a thing easily done; and it is not the small teeth will be so broken, but their very grinders; for, *"He shall break the grinders of the lions,"* the largest and most durable of all the teeth.

7. Another simile, teaching us that the power of the wicked would be very brief, and, after a very short time, would be so extirpated that not a trace of it would be found; like a sudden fall of rain, that creates, for the moment, a great inundation, of which, in a few hours, not a trace can be found. Such

was the case with Saul, Achab, Jeroboam, Nero, Caius, Domitian, and, with the great heresiarchs, Arius, Nestorius, and others. *"They shall come to nothing, like water running down;"* that runs with great velocity, leaving not a trace of itself. And lest we may suppose this happened in an ordinary way, he adds, *"He hath bent his bow till they be weakened;"* to show it was all God's work, all his doings; for it was he who bent his bow against them, and kept it bent against them until they were utterly ruined.

8. The third simile, showing that it is as easy for God to destroy the power of the tyrant or the sinner, as it is for the fire or the sun to melt wax, which, however hard it may be, readily yields to the action of either. *"Like wax that melteth away,"* when the fire or the sun comes to act upon it, so shall the sinners *"be taken away,"* and utterly destroyed. *"For fire hath fallen on them;"* the fire of the anger of God; and being thus melted, they disappeared; *"and they shall not see the sun;"* a thing they could not do when they were utterly destroyed.

9. The last simile through which the prophet teaches us that the wicked will be uprooted and cut down by God, before they can carry out their wicked designs against the just, and thus balk them of the gratification they calculated on from their ruin. Thus Saul had an unhappy end, before he could rejoice on David's death; so with Diocletian and the other persecutors of the Church, who had a miserable exit before they could witness the extirpation of Christianity they were so bent on. The simile is taken from thorns, which, when young, are easily cut down, but when they grow to any age, so as to get into timber, or, as the verse expresses it, *"To know the briar,"* cannot be rooted out but with great difficulty. *"He swalloweth them up as alive in his wrath."* He will annihilate them as completely as if the earth opened and swallowed them up alive.

10. When the sinners shall have been so signally punished, *"the just shall rejoice when he shall see the revenge;"* not through love of revenge, but from a love of justice, seeing it was God's goodness that prevented himself from falling into such sins and meriting such punishment; and he will not only rejoice, but *"he shall wash his hands in the blood of the sinner;"* that is, his own good works will shine forth in bright contrast to the wickedness of the sinner. Contraries show more clearly when placed in juxtaposition; and the Scripture not infrequently uses the term *"blood"* to signify sin.

11. When the wicked shall be punished and the just shall rejoice, then, in reality, *"man shall say;"* the men, witnessing those things, will say. If justice brings any advantage with it, the greatest is, that God, the supreme Judge, does not let the wicked go unpunished, nor the just unrewarded; but he reverses all unjust judgments, and judges all, both good and bad, rewarding the good for all the good works they did, and for all the persecutions they

suffered; and inflicting condign punishment on the wicked for all their bad acts, and for all the wantonness in which they reveled; and thus is fulfilled the sentence in the Apocalypse 18, *"As much as she hath glorified herself; and hath been in delicacies, so much torment and sorrow give unto her."*

PSALM 58

A prayer to be delivered from the wicked, with confidence in God's help and protection. It agrees to Christ and his enemies the Jews.

1 Deliver me from my enemies, O my God; and defend me from them that rise up against me.

2 Deliver me from them that work iniquity, and save me from bloody men.

3 For behold they have caught my soul: the mighty have rushed in upon me:

4 Neither is it my iniquity, nor my sin, O Lord: without iniquity have I run, and directed my steps.

5 Rise up thou to meet me, and behold: even thou, O Lord, the God of hosts, the God of Israel. Attend to visit all the nations: have no mercy on all them that work iniquity.

6 They shall return at evening, and shall suffer hunger like dogs: and shall go round about the city.

7 Behold they shall speak with their mouth, and a sword is in their lips: for who, say they, hath heard us?

8 But thou, O Lord, shalt laugh at them: thou shalt bring all the nations to nothing.

9 I will keep my strength to thee: for thou art my protector:

10 My God, his mercy shall prevent me.

11 God shall let me see over my enemies: slay them not, lest at any time my people forget. Scatter them by thy power; and bring them down, O Lord, my protector:

12 For the sin of their mouth, and the word of their lips: and let them be taken in their pride. And for their cursing and lying they shall be talked of,

13 When they are consumed: when they are consumed by thy wrath, and they shall be no more. And they shall know that God will rule Jacob, and all the ends of the earth.

14 They shall return at evening and shall suffer hunger like dogs: and shall go round about the city.

15 They shall be scattered abroad to eat, and shall murmur if they be not filled.

16 But I will sing thy strength: and will extol thy mercy in the morning. For thou art become my support, and my refuge, in the day of my trouble.

17 Unto thee, O my helper, will I sing, for thou art God my defence: my God my mercy.

EXPLANATION OF THE PSALM

1. David, hemmed in by the soldiers of Saul in his own house, as if he were in a prison, prays to Almighty God. It is also applicable to Christ as he lay in the sepulchre, with guards on it; and is also applicable to any just person in danger of death.

2. An explanation of the preceding verse. *"My enemies,"* in the first verse, are here called the *"workers of iniquity,"* for the just have no other enemies than such persons who can assign no reason for being so, but that they are wicked, and the others just. *"They that rise up against me,"* in the first verse, are called here *"bloody men;"* homicides, who rise up against their neighbor to spill their blood.

3. He assigns a reason for asking for deliverance, being in extreme danger, as he was, of losing his life. He was like a wild beast *"caught"* in the toils, and about to be destroyed. *"The mighty have rushed in upon me;"* such as Saul, Abner his general, and people of that class, to show he was persecuted, not by a few soldiers, but by a most powerful king, having a numerous army at his command.

4. These words, when referred to David, do not convey that he was absolutely free from sin, but that he was not guilty of the sin laid to his charge, that of rebellion against Saul. If referred to Christ, they are absolutely true, for *"He did no sin, neither was guile found in his mouth;"* 1 Peter 2. *"Neither is it my iniquity nor my sin, O Lord; that is to say, "Though the mighty have rushed in upon me,"* it is not my iniquity, nor my sins, nor any injury offered them by me that has provoked them. Because *"without iniquity have I run;"* my life has been a most inoffensive one. *"And directed my steps;"* have turned neither to the right nor to the left: to the right, to ingratiate myself with the rich; to the left, to oppress the poor and the humble.

5. He said that *"he ran,"* and that *"he directed his steps."* Now, he that *"directs his steps"* will, undoubtedly, run to God, to whom, as to their last end, all good things are directed; and he, therefore, says, I, by my good acts, have directed my course to you; and do you, therefore, in return, protect me *"by rising up to meet me." "And behold"* the danger I am in, and consider for the trouble I am in; nor can you plead inability or ignorance for you are the *"Lord God of hosts;"* and, as Lord, you can do everything; and, as God, you see and know everything; as Lord of Hosts you have thousands of Angels to do your bidding, and whom you can employ in helping me; you are, finally, *"the God of Israel;"* and, therefore, we have a special claim on your protection, by virtue of the compact you entered into with our fathers. *"Attend to visit all the nations."* Let the day of universal judgment arrive, and then *"have no mercy on all them that work iniquity;"* spare no sinner; punish them all according to their deserts. These expressions should be understood in a prophetic, rather than an imprecatory sense, making the meaning to be, the great day of general retribution will come, at length, when all shall have to render an account to God, the supreme Judge; and God wilt then spare no wicked person, but *"will bring all evil men to an evil end."* Hereon, however, St. Augustine raises question; how can it be true that God *"will have no mercy on them that work iniquity,"* when it is certain that he had mercy on David himself, though guilty of adultery and homicide; on Peter, who denied Christ; and on Paul, who so persecuted the Church. In thus extending his mercy, God acts, not as a Judge, but as the Father of mercies: through which mercy he softens the heart, and moves it to penance. But in this passage David speaks of God purely as Judge, *"who will render unto every one according to their works;"* and especially, on the last day, when he will neither spare nor have mercy on any wicked person.

6. He continues describing the wretched condition of the wicked on the last day, *"They shall return at evening;"* their conversion will be too late; they let the day pass, in which they might have worked and been converted, and now turn to penance of no value; such penance as Wisdom 5 describes, *"Saying within themselves repenting, and groaning for anguish of spirit."* *"And shall hunger like dogs;"* for that justice they disregarded, when they could have had their fill of it, or for the rest and quiet they cannot now hope for; *"And shall go round,"* as the dogs do, *"about the city"* of God; the assembly of the elect, seeking in vain for admission; trying to move those within to look with mercy on them, but to no purpose; for none of the saints will, on that day, have the slightest pity on the workers of iniquity. Such retribution will be an essentially just one; for, in this life, the wicked *"returned at evening;"* sought the darkness of night, instead of the light of day. *"And suffered hunger;"* indulged in carnal passions with all the eagerness that hungry dogs devour their meat; and as the dogs *"go round about the city"* in quest of the carrion thrown into the trenches, so did they seek in all quarters for the gratification of their carnal desires. Others explain this passage as applying to the soldiers coming, like dogs, in the evening to destroy David. Others apply it to the conversion of the Jews in the end of the world.

7. He reverts to the malice of the wicked, speaking of it alternately with their punishment. *"Behold,"* they who sought my life *"shall speak with their mouth,"* in an under tone, for fear they may be heard; *"And a sword is in their lips,"* for it all turned on my death, and they did so with the greatest security, for they said to each other, *"Who hath heard us?"* Nobody.

8. They thought they were not heard, when they plotted so privately, and proposed doing wonders. *"But thou, O Lord,"* from whom nothing is secret, *"shalt laugh at them,"* for their folly; for you can not only baffle their designs with the greatest ease, but, even though they had the whole world to support them, *"thou shalt bring all the nations to nothing."*

9-10. Remembering God's omnipotence, compared with which all nations are reputed as nothing, he humbles himself before him with a view to merit his grace. *"I will keep my strength to thee,"* whatever strength I have is from you, and not from myself; and it is not possible, therefore, for me to keep it, but you will keep it because you gave it, *"for thou art my protector."* I have the best reasons for thus confiding in you, for you have undertaken my protection from my infancy, being peculiarly my God, who alone I worship. *"His mercy shall prevent me."* I do not speak idly, for God's mercy, as it has hitherto attended me, will (as I trust) continue to attend me, and not allow me to be oppressed by my enemies. David could say so, with great justice, for, from his very youth, the grace of God was with him, and it strengthened him, especially when he killed the bear and the lion, and afterwards Goliath the giant, without a weapon, and while still a boy when he was anointed king by Samuel. All this is much more applicable to Christ, because not only from his boyhood or his infancy was he anointed, but even from his very conception. *"He was anointed with the Holy Ghost, and with power,"* Acts 10.

11. He now reverts to his enemies, and predicts their punishment, speaking in the person of Christ. *"God shall let me see over my enemies;"* will let me see the punishment in store for them. He has already revealed it to me, and when it shall have been accomplished, I will see the punishment they shall justly suffer. But I pray God to *"slay them not,"* not to extinguish the Jewish race entirely. *"Lest at any time my people may forget,"* he still has regard to his people, and wishes them not to be forgotten entirely. What I ask, therefore, is, that you would *"scatter them by your power,"* by that power that no one can resist; to scatter them all over the world, and *"bring them down"* from that pitch of glory they enjoyed when they were God's peculiar people, and had their kings and their priesthood. All of which was literally accomplished in regard of the Jews.

12. He tells us now why the Jews were so scattered, *"For the sin of their mouth,"* when they said, *"We have no king but Ceasar,"* and *"His blood be on us and on our children,"* for God, with great justice, gave them the benefit of their prayer, according to Daniel 9, *"And the people that shall deny him shall not be his."* *"And let them be taken in their pride,"* be led captives by the Romans, humbled and cast down on account of their pride, that made them boast of being children of Abraham, and of never having been slaves to any one, as may be seen in John 8. It was, in fact, their pride and contumacy that provoked the anger of the Roman people, as appears from Josephus. That, however, was the occasion; the real cause of their ruin was their pride, that made them despise the Son of God. *"And for their cursing and lying they shall be talked of."* The cursing consisted in that dreadful imprecation quoted above, *"His blood be on us;"* and the other expression, *"We have no king but*

Caesar," was a palpable lie and a falsehood, for it is certain that they resisted paying tribute to him, and boasted they were a free people, never subject to any one, which was a downright falsehood, for they were subject to Pharao in Egypt, to Nabuchodonosor in Babylon, to the Philistines in the land of promise, and, at the very time of their boasting, to the Romans.

13. The prophet predicts that, in consequence of their cursing and lying, *"they will be talked of;"* published, proclaimed all over the world as such. *"When they are consumed;"* when, on the destruction of the city, all the power and glory of the Jewish people will be destroyed forever. *"When they are consumed by the wrath;"* not by any chance or fortuitous destruction, but by the destruction arising from God's anger; which will, therefore, be a destruction so complete and entire, that the Jews can never again hope for a king or a seat of government; and, therefore, he adds, *"and they shall be no more;"* there will be no trace of them, neither of kingdom nor of people; they will be miserably dispersed and scattered, as we actually see accomplished. *"And they shall know that God will rule Jacob;"* when the Jews shall have been scattered throughout the world, then *"they shall know"* and clearly see that the true God is the God not only of Jacob, of the people of Israel, but he is also the God of *"all the ends of the earth,"* of the whole world, and all the nations thereon. Hitherto *"God was known to Judea and in Israel, great was his name,"* Psalm 95; and, in Psalm 78, was said, *"Pour out thy wrath upon the nations that have not known thee; and upon the kingdoms that have not called upon thy name;"* but, after the destruction of Jerusalem, and the preaching of Christ's Gospel through the world, the dispersed Jews saw the true God worshipped everywhere, idols broken, the Psalms of David chanted; and thus they learned that God was not the God of the Jews alone, but also of the gentiles.

14. They will never see more clearly the truth of the preceding verse, *"that God rules Jacob and the ends of the earth,"* than on the last day, when *"we shall all stand before the tribunal of Christ,"* and *"every knee shall bend to him;"* then *"they shall return"* to penance, but too late; for it will be in the *"evening,"* when the hour of mercy shall have passed; *"they shall suffer hunger like dogs,"* prowling and *"going round about the city"* of the elect, looking in vain for admission or consolation.

15. The same Jews, in their appeal to their patriarchs and prophets, will not be heard by them; but will be dispersed, looking for food like so many dogs; and, when they meet no consolation, get nothing, and are not acknowledged as children, they will begin to murmur and complain of their unhappy state.

16. Hitherto those impious persecutors had been his subject; he now, in his own person, or rather, in the person of Christ and the Church, which is his body, gives expression to his joy and gladness, accompanied by thanksgiving and praise of God. *"but I will sing thy strength."* Those wretched beings may howl and grumble; but I, on the other hand, *"will sing"* and praise *"thy strength,"* so displayed by you in the total destruction of the wicked; *"And will extol thy mercy;"* with great delight will I praise thee for the mercy you displayed in the liberation and glorification of the just, and I will do so *"in the morning,"* before I turn to any other business or occupation. *"For thou art become my support and my refuge in the day of my trouble."* He tells the effect of the mercy he promised to sing of, and that is, God becoming *"his support;"* undertaking to protect him, and affording him *"a refuge in the day of his trouble."*

17. The same repeated, but differently expressed, to show his affection and gratitude to so great a benefactor. The word *"helper"* implies God's power; *"my defense"* refers to his goodness, which causes him to take his elect under his protection. The words *"my God"* imply that he is our supreme good, and the final object of all our desires; finally, *"my mercy"* comprehends all God's gifts, that enable us to come to him as the supreme good; for, as St. Augustine properly observes, it is of much more importance to us that he should be *"our mercy,"* than our salvation, our life, or our hope. For it was his mercy that made us to live and to exist, to be delivered from evil, and advance in virtue. By the mercy of God we were predestinated, called, justified, and will be finally glorified; for, though glorification depends on merit, our very merits are gifts of God, because, without his previous grace, they would be of no value. Justly, therefore, the prophet, in Psalm 102, says, *"Who crowneth thee with mercy and compassion."*

PSALM 59

After many afflictions, the Church of Christ shall prevail.

1 God, thou hast cast us off, and hast destroyed us; thou hast been angry, and hast had mercy on us.
2 Thou hast moved the earth, and hast troubled it: heal thou the breaches thereof, for it has been moved.
3 Thou hast shewn thy people hard things; thou hast made us drink wine of sorrow.
4 Thou hast given a warning to them that fear thee: that they may flee from before the bow: That thy beloved may be delivered.
5 Save me with thy right hand, and hear me.
6 God hath spoken in his holy place: I will rejoice, and I will divide Sichem; and will mete out the vale of tabernacles.
7 Galaad is mine, and Manasses is mine: and Ephraim is the strength of my head. Juda is my king:

8 Moab is the pot of my hope. Into Edom will I stretch out my shoe: to me the foreigners are made subject.
9 Who will bring me into the strong city? who will lead me into Edom?
10 Wilt not thou, O God, who hast cast us off? and wilt not thou, O God, go out with our armies?
11 Give us help from trouble: for vain is the salvation of man.
12 Through God we shall do mightily: and he shall bring to nothing them that afflict us.

EXPLANATION OF THE PSALM

1. He begins by a narration of the past afflictions of the people of Israel; *"O God, thou hast cast us off,"* from your fatherly care and protection, *"and hast destroyed us,"* allowing us to be harassed, oppressed, and destroyed by the Philistines, the Idumeans, the Moabites, and other enemies. *"Thou hast been angry, and hast had mercy on us."* Thou hast been angry with us for our sins that provoked you, and therefore given us up to our enemies; but, shortly after thou *"hast had mercy on us;"* when, through your grace, you inspired us to do penance, and, after having done penance, delivered us from captivity and persecution. The truth of these expressions will at once appear to any one reading the book of Judges, and the first book of Kings. The Jews were left in the hands of their enemies by reason of their sins; on doing penance they were liberated. So with the Church of Christ. St. Cyprian attributes the persecution of the early Christians to their sins, which was sometimes so severe, that this verse was quite appropriate to them. The expression, *"Hast had mercy on us,"* refers especially to the fortitude of the martyrs; for, though God, angry with Christians for their sins, may permit persecution, he still had great mercy on the Church, in giving the grace of fortitude to so many Christians; and its glory, from the crowns of innumerable martyrs, was much greater than its depression from rapine or the ruin of its sacred edifices.

2. He explains the greatness of the persecution, for it was not one, or two, or many cities that were moved, but *"the whole earth was moved."* If we take these words in reference to the Jews, the meaning will be, the whole land of promise was moved; if in reference to the persecution of the Christians, the meaning will be, the Church diffused over the whole earth. *"Heal thou the breaches thereof, for it has been moved;"* you who strike with fire and sword, not as an enemy, but as a physician, heal her wounds and *"breaches,"* for *"it has been moved;"* admonished by the scourge, it has been moved to penance; and she that, from a continued prosperity, had begun to halt and to falter, has now taken to run in the way of your commandments.

3. He goes on with the same subject, and says, *"thou hast shown thy people hard things;"* made your people to see and to feel severe persecution. *"Thou hast made us drink the wine of sorrow;"* taking advantage of this persecution, you have made us enter into ourselves, and drink the bitter, but wholesome cup of holy sorrow. The word *"shown"* conveys the idea of God's kindness, who rather shows than inflicts trouble; and that with a view more of deterring than of punishing us; whence his chastisements are not at all as severe as they appear to be to the carnal; and therefore, the Apostle says, *"Our present tribulation, which is momentary and light."* The words, *"Thou hast made us drink,"* convey to us also an idea of God's goodness, who does not show us that most wholesome gift of penance, but pours it into our hearts, into the very depth of our hearts, and thus warms us, as wine warms the whole interior.

4. Through all those *"hard things"* meaning the persecutions and afflictions by which the just are harassed here below. God gives a warning to them that fear him, *"To flee from before the bow,"* that will shoot deadly arrows at the wicked on the last day; for the tribulations the just suffer here, in order to purge them from venial sin, are signs of the grievous punishments that await the wicked after this life, of which the Apostle Peter writes in his 1st Epistle, chap. 4, *"For the time is that judgment should begin at the house of God. And if first at us, what shall be the end of those who believe not the gospel of God?"* And his fellow Apostle Paul, 1 Cor. 11, *"But whilst we are judged, we are chastised by the Lord, that we may not be damned with this world."* God, then, while he purges the elect, leads them to infer, from their own trouble, how great are the punishments in store for the wicked; and therefore, that they should by leading a pious and holy life, *"Flee from before the bow;"* which is now drawn, but, on the last day, will be let fly with such force as will destroy the wicked for all eternity. *"That thy beloved may be delivered;"* a prayer for the deliverance of his beloved from their troubles and persecutions.

5-7. He now begins to show that his prayer was heard, that he conquered all his enemies, and that he made a considerable addition to his kingdom. *"God hath spoken in his holy place,"* through me his holy prophet, to whom he has revealed what is to happen, most of which is already accomplished. The prophecy was a well known one, for Abner, Saul's general, said to the people, 2 Kings 3, *"The Lord hath spoken to David, saying: By the hand of my servant David I will save my people Israel from the hands of the Philistines, and of all their enemies." "I will rejoice, and I will divide Sichem."* Having mentioned the prophecy, he now comes to prove that it was already, in a great degree, fulfilled. *"I will rejoice,"* like a conqueror after a victory, with an extension of his kingdom, and first of all, *"I will divide Sichem,"* that is, Samaria; as master of it, I will form it into districts, make a census of its cities, towns, and villages, and appoint judges and magistrates in them; *"And I will mete out the vale of tabernacles,"* I will do the same in the country next it, called the vale of tabernacles from the fact of Jacob having first pitched his tent there, and bought part of the land of Sichem. Observe here, that David, in enumerating the provinces of his kingdom, begins with Sichem, a part of Samaria, and is generally applied to Samaria; as also from the vale of tabernacles, called also Sochot, because it was there Jacob and his sons got first hold of the land of promise. It is to be observed also, that he mentions here not more than Sichem, Sochot, Galaad, Manasses, and Ephraim, all of which belonged to the tribe of Joseph, because that was the greatest tribe of all, and thus he made it to signify all the tribes of Israel, or the kingdom of Israel. He makes separate mention afterwards of the tribe of Juda, uniting with it the tribe of Benjamin, and was called the kingdom of Juda, when the division was made under Roboam. He, therefore, adds, *"Galaad is mine, and Manasses is mine,"* mine is the country called after the man named Galaad, and mine is the country called after Manasses the son of Joseph. *"And Ephraim is the strength of my head;"* mine is the country named after Ephraim, another son of Joseph, a country full of brave men, the principal defense, strength, and support of my kingdom. *"Juda is my king."* Having enumerated the provinces of the ten tribes, under the name of Manasses and Ephraim, he now adds the tribe of Juda, to which, as we said before, was united the tribe of Benjamin. *"Juda is my king."* The whole country called Juda, from Juda the son of Jacob, is mine too. Juda is a royal tribe, as we read in 1 Paralipomenon 28, *"For of Juda he chose the princes;"* and Jacob himself, at his death, when blessing his sons, said of Juda. *"The scepter shall not be taken away from Juda, nor a ruler from his thigh;"* alluding to which promise David makes use of the word used by Jacob, that signifies either a king or a leader. He therefore says, *"Juda is my king;"* that is to say, the tribe of Juda, that always held the first place, and from which the kings, my fathers, sprung, is mine, and will supply the future kings.

8. Having enumerated the provinces of his own kingdom, he now enumerates the provinces of the enemy become tributary to him, first of which he names that of the Moabites, called Moab, after Moab, the son of Lot, the nephew of Abraham. *"Moab is the pot of my hope."* The province of Moab, now subject to me, is like a pot full of meat, abounding in riches and plenty, and giving me great hopes. *"Into Idumea will I stretch out my shoe;"* Idumea is the country possessed by the descendants of Esau, brother to Jacob, and at the time this Psalm was written, though David had obtained a victory over them, having killed twelve thousand of them, he had not yet conquered the whole of Idumea. That he did so afterwards appears from 2 Kings 8, where we read, *"And all Idumea became subject to David."* He therefore says, *"Into

Edom I will stretch my shoe." I will proceed to wage war, and trample on Idumea. *"To me the foreigners are made subject."* I have already subdued the Philistines, who are foreigners, so called having had no connection or affinity with the Israelites. The Idumeans, the Ammonites, and the Moabites, though not children of Jacob, were connected with the Israelites, for the Idumeans were descended from Esau or Edom, who was brother to Jacob; and the Ammonites and Moabites were descended from Lot.

9. Edom being the only nation not entirely subdued by David, and being the best fortified of all, he now says, *"Who will lead me into the strong city?"* Idumea was a real stronghold, and he asks who will be the leader of the expedition to subdue it; of its strength the prophet Abdias says, *"The pride of thy heart hath lifted thee up, who dwellest in the clefts of the rocks, and settest up thy throne on high, who sayest in thy heart, Who shall bring me down to the ground? Though thou be exalted as an eagle, and though thou set thy nest among the stars, thence I will bring thee down, saith the Lord."* And he tells us of what strong city he speaks, when he adds, *"Who will lead me into Edom?"* Who will help me to conquer Idumea? All this is most applicable to Christ and the Church. The kingdom of Juda means the Church, the Sichemites or Samaritans mean its enemies, who will, with great trouble, but with great certainty, be ultimately subdued. Ephraim and Manasses, typify the schismatics, inasmuch as Jeroboam drew them off from Jerusalem and the temple, and set up another altar; and they too will, at a fitting time, be subdued. The Idumeans are the type of the Jews, the last to submit, like the Jews, who, however, in the end will be brought to Christ.

10. He answers a question by asking another. Nobody can possibly bring us into the strongholds of the Idumeans, but you, *"O God, who hast cast us off."* *"And wilt not thou, O God, go out with our armies?"* If you do, we must needs conquer; without your help, we will be the conquered.

11. You, therefore, who are alone the all powerful, give us that help that will free us from all trouble; for any human help is of no value.

12. Relying on God's help we can do anything, and we will frustrate the designs of all those who seek to harm us.

PSALM 60

A prayer for the coming of the kingdom of Christ, which shall have no end.

1 Hear, O God, my supplication: be attentive to my prayer,
2 To thee have I cried from the ends of the earth: when my heart was in anguish, thou hast exalted me on a rock. Thou hast conducted me;
3 For thou hast been my hope; a tower of strength against the face of the enemy.
4 In thy tabernacle I shall dwell for ever: I shall be protected under the covert of thy wings.

5 For thou, my God, hast heard my prayer: thou hast given an inheritance to them that fear thy name.
6 Thou wilt add days to the days of the king: his years even to generation and generation.
7 He abideth for ever in the sight of God: his mercy and truth who shall search?
8 So will I sing a psalm to thy name for ever and ever: that I may pay my vows from day to day.

Explanation of the psalm

1. A very brief preface, because it is the prayer of a just man or a Christian people, asking to be heard by God; not to turn away from them, but to take a considerate view of their case. The Hebrew for *"supplication"* conveys the idea of its being not an ordinary one put up in silence, but an ardent, loudly expressed appeal to God; and, therefore, more likely to arrest his attention. A cold prayer, coming from the lips alone, will hardly penetrate the clouds, much less the heaven of heavens.

2. David was never an exile in *"The ends of the earth,"* nor were the children of Israel; and, therefore, he must speak here in the person of the Church, which has spread over the whole world, to its very extremities, according to Psalm 2, *"Ask of me, and I will give thee the gentiles for thy inheritance, and the utmost parts of the earth for thy possession."* He therefore says, I (the Church) having been propagated to the ends of the earth, from those extremities of the earth, through the voice of all my members, *"Have cried to thee"* with a loud and earnest voice. The words, *"Ends of the earth,"* seem also to convey an idea of the distance between him who asks and him from whom he expects. God, to whom the appeal is made, is in heaven, and he who asks it in *"The ends of the earth;"* and hence he should needs cry aloud. The same idea is conveyed in the expression, *"From the depths have I cried to thee, O Lord."* He should have a loud voice who, from the depths, expects that God, who sits aloft in the highest heavens, nay, even on the Cherubim, should hear him; in other words, the person who, cognizant of his own nothingness, when compared to the divine perfections, yet presumes to commune with God in prayer. *"When my heart was in anguish thou hast exalted me on a rock."* He assigns a reason for appealing to God with such confidence, because he found the divine assistance never withheld from him when in trouble. *"When,"* on various other occasions, *"my heart was in anguish,"* by reason of various temptations that beset me, you heard me when I cried to you, and *"exalted me on a rock;"* the safest possible place I could be lodged in, afterwards called *"a tower of strength."* That lofty rock is Christ; and anyone that will raise himself up to him in contemplation, considering how much he suffered for us, and what an end he had, will easily conquer, and despise the whole world beside.

3. He explains the expression, *"Thou hast exalted me on a rock,"* by the words, *"Thou hast conducted me;"* became my guide when I fled from the enemy, who assailed me with temptation. *"For thou hast been my hope;"* your escort and guidance consisted in inspiring me with hope, which not only upheld me, but made me bear everything with the greatest courage. And thus, you became *"a tower of strength against the face of the enemy;"* for he who trusts in God, and reflects on the sufferings of Christ, to what glory he came on his resurrection, that he is our head, from looking on whom we are to learn what we have to suffer on earth, and what we have a right to expect and desire in heaven; he undoubtedly stands on a highly fortified tower, where he can not only avoid the weapons of the enemy, but even hurl weapons at them.

4. He now tells us that, by the stronghold in the preceding verse, he does not mean the kingdom of heaven, but the resting place of the pilgrim here below; such is the force of the word in the Hebrew; and he says, I will take up my lodging in *"that tower of strength;"* and in the meantime, while there, *"I shall be protected under the covert of thy wings,"* as the hen protects her chickens from the birds of prey.

5. His confidence arises from the fact that, at all times, *"Thou, my God, hast heard my prayer;"* and that because, *"Thou hast given an inheritance to them that fear thy name;"* made me one of your heirs, your children. For if God has an everlasting inheritance for his children that fear him, will he not protect them on their journey thereto? What father ever despised or deserted his deserving children? *"And if God be for us, who is against us?"* We are absolutely sure and certain of the eternal inheritance in heaven, and God's protection in this world, if we truly fear him.

6. The Prophet, bearing in mind that the inheritance of the saints is life everlasting, now informs us that this inheritance, so promised to the Church, should commence with its head; and, therefore, says, *"Thou wilt add days to the days of the king;"* you will multiply the days of Christ our king without end, *"even to generation and generation;"* to the day of eternity, which, though designated as a day, is equivalent to generation and generation, to ages of ages, and times of times without end. That the expression means eternity is evident from Psalm 118, where he says, *"Forever, O Lord, thy word standeth firm in heaven. Thy truth unto all generations."* Which is similar to the expression in Psalm 134, *"Thy name, O Lord, is forever; thy memorial, O Lord, unto all generations."* From which we clearly see that the Psalm is not applicable to David as king, but to Christ as king; for David did not live more than seventy years, nor did the sovereignty remain in his family. The eternity, then,

of both king and kingdom, foretold in the Scriptures, is accomplished in Christ alone, for *"There will be no end of his kingdom,"* Luke 1 *"And he, rising from the dead, shall die no more. Death shall have no more dominion over him."* Rom. 6.

7. Christ, the head of the Church, *"abideth forever in the sight of God"* for us; the Apostle testifies it was for such purpose he *"entered into heaven itself, that he may appear now in the presence of God for us."* Instead of *"abideth,"* the Hebrew word has *"he sitteth;"* to show that he sits as a Judge, instead of standing as a servant. *"His mercy and truth who shall search?"* His mercy, in redeeming fallen man; and his truth, by virtue of which he has kept and will adhere to his promises. *"Who shall search them,"* for they are a great abyss; and, as the Apostle to the Ephesians says, *"The charity of Christ surpasseth knowledge;"* is beyond our comprehension.

8. As God's mercy has been poured upon me in abundance, and his truth is so certain that I have no need of inquiring into it, *"I will sing a psalm to thy name forever and ever;"* I will praise you, my God, not only here on earth, but forever, with loud canticles and shouts of praise in heaven; that by doing so *"I may pay my vows"* of thanksgiving *"from day to day,"* all the days of my life, to the day that will not be succeeded by night.

PSALM 61

The prophet encourages himself and all others to trust in God, and serve him.

1 Shall not my soul be subject to God? for from him is my salvation.
2 For he is my God and my saviour: he is my protector, I shall be moved no more.
3 How long do you rush in upon a man? you all kill, as if you were thrusting down a leaning wall, and a tottering fence.
4 But they have thought to cast away my price; I ran in thirst: they blessed with their mouth, but cursed with their heart.
5 But be thou, O my soul, subject to God: for from him is my patience.
6 For he is my God and my saviour: he is my helper, I shall not be moved.
7 In God is my salvation and my glory: he is the God of my help, and my hope is in God.
8 Trust in him, all ye congregation of people: pour out your hearts before him. God is our helper for ever.
9 But vain are the sons of men, the sons of men are liars in the balances: that by vanity they may together deceive.
10 Trust not in iniquity, and cover not robberies: if riches abound, set not your heart upon them.
11 God hath spoken once, these two things have I heard, that power belongeth to God,

12 And mercy to thee, O Lord; for thou wilt render to every man according to his works.

EXPLANATION OF THE PSALM

1. A just man, fiercely assailed by various concupiscences, every one of which contend for a mastery over him, in his brave struggle, exclaims, *"Shall not my soul be subject to God?"* Is it not better and fitter for me to serve God than be a slave to avarice, pride, or concupiscence? *"For from him is my salvation."* Those evil passions and desires offer me nothing but death everlasting; but God promises, and will certainly confer, eternal happiness, if I remain faithful to him.

2. My salvation not only depends on him, but *"he is my God and my Savior."* The Hebrew has the word *"rock"* for God, to signify that in this world he is the rock we are to build upon, to take refuge on, and in the other world to be our Savior. In both he will be our protector here to defend us, hereafter to crown us; and, therefore, *"I shall be moved no more."* I will not be much concerned or troubled, but remain firm, however grievous the temptations may be.

3. Having spoken of himself, he now turns to deplore the dreadful ruin of souls by the evil spirits through the agency of the various concupiscences. In truth, nobody can calculate the numbers brought to ruin by the evil spirits, through the agency of avarice, ambition, lust, anger, envy, and such evil passions. Full of indignation, therefore, against the evil spirits, he exclaims, *"How long do you rush in upon a man?"* will you never cease from persecuting man? *"You will kill;"* you all seek to destroy souls in various places and by various means, but with one common object. *"As if a leaning wall and a tottering fence;"* waging war upon poor, fallen human nature, so weak and corrupt, that it may aptly be compared to a tumbling wall and a rotten fence. A beautiful description of the malice and power of the demons, as well as of the frailty and weakness of human nature; for, in truth, since his fall, man may be compared to a tottering wall or heap, that requires the very smallest push to tumble it; for he is frail, and, as Genesis, chap. 8, has it, *"Prone to evil from his youth;"* and, therefore, the Apostle justly exclaims, *"Unhappy man that I am, who shall deliver me from the body of this death?"* and he immediately answers the question thus, *"The grace of God by Jesus Christ our Lord."*

4. He returns to the subject he began with, and shows that the object of our spiritual enemies, in their attacks upon the just, is to deprive them of the everlasting rewards for which they envy them, and which they themselves lost through their own fault. *"But they have thought to cast away my price."* They tempt, assault, excite my concupiscence to balk me of *"my price;"* that price by which I was redeemed, and thus deprive me of the dignity and great honor of everlasting glory. But I, on the contrary, *"ran in thirst."* The more they sought to keep me back, the more ardently and thirstily I ran; for *"The prize of the supernal vocation,"* Phil. 3:14; *"They blessed with their mouth, but cursed with their heart."* Their words were those of kindness, gently alluring to enjoy the present, and yield to pleasure; but, meanwhile, *"They cursed with their heart,"* knowing those very pleasures to be poison to the soul, and the most direct means of marring me in the pursuit of eternal happiness.

5-7. He now repeats the two first verses, to show the greatness of the temptations by which he was assailed; and that he so confided in God that he was in no way afraid of them. *"But be thou, O my soul, subject to God."* However the enemy may rage do you, my soul, in silence and subjection, be obedient to God, *"for from him is my patience;"* say nothing, for he will certainly help you. *"For he is my God;"* this is word for word in the Hebrew with verse 2, which see. In verse 7 he concludes by saying he expects everything from God; that is, our true end, and the means to obtain it. Our true end consists in being delivered from all evils, and the possession of the supreme good; salvation implying the one, and glory the other: the means are God's assistance and our own hope, as they are properly named in the text, *"In God is my salvation and my glory."* From God I expect salvation and deliverance from all harm, and eternal glory, the supreme good; for when we shall see God, and become like him, and perfectly united to him, we shall be truly safe and happy.

8. He now exhorts everyone to the practice of that virtue, that God had so bounteously and gratuitously granted him to practice; first reminding them to put their trust in God alone, and not in anything created. *"Trust in him, all ye congregation of people;"* including every family, assembly, people, all men, not only Jews, but gentiles. *"Pour out your hearts before him."* Make a sincere and open confession of your sins and wretchedness; make all your wants known to him; pray to him to have mercy on you, as Anna did, when she said, *"I have poured forth my soul in the sight of the Lord;"* and, as a matter of course, *"God is our helper forever;"* there is no doubt but he will help you.

9. Conscious of the smallness of the number that would follow his advice, he, therefore, inveighs now against the multitude of the wicked, saying, the greater part of men are quite devoid of true wisdom though they apparently abound in it; but it is that wisdom designated by the Scriptures as *"the prudence of the flesh;"* and, therefore, most men are vain, senseless, and imprudent; because *"They are liars in the balances;"* in false and fraudulent weights and measures. This observation applies not only to those who are engaged in trade and commerce, but to all mankind; for we, all of us gifted with reason, get that reason as a sort of balance or measure wherewith to

distinguish real from apparent good, and then to choose the one, and reject the other. Now, the greater part of mankind, in doing so, miserably deceive themselves and others, by making use of such false measures, and what is worse, by doing so willfully. No one can deny that the greatest evil that can befall man is to commit sin, and thereby deserve hell's torments; and that the greatest good that can be secured is grace in this life, and happiness in the next; and yet, when we come to weigh to measure one with the other in the balance, temporal gain will generally preponderate; and to secure it, the risk of eternal punishment will be incurred. *"That by vanity they may together deceive;"* though lies and vanity assume various shapes and forms, they agree in one point, in deceit.

10. He comes again to exhort, and especially against avarice, it being *"the root of all evil;"* secret frauds being expressed by the word *"iniquity,"* and open wrongs by the term *"robberies;"* and he goes farther, in prohibiting even an affection for riches, saying, *"If riches abound, set not your heart on them."* St. Augustine beautifully remarks, that they who rob, see their plunder, but they do not see who, at the very moment, robs themselves; that is, the devil, who robs them of their soul. The same Augustine and Basil remark, that when riches abound, they begin to overflow and run away, and the blind and the covetous look only to their abundance, and never consider their flowing, nor perceive it. We are, therefore, reminded *"not to set our heart on them,"* for fear it, too, may flow with them, and be lost. When riches abound, then, having our hearts firmly and securely fixed on God, we should take care to let the riches flow, but to flow to advantage; like the prudent farmer, who directs the course of the stream to irrigate and enrich his land, but will be most careful in not allowing it to carry himself along.

11-12. He concludes by assigning a reason for not wishing for riches, and for guarding against all manner of sin; God, once for all, in one word, comprising everything. The two things announced to David are God's power and mercy, for us to fear the one, and love the other; and, secondly, that he will *"render to every man according to his works;"* that his power will not unjustly oppress anyone nor will his mercy obstruct his justice; and they who seriously reflect on those two points, *"and set their hearts on them"* may be called the truly wise.

PSALM 62

The prophet aspireth after God.

1 God, my God, to thee do I watch at break of day. For thee my soul hath thirsted; for thee my flesh, O how many ways!
2 In a desert land, and where there is no way, and no water: so in the sanctuary have I come before thee, to see thy power and thy glory.

3 For thy mercy is better than lives: thee my lips shall praise.
4 Thus will I bless thee all my life long: and in thy name I will lift up my hands.
5 Let my soul be filled as with marrow and fatness: and my mouth shall praise thee with joyful lips.
6 If I have remembered thee upon my bed, I will meditate on thee in the morning:
7 Because thou hast been my helper. And I will rejoice under the covert of thy wings:
8 My soul hath stuck close to thee: thy right hand hath received me.
9 But they have sought my soul in vain, they shall go into the lower parts of the earth:
10 They shall be delivered into the hands of the sword, they shall be the portions of foxes.
11 But the king shall rejoice in God, all they shall be praised that swear by him: because the mouth is stopped of them that speak wicked things.

Explanation of the Psalm

1. A just man tells us his first impulse at the dawn of day, and that is to seek God, to desire God, to confess his misery to him. *"O God, my God;"* my help, my strength, for without you I am nothing, can do nothing. *"To thee do I watch by break of day."* The moment I open the eyes of my body, I open those of my mind, to behold you, the increased light; and thus I watch to look for you, instead of looking for the things of this world. I do so, because *"For thee my soul hath thirsted;"* it longs for thee as its meat and drink; its light and gladness. My flesh thirsts in various ways for thee, the fountain of all good. Though the flesh, properly speaking, cannot be said to thirst for God, it is said to thirst, because by reason of its manifold miseries, it needs his mercy, just as parched land is said to thirst for rain, without which it can produce nothing. Everyone has experienced the necessities, wants, and miseries of our corruptible flesh, which he alone, of whom it is said, *"Who heals all your infirmities,"* can heal.

2. The characteristics of a desert are three, uninhabited, inaccessible, without water; the second being the effect, and the third the cause, of the first; for a country is generally deserted by reason of a want of water; for that makes the ground dry and barren, and when so deserted and barren, it becomes inaccessible. The prophet means to convey that such uncultivated land, wanting not only the luxuries, but even the necessaries of life, was of great use to him in finding God. For the more the soul is destitute of the goods of this world, or, certainly, the more it takes its affections off them, and betakes itself to a spiritual desert, the more easily it ascends to the contemplation and enjoyment of things celestial. *"In that desert land, and where there is no way and no water;"* here I come to thee in spirit, raising up my soul to thee, as if I were *"in thy sanctuary,"* so that the desert became a sanctuary to me, *"to see thy power and thy glory."*

3. The word *"For"* must be referred to the following, and not to the preceding; and the meaning is, I will not only see thy power and thy glory, but my lips shall daily praise you, for your mercy is better to me than life itself; for it was your mercy that gave me that life, that preserves that life; and the same mercy will make that life a much happier one to me, should I lose it for your sake; but if, for the purpose of preserving that life, I should fall from your grace and mercy, I will lose both my life and your mercy.

4. With such daily praise: *"I will bless thee my life long;"* whatever may befall me, whether in prosperity or adversity, I will bless you forever; *"And in thy name I will lift up my hands."* Whenever I invoke your name, I will raise up my hands in prayer, expecting help from you alone in adversity; and, on the other hand, thanking you alone in my prosperity. The custom of raising the hands in prayer was practiced in both the old and the new law; for, when Moses lifted up his hands to God, the people conquered. And the Apostle, 1 Tim. 2, says, *"Raising their pure hands."* St. Augustine reminds those who raise their hands to God in prayer, that if they wish to be heard, they should also raise their hands to do good works. Raising the hand also was used by the Jews as a form of oath; thus, we find Abraham saying *"I lift up my hand to the Lord God, the Most High, the possessor of heaven and earth, that from the very woof thread unto the shoe latchet, I will not take of anything that are thine."* And, in the Apocalypse 10, *"He lifted up his hand to heaven, and swore by him that liveth forever and ever."* The expression, then, may mean, I will swear by your name, and thus worship you alone as the true God.

5. Here is what he asked when he lifted his hands in prayer to God, that his *"soul should be filled as with marrow and fatness;"* that his soul should become replete with that spiritual marrow and fatness that acts upon the soul as the natural marrow and fatness do upon the body. Those who enjoy it are generally sound, strong, active, ruddy, and good humored; on the other hand, those who lack it are shriveled, weak, deformed, and gloomy; so those who are full of grace, of the spiritual richness here described, are devout, fervent, always in good temper; while, on the contrary, those who have it not, nauseate everything spiritual, are wasted away by listlessness; being quite weak and infirm, they can neither resist anything bad, nor do anything good. St. Augustine properly observes, that while we are in this desert, we cannot ask for and desire the feast of wisdom and justice, which we can only enjoy when we shall have arrived at our country; then will the expression of the Psalm, *"And filleth thee with the fat of corn,"* be fulfilled, as also that in Mat. 8, *"Blessed are they that hunger and thirst after justice, for they shall be filled;"* and then, *"my mouth,"* for praise shall succeed to prayer, shall

perfectly, without end, without tiring, praise God, *"with joyful lips;"* when we shall be so full that we shall want nothing; for, at present, no matter what we have, we always want something still; and thus we must have recourse to daily and constant prayer.

6. Not only in the next life, when *"filled with marrow and fatness,"* he will praise God with exultation, but also, while in this world, will he remember God and his gifts. *"If I have remembered thee upon my bed;"* in the depth of the night, as I lay thereon, much more so will I do it by day; and, therefore, *"I will meditate on thee in the morning;"* I will think and reflect on your power and glory for the following reason:

7-8. No wonder I should always reflect on your power and glory, *"because thou hast been my helper,"* always remembered me by helping and protecting me. St. Augustine gathers a useful lesson from this passage, for those who, while at their work, wish to remember God and to keep his fear and love before their eyes. To do that, they must, while lying on their bed at night, remember him, and reflect on his mercy and his promises. Most people go through their daily work as if God were not over them at all, and that because they have no fixed time for reflection or meditation. *"And I will rejoice under the covert of thy wings."* Having said, *"because thou hast been my helper,"* for fear he may be considered as looking upon himself as now secure and indifferent as to God's protection, he now adds, *"And I will rejoice under the covert of thy wings."* I will keep myself under the cover of your wings, trusting in your protection. *"I will rejoice,"* being perfectly secure from the birds of prey. *"My soul hath stuck close to thee."* Such protection, so many favors so moved me, that *"my soul hath stuck close to thee,"* united by a tie of charity so strong, that nothing can separate it; and for fear it may be supposed he was taking credit to himself for being so ardently attached to God, he adds, *"Thy right hand hath received me."* I follow you, because you draw me; I love you, because you first loved me, and by loving me made me love you. Happy is he, who, however perfect he may be, ascribes all to God, and like a chicken, shelters himself under God's wings. More happy is he who can truly say, *"my soul hath stuck close to thee,"* who, not only puts his trust in the covering of God's wings, but also loves him so entirely, with his whole heart, that he can say with the Apostle, *"Who shall separate me from the love of Christ?"* and more happy than that again is he, who, by his own experience, or by the testimony of his conscience, has learned *"that thy right hand received me,"* for of such the Lord says, *"And no man shall snatch them out of my hand. And no one can snatch them out of the hand of my Father, I and the Father are one."*

9-10. In the three last verses the prophet foretells the ultimate destruction and extermination of the persecutors of the just, and the everlasting happiness and felicity of the same just. *"But they,"* the wicked persecutors, *"have sought my soul in vain,"* endeavored in vain to have my life, to put me to death; for the wicked persecute the just, with a view of becoming masters of everything, and revel in pleasure and power; but to no purpose, for instead of being masters of the earth, they will be swallowed up by it: and when so condemned to hell, instead of the luxuries, the ease, and enjoyment they set their hearts on, they will never be allowed even a moment's rest, but will be consigned to eternal punishment, inflicted by the demons who tear them more cruelly than so many ravenous wolves and foxes. *"They shall go into the lowest parts of the earth."* See why they labored in vain, they thought to become masters, but instead of that, they will be hurled beneath the earth, into its very heart, and compelled to take up their abode forever in hell. *"They shall be delivered into the hands of the sword."* They will have no rest in hell, much less will they enjoy the blessings of the earth, but will be *"delivered into the hands of the sword,"* given up for torment; for God's punishments, as coming from a supreme and angry Judge, will be both grievous and interminable *"They shall be the portion of foxes."* Instead of lording it over the just, they will be lorded over by the unjust demons, as being now their *"lot and inheritance."* These demons are styled foxes, rather than lions or wolves, because they entrap sinners, and enslave them more by the cunning of the fox, than the strength of the lion.

11. How vain have been all the labors of the wicked! They will not only be disappointed in what they set their hearts upon, but they will not be able to deprive the just of their own, for *"their king,"* Christ, of whom the Jews said, *"Away with him, away with him, crucify him,"* whose name the pagans, with all their power, endeavored to eradicate, and which is blasphemed by all the wicked, will live and reign forever, and *"shall rejoice in God"*, sitting in glory on the right hand of the father; and *"all they shall be praised (on the day of judgment) that swear by him,"* they, who in this life, in spite of all persecution, religiously worship him as the true God, and swear by his name, or rather swear faithful obedience to him. All Christ's faithful *"will be praised," "because the mouth is stopped of them that speak wicked things."* In the day of judgment, the mouth of all the wicked will be stopped, for then the truth will be manifest, and cannot be demurred to or gainsaid; and then the wicked will exclaim, as we read in Wisdom 5, *"Therefore we have erred from the way of truth, and the light of justice hath not shined unto us, and the sun of understanding hath not risen upon us. Behold, how they are numbered among the children of God, and their lot is among the saints."* Thus the just will be praised by their very enemies, when the truth, having been exposed by God's judgment, shall shut up the mouths of those who now, by their blasphemies, maledictions, calumnies, detractions, reproaches, and lies, *"speak evil things."* Some apply those verses to David, others to Christ. Saul and

the other enemies of David, who sought to kill him, that they might reign in security, truly *"labored in vain,"* for they were destroyed, and David had a glorious reign of it. So with the Jews, who sought to put Christ to death, *"lest the Romans should come and take away their place and their nation,"* they would not have a Lamb for their King, they preferred a fox and a lion together, for the Romans sacked their city, took away their kingdom, nearly annihilated themselves; while Christ rose again, had a glorious reign of it, *"and of his kingdom there shall be no end."*

PSALM 63

A prayer in affliction, with confidence in God that he will bring to naught the machinations of persecutors.

1 Hear, O God, my prayer, when I make supplication to thee: deliver my soul from the fear of the enemy.
2 Thou hast protected me from the assembly of the malignant; from the multitude of the workers of iniquity.
3 For they have whetted their tongues like a sword; they have bent their bow a bitter thing,
4 To shoot in secret the undefiled.
5 They will shoot at him on a sudden, and will not fear: they are resolute in wickedness. They have talked of hiding snares; they have said: Who shall see them?
6 They have searched after iniquities: they have failed in their search. Man shall come to a deep heart:
7 And God shall be exalted. The arrows of children are their wounds:
8 And their tongues against them are made weak. All that saw them were troubled;
9 And every man was afraid. And they declared the works of God: and understood his doings.
10 The just shall rejoice in the Lord, and shall hope in him: and all the upright in heart shall be praised.

Explanation of the psalm

1. As usual, the prophet asks to be heard, and then tells what he wants. *"Hear, O God, my prayer, when I make supplication to thee;"* grant I may pray not in vain. *"Deliver my soul, from the fear of the enemy."* A petition that may be understood in two ways; the first, making him ask to be delivered from the fear of the enemy about to kill him, by removing the cause of his fear; that is, by rendering the enemy either unable or unwilling to kill him, which seems to be the literal explanation. The second explanation makes him ask to be freed from this fear, not by removing the cause of it, but by such an increase of love and constancy as will make him rise above fear, to render him insensible to fear any death but the death by sin, or in other words, that he may *"not fear men, that can kill the body and cannot kill the soul, but rather fear him that can destroy both body and soul in hell."* Such is the explanation of St. Augustine, a most useful and spiritual one, for in any tribulation nothing can be better than to be free from the fear of the world, and rooted in the fear of the Lord. In the latter view of it, Christ speaks in the person of his weak members; in the former view of the passage, he seems to have spoken in his own person; for as on the day before his passion, he let himself down to tremble, to fear, and to pray in the garden, saying, *"Father, if it be possible, let this cup pass from me;"* so he wished it to be here predicted.

2. Christ now shows that his prayer was heard, and that, as well as he was heard in times past, his members would, in time to come. *"Thou hast protected me from the assembly of the malignant."* We know from the Gospel, how often *"the princes of the Jews assembled against Jesus to put him to death,"* and to extinguish his name and his religion. This was not confined to the princes, for the very soldiers and satellites, *"assembled to work iniquity;"* that is, to mock, to scourge, to crucify our Savior. Yet God so protected him, that neither the assembly of the malicious Jews, nor the host of gentiles, *"workers of iniquity,"* could harm him. God, to be sure, suffered Christ's person to be scourged and flayed, but those scourges and temporal death wrought our salvation, and were turned into glory and triumph, and the beginning made by the head, has been followed up by the members, and will continue to go on, for God protected the martyrs, so that the loss of their lives was not only of no harm to them, but even turned to their everlasting glory; and God will equally protect all the pious, by causing their tribulations and persecutions always to turn to their benefit.

3-4. These verses refer to *"the assembly of the malignant,"* who fought not with their hands, but with their tongues, that is, by their consultations, accusations, importunities with Pilate to destroy Christ. He compares the language of the malicious Jews to swords and arrows; the former striking openly and close to hand, the latter, from a distance, and without being seen. So with the Jews, they openly slew Christ with the sword of their tongue, when they brought him before the council, and accused him, and condemned him, as if he had been convicted saying, *"He is guilty of death;"* and afterwards, when they again accused him before Pilate, and over and over insisted on his being crucified. *"For they have whetted their tongues like a sword,"* to strike him by their cross questions in their examination. *"They have bent their bow, a bitter thing."* They not only struck openly at him with the sword, but even in his absence, by private snares and plots they shot their arrows at hire, when they sent so many to him to take advantage of what he said, when they held private conference with Judas the traitor, and when they suborned false witnesses against him. *"They have bent their bow a bitter thing,"* laid snares that are nothing else but bitter and deadly things. *"To shoot in secret the undefiled."* Such was the end, scope, and object of their conspiracy, to show that Christ was a sinner and a false one, which they sought to prove by false and suborned witnesses; that Christ, who was truly immaculate, and came into the world to wipe away the stain of sin from others.

5. Having said that the *"assembly of the malignant"* had *"bent their bow"* *"to shoot at the undefiled,"* he now predicts the certainty of it, from the fact of their being hardened and confirmed in wickedness; for the Holy Ghost foresaw and foretold, the more than incredible obstinacy of the Jews; which prophecy Isaias also predicted, chap. 6, to which St. John alludes in the 12 chap., *"They will shoot at him on a sudden."* They will quite unexpectedly shoot their arrows from their ambush, *"and will not fear;"* will shoot boldly, having no fear of the Lord before them, and no respect for the all seeing eye of God. *"They are resolute in wickedness."* They will have no fear in so shooting at the innocent, because they are obstinate and hardened, and have made up their minds to it in the very spirit in which they cried out to Pilate, *"He is guilty of death;"* and hence, when Pilate afterwards tried all means to divert them from such a crime, they only obstinately cried out, *"Crucify him."* *"They have talked of hiding snares."* To the obstinacy of the wicked Jews, he now adds their hypocrisy, through which they sought to cover their wickedness and malice, under pretence of allegiance to Caesar. Pilate knew that well; for, as St. Mat. says, *"he knew that through envy they had delivered him up;"* which they sought to conceal, saying, *"We found this man perverting our nation, and forbidding to pay tribute to Caesar,"* Luke 23; and again, *"If thou release this man, thou art not Caesar's friend; for, whosoever maketh himself a king, speaketh against Caesar."* The meaning, then, of *"They have talked of hiding snares,"* is, They said to each other, let us enter into a plot, pretending that we are concerned only for the injury done to Caesar by this man. *"Who shall see them?"* Who will ever find out what we are at? Who, therefore, shall punish us? As if God does not see everything or as if it were of no consequence to be seen by him, who is the supreme Judge of all.

6. The prophet proceeds in relating and enlarging on the malice of the Jews, who, not content with having recourse to treachery and hypocrisy, had recourse to a most searching investigation to try and make a case out against Christ. Hence, *"The chief priest and all the council sought for false testimony against Jesus,"* and, though the witnesses did not agree, they said to him, *"Do you make no answer to what these testify against you?"* *"They have searched after iniquities,"* then, means, to look out for false testimony, and then,

knowingly to act on it, as if it were true. *"They have failed in their search,"* because they found nothing that bore even the semblance of truth; and, because, through God's providence they were so struck with blindness, that they should make themselves an object of derision to every one, by bringing forward witnesses to prove to a fact that occurred while the witnesses were asleep; for, they said to the guards on the sepulchre, *"Say you, that his disciples came by night, and stole him away when we were asleep." "Man shall come to a deep heart."* Having entered into the perversity of the wicked enemies of Christ, he now predicts the part Christ himself was to take in these persecutions. *"Man shall come to a deep heart;"* that is, Christ, as man, *"shall come to"* offer and give himself up, as one ignorant and infirm, yet having an intimate knowledge of the secrets of their hearts. *"Shall come to"* all the sufferings they planned in their hearts for him; that is, will patiently and humbly bear all the injuries they, in *"a deep heart,"* with consummate and deep malice prepared for him. The *"deep heart"* may be also referred to Christ's own heart; thus, He will enter into his own deep and profound heart, the heart in which he determined, in the form of a servant, to be abused and ill treated by the Jews, while the form of God, who was to raise him up, lay hid within.

7. While he humbles himself as man, he will be exalted as God; for then, especially, will the wisdom of God be seen superior to the malice of man, when it shall appear that Christ, by his death, conquered death, and by his resurrection, repaired life. *"The arrows of children are their wounds."* The power and wisdom of God caused the wounds inflicted on the Savior to harm him just as little as would so many arrows shot from the hands of babies, whose weak and infirm hands can injure no one. And, in fact, what signifies the wounds that were perfectly healed in three days, or rather immediately? for his body rose impassible and immortal.

8. Their calumnies and blasphemies were of no more avail, than if they were so many swords of lead; *"they are made weak,"* against themselves, to their own detriment and danger, alluding to what he already said of them in the third verse, *"For they have whetted their tongues like a sword; they have bent their bow, a bitter thing;"* in other words, they labored to whet the sword of their tongue, and to shoot their deadly arrows from their bow; but their tongue became like a sword of lead, and their arrows like those of children. The same may be said of all the persecutors of the martyrs and of the just; for the day of judgment will show how little the cruelty of their persecutors harmed them. *"When they shall stand with great constancy against those that have afflicted them."* Wisdom 5. *"All that saw them were troubled."* He now tells us the consequence of the arrows of the Jews becoming arrows of children, and their calumnies and contumelies being all refuted by the

resurrection of Christ; it was, that *"All that saw them were troubled."* The Jews were astonished and confounded when they heard from the Apostles that he whom they had put to death had risen from the dead, and ascended into heaven, would come to judge the living and the dead; and saw what they heard confirmed by great signs from heaven.

9. All who had the right use of their reason began to tremble, to fear, and to say, *"Men brethren what shall we do?"* Of such holy fear St. Luke writes, Acts 2. *"And fear came upon every soul; and many wonders and signs were done by the Apostles in Jerusalem, and there was great fear in all." "And they declared the works of God."* Those seized with such holy fear, especially the Apostles, who were in such terror when Christ arose and first appeared to them. *"They declared the works of God;"* began at once to preach his incarnation, passion, resurrection, doctrine, and miracles, *"and understood his doings."* The word *"and"* is often used in the Scripture as it is here, to signify *"because."* The Apostles, then, instructed by Christ, who after his resurrection, *"opened their understanding that they might understand the Scriptures,"* as also by the Holy Ghost, who descending on them, *"taught them all truth,"* John 16; they *"understood his doings,"* and announced them to the whole world.

10. The consequence of such preaching by the Apostles will be, that every one truly justified, that is, every one changed from a wicked to a just man, will thenceforth *"rejoice in the Lord, and shall hope in him;"* having shaken off all servile and worldly fear, *"for the fruit of the spirit is charity, joy, peace, patience, benignity,"* Gal. 5; and, ultimately, *"all the upright in heart shall be praised;"* all who shall have persevered in justice, and thus, had their hearts directed to God; who relished nothing, sought nothing, but what was pleasing to him; they will be praised by God in the great theater of the whole world; while, on the contrary, in the very same theater will the perverse in heart, be overwhelmed with intolerable confusion.

PSALM 64

God is to be praised in his Church, to which all nations shall be called.

1 A Hymn, O God, becometh thee in Sion: and a vow shall be paid to thee in Jerusalem.

2 hear my prayer: all flesh shall come to thee.

3 The words of the wicked have prevailed over us: and thou wilt pardon our transgressions.

4 Blessed is he whom thou hast chosen and taken to thee: he shall dwell in thy courts. We shall be filled with the good things of thy house; holy is thy temple,

5 Wonderful in justice. Hear us, O God our saviour, who art the hope of all the ends of the earth, and in the sea afar off.

6 Thou who preparest the mountains by thy strength, being girded with power:

7 Who troublest the depth of the sea, the noise of its waves. The Gentiles shall be troubled,
8 And they that dwell in the uttermost borders shall be afraid at thy signs: thou shalt make the outgoings of the morning and of the evening to be joyful.
9 Thou hast visited the earth, and hast plentifully watered it; thou hast many ways enriched it. The river of God is filled with water, thou hast prepared their food: for so is its preparation.
10 Fill up plentifully the streams thereof, multiply its fruits; it shall spring up and rejoice in its showers.
11 Thou shalt bless the crown of the year of thy goodness: and thy fields shall be filled with plenty.
12 The beautiful places of the wilderness shall grow fat: and the hills shall be girded about with joy,
13 The rams of the flock are clothed, and the vales shall abound with corn: they shall shout, yea they shall sing a hymn.

EXPLANATION OF THE PSALM

1. Speaking in the person of the prophet of God, the prophet sets out from a principle most true in itself, from which he infers that their desire of returning to their own country is most just and rational. The principle is, that it is right for them to praise God, and pay their vows in Jerusalem. Praise is due to a good thing, and the highest praise to the supreme good; and this praise ought to be given where this supreme good is well known. Now, God was not known in Babylon, but he was known in Jerusalem; and it was, therefore, there the people ought to praise him. In like manner, vows, especially those which promised sacrifices, should be paid where there was a temple and an altar on which to offer them, which were to be found in Jerusalem only; and there therefore, should their vows be paid. Hence, he justly infers that God's people have a right to long for, and to ask for, a return to their country. If such be true as regards a return to the terrestrial Jerusalem, much more true is it in reference to that celestial Jerusalem, where there is a much clearer idea of the extent of God's goodness; where the tabernacle is not made by the hands, nor the altar of gold; but one on which all the citizens of Jerusalem offer themselves, lighting up with the fire of the most ardent love, as a holocaust to God. *"A hymn, O God, becometh thee in Sion."* It is most meet that your people should sing your praises *"in Sion,"* where your greatness is well known, and not in a foreign land, where gods of sticks and stones, of gold and silver, are praised. *"And a vow shall be paid to thee in Jerusalem."* It is meet that the same people should pay their vows of thanksgiving in Jerusalem, where your favors, and the vows of sacrifices are understood, where there is a temple and an altar dedicated to your name; and not in Babylon, where your favors are not acknowledged, and where there are neither altars nor temples, but those of idols; *"For all the gods of the gentiles are devils,"* Psalm 95.

2. From the fact of praise in Jerusalem being due to God, the people pray that God may grant them to return from captivity to praise him in Jerusalem; and not only that, but that all mankind may be converted to God, and come by faith to the terrestrial Jerusalem, the Church, and afterwards (in reality) to the celestial Jerusalem; for, as God *"wishes all men to be saved, and to come to a knowledge of the truth,"* so his people desire and pray that all men may come to know and praise him. *"Hear my prayer;"* asking that, through your help, I may, as quickly as possible, sing a hymn to you in Sion, and pay you a vow in Jerusalem. *"All flesh shall come to thee."* If you hear me I will not be alone, but all men will come and praise you, and pay you their vows. That is my wish and my desire, and, as far as in me lies, I will labor to carry it out, by my words and by my example. *"All flesh"* means all men, as is clear from many passages in Scripture, Gen. 6, *"All flesh hath corrupted its way;"* Joel 2, *"I will pour out from my spirit on all flesh;"* Isaias 40, *"All flesh shall see the salvation of God;"* Mat. 24, *"If those days had not been shortened, all flesh would not be saved."*

3. Another reason for God's people asking to be released from their captivity, and to be restored to their country, and that is, because it was the sins of their parents, and not their own, that brought such a calamity on them. At the end of the captivity, nearly all the Jews then in Babylon had been born there; and thus, it was only to the sins of their parents that the punishment could be attributed; just as we are indebted to our first parents for the captivity we are in to the devil. *"The words of the wicked have prevailed over us;"* that means, the wickedness of our progenitors has lighted on our heads, and weighed us down under the yoke of a most severe captivity; but you, most merciful Father, *"wilt pardon our transgressions;"* both those we have inherited from our parents, and to which, in imitation of their example, ourselves have made considerable additions. We have interpreted the, *"words of the wicked,"* as if read *"the works of the wicked;"* the former being not infrequently used in the Scripture to signify the latter. Thus, in Luke 2, *"Let us see this word that is come to pass, which the Lord hath showed to us;"* and in Psalm 21, *"The words of my sins;"* Psalm 104, *"And he gave them words of signs;"* and 2 Kings 1, *"What is the word that is come to pass, tell me."*

4. A third reason for God's people desiring and praying to be brought back to their country, taken from the happiness to be enjoyed there. *"Happy is he whom thou hast chosen"* from eternity, and in time raised to the dignity of becoming *"fellow citizens with the saints and the domestics of God,"* for *"he shall dwell in thy courts;"* that is, in thy house, a part being put for the whole.

"We shall be filled with the good things of thy house, holy is thy temple." Buoyed up now with hope, God's people already number themselves among the blessed who dwell in his house, and say, that in that house they will have blessings in abundance, to such an extent, that nothing will be left to look for, which, applicable as it may be, either to the terrestrial Jerusalem, or to the Church militant, still, absolutely speaking, is applicable alone to our home in heaven. *"We shall be filled with the good things of thy house;"* we shall be so filled, that nothing can be said to be wanting, we shall have nothing to look for outside. What can be wanting in the house of him who made everything, who is the master of everything, who will be *"all unto all,"* in whom is an inexhaustible treasure of good? Of him is said, in Psalm 102, *"Who satisfieth thy desire with good things;"* and in Psalm 16, *"We shall be satisfied when thy glory shall appear."* *"Holy is thy temple."* In that holy city of Jerusalem, what will be most wonderful and worthy of love will be, that we will dwell in God as if in a house, and he will dwell in his temple; and thus, we will be his house, and he our house, according to the expression in John 15, *"Remain in me and I in you;"* and again, 1 John 4, *"And he that abideth in charity abideth in God, and God in him."* And if such reciprocity of habitation commences in this world, on the way, it will certainly be carried to a much greater extent in the other world, our true country.

5. It is a really wonderful thing to see men born in sin, and so prone to sin, that Psalm 8 says of them, *"They are corrupt, and become abominable in their ways, there is none that doeth good, no not one;"* and Prov. 24, *"For a just man shall fall seven times;"* and in Psalm 142, *"For in thy sight no man living shall be justified;"* who, however, afterwards arrives at such a degree of sanctity and justice as not only to have no sin to account for, but even will never have any to account for; and thus becoming a holy temple on which the very Angels in heaven look with admiration. *"Hear us, O God our Savior, the hope of all the ends of the earth, and in the sea afar off."* He returns to prayer, assigning a fresh reason for his being heard, because God is a Savior, and all nations hope in him. *"Hear us, O God,"* when we ask to be freed from captivity, and brought back to our country, and we ask with confidence, for you are *"our Savior,"* who often saved us from our enemies and our persecutors; you are also *"the hope of all the ends of the earth;"* all nations hope in thee, even in the islands, *"in the sea afar off."* The prophet had the conversion of all nations in view when he spoke thus, and speaks in the present tense, as if the thing were actually accomplished.

6-7. Another reason, drawn from the great power of God, who can easily, if he will deliver his people from captivity, and bring them back to their country, from which they had been expelled. He proves God's omnipotence, from two contraries. From his having so firmly founded the earth, that no storm can stir its mountains; and, on the contrary, made the waters so liquid and moveable that every breeze, however slight, will stir them. *"Thou who prepares"* the mountains by thy strength," raising the highest mountains by your power; *"being girded with power,"* having power on all sides, all round you, to raise those mountains. *"Who troubles"* the depth of the sea, the noise of its waves," stirring up the depths of the sea, and making its billows to roar. *"The gentiles shall be troubled."* As well as God's power is seen in the stability of the mountains and the fluctuation of the sea, so his wisdom is displayed in now terrifying, now gladdening the human race. *"The gentiles shall be troubled,"* the whole human race, as he explains more fully in the next verse.

8. All manner of people, even to the remotest quarter of the globe, will be confused and will be afraid *"at thy signs,"* at your coruscations, thunder and lightning, as we read in 1 Kings 2, *"The adversaries of the Lord shall fear him; and upon them shall be thunder in the heavens;"* for nothing is more terrific, more alarming, no one thing makes the stoutest heart quail more than God's thunder. Yet, that same God, by the rising and setting of the sun, gives wonderful gladness to man. When the sun rises, with what glee do they not turn out to their work? and when it sets, how sweet for them to rest and draw their breath! Again, what can be more beautiful than a glorious sunrise; nothing but the same sky, studded in the evening with countless stars, like so many precious jewels. *"Thou shalt make the out goings of the morning and of the evening to be joyful."*

9. Having praised the power and the wisdom of God, he now comes to praise his goodness, especially shown in the admixture of earth and water; from which all the fruits of the earth spring, and without which life cannot be supported. The earth without water, and the water without earth, are quite unproductive. *"Thou hast visited the earth,"* which of itself *"was empty and void;"* but by your visit became rich and full. God's visit was effective, and was not simply a vision of it, but a provision for it; and he tells how, when he adds, *"and hast plentifully watered it;"* abundantly irrigated it, and, by such irrigation, *"Thou hast many ways enriched it;"* made it exceedingly rich, and stored with abundance of good things. *"The river of God is filled with water;"* a fuller explanation of the manner in which the earth was enriched. The rivulets were filled with water, which nourished and fertilized the fields, and made them yield their fruits to support man and beast.

10. The same goodness of God extolled in different language; as much as to say, Go on, O Lord, saturate the fields, and thereby multiply the fruits of the earth, so as to be glad itself, and to gladden others.

11. By thy blessing thou shalt so benefit the whole circle of the year, that it will be like a crown daily ornamented with fresh flowers; and thus, always

renewed, and, through such blessing, *"thy fields,"* thus enriched, *"will be filled with plenty;"* with an abundance of all good things.

12. Not only will the plains and the arable lands yield abundant crops, but even the desert, fit for pasture only, and beautiful by reason of the multitude of herbs and natural flowers, will be enriched, and *"grow fat,"* by the dews of heaven; and so will the *"hills,"* hitherto barren and uncultivated, they too will be clothed with such verdant herbage that on all sides all things will seem to be glad and to rejoice.

13. To sum up; there will be the greatest abundance and multiplication of cattle, as well as of the fruits of the earth. The lambs are now become sheep, the desert places now abound in sheep, and the valleys in corn; and all places, whether hills or valleys, whether cultivated or uncultivated, whether cattle or corn, all, in their own way, cry out in praise of God, and in their own language, sing their hymn of praise to their creator and benefactor. Now, all created things, in their own way, cry out and sing God's praise, in order that man, for whose use and benefit they were created; may, mentally and orally, praise the same God, and return him thanks without ceasing. All these things were chanted by the holy prophet, in praise of the power, wisdom, and goodness of God, in order that he may be able to argue from thence that he ought to hope for, and to ask for, the delivery of his people from captivity, and their restoration to their country.

PSALM 65

An invitation to praise God.

1 Shout with joy to God, all the earth,
2 Sing ye a psalm to his name; give glory to his praise.
3 Say unto God, How terrible are thy works, O Lord! in the multitude of thy strength thy enemies shall lie to thee.
4 Let all the earth adore thee, and sing to thee: let it sing a psalm to thy name.
5 Come and see the works of God; who is terrible in his counsels over the sons of men.
6 Who turneth the sea into dry land, in the river they shall pass on foot: there shall we rejoice in him.
7 Who by his power ruleth for ever: his eyes behold the nations; let not them that provoke him be exalted in themselves.
8 bless our God, ye Gentiles: and make the voice of his praise to be heard.
9 Who hath set my soul to live: and hath not suffered my feet to be moved:
10 For thou, O God, hast proved us: thou hast tried us by fire, as silver is tried.
11 Thou hast brought us into a net, thou hast laid afflictions on our back:
12 Thou hast set men over our heads. We have passed through fire and water, and thou hast brought us out into a refreshment.

13 I will go into thy house with burnt offerings: I will pay thee my vows,
14 Which my lips have uttered, And my mouth hath spoken, when I was in trouble.
15 I will offer up to thee holocausts full of marrow, with burnt offerings of rams: I will offer to thee bullocks with goats.
16 Come and hear, all ye that fear God, and I will tell you what great things he hath done for my soul.
17 I cried to him with my mouth: and I extolled him with my tongue.
18 If I have looked at iniquity in my heart, the Lord will not hear me.
19 Therefore hath God heard me, and hath attended to the voice of my supplication.
20 Blessed be God, who hath not turned away my prayer, nor his mercy from me.

EXPLANATION OF THE PSALM

1-2. He invites the whole earth, that is, all the elect therein, to be glad, and to sing to God; all having common reason to rejoice in the resurrection of the just. He wishes three things to be exhibited in doing so: jubilation or gladness; the sound of the psaltery; and the human voice. Jubilation or gladness, which consists more in the interior affections than in words, is properly given to God. *"Shout with joy to God;"* for God, being a spirit, naturally regards such spiritual desire. The sound of the psaltery is due to his name; that is, to his fame, his glory. Finally, the human voice is to be employed in his praise. *"Give glory to his praise;"* take no glory to yourselves, give all to his praise.

3. The subject of God's praise is to be the works of his supreme power and wisdom. *"Say unto God,"* when you wish to praise him, *"How terrible are thy works, O Lord!"* that is, thy works, by reason of their magnitude, strike terror into all. *"In the multitude of thy strength thy enemies shall lie to thee;"* such is thy power and strength, that you make liars of all your enemies, who boasted of your inability to do things of no great consequence. Numerous examples of this occur in the Scriptures. In Psalm 77 we read, *"And they spoke ill of God, they said: Can God furnish a table in the wilderness?"* Yet God, in his supreme power, sent such a quantity of quails into the desert as abundantly sufficed to feed them all; thus proving them liars, and for which he inflicted dreadful punishment on them. In like manner, when Eliseus the prophet, on the occasion of a most grievous famine, said, *"Hear ye the word of the Lord: tomorrow, about this time, a bushel of fine flour shall be sold for a stater, in the gate of Samaria;"* and one of the lords replied, *"If the Lord should make flood gates in heaven, can that possibly be which thou sayest?"* Yet God in his power proved him a liar, too; for it turned up that on the following day a bushel of fine flour was actually sold for a stater, and that lord, who so contradicted the prophet, was trampled on at the gate by the people, and met a miserable end. Such also were the lies of the Jews, when they insulted the Savior, as he hung on his cross, saying, *"If thou art the Son of God, come down from the cross."* Yet he, in his supreme power, wrought a much greater miracle; for he rose from the grave, which was a much greater work than to descend from the cross.

4-5. The prophet again stirs up all mankind to adore and praise God in the sincerity of their hearts; and, to do so with greater affection, he exhorts them to reflect on God's works, and how terrible he is in his dealings with mankind.

6. He gives two examples of God's wonderful acts, such as never could have been accomplished by human design. *"Who turneth the sea into dry land."* The first miracle, recorded in Exodus, *"And the children of Israel went through the midst of the sea dried up;" "In the river they shall pass on foot."* The second miracle, recorded in Josue 3, where God so dried up the Jordan, that the children of Israel required neither bridge nor boat to pass over, but went across dry on foot. *"There shall we rejoice in him;"* where those things have been done; there we have rejoiced in him, not taking any credit to ourselves as if they were our acts, but rejoicing and glorying in God, and have praised him, as may be seen in Exod. 15 and Josue 3. The prophet uses the future for the past, unless, perhaps, he meant to insinuate that these miracles would be succeeded by much greater ones, of which they were only the types and figures. A much greater miracle is that men should pass over the bitter sea of this life, and cross the river of mortality, that never ceases to run, and which swallow up and drown so many; and still come safe and alive to the land of eternal promise, and there rejoice in God himself, beholding him face to face; and yet this greater miracle is so accomplished by God, that many pass through this sea as if it were dry land, and cross this river with dry feet; that is to say, having no difficulty in despising all things temporal, be they good or be they bad; that is to say, being neither attached to the good things, nor fearing the evil things of this world, that they may arrive in security at the heavenly Jerusalem, where we will rejoice in him, not in hope, but in complete possession, for eternity.

7. This seems a digression addressed to the wicked, who despise submission to God, and refuse to praise him, for he reminds them of the omnipotence and the omniscience of God, *"who by his power ruleth forever."* He rules with universal sway, and that of himself, and not by reason of having received power from any other; and also, *"his eyes behold the nations,"* sees them all, and from aloft notes what they are doing; and, therefore, *"let not them that provoke him be exalted in themselves,"* let them not be proud, or glory in their

own strength, because they will not escape the hands of an all powerful, all seeing God.

8. After such digression, he now repeats the exhortation he made in the first and fourth verses, and now (the third time) he invites all nations to bless our God, who is the only true God, and to chant his praise with a voice so loud that it may be heard by all.

9. He now tells us the reason why he is so extremely anxious that God should be praised by all, and that is, because he saved him from the greatest dangers. *"Who hath set my soul to live."* I wish God should be praised, because he saved my soul, and suffered me not to stumble or to fall. Such is the language of the elect on their arrival, through many and various temptations, at the port of safety. *"My soul,"* means the entire man, which is a most common expression in the Scriptures. *"Who hath set,"* signifies, preordained or predestinated to life eternal, or set me in the number of those who are to live forever. *"And hath not suffered my feet to be moved;"* has given me the gift of perseverance, which especially belongs to the predestined, for God protects and directs, so that they may not fall to the right or to the left, those whom he predestines.

10. The prophet explains the tribulations of the just by various metaphors, the first taken from the furnace in which silver is refined, to show that God suffers the just to undergo persecution, not for the purpose of harming them, but to prove them, that they may be shown to be proved, and pure, faithful, and sincere. For fire consumes straw, makes gold and silver more pure. Straw smokes in the fire, silver shines. Hence, the Angel said to Tobias, *"Because thou wert acceptable to God, it was necessary that temptation should prove thee;"* and in Wisdom 3, *"God tempted them and found them worthy of him, like gold in a furnace he proved them;"* and in Eccli. 27, *"The furnace trieth the potter's vessels, and the trial of affliction just men;"* and 1 St. Peter 1, *"That the trial of your faith, much more precious than gold which is tried by the fire, may be found unto praise, and glory, and honor, at the appearing of Jesus Christ."*

11. He now enters into particular afflictions, making use of various metaphors. *"Thou hast brought us into a net,"* you have handed us over to our enemies, who bound us with chains, manacles, and fetters, and threw us into prison; for as birds and wild beasts, when caught in a snare, are deprived of their liberty, so it may be said, that men, when deprived of their liberty, and shut up in prison, are bound with chains and fetters, *"Thou hast laid afflictions on our back;"* suffered us to be loaded and lashed, like so many wild beasts of burden, alluding to the various labors and hardships imposed by the wicked on the just, when they were forced to go down into mines, to hew marble, to carry heavy loads, and be stripped and lashed while so harassed and tormented.

12. You made men trample on our heads, as if we were captives of war; which also is metaphorical, to give us an idea of the tyranny and cruelty exercised by princes over their wretched subjects. Just and considerate princes are placed on the heads, or rather over their subjects; but they press so lightly on them, that the weight of obedience is scarcely felt; while cruel tyrants and inhuman princes, such as were the early persecutors of the Christians, such as Pharao of Egypt, and Nabuchodonosor of Assyria, so oppress their subjects by exactions, by edicts, pains and punishments, that they can scarcely breathe. The prophet shows most skillfully in this verse, how no part of the persons of the just is free from suffering; the hands and feet suffer from the snares; the back from the heavy loads; and the head from being trampled on. *"We have passed through fire and water;"* the last of those beautiful figures made use of by the prophet, to give us an idea of the sufferings of the saints. Fire and water are too opposites; fire burns, water gets congealed; the former is most active; the latter, most soft and easy. Fire dries up water, and water extinguishes fire; and therefore, when a man gets burned, water is applied to cool and to heal him; and yet, where there is question of afflicting the servants of God, both fire and water seem to conspire; the one to consume him, the other to suffocate him. By fire, then, we are to understand the more active punishments, such as stripes, wounds, burning, etc.; and by water, the slow, but constant punishments, such as exile, imprisonment, nakedness, hunger. But, as fire will consume wood, and will not consume gold, so also water will cause wood to rot and decay, and will not harm gold; and, as gold is purged of its dross by fire, so it is cleansed of all exterior dirt by fire. The just and the holy, then, who may be compared to gold, pass through fire and water without suffering any harm; because, in their tribulation, they keep their patience; and in their prosperity, their moderation; but the children of this world, like rotten timber, are consumed in the fire, or crumbled in the water; because, being unable to bear their troubles with patience, they murmur, they rail, they blaspheme; while, in their prosperity, they revel in all manner of luxury, pride, and effeminacy. The elect, therefore, say, *"We have passed through fire and water, and thou hast brought us out into a refreshment;"* because in our heavenly country there will be no lack of fire and water; that fire, however, in warming will refresh us, instead of destroying us in its fury; and that water, while it extinguishes our thirst, will not take away our life. We will thus be refreshed by both in their own way; that is to say, in heaven we shall have the fire of charity, which will heat without harming, perfecting instead of destroying; transforming us into God, instead of turning us into ashes. There will be an abundance

of water; the real and eternal truths, the immense joys, and the ineffable pleasures; but such as will not enervate or weaken the soul, or stir up the concupiscence of the flesh against the spirit; and finally, will delight it by refreshing it, without suffocating it by excess.

13. This verse seems to be a conclusion from the preceding; as if he said, As you have brought us through fire and water, into a place of refreshment, *"I will go into thy house,"* for you led me to it, protected me in the way; and I will go *"with burnt offerings;"* I will offer you the sacrifice of thanksgiving, for holocausts were offered only in thanksgiving. And, in fact, in no place is a more perfect holocaust offered than in heaven, where all the saints, lighted up with the fire of the purest love, and with the full affections of the soul, offer themselves unreservedly to God; for the whole study, the whole business of the just in heaven will be to praise God. *"I will pay thee my vows."* Such a holocaust is due to you, for I promised it when I was in trouble. I will, therefore, enter into your house with burnt offerings, that I may discharge the vows that have been made; not by any one else, but which I distinctly promised with my own lips.

14-15. He tells what were the vows he promised in his trouble, and says he promised the richest sacrifices of cattle that could be made according to the law. These were three, rams, cows, and goats. Rams included lambs, cows included heifers, and goats, kids. *"And my mouth had spoken when I was in trouble;"* that is to say, I said *"I will pay thee my vows,"* which my lips have uttered when I was in trouble, and needed the divine assistance, and, with tears, implored his help. *"Holocausts full of marrow, with burnt offerings of rams."* I will sacrifice fat lambs full of marrow, with a fragrant odor from the rams that will be slain along with them, and burnt as a holocaust. *"I will offer to thee bullocks with goats;"* to the holocaust of lambs and rams I will add another of bullocks and goats.

16. Speaking in the person of God's elect, the prophet now exhorts us all to understand God's favors, conferred by him on the saints, and their return for them, that in imitation of them we, too, may receive similar favors, and thus, in the end, arrive at the same rest and glory. *"Come and hear, all ye that fear God, and I will tell you what great things he hath done for my soul."* Come, all you who fear God, and hear me, and I will tell you what he has done for me. Observe the invitation given to those only *"who fear God"*, because, *"the fear of the Lord is the beginning of wisdom;"* he loosens the feet, opens the ears; and, therefore, he who has no fear of God will be called to no purpose, either to come or to hear.

17. Here is the first gift of God conferred on the soul, as announced by the assembly of the elect, supposed to speak here. This much God *"has done for my soul;"* given me faith and the spirit of prayer. For, *"how shall they invoke* him in whom they have not believed?" Through faith, then, I learned the wretched captivity in which I was held, and I learned who was my Savior and my Redeemer; and thus, *"I cried to him with my mouth."* He now mentions a second favor, *"And I extolled him with my tongue;"* I not only prayed to my God, but I praised him, returned him thanks for the favors conferred, that thereby I may get fresh ones, sadly wanting to me. And all these acts of prayer, praise, and thanksgiving were the work of God's own grace.

18. The third favor received from the Lord consisted in light to know the obstacles to his prayers being heard. *"If I have looked at iniquity in my heart, the Lord will not hear me."* To look at iniquity in the heart means to love it in secret, or to indulge in secret concupiscence, as we find in the Gospel, *"Whosoever shall look upon a woman to lust after her."* For very many, both by their words and their acts, seem to have a thorough horror of sin, reprove and chastise sinners, and yet, in their hearts, where nobody can be a witness, they cherish sinful desires, and would gratify them if they could with impunity. Such hypocrites are not heard by God; he hears those only who hate iniquity in their heart, and, if they should chance to sin, confess it, and seek the physician who can heal them; and, whereas all the elect consist of such persons, the prophet therefore adds, in their name:

19. Because he is a searcher of hearts, God saw me sincerely sorry for my sins, and, so far from *"looking at iniquity in my heart,"* that I turned away from it in perfect horror. *"And hath attended to the voice of my supplication;"* because he saw me attending to the voice of his commandments, and not to the voice of the evil one, prompting me to wickedness.

20. May that God be praised and blessed forever who heaped such unbounded favors on me, the principal one being that he *"hath not turned away my prayer,"* nor taken away *"his mercy from me."* Thus, through his mercy, I have persevered in the way of his commandments, have already obtained the reward of such perseverance, namely, deliverance from captivity, and a return to the heavenly Jerusalem.

PSALM 66

A prayer for the propagation of the Church.

1 May God have mercy on us, and bless us: may he cause the light of his countenance to shine upon us, and may he have mercy on us.
2 That we may know thy way upon earth: thy salvation in all nations.
3 Let people confess to thee, O God: let all people give praise to thee.
4 Let the nations be glad and rejoice: for thou judgest the people with justice, and directest the nations upon earth.
5 Let the people, O God, confess to thee: let all the people give praise to thee:
6 The earth hath yielded her fruit. May God, our God bless us,

7 May God bless us: and all the ends of the earth fear him.

EXPLANATION OF THE PSALM

1. With desire and earnestness David exclaims, *"May God have mercy on us,"* according to the great mercy that prompts him to send a Savior to us; and may he in such mercy *"bless us,"* which blessing we pray may not be confined to the things of this world, but *"may he cause the light of his countenance to shine upon us,"* which may be variously interpreted. First, God is said to make *"the light of his countenance shine upon us,"* when, having removed the clouds of his anger and indignation, he regards us with a look of benignity, as children, as friends, as restored to grace. Again, he is said to *"cause the light of his countenance to shine upon us,"* when, by the infusion of wisdom and love, he enlightens and warms us, as the sun is wont to do when no cloud intervenes. Finally, he is said to cause the light of his countenance to shine upon us when it pleases him to let us see him to a certain extent; which he did through the mystery of the Incarnation, when *"He was seen upon earth, and conversed with men,"* Baruch 3. And such seems to be the prayer of the prophet here, that God should show his countenance, if not in the form of God, at least in the form of man. He puts up the same petition in Psalm 79, where he says, *"Thou that sittest upon the Cherubim shine forth before Ephraim, Benjamin, and Manasses."* And this being the mercy he originally asked, he, therefore, repeats, *"and may he have mercy on us;"* that means, may he, by such light, have mercy on us.

2. The reason why he so ardently longs for the light of God's countenance is, that through that divine light we may, in this land of darkness know the way to God, to our country from which we have been so long exiled in darkness and the shade of death; which way most undoubtedly is Christ himself, who says, *"I am the way;"* and not only the way, but the light through which it is to be known, of which Isaias, chap. 9, says, *"The people that walked in darkness have seen a great light: to them that dwelt in the region of the shadow of death light is risen."*—*"Thy salvation in all nations"* explains the first part of the verse, that the Savior may be known among all nations.

3. The prophet's desires being in accordance with true charity, he wished that Christ should come upon earth; first, for the glory of God, then, for the benefit of mankind; and in this verse, therefore, he prays that all manner of people should praise, thank, and glorify him for so great and so universal a favor; that all worship and veneration of false gods should cease, and the one true God alone be acknowledged by all.

4. Next to the glory of God, let the benefit of mankind be acknowledged; and, therefore, *"let the nations be glad and rejoice;"* let all manner of people rejoice; *"for thou,"* through Christ, *"judgest the people with justice;"* you have

destroyed the power of the tyrannical prince of darkness, and established the just authority of the Church in its stead. *"And directest the nations upon earth;"* governing and guiding them, by your most wholesome laws, to the harbor of life everlasting.

5-6. He again exhorts the people to praise God, assigning as an additional reason, that *"the earth hath yielded her fruit;"* that means, that the earth had at length yielded that fruit, to yield which she was created, namely, Christ in the flesh. For this is the fruit of which Isaias speaks when he says, *"In that day the bud of the Lord shall be in magnificence and glory, and the fruit of the earth shall be high;"* and in Psalm 84, *"Our earth hath yielded its fruit;"* fruit of such value, that, when compared to it, the earth seems never before to have yielded anything but thorns and briars.

7. Henceforth will come the agreeable change, that God will open his hands, and replenish us with all manner of blessings, spiritual ones especially; and, on the other hand, all men, in the utmost quarters of the globe, will fear the true God with a holy fear, and will pay him the tribute of obedience and praise. The name of God, three times repeated here, while it shows the strong affections of the prophet, would also seem to foreshadow the mystery of the Most Holy Trinity, which was so clearly preached by Christ and his Apostles.

PSALM 67

The glorious establishment of the Church of the New Testament, prefigured by the benefits bestowed on the people of Israel.

1 Let God arise, and let his enemies be scattered: and let them that hate him flee from before his face.
2 As smoke vanisheth, so let them vanish away: as wax melteth before the fire, so let the wicked perish at the presence of God.
3 And let the just feast, and rejoice before God: and be delighted with gladness.
4 Sing ye to God, sing a psalm to his name, make a way for him who ascendeth upon the west: the Lord is his name. Rejoice ye before him: but the wicked shall be troubled at his presence,
5 Who is the father of orphans, and the judge of widows. God in his holy place:
6 God who maketh men of one manner to dwell in a house: Who bringeth out them that were bound in strength; in like manner them that provoke, that dwell in sepulchres.
7 God, when thou didst go forth in the sight of thy people, when thou didst pass through the desert:
8 The earth was moved, and the heavens dropped at the presence of the God of Sina, at the presence of the God of Israel.
9 Thou shalt set aside for thy inheritance a free rain, O God: and it was weakened,

but thou hast made it perfect.
10 In it shall thy animals dwell; in thy sweetness, O God, thou hast provided for the poor.
11 The Lord shall give the word to them that preach good tidings with great power.
12 The king of powers is of the beloved, of the beloved; and the beauty of the house shall divide spoils.
13 If you sleep among the midst of lots, you shall be as the wings of a dove covered with silver, and the hinder parts of her back with the paleness of gold.
14 When he that is in heaven appointeth kings over her, they shall be whited with snow in Selmon.
15 The mountain of God is a fat mountain. A curdled mountain, a fat mountain.
16 Why suspect, ye curdled mountains? A mountain in which God is well pleased to dwell: for there the Lord shall dwell unto the end.
17 The chariot of God is attended by ten thousands; thousands of them that rejoice: the Lord is among them in Sina, in the holy place.
18 Thou hast ascended on high, thou hast led captivity captive; thou hast received gifts in men. Yea for those also that do not believe, the dwelling of the Lord God.
19 Blessed be the Lord day by day: the God of our salvation will make our journey prosperous to us.
20 Our God is the God of salvation: and of the Lord, of the Lord are the issues from death.
21 But God shall break the heads of his enemies: the hairy crown of them that walk on in their sins.
22 The Lord said: I will turn them from Basan, I will turn them into the depth of the sea:
23 That thy foot may be dipped in the blood of thy enemies; the tongue of thy dogs be red with the same.
24 They have seen thy goings, O God, the goings of my God: of my king who is in his sanctuary.
25 Princes went before joined with singers, in the midst of young damsels playing on timbrels.
26 In the churches bless ye God the Lord, from the fountains of Israel.
27 There is Benjamin a youth, in ecstasy of mind. The princes of Juda are their leaders: the princes of Zabulon, the princes of Nephthali.
28 Command thy strength, O God: confirm, O God, what thou hast wrought in us.
29 From thy temple in Jerusalem, kings shall offer presents to thee.
30 Rebuke the wild beasts of the reeds, the congregation of bulls with the kine of the people; who seek to exclude them who are tried with silver. Scatter thou the nations that delight in wars:

31 Ambassadors shall come out of Egypt: Ethiopia shall soon stretch out her hands to God.
32 Sing to God, ye kingdoms of the earth: sing ye to the Lord: Sing ye to God,
33 Who mounteth above the heaven of heavens, to the east. Behold he will give to his voice the voice of power:
34 Give ye glory to God for Israel, his magnificence, and his power is in the clouds.
35 God is wonderful in his saints: the God of Israel is he who will give power and strength to his people. Blessed be God.

Explanation of the psalm

1. Such were the words used by Moses on the raising of the ark when the people were about to proceed on their journey, containing a prayer to God, that as the ark was raised and was carried before the people, he too may deign to rise up and defend and protect his people on their journey. David, then, in imitation of Moses, and having a prophetic knowledge of Christ's resurrection, through which his human nature was to be raised, and to make him the future leader of all the elect to the land of promise, exclaims, *"Let God arise."* Let Christ, who is God, arise from the dead, and precede his people to the heavenly Jerusalem. *"Let his enemies be scattered;"* that is, the Jews, who said, *"We will not have this man to reign over us;"* which has been literally carried out; for no nation was ever so scattered over the world as that of the Jews. *"And let them that hate him flee from before his face."* Let his enemies, the demons now conquered and routed, fly before the face of God, now in triumph, and proving by his resurrection that he is the real true God.

2. The celerity and facility with which the presence of Christ scatters sinners could not be more expressively conveyed than by comparing them to the smoke that is dispelled by the wind, or wax that melts before the fire, and is consumed by it. If we understand the *"wicked"* here to apply to the demons, then we must not take it that they *"perish,"* strictly speaking; but, that they are so deprived of all strength and power as to render them perfectly harmless. If we apply the word *"wicked"* to men, the meaning will be, that the oppressors of the just will be quickly and severely punished by God.

3. The consequence of this signal punishment of the wicked will be, that the just, who have been so supported by God, *"will feast;"* will be refreshed in soul and body, and will *"rejoice before God;"* will give full vent to their joy; but, with such modesty and gravity, as becomes those who know that God's eyes are always on them; *"and be delighted with gladness;"* will find such pleasure in their gladness, that they will have no occasion to turn to any carnal or dangerous pleasure.

4. These words are addressed to the Apostles and the first converts to Christianity. *"Sing ye to God,"* ye the first of the believers. *"Sing a psalm to his name;"* praise God by works and words for having deigned to make you cognizant of such mysteries; *"make a way for him who ascendeth upon the west."* By your preaching prepare the way of the Lord, so that he who has already ascended upon the west, and has risen above all corruption and mortality, and is about to take up his abode, through faith, in the hearts of all nations, may, through your preaching, find the way prepared and open. *"The Lord is his name;"* and, therefore, has a right to rule; and he is Lord by right of creation, as well as of redemption. The words, *"make a way,"* do not mean, retire, but they mean, to make a road, a passage, where there was none before; by removing every obstacle, as it is said in Isaias, *"Prepare ye the way of the Lord;"* which he explains when he adds, *"Every valley shall be filled, and every mountain and hill shall be lowered;"* thereby inspiring the timid with confidence to raise themselves up in the hope of salvation; and taking down the proud through the fear of God's judgments. The word *"ascendeth"* does not mean to ascend or rise up, but to be carried along on an exalted, elevated place, as appears from the Hebrew, from which, too, we learn that the words, *"upon the west,"* signify darkness, or a desert; to signify the corruption of human nature, that is full of drought and darkness. Christ, then, in his resurrection, is said *"to ascend upon the west;"* because, to a certain extent he is carried along, and rides triumphantly over death, darkness, and the desert of this world below. Such is the explanation of most of the holy fathers. *"Rejoice ye before him;"* you who have prepared his way, do not fear your persecutors, for *"they shall be troubled;"* at the fitting time, on the day of judgment, or, perhaps before, when God shall see it fit and opportune, *"they shall be troubled,"* and that severely.

5. No wonder they should be punished severely, for God has special charge of the oppressed, the orphan, the widow, and all afflicted; but especially the orphan and the widow; in a spiritual sense, that is, those who acknowledge no father, no spouse, in this world, but God alone, confide in him alone, love him alone, and long for the day when they shall see him; and, therefore, it is with them that he mostly dwells, and their hearts are *"his holy place."*

6. Such as the primitive Christians, of one mind, one will, one faith, hope, and love, of whom the Acts say, they were *"One soul, one heart;" "who bringeth out them that were bound in strength."* Behold God's great love, who not only *"maketh men of one manner to dwell in a house,"* but he also *"bringeth out them that were bound in strength;"* that is, by the strength of his arm brings from captivity those that were bound in the chains of sin; and, what is more wonderful, *"them that provoke"* God by their incredulity; *"that dwell,"* as if they were dead, *"in sepulchres"* of the deepest iniquity; even such people, by

the power of his grace, he brings out of their sepulchres, restores them to life, and *"makes them to dwell of one manner in a house."* St. Augustine notes a difference between the bound and the buried. The bound are they who are caught in the chains of concupiscence; but, are anxious to be loosed, and pray for help thereto. The buried are they who come to the very lowest grade of iniquity, and when they do, despise salvation altogether, and exasperate God greatly thereby; and still God's great love sometimes softens both one and the other, brings them to penance, and frees them from the slavery of the devil, the greatest ever known or thought of.

7-8. To make the benefits of the redemption of Christ more credible, he reminds them of past benefits, which were only types of the future. *"O God, when thou didst go forth in the sight of thy people;"* when you went before your people as a pillar of cloud by day, and as a pillar of fire by night; when you were going through the desert, after having passed the Red Sea, then *"the earth was moved, and the heavens dropped."* It was moved when it began to tremble at the sight of God descending on mount Sinai, as we read in Exodus 19, where it is said, *"And all the mount was terrible,"* the Hebrew for which means trembling, or leaping. He is God of Sinai, by reason of his having appeared thereon. *"The heavens dropped,"* when manna fell from them; *"at the presence of the God of Israel,"* to show it was for the use of the people that the heavens did so drop.

9. The heavens dropped a certain rain, the manna, to our fathers in the desert; but you *"have set aside a free rain;"* a rain that descends freely; the grace of the Holy Ghost, which is called free or voluntary, because it does not descend by reason of our merits, as the rain is collected through exhalations from the earth; but is freely poured into the hearts of the faithful by the influence of the Holy Ghost; and it is said to be *"set aside for thy inheritance,"* because temporal blessings are common to all, faithful and infidels; but the grace of the Holy Ghost is set aside that it may be imparted to the faithful only, members of the Church, out of which there is no salvation. *"And it was weakened, but thou hast made it perfect."* The word *"and"* has the force of the word *"because;"* and thus, the meaning is, because your inheritance was weakened through ignorance, and through concupiscence, in the worship of idols, and in the indulgence in all manner of vice, you have, through the grace of the Holy Ghost, confirmed and strengthened it by a salutary rain.

10. In that inheritance, the Church, which is irrigated by the water of heaven, *"shall thy animals dwell;"* the sheep of your flock, that you undertook to provide for and to feed; for you, O God, *"hast provided"* food, for instance, *"for the poor,"* for your people in want; *"in thy sweetness,"* agreeable to your goodness and mercy, that is always most sweet to the wretched and the needy.

11. He informs them what sort is the food that the Lord had prepared for his poor people; and says the food is his word. *"The Lord shall give the word to them that preach good tidings;"* the Lord will confer fluency of speech on those who preach his word, which is the food of souls; *"with great power;"* with such strength and efficacy that their adversaries will not be able to resist or to contradict them.

12. The king of great armies is also the king of the beloved of the beloved; that means of the most beloved, meaning Christ, most beloved by God and man; *"and the beauty of the house,"* in order to decorate and beautify his house, the Church; *"shall divide spoils,"* the spoils of the gentiles, brought to the true faith by the preaching of the Apostles.

13. A most obscure verse; but the general opinion of the fathers seems to be, that *"lots"* mean an inheritance, a possession; and that he thus addresses the Apostles, *"If you,"* who preach the Gospel, *"sleep,"* that is, rest between the two Testaments, the Old and New; acknowledging the authority of the prophets, as well as of the Apostles; then the *"wings of the dove,"* the faith and morals of the Church, shall *"be covered with silver,"* in the purity of wisdom, and *"gilded"* with the fervor of charity.

14-16. The prophet having compared the preachers of the Old and New Testament to *"those who sleep among the lots,"* and having compared the Church to a silvered and gilded dove, now compares the same preachers to a number of princes appointed by the supreme King, and the Church to a very high mountain, whitened with snow, and abounding in cattle giving milk. Mount Selmon is a very high mountain, having its summit always covered with snow, but in the bottom exceedingly rich and fertile. He therefore says, *"When he that is in heaven,"* Christ, who is God, the celestial, all powerful King, *"appointeth,"* divides and separates the provinces, appointing a prince over each; *"kings over her;"* the Apostles, who were placed over the Church, called previously the silvered dove; for, as he said in Psalm 44, *"Thou shalt make them princes over all the earth,"* to guide and govern the people. *"They shall be whited with snow in Selmon;"* then many people will be converted, and the darkness of their sins having been changed into the brightness of virtue, they shall be made more white than the snow on mount Selmon, the type of the Church. The same mount Selmon is *"the mountain of God, a fat mountain;"* for the Church, by reason of its dignity is like a mountain, it is the *"mountain of God,"* for God dwelleth in her, and chose a habitation for himself in her, and she is *"a fat mountain,"* abounding in the graces and gifts of the Holy Ghost. She is also *"a curdled mountain,"* because the milk of divine grace never fails or flows away, but remains as it were, curdled in her. *"Why suspect, ye curdled mountains?"* Why do ye suspect or imagine that there are any other mountains equally rich or curdled?

There are no mountains as rich or as curdled as Selmon. For this is the only *"mountain in which God is well pleased to dwell;"* for his abode in it will not be temporary, as it was in Sinai, but *"There the Lord shall dwell unto the end;"* that is, forever. Hence it is vain for other mountains to rival, or to contend with it, or to envy it. Of this mountain we read in Isaias, chap. 2, *"And in the last days the mountain of the house of the Lord shall be prepared on the top of mountains, and it shall be exalted above the hills, and all nations shall flow unto it: and many people shall go and say: Come, and let us go up to the mountain of the Lord, and to the house of the God of Jacob; and he will teach us his ways, and we will walk in his paths;"* all of which certainly applies to the Church.

17–18. The prophet now draws a comparison between God's descent on mount Sinai, to give the old law to the Jewish people; and Christ's ascension to heaven, to send from thence the gifts of the Holy Ghost and the new law to Christians; with a view to show the source of so much milk and brightness in the Church. *"The chariot of God is attended by ten thousands."* The chariot in which God rode when he descended on Sinai was drawn by an infinite number of Angels, not groaning or laboring under the load, but, *"of them that rejoice,"* delighted at having the honor of bearing their Master; *"for the Lord is among them;"* he was sitting *"in Sinai in the holy place."* Of those holy Angels who descended with him, Moses speaks more plainly in Deut. 33, when he says, *"The Lord came from Sinai, and from Seir he rose up to us; He hath appeared from mount Pharan, and with him thousands of saints."* The Angels are frequently called God's chariot in the Scriptures, as in Psalm 79, *"Who sittest on the Cherubim." "Thou hast ascended on high."* St. Paul, Ephes. 4, applies this passage to Christ's ascension; and the meaning is, the Lord formerly descended on Sinai, accompanied by many millions of Angels; but thou, the Messias, is forever ascended on high," to the highest heavens; *"hast led captivity captive;"* made those who had been captives to the devils captives to yourself, commuted a most miserable captivity into a most glorious one; and thus, in triumph, accompanied by the countless myriads of the saints so redeemed, you entered into your kingdom. *"Thou hast received gifts in men;"* you have got the gifts of the Holy Ghost from your Father, for the men so redeemed, to whom you have given them. Such is the explanation of St. Paul, who thus quotes the passage, *"Ascending on high, he led captivity captive, he gave gifts to men;"* and this explanation agrees with the Gospel; for in John 14, we read, *"I will ask the Father, and he will send you another Paraclete;"* and, in chap. 15, *"When the Paraclete shall come, whom I shall send you from the Father."* Now, among the gifts conferred by Christ on mankind the principal is charity, in which, according to the Apostle, consists the new law, Rom. 5, *"Because the charity of God is poured into our hearts by the Holy Ghost, who is given to us."* And, in Gal. 5, *"But the fruit of the Spirit* is charity, joy, peace, patience, benignity, goodness, longanimity, mildness, faith, modesty, continence, chastity." "For those also that do not believe, the dwelling of the Lord God," means that unbelievers even were converted through those gifts of the Holy Ghost, and got to be numbered among the happy captives.

19-20. Having described the ascension of Christ, who was our guide, to the kingdom of heaven, he gives thanks to God, saying, *"Blessed be the Lord day by day,"* which means every day. We bless God every day, because he blesses us every day, and showers his favors on us. *"The God of our salvation;"* the God on whom our salvation depends; for it is not simple protection we need, exposed, as we are, to a multiplicity of dangers. *"Will make our journey prosperous to us;"* will bless us every day; for he will not desert us on the road that we daily travel, until we shall have come to the day of eternity. We are thus promised daily, constant, protection from God while here below on our pilgrimage. *"Our God is the God of salvation."* I had reason to say, God would make our journey prosperous, and protect us in more ways than one; for such are his characteristics, such is his nature; for our God is a God of salvation, of mercy, and of love. *"And of the Lord, of the Lord, are the issues of death;"* and through him we evade, or come out from, death; God alone can help us to escape everlasting death.

21. Having told what the Lord would do for his friends, he now tells us how he will deal with his enemies, who remained incredulous and refused to be subject to him. *"God shall break the heads of his enemies;"* he will humble their pride when he shall condemn them to hell to be punished with everlasting torments. *"The hairy crown of them that walk in their sins."* The same idea, in different language; the *"hairy crown"* here being synonymous with the *"heads,"* and his *"enemies"* being called here *"those that walk in their sins,"* for they alone are enemies of God, who, instead of walking in his law, walk in their own sins; that is to say, spend their whole life in the commission of sin.

22-23. God here confirms the sentence pronounced by the prophet on the destruction of the wicked. I will turn them out of Basan, a rich and fertile country, and I will cast them into the depths of the sea, as I formerly did to Pharao. I will turn the wicked from their enjoyment and pleasure to final destruction; and such will be the carnage of the enemy, *"that thy foot,"* my people, *"may be dipped in their blood, and the tongue of thy dogs be red with the same;"* with their blood shed by the enemy.

24. Having related Christ's victory and triumph over his enemies, he now informs us that they who witnessed such wonders began to publish them to the whole world, with great joy and acclamation. *"They have seen thy going, O God;"* that is, many witnessed what you did, your battles and your victories. *"The goings (I say) of you who are my God and my king, who are now in your sanctuary;"* whether that be heaven or the Church, for it may apply to either, Christ being visibly present in the one, and in the other, through faith and providence.

25. He alludes to the conduct of the children of Israel on their delivery from Pharao, when Moses, their leader, with other sons of Israel, sung the canticle, *"Let us sing to the Lord for he is gloriously magnified. So Mary, the prophetess, the sister of Aaron, took a timbrel in her hand, and all the women went after her with timbrel and with dances."* Thus, too, when the princes of the Church saw the triumph and victory of Christ, that freed us from the power of Satan, they *"went before"* other nations and people in proclaiming and announcing the praises of Christ. *"Joined with singers;"* in union with the holy Angels in heaven, singing God's praises, by reason of the same victory, *"in the midst of young damsels;"* in the midst of the holy souls who ascended with Christ, and so are named, by reason of their being so lately admitted to eternal life, and to the society of the Angels, so chanting God's praises.

26. This verse is to be read as if in a parenthesis. The prophet, foreseeing the future joy of the princes of the Church, exhorts them, *"Bless ye God the Lord in the churches"* they were about to establish, taking the subject of their praise *"from the fountains of Israel;"* namely, the promises of God to the patriarchs, and the prophecies that we now see fulfilled, and for which we rejoice.

27. He now returns to the former narration, and tells who are the princes he alluded to when he said, *"Princes went before,"* and says they were *"Benjamin a youth,"* the princes of Juda, of Zabulon, and of Nephthali, which, by the general consent of the fathers, mean the Apostles, who *"are appointed princes over all the earth."* Benjamin, the youth, is named first, by whom the Apostle Paul is meant; he being of the tribe of Benjamin, and the last in point of call, labored more than all the rest in preaching, and praising the victories of Christ; and he, *"in excess of mind,"* was so united with the singers in the third heaven as not to know *"whether he was in the body or out of the body,"* as he testifies himself. By the princes of Juda are meant the Apostles, who belonged to that tribe, and are called Christ's brethren in the Gospel, by reason of their being the Sons of Cleophas, the brother of Joseph the spouse of the Blessed Virgin; they were James and Simon. The other Apostles, are included in the princes of Zabulon and Nephthali, such as Peter and Andrew, James and John, Philip and Matthew, who were from Bethsaida or Capharnaum, and the neighboring towns that belonged to Zabulon and Nephthali, as may be inferred from the passage in Mat. 4, *"Now when Jesus had heard that John was delivered up, he retired into Galilee, and leaving the city of Nazareth, he came and dwelt in Capharnaum on the sea coast, in the confines of Zabulon and Nephthalim, that what was said by Isaias*

the prophet might be fulfilled. The land of Zabulon and the land of Nephthali, the way of the sea beyond the Jordan, Galilee of the gentiles. The people that sat in darkness saw great light, and to them that sat in the region of the shadow of death light is sprung up;" but, as the ten tribes did not return from captivity, as we read in the first book of Esdras, Juda and Benjamin, with the Levites, the Apostles are called princes of Zabulon and Nephthali, either because they were natives of the country of those two tribes, or because, perhaps, a few of those tribes did return in the company of the other Jews, which must have been the case, for Anna the prophetess was of the tribe of Asser.

28. The prophet now, after having described the victory of Christ, and the consequent joy of the Apostles, asks of God that the power so exercised by him in conquering his enemies, and founding his Church, may still be exercised in protecting and preserving his work. *"Command thy strength"* to look after the work you commenced, to strengthen and fortify it; which he explains more clearly when he says, *"Confirm, O God, what thou hast wrought in us;"* as much as, to say, you have delivered us from the power of Satan, you have brought us into the kingdom of your Son, you have planted the Church with the blood of the same Son, you have poured on us *"the spirit of adoption of sons;" "confirm"* all these things, the works of thy mercy.

29. This verse may apply to those who reign in heaven; because, in the temple of heaven, the saints offer God perpetual presents of praise; or it may apply to the spiritual kings, the priests of the Church, who daily offer their *"presents,"* the sacrifice of the Eucharist, the sacrifice of praise and prayer; and, finally, that of the conversion of souls; or it may apply to the temporal kings of the earth, who, to maintain public worship, and to support the ministers thereof, generously contribute thereto from their own revenue, of which the Prophet Isaias, chap. 60 and 66, spoke at length.

30-31. He now directs his prayer against the enemies of the Church, who seek to disturb its peace, and to impede the offerings of praise and the sacrifices of good works; and first, against her invisible enemies, saying, *"Rebuke,"* frighten, coerce, restrain *"the wild beasts of the reeds;"* the wild beasts that usually shelter themselves among the reeds, the demons, who are usually found among vain and light headed people, and in most places where rank weeds, the type of luxury, abound. In such terms does the Lord speak of the devil, under the title of Behemoth, in the Book of Job, chap. 40, where he says, *"He sleepeth under the shadow, in the covert of the reed, and in moist places."* Then he adds concerning the enemies to be found among men, *"The congregation of bulls, with the kine of the people,"* meaning the assemblage of wicked princes raging like so many bulls, *"with the kine of the people;"* among a people without guile, and running wanton, like so many young heifers, *"to exclude them who are tried with silver;"* meaning that those impious princes and people, at the instigation and under the impulse of Satan, assembled to exclude, reject, and reduce to nothing the preachers of the Gospel, who had been proved like silver in a furnace, and found most faithful and pure. Here is clearly foreshown the grievous persecutions both by Jews and Pagans, after the ascent of Christ to heaven. *"Scatter thou the nations that delight in wars."* He now foretells the victory they were to gain over their persecutors. *"Scatter,"* you will scatter all those who shall wage war against your people; and then *"Ambassadors shall come out of Egypt,"* asking for peace, and proffering submission. *"Ethiopia,"* which is farther off, *"shall soon stretch out her hands to God;"* will get before Egypt in the tender of her offerings and her homage to God. He specifies Egypt and Ethiopia, the former as being very hostile to the true religion, and the latter as being a very remote country. The fathers think that in the expression, *"Ethiopia stretching out her hands,"* he alludes to the eunuch of Queen Candace, who was converted to the Christian religion long before any one from Egypt, or any other country of the gentiles. Read Acts, chap. 8

32. He proceeds to foretell, in the shape of an exhortation, the conversion of the gentiles to the Christian religion. *"Ye kingdoms of the earth,"* of the whole world irrespective of Israel or Juda; *"sing to God,"* in faith acknowledging him as the true God, sing his praises. *"Sing ye to the Lord,"* not only in words but by good works.

33. He who, after his ascension on high, sits on the highest heaven, the fountain of light, whence all light has its source and origin. The words *"who mounteth above the heaven of heavens,"* do not imply ascent, but the act of sitting on them, as on a throne; such is the force of the Hebrew word, as we explained in regard of the words, *"who ascendeth upon the west."* The prophet then means to convey that Christ our Lord, after his ascension to heaven, of which he spoke when he said, *"Thou hast ascended on high,"* came to be higher and more elevated than heaven itself, sitting thereon as a man would on a horse or a chariot, or as a king upon his throne. The words, *"to the east,"* correspond exactly with what he said before, *"who ascendeth upon the west;"* that is, because he has all darkness beneath him, while he is himself in light, in light inaccessible, the source of all light that is communicated to Angels and to men. *"Behold he will give to his voice the voice of power."* He that appeared so humble and *"was dumb as a lamb before his shearer,"* now sits on the heaven of heavens, and will shortly *"give to his voice the voice of power;"* make it most powerful and effective, which shall come to pass, *"when all that are in the graves shall hear the voice of the Son of God. And they that have done good shall come forth unto the resurrection of life; but they that have done evil, unto the resurrection of judgment."* No more powerful voice can be imagined. It was the voice of power that said, *"Young man, I say unto thee,*

arise;" as also, *"Lazaras, come forth."* Imagine, then, if possible, the power of that voice that will, on the last day, in one moment, bring together, animate, and raise up the ashes of all the dead from the beginning of the world! It will also be a voice of power that will on that day pronounce, *"Go, ye cursed, into eternal fire;"* and *"Come, ye blessed, possess the kingdom prepared for you;"* Which voice, in both cases, will be obeyed without the slightest effort at resistance. In truth, when compared to such a voice, all the laws, edicts, and commands of the rulers of this world sink into insignificance. Hence he most properly adds,

34. "Give ye glory to God for Israel." Glorify God for the favors conferred on his elect; *"all things for the elect;" "his magnificence and his power is in the clouds;"* a reason for glorifying him, for God's magnificence and power will be especially displayed to Israel; when they shall be *"caught up together in the clouds to meet Christ in the air;"* and shall sit on the clouds, like so many princes on splendid and elevated thrones, on the right and on the left of the Almighty Judge. Then may it well be said, *"God is wonderful in his saints;"* for then will the whole world clearly understand that God, in raising his saints from the lowest depths to the greatest height, from profound abasement to the highest and most exalted glory, was truly *"wonderful;"* for *"the God of Israel,"* of his chosen people, will then *"give power and strength to his people,"* will endow his elect with true and real immortality. *"Blessed be God."* The consequence of what he related, for with great justice all should bless that God whose mercy, justice, power, and wisdom so wonderfully appear in so many mysteries.

PSALM 68

Christ in his Passion declareth the greatness of his sufferings, and the malice of his persecutors the Jews; and foretelleth their reprobation.

1 Save me, O God: for the waters are come in even unto my soul.
2 I stick fast in the mire of the deep: and there is no sure standing. I am come into the depth of the sea: and a tempest hath overwhelmed me.
3 I have laboured with crying; my jaws are become hoarse: my eyes have failed, whilst I hope in my God.
4 They are multiplied above the hairs of my head, who hate me without cause. My enemies are grown strong who have wrongfully persecuted me: then did I pay that which I took not away.
5 God, thou knowest my foolishness; and my offences are not hidden from thee:
6 Let not them be ashamed for me, who look for thee, O Lord, the Lord of hosts. Let them not be confounded on my account, who seek thee, O God of Israel.
7 Because for thy sake I have borne reproach; shame hath covered my face.
8 I am become a stranger to my brethren, and an alien to the sons of my mother.

9 For the zeal of thy house hath eaten me up: and the reproaches of them that reproached thee are fallen upon me.
10 And I covered my soul in fasting: and it was made a reproach to me.
11 And I made haircloth my garment: and I became a byword to them.
12 They that sat in the gate spoke against me: and they that drank wine made me their song.
13 But as for me, my prayer is to thee, O Lord; for the time of thy good pleasure, O God. In the multitude of thy mercy hear me, in the truth of thy salvation.
14 Draw me out of the mire, that I may not stick fast: deliver me from them that hate me, and out of the deep waters.
15 Let not the tempest of water drown me, nor the deep swallow me up: and let not the pit shut her mouth upon me.
16 Hear me, O Lord, for thy mercy is kind; look upon me according to the multitude of thy tender mercies.
17 And turn not away thy face from thy servant: for I am in trouble, hear me speedily.
18 Attend to my soul, and deliver it: save me because of my enemies.
19 Thou knowest my reproach, and my confusion, and my shame.
20 In thy sight are all they that afflict me; my heart hath expected reproach and misery. And I looked for one that would grieve together with me, but there was none: and for one that would comfort me, and I found none.
21 And they gave me gall for my food, and in my thirst they gave me vinegar to drink.
22 Let their table become as a snare before them, and a recompense, and a stumblingblock.
23 Let their eyes be darkened that they see not; and their back bend thou down always.
24 Pour out thy indignation upon them: and let thy wrathful anger take hold of them.
25 Let their habitation be made desolate: and let there be none to dwell in their tabernacles.
26 Because they have persecuted him whom thou hast smitten; and they have added to the grief of my wounds.
27 Add thou iniquity upon their iniquity: and let them not come into thy justice.
28 Let them be blotted out of the book of the living; and with the just let them not be written.
29 But I am poor and sorrowful: thy salvation, O God, hath set me up.
30 I will praise the name of God with a canticle: and I will magnify him with praise.
31 And it shall please God better than a young calf, that bringeth forth horns and hoofs.

32 Let the poor see and rejoice: seek ye God, and your soul shall live.
33 For the Lord hath heard the poor: and hath not despised his prisoners.
34 Let the heavens and the earth praise him; the sea, and every thing that creepeth therein.
35 For God will save Sion, and the cities of Juda shall be built up. And they shall dwell there, and acquire it by inheritance.
36 And the seed of his servants shall possess it; and they that love his name shall dwell therein.

Explanation of the psalm

1-2. The history of the passion of our Lord Jesus Christ, in the Gospel, takes very little notice of the intensity of his sufferings, because the evangelists wished to show that it was quite voluntary, and borne with the greatest fortitude. But, as it was right that the world should know that the sufferings of Christ were intense beyond measure, and learn from thence the extent of their debt to the Redeemer, the Holy Ghost was pleased to reveal the intensity of his sufferings, long before, to the prophets, and, through them, as trustworthy witnesses and above suspicion, to be narrated to us. Isaias, therefore, wrote much about them, so did Jeremias, but none more than David. In the two first verses, then, of this Psalm the passion of Christ is compared to immersion of one into most deep and muddy water. *"Save me, O God."* Not as regards my soul, for that he could not lose, but my body; and he does not ask that absolutely, but to express the intensity of the pains he was suffering, and the natural repugnance of man to death; in the same spirit in which he said in the garden, *"Father, if it be possible, let this cup pass from me." "For the waters have come in even unto my soul."* He now begins the simile of one tossed into the water. Because I am like one cast into the water, and just feeling it so to enter into his vitals as to prevent his further breathing, and, consequently, living. *"I stick fast in the mire of the deep, and there is no sure standing."* I am like a man not only thrown into the deep, but even into a muddy deep, where there is no bottom, no standing. *"I am come into the depth of the sea."* It is not into a small pool I have been thrown, but into a great and deep sea, overwhelmed by a heap of water over me; *"and a tempest hath overwhelmed me,"* because, a fierce storm of winds and waves has completely sunk me. This gives us some idea of the extent and the severity of Christ's sufferings; for they were not confined to the simple death on the cross; his pains and his sufferings were all but innumerable. The *"mire of the deep,"* signifies the sins of the human race that kept him in punishment. The *"tempest that overwhelmed him,"* signifies God's justice and decree that man's sins should be atoned for, as also the rage and cruelty of the Jews, and it may also signify his own ardent love for mankind. That storm was the immediate cause of his passion, inasmuch as his love for us caused him to suffer, as the Apostle says, *"Who did not spare his own Son, but delivered him up for us all;"* and as St. Peter said to the Jews, *"You have killed the author of life;"* and St. Paul again, *"Christ loved the church and delivered himself up for it."* The powerful storm then that sunk Christ into the depths of his death and passion, was partly good and laudable, partly bad and deserving extreme censure.

3. From this verse we can infer, that what he said in the two previous verses are not to be taken in the strict sense of the words, for if he had been drowned, he certainly could not cry out. This verse is also to be read under similar limitation, for Christ cried out in his passion, when he said, *"My God, my God, why hast thou forsaken me?"* and again, when he said, *"Into thy hands, Father, I commend my spirit."* These cries could hardly have made him hoarse. Nor is it the fact that *"his eyes failed,"* expecting help from God. The meaning then is, that his sufferings were as intense and as continuous as with those whose pains make them hoarse in calling for help, and whose sight has failed in looking up to God for assistance in their sufferings. If Christ, then, was always silent, and *"like a lamb led to the slaughter,"* sought for no help, as if he were suffering nothing, it was all owing, not to the lightness of his sufferings, but to his own firmness, his power of endurance, and the extent of his love. Had his lamentations been at all commensurate to his sufferings, his jaws would certainly have become hoarse through constant vociferation, and his eyes would have become dim in his searches for one to help him; and, therefore, as we said at first, the prophet expresses the intensity of his sufferings, while the evangelist glanced at the extent of his constancy under them.

4. Speaking now in the person of Christ, he explains, in plain language, what he had figuratively expressed before. He compared Christ's persecutors to a swell of waters, and to a violent tempest; he now plainly says they were most violent, and almost innumerable, and were thus fierce and violent without any provocation whatever. *"They are multiplied above the hairs of my head."* They were more numerous than the hairs of my head, that can scarcely be counted. *"Who hate me without cause."* Their number is clear from the Gospel, for beside the counsel of the Elders, Priests, Scribes, and Pharisees, there was the great body of the people, *"who cried out, Crucify him."* Whole cohorts of the pagan soldiers joined them, for *"Herod with his army mocked him."* In Pilate's house, an entire company of soldiers assembled to deride him, to whom was added Judas the traitor, to betray him. And that *"they hated him without cause,"* cannot be questioned, for *"he went about doing good, and healing all that were oppressed by the devil,"* and never harmed or injured any one. The excuse they put forth in the council, namely, *"If we let him*

alone, so the Romans will come and take away our place and our nation," was proved, by the event, to have been dictated by a false and a mistaken prudence; for though they did not let him alone, though they obstructed, as far as in them lay, the progress of the Gospel, still the Romans came, took their place and their nation away, which would not have befallen them, had they given a favorable reception to Christ the teacher and the source of peace, mildness, and love. The prophet gives an additional instance of their violence. *"My enemies are grown strong who have wrongfully persecuted me."* My unjust persecutors are strengthened, have taken courage, have succeeded, and that through their injustice, for they compelled me to pay *"that which I took not away,"* to suffer punishment without deserving it. Every unjust man may be called a robber, because he robs God of his glory; and therefore, when he is punished, he pays for what he so took away. Now, Christ never robbed nor took away, for he never sinned, and yet underwent the severest punishment. That the thief hanging on the cross acknowledged, when he said, *"And we indeed, justly, for we receive the due reward of our deeds, but this man hath done no evil."* Luke 23.

5. Having said that he suffered unjustly, and that he had to pay what he did not take away, he now assigns a reason for his having chosen so to suffer, when he might have easily delivered himself from such unjust persecution; and the reason he assigns is his own foolishness, and his offences, however hidden from the world, being well known to God. *"My foolishness;"* that is, the foolishness of Adam that he took upon himself, *"and my offences,"* the offences of Adam and his posterity, which he bore without committing. *"O God, thou knowest my foolishness,"* you know that I am suffering for the folly of the first man, who believed the deceiver when he told him, that by eating the forbidden fruit he would become equal to God; and through his disobedience what has been the result of his foolishness! St. Augustine adds, that the foolishness of Christ may be said to be that which may be looked upon as such by men, and may still be the height of wisdom, namely, that when by one word he may have delivered himself from death, still he preferred suffering the most bitter torments, and the death of the cross itself, to redeem his servants and even his enemies from torments and death. That seemed folly to men, but God knows that such folly is wiser than all human wisdom. Just as to those who know nothing of agriculture, it seems folly and an irreparable loss to throw a quantity of the best grain into the earth; but when the same grains are multiplied and gathered in the harvest, then, instead of its appearing to have been folly, it turns up to have been the height of wisdom.

6-7. In his solicitude for the members of his Church, and that his passion may not be a source of scandal to them, or perhaps of despair, in spite of his promise, he says, *"Blessed is he who shall not be scandalized in me;"* and on the eve of his passion, *"You will be all scandalized in me this night;"* he therefore now says, *"Let them not be ashamed for me who look for thee;"* that is to say, let not those who confide in thee be ashamed on my account, as if I had been abandoned by thee, and my hope had been vain. Let them not say, who will ever expect the Lord, or confide in the Lord, after his thus deserting and abandoning his only Son? which he repeats and explains, when he says, *"Let them not be confounded on my account, who seek thee, O God of Israel;"* the words being an explanation of the words, *"Let them not be ashamed,"* and the words, *"who seek thee,"* being synonymous with, *"who look for thee."* Instead of Lord of Hosts, he has now O God of Israel, to show that men have just reason for confiding in him, he being Lord of Hosts, and therefore supreme in power; and at the same time he is the God of Israel, and in consequence, the friend and protector of his people, and therefore kind to them; and not only all powerful, but most willing, and ready to defend his own. He finally assigns his reason for this just demand. *"Because for thy sake I have borne reproach;"* it was for your honor, and not for my own sins, that I have suffered so much ignominy. It was on your account, that *"shame hath covered my face,"* for the same glory, your glory, I suffered contumely, stripes, derision, spits in the face, and the like, that truly filled my face with shame and confusion.

8-9. The prophet, speaking in the person of Christ, explains the cause of the persecution of the Jews. It was because the Lord censured and reproved their evil doings, as he himself says, John 7, *"The world cannot hate you, but me it hateth, because I give testimony of it, that the works thereof are evil;"* and in Wisdom, chap. 2, we read, *"Let us lie in wait for the just, because he is not for our turn, and he is contrary to our doings, and upbraideth us with transgressions of the law, and divulgeth against us the sins of our way of life."* He therefore says, *"I am become a stranger to my brethren;"* my brethren the Jews look upon me as a stranger, *"and an alien to the sons of my mother;"* I am looked upon as a foreigner and an alien by the sons of my mother, the synagogue. The very thing that John wrote in the beginning of his Gospel, *"He came unto his own, and his own received him not."* For though they once said, *"We know him and whence he is;"* and the Lord himself said to them, *"You know me and whence I am;"* still, at another time, they said, *"We know that the Lord hath spoken to Moses; but as to this man, we know not from whence he is;"* that is, we know him not, he is a foreigner; and he tells why they looked upon him as a foreigner, when he says, *"For the zeal of thy house hath eaten me up;"* because zeal for God's temporal house, the temple which the Jews were in the habit of daily profaning by secular business; as also for God's spiritual house, the congregation of the faithful, that they were daily defiling by their vices; *"eat me up;"* consumed, fired, and pained him; and, under the influence of such zeal, he reproved the Jews grievously, as may be seen in different parts of the four evangelists; and, while he justly reproved them, with a view to their correction, they, in return, abused and blasphemed him, saying, *"Thou hast a devil. Thou art a Samaritan. In Beelzebub the prince of devils, he casteth out devils; we know that this man is a sinner;"* and he, therefore, now adds, *"And the reproaches of them that reproached thee, are fallen upon me."* Any offence against the Son constitutes one against the Father, they being essentially one; and though all sins may be looked upon as common offences to the Father as well as to the Son, those connected with miracles may be said specially to touch the Father, on which Christ himself said, *"The works which the Father hath given me to perfect, give testimony of me,"* John 5; and in John 14, *"The Father who abideth in me, he doth the works."* The calumny, then, in the reproach, *"In Beelzebub the prince of devils, he casteth out devils,"* offered special injury to the Father, inasmuch as it attributed those works of God, which the Son was performing in the name of his Father, and which the Father was producing through the Son, to the devil. Those *"reproaches of them that reproached thee,"* the Father, fell upon the Son, because it was him the Jews intended to calumniate, and not the Father, as also because the Son cheerfully suffered those calumnies that assailed the Father; and in this sense the verse is quoted by St. Paul, Rom. 15.

10-11. This is a very obscure passage, and the more so by reason of the difference between the Septuagint and the Hebrew versions. The most probable explanation of it seems to be as follows. The soul is taken here for the entire man, so that when David says, he *"covered his soul,"* he means, he covered himself, or covered his head, in fasting. Now, among the Jews, the covering one's head was a sign of great grief and sorrow, and generally accompanied their fasts; hence we read in Psalm 34, *"I humbled my soul in fasting;"* and the practice of covering the head when in grief and trouble appears from many passages in the Scriptures; for instance, 2 Kings 13, *"But David went up by the ascent of mount Olivet, going up and weeping, walking barefoot, and with his head covered."* And in chap. 19, *"And the king covered his head, and cried with a loud voice: O my son Absalom, O Absalom, my son, O my son;"* and in Esther 6, *"Aman hastened into his house, with his head covered."* And Isaias, speaking of the manner of fasting, has, chap. 58, *"Is this such a fast as I have chosen for a man to afflict his soul for a day? is this it to wind his head about like a circle, and to spread sackcloth and ashes?"* In this passage, *"to wind his head about like a circle,"* means to wind the covering about it, and bind his head all round tightly with it. Now, we don't read that Christ fasted with his head covered, nor that he wore sackcloth, much less that he was derided for so doing; on the contrary, it was objected to him that he was, *"Behold, a man that is a glutton and a wine drinker;"* and his disciples were found fault with because they did not fast like the disciples of St. John and the Pharisees. It is true, the Lord fasted forty days in the desert, but that was a private fast, with which he could not be reproached. He also fasted several days while he was taken up in preaching, as he watched several nights while absorbed in prayer; but we do not read that they were made a matter of reproach to him either. Finally, in his passion, he fasted from the vespers of Thursday to the ninth hour on Friday, and, from exhaustion and the punishment, no doubt, both hungered and thirsted; nor was his head without being covered, for, covered with a helmet of thorns, he fasted severely and bitterly, with no other food than gall, and no drink but vinegar; and still we find no mention whatever in the Gospel of the sackcloth and ashes. We must, then, with St. Augustine, allow that these verses have a spiritual meaning, and are so to be explained; and then we are to understand the fasting in tears and sorrow to signify the ardent hunger and thirst for the salvation of souls that afflicted him so deeply; and the sackcloth to represent the mortal and frail flesh he chose to assume, that, by such humility, he may induce mortals to despise the things of this world, and long for those of the next; and, for such reasons, he became *"a reproach,"* and became also a *"by word;"* that is, a thing to be scoffed at among the Jews. And that Christ was derided and scoffed at is plain, from Mark 5; for, when he said, *"The girl is not dead, but sleepeth, they laughed him to scorn;"* and when he spoke of the necessity of giving alms, *"Now, the Pharisees, who were covetous, heard all these things, and they derided him."* And, in his passion, he was derided by the soldiers, by Herod, by the high priests, and many others.

12. By way of appendix to the foregoing persecutions, he adds, The judges and the princes, in their councils, sought my death, suborned false witnesses against me; and, finally, condemned me. Judgment was generally delivered at the gates; hence we have, in Proverbs 31, *"Her husband is honorable in the gates, when he sitteth among the senators of the land." "And they that drank wine made me their song;"* not only in their public assemblies, but even in their private parties of pleasure, did they talk of me, making me the butt of their mirth and ridicule.

13. The prophet having hitherto explained the extent and the greatness of the sufferings of Christ, now enters into Christ's prayer to his Father, to be delivered from such calamities, of which St. Paul writes, Heb. 5, *"Who in the days of his flesh, offering up prayers and supplications with a strong cry and tears to him, that was able to save him from death, was heard for his reverence."* Whence we gather that Christ's prayer was not an absolute prayer that he should not suffer, or that he should not die, but that he should not be detained in his passion or in death, in which *"he was heard,"* for that prayer

was put up while he hung on the cross, and after three days, by a glorious resurrection, he was delivered from death, and every other tribulation. *"But as for me, my prayer is to thee,"* while they insulted and abused me, *"my prayer is to thee."* I offered myself to thee, God the Father, for them, saying, *"The time of thy good pleasure, O God,"* the time defined by you, when it would be your good pleasure to deliver me from such torments, and to reconcile the whole world by such an oblation, has now arrived. We read the same in John 18, *"Father, the hour is come, glorify thy Son;"* and John 19, *"It is consummated."*—*"In the multitude of thy mercy hear me, in the truth of thy salvation."* He goes on with his prayer, and asks, that as *"the time of his good pleasure is come,"* his prayer may be heard. *"In the multitude of thy mercy hear me, in the truth of thy salvation;"* that is, through the immense mercy that prompted you to promise reconciliation through the passion of your Son. *"In the truth of thy salvation,"* and by reason of the truth; that is, the veracity and the certainty of salvation, for God is no less pious and merciful in promising that salvation which he did promise.

14-15. He asks to be delivered in the same figurative language that he used in the three first verses, under the figures of water, mud, and storm. *"Draw me out of the mire, that I may not stick fast,"* that I may not sink so deep in it, that I could not be pulled out, for he said previously, *"I stick fast in the mire."* He now prays that he may not be kept fast in it. *"Deliver me from them that hate me,"* from my wicked persecutors, *"and out of the deep waters,"* from the grievous tribulations into which they have plunged me. *"Let not the tempest of water drown me."* Having previously said, *"a tempest hath overwhelmed me;"* he, therefore, now asks that he may not be drowned in it, that he may not be detained in the deluge of water, which he explains by the expression, *"nor the deep swallow me up,"* so that I may never rise again. *"And let not the pit shut her mouth upon me."* Let not the pit into which I have fallen close upon me; while it is open, there is some hope of escape, once it closes there is none.

16-18. In order to show the greatness and the extent of Christ's sufferings, he now, speaking in the person of Christ, prays at greater length. *"Hear me, O Lord, for thy mercy is kind;"* and he offers three reasons for being heard, because of God's mercy, by reason of the greatness of his pain; and the third by reason of his relentless enemies. The first is taken from the mercy of God, who is always most kind and merciful to those who are in trouble. The second reason is found in the verse, *"And turn not away thy face."* God never turned away his face from his Son, though he seemed to do so when he left him hanging on the cross in the most intense pain, forcing him to exclaim, *"O God, my God, why hast thou abandoned me?"* and it is the same he has in view, when he says here, *"Turn not away thy face from thy servant;"* that is to say, leave me no longer in those torments. The third reason is found in the expressions *"Attend to my soul and deliver it."* He asked in the previous verse to be *"heard speedily,"* and he now explains what he wanted, saying, *"Attend to my soul;"* that is, to my course of life now run, and deliver my soul by a speedy resurrection; and he assigns a reason for his so doing, which is the third, as we have already said, namely, *"Save me because of my enemies;"* take me from death and sorrow, restore me to life everlasting, that my enemies, when they shall have seen their efforts against me were fruitless, may be either confounded or converted; which really happened; for when the people heard that Christ arose from the grave, and saw the fact confirmed by evident signs and prodigies, many in sorrow began to say, *"What shall we do men, brethren?"* and three thousand were at once converted. More of them in their obstinacy were so confounded as to say, *"What shall we do to those men? for a miracle indeed hath been done by them, conspicuous to all the inhabitants of Jerusalem; it is manifest, and we cannot deny it."*

19-20. He calls God himself to witness the extent of his sufferings, and especially what he was suffering from slander and calumny, for high minded souls feel more thereon than they do from any corporal sufferings. *"Thou knowest my reproach;"* the calumnies they are heaping on me, *"and my confusion,"* the shame I suffer in consequence, for the innocent, in such cases, suffer as well as the guilty, when they see credit attached to the false accusations that are made against them; *"and my shame,"* the shame that follows confusion, however unjust it may be. *"In thy sight are all they that afflict me."* As well as my afflictions cannot escape your notice, so you must see those who inflict them, from whom I can expect nothing but reproaches and misery, a thing my heart long since expected. *"And I looked for one that would grieve together with me, and there was none."* He finally adds, that he not only had no one to console him under such sufferings, but in his hunger he got gall, and in his thirst vinegar. There were many at the time sorry for the death of Christ, but there were not many *"grieving together with him;"* that is, whose sorrow sprung from the same source as that of Christ's. The Apostles and the pious women, to be sure, grieved for Christ's death, for the death of his body, but Christ himself grieved the spiritual death, and the spiritual blindness of the Jews, who madly raged against the physician who came to cure them. In like manner, he looked for *"one that would comfort me, and I found none;"* because the comfort he looked for was the conversion of the wicked. During his passion many were hardened, few or none converted. The thief was converted, but it was in the very end of his passion; but in his very passion, the crowd cried out, *"Away with him, away with him, crucify him;"* the Apostles were scandalized and fled; Peter denied him, Judas fell into despair.

21. It does not appear from the Scriptures that they gave him gall to eat, for St. Matthew, who mentions the gall, said it was given him to drink, and not to eat. *"They gave him wine mixed with gall to drink,"* which perhaps was not, properly speaking, gall at all, for it was a bitter drink; and St. Mark, relating the same, says it was wine mixed with myrrh, which possibly was the reason why St. Matthew did not quote this verse of the Psalm, as is his wont, when any passage is fulfilled by the life or doings of Christ. It is, therefore, probable that the word food is to be understood, in a spiritual sense, to signify to us the bitterness of the sins our blessed Savior had to digest in his passion. As regards the vinegar, it was not only spiritually but literally fulfilled, as is clear from John 10, where the evangelist states, that on Christ's saying, *"I thirst,"* they offered him vinegar on a sponge, that the Scripture may be fulfilled, which was the passage here.

22-25. The prophet begins now, by way of imprecation, to foretell the calamities that were to fall on the Jews, by reason of their ingratitude and cruelty to Christ, who had been sent to them as a Savior and a Redeemer, and he enumerates the spiritual as well as the temporal punishments, of which we have daily instances." *"Let their table become as a snare before them."* The fathers say that *"their table"* means the reading of the Scriptures, being the table from which pious souls are fed with God's truths; and he calls it a table, to place it in contrast with the gall they gave him for food; as if he said, They gave me gall for my food, and you will make their food and their table a snare before them. That table is daily before the Jews, for they daily read Moses and the prophets, but it is quite a snare to them, because by false and wrong interpretations they misunderstand it, and thus the very Scriptures, which, if faithfully studied, may bring them to life everlasting, leads them to eternal perdition, keeping them, as it does, in their incredulity. The same applies to them as *"a recompense"* for their wickedness, for it is right that they who do not wish to see the light should remain in the dark. It is also *"a stumbling block"* to them; for, instead of recognizing the corner stone sent to them by God, they rather dashed up and knocked themselves against it; and hence, it has become too, as Isaias 8 says, *"a stone of stumbling, and a rock of offense." "Let their eyes be darkened that they see not."* The root of the aforesaid evils is, God's having allowed both their understanding and their affections, to be depraved. The eyes of their soul are darkened, nay more, according to St. Paul, *"There is a veil upon their heart,"* and furthermore, *"They are blinded,"* Isaias 6, Mat. 13, John 12, Rom. 11. Their affections, too, are depraved, for they have no taste for anything but the things of this world, which is conveyed in the words, *"And their back bend thou down always;"* that is to say, allow them to be ungrateful, and punish them for it, that they may be always groveling and bent down, so that they may see nothing but the earth. That we may understand such blindness and perversity to be the effect of God's anger, he now adds, *"Pour out thy indignation on them;"* plain language enough, which the Apostle confirms, 1 Thess. 2, *"Who both killed the Lord Jesus, and the prophets, and have persecuted us, and they please not God,"* and in the next verse he adds, *"for the wrath of God has come upon them to the end."* That wrath of God brought a spiritual plague on them first, and then a temporal one, for they were exiled from the land of promise, and scattered all over the world; to which the prophet alludes when be says, *"Let their habitation be made desolate;"* which was literally fulfilled when, by the orders of the Emperor Titus, Jerusalem was pulled down and rendered uninhabitable; it was, to be sure, afterwards rebuilt and inhabited, by gentiles, Christians, or Saracens, but not by the Jews. As far as the Jews, then, are concerned, it is still a desert, for a few only of them are allowed to live there, a thing predicted by our Lord himself, when he said, *"Behold, your houses shall be left to you desolate."*

26-28. As the Jews were punished for having given gall for food to Christ, by having their own table turned into a snare for them, so the prophet says they will now be punished by adding iniquity upon their iniquity, in the same way that they heaped punishment upon punishment, and pains upon pains on Christ. But we have to explain how the Jews persecuted him whom God hath smitten, and how they added to the grief of his wounds. God does not seem to have smitten Christ, except in his allowing the Jews to smite him; and whatever he suffered seems to be from God as well as from the Jews. We are to understand, then, that Christ was smitten to a certain extent, in which the Jews had no part; and smitten, in other respects, by the Jews, with God's permission. He was smitten by God, and the Jews had no part whatever in it, when he assumed mortal, frail, suffering flesh, subject to hunger, thirst, fatigue, heat, and cold, and many other grievances. Now, the Incarnation, that brought all those things on him, was the act of the Holy Ghost; and, in this way, God alone struck Christ, when, without any fault on his part, he was made subject to so many consequences of original sin. The Jews added to these inflictions when they wounded and persecuted Christ. For, though God advisedly meant and intended Christ so to suffer, and took advantage of the perversity of the Jews to bring it about, still, the Jews themselves, in their own malice and wickedness, persecuted and took away the life of the Redeemer. The prophet, therefore, says, *"Because they have persecuted him whom thou hast smitten;"* for smite him you did when you sent him into the world, *"in the likeness of sinful flesh;"* subject to hunger and thirst to heat and cold, and other innumerable inconveniences; him *"they persecuted,"* by calumnies, reproaches, and false testimonies; *"and they have added to the grief of my wounds;"* to the intense grief I felt at the consideration of their sins innumerable, and which I had undertaken to heal and to cure, as if the wounds were my own, they *"added"* the pain of the lash, the thorns, and the nails; and, even when I was dead, they *"added"* the wound in my side; and even when I had risen from the grave, and would seem to have been beyond their persecution, they followed it up by wounding me through my members, by stoning and slaying my disciples. *"Add thou iniquity upon their iniquity."* As they have *"added to the grief of my wounds,"* so do you, O just Judge, *"add iniquity upon their iniquity;"* in thy justice, instead of delivering them from their first iniquity, let them accumulate iniquities. *"Let them fill up the measure of their fathers,"* that *"upon them may come all the just blood that has been shed upon the earth."* God is said to do a thing when he permits it, and that not by chance, but by a fixed decree, to punish the sins of those who deserve so to be blinded and deserted; for no punishment is more severe than the causing one sin to be the punishment of another. *"And let them not come into thy justice."* An explanation of the preceding sentence; for they who do *"not enter into the justice"* of God; that is, they who are not justified, who are not admitted to that justification which God gratuitously works in the vessels of mercy, they rush from sin to sin, adding sin to sin. *"Let them be blotted out of the book of the living."* Some will have this to mean, let them be put to death; but the following sentence, *"and with the just let them not be written,"* altogether forbids that explanation. In the holy Scriptures nothing is more usual than for one member of a verse to be an explanation of the other; and thus, *"with the just let them not be written,"* is one and the same with *"let them be blotted out of the book of the living,"* which forbids any other interpretation of the living than those who alone have real life in them; that is, the just, the wicked being truly dead in their reins. The book of the living means that book in which the names of God's true servants, who alone have got real justification, and who, as being children and heirs, are enrolled. For, in fact, the Jews, who were formerly God's people, being now blotted out of the book of the living and the just, are no longer God's people nor have they a part in the inheritance of the children of God; and, on the contrary, the gentiles, who were not God's people, by faith in Christ came to be God's people, and have a share in the kingdom of God. That was predicted by Ezechiel, chap. 13, *"They shall not be in the council of my people, nor shall they be written in the writing of the house of Israel;"* and Daniel 9, *"And the people that shall deny him, shall not be his;"* and Osee 1, *"For you are not my people, and I will not be yours;"* and the Lord himself, in the Gospel, frequently promised the same to the Jews, saying, *"The kingdom of God would be taken from them, and the children of the kingdom would be cast out;"* And that, in their place, *"many would come from the east and from the west, and repose with Abraham, and Isaac, and Jacob, in the kingdom of heaven."*

29. He now, at length, in the end of the Psalm, predicts the glory of Christ, and the edification of his Church, speaking as he did hitherto in the person of Christ. *"I am poor and sorrowful;"* so I was while I hung naked on the cross, covered all over with wounds. He thus, in leaving this world, took nothing with him but our sins and miseries; thus giving us an example, how by gladly despising the good things of this world, and bearing all its crosses with patience, we may tread in his footsteps. *"Thy salvation, O God, hath set me up;"* when I was in such a state, in need of everything good, overwhelmed with everything evil and bad, *"thy salvation"* raised me up from the dead, wiped away all my misery, and replenished me with blessings and happiness. For, how can unhappiness find a place in him, adopted by salvation itself, and circled all round by it.

30. Christ, in the form of man, raised up and glorified by God the Father, now returns him thanks, and will do so forever, saying, having now discharged my labors, and free as I am from all pain, I will never cease praising the name of God; that is, his power, *"with a canticle,"* that is, with joy and gladness; *"and I will magnify him with praise;"* a repetition of the same to produce effect.

31. The sacrifice of praise offered to God in heaven, is far and away beyond the most valuable sacrifices offered in the law, among which the most superior was that of a young heifer, whose hoofs and horns were just beginning to shoot; and yet my canticle of praise will be more acceptable in the sight of God than such a sacrifice.

32. He now mingles exhortation with his praises. Let the poor understand and consider those things, that they may learn to rejoice in their poverty. He speaks to those who are poor, as he is; that is, poor from choice, and not from necessity, and who, though they may be rich, dispense their riches as stewards and not as masters, agreeable to God's will; that they may indulge, and not in a spirit of pride, in works of charity and not in the gratification of their passions; and, finally, who repeat the expression, *"Blessed be the name of the Lord,"* with equal devotion, whether in prosperity or in adversity. *"Seek ye God, and your soul shall live."* You poor in spirit, who despise everything earthly, as you are disencumbered of such a load, raise up your spirits, seek God, and your soul, which, as a perishable thing, cannot live, will then truly live. *"Take heed, says Christ, and beware of all covetousness, for a man's life doth not consist in the abundance of things which he possesseth."* Whereas, on the contrary, it is said of God, *"In him was life"* John 1; and in Psalm 35, *"For with thee is the fountain of life;"* and in Eccli. 1, *"The word of God is high in the fountain of wisdom;"* and in Prov. 8, *"He that shall find me shall find life."* For wisdom is the life of a rational soul, and the soul is then most wise and most perfect, when it sees its first and supreme cause in itself, without

anything coming between them. Seek God, then, by walking in the way of his commandments, diverging neither to the right nor to the left, and when you shall have come to him, then *"your soul shall live."*

33. He assigns a reason for its being a good thing to seek God, that we may live, because the holy fathers visited by Christ, in his descent into Limbo, experienced the truth of it. They sought God for a long time, and were the first to find him; the way to eternal life having been opened by Christ, and they having been introduced thereto by him. *"For the Lord hath heard the poor."* All the patriarchs and prophets were poor in spirit, dwelt in this world as so many strangers and pilgrims in search of their heavenly country. Such poor were heard by the Lord, and having heard them, *"he hath not despised his prisoners,"* for prisoners they were, inasmuch as they could not have passed from their prison to their heavenly country, had not Christ, by his death, burst the gates of hell, and broke its chains of iron.

34. He invites the whole universe to return thanks for the favors conferred on it, making special mention even of the reptiles, without mentioning men and Angels at all, of whose readiness to praise God he had no doubt.

35. The establishment of the Church, through the passion and resurrection of Christ, is now predicted, or, as some will have it, the establishment of the celestial Jerusalem, or perhaps both. *"For God will save Sion."* He will protect from every danger and persecution on earth, and will afterwards endow with immortality, his primitive Church, formed out of the Jews; that is, the assembly of the Apostles and primitive disciples. *"And the cities of Juda, shall be built up;"* that is, that primitive Church will be propagated by the accession of many living stones, and many Churches will be built all over the world, called cities of Juda, that is, of confession, because the confession of the true faith builds up and propagates the Church, for Juda signifies confession. *"And they shall dwell there."* He now foretells the solidity and the happiness of the Church. For the cities, that is, the inhabitants of the cities of Juda, *"shall dwell there;"* that is, in Sion, *"and acquire it by inheritance;"* for all the real faithful of the several churches acknowledge the Apostolic Church, that of Sion, excluding of course, heretics and schismatics. And the same true faithful, if they remain in the faith, *"which worketh by charity,"* will also inhabit the celestial Sion, and will *"acquire it by inheritance,"* because, *"if sons, they are heirs also."* Rom. 8.

36. That means, not only will the primitive faithful, but even their posterity, possess that Sion, whether on earth or in heaven; for the Church of Christ, which is built on a rock, never dies. *"And they that shall love his name shall dwell therein;"* as many as shall be found to love his name shall permanently live in his Church, and afterwards in the celestial Sion. Those who shall be found on the last day to have had no charity, like chaff, will be separated from the corn, cast into the fire, and burned. Life everlasting is the reward of charity, according to St. James 1, who says, *"Blessed is the man that endureth temptation; for, when he hath been proved, he shall receive the crown of life, which God hath promised to them that love him."* Sinners, then, having faith alone, without charity, may belong to the Church as well as the just, in the way that the chaff lies in the barn as well as the grain; as good and bad fish are found together in a net; but they will not be so always, nor will they *"acquire by inheritance"* the heavenly Sion, that they may dwell forever therein.

PSALM 69

A prayer in persecution.

1 God, come to my assistance; O Lord, make haste to help me.
2 Let them be confounded and ashamed that seek my soul:
3 Let them be turned backward, and blush for shame that desire evils to me: Let them be presently turned away blushing for shame that say to me: Tis well, tis well.
4 Let all that seek thee rejoice and be glad in thee; and let such as love thy salvation say always: The Lord be magnified.
5 But I am needy and poor; O God, help me. Thou art my helper and my deliverer: O Lord, make no delay.

EXPLANATION OF THE PSALM

1. A verse celebrated in the Catholic Church, as all the divine offices commence with it. For though it is peculiarly applicable to Christ hanging on the cross, it may be used by all the faithful in any danger whatever; and as we are in daily and great danger while we are on our pilgrimage here, and while *"our adversary the devil goes about like a roaring lion, seeking whom he may devour;"* it is not only lawful, but expedient to repeat this verse very frequently. In this verse we ask great and speedy help to avert a great and imminent danger.

The remainder of the Psalm is almost word for word with Ps. 39, which see.

PSALM 70

A prayer for perseverance.

1 In thee, O Lord, I have hoped, let me never be put to confusion:
2 Deliver me in thy justice, and rescue me. Incline thy ear unto me, and save me.
3 Be thou unto me a God, a protector, and a place of strength: that thou mayst make me safe. For thou art my firmament and my refuge.
4 Deliver me, O my God, out of the hand of the sinner, and out of the hand of the transgressor of the law and of the unjust.

5 For thou art my patience, O Lord: my hope, O Lord, from my youth;
6 By thee have I been confirmed from the womb: from my mother's womb thou art my protector. Of thee shall I continually sing:
7 I run become unto many as a wonder, but thou art a strong helper.
8 Let my mouth be filled with praise, that I may sing thy glory; thy greatness all the day long.
9 Cast me not off in the time of old age: when my strength shall fail, do not thou forsake me.
10 For my enemies have spoken against me; and they that watched my soul have consulted together,
11 Saying: God hath forsaken him: pursue and take him, for there is none to deliver him.
12 God, be not thou far from me: O my God, make haste to my help.
13 Let them be confounded and come to nothing that detract my soul; let them be covered with confusion and shame that seek my hurt.
14 But I will always hope; and will add to all thy praise.
15 My mouth shall shew forth thy justice; thy salvation all the day long. Because I have not known learning,
16 I will enter into the powers of the Lord: O Lord, I will be mindful of thy justice alone.
17 Thou hast taught me, O God, from my youth: and till now I will declare thy wonderful works.
18 And unto old age and grey hairs: O God, forsake me not, Until I shew forth thy arm to all the generation that is to come: Thy power,
19 And thy justice, O God, even to the highest great things thou hast done: O God, who is like to thee?
20 How great troubles hast thou shewn me, many and grievous: and turning thou hast brought me to life, and hast brought me back again from the depths of the earth:
21 Thou hast multiplied thy magnificence; and turning to me thou hast comforted me.
22 For I will also confess to thee thy truth with the instruments of psaltery: O God, I will sing to thee with the harp, thou holy one of Israel.
23 My lips shall greatly rejoice, when I shall sing to thee; and my soul which thou hast redeemed.
24 Yea and my tongue shall meditate on thy justice all the day; when they shall be confounded and put to shame that seek evils to me.

Explanation of the psalm

1-2. The holy prophet, mindful of God's promises to those who put their trust in him, and not presuming on his own strength, exclaims, *"In thee, O*

Lord," and not in myself nor in any other creature, *"I have hoped,"* certain, therefore, that I will *"never be put to confusion."* I fly to you in my present trouble, and ask of you *"to deliver and rescue me"* from the hands of my persecutors; *"in thy justice,"* with that justice that prompts you to punish the wicked, and free the innocent. And, for effect, he repeats the prayer, saying, *"Incline thy ear unto me, and save me;"* hear my humble voice, save me in the present danger.

3. He now explains more clearly what he wants from God, and that is, that God should protect him like a city strongly fortified, and incapable of being penetrated by the enemy. The Hebrew implies that this fortified place was on a lofty rock and, in truth, there is no easier way of overcoming all troubles than the knowing how to ascend in spirit to God, and there to contemplate the everlasting happiness; and there one will at once despise everything human; thus, the tribulations, which otherwise would be counted severe and heavy, St. Paul calls *"momentary and light." "While we look not at the things which are seen, but at the things which are not seen. For the things which are seen are temporal; but the things which are not seen are eternal."* 2 Cor. 4. *"For thou art my firmament and my refuge."* Be my protector, for you alone *"are my firmament;"* my firm and well built house, built of stone, as the Hebrew implies, to which I can fly; and *"my refuge."*

Everything else, the favors of man, my own industry and exertions, are houses of mud or of straw, built on the sand; for what are all the goods of this world but frail, perishable things, in which fools alone confide? Happy they who understand so much; happier they who put them into practice.

4. He now descends to particulars, and asks to be delivered out of *"the hand,"* that is, from the power of the sinner, *"the transgressor of the law, and of the unjust;"* all of which literally apply to Absalom, Achitophel, and their servants, for this Psalm altogether corresponds with Psalm 30, which, by general consent, treats of Absalom's persecution. *"The hand of the sinner,"* then, seems to be intended for Absalom, a perverse, wicked man; *"the transgressors of the law"* are the people who rise up in arms against their lawful king, and the *"unjust"* alludes to Achitophel, who in private, had fraudulently sought to injure David. Looking at the passage in a spiritual sense, the sinner may mean the devil, the unjust may mean heretics, and the transgressors of the law, tyrants and persecutors. The just man, however, desires to be freed not only from corporal trouble, but much more so from any danger to his soul, for fear he may, through fear of persecution, consent to sin, and run the risk of eternal death.

5-6. The Hebrew for patience here implies patience in hope, rather than in endurance, as we have it in Rom. 8, *"We wait for it with patience;"* and in James 5, *"Behold, the husbandman waiteth for the precious fruit of the earth, patiently bearing till he receive the early and the later rain. Be you, therefore, also patient, and strengthen your hearts, for the coming of the Lord draweth near."* *"For thou art my patience,"* then, means, for it is from thee I am patiently expecting help. *"My hope, O Lord, from my youth;"* because I began to hope in you from the time that I first knew you, nay more, long before I was capable of knowing you, in your mercy you were my protector; because, *"By thee have I been confirmed from the womb;"* scarce had I come into the world, when I was in a most infirm state, incapable of invoking you, you extended your protection to me. Such favors God is wont to confer on all men, especially when they are of an age when they cannot help themselves; while very few are they who acknowledge such favors, or thank God sufficiently for them; and the prophet, therefore, who, by the light of the Holy Ghost, knew such to be the case, with great devotion exclaims, *"By thee I have been confirmed from the womb; from my mother's womb thou art my protector;"* as much as to say, I know and confess, O Lord, that you cared me from my very infancy, which makes me now confidently hope that you will be my protector when I shall call upon you. *"Of thee shall I continuously sing."* For such reasons, for such favors, I will always chant thy praises, in prosperity and adversity, in this world, and in the next.

7. Banished from my kingdom by my own son, a wretched fugitive instead of a glorious conqueror, I am the wonder of every one, especially when I seem to be so deserted by you whom I always worshipped, in whom I always trusted; but, however, you are a *"strong helper,"* and a steady one; and though, for a time, in your wisdom, you may appear to have deserted me, and allowed my enemies to get the better of me, still, when the proper time comes, you will be a *"strong helper."* St. Augustine, taking a spiritual view of this passage, says, that he who despises the things of this world, patiently submits to injury, and thus goes in a contrary direction to that of mankind, may be called a wonder and a prodigy. Such was John the Baptist, Christ himself, Peter, Paul, and the other Apostles; such were all the martyrs and confessors, and others, who were looked upon by the wise ones of the world as fools, yet could truly say, I am become as a wonder to many, yet you are a strong helper, to carry me through the narrow gate, and to offer violence to the kingdom of heaven, when it will appear whether I was a fool or a wise man.

8. Whatever men may think or say of me, I therefore, wish that *"my mouth may be filled with praise,"* that nothing else may please me, may delight me, but to love thee and praise thy glory; and *"the whole day,"* that is, at all times, *"to sing thy greatness and thy glory."* All they, and they alone, are like this holy king and prophet, who think, and feel, and deeply consider that there is nothing great, nothing worthy our admiration but God alone.

9. David was an old man when he was persecuted by Absalom; and, therefore, calling to mind the victories of his youth, nay, even of his boyhood, he says, *"Cast me not off in the time of old age;"* do not desert him you always stood by, now at the last moment. *"When my strength shall fail;"* when I am become weak and feeble, *"do not thou forsake me;"* when I want your help more than ever I did before.

10-11. Such was literally true of David, against whom his people, with Absalom at their head, and Achitophel as his counselor, rebelled; a thing they did under the impression that he was now grown old and weak, and abandoned by God. *"And they that watched my soul,"* my former counselors and guards, *"have consulted together;"* took counsel how they may destroy me, saying, as *"God hath forsaken him, pursue and take him;"* the very advice that Achitophel gave, which, however, had no effect, as God did not suffer it to be carried out. See 2 Kings 17.

12-13. While they were taking measures against David, he had recourse to God, who, without any trouble, could mar them all, as he really did. *"O God, be not thou far from me,"* as they boast you are, but rather *"make haste to my help,"* to save me from them. *"Let them be confounded and come to nothing that detract my soul,"* by your hastening to help me, let Absalom's counselors be confounded, their plots fail, disappear, and vanish; and let those *"that detract my soul,"* that calumniate me, be rendered senseless. *"Let them be covered with confusion and shame that seek my hurt;"* a repetition of the foregoing.

14-15. Let them be confounded and come to nothing; *"But I will always hope;"* will confide more and more in you, having learned by experience the efficacy of your assistance, and will always *"add to all thy praise;"* singing new hymns to you for your new and repeated favors. *"My mouth shall show forth thy justice,"* with which you punish the wicked; and *"thy salvation,"* through which you free and save the innocent, *"all day long;"* that is, constantly. *"Because I have not known learning."* How could David say this of himself, when he says, in Psalm 118, *"I have understood more than all my teachers;"* and the Psalms prove him to have been well up in both human and divine knowledge; for, though he was a shepherd and a soldier, he may not have been so entirely devoted to caring his flocks, or waging war, as not to be able to devote some time to literature and study? By the word *"learning,"* then, I take it that David means that human craft and cunning in which Achitophel, who had given counsel against him, abounded; and, by the words, *"I have not known,"* that he does not simply mean knowledge, but approbation and use; as we commonly say, *"I don't know you;"* and, as St. Paul says, *"that he knows nothing but Christ, and him crucified."* The meaning, then, is, *"I have not known learning."* I know not the wisdom of this world; I confide not in the counsels of man; I approve not of human craft and cunning; but,

16. I will cling entirely to God's omnipotence; in it will I confide, and will hide myself in it as I would in an impregnable fortress; and thus, *"I will be mindful of thy justice alone;"* I will lose sight completely of human counsel, of my own strength, or of my friends; but I will remember and bear in mind *"thy justice alone,"* by virtue of which you keep your promises and through which you punish the wicked, and crown the pious.

17. You taught me to despise human literature, and to trust in your power; and it was in consequence, that I, an unarmed youth, fought with a bear and a lion, and conquered both them and the giant Goliath. *"And till now I will declare thy wonderful works;"* while I live, to the last day of my life, I will record *"the wonderful works"* you enabled me to do in my youth.

18. And I ask, at the same time, that *"unto old age you forsake me not,"* but that you always may come to my aid, *"until I show forth,"* until I shall have finished the book of Psalms, through which I will show forth *"thy arm,"* thy strength, to all posterity. How David could say that he would announce God's power to all posterity we have already explained, for he foresaw that the Psalms composed by him would be chanted all over the world to the end of time. *"Thy power."* He explains what arm he is to announce, when he says, *"thy power."*

19. He explains the meaning of the showing forth thy arm to the generation that is to come, and says, *"thy power and thy justice;"* that is to say, I will announce thy arm, which signifies your power united with your justice. God is all powerful, but he is still most just; he can do what he wills, but he wills nothing unjust. Now, such power and justice reaches even *"to the highest great things"* among God's creatures, for God created by his power, not only the earth, and the sea, and all their inhabitants, but he also created the heavens, and the heavens of heavens, and the countless millions of Angels that dwell therein. Thus the arm of God's power reaches even those highest great things. God's justice also has not only punished sinful man, who is but dust and ashes, but he has also punished the most exalted among the Angels, who, for their pride, he hurled from heaven into the abyss. The arm of divine justice, then, has reached *"the highest things,"* so that one may well exclaim, *"O God, who is like to thee?"* Nor does this contradict the Scripture that says, *"God made man to his likeness;"* and 1 John 3, *"We know that when he shall appear we shall be like to him; because we shall see him as he is."* For when David says here, *"Who is like to thee?"* he means, is equal to thee, equally wise, powerful, depending on no one, while all depend on him.

20-21. David consoles himself in his present calamity, by the fact of having escaped, through God's assistance, from other calamities. *"How many*

troubles hast thou shown me, many and grievous;" great in their variety and bitterness, borne by me in Saul's persecution, *"and turning, thou hast brought me to life,"* when I was all but in the jaws of death, *"and hast brought me back again from the depths of the earth;"* deliver me from the height of misery, that nearly drove me to the other world. For *"thou hast multiplied thy magnificence,"* in accordance with the extent of my troubles, *"and turning to me,"* in mercy, while you chastised me, as a father you have wonderfully *"comforted me,"* when from a wretched exile you made me a prosperous king.

22-24. The prophet now predicts his delivery from the power of Absalom, and promises all manner of thanks in his heart, with his lips, and with all sorts of musical instruments. *"For I will also,"* when I shall have obtained the victory, *"confess thy truth to thee;"* will praise your justice and your fidelity, *"with the instruments of psaltery,"* with the musical instrument called the psaltery. And I will use the harp too, *"thou Holy One of Israel;"* a name applied to God, whom the people of Israel were bound to sanctify by public worship and due honor, for which he in return sanctified them by the sanctity of his grace. And I will not only thank and praise you with the harp and psaltery, but *"my lips shall greatly rejoice,"* my mouth shall send forth its notes, *"when I shall sing to thee;" "and my soul,"* my life, *"which thou hast redeemed,"* shall also praise thee. And it is not once or twice that *"my tongue shall meditate on thy justice,"* but *"all the day,"* at all times *"it shall meditate,"* exercise itself in chanting the praises of thy justice, *"when they shall be confounded and put to shame that seek evils to me."*

PSALM 71

A prophecy of the coming of Christ, and of his kingdom: prefigured by Solomon and his happy reign.

1 Give to the king thy judgment, O God: and to the king's son thy justice: To judge thy people with justice, and thy poor with judgment.
2 Let the mountains receive peace for the people: and the hills justice.
3 He shall judge the poor of the people, and he shall save the children of the poor: and he shall humble the oppressor.
4 And he shall continue with the sun, and before the moon, throughout all generations.
5 He shall come down like rain upon the fleece; and as showers falling gently upon the earth.
6 In his days shall justice spring up, and abundance of peace, till the moon be taken sway.
7 And he shall rule from sea to sea, and from the river unto the ends of the earth.
8 Before him the Ethiopians shall fall down: and his enemies shall lick the ground.
9 The kings of Tharsis and the islands shall offer presents: the kings of the

Arabians and of Saba shall bring gifts:
10 And all kings of the earth shall adore him: all nations shall serve him.
11 For he shall deliver the poor from the mighty: and the needy that had no helper.
12 He shall spare the poor and needy: and he shall save the souls of the poor.
13 He shall redeem their souls from usuries and iniquity: and their names shall be honourable in his sight.
14 And he shall live, and to him shall be given of the gold of Arabia, for him they shall always adore: they shall bless him all the day.
15 And there shall be a firmament on the earth on the tops of mountains, above Libanus shall the fruit thereof be exalted: and they of the city shall flourish like the grass of the earth.
16 Let his name be blessed for evermore: his name continueth before the sun. And in him shall all the tribes of the earth be blessed: all nations shall magnify him.
17 Blessed be the Lord, the God of Israel, who alone doth wonderful things.
18 And blessed be the name of his majesty for ever: and the whole earth shall be filled with his majesty. So be it. So be it.
19 The praises of David, the son of Jesse, are ended.

EXPLANATION OF THE PSALM

1. A kind prayer of David's, imploring the divine assistance on his son Solomon to judge with justice. The holy man does not ask for riches or power for his son, as the children of this world are wont to ask; but he asks to give him the grace of properly discharging his duties. He knew that kings were created for the people, not the people for kings; and, therefore, that he alone could be called a good king who ruled the people with justice. Solomon himself, no doubt, instructed by his father, asked the very same thing of God, as we read in 3 Kings 3. He, therefore, says, *"Give to the king thy judgment."* Give my son Solomon, just anointed king, *"thy judgment;"* judgment like your own, right, wise, just; or rather the grace of judgment, of judging agreeable to your wish, according to your laws; and repeating the same, he adds, *"and to the king's son thy justice."* Give it to him, that he may *"judge thy people with justice;" "and thy poor;"* that is, thy people, *"with judgment."* A mere repetition of the first sentence. He designates God's people as God's poor; for all men, however rich they may appear to be, are poor in God's sight. They need his assistance in everything, and whatever they have, they have from God, not as a gift, but as a loan; and, therefore God can demand it back, and take it away from them without offering them any injury; and though the heathens do not understand these things, God's people should understand it, and profit by it. This seems to me to be the literal sense of this passage, still I will not say that it may not be taken to apply to Solomon's authority as a king and a judge, so that the meaning would be, grant, O my God, to me, and to my son, the king elect, such judiciary power that he may justly judge your people; or if one choose to apply the passage to Christ, the meaning will be, O God the Father, grant to Christ your Son, the King, the grace of judgment; for according to John 3, *"The Father does not judge any one, but has given all judgment to the Son."* Between judgment and justice there is a difference, justice being a virtue, and judgment is an act of justice; here, however, they are synonymous, are taken for the same thing, for the power or the grace of judging rightly, or the actual judgment. St. Augustine remarks that in this Psalm, and throughout the Psalms, the same idea is repeated in different words, and thus not only here, but in various other parts of the Scriptures, justice and judgment are used to convey the same idea. Titus, in 2 Kings 8, *"And David did justice and judgment to all his people;"* and in Psalm 118, *"I have done judgment and justice, give me not up to them that slander me."*

2-3. He continues to pray for his son king Solomon, begging that during his reign peace and justice may settle on the land, and on all its inhabitants; and as the country was a hilly, mountainous country, he says, *"Let the mountains receive peace;"* that is, may peace descend on all its hills and mountains, and may all its inhabitants receive it. *"He shall judge the poor of the people;"* where peace and justice reign, few are found to injure their neighbor by word or deed; and, therefore, the king of such a place will have no great trouble in protecting the poor from the few oppressors, who must, of necessity, be found in every community.

4. He now begins to pass from Solomon to Christ, this verse being quite inapplicable to Solomon, but not so to Christ, a descendant of Solomon, whose kingdom is to flourish for all eternity. And Christ, of the family of Solomon, *"shall continue;"* shall govern the world *"with the sun;"* so long as the sun shall shine, *"and before the moon,"* which means in presence of the moon; *"throughout all generations;"* to the end of time. We are to observe here, that when the prophet says, that Christ's kingdom would continue as long as the sun would shine, he by no means implies that there would be an end to it when the sun would cease to shine, for Christ's kingdom will endure forever, though the sun will one day cease to shine. The expression, *"throughout all generations,"* is to be understood in a similar sense; when all generations shall have passed away, Christ's kingdom will not also pass away, no more than Christ meant to tell his Apostles he would desert them at a given time, when he said, *"Behold, I am with you all days, to the end of the world;"* which meant, that as he would be with them here, through his grace and his help, so they would be with him in the world to come, in happiness and glory.

5. As he said that Solomon's reign was to continue to the end of the world; looking upon Solomon as the type of Christ, he now describes the coming of Christ, the propagation and the peculiarities of his kingdom; and he describes his coming, first to the Jews, and then to the gentiles, under the figures of rain, a fleece, and earth; such as the signs Gedeon got formerly of the liberation of the people; for, when he asked a sign from God, it happened that the fleece of wool, placed on the floor for the purpose, was completely saturated by dew from heaven, the whole floor around remaining perfectly dry; while, on the following night, the fleece remained quite dry, while the whole floor around was completely wet; in like manner, Christ first descended on or came to the Jews, represented by the fleece of wool; while the whole world beside was perfectly arid and dry; for Christ himself said, "*I am not sent to the lost sheep of the house of Israel.*" Then he came to the gentiles, through the preaching of the Apostles, and then the earth all round was saturated with the rain of the truths of salvation; for the same Lord said, "*Go teach all nations, baptizing them in the name of the Father, and of the Son, and of the Holy Ghost;*" and the fleece alone remained dry, in the dryness of incredulity, even to the present day. Such is the interpretation of St. Augustine, to which St. Bernard adds, that Christ came "*like rain upon the fleece;*" when he came silently into his mother's womb, as rain would upon the purest wool, by virtue of his heavenly power, and that he came "*as showers falling gently upon the earth,*" when, through the miracles of the Apostles, and through their preaching, he made the earth resound as it would under a torrent of rain.

6. The first fruit of Christ's coming will be true justification, and the most perfect peace with God and with all men. "*In his days shall justice spring up,*" which means, when the Savior shall have come all sin will be destroyed, and instead of it, "*everlasting justice will be brought.*" For, though truly just persons appeared from the beginning of the world, such as Abel, Henock, Noe, Abraham, and others; they were all, however, justified through the merits of Christ; for the Angel truly said to Joseph, "*Thou shalt call his name Jesus, for he will save his people from their sins;*" and that was the joy the Angel announced to the shepherds when he said, "*For today is born a Savior unto you.*" "*Justice,*" then, will "*spring up*" in the hearts of men, through faith in Jesus Christ; and thence will follow "*an abundance of peace,*" because real justice consists in love, and the offspring of love is peace, that peace which the world cannot give, but true, permanent peace; and in such abundance as to fill the heavens and the earth; and as a sign of it, universal peace existed under Augustus Caesar at the time of the birth of Christ. That justice and peace will continue in the world "*till the moon be taken away,*" that is to say, the justice of faith and peace with the conscience, but not without

persecution from abroad, will continue as long as the moon, that is, to the end of the world.

7. The propagation of Christ's kingdom, which is the Church spread all over the world, is now described; taking it as to length, from the Indian Ocean to the Sea of Gibraltar; and as to breadth, from the river Tanais in the north, to the extreme boundaries of Ethiopia on the south. Others say the river means the Euphrates, which is not probable, because Christ's kingdom neither begins nor ends at it; but lies at both sides of it. A better interpretation is that which makes the river to be the Jordan, where Christ was called *"my beloved Son,"* where he was baptized, where he commenced his preaching, and where his kingdom had its rise; and thus, according to St. Augustine, the words, *"from the river unto the ends of the earth,"* are only an explanation of *"from sea to sea;"* as if he said, he will rule over the whole world, from sea to sea; for the earth is everywhere surrounded by the ocean; and that will come to pass, because the preaching will commence at the river Jordan, and will be spread throughout all countries, even to the ocean that surrounds it on every side.

8. The Ethiopians are specially named, either because Ethiopia lies in the ends of the earth, and to which he alluded in the preceding verse, or because the Ethiopian eunuch was the first convert among the gentiles, or because the Ethiopians, looking at the darkness of their color, and the savageness of their manners, seemed to be the farthest removed from the worship of the true God. The next sentence, *"And his enemies shall lick the ground,"* is a mere explanation of the preceding, for they who fall down become as prostrate as if they were licking the ground; and it conveys to us the total subjection and prostration of Christ's enemies; that is, of the sinners and infidels, converted through faith to do penance. And they who will not willingly fall down before Christ, and piously, and faithfully adore him, will be compelled, on the last day, to fall down before him, and *"to lie under his footstool."*

9. Having said that Christ would rule from sea to sea; that is, throughout the whole earth surrounded by the sea, lest it may be supposed that the islands were excluded, he adds, *"The kings of Tharsis and the islands shall offer presents."* The meaning of the *"kings of Tharsis"* has been explained in Psalm 47, and the most probable opinion is, that the islands alluded to are those in the eastern sea, which are very large and very numerous, and from which a great quantity of gold and spices were, every third year, brought to Solomon, as we read in 3 Kings 18; and the meaning is, *"the kings of Tharsis;"* that is, of the islands in the east; *"and the islands;"* that is, the people of the islands also, shall offer precious gifts to Christ their king. To these kings and people he then unites *"the kings of the Arabians and of Saba,"* these being the countries from whence was had the greatest quantity of gold, silver,

precious stones, and all sorts of spices; for, as we read in the passage just cited, 3 Kings 18, *"The queen of Saba brought Solomon an immense quantity of gold, silver, precious stones, and spices."* We cannot avoid considering here what presents we should offer to Christ, and what presents are most agreeable to him; and they are the gold of love, the incense of prayer, and the myrrh of patience, or rather, faith united with prayer, hope with a longing for the things above, charity with the fruit of good works, which charity causes those who are inflamed by it to offer, without difficulty, not only the wealth of this world, and all manner of hardships, but even their very life to Christ their master.

10. All this, to a certain extent, has been accomplished as regards Christ, and will, unquestionably, to the letter, be ultimately accomplished. It is not unusual in the Scriptures to speak in such general terms, though there may be many exceptions. Thus, we read in Genesis, *"that all flesh had corrupted its way;"* and yet, in the very same place, we find Noe called *"a just and perfect man;"* so we read in Matthew, that *"Herod was troubled, and all Jerusalem with him;"* still we know that Simeon the just man, and Anna the prophetess, and many other just people, so far from being troubled, were just as glad as the wise men who came in search of the Redeemer. In a similar manner, then, it is said, that all the kings of the earth will adore Christ, and all nations will serve him; because a great many princes and nations will be converted to the service and worship of Christ. If we refer the passage to the day of judgment, it is true to the letter; for then every knee will be bent to Christ. Finally, if we refer it to the actual power that Christ has over all princes and all nations, so that, with or without their knowledge, with or without their consent, he may deal as he pleases with them, treat them as he likes, and compel them to do his bidding, the prophecy will be always fulfilled in him; *"For all power is given to him in heaven and on earth,"* Mat. 28. And Apoc. 1, *"He is the prince of the kings of the earth;"* and Apoc. 19, *"And he hath on his garment and on his thigh written king of kings, and Lord of Lords."*

11. Kings and people will serve Christ for this reason, because, through him they will be delivered from the power of the devil, from the cruel tyranny of the prince of darkness, and will be introduced to his own most peaceful kingdom. The poor man named here signifies the human race, despoiled of all the blessings enjoyed in a state of innocence, by the devil. The mighty is the devil, turned from a crafty into a mighty one by our iniquity; for, if man had not yielded to temptation he never could have been subdued by the devil. By his sin, though, he became the captive of the devil, and the devil acquired a mastery over him. Now, man begins to acquire his liberty when he begins to see his own poverty, and thereby to humble himself, and to trust in the Lord, and not in himself. He will, therefore, deliver the poor man from the powerful devil; *"and the needy that hath no helper;"* whom neither man nor Angel, nor any other creature could have helped.

12. He now tells us in what manner, Christ will deliver men from the devil, by forgiveness of their sins, and restoration of grace; for, when the sins are forgiven, the chain which held them captives to the devil is broken. Our king, therefore, *"shall spare the poor and the needy;"* will forgive the sins of those who acknowledge them, avowing their inability of discharging their debts, and he will, along with it, bestow grace and justice on them, and so *"save the souls of the poor."*

13. Man, through original sin, became a debtor to the extent of everlasting death. Such was the original debt, and so long as it remains unpaid, the devil, a remorseless creditor, exacts usury thereon, daily urging us to the commission of fresh sin, that being the punishment of the first sin; and, so long as the punishment of those sins is deferred, the interest is added to the principal. Thus, the longer the sinner lives, the more the debt increases. Christ, then, that kindest of masters, not only remits, through his grace, the original sin, which may be called the original debt, but he even frees from the usury; that is, from the actual sins added thereto, and from the iniquity of so severe an exactor. This was foretold by Isaias when he said, *"for the yoke of their burden, and the rod of their shoulders, and the scepter of their oppressor thou hast overcome."* *"And their name shall he honorable in his sight."* The word *"and"* is to be read as *"because;"* for the meaning is, God has such love for man, because the very name of the poor is honorable in the sight of God; and by their *"name"* we are to understand men created to God's image. For, though man became very wretched and despicable through sin, still, human nature and man's name is not vile before God, nor does he despise his own image. And, in truth, the Incarnation of the Son of God is a manifest proof how precious is human nature in his sight, a consideration that should move all mankind to love him, when they see themselves so dealt with, beyond their merits far and away.

14. Having alluded to Christ's death in the preceding verse, which was the redemption and a propitiation for our sins, he now thinks proper to allude to his resurrection, and his life eternal; and, therefore, he says, and *"he shall live;"* that is, after he shall have redeemed them by his death, he shall live again. *"And to him shall be given of the gold of Arabia;"* he shall be worshipped with most costly presents; *"for him they shall always adore;"* those that shall have been redeemed by him will adore the true God according to his own rite, doctrine, and institution, to the end of the world. *"They shall bless him all the day;"* constantly praise and glorify him.

15. He now describes the fruit of the Apostle's preaching after Christ's resurrection and ascension. The word *"firmament,"* however, requires some

notice previous to an explanation of the text. It means such a supply of corn, oil, and other necessaries as may supply a family; but here it is to be understood in a spiritual sense, and means an abundance of spiritual graces, as may be inferred from the words, *"and they of the city shall flourish like the grass of the earth,"* where the metaphor contained in the preceding words is explained. The meaning of the passage, then, obscure enough as it is, seems to be, *"There shall be a firmament on the earth;"* an abundance of spiritual food, the word of God; *"on the tops of the mountains;"* in places naturally barren; for it is in the valleys, and not on the tops of mountains, that corn usually abounds. *"The fruit thereof shall be exalted;"* the fruit of such corn, when sown, shall increase and multiply *"above Libanus."* The fruit of this seed so committed to the earth will rise higher than the cedars of Libanus, the tallest in the world; *"and they of the city shall flourish like the grass of the earth,"* and such fruit will not consist in mere ears of corn, but in the crowd of believers; for, out of the city of God, Jerusalem, of which Isaias, chap. 2, says, *"From Sion will go forth a law, and the word of the Lord from Jerusalem;"* and the believers will flourish, and be multiplied in such numbers as to resemble the growth of the grass on the land. And that such was the case St. Luke tells us, Acts 6, where he says, *"And the word of God increased, and the number of believers was greatly multiplied."*

16. The prophet concludes the Psalm with prayer and praise of the future Messias. *"Let his name be blessed forevermore."* Let Christ's name be blessed by all, everywhere and at all times. *"His name continueth before the sun;"* will continue as long as the sun exists. His persecutors may endeavor to extinguish that name, but they never will succeed. *"And in him shall all the tribes of the earth be blessed;"* words taken from Genesis 22. *"And in thy seed shall the nations of the earth be blessed;"* and explained by the Apostle, in Gal. 3, *"He saith not And to his seeds, as of many, but as of one, And to thy seed, who is Christ;"* all nations, then, will be blessed by Christ, who is God; that is to say, nobody will be blessed but through Christ, and in him will be blessed as many as shall have been regenerated, and persevered in him. To them will be said on the judgment day, *"Come, you blessed of my Father, possess the kingdom prepared for you from the beginning of the world,"* That benediction, then, is justification and adoption of children, through Christ. And, as all the tribes of the earth shall be blessed in him, so, on the other hand, *"all nations shall magnify him;"* will praise and glorify him.

17. Such is the praise in which all nations will magnify him, for they will acknowledge and proclaim that the wonders Christ did in justifying the wicked, rescuing them from the power of darkness, and transferring them to his own kingdom could have been done but by him alone.

18. *"And blessed be the name of his majesty forever: and the whole earth shall be filled with his majesty. So be it. So be it."* The prophet ultimately wishes, that the name of the Divine Majesty may be blessed to all eternity by all, not only in heaven, where he is constantly blessed by the Angels, but also on earth, so that all the earth may be filled with the glory of the Lord; and that all men may acknowledge and praise the Lord; and he concludes with great affection, by repeating: So be it. So be it.

PSALM 72

The temptation of the weak, upon seeing the prosperity of the wicked, is overcome by the consideration of the justice of God, who will quickly render to every one according to his works.

1 How good is God to Israel, to them that are of a right heart!
2 But my feet were almost moved; my steps had well nigh slipped.
3 Because I had a zeal on occasion of the wicked, seeing the prosperity of sinners.
4 For there is no regard to their death, nor is there strength in their stripes.
5 They are not in the labour of men: neither shall they be scourged like other men.
6 Therefore pride hath held them fast: they are covered with their iniquity and their wickedness.
7 Their iniquity hath come forth, as it were from fatness: they have passed into the affection of the heart.
8 They have thought and spoken wickedness: they have spoken iniquity on high.
9 They have set their mouth against heaven: and their tongue hath passed through the earth.
10 Therefore will my people return here and full days shall be found in them.
11 And they said: How doth God know? and is there knowledge in the most High?
12 Behold these are sinners; and yet abounding in the world they have obtained riches.
13 And I said: Then have I in vain justified my heart, and washed my hands among the innocent.
14 And I have been scourged all the day; and my chastisement hath been in the mornings.
15 If I said: I will speak thus; behold I should condemn the generation of thy children.
16 I studied that I might know this thing, it is a labour in my sight:
17 Until I go into the sanctuary of God, and understand concerning their last ends.
18 But indeed for deceits thou hast put it to them: when they were lifted up thou hast cast them down.
19 How are they brought to desolation? they have suddenly ceased to be: they

have perished by reason of their iniquity.
20 As the dream of them that awake, O Lord; so in thy city thou shalt bring their image to nothing.
21 For my heart hath been inflamed, and my reins have been changed:
22 And I am brought to nothing, and I knew not.
23 I am become as a beast before thee: and I am always with thee.
24 Thou hast held me by my right hand; and by thy will thou hast conducted me, and with thy glory thou hast received me.
25 For what have I in heaven? and besides thee what do I desire upon earth?
26 For thee my flesh and my heart hath fainted away: thou art the God of my heart, and the God that is my portion for ever.
27 For behold they that go far from thee shall perish: thou hast destroyed all them that are disloyal to thee.
28 But it is good for me to adhere to my God, to put my hope in the Lord God: That I may declare all thy praises, in the gates of the daughter of Sion

Explanation of the psalm

1. Jeremias did the same, for in chap. 12 he first says, *"Thou indeed, O Lord, art just, if I plead with thee;"* and having laid so much down as a foundation, he adds, *"But yet I will speak what is just to thee. Why doth the way of the wicked prosper? Why is it well with all them that transgress?"* In like manner, David first affirms here that God is good, and therefore just, but that it is only those who are endowed with sound judgment that see his goodness, while the wicked look upon him as perverse. He says then, not by way of interrogation, but of affirmation, *"How good is God to Israel, to them that are of a right heart;"* that is to say, God is exceedingly good to the Israelites, to those that are of a right heart. Thus God, who in himself is always good, upright, and just, is so in the opinion of Israel; still not of all Israel, but of those in Israel who have a pure heart, unclouded by passion, so that they can form a correct judgment; or, perhaps, *"are of a right heart"* means those whose heart is conformable to God's righteousness, for those who have a crooked heart look upon everything straight as crooked.

2. He now begins to explain the temptations to which the weak are subject, speaking in their person, as we observed already. He says, the pious faithful, who have a pure and upright heart, have no doubt in God's justice and goodness, in any position he may place them; but I am not so, for with a heart by no means pure and upright, I nearly fell into doubting God's justice. Such doubt he expresses figuratively by the movement of the hands and feet. When the feet begin to grow weak, and when one slips in walking, it is a sign of infirmity and weakness; and so with him who is tormented with doubts about the truth, he, too begins to totter, and, as it were, fall

from the faith. *"But my feet were almost moved."* I began to totter, though I did not fall entirely. *"My steps had well nigh slipt."* I began to trip in my walking without coming to the ground, giving us to understand that he all but fell into doubt of God's justice and providence.

3. He tells us now whence those temptations proceeded, and says it arose from seeing the wicked, who should have been punished by God, enjoying the most profound peace, and many other blessings.

4. He goes on recounting the various blessings of the wicked. They enjoy all manner of peace and prosperity, because such is their health that they never think of death, they fancy that they are to live forever; and though they may now and then be struck by sickness, it is one of no great duration, but quickly passes away. *"There is no regard to their death."* They never think of death themselves, nor do others think of it, when they see them always so robust, so happy, so healthy. *"Nor is there strength in their stripes."* When they do suffer any stripes of tribulation, there is no strength in such stripes, for they quickly disappear, leaving the wicked at once just as happy as ever.

5. To add to the happiness enjoyed by the wicked, in exemption from disease and bodily afflictions, they enjoy beside an abundance of all manner of things, so that they have not to contend with want, fatigue, litigation, griefs, and other troubles, the lot of man in general, *"who eat their bread in the sweat of their brow,"* and are oppressed by the stronger. But St. Bernard justly observes that the case will be otherwise with them in hell; for, the saying of the Apostle *"All who wish to live piously in Christ Jesus shall suffer persecution,"* 2 Tim. 3; and, *"For whom the Lord loveth he chastiseth; and he scourgeth every son whom he receiveth,"* Heb. 12.

6. The prophet now tells us the fruit produced in the wicked by prosperity—pride, and a mass of iniquity. For they spend their superfluities in gratifiyng their lust and oppressing the poor; while, on the contrary, very pious people are full of fear, and tremble in the days of their prosperity; they are afraid of prosperity, for fear it may be their reward, instead of the eternal reward they so ardently long for. *"Pride hath held them;"* instead of their holding pride, it holds them as if with a chain. *"For he that committeth sin is the slave of sin." "They are covered with their iniquity and their wickedness;"* implying that the wicked, in their prosperity, commit sin, not only in private, that is, in their heart, as do the poor and wretched sinners who, in thought, are guilty of theft, adultery, vanity, which they commit not, not from want of will, but from want of means; (and thus, their sins are all interior;) but the wicked alluded to in this verse, who have the wealth of this world at their command, are so steeped in iniquity that they sin not only in thought and desire, but they use their eyes, hands, tongue, feet, and all the members of the body, to transgress in word and deed.

7. He now shows that their iniquity arose from the bad use of the temporalities so abundantly bestowed on them by God. They did not share them with the poor, as they should have done; they kept all to themselves, and, becoming fat in consequence, they oppressed the poor like so many untamed horses or bulls. St. Augustine appositely remarks, that the poor become wicked from leanness, the rich from fat. Ask the poor why they steal, and they will tell you want drove them to it; ask the rich why they unjustly seize another's land, and they will answer, if they will condescend to give an explanation at all, that they have land adjoining, which absolutely requires the addition of that of their neighbor. Thus, Achab took away Naboth's vineyard, not because he wanted it, but because it bounded his palace. And that the wealth of this world, when not shared with our needy neighbors, is the cause of much wickedness, we read in Ezechiel 16, where he says, *"Behold, this was the iniquity of Sodom;"* that is, the iniquity that brought fire from heaven on it, *"Pride, fullness of bread, and abundance, and the idleness of her and of her daughters: and they did not put forth their hand to the needy and to the poor. And they were lifted up, and committed abominations before me, and I took them away, as thou hast seen." "They have passed into the affection of the heart."* A difficult passage, and variously explained. My opinion is, that *"passing into the affection of the heart"* means to be so transformed and possessed by carnal desires that the whole man becomes animal; as St. Paul says, when *"God gave them up to the desires of their heart;"* and in the end of the same chapter where he says, *"For this cause God delivered them up to shameful affections,"* Rom. 1; for the thoughts and the affections are most united, and taken for the same. Man desires nothing but what he thinks on and what he knows. Thus, the adulterer, who places all his affections on a woman, and prefers her even to eternal happiness, is not actuated by the fact of her being the fairest and most beautiful person in existence, but because he thinks she is, and paints her to himself as such; thus, the sinners, in the abundance of the goods of this life, *"passed into the affection,"* and thoughts, and pictures of their own heart, because they have devoted themselves entirely to the creations and the concupiscences of their hearts.

8. He goes on to show the perversity of the wicked, who enjoyed so much prosperity, says they entertained blasphemous thoughts against God and man, were not afraid to proclaim it publicly, and derided God's majesty and his servants; and those who *"were on high,"* were most forward in doing so; that is, those who were in the highest positions among them.

9. Such was the wickedness of the impious that they were not afraid to blaspheme, to open their mouth against heaven, fearing neither God nor Angels; and their tongue hath passed through the earth, detracting, deriding God's servants, as if their *"hope were vain."*

10-11. The prophet again speaks in the person of those weak in faith, to explain the temptations that assail them, in consequence of the happiness enjoyed by sinners *"Therefore will my people return here."* In consequence of the crimes and the prosperity of the wicked, my people, a faithful and God fearing people, *"will return here,"* to reflect and consider on those matters. *"And full days shall be found in them;"* which means, they will find that the wicked are truly happy, and they even enjoy the longest life, so that their days are full when they come to old age. *"And they said: How doth God know? and is there knowledge in the Most High?"* Those wavering in the faith said, how can God know and permit such things? has God on high any knowledge? or, which is he ignorant of, or does not reflect on such things?

12-14. He assigns his reason for doubting in God's knowledge of what happens on earth, and still speaks in the person of one of the infirm, but with a view to the easier relief of them. *"Behold, these are sinners; and yet, abounding in the world, they have obtained riches."* The reason for my doubts in God's providence were, that sinners, who deserved to be afflicted, have all the good things of the world and abound in riches. *"And I said,"* turning the thing in my mind, *"then have I in vain justified my heart;"* in vain have I kept my heart free from sin, and in vain have I *"washed my hands among the innocent;"* leading a life of innocence in vain, I say, for God favors the sinner, and not the just; nay, more, he afflicts them; for I, always desirous of justice, *"have been scourged all the day;"* have been always in trouble; *"and my chastisement hath been in the mornings;"* begins at dawn of day, and never stays or allows me a moment's rest.

15. He now begins to administer medicine, as it were, to the infirm. Hitherto he entered into their complaints, and their cause of being scandalized by reason of the prosperity of the sinner, and the adversity of the just; and now, as if in a spirit of compunction and penitence, he says, *"If I said"* to myself, *"I will speak thus;"* I will go to show how unjust is the prosperity of the wicked, and I will charge God with it. *"Behold, I should condemn the generation of thy children;"* by that very fact I should condemn and reprobate all thy children, Abraham, Isaac, Jacob, Moses, and the rest of thy servants; for all those acknowledged that God directed all the affairs of men, and by a just judgment permitted the wicked sometimes to prosper, and the just to be afflicted. Or the meaning may be, I have condemned all the children of God as so many fools, who idly seek to lead a righteous life. Or another interpretation, I have condemned the generation of thy children, because I looked upon them all as abandoned by God, which was most false and worthy of censure. And this is the first reason the prophet assigns, to persuade the infirm to have no doubt in God's providence, that they may not be setting themselves up against all the children of God, the saints, prophets, and patriarchs; nor imagine that they were either foolish or deserted by God.

16-17. To the first reason he now adds a second, taken from the difficulty of the question, which should make people be slow in condemning things they do not understand. *"I studied that I might know this thing."* I thought within myself that by investigation I might come at the bottom of this matter; but *"it is a labor in my sight;"* a great difficulty presented itself, *"until I go into the sanctuary of God;"* and through prayer obtain light from him, and by that light *"understand concerning their last ends;"* get a view of the last end of those wicked people; for then, only, will it clearly appear that they had by no means all the happiness they appeared to have.

18. The prophet now shows that the last end of the wicked proves they could not have been happy in this world, and that God is a just judge. The very snares and artifices those wicked people employed to injure their neighbors, and get possession of their substance, have been, through your divine providence, O Lord, turned back upon themselves with a vengeance; for, though they may have got hold of their neighbor's money by such schemes, they lost eternal life to them. *"When they were lifted up, thou hast cast them down;"* when they rose to the enjoyment of honors and dignities, they were the cause of their being, through your just judgment, hurled down the precipice of everlasting death.

19. He now explains what he had just rather obscurely expressed; and, in astonishment at the rapid destruction of the wicked, whose happiness had only begun when it ended; had only just shot forth, when it died away; he exclaims, *"How are they brought to desolation!"* They who had such an abundance of all things, are become like a desolate city, where nothing but ruins are to be seen; *"they have ceased to be,"* though they thought they were to live forever.

20. He most happily compares the prosperity of the wicked to a dream. Dreams are merely the appearance, not the reality. The dreamer who fancied himself in possession of a large sum of money finds, on his waking, that he was deluded by an empty phantom; so with the wicked in this world, who abound in its riches, they think themselves happy, but when the night of this world shall have passed away, then they will understand that they were not truly happy, and then *"their image,"* their imaginary happiness, *"shall be brought to nothing;"* for that imaginary and momentary happiness, derived from gold and silver, servants and horses, palaces and gardens, honors and dignities, feasting and luxury, has no room in heaven, for all these things will perish, and leave their wretched votaries most unhappy. Justly, then, does the Apostle admonish us, *"That they who have the good things of* this world should be as if they had them not, that they should not glory nor confide in them, for the fashion of this world passeth away." "As the dream of them that awake," which vanishes on awaking, "so in thy city, O Lord," which will be made visible and manifest on the last day, "thou shalt bring their image to nothing;" prove all their happiness to have been baseless and imaginary; for then will appear in what true happiness consists. Justly, says St. Augustine, will God in his heavenly kingdom reduce to nothing the image of those wicked beings, who on earth sought to reduce his image to nothing.

21-24. He now explains how he got at the solution of the question, and made great proficiency with God. The causative particle, *"for,"* does not refer to the preceding, it refers to the 24th verse. *"For my heart hath been inflamed"* towards God, *"and my reins have been changed,"* my carnal affections changed into spiritual ones. *"And I am brought to nothing, and I knew not."* I have been humbled, and confessed my ignorance; nay, more, like a fool, *"I am become as a beast before thee,"* determined to obey without a single murmur, and like a beast to submit to any burden, however grievous. *"And I am always with thee;"* from your faith and charity I will never depart, and for all these my virtues, gifts, of yours, *"thou hast held me by my right hand,"* for fear those grievous temptations may cause me to stray from you; *"and by thy will,"* in the spirit of your great kindness, *"thou hast conducted me"* in the right path; *"and with glory hast thou received me"* into your city, in hope here, and in reality hereafter.

25 Having said, *"With glory thou hast received me,"* he now, with his mind's eye fixed on that glory, is so wrapt in spirit as to despise all created things. *"For what have I in heaven?"* what is there beautiful? what is there precious? that I could desire in heaven; *"and besides thee what do I desire on earth?"* what is there beautiful or precious that I could ask or desire upon earth? Nothing, positively nothing, I find nothing created to satisfy me, nothing with which my heart can rest perfectly content, either in heaven or on earth

26. He assigns a reason for desiring nothing but God, because, wherever he may place his heart or his flesh, they will rot and moulder, if not placed on God. *"My flesh and heart have fainted away."* They have become corrupted and rotten whenever I allowed them to rest on created things. *"The God of my heart, and the God that is my portion forever."* The Hebrew makes it *"the rock of my heart;"* as much as to say, God alone is the rock on which my heart can securely rest, so that it can neither sink nor fall; he is the center of all my desires, he is my portion, my lot, my inheritance, the only thing I can hold for all eternity; let others have other portions, be they gold or silver, be they carnal desires or stately palaces, be they empires or kingdoms; God will suffice for me both for this world and for the next.

27. He made a good choice in standing on God as his rock, because all who are separated by sin from him will perish altogether; just as the body perishes when the spirit leaves it, or as a house tumbles when the foundation is taken from it. *"Thou hast destroyed all them that are disloyal to thee;"* not only will those who estrange themselves from God perish, for want of that grace that is the life of the soul, but, with that, God having espoused those souls to himself, and being essentially a jealous God, he, therefore, most grievously punishes with eternal death those who are unfaithful to a spouse of such power and goodness.

28. He concludes the Psalm by saying, *"It is good for me to adhere to my God."* Let others judge as to what may be good for themselves, for me it certainly is good, useful, and honorable to stick close to my God; and, as I cannot embrace him, or lay hold of him in this life, it is good also, now *"to put my hope in him,"* to stick to him through hope, and, meantime, to rejoice in the hope of perfect adhesion to him. *"That I may declare all thy praises in the gates of Sion."* That, having been freed from all earthly desires by such perfect adhesion to God, I may be totally taken up in praising him, and that, *"in the gates of the daughter of Sion,"* before the multitude of the faithful, I may teach the many how idle, nay, even hurtful it is to cling to the things of this world, and how good it is *"to adhere"* to God, and to put their hopes in the Lord their God.

PSALM 73

A prayer of the Church under grievous persecutions.

1 God, why hast thou cast us off unto the end: why is thy wrath enkindled against the sheep of thy pasture?

2 Remember thy congregation, which thou hast possessed from the beginning. The sceptre of thy inheritance which thou hast redeemed: mount Sion in which thou hast dwelt.

3 Lift up thy hands against their pride unto the end; see what things the enemy hath done wickedly in the sanctuary.

4 And they that hate thee have made their boasts, in the midst of thy solemnity. They have set up their ensigns for signs,

5 And they knew not both in the going out and on the highest top. As with axes in a wood of trees,

6 They have cut down at once the gates thereof, with axe and hatchet they have brought it down.

7 They have set fire to thy sanctuary: they have defiled the dwelling place of thy name on the earth.

8 They said in their heart, the whole kindred of them together: Let us abolish all the festival days of God from the land.

9 Our signs we have not seen, there is now no prophet: and he will know us no more.
10 How long, O God, shall the enemy reproach: is the adversary to provoke thy name for ever?
11 Why dost thou turn away thy hand: and thy right hand out of the midst of thy bosom for ever?
12 But God is our king before ages: he hath wrought salvation in the midst of the earth.
13 Thou by thy strength didst make the sea firm: thou didst crush the heads of the dragons in the waters.
14 Thou hast broken the heads of the dragon: thou hast given him to be meat for the people of the Ethiopians.
15 Thou hast broken up the fountains and the torrents: thou hast dried up the Ethan rivers.
16 Thine is the day, and thine is the night: thou hast made the morning light and the sun.
17 Thou hast made all the borders of the earth: the summer and the spring were formed by thee.
18 Remember this, the enemy hath reproached the Lord: and a foolish people hath provoked thy name.
19 Deliver not up to beasts the souls that confess to thee: and forget not to the end the souls of thy poor.
20 Have regard to thy covenant: for they that are the obscure of the earth have been filled with dwellings of iniquity.
21 Let not the humble be turned away with confusion: the poor and needy shall praise thy name.
22 Arise, O God, judge thy own cause: remember thy reproaches with which the foolish man hath reproached thee all the day.
23 Forget not the voices of thy enemies: the pride of them that hate thee ascendeth continually.

Explanation of the psalm

1. The holy prophet, speaking in the person of the Jewish people, deplores that universal calamity that was inflicted on them by the gentiles, under king Antiochus, who was called Epiphanes. *"O God, why hast thou cast us off,"* us thy people, *"to the end?"* as if you were never more to care for or to regard us; *"why is thy wrath enkindled,"* is thy anger excited, *"against the sheep of thy pasture?"* against that people you were wont to protect with as much care as a shepherd does his flock. The words, *"thou hast cast us off unto the end,"* do not imply that God, in reality, by a fixed decree, cast off his people forever; but that the people thought he had done so, and were fearful for the

consequence; and, therefore, in a pitiable voice, exclaimed, *"Why have you cast us off forever?"* that is, you deal with us as if you had cast us off; for, when he says in a subsequent verse of this same Psalm, *"and forget not the souls of thy poor,"* he shows that he was not at all so sure of their having been cast off.
2. They now pray to God not *"to cast them off,"* inasmuch as they are the people he formerly brought out of Egypt, formed them into a peculiar congregation, by giving them magistrates, laws, and rites, and, therefore, that it would seem incongruous that he who had so formed and established them should now desert them. *"Remember thy congregation,"* the people you congregated, *"which thou hast possessed from the beginning;"* who acknowledged no king or lord before you; you were the first to possess it as its Lord and Master. *"The scepter of thy inheritance which thou hast redeemed, mount Sion, in which thou forever dwells."* Another argument to prove it was not right that God should cast them off; because he not only first called them as his congregation together, and possessed these; but he also raised them into a kingdom, turned the Chananeans out of the land of promise for them, and gave the land to them as being his people. *"The scepter of thy inheritance which thou hast redeemed."* The scepter of the kingdom of the land of promise, which you have acquired by right of war, having ejected the unlawful possessors of it from the land you promised to Abraham and his descendants, the children of Israel. He calls it *"the scepter of his inheritance,"* because God took that scepter, that kingdom of the land of promise as his own, for his inheritance, as it were, to indicate they were his own peculiar people. *"Mount Sion, in which thou hast dwelt;"* Sion being the capital of the kingdom you have thus chosen.
3. For the reasons aforesaid, God's people now pray that he may turn his hand against their enemies, and so confound their pride forever, that they would never again dare to rise up against God's servants. The extravagance of Antiochus's pride appears from Mac. 1, where we read, *"He proudly entered into the sanctuary;"* and in a few verses after, *"that he spoke with great pride."* *"See what things the enemy hath done wickedly in the sanctuary."* Assigning a reason for the justice of God's punishing the pride of the enemy, because he had offered grievous injuries to the sanctuary of God, which is most applicable to king Antiochus, who, as we read in Machabees, *"despoiled and profaned the sanctuary."*
4. Antiochus, to whom only this passage can apply, hated the Jews and their God, and the ceremonies of the law, and did everything in his power to induce the Jews to worship idols; and, therefore, to him and his soldiers properly applies the expression, *"that they made their boasts,"* and that like so many barbarians, for such is the force of the word in Hebrew; *"they that hate thee,"* who hated your sacred rites and the ceremonies of your law; *"in

the midst of thy solemnity," who, while public worship was going on in your sanctuary, entered, profaned, and despoiled it, and in triumph carried off the spoils, like so many conquerors after seizing their booty. *"They have set up their ensigns for signs."* They erected their own banners in the most conspicuous parts of the city, to show they had conquered and taken it.

5-6. The words, *"and they knew it not,"* should be read as if in a parenthesis; that is, while they were so profaning the sanctuary, they knew not what wrath they were stirring up for themselves. The words, *"both in going out, and on the highest top,"* refer to the 4th verse, showing that their ensigns were most conspicuous, on the highest towers and the most public passages. *"As with axes in a wood of trees."* He goes on to recount the injuries offered to the city by its enemies. They tumbled its gates, as if they were cutting down so many trees with axes, and that *"at once"* they were all ready, willing, and egged each other on to the work. *"With axe and hatchet they have brought it down;"* the very thing we read of king Antiochus, who leveled the gates and walls of the city.

7. This seems to be the only passage forbidding the application of this Psalm to the persecution of Antiochus, which, however, in my opinion, can be explained in accordance with it; for, though the entire temple was burnt and razed down by Nabuchodonosor and by Titus, and was not burnt by Antiochus; still the gates of the temple were burned by him, so we read in 1 Mac 4, *"And they saw the sanctuary desolate, and the altar profaned, and the gates burned, and shrubs growing up in the courts, as in a forest or on the mountains, and the chambers adjoining to the temple thrown down;"* and immediately after, in speaking of the renewal of the temple, he says, *"and they renewed the gates and the chambers, and hanged doors upon them."* The expression, then, *"They have set fire to thy sanctuary,"* may be understood of a part of it, and not of the entire, which seems likely too, from the following; for, if they had burned the whole of the sanctuary, David could not say, as he does say, in the same verse, *"they have defiled the name of thy dwelling place on earth;"* for, what had been burned could not be defiled. They burned the gates, then, and they defiled the temple and the tabernacle, by placing therein the idol of abomination, and sacrificing to it, as we read in Machabees.

8. This seems to apply to the pagans, who, in the time of Antiochus, endeavored with all their might to extinguish the religion of the true God, as appears from Machabees. *"They said in their heart:"* the whole nation of the gentiles subject to Antiochus came to a resolution, saying, *"Let us abolish all the festival days of God from the land;"* that is, let us contaminate the sanctuary, fill every place with idols, remove all signs of religion, and thus we will abolish; that is, we will put an end to, and stop all the festivals of God in the land of Israel.

9. He gives us now the expressions of a faithful, though desponding people, under such afflictions, These are most applicable to the days of Antiochus, when the old miracles and the voice of the prophets were so lost that God would seem to have deserted his people entirely.

10. God's people go on to implore God's clemency, that, mindful of them, he may turn his anger on his enemies, who reproached him with infirmity, as if he were not able to save his people. He seems to have Nicanor in view, *"who mocked and despised God's people;"* and also king Antiochus and king Demetrius, and their generals, who were so hostile to God and his people, as may be seen in the first book of Machabees.

11. The people having prayed to God to turn his anger against his enemies, they now pray to him to embrace his people, as he was wont to do, and not to exclude his children from the bosom of their Father. Why do you keep your hands to yourself; keep them in your bosom, instead of extending them to embrace your children.

12. The general explanation of this and the five following verses is the literal one, in which the power of God is explained, both in the case of the children of Israel, who were delivered, as well as the creation of the world; in order to show that he can, if he will, now free the children of Israel from the present calamity. *"But God is our king, before ages he hath wrought salvation;"* namely, of the Jews, *"in the midst of the earth,"* in the land of promise, to which he introduced them, after delivering them from Pharao. *"In the midst of the earth;"* some interpret this to mean, publicly, openly, which I would not condemn. It is true, however, to say, Palestine was *"in the midst of the earth;"* it was in the midst of the habitable world, then known, being quite contiguous to Europe, Asia, and Africa; and it was for such reason our Savior selected it for the spread of his Gospel, as being the most central place from whence it may be promulgated.

13. He now explains how God accomplished the salvation of the Jews. *"Thou by thy strength didst make the sea firm."* By your power you made the Red Sea stand up like a wall, to afford a dry passage through to the children of Israel; and by the same power you brought the same waters back in a heap on the heads of the Egyptians, who, like so many dragons, pursued the children of Israel.

14. Nearly all commentators say that Pharao is alluded to in this verse; for the Hebrew for dragon in this verse, is not the same as for it as in the preceding verse; here it implies a great chief, or prince of dragons. Thou hast given him to be meat for the people of the Ethiopians. Some say that upon Pharao's being drowned, his kingdom was plundered by the Ethiopians. Some say that the bodies of Pharao and his army were cast ashore on the coast of the Arabs, who are also called Ethiopians, and stripped by them; while others say that the crows, who, from their color may be called Ethiopians, fed on the carcasses of the drowned Egyptians; but it matters not which, when it is clear that signal punishment was inflicted on Pharao.

15. He now describes God's power, who, shortly after made a stream of water to gush from the rock, widened a rivulet to the breadth of a river, and then, dried up the Jordan to pass the people over to the land of promise. *"Thou hast broken up the fountains;"* you broke the rocks and made fountains and torrents of pure water to issue from them. *"Thou hast dried up the Ethan rivers;"* the river Jordan, a very large river, as the word *"Ethan"* signifies.

16. He now passes to the power displayed by God in creation, and as creation comprises two principal divisions, the heavens and the earth, according to Genesis; *"In the beginning God created the heavens and the earth."* He speaks here of the two only, saying, *"Thine is the day, and thine is the night;"* and he assigns a reason for calling them his, when he says, *"thou hast made the moon and the sun,"* the one to light the night, the other the day.

17. He touched upon the creation of heaven by speaking of the light and of the sun; and now he alludes to the creation of the earth, by saying, *"Thou hast made all the borders of the earth;"* you have created the whole earth, even to its remotest bounds, from east to west, from north to south. *"The summer and the spring were formed by thee;"* you established the changes in the seasons by virtue of which the earth now conceives, and then brings forth her fruit; and no sooner does she yield her fruit, than, by such changes in the seasons, she is prepared for another yield.

18. Having dilated on God's power, he now returns to prayer, asking of God to remember how his enemy blasphemed him, as if he were impotent and infirm. This, and the following verses, seem to allude to the pride of Antiochus, of which Machabees says, that *"He spoke with great pride;"* and in 2 Mac. 5, having said that Antiochus *"took in his wicked hands the holy vessels, and unworthily handled and profaned them;"* he afterwards adds, *"So when Antiochus had taken away out of the temple a thousand and eight hundred talents, he went back in all haste to Antioch, thinking through pride, that he might make the land now navigable, and the sea passable on foot; such was the haughtiness of his mind."* The Psalmist, therefore, says, *"Remember this;"* remember, O Lord, what I am about to say, *"the enemy hath reproached the Lord;"* has reproached him with impotence to save his people; *"and a foolish people hath provoked thy name,"* by blaspheming it.

19. This verse should decide on Antiochus being the one the Psalmist had in view. It was in the persecution of Antiochus that such prayer was most appropriate; because he never succeeded in entirely annihilating them as did Nabuchodonosor, Titus, and Vespasian. *"Deliver not up to beasts,"* to cruel men as ferocious as beasts, *"the souls that confess to thee;"* who worship thee

and chant thy praises; *"and forget not, to the end, the souls of thy poor;"* forget not to defend and deliver the souls of your poor, who daily beg at the gate of your mercy.

20. He brings forward two other arguments to appease God; one from the covenant entered into with the fathers; the other drawn from the iniquity of their adversaries, who, though of the vilest of the vile, had unjustly gotten possession of their mansions. *"Have regard to thy covenant."* If you will not regard us, regard, at least, thy covenant or testament which you made with our fathers, that you would be a God to us, and that you would protect and defend us in the land you gave us; *"for they that are the obscure of the earth,"* an obscure, wretched set of barbarians, *"have been filled with dwellings of iniquity";* have an abundance of the houses and palaces they have most iniquitously deprived us of.

21. He follows up his prayer, and begs that a prostrate people may not be obliged to retire in confusion at not having their prayer attended to. *"Let not the humble be turned away with confusion"* at his prayer being rejected; *"the poor and the needy shall praise thy name;"* that is, those despised by the rich and the proud.

22. He now assigns a fresh reason, because the people's cause is God's cause, for the reproaches heaped upon them actually fall on God himself. *"Arise, O God, judge thy own cause,"* defend it; the Hebrew has, plead your own cause; *"remember thy reproaches"* that are daily heaped upon you by your enemies: this proud ignorant people.

23. He concludes by asking God not to forget punishing his enemies, because they do not forget to punish him. Do not let the blasphemies of your enemies go unpunished, for *"the pride of them that hate thee, ascendeth continually,"* the proud voices of your enemies will never cease, but daily ascend from their tongues, like sparks from the furnace of their malignant hearts.

PSALM 74

There is a just judgment to come: therefore let the wicked take care.

1 We will praise thee, O God: we will praise, and we will call upon thy name. We will relate thy wondrous works:
2 When I shall take a time, I will judge justices.
3 The earth is melted, and all that dwell therein: I have established the pillars thereof.
4 I said to the wicked: Do not act wickedly: and to the sinners: Lift not up the horn.
5 Lift not up your horn on high: speak not iniquity against God.
6 For neither from the east, nor from the west, nor from the desert hills:
7 For God is the judge. One he putteth down, and another he lifteth up:

8 For in the hand of the Lord there is a cup of strong wine full of mixture. And he hath poured it out from this to that: but the dregs thereof are not emptied: all the sinners of the earth shall drink.
9 But I will declare for ever: I will sing to the God of Jacob.
10 And I will break all the horns of sinners: but the horns of the just shall be exalted.

Explanation of the psalm

1-2. The elect of God, who, from the superior knowledge of God enjoyed by them, say it is their duty to pray to, to praise; and to announce God to others, speak here, saying, *"We will praise thee, O God, we will call upon thy name;"* we will not only praise thee in this life, but we will invoke thy name, for pure praise does not belong to this life, but to the next. *"We will relate thy wondrous works."* We will not only praise you in our heart, and pray to you, but we will also announce your wonderful works to all beside, that they too may learn to fear and to love you. *"When I shall take a time, I will judge justices."* These words come from the supreme judge, in approbation of the preceding, promising the just their reward in due season, as well as condign punishment to the wicked, who neither confess to nor invoke him. *"When I shall take a time,"* the time of judgment determined from all eternity; then, *"I will judge justices;"* judge with the greatest candor and justice. That not only the day, but even the hour of judgment has been definitively laid down, is taught by the Apostle, Acts 17, where he says, *"Because he hath appointed a day wherein he will judge the world in equity by the man who he hath appointed, giving faith to all by raising him up from the dead;"* and St. John teaches, in the Apocalypse, *"Fear the Lord, and give him honor, because the hour of his judgment is come."* Great thanks, says St. Augustine, should be given to God, who does not pronounce judgment immediately after the commission of the sin, but waits for mortals to do penance, never ceasing, in many and various ways, in the meantime to invite and exhort them until the appointed day and hour arrive.

3. The just speak again, saying, If you judge justly, O Lord, who can stand it? for, *"the earth is melted;"* gone to the bad, corrupted, become dissipated by the vices of its inhabitants; *"and all that dwell therein"* have also gone to the bad, there is no one, not even one, there to do good. The Lord answers, *"I have established the pillars thereof."* It is not gone entirely, for I have established the pillars of it, perfect souls, who are allowed to exist; for God always had perfect and faithful servants, though it is said in Genesis that, *"the earth was corrupt through the iniquities of its inhabitants;"* yet in the very same chapter it is stated that *"Noe was a just and perfect man."*

4. The prophet now, in the person of one of the just, admonishes the wicked to cease from their iniquity, while a hope of salvation remains; and that judgment is only deferred to give them an opportunity of doing penance. *"And to the sinners, lift not up the horn;"* that is, I said to the sinners, do not glory in your iniquity, do not proudly defend your sins. The horn is an emblem of pride, and they who not only commit sin, but even glory in their crimes, and seek to be praised for them, are the farthest from salvation. *"Lift not up the horn;"* do not allow yourselves to be so deeply immersed in sin as to despise and to blaspheme the Almighty.

5-6. He assigns a reason why we should not *"speak iniquity against God,"* because there will be no escaping his judgment; for he will not judge from the east, so that one may fly to the west; nor from the west, so that one may conceal himself in the east; nor from the desert mountains, where one may hide himself among the trees, or shelter himself in the valleys.

7-8. And he hath poured it out from this to that; but the dregs thereof are not emptied; all the sinners of the earth shall drink. *"For God is the judge,"* who is everywhere, and, therefore, there is no escaping him; *"one he putteth down,"* the proud man; *"and another he lifteth up,"* the humble man. *"For in the hand of the Lord there is a cup of strong wine;"* for God has the attribute of retributive justice, by virtue of which, while he punishes the haughty sinner, he, at the same time, raises up and consoles the just, after freeing them from the persecution of the wicked. Retributive justice is called a cup of strong wine in various parts of the Scripture, as Isaias 51, Jeremias 25, Lamentations 4, Ezechiel 23, Apocalypse 14, and in various other places. The metaphor is derived from the fact of man being so weakened by an excess of strong wine that he neither knows how, nor is he able, to help himself. The drunken man loses all power of judgment, totters, falls, is buried in sleep. He that is punished by his fellow man, generally speaking, has some remedy, either by seeking to regain the favor of the person who so punishes him, or by flying from him, or by resisting him; but he that is punished by God has no remedy, but, like a drunken man, suddenly falls down insensible under God's judgments. He adds, *"full of mixture;"* that is, the cup of strong wine prepared by the Lord will not be simply a cup of strong wine, but various strong wines will be mixed up in it, to make it stronger again, thereby giving us to understand the severity and strength of God's judgments, and the variety of punishments it has at command; as we read in Psalm 10, *"fire and sulphur, and the spirit of storms is the portion of their cup."* *"And he hath poured it out from this to that;"* God has already poured out the cup of his anger on many, pouring it on this nation now, on another at another time; going from the Sodomites to the Chaldeans, from them to the Egyptians, and to other nations; *"but the dregs thereof are not emptied;"*

the heaviest portion of his retributive justice has not been yet applied, it is reserved for the day of judgment, and then *"all the sinners of the earth shall drink."* For then there will no longer be any room for mercy; but all who shall be found among the sinners on that day shall be compelled to drink the dregs of the cup of the anger of the Lord.

9. The prophet now speaks, after having described God's judgment, and the punishment of the wicked, and promises that he will publish God's praise forever. They may drink of the cup of the anger of God; but I, delivered through his grace, *"will declare forever,"* how? *"I will sing to the God of Jacob;"* what I will declare forever will be a hymn of praise and thanks to the God of Jacob, which I will sing forever.

10. God speaks here, and says, *"I will break all the horns of sinners;"* all their pride, all their glory, all their power; *"but the horns of the just shall be exalted."* I will cause the power and the glory of every just man, and especially of Christ, who was so eminently just as to justify many, to be exalted, as it is said in Isaias 53, *"My just servant shall justify many."* St. Jerome observes that this Psalm was composed in the form of a dialogue.

PSALM 75

God is known in his Church: and exerts his power in protecting it. It alludes to the slaughter of the Assyrians, in the days of King Ezechias.

1 In Judea God is known: his name is great in Israel.
2 And his place is in peace: and his abode in Sion:
3 There hath he broken the powers of bows, the shield, the sword, and the battle.
4 Thou enlightenest wonderfully from the everlasting hills.
5 All the foolish of heart were troubled. They have slept their sleep; and all the men of riches have found nothing in their hands.
6 At thy rebuke, O God of Jacob, they have all slumbered that mounted on horseback.
7 Thou art terrible, and who shall resist thee? from that time thy wrath.
8 Thou hast caused judgment to be heard from heaven: the earth trembled and was still,
9 When God arose in judgment, to save all the meek of the earth.
10 For the thought of man shall give praise to thee: and the remainders of the thought shall keep holiday to thee.
11 Vow ye, and pay to the Lord your God: all you that are round about him bring presents. To him that is terrible,
12 Even to him who taketh away the spirit of princes: to the terrible with the kings of the earth.

EXPLANATION OF THE PSALM

1. The carnal Jews are very proud of this expression, but without any reason. God certainly was known in Judea when it had the prophets, and the people obedient to them; and God's name was great in Israel when the people were circumcised, not only in the flesh, but in their hearts; but once they denied God the Son, foretold by all the prophets, and ceased to be his people; God is no longer known in Judea, nor is his name great in Israel, according to the flesh. But, as this Psalm has *"to the end"* in its title, and, therefore, has reference to Christ, who is the end of the law, and will be praised to the end of the world, it is now true to say, and will be forever true to say, *"God is known in Judea, great is his name in Israel."* By Judea, however, we are to understand the Church, in which are to be found the true children of Juda, circumcised in the heart, and not in the flesh; of whom the Apostle, Romans 2, says, *"For it is not he is a Jew that is so outwardly, nor is that circumcision that is outward in the flesh; the circumcision is that of the heart in the spirit, not in the letter;"* and in chap. 9, *"For all are not Israelites that are of Israel."* God, then, is known in the Church of Christ, and great is his name among the people of Christ; for greater wisdom is to be found in children instructed in the shortest catechism, than was formerly to be found among the pagan philosophers, or the Jewish rabbis. God, however, is principally known to those perfect souls who devote themselves to contemplation, and from contemplation, burst forth with all their hearts to celebrate the divine praise.

2. He assigns a reason for God being better known in Judea than in any other place, because he chose Jerusalem as his royal residence, and Sion as his citadel. *"And his place is in peace;"* God chose a particular spot for himself, in which to place his tabernacle, the city of Salem, which signifies peace; *"and his abode is in Sion;"* he chose Sion for his habitation, it being the best and the most elevated part of Jerusalem.

3. He now describes the victory over the Assyrians, of which there is mention in the title of the Psalm. It is to be found in 1 King 19, where God delivered Jerusalem from the blockade of king Sennacherib, without the Jews striking a single blow; for the Angel of the Lord killed, in one night, one hundred and eighty-five thousand of the Assyrians, and thus *"broke the powers of bows"* the Assyrians had ready to shoot the Hebrews, and *"the shield"* they had ready to defend themselves from the Hebrews, and the *"sword"* they had sharpened to fight hand to hand, after having discharged the arrows; and, finally, put down the entire *"war,"* diverted it from Jerusalem.

4. The prophet explains how the Jews accomplished the victory over the Assyrians, which he does by an appeal to God. *"Thou enlightenest wonderfully from the everlasting hills;"* the Lord destroyed the weapons of offence and defence carried by the Assyrians, before Jerusalem; and you are the Lord that did so, when from the heavens, *"the everlasting hills"* as if from a lofty tower, you *"enlightened wonderfully;"* sent forth your Angel like lightning from heaven to destroy the army of the Assyrians.

5. In consequence of such havoc by the destroying Angel, *"all the foolish of heart were troubled;"* all the soldiers of Sennacherib, who hoped to have taken the city. *"They have slept their sleep,"* instead of taking the city, however, they are buried in the sleep of death; *"and all the men of riches have found nothing in their hands;"* the richest of the Assyrians, who coveted more than the poorest, instead of adding to their riches, lost what they had; and thus, *"they found nothing in their hands,"* neither of what they expected nor what they brought with them.

6. He asserts that the death of the Assyrians was not a natural death, but one inflicted by God in his anger. *"At thy rebuke, O God of Jacob, they have all slumbered;"* they were said in the preceding verse *"to have slept their sleep."* They have slept their sleep, *"prostrated by thy rebuke;"* they have slept the sleep of death; for God's rebuke is most effective, and produces its effect at once. If the rebuke of St. Peter put Ananias and Sapphira to instant death, how much more fearful must not the rebuke of Almighty God be? *"Mounted on horseback"* alludes to the confidence and arrogance of the Assyrians, who trusted so much in their cavalry.

7. The prophet now addresses Almighty God in admiration of his power, so displayed in the punishment of, and vengeance indicted on, the Assyrians, teaching us to fear and admire him in like manner. *"Thou art terrible, and who shall resist thee in thy anger?"* such is the meaning of *"from that time thy wrath."*

8-9. Taking advantage of God's anger towards the Assyrians, he passes to the anger that will be displayed by the same Judge on the day of general judgment; for it is then in reality that none of the wicked will be able to stand the countenance of the angry Judge, making use, as is wont with the prophets, of the past tense to indicate the future. *"Thou hast caused judgement to be heard from heaven;"* that means, you will announce, by various signs from heaven, that will appear in the sun, the moon, and the stars; and, finally, by that dreadful trumpet of the Angels, that you are about to come to the last judgment; and then the earth will *"tremble,"* will *"be silent,"* through fear; meaning all its inhabitants, who will *"be withered up through fear, in expectation of what is to come on the whole world."* *"When God arose in judgment, you will cause judgment to be heard from heaven;"* when you shall arise to judge, rise from your throne in heaven, and come to judge the world, *"to save all the meek of the earth;"* for such will be the end and object of judgment, that all the meek in the world may be no longer harassed by their proud and cruel persecutors, but that, upon their just condemnation, all the pious and the just may obtain eternal salvation, peace, and happiness.

10. The consequence of the last judgment will be that the meek, now delivered from all oppression on the part of their persecutors, will bear such kindness in mind, will perpetually praise God, and will keep holy days in heaven, in memory of such kindness. Man, when he thinks on those matters, will constantly praise thee; *"and the remainders of the thought;"* the very recollection of the pleasure imparted by such thoughts, will make man as joyful as he is in times of holiday.

11-12. The prophet concludes the Psalm by exhorting the faithful to make vows, in order to appease God who is so terrible, that he deprives kings themselves of life, when he wills it. *"Vow ye, and pay;"* promise God those gifts and sacrifices that you know are agreeable to him; but, be sure faithfully to discharge what you shall have promised. Vow and pay, I say, *"all you that round about him bring presents;"* all you that are in the habit of approaching his altars and offering your gifts upon them. Vow then, and pay your vows to that true God, *"who is terrible"* in his judgments, and can neither be deceived nor derided by any one; and is terrible, not only to ordinary men, but even to kings and princes, who are usually terrible to others. From the words vow ye, and pay to the Lord, we refute the heresy of those who question the legitimacy of vows regarding matters not commanded by God.

PSALM 76

The faithful have recourse to God in trouble of mind, with confidence in his mercy and power.

1 I cried to the Lord with my voice; to God with my voice, and he gave ear to me.
2 In the day of my trouble I sought God, with my hands lifted up to him in the night, and I was not deceived. My soul refused to be comforted:
3 I remembered God, and was delighted, and was exercised, and my spirit swooned away.
4 My eyes prevented the watches: I was troubled, and I spoke not.
5 I thought upon the days of old: and I had in my mind the eternal years.
6 And I meditated in the night with my own heart: and I was exercised and I swept my spirit.
7 Will God then cast off for ever? or will he never be more favourable again?
8 Or will he cut off his mercy for ever, from generation to generation?
9 Or will God forget to shew mercy? or will he in his anger shut up his mercies?
10 And I said, Now have I begun: this is the change of the right hand of the most High.
11 I remembered the works of the Lord: for I will be mindful of thy wonders from the beginning.
12 And I will meditate on all thy works: and will be employed in thy inventions.
13 Thy way, O God, is in the holy place: who is the great God like our God?

14 Thou art the God that dost wonders. Thou hast made thy power known among the nations:
15 With thy arm thou hast redeemed thy people the children of Jacob and of Joseph.
16 The waters saw thee, O God, the waters saw thee: and they were afraid, and the depths were troubled.
17 Great was the noise of the waters: the clouds sent out a sound. For thy arrows pass:
18 The voice of thy thunder in a wheel. Thy lightnings enlightened the world: the earth shook and trembled.
19 Thy way is in the sea, and thy paths in many waters: and thy footsteps shall not be known.
20 Thou hast conducted thy people like sheep, by the hand of Moses and Aaron.

Explanation of the psalm

1. The effusions of soul of a holy person expressing how heavily the delay and the dangers of his pilgrimage here below bear on him. For he says, *"I cried with my voice;"* not through a message, nor through my friends, nor even with my tongue, but with my voice; with the whole power of my body, I cried to God. He says he cried to the Lord, and to God, because he saw no created being or thing could confer on him what he wanted; and therefore, without applying to anyone he appeals directly to God himself. He says, *"I cried,"* because seeing himself in a strange country, far removed from God, he required to speak with a loud and an impassioned voice, to transmit it from the abyss in which he lay to the elevation on which God was placed; *"and he gave ear to me;"* his prayer then was heard.

2. He tells here why and how he sought and found God. *"In the day of my trouble I sought God."* During my lifetime, which, according to Job, is *"a warfare;"* that is, according to St. Paul, a constant *"wrestling with our vices and concupiscence, as well as with the principalities and powers of the air;"* hence, he exclaims, *"Who shall deliver me from the body of this death?" "With my hands to him in the night."* In the night of this life I stretched out my hands to him, seeking to grasp and hold him; and I was not deceived. This life does not deserve the name of day, but of night; *"For we walk by faith, and not by sight,"* 2 Cor. 5; and we, therefore, require the light of Scripture, shining like a lamp in a dark place." In the night time we succeed better by groping with our hands, than by searching with our eyes; hence, the Apostle says, that men were created *"that they should seek God; if happily they may feel after him, or find him."* Now, to seek God with one's hands in the night, means nothing more than to seek God in this dark exile of ours, by good works, by observance of the commandments, and by holiness of life; and it often happens that they who seek God in such manner will attain the object of their wishes, a thing they could never accomplish by reading and study; for, the testimony of a good conscience, patience in sufferings, frequent victories over temptation, cause the soul to feel a certain divine and interior sweetness, that is a sort of testimony to its being a child of God. *"My soul refused to be comforted."* As he was not deceived in his search for God, his soul refused all human consolation, knowing how empty it was. *"My soul refused to be comforted."* Though the pleasures of the world surrounded me, I could not enjoy them, knowing what consequent sorrow they always entailed.

3. However, that I should not be without comfort in some shape, *"I remembered God,"* who deceives nobody, in whom alone that solid joy, that no one can deprive us of, is to be found. *"And I was delighted."* Here is the great secret of God's wisdom, that in this our exile, the recollection of God delights us more than the carnal pleasures around us; and, if the recollection of God delights us so much in the midst of the carnal allurements about us, how much more still not the actual presence of God delights us, when those allurements of the flesh shall have passed away? *"And was exercised, and my spirit passed away."* After calling God to mind, and the pleasure I derived from doing so, I turned to meditation, and talked over with myself the miseries of our exile, and the joys of heaven until I fainted away in my desires for it.

4. He explains the meaning of the expression, *"I was exercised,"* by saying, *"my eyes prevented the watches;"* that is, I rose at night for meditation, before the military watches turned out for guard. We have a similar phrase in Psalm 118, *"My eyes to thee have prevented the morning; that I might meditate on thy words." "I was troubled and I spoke not;"* he was terribly confused from meditating on the dangers of this life, but did not attempt to say one word, knowing that the judgments of God, however occult, are always most just.

5. Such was the subject of my meditation when I got up before the watch, *"the days of old;"* the days of this life, from the beginning to the end; and *"the eternal years"* of futurity, that do not pass away, but remain fixed and permanent; thus, he thought not only of the things of the present day, that presently grow old and perish, but also of what we shall be doing and engaged in for the years of eternity, that always remain in the same state. Reflections worthy of occupying one in meditation during the whole night.

6. The same idea repeated and inculcated. I spent, he says, long nights turning the thing in my mind *"and I was exercised"* in my thoughts and my reflections, *"and I swept my spirit."* I put my mind to and fro, as if I were sweeping it with a broom. Like the woman in the Gospel, who swept the whole house diligently in search of the lost piece of money; so he searched his spirit, and brushed it up, as with a broom, in search of the hidden truth.

7-9. Here is the subject of his meditation, and the cause of his agitation during the night. Looking at the countless number of sinners, will scarcely one to be found doing good, he said to himself, Will God consign all men to eternal perdition? Where, then, is His infinite mercy? But from such interrogatory, he draws the very contrary conclusion, asserting that the time for the redemption of mankind would come, when not only the remnants of the Jews, but even the multitude of the gentiles, would be saved. He says, therefore, *"Will God then cast off forever?"* Will God cast off forever from his mercy, and leave in their blindness and their infidelity, such a multitude of the human race? in other words, he will not cast them off, but he will visit them in his own time. *"Or will he never be more favorable again?"* that means, will he not add his mercy to his anger, so that he may begin to look with more favor on those whom he seems now so to hate. He says he will be pacified, for in the next verse he has, *"Or will he cut off his mercy forever, from generation to generation?"* Will he withdraw his mercy from man forever? he will not. *"Or will God forget to show mercy? or will he in his anger shut up his mercies?"* He will not forget, nor shut up his mercy, for it is easier for God to repress his anger than his mercy; and, therefore, however justly he may be angry with sinners, in his anger he will not withhold his mercy but will pour it out to mitigate his anger.

10. The prophet having both foreseen and foretold the redemption of man, he says that he began thereon to draw his breath after the grief and sorrow that previously held him captive. *"And I said, now have I begun;"* begun to breathe, when by meditation and watchings, I ascertained that God's mercy would be poured out on the human race. *"This is the change of the right hand of the Most High;"* the change which I foresee and foretell, that of God's anger into mercy, of man's wickedness to holiness, of his captivity to redemption, of everlasting punishment to eternal glory, is a wonderful change, that no one, but Christ, who is the right hand of the Most High, could accomplish, for it was he who appeased the Father's anger, by turning it to mercy; it was he that justified the wicked, redeemed the captive, and glorified the wicked; and, what is more wonderful, the right hand of the Most High effected this change, by changing himself to a certain extent; for his right hand was weakened, in order to strengthen us; and *"when he was in the form of God he took the form of a servant."*

11-12. The prophet now breathing in the hope of a future redemption, says he will call to mind the wonderful works of the Lord, and proceeds to relate some of them, saying, Hitherto I called to mind some of the wonderful things the Lord did in Egypt for our fathers, but now, O Lord, I will call up all your wonderful works from the beginning of the world, *"and I will meditate on all your works,"* your works of justice and mercy, of power and wisdom; of nature and grace; *"and will be employed in your inventions;"* turning over in my mind, with profound admiration, the secret counsels and wonderful designs struck out by your wisdom for the salvation of the human race.

13. He now begins to praise those wonderful works of God on which he was accustomed to reflect, saying first in general, that the works of God are holy, great, and admirable; that is, that they are done with holiness, power, and wisdom, he himself being holy, omnipotent, and wise. *"Thy way, O God, is in the holy place;"* your action or your works, which may be looked upon as your way to us, are all done in holiness, for you do nothing but what is right and just; *"Who is the great God like our God?"* not only are our God and his way holy, but he is also great, and great are his works.

14. You are not only holy and great in your works, but they are also wonderful, by reason of the depth of wisdom displayed in them. *"Thou hast made thy power known among the nations."* He now descends to a special, great, and wonderful work of God, the deliverance of his people from Egypt, and says he has made known his power, not only to the people of Egypt, but to all the other nations that heard of the plagues of Egypt.

15. By your own power and strength, for you need no help from anyone, you have delivered your people, the descendants of Jacob and of Joseph. Joseph and his father are named, because the people of Israel consisted of thirteen tribes, eleven of whom sprung from eleven sons of Jacob, and two, that of Ephraim and Manasses, from the sons of Joseph. In a spiritual sense, God *"made his power known"* to all nations, when he delivered them from the power of the devil, *"with the arm,"* meaning Christ, of whom Isaias says, *"The arm of the Lord, to whom is it revealed?"* St. Augustine says that in God's people two families are to be found, the children of Jacob and the children of Joseph, who are the Jews, and the converted gentiles. By the children of Jacob we understand the carnal Israelites; by the children of Joseph, they who are regenerated in Christ. Joseph, sold by his brethren through envy, humbled everywhere at first, but ultimately exalted, represents Christ, who, through the envy of the Jews, was cast out of the synagogue, sold and humbled, but in the end, through his resurrection and ascension, was so exalted as to fulfill what is written of him in Psalm 71, *"All the kings of the earth shall adore him: all nations shall serve him."*

16. He now describes the separation of the waters of the Red Sea, when God delivered his people from the slavery of Pharao, and he does it in a poetical manner, investing the water with fear and trembling, as if they felt such at the presence of God, as he says also in Psalm 113, *"The sea saw and fled."* *"The waters saw thee, O God, the waters saw thee."* The waters of the Red Sea, at thy command, were dried up as if they had seen thy majesty, and ran away in fear and reverence, *"and the depths were troubled."* It was not only on the surface, but in the very lowest bottom, that the waters, affrighted at your presence, disappeared.

17. Having described God's wonderful doings in the separation of the waters of the Red Sea, he now speaks of the return of the waters, and the storm to destroy the Egyptians, which, too, was a wonderful work, *"Great was the noise of the waters."* Great confusion and roaring of the waters succeeded, when, at God's command, the waters that stood up like two walls, while God's people were passing through, fell in with a tremendous crash, to drown and suffocate the Egyptians, as also when *"thy arrows pass,"* your lightning shot like arrows at them.

18. The voice of your thunder rattled in the wheels of Pharao's chariots, and upset them. *"Thy lightnings enlightened the world."* The prophet adds, that such vengeance inflicted on Pharao was made known not only to the Jews then present, but even, like lightning in heaven, was made known to the whole world, and caused great fear and commotion among the nations far removed, the truth of which we read in Josue 3, where Racab says, *"We heard that the Lord dried up the waters of the Red Sea at your approach, and we were very much afraid."*—*"Thy lightnings enlightened the world;"* your lightnings, signs, and miracles, enlightened not only the Jews and Egyptians then and there, but the whole world heard of them, they were known far and near; and, therefore, *"the earth shook and trembled;"* its inhabitants were frightened and alarmed, and began to fear the people of Israel.

19. He now plainly describes the passage of the children of Israel, under God's guidance, through a new and unusual path, through the middle of the sea, without wetting their feet. *"Thy way is in the sea;"* you have discovered a new and unheard of way through the sea for your people; *"and thy paths in many waters;"* made a path for the same people through the deep sea, *"and thy footsteps shall not be known;"* you have brought your people through that passage in the sea in so wonderful a manner that nobody could ever discover a trace of said passage.

20. The object of all the wonderful works of God in Egypt and the Red Sea was to free his people, and introduce them to the land of promise, which he did through Moses and Aaron, the first pastors of the synagogue. *"Thou hast conducted thy people like sheep;"* brought the people, as you would so many sheep, through the desert, into the land of promise, as it were, to the richest pastures, with the greatest ease, the greatest love, and untiring providence *"by the hand of Moses and Aaron;"* under the guidance and authority of Moses and Aaron, two most excellent leaders.

PSALM 77

God's great benefits to the people of Israel, notwithstanding their ingratitude.

1 Attend, O my people, to my law: incline your ears to the words of my mouth.
2 I will open my mouth in parables: I will utter propositions from the beginning.
3 How great things have we heard and known, and our fathers have told us.
4 They have not been hidden from their children, in another generation. Declaring the praises of the Lord, and his powers, and his wonders which he hath done.
5 And he set up a testimony in Jacob: and made a law in Israel. How great things he commanded our fathers, that they should make the same known to their children:
6 That another generation might know them. The children that should be born and should rise up, and declare them to their children.
7 That they may put their hope in God and may not forget the works of God: and may seek his commandments.
8 That they may not become like their fathers, a perverse and exasperating generation. A generation that set not their heart aright: and whose spirit was not faithful to God.
9 The sons of Ephraim who bend and shoot with the bow: they have turned back in the day of battle.
10 They kept not the covenant of God: and in his law they would not walk.
11 And they forgot his benefits, and his wonders that he had shewn them.
12 Wonderful things did he do in the sight of their fathers, in the land of Egypt, in the field of Tanis.
13 He divided the sea and brought them through: and he made the waters to stand as in a vessel.
14 And he conducted them with a cloud by day: and all the night with a light of fire.
15 He struck the rock in the wilderness: and gave them to drink, as out of the great deep.
16 He brought forth water out of the rock: and made streams run down as rivers.
17 And they added yet more sin against him: they provoked the most High to wrath in the place without water.
18 And they tempted God in their hearts, by asking meat for their desires.
19 And they spoke ill of God: they said: Can God furnish a table in the wilderness?
20 Because he struck the rock, and the waters gushed out, and the streams overflowed. Can he also give bread, or provide a table for his people?
21 Therefore the Lord heard, and was angry: and a fire was kindled against Jacob, and wrath came up against Israel.
22 Because they believed not in God: and trusted not in his salvation.

23 And he had commanded the clouds from above, and had opened the doors of heaven.
24 And had rained down manna upon them to eat, and had given them the bread of heaven.
25 Man ate the bread of angels: he sent them provisions in abundance.
26 He removed the south wind from heaven: and by his power brought in the southwest wind.
27 And he rained upon them flesh as dust: and feathered fowls like as the sand of the sea.
28 And they fell in the midst of their camp, round about their pavilions.
29 So they did eat, and were filled exceedingly, and he gave them their desire:
30 They were not defrauded of that which they craved. As yet their meat was in their mouth:
31 And the wrath of God came upon them. And he slew the fat ones amongst them, and brought down the chosen men of Israel.
32 In all these things they sinned still: and they believed not for his wondrous works.
33 And their days were consumed in vanity, and their years in haste.
34 When he slew them, then they sought him: and they returned, and came to him early in the morning.
35 And they remembered that God was their helper: and the most high God their redeemer.
36 And they loved him with their mouth: and with their tongue they lied unto him:
37 But their heart was not right with him: nor were they counted faithful in his covenant.
38 But he is merciful, and will forgive their sins: and will not destroy them. And many a time did he turn away his anger: and did not kindle all his wrath.
39 And he remembered that they are flesh: a wind that goeth and returneth not.
40 How often did they provoke him in the desert: and move him to wrath in the place without water?
41 And they turned back and tempted God: and grieved the holy one of Israel.
42 They remembered not his hand, in the day that he redeemed them from the hand of him that afflicted them:
43 How he wrought his signs in Egypt, and his wonders in the field of Tanis.
44 And he turned their rivers into blood, and their showers that they might, not drink.
45 He sent amongst them divers sores of flies, which devoured them: and frogs which destroyed them.
46 And he gave up their fruits to the blast, and their labours to the locust.
47 And he destroyed their vineyards with hail, and their mulberry trees with

hoarfrost.

48 And he gave up their cattle to the hail, and their stock to the fire.

49 And he sent upon them the wrath of his indignation: indignation and wrath and trouble, which he sent by evil angels.

50 He made a way for a path to his anger: he spared not their souls from death, and their cattle he shut up in death.

51 And he killed all the firstborn in the land of Egypt: the firstfruits of all their labour in the tabernacles of Cham.

52 And he took away his own people as sheep: and guided them in the wilderness like a flock.

53 And he brought them out in hope, and they feared not: band the sea overwhelmed their enemies.

54 And he brought them into the mountain of his sanctuary: the mountain which his right hand had purchased. And he cast out the Gentiles before them: and by lot divided to them their land by a line of distribution.

55 And he made the tribes of Israel to dwell in their tabernacles.

56 Yet they tempted, and provoked the most high God: and they kept not his testimonies.

57 And they turned away, and kept not the covenant: even like their fathers they were turned aside as a crooked bow.

58 They provoked him to anger on their hills: and moved him to jealousy with their graven things.

59 God heard, and despised them, and he reduced Israel exceedingly as it were to nothing.

60 And he put away the tabernacle of Silo, his tabernacle where he dwelt among men.

61 And he delivered their strength into captivity: and their beauty into the hands of the enemy.

62 And he shut up his people under the sword: and he despised his inheritance.

63 Fire consumed their young men: and their maidens were not lamented.

64 Their priests fell by the sword: and their widows did not mourn.

65 And the Lord was awaked as one out of sleep, and like a mighty man that hath been surfeited with wine.

66 And he smote his enemies on the hinder parts: he put them to an everlasting reproach.

67 And he rejected the tabernacle of Joseph: and chose not the tribe of Ephraim:

68 But he chose the tribe of Juda, mount Sion which he loved.

69 And he built his sanctuary as of unicorns, in the land which he founded for ever.

70 And he chose his servant David, and took him from the flocks of sheep: he brought him from following the ewes great with young,

71 *To feed Jacob his servant, and Israel his inheritance.*
72 *And he fed them in the innocence of his heart: and conducted them by the skillfulness of his hands.*

Explanation of the Psalm

1. David, being about to exhort the people, in rather a long discourse, endeavors, at the outset, to arrest their attention by saying he is going to speak on matters of utility and importance. *"Attend to my law;"* to my precepts, which, like good and most wise laws, will direct you to happiness. And he repeats the same at greater length when he says, *"incline your ears;"* and what he expressed at first by the words, *"my law,"* he now expresses by the words, *"to the words of my mouth;"* thereby insinuating that when he mentioned the law, he did not mean the law of Moses, though often called simply the law, but his own words, with which he meant to instruct and to exhort his people; in which sense Christ himself uses the term when he said, John 15, *"But that the word may be fulfilled, which is written in their Law, they have hated me without cause."* To incline the ear, when applied to the people, means to hear with humility and obedience, but, when applied to God, means to hear with clemency and mercy. Some will have this Psalm spoken in the person of God, others, of Christ; but verse 3, "and our fathers have told us' " shows that David speaks in his own person, and no other.

2. The reason why David asks that what he says may be listened to with attention and humility is, that he is about to enter on difficult and obscure matters, that require attention and humility. By parables is understood here proverbs or similes that are usually short and figurative. Propositions mean enigmas that are most obscure, for such is the meaning of the word in Hebrew, as is clear from that passage in the book of Judges, where Samson's enigma, *"out of the eater came forth meat, and out of the strong came forth sweetness,"* is called an enigma, and in Greek a problem. There are many proverbs and enigmas in this Psalm, as we shall see hereafter; but the one particularly alluded to here seems to be the kingdom of Christ, of which David's kingdom is the figure; and the Church, of which Mount Sion is the figure. The words, *"from the beginning,"* looking at the text of the Psalm, would seem to apply to the date of the liberation of the people from the captivity of Egypt, when the people of Israel began to assume the form of a republic, and to be subject to laws and judges; and verse 5, *"and he set up a testimony in Jacob; and made a law in Israel,"* favors that view; but Mt. chap. 13, in quoting this passage, says that *"the beginning"* refers to the beginning of the world; for he says, *"That the word might be fulfilled which was spoken by the prophet, saying: I will open my mouth in parables, I will utter things hidden from the foundation of the world."* The meaning, then, is, I will lay before you ideas that were hidden, and like so many enigmas, from the beginning of the world; for, though the mysteries of Christ were at all times foretold and foreshadowed, still they were veiled, and openly revealed to very few. St. Paul, writing of them, says, Ephes. 3, *"To me, the least of all the saints, is given this grace to preach among the gentiles the unsearchable riches of Christ, and to enlighten all men what is the dispensation of the mystery which hath been hidden from eternity in God who created all things."*

3–4. Being about to write a history of matters that had within them mysteries hidden from the beginning of the world, he tells us he got the history of these from the fathers, who got them from their ancestors; I will, he says, utter propositions from the beginning. *"What great things we have heard and known,"* because *"our fathers have told us,"* both by their writings and word of mouth, for they did not wish them *"to be hidden from their children"* they were to leave after them *"in another generation;"* and what they had to tell was God's praises and virtues; that is, his wonderful power and his wonderful works, for which he deserves the highest meed of praise. *"They have not been hidden."* St. Matthew says *"I will utter things hidden,"* which would seem like a contradiction, but it is not, for the things that were done were not hidden from the children of those who related them, though their mystical signification was.

5–6. He now begins to relate the things done by God, as he heard from the fathers, and he places first the fact of God's having given the people of Israel the law and the commandments through Moses, and having ordered that law to be given by the parents to their children, and so to be handed down to posterity. The law of God is called a *"testimony,"* because it testifies God's will to man, as we have explained at length in Psalm 18, *"Setting up a testimony in Jacob;"* that is, God gave his law to the children of Jacob, who was also called Israel. The expression, *"how great things he commanded,"* means no more than what he commanded, according to the Hebrew, from which we gather that *"the law"* does not simply mean here, the decalogue, but all the commands, both moral, ceremonial, and judicial in the five books of Moses.

7–8. He now explains why God gave the law to his people, and ordered the parents to teach it to children, and the children to hand it down to their posterity. To make them put no trust in false gods, or the idols of the gentiles, but to trust alone in the true God, who gave them a holy law from heaven, accompanied by great signs and prodigies; and also that they should not forget God's wonderful doings in delivering them from the bondage of Pharao; furthermore, that they should anxiously seek to know, and studiously put into practice, God's wishes; and, finally, that they should not imitate the ingratitude and the infidelity of their fathers, who, after all the favors conferred on them through Moses, proved most ungrateful. For, while they were in Egypt, they could hardly be brought to trust Moses, and after having left Egypt, they several times rebelled against Moses and against God; were forever murmuring, and (what is much worse) adoring the golden calf: *"A generation that set not their heart aright,"* did not keep their heart firmly directed to God, but rather regarded other help. *"Whose spirit was not faithful to God,"* for it often fell away from faith and obedience.

9. Many suppose that some unsuccessful battle of the tribe of Ephraim is alluded to here; now, there is no trace of any such battle in Holy Writ, nor is it probable that the prophet, in giving a general description of the vices of the people, miraculously brought out of Egypt, and freed from slavery, would digress to an isolated fact such as this. It is, therefore, much more probable that he explains, by a sort of simile, how inconstant the Hebrews were, in their faith and their obedience to God, making the meaning of the passage to be *"the sons of Ephraim;"* that is, the Israelites were like soldiers who began to fight with the enemy, and at once turned their backs and fled; so the Israelites, in the desert, more than once promised God they would obey him, and observe his commandments, and in a minute they would change their minds, think of returning to Egypt, and murmur against Moses and against God. David specifies the sons, that is, the tribe of Ephraim, by it meaning the whole assembly of the Israelites; for, next to Juda, the tribe of Ephraim was most numerous and powerful, and thus a rival of Juda, and in the Scripture Ephraim is generally censured, while Juda is praised; and thus the calamities of the whole people were attributed to Ephraim rather than to any of the other tribes, and in the end of this very Psalm, he says, *"And chose not the tribe of Ephraim, but he chose the tribe of Juda."* See Osee the prophet.

10-12. He now explains what he had figuratively expressed, that the children of Ephraim, the Israelites, were turned back; for when they undertook to obey God, they did not keep the compact, nor did they observe the law of God; and they at once forgot God's kindness to them, and the wonderful works he did for them in Egypt, which had been related to them by their fathers. The field of Tanis means Egypt, of which Tanis was the royal residence, to show that the wonderful things done by Moses were not done in a nook or corner, but in a most public place, up to the king's palace.

13-17. Having touched upon the wonderful things that were done in Egypt before Pharao; he now describes the other miracles that were performed in the departure of the Israelites, viz., the separation of the waters of the Red Sea, to afford them a dry passage through it; and, then, after their departure from Egypt, the miracles that were performed in the desert, viz., the pillar of cloud to precede, and show them the way by day, and the pillar of fire by night; and the abundance of water drawn from the rock to slake their thirst. And he adds, that, notwithstanding all those miracles, the incredulous people again provoked God to anger, when they found themselves without water in the desert, which had to be struck a second time for them from the rock; for the first supply of water was given them the year before, as we read in Num. 17, while mention is made of the second in Num. 20. *"He made the waters to stand as in a vessel;"* means, that God made the waters of the sea to stand up at both sides, as perpendicularly as if they were shut up in a vessel, while the children of Israel were passing through. *"And gave them to drink as out of the great deep;"* means, that when the rock was struck, as great a quantity of water issued from it as if the rock had been turned into a deep lake or a great ocean of water.

18-29. The prophet unites the miracles of the bread from heaven and the water from the rock; they being types of Christ's passion, and of the Eucharist, as the Lord himself explains in John 6, and the Apostle in 1 Cor. 10. Water from a rock, is the same as bringing wisdom from folly; for wisdom is no less opposed to folly than is a rock, a hard and solid substance, to water, which is a fluid. The mystery of the crucifixion is wisdom, it is the rock which was struck; a folly to the gentiles, and a scandal to the Jews; but the height of wisdom to the faithful, as St. Paul writes 1 Cor. 1, *"For seeing that in the wisdom of God, the world by wisdom knew not God; it pleased God by the foolishness of preaching, to save them that believe."* Now the real bread from heaven was not the manna that fell from the sky, but the flesh of Christ that comes from the heaven of heavens, and gives life to the world. The manna, however, was a type of this true bread, and the prophet had that in view when he said, in the beginning of the Psalm, that he was about to speak in parables and propositions. Now to explain the passage. Having alluded to the miracle of the water brought from the rock and the infidelity of the people, he comes to the miracle of the bread and the meat, another incredulity of theirs. We must bear in mind that the Israelites got meat in a miraculous manner twice, once along with manna, Exodus 16, and a second time without any manna, Numbers 11; and that they got the meat and manna previous to the water from the rock, and the meat alone subsequent to the water. David, however, unites both miracles, and thus renders the matter somewhat confused; but, bearing what we said in mind, it will be easily understood. *"And they tempted God in their hearts."* They wished to try if God was really omnipotent and was concerned for his people; and, therefore, *"they asked meat for their desires;"* bread and meat they were longing for, as we read in Exodus 16 and Num. 11. *"And they spoke ill of God,"* doubting whether he could give them to eat as well as he gave them to drink in the desert; this alludes to the second time they murmured, for the first murmur was previous to striking water from the rock. *"Therefore the Lord heard"* their murmurs, proceeding from their incredulity, *"and was angry;"* so that he sent fire into their camp, and destroyed numbers of them. Yet, he wished to convince an unfaithful people, and to prove his power; and, therefore, *"he commanded the clouds from above, and had opened the doors of heaven. And had rained down manna upon them to eat; and had given them the bread of heaven. Man ate the bread of Angels."* This refers to the first time they murmured; for they got the manna before they got the water. The manna is called bread from heaven, having fallen from thence; and it is called the bread of Angels, being made and produced by them. The word manna is derived from two Hebrew words, that mean, *"What is it?"* which the Jews said when first they saw it.

30-37. The prophet goes on to show in these verses that God, to satisfy the Jews, showed his great power by great miracles; still, that he did not let their contumacy and infidelity go unpunished; and, that the Jews were brought to faith and to obedience, both by the miracles and the punishments inflicted on them, but still, without that perseverance, or that sincerity of heart that God required. *"As yet their meat was in their mouth."* They had scarcely finished the quails, *"and the wrath of God came upon them,"* and destroyed such a number of them, that the place got the name of *"The graves of lust."* The Scripture does not tell us how God destroyed them, but, it is likely, through some disease arising from gluttony. And the Lord singled out *"the fat ones,"* and *"the chosen men of Israel;"* those most devoted to pleasure, they who exulted in their youth and their strength; *"and brought down,"* laid them so prostrate by disease, that they could not possibly escape. All this came upon them by reason of their infidelity, for they did not believe that the quails were sent by providence, but came by chance. They were, therefore, punished so quickly, that *"their days were consumed in vanity,"* and *"their years in haste;"* for they passed away like a shadow or like smoke, without a trace after them. But they, *"when he slew them,"* when they were scourged by God, and put to death by him, *"they returned"* to their senses, and asked God's help, and that *"early in the morning;"* as soon as ever they felt the scourge they came to implore God's mercy, converted, but through fear; and their conversion was feigned, for *"with their mouth they called to mind God's previous goodness; but while they so professed their devotion to him, they lied in their heart; "for their heart was not right with him, nor were they counted faithful in his covenant."* Would that we Christians would not imitate this inconsistency of the Jews. How many among us, when in danger of death, promise God and his saints to amend our lives, and the moment they recover resume their old habits? But God will not be mocked; and such people will not escape his judgment.

38-42. The prophet now compares God's goodness with man's wickedness, and says, that though God scourged his people, he did not forget his mercy; and, therefore, that he did not chastise them as heavily as their sins deserved, for he had mercy on them, and did not utterly destroy them. They certainly deserved utter extermination, but, through the mercy of God, some were spared; as, in fact, of those that left Egypt, two, Josue and Caleb, survived, types of the elect, who will be saved; for, as the Apostle says, *"God hath not cast away his people, which he foreknew, but there is a remnant saved, according to the election of grace."* This verse, then, does not contradict the dispersion of the Jews that we daily see, for the promise was fulfilled in the Apostles, who were Jews; and, so far from being dispersed, have gathered together a great multitude of people, elect in God, a fact foretold by Osee, chap. 1, and explained by 1 St. Peter 2, where he says, *"Who in time past were not a people, but are now the people of God: who had not obtained mercy, but now have obtained mercy."* The prophet goes on and says, *"And many a time did he turn away his anger;"* for he forgave a great share of the punishment due to their sins, and thus turned away his anger; because he *"did not kindle all his wrath,"* as he may justly have done. *"And he remembered that they are flesh: a wind that goeth and returneth not."* In addition to his motives for mercy, man's infirm nature, weakened by the fall of our first parents, mortal and subject to concupiscence, presented itself. For he knows what we are made of; *"that they are flesh,"* carnal, weak, and feeble; and that we are *"a wind that goeth and returneth not;"* that is, that our life is a passing one—passing from boyhood to youth, without ever coming back to boyhood; passing from youth to old age, without ever returning to youth, but quickly ending in death. Thus, it is like the flowers and other perishable things, and not like the sun, moon and stars that revolve in their orbits, and are always the same by reason of their being solid and eternal. By the word *"wind"* we are to understand that spirit or breath of life that quickens and enlivens us, which in its progress grows weaker, and is frail and changeable; and that such is the life of man, the prophet proves in the following verse, *"How often did they provoke him in the desert? and move him to wrath in the place without water?"* by their want of purpose, promising faith and obedience at one time, and, in a moment after, by heaping obloquy on him, and by rebellion; for, *"they turned back"* from all their faithful promises, *"and tempted God,"* to try if he were truly omnipotent; and thus *"grieved"* God, who is *"the Holy One of Israel."* The God of Israel is called *"the Holy One,"* not only by David, but by Isaias, in various places; for God alone is truly holy, that is, pure and inviolate; while the gods of the gentiles are unclean demons. Finally, such was the fickleness and folly of the Jews so brought by God out of Egypt, that they at once forgot the countless and most wonderful signs and prodigies that God wrought in their favor while he was bringing them out from the bondage of Egypt.

43-53. Having said, in verse 42, that the Jews forgot all the miracles God wrought in their favor, when he was bringing them out of the land of Egypt, he now describes, in the above verses, how God afflicted Pharao, until he ultimately overwhelmed him and his whole army in the sea, all of which is to be found in Exodus, from chaps. 7 to 14. Now, David does not record all the miracles, he merely gives the principal ones, and that in a different order from that in which they happened. *"They remembered not,"* meaning the Jews in the wilderness, *"his hand,"* the power of the Lord that delivered them from Pharao in his persecution. *"How he wrought his signs in Egypt."* They did not remember the wonderful miracles, signs of his power, that he wrought in Egypt, especially those he did in the fairest part of it, Tanis, nigh the royal residence. *"And he turned,"* for he turned *"their rivers into blood, and their showers that they might not drink,"* Exod., chap. 7. By the rivers of Egypt we understand the branches of the Nile that flow through it; by their showers we are not to understand the rain that falls, which seldom happens in Egypt, but the water itself, and it is not unusual with David to repeat the same idea, and thus, what he calls their rivers in the first part of the verse, he calls showers in the second. *"He sent among them diverse sort of flies which devoured them, and frogs which destroyed them,"* Exod., chap. 8. He goes on to enumerate the principal scourges inflicted on the Egyptians; and, finally, to include any he may have omitted, as, in fact, he did, he says in verse 49, *"And he sent upon them the wrath of his indignation: indignation and wrath and troubles which he sent by evil angels."* Touching, in the latter part of it, on the most grievous of all the plagues, the slaughter of the first born by the destroying angel. From this, we infer, that the plagues of Egypt, especially the slaughter of the first born, was effected through the agency of the fallen angels, who cannot injure us, but as far as God will suffer them, they being his ministers. The holy Angels even may be called evil angels, from the punishments they inflict when God so employs them. The impure demons may also be called evil angels, they being so in reality, and hostile to man, and God employs both; for, through the former he punished the Sodomites, by fire from heaven; and through the latter, with similar fire, he chastised Job. *"He made a way for a path to his anger."* A beautiful figure. It means, God's anger prompting him to revenge, was restrained by his mercy, urging him not to destroy them entirely, but at length he set aside his mercy, and *"made a way for a path to his anger,"* and he did not spare them, for he killed all the first born of men and beasts, which were the first fruits of their labor; that is, of the Egyptians, for men generally labor in rearing their children and their cattle, but the first of their labor is directed to their first born, which thus get the appellation of the first fruits of their labor. *"In the tabernacle of Cham;"* means, in Egypt, which was so called after Mizraim the son of Cham, the son of Noe, he having been the first to inhabit and possess Egypt. *"And he took away his own people like sheep."* Upon the slaughter of the first born of Egypt, Pharao allowed the Jews to go away, and then God brought them into the desert of Arabia. *"And he brought them out in hope, and they feared not;"* they went out with great confidence, *"and the sea overwhelmed their enemies;"* the last plague inflicted on the Egyptians, and the end of the captivity of the children of Israel.

54-58. The prophet now passes to the facts related in the books of Josue and Judges, and shows that the Jews were brought by God into the land of promise, which he calls *"the mountain of his sanctuary,"* because it was a mountainous country, and one which God had sanctified and dedicated to himself to be worshipped there by his people; he also calls it *"the mountain which his right hand had purchased,"* because God caused the Israelites under Josue, to conquer the old inhabitants who were most devoted to idolatry, and to banish them by the aid of most signal miracles. He adds, however, that the Jews so introduced by God into the land of promise, proved to be not a whit better than their fathers who had perished in the desert, for they too *"tempted and provoked the Most High God,"* by abandoning his worship, and by the service of idols. The expression, *"They were turned aside as a crooked bow,"* means that they were like a bow out of shape, sending the arrows where they should not be sent; for the Jews promised to observe God's commandments, and apparently directed their arrows to the worship of the true God, while they were, meanwhile, offering sacrifices to false gods; which the prophet expresses in plain language, when he says, *"They provoked him to anger on their hills; and moved him to jealousy with their graven things:"* for it was on lofty hills, especially wooded ones, that they erected altars to their idols, and sacrificed thereon to them.

59-64. The prophet now enters into the vengeance inflicted by God on the sins of his people, making special mention of the time when the Philistines routed the Jewish army, and carried the Ark of the Lord away with them, after having slain the priests who were in charge of it, 1 Kings 4. *"God heard,"* or rather he knew the sins of his people crying unto heaven, *"and despised them,"* as an useless people, and deserving of death, *"and he reduced Israel exceedingly,"* humbled them to nothing, allowing their enemies to triumph over them. *"And he put away the tabernacle of Silo."* He rejected the tabernacle containing the Ark, which was then in Silo, in which tabernacle, God, to a certain extent *"dwelt among men;"* because from thence he gave his answers to men. *"And he delivered their strength into captivity, and their beauty into the hands of the enemy;"* he allowed that people that he had chosen for his inheritance, as his own and favored people to be surrounded and circumvented by the swords of the enemy. *"Fire consumed their young men;"* the fire of war, or the fire of God's anger destroyed the flower of them, for such are always the young; *"and their maidens were not lamented,"* because there was nobody left to deplore them. *"Their priests fell by the sword,"* Ophni and Phinees the sons of Heli, who are specially named among the dead; *"and their widows did not mourn,"* for all were occupied in their own private and peculiar losses.

65-72. In this, the latter part of the Psalm, David shows that God was pleased at his people being punished as they were, inasmuch as their sins called for such punishment; but that he was not pleased with the pride and malice of the Philistines, who so afflicted them; and, therefore, that he signally punished the Philistines, as we read in the same book of Kings, chap. 5. God often uses the wickedness of some to punish others, and then punishes the wicked for doing so, not looking to the good effected through them, but to the malicious motives that prompted them, in which he had no share. He then goes on to say that God would not have the tabernacle any longer in Silo, a city of the tribe of Ephraim, nor that the supreme power should be in the tribe of Joseph; but that he wished the tabernacle to be placed on mount Sion, and that the supreme rule should belong to the tribe of Juda, from which tribe he had chosen David to be king over his people; a prophecy regarding Christ and his Church, as we said in the beginning of the Psalm. For, as St. Augustine well remarks, God did not reject Joseph, and select Juda by reason of their personal merits; had he done so, he would have chosen Joseph, who excelled very much, whether one regards his chastity, his patience, his wisdom, his prudence, or his love of his enemies; but he chose Juda on account of David, and David on account of Christ, and he destroyed the synagogue to build up the Church. To come now to the explanation of the text. *"And the Lord was awaked as one out of sleep."* The Philistines had overpowered the Jews, not by their own strength, nor by reason of want of strength on the part of the Lord, but because he slept, and slept, too, *"like a mighty man that hath been surfeited with wine;"* wine makes one sleep. But when he was awaked from that sleep, he made a grand display of his power against the Philistines. God is said, figuratively, to sleep when he does not seem to notice the evil doings of the wicked; and he is said to sleep *"like one surfeited with wine,"* when he deals with the most grievous sinners as if he were in a profound sleep, and was insensible to the grievous injuries offered him, such as the taking away of the Ark. *"And he smote his enemies on the hinder parts."* He afflicted them with a most painful disease, that of the emerods in their private parts; *"he put them to an everlasting reproach;"* for God, in his wisdom, caused them to make golden emerods, and hang them on the Ark, to their own everlasting shame, to hand down the disease with which God had afflicted them. *"And he rejected the tabernacle of Joseph;"* he would not have the tabernacle in which was kept the Ark, to remain any longer in Silo, a city in the tribe of Ephraim, the son of Joseph; *"and chose not the tribe of Ephraim;"* when about to establish a sovereignty in his people, he did not choose a king from Ephraim, the most numerous and powerful of the tribes, *"But he chose the tribe of Juda, mount Sion which he loved."* He chose the tribe of Juda, from which his rulers were to be selected, and mount Sion on which to place his tabernacle, and afterwards his temple, to hold his Ark, and to offer his sacrifices therein. *"And he built his sanctuary as of unicorns in the land which he founded forever;"* God built on mount Sion, or in Jerusalem, which is to exist, his sanctuary, as firm as the horn of a unicorn. Here is the principle, or parable, or, rather, enigma, which the prophet promised in the beginning of the Psalm; for the sanctuary of the Old Testament was not as firm as the horn of a unicorn, only inasmuch as it was the type of the sanctuary of the New Testament; nor was mount Sion or Jerusalem founded, (for it was soon after destroyed,) only inasmuch as it was the type of the Church of Christ, *"against which the gates of hell shall not prevail,"* and whose worship and sacraments will suffer no change to the end of the world. *"And he chose his servant David, and took him from the flocks of sheep; he brought him from following the ewes great with young."* He passes over the reign of Saul, for it was to be a short time, and, in a manner, extorted from God by the clamors of the people; but he mentions the kingdom of David, who was a type of Christ, and which, through the pure will of God, was to last. He, therefore, *"chose his servant David"* from a humble position, for fear he should attribute his elevation to any merits of his own; *"he took him from the flocks of sheep;"* from being a shepherd, as he really was, *"to feed Jacob his servant, and Israel his inheritance;"* from feeding sheep, took him to feed men; for he placed him over the kingdom of Israel and of Jacob, his people and his inheritance. *"And he fed them in the innocence of his heart; and conducted them by the skillfulness of his hands."* The event proved the soundness of God's judgment, for David fed and governed God's people in the innocence of his heart, and the wisdom of his acts. In the innocence of his heart, because, with a pure and immaculate heart, he never sought his own glory, but that of God; not his own benefit, but that of the people; he was more anxious to serve than to rule; he fed the sheep, not as his own, but as belonging to his Master, as a servant, and not as an heir. In his wisdom, or, as he expresses it, *"in the skillfulness of his hands,"* he guided the people; because, whatever he did, he did it on due reflection, not rashly, not without taking counsel, or inconsiderately. All which perfections, however applicable they may be to David, are, absolutely speaking, to be found completely in Christ alone. Had David been so perfect in them, he would not have been so severely condemned for coveting the wife of another, for the commission of murder and adultery, for wantonly making a census of the people; for condemning Mephiboseth, and giving his property to the false informer, without any manner of trial. Christ, though, was truly innocent in heart, and wise in his works, *"for he committed no sin, nor was there guile found in his mouth;"* and he alone could boldly say, *"Which of you shall convince me of sin?"*

PSALM 78

The Church in time of persecution prayeth for relief. It seems to belong to the time of the Machabees.

1 God, the heathens are come into thy inheritance, they have defiled thy holy temple: they have made Jerusalem as a place to keep fruit.
2 They have given the dead bodies of thy servants to be meat for the fowls of the air: the flesh of thy saints for the beasts of the earth.
3 They have poured out their blood as water, round about Jerusalem and there was none to bury them.
4 We are become a reproach to our neighbours: a scorn and derision to them that are round about us.
5 How long, O Lord, wilt thou be angry for ever: shall thy zeal be kindled like a fire?
6 Pour out thy wrath upon the nations that have not known thee: and upon the kingdoms that have not called upon thy name.
7 Because they have devoured Jacob; and have laid waste his place.
8 Remember not our former iniquities: let thy mercies speedily prevent us, for we are become exceeding poor.
9 Help us, O God, our saviour: and for the glory of thy name, O Lord, deliver us: and forgive us our sins for thy name's sake:
10 Lest they should say among the Gentiles: Where is their God? And let him be made known among the nations before our eyes, By the revenging the blood of thy servants, which hath been shed:
11 Let the sighing of the prisoners come in before thee. According to the greatness of thy arm, take possession of the children of them that have been put to death.
12 And render to our neighbours sevenfold in their bosom: the reproach wherewith they have reproached thee, O Lord.
13 But we thy people, and the sheep of thy pasture, will give thanks to thee for ever. We will shew forth thy praise, unto generation and generation.

EXPLANATION OF THE PSALM

1. The prophet, putting himself in the position of the people in the time of the Machabees, addresses God, complaining of the destruction of the temple and of the city. *"O God, the heathens are come;"* the pagan idolaters, *"into thy inheritance;"* to that city and province which you have selected from the entire world to be your own. Inheritance and possession are synonymous in the Scriptures. He tells, then, for what purpose the heathens came into his inheritance. *"They have defiled thy holy temple,"* which they did in the time of Antiochus, when they set up an idol in the temple, and profaned the altars by offering sacrifices to idols on them. *"They have made Jerusalem as a place to keep fruit;"* they left the royal city so desolate that it had no longer the look of a city, but looked rather like a hut set up to watch the fruit in a garden or vineyard; that such was the case is stated in 1 Mac. 3, where we read, *"And Jerusalem was not inhabited, but was like a desert."*

2-3. Having deplored the devastation of the temple and the city, he now deplores the slaughter of the people, and the cruelty and the barbarity of the enemy who would not suffer the corpses of the slain to be buried. *"They have given the dead bodies"* of the Jews that were killed, not for interment, but exposed them to be eaten by the crows and the dogs. *"They hare poured out their blood as water;"* in great abundance, without regard to time or person; *"and there was none to bury them;"* and their bodies, therefore, were left to the birds of the air and the beasts of the fields. This was accomplished several times, and especially in the slaughter of three score of the leading men of the Jews, who were put to death in one day by Alcimus, as we read in 1 Mach. 7, where this very verse is quoted, when speaking of the slaughter.

4. He now deplores the infamy attached to them by such persecution. *"We are become a reproach to our neighbors,"* to the neighboring kingdoms of the Moabites, Ammonites, and others, who despise and mock us as weak and contemptible fellows.

5. The prophet, seeing God's anger so terribly excited against his people, that he feared for their total destruction, in deprecation of which he earnestly asks, *"How long wilt thou be angry?"* and he repeats it, saying, *"shall thy zeal be kindled like a fire?"* when he compares God's anger to a fire, which if not extinguished at once, rapidly spreads and consumes everything before it.

6. He prays here that God's anger may be turned on the enemies of his people. We thy children, bad as we may be, are still thy children; we know you to be the true God, we worship you, we invoke you; rather, then, *"pour forth thy wrath upon the nations that have not known thee;"* who have not thee for their God, who do not invoke your name, who do not believe you to be omnipotent. This would seem to contradict the saying of our Savior, Luke 12, *"And that servant who knew the will of his Lord, and did not according to his will, shall be beaten with many stripes. But he that knew not, and did things worthy of stripes, shall be beaten with few stripes."* St. Augustine replies, that the Gospel speaks of servants belonging to the same family, with whom the fault, and, consequently, the punishment is greater in proportion to their cognizance of the extent of it; but much more grievously do they sin, and much more severe will be the punishment of those who do not belong to the family; nay more, but are sworn enemies, *"serving the creature rather than the Creator,"* and grievously persecute the entire family; and it is of such persons the following verse speaks.

7. Not only have they paid no regard to the invocation of the Almighty, but they eat up his people as they would so much bread, robbing them, banishing them, putting them to death, seeking to drive them to apostasy, by threats and torments; *"and have laid waste his place,"* the city of Jerusalem which they left waste and desolate.

8. For fear God's people, in accusing their enemies, and deeming them worthy of punishment, would appear to be justifying themselves, as if their own punishment were not deserved, and that they were afflicted more through the power of their enemies than through the justice of God, in this verse they confess their own sins, and the sins of their fathers, and appeal to the mercy of a Father instead of the justice of a judge. *"Remember not our former iniquities."* Punish us not for our old sins, nor for those of our fathers. God sometimes revenges the sins of the fathers on the children to the third and fourth generation, as we read in Exod. 20. Even the Lord himself says, Mt. 23, *"Fill ye up then the measure of your fathers;"* and, in few verses after, *"That upon you may come all the just blood that hath been shed upon the earth, from the blood of Abel the just, even unto the blood of Zacharias the son of Barachias."* Nor does this contradict Ezechiel, who says, *"The son shall not bear the iniquity of his father;"* for the son, strictly speaking, is punished for his own sins, but he is said sometimes to be punished for the sins of his parents, for God would not have punished him, though he might have done so in justice, but for the sins of his parents. *"Let thy mercies speedily prevent us;"* we are rushing to destruction if your mercy will not speedily interfere; and he tells why, when he says, *"for we are become exceeding poor;"* afflicted, humbled, attenuated, wanting; not only the riches of this world, but also help and assistance.

9. The prophet now explains how *"God's mercies prevent us,"* which he does in the shape of a prayer rather than an instruction. *"Help us, O God, our Savior;"* may your mercies prevent us, by helping us in doing what is right, so as to avoid sins of the future, and in doing penance to atone for sins of the past. He says, *"help us,"* to show that free will, instead of being suspended by grace, is only helped by it; for no one can be said to be helped but he who

does something through the cooperation of grace. He then explains both by saying, *"And for the glory of thy name, O Lord, deliver us."* Deliver us from the death of future sin, by helping us in doing what is right; not on account of our merits, but for your own glory. *"And forgive us our sins, for thy name's sake;"* and for the sake of the same glory, and not for our sake, forgive us our past sins, by helping us to do penance.

10. Here is the reason why, in the preceding verse, he appealed to God by the glory of his name, *"lest they should say among the gentiles: Where is their God?"* where is the God that was wont to protect the Jews? He must have deserted them like an imbecile or a coward, or he is quite ignorant of what they have come to. *"And let him be made known among the nations before our eyes;"* such blasphemies will be uttered not only here, but they will spread among the surrounding nations; and when we hear and see them, we must needs be the more grievously afflicted. *"By the revenging the blood of thy servant which hath been shed."* That your name, then, be not blasphemed, revenge the blood of your servants so cruelly spilled.

11. Let the groans of thy servants in captivity, and even in chains, come before thee. *"According to the greatness of thy arm, take possession of the children of them that have been put to death."* The prophet, speaking in the person of God's people, had previously asked two things, namely, that vengeance may be inflicted for the slain, and that the captives doomed to death may be freed; he now repeats the prayer, but inverts it, first asking for protection for the living, then vengeance for the dead. *"According to the greatness of thy arm, take possession of the children of them that have been put to death."* As your arm is most powerful, bravely resist our persecutors, and take possession (it being your peculiar inheritance) of the remnants of your people, to wit, the children of those who have been slain by the enemy. *"And render to our neighbors seven fold in their bosom,"* punish our neighbors seven fold, and hide it in their bosom, so that it will not be easy for them to get quit of it: *"the reproach wherewith they have reproached thee, O Lord;"* as they reproached you with imbecility and folly, as if you were not the true God, show them that they were the real imbeciles and fools, and, instead of being men, were rather the vermin of the earth, or dust and ashes.

12-13. St. Augustine, writing on the words, *"render to our neighbor,"* says, with much truth, that such and similar expressions are to be read rather as predictions than imprecations; for the Psalm is concluded by the certain prediction that God's praise would have no end. They, says he, (and they deserve it) will get seven fold punishment in their bosom; but we will give thanks to thee;" we will praise thee, and preach up thy glory to all ages. That was foreshadowed to the Jews, with whom the Machabees held sway for many years after the persecution of Antiochus; but will be more completely accomplished in the Church of Christ, which, after many and varied persecutions, will, on the day of judgment, see all her persecutors receive in their bosom the reward of their iniquity, while she, with Christ her King, will, in the heavenly Jerusalem, praise her God through ages of ages.

PSALM 79

A prayer for the Church in tribulation, commemorating God's former favors.

1 Give ear, O thou that rulest Israel: thou that leadest Joseph like a sheep. Thou that sittest upon the cherubims, shine forth

2 Before Ephraim, Benjamin, and Manasses. Stir up thy might, and come to save us.

3 Convert us, O God: and shew us thy face, and we shall be saved.

4 Lord God of hosts, how long wilt thou be angry against the prayer of thy servant?

5 How long wilt thou feed us with the bread of tears: and give us for our drink tears in measure?

6 Thou hast made us to be a contradiction to our neighbours: and our enemies have scoffed at us.

7 God of hosts, convert us: and shew thy face, and we shall be saved.

8 Thou hast brought a vineyard out of Egypt: thou hast cast cut the Gentiles and planted it.

9 Thou wast the guide of its journey in its sight: thou plantedst the roots thereof, and it filled the land.

10 The shadow of it covered the hills: and the branches thereof the cedars of God.

11 It stretched forth its branches unto the sea, and its boughs unto the river.

12 Why hast thou broken down the hedge thereof, so that all they who pass by the way do pluck it?

13 The boar out of the wood hath laid it waste: and a singular wild beast hath devoured it.

14 Turn again, O God of hosts, look down from heaven, and see, and visit this vineyard:

15 And perfect the same which thy right hand hath planted: and upon the son of man whom thou hast confirmed for thyself.

16 Things set on fire and dug down shall perish at the rebuke of thy countenance.

17 Let thy hand be upon the man of thy right hand: and upon the son of man whom thou hast confirmed for thyself.

18 And we depart not from thee, thou shalt quicken us: and we will call upon thy name.

19 Lord God of hosts, convert us: and shew thy face, and we shall be saved.

Explanation of the psalm

1. The prophet commences this Psalm with a prayer to God, that he may hear him, and cast a favorable eye on his people. *"Give ear, O thou that rulest Israel; O God,* who art the ruler and the guide of the people of Israel, hear the prayer I pour forth for your own people. He then repeats the first part of the prayer, leaving the second to be understood; *"thou that leadest Joseph like a sheep;"* O God, who leadest the descendants of Joseph as a shepherd would his flock, hear the prayer which I pour forth for your people, who are called Israel and Joseph. The reason for his mentioning Israel and Joseph is, that the name Israel comprehended all the tribes, and the name Joseph does the same. We can easily understand why Israel includes all the tribes, for they were all descended from Israel; and the reason why Joseph also comprehends all the tribes is, because he fed the whole of them, and ruled over them in Egypt, and his two sons, Ephraim and Manasses, became the heads of two distinct tribes, the only instance of the like. Each of the sons of Israel became the head of a separate tribe, with the exception of Joseph, who got the privilege of founding two tribes; and, upon the death of Solomon, when his kingdom was divided into the kingdom of Israel and the kingdom of Juda, the first who reigned as king over the ten tribes of Israel was Jeroboam, of the tribe of Ephraim, the son of Joseph. *"Thou that sittest upon the Cherubim shine forth."* Having asked God to hear the prayers of his people favorably, he now begs that he may turn his eyes on them, and regard them with a look of complacency. God is said to look on one when he is pleased with him, and to turn away his eyes, or to cover them with a cloud, when he is displeased. *"Thou that sittest upon the Cherubim;"* O God, who sittest in heaven, above the Angels of the first rank, called Cherubim, and as a type thereof you have in your sanctuary, the mercy seat resting on the images of the Cherubim for your throne, and where the Ark is, as it were, the footstool of your feet, attend to us.

2. Show thy face and look with pity on us, the people of Israel. Why the three tribes just named should stand for the whole people of Israel, the reason seems to be that which we have assigned in the preceding verse, for Ephraim and Manasses, to whom he unites Benjamin here, because he was uterine brother to Joseph; and when the tribes were marshalled in array of battle, Ephraim, Manasses, and Benjamin always went together. The prophet had also, possibly, in view the fact of these three tribes being in possession of the principal parts of the land of promise. Ephraim held Samaria, the capital of the kingdom of Israel; Benjamin had Jerusalem, the capital of the kingdom of Juda; and Manasses had the country beyond the Jordan. The reason for his placing Benjamin between the brothers, seems to be for distinction sake, he having been their uncle. *"Stir up thy might and come to save* us." He tells now, more plainly, why he asked God to direct his ears and his eyes towards them, that he may save them. *"Stir up thy might,"* your power which looks as if it were buried, when you so allowed us to be harassed by our unjust persecutors; *"come,"* therefore, with your most powerful help *"to save us."*

3. The reason why God often does not look upon us is, because we turn away from him, and turn to creatures; but as we cannot turn to him without his aid, the prophet asks for both for God's people. *"Convert us, O God,"* inspire us with your love, that we may turn away from the things of this world, and turn back to you: *"and show us thy face; turn your face to us, at the same time, that thus united to you by the bonds of holy charity, "we will be saved"* from all the enemies that assail us, for when you turn your face away, we languish and perish; when you look upon us, we revive and recover.

4. The prophet, seeing that God's anger towards his sinning people was very great, and that he was not likely to be heard, renews his prayer with greater force, saying, Lord God of armies, who art terrible, (for such is the force of the Hebrew,) how long will you be angry, even with me who am praying to you.

5. How long will you leave us in such affliction, that we can do nothing but shed tears in abundance, which will thus seem to be the only meat and drink we have to support us?

6. He tells why they are overwhelmed with so much grief, and shed so many tears, because they are beset and trampled on by all their neighbors, and scoffed at and insulted when so subdued. *"Thou hast made us to be a contradiction to our neighbors;"* when you took your protection from us, you encouraged all our neighbors to rise up against us and to *"contradict us,"* not only by word of mouth, but by open assaults and violence. *"And our enemies have scoffed at us;"* they conquered and subdued us, and then insulted and scoffed at us.

7. This verse is the same as the third, and it is repeated again in the end of the Psalm, with this difference, that we have the word *"of hosts;"* that is, of armies here, and we have *"Lord God,"* in the last verse, instead of *"God"* here. Such repetition indicates the principal object of the Psalm. And as nothing more valuable can be asked of God than *"to turn us to him, and turn himself to us,"* such grace is the source of all good. The addition of one word in the first, and two in the second repetition, expresses the increase and the earnestness of his prayer as he advances in it.

8. In order to succeed in his prayers, he falls back upon God's favors to the Jews, whom he had delivered from the bondage of Egypt, and introduced into the lands of the Chananeans, making use of the figure of the wine, as was afterwards adopted by Isaias and Ezechiel, and even by the Savior

himself. The application is most appropriate, for many reasons; but mainly because the vine will either produce fine and well flavored fruit, and then it is most valued by its owner, and tended with the greatest care, or it will be barren and unproductive, in which case it will be thrown into the fire. Such will be the case with everyone of us; if we shall have the fruit of good works to produce, we shall inherit the kingdom of heaven, if we lack them we shall be sent into hell fire. *"Thou hast brought a vineyard out of Egypt;"* you brought your people like a vine from the barren land of Egypt, and planted them in the rich land of Palestine. And as that beautiful land was previously occupied by wild and useless vines, *"you cast them out,"* and *"planted"* your own vine in their stead.

9. That we may understand clearly what the prophet says here about this vine, meaning man, he uses indiscriminately plain and figurative language. *"Thou wast the guide of its journey in its sight;"* when you were bringing that vine of yours from Egypt to Palestine, and the vine, as being endowed with reason, was on its journey, you were its guide, preceding it by day as a pillar of cloud, and by night as a pillar of fire. God was, in a moral sense also, the guide of his vineyard, of his people on their journey to the land of promise, when he gave them the law. *"Thou planted the roots thereof, and tilled the land;"* you established your people in the land of promise, and so propagated them, that the whole country became replete with inhabitants.

10-11. He now describes the increase and propagation of the people of Israel as to length and breadth; that is, as to glory and numbers, mixing up much high flown language with his metaphors. *"The shadow of it covered the hills."* This vine grew to such an enormous height, that it rose above the mountains and overshadowed them, nay, even to such a height did it rise, that its branches rose higher than the cedars of Libanus, the highest trees in the world, and standing on one of its highest mountains. Such height was typical of the power and glory of the kingdom of Israel, that it exceeded the power and glory of many kingdoms. For Israel subdued the Amorrheans, in the time of Moses, and under Josue they conquered thirty-one kings, and under David they subdued the Philistines, the Idumeans, and the Moabites. He now describes the propagation of the kingdom, saying, *"It stretched forth its branches unto the sea, and its boughs unto the river."* Israel was so extended and propagated as to fill the land of promise, from the west to the Mediterranean, and from the east to the great river Euphrates; and thus was God's promise, Deut. 11, fulfilled. *"From the great river Euphrates, unto the western sea, shall be your borders."*

12. Having described the greatness and the excellence of the Jewish people, under the figure of a vine, helping up the same idea, he now deplores the miserable state of the people, by reason of God's anger. *"Why hast thou*

broken down the fence thereof?" why have you withdrawn your protection, which was like a fence round about it? *"so that all they who pass by the way do pluck it?"* why do you allow all the enemies of your people to conquer her and plunder her, as people do a vineyard when the fences are all leveled? More than once were the Israelites persecuted and plundered by the Philistines, and the Madianites, when God, provoked by their sins, was pleased to abandon them.

13. Following up the metaphor of the vine, he now deplores, in particular, the severe captivity inflicted on them by the kings of the Assyrians, whether it was Salmanasar, who carried away ten whole tribes captives, or Nabuchodonosor, who carried off the remaining two tribes captives, having totally demolished the city, burned the temple, and dethroned the king; and this latter king he calls *"the boar out of the wood,"* and *"a singular wild beast,"* who not only leveled the fences, but thoroughly rooted out the vine.

14. He now, by way of a prayer, foretells the coming of Christ, who made up the breaches in the hedge, and gave the vineyard to be managed by other hands, as we read in Mt. 21, *"He will bring those evil men to an evil end, and will let out his vineyard to other husbandmen;"* which he at once explains more clearly in the following verses, where he says, *"The kingdom of God shall be taken from you, and shall be given to a nation, bringing forth the fruits thereof."* For the Church of the Old Testament, which was at one time God's vineyard, was never thoroughly destroyed, but it was reformed. The Apostles, the first fruits of the Church, belonged to Israel, and so did the many thousands who were converted by the preaching of Peter; and St, Paul, Rom. 11, clearly proves the gentiles to be *"the branches ingrafted into the good olive tree;"* that is, the Church originally formed of the Jews. He therefore says, *"God of hosts,"* who hast many thousands of Angels, nay, even all created things, serving thee, and art, therefore, all powerful, *"turn again,"* in your mercy, to your vineyard, your people, for whom you have so long entertained a just and deserved hatred; *"look down from heaven and see;"* when you shall have retired far from your vineyard, deign, at least, to look down from your throne in heaven, *"and see"* how disfigured your vineyard has been by the wild boar; *"and visit this vineyard;"* come and make a personal inspection of this vineyard. When he did so, Zacharias said, *"He hath visited and wrought the redemption of his people;"* and Christ himself, when he wept over Jerusalem, and foretold its destruction, attributed it to, *"because thou hast not known the time of thy visitation."*

15. He now foretells the coming of the Messias more clearly. *"And perfect the same which thy right hand hath planted."* Finish the work you began. Reform the Church of the Old Testament, now nearly defunct, and give a better one in its stead; as it was you that originally founded it, and planted it as a

vineyard, not to perish, but to yield fruit; *"and upon the Son of man;"* look down also upon the Son of man, who is thy Son also, the Messiah, *"whom thou hast confirmed for thyself,"* as the principal husbandman in charge of your vineyard, as the head and guide of your Church. All agree that this passage refers literally to Christ, because, after the Babylonian captivity, the Jewish people never recovered their former position, and, therefore, the vineyard was never made perfect, as regards them; and it was only under Christ, as its Savior and its Lord, that it could have been said to have been made perfect.

16. He now explains the effects likely to follow from the coming of the Messias, namely, that the vineyard of the Lord, though burned down and rooted up, shall flourish and grow up again; for one rebuke from him will stop the devastation of the vineyard; just as when he rebuked the storm there was an immediate calm; and, when he commanded death and disease, they immediately disappeared, and were succeeded by life and health.

17. Certain of the coming of the Messias, he prays all manner of blessings on him. *"Let thy hand be upon the man of thy right hand;"* may your hand be extended to protect at all times, and in all places, the man of your right hand, the man who was formed by your right hand alone, without any co-operation on the part of man; for that Christ was so formed is certain, as we read in Luke 1, *"The Holy Ghost shall come upon thee, and the power of the Most High shall overshadow thee;"* and the same Christ was placed over the Church, not by the choice of man, but by the decree of God. *"But I am appointed king by him over Sion his holy mountain."*

18. While Christ is our ruler, *"we depart not from thee;"* because Christ's kingdom will last forever, and the gates of hell will not prevail against his Church. *"Thou shalt quicken us"* with the life of grace here on earth, and of glory hereafter in heaven; *"and we will call upon thy name;"* offering our tribute of invocation, praise, and thanks forever.

19. See verse 7.

PSALM 80

An invitation to a solemn praising of God.

1 Rejoice to God our helper: sing aloud to the God of Jacob.
2 Take a psalm, and bring hither the timbrel: the pleasant psaltery with the harp.
3 Blow up the trumpet on the new moon, on the noted day of your solemnity.
4 For it is a commandment in Israel, and a judgment to the God of Jacob.
5 He ordained it for a testimony in Joseph, when he came out of the land of Egypt: he heard a tongue which he knew not.
6 He removed his back from the burdens: his hands had served in baskets.
7 Thou calledst upon me in affliction, and I delivered thee: I heard thee in the

secret place of tempest: I proved thee at the waters of contradiction.
8 Hear, O my people, and I will testify to thee: O Israel, if thou wilt hearken to me,
9 There shall be no new god in thee: neither shalt thou adore a strange god.
10 For I am the Lord thy God, who brought thee out of the land of Egypt: open thy mouth wide, and I will fill it.
11 But my people heard not my voice: and Israel hearkened not to me.
12 So I let them go according to the desires of their heart: they shall walk in their own inventions.
13 If my people had heard me: if Israel had walked in my ways:
14 I should soon have humbled their enemies, and laid my hand on them that troubled them.
15 The enemies of the Lord have lied to him: and their time shall be for ever.
16 And he fed them with the fat of wheat, and filled them with honey out of the rock.

Explanation of the Psalm

1. The prophet exhorts us, when we praise God, that we should do it with great interior joy; *"for God loveth a cheerful giver;"* and if he loves the one who gives cheerfully, much more does he love him who praises cheerfully. Cheerfulness comes from love and from desire; and, therefore, he who sings moodily, and who looks upon the divine office as an intolerable burden, rather than a sweet canticle, gives to understand that he has very little affection for him whose praises he chants. *"Rejoice to God our helper."* Praise God in great exultation, for it is he who can help us on all occasions. *"Sing aloud to the God of Jacob;"* give your mind to it, and sing his praises with a loud voice.

2-3. He tells them when they are especially to sing their hymns of praise, at the time of new moon; for then the Jews began the month, and held their festivals. *"On the noted day of your solemnity,"* which some will have to be the new moon of September, the most solemn feast of the Jews, while others will have it to be the first of each month; but it matters little which, as the sense is the same.

4-5. He assigns a reason for singing with such joy, and bringing in the aid of musical instruments, and that is, because God himself commanded it, when he brought the people out of Egypt. For God, who needs nothing, still wishes for such tribute of praise, and that we should keep up the memory of his benefits. *"For it is a command in Israel."* We must sing and play on musical instruments, as a mark of joy and thanksgiving, because it has been commanded by God, and the commandment is kept in Israel by God's people, who are so called from their parent Israel. *"And a judgment to the God of Jacob;"* a repetition of the same idea, for judgment and commandment, and Israel and Jacob, are frequently used in the Scriptures, to express the same idea. He ordained it for a testimony in Joseph, *"when he came out of the land of Egypt;"* another repetition, testimony, commandment, and judgment, signifying the same thing, as is also the case with Israel, Jacob, and Joseph. *"He heard a tongue which he knew not;"* for, up to the delivery of the commandments on mount Sinai, the people never heard the voice of God speaking to them.

6. Another favor conferred by God on the Jews in their departure from Egypt. They had been compelled by the Egyptians to the severest labor, in making and burning brick; that was *"removed from their backs,"* they were no longer obliged to bear the heavy loads they had been subjected to in brick making. *"His hands had served in baskets,"* fetching the clay, from which slavery God delivered them.

7. From this verse to the end, God alternately puts before them his own kindness and their ingratitude. *"Thou callest upon me in affliction; and I delivered thee;"* when you were laboring under most grievous persecutions in Egypt you called upon me, and I heard you, and I delivered you from such slavery, and brought you out of the country. *"I heard thee in the secret place of tempest."* I heard you, not only when you dreaded Pharao's anger; but also when you dreaded the tempests and plagues you saw inflicted on the Egyptians, for then I put you in a secret place, and protected you, so that the plagues did not harm you. Others will apply it to the invisible protection afforded by God in their passage through the Red Sea, and afterwards in the desert. *"I proved thee at the waters of contradiction."* After such great favors I tried you, in order to prove your patience and fidelity, by depriving you of water, and I found you impatient and unfaithful, see Num. 17 and 20, where God deprived them of water for a short time, and, when they murmured and became seditious, brought an abundance of it from the rock for them. The place was called *"The waters of contradiction,"* the people having rebelled against Moses, and contradicted him there.

10. The prophet, speaking in the person of God, relates what fair conditions he offered, and what ample promises he made his people, if they would adhere to their promises, from which we can judge of the unspeakable goodness of God. *"Hear,"* you Jews, who are *"my people,"* and I will tell you plainly, *"I will testify to thee"* what I require of you, and what I will give you in return. This much I require of you, and beyond and above all things command, *"There shall be no new god in thee,"* no god who was not worshipped by your fathers. *"Neither shalt thou adore a strange god;"* a repetition of the same thing. *"For I am the Lord God who brought thee out of the land of Egypt."* No better reason could be assigned for the Jewish people not worshipping

strange gods, for it was he who redeemed them from captivity, and transferred them from the bondage of Pharao, to be his own servants. A consideration that should weigh much more powerfully with Christians and attach them to that God who delivered them from the slavery of the devil, and brought them into the kingdom of his beloved Son. *"Open thy mouth wide and I will fill it."* A most ample promise, on the part of God, to those who serve him. *"Open your mouth"* as wide as you can, and the jaws of your desires, and I will satisfy the cravings of your hunger with most delicious food. God alone could make such promise, for nothing created can satisfy the cravings of man's heart. The sight and enjoyment of God, who is the infinite good, and comprehends all good, can thoroughly satisfy us.

11. God now complains of the ingratitude of his people, in not accepting such favorable offers. And how truly wonderful is it not, that slaves in this world will fawn to such an extent upon their masters, and think it great condescension on his part to speak to them, or even to look upon them; and yet, Israel, dust and ashes, will not condescend to hear or to attend to the Lord of Lords? How truly, then, he said, in Lk. 16, *"For the children of this world are wiser in their generation than the children of light."*

12. A dreadful, but most just, scourge is here held out by God, to those who despise him; and that is, that sin shall be the punishment of sin to them; that means, they will be suffered continually to lapse into greater sins, until they shall have, at length, come to the lowest depths of misery, of which the Apostle thus speaks, Rom. 1, *"Wherefore, God gave them up to the desires of their hearts;"* and immediately after he adds, *"For this cause God delivered them up to shameful affections;"* and again, *"God delivered them up to a reprobate sense to do those things which are not convenient."* This is the hardness of heart, of which Eccli. chap. 7, speaks, *"Consider the works of God, that no man can correct whom he hath despised."* *"So I let them go according to the desires of their own hearts."* I let them walk and work, in accordance with their own concupiscence; gave them no discipline, as I would to a child; but, as strangers, I allowed them to tumble down the precipice and be destroyed. *"They shall walk in their own inventions."* They will not follow the paths of their fathers, nor the straight ways of my law, but they will follow whatever their own inventions or human curiosity may suggest, in the worship of false gods, and will thus fall into all the vices that disgrace human nature, when they are not directed by God's light, supported by his hand, or assisted by his efficacious grace.

13-14. To show the abundance of the innate mercy of God, he returns now to the promises he made them, which, in the Hebrew, are accompanied by a wish, as if he said, Oh, that my people had heard me; for truly God is *"the Father of mercies, and the God of all consolation."* Had they heard me, I would have humbled and cast down all those that now afflict her, in such a way that they would never be able to raise their heads again.

15. The prophet speaks here, and confirms what God had asserted, *"But my people heard not my voice."* By his enemies he means the Jews, who from children became enemies, especially when they denied, in presence of Pilate, that Christ was their king; on which Daniel distinctly says, chap. 9, *"And the people that shall deny him shall not be his."*—*"The enemies of the Lord (the rebellious, incredulous Jews) have lied to him;"* for they promised, at the foot of mount Sinai, that they would carry out all his commands; for *"the people answered with one voice: We will do all the words of the Lord, which he hath spoken,"* Exod. 24; and yet they did not do one of them; *"and their time shall be;"* their punishment will be everlasting, for the fire of hell will never be extinguished.

16. Behold the great ingratitude of the Jews, who had received so many favors from God, and still *"have lied to him."* These words may have reference, to the manna that rained down to them in the desert, and the water that gushed from the rock; for that food might have been properly called *"the fat of wheat;"* because it was the bread of Angels, as it is called in Psalm 77; and it had, as we read in Wisdom 16, *"The sweetness of every taste;"* the honey out of the rock may have been the water; which, to the thirsty Hebrews, was then sweeter than any honey. The whole verse may refer to the land of promise, which, though rocky and mountainous, abounded in wheat, wine, and oil; so Moses writes, Deut. 32, *"He sat him upon the high land, that he might eat the fruits of the fields, that he might suck honey out of the rock, and oil out of the hardest stone."* The fat of wheat and the honey out of the rock are, however, in much more esteem with Christians, who have, under the appearance of bread, the body of the Redeemer, and the honey of heavenly wisdom from the rock, no other than the same Christ; and yet, how many, after renouncing the devil, his works, and his pomps in baptism, prove false to God, by returning to those very things they renounced; and, after partaking of bread from heaven, and honey from the rock, returns like unclean dogs, to their vomit. They ought to fear the eternity of the punishment in store for them, of the fire that will never be extinguished, of the worm that will never die.

PSALM 81

An exhortation to judges and men in power.

1 God hath stood in the congregation of gods: and being in the midst of them he judgeth gods.
2 How long will you judge unjustly: and accept the persons of the wicked?
3 Judge for the needy and fatherless: do justice to the humble and the poor.

4 Rescue the poor; and deliver the needy out of the hand of the sinner.
5 They have not known nor understood: they walk on in darkness: all the foundations of the earth shall be moved.
6 I have said: You are gods and all of you the sons of the most High.
7 But you like men shall die: and shall fall like one of the princes.
8 Arise, O God, judge thou the earth: for thou shalt inherit among all the nations.

Explanation of the psalm

1. The holy prophet pronounces that God is always present with judges when they are delivering their judgment, and that he sits in judgment on theirs. A consideration that would prove highly useful to judges, if they would seriously consider that all causes will be judged in the sight of the supreme Judge. *"God hath stood;"* is always present in his majesty, though invisible; *"in the congregation of gods;"* in the assembly of the judges when they meet to sit in judgment; and, while they are judging the people, he, *"in the midst"* of them standing by, judges the judges themselves.

2. Whether this is the language of the prophet reproving the judges for not reflecting on the fact of God's presence at their judgments, and thus judge wrongfully; or whether it is the language of God, who, on assisting at the trials, and examining the decisions, reproves the corrupt judges for their principal and most frequent crime, their regard of persons, which causes them to decide unjustly, is uncertain, but, whether spoken by God or by the prophet, is immaterial; because it is the Holy Ghost who speaks through the mouth of the prophet, and because it seldom happens that a poor man, however just, meets with favor or partiality; and it is quite the other way with the rich man, no matter how much in the wrong; he, therefore, censures them most severely for such regard of persons. *"How long will you judge unjustly?"* How long will you persevere in this sin of unjust judgment? and he assigns the principal cause of their doing so when he says, *"and accept the persons of the wicked;"* for, hence all the unjust judgments, the judges not looking to the merits of the case, but to the favor of the rich and powerful, who themselves sin by the fact of wishing the judges to lean to them instead of to justice. To *"accept the persons of the wicked,"* then, means to pronounce sentence, not according to the justice of the case, but according to the wishes of one party, be he friend, benefactor, or relation.

3. Having censured the vice of regard of person, he now adverts to the oppression of the poor, which judges are guilty of when they defer justice to the poor, or when they decide unjustly against them, for fear of displeasing their more powerful adversaries. *"Judge for the needy and the fatherless."* Freely entertain, diligently discuss, and, for fear they may suffer by protracted litigation, decide as quickly as possible on the case of the poor; and

especially of the orphan. This, however; supposes that they have justice at their side; for, in Lev. 19, we read, *"Respect not the person of the poor nor honor the countenance of the mighty, but judge thy neighbor according to justice."* The meaning, then, is, not to judge at all times in favor of the poor; but, when he shall have justice at his side, that the judge shall take care to make it appear, and not to allow him to be oppressed by the influence of his adversaries.

4. The judge does not discharge his duty by giving a just decision if he does not compel the rich and the powerful to make restitution to the poor and the needy, either by restoring what they took from them, or by compensating them for their losses through defamation or litigation; and he therefore says, *"Rescue the poor"* from the powerful, *"and the needy"* from the same sinner. A repetition for the sake of impression. In this point especially, should judges and princes show their power in protecting the poor. By so doing, they conciliate God and the people; but as they generally do not, the prophet adds:

5. He now deplores the willful blindness of those judges, whose injustice is the cause of all the confusion all over the world. For, as the Lord himself says, *"If the salt lose its flavor, with what shall it be salted?"* and again, *"If the light that is in thee be darkness, how great will the darkness itself be?"* so we can say of those who administer justice, If justice be not found in them, where will it be found? Injustice will reign supreme. *"They have not known nor understood."* They took no trouble to inquire into the facts nor the law of the case. Such ignorance caused them *"to walk on in darkness;"* to give erroneous decisions, like one going astray in the dark; and from erroneous decisions, from such ignorance, arose confusion, tumult, sedition and rebellion, on the part of the people; as is signified in the next sentence, *"all the foundations of the earth shall be moved;"* that means, the whole world will be confused, and knocked about. When the whole kingdom of Israel revolted from David, no other reason could be assigned for such revolt but Absalom's having persuaded the people that David took no trouble in hearing their complaints, and doing them justice, 2 Kings 13. The holy Scripture assigns bribery as the cause of so much corruption among judges. Thus, Isaias 1, *"They all love bribes, they run after rewards; they judge not for the fatherless, and the widow's cause cometh not in to them;"* and in Exod. 23, *"Neither shalt thou take bribes, which blind the wise;"* and in Deut. 16, *"Thou shalt not accept gifts: for gifts blind the eyes of the wise, and change the words of the just;"* and finally, Eccli. 20, *"Presents and gifts blind the eyes of judges, and make them dumb in the mouth, so that they cannot correct."*

6. Having hitherto censured those judges for their respect of persons, their injustice, and their ignorance, he now shows how derogatory such vices are to the high position in which God had placed them. *"I have said;"* I have

asserted, that you judges and princes *"are gods, and all of you the sons of the Most High."* He calls them the sons of the Most High; either, because they were nearly equal to the Angels who, in Job, are called *"sons of God;"* or to show that these judges were not gods, strictly speaking, as is the true supreme God, who has neither beginning nor end; but that they may be called gods, inasmuch as they are sons of God, of the one true God; and made, to a certain extent, gods by him when he gave them a share in his authority, and power of sitting in judgment. In the Gospel of St. John, our Lord, in quoting this passage, says, that they are called gods, because *"the word of God was spoken to them."* Then said he, *"If he called them gods, to whom the word of God was spoken; Do you say of him, whom the Father hath sanctified, and sent into the world: Thou blasphemest; because I said, I am the Son of God?"* The meaning of the expression, *"To whom the word of God was spoken,"* is the being appointed to, or entrusted with, some particular duty by God. Thus, *"The word of God came to the prophets whom he sent to preach;"* and in Luke 3, *"The word of the Lord came to John."* Hence, we see the force of Christ's argument. If those whom God entrusted with any particular duty or mission were called gods, how much a better title thereto have I not, who am the Son of God, sent with all power into the world by my heavenly Father? We are not, however, to infer from this passage that all princes and judges have their power immediately from God. Some have, such as Moses in the Old, and Peter in the New Testament. Others have it through the consent of the people, who give up the power of the natural law conferred on them, which power had its origin in God, *"For there is no power but from God,"* Rom. 13.

7. I have told you what you were through God's mercy. I will now tell you what you are through your own perversity. Through God's mercy you were gods, and like Angels; but, from the sin you inherit from your first parent, *"like men you shall die;"* and, from your own wickedness in abusing the power committed to you, *"you shall fall"* from the highest pinnacle of glory to the lowest pit of hell, *"like one of the princes,"* the fallen angels.

8. The prophet concludes by asking God's assistance against the injustice of the princes and judges of this world, and prays that he who is the real master and owner of this world may correct the judgments of man, may punish unjust judges, and relieve the oppressed poor according to his own power and wisdom; the prayer being a prophetic one, in which he predicts the coming of the Messias, who, as he will come in for the inheritance of the world, will also see that justice be fairly administered therein, through his princes and judges, and afterwards by himself on the day of judgment. *"Arise, O God, judge the earth;"* since the judges so abuse their authority, you, that are the supreme Judge, arise and *"judge the earth,"* including the judges themselves,

and deliver the suffering poor from their unjust oppressors; *"for thou shalt inherit among all the nations;"* because all nations, as they ever did, so they ever will belong to you; because you never placed any one in power here below without reserving the supreme authority to yourself above.

PSALM 82

A prayer against the enemies of God's Church.

1 God, who shall be like to thee? hold not thy peace, neither be thou still, O God.
2 For lo, thy enemies have made a noise: and they that hate thee have lifted up the head.
3 They have taken a malicious counsel against thy people, and have consulted against thy saints.
4 They have said: Come and let us destroy them, so that they be not a nation: and let the name of Israel be remembered no more.
5 For they have contrived with one consent: they have made a covenant together against thee,
6 The tabernacles of the Edomites, and the Ismahelites: Moab, and the Agarens,
7 Gebal, and Ammon and Amalec: the Philistines, with the inhabitants of Tyre.
8 Yea, and the Assyrian also is joined with them: they are come to the aid of the sons of Lot.
9 Do to them as thou didst to Madian and to Sisara: as to Jabin at the brook of Cisson.
10 Who perished at Endor: and became as dung for the earth.
11 Make their princes like Oreb, and Zeb, and Zebee, and Salmana. All their princes,
12 Who have said: Let us possess the sanctuary of God for an inheritance.
13 my God, make them like a wheel; and as stubble before the wind.
14 As fire which burneth the wood: and as a flame burning mountains:
15 So shalt thou pursue them with thy tempest: and shalt trouble them in thy wrath.
16 Fill their faces with shame; and they shall seek thy name, O Lord.
17 Let them be ashamed and troubled for ever and ever: and let them be confounded and perish.
18 And let them know that the Lord is thy name: thou alone art the most High over all the earth.

Explanation of the psalm

1. The prophet, assuming the person of the people, prays to God that, as he is more powerful than all their enemies, he should no longer defer taking vengeance on their persecutors. *"O God, who shall be like to thee?"* No one can be compared in power and strength to you, the only all powerful.

Therefore, *"hold not thy peace;"* have no further patience with them; wreak the vengeance they deserve on them, in which no one can resist you. St. Augustine very properly applies this passage to Christ, who, while in this world, seemed like other men, but will have no one like him on the day of judgment, *"when he shall appear in the glory of his Father, and sit on the throne of his majesty."* Who also, during his passion, was silent, and, *"like a meek lamb,"* restrained himself; but will not be silent on the day of judgment, nor suppress his most just anger when he shall say, *"Go, ye cursed, into everlasting fire."*

2. A strong reason is offered here for God's being no longer silent, and that is, because his enemies, assembling in a great body, and from various nations, raised a most unusual tumult; and they who had hitherto been enemies in private, now openly professed themselves as such. The expression, *"have made a noise,"* signifies, in the Hebrew, the discontented growl of a multitude. *"Have lifted up the head,"* St. Augustine says, refers to Antichrist, who will be the head of Christ's enemies; for, when he shall appear, many, who did not dare to profess themselves enemies of the Church, will openly attach themselves to Antichrist, will boldly *"lift up their own head,"* and will also lift up the common head of all the wicked, Antichrist.

3-4. He now explains the greatness of the danger, so that God may not wait or defer his help any longer, inasmuch as the enemy were not preparing for a raid or an incursion, but for the thorough annihilation and complete desolation of the Church of God. Hence it is probable that this was fulfilled to some extent, as it were, in type and figure in the time of the Machabees; for, we read in the first book of the Machabees, that all the nations around assembled to destroy the house of Jacob. It refers, however, principally to the time of Antichrist, for then all the wicked will, simultaneously, with all their might, endeavor to destroy the strongholds of the saints. *"They have taken a malicious counsel against thy people;"* by a malicious counsel we are to understand one not only full of craft, but also taken in private, such being the force of the Hebrew; and such will be the counsels of Antichrist; private, because he will take counsel with the devil, whom he worships in private; and crafty, for he will pretend to be Christ, in order to deceive Christians; and, at the same time, in order to seduce the Jews, he will introduce circumcisions and other rites of theirs. *"And have consulted against thy saints."* They have entered into a wicked conspiracy against the faithful, who have been sanctified by the blood of your only begotten Son. *"Let us destroy them so that they be not a nation;"* utterly crush and annihilate them; *"and let the name of Israel be remembered no more;"* no trace of their name, no recollection of themselves.

5-8. An enumeration of the nations who sought to extinguish God's people. *"For they have contrived with one consent."* All the enemies of Israel unanimously conspired; *"they have made a covenant together against thee;"* entered into a common treaty against your people. Here they are: first, the tabernacles of the Edomites; that is, the whole body of them. The Edomites were the descendants of Esau, who was also called Edom. Secondly, the Ishmaelites, the descendants of Ishmael the son of Abraham by Agar his handmaid. Thirdly, Moab, the people sprung from Moab, the son of Lot. Fourthly, the Agarens, the people coming from Agar, the handmaid of Abraham, but from another husband, to whom she was married, after having been dismissed by Abraham. Fifthly, Gebal, the people descended from Gebal, but whether that be the name of a place or a person is quite uncertain, as the name occurs in no other part of the Scriptures. Sixthly, Ammon, the people sprung from Ammon, the son of Lot, and brother to Moab; both of whom Lot begot from his daughters. Seventhly, Amalec, the people descended from Amalec, the grandson of Esau. Eighthly, the Philistines, frequent mention of whom is made in the book of Kings. Ninthly, with the inhabitants of Tyre, a town of extensive commerce. Tenthly, the Assyrians, who came to aid the sons of Lot, viz., the Moabites and Ammonites, against the Jews. Those ten different nations or people represent the nations that fought against the Jews, or rather, the multitude of the eastern barbarians, who, with Antichrist, will hereafter raise up a bitter persecution against the Church.

9. The prophet now predicts, in the shape of an imprecation, the extermination of those nations who fought against the Machabees, and particularly of Antichrist and his army, comparing them to other persecutors who met a similar end. *"Go to them as thou didst to Madian."* Scatter and rout them as you formerly scattered the Madianites in the time of Gedeon, Judges 6 and 7; *"as to Sisara,"* the leader of king Jabin's army; *"as to Jabin at the brook of Cisson;"* and as you destroyed Jabin himself, the king of Chanaan, near the torrent called Cisson, Judges 4 and 5. The prophet quotes these especially, their defeat having been miraculous, having been conquered by a few, and rather through fear inspired by God than by the bravery of the Jews.

10. They were conquered at Endor, Josue 16, and became as dung for the earth, for their bodies remained unburied and rotted, thereby enriching the ground; being thus reduced from the height of glory to the depth of infamy.

11. He reverts to Gedeon's history, who not only routed the army of the Madianites, but soon after killed two of their princes, Oreb and Zeb; and two of their kings, Zebee and Salmana, Judges 7 and 8.

12. All these princes and kings said, Let us possess the sanctuary of God, as if it were our own, and came to us by inheritance; that place that was sanctified by God as his own dwelling place. The Jerusalem alluded to here means the Church of God; which Antichrist will endeavor to subdue and lead captive with all his might.

13. The prophet describes the instability and the death of the wicked, by a most appropriate simile. A wheel when rolling down a precipice is constantly turning about, cannot stop for a moment, and is ultimately smashed in pieces. Straws carried by the wind are repeatedly tossed to and fro, until they ultimately disappear; and so, the prophet predicts God will deal with the wicked persecutors of the just; as, in fact, we learn from daily experience, for nothing is more uncertain than the prosperity of the wicked, and their end is death everlasting.

14-15. He prophesied that the wicked would be punished, their uncertainty in this world, and their utter destruction in the next; he now predicts the quickness and the ease with which God will punish them; for, though he did so in the previous verse, where he said they would be scattered like the straws blown about by the wind, he now likens God's anger to a raging fire that destroys the trees of the forest, and the herbage of the plains. *"As fire which burneth the wood;"* the trees of the forest, many of which are withered, readily take fire, and extend the conflagration; *"and as a flame burning mountains,"* especially when the grass is dry in parching seasons. *"So shalt thou pursue them with thy tempest;"* you will just as easily pursue and destroy them; which he explains by adding, *"and shalt trouble them in thy wrath;"* tempest and wrath being the same, for both signify the just judgment of God, which, like a vehement irresistible storm, will strike down, confound, and scatter the wicked.

16-18. In the conclusion of the Psalm he prophesies that some of his persecutors would be so taught by the scourges inflicted on them, that they would be converted; as will many of the Jews, who will ultimately acknowledge their error, and in shame will be brought to God. Some will persevere and remain obdurate, but they, too, will be confounded, and will, even against their will, be brought to know the singular power of God, and that he is the true Lord of all things. *"Fill their faces with shame;"* with confusion, that when they understand the disgraceful position in which they have placed themselves *"they shall seek thy name;"* call upon you to help them. But as to those who will not be moved by such scourges, but get rather, like Pharao, to be more hardened, *"Let them be ashamed and troubled;"* filled with eternal confusion; for *"let them be confounded and perish." "And let them know,"* (against their will,) *"that the Lord is thy name."* Having now learned it by experience, let them understand that the name of Lord belongs to you exclusively, that all things depend on your nod, and are subservient to you; while you serve nobody, and want nothing, having everything within yourself.

While all those who are called Lords, have usurped a name that does not belong to them; or at least, who deserve no such name, while they need many things; and must, therefore, yield to many necessities; *"thou alone art the Most High over all the earth."* Let them also know that your power is preeminently beyond that of all the princes of the earth; nor is there one who can cope with you, or be in anywise compared to you. This prophecy is already fulfilled to some extent, but will be thoroughly accomplished on the day of judgment.

PSALM 83

The soul aspireth after heaven; rejoicing in the meantime, in being in the communion of God's Church upon earth.

1 How lovely are thy tabernacles, O Lord of host!
2 My soul longeth and fainteth for the courts of the Lord. My heart and my flesh have rejoiced in the living God.
3 For the sparrow hath found herself a house, and the turtle a nest for herself where she may lay her young ones: Thy altars, O Lord of hosts, my king and my God.
4 Blessed are they that dwell in thy house, O Lord: they shall praise thee for ever and ever.
5 Blessed is the man whose help is from thee: in his heart he hath disposed to ascend by steps,
6 In the vale of tears, in the place which be hath set.
7 For the lawgiver shall give a blessing, they shall go from virtue to virtue: the God of gods shall be seen in Sion.
8 Lord God of hosts, hear my prayer: give ear, O God of Jacob.
9 Behold, O God our protector: and look on the face of thy Christ.
10 For better is one day in thy courts above thousands. I have chosen to be an abject in the house of my God, rather than to dwell in the tabernacles of sinners.
11 For God loveth mercy and truth: the Lord will give grace and glory.
12 He will not deprive of good things them that walk in innocence: O Lord of hosts, blessed is the man that trusteth in thee.

Explanation of the psalm

1-2. Such are the effusions of a pious soul making for its country, and expressing its desire of coming to its journey's end; such desires proceeding from the happiness to be found in its home, as well as from the troubles to be encountered in its pilgrimage. For the pious soul, whatever may be the amount of its happiness here below, always looks upon itself as miserable and *"suffering persecution."* For the prosperity of this world is a great temptation, and a persecution. He exclaims, then and that in admiration, *"How lovely are thy tabernacles, O Lord of Hosts!"* Oh, what an amount of love have not the pious for your tabernacles, those heavenly mansions of yours, O Lord of Hosts! *"Lord of Hosts,"* what can make your tabernacles more beautiful, or more delightful than the innumerable hosts of Angels, endowed with all wisdom, perfection, power, and beauty, the least glimpse of one of whom would suffice to gladden one's whole pilgrimage here below; while the combined brightness and splendor of the entire is but as darkness when compared to the brightness of Him whom we hope there to behold face to face. In the Jerusalem of the Jews there was only one tabernacle; and therefore, as he speaks here of many, he cannot possibly be supposed to refer to that one of timber, gilded over and made by the hands of man; but to those heavenly *"tabernacles not made by human hands,"* of which the Lord speaks when he says, *"There are many mansions in my Father's house."* *"My soul longeth and fainteth for the courts of the Lord."* Having said that the tabernacles of the Lord were an object of great affection to the pious in their exile, he now ranks himself amongst them, saying, *"My soul longeth and fainteth,"* when I reflect on the courts of the Lord, and consider their beauty; I so long for them, that I languish, decline, and faint away. *"My heart and my flesh have rejoiced in the living God."* To give us an idea of the extent of his longings and of his love, he tells the effects produced by them; for when one is stricken by a vehement love or desire, they not only turn over in their mind, but they express their admiration of the object of their love. *"My heart and my flesh;"* that is, my mind and my tongue have united in the praise of the living God, the increate and infinite beauty, for whom I sigh. This latter part of the verse by no means contradicts the first; though he speaks of his soul fainting there, rejoicing here, for various are the feelings of those in love; they one time deplore the absence of the one beloved, and faint away; and soon again they rejoice when they have got back their beloved, and burst forth in praise of it or him. He calls him *"the living God,"* not only to distinguish him from the idols, *"that have eyes, and see not; who have ears and hear not,"* by reason of their being inanimate things; but also because God alone can be said, strictly speaking, to live; for, to live is to have the power of motion from one's self, and not from another; but created things are said to live, because they have in them a certain principle of motion, yet without God they have none; for, *"in him we live, and move, and have our being."* His life, then, is such as to require no impulse from any other being, that is to say, he has from himself alone the power of understanding and willing; being himself the source of life, not deriving it from any one, but bestowing it on all. *"In him was life, and the life was the light of men."*

3. The holy pilgrim's anxious wish was for a home in heaven; but, as he will have to wait awhile for that, he consoles himself with having found a little

nest on earth, the altars of his Lord; for we have nothing in this world so calculated to give us an idea of the tabernacle above as the holy altar. It brings before the memory a host of heavenly recollections. There is daily offered that Lamb of God, who, by his blood, opened the kingdom of heaven to believers. There a pledge of the glory to come is given us. There we stand nearer to God, and I pray to him with more earnestness. There we pour forth our whole hearts, and chant his praises more devoutly and more attentively than in any other place, or at any other time. He therefore says, *"The sparrow hath found herself a house."* All animals look for some place of rest for themselves, and even the little sparrow has found a house for itself; its little nest, *"and the turtle, a nest for itself;"* not only have those animals, such as the sparrow, accustomed to the society of man, got a dwelling for themselves, but even the turtle, a solitary animal, has too her nest, in which to place her young ones, and rest in security with them. *"Thy altars,"* as for my part, whether my life be an active one, like that of the sparrow, or contemplative like that of the turtle, *"thy altars"* are my nest, where I may securely rest for a while, and lay up my vows, my chaste desires and pious meditations, my prayers and hymns of praise, as so many young ones. *"My God and my King,"* you who direct me while I stray here and there, like a sparrow, and who consoles me, while I mourn like the solitary turtle.

4. He said he found a nest wherein to rest for a while, but being admonished from that very nest, of the superiority of the house of eternity to any temporary rest, he exclaims, *"Blessed are they that dwell in thy house, O Lord."* However happy I may be for a brief moment in this little nest of mine, they alone are truly happy, they alone enjoy perfect rest, *"who dwell in that house of yours,"* where alone are to be found riches, glory, many mansions, and everlasting rest and peace.

5-6. Having spoken of the happiness of him who dwells in the house of the Lord, he adds, that he, too, is happy, if not actually so, at least, by reason of the hope that is in him, when, depending on the divine assistance, he firmly resolves in his heart not to remain in this valley here below, but to be always ascending higher and higher, through successive grades of virtue, until he shall have arrived at the place which God has marked out as the end of his labor, eternal happiness. *"Blessed is the man whose help"* is not a reliance on his own strength, but *"from thee,"* O Lord. *"In his heart he hath disposed to ascend by steps in the vale of tears,"* made up his mind while a mortal in this valley of tears, to seek daily to arrive at a higher degree of perfection *"in the place which he hath set"* in this valley of tears in which he set himself by sin; for God set him in Paradise, but he set himself in the valley of tears by sin.

7. The prophet now explains how the just man, in ascending through the valley of tears, will arrive at that place of rest that is established by God,

and points out the beginning, the means and the end of such ascension. Justification is the beginning, for without it the law cannot be fulfilled, the observance of the law is the means, and the beatific vision the end. *"For the lawgiver shall give a blessing;"* God, who gave the law, and made it the way to life, for he said, *"If thou wilt enter into life, keep the commandments:"* he will also *"give a blessing,"* an abundance of grace through the Holy Ghost, by justifying us from sin, pouring his love into us, and expelling all fear. *"They shall go from virtue to virtue."* Having received his grace and his blessing, they will make daily advances in virtue, and acquire more strength to resist every temptation and overcome every difficulty; for virtue is to be understood here as strength or power. *"The God of gods shall be seen in Sion,"* and thus they will, at length, arrive at the heavenly mountain Sion, where they shall see, face to face, the one true God, who is not only the God of heaven and earth, but also of the Angels, of the blessed, who, to a certain extent, are gods.

8. He now returns to his original longings to form one of those who ascend from the valley of tears, and happily proceed on their road, going from virtue to virtue. *"O Lord, God of Hosts,"* who aboundest in power, strength, and virtue, *"hear my prayer,"* in which I ask you for the grace of going from virtue to virtue, and by such virtue to be strengthened in the interior man. *"Give ear, O God of Jacob,"* you that are the God of your faithful, the children of Jacob, hear one who is in spirit one of the children of Jacob.

9. He had already implored the divine assistance, on the grounds of God's power being boundless, and his being most concerned for the welfare of his people; he now repeats the prayer in a different form, but with greater emphasis. Instead of *"God of Hosts,"* he now calls him *"our protector,"* or, as it is in the Hebrew, *"our shield,"* indicating that God is all powerful to protect his people, and that he is like a shield to defend them. Instead of *"hear my prayer,"* he says here, *"behold,"* as much as to say, not only hear me, but look on me, and see the dangers by which I am surrounded. In the previous verse he said, *"Give ear, O God of Jacob;"* for which he now says, *"Look on the face of thy Christ,"* look on the true Prince of your people, the Messias, the Lamb without spot, who taketh away the sins of the world, and, for his sake, protect us. How could David thus refer to Christ, who was not then incarnate? He had not then, as *"Mediator of God and men, the man Christ Jesus, given himself a redemption for all,"* 1 Tim. 2. Christ's merits were before God from eternity, hence he is called in the Apocalypse, *"The Lamb slain from the beginning of the world,"* because, from the very beginning of the world, God granted many favors, especially spiritual ones, to his servants, through the previous merits of the passion of Christ. *"Who hath blessed us with all*

spiritual blessings in heavenly places in Christ, as he hath chosen us in him before the foundation of the world," Ephes. 1.

10. The holy soul, in his exile from God, in order to show that he did not ask for protection against the evils of this world, but against the temptations and spiritual dangers that beset us on our journey to the house of God, now adds, that such is the happiness of that heavenly country, that one day in it would be preferable to a thousand days elsewhere, and that he would prefer the last place in it, to the first in any other place; two reflections that cannot, if seriously considered, fail to produce the most lively affections in a pure heart. The word *"for"* assigns a reason for his having expressed with so much affection, *"Behold, O God, our protector,"* as if he said, I am so extremely anxious for your protection in this my journey to my country; for, should I fail in getting there, the loss would be too great, *"for better is one day"* in those heavenly courts, than days without end elsewhere. *"I have chosen to be an abject in the house of my God."* So sublime and grand is the everlasting house prepared for us in heaven, that I would prefer the last place in it, even at the very door of it, *"rather than to dwell in the tabernacles of sinners,"* in the palaces of the great, because while no iniquity will find a place in one house, it abounds in the other; and, when we compare all these grand mansions to the everlasting house of heaven, they may truly be called so many tents or tabernacles, without a sure foundation, without permanence, for these are not the tabernacles alluded to in the first verse of the Psalm, the Hebrew for both being quite different.

11. In this and the following verse the prophet consoles the just man in his journey up through the valley of tears, and longing for his true country; for he promises him grace and glory from God; grace through which he will be justified, and an advance in justice, as he ascends from virtue to virtue; and glory, through which he will be glorified, when he shall have arrived at mount Sion, where he shall behold God face to face, and no longer through faith; and he proves that God will give such grace and glory, because *"he loves mercy and truth."* For he that *"loves mercy"* shows mercy, and that mercy makes him confer grace; and he that loves truth, or, in other words, justice, will faithfully render what he has promised to those that love him.

12. He repeats his assertion, but restricts the promise of grace and glory to those who tread the path of innocence; as if he said, God, who abounds in mercy and justice, will not deprive those who, once justified, tread the path of innocence, and who persevere and advance in faith, hope, and charity, of those blessings of grace and glory which alone deserve the name of blessings. If they do not, if they retrograde and tread the path of iniquity, they will fall from grace, and come to confusion instead of glory. He concludes the Psalm by turning to God, saying, *"Lord of hosts,"* of armies, *"blessed is* the man who trusteth in thee," with that true, solid confidence that usually springs from true faith and a good conscience.

PSALM 84

The coming of Christ to bring peace and salvation to man.

1 Lord, thou hast blessed thy land: thou hast turned away the captivity of Jacob.
2 Thou hast forgiven the iniquity of thy people: thou hast covered all their sins.
3 Thou hast mitigated all thy anger: thou hast turned away from the wrath of thy indignation.
4 Convert us, O God our saviour: and turn off thy anger from us.
5 Wilt thou be angry with us for ever: or wilt thou extend thy wrath from generation to generation?
6 Thou wilt turn, O God, and bring us to life: and thy people shall rejoice in thee.
7 shew us, O Lord, thy mercy; and grant us thy salvation.
8 I will hear what the Lord God will speak in me: for he will speak peace unto his people: And unto his saints: and unto them that are converted to the heart.
9 Surely his salvation is near to them that fear him: that glory may dwell in our land.
10 Mercy and truth have met each other: justice and peace have kissed.
11 Truth is sprung out of the earth: and justice hath looked down from heaven.
12 For the Lord will give goodness: and our earth shall yield her fruit.
13 Justice shall walk before him: and shall set his steps in the way.

Explanation of the psalm

1. The prophet, through the inspiration of the Holy Ghost, discloses the eternal decree of God regarding the future salvation of man, in the beginning of the Psalm, telling us the first cause and ultimate effect of such salvation. Love was the first cause—that love through which God loved mankind. For no reason can be assigned why *"God so loved the world as to give his only begotten Son,"* John 3, through whom we may be redeemed, *"and blessed with all spiritual blessings,"* Ephes. 1, but the will of God alone, or, rather, his good pleasure and mercy. The ultimate effect of such salvation will consist in complete delivery from captivity, which will be thoroughly accomplished in the resurrection only, when we shall arrive at the liberty of the glory of the children of God. We are at present only partially free; but we are in expectation of the redemption of our bodies that is to set us free from all corruption and necessity. He, therefore, begins by saying, *"Lord, thou hast blessed thy land;"* you cursed the land you created and gave to man to inhabit, on account of the sin of the first man; but I know, from revelation, that you also, in your own mind, by your own decree, *"blessed thy land;"* decreed in your own good pleasure to visit and bless it with all manner of blessings and graces, by sending your only begotten, *"full of grace and truth,"* into that land which you created. *"Thou hast turned away the captivity of Jacob."* In the same eternal decree, having been appeased by the death of your Son, which you foresaw, thou hast turned away, or put an end to the captivity of Jacob, your people, so that they may thenceforth enjoy the liberty of the glory of the children of God. By Jacob the prophet means, not only the people of Israel, but the whole human race, *"who are, like the branches of the wild olive tree, engrafted into the good olive tree;"* and, like *"living stones, built upon the foundation of the Apostles and prophets."*

2. He now explains the manner in which God, by his blessing the land, put an end to the captivity of Jacob, and says it was by remitting the sins of his people. For, as sin was the cause of their being held in bondage, the remission of the sin procured their liberty. *"Thou hast forgiven the iniquity of thy people."* In your own mind, and by your own decree, thou hast forgiven the iniquity of thy people, for which iniquity you had given them up to the devil, as you would to the minister of justice. *"Thou hast covered all their sins;"* the same idea repeated; *"thou hast covered;"* hidden them, wrapt them up, so that you may not see and punish them: but, as nothing can be hid or concealed from God, when he, therefore, forgives sin, he extinguishes it altogether; so that it has no longer any existence whatever; and when God is said to cover sin, he does so, not as one would cover a sore with a plaster, thereby merely hiding it only; but he covers it with a plaster that effectually cures and removes it altogether. *"All their sins;"* to show it was not one sin, such as original sin, common to all, that was forgiven, but that the personal and peculiar sins of each individual were included.

3. He now assigns a reason for God's having forgiven the iniquity of his people, and says it arose from his having been appeased, and having laid aside his anger. For, as it was anger that prompted God thus to revenge himself, so, when he was appeased, he was led to forgive us; and that was effected *"by the lamb that was slain from the beginning of the world;"* and that immaculate Lamb was given to us through the good pleasure and mercy of him *"who so loved the world as to give his only begotten Son for it."* Here, then, is the order of our redemption. The benediction, or the good pleasure of God, gave us his Son as a Savior; the son, by his death, appeased God's anger, and made satisfaction to his justice for the sins of the whole world; God, having been thus appeased, forgave the sins, and the remission of the sins put an end to the captivity; and the Holy Ghost revealed the whole of this mystery, so concealed in the mind of God, to his prophet; and he describes it to us in those three verses. The expression, *"all thy anger,"* signifies that the redemption effected by our Savior was all sufficient and most effectual, and it also conveys that the liberty we shall enjoy hereafter will be most full, complete,

and entire, leaving not a trace of punishment or misery, for such proceed from God's anger. *"Thou hast turned away from the wrath of thy indignation,"* is a repetition of the same idea.

4. The prophet, speaking in the person of God's people, begins now to pray for the execution and completion of the divine decree, and first begs of God to mitigate his anger; the first effect of which would be the beginning of our salvation; that is to say, his divine assistance, through which our conversion to God commences; for we cannot be converted to God, unless his grace go before us, and by calling, enlightening, assisting, and moving, convert us. He, therefore, says, *"Convert us, O God our Savior."* O God our Savior, begin the work of our salvation, by inspiring us with the holy desire of conversion. And that, in your mercy, you may commence it, *"turn off thy anger from us."* Be reconciled to us, and forget the offences that have estranged us from you.

5. He perseveres in the petition, saying, we have borne your anger long enough; do not defer the gift of your mercy, and the restoration of your peace. *"Wilt thou be angry with us?"* Will your enmity to the human race be everlasting? *"or wilt thou extend thy wrath from generation to generation?"* a thing that does not accord with your infinite clemency.

6. He tells us the effects that will follow from being reconciled with God; to man will come life, to God praise. *"Thou wilt turn, O God;"* by laying aside your anger, and on being reconciled, will *"bring us to life;"* for *"the wages of sin is death; but the grace of God everlasting life, in Christ Jesus our Lord;" "and thy people,"* come to life and strength through so great a favor, *"shall rejoice in thee,"* and joyously chant your praise.

7. Having asked that the divine wrath may be mitigated; and having asked for that reconciliation and regeneration that always accompanies remission of sin, he now asks for the coming of the Savior, through whom we were brought clearly to see and to behold God's kindness and mercy to us, of which the Apostle says, *"The grace of God hath appeared to all men;"* and again, *"the goodness and kindness of our Savior God appeared."* For who can for a moment doubt of the care that God has for mankind, and the extent of his warmest love, when he sent his only begotten Son to redeem us by his precious blood from the captivity of the devil? *"Show us, O Lord, thy mercy;"* make us plainly see and feel by experience, that mercy through which you determined in your mind, from eternity, to bless thy land; *"and grant us thy salvation."* Send us your Son for a Savior, for then you will clearly show unto all the extent of your mercy, goodness, and grace. St. Augustine, taking a moral view of this passage, says that God shows us his mercy when he persuades us, and makes us see and understand that we are nothing, and can do nothing, of ourselves; but that it is through his mercy we exist at all, or

can do anything we go through; we thus are neither proud nor puffed up, but are humble in our own eyes; and it is to such people the Savior gives his grace.

8. To convince us of the truth of what he now means to express, the prophet here reminds us that he speaks not from himself, but what has been revealed to him, and that he is only announcing what he has heard from the Lord. *"I will hear what the Lord God will speak in me;"* that is, I will tell whatever I shall hear; and, therefore, having laid my petition before him, I will hear his answer to make it known to others. *"What he will speak in me;"* to give us to understand that when God speaks to the prophet, he does it interiorly, and spiritually. For the Holy Ghost, who abides in the prophets, speaks to them through their heart, and then, through their tongues, to the ears of mankind. The expression, *"I will hear,"* besides attention, signifies a desire to hear as it were, to say, I will most willingly and attentively hear; for God usually says nothing but what is good and useful; *"for he will speak peace unto his people."* The reason I have for hearing him with pleasure and with attention is, because I know he will speak peace to his people. The summary, then, of God's message to his people is the announcement and promise of peace through the coming of the Messias, for which the prophet asked when he said, *"Show us, O Lord, thy mercy, and grant us thy salvation."* God, then, will grant a Savior, and through him, will announce and establish a most perfect peace; hence he is styled *"the Prince of Peace;"* and, as the Apostle says, *"making peace through the blood of his cross, both as to the things that are on earth and the things that are in heaven."* Now peace comprehends all God's favors; and we shall never be in perfect possession of it until we shall have arrived at the heavenly Jerusalem, which is interpreted the vision of peace. Peace is opposed to war, in which we shall be mixed up, until *"death is swallowed up in victory, and this mortal shall have put on immortality."* Then there will be an end to that war with our vices and concupiscences, with the princes of darkness, with all our difficulties and necessities. For, while we live here below, *"the life of man is a warfare upon earth,"* however we may desire, as far as in ourselves lies, to be at peace with all men. *"And unto his saints, and unto them that are converted to the heart.* He now explains the expression, *"to his people;"* God promised peace to his people, but not to the whole of them; for they are composed of good and bad, and the bad can have no peace. For, *"much peace have they that love thy law;"* while, *"the wicked have no peace, saith the Lord;"* and, when he says, *"unto them that are converted to the heart,"* he tells us who the saints are to whom peace is promised. For sanctity, and consequently peace, then begins when man turns from exterior to interior matters; and, therefore, Isaias says, *"Return ye transgressors to the heart;"* and of the prodigal son is

said, *"and returning to himself, he said."* Man begins to return to himself, or to return, if you will, to his heart, when he begins to reflect within himself on the vanity of all things here below, and how trifling and how short lived is the pleasure to be derived from sin; and on the contrary, how noble virtue is, and of what value are the goods of eternity. In a little while man begins to advance by degrees, when he comes to consider and judge of externals, not by the aid of his own sense, or the discourses of the children of the world; but, *"returning to his heart,"* he consults sound reason on everything, consults the faith that has been divinely inspired, consults the truth itself, which is God. Finally, that man is truly converted to the heart, and begins to taste that peace *"that surpasses all understanding,"* who raises a tabernacle in his heart to God, and, on the wings of contemplation, rises from the image, the soul of man, to the reality, God himself; and there, beholding the infinite beauty of his Creator, is so inflamed and carried away by his love as to despise the whole world beside, and unite himself to God exclusively in the bonds of love, totally indifferent to, and forgetful of, the whole world. No pressure from abroad can disturb one so disposed.

9. On the coming of the Messias peace will be preached, but the establishment will be delayed for some time. However, salvation, which means the power of healing and of performing other miracles, will be always at hand, and available to those who believe in him, and have a pious and reverential fear of him. Hence, great glory will accrue to God, for all who see his wonderful works will praise and magnify him; many proofs of which can be read in the Gospels; and it is to it the prophet alludes when he says, *"Surely his salvation is near to them that fear him;"* that is to say, the salvation of God, or Christ himself, the Savior, will be at hand to save, through his power, all that fear him; all that worship him with a holy fear; *"that glory may dwell in our land;"* those numerous miracles will be performed with a view to make God's glory known, and to dwell in that land of promise to which the Savior will be sent specially. And if the salvation of the body be near to them that fear him, and God's glory be thereby greatly augmented, with much more reason will the salvation of the soul be near to those that fear him. *"For to those who will receive him, he will give power to become sons of God,"* 1 John; and thence his glory will be made manifest, *"as the only begotten of the Father, full of grace and truth."*

10. He now reveals another mystery that will be accomplished on the coming of the Messias; that is, the union of mercy and justice, which seem so opposed to each other; the one prompting to punish, the other to forgive; for Christ's passion and suffering was meant to deliver the human race in mercy, while it made the fullest satisfaction to the divine justice. *"Mercy and truth have met each other."* They met in the time of the Messias, whereas at

other times they seemed to move in contrary directions. *"Justice and peace have kissed;"* the justice that inflicts punishment, previously called truth and peace, which then was called mercy, will be joined in the bonds of the strictest friendship; and, as it were, kissed each other.

11. He now touches on the mystery of the Incarnation, making use of the past for the future tense, as is usual with the prophets. *"Truth is sprung out of the earth."* Christ, who is the truth, will be born of the Virgin Mary, *"and justice hath looked down from heaven."* Then also justice from heaven will be made manifest, because, on the birth of Christ, true justice began to come down from heaven, and man began to be justified by faith in Christ; as also, because by the coming of Christ, *"The wrath of God is revealed from heaven against all impiety and injustice,"* for the extent of God's anger and hatred of sin would never have been thoroughly known, had not God decreed that it should be expiated by the death of his only Son; and, even, we should never have known the extent of God's anger to the sinner on the day of judgment, had we not seen the amount and the extent of Christ's sufferings in atoning for the sins of others, *"For if in the green wood they do these things, what shall be done in the dry?"* says our Lord, Luke 23.

12. He still treats of the mystery of the Incarnation, showing that truth could spring out of the earth; not in the manner of the seed that we sow and cultivate, but in the manner of the natural flowers that grow spontaneously, with no other culture than the beams of the sun, and the rains of heaven. *"For the Lord will give goodness,"* he will send his Holy Spirit from heaven, who will overshadow a virgin, and thus our land, which was never ploughed nor sown, and was altogether an untouched virgin, will yield her fruit. Hence, he says, in the canticle of canticles, *"I am the flower of the field, and the lily of the valleys."*

13. The prophet concludes by showing that Christ would be so replete with justice and sanctity, that the rays of his justice would go before him, and by their light shed the way to complete progress in this gloomy valley of our mortality. *"Justice shall walk before him."* Christ, the sun and true light of the world, will send the rays of his justice and wisdom before him, as it is in Psalm 88, *"Mercy and truth shall go before thy face;"* and in Isaias 58, *"And thy justice shall go before thy face;"* and thus *"shall set his steps in the way,"* shall enter on his pilgrimage to bring many pilgrims back to their country.

PSALM 85

A prayer for God's grace to assist us to the end.

1 Incline thy ear, O Lord, and hear me: for I am needy and poor.

2 Preserve my soul, for I am holy: save thy servant, O my God, that trusteth in thee.

3 Have mercy on me, O Lord, for I have cried to thee all the day.
4 Give joy to the soul of thy servant, for to thee, O Lord, I have lifted up my soul.
5 For thou, O Lord, art sweet and mild: and plenteous in mercy to all that call upon thee.
6 Give ear, O Lord, to my prayer: and attend to the voice of my petition.
7 I have called upon thee in the day of my trouble: because thou hast heard me.
8 There is none among the gods like unto thee, O Lord: and there is none according to thy works.
9 All the nations thou hast made shall come and adore before thee, O Lord: and they shall glorify thy name.
10 For thou art great and dost wonderful things: thou art God alone.
11 Conduct me, O Lord, in thy way, and I will walk in thy truth: let my heart rejoice that it may fear thy name.
12 I will praise thee, O Lord my God: with my whole heart, and I will glorify thy name for ever:
13 For thy mercy is great towards me: and thou hast delivered my soul out of the lower hell.
14 God, the wicked are risen up against me, and the assembly of the mighty have sought my soul: and they have not set thee before their eyes.
15 And thou, O Lord, art a God of compassion, and merciful, patient, and of much mercy, and true.
16 look upon me, and have mercy on me: give thy command to thy servant, and save the son of thy handmaid.
17 Shew me a token for good: that they who hate me may see, and be confounded, because thou, O Lord, hast helped me and hast comforted me.

Explanation of the Psalm

1. He begins his prayer by touching on God's greatness and his own poverty, an excellent form of prayer, and calculated to get what we want; for, "*the prayer of him that humbleth himself shall pierce the clouds,*" Eccli. 35. "*Incline thy ear,*" for you sit so high, you have need to do so, in order to hear me, who lie so low, "*for I am needy and poor.*" As I am the beggar sitting at the rich man's gate, incline thy ear to your poor servant, and hear him. By the poor and the needy he means the person, who, though he may abound in the riches of the world, still does not put his trust in them, takes no pride in them, does not despise others, but rather despises the wealth itself; and does not look upon himself one bit better or greater than those who are not possessed of such wealth. St. Augustine very properly remarks, that Lazarus was not taken up into Abraham's bosom by reason of his poverty, but on account of his humility; nor was the rich glutton hurried in hell for his riches, but for his pride. Had such been the case, Abraham too, who abounded in riches, would have been buried in hell. But, as Abraham looked upon himself, and called himself *"dust and ashes,"* Gen. 18, and observed the commandments of God so faithfuly, that he was most ready to sacrifice, not only all his wealth, but even his only son for whom he had it in store, at the command of God, he was, therefore, not only himself brought to the place of rest after his death, but in his bosom were gathered together all who then died in the Lord. David, too, abounded in the riches of this world; but, as he took no pride in them, set no value on them, but depended entirely on God, in whom he had placed his entire hope, his strength, and his riches, and without whom he knew he was nothing, and could do nothing; he, therefore, with great truth, proclaimed himself really poor and needy.

2. He tells in what respect he wishes to be heard, and first proposes what is really uppermost in his mind, and which the Lord himself directed should be sought for in preference to everything, and that is, *"Seek first the kingdom of God and his justice, and all these things shall be added unto you." "Preserve my soul,"* that so many enemies lie in wait for, in this my exile, *"for I am holy."* I ask for the safety of my soul, because I got it from you, and you have justified me who was dead in sin, through the blood of your Son, and you have sanctified me, and enlivened me. For, as St. Augustine says, when one feels a confidence that he has been justified through the sacraments, and calls himself holy, through the grace of God; such is not to be looked upon as the pride of a vain man, but the confession of one who is not ungrateful; but if one cannot venture to say, I am justified and cleansed, he can at least say, *"I am holy;"* that is, I am one of the faithful, a professor of our holy faith and religion, dedicated and consecrated to God through baptism. *"Save thy servant, O my God, that trusteth in thee."* A repetition of the preceding. The reason he wishes his soul to be saved is, that he may not lose life everlasting. St. Peter, in his first Epistle, uses similar language, when he says, *"Who, by the power of God are kept by faith unto salvation, ready to be revealed in the last time."* He asks, then, for life everlasting, for fear of losing which, he asks for the safety of his soul, assigning a reason, when he says, *"thy servant that trusteth in thee;"* because, when God saves his servant, he saves what belongs to himself; and, when he saves him that trusts in him, he shows himself to be just and faithful, in carrying out what he promised.

3-4. He had asked, in the second verse, for supreme happiness; that is, the salvation of his soul, the object of all his desires; and he now most properly asks for the means of arriving at such an end, namely, that interior joy that manfully bears up against the temptations and the dangers of this our exile, until it comes to that harbor of safety, where there will be no temptations, no dangers. *"Have mercy on me, O Lord."* In mercy hear my prayer, *"for I hare cried to thee all the day;"* I have put up my prayers with the greatest fervor and perseverance, for nothing is more necessary in prayer than great fervor, which the expression, *"I have cried,"* implies, and with perseverance, which the words, *"all the day,"* convey. Here is the petition, which, in mercy, he asked should be listened to, and for which he cried the whole day, *"Give joy to the soul of thy servant."* I am hemmed in on all sides by temptations, nothing but what is bitter presents itself to me in this valley of tears, while my very prosperity terrifies me as much as my adversity saddens me; therefore, *"Give joy to the soul of thy servant, for to thee, O Lord, I have lifted up my soul."* As I have not found rest in anything created, I have raised up my soul on the wings of thought and desire to thee my Creator. Love bears one's soul up; and it has been truly said, that the soul is more where it loves, than where it actually is. Thought and desire are the wings of love; for he that loves is borne on to, and abides in, what he loves, by thinking constantly on, and longing for, the object of his love. Whoever truly, and from his heart, loves God, by thinking on him and longing for him, lifts up his soul to God; while, on the contrary, whoever loves the earth, by thinking on and coveting the things of the earth, lets his soul down to its level. Thus he alone, with the prophet, can truly say, *"To thee, O Lord, I have lifted up my soul,"* and can with justice ask for consolation, saying, *"Give joy to the soul of thy servant,"* who has no inordinate affection for anything created, and is in no way stuck in the mud of this world.

5. A reason assigned for having raised up his soul to God in order to obtain consolation; because *"God is sweet and mild;"* and as St. John says, *"God is light, and in him there is no darkness."* So we can say God is sweet, and in him there is no bitterness; whereas in the consolations of this world there is an abundance of bitterness with little or no sweetness And not only is God sweet, but he is also mild, offering no repulse to those who approach him, and bearing with our imperfections. St. Augustine observes that God's mildness is most remarkable in bearing with us when we pray; when, during our prayers, we divert our attention to so many different subjects. The judge would hardly have patience with the culprit who, while laying his petition before the court, would turn about to talk with his friends, especially on matters of no moment. And not only is God sweet and mild in himself, inasmuch as he repels no one approaching the fountain of his sweetness; but he is also *"plenteous in mercy,"* for he freely admits and receives, and offers himself to be tasted of by all that call upon him, having no regard to rich or poor, Jew or gentile *"For whosoever shall call upon the name of the Lord shall be saved."* If he sometimes does not hear or have mercy on those who pray to him, the reason is because they do not really call upon him, or do not call upon him as they ought. He very often hears us, but at the fitting time; and he very often hears the wish of him who prays, instead of the words he

utters; for instance, when the petitioner asks a thing quite unsuited to him, and which he would not have asked had he known it to be so.

6. A repetition of the first part of the first verse, in different language, in order to express his great desire for what he asks.

7. This verse would seem to have been introduced as an explanation of the preceding. He said therein, *"give ear, O Lord, to my prayer,"* and God may fairly have asked him, When did you pray? When will you have me give ear to your prayer? The prophet answers, I have prayed every day, and I will pray every day while I stray about in this exile. Every day of my exile is a day of trouble, for he who loves his country cannot but loathe his exile. *"In the day of my trouble;"* during the whole time of my exile, I found nought but trouble and sorrow; and therefore I have always *"called upon thee,"* and with so much confidence, *"because thou hast heard me."*

8. He assigns a reason for flying to God alone, for invoking him, and for seeking to lift up his soul to him, because there is no one, not only among men, but even among gods, like God; either in essence or in power, or in wisdom, or in goodness. If by the word *"gods"* we understand false gods, idols, and demons, of which it is said in Psalm 95, *"All the gods of the gentiles are devils;"* then, what he says here is absolutely true; for idols have eyes and do not see, and depend on man both for motion and protection; but the true God sees without corporeal eyes, depends on no one, but all things depend on him; *"For in him we live, move, and have our being."* The demons, it is true, were made to God's image, but they lost it by sin. *"And there is none according to thy works."* Not only is there no god like unto thee, O Lord, but none of them have produced any one work equal to any of yours; for God made the heavens, and the earth, and everything in them, from nothing; other gods only work from the matter which our God created.

9. From this verse we learn that, in the preceding one, he referred to the false gods, who were adored by the sinners as true and supreme gods; for the prophet proves that none of those gods are like our God, that their worship will one day cease, and their falsity and vanity be made perfectly clear; while the worship of our God will be everlasting, a fact partly accomplished in the Church of Christ, and fully so on the day of judgment. For, though in the days of David there were gods of the Moabites, of the Ammonites, of the Philistines, and of various nations, still, on the promulgation of the Gospel of Christ, idolatry began to disappear, and the worship of the true God to be introduced among all nations. Thus, *"all the nations shall come;"* that is, they came from all nations, and, after abandoning their false gods, they adored the true one; but, on the day of judgment, all men, without any exception, shall know that the gods of the gentiles were demons, or empty images, and, whether they will or will not, shall bow the knee before the

Lord, fulfilling the prophecy of Isaias *"For every knee shall be bowed to me,"* a text applied by St. Paul, Rom. 14, and Phil. 2, to Christ as the true God. *"And they shall glorify thy name;"* but in a different manner; the just will from love, and with pleasure; but the wicked will through fear, and against their will, glorify the Lord on the day of judgment, and will say, *"Thou, art just, O Lord, and righteous is thy judgment."*

10. The reason why the worship of false gods will cease, and all nations will adore and glorify the Lord is, *"for he is God alone,"* truly great, *"and does wonderful things,"* that nobody else can do; a thing that will be well known on the day of judgment, especially when, at his nod, all the dead shall arise, and be gathered before the tribunal of Christ, when, without the slightest resistance or opposition, the just shall be exalted to their kingdom, and the wicked shoved down to everlasting punishment. Hence the Apostle, when speaking of said judgment, uses the expression, *"of the great God,"* for it is in the last judgment that his greatness is most clearly exhibited, *"waiting for the blessed hope and coming of the glory of the great God, and our Savior Jesus Christ."*

11. For fear of straying from the path that leads to his country, he has again recourse to prayer, in which he asks for guidance in this his wandering and his exile, and at the same time, asks for spiritual help and succour, for fear he may faint on the way. *"Conduct me, O Lord, in thy way."* Show one the way, through the assistance of your grace, not only by enlightening my mind, but by moving my will; and thus, *"I will walk in thy truth,"* according to the truth of your law and of your faith. *"Let my heart rejoice;"* he asked in the third verse *"that his soul should have joy;"* let it, then, rejoice when you gladden and console my heart, *"that it may fear thy name;"* I do not seek consolation for consolation's sake, but in order that, being refreshed by it as if with food, I may persevere in thy holy fear. By fearing to offend you I will be sure to proceed in the direct road of your commandments, to that country where I will serve you without any fear.

12. To prayer he adds thanksgiving, for nothing tends more to obtain fresh favors than to appear mindful on and grateful for, the past. *"I will praise thee, O Lord, my God;"* I will render you the tribute of praise and thanksgiving, *"with my whole heart,"* with the full tide of my affections. *"And I will glorify thy name;"* that is, thy power, *"forever,"* while I live, incessantly.

13. The favor for which he returns thanks is, that God, in his great mercy, and not through the merits of the supplicant, should have delivered his soul from the lowest hell; that is, should have justified him from the sins that would have carried him to hell, had he not been delivered through grace. And, in truth, the mercy of God, which converts the sinner into a just man, is as great as the punishment of eternal fire from which we are saved, or the everlasting happiness to which we get a right and free access. Hence St. Peter says, *"Who, according to his great mercy, hath regenerated us unto a lively hope."* Various explanations are offered of the words, *"lowest hell."* We adopt that of Saints Augustine, Jerome, and Bernard, who say it means that part of hell where no one praises the Lord, and from which there is no egress.

14. Having returned thanks, he comes again to pray, asking to be delivered from the multitude of the enemies that sought his life; and though some make him allude to his corporal enemies, or to those of Ezechias, some will have him allude to the enemies of Christ, who caused his death; the explanation of St. Augustine is more in accordance with the rest of the Psalm; and he says it is to be understood of the members of Christ's body of the just, or any person suffering persecution from their spiritual enemies, be they heretics or schismatics, or bad Christians. The man of God, then, delivered through the grace of Christ from the lower hell, fighting in the meantime with his spiritual enemies, in heavy groans exclaims, O my God, *"behold the wicked are risen up against me;"* neither few in number, nor weak in strength, but *"an assembly of the mighty;"* a great congregation of most powerful enemies *"have sought my soul"* to destroy it; and in their blindness and obduracy *"have not set thee before their eyes;"* have not considered that you are the protector of the just, and they presume to wage war, not with weak mortals, but with the Lord God of armies.

15. Having mentioned the quantity and the quality of his enemies, he now asks for help against them, and in various terms proclaims God's goodness, to show he was not rash in hoping for assistance from so good a God. He is a God of compassion, which in Hebrew signifies the regard a parent has for his child. *"Merciful,"* which means a bestower of grace, or the making one acceptable, as St. Paul says, *"by which he made us acceptable through his beloved Son;"* that is, made us acceptable to him or received us into grace. *"Patient,"* the word in Hebrew signifies long nosed, not easily provoked to anger, for with the Hebrews a long nose was looked upon as a sign of much patience; *"and of much mercy,"* abounding in mercy, *"and true,"* or faithful. Hence we learn that God loves us with the affection of a father, and, therefore, most ready to forgive, most slow to be provoked, liberal, and ready to promise in his mercy, and faithful to carry out such promises; all of which afford incalculable consolation and confidence to pious souls, who, from their heart, attach themselves to God; for all this applies only to those who fear God, as is more clearly explained in Psalm 102. They who abuse God's goodness *"treasure up to themselves wrath against the day of wrath, and revelation of the just judgment of God,"* Rom. 2; to whom he says in Heb. 10, *"It is a dreadful thing to fall into the hands of the living God."*

16. Having explained God's goodness in so many terms, he now begs that he may have a share in it. *"O look on me"* with the eyes of your infinite goodness, and prodigal as you are of your mercies, *"have mercy on me."*—*"Give thy command to thy servant."* Grant that my numerous enemies may not prevail over me, but, on the contrary, give thy servant strength and power to subdue and command them, and thereby *"save the son of thy handmaid,"* whether from their secret snares or open persecutions.

17. He concludes by asking for some external sign that may let even his enemies see that God always consoles and assists his faithful servants. *"Show me a token for good;"* give me some sign that will assure me of something good, that is, of your grace and favor, *"that they who hate me may see,"* that my enemies may see it, be confounded, and despair of subduing me, *"because thou, O Lord, hast helped me and hast comforted me."* As you have really helped me in the combat, and by your interior grace consoled me in my trouble, show also some external sign of your favor, that my enemies, on seeing it, may be confounded. A question has been raised, what is the sign he asks for? St. Jerome says, it is the sign of the cross of Christ, for it is a token for good, it being the token of redemption, and when the evil spirits, who hate us, behold it, they are confounded. St. Augustine explains it of the sign that will appear on the last day, which will be for good to the elect, and on the sight of which all their enemies will be confounded. Others interpret it of the sign given by Isaias to king Achaz when he said to him, *"The Lord himself will give you a sign, behold, a virgin will conceive, and will bring forth a son."* That was truly a token for good to David, to have the Messias descended from him, and to the whole world that was to be delivered, through Christ, from all its enemies. Perhaps, the token for good means that spiritual joy, which he asked for in the beginning of the Psalm, when he said, *"Give joy to the soul of thy servant;"* for such joy to a holy soul in tribulation is the clearest sign of the grace of God, and on the sight of it, all manner of persecutors are confounded, and then the meaning would be, *"show me a token for good;"* give me the grace of that spiritual joy that will appear exteriorly in my countenance, *"that they who hate me may see"* such calmness and tranquillity of soul, *"and be confounded;"* for you, Lord, have helped me in the struggle, consoled me in my sorrow, and have already converted my sadness into interior joy and gladness.

PSALM 86

The glory of the Church of Christ.

1 *The foundations thereof are in the holy mountains.*
2 *The Lord loveth the gates of Sion above all the tabernacles of Jacob.*
3 *Glorious things are said of thee, O city of God.*

4 I will be mindful of Rahab and of Babylon knowing me. Behold the foreigners, and Tyre, and the people of the Ethiopians, these were there.
5 Shall not Sion say: This man and that man is born in her? and the Highest himself hath founded her.
6 The Lord shall tell in his writings of peoples and of princes, of them that have been in her.
7 The dwelling in thee is as it were of all rejoicing.

EXPLANATION OF THE PSALM

1. The prophet commences by praising the city, by reason of the holy mountains it has for a foundation. He names not the city, so wrapt in admiration is he with the beauty of the new city he sees descending from heaven, the Church of Christ, whose foundations may be considered in various lights. If we regard the first founders and propagators of the Christian religion, the foundations signify the twelve Apostles, as we read in Apoc. 21, *"And the wall of the city had twelve foundations, and in them the names of the twelve Apostles of the Lamb."* If we consider the doctrine on which the faith of the Church is founded, the foundations are the Apostles and the prophets, who were the immediate ministers of the word of God, of whom the Apostle says, *"Built upon the foundations of the Apostles and the prophets."* Finally, if we regard ecclesiastical power and authority, according to which the foundation in a house corresponds with the head in a body, Christ and Peter are the foundations, Christ being the primary. Of Christ the Apostle says, *"For no one can lay any other foundation but that which is laid, which is Christ Jesus;"* and of Peter, Christ himself says *"Thou art Peter, and upon this rock I will build my Church."* Those, then, are the holy mountains, upon which the city of God is built, getting the name of mountains by reason of their altitude and excellence; and holy, for their elevation is not by reason of their pride, but by reason of their sanctity, wisdom, and authority. The objection of Christ's being called the cornerstone surmounting the edifice, viz., *"The stone which the builders rejected, the same is become the head of the corner;"* and also, *"Jesus Christ himself being the chief cornerstone,"* is of no consequence, for there are two cornerstones, one in the foundation, the other in the summit of the building, and both connecting two walls; and though, in an ordinary building, the same stone cannot be in the foundation supporting the entire building, and on the top supported by the building; still, in the spiritual edifice, one and the same stone, that is, one and the same prelate, supports and bears the whole edifice by his authority, while, at the same time, he presides over and is borne, through obedience, by the whole edifice, by all the living stones, which two duties apply principally, to Christ, who is absolutely the head and ruler of the whole Church; and they also apply to the supreme pontiff, who is Christ's vicar on earth; and, to a certain extent, to all prelates, in regard of those over whom they preside, for all prelates should bear and be borne; bear with the infirmities of those over whom they are placed, and be borne with when they correct or command. The city has another subject of praise in its gates.

2. Having said that the city of God had holy mountains for its foundations, so that there was no fear of its falling, like buildings erected on sand; he now adds, that, with its being exempt from danger on that score, it also is incapable of being stormed by the enemy, so strongly are the gates of it fortified; Psalm 147 saying of them *"because he hath strengthened the bolts of thy gates."* *"The Lord loveth the gates of Sion,"* by reason of the strength of its gates, that render it impregnable *"above all the tabernacles of Jacob;"* loves those gates more than the tabernacles of Jacob; for, however beautiful and elegantly laid out those tabernacles may have been when the Jews were on their journey from Egypt to the land of promise, still they had neither gates nor foundations, and, therefore, were frail and temporary. These words refer to the stability and permanence of the Church, against which the gates of hell shall not prevail; and especially to the time when it shall arrive at its heavenly country, for which the patriarch sighed, and of whom the Apostle says, *"For he looked for a city that hath foundations, whose builder and maker is God;"* and, in the Apocalypse, the new Jerusalem is said to have *"twelve gates, and in the gates twelve Angels, and names written thereon, which are the names of the twelve tribes of the children of Israel."* By the twelve gates we understand the twelve Apostles; for it is through their true and sound preaching that we all enter into the Church of God: their being called the foundations in another place is of no moment, for they are gates and foundations together; gates by their preaching, foundations by their support of the faithful. Christ, to be sure, said, *"I am the gate;"* Christ is the gate, no doubt, because it is through his merits we all enter, and are saved; but the city has twelve gates and one gate, as well as it has one foundation and twelve foundations, for Christ was in the Apostles, and spoke through the Apostles, as St. Paul says, *"Do you seek a proof of Christ who speaketh in me?"* Thus, when we enter through the Apostles, we enter through Christ, because the Apostles did not preach up themselves, but through Christ, and Christ preached through them; and, when we are founded and built upon the Apostles, we are founded and built on Christ. The names of the twelve tribes of Israel being written on the gates signifies that the first members of the Church came from the children of Israel, to whom the Apostles themselves belonged; then came the fullness of the gentiles. In the Apocalypse, when mention is made of the elect, and of those to be saved, mention is first made of twelve thousand from each of the twelve tribes of the children of

Israel; and then follows *"a great multitude; which no man could number, of all nations and tribes, and peoples, and tongues."*

3. The prophet, as it were, intoxicated with the spirit, as he began abruptly by admiring the excellence of the city, saying, *"The foundations thereof are in the holy mountain,"* now just as abruptly changes his mode of speech and addresses the city itself, saying, *"Glorious things are said of thee, O city of God;"* as much as to say, Holy city, don't wonder if I began incoherently, for I am overwhelmed by the multitude of your praises; for the Holy Ghost has been telling me many glorious, grand, and wonderful things about you. And, in fact, who could observe any order in narrating the praises of a city where God will be all unto all, and where those blessings are reserved for the elect, *"which eye hath not seen, ear hath not heard, and which hath not entered into the heart of man to conceive."* And though, strictly speaking, the city of God in heaven, and, to a certain extent, his Church, spread over the earth, are alluded to here, even of that earthly Jerusalem, type, as it was, of the Church, *"glorious things are said."* It was a royal and sacerdotal city, the temple of the Lord, the Ark of the covenant, and many things belonging to both were there; and what is more, there it was that the King of Angels and the Lord of all nature gave his instructions, performed his miracles, effected the redemption of the human race, was buried there, sent the Holy Ghost from heaven there, and there laid the foundations of his Church to endure.

4. He now praises the holy city, by reason of the number and the variety of the nations who inhabit it, for it is not confined to the Jews alone, as was the case in the Old Testament; but all nations are to inhabit the Catholic Church, which is the true Jerusalem, so praised in this Psalm. He mentions Rahab and Babylon, Palestine, Tyre, and the Ethiopians, all gentiles, but well known to the Jews. Rahab means proud, and by it he means the Egyptians; and the meaning is, in calling and enrolling the elect of the new Jerusalem, I will bear in mind, not only the Jews, but even the Egyptians and Babylonians, who know me through faith and religious worship. For behold, the foreigners, the nations of Palestine, and the people of Tyre, and the Ethiopians *"were there,"* that is, those nations called and invited by me, will be there too; for he makes use, of the past tense, as usual, to signify the future.

5. The prophet now adds, as the chief praise of Sion, that the Highest, the Son of God, who founded her, was born in her. For the most glorious thing that could be said of her was, that he who, in his divine nature, founded her, chose, in his human nature, to be born in her. The text should be read thus, according to the Hebrew, *"Shall not this man say to Sion?"* Is it possible that any one will say to Sion a thing so wonderful and so unheard of, *"that a man is born in her; and the Highest himself hath founded her?"* will anyone

tell Sion that there is one born in her, her very Creator? This very evident prophecy has been carped at by the Jews, who cannot possibly get over it. Christ, however, was born in Bethlehem, and not in Sion; to which we reply, that the Sion spoken of here means the Church of God's people, and that Christ, as man, was born therein, while, as God, he is the founder of it. It may also be fairly said that Christ was born in Sion, inasmuch as his parents, Solomon and David, his ancestors, belonged to Sion.

6. He answers the question he put when he said, *"Will any one say to Sion?"* for he says the Lord himself will put the question; nay more, in order that it may be kept in eternal memory, that he will write it in the book in which are the people and the princes, who through regeneration have been in the city. *"The Lord shall tell;"* will announce that in Sion one has been born who is the very founder of the city of Sion; and he will tell it *"in his writings of peoples and of princes;"* in the rolls of those people and princes who have been regenerated in the city, for he who is the head of them all, is also the founder of the city; and will, therefore, be written in the head of the book. That book will be published on the day of judgment, for then the books will be opened with another book, the book of life, of which our Savior says, *"Rejoice because your names are written in heaven."* By princes we understand the Apostles whom God appointed princes over all the earth.

7. The conclusion of the Psalm, declaring the supreme happiness of all the inhabitants of that city, whose foundations were alluded to in the beginning of the Psalm; for the peculiar happiness of the holy city of Jerusalem is, that in it no poor, no sad, no miserable person is to be found, for *"God will wipe away every tear from their eyes;"* and though this is to be accomplished in the heavenly Jerusalem only, still in the Church militant, those who are enrolled citizens in heaven are all rejoicing in hope, and to them the Savior says, *"Nobody shall take your joy from you;"* and the Apostle, *"Always rejoicing;"* and in fact, if God's servants rejoice even in tribulation, when can they be sad? St. Augustine remarks that the Psalmist does not use the word *"rejoicing"* absolutely, but *"as it were of all rejoicing,"* lest we should suppose that the joy spoken of here was such as we see with the children of this world, who rejoice in the acquisition of gold or silver, or in carnal pleasures, or the like. The dwelling in the heavenly Jerusalem will be, to a certain extent, like a dwelling where a banquet or a wedding feast is celebrated with music, songs, and pleasure; but no such things will have a place there, nor will the cause be the same for such joy and gladness.

PSALM 87

A prayer of one under grievous affliction: it agrees to Christ in his Passion, and alludes to his death and burial.

1 Lord, the God of my salvation: I have cried in the day, and in the night before thee.
2 Let my prayer come in before thee: incline thy ear to my petition.
3 For my soul is filled with evils: and my life hath drawn nigh to hell.
4 I am counted among them that go down to the pit: I am become as a man without help,
5 Free among the dead. Like the slain sleeping in the sepulchres, whom thou rememberest no more: and they are cast off from thy hand.
6 They have laid me in the lower pit: in the dark places, and in the shadow of death.
7 Thy wrath is strong over me: and all thy waves thou hast brought in upon me.
8 Thou hast put away my acquaintance far from me: they have set me an abomination to themselves. I was delivered up, and came not forth:
9 My eyes languished through poverty. All the day I cried to thee, O Lord: I stretched out my hands to thee.
10 Wilt thou shew wonders to the dead? or shall physicians raise to life, and give praise to thee?
11 Shall any one in the sepulchre declare thy mercy: and thy truth in destruction?
12 Shall thy wonders be known in the dark; and thy justice in the land of forgetfulness?
13 But I, O Lord, have cried to thee: and in the morning my prayer shall prevent thee.
14 Lord, why castest thou off my prayer: why turnest thou away thy face from me?
15 I am poor, and in labours from my youth: and being exalted have been humbled and troubled.
16 Thy wrath hath come upon me: and thy terrors have troubled me.
17 They have come round about me like water all the day: they have compassed me about together.
18 Friend and neighbour thou hast put far from me: and my acquaintance, because of misery.

EXPLANATION OF THE PSALM

1. The prophet, speaking in the person of Christ, repeats and expresses in various terms what our Lord expressed when hanging on the cross, "My God, my God, why hast thou forsaken me?" in order to show the greatness of his sufferings. He, then, begins with a prayer to God the Father, saying, "O Lord, the God of my salvation," from whom, through a speedy resurrection, I hope for salvation. "I have cried in the day and in the night before thee." He did so on the day of his passion, when he cried on the cross, "My God, my God, *why hast thou forsaken me?"* and on the night before, when he thrice cried out in the garden, *"Father, if it be possible, let this cup pass from me."*

2. Hear my prayer, I beseech you. Such is the meaning of this verse, full of metaphorical language. *"Let my prayer come in before you;"* as an orator would be admitted to plead a cause. *"Incline thy ear to my petition."* Give a favorable audience to said orator when he shall have been admitted.

3. This refers to the time when our Savior exclaimed, *"My God, my God, why hast thou forsaken me?"* for, then, Christ's soul was evidently *"full of evils,"* by reason of the great pains all over his body, by reason of his feeling for his mother, who stood by; and then, especially, *"his life was drawn nigh to hell;"* for he was just about to die, and to go down to the hell where all the souls of the faithful were shut up.

4. Having mentioned the grievous bodily pains that brought him nigh unto death, he now alludes to the contempt and ignominy he suffered in man's opinion on his death; for they looked upon him as an ordinary mortal, who died reluctantly, who could in nowise help himself, and had nobody else to help him; whereas, though among the dead, he was not subject to death, nor to the captivity of the devil, and could die when he chose, and rise when he chose. *"I am counted among them that go down to the pit."* People thought that l had gone down to where the souls are, as all mortals have gone down, forcibly and against my will, and, therefore, looked upon me as no more than any other mortal. *"I am become,"* in the opinion of the world, *"as a man without help;"* for they insulted me, wagging their heads, and saying, *"He saved others, himself he cannot save."*

5. Death has dominion over all except myself, I alone am free, and nobody can put me to death against my will; as our Savior says, John 10, *"And I have power to lay my life down, and I have power to take it up again."* *"Like the slain."* He tells further what men thought about him. They looked upon him *"like the slain sleeping in the sepulchres;"* like so many who died of their wounds, and lay in their graves in the sleep of death." *"Whom thou rememberest no more;"* whom you, O Lord, care for no longer, as being no longer under your charge as human beings, which he repeats and explains by saying, *"And they are cast off from thy hand;"* you have forgotten them, and think no more of them, for they are cast off from your providential hand, as having no further existence.

6. My enemies, who put me to death, caused my soul to descend to the lower pit, while my body lay in the sepulchre, and the lower pit may be described as *"the dark places, and in the shadow of death."* See Psalm 22:4. hereon.

7. Speaking still in the person of Christ, he now makes use of two metaphors to explain the extent of his sufferings. *"Thy wrath is strong over me;"*

your anger at the sins of mankind, or rather the justice that prompted you to inflict condign punishment on the sinner, was not only poured out upon me, but was made strong and was increased upon me, never to lose hold of me until satisfaction to the last farthing should have been exacted. This is the first metaphor by which we are given to understand that the sufferings of our Lord were as intense as was the anger of Almighty God, by reason of the sins of the whole world. A serious matter for all of us who have been redeemed to reflect on; *"and all thy waves thou hast brought in upon me."* Another metaphor, in which the passion of our Lord is compared to all the billows of the sea tumbling in upon, overwhelming, and dashing on the rock, one unfortunate creature struggling in the sea. For as our Lord Jesus Christ had undertaken to wipe away the sins of the whole world, it was not one or two tides of sorrow he had to bear up against, but a universal inundation of the sins of mankind.

8. In addition to his sufferings came the aversion of his acquaintance, and by acquaintance we are to understand all who knew him through his conversation and his teaching, but did not believe him to be either God or the Messias, of whom it is said in John, *"He came unto his own and has own received him not." "Thou hast put away my acquaintance far from me,"* allowed those who knew me to shun and avoid me; they have set me an abomination to themselves," they not only held back from me as if they did not know me, but they even execrated me as a deceiver, as a Samaritan, as one possessed by a devil, as a friend of publicans and sinners, all of which we read in the Gospels. This verse may also be applied to his disciples, who may be called his acquaintance; for St. Luke says, chap. 23, *"And all his acquaintance stood afar off;"* and in St. Mat. 26, *"And all the disciples leaving him, fled away." "They have set me an abomination to themselves,"* was accomplished in Peter, *"who began to curse and swear that he knew not the man;"* for, though St. Peter in reality had no such hatred of Christ in his heart, he professed it, however, when he swore so vehemently that he had no knowledge of him. Even his disciples, before they understood the mystery of his passion, and when they looked upon it as fraught with evil to him and to themselves, considered it an abomination; hence they said to him, *"Rabbi, the Jews but just now sought to stone thee, and goest thou thither again?"* And when St. Peter heard of his intended passion, he too looked upon it as an abomination, saying, *"Lord, be it far from thee; this shall not be unto thee." "I was delivered up, and came not forth."* I was like one shut up in a prison, without the power of leaving it until I should have suffered what had been decreed by you.

9. The abundance of tears shed by me weakened and impoverished my eyes. *"All the day I cried to thee,"* a repetition of the first verse, which is explained more fully by St. Paul, when he says, Heb. 5, *"Who in the days of his flesh, offering up prayers and supplications with a strong cry and tears to him that was able to save him from death, was heard for his reverence."* He is said to have cried out *"all the day,"* because it is explained in the first verse, he cried out both by day and by night; for as the natural day is composed of night and day, so both parts of it may be termed the whole day, though each part may not be entire. *"I stretched out my hands to thee"* in prayer; or, perhaps, on the cross, that by such an oblation I may obtain a speedy resurrection for myself, and freedom from death everlasting, for my mystical body, the Church.

10-12. Speaking still in the person of Christ, he assigns a reason for having asked to be saved from death. These three verses are differently explained. They may be referred to that everlasting death which Christ wished to avert from his faithful; for a reason is assigned why he prays, and wishes for the aversion of such an evil, because God does not, nor ought he, show his wonders to the damned; neither ought they rise to life everlasting, nor will they relate with praise the mercy and truth of God; and, finally, they not only will not declare them, but they will not even know them. An objection to this explanation is, the introduction of sepulchres and physicians; sepulchres seem connected with dead bodies, and not with damned souls; and physicians have more connection with the body than with the soul. Another explanation refers these verses to the death of the body, which Christ for himself and for his faithful disciples deprecates, while he prays for, and wishes a speedy resurrection for himself and for them; and then the meaning would be, *"Wilt thou show wonders to the dead?"* I fear death, I desire to live, or that my life may be quickly restored to me and to my faithful; for, the dead, devoid of life or feeling, would in vain behold your wonderful works, that tend so much to your glory, and for which you should so deservedly be thanked, honored, and praised. *"Or shall physicians arise to life, and give praise to thee?"* the dead are not only devoid of life and feeling, but even all the art and skill of medicine will not raise them or give them life and feeling to render you the tribute of praise. *"Shall any one in the sepulchre declare thy mercy; and thy truth in destruction?"* You do not show your wonders to the dead, because they are lying inanimate in their sepulchres, they cannot appreciate them, and therefore, you do not declare your mercy to them, or your wonders, the works of your mercy and your truth. *"In destruction,"* signifies here, the losing one's life, and therefore, it is synonymous with lying in the sepulchre, where alone lie the dead. *"Shall thy wonders be known in the dark, and thy justice in the land of forgetfulness;"* The dead in their sepulchres will not declare your mercy or relate your wonderful things, because they know them not; nor can they know them for they live in the darkness of death, and in the land of forgetfulness, where there is no memory of the past, and consequently no sense of the present. This exclamation is confirmed by the words of king Ezechias, who certainly asked for life in this world, when he said, Isaias 38, *"For hell shall not confess to thee; neither shall death praise thee, the living, the living shall give praise to thee, as I do this day."* We have a similar passage in Psalm 113, *"The dead shall not praise thee, O Lord, nor any of them that go down to hell, but we that live bless the Lord."*

13-14. He now shows that the passion of Christ was so decided on by a divine decree, that it could not be changed; and explains at greater length the brief exclamation of our Savior on the cross, *"My God, why hast thou forsaken me?" "But I, Lord, have cried to thee,"* that the chalice of my passion may pass from me; *"and in the morning my prayer shall prevent thee;"* early enough, in the very morning or beginning of my passion, my prayer shall prevent or anticipate thee; for, though Christ's prayer in the garden was offered in the night, still, that night was the morning or the beginning of his passion. *"Why casteth thou off my prayer?"* Why don't you hear me? Why don't you cause this chalice to pass from me? *"Why turnest thou away thy face from me?"* Why do you turn away from me as if I were a stranger? Why do you abandon me? He makes use of all these expressions to give us some idea of the enormity of the sufferings, so repugnant to his human nature; for, absolutely speaking, the Lord wished for and chose such sufferings as a remedy for the sins of mankind; and the Father always heard him in what he wished and asked for.

15. For fear it may be supposed that the passion of Christ lasted only for three hours, or for one day, the Holy Ghost reveals here that his passion was constant during the whole period of his life. For, to say nothing of the chalice of his most bitter death, that was always before his eyes, he was at all times in troubles and difficulties; *"I am poor and in labors from my youth;"* though in the form of God I was rich and happy, for you, mankind, have I become poor and in difficulties from my childhood. And so he was; witness his birth in a stable, and his flight into Egypt; *"and being exalted"* on my cross, as on a throne, with my title written over my head, *"Jesus of Nazareth, the king of the Jews,"* still *"have been humbled,"* even unto death, *"and troubled,"* at the blindness and the ruin of my people; or, *"being exalted,"* by the people crying out and saying, *"Blessed is the king, who cometh in the name of the Lord;"* and, for that reason, *"have been humbled,"* so as to be scourged, and suffer death on the cross; and *"have been troubled,"* seeing the blindness of my people.

16. He assigns a reason for having been humbled after having been so exalted, because God's anger, by reason of the many and multifarious sins of mankind, came upon him, on Christ himself; for, as Isaias 63, says, *"For the wickedness of my people have I struck him;"* and, as 1 St. Peter 2 says, *"Who his own self bore our sins in his body upon the tree." "Thy wrath hath come upon me*," that was about to come on the wicked, *"and thy terrors,"* intended for them, *"have troubled me;"* and hence it was that in the garden he began to fear, and to be sad, and to be heavy, terrified, as he was, by what he was about to undergo for the expiation of sin, and the satisfaction of divine justice.

17. He says that the anger of God, and the terror inspired by him, was like the absorbing and swallowing up a human being, as he briefly expressed before when he said, *"My soul is filled with evils,"* which is more fully expressed here, when he says, they were like a sea all round about him, overwhelming and absorbing him.

18. To this heap of misery is added the intolerable one of being alone obliged to drink the bitter chalice, with no one to share with him, to help him in this dreadful calamity. *"Thou hast put far from one,"* in the height of my sufferings, the *"friend and neighbor;"* Judas, who went farthest from him, and, from a friend and neighbor, proved an enemy. *"And my acquaintance because of misery;"* the Apostles themselves, for, *"leaving him, they all fled;"* and, though St. John and some of the women came to him, instead of diminishing, they only augmented his sorrows. How justly, then, the Lord complains in Isaias 63, *"I have trodden the winepress alone, and of the gentiles there is not a man with me. I looked about, and there was none to help; I sought, and there was none to give aid."*

PSALM 88

The perpetuity of the Church of Christ, in consequence of the promises of God: which, notwithstanding, God permits her to suffer sometimes most grievous afflictions.

1 The mercies of the Lord I will sing for ever. I will shew forth thy truth with my mouth to generation and generation.

2 For thou hast said: Mercy shall be built up for ever in the heavens: thy truth shall be prepared in them.

3 I have made a covenant with my elect: I have sworn to David my servant:

4 Thy seed will I settle for ever. And I will build up thy throne unto generation and generation.

5 The heavens shall confess thy wonders, O Lord: and thy truth in the church of the saints.

6 For who in the clouds can be compared to the Lord: or who among the sons of God shall be like to God?

7 God, who is glorified in the assembly of the saints: great and terrible above all them that are about him.

8 Lord God of hosts, who is like to thee? thou art mighty, O Lord, and thy truth is round about thee.

9 Thou rulest the power of the sea: and appeasest the motion of the waves thereof.

10 Thou hast humbled the proud one, as one that is slain: with the arm of thy strength thou hast scattered thy enemies.
11 Thine are the heavens, and thine is the earth: the world and the fulness thereof thou hast founded:
12 The north and the sea thou hast created. Thabor and Hermon shall rejoice in thy name:
13 Thy arm is with might. Let thy hand be strengthened, and thy right hand exalted:
14 Justice and judgment are the preparation of thy throne. Mercy and truth shall go before thy face:
15 Blessed is the people that knoweth jubilation. They shall walk, O Lord, in the light of thy countenance:
16 And in thy name they shall rejoice all the day, and in thy justice they shall be exalted.
17 For thou art the glory of their strength: and in thy good pleasure shall our horn be exalted.
18 For our protection is of the Lord, and of our king the holy one of Israel.
19 Then thou spokest in a vision to thy saints, and saidst: I have laid help upon one that is mighty, and have exalted one chosen out of my people.
20 I have found David my servant: with my holy oil I have anointed him.
21 For my hand shall help him: and my arm shall strengthen him.
22 The enemy shall have no advantage over him: nor the son of iniquity have power to hurt him.
23 And I will cut down his enemies before his face; and them that hate him I will put to flight.
24 And my truth and my mercy shall be with him: and in my name shall his horn be exalted.
25 And I will set his hand in the sea; and his right hand in the rivers.
26 He shall cry out to me: Thou art my father: my God, and the support of my salvation.
27 And I will make him my firstborn, high above the kings of the earth.
28 I will keep my mercy for him for ever: and my covenant faithful to him.
29 And I will make his seed to endure for evermore: and his throne as the days of heaven.
30 And if his children forsake my law, and walk not in my judgments:
31 If they profane my justices: and keep not my commandments:
32 I will visit their iniquities with a rod: and their sins with stripes.
33 But my mercy I will not take away from him: nor will I suffer my truth to fail.
34 Neither will I profane my covenant: and the words that proceed from my mouth I will not make void.
35 Once have I sworn by my holiness: I will not lie unto David:

36 His seed shall endure for ever.

37 And his throne as the sun before me: and as the moon perfect for ever, and a faithful witness in heaven.

38 But thou hast rejected and despised: thou hast been angry with thy anointed.

39 Thou hast overthrown the covenant of thy servant: thou hast profaned his sanctuary on the earth.

40 Thou hast broken down all his hedges: thou hast made his strength fear.

41 All that pass by the way have robbed him: he is become a reproach to his neighbours.

42 Thou hast set up the right hand of them that oppress him: thou hast made all his enemies to rejoice.

43 Thou hast turned away the help of his sword; and hast not assisted him in battle.

44 Thou hast made his purification to cease: and thou hast cast his throne down to the ground.

45 Thou hast shortened the days of his time: thou hast covered him with confusion.

46 How long, O Lord, turnest thou away unto the end? shall thy anger burn like fire?

47 Remember what my substance is for hast thou made all the children of men in vain?

48 Who is the man that shall live, and not see death: that shall deliver his soul from the hand of hell?

49 Lord, where are thy ancient mercies, according to what thou didst swear to David in thy truth?

50 Be mindful, O Lord, of the reproach of thy servants (which I have held in my bosom) of many nations:

51 Wherewith thy enemies have reproached, O Lord; wherewith they have reproached the change of thy anointed.

52 Blessed be the Lord for evermore. So be it. So be it.

Explanation of the psalm

1. God's mercy is the entire subject of this Psalm. The prophet at once tells us that he is about to sing of the sure and certain mercies of God; that is, the favors that were promised in his mercy, and which will never fail, which are called in Isaias 55, *"the faithful mercies of David."* The word forever is not to be connected with the verb sing, but with the noun mercies; for David, who was then near his end, could not say he would sing forever; but he could say that he would sing of the mercies of the Lord that were to endure forever. *"I will show forth with my mouth thy truth to generation and generation."* A repetition and an explanation of the first part of the verse; for *"to generation*

and generation" signifies the same as *"forever." "I will sing"* and *"show forth"* are clearly the same, and *"the mercies of the Lord"* seem to be the same as *"his truth."* In the first part of the verse he says he will sing of the mercies of the Lord that will exist forever; in the second part of the verse he says he will sing of the truth of the Lord; that is, his observance of what he promises, which will remain from generation to generation. The words, *"to generation and generation,"* like the word *"mercies,"* in the first part of the verse, are to be connected with the noun, *"thy truth,"* and not with the verb *"show forth,"* as is clear from his adding *"with my mouth,"* unless we will have it, that David meant to convey that his Psalms would be chanted by the faithful to the end of time; and therefore, that through the faithful he may be said *"to sing forever,"* and *"to show forth his truth."*

2. He proves that God's mercy and truth will be everlasting, God, who cannot speak a falsehood, having said so; I will sing of your truth and mercy which will be everlasting, *"for thou hast said so,"* and revealed it to me your prophet. *"Mercy shall be built up forever in the heavens,"* the favors mercifully promised to David will rise up like an everlasting edifice in heaven; that is, will be as firm and stable as an immoveable edifice, that no time can damage. And this edifice of mercy will be *"in heaven,"* where everything is eternal. For the event will not depend on the caprice of mortals, nor on mutable counsels and decrees, but will have its foundations in heaven. *"Thy truth shall be prepared in them."* In the same heavens your faithful accomplishment of your promises will be prepared. The Hebrew for prepared implies direction and adjustment, and thus the meaning of the sentence is, the pledges you have given are certain, can be tampered with by no inferior authority, because they will be confirmed and strengthened in heaven and will be like unto heaven, which endureth forever and ever.

3. He now begins to unveil the faithful mercy he proposed to sing of in the beginning of the Psalm. That mercy was a certain promise, confirmed by an agreement and an oath, regarding David's posterity, and the supreme power to be continued in his family; an account of which we have in 2 Kings 7, where David desired to build a house for the Lord, that is, a temple for the reception of the Ark, and for divine sacrifice; and God, through Nathan the prophet, rewarded David for his good intentions, by a promise of raising his house; that is, by the propagation of his posterity, and establishing the sovereignty in his family. This he conveys when he says, *"I have made a covenant with my elect;"* I have entered into a treaty with my chosen people; *"I have sworn to David my servant;"* I have made a promise, an oath, to David the prince of my people elect. *"Thy seed will I settle."* I have sworn to establish his descendants, so that a son of David shall never be wanted. *"And I will build up thy throne unto generation and generation."* I will keep up your kingdom,

which is the meaning of from generation to generation. There can be no doubt but all these things apply to Christ alone, who was to come from the family of David, and whose reign was to be everlasting. Isaias alludes to it when he says, chap. 9, *"His empire shall be multiplied, and there shall be no end of peace; he shall sit upon the throne of David and on his kingdom, to establish it and strengthen it with judgment and with justice, from henceforth and forever."* The Angel Gabriel announced the same when he said, *"And the Lord God shall give unto him the throne of David his father, and he shall reign in the house of Jacob forever, and of his kingdom there shall be no end."* These prophecies cannot possibly apply to a temporal kingdom that has long ceased to exist, and of which there is now no trace, but to a spiritual, and an eternal kingdom; and hence, the Jews, who still look out for the Messias, who, they expect, will rule yet in Jerusalem, are grievously mistaken.

4-5. Before he enters into detail of the promises of God, a summary of which he had already given, he digresses for the purpose of praising him, and offering him a sacrifice of thanksgiving. And first of all, the holy man, seeing himself incompetent to return adequate thanks for all the favors conferred on him, calls upon the Angels to do it for him, to praise and thank God for him. *"The heavens shall confess thy wonders, O Lord."* I am not equal to the task, I am unable to praise them as they merit, but the *"heavens,"* the Angels dwelling therein will do it for me, will recount *"thy wonders,"* the extent of your wonderful mercy, *"and thy truth in the Church of the saints."* The same Angels, who surround your throne in such numbers, will praise and glorify your mercy and your truth. They know the extent of that *"mercy"* that is built up forever in the heavens, better than we do who lie groveling on the earth.

6. He proves that the Angels will not object to such an office, because they are inferior to God. *"For who in the clouds can be compared to the Lord?"* Not one of those in heaven, which is over the clouds, can be compared to him who created them and heaven. They are all subjects, all servants, which he repeats by asking, *"Or who among the sons of God shall be like to God?"* which of the sons of God who are his Angels is like to God in point of equality, he alone being essentially God, and not by participation.

7. He now proves that none of the Angels can be compared to God, because God is *"glorified in the assembly of the saints;"* he is acknowledged by the saints themselves in their assembly as worthy of all glory, and he is *"great"* in power and wisdom; and therefore, more dreaded and revered, than all the Angels who surround his throne like so many soldiers or servants.

8. He had hitherto narrated God's praises, he now continues the subject, by addressing God, and descanting more at length on his praise. *"Lord God of Ghosts, who is like to thee?"* You, O Lord, are the Lord of armies, of many

thousands of Angels, and so outshine them all that no one is like you. *"Thou art mighty, O Lord, and thy truth is round about thee;"* the reason why nobody is perfectly like you arises from your being alone all powerful, able to do not this one thing, or that one thing, but to do every, all things, and nothing can resist your power; and you are not only able to do all things, but you actually do what you promise, for you are faithful in all your promises. Truth, or veracity, the faithful carrying out what was promised, is said to be *"round about"* God, because it is like a cincture to him, according to Isaias, *"And justice shall be the girdle of his loins, and faith the girdle of his reins;"* for, as a cincture ties up one's robes, and binds them firmly to his person; so truth binds one to his promise, so that he will not swerve from it, but carry it out; and as a cincture adjusts one's clothes, and fits him for a journey, whence the Angel Raphael is said to have appeared to Tobias in the shape of a young man, with his robes tied up and prepared for a journey, so truth or veracity, causes a man to remove every obstacle, and proceed without delay to carry out what he may have promised.

9. Having said that God was both powerful and faithful, he now proves the former by the fact of his ruling the sea, and calming its billows. The sea is sometimes dreadfully agitated and uproarious, being of immense length and breadth, and sometimes raising its billows, apparently to the very skies; and, therefore, nowhere is God's omnipotence more clearly manifested than when he quiets and composes it. The Lord himself, speaking hereon, says, Job 38, *"I set my bounds round about it, and made it bars and doors. And I said: Hitherto shalt thou come, and shalt go no further; and here thou shalt break thy swelling waves;"* and, in Jeremias 5, *"Will you not, then, fear me saith the Lord, and will you not repent at my presence? I have set the sand a bound for the sea, an everlasting ordinance, which it shall not pass over; and the waves thereof shall toss themselves, and shall not prevail: they shall swell, and shall not pass over it."* But God especially showed his command of the sea, when he dried up the Red Sea, and stayed its billows, so that the water stood up like a wall on each side, while the children of Israel were passing through.

10. This verse is to be literally understood of Pharao and his army, and is justly connected with the preceding verse; for, at one and the same moment, God thoroughly dried up the sea, and destroyed Pharao the proud and his army, leaving him as one that is slain, and the enemies of God's people scattered; which is more fully expressed in Isaias 51, *"hast thou not struck the proud one, and wounded the dragon? Hast thou not dried up the sea, the water of the mighty deep, who madest the depth of the sea a way, that the delivered might pass over."* He, therefore, says, *"Thou hast humbled the proud one,"* by stretching him in the depth of the sea, and that without any trouble, as easily as *"one that is slain; with the arm of thy strength;"* with your most powerful arm you have *"scattered your enemies,"* Pharao's army, in the Red Sea.

11. He now informs us that it is no wonder that God so easily calmed the sea, and humbled the proud one; for he is the Lord of all, and that by reason of his having created everything. *"Thine are the heavens,"* and every one in them; *"thine is the earth,"* and everything in it; *"the world and the fullness thereof thou hast founded;"* you are the absolute owner of the world and everything in it, because it is your creation, without the help or assistance of any other person.

12. You have made the foundations of the globe, north, south, east, and west. The north requires no comment; the sea means the south, for the greater part of the sea lay in that direction. Thabor and Hermon signify the east and west, those mountains lying east and west of Jerusalem; and they, that is, their inhabitants, will rejoice in the great goodness and mercy of the Lord.

13. That your hand is a strong one, in nowise feeble or weak, but full of strength and power, can be inferred from your dominion over the sea, from your humiliation of the proud, and the scattering of your enemies. *"Let thy hand be strengthened, and thy right hand exalted."* The holy prophet had spoken of two of God's attributes, power and truth, in verse 7; he discussed his power in the five following verses, and he now has to speak of and to extol his truth, which is also called justice and judgment, and is usually united to mercy. *"Let thy hand be strengthened;"* I sincerely pray and rejoice that your hand may be strengthened, and become most powerful; *"and thy right hand exalted;"* praised and magnified by all, as is right it should; but, at the same time,

14. Let your throne be prepared, decorated, and founded on mercy and justice. I consider that justice means here goodness and mercy, in the sense it is taken in Mat. 5, *"Unless your justice abound more than that of the Scribes and Pharisees;"* and again, chap. 6, *"Take heed that you do not your justice before men;"* in both of which justice means the giving of alms; and, in the same chapter, we read, *"Seek first the kingdom of God, and his justice;"* for he repeats it when he says, *"Mercy and truth shall go before thy face;"* that is to say, justice shall go before thy face to prepare your throne when you are about to come to administer justice; which means, we are quite certain that you will not judge but with the greatest justice, tempered with mercy, administering as little punishment as possible, and faithfully rendering to every one according to their works. We have here a metaphor taken from the king's throne. Before the king seats himself thereon for judgment, the servants usually precede him, in order to dust, arrange, and dispose in order everything connected with it. Mercy and justice are supposed here to do the same, for they cause God's decisions to be most just, and, by no

possibility, unjust. For God, in the first instance, exhibits great mercy to all men, by teaching them through his laws, by helping them through his grace, by encouraging them to virtue through the promise of reward, by deterring them from sin through the threats of punishment, and afterwards proves his justice by rewarding the good, and punishing the wicked; for, had not his mercy preceded his justice, we would have been all lost. Hence, the rulers and authorities of this world may learn that their thrones are more highly ornamented, and more firmly established by mercy and justice than by gold and precious stones; and that they are bound to prevent rather than to punish crime. If not the princes themselves, at least many deriving authority under them, will glory in having crime committed, that they may have an opportunity of showing their zeal in bringing the offenders to justice; and they will feel indignant at the efforts of the pious in devising means for the diminution of crime, as if the lawyers or the judges were to suffer thereby; but where mercy and justice prepare the throne, avarice and iniquity have no room whatever.

15. Having explained the union of God's power and truth with his mercy, he applies them to the people of Israel, and particularly to himself, showing that he and they fully experienced God's power, mercy, and justice. *"Blessed is the people that knoweth jubilation."* Truly happy, beyond all others, are the people of Israel, who know by experience and practice, how to praise God, and *"jubilation,"* to praise him with great affection. Hence, we can infer that he is not blessed who with his lips alone praises God unless he also truly understands and thinks that God is most worthy, nay, even more worthy than can be expressed, of all praise and glory; and therefore, that the whole feelings of our heart must accompany the motion of our lips and of our voice, when we turn to praise or to pray to him. *"They shall walk, O Lord, in the light of thy countenance."* He tells us why they who *"know jubilation"* are happy; it is because they do not walk in darkness, like the gentiles who know not God; but, having been converted to God, *"in the light of his countenance,"* walk the way of this life. The light of God's countenance comprehends the enlightenment of the understanding by the knowledge of the law and of the will of God, as well as the gift of grace, that inflames the affections. The joy of a good conscience and thanksgiving, is the consequence of such walking in the light of God's countenance; and therefore,

16. That means they will daily exult praising and thanking God for his mercies. And, as they who tread in such a path will daily advance more and more, and come to a closer friendship with, and more intimate knowledge of God and will be, consequently, favored with fresh gifts, he therefore adds, *"and in thy justice they shall be exalted;"* will arrive at greater perfection, and afterwards come to eternal glory, through the justice that causes God to keep his promises, or through the justice he gives us when he daily justifies us more and more, or makes us more just. And here we are reminded that we are not to confide either in our own strength, or in our learning; either when we begin to walk, or when we have made a proficiency in walking.

17. He now proceeds to humble man's pride that is so ready to assume to itself what belongs to God, thereby deserving to lose what it already had received. I had reason for saying *"that it is in thy justice they shall be exalted,"* because *"thou art the glory of their strength."* Whatever power and strength they have is from you, and not from themselves; and, therefore, it is in you, and not in themselves, they should glory; and that you do, not because they deserve it, but because you will it; for it is through *"thy good pleasure"* your pure will and pleasure, that *"our horn shall be exalted,"* we shall be rendered valiant and brave, to meet and confound our enemies.

18. Herein appeared the good pleasure of God, that out of all the people on the face of the earth it pleased him to select the people of Israel for his own. *"Our protection is of the Lord."* The Lord, through his good pleasure, and not from our own merits, selected us as his own people, and deigned to become our king, in order to protect us. God is called *"the Holy One of Israel"* by David, as well as by the other prophets, because his name was regarded by the Israelites with peculiar veneration, and was strictly forbidden to be taken in vain, blasphemed, or dishonored.

19. He now begins to descend to himself, as the head of a people specially beloved by God. A serious question, however, arises here, viz., whether this and the following verses apply to Christ or to David, or partly to Christ, and partly to David. St. Augustine applies them to Christ; but the words of the Apostle, Acts 13, *"I have found David the son of Jesse, man according to my own heart,"* apply those words to David, which are partly taken from this passages and partly from 1 kings 13; with that, the expression, *"I will make his seed to endure forevermore,"* ver. 29, can hardly be applied to Christ; while it is most applicable to David, to whom God promised, that he would place his seed on his throne, and that his kingdom would endure. Others apply the whole to David himself; but verse 27, *"I will make him my first born,"* forbids that. Others will have it apply partly to Christ, and partly to David; but the continuity of the subject, and the connection of the language and of the ideas, clearly indicate that one or either only was intended. My opinion is, that the whole was intended for David himself, but that a great part was to be fulfilled only in Christ, so that David may be called the first born, high above the kings of the earth, but only inasmuch as he was the type of Christ, his son. If this explanation be not approved of, we must adopt St. Augustine's, who applies it exclusively to Christ, thus: When you adopted the Jewish people as your own you gave them a king highly agreeable to

yourself, for you spoke in a vision or revelation to your saints to Samuel, and afterwards to Nathan, and you said *"I have laid help upon one that is mighty."* I have given my people, as a helper, one that is stout and resolute in mind and body, *"and have exalted one chosen out of my people."* I have set up a powerful help for my people, because I have exalted him whom I have chosen from among them to be a king and a protector and a defender of my people.

20. He now tells us who the powerful man is, and says it was David himself, whom he had found worthy to be elected and anointed king, and thus, this verse can be literary applied to David, who was anointed by Samuel. However, St. Augustine maintains that Christ was intended here, though named as David, as is the case in chaps. 34 and 37 of Ezechiel; and of whose anointing we read in Psalm 44, where he says, *"Therefore God, thy God, hath anointed thee."* The expression, *"I have found David,"* is purely metaphorical; for God, who sees everything, however secret, at one glance, has no need of seeking after any one; hut he is said to seek, because he does not choose at random, nor take the next to hand; but he finds without the labor and trouble that mortals must have recourse to, and chooses him who is most fit for, and worthy of, the position in question.

21-23. However true all this may be of David, who, through God's assistance had many victories over his enemies, they apply much more forcibly to Christ, *"for the enemy had an advantage over"* David, when he induced him to commit the sin of murder and adultery; and his enemy Absalom, had an advantage over him, when he banished and drove him out of his kingdom. Such was not the case with Christ, for *"the hand and the arm"* of the Lord, which means the very Word of God, the power and wisdom of the Father, so strengthened the human nature of Christ, hypostatically united to it, that no enemy could possibly *"have an advantage over him,"* nor deceive nor circumvent him in any shape; but, on the contrary, all who hated him *"were cut down before his face,"* and were conquered and routed. For, though Christ was scourged and crucified by his enemies, yet, it was with his own consent, and it was through that passion of his that he conquered the devil, rescued those who were captives to him, and had a most glorious triumph over him; and we see the Jews, his enemies, dispersed through the whole world, like a routed and scattered army.

24. This was rather obscurely foreshadowed in David but accomplished most fully in Christ; for the truth and mercy of God always remained with Christ. The hypostatic union, that could never be dissolved, was the effect of his mercy; and his truth appeared from having faithfully carried out what the Angel promised, Luke 1, *"He shall reign in the house of Jacob forever; and of his kingdom there shall be no end."* And, from the fact of truth and mercy

always remaining with him, *"in my name shall his horn be exalted;"* his power will be extended until, *"at his name, every knee shall bend of those that are in heaven, on earth, and in hell."* Christ's power is said to be exalted in the name of God, because his glory is *"as that of the only begotten of the Father;"* and he is adored by all as the Son of the eternal Father, and he came in the name of the Father, and *"God the Father also hath exalted him, and hath given him name which is above every name."*

25. From this verse to the end cannot possibly be applied to any but Christ, or to David, through his descendant Christ, so that David may be named, while Christ, his son, was understood; for David never had any power at sea, his power was limited to the land, and that confined enough, for the land of promise lay between the sea and the river Euphrates; while the king spoken of here is to have *"his hand set in the sea;"* to have the command of the sea, and *"his right hand in the rivers,"* and, consequently, all over the world; for the sea surrounds the land, and the rivers intersect it, so that the sea and the rivers comprehend the globe, which is expressed in other words in Psalm 71, where he says *"He shall rule from sea to sea;"* from one extremity of the world to the other.

26. He now speaks more plainly of Christ, and not of himself, unless these words may be applied to David as representing his Son, Christ; for David, throughout the Psalms, never addresses God as his Father; and, therefore, he cannot mean himself when he says, *"He shall cry out to me: Thou art my Father."* And, perhaps, it was by God's special providence that David should never have invoked God by the name of Father, in order to show that this passage could not possibly apply to David, save and except through Christ. Now, Christ commenced his labors by referring to his Father, for, in Luke 2, he says, *"Did you not know that I must be about the things that are my Father's;"* and his last words upon earth were, *"Father, into thy hands I commend my spirit;"* and, through his whole life, he most constantly addressed God as his Father. *"He shall cry out to me: Thou art my Father,"* as far as my divinity is concerned. *"My God,"* as far my humanity is concerned; *"the support of my salvation,"* as regards my mortality.

27. He now speaks of Christ in the plainest manner; for Christ, who, as regards the divinity, is only begotten, as regards the humanity, is first born among many brothers; and there are three reasons for calling him first born. First, because he is first in the order of predestination, for it is through him, as through the head, that we are predestinated, as we read in Ephes 1. Secondly, because he is first in the second generation to life everlasting, whence he is called, Colos. 1, *"the first born from the dead;"* and in Apoc. 1, *"the first begotten of the dead;"* and, thirdly, because he had the rights of the first born; for *"he was appointed heir of all things;"* and he was made not only

first born, but also *"high above the kings of the earth;"* that is, Prince of the kings of the earth, and King of kings.

28. As well as he had before predicted the excellence of the kingdom of Christ, he now predicts its eternity, which does not apply to David, nor to Solomon, nor to his posterity for the kingdom had an end under Jechonias. *"I will keep my mercy for him; the mercy through which I promised David a son, through him his kingdom should be everlasting, shall always keep and remain to him; for "my covenant,"* my agreement and promise made to Nathan, shall be observed most faithfully. But, if we are to apply this verse to Christ, the meaning would be, *"I will keep my mercy for him forever;"* that is, the mercy, through which I predestinated and chose him from eternity to be the Son of God in power, and high above the kings of the earth, will always be kept with him; for the hypostatic union of the humanity with the Word will never be dissolved, and, through it, the man Christ will always be the Son of God, *"first born,"* and *"high above the kings of the earth;" "and my covenant faithful to him;"* my agreement to establish his kingdom forever will be always faithfully observed, which promise the Angel Gabriel expressed when he said, *"And of his kingdom there shall be no end."*

29. He now explains how God intends to keep his mercy forever for David; for he will give him seed, that is, a son, meaning Christ, who *"will endure forevermore;"* and thus, *"his throne,"* his kingdom, will never have an end, but will be *"as the days of heaven,"* as long as there shall be a heaven, which God *"has established forever and for ages of ages."*

30-34. He answers an objection that may be made, and says, that if the sons of David should provoke the anger of the Lord by their evil doings, that he will punish the delinquents, but that it will not cause him to break his promise, a promise that he made upon oath. *"And if his children forsake my law."* If David's posterity should break my laws, whether judicial, ceremonial, or moral, *"and walk not in my judgements;"* if they break even the judicial law alone. *"If they profane my justices,"* if they even infringe on the ceremonial law, *"and keep not my commandment;"* if they fail in observing my moral code, *"I will visit their iniquities with a rod, and their sins with stripes;"* I will not let their crimes go unpunished, but I will chastise them as a father would his children. *"But my mercy I wall not take away from him."* The sins of the children, however, will not cause me to withdraw the favors I promised, in my mercy, to the father. *"Nor will I suffer my truth to fail."* I will not go against the truth, a thing I should do were I to injure him after the promises I made him. There are two observations to be made here; one is, that David's children may be read literally; and the opinion of St. Augustine, who understands the passage as applying to Christ, is also admissible; and, in such case, the children of David must be taken to represent all Christians regenerated in Christ. The second is, that we are not to infer from this passage that the children of David, whether Jews or Christians, however wicked they may be, can never be lost; for God does not say, through the Psalmist, *"My mercy I will not take"* from them, but from him. If the wicked, then, upon being paternally corrected, choose to reform, they will not lose the inheritance; nay, even like the prodigal child, they will be taken back to favor most affectionately; but, if they obstinately persevere in sin, they will certainly lose the inheritance; but the truth of the Lord will hold; nor will the kingdom of Christ fail; for *"he is able of these stones to raise up children to Abraham,"* although those, who are previously known and predestined in Christ before the constitution of the world, will, most unquestionably, persevere to the end in faith, hope and charity.

35-37. He assigns a reason for his wishing to fulfill the promise he made of establishing David's kingdom, even though his children should not observe his commandments; and the reason is, because he swore thereto; promised firmly, without the power of retracting. *"Once have I sworn by my holiness."* I have irrevocably and solely sworn by my holiness. The word *"once,"* implies immutability, for one oath of God's is equivalent to innumerable oaths of others. *"I will not lie unto David;"* as he says in Psalm 131, *"the Lord hath sworn truth to David, and he will not make it void."* A similar expression occurs in Isaias 22, *"Surely this iniquity shall not be forgiven you till you die, saith the Lord of Hosts."* Here are the words of the oath. *"His seed shall endure, and his throne as the sun before me."* I have sworn, and I will not deceive David, that his son, Christ, shall live forever; and that his kingdom will be everlasting; and he illustrates this sworn promise of his by three comparisons; with the sun, the full moon, and the rainbow. *"His throne as the sun before me; and as the moon, perfect forever; and a faithful witness in heaven;"* which signify that the kingdom of Christ, and through it, his Church, would be always visible and conspicuous; for nothing is brighter or more beautiful than the sun by day, or the rainbow betimes in the clouds, that has been given by God as a faithful witness to man, of the earth being nevermore to be destroyed by a deluge,

38. This is the second part of the Psalm, in which the prophet, speaking in the person of the people in their captivity, asks that God's promises may be fulfilled; for, though God may have solemnly, and even with an oath, made a promise; still, he wishes to be asked to do what he so promised; thus, *"Isaac besought the Lord for his wife, because she was barren,"* though God had promised a numerous progeny to Abraham through his son Isaac. *"I will multiply your seed; as the stars of heaven"* and again, *"In thy seed shall all nations be blessed."* In his prayer the prophet seems to give a gentle hint to the Almighty, that if he defer the fulfillment of his Promise so long, he will

appear to have no idea of observing this bargain and his oath. The meaning, then, of this and the following verses is: You have promised, O Lord, with an oath, that the son of David would reign, but now we see the kingdom taken from the children of David, and seized upon by the king of the Assyrians; to carry out your promise, then, send that son of David you promised, and give him that everlasting kingdom you swore to give him, for otherwise, our enemies will laugh at us, and our disgrace will be attributed to you. *"But thou hast rejected and despised;"* you promised all manner of favors, but now you only heap misery on us, for you have *"rejected us"* from your protection, *"and despised"* those you previously made so much of; *"thou hast been angry with thy anointed;"* you have in your anger allowed your anointed kings Jechonias and Sedecias, to be led away captives to Babylon.

39. He now explains how God did reject and despise his people; and first he lays down, that God *"overthrew the covenant of his servant,"* backed out of the bargain he entered into with his servant David, which must be understood as if he did so in appearance, and not in reality; for God, in suffering the city of Jerusalem, as well as all Palestine, to fall into the hands of the king of the Assyrians, would seem to be unwilling that David's kingdom should be everlasting; whereas the promise applied to the spiritual and celestial kingdom of David, and not to his kingdom of this world. *"Thou hast profaned his sanctuary on the earth,"* you have brought to the ground and thus profaned his holy diadem, which happened when David's kingdom terminated, Jechonias and Sedecias having beep deposed, and the royal diadem carried away.

40-41. He compares the Jewish People, represented by David, to a vineyard, whose fences are broken down and plundered indiscriminately by every passer by; a thing of frequent occurrence to the Jews, who were more than once conquered and despoiled by the Assyrians, when God withdrew his protection from them. Read the 4th book of Kings hereon. *"Thou hast broken down all his hedges,"* you have deprived us, O Lord, of your help and protection so that, like a vineyard whose fences are destroyed, we have been indiscriminately plundered by the enemy. *"Thou hast made his strength fear."* In David's kingdom his soldiers, who were full of life and courage, and were the strength of his kingdom, now became so timid, so full of fear, that they could not for a moment withstand the enemy, and the people attribute all this to God, because they knew such could not befall them without God's will, and that he might, had he so willed, easily have prevented the entire. *"All that passed by the way have robbed him,"* all the enemies of God's people have plundered and pillaged them, just as the passersby plunder a vineyard they see without a wall or a hedge, or any one in care of it. *"He is become a reproach to his neighbors."* Hence, all the neighboring people mock and jest at the people of God, now become so feeble, as to be incapable of resisting any one.

42-43. He continues to describe the calamities into which the people fell, when they were deserted by God. *"Thou hast set up the right hand of them that oppress him,"* you have assisted the enemies of your people to obtain a more easy victory over them. The enemies' joy, then, was unbounded on so cheap a victory, and he, therefore, adds, *"Thou hast made all his enemies rejoice,"* while, on the other hand *"thou hast turned away the help of the sword,"* or rather you have withdrawn your own help from his, the king's sword, and from his people, which he expresses more plainly when he adds, *"and hast not assisted him in battle,"* and hence the kings of Juda were unable to resist their enemies the Assyrians.

44. An obscure passage, but the end of the verse seems to indicate that he alludes to the king being deprived of that regal splendor and mode of living princes are usually accustomed to; and the meaning would seem to be, you have deprived the king of his royal apparel, you have made his cleanness and his purification to disappear, by compelling him to submit to filthy and uncared for garments; and *"you have so cast his throne to the ground"* that there is no trace either of it, or of the respect and submission due to the king himself.

45. The last and principal calamity was, that though God had promised David that his kingdom would be everlasting, it would now appear that the everlasting term so promised had been reduced to a very limited period, for that temporal kingdom of David, that he hoped would have had no end, was terminated in the time of Jechonias and Sedecias; and, from such *"shortening of the days of his time,"* David, through his posterity, *"was covered with confusion."*

46. He now begins a prayer for the acceleration of the Messias, in order that the sworn promises of God nay be fulfilled. *"How long, O Lord, turnest thou away unto the end?"* How long will you turn away your face from us? Will it be to the end, until we shall have been totally ruined and swept away? *"Shall thy anger burn like fire?"* that never ceases until it consumes everything within its reach.

47-48. Those verses have been variously interpreted, but, in my mind, the true interpretation is as follows: The prophet being an extremely spiritual person, from reflecting on the extreme shortness of human life, and the uncertainty of human affairs, was carried away by a burning desire for life everlasting in the world to come, and prayed to God to send the Messias, the Father of the world to come, who was to open the kingdom of heaven to believers, at once; for if some part, at least, of the human race were not to come to a happy and eternal life, through Christ, in fact, God would seem to have made all the children of men in vain. He, therefore, says, *"Remember what my salvation is,"* how brief, how frail, how full of troubles is my existence on earth. *"For hast thou made all the children of men in vain?"* Have you made and created mankind to enjoy this life alone, and that a life of such short duration, and so full of misery? that would amount to the creation of man in vain, when no part of mankind would have arrived at its ultimate end. *"Who is the man that shall live and shall not see death?"* The shortness and the misery of this life is clear from the fact, that no one can escape death, *"or deliver his soul from the hand of hell."* For the other world hurries all men, without exception, to itself.

49. He now openly prays to God to send that king, from the seed of David, who was to rule over his people, saying, where are those promises you formerly made in your mercy to David, promises you confirmed by an oath, when you swore, *"And I will make his seed to endure more, and his throne as the days Heaven."*

50. He assigns another reason for asking so urgently for the coming of the Messias, because the infidels were constantly reproaching God's people with the folly of their expecting a king from the seed of David, who was to reign. *"Be mindful, O Lord, of the reproach of thy servants,"* of the constant reproaches heaped upon them by the infidels, *"which I have held in my bosom,"* which your people have been obliged to bear in silence, having no reply to make, when *"many nations"* reproached them, and not being able to show that God's promises were either fulfilled, or would be fulfilled in any given time, or with any certainty.

51. Here is the reproach he carried in his bosom, that the enemies of the Lord upbraided God's people with having exchanged the anointed, that is, with David having received no compensation whatever for the loss of his kingdom, notwithstanding all the ample promises.

52. This conclusion of the Psalm clearly shows that the prophet understood the promise made to David was sure and certain, and would be accomplished in the proper time, however unlikely it may have appeared to have been in the time of Nabuchodonosor. Nay, even this very conclusion shows that David knew that it was a part of the divine policy to allow that temporal kingdom to be abolished, for fear the carnal Jews may suppose that the divine promises were accomplished in Solomon or any of the kings of Juda. He, therefore, says, *"Blessed be the Lord forevermore. So be it, so bet it."* May praise and thanks be always given to God, for he does everything well, is just in all his words, and holy in all his acts. *"So be it; so be it."* I earnestly pray it may be so, viz., that the Lord may be blessed evermore. This is the end of the third book, according to the Hebrews.

PSALM 89

A prayer for the mercy of God: recounting the shortness and miseries of the days of man.

1 Lord, thou hast been our refuge from generation to generation.
2 Before the mountains were made, or the earth and the world was formed; from eternity and to eternity thou art God.
3 Turn not man away to be brought low: and thou hast said: Be converted, O ye sons of men.
4 For a thousand years in thy sight are as yesterday, which is past. And as a watch in the night,
5 Things that are counted nothing, shall their years be.
6 In the morning man shall grow up like grass; in the morning he shall flourish and pass away: in the evening he shall fall, grow dry, and wither.
7 For in thy wrath we have fainted away: and are troubled in thy indignation.
8 Thou hast set our iniquities before thy eyes: our life in the light of thy countenance.
9 For all our days are spent; and in thy wrath we have fainted away. Our years shall be considered as a spider:
10 The days of our years in them are threescore and ten years. But if in the strong they be fourscore years: and what is more of them is labour and sorrow. For mildness is come upon us: and we shall be corrected.
11 Who knoweth the power of thy anger, and for thy fear
12 Can number thy wrath? So make thy right hand known: and men learned in heart, in wisdom.
13 Return, O Lord, how long? and be entreated in favour of thy servants.
14 We are filled in the morning with thy mercy: and we have rejoiced, and are delighted all our days.
15 We have rejoiced for the days in which thou hast humbled us: for the years in which we have seen evils.
16 Look upon thy servants and upon their works: and direct their children.
17 And let the brightness of the Lord our God be upon us: and direct thou the works of our hands over us; yea, the work of our hands do thou direct.

Explanation of the Psalm

1. The prophet begins his prayer by returning thanks for past favors; for he that seeks for fresh favors can make use of no argument so convincing as the showing himself grateful for the past. *"Lord, thou hast been our refuge."* We allow we are subject to many and various dangers, but we have found a helper and a protector in you, and that not once or twice, but always, *"from generation to generation."* The Hebrew for refuge signifies a well fortified house, placed on an eminence, the tenants of which are quite secure from their enemies, from beasts, from flood and from storms. And, in fact, they have recourse to God, and dwell in him, by constant reflection and daily desire for him, dwell as they would in a city fortified by faith, hope, and charity, and are most secure from all evil; for, with such persons, *"all things work together unto good."*

2. He proves that the very same God might have been a refuge to those who hoped in him at all times; for he is always the same, especially powerful, wise, and kind; and, to show that God existed before all these things that man confides so much in, he first names the mountains. *"Before the mountains were made;"* for the mountains, being of great altitude and solidity, afford man a refuge in many ways; or, perhaps, he names the mountains first, by reason of their having been the first to appear when the waters that covered them at the creation began to recede; or, perhaps, because the mountains form a conspicuous and considerable portion of the earth. *"From eternity and to eternity thou art God;"* you existed not only before the earth and the mountains, but from eternity thou art, and to eternity thou art God. And, observe, he does not say, Thou hast been, and will be God, but, Thou art God, in order to show the true eternity of God, in which there is no past or future, but one continuity of existence, without any change or variety, to which he alludes in Psalm 101, where he says, *"But thou art always the self same, and thy years shall not fail."*

3. Now begins the prayer the prophet puts up to God, begging of him not to allow mankind to lapse into extreme degradation and ruin. For he saw that man, estranged from God by the sin of our first parents, was rushing headlong to destruction, and he, therefore, exclaims, *"Turn not man away to be brought low."* Do not suffer mankind to be turned away from the light of your countenance, to extreme wretchedness and meanness, so as to forget what is really good, and to turn to the things of the earth and the clay of secular desires, and thus be consigned to eternal perdition. And he assigns a reason for its not being meet that God should suffer a creature so noble as man to be lost. For *"Thou hast said: Be converted, O ye sons of men;"* that is to say, by the preaching of your prophets, and by your own secret inspirations, you have invited sinners; and you, therefore, by the powerful succor of your grace, should help the sinner in the way of his conversion, and not suffer him to sink to the depth of wretchedness.

4-5. He now describes the abject state of the human race after the fall of man, by comparing the shortness of man's life with God's eternity. God's eternity is so immense that a thousand years with him are but as part of a day with us; and yet, by reason of the fall of man, our life is not one of a thousand years, nor of a hundred, but scarcely of seventy, or with the more robust, of eighty. Our life, then, as compared with the existence of God, is less than that of one day, nay more, of even part of a day; and yet, had man not fallen into sin, he would have lived to eternity. *"For a thousand years in thy sight are as yesterday, which is past."* We are come to the lowest degree of wretchedness; for, while your existence is that of eternity, so that a thousand years are as but one day, that quickly passes with you, or, *"as a watch in the night,"* three hours; the life of man, who was created to your image, and, therefore, should have been everlasting, is now so brief that it may be looked upon as nothing; for *"things that are counted nothing, shall their years be;"* very short and next to nothing.

6. To show how contemptible is the life of man, he compares it to grass, that in one day springs up, flowers, withers, and perishes. *"In the morning,"* in the early part of the day, man will appear in his youth, like the verdant grass, and will not stop there, but will pass on; in the morning again, in the early part of the day, *"he will flourish"* in the vigor of youth; and will again pass on; *"in the evening,"* in another part of the same day, *"he shall fall;"* his strength will begin to fail, *"grow dry and wither"* in his old age, in death, when all his bodily powers shall have been wasted. Alas, the blindness of mankind, who love the existence of one day, that ought to be looked upon as of no value, as if it were eternity! David is not alone in denouncing such folly; for in Job, chap. 14, we read, *"Man, born of a woman, living for a short time, is filled with many miseries. Who cometh forth like a flower, and is destroyed, and fleeth as a shadow, and never continueth in the same state."* And after him, Isaias, on the same subject, says, *"All flesh is grass, and all the glory thereof as the flower of the field. The grass is withered, and the flower is fallen, because the Spirit of the Lord hath blown upon it."*

7. He assigns a cause for the shortness of human life, and says, it proceeds from the just anger of God, roused by the perversity of man. *"For in thy wrath we have fainted away;"* we have been consumed and become mortal, by having provoked your anger; *"and are troubled;"* we, who previously led a life of quiet and security, are now troubled with the fear and horror of death, by reason of your anger. God does not get into anger or into rage, or into any excitement, but he is said figuratively to be so when he does not spare the sinner, but punishes him according to his merits.

8. Having said that God's anger was the cause of the shortness of our life, he now says that our sins are the cause of God's anger. He calls the sin of our first parents our sin, because it was common to us, and comprised many sins, pride, disobedience, infidelity, curiosity, and other sins. Perhaps David also took in the sins of posterity as the cause of our life being shortened; for, up to the deluge, men lived to be nine hundred years; after the deluge, to two and three hundred years; and, in Moses' time, to a hundred and twenty; and, finally, in the time of David, to eighty years. He, therefore, says, *"Thou hast set our iniquities before thy eyes;"* you would not, in your mercy, hide our

sins, but you put them right before you, that you may consider on them and punish them. For God is considered as forgiving sin when he turns his face away from it, as the prophet says, in Psalm 1, *"Turn away thy face from my sins, and blot out all my iniquities."*—*"Our life in the light of thy countenance;"* is only a repetition of the first part of this verse; for *"our life"* means the iniquities of our life, which God, for fear they should escape him, placed *"in the light of his countenance;"* so lighted and showed up that their hideousness may be apparent to all, and punished by the just judgment of God.

9. The very punishment of death inflicted on us proves that God saw and condemned our delinquencies. *"For all our days are spent;"* our life has passed away, none of it now remains; *"and in thy wrath we have fainted away;"* not only have our days been spent, but ourselves are spent with them; for, if Adam had not revolted, our days would have passed away, but they would have been succeeded by other days, and we would not have fainted away; but, at present, our days flow on so as to come to an end by the intervention of death; and we come to an end with them, and are destroyed by the anger of God, justly punishing us for our sins. *"Our years shall be considered as a spider."* Having said that death is the punishment of sin, he now adds that life itself, previous to death, is both wretched and short, according to the patriarch Jacob. *"The days of my pilgrimage are a hundred and thirty years, few and evil;"* and of their wretchedness he says, *"Our years shall be considered as a spider;"* as the spider's whole occupation consists in weaving flimsy webs, that have no substance or duration, and which waste the body of the spider itself, so is the whole period of our life devoted to idle labor and pain, harassed by fear and suspicions, in running after the imaginary goods of this world, and guarding against its evils.

10. He now passes from the misery to the shortness of our life, saying, The term of our life is marked and defined, averaging seventy years; a few of the more robust may reach eighty; but if they go beyond that, their life is one of infirmity, pain, and trouble. Hale and robust people are to be found after their eightieth year, to be sure, but there is no rule without an exception; and if; previous to the deluge, men lived to be eight and nine hundred years, that was necessary for the propagation of the human race, as it afterwards, in God's providence, became necessary to curtail the life of man, in order to prevent an excess of population, as well as to punish men for their sins. *"For mildness is come upon us, and we shall be corrected."* The evils of old age bring this much good with them, that they make us lay aside our pride and the vanity of youth, they make us conscious of our own infirmity, and thus we become humbled, mild, and corrected under the powerful hand of God.

11-12. The prophet infers from the severity of the punishment inflicted for the sin of our first father, that God's anger and severity, in regard of sin, is very great, and makes use of a beautiful figure of speech to express it. *"Who knoweth the power of thy anger?"* Who can possibly conceive the force, power, and effects of your anger? *"And for thy fear can number thy wrath?"* who can fear you as you ought to be feared, and in such fear to measure the extent of your anger, or enumerate the various modes of punishment? For as God was so incensed against all mankind for the one sin of our first parents, so as to condemn them to a life of pain, labor, and trouble here, and afterwards to death, to a return to the dust from whence they came, it certainly may be fairly inferred, that God's anger to the sinner must be boundless, and that he has countless modes of punishing the sinner. And if the magnitude of God's anger to the sinner is to be inferred from the corporeal death so inflicted on him, who can possibly conceive or comprehend the extent of that anger, not satisfied with the death of that wretched body, without consigning both soul and body, on the day of judgment, to everlasting and inextinguishable fire? It far exceeds the understanding of man! *"So make thy right hand known: and men learned in heart, in wisdom."* From hence to the end of the Psalm the prophet prays to God, that as he was pleased, in his justice, to shorten the life of man, he may now, in his mercy, look down upon and help man in his pilgrimage here below. *"So make thy right hand known."* Do, O Lord, at last stretch out your right hand to us, to sustain and support us, and to give us, in abundance, the gifts of your grace. *"And men learned in heart, in wisdom."* Prophets and Apostles with hearts fully imbued with the true wisdom, not like the wise ones of this world, whose tongue may be polished, but whose heart is not; or, if it be, it is not with wholesome and salutary wisdom, but with the pernicious wisdom of the world, *"which puffeth up, and does not edify."*

13. He repeats the same prayer, but in more general terms, saying, Having been angry with us, by reason of our sins, you have turned your face away from us; but, as you have been appeased, turn to us at length and look upon us with an eye of kindness. *"And be intreated in favor of thy servants."* Do not be inexorable, but listen to your servants, whom you have created, and whom you nourish and support for your service.

14-15. When we shall have been reconciled to God, when he shall have been *"intreated in favor of his servants,"* then we can justly say, *"we are filled in the morning with thy mercy;"* that is to say, in the beginning of that real day that we began to see the sun of Justice, without any cloud to hide it from us, and the night and the darkness of this life had disappeared, we have been filled with that great mercy of yours, that totally excluded all misery and trouble, of which it is written in Psalm 102, *"Who crowneth thee with mercy and compassion, who healeth all thy diseases, who satisfieth thy desire with good things;"* therefore, *"we have rejoiced and are delighted;"* for all that is left to the blessed, when freed from their sins, is to exult in praising God, and revel in the delight of having got possession of him. And we have rejoiced, not only for such a load of favors, but we have even *"rejoiced for the days in which thou hast humbled us,"* and for *"the years in which we have seen evils;"* both because prosperity is much sweeter to those who have tasted of adversity, and because our own patience in adversity had some share in this return of prosperity, according to the Apostle, 2 Cor. 4, *"For our present tribulation, which is momentary and light, worketh for us above measure exceedingly an eternal weight of glory."* Thus, we now bless those days and years in which our patience was tested, and we thank God, who did not spare us here below, that he may be able to do so for eternity.

16. After he had asked for that supreme good that is the ultimate end of man's life, and of all our actions, he now asks for the means of acquiring it; that is to say, the grace of doing good. For, according to our Lord, we must *"Seek first the kingdom of God and his justice;"* he, therefore, says, *"Look upon thy servants;"* enlighten thy servants and inflame them with thy love; for God is the increate sun, who by one look both illuminates and enlivens. Also, *"Look upon thy servants"* with an eye of favor and benevolence, and direct, protect, and further them, as belonging to you; *"and upon their works;"* the good works you have caused them to commence; for God is said to perform all our good works in us, because it is by his help and assistance they are done, and without his grace, both preceding them and accompanying them, they would be of no value whatever. And look upon, not only thy servants, but *"direct their children"* also; whether their natural, or their spiritual children; that under thy guidance, both parents and children may persevere in the path of your commandments, and thus deserve to reach life everlasting.

17. In order to show how extremely desirous he is to get what he asks, he repeats the same petition in different language, for the expression, *"Let the brightness of our Lord be upon us,"* is the same as *"Look upon thy servants;"* for God, as we already said, when he looks on us enlightens us; when he turns his face away, he leaves us in darkness; and the expression, *"and upon their works,"* in the previous verse, he repeats here when he says, *"and direct thou the works of our hands over us;"* that is to say, by overseeing us, makes us to work as we ought, and always to follow that most correct rule, thy will and thy law. He adds, *"Yea, the works of our hands do thou direct;"* to show that all our works may be brought under one head, that is, charity, the root of all, and containing all, *"for he that loveth his neighbors hath fulfilled the law,"* and, *"Charity is kind, is patient."*

PSALM 90

The just is secure under the protection of God.

1 He shall say to the Lord: Thou art my protector, and my refuge: my God, in him will I trust.
2 He shall say to the Lord: Thou art my protector, and my refuge: my God, in him will I trust.
3 For he hath delivered me from the snare of the hunters: and from the sharp word.
4 He will overshadow thee with his shoulders: and under his wings thou shalt trust.
5 His truth shall compass thee with a shield: thou shalt not be afraid of the terror of the night.
6 Of the arrow that flieth in the day, of the business that walketh about in the dark: of invasion, or of the noonday devil.
7 A thousand shall fall at thy side, and ten thousand at thy right hand: but it shall not come nigh thee.
8 But thou shalt consider with thy eyes: and shalt see the reward of the wicked.
9 Because thou, O Lord, art my hope: thou hast made the most High thy refuge.
10 There shall no evil come to thee: nor shall the scourge come near thy dwelling.
11 For he hath given his angels charge over thee; to keep thee in all thy ways.
12 In their hands they shall bear thee up: lest thou dash thy foot against a stone.
13 Thou shalt walk upon the asp and the basilisk: and thou shalt trample under foot the lion and the dragon.
14 Because he hoped in me I will deliver him: I will protect him because he hath known my name.
15 He shall cry to me, and I will hear him: I am with him in tribulation, I will deliver him, and I will glorify him.
16 I will fill him with length of days; and I will shew him my salvation.

Explanation of the psalm

1. The first verse contains a remarkable promise, in which the Holy Ghost assures us that the divine assistance will never be wanting to those who really put their trust in God. To explain the words. "He," no matter who he may be, rich or poor, learned or unlearned, patrician or plebeian, young or old, for *"God is no respecter of persons,"* but he is *"rich to all that call upon him"*—"that dwelleth," to give us to understand that this liberal promise does not apply to those who put only a certain amount of trust in God, but that this trust must be continuous, constant, and firm, so that man may be said to dwell in God, through faith and confidence, and to carry it about with him, like a house, like a turtle, *"in the aid,"* for God's aid is not like one of the strongholds of this world, to which people fly for defense, but consists in an invisible and most secret tower that can be found, and entered by faith alone. However, the expression in the Greek as well as the Latin conveys, that we must place the most entire confidence in God, but still we are not to neglect the ordinary means that man can avail himself of. The husbandman puts his trust in him who gives the rain from heaven, and makes his sun to rise, but in the meantime he will be sure to plough, to sow, and to reap, knowing that God helps those who help themselves. *"Of the Most High,"* God has been called by many names, but that of the *"Most High"* seems the most apposite in this passage, both because God is really most high, sits in the highest place, sees everything, and is aware of every danger around us. And again, not only is he Most High, and sees everything, but all things are subject to him, and therefore, he can deliver us from all manner of danger. *"Shall abide under the protection of the God of Jacob."* The second part of the verse, in which a reward is promised to those who put their trust in God, and the meaning is, He that really trusts in the divine assistance will not be disappointed in his hope, but will be completely protected by the Lord. The several words in each member of the verse beautifully correspond with each other. The word *"dwelleth"* corresponds with *"abide under;"* the word, *"in the aid,"* with *"protection,"* and *"the Most High,"* with *"the God of heavens."* To come now to the several words. The Hebrew for protection signifies shade or shadow, implying that God protects those that trust in him, as the hen that gathers her chickens under the shadow of her wings. Shadow may also signify the grace and favor of princes, a shade that easily, and from a great distance, affords protection, as are read of a stag that roamed about in the greatest security, by reason of its having a label on its neck, *"Touch me not, I belong to Caesar;"* thus, the true servants of God are always safe, even among lions, bears, serpents, fire, water, thunder, and tempests, for all creatures know and reverence the shadow of God. Even the Latin word *"protection"* is very significant. To protect means to cover from a distance, and one may be covered from a distance in two ways, by the person standing nigh, and warding off the weapons that are shot from a distance; or by standing afar off, and still warding off the weapons of close combat. God does both, for, abiding in us, he wards off the weapons that are shot from afar, for he sees the very first beginning of the danger; and, by his wonderful power, stifles it in the bud, if he thinks proper; he also, though seated in heaven, puts aside all dangers, however proximate to us, for he has far seeing eyes and long reaching hands, so that he can easily cut short all impending dangers, his eye is his intelligence, his hand is his power, and his power his will. *"The God of heaven;"* for nobody is all sufficient, needing nothing, and through and in himself omnipotent, but the true God, who made the heavens, *"For all the gods of the gentiles are devils; but the Lord made the heavens;"* and though the earth, and the sea, and the air are great and wonderful works of God, still, among things created there is nothing greater or more wonderful than the heavens, whether we regard its size, its beauty, its efficacy, its velocity, or its stability; and no wonder the prophet should exclaim in another place, *"The heavens show forth the glory of God."*—*"Shall abide."* This expression conveys that the person trusting in God will be protected by him, not now and then, or casually, but will be constantly protected by him, that the protection of God will not be like a hut on the roadsides but like one's own or his father's house. Here we cannot but wonder at the folly of mankind, who make so little of such a promise. Those in power spend much money on their fortresses and body guards, and yet are often betrayed by them; but here it is not frail and deceitful man, but the Almighty and truthful God that says, *"Trust in me, and I will protect you,"* and yet scarce can one be found to trust himself to God as he ought.

2. The prophet now proves and explains his assertion by the testimony of a just man confiding in God, who gives his testimony from experience. *"He shall say to the Lord;"* that is, the just man, who dwells in the aid of the Most High, will acknowledge the favor of the protection he had from God. He calls God absolutely Lord, because God alone is truly and strictly Lord, both because he has neither equal nor superior, is subject to no necessity, wants nothing; as also, because all things are at his beck, without him they can neither move nor exist; and finally, because he alone can change, destroy, or repair all things as he pleases. *"Thou art my protector, my refuge, my God."* These words represent three of God's favors, for which the just man returns thanks; one, a past favor; the second, a present; and the third, a future favor. The first favor is that unspeakable mercy of God, through which he supports man after falling into mortal sin, and rushing headlong to hell; of whom is said in Psalm 117, *"Being pushed, I was overturned that I might fall; but the Lord supported me;"* so St. Bernard explains the passage, and says, *"A sign of such support is, when the person who fell rises up more humble, more resolute, and more cautious, as did David, and Peter, and Magdalen."* The just man, then, who confides in God, mentions this favor first, not that it arises from confidence, (for it precedes instead of coming from confidence), but because he says to himself, if God be so good as to protect the enemy who does not confide in him, and to inspire him with penance and confidence, how good and kind must he not be to the friend and child who does confide in him. The second favor is one of the present time, and is contained in the expression, *"and my refuge."* For, when God protects anyone through the grace of justification, he does not, at once, take him up to heaven, but he places him in the line of his soldiers, who are fighting here below, but if he trust in the Lord, he will prove *"a refuge"* to him in every temptation

and difficulty, and a most safe and secure refuge, as the Hebrew word for refuge implies. The third favor is a future one, and the greatest of all, and is contained in the words, *"my God,"* for God is the supreme good, and God is always God in himself, and, therefore, the supreme good; and he will be peculiarly so *"when we shall see him as he is,"* for then we shall enjoy the supreme good. The just man, therefore, reflecting and allowing that God was one time his protector, then his refuge, and, after this life, will constitute his happiness, comes to the conclusion, *"in him will I trust;"* that is, I am firmly determined to put my trust in him, through every danger and temptation, as did holy Job, when he said, *"Although he should kill me, I will trust in him."*

3. Having said, in the previous verse, that he would put his trust in God, he now assigns a reason for doing so, *"For he hath delivered me from the snare of the hunters, and from the sharp word,"* in which he alludes to two favors conferred on him, one temporal, the other spiritual. The temporal blessing consists in immunity from snares, stratagems, and frauds of the wicked, the source of much temporal injury; the frauds being designated by the *"snares of the hunters,"* and the *"sharp word"* implies the injuries consequent on the frauds. And, as frauds and stratagems are generally effected through the tongue, Eccli. 51 says, *"Thou hast preserved me from the snare of an unjust tongue."* God, then, in his singular providence, has caused, and always will cause, the frauds and schemes of the wicked to do no harm to the just, who confide in the aid of the Most High. Another favor, and much a greater one, is an exemption from the temptations of the evil spirits; for such is their craft, that men, however prudent they may be, when compared with them, may be looked upon as half fools. Those demons, then, are the hunters of whom the Apostle says, *"For they who would become rich, fall into temptation, and into the snare of the devil;"* and again, *"And they recover themselves from the snares of the devil, by whom they are held captives, at his will."* Those demons are so numerous as nearly to fill completely the dark prison in which they are confined, and, according to St. Jerome, they are so powerful and so ferocious as to be compared, in the Scriptures, *"to lions and dragons;"* and they have no other study but constantly *"going about roaring, seeking whom they may devour;"* and, if we would seriously and attentively keep this fact before us, we would watch with as much fear and trembling in our prayers as it is probable Daniel did in the lions' den, or the three children in the fiery furnace. All created things are so many snares, which catch the heart of man either through the concupiscence of the flesh, the concupiscence of the eyes, or the pride of life. The wise man says of them, *"The creatures of God are made a snare to the feet of the unwise,"* Wisdom 14; and Eccli. 9 has, *"For thou art going in the midst of snares,"* *"The sharp word"* is that spiritual death incurred by the person caught in such snares, or, if you will, it may mean

that sentence that will be pronounced on the wicked, *"Go, ye cursed, into everlasting fire;"* for what can be rougher or more severe than such a sentence, when it conveys the loss of all that is bright and good, and an accumulation of all that is evil, not for a time, but for eternity. Such sentence of a most just judge will be justly pronounced on those who voluntarily suffer themselves to be tangled in the snares of the hunters, the demons.

4. The prophet now speaks in his own person, and addresses the just man, who spoke hitherto, saying, you were right in saying I will trust in him, for *"he hath delivered me from the snare of the hunters;"* for he really did deliver you, and will always deliver you from every danger, for while you will be but a little one, and no match for your enemies, he will foster you under his wings, like a hen or an eagle. God has been compared to two birds in the Holy Scriptures, the eagle and the hen; to the former in Deut. 32, *"As the eagle enticing her young to fly, and hovering over them;"* to the latter in Mat. 23, *"How often would I have gathered together thy children, as the hen gathereth her chickens under her wings."* God was an eagle before, a hen after the incarnation; or, if it be referred to Christ alone, as God he is an eagle, as man a hen; or he was a hen previous to an eagle after his resurrection. He, therefore, says, *"He will overshadow thee with his shoulders."* God, like an eagle or a hen, will gather you under his wings, and will so *"overshadow"* and protect you, that you will have nothing to fear from the heat of the sun, nor the severity of the rain or the storm, or from birds of prey; lodged, therefore, in the greatest safety *"under his wings,"* under his care and protection, *"thou shalt trust"* for deliverance and safety.

5-6. The prophet now explains another figure in regard of the more advanced in years, who can defend themselves; for God arms them with an extraordinary shield. The poets record the shields of Aeneas and Achilles, which were said to have been gifts from heaven, and through which they became invulnerable; but that was all a fable; but the shield of which David speaks is really celestial, and truly renders those invulnerable who know how to make proper use of it; and the prophet says, *"He shall compass thee with a shield;"* not with a helmet which protects the head only, nor with a coat of mail that protects the breast and shoulders only, but with a shield that may be used for the protection of the entire body, for it may be raised or lowered, turned to all sides, and opposed to every blow. *"In all things taking the shield of faith, wherewith you may be able to extinguish all the fiery darts of the most wicked one,"* says St. Paul, Ephes. 6. That shield is truth, so the passage says, *"His truth shall compass thee with a shield;"* as if he said, The truth of the Lord shall encompass thee like a shield. The truth of the Lord has two acceptations in the Scripture. In one sense it means God's strict observance of his promises, as in Psalm 88, *"My truth and my mercy* shall be with him;" and in another part of the Psalm, *"But my mercy I will not take from him; nor will I suffer my truth to fail."* In another sense it means the truths revealed to the prophets and Apostles, on which we have, in John 17, *"Thy word is truth;"* and in Proverbs 30, *"Every word of God is fire tried; he is a buckler to them that hope in him;"* and in Ephes. 6, *"In all things taking the shield of faith;"* that is, of truth, which is had through faith alone, that being a supernatural truth. Both sorts of truth form the best possible shield to repel all the weapons of the enemy, whether in adversity or prosperity, for God's promises are so fixed and unalterable, that of them may be said, *"Heaven and earth shall pass away, but my words shall not pass away;"* for the truth of God is like holding ground in which the anchor of hope is firmly fixed. While the anchor is passing through the water it does not hold the ship, for water is a liquid and unsteady element, but once the anchor takes hold in the ground, it keeps the ship in her place. Thus our hope, when it is built on the promise of man, cannot but totter and waver; but when fixed in God's truth, it remains firm and steady; *"For God is true, and every man a liar,"* Rom. 3. And who can injure him who has been promised the protection of that God who cannot deceive him? The truth of faith protects us like a shield also when it gives us a certainty that eternal happiness is prepared for the just, and torments everlasting for the sinner after this life; and that judgment will be held on the last day, when all men shall have to render the most exact account of all their deeds, words, thoughts, desires, omissions; in short, of every idle word, however brief, they may have uttered. Such and similar reflections, disclosed to us by the truth of faith, would easily protect us from all temptations, both in adversity and prosperity, if we would daily use them as a shield; that is, if we daily and faithfully meditate on these truths of our religion. Who is he that would not bravely bear up against any terror whatever, by reflecting seriously on those words of our Lord? *"And fear not those that kill the body, and cannot kill the soul; but rather fear him that can destroy both soul and body in hell."* And who is there that will not despise the empty pleasures of this world, and the occasions of wronging their neighbor, when they seriously reflect on the following words of our Divine Master? *"For what doth it profit a man if he gain the whole world, and lose his own soul? Or what shall a man give in exchange for his soul?"*—*"Thou shalt not be afraid of the terror of the night; of the arrow that flieth in the day."* He now tells us what the dangers are against which we need the shield of truth. The passage is a very obscure one, and variously explained, but of the various ones offered, we consider one to be the most simple and literal, as follows: You will have no dangers to fear, either by day or by night. *"Thou shalt not be afraid of the terror of the night,"* you need not fear anything that may frighten you by night; fear, here, being used for the thing that causes it; as it is also in 1 Peter 3, *"And be not afraid of their terror;"* just as hope is used for the thing hoped for, and desire for the thing desired, as in Titus 2, *"Waiting for the blessed hope;"* and in Psalm 77, *"And he gave them their desire;"* that is, the thing they desired. The words, *"of the arrow that flieth in the day,"* mean, you will have to fear no dangers in the day time; *"of the business that walketh about in the dark,"* is only a repetition and explanation of *"the terror of the night;" "of invasion or of the noonday devil,"* is a mere repetition of *"the arrow that flieth in the day."* In fine, in these words we have a general promise of security, both by day and by night, to those who trust in God, and are armed with the shield of truth; *"For if God be for us, who is against us?"* Rom. 8; as also, *"And who is he that can hurt you, if you be zealous of good?"* 1 Peter 3.

7. The prophet follows up the description of the victory of the just man who confides in God, and makes proper use of the shield of truth. He reminds the just of the great value they should set upon such a victory, it being a rare one, and that of the few over the many. For in this fight *"a thousand shall fall at thy side, and ten thousand at thy right hand; but it shall not come nigh to thee;"* neither the terror of the night, nor the arrow that flieth in the day, nor the business that walketh about in the dark, nor the noon day devil shall come nigh to thee. *"Thy side"* means thy left side, being opposed to the right, and signifies adversity; whilst the right stands for prosperity; and many more fall from the latter than from the former; for prosperity is the source of pride, usury, licentiousness, impudence, and other like vices; while adversity renders men humble, chaste, and patient; for, as the Apostle says, *"Tribulation worketh patience."* The numbers, a thousand and ten thousand, merely signify that many will fall on the left, but a great many more on the right hand; and it is in such sense these numbers are understood in Kings, *"Saul slew his thousands, and David his ten thousands;"* and, in Deut. 32, *"How should one pursue after a thousand, and two chase ten thousand?"*

8. A fresh source of joy to the just man, who not only has been promised a victory, but that he will, furthermore, have great pleasure in seeing his enemies laid low, and punished according to their deserts, a promise that is sometimes fulfilled even in this world. Thus, the children of Israel saw the Egyptians cast dead on the shores of the Red Sea; Moses and Aaron saw Dathan and Abiron swallowed up alive; Ezechias saw the prostrate corpses of Sennacherib's army; and Judith, with God's people, saw the head of Holofernes cut off, and his whole army scattered and routed; but this promise will be completely fulfilled on the day of judgment, when we shall see all our enemies prostrate on the ground, naked and unarmed, without any strength whatever, and consigned to eternal punishment. *"But thou shalt consider,"* not in a cursory way, or in a hurry, but with diligence and accuracy, you will consider all your enemies, their number, their position, what

they deserved, and what they are suffering; *"with thy eyes;"* you will not take it from hearsay or report, but you shall see with those very eyes with which you saw the arms and the dangers of your enemies: for your eyes will then be your own property, a thing they are not now, while curiosity opens them, sleep closes them, old age dims them, and death destroys them; and all in spite of you. *"And shall see the reward of the wicked;"* you will then see plainly the reward the wicked get for all their labor. Hence will arise a beautiful order of things, that now seem in general disorder and confusion. For, while punishment should follow sin, and virtue should be rewarded, it often happens that the just are afflicted, and bad men honored; and thus sorrow comes from virtue, joy from sin; but, on the last day, all things will be righted and put in their proper place; guilt will meet its punishment, and that in proportion to its enormity; while, on the contrary, justice shall be rewarded in proportion to its merits, too; and then will be accomplished what is prophesied in Psalm 57, *"The just shall rejoice when he shall see the revenge;"* that is, when he shall see the sinner duly punished; not that he will rejoice in their misfortunes, but for the vindication of the divine justice and wisdom, that will appear so conspicuous in the punishment of the wicked.

9. This verse is very easy, as far as the words are concerned, all of which have been explained when we discussed the first and second verses; but the connection is not so apparent; because, in the preceding verse, the prophet seems to have addressed the just man; he now seems to speak to God, saying, *"Because thou, O Lord, art my hope;"* and we don't see why he says so; and then the second part of the verse, *"thou hast made the Most High thy refuge,"* is addressed to the just man again, but without any connection between the members of the sentence. The first part of the sentence is the voice of the just man speaking to God; the second part are the words of the prophet; we have already observed that this Psalm is, to a certain extent, dramatic, in the form of a dialogue, though the characters are not named, however; that the prophet speaks at one time, the just man at another, and God at another time. The prophet, then, having said to the just man, *"God will overshadow thee with his shoulders,"* as the hen does her young; *"will compass thee with a shield,"* as a general would his soldiers; *"you shall not be afraid of the terror of the night, nor of the day;"* and hence many will fall on your right and left, but the danger will not come near you, but you will rather see your enemies conquered before your face—the just man, on hearing all this, turns to God, and says, *"Because thou, O Lord, art my hope,"* I believe every word of it; it's all true, and that because you, O Lord, art my hope; I trust not in my own strength or arm, nor in the strength nor in the arms of my friends; but in thee alone, who art my whole and sole hope, and in whom alone I confide. Now, God is said to be the hope of the just, because they not only

hope for help from him, but they hope he will prove himself a strong citadel in their regard, to which they fly for protection in time of persecution; and dwelling in which, through faith, hope, and charity, through prayer and contemplation, they can suffer no injury. The prophet understood that well, and, therefore, he adds, *"thou hast made the Most High thy refuge;"* as much as to say, you have acted most wisely and properly in placing your hope in God; for thus you have selected your place of refuge in the highest possible and best fortified citadel you could select, God himself, where (as will be said in the following verse) no harm can possibly reach you.

10. The prophet now tells what good the just man is to derive from having made the Most High his refuge, and says it consists in his being most safe from all evil. Evil is two fold, that arising from sin, and that arising from the punishment consequent on sin. The evil of sin is absolutely and radically evil, and to it applies the first part of the verse, *"There shall no evil come to thee;"* the evil of punishment is not simply evil, and, therefore, to it applies the second part of the verse, *"nor shall the scourge come near thy dwelling."* That the evil of sin is simply and absolutely evil, and that such is not the case with the evil of punishment, is clear from the fact that the former renders man absolutely evil, while the latter makes him only miserable; nobody can turn the evil of sin to good account; not so as regards the evil of punishment. The evil of sin cannot be called good, for it is not right to call it so, it being iniquity; nor is it of any use, when he who sins always loses more than he gains; the evil of punishment may be called good, for it is frequently both good and useful. God, being the author of all good, is not the author of the evil of sin; while the evil of punishment has God, as being a just Judge, for its author. That can be inferred from the words of the prophet; for; when, he says, *"There shall no evil come to thee,"* he speaks of the evil that is in us, and cannot be outside us; such is the evil of sin, which must of necessity be within us, that is, in the power of our free will; and when he adds, *"nor shall the scourge come near thy dwelling,"* he speaks of the evil that may happen to our property, our children, our house, our land; and such is the evil of punishment. A serious doubt arises here regarding the truth of this promise; for David was certainly one of those just who trusted in God, and still the evil of sin; adultery, murder, and the scourge, nay, even many scourges, *"came near his dwelling;"* for he says himself, *"I washed my hands among the innocent, and I have been scourged all the day;"* which may also be said of Job, Tobias, of the prophets and Apostles, nay, even of Christ himself, who, too, was scourged; nay, even the Lord *"scourgeth every son whom he receiveth,"* Heb. 12. To this objection two answers may be made; the first is, that the promise does not regard this life, but the next, when that prophecy will be fulfilled, *"Thou shalt consider with thy eyes; and shalt see the reward of the wicked;"* for then, when we shall have entered the heavenly tabernacle, we will be quite safe from all the evil of sin, as well as of punishment; for God's reason for *"strengthening the bolts of the heavenly Jerusalem, and "placing peace in its borders,"* was that the scourge may not possibly come near it. The second answer is, that the promise does regard this life, but that is to be understood with some restriction; for the evil of sin will not come near the elect and those who trust in God; not that they cannot possibly fall into sin, but because, through God's singular providence, their very sins will tend to their improvement, making them more humble and cautious, and more inflamed by the love of God, in proportion to the extent they are indebted to his grace and mercy. So St. Gregory applies it to St. Peter, which also holds in the case of St. Thomas, Mary Magdalen, and many others. The scourge, that is, the evil of punishment, will not *"come near their dwelling,"* because, in spirit, they are dwelling in the heavenly tabernacles, and, with the Apostle Paul, engrossed entirely in meditation, they scarcely feel such temporal evils, or if they do, they despise them; nay, more, so far from looking upon them as evils, they consider them positive blessings and graces, from which they hope to reap an abundant crop of glory; such were the feelings of the Apostle when he said, *"I am filled with comfort. I exceedingly abound with joy in all our tribulation."*

11. The just man might have said, I am quite sure that no evil can possibly happen to me, when I shall have got within that heavenly tabernacle; but I would like to know who is to guard me on the way to it, to prevent my going astray, or falling in with robbers, or into a pit? The prophet replies, Never fear, *"For he hath given his Angels charge over thee: to keep thee in all thy ways."* Each word in which requires an explanation. *"For"* does not refer to the preceding, but to the following sentence the meaning being, whereas God gave you in charge to his Angels, to guard you on the way, the Angels will take you in their hands, for fear you should knock against a stone. *"Angels"*— Angels are blessed spirits, most noble princes, who guard with the greatest care, being most powerful, wise, and excellent, showing us how God values the human race in assigning such guardians to it. But why Angels, instead of an Angel? According to our Lord, we have a guardian Angel every one of us; for he says, *"Their Angels always see the face of my Father;"* and when St. Peter knocked at the door, those within said, *"It is as Angel."* Granted; but we still have Angels who have common charge of us, such as those who are in charge of towns, states, and kingdoms; on which see chap. 10 of Daniel. *"His;"* they are called *"his"* Angels because there are fallen angels also, of whom is said in the Apocalypse, *"And the dragon fought and his angels."* God, then, gave you in charge to *"his Angels,"* and not to those angels who, instead of protecting you, would have sought to destroy you. *"Hath given charge;"*

the reason why the Angels take such care of us is, because God ordered them to do so, gave us in charge to them; for, though they guard us with right good will, loving us as they do, and though they have a horror of the evil angels, and wish the heavenly Jerusalem to be renewed as soon as possible; and though they know all this to be most agreeable to their King, Christ our Lord, still God's command is uppermost, is their ruling motive for the whole; for they are conscious of being God's servants, and there is nothing that he requires more strictly from his servants than prompt and implicit obedience; *"over thee,"* which means that God's providence extends to all, and that he has given a guardian Angel to each and every human being; but still that he has a peculiar regard for the just, for those that confide in him; and, therefore, that he has given special orders to his Angels to look *"over thee,"* the just man, who trusts in his help, *"to keep thee;"* the charge God gave his Angels regarding the just was to preserve him from his enemies, the evil angels; for man, by reason of the flesh that envelopes him, can see nothing save through the eyes of the flesh, and, therefore, is no match for the evil spirits, unless he get help from someone more powerful; *"in all thy ways;"* not on thy way, but in all thy ways; for numerous are the ways of man, and in every one of them he needs the help of his guardian Angel. The law is the way, according to Psalm 118, *"Blessed are the undefiled in the way, who walk in the law of the Lord;"* and in the same Psalm, *"I have run the way of thy commandments."* The way also means the works, as in Proverbs 8, *"The Lord possessed me in the beginning of his ways before he made anything."* Finally, this life is a way to a certain extent. The way of the law is varied, for there are many laws; the way of the works is equally so, for there are many works; the way of life is also varied, for there are many parts, ages, and states of life. We require assistance in every one of them, since we are liable to fall in every law, work, age, and state of our life.

12. A verse full of metaphors, but otherwise easily explained; we, therefore, have merely to explain what he means by the *"Angels' hands,"* what the *"stones"* and the *"feet"* signify. The Angels' hands signify the intellect and the will, or wisdom and power, for it is by understanding and by willing they do everything. The stones, all the obstacles that we meet in this life, be they temporal or spiritual, such as scandals, temptations, persecutions, and the like. The feet mean our affections, that very often knock against the stones; and, as St. Augustine, treating of this passage, says, Our feet are two affections, fear and love; and, whenever man proceeds in his actions, words, or desires, he is carried by one or the other, by the desire of acquiring one thing or losing something else, or by a desire of avoiding evil, or the fear of falling into it; we then knock our foot against the stone, when we fall into sin, on an occasion offering of acquiring some temporal good, or of

avoiding some temporal evil, whence we lose eternal happiness, and incur eternal punishment; but they *"who dwell in the aid of the Most High"* are so assisted by the Angel guardian, that the occasion is altogether removed; that is, the stone is taken out of the way, or the mind is so enlightened as to distinguish good from evil; that the feet, that is, the affections are so raised from the earth that the temporal advantage, that could not be had without sin, is easily despised; and the temporal evil, that could not be avoided without sin, is most patiently endured.

13. Having made mention of the good Angels who have charge of the just man that trusts in God, he now alludes to the bad angels, and says, so far from their harming the just man, that he, on the contrary, will trample on and crush them, as the Apostle says, *"And may the God of peace crush Satan speedily under your feet."* He calls Satan a serpent, by reason of his cunning, and a lion, by reason of his ferocity; and, as there are various sorts of serpents, he calls him an asp, a basilisk, and a dragon, for to the cunning that is common to all serpents, the asp unites obstinacy, the basilisk cruelty, and the dragon great strength and power, for all of which Satan is remarkable. This is not the only passage in which the devil is called a serpent and a lion. In Job 26, and Isaias 27, he is called *"the winding snake"* and *"the crooked serpent."* The Apocalypse calls him *"the dragon"* and *"the old serpent;"* and St. Peter calls him *"the roaring lion,"*

14. As we read in Deuteronomy, that *"in the mouth of two or three witnesses every word shall stand,"* the holy prophet would have three witnesses to prove what he promised in the beginning of the Psalm, viz., that all who truly trust in God would be protected by him. The first witness was the just man, who, from his own experience gave testimony to the truth of it, when he said, *"For he hath delivered me from the snare of the hunters."* The second witness was the prophet himself, who, as the organ or voice of the Holy Ghost declared, *"He will overshadow thee with his shoulders."* The third witness is God himself, who, in the last three verses, confirms all that had been said, and adds a great deal more, for these three verses contain eight promises of God, which most appropriately commence with deliverance from evil, and advance up to elevation, to supreme happiness. Four of them, *"I will deliver him, protect him, hear him, am with him in tribulation,"* belong to this life; and the four others, *"I will deliver him, glorify him, fill him with length of days, and I will show him my salvation,"* belong to the next life. *"Because he hoped in me I will deliver him."* The deliverance that is promised here refers to deliverance from all evil, and may be referred to the deliverance previously mentioned through the Angels, or the shield, or in any other way, so that the meaning is, Let not the just man imagine for a moment that he can be delivered by the Angels, or by a shield, or by any means without me;

they can do nothing without me, and it is I that will deliver him through them, and frequently without them, since it was in me principally, and not in them, that he trusted. Looking at the passage from a higher point of view, the deliverance here promised may be said to mean deliverance from the tyranny of sin, which may be said specially to be a mark of the perfect, and a most desirable one; our Savior himself, speaking thereon, says, *"Whosoever committeth sin, is the servant of sin. If, therefore, the Son shall make you free, you shall be free indeed."* Now such liberty is not granted unto all, but to those that hope in God, *"Because he hoped in me I will deliver him."* It is not, then, every hope, but that confidence that is the fruit of a good conscience, and springs from filial love and affection, that frees man from the vices that tyrannize over him; for, as avarice ties him down, and holds him captive, and the more he advances in charity, the more is his avarice diminished; and when his charity and attachment to the supreme good shall be most perfect, then, too, will his liberty be most complete, that liberty that is styled by the Apostles *"the liberty of the glory of the children of God."* The next promise is, *"I will protect him, because he hath known my name."* For he that is freed from the tyranny of vice in this world, still is not perfectly free, he needs God's help to advance in grace until he shall have come to glory. God, therefore, promises continual protection to those *"who have known his name;"* that is, to those who have come to the knowledge of his power, wisdom and goodness which raises up in them the most firm hope and confidence. They, too, are said *"to know his name,"* who are on familiar terms with God, and know him as a pastor, a friend, and a father, speaking of which our Savior says, *"I am the good shepherd, I know my sheep, and my sheep know me;"* and, on the other hand, speaking of the others, he says, *"I know you not;"* and in 2 Thess. 1, *"In a flame of fire, giving vengeance to them who know not God."* Wonderful altogether is God's kindness to man, when he speaks to him not only as a Lord but as a friend, and no wonder David should exclaim: *"Lord, what is man that thou art made known to him?"*

15. There are four promises in this verse; the first is a general promise of being heard, a promise which God alone can make; and that there is no restriction whatever to the promise of hearing the prayer of all who confide in God, is clear from the words, *"and I will hear him;"* other passages of Scripture confirm it. Deut. 4, *"Neither is there any other nation so great, that hath God so nigh to them, as our God is present to all our petitions."* John 13, *"You shall ask whatever you will and it shall be done to you;"* and in Mark 11, *"All things whatsoever you ask, when ye pray, believe that you shall receive, and they shall come unto you;"* and finally, in 1 John 3, *"We have confidence towards God, and whatsoever we shall ask we shall receive of him;"* and though certain conditions are necessary to have our prayer heard, the principal one

is that which is expressed here, when he says, *"he shall cry to me;"* which implies a vehement desire, springing from confidence and love. The three other promises come next. *"I am with him in tribulation, I will deliver him, and I will glorify him."* Three promises correspond most exactly to the three most remarkable days in the year: the Friday on which the Lord, hanging on his cross, was in his greatest tribulation; the Saturday on which he rested in peace from all his troubles; and the Sunday on which, by rising from the dead, he had a most glorious triumph. All the just and the elect have three such days before them; for, with Christ, we must all go through our own tribulations on Friday, that is, in this life, which is the shortest, and is counted but as one day; we must rest in the sepulchre on the Saturday; and, finally, rise on Sunday, and be glorified with Christ. The Lord, therefore, says, *"I am with him in tribulation;"* for the person praying asked for the gift of patience above all things, *"which is necessary for you, that you may receive the promise,"* Heb. 10. Now, the Lord who said, *"I will hear him,"* promises him, in the first place, the gift of patience, when he says, *"I am with him in tribulation,"* each word of which has a peculiar force of its own. *"I am,"* in the present tense, whereas everything else was expressed in the future; *"I will deliver, I will protect, I will hear, I will glorify, I will fill;"* and this was so expressed, with a view to show us that the troubles of this world are momentary, as the Apostle, 2 Cor. 4, says, *"For our present tribulation, which is momentary and light, worketh for us above measure exceedingly an eternal weight of glory;"* and, therefore, God's mercy causes our tribulations to fall upon us, as it were, drop by drop, whereas our future glory will flow upon us like the inundation of a river; as the Psalm expresses it, *"Thou shalt make them drink of the torrent of thy pleasure;"*—*"with him"* conveys that God is present with everyone, in various ways, but that he is specially, through his interior consolations, and the influx of his unspeakable sweetness, with those who are in trouble; like a fond mother, whose entire care, even to the neglect of the others, is bestowed on the child in sickness; or as we ourselves, who nurse and care the ailing members of our body, and care not for the others. *"In tribulation;"* this gives us to understand that, however great the consolations, whether temporal or spiritual, bestowed by God upon his friends here below, that they are not without a certain admixture of tribulation. Some, especially among sinners, have their troubles without any consolation; but none, neither just nor wicked, have their consolations without some mixture of trouble; but there is this difference between the good and the bad; that the former, with few tribulations, more apparent than real, get true and solid consolations, for *"the fruit of the spirit is charity and joy,"* Gal. 6; but as to those who have not the Spirit, how can they expect its fruits? *"I will deliver him;"* this promise regards the future life, for it is at their death that the just are delivered from all present and future troubles, as St. John has it in the Apocalypse, *"Blessed are the dead who die in the Lord, from henceforth, now and forever; that they may rest from the labors;"* and again, chap. 21, *"And God shall wipe away all tears from their eyes; and death shall be no more, nor mourning, nor crying, nor sorrow shall be any more."* The wicked appear to be delivered from the troubles of this world by death, but it is by no means the fact; for they only pass from temporary to eternal tribulation; they are no more delivered than is the wretch who is brought out of jail to the place of execution. Sometimes, however, the just, even in this life, are delivered from their tribulation. Such was the case with Joseph, Job, David, Tobias, Daniel, the three children, Susanna, and others; but it was only a short and brief delivery. The fourth promise is, *"and I will glorify him;"* that, to a certain extent, sometimes happens also in this life, for holy Job was not only delivered from many and grievous tribulations, but was even raised to great glory afterwards; so was the patriarch Joseph; so was king David; but, beyond yea or nay, the real and true glorification will be accomplished in the other world only, for *"Then shall the just shine as the sun in the kingdom of their Father,"* Matt. 13; and he says to the Apostles, *"you also shall sit on twelve seats, judging the twelve tribes of Israel;"* and, to express their glorious position, the Psalmist says, *"Their principality is exceedingly strengthened;"* and the Apostle, in speaking on the matter, says, *"The sufferings of this present time are not worthy to be compared with the glory to come that shall be revealed in us."*

16. These are the two last favors promised to those *"who dwell in the aid of the Most High,"* and may be looked upon as an explanation of the sixth favor. *"I will glorify him,"* for the glory of the saints consists in their having secured supreme happiness; now, supreme happiness must be everlasting, for happiness, without being everlasting, is nothing more than misery; and eternity, without happiness, is eternal misery. He, therefore, describes real eternity; first, by the expression, *"I will fill him with length of days,"* and then true happiness by the words, *"and I will shed him my salvation."* By length of days is meant a space of time, so extended as fully to satisfy man's desire, for that is what he promises when he says, *"I will fill him with length of days;"* and, as man's desires cannot be satiated but by a continuance of what he desires, this length of days must be taken to mean eternity. The Scripture makes use of such expressions to designate eternity, because it speaks to those who can form no idea of eternity, but from the length or the number of days. In eternity there is no succession of days, but one day always going on, or rather one moment lasting without change, succession, or vicissitude. But it may be said, the vicissitudes of the seasons bring their pleasure with them, and we find men beguiling the length of the day in summer, and of the night

in winter; by various amusements. That arises from all the stages of this life being full of various inconveniences and troubles, which make us look forward with impatience to the future, but when the day, than which no better can be expected, shall have come, the wish, then, that it may always last, will be the wish of all. *"And I will show him my salvation."* I will cause the just man to live no longer by faith, by belief in what he sees not, but that he may clearly see and feel, and know by experience the salvation I offer him. That salvation consists in the beatific vision promised to us, which renders man's salvation both perfect and perpetual. The mind will then be cleared of all error and ignorance, when it shall have arrived at the summit of wisdom, which consists in viewing the supreme and sovereign author of all things. From such wisdom there will spring up in the will a most ardent and steadfast love of the supreme good, that will completely take the affections from anything gross or unworthy, and such salvation will have its own effect on the inferior part of man, that thus will become subject to the superior without resistance or rebellion; and on the body itself, which will rise again immortal, impassible, most beautiful, and brighter than the sun. Here we cannot but wonder at the blindness of mankind; for while all wish for eternal happiness, and cannot avoid wishing intensely for it, they will, however, for some temporal or trifling advantage, whether in grasping and hoarding riches, or obtaining and keeping honors and preferments, or in gratifying and indulging their carnal and sensual desires, leave no stone unturned, will run backwards and forwards, watch, labor, sweat, exercise all ingenuity, draw upon their eloquence, apply all their talents; and still, where true, solid, and eternal happiness, real riches, the highest honors, unspeakable happiness that has been prepared for those that love God, are in question, they are so lazy that they will not even condescend to stir one finger for them. It is dreadful to reflect that man, endowed with reason and understanding, should so devote his whole life to the pursuit of things the most likely to shut him out from eternal happiness. We should pray to God, that as he has deigned to promise us such blessings, he may infuse his Holy Spirit into us, so as to enlighten our hearts, that we may know *"what is the hope of his calling, and what are the riches of the glory of his inheritance in the saints,"* Eph. 1.

PSALM 91

God is to be praised for his wondrous works.

1 It is good to give praise to the Lord: and to sing to thy name, O most High.
2 To shew forth thy mercy in the morning, and thy truth in the night:
3 Upon an instrument of ten strings, upon the psaltery: with a canticle upon the harp.

4 For thou hast given me, O Lord, a delight in thy doings: and in the works of thy hands I shall rejoice.
5 Lord, how great are thy works! thy thoughts are exceeding deep.
6 The senseless man shall not know: nor will the fool understand these things.
7 When the wicked shall spring up as grass: and all the workers of iniquity shall appear: That they may perish for ever and ever:
8 But thou, O Lord, art most high for evermore.
9 For behold thy enemies, O Lord, for behold thy enemies shall perish: and all the workers of iniquity shall be scattered.
10 But my horn shall be exalted like that of the unicorn: and my old age in plentiful mercy.
11 My eye also hath looked down upon my enemies: and my ear shall hear of the downfall of the malignant that rise up against me.
12 The just shall flourish like the palm tree: he shall grow up like the cedar of Libanus.
13 They that are planted in the house of the Lord shall flourish in the courts of the house of our God.
14 They shall still increase in a fruitful old age: and shall be well treated.
15 That they may shew, That the Lord our God is righteous, and there is no iniquity in him.

EXPLANATION OF THE PSALM

1. An exhortation to praise God with instrumental and vocal music. He says it is right, useful, delightful, and honorable to give God his need of praise; right, because it is due to him; useful, because we save ourselves by it; delightful, for the lover always delights in praising the beloved; and honorable, because the office belongs to the celestial spirits; *"and to sing to thy name, O Lord."* It is good to praise you, not only with our hearts and lips, but also to use musical instruments, such as the psaltery, whereon to make your praises resound, O Most High God.

2. Such must be the subject of our praise, to announce and proclaim to all the mercy in which you created the world, and the truth or the justice with which you rule it. And, as the work of mercy appears to every one, let it be announced in the day; for who is there that does not know that the heavens and the earth, and all things in them were created by God, through his goodness and mercy, and not from necessity or compulsion. And, as the works of justice are occult; for, through God's secret designs, the just are often afflicted, and the wicked exalted; let such works be announced at night, in the darkness of faith, and not in the light of knowledge. In like manner, let mercy be announced in the morning, and justice at night, that men may, in the light of their prosperity, return thanks to God for his mercy, and in the

darkness of tribulation for his justice; for, as St. Augustine observes on this passage, the father loves his children no less when he threatens than when he caresses them; nor should we be less grateful to God when he chastises us in the time of trouble, than when he heaps favors on us in our prosperity. We should imitate the prophet, who says, in another Psalm, *"I will bless the Lord at all times; his praise shall be ever in my mouth."*

3. As well as he explained the subject of his praise, when he said, *"It is good to give praise to the Lord,"* he now explains the second part of the same verse; *"and to sing to thy name;"* for he says he is to sing with the harp and psaltery, but not without the sweet sounds of the human voice.

4. He now opens on the work of creation, one of God's mercies. I have been studying the beauty, variety, excellence, strength, and the uses of your works; of the heavens, the earth, the waters, the stars, animals, and plants: I have been delighted beyond measure with them; but it was not your works that delighted me, for I did not dwell upon them, but it was in yourself I delighted; for your works led me to reflect on your own infinite beauty; and, carried away by the love of such extraordinary beauty, I was delighted and lost in admiration; and will, therefore, daily exult and praise thee *"in the works of thy hands."*

5. Having said that he was delighted so much with the works of God, for fear he should be supposed to have comprehended them thoroughly, or to have an intimate knowledge of the excellence of all God's works, he now adds, that the works of the Lord are too great, and his wisdom in producing them too profound for any one in this life to comprehend. *"How great are thy works!"* I am lost in admiration at the greatness and the excellence of your works; I cannot comprehend the magnitude of them, for truly did Ecclesiasticus say, *"Who hath numbered the sand of the sea, and the drops of rain, and the days of the world? Who hath measured the height of heaven, and the breadth of the earth, and the depth of the abyss?"* yet however great they may be, greater beyond comparison is the wisdom that created them; of which the same inspired writer immediately adds, *"Who hath searched out the wisdom of God, that goeth before all things;"* and David here adds, *"thy thoughts are exceeding deep;"* that is to say, those thoughts of yours so full of wisdom, through which you have devised so many wonderful things, and so perfect that nothing can be added to or taken from them, are so occult as to surpass all human understanding. To give an instance of it in most trifling and common things. Who can comprehend how in one small seed is contained an enormous tree with large and numerous branches, verdant foliage, beautiful blossoms, and its own seed for its own propagation? Who can comprehend by what art God contrived to infuse life, sense, and motion into the minutest insects, and with it endowing the ant with such prudence,

the spider with such cunning, and the gnats and the fleas with such a power of incision with so poor an instrument?

6. He concludes this part of the Psalm, that treats on creation, by asserting, that it is only the wise, and not the senseless or the fool, that can know how great and inscrutable are the works of the Lord. For fools never look for anything in things created but the pleasure or the advantage they derive from them, just as the brute beasts do, who have no understanding, and know not their own ignorance. But the wise, though they do not comprehend the greatness of God's works, still, they feel they are unequal to comprehending them, and are sensible of their ignorance therein; and the more they are sensible of it, the more they admire God's works, and come near true wisdom. *"The senseless man shall not know"* how wonderful are the works of the Lord; *"nor will the fool understand"* how profound are his thoughts; for a knowledge of one's own ignorance is only to be met with in the wise.

7. He now passes to direction and the providence of God, in which his justice or his truth is most conspicuous, and especially so in the fact of the wicked being allowed to flourish for a time, that they may be condemned to eternal punishment; while the just, on the contrary, suffer here for a while, that they may be crowned hereafter. *"When the wicked shall spring up as grass;"* when they shall flourish and multiply as quickly as the grass grows and in as great abundance; *"and all the workers of iniquity shall appear"* most conspicuous, in high situations, and abounding in riches, *"that they may perish forever and ever."* All this prosperity of theirs will be suffered by God as a reward for some of their works, while they are sure to be punished with everlasting death for their crimes.

8. Your position, O Lord, is quite different from that of the wicked, for their elevation is only temporary, but you are *"Most High"* forever and ever.

9. He proves that the wicked will prosper for a time only, and that a short one. The word *"behold,"* implies the suddenness of the change, as if he said, They that so thrived and flourished will perish all at once; and the repetition of the expression is with a view to express his execration of them; just as a similar repetition is used by him in Psalm 125, to express his devotion, *"O Lord, for I am thy servant; I am thy servant, and the son of thy handmaid."* Worthy of all execration is he who fears not becoming an enemy to God, that he may be a friend to the world; for thus writes St. James, *"whosoever therefore will be a friend of this world, becometh an enemy of God."* What an amount of perversity to despise the friendship of the Creator for that of the creature. *"And all the workers of iniquity shall be scattered."* This is but a repetition and explanation of the first part of the verse. Those he called *"enemies"* there, he calls *"workers of iniquity"* here; and those he said there *"shall*

perish," he says here *"shall be scattered;"* for men become enemies to God by the fact of their contradicting his will that has been made known to us through his law; and they who *"work iniquity,"* contradict his law; for the law of God is most direct and straight, and the rule of rectitude; but iniquity is nothing else than crookedness, and a departure from that rule. The wicked *"shall be scattered"* like the dry grass, to which he compared them; for as the dry grass is hurried away and scattered by the wind, and no trace of it found after; thus, the wicked, when they shall have prospered and flourished for a while, by God's will, are sure to be cut down and carried off, leaving not even a trace of their memory.

10. He now contrasts the lot of the just with that of the wicked, and shows that they will one day be exalted by the divine providence and justice; and he speaks in his own person, piously hoping he will one day be numbered among them. *"My horn;"* that is, my power, happiness, and glory will rise aloft; not like the frail grass, but like the horn of the unicorn, an animal having only one horn, but that a large, straight, and powerful one, *"and my old age in plentiful mercy;"* that is, not only will my power, happiness, and glory be great, but it will be continued and constant, following me to my old age, for my *"old age will be in plentiful mercy"* before God.

11. An addition to the just man's happiness will be that he will no longer have any fear of his enemies; he says, I have seen and despised them, for divine providence rendered them incapable of doing me any harm. *"And my ear shall hear of the malignant that rise up against me,"* and as regards my absent enemies who, in their malignity, would rise up against me, *"my ear shall hear"* of their downfall too.

12. The prophet now applies to other just men what he had said of himself, gracefully comparing them to the palm and cedar trees, in contrast to the wicked he had compared to grass. Grass springs up in the morning, withers during the day, or is cut down by the mowers, is a thing of no permanence or endurance; whereas the palm tree lives a long time, and gives forth its fruit and its leaves for a long time; so does the cedar, the highest and the longest lived among trees, and in great request for the ornamentation of royal palaces and ceilings. Thus the wicked thrive and prosper for a while, and are then thrown into the fire; but the just, like the palm tree, will flourish and hold verdant, and bear the sweetest fruits forever; nor will they sink under any burden, but will overcome all difficulties, and, furthermore, *"shall grow up, like the cedar of Libanus,"* to an enormous height, sending out its branches of good works and roots of perseverance, which will enable them to resist any storm, however great, of temptation, and in the end, like the cedars, will be an ornament in the heavenly palace of the new Jerusalem.

13. He assigns a reason for having compared the just to the palm and the cedar, because they will not be planted in the woods or the wild mountains, but will be planted in God's own house, and will flourish in God's own courts; that is to say, they will be planted in his Church by true faith, watered by his sacraments and his word, fixed and rooted in charity, they will not fail to give out in abundance the flowers of virtue and the fruit of good works. For, outside the Church, and without the foundation of faith, every plantation will be rooted up, inasmuch as it was not planted by the Heavenly Father.

14. What the prophet previously promised himself, viz., *"that his old age should be in plentiful mercy,"* he now promises to all the other just; that they will prosper, not only in their youth and vigor, but that they will have a long and happy old age. *"They shall still increase in a fruitful old age;"* and, furthermore, *"they shall be well treated;"* enjoying the blessings of this life, and hoping for the next.

15. All this will turn up, that the just may show and make known to all by word or by example, *"that the Lord our God is righteous;"* for, though he suffers the wicked to prosper for a while, he will, in his own time, exercise the judgments of his justice, by rewarding the good, and punishing the wicked.

PSALM 92

The glory and stability of the kingdom, that is of the Church of Christ.

1 The Lord hath reigned, he is clothed with beauty: the Lord is clothed with strength, and hath girded himself. For he hath established the world which shall not be moved.
2 Thy throne is prepared from of old: thou art from everlasting.
3 The floods have lifted up, O Lord: the floods have lifted up their voice. The floods have lifted up their waves,
4 With the noise of many waters. Wonderful are the surges of the sea: wonderful is the Lord on high.
5 Thy testimonies are become exceedingly credible: holiness becometh thy house, O Lord, unto length of days.

Explanation of the Psalm

1. The beginning of this Psalm may apply either to the creation or the redemption, and it is not unusual for passages in the Scripture to have more literal meanings than one. *"The Lord hath reigned;"* has got possession of his kingdom, has begun to reign; *"he is clothed with beauty;"* has assumed his beautiful robes of office. *"The Lord is clothed with strength;"* he has not only got possession of the throne, but he has got strength and power to hold it, a matter of great consequence to one in power; *"and hath girded himself,"* to govern and to rule. If this be referred to creation, God may be said to have begun to govern when he created the world, and peopled it. If it be referred to the reparation, it was in the resurrection that Christ began to reign, and then he was clothed with the beauty of his glorious body, as well as with strength; for all power in heaven and on earth was given unto him, so that he should no longer be subject to any creature, but have everything under his feet. Finally, he girded himself to extend his kingdom to the bounds of the earth, through the preaching of his Apostles. *"For he hath established the world, which shall not be moved;"* God began to reign from the beginning of the world, for he then founded it from its very lowest foundations, and he established and settled it so that it cannot be moved; and thus gave a fixed habitation to men, who are bound to obey and to acknowledge him as their King. Christ, too, by his passion and resurrection, established and settled the world, that was hitherto harassed by demons, and by the worship of many false gods, in one true faith and religion.

2. Though your reign commenced with the creation of the world, or with the resurrection, your existence did not date from it; for, *"thou art from everlasting;"* which means that he not only existed, but that he had within him the fullness of existence, which contains everything; for, before the creation, God was not a pauper, nor did he need anything, nor did he become richer or more wealthy by the creation of the world, for God did not create the world to enrich himself, but to share his riches with us. Thus, it was not from coercion that he created the world, but from mercy and love, which same mercy and love led him to make atonement for the world. *"For God so loved the world as to give his only begotten Son, that whosoever believeth in him may not perish, but may have life everlasting,"* John 3.

3-4. If these verses be referred to the creation, they explain the manner in which God made the earth habitable, so as to be the fixed residence of mankind. In the beginning of creation the waters covered the whole earth, and in consequence of a great inundation were raised considerably above it; but God, being brighter and more elevated again, and infinitely more powerful than them, rebuked and restrained the waters, and shut them up in the caverns of the earth, with strict orders never to return thence. This is expressed more clearly in Psalm 103, where he says, *"Who hast founded the earth upon its own basis, it shall not be moved forever and ever. The deep like a garment is its clothing; above the mountains shall the waters stand;"* that is to say, the earth was originally so formed that an abyss of water completely enveloped it, covering even the tops of the highest mountains; but, *"At thy rebuke they shall flee, at the voice of thy thunder they shall fear;"* that means, but you, O Almighty, rebuked the waters and so confused them by your thunder, that they fled and hid themselves in the depths of the earth; and then *"you set a bound which they shall not pass over; neither shall they return to cover the earth."* A description of the same is to be found in Job 38, and has been beautifully condensed here by the Prophet, *"Wonderful are the surges of the sea; wonderful is the Lord on high;"* all the waters of the sea and the great abyss of waters raged and roared at a great elevation over the earth; but the Lord, who is wonderful, who dwelleth on high, and who is higher than anything created, confined the waters, and made the earth habitable. If we interpret this in reference to the redemption, we must take it as a description of the extent of the persecutions got up by the Jews and Pagans against the kingdom of Christ, just commenced at his resurrection, and his victory over all his enemies. *"The floods have lifted up their voice; the floods have lifted up their waves."* The Jews lifted up their voices when they began to speak out against the Gospel and to thwart it. *"Wonderful are the surges of the sea;"* the persecutions of Nero, Domitian, and the other Roman emperors, that were seas as compared to rivers, when set alongside the persecutions of the Jews. *"Wonderful is the Lord on high;"* more wonderful than them all is the Lord who dwells on high, having obtained a victory over all his persecutors; and having, in spite of them all, propagated his kingdom throughout the entire world.

5. If this verse be referred to creation, it must be taken as a reply to an objection that may be raised, for one may say, how do we know that what has been said about the founding of the earth, the abyss of waters, and their being restrained and confined, took place at all; for this happened before the creation of man, when there was no one to witness it? The prophet replies that he has it from God's own testimony, who revealed it to his servant Moses, and that such testimony is worthy of all belief, by reason of Moses having proved himself a faithful servant of God, and a true prophet, by many signs and prodigies. The same may be said if we refer the verse to the redemption, for the testimonies to Christ, conveyed to us through his Apostles, are become so exceedingly credible, through the miracles of both, and through the accomplishment of the prophecies, and for various other reasons without end, that so established Christianity, that no one, having heard them, can possibly gainsay it. From which the prophet concludes that *"holiness,"* that is, that it should be regarded as holy, and that all who dwell in it should lead a holy life; and by the holiness of their lives, correspond with the holiness of *"thy house,"* the Church of God which has, and in which are preached, such testimonies; *"unto length of days;"* that it is right the Church should be saved and preserved by you, O Lord, unto length of days; *"that the gates of hell may not prevail against her."*

PSALM 93

God shall judge and punish the oppressors of his people.

1 The Lord is the God to whom revenge belongeth: the God of revenge hath acted freely.
2 Lift up thyself, thou that judgest the earth: render a reward to the proud.
3 How long shall sinners, O Lord: how long shall sinners glory?
4 Shall they utter, and speak iniquity: shall all speak who work injustice?
5 Thy people, O Lord, they have brought low: and they have afflicted thy inheritance.
6 They have slain the widow and the stranger: and they have murdered the fatherless.
7 And they have said: The Lord shall not see: neither shall the God of Jacob understand.
8 Understand, ye senseless among the people: and, you fools, be wise at last.
9 He that planted the ear, shall he not hear? or he that formed the eye, doth he not consider?
10 He that chastiseth nations, shall he not rebuke: he that teacheth man knowledge?
11 The Lord knoweth the thoughts of men, that they are vain.
12 Blessed is the man whom thou shalt instruct, O Lord: and shalt teach him out of thy law.
13 That thou mayst give him rest from the evil days: till a pit be dug for the wicked.
14 For the Lord will not cast off his people: neither will he forsake his own inheritance.
15 Until justice be turned into judgment: and they that are near it are all the upright in heart.
16 Who shall rise up for me against the evildoers? or who shall stand with me against the workers of iniquity?
17 Unless the Lord had been my helper, my soul had almost dwelt in hell.
18 If I said: My foot is moved: thy mercy, O Lord, assisted me.
19 According to the multitude of my sorrows in my heart, thy comforts have given joy to my soul.
20 Doth the seat of iniquity stick to thee, who framest labour in commandment?
21 They will hunt after the soul of the just, and will condemn innocent blood.
22 But the Lord is my refuge: and my God the help of my hope.
23 And he will render them their iniquity: and in their malice he will destroy them: the Lord our God will destroy them.

EXPLANATION OF THE PSALM

1. In the beginning of this Psalm David lays down one proposition, from which all, if they choose, can plainly learn that not one of the wicked will go unpunished. Here is the proposition: The Lord God is the supreme Judge, most just and most powerful, so that none can resist him. For vengeance is the province of the Judge, and is, therefore, prohibited to private individuals. And though all judges are authorized to punish guilt and crime, yet vengeance, absolutely speaking belongs to God, who will punish the crimes not only of all people, but even of judges, princes, and kings. He, therefore, says, *"The Lord is the God to whom revenge belongeth;"* that is, our Lord, who, strictly speaking, is the only Lord, who is obeyed by all in heaven and on earth; he is the God *"to whom revenge belongeth;"* that is, the supreme Judge, who will punish all crime; *"the God of revenge hath acted freely;"* punished when he liked, for he fears no one, is not an acceptor of persons, no one can impede him, no one can resist him. That appeared in his ejecting the devil and his angels from heaven; in the deluge, through which he destroyed the human race, with the exception of a few; in the burning of Sodom and Gomorrah; in the overwhelming of Pharao and his host in the Red Sea; and in various other signal judgments. I come now to explain the words. The Hebrew for God, in this passage, implies that he is stout, brave, strong, to signify that he takes vengeance on crime with great severity. He is called *"the God of revenge,"* to give us to understand that vengeance proceeds from him, just as he is called the God of peace, the God of hope, the God of salvation. For God is really a God of revenge, because he not only punishes the guilty, when he sits in judgment on them, but he also takes vengeance on his creatures in innumerable and occult ways. For, through the justice of God, sin often becomes the punishment of sin, and the very things that men most desire and seek for become sources of punishment to them, through God's justice. *"Hath acted freely;"* for he that is afraid cannot act freely, and the meaning is, that when God chooses to avenge the sins of mankind, he does so freely, and before the whole world.

2. Having said that God was the avenger of crime, he now calls upon him to do his duty, and, by punishing the wicked, to close the mouths of those who question his providence. *"Lift up thyself, thou that judgest the earth;"* you that are Judge of the whole world, rise, and ascend thy throne; *"render a reward to the proud;"* pass sentence of damnation on them, and thus punish the principal crime of mankind; for pride is the queen of vices, and once it is subdued, vice in general is conquered. Another reason for specifying the proud here is, that they alone who will not humble themselves through penance, will be punished on the last day; *"for all have sinned, and need the glory of God,"* but those who humble themselves under the powerful hand of God, and have a contrite and humble heart, will be saved; but the stiff necked, who only excuse their sins, shall be severely punished.

3. He assigns a reason for calling for judgment on the wicked and the proud, and that is the long continuance of their pride and wickedness. This, however, is not to be read as an imprecation, but as a prediction, and that in order to console the just and the afflicted, to whom the prophet says that the wicked and the proud will quickly perish, however established their happiness and power may seem to be now. *"How long shall sinners O Lord, how long shall sinners glory"* in their strength, their prosperity, and their crimes? *"Shall they utter and speak iniquity?"* boast of their iniquitous doings, without any shame or fear whatever.

4-6. He tells what an amount of crime they perpetrated while they were suffered to run riot. *"Thy people, O Lord, they have brought low."* The assembly of the pious, your people, chosen and set aside by you, and devoted to you alone, has been humbled, laid low, afflicted, and persecuted by them; *"They have afflicted thy inheritance;"* they have most unjustly oppressed the same assembly of the pious, your peculiar inheritance. And they have afflicted the community in general, but they have specially vented their fury on wretched people, destitute of all help; for they killed *"the widows"* who lost their husbands, and *"the strangers,"* who were far from their own country, and unknown; and *"the fatherless,"* who were left without the parent's help when most they needed it.

7. He assigns a reason for those wicked people having committed sin with such effrontery; for they were so foolish as to suppose that God took no cognizance of human affairs, and that there was no judge to whom they would be bound to render an account of their works. *"And they have said"* to each other *"the Lord shall not see, neither shall the God of Jacob understand;"* he will neither see nor hear, and thus will not know what we are doing, and, therefore, cannot examine or understand what we are about.

8-10. The verse, *"He that planted the ear, shall he not hear?"* is a refutation of the verse, *"The Lord shall not see,"* where seeing is used for the knowledge derived from either eyes or ears. The prophet proves that God both sees and hears, from the fact of having given men eyes to see and ears to hear, and, therefore, must, of necessity, see and hear; for no one can give what he has not. The verse, *"he that chastiseth nations, shall he not rebuke?"* is a reply to the wicked, who said, *"Neither shall the God of Jacob understand;"* for the prophet proves that God is endowed with intelligence and reflection, for it was he gave both to man; for he both teaches and instructs them when he creates them with a mind able to reason, and infuses the light of intelligence into their minds. *"Ye senseless among the people,"* gives us to understand that the wicked are the most brainless set among the entire people, in preferring false to true happiness, and temporary to eternal. *"He that planted the ear"* is a beautiful figure, giving us to understand that the sense of hearing, as well as the other senses, did not spring from the body itself, but were planted in it by God, as the trees, that do not spring from the earth itself, which is inanimate, but from the seed which man puts into the earth. *"Shall he not hear?"* This does not imply that God enjoys the corporeal sense of hearing, but that he, essentially, knows what we know only through the sense of hearing. The expression, *"he that formed the eye,"* is another figure, through which we are given to understand that the beautiful mechanism of the eye, and the more extraordinary power it has to see objects, was made by God with as much facility as the potter forms any vessel whatever. *"He that chastiseth nations, shall he not rebuke?"* He that chastises all nations, by smiting their conscience, and admonishing them to desist from evil, and often punishing them openly, shall he not also rebuke his people, through the prophets, or through the scourge of tribulation? and if God corrects and reproves, he certainly knows and understands what men are doing, and, therefore, falsely do the wicked say, *"Neither shall the God of Jacob understand?"*

11. Having refuted the assertions of the wicked, he says this is no new calumny of theirs, nor unknown to God. For *"he knoweth the thoughts of men that they are vain."* For man, after his nature was corrupted by the fall of the first man, became vain and like the senseless brutes that think of nothing but the present. We are, therefore, reminded here not to presume on ourselves, but, in all humility, to ask God for wisdom; for, *"all men are vain in whom there is not the knowledge of God;"* and St. James, therefore, admonishes us, *"But if any of you want wisdom, let him ask of God, who giveth to all abundantly, and upbraideth not;"* that is, he never upbraids us with our importunity for asking too often or too much; for he is rich in mercy, and so generous and liberal that he not only gives us what we ask, but rewards us for asking it. *"Pray to thy Father in secret; and thy Father, who seeth in secret, will reward thee."*

12. This is a consequence of the preceding verse, for, if the thoughts of man, as far as they spring from himself, are vain, it certainly follows that he alone, whom God deigns to instruct, that is, whose eyes are opened by God to see and arrive at what is really good, is truly happy; that is to say, not vain, nor puffed up, but full of true and solid virtue. *"And shalt teach him out of thy law;"* that is, make him fully persuaded that he must give all the affections of his heart to the observance of God's law; for he cannot be said to have learned God's law who can merely repeat the commandments; it is he alone whose heart and affections, moved by the infusion of divine grace, are so devoted to the observance of them, that he keeps them through the love of

justice, rather than the fear of punishment; and the law becomes to him a yoke that is sweet, and a burden that is light.

13. The prophet now instances one of the fruits of God's teaching, for the man so instructed by God will feel the persecution of the wicked less acutely, until their own ruin shall have come about. *"That thou mayest give him rest from the evil days."* The advantage your teaching will confer on the just man will sensibly mitigate the sadness consequent on the evil days, the days of tribulation and persecution. How long, though, are those days to last? *"Till a pit be dug for the wicked;"* until the digging of that pit, in which the wicked are to be cast, shall have been finished, for then there will be an end to the evil days, as there will be no wicked to harass the just, as all grief and pain shall then have left them, and recoiled upon the wicked. We must here observe that this delight in the law, and the spiritual gladness that characterizes the just in this life, is not pure and simple, as it is in the kingdom of heaven, but it is mixed to a certain degree with sadness; for the sadness is only mitigated, and not entirely removed, as St. Paul says, 2 Cor. 1, *"For, as the sufferings of Christ abound in us, so also by Christ doth our comfort abound;"* and again, in chap. 6, *"as sorrowful, yet always rejoicing,"* where he does not say absolutely sorrowful, but *"as sorrowful,"* because his joy exceeded it, as he says, in chap. 7, *"I am filled with comfort, I exceedingly abound with joy in all our tribulation."* We have to observe also that while a crown is being woven for the just, a pit is being dug for the wicked, and that we must not be surprised at their punishment being sometimes deferred, when their pit, perhaps, is not entirely dug; as we are also not to wonder if the just be not crowned at once, when, perhaps, their crown is not completely woven. A matter of much wonder, though, is that the happiness and rise of the wicked should be the actual digging of their pit, and the higher they rise, the deeper they are sure to be buried; for the higher the wicked are exalted, the prouder they become; and by the very fact, the deeper they fall before God, according to Psalm 72, *"when they were lifted up, thou hast cast them down."*

14. He assigns a reason for having said, *"Till a pit be dug for the wicked;"* such a death is prepared by divine providence for the wicked; *"for the Lord will not cast off his people,"* however angry he may appear to be for a time, and suffer them to be afflicted, which he repeats when he says, *"Neither will he forsake his own inheritance."* He calls the assembly of the elect his people and his inheritance, for they are truly the people of Israel, chosen to be his inheritance.

15. The prophet now informs us that the assembly of the just would not be repulsed nor deserted by God to the day of judgment, that is, so long as we shall be surrounded by temptation, *"until justice be turned into judgment;"* that is, until the day when the justice of God, that now seems to be dormant, inasmuch as it does not reward the good, nor punish the wicked, comes into play; and that which was previously justice in the name comes now to take action and reward the good, while it punishes the wicked with a crown of justice, or the stipend of death everlasting. *"And they that are near it are all the upright of heart;"* and then, according to the justice of God, which will appear admirable in the clouds, they who will sit near him will be all they who loved him; who then will not fear but love him, being *"upright of heart;"* that is, conformable to his uprightness, and thereby just.

16. He said that there would be an end of all injustice; and, on the contrary, that justice would reign forever, after the last judgment; he now says that, in the meantime, in the interval of converting justice into judgment, that the divine assistance was of absolute necessity to the just, to protect them from the persecutions of the wicked. *"Who shall rise up for me against the evil doers?"* Who will protect me from such a number of wicked men and angels? *"or who shall stand with me, to defend me against the workers of iniquity?"* the second part of this verse being a mere repetition of the first.

17. He tells the greatness of the danger we are in by reason of the multitude of the malignant that meet us everywhere; in saying so he speaks in the person of the pious, and says *"Unless the Lord had been my helper,"* were it not for his help and assistance, *"my soul had almost dwelt in hell;"* I was within an ace of everlasting death, for I would have fallen under the temptations, and doubted of the providence of God. From this passage it will be objected that God's help is not absolutely necessary to overcome temptation, but that it enables us to overcome them with more facility; for he would seem to say, If the Lord had not helped me I would hardly have escaped death, which would appear to imply, that he would have escaped death, but with some trouble and difficulty. The answer is, that the expression, *"had almost,"* refers not to the difficulty of the matter, but to the shortness of the time, making the meaning to be, Had not the Lord assisted me my soul had been in a few minutes after in hell.

18. He explains the nature of the mercy without which his soul had almost dwelt in hell, and it was this that the moment I acknowledged my weakness, and my inability to meet temptation *"thy mercy, O Lord assisted me,"* for it enlightened my understanding, purified my affections, etc., strengthened my will, all which enabled me to place the powers of my soul in the way of your commandments.

19. God, in his providence, not only gives the virtue of patience to the just, but with it great and unspeakable consolation; which, though it does not remove tribulations, finds a place with them, and converts them into a subject of joy. So the Apostle says, 2 Cor. 7, *"I exceedingly abound with joy in all our tribulation."* Because when the just man suffers any tribulation, he feels that

he is only purged of the dross of his faults, should he have any to be purged of; or, if he has not, that he is only being tried by the Lord: he feels that he is only suffering with Christ that he may be afterwards glorified with him; and, finally, he feels and understands that the reward of patience is great and valuable beyond measure, according to the Apostle, 2 Cor. 4, *"For our present tribulation, which is momentary and light, worketh for us above measure exceedingly an eternal weight of glory."* He, therefore, says, *"According to the multitude of my sorrows in my heart."* In proportion to the sorrows that produced sadness in my heart, *"thy consolations have given joy to my soul;"* for it is not according to the sufferings in the flesh that God gives consolations in the flesh to the just in this world; but in proportion to their corporal sufferings God gives them spiritual consolations, that subdues the sadness arising from their corporal sufferings. Nor does this expression of the prophet, *"According to the multitude of my sorrows in my heart, thy comforts have given joy to my soul,"* contradict the saying of the Apostle, *"I exceedingly abound in joy;"* for spiritual joy is far and away beyond any corporal sadness, but is always in proportion to the extent of the tribulation.

20. He assigns a reason why God should console the just in their trouble, and that is, when God, who is all justice, gave men his commandments, which are troublesome to observe, it was meet that he should, with the oil of his sweet consolation, soften down and modify the burden of a law in other respects heavy and severe. *"Doth the seat of iniquity stick to thee?"* Have you chosen for a companion the judgment seat of those who judge unjustly, *"who framest labor in commandment,"* you who have made your commandments so difficult of observance.

21. He concludes the Psalm by affirming that the wicked would deal unfairly with the just, but that God, in his providence, would watch them, and give both their deserts. *"They will hunt after the soul of the just;"* the wicked will, as usual, try to ensnare the just, as the hunter seeks to catch his prey; *"and will condemn innocent blood,"* when they shall have ensnared him they will condemn him to death, however conscious they may be of his perfect innocence; which may be understood of corrupt judges, false accusers, and all ill disposed characters.

22. The prophet now speaks in the person of the just; and, in reference to the expression, *"They will hunt after the soul of the just,"* the just man replies, So they may; they may hunt after me, and condemn me to death, *"but the Lord is my refuge,"* so that their treachery cannot reach me. *"And my God, the help of my hope."* In the Hebrew it is *"my rock;"* on which I firmly stand and build.

23. The most just providence of God consists in finally helping the just, and scattering the wicked. *"He will render them their iniquity."* He will cause their

wickedness to recoil on themselves, for it will not harm the just, who will be rewarded with a crown for his patience; while it will damage the impious, who will be punished for his malice, which is explained in the next sentence; *"and in their malice he will destroy them."* St. Augustine observes the force of *"in their malice,"* because God punishes them, not so much for what they did, but for the spirit, the malice in which they did it. Judas gave Christ to death, so did God the Father; but we thank him because, in the excess of his love, *"He spared not even his own Son, but delivered him up for us all;"* but we execrate Judas, who delivered up the Lord, not through love, but through avarice; not for our salvation, but for his own purse. The prophet adds, *"The Lord our God will destroy them;"* to explain who it was would destroy them, for though he said, in the beginning of the verse, that they would be destroyed, he did not say by whom, and he now says they will be destroyed by *"the Lord our God,"* whose providence they either denied or despised.

PSALM 94

An invitation to adore and serve God, and to hear his voice.

1 Come let us praise the Lord with joy: let us joyfully sing to God our saviour.
2 Let us come before his presence with thanksgiving; and make a joyful noise to him with psalms.
3 For the Lord is a great God, and a great King above all gods.
4 For in his hand are all the ends of the earth: and the heights of the mountains are his.
5 For the sea is his, and he made it: and his hands formed the dry land.
6 Come let us adore and fall down: and weep before the Lord that made us.
7 For he is the Lord our God: and we are the people of his pasture and the sheep of his hand.
8 To day if you shall hear his voice, harden not your hearts:
9 As in the provocation, according to the day of temptation in the wilderness: where your fathers tempted me, they proved me, and saw my works.
10 Forty years long was I offended with that generation, and I said: These always err in heart.
11 And these men have not known my ways: so I swore in my wrath that they shall not enter into my rest.

Explanation of the Psalm

1. An invitation and an exhortation to praise God. The word *"come"* contains an exhortation, exciting them to join heart and lips in praising God; just as the word is used in Genesis, where the people, exciting and encouraging each other, say, *"Come, let as make bricks;"* and *"Come, let us make a city and a tower;"* and, in the same chapter, the Lord says, *"Come, let us go down, and there confound their tongue." "Let us praise the Lord with joy."* He invites them first to exult in the spirit, and then to compress their joy in song; for song is of little value unless the mind be previously raised up to God in interior joy and admiration. Hence, it is written of the Lord himself, that *"he rejoiced in the Holy Ghost, and said, I give thanks to thee, O Father;"* and the Mother of the Lord said, *"My soul doth magnify the Lord, and my spirit hath rejoiced."* The prophet, then, says, *"Come, let us praise the Lord with joy."* Let us all unite in praising the Lord, giving full expression to our joy, and chanting hymns of praise to him who is our hope and salvation.

2. This verse may be understood in two ways—one making the prophet summon us to rise early in the morning to praise God, as if he said, Before others rise let us be first before God; and in such spirit does the Church put this Psalm in the beginning of matins. The second explanation makes the prophet tell us to unite an avowal of our own misery with God's mercy, making us come before him by acknowledging our sins, previous to his sitting in judgment on them, and punishing us for them; *"and make a joyful noise with psalms,"* in praising the great mercy so extended to us.

3. He assigns five reasons why God should be praised by us. The first is, because our Lord is a great God, far above all other gods; and he is a great King, far higher than all other kings, who are sometimes called gods.

4. The second reason is, because God's power is supreme throughout the entire world, whether as to its length, or breadth, or height; and, therefore, all who inhabit the earth are subject to him, and owe him the sacrifice of praise. *"For in his hand,"* in his power, *"are all the ends of the earth;"* the whole world to its extreme boundaries; *"and the heights of the mountains are his;"* not only does the whole length and breadth of the land belong to him, but even up to the top of the highest mountains are subject to him. In a very old manuscript, after these words is read a verse from the preceding Psalm, *"For the Lord will not cast off his people;"* which verse is daily read in the divine office, but it is not in the Hebrew, the Greek, nor in the Vulgate. In the same copy, instead of the words, *"the heights of the mountains are his,"* the version is, *"he sees the heights of the mountains;"* indicating God's elevation and power.

5. The third reason is, because our God is Lord, not only of the land but of the sea; for it is he who made it, and surrounded it with its sands that confine it as if in a bowl. It is, therefore, most meet that mankind, who derive so many benefits from the sea, should thank and praise him who gave it to them.

6. The fourth reason is, because the same Lord that created the earth and the sea created us men, too, though we are daily offending our Creator by

our sins. Come let us adore and fall down and weep, deploring our ingratitude and our sins, *"before the Lord that made us;"* and, therefore, our Lord by every title, to whom we owe implicit obedience.

7. This is the fifth and last reason, because the Lord not only made us, but he governs us by a special providence, as a shepherd would the flock that belonged to himself. St. Augustine notices an elegant transposition of words here, for instead of saying we are the people of his hand, and the sheep of his pasture, he connects people with pasture, and sheep with hand; to give us to understand that the people, in respect of God, are like sheep that need a shepherd; yet, still, that they are not sheep devoid of reason, that need to be driven with a staff; and they are called the sheep of his hand, either because he made them, or because he guides them with his hand; for though God's people have shepherds and teachers to feed and to direct them, still God has a peculiar care for them, and does not let them suffer from the negligence or the ignorance, or even the malice of the pastors. Whence we infer that God's people should put great confidence in God, their supreme Pastor, and have recourse to him, through prayer, when they fall in with an unworthy pastor, for God himself says, *"I will feed my sheep,"* Ezec. 34.

8. This is the second part of the Psalm, in which the prophet exhorts God's people to praise God, not only by word of mouth, but also by their works. Now, the most agreeable sacrifice we can offer to God is the observance of his commandments, according to 1 Kings 15, *"Doth the Lord desire holocausts and victims, and not rather that the voice of the Lord should be obeyed?"* He introduces God speaking here, in order to give greater effect to his exhortation; for the use of the pronoun *"his"* would lead one to suppose it was other than God was speaking; still, in the Scripture, it is not unusual for God so to speak of himself as in the passage last quoted, *"Doth the Lord desire holocausts?"* for it is God himself who puts the question; so also the Holy Ghost in this passage says, *"Today if you shall hear his voice,"* if you will hear my voice, who am your Lord, *"harden not your hearts."* The word *"today"* means, at present; and, as the Apostle, Heb. 3, explains, holds good or stands *"whilst today is named;"* that is, during the whole time of this life, for after this life time will be no longer, it will be eternity. The word *"if"* seems to mean, that God does not speak to us every moment, but that he advises in fitting time and place, either through his preachers, or through the reading of the Scriptures, or in some other mode to make his will known to us. The expression, *"harden not your hearts,"* signifies that the hearing of the voice of the Lord is of very little value, unless it penetrate the very inmost recesses of our hearts. The hardening of the heart is sometimes ascribed to God, sometimes to man, for the Lord says, Exod. 7, *"I will harden Pharao's heart;"* and yet, in 1 Kings 6, it is said, *"Why do you harden your hearts, as Egypt and*

Pharao hardened their hearts?" Now, God hardens the heart, not by the infusion of malice, but by withholding his mercy; for as St. Augustine says, God hardens, by deserting, by not helping; a thing he can do in his secret dispensations, but not by way of injustice. God is said to harden the heart justly, when he does not, by his grace, soften the reprobate; and man hardens his own heart when he resists the voice and the inspirations of God, according to Acts 7, *"You always resist the Holy Ghost;"* and by the passing pleasure of sin, which the Apostle calls *"the deceitfulness of sin,"* when he says, *"Lest any of you be hardened by the deceitfulness of sin,"* which induces man to resist God, and to close the ears of his conscience against him.

9. He gives an example of the obduracy. For the fathers of old, who were led out of Egypt by Moses, while they were on the way, and were passing through the desert, hardened their hearts, and refused to believe in God's promises or to obey him, more than once; and, therefore, they tempted him and got a proof of, and saw, his wonderful works; such as the manna that rained from heaven, and the water that spouted from the rock. He then says, *"As in the provocation,"* when they provoked God to anger; *"according to the day of temptation in the wilderness,"* at the time they were in the habit of tempting him, for it is not necessary to point out any one specific day, because they frequently rebelled against, and tempted, him; and the day, therefore, comprehends the whole term of their journey through the desert. *"Where your fathers tempted me;"* when they wanted to find out if I were truly God, and whether I could procure bread and water for them in the desert, of which the place seemed totally void. *"They proved me, and saw my works,"* where they had a proof of my omnipotence, seeing the things done by me could be done only by one truly divine, truly omnipotent.

10. He tells the length of time during which he was provoked and tempted. *"Forty years long,"* during the whole time that he was conducting them through the desert to the land of promise; *"and I said, These always err in heart;"* are carried away by various desires, and, therefore, wander and stray from the right path of salvation.

11. He explains why they should have erred in their heart, *"because they have not known my ways,"* my laws which are the straight path, and anyone walking therein cannot possibly go astray; and when he says they have not known his laws, he means knowing them so as to observe them. The meaning, then, is, They who always err in heart have not known my ways, that lead to rest, and, therefore, have not come into rest. *"So I swore in my wrath that they shall not enter into it."* The rest, in a historical sense, was the land of promise, which very few of those who left Egypt saw at all, as the Lord swore, Num. 14, *"As I live, saith the Lord; according as you have spoken in my hearing, so will I do to you. In the wilderness shall your carcasses lie."* In a higher

PSALM 95

An exhortation to praise God for the coming of Christ and his kingdom.

1 Sing ye to the Lord a new canticle: sing to the Lord, all the earth.
2 Sing ye to the Lord and bless his name: shew forth his salvation from day to day.
3 Declare his glory among the Gentiles: his wonders among all people.
4 For the Lord is great, and exceedingly to be praised: he is to be feared above all gods.
5 For all the gods of the Gentiles are devils: but the Lord made the heavens.
6 Praise and beauty are before him: holiness and majesty in his sanctuary.
7 Bring ye to the Lord, O ye kindreds of the Gentiles, bring ye to the Lord glory and honour:
8 Bring to the Lord glory unto his name. Bring up sacrifices, and come into his courts:
9 Adore ye the Lord in his holy court. Let all the earth be moved at his presence.
10 Say ye among the Gentiles, the Lord hath reigned. For he hath corrected the world, which shall not be moved: he will judge the people with justice.
11 Let the heavens rejoice, and let the earth be glad, let the sea be moved, and the fulness thereof:
12 The fields and all things that are in them shall be joyful. Then shall all the trees of the woods rejoice
13 Before the face of the Lord, because he cometh: because he cometh to judge the earth. He shall judge the world with justice, and the people with his truth.

Explanation of the psalm

1. He begins by exhorting the whole world to unite in thanksgiving to God for the favors bestowed on them in general. He repeats the expression, *"Sing ye,"* three times, as he also in a subsequent part of the Psalm repeats another expression, *"Bring ye to the Lord,"* three times, in order to glance remotely at a mystery, that of the Most Holy Trinity, that was to be openly promulgated in the new testament. *"Sing ye to the Lord a new canticle,"* praise and thank him in joy and song, and it must be *"a new canticle,"* a beautiful canticle, and elegantly composed; also a canticle for fresh favors; in like manner, a canticle befitting men who have been regenerated, in whom avarice has been supplanted by charity; and, finally, a canticle not like that of Moses, or Deborah, or any of the old canticles that could not be sung outside the land of promise according to Psalm 136, *"How shall we sing the song of the Lord in a strange land?"* but a new canticle that may be sung all over the world; and he, therefore, adds, *"Sing to the Lord all the earth,"* not only Judea, but the whole world.

2. Having promised this general exhortation, he proceeds to tell the subject of his praise and song, which is the advent of the Savior. *"Sing to the Lord and bless his name,"* in song, praise the power and bless the name of him, *"whose salvation you are to show forth from day to day;"* that is, every day be sure to celebrate the coming salvation or Savior.

3. Having said he should be praised at all times, he now adds, that he should be praised in all places. *"Declare his glory among the gentiles."* Make known God's glory, not only to the Jews, as did the prophets of old, but also to the gentiles, which he expresses more clearly, when he says, *"his wonders among all people,"* tell all nations of the wonderful works of God, that so manifest his glory. Though this exhortation applies to all who know his wonders, it specially applies to the Apostles of the Lord, for it was they that made God's glory known to all nations, as well as the wonderful works, not only of the Creator, but also of the Redeemer, and of the sanctifier; that is, of the Father, Son, and Holy Ghost.

4-5. He now informs us what glory of the Lord, and what wonderful works of his deserve such praise as he just spoke of. *"For the Lord is great and exceedingly to be praised."* In this consists his glory, that he is absolutely great, whether in regard of his power, his wisdom, his goodness, his authority, his riches, or in any other point of view; and that he should be, and is actually praised in proportion to such greatness, and hence the heavens and the earth are full of his glory. Then, *"he is to be feared above all gods;"* that is, that he rises so far above all who have the remotest claim to be called gods, that so far from their presuming to compare themselves to him, they rather tremble like slaves or serfs before his majesty. The Church, in speaking of the good Angels, who are sometimes called gods, says, *"The Angels praise, the dominations adore, the powers tremble before thy majesty;"* and of the fallen angels, who, too, are improperly called gods by the ignorant, St. James says, *"the devils also believe and tremble;"* and, as David alludes to false gods, especially in this Psalm, he, therefore, assigns a reason for our God being feared above all gods, when he says, *"For all the gods of the gentiles are devils; but the Lord made the heavens;"* that is to say, God is to be feared above all false gods, erroneously adored by the gentiles, because the gods of the gentiles are not true gods, but demons, who, through pride, have revolted from the God who created them, and have been doomed by him to eternal punishment; *"but the Lord,"* instead of being a spirit created, is a creating spirit, who *"made the heavens,"* the greatest and the most beautiful things in nature, as well as everything under its canopy, that is, all things created.

6. Having said that God was great and to be feared; he now adds, that he is most worthy of praise in all points of view, that he is most beautiful, glorious, and holy; and that all this is particularly seen in his heavenly sanctuary, where he shows himself to the Angels and other blessed spirits. The second verse of Psalm 103 will throw some light on this verse, which is rather obscure; that verse is, *"Thou hast put on praise and beauty, and art clothed with light like a garment;"* for God is said to have put on praise and beauty, because from every point of view he is seen to be worthy of praise, and that by reason of his being all fair and beautiful, both in his essence, his attributes, his judgments, his thoughts, or his works; which St. John briefly summed up, when he said, *"God is light and there is no darkness in him."* The prophet, then, says of God, *"Praise and beauty are before him;"* that is, praise, or matter of praise, and beauty, or comeliness, and glory, are encircling God, for he has put on praise and beauty, and, therefore, sees his own praise and beauty about him, and it is seen by all; just as the sun, if it had the sense of seeing, would see all the rays of his own light; as they are seen by all, bright and beautiful. *"Holiness and majesty in his sanctuary;"* the holiness, or the purity, and magnificence, or the majesty and glory, with which God is clothed, as it were, with vestments, is seen in his sanctuary, or in the holy temple which he has in heaven.

7. He had already prophesied that the knowledge of God would be preached to all nations, through the coming of Christ; and he now predicts that all nations will be converted, and will glorify God. And, as he predicted the former by way of exhortation, saying, *"Declare his glory among the gentiles,"* he now predicts the latter in the same form, saying, *"Bring to the Lord, O ye kindreds of the gentiles;"* ye families of gentiles scattered all over the world, so soon as the glory of the Lord, who descended from heaven, and, after having accomplished your redemption, returned again in glory to heaven, shall have been announced to you, be not incredulous, nor slow in acting thereon, but run in all haste to the tabernacle of the Lord, and bring to him glory and honor, by glorifying and honoring God and his holy name in your actions and in your words. He calls upon them to come in kindreds or families, in allusion to the Jewish custom of families coming by themselves on the several festival days to worship in Jerusalem; and the Holy Ghost gives us here to understand that such custom was to serve as a model for Christians, whose families should unite in coming to the Church to give glory and honor to God for all the wonderful things he accomplished in the redemption of man; for it was not by our own industry, or by our merits, that we have come to grace, and to be the adopted children of God, but through God's mercy, to whom, therefore, is due all honor and glory.

8. He alludes here to a custom of the Jews, who, when they went up to the temple, offered their victims, and after having adored God, returned to their homes. Now, as the gentiles are here invited to come to the Church of the Lord, such sacrifices are to be understood of those spiritual sacrifices of which St. Peter speaks, *"to offer up spiritual sacrifices, acceptable to God by Jesus Christ."* Those spiritual sacrifices are, the sacrifices of a contrite heart, confession of sins, prayer, fasting, alms, and the like. This may also apply to the Eucharistic sacrifice, that took the place of all the Jewish sacrifices, according to the prophecy of Malachy, and which is offered, *"from the rising of the sun even to the going down,"* to God, by the converted gentiles, through the hands of the priests of the New Testament.

9. He had hitherto seen, as it were, from afar, the kingdom of the Messias, and he exhorted preachers to announce, and people to acknowledge, the coming King; he now beholds him, as it were, at hand, sees him approaching; and, exulting in spirit, he calls upon not only all nations, but even the heavens and the earth, the seas, the very trees, to exult, and to adore him; not that he looked upon such things as imbued with reason, but in order to express the extent of his own feelings, and the universal joy that would be felt all over the world on the coming of Christ. Some will refer this passage to the first, others to the second, coming of Christ; but we see no reason why it should not take in both. He, therefore, says, *"Let all the earth be moved at his presence."* Let all the inhabitants of the earth be full of fear and reverence on the approach of the Lord.

10. In order to stir the people up, preach to them that the coming Lord has taken possession of his kingdom, which kingdom means his spiritual one, through which he reigns by faith in the hearts of men. God always reigns in heaven, and he reigns on earth through his power and majesty; but he began to reign, through faith, among the gentiles, from the coming of the Messias, where the devil previously reigned, through the errors of idolatry; hence the Lord himself said, *"Now is the prince of this world cast out." "For he hath corrected the world, which shall not be moved."* He proves that this kingdom belongs to Christ, by two arguments. The first is, because it was Christ, as God, that made, confirmed, and established the world, so that it cannot be moved, and that it is only just that he who made it should reign in it. This, then, may have reference to the creation of the world; and the word *"corrected"* means that he established the world so firmly that it cannot, even for a minute, go out of its place. The word *"corrected"* may also apply to correction of morals, and the wholesome reformations introduced by the Gospel, and then the meaning would be, that Christ should justly and deservedly reign upon earth, because, when it had gone astray, and fallen into the pernicious errors of the gentiles, he, by his evangelical precepts, that prohibit all manner of vices, corrected, reformed, and so established it that it can never possibly lapse into error, so long as his rules and precepts shall be observed. One precept alone, that of love, if properly observed, would correct the whole world, and keep it in profound peace. The second reason is contained in the words, *"he will judge the people with justice;"* that is, he has not only corrected the world by his most holy laws, but he will also, in the fitting time, judge the world with the greatest justice; for, to those who shall have observed the precepts of the Gospel, he will give most ample rewards, and to those who shall not, most condign punishment.

11-12. He calls upon all creation to be glad and to rejoice, by reason of the first as well as the second coming of the Messias; for while the first coming consecrated, the second will glorify, all things. *"For we know that every creature groaneth and is in labor even till now, but it shall afterwards be delivered from the servitude of corruption into the liberty of the glory of the children of God."* Therefore *"Let the heavens rejoice and the earth be glad,"* as being the principal parts of the world; *"let the sea be moved"* with the same feelings of joy and exultation; *"and the fulness thereof,"* all the living things of which it is full, the fishes. *"The fields and all things that are in them shall be joyful,"* whether cattle or plants, nay, even the very *"trees of the woods,"* however barren and uncultivated, *"shall rejoice."*

13. All the things above named will rejoice in the presence of the Lord, *"because he cometh"* to redeem the world in his mercy, and because he will come again to judge it in his justice. Then they will have to say that the last judgment will be, at once, most terrible and most joyous; terrible to the wicked, a source of unbounded joy to the just. Hence, in the sacred Scripture, the last judgment is sometimes described as a fearful, frightful, and saddening occasion, for, according to St. Luke, *"There will be signs in the sun and in the moon and in the stars; and upon the earth distress of nations, by reason of the confusion of the roaring of the sea and of the waves. Men withering away for fear and expectation of what shall come upon the whole world. For the powers of heaven shall be moved."* At other times it is described as something pleasant and delightful, by reason of the glory of the elect, which will produce a certain effect on the very heavens, earth, and sea, all of which will be renovated and placed in a better position, and, therefore, in a few verses after, in the same chapter, our Savior says, *"But when these things come to pass, look up, and lift up your head, because your redemption is at hand."*—*"He shall judge the world with justice, and the people with his truth."* He concludes by predicting what sort the judgment will be; one that will be in accordance with the justice and the truth that always characterized him, and by virtue of which he always fulfills what he promises, and he has promised to reward every one according to his works; to have no regard of persons, and to judge in all justice. Such will be his mode of judging, and in no other way will he judge. Such an expression ought to knock the sleep out of men's eyes and arouse them; nor should we imagine, for a moment, that because God deals patiently with us, and defers the sentence, that we will escape the judgment; for he that promised so much, and was so true to his promises, cannot possibly lead us astray in this one thing of so much importance. Is it possible, says St. Augustine, that God could have been so faithful in everything, and so false as to the day of judgment?

PSALM 96

All are invited to rejoice at the glorious coming and reign of Christ.

1 The Lord hath reigned, let the earth rejoice: let many islands be glad.
2 Clouds and darkness are round about him: justice and judgment are the establishment of his throne.
3 A fire shall go before him, and shall burn his enemies round about.
4 His lightnings have shone forth to the world: the earth saw and trembled.
5 The mountains melted like wax, at the presence of the Lord: at the presence of the Lord of all the earth.
6 The heavens declared his justice: and all people saw his glory.
7 Let them be all confounded that adore graven things, and that glory in their idols. Adore him, all you his angels:
8 Sion heard, and was glad. And the daughters of Juda rejoiced, because of thy judgments, O Lord.
9 For thou art the most high Lord over all the earth: thou art exalted exceedingly above all gods.
10 You that love the Lord, hate evil: the Lord preserveth the souls of his saints, he will deliver them out of the hand of the sinner.
11 Light is risen to the just, and joy to the right of heart.
12 Rejoice, ye just, in the Lord: and give praise to the remembrance of his holiness.

EXPLANATION OF THE PSALM

1. This Psalm admits of two literal explanations. Some refer it to the kingdom of God absolutely; others to the kingdom of Christ after his resurrection. Read according to the first the meaning of this verse is, *"The Lord hath reigned."* The Lord God is the true and supreme King, and all other kings are but his servants; therefore, *"let the earth rejoice; let many islands be glad;"* let all the inhabitants of the earth, and of the islands that are so numerous in the sea, rejoice and be glad; for should they be oppressed by any of the kings here below, the Lord, who is the supreme King, and can easily control and bring them to order, will not fail to protect and to shield them. In the second sense, the meaning is, Christ our Lord, who at one time humbly appeared before the kings of this world, for judgment, *"hath reigned,"* for *"all power on earth and in heaven hath been given unto him,"* so that he is subject to no one, nor can any one claim any authority over him; but, on the contrary, he governs all as *"Prince of the kings of the earth, as King of kings, and Lord of lords;"* and therefore, *"let the earth rejoice, let many islands be glad,"* because the Lord, who has got possession of his kingdom, has let himself down to be our brother, though he is our God, by having created us, and our Lord, by having redeemed us.

2. According to meaning the first, the nature of God is touched upon here, who, though invisible, governs and rules the visible world with extreme justice. *"Clouds and darkness are round about him."* Our King, the Lord, is invisible, for *"he inhabits light inaccessible,"* and is like the sun concealed by a cloud, yet still diffusing its light and heat. God is also described similarly in Psalm 17, *"And he made darkness his covert, his pavilion round about him; dark waters in the clouds of the air."* In like manner, when God gave the ten commandments on mount Sinai, he was covered with a dark cloud; *"justice and judgment are the establishment of his throne."* However invisible he may appear to be, he still is really present, and judges his people with extreme justice. Meaning the second is, Christ's coming to the general judgment; for *"he will come on the clouds of heaven,"* in great splendor, as he has in Mat. 25, and in the Apocalypse.

3. According to meaning the first the admirable power, efficacy, and celerity of the punishment that God inflicts on the wicked, when he chooses to punish them in this world, is here detailed. *"A fire shall go before him."* He will send a fire before him whenever he may wish to judge and punish the wicked, and that will be most effective and immediate, for it will suddenly *"burn his enemies,"* and consume all *"round about him,"* so that a trace of them will not remain. This fire may also mean his ministering Angels, as we read in Psalm 103, *"Who maketh thy Angels spirits; and thy ministers a burning fire,"* of which fire Psalm 17 says, *"A fire flamed from his face;"* and Daniel 7, *"A swift stream of fire issued forth from before him."* The second interpretation refers it to that fire that will precede the general judgment, and burn men, houses, gardens, vineyards, and all manner of living things on the face of the earth, concerning which, St. Peter says, as in Noe's time, *"The world that there was, being overflowed with water, perished;"* so in the coming of Christ, *"The heavens which now are, and the earth, are reserved unto fire against the day of judgment,"* and will be consumed. And the Psalm says that said fire will hurt God's enemies only, because it is for them only it is intended; for those who have their heart and their treasure in this world. It will be a heavy load on them to have themselves, and the wealth they so loved, consumed by the fire. The just will suffer nothing from it, for they long since despised

the goods of this world, seeing that death would only put them in a better position.

4. According to the first interpretation, David goes on with the relation of God's power over the wicked. God, when he chooses, terrifies his enemies, not only with his fire, or that of his Angels, but even with the ordinary lightning, and cuts them down so unexpectedly, that they cannot possibly protect themselves. He says the same in Psalm 17, *"And the Lord thundered from heaven, and the highest gave his voice, and he sent forth his arrows, and he scattered them, he multiplied lightnings, and troubled them."* He then says, *"His lightnings have shone forth to the world;"* he had his winged lightning, wherewith to rouse the world, which so *"shone forth as to terrify all who saw them,"* and hence, *"the earth,"* as if it had sense and feeling, *"saw and trembled."* A most poetic description to give an idea of the effects of God's lightning. In the second explanation, he explains how an enormous fire, that will consume everything, will precede the last judgment, and will be caused by lightning, of which Wisdom, chap. 5., says, *"Their shafts of lightning shall go directly from the clouds, as from a bow well bent, they shall be shot out, and shall fly to the mark."*

5. The prophet now shows the extent of God's power from its effects, and again compares it to fire, for as wax cannot be brought near the fire without liquefying and melting, thus the mountains, however lofty and durable, nay, even the very earth, the most solid of all the elements, cannot stand for a moment, should God wish to consume and destroy them. We are not to understand, then, that the mountains did, or will run like wax, but that God could cause them, if he chose, to melt, and be dissolved like wax.

6. According to the first interpretation, *"the heavens declared his justice,"* because men could easily infer from the appearance of the sun, moon, and stars, and their continual changes, that God was a most just director of the whole world, as is also said in Psalm 18., *"The heavens declare the glory of God;"* St. Paul, Rom. 1, and Wisdom, chap. 14., say the same. According to the second interpretation, these words allude to the Angel's trumpet, that will announce from heaven the Judge about to sit in judgment on the whole world, and the severity of his justice on those who rejected a merciful Redeemer; and then, *"all people will see his glory,"* when he shall appear in the clouds in his majesty, with all his Angels. The Apostle says of such coming, *"For the Lord himself shall come down from heaven with commandment, and with the voice of the Archangel, and with the trumpet of God;"* and the Lord himself says, *"And he shall send his Angels with a trumpet and a great voice;"* and in the Apocalypse, St. John writes, *"Behold, he cometh with the clouds, and every eye shall see him, and they that pierced him."* *"The heavens declared"* the Angels from heaven, *"his justice,"* for he will come to render unto every one according to his works, *"then all people saw,"* without any exception, *"his glory,"* for every knee will bend of those that are in heaven, on earth, and in hell.

7. According to the first interpretation, the prophet infers from what has been said, that all worshippers of idols should be justly confounded, when it is sufficiently clear that there is only one true God, who rules and governs in heaven and on earth, and who is endowed with the greatest power, wisdom, and justice to direct everything. *"Let them be all confounded that adore graven things,"* that are vain and empty gods, that cannot help themselves nor anyone else; and much more confusion to those *"that glory in their idols,"* for glorying in what, above all other things, they should be ashamed of. According to the second interpretation, this is a prediction, in the form of a prayer, of the immense confusion that will overwhelm all idolaters on the day of judgment; for they will then most clearly see that their idols were nothing, that they who spoke through them were unclean spirits, with whom they will be condemned to eternal punishment. *"Adore him, all you his Angels."* According to the first interpretation, the prophet, in order to prove how justly he said, *"Let them be all confounded that adore graven things, and that glory in their idols,"* turns to the Angels, and invites them to adore God; for, if even the Angels, who are the most noble of created things, so far from being adored, should, like so many servants, adore God, how much less are demons or idols to be adored. According to the second interpretation, the prophet proves the majesty of Christ coming to judgment, from the fact that it will appear on that day that he is the true God, from the homage that will be rendered to him by the Angels. For the Angels will stand by like so many servants, will adore him, and will execute all his commands, which will be a source of the greatest joy and gladness to the true faithful, seeing their Lord so honored and glorified before the whole world. He appeals to the Angels, as if he were exhorting them to do what he foresaw would certainly be done by them. *"Adore him, all you his Angels,"* sitting on his throne for judgment. The Apostle bears out this exposition, when he says, in Heb. 1., *"And again, when he introduceth the first begotten into the world, he saith: And let all the Angels of God adore him;"* for the Apostle would appear by the word *"again"* to mean his second coming, and to apply these words to it, for no other words of the sort are found in the entire Scripture.

8. When God's people heard that he reigned supreme everywhere, that idols had disappeared, that the very Angels were subject to God, they were greatly rejoiced at having such a king. *"And the daughters of Juda rejoiced, because of thy judgments, O Lord;"* the same people, now called Sion, now Juda, rejoiced to find the Lord sitting in judgment with so much justice.

9. He assigns a reason for God's people beginning to exult and be glad on hearing those things, and the reason is, because they inferred from them, that the God of God's people was really the supreme Lord of all, *"the Most High Lord over all the earth,"* over all kings and princes, and *"exalted exceedingly,"* especially over the false gods erroneously worshipped by the gentiles; and, however true this may be, according to interpretation No. 1, for God proved himself, by various miracles, to be superior to all the kings of the earth, and all their false gods; it is no less true, when we read by interpretation No. 2, for God never displayed his glory so openly as he will on the last day, when, as we said above, all men and Angels, bad as well as good, will bend the knee before him.

10. He concludes the Psalm, by exhorting the people to lead a life of holiness and purity, for which they will get a great reward, both in this world and in the next. *"You that love the Lord, hate evil."* The holy prophet could not possibly address God's chosen people more briefly, yet more comprehensively; for, when he says, *"You that love the Lord,"* he appeals to all the truly just, for charity comprehends all virtues; for, *"he that loveth his neighbor hath fulfilled the law, and love, therefore, is the fulfilling of the law,"* Rom. 13: *"you that love the Lord,"* then, means, All you just and holy souls, that fear the Lord really, and not feignedly, not only with your lips, but in your heart, according to the substance, and not the shadow of the law, *"hate evil:"* which is the essence of perfection, for he does not say, Fly from, or decline from evil, which may be done externally, but *"hate evil,"* which can only proceed from the heart. The heart is the source of all our actions, good and bad; for, as the love of the supreme good comes from the heart, so, in like manner, *"out of the heart proceed evil thoughts, murders, adulteries, fornications, thefts, false testimonies, blasphemies."* He then announces the reward for having done so, saying, *"The Lord preserveth the souls of his saints, he will deliver them out of the hand of the sinner."* The Lord is a faithful, diligent, powerful, and prudent guardian of those that love him, and he will defend and deliver them from the power of the wicked, who are, generally speaking, deadly enemies of the just. According to interpretation No. 1, this promise is fulfilled even in this life, in regard of the just, for God often saves their lives, but will certainly save their souls, which is a far greater blessing; and hence, the expression, *"preserveth the souls,"* for he causes *"all things to work together unto good, to such as according to his purpose are called to be saints."* According to explanation No. 2, the meaning would be, He will preserve the souls of his saints on the last day, so that they will not be injured by the accusations of the enemy; he will most completely deliver them from the hand of the sinner, for once the last sentence shall have been passed, the sinner can no longer harm the just.

11. Another reward of the just is, that they will not only be delivered from all evils, but they will be replenished with blessings. By light, here, may be understood the light of divine grace, or what seems more likely, the light of justice, of which Wisdom, chap. 5., says, *"Therefore, we have erred from the way of truth, and the light of justice hath not shined unto us, and the sun of understanding hath not risen upon us."* Now, the light of justice and of understanding is said to rise on a person when he begins to know, not only in theory but in practice, what is just and what is unjust, what is good and what is evil; and forms a correct judgment, and makes a judicious choice of what is really good and just, and not of what is apparently so to a badly formed and irregular mind. The light, then, that has risen to the just, is that which constitutes him a just man; and as the just take the greatest pleasure in doing what is just, he very properly adds, *"and joy to the right of heart;"* for justice directs the heart, and an unspeakable amount of joy is poured into the upright of heart from the fact of its conformity to the will of God, and everything that pleases God, on whose nod all creation hangs, pleases that soul. Nothing, then, can sadden the just; they rejoice and are joyful under the most grievous tribulations, *"and nobody taketh their joy from them."*

12. This is a consequence of what has been said in the preceding verse; for if joy has arisen to those right of heart, it follows that they should not rejoice in the vanities of the wicked, but *"in the Lord,"* who bestows justice and gladness on them; nay, who himself is their real and solid joy, being most beautiful to the eyes of the soul, and sweet to the interior; and not only should *"the just rejoice in the Lord,"* but they should also *"give praise to the remembrance of his holiness;"* they should ever celebrate with thanksgiving the memory of the sanctification they received from God, for they should never forget so great a favor as that which transformed them from being impious and wicked, to be holy and just. By holiness also may be understood God's own holiness, for he is supremely holy; hence, Isaias calls him *"Holy, Holy, Holy,"* and we give praise to the remembrance of his holiness, when with praises we always remember that our God is most holy; and, therefore, that we should with all earnestness endeavor to make ourselves holy too. *"For this is the will of God your sanctification;"* and *"Be ye holy,"* saith the Lord, *"for I am holy."*

PSALM 97

All are again invited to praise the Lord, for the victories of Christ.

1 Sing ye to the Lord anew canticle: because he hath done wonderful things. His right hand hath wrought for him salvation, and his arm is holy.
2 The Lord hath made known his salvation: he hath revealed his justice in the sight of the Gentiles.

3 He hath remembered his mercy his truth toward the house of Israel. All the ends of the earth have seen the salvation of our God.
4 Sing joyfully to God, all the earth; make melody, rejoice and sing.
5 Sing praise to the Lord on the harp, on the harp, and with the voice of a psalm:
6 With long trumpets, and sound of cornet. Make a joyful noise before the Lord our king:
7 Let the sea be moved and the fulness thereof: the world and they that dwell therein.
8 The rivers shall clap their hands, the mountains shall rejoice together
9 At the presence of the Lord: because he cometh to judge the earth. He shall judge the world with justice, and the people with equity.

EXPLANATION OF THE PSALM

1. He invites all men to praise God for his wonderful works. *"Sing ye to the Lord a new canticle,"* for there is not only new but great and wonderful matter for it, *"because he hath done wonderful things;"* for he was wonderfully, and in an unheard of manner, conceived of the Holy Ghost, born of a virgin, committed no sin, justified sinners, made the deaf to hear, and the dumb to speak, nay, even the blind to see, the lame to walk, cured the sick, raised the dead; and, what is the most strange and wonderful of all, showed himself alive within three days after he was buried, took his body up to heaven, sent the Holy Ghost from heaven, and through the agency of poor, humble men, persuaded the prudent and the wise to worship the crucified, to despise the things of the present, and to look forward to the things of the future; and, finally, as St. Augustine says, conquered the world, not by the sword but by the cross. All this may be referred to the Father, who in the Son, and through the Son, effected all these wonderful things; for the Lord says, *"But the Father, who abideth in me, he doth the works." "His right hand hath wrought for him salvation, and his arm is holy."* He explains what those wonderful things are, and instances one of them that comprehends the whole. The wonderful thing God did consisted in his having saved the world purely by his own power, without associates, without an army, without arms; he alone cast out the prince of this world, and delivered mankind from his power. Such was the object of all the wonderful things enumerated above; and thus, this one thing comprehends all. The expression, *"hath wrought for him salvation,"* may apply to the Son, who saved the world by his own power; and to the Father who, through Christ, his right hand, saved it; but it comes to the same thing; *"and his arm is holy,"* is merely a repetition of the foregoing; right hand and arm being nearly synonymous, and they signify virtue and power; but the word *"holy"* is added, for fear we should suppose carnal, not spiritual, strength is intended; for Christ did not overcome his enemy by the force of arms or by bodily strength, but by love and patience, by humility and obedience, by the merits of his most holy life, by his most precious blood spilled for love of us, and not by the spear or the sword, and obtained a signal victory over a most powerful enemy. So, says the Apostle, *"He humbled himself, becoming obedient unto death, even the death of the cross."*

2. This verse, too, may be referred to the Father, *"who made known his salvation;"* that is, the Savior he sent; first, through the prophets, then through the Apostles, and through the same *"revealeth his justice."* It may also be referred to the Son, who made known the salvation effected by himself, through himself, and through his Apostles; for he preached it openly for three entire years and more, and then he sent his Apostles, who announced his Gospel to the entire world. The Lord, therefore, by his own preaching, *"made his salvation known;"* that is, the salvation he brought on earth to confer on those who would believe in him; then, *"in the sight of the gentiles,"* through his Apostles, *"he hath revealed his justice;"* that is, he made known and revealed to the gentiles that mystery that was hidden from the world; and the mystery is his own justice; that is, the fulfillment of that promise that was formerly made to the fathers concerning the redemption of the human race. This I consider to be the meaning of justice here; for in the following verse it means truth, as we shall see. However, if anyone wishes justice to be understood of the satisfaction Christ had to offer, in the rigor of justice, for the sins of the whole world, I do not object, whether in reference to the Father, or to the Son. For truly did the Father, through the passion of the Son, and the Son through his own sufferings, *"reveal"* how iniquity required to be punished, and how rigorously God's justice required satisfaction. On this mystery the Apostle writes as follows to the Ephesians, *"To me, the least of all the saints, is given this grace to preach among the gentiles the unsearchable riches of Christ. And to enlighten all men what is the dispensation of the mystery, which hath been hidden from eternity in God."*

3. He assigns a reason for God's having *"made known his salvation,"* and *"revealed his justice."* Because he promised such to the fathers; and though he delayed the fulfillment of his promise for some time, he at length *"remembered"* it; that is, he acted as those do who remember a thing. God cannot forget, but he is figuratively said to remember when he does a thing after a while, as if he had forgotten it. The expression often occurs in the Scriptures; thus, *"The Lord remembered Noe;"* and, Luke 1, *"He hath remembered his mercy."* God the Father, then, *"remembered his mercy,"* through which he promised a Savior to the fathers; and God the Son *"remembered his mercy,"* that induced him to promise to come as a Savior; and both remembered *"their truth,"* their honor and justice in fulfilling the promise *"toward the house of Israel;"* for the promise was made to them, and not to the gentiles; although

God had determined, and often announced it through the prophets, that he would have mercy on the gentiles, too. Hence our Savior, Mat. 15, says, *"I was not sent out to the sheep that are lost of the house of Israel."* And the Apostle, Rom. 15, *"For I say that Christ Jesus was minister of the circumcision for the truth of God, to confirm the promises made to the fathers; but that the gentiles are to glorify God for his mercy, as it is written. Therefore will I confess to thee, O Lord, among the gentiles."*—*"All the ends of the earth have seen the salvation of our God."* See the fruit of the preaching of the Apostles! It was not in vain that God made his salvation known through their preaching, for the gentiles heard them, and believed in Christ; and thus the interior eye of the heart having been purified through faith and grace, *"all the ends of the earth,"* the whole world, to its remotest boundaries, *"have seen the salvation of our God,"* or the Savior sent by him. There is a degree of point in the expression, *"have seen;"* it implies actual faith, united with knowledge, that moves the will to love and to desire; for they cannot be said to have seen God's salvation, who, content with habitual faith, never bestow a thought on the Savior, and take no trouble whatever in accomplishing the salvation to be had through him. The expression, *"all the ends of the earth,"* is not to be read literally, for it does not mean each and every individual, but a great many from every nation and people.

4. The giving thanks to God, and exulting and singing in spiritual joy, is a sign of faith. Thus, he that found the treasure *"went, and, through joy, sold all he had."* Thus when Philip preached in Samaria, and the inhabitants received the word of God, *"there was great joy in that city;"* and the eunuch, when converted and baptized, *"went his way rejoicing"* thus also St. Peter says, *"And believing, shall rejoice with an unspeakable and glorious joy."* This joy is now predicted by the prophet, as if he were inviting and exhorting the faithful to it, *"Sing joyfully to God, all the earth."* All you faithful, all over the world, who have been brought from darkness to *"the admirable light,"* to the knowledge of the true God and our Savior Jesus Christ, praise and thank with a loud voice; sing, exult, and play upon musical instruments.

5-6. Four instruments are enumerated for those who have seen God by faith, and, desire to see him by sight; they are the harp, the psaltery, long trumpets, and sound of cornet. These were, literally, the instruments most in use among the Jews, and a spiritual signification has been attached to each instrument. They seem to be to represent the cardinal virtues, the harp implying prudence; the psaltery, justice; the long trumpet, fortitude, and the cornet temperance. The harp, having various strings, blends their sounds together, and produces a sweet harmony; and thus prudence unites good works with various circumstances, and produces a perfect work. The psaltery of ten strings represents the decalogue, containing all the precepts of justice. The long trumpet is beaten out and formed by repeated blows of the hammer, until it produces the sweet sounds required; thus, fortitude, by patiently bearing all trials and tribulations, so draws out and perfects the man of God, that, with holy Job, it is no trouble to him to give out that sweet sound, *"If we have received good things at the hand of God, why should we not receive evil?"* Finally, temperance, like a hard horn, from which the cornet was made, rising above and out topping the flesh; that is, chastising the body, by fasting and watching, and by bringing it under subjection to the spirit, forms it into a spiritual cornet. Such was the precursor of our Lord, who, with wild honey and locusts for his food, and a garment of camel's hair with a leathern girdle for his dress, called out, *"A voice of one crying in the desert."* Such, too, was the most blessed Paul, who, instructed as he was by long continued temperance, gave out the following sweet sounds, *"But having food and wherewith to be covered, with these we are content;"* and again, *"The meat for the belly, and the belly for the meats; but God shall destroy both it and them."* And truly, *"piety with sufficiency is great gain." "Make a joyful noise before our King."* Be sure to strike up all the aforesaid instruments the moment the great King, who is Lord of all, shall have made his appearance.

7. As the coming of the Lord was a blessing to all in general, the prophet calls, not only on the whole earth, but on all its parts, separately, to praise and sing to God. *"Let the sea be moved,"* heaving and swelling with exultation, as if it were animated; *"and the fulness thereof;"* its waters, islands, fishes; *"the world, and they that dwell therein."* Let them, too, rejoice and exult because the Lord is the Savior of all men, especially of the faithful.

8. Having invited the sea and the earth, he now summons the rivers and the mountains to unite in their expressions of joy. He said, however, *"Let the sea be moved,"* in the Hebrew, let it thunder; whereas to the rivers he says, they shall *"clap their hands,"* thereby expressing the difference between the noise of the one and of the other; and when he calls upon *"the mountains to rejoice together,"* we can easily understand that the prophet does not ask those inanimate things to speak, to praise, or to sing, but that he is so carried away and inflamed with love for the coming Messias, that he calls upon and wishes all created things to unite with him, as far as possible, in praising and thanking God.

9. *"Because he cometh to judge the earth"* may be referred either to his first or his second coming. If to his first, the meaning will be, Let all the aforesaid rejoice, *"because he cometh to judge the earth,"* to rule and govern the earth through most just and wise laws, not only as of old, in the majesty of his invisible divinity, but in visible and corporal appearance, *"being made to the likeness of men, and in shape found as a man."*—If we refer it to his second coming, the meaning would be, Let all these rejoice, because *"the Lord*

cometh to judge the earth," and he will exterminate all the sinners in it, and renew all its elements, *"and he will deliver it from the servitude of corruption, under which it now groans and is in labor."*—*"He shall judge the world with justice."* The same as the conclusion of Psalm 95, which see.

PSALM 98

The reign of the Lord in Sion; that is, of Christ in his Church.

1 The Lord hath reigned, let the people be angry: he that sitteth on the cherubims: let the earth be moved.
2 The Lord is great in Sion, and high above all people.
3 Let them give praise to thy great name: for it is terrible and holy:
4 And the king's honour loveth judgment. Thou hast prepared directions: thou hast done judgment and justice in Jacob.
5 Exalt ye the Lord our God, and adore his footstool, for it is holy.
6 Moses and Aaron among his priests: and Samuel among them that call upon his name. They called upon the Lord, and he heard them:
7 He spoke to them in the pillar of the cloud. They kept his testimonies, and the commandment which he gave them.
8 Thou didst hear them, O Lord our God: thou wast a merciful God to them, and taking vengeance on all their inventions.
9 Exalt ye the Lord our God, and adore at his holy mountain: for the Lord our God is holy.

EXPLANATION OF THE PSALM

1. According to the first interpretation, we are given to understand, in this first verse, that the kingdom of God was established in Jerusalem in David's time, notwithstanding the indignation and annoyance of its idolatrous enemies. *"The Lord hath reigned."* The Lord, after having expelled the idolatrous Jebusans and Chanaaneans, established his kingdom in Jerusalem. Though David was king, he felt he had his power from God, and owed him his kingdom. *"Let the people be angry,"* in spite of the pagans and idolaters. *"He that sitteth on the Cherubim;"* the same Lord that sits on the Cherubim, hath reigned, no matter how the earth, that is, the idolaters therein, may be troubled at it. God literally sits on the Cherubim, because he chose the propitiatory for his seat, which was supported by two gilded Cherubim, under which was the Ark, which formed the footstool of the Lord. In a spiritual sense, God is said to sit on the Cherubim, because he presides over all the choirs of Angels, or because Cherubim signify fulness of knowledge, in which God excels all created beings. We, too, may become Cherubim, and have God presiding over us, if we can obtain that fulness of knowledge that God requires, the knowledge of his will, the knowledge of his law, and, since *"love is the fulfilling of his law,"* we will become Cherubim, and have God sitting on us, when we shall have that love, as it is written, *"The soul of the just man is the seat of wisdom."*—*"Let the earth be moved"* is only a repetition of *"Let the People be angry;"* for the Holy Spirit wished to show that they who feel anger towards God are no more than earth, and cannot harm God, who sits in heaven on the Cherubim; nor need we fear, if we, too, become Cherubim, and have God sitting on us. Referring the verse to Christ, the meaning would be, that his kingdom was declared after his resurrection and ascension, for then it began to be preached through the world, and at once the people got angry, and the earth was moved, at their fighting against their Lord for their idols; but, in spite of all their opposition, Christ our Lord reigned, and the idols were destroyed. And though it would appear that the anger of the idolaters had the victory over the bodies of the saints, it was only an apparent victory; for the bodies of the saints will be newly formed by him who conquered death in his own person, and they will live; but the idols, once demolished, will never be put together again.

2. In the first exposition, a reason is assigned here for the inutility of the anger of those people against God, who established his kingdom in Sion, and the reason is, because he is *"great,"* *"and high above all people;"* that is, he excels all in greatness, power, and wisdom, so as to be excelled by no one. According to the second interpretation, it means that Christ, who reigns supreme in the Church, militant as well as triumphant, represented by Sion and Jerusalem, is great and high above all people, so that nobody can resist him.

3. The prophet now exhorts the people, instead of being angry with God, to turn to him, and celebrate his name with praise; for his name *"is terrible and holy."* His name is said to be terrible and holy, because it is the name of a most powerful and just Judge or King, terrible by reason of his power, just by reason of his holiness.

4. A reason assigned for God's or Christ's name being terrible and holy. The name of the Lord, who is a most just King, is terrible and holy, because his dignity, his holiness, his authority requires that he should love justice, and that all his judgments should proceed from a pure love of justice, and not from anger, from fear, or from any pressure from without. Thou hast prepared directions; thou hast done judgments and justice in Jacob." To prove that what he said regarding the king's love for justice was true, he addresses Christ or God, saying, It must be true that you do love justice, for, you have *"prepared directions;"* wholesome and salutary laws calculated to direct the people and to reform their manners; and, with that, you have shown your love for justice; for, *"thou hast done judgment and justice in Jacob,"* by punishing sin, and rewarding virtue; many examples of which are to be found in

the Old and New Testament. For, though God suffers the pious to be afflicted, and the wicked to prosper in this world, he, however, ultimately delivers and crowns the former, and condemns and torments the latter, certainly in the other world, and not unfrequently in this.

5. From what has been said the prophet infers that God ought to be adored, and exhorts all to do it diligently. According to the first interpretation, he exhorts them to adore God not only as God, but also in the Ark of the covenant, which was his footstool, for we read in Paralipomenon 28, *"In which the Ark of the Lord, and the footstool of our God might rest;"* and no wonder it should be called the footstool of the Lord, for the propitiatory that was supported by the Cherubim was God's seat, and the Ark being under that was naturally called his footstool. He, therefore, says, *"Exalt ye the Lord our God,"* by praising and magnifying his majesty with heart and voice. *"And adore his footstool,"* by bowing and prostrating yourselves before the Ark of the Covenant, which is his footstool; *"for it is holy,"* by reason of its relation to God, to whom it is dedicated, and in honor of whom it is adored. Hence, we justly infer that sacred things, such as the images of Christ and of his saints, their relics and altars, sacred vessels, and the like, are, by reason of their relation to God, worthy of a certain degree of reverence and adoration. According to the second interpretation, the prophet exhorts all to adore the human nature of Christ, that was the footstool of the divinity in a much more intimate and noble manner than was the wooden Ark. The latter contained the word of God on tables of stone; but the Word itself was contained in the other. The one merely contained the tables of the law, as a vessel would hold its contents; while the other was hypostatically united to its contents, the Word; so that John truly expressed it when he said, *"The Word was made flesh."* And we are to adore Christ not only as man, but also under the sacramental species, as has been justly proved by the fathers from this same passage.

6. The prophet now proposes a model for our imitation in three celebrated characters, who *"exalted"* God, and *"adored his footstool,"* and *"invoked his name,"* and were, in consequence, heard by him, and got the power of working many miracles through him. He names three of the principal persons who were so remarkable among the Jews. Moses, who was the leader, and at the same time a high priest; Aaron, who was high priest only; and Samuel, who was a civil ruler only; for though Samuel is sometimes called a priest by the holy fathers; he in reality was not a priest, he was only a Levite. In the first place, he was not of the family of Aaron, to whom the priesthood was confined. Secondly, when Samuel ministered, he was dressed in a linen ephod, the peculiar dress of the Levites. Thirdly, his father, Elcana, was only a Levite, and not a priest. Fourthly, David himself evidently distinguishes

him from Moses and Aaron, whom he classes among the priests, while he designates Samuel as merely among those that called upon the name of the Lord. *"They called upon the name of the Lord."* He proves that they were friends of God, for they prayed to him for themselves and for their people, and he heard them as being faithful friends. The Scriptures bear testimony to that, as far as Moses and Aaron are concerned most clearly; as also to Samuel, to whom he addressed himself in the night, and heard Samuel in reply.

7. Though he did not speak to Samuel in the pillar of the cloud, he spoke to Moses and Aaron; and thus, the expression applies to the majority of those named. *"They kept his testimonies."* The reason why they were so promptly heard, for as the Lord himself says, *"If any one love me he will keep my word;"* and, therefore, he that wishes God to hear his prayer, must hear God in his commandments, *"They kept his testimonies;"* all his commandments which regarded all men, *"and the commandment which he gave them;"* they not only observed the precepts that bind men in general, but the peculiar obligation of governing and directing and teaching the people committed to them; for princes and rulers are not exempt from the commandments, but they should rather be remarkable for their observance of them, to show a good example to those they govern.

8. When Moses and Aaron invoked you, you heard them in your mercy, and took vengeance on their enemies, and on all their wicked inventions.

9. The prophet concludes by a repetition of the fifth verse, it being the essence of the Psalm, and containing the whole object of it. There is a slight difference however, for, in the fifth verse, *"adore his footstool,"* is here, *"adore at his holy mountain;"* and *"for it is holy,"* is here, *"for the Lord our God is holy."* According to interpretation No. 1, the meaning is, David exhorts the Jews to adore the Lord on mount Sion where the tabernacle was, and the temple was to be. According to interpretation No. 2, he exhorts Christians to adore God in the Catholic Church, the holy mountain, the spiritual Sion, and to avoid the conventicles of heretics and schismatics, because the Lord our God is holy, and, in consequence, hates the mountains polluted by the filth of false religions; and, as he is himself holy, so he wishes to be adored in his holy mountain, the assembly of the faithful.

PSALM 99

All are invited to rejoice in God the creator of all.

1 Sing joyfully to God, all the earth: serve ye the Lord with gladness. Come in before his presence with exceeding great joy.
2 Know ye that the Lord he is God: he made us, and not we ourselves. We are his people and the sheep of his pasture.

3 Go ye into his gates with praise, into his courts with hymns: and give glory to him. Praise ye his name:
4 For the Lord is sweet, his mercy endureth for ever, and his truth to generation and generation.

EXPLANATION OF THE PSALM

1. To sing joyfully means, as we have frequently repeated, to praise with loud and joyful voice and to serve with gladness means to be obedient through love, and not through fear. *"Sing joyfully to God all the earth."* All you worshippers of the true God, in whatever part of the world you may be cast, praise him. Good and bad are to be found all over the world: in the wheat will be found the cockle, and thorns among the lilies. And as the wicked, when they do not succeed according to their wishes, are always ready to blaspheme and murmur against God, so it is meet that the good throughout the world, whatever may happen to them, whether for or against them, should praise and bless him; for, as St. Paul says, *"we know that to them that love God all things work together unto good, to such as, according to his purpose, are called to be saints."*—*"Serve ye the Lord with gladness."* Serve him by obeying him freely, and not as if you were under coercion—with the joy of freemen, and not with the bitterness of slaves. For, as St. Augustine expresses it, Truth delivered us, but love has made us slaves; and he that is a slave from love is one with pleasure. The principal reason, however, for serving God with pleasure consists in love being the summary of his precepts, and nothing is sweeter than love. Besides, the service of God is a profitable thing to us, of no profit to him. *"Come in before his presence with exceeding great joy."* We are bound to praise God everywhere, but especially when we enter his house, *"a house of prayer,"* where we see God himself in his sacred things, and he, by a special providence, looks on and hears us, according to 2 Paralip. 7, *"My eyes also shall be open, and my ears attentive to the prayer of him that shall pray in this place."* The prophet, therefore, admonishes them *"to come in before his presence,"* into the house of God, where they can specially see him, and he them, and to come *"with exceeding great joy,"* in high spirits, so that God may see their ardent desire for him.

2. Nothing tends so much to stir up that devotion suited to the house of God, as an attentive consideration of God's greatness and his gifts. *"Know ye that the Lord he is God."* Consider, and, after serious consideration, be it known to you, that the God you worship, and to whom you come to offer your tribute of prayer and praise, is the true God, than whom nothing greater or better can be imagined. To him you owe your whole life and existence; for *"he made us, and not we ourselves;"* he is the primary source of our being; for though parents beget children, they get them through God's will

only. How many in the world sigh and long for children, and are still denied them; and, on the other hand, how many would enjoy the married state without the burden of children, and still have children thrust upon them. Most justly, then, did the holy mother of the Machabees say to her sons, *"I know not how you were formed in my womb, for I neither gave you breath, nor soul, nor life; neither did I frame the limbs of every one of you, but the Creator of the world that formed the nativity of man, and that formed out the origin of all."*—*"We are his people, and the sheep of his pasture."* He now reminds them of another of God's favors, for which they are bound to thank and praise him, because he not only created us, but he also directs and supports us. *"We are his people,"* directed by God's special providence; *"and the sheep of his pasture;"* supported by the food of his word, that nourishes us as rich pastures support the sheep that feed on them.

3. Enter into his house with praise and thanksgiving, acknowledging you owe all to him, and have received everything from him.

4. The prophet now enumerates three of God's attributes as a further reason for being praised and glorified by all. God's sweetness, mercy and veracity which so connected that one would seem to be the source of the other. *"The Lord is sweet,"* and, therefore, inclined to mercy; his mercy causes him to promise pardon, and his veracity causes him to fulfill his promise. *"For the Lord is sweet."* An extraordinary attribute of that omnipotent and tremendous majesty that dwells in light inaccessible, that is terrible above all gods, who taketh away the spirit of the princes, and of whom the Apostle says, *"It is a dreadful thing to fall into the hands of the living God;"* and yet, most truly is it said of him, *"The Lord is sweet."* This is not the only passage that says so. It is frequently repeated in the Scriptures, Psalm 33, *"O taste and see that the Lord is sweet;"* and in Psalm 85, *"For thou, O Lord, art sweet, and mild, and plenteous in mercy;"* and, 1 Peter 2, *"If yet you have tasted that the Lord is sweet;"* and in 2 Cor. 1, *"The Father of mercies, and the God of all consolation."* These two apparently contradictory attributes of God are, however, easily reconciled. God is sweet to the upright of heart, to those that fear him; he is rough and terrible to the crooked of heart, and to those that despise him. Hence the prophet, in another Psalm, exclaims, *"How good is God to Israel, to them that are of a right heart;"* for what is quite level seems rough to one with a crooked heart, and all those are crooked in heart, who will not conform themselves to the will of God; and hence we read in Psalm 102, *"As a father hath compassion on his children, so hath the Lord compassion on them that fear him; his mercy is from eternity, and unto eternity upon them that fear him;"* an expression used by the Virgin, in her canticle, when she sang, *"And his mercy is from generation to generation, to them that fear him."* If anyone, then, will begin to direct his heart, and make it conformable to God's will,

and to fear nothing so much as offending God, he will, at once, begin to taste how sweet God is; and in him will be realized the conclusion of the Psalm, *"his mercy endureth forever, and his truth to generation and generation."*

PSALM 100

The prophet exhorteth all by his example, to follow mercy and justice.

1 Mercy and judgment I will sing to thee, O Lord: I will sing,
2 And I will understand in the unspotted way, when thou shalt come to me. I walked in the innocence of my heart, in the midst of my house.
3 I did not set before my eyes any unjust thing: I hated the workers of iniquities.
4 The perverse heart did not cleave to me: and the malignant, that turned aside from me, I would not know.
5 The man that in private detracted his neighbour, him did I persecute. With him that had a proud eye, and an unsatiable heart, I would not eat.
6 My eyes were upon the faithful of the earth, to sit with me: the man that walked in the perfect way, he served me.
7 He that worketh pride shall not dwell in the midst of my house: he that speaketh unjust things did not prosper before my eyes.
8 In the morning I put to death all the wicked of the land: that I might cut off all the workers of iniquity from the city of the Lord.

Explanation of the psalm

1. This is a sort of preface to the Psalm, in which David gives us to understand that he is about to sing of the mercy and judgment of God, for which he has many reasons; first, that all may understand that his own good works proceed from the mercy of God, and will be crowned hereafter by the judgment of God. Secondly, to admonish princes that nothing pleases God so much as mercy and judgment; and, therefore, that it behoved them to be merciful without being unjust, to be just without being cruel. Thirdly, that all men should hope in God's mercy, while they dread his judgment; but to hope, without presuming, and to fear, without despairing. He names mercy first, for the present life is that of mercy, the future that of judgment; so that no one need be surprised if, for the present, *"he makes his sun to rise upon the good and the bad, and raineth upon the just and the unjust."*
2. I will consider on, reflect, and think upon the perfect and unspotted way, that consists in mercy and judgment; for *"all the ways of the Lord are mercy and truth."* A similar expression occurs in Psalm 40, Blessed is he that understandeth concerning the needy and the poor;" which means, he considers the misery of the poor with a view of relieving them; thus also, *"I will understand in the unspotted way"* means, I will consider it attentively, with the view of walking in it. That I never will be able to do of myself, by my

own strength, but by the help of your grace, *"when you shall come to me,"* to enlighten, teach, inflame, and move me. *"I walked in the innocence of my heart, in the midst of my house."* He now commences relating his mode of life, as worthy of imitation both by his successors and by his subjects; for it is for this purpose that the king sits on an elevated seat, *"that, like a candle placed on a candlestick, he may shine unto all."* He first explains his position with himself and with God; next, with others, and in the eyes of his people. *"I walked in the innocence of my heart;"* I led or walked the life of this world, preserving my innocence most completely; thinking of nothing, seeking nothing, delighting in nothing but what was good; most careful in keeping my heart from being polluted by sinful thoughts or desires; for I knew the heart to be the source of life and of death. Hence his son Solomon, educated by such a father, afterwards wrote, *"With all watchfulness keep thy heart, because life issueth out from it."*—*"In the midst of my house."* Where there was no one to censure me; for many will conduct themselves with great gravity and decorum in the streets or market place, while they revel in all manner of licentiousness in their houses or their chambers, especially in the chambers of their hearts; while David kept his innocence unstained, not only in his house, but also in his heart.

3. What he said of the innocence of his heart he now says of his eyes and of his hands. *"I did not set before my eyes any unjust thing;"* I turned away the eyes of my mind as well as of my body from all injustice, whether in deciding between my subjects or in the distribution of honors and promotions, or in bargains and contracts; and furthermore, from all sinful objects, illicit sports, impure revels, and from all manner of objects that could possibly defile the soul. *"I hated the workers of iniquity."* I not only turned away my eyes from forbidden objects, and did no manner of iniquity, but I even hated all those guilty of it; and thus, got a thorough detestation of iniquity itself.

4. After telling his position in regard of himself, he now tells us how he stood in regard of others; and such was his position that the wicked would not even dare to approach him. Great must be the virtue of anyone, when others have such an opinion of his sanctity, that the wicked shrink from even appearing in his presence. Such should all princes and prelates be, who are set up by God to give good example to others. *"The perverse heart did not cleave to me."* The ill disposed avoided me, *"and the malignant, that hath turned aside from me, I would not know."* When the wicked would cut and fly from me, I took no trouble about them and sought not their acquaintance.

5. Another royal virtue, in which mercy and judgment are most conspicuous, is now touched upon. For kings have power to punish the wicked; and many, more through hatred of their neighbor than from a love of justice,

bring charges against those they wish to injure and seek to oppress them by falsehood and calumny; and King David, in his wisdom and justice, most severely punished such unjust complainants, and thus exercised his mercy on the unjustly accused and his justice on the false accusers. *"The man that in private detracted his neighbor,"* when anyone falsely accused his innocent neighbor, and in private would take from him his character with me, I not only gave no ear to him but I punished him severely. *"Him did I persecute."*—*"With him that had a proud eye and unsatiable heart I would not eat."* David had a thorough hatred not only of detractors, but of the proud and the avaricious, and justly. For no greater misfortune can befall a people than to have the king's ministers proud or avaricious. They abuse their power in satisfying their avarice, to the great injury of those under them. The meaning, then, is, I never admitted to my table, or used the slightest familiarity with him *"that had a proud eye,"* one who by his looks and his bearing betrayed his pride: *"and an unsatiable heart,"* to whose avarice and cupidity there were no bounds. That the king's principal ministers were accustomed to sit at the same table with him may be seen in 1 Kings 20, where David, who was then general, and even Abner, who was a subaltern officer, sat at table with Saul the king.

6. Having shut out detractors, the proud, and the avaricious from his friendship and from his service, David now adds that he was wont to relent the faithful and the upright, two qualities absolutely necessary in good ministers, to be faithful to their master, and upright in everything that regarded their own and their neighbor's salvation. It often happens that ministers are kept in the employment of their sovereigns, and are much regarded by them by reason of their being so faithful to them, no matter how depraved and abandoned they may be in other respects, or how much harm they may be doing to themselves and to others through their bad example: but holy David's ministers should be not only faithful to him, but unstained and unblemished, and like himself in every respect. He, therefore, says, *"My eyes were upon the faithful of the earth."* I looked about and sought for the faithful; or I looked with an eye of favor on those whom I knew to be faithful, and selected them; *"to sit with me,"* at my table, as so many friends and companions. *"The man that walked with me in the perfect way, he served me."* And furthermore, if there was any other subject or citizen however unknown to or unacquainted with me, provided he bore a good character, and led an irreproachable life, he was adopted as my prime minister.

7. Having expressed his horror of those who displayed their arrogance by the pride of their eyes, he now declares his disgust with those whose actions savored of pride; that is, with those who proudly oppressed their neighbor. And as he previously reprehended those who secretly detracted

their neighbor, he now censures and excludes from his company all those who have recourse to lies, in order to deceive any manner of people. *"He that worketh pride,"* whose actions savor of pride, who proudly insults or oppresses others, *"shall not dwell in the midst of my house,"* shall not be reckoned among my friends or domestics. *"He that speaketh unjust things,"* lies, by which he deceives others in business transactions, or in anything else, *"did not prosper before my eyes;"* did not please me, and therefore, got no grace from me to make him prosper.

8. He concludes the Psalm by showing the amount of his zeal in purging the city of the Lord, therein dealing mercifully with the good, who had been hitherto crushed and oppressed by the wicked, and inflicting condign punishment from the latter for their oppressions. *"In the mornings"* speedily, quickly, before vice could have taken root; *"I put to death all the wicked in the land,"* all those who deserved death, and whose life could not be spared without danger to the innocent. And that was done by me in order *"that I might cut off all the workers of iniquity,"* to restore peace and tranquillity to the inhabitants of God's holy city, by weeding out all the disturbers therein. All the Psalm, though spoken by David in his own person, is more applicable to Christ, especially this last verse; for David did all in him lay to banish all bad members from the city of the Lord, but he did not succeed, and never could succeed therein; but Christ, in the morning of the world to come, will really and truly cut off and scatter all the workers of iniquity, and thenceforward the holy city of the heavenly Jerusalem will be what its name implies, a vision of peace.

PSALM 101

A prayer for one in affliction: the fifth penitential psalm.

1 Hear, O Lord, my prayer: and let my cry come to thee.
2 Turn not away thy face from me: in the day when I am in trouble, incline thy ear to me. In what day soever I shall call upon thee, hear me speedily.
3 For my days are vanished like smoke: and my bones are grown dry like fuel for the fire.
4 I am smitten as grass, and my heart is withered: because I forgot to eat my bread.
5 Through the voice of my groaning, my bone hath cleaved to my flesh.
6 I am become like to a pelican of the wilderness: I am like a night raven in the house.
7 I have watched, and am become as a sparrow all alone on the housetop.
8 All the day long my enemies reproached me: and they that praised me did swear against me.
9 For I did eat ashes like bread, and mingled my drink with weeping.

10 Because of thy anger and indignation: for having lifted me up thou hast thrown me down.
11 My days have declined like a shadow, and I am withered like grass.
12 But thou, O Lord, endurest for ever: and thy memorial to all generations.
13 Thou shalt arise and have mercy on Sion: for it is time to have mercy on it, for the time is come.
14 For the stones thereof have pleased thy servants: and they shall have pity on the earth thereof.
15 And the Gentiles shall fear thy name, O Lord, and all the kings of the earth thy glory.
16 For the Lord hath built up Sion: and he shall be seen in his glory.
17 He hath had regard to the prayer of the humble: and he hath not despised their petition.
18 Let these things be written unto another generation: and the people that shall be created shall praise the Lord:
19 Because he hath looked forth from his high sanctuary: from heaven the Lord hath looked upon the earth.
20 That he might hear the groans of them that are in fetters: that he might release the children of the slain:
21 That they may declare the name of the Lord in Sion: and his praise in Jerusalem;
22 When the people assemble together, and kings, to serve the Lord.
23 He answered him in the way of his strength: Declare unto me the fewness of my days.
24 Call me not away in the midst of my days: thy years are unto generation and generation.
25 In the beginning, O Lord, thou foundedst the earth: and the heavens are the works of thy hands.
26 They shall perish but thou remainest: and all of them shall grow old like a garment: And as a vesture thou shalt change them, and they shall be changed.
27 But thou art always the selfsame, and thy years shall not fail.
28 The children of thy servants shall continue: and their seed shall be directed for ever.

Explanation of the psalm

1. This verse is used daily by the Church as a preparation to any other petitions she may need to put up to the Creator; for, she learned from the prophet that we should ask for an audience from God before we put any petition in particular before him; not that God, as if he were otherwise engaged, needs being roused or having his attention called, but because we need that God should give us the spirit of prayer; nay, even it is *"the Spirit himself that asketh for us with unspeakable groanings,"* Rom. 8, *"Hear, O Lord, my prayer;"* that is, make me so pray that I may be worthy of being heard. And, to express his delight, he repeats it by saying, *"and let my cry come to thee."* Make me pray in such a manner that my prayer may be the earnest cry of my heart; so full of fire and devotion, that, though sent up from the lowest depth, it may not falter on the way, but ultimately reach you sitting on your lofty throne. Many things prevent our prayers from penetrating the clouds, such as want of faith, of confidence, of humility, desire, and the like; and he, therefore, asks for the grace of praying well, that is, in a manner likely to obtain what we want.

2. This is the primary and principal petition of a poor man in trouble, or of a repentant sinner; for *"No man can correct whom God hath despised;"* and as God's regarding us is both the first grace and the fountain of grace, he, at the very outset, asks God to look on him, saying, *"Turn not away thy face from me,"* however foul and filthy I may be; and if your own image, by reason of my having so befouled it, will not induce you to look upon me, let you mercy prevail upon you, for the fouler I am, the more wretched and miserable I am, and unless you look upon me, I will never be brought to look upon you, but daily wallowing deeper and deeper in my sins, I must, of necessity, be always getting more filthy and more foul. Anyone that speaks in such manner begins to be already looked upon by God, but, as it were, with only half his anger laid aside, and still averting his face; however, having got any glimpse of God's light and countenance, he cries out, *"Turn not away thy face from me;"* cast me not away from thy face; finish what you have begun, by turning yourself to me, that I may be perfectly and completely turned to thee. *"In the day when I am in trouble, incline thy ear to me."* This is a second petition, but a consequence of the first; for, the moment God begins to look upon anyone, that moment man begins to see his own filth and nakedness, and, through it, his real poverty. He then begins to be troubled and afflicted, and to recur to the supreme Physician, who is rich in mercy; for he knows that God never despises an afflicted spirit and a contrite heart. He, therefore, says, with confidence, *"In the day when I am in trouble, incline thy ear to me;"* whenever, through the influence of your grace, I shall feel troubled for my sins, and, in consequence, cry to you, hear me kindly, I pray you; and he repeats it, *"In whatsoever day I shall call upon thee, hear me speedily;"* whenever I shall be in trouble, and call upon you, my all powerful Physician, hear me, and that quickly, for fear a delay may lose you the one you seek to heal.

3. He assigns a reason for having said, *"hear me quickly,"* and the reason is, that man's life draws to a close with the greatest rapidity; and if the wounds inflicted by sin be not cured at once, there is a chance of their never being cured. *"For my days are vanished like smoke."* The time I have spent in this

world has passed away like a body of smoke, that seems large and bulky on its first ascending, but immediately gets thinner and evaporates altogether; and thus, too, will the remainder of me; my bones, the pillars, as it were, of my whole body, *"they are grown dry,"* and thus weakened and verging to ruin.

4. He continues deploring his past state, and says, *"I am smitten as grass."* The sun so shone on me in my prosperity that I am stricken down like so much withered grass; *"and any heart is withered;"* for I have been so overwhelmed by the cares of the world that *"I forgot to eat my bread;"* the bread of heavenly truth, which, strictly speaking, is our bread, and not shared in by the brutes; for the food of the body is not, strictly speaking, our food. Nothing can be truer; and it is a reflection that should be always before those who are well to do in the world; for, if they dwell under the shadow of God's wings, or constantly bedew themselves with the showers of his grace, they must, of necessity, *"be smitten as grass;"* and their heart, that so sickens at the food of heaven, must become quite *"withered."* *"Take heed to yourselves lest, perhaps, your hearts be overcharged with surfeiting, and drunkenness, and the cares of this life;"* for such people always forget to eat the true bread, and become dried up of all the grace of devotion.

5. He now tells how sorry he is for his past life, and shows fruit worthy of penance; for as his flesh formerly reveled in luxuries, and his heart withered by reason of his having forgotten his daily spiritual food, so now, on the contrary, *"through the voice of his groaning,"* from his constant lamentations, his flesh neglects its daily food; and thus, *"my bone hath cleaved to my flesh;"* that is, to the skin, being all wasted and worn—an evident approval of fasting and penance, being both the signs and the fruit of true penance.

6-7. To tears and fasting he unites solitude and watching, the marks of true penance. For if one will not seriously withdraw himself awhile from the world, and, in serious watchings, call up the number and the greatness of his sins, it is hardly possible to deplore them sufficiently. He compares the penitent to three birds; the pelican, living exclusively in the desert; the night raven or the owl, an inhabitant of old dismantled houses; and the sparrow, dwelling on, rather than in, houses. For, as St. Jerome remarks, the houses in Palestine were built with flat and not pointed roofs like ours, on which the people were wont to enjoy themselves, to sun themselves, and frequently to have their meals there. Hence, in Mt. 10, we have *"Preach ye upon the house tops;"* that is, standing on such flat housetops; and in Acts 10, we read of St. Peter, that *"He went up to the higher parts of the house to pray."* These three birds represent three classes of penitents. Some repair altogether to the desert, such as Mary Magdalen, Mary of Egypt, Paul the first hermit, Anthony, Hilarion, and many others, who can say with the prophet,

Psalm 5, *"So I have gone afar off, flying away; and I abode in the wilderness;"* and as the pelican wages constant war on noxious animals, especially on serpents, so the Anchorets constantly combat with the demons, and live, as it were, on the victories acquired over them. Others do penance in the cities and towns, cooped up in narrow cells and cloisters, and, separated from the world, come out like the owl in the night, and spend the most of it in chanting the divine praises in hymns and sacred music. Finally, others, encumbered with families, or public duties, who cannot retire from the world, still, like the solitary sparrow on the housetop, manage to rise above the world and its cares. These are they who, while they are in the world, are not of the world; being slaves neither to the wealth nor the honors, nor the cares of the world. They make such things slaves to them; they master, they dispose of, and they dispense them, and they do not suffer themselves to be entangled or ensnared by them; so that their minds can revel freely in solitude here, and thus, enjoy heaven hereafter. To such persons it belongs to watch and preach from the housetops, to watch their own temptations and dangers, and to preach both by word and by example to those over whom they may be placed. No penance can be more valuable than for those in high rank to observe the greatest humility, for those who have the wealth of the world to content themselves with moderate food and clothing, that thereby they may be the better able to help those in want; for those who are prone to concupiscence, to chastise their body, and bring it under subjection, by fasting and spare living; and finally, to serve our neighbors from love, to compassionate their sufferings, and to bear with their annoyances and scandals.

8. They who seriously turn to penance are always objects of hatred to those sinners who choose to remain in their sins. *"He is grievous unto us even to behold; for his life is not like other men's, and his ways are very different,"* Wisdom 2; and, though that was said of the just man, it applies to the penitent sinner, seeking to be reconciled also. He, therefore, says, *"All the day long my enemies reproached me."* All those who previously, by reason of our union in wickedness, had been my friends, when they saw me become another man, turned out most bitter enemies, and upbraided and reproached me with my conversion, as if I were doing a foolish act; *"and they who praised me"* as a brave and boon companion, for the wicked are praised for their bad acts, afterwards *"did swear against me,"* conspired to injure me.

9. He tells why his enemies reproached him: it was because *"I eat ashes like bread, and mingled my drink with weeping;"* that is to say, they thought it the height of madness for me to adopt so severe a rule of life of my own accord. The eating of ashes like bread means that the bread he ate was coarse, and rudely baked, being baked in the ashes, which clung to it; such bread being in use with those doing penance. *"And mingled my drink with weeping,"* wept while I remembered how often I had offended God.

10. See why the true penitent chooses to begrime himself with ashes and quench his thirst with his tears! He does not do so for want of reason, or because he cannot help it through his poverty, but because he has the Divine anger before his mind, and by such humiliations and signs of true repentance he hopes to satisfy him in some degree. He so punished himself because he saw God's anger and indignation were lighted up against him for the sins he had committed; and that he saw, because *"having lifted me up thou hast thrown me down."* Having, through your grace, raised me to the highest dignity by your friendship and adoption, you afterwards, by reason of my own sins, degraded me from the rank of a friend and a child to that of an enemy or a rebellious fugitive slave. For fear sinners may imagine that the loss they suffer by the commission of sin is a trifling one, the Scripture makes use of a word, translated *"thou hast cast me down,"* that signifies complete demolition. It alludes to a vessel thrown on the ground from a high place, and thereby shivered into a thousand atoms along with losing its high position. And so with the sinner, who, blinded by the desires of the flesh, does not see the injury done to him, yet truly loses his all when both body and soul are consigned to hell by him who cannot be resisted.

11. Our own mortality is a part and a sign of the aforesaid demolition; for, when our first parent was placed in so glorious a position that he might have lived forever, by reason of his sin he *"was thrown down,"* with all his posterity, and the effect of that was, *"that his days declined like a shadow, and he became withered as grass."* The prophet, then, speaking in the person of the penitent, says, I am *"thrown down"* by you in your anger. Not only by reason of my own sins, but by reason of the old fall, that is, common to us all; *"my days have declined like a shadow,"* quietly, insensibly, but steadily, until at sunset it disappears and passes into the shadow of night. *"And I am withered like grass."* I, who was created to flourish like the palm forever, am now prostrate and withered, like the grass that dries up immediately.

12. This is the second part of the Psalm, in which the prophet, in the person of a poor penitent, after having recounted his wretchedness, now conceives a hope of reconciliation; and, inspired by the Holy Ghost, predicts the future restoration and renovation of the Church through Christ, as the Apostle explains in the first chapter of the Hebrews. The Apostle, wishing in that chapter to prove the divinity of Christ, first quotes the words in Psalm 44, *"Thy throne, O God, is forever and ever;"* then those of Psalm 95, *"Adore him all you his Angels;"* and lastly, the words of this present Psalm, saying, *"Thou, O Lord, in the beginning hast founded the earth;"* which words are addressed to the same person as those words before us, *"But thou, O*

Lord, endurest forever." If the former, then, be addressed to the Son, so are the latter. They who say these words apply to God directly, and to Christ indirectly as the Son of God, do not meet the objection; for in that case the Apostle, instead of proving Christ to be God, would be only taking for granted he was God. The meaning of the passage, then, is: I, indeed, have withered away like grass, but thou, O Lord, the Messias we expect, remainest forever; our memory passes away like a sound, but your memorial—that is, your memory—will pass from generation to generation, because, in the succession of ages, there shall be always those to hand down your wonderful doings.

13. The reason why *"thy memorial shall be propagated to all generations"* is, because you will not forget dealing mercifully with your people; but *"thou shalt arise"* as if from a long sleep, *"and have mercy on Sion,"* wilt come in mercy and save us; for in spirit I see *"the time is come to have mercy on it;"* that is, it is nigh, just at hand, nay, even has already come; for, with the eye of a prophet, I see the future as if it were really present. This is the time of which the Apostle speaks when he says, *"But when the fullness of the time was come, God sent his Son,"* of whom Isaias says, *"In an acceptable time I have heard thee, and in the day of salvation I have helped thee;"* in explaining which St. Paul, 2 Cor. 6, says, *"Behold, now is the acceptable time; behold, now is the day of salvation."*

14. The prophet foresaw and foretold the renovation of the holy Sion, from the fact of foreseeing God's servants, his holy Apostles, who hitherto had been devoted to fishing and such humble pursuits, now, after having been instructed by Christ, and filled with the Holy Ghost, inflamed with the most ardent desire of establishing the Church, and having abandoned all the cares of this world, devoting themselves to that one object alone. *"For the stones thereof,"* the building of the new Jerusalem, the collecting and placing the living stones together that were to be built upon the foundation already laid, *"pleased thy servants,"* those whom you chose and predestined for the purpose; *"and they shall have pity on the earth thereof,"* they will foster and cherish the land of the new Jerusalem, as the mother clings to the child in her womb (for such is the force of the Hebrew), as in Isaias, *"Can a woman forget her infant so as not to have pity on the son of her womb?"* By stones are meant in this verse the steady and the perfect, while the earth represents the weak and the infirm of whom the Apostle says, *"Him that is weak in faith take unto you;"* and again, *"Now, we that are stronger ought to bear the infirmities of the weak;"* and again, *"Who is weak, and I am not weak."*

15. When the new Sion shall be in progress of building, the gentiles will be converted, and *"shall fear"* with a holy fear and pious veneration, *"thy name, O Lord,"* Jesus Christ; *"and all the kings of the earth"* will also be converted,

and will fear *"thy glory;"* that is, thy majesty, as King of kings and Lord of lords of the earth, sitting at the right hand of the Father, until all your enemies shall be put under the footstool of your feet; and afterwards as the Judge that will come to judge the living and the dead, and render to everyone according to his works.

16. See why all nations and all their kings shall fear Christ's glory! *"For the Lord hath built up Sion"* in the present day, having established his Church in spite of all kings and nations, and *"the gates of hell will not prevail against it;" "and he shall be seen in his glory,"* in the time to come, when he shall come with all his Angels, in the clouds of heaven, with great power to judge the world. When he began to build up Sion he was seen in his lowliness. *"We have seen him, and there was no sightliness, that we should be desirous of him;"* but when he shall come to pass judgment, then *"he shall be seen in his glory."*

17. This verse alludes to the prayers of the holy martyrs, who in Apocalypse 6, say, *"How long, O Lord, dost thou not judge and revenge our blood on them that dwell on the earth?"* The Son of God, then, will be seen in his glory, for he hath *"had regard to the prayer"* of all the martyrs, and all his other pious servants; *"and he hath not despised their petitions;"* and, therefore, he will come to judge, and to avenge their blood on those who are still in this world.

18. For fear the Jews may suppose that this prophecy applied to themselves, and take it as in reference to the termination of the captivity of Babylon, and the building of Jerusalem, the Holy Ghost was pleased to remind them distinctly, as St. Peter afterwards clearly explains in his first Epistle, chap. 1, *"The prophets who prophesied of the grace to come in you;"* and further on, *"To whom it was revealed, that not to themselves but to you they ministered those things which are now declared to you by those who have preached the Gospel to you."* The Holy Ghost, then, speaking through David, says, *"Let these things be written unto another generation."* These things will be understood hereafter, *"and the people that shall be created,"* the people then in existence, *"shall praise the Lord,"* by reason of seeing all those things accomplished.

19. The reason why the people of the New Testament will praise the Lord is, because God has designed to look down from his holy place on high on this vale of our wretchedness; and that, not with an uninterested or indifferent eye, but with a view to let himself down, to be seen on earth, and to converse with men.

20. God Almighty so humbled himself to have an opportunity in that he might hear the groans of them that are in fetters," imposed upon them by the prince of darkness, and held in captivity by him; and that he might, on hearing their groans, release them and send them away in freedom. That was accomplished, as the Lord himself testifies, by his own coming, as we

read in Lk. 4. By those *"that are in fetters,"* we are to understand those who are slaves to concupiscence, mastered and fettered by their own passions. *"The children of the slain,"* are the old children of Adam and Eve, who were slain by the craft of the serpent, for, as we read in Wisdom 2, *"By the envy of the devil, death came into the world;"* and the Lord himself, speaking of the devil, says, Jn. 8, *"He was a murderer from the beginning, and he abode not in the truth."*

21. The Lord came to break the bonds of those that were in fetters, and to rescue them from the power of darkness, in that they may declare the name of the Lord in Sion;" that is, that by their conversion to the true and living God, they may glorify the name of the Lord in the Church, which is the spiritual Sion; which he repeats when he says, *"and his praise in Jerusalem,"* praising and thanking God, and blessing him for the great favor of calling them to the Catholic Church, which is the new Jerusalem, as St. Peter explains in his first Epistle, *"But you are a chosen generation, a royal priesthood, a holy nation, a purchased people; that you may declare his virtues, who hath called you out of darkness into his admirable light."*

22. He now tells when those who have been delivered from the powers of darkness ought to praise the name of the Lord. *"When the people assemble together."* When the various nations all over the world, who hitherto had been worshipping various and different false gods, *"shall assemble together,"* and be formed into one body, and there shall be one spirit, one God, one faith, one baptism; nay more, when, through charity, there shall be one heart and one soul; when not only the people, but those who are placed over them, shall come together in the one body of the Church, that they, too, may serve God.

23. This is a most obscure passage, and the most probable interpretation of it is that which makes it an answer of the prophet to him who commanded him to write those things to another generation. The prophet *"answers in the way of his strength;"* that is, when he was in the flower of his youth, in robust health: *"Declare unto me the fewness of my days."* Make me understand and seriously persuade myself, that my days are numbered, and short is the term of my life, for fear I may be deceived by calculating, from the present vigor of my youth, on a long and hale old age, and be hurried off when I least expect it, unforeseen and unprepared; and thus fail in being numbered among that people that will be created to praise thee forever in the heavenly Jerusalem.

21. The first half of this verse refers to the preceding; the last half to the following verse. Having said, *"Declare unto me the fewness of my days,"* he adds another prayer, saying, *"Call me not away in the midst of my days."* Do not cut my course short by hurrying me off on a sudden, when I may be quite

unprepared, and the call most unexpected. *"Thy years are unto generation and generation."* A reason why God should allow man to live as long as may be necessary to meet a holy and happy death. In other words, your years, O Lord, are everlasting, from generation to generation, without end; and it is, therefore, only meet that the creature formed to your image should be favored with a life long enough to secure an everlasting life.

25-27. He proves that God alone is eternal from the fact of his being alone immutable, a proof from first principles. And he proves God to be immutable, from the fact of his having brought the heavens from nonexistence into existence, and will again bring them back to their original nonexistence, while he always remains the same, without any change, and what he says of the heavens applies to all creation, of which the heavens form the noblest part. *"In the beginning, O Lord, thou foundest the earth;"* you, O Lord, existed in the beginning, before the earth, an inferior part of the world, and you laid its foundations, without any preexisting matter whereon to lay them. *"And the heavens are the work of thy hands."* You made not only the earth, but even the heavens, the most excellent part of the world, without any help, from Angels or anyone else, but with your own hands, by your own power and wisdom; and thus brought the whole world from nonexistence into existence. *"They (the heavens) shall perish, but thou remainest."* Even though the heavens should grow old, should change and perish, you will always remain the same, as we read in Mt. 5, *"Till heaven and earth shall pass, one jot or tittle shall not pass from the law, till all be fulfilled;"* which is explained in Lk. 16, *"It is easier for heaven and earth to pass, than for one tittle of the law to fail."* Another explanation of this sentence makes it absolutely apply to what he names. For the heavens will perish, will grow old, will be subject to changes, as regards the motion of the heavenly bodies, the influence of heat, the production of inferior bodies; the earth, too, will perish as regards the production of herbs and animals, and the world will be consumed as regards the figure and shape it now has for the Apostle writes, *"For the figure of this world passeth away;"* and again, *"For the things which are seen are temporal; but the things which are not seen are eternal."* Here he gives the name of temporal to everything we see, because the very elements, and the heavens, as we see them, will have an end. We see the earth clothed with trees, full of cattle, ornamented with buildings; the rivers now placidly rolling along, now swollen and muddy; the sky now clouded, now serene; the stars in perpetual motion; all of which are temporal, and sure to come to an end; for, as St. Peter writes, *"We look for new heavens and a new earth, according to his promise."*—*"And all of them shall grow old like a garment."* All the heavens, as regards their shape and form, shall be consumed. *"And as a vesture thou shalt change them, and they shall be changed;"* you will remove the external clothing the heavens now have, and put a new one on them, as if you took off a man's old clothes, and dressed him in a new suit. *"But thou art always the self same, and thy years shall not fail."* No length of years will make any impression on you. God can suffer no change, for changes are made with a view to further acquisitions, which does not apply to God, he being most pure, most perfect, nay, even infinitely perfect, and, therefore, can acquire nothing when he wants nothing.

28. Having discussed the eternity of God, the destruction and renovation of the world, he now predicts that God's servants and children, and the children of his servants forever, would be sharers in his eternity in that world so renovated; not that there would be a propagation of children in that world, but that all the faithful servants of God, with all their posterity, who may share in their piety, will certainly arrive at that happy rest; and such was the promise formerly made to Abraham, *"And I will establish my covenant between me and thee, and between thy seed after thee in their generations, by a perpetual covenant."* The servants of God here represent the patriarchs; their sons represent the Apostles; and their sons again represent all other Christians. *"The children of thy servants shall continue."* The Apostles, with their parents the patriarchs, shall continue in thy kingdom, that renewed heaven, that heavenly Jerusalem; *"and their seed shall be directed forever;"* and it will not be confined to them, but those also begotten by them through the Gospel, if they persevere in faith and love, *"shall be directed forever;"* will remain to all eternity upright and steady in all prosperity.

PSALM 102

Thanksgiving to God for his mercies.

1 Bless the Lord, O my soul: and let all that is within me bless his holy name.
2 Bless the Lord, O my soul, and never forget all he hath done for thee.
3 Who forgiveth all thy iniquities: who healeth all thy diseases.
4 Who redeemeth thy life from destruction: who crowneth thee with mercy and compassion.
5 Who satisfieth thy desire with good things: thy youth shall be renewed like the eagle's.
6 The Lord doth mercies, and judgment for all that suffer wrong.
7 He hath made his ways known to Moses: his wills to the children of Israel.
8 The Lord is compassionate and merciful: longsuffering and plenteous in mercy.
9 He will not always be angry: nor will he threaten for ever.
10 He hath not dealt with us according to our sins: nor rewarded us according to our iniquities.
11 For according to the height of the heaven above the earth: he hath strengthened his mercy towards them that fear him.

12 As far as the east is from the west, so far hath he removed our iniquities from us.
13 As a father hath compassion on his children, so hath the Lord compassion on them that fear him:
14 For he knoweth our frame. He remembereth that we are dust:
15 Man's days are as grass, as the flower of the field so shall he flourish.
16 For the spirit shall pass in him, and he shall not be: and he shall know his place no more.
17 But the mercy of the Lord is from eternity and unto eternity upon them that fear him: And his justice unto children's children,
18 To such as keep his covenant, And are mindful of his commandments to do them.
19 The Lord hath prepared his throne in heaven: and his kingdom shall rule over all.
20 Bless the Lord, all ye his angels: you that are mighty in strength, and execute his word, hearkening to the voice of his orders.
21 Bless the Lord, all ye his hosts: you ministers of his that do his will.
22 Bless the Lord, all his works: in every place of his dominion, O my soul, bless thou the Lord.

EXPLANATION OF THE PSALM

1. David piously believing himself to be one of the elect, stirs himself up, in the person of all the elect, to bless the Lord, *"Bless the Lord, O my soul;"* reflect on his favors and praise him who conferred them on you; you, my soul, who through God's gift have not only deserved to get such favors, but also to acknowledge them. And let not you alone, my soul, praise the Lord, but, *"let all that is within me"* be turned into so many tongues, *"to bless the Lord."* St. Augustine considers the second part of this verse to be a mere repetition, or perhaps, an explanation of the first part; as much as to say, let all my thoughts and affections, the very deepest within me, bless his holy name. That may be very true; but there is nothing to prevent our applying the words, *"all that is within me,"* to all that is in man, and enclosed in this outward skin of ours; in the same sense as we have, in Psalm 83, *"My heart and flesh have rejoiced in the living God;"* and in Psalm 34, *"All my bones shall say, Lord, who is like to thee?"* Inanimate and senseless things contribute to God's praise, just as a piece of work does to its maker; or through the affections of our soul, that should wish all creation, if it were possible, should know and praise God.

2. He repeats the expression, to shed the intensity of his affection, as also from a consciousness of human infirmity, that is very apt to cool in matters that do not come under cognizance of the senses, especially such as God, *"who dwelleth in light inaccessible"* and he, therefore, adds, *"and never forget all he hath done for thee;"* meaning all his gifts, which are not simply gifts, but gifts (to use the expression) on the double. A great gift is his not exacting from us the punishment our daily sins deserve; and a double gift is the bestowal of so many favors on us for all our wickedness. He that can recount the sins of mankind, by which we daily offend God, can form a remote idea of the extent of God's love for us in daily conferring so many favors on us; *"for he is kind to the unthankful and to the evil,"* Lk. 6.

3. He now proceeds to enumerate God's favors, beginning in order from the first to the last. The first is remission of sin, through which he makes us just, from being sinners; friends, from enemies; children, from slaves, *"who forgiveth all thy iniquities,"* pardoning them gratuitously, however innumerable they may be; and not only that, but *"who healeth all thy diseases,"* to cut off the root of sin; *"for covetousness is the root of all evils,"* 1 Tim. 6; or, as St. John expresses it, *"the concupiscence of the flesh, the concupiscence of the eyes, and the pride of life."* This weakness or infirmity, attached to man by the fall of our first parent, is, to a certain extent, cured and relieved by God in this world; but the complete cure will be effected in the world to come only. Everyone, then, should ask himself if he feels a diminution in his own infirmity—if he bears the touch of the heavenly physician patiently; for they who refuse the physician's prescriptions, and suffer the language of concupiscence to rest in them, cannot apply those words, *"who healeth all thy diseases,"* to themselves; and they who are not in a position to do that cannot possibly expect the following gifts of God.

4. From the gifts of grace he passes to those of glory. *"Who redeemeth thy life from destruction,"* who, through the redemption that is in Christ, delivers you from eternal death and transfers you into his own kingdom, crowning you with a crown of glory, *"with mercy and compassion."* Because, in order to merit that crown of glory, mercy had to go before you, justifying you gratuitously, and compassion had to direct and protect you on the way; for otherwise you would not have persevered in the grace so conferred on you.

5. He tells us here what that crown of glory contains. Two things, the satisfaction of all our desires and the immortality of our bodies, or, in other words, perfect happiness, as regards body and soul; for the soul ceases to desire, and the heart to hunger, once it gets possession of the supreme happiness, which is so comprehensive of everything good that it has nothing further to seek or desire. To this glorious resurrection will be added a thorough renovation of the body itself, a happy and never decaying youth. This renovation is compared to that of the eagle, not that the eagle can possibly be supposed to renew its youth forever, but because it in some degree represents the resurrection of the just, by reason of its soaring so high, its

acuteness of ken, and its length of life, correspondent to the happiness of the just, who will soar above the heavens, will behold light inaccessible, and behold it forever. How the eagle is renewed is quite uncertain; St. Jerome says that they frequently get new wings, and are thus renewed; St. Augustine says it alludes to the renewal of their beaks, that grow so hooked by age that they cannot take up their food, until they rub it and grind it against a stone, and by thus wearing it away form themselves a new one.

6. Having told us of all the blessings in store for the just, he now tells us that God's mercy is the source of them all, and that for fear anyone should be mad enough to attribute to himself what belongs to God, and lose, through his pride, what he should have received in all humility. *"The Lord doeth mercies."* It is the Lord himself who behaves kindly to us, pours down his favors on us, liberally sharing every blessing he has with us, and also in his goodness delivering us from every trouble, and from the hands of the unjust; and one of his peculiar mercies is, that he shows *"judgment to all that suffer wrong,"* for he delivers those that suffer it, and punishes those that inflict it.

7. A proof of what he said in the preceding verse; for God made his ways, which are mercy and truth, according to the Psalm, *"All the ways of the Lord are mercy and truth,"* according to Moses his special servant; for he gave him a most holy law, through which he made known his will, not only to Moses but to all the people of Israel; the essence of which was, that as well as he himself was merciful and just, we should be so too; and the very fact of God's so deigning to instruct us was a great mercy. He also *"made his way known to Moses,"* when in his mercy he delivered the people from the captivity of Pharao, and slew him and his army in his justice; and thus gave a clear proof of his mercy and his justice.

8. These epithets, so applied by that Scripture that cannot deceive us to the Almighty, should prove a great source of consolation to all pious souls. He is called *"compassionate,"* which, in Hebrew, signifies the tender and the intimate love a parent feels for its own children; *"merciful,"* which in the same language implies a giver of all grace and favors, which is a consequence of the paternal love one feels for his children. And such was the case with God. Having taken delight in his elect from eternity, and having foreseen and predestined them to be agreeable to the image of his Son, he, at the fitting time, poured down innumerable blessings on them, both of nature and of grace. He is also styled *"long suffering"*—patient, tolerant, not easily provoked; for God bears with our infirmity and our imperfections in this our journey to our country as a parent, especially a mother, would bear with the folly and trifling, the insults and the ingratitude of the infancy and the childhood of those who call her mother. Who can enumerate the distractions that seize on us while we are speaking to God in prayer? Who can form

a proper estimate of our unsteadiness, our various desires, concupiscences, ingratitude, lapses and crimes? And yet God, in his goodness, bears with us, for which we should most constantly and heartfully thank him. Finally, he is *"plenteous in mercy,"* which seems to have reference to that great and unspeakable mercy, through which God will raise us to a level with the Angels, and to his own likeness, which will happen when we shall see him as he is. Those four epithets, then, include all God's favors from first to last. The first is the grace of predestination, or the eternal love of God; then follow the gifts of justification and the remission of various sins into which, finally, is added a crown of glory?

9. He now explains in detail the epithets he applied to God in the preceding verse. First, the tender affection God has for those that fear him. *"He will not always be angry."* God, to be sure, is sometimes angry with his elect, when they fall into sin, and he will scourge them for it, but he will not be long without being reconciled to them. The affection of the parent remains in that very heart that prompts him to scourge them, which he repeats when he says, *"Nor will he threaten forever."* He will not always threaten in his anger, but will in due time administer his sweet consolations. This is not to be quoted in favor of the heresy that would make hell's pains to be but temporary, because there is question here solely of the elect.

10. He comes now to the second epithet, and says that God, in his infinite mercy, instead of visiting us with the punishment we deserved for our sins, overwhelmed us with gifts we did not deserve. For what did the sinner and the unjust deserve but death? *"For the wages of sin is death."* Now God not only withheld such wages from us, but he even gave us the life of grace, promised us eternal life, and meanwhile furnished us with a liberal supply of all necessaries in this our pilgrimage.

11-12. These verses also apply to the second epithet, (merciful,) for the prophet proves that God did not deal with the elect according to their sins; for *"he strengthened his mercy,"* in pouring down all manner of grace on them, and removing all manner of harm from them. He compares his mercy to the distance between the earth and the sky, the far east and far west, to show how boundless it is; and, therefore, that the remission of sin and the infusion of grace is real and substantial, and not imputative, as some heretics will have it.

13. The prophet enters into the third appellation (long suffering) in this and the two following verses, making use of a happy comparison. No people are more patient or *"long suffering"* than parents, in bearing with the follies and frivolities of their younger children. Paternal or maternal love brings them to labor severely and incessantly for them, and to bear up against their ingratitude and even their violence in a most extraordinary manner. Such is the meaning of God's mercy to *"them that fear him,"* in regarding their daily transgressions not as so many offences against himself, but as so many filial wanderings.

14-16. God's great mercy arises from the fact of his knowing of what we are composed, of earth, of flesh that is corruptible and exposed to all manner of concupiscences, and that we are, therefore, a pitiable set indeed. He remembereth that we are dust; composed of and formed from it, and, therefore, from our frailty, deserving of all mercy and compassion; and, when he did *"remember,"* it does not imply that he ever forgot it, (for that he could not,) but that he sometimes acted as if he had forgotten it. In further elucidation of our frailty, he draws another comparison, *"Men's days are as grass;"* most brief, as brief as those of the grass that never remains an entire year on the ground, for it grows up in the spring, and in the following summer is cut down and gathered up; and as the grass is not in flower even all that time, but flowers in the morning, and withers in the evening; so it is with man, who lives for a short time, and is still a shorter time in the flower of his youth when he withers into old age. *"For the spirit shall pass in him, and he shall not be;"* that is, the spirit of life, or his corporeal life, will not be permanent in him, will be always transient, and never remain in the same state; for it will be always changing; from infancy to childhood; from childhood to puberty; from puberty to youth; from youth to manhood; from manhood to old age, from old age to death. *"And he shall know his place no more;"* he will not return to the place from whence he set out, and will never again see the age he has passed. In this respect a great difference exists between things corruptible and things incorruptible, celestial and terrestrial bodies; for the sun, moon, and stars rise in the morning, and set in the west in the evening, but return again in the morning to the spot from whence they set out, without appearing to have undergone the slightest change, but the terrestrial, or the things of this earth, perform their course, undergo various changes therein, and never return to the starting points but grow old and decay. By the spirit here we are not to understand the soul of man, which is immortal, and will return to the body it inhabited on the last day, but the spirit of life, or corporeal existence.

17. We now come to the fourth epithet in verse 8, *"and plenteous in mercy,"* which applies to the gift of glorification, which is the last and the greatest. *"The mercy of the Lord,"* then, which in the beginning, extended by predestination to those that fear him, *"is from eternity"* with them in their glory, and thus, God will be *"plenteous in mercy,"* whether we consider the number, the greatness or the duration of his favors. Where is the man, then, that will seriously reflect on himself, and on the Lord of the universe, who does not want us, having resolved in his mercy, to take pity on a handful of dust, to raise it to a level with the Angels, and to attach it to himself, the supreme good, in the enjoyment of the most perfect happiness for all eternity? We certainly should not forget such mercy for even one moment, and we should return thanks for it forever. *"And his justice unto children's children, to such as keep his covenant."* This is a sort of appendix to God's mercy, in regard of those that fear him. The prophet adds, that they who fear God will not only be exalted and protected by the eternal mercy of God, but that the same mercy will be extended to their posterity, if they follow in the pious steps of their parents and ancestors. *"And his justice;"* his veracity and fidelity, by virtue of which he always carries out what he promises, will be observed towards the *"children's children, to such as keep his covenant;"* who observe the covenant entered into by God, that they should be his people, and he their God: *"and are mindful of his commandments;"* not only to turn them in their mind and to think on them, but also *"to do them."*

18-19. He now proves that God is able to carry out all he promised to those that fear him, and to their children's children, because he is the supreme Judge of all; and therefore, *"he prepared his throne in heaven,"* his judgment seat, on an elevated spot, in the highest heaven, whence he can see everything and judge everything; and for fear we should suspect him to be a judge delegated by another, he adds, *"and his kingdom shall reign over all;"* that is, he sits in heaven, not as a judge appointed by a king, but as a Judge supreme, a King over all kings, for his kingdom, that is, his power as a king, extends to all created things.

20. In the end of the Psalm the prophet, finding himself quite unable to return adequate thanks to God for all his favors, invites other creatures to bless him and give him praise; and he first invites the Angels, as being creatures of the highest order; and, therefore, most suited to praise God. We are less suited by reason of our weakness and frailty, and by reason of our frequent lapses into sin, and *"praise is not seemly in the mouth of a sinner;"* while the Angels are always untiring, endowed with great vigor, are always obedient to God, and thus, never fall into sin, but are agreeable and fair in the sight of God. *"Bless the Lord, all ye his Angels;"* all you his Angels who surround him, and thus have a more thorough knowledge and conception of his greatness, praise our common Lord; and let it not be confined to one or two, but let the whole of you, however innumerable you may be, unite in his praise. *"You that are mighty in strength;"* you that have been endowed with super excellent strength, in order to execute all God's commands, who have, therefore, nothing to fear, and can be prevented by nobody from praising God. *"And execute his word;"* carry out his commands to the letter; *"hearkening to the voice of his orders,"* and thus proving themselves most faithful and diligent servants.

21. For fear we should suppose that the invitation addressed to the Angels included those only in the lower grade, he now summons *"all his hosts,"* everyone of them, Archangels, principalities, dominions, and the other superior orders, who all are God's servants, and carefully and diligently carry out his behests.

22. Having invited men and the Angels, who, from their knowledge of God, know best how to do it, to praise God, he now summons all created things, however mute and insensible, to praise their Maker in their own way. And for fear any exception should be made, or that it may be thought the prophet did not include all created things, whether in sky, earth, or sea, he says, *"in every place of his dominion;"* that is to say, bless him, all ye his works, everyone of you, wherever you may be; for he made all things, governs all things, is with them everywhere, filling, bearing, preserving, moving everything. And you, my soul, who have thus invited them, bless you the Lord at all times, and let his praise be forever in thy mouth.

PSALM 103

God is to be praised for his mighty works; and wonderful providence.

1 Bless the Lord, O my soul: O Lord my God, thou art exceedingly great. Thou hast put on praise and beauty:

2 And art clothed with light as with a garment. Who stretchest out the heaven like a pavilion:

3 Who coverest the higher rooms thereof with water. Who makest the clouds thy chariot: who walkest upon the wings of the winds.

4 Who makest thy angels spirits: and thy ministers a burning fire.

5 Who hast founded the earth upon its own bases: it shall not be moved for ever and ever.

6 The deep like a garment is its clothing: above the mountains shall the waters stand.

7 At thy rebuke they shall flee: at the voice of thy thunder they shall fear.

8 The mountains ascend, and the plains descend into the place which thou hast founded for them.

9 Thou hast set a bound which they shall not pass over; neither shall they return to cover the earth.

10 Thou sendest forth springs in the vales: between the midst of the hills the waters shall pass.

11 All the beasts of the field shall drink: the wild asses shall expect in their thirst.

12 Over them the birds of the air shall dwell: from the midst of the rocks they shall give forth their voices.

13 Thou waterest the hills from thy upper rooms: the earth shall be filled with the fruit of thy works:

14 Bringing forth grass for cattle, and herb for the service of men. That thou mayst bring bread out of the earth:
15 And that wine may cheer the heart of man. That he may make the face cheerful with oil: and that bread may strengthen man's heart.
16 The trees of the field shall be filled, and the cedars of Libanus which he hath planted:
17 There the sparrows shall make their nests. The highest of them is the house of the heron.
18 The high hills are a refuge for the harts, the rock for the irchins.
19 He hath made the moon for seasons: the sun knoweth his going down.
20 Thou hast appointed darkness, and it is night: in it shall all the beasts of the woods go about:
21 The young lions roaring after their prey, and seeking their meat from God.
22 The sun ariseth, and they are gathered together: and they shall lie down in their dens.
23 Man shall go forth to his work, and to his labour until the evening.
24 How great are thy works, O Lord? thou hast made all things in wisdom: the earth is filled with thy riches.
25 So is this great sea, which stretcheth wide its arms: there are creeping things without number: Creatures little and great.
26 There the ships shall go. This sea dragon which thou hast formed to play therein.
27 All expect of thee that thou give them food in season.
28 What thou givest to them they shall gather up: when thou openest thy hand, they shall all be filled with good.
29 But if thou turnest away thy face, they shall be troubled: thou shalt take away their breath, and they shall fail, and shall return to their dust.
30 Thou shalt send forth thy spirit, and they shall be created: and thou shalt renew the face of the earth.
31 May the glory of the Lord endure for ever: the Lord shall rejoice in his works.
32 He looketh upon the earth, and maketh it tremble: he toucheth the mountains, and they smoke.
33 I will sing to the Lord as long as I live: I will sing praise to my God while I have my being.
34 Let my speech be acceptable to him: but I will take delight in the Lord.
35 Let sinners be consumed out of the earth, and the unjust, so that they be no more: O my soul, bless thou the Lord.

EXPLANATION OF THE PSALM

1. The prophet stirs up his soul to bless, that is, to praise God, and at once his soul, so excited, bursts forth into admiration and praise, saying, "O Lord *my God, thou art exceedingly great."* Your works have made you exceedingly great in the eyes of all those who got a glimpse of them. God being infinite and immense, cannot increase in any way, but he can increase in the opinion of men and Angels by their coming to a greater knowledge of the power, wisdom, and goodness that shines forth in his works. *"Thou hast put on praise and beauty,"* an explanation of how God is so exceeding great. As we recognize a king or a judge, or anyone in authority, from the beauty and costliness of their dress, so we perceive God's wisdom and power from the glory in which he is enveloped. Now, *"God is light, and in him there is no darkness,"* still *"he inhabits light inaccessible, which no man hath seen, nor can see."* But, independent of that light, there is another light of glory, a certain splendor that shines forth from God's works, of which the prophet speaks when he says, *"Thou hast put on praise and beauty."*

2. As nothing is more beautiful than light or glory, you have assumed both as a robe, being clothed with that light of glory that shines forth in all your works. Here we must remind our readers how strange it is that, though we cannot look upon the sun, yet, from the light that surrounds it, we readily form an idea of its presence and its beauty; and still we find such a difficulty in raising the eyes of our interior to God that we form but a very faint idea of his boundless beauty, however surrounded he may be by the splendid and extraordinary light that shines in all his works, himself being the light *"that enlightens every man coming into this world."* The only reason that can be assigned for it is, that our hearts are blinded by the dust of carnal thoughts and affections; for *"blessed are the clean of heart, for they shall see God."* For certainly, if we had a clean heart we would readily behold God in all his works, and his glory filling everything, and, with Abraham, Elias, and Eliseus, we would exclaim, *"God, in whose sight I stand,"*—*"Who stretchest out the heaven like a pavilion."* He now begins to draw our attention to the light of the power and wisdom of God, as visible in the creation of the firmament or the heavens, and proposes two points for our consideration, as being worthy of great admiration in them. The first is, that God so dexterously spread out the immense mass of the firmament, and enveloped all created things with it, with as much ease as men will erect and spread out a tent usually made of skins to protect themselves.

3. The second point for our consideration, God's wonderful skill in placing the waters above the heavens, as if he put them on so much fire without the fire being quenched by the waters, or the waters being dried up by the fire. Without entering into the various theories propounded to explain this passage, let it suffice to say, that the general opinion of the holy fathers is, that there is water above the ethereal sky called the firmament, and they are the waters alluded to, and not the water in the clouds. *"Who makest*

the clouds thy chariot." Descending from the ethereal sky to the clouds, he chants forth the admirable wisdom of God in their construction, endowing them with such velocity that when impelled by the wind they travel with marvelous celerity from one part of the world to the other. At one time we behold the sky all serene, and in the twinkling of an eye, on the change of the wind, we behold it veiled with clouds; and, on the other hand, we behold it now murky and gloomy, and in a moment, on another change of wind, away with the clouds, and all becomes bright and cheerful again. This is all described in a most poetical manner, making God, as it were, to sit on the clouds as he would on a chariot, with the winds for so many winged horses; the meaning of the whole being, that God is the primary author of all things, and that the winds and the clouds are moved, and directed, and governed at his pleasure.

4. Only for St. Paul this verse could be easily explained by applying it to the storms and lightnings, and the meaning would be, You who use the storms as your messengers to admonish mankind, and the lightning to punish them: but as the Apostle, in the epistle to the Hebrews, quotes this passage in allusion to the Angels, and argues from it in favor of the divinity of Christ, and his superiority to the Angels, we must say that the prophet speaks here of them, telling us, that God has not only the winds and the clouds at his command, but also far superior and more exalted messengers, the Angels, to send to mankind when he chooses to admonish or to punish them. The meaning, then, of the passage is, When you employ your Angels on any mission, you endow them with the velocity of the wind to execute your commands, with as little delay as possible; and you give them the force of burning fire, so that nothing can resist them.

5. From the air the prophet now comes to the earth; and, from the fact of its being inhabited by us, and consequently, better known to us than the other parts of the world, he devotes more time to description of, and reflection on, the wonderful works of God to be found there. He begins with the creation, and proposes for consideration God's wonderful power, that could produce such an enormous and ponderous mass, and place it aloft without any support or foundation, having nothing but itself to rest on. *"Who hast formed the earth upon its own bases;"* you have built the earth on no foundation whatever, but on itself, without anything to support it. *"It shall not be moved forever and ever;"* your command is surer than any foundation, and such being your orders, the earth, dependent on its own gravity, will remain undisturbed forever.

6-9. He now comes to the consideration of the state of the earth at the creation, being then enveloped, as if by a robe, with water; and yet, by the mere expression of his will, God shut up the water in the lower parts of the earth; by his power and wisdom made the land to rise up, and made it fit for producing grass and grain for the support and nourishment of animal life. That was effected by condensing the water, which hardly deserved the name of water at the time, being rather a sort of watery vapor that upon condensation fell down to the hollows of the earth, to which, possibly, allusion is made in Ecclesiasticus, chap. 24, where he says, *"And as a cloud I covered all the earth;"* which David describes more poetically when he says, *"The deep like a garment is its clothing;"* that is, in the beginning of creation, the earth was all surrounded with water, as if with a garment, that completely envelopes one. He calls the depth of waters an abyss, as it is styled in Genesis, where we read that, darkness was over the face of the abyss; and then, *"above the mountains shall the waters stand;"* that is to say, that the vapors of water, or that very deep cloud that was all but water, covered the very mountains. He uses the future shall, for the preterimperfect tense, a thing not uncommon with the Hebrews when they spoke or wrote of anything in actual progress. By the same rule the expression, *"at thy rebuke they shall flee;"* that is, they did flee, for at the voice of God's thunder the waters that previously covered the whole earth, on being condensed at God's nod alone, descended to the hollows; for the divine intimation was something terrible, having the effect of thunder on thinking beings. *"The mountains ascend, and the plains descend, into the place which thou hast formed for them."* The mountains then began to appear aloft, as if they had ascended, and the fields in the low grounds, as if they had descended; but they all rested *"in the place which thou hast founded for them,"* being over awed by God's reprimands and thunder. *"Thou hast set a bound which they shall not pass over; neither shall they return to cover the earth."* When the waters did recede and were shut up in the caverns of the earth, you put bounds to them they can never transgress, nor can they come back again of themselves by their own power to cover the earth again. They did come back, to be sure, at the time of the deluge, but that was by God's orders and permission. The bounds that God put to the waters was the sand, as we read in Job 39 and Jer. 5, *"The sands of the shore,"* which he did when he created the elements, for the water being heavier that the air, always descends to the lower parts, leaving the higher to the air.

10-12. In the third place, the prophet now comes to consider God's wonderful wisdom in the formation of fountains and rivers. If the waters, when they receded from the earth, had left it dry entirely, the animals thereon could have died of thirst; and, therefore, God, in his wisdom, formed fountains of sweet water, from which the rivers flow in all directions, to supply all animals with drink. These fountains generally have their source in the mountains, and the streams from them run down to the valleys; and thus, the meaning of the words, *"Thou sendest forth springs in the vales,"* seems to be, you who made the streams from the springs in the mountains to run down into the valleys, and the rivulets to pass between the mountains. *"All the beasts of the field shall drink,"* especially *"the wild asses,"* who inhabit the mountains, and, being naturally thirsty, long very much for water. And these fountains will be available not only to the four footed animals, but even the birds of the air will build their nests near them, so as to be able to have recourse to them, and, from the midst of the rocks in which they have their nests, *"shall give forth their voices,"* chanting, in their own way, the praises of the Lord.

13-15. In the fourth place, the prophet proposes for consideration, and sings of another admirable gift of God's providence. When he saw that many elevated places in the hills and mountains could not be reached by the fountains and the rivers, and that they would be even unavailable to many of the fields, he thought of rain, which, coming from the clouds, as if from so many fountains, might irrigate any land, however elevated; and that the land so enriched may produce grass and grain to support all those living on it. *"Thou waterest the hills from thy upper rooms;"* that is to say, God it is who waters or irrigates the hills, that cannot be reached by the rivers; *"from his upper rooms;"* from the clouds. *"The earth shall be filled with the fruits of thy works."* The dry and thirsty earth shall be satiated with the water you express from the clouds. *"Bringing forth grass for cattle, and herb for the service of men."* By that providence of God, you bring forth food for man and beast. *"That thou mayest bring bread out of the earth;"* bread being taken for the food of man in general; *"and that wine may cheer the heart of man,"* intelligible enough. *"That he may make the face cheerful with oil;"* for the Jews were much pleased with oil at their repasts; *"and that bread may strengthen man's heart;"* may support and keep up nature. We have a few remarks to make here. First, that God is the source of all good things that appertain to the support and the enjoyment of corporal life; for, however man may labor in digging up the ground, putting the seed into it, planting trees, and fixing and pruning vines, if God will not make his sun shine on them, and his rain fall on them, cause them to fructify, and give man strength to labor on them, all will be of no avail. And, as God can do everything of himself, without the intervention of secondary causes, as he did in the beginning of the world; while the secondary causes, without God, can do nothing; with the greatest truth does the Apostle say, *"Neither he that planteth is anything, nor he that watereth; but God who giveth the increase;"* and in Acts 14, *"Nevertheless, he left not himself without testimony, doing good from heaven, giving rains, and fruitful seasons, filling our hearts with food and gladness;"* and again, Acts 17, *"Seeing it is he who giveth to all life and breath, and all things; for in him we live, and we move, and we are."* Most truly also does the Psalmist sing in this passage, that it is God who brings forth grass for the cattle; bread, wine, and oil for mankind. Hence appears the incredible ingratitude of many, who, while they are in the receipt of so many favors from God, never raise their thoughts to heaven to thank their most loving Father, by whom they are so paternally and fondly supported. Secondly, it is to be remarked, that, in the spirit of a truly fond and loving Father, he has given us, not only the necessaries of life, represented by bread and water, but even the luxuries of life, in order to savor the necessaries, and make them more agreeable to us; for he gave us wine to gladden our hearts, according to Proverbs 31, *"Give wine to them that are grieved in mind,"* and oils which serves to beautify the face, and also to season our food, for when mixed with herbs or vegetables, it makes them much more palatable, and thus tends to make the face cheerful. Hence the monks of old, when they would be hospitable to a stranger, always served up the herbs or vegetables with oil. Thirdly, we should remark that man ought to be content with frugal meals, and moderate drink, such moderation is a gift from God, while expensive delicacies and the various condiments of luxury, and, of course, much more so excess and drunkenness, are from the devil.

16-18. In the fifth place, the prophet turns to the consideration of the divine providence, in his producing and nourishing, without any human aid, trees of enormous size, such as the cedars of Lebanon, that serve as a dwelling and a refuge for certain birds, as the mountains do for the stags, and the rocks for the irchins. *"The trees of the fields shall be filled."* The rain that falls will supply sufficient moisture to nourish those great cedar trees, which God *"himself hath planted,"* because the seed of them was not set by man, for they grew spontaneously. *"There the sparrows shall make their nests;"* the sparrow is a term for all small birds that nestle there. *"The highest of them is the house of the heron."* The heron, being the largest of the birds that nestle therein, inhabits the highest branches. *"The high hills are a refuge for the harts;"* as these tall trees protect the heron and the sparrow, so the high hills shelter the deer, and the rocks protect the irchins (a species of hedge hog), into whose crevices they run for shelter.

19-23. In the sixth place, the prophet praises and reviews God's providence, in his division of time for labor, both of man and beast; for he gave the night to the beasts to go in quest of their prey, and the day to man to labor for his food. *"He made the moon for seasons; the sun knoweth his going down."* The Lord God made the moon for the use of man and beasts to give them light at certain seasons in the night. *"The sun knoweth his going down;"* when he ought to set and give way to the night. *"Thou hast appointed darkness and it is night; in it shall the beasts of the wood go about;"* from such alternation of moon and sunshine you have caused darkness to ensue on the setting of the sun, to enable the wild beasts to emerge from their hiding places, and go abroad in quest of food and especially *"the young lions roaring after their prey,"* through hunger, and thus *"seeking their meat from God,"* seeking it in the way ordained by divine providence. *"The sun ariseth, and they have gathered together, and they shall lie down in their dens."* The same divine providence causes those wild beasts who roamed about so ferociously during the nights to return to their dens towards morning, and lie down in quiet there. *"Man shall go forth to his work and to his labor till the evening."* The wild beasts having retired to their lairs, man arises and goes out in safety to his labor. Here we are reminded that the beasts who have got no hand, and are not endowed with reason, are prompted by nature to live on the plunder acquired in the night; but that such plunder is positively prohibited to mankind, that has got hands wherewith to labor, and reason to guide and direct that labor; and, therefore, that all thieves, robbers, or those who are engaged in deception, lying, fraud, or other such sinful practices, disturb, as far as in them lies, the order of divine providence; and to them may properly be applied that verse of the Psalm, *"Man when he was in honor did not understand: he hath been compared to senseless beasts, and made like to them."*

24. An exclamation in admiration of the works of God all over the earth, and a sort of conclusion from the six foregoing considerations. His admiration turns on the excellence, wisdom, and multitude of God's works. In regard of their excellence he says, *"how great are thy works!"* how splendid, noble, superior, and worthy of all praise are thy works, O Lord! In regard of their wisdom he says, *"Thou hast made all things in wisdom;"* nothing has been done by chance or at random; everything has been done, with consummate prudence and judgment, so that there is not too much or too little to be found anywhere; in fine, there is no one thing where God's wisdom does not shine forth and appear, and especially in the formation and construction of the human frame, and of all its minutest parts. In regard of the number of his works he says, *"The earth is filled with thy riches."* These beautiful, valuable, extraordinary works, formed with such consummate skill, are not few in number, for they are innumerable; they fill the whole world, they are to be found everywhere, so that the earth may be truly said to be *"filled with thy riches."*

25-27. Having praised God's wisdom by reason of his works in the heavens, the air, and on the earth, he, at length, comes to the sea, and sings of God's wisdom as displayed therein, by reason of its extent, the multitude and variety of its fishes, its utility as a highway for shipping, and the magnitude of one of its denizens, the whale; and comes to the conclusion that all those animals, and not only those of the deep, but all animals in general, however innumerable, are supported and maintained by God. *"This great sea which stretcheth wide its arms."* This great sea, too, is one of the wonderful works of God, great in its depth, great in its extent, and as the strength of a man is judged by the extent to which he can stretch out his arms, we can infer what the power and might of the sea is, when we look at its various and extensive ramifications. *"There are the creeping things without number."* Another of the wonderful works of God to be found in the sea is, that notwithstanding the incredible and daily capture of fish over the world, they still so abound that they are *"without number,"* which fecundity was alluded to when the Creator said to them, *"Increase and multiply and fill the waters of the sea."* Add to this their variety, which is nearly infinite, to which he alludes when he says, *"Creatures little and great."*—*"There the ship shall go."* Another wonderful attribute of the sea is its being able to bear up ships laden with the heaviest materials, transporting them with facility from one part of the world to the other, and thus promoting man's comforts by the blessings of trade and commerce. *"This sea dragon which thou hast formed to play therein."* Great and heavy as the ships may be, a greater and a heavier burden still is borne by the same waters, and not only borne by them, but this great sea dragon skips about and *"plays therein."* And all these animals, great and small, so living in the sea, were not only created, but are even fed and supported daily by God. *"All expect of thee that thou give them their food in season."*

28-29. He repeats, at greater length, that all animals are so dependent on God, that when he opens his hand to give them food, they all live, and when he closes his hand, in refusal of the food, they die; and though, strictly speaking, this is said of those in the deep, it is true in regard of all animals, who equally depend upon God. *"What thou givest to them they shall gather up."* If you cooperate with them through secondary causes, or rather yourself move the secondary causes, and by your assistance help them to procure their food, *"they shall gather up,"* and, therefore, live. *"When thou openest thy hand they shall be all filled with good;"* a repetition, in different language, of the same idea, which clearly proves God to be the author of all good, and without whose assistance neither the art of man, nor the fertility of the soil, can be of any avail. *"But if thou turnest away thy face they shall be troubled."* If you turn from them in anger they will feel it severely, they will be troubled; *"they will fail,"* die away, for *"you will take away their breath,"* the spirit of life you infused into them; *"and shall return to their dust,"* the mother earth from whence they sprang.

30. He proves that God's power should be greatly praised and extolled from the fact of his being able to restore life to things he had deprived of life, a thing he can do even in individual cases, as he actually will do in the resurrection of the dead on the day of judgment; however, he speaks here of

resurrection, not in the individual, but in the species, for God deprives a thing of life, when, by various ways, he suffers it to die; and, again, he infuses the spirit of vitality into animals, by a new generation; and thus, *"he renews the face of the earth,"* by filling it with all manner of animals.

31. Having explained the wonderful works of God in the heavens, the air, the land, and the sea, he concludes the Psalm with prayer, using the first petition in the Lord's prayer. *"May the glory of the Lord endure forever."* May the Lord always be praised, not only by the words, but also by the life and conduct of his servants. *"The Lord shall rejoice in his works;"* hence will come to pass, that God will always be glad of what he shall have done, and will have no occasion to regret or be sorry for it, as he did in Genesis, where we read that *"God, seeing the wickedness of men upon the earth was great, and being touched inwardly with sorrow of heart, he said, I will destroy man whom I have created from the face of the earth, from man even to beasts, from the creeping thing even to the fowls of the air; for it repenteth me that I have made them."* God cannot suffer sorrow, nor regret, nor joy; but the prophet uses the ordinary mode of expression, to convey to us, that God, in order to punish sinners, destroys his own work, just as those do who regret having produced a work; while, on the contrary, he cherishes and regards with fondness other works of his, to reward the just, as those who are proud of having produced them.

32. Having said that all created things were the works of the Lord, he proves it briefly, from the fact that such is the power of God over all creation, that a single look of his makes the earth tremble, and a touch of his ignites the very mountains, alluding to God's descent on mount Sinai, when the whole mountain smoked and trembled.

33-34. Another petition, that his praise may be pleasing to God. As I wish that God should be praised by all, I too, *"will sing to the Lord as long as I live,"* and will celebrate his praise, not only with my voice, but also with the psaltery. But this I ask and pray for, *"that my speech be acceptable to him;"* that is, that the hymn I shall constantly chant to his praise may be agreeable to his Majesty, and I, too, *"will take delight in the Lord;"* will be delighted in loving him, and in constantly reflecting on his goodness.

35. This is the last petition, praying that those sinners who know not how to praise God *"be consumed out of the earth,"* either that they be no longer sinners, by being converted, or if they will not be converted, that they be cast beneath the earth, never again to appear.

PSALM 104

A thanksgiving to God for his benefits to his people of Israel.

1 Give glory to the Lord, and call upon his name: declare his deeds among the Gentiles.

PSALM 104

2 Sing to him, yea sing praises to him: relate all his wondrous works.

3 Glory ye in his holy name: let the heart of them rejoice that seek the Lord.

4 Seek ye the Lord, and be strengthened: seek his face evermore.

5 Remember his marvellous works which he hath done; his wonders, and the judgments of his mouth.

6 ye seed of Abraham his servant; ye sons of Jacob his chosen.

7 He is the Lord our God: his judgments are in all the earth.

8 He hath remembered his covenant for ever: the word which he commanded to a thousand generations.

9 Which he made to Abraham; and his oath to Isaac:

10 And he appointed the same to Jacob for a law, and to Israel for an everlasting testament:

11 Saying: To thee will I give the land of Chanaan, the lot of your inheritance.

12 When they were but a small number: yea very few, and sojourners therein:

13 And they passed from nation to nation, and from one kingdom to another people.

14 He suffered no man to hurt them: and he reproved kings for their sakes.

15 Touch ye not my anointed: and do no evil to my prophets.

16 And he called a famine upon the land: and he broke in pieces all the support of bread.

17 He sent a man before them: Joseph, who was sold for a slave.

18 They humbled his feet in fetters: the iron pierced his soul,

19 Until his word came. The word of the Lord inflamed him.

20 The king sent, and he released him: the ruler of the people, and he set him at liberty.

21 He made him master of his house, and ruler of all his possession.

22 That he might instruct his princes as himself, and teach his ancients wisdom.

23 And Israel went into Egypt: and Jacob was a sojourner in the land of Cham.

24 And he increased his people exceedingly: and strengthened them over their enemies,

25 He turned their heart to hate his people: and to deal deceitfully with his servants.

26 He sent Moses his servant: Aaron the man whom he had chosen.

27 He gave them power to shew his signs, and his wonders in the land of Cham.

28 He sent darkness, and made it obscure: and grieved not his words.

29 He turned their waters into blood, and destroyed their fish.

30 Their land brought forth frogs, in the inner chambers of their kings.

31 He spoke, and there came divers sorts of flies and sciniphs in all their coasts.

32 He gave them hail for rain, a burning fire in the land.

33 And he destroyed their vineyards and their fig trees: and he broke in pieces the trees of their coasts.

34 He spoke, and the locust came, and the bruchus, of which there was no number.
35 And they devoured all the grass in their land, and consumed all the fruit of their ground.
36 And he slew all the firstborn in their land: the firstfruits of all their labour.
37 And he brought them out with silver and gold: and there was not among their tribes one that was feeble.
38 Egypt was glad when they departed: for the fear of them lay upon them.
39 He spread a cloud for their protection, and fire to give them light in the night.
40 They asked, and the quail came: and he filled them with the bread of heaven.
41 He opened the rock, and waters flowed: rivers ran down in the dry land.
42 Because he remembered his holy word, which he had spoken to his servant Abraham.
43 And he brought forth his people with joy, and his chosen with gladness.
44 And he gave them the lands of the Gentiles: and they possessed the labours of the people:
45 That they might observe his justifications, and seek after his law.

Explanation of the psalm

1. The prophet, in the spirit of his fervor, invites God's people to praise and invoke God, and to announce his wonderful works to other nations, that his praise and worship may be extended thereby. The true lover does not wish the praise and knowledge of his beloved should be confined to himself, but wishes that many, nay even all, should know her perfections and praise them. He, therefore, says, *"Give glory to the Lord,"* give him the just tribute of praise, *"and call upon his name,"* to help you to do it properly; for without his assistance you will not be able to accomplish it. *"Declare his deeds among the gentiles;"* speak in all directions among the gentiles of the wonderful works of God, that they, too, from a knowledge of his works, may begin to know, praise, and invoke their Creator.

2. An explanation of the previous verse, as much as to say, you are not only to sing to him, but also to sing with musical instruments, praising him in word and deed, by extolling him in your words and living up to the standard laid down by him as your rule of life, *"relate all his wonderful works,"* a repetition of the latter part of the previous verse; that is, announce to the gentiles God's works, all of which are most astounding and sublime.

3. Having invited them to an expression of praise, united with chant, he now invites them to rejoice and be glad internally, first saying, *"Glory ye in his holy name."* Glory in your heart for having come to the knowledge of God, the author of all good. *"Let the heart of them rejoice that seek the Lord."* Do not seek the Lord in grief and sorrow, but in joy and gladness; for the getting hold of him surpasses all other earthly treasures.

4. He impresses on us the necessity of having constant recourse to God, *"seek his face evermore."* If we refer this advice to those of the Old Testament, the meaning would be, seek to have God always present with you; through his grace and his favors endeavor that he may always look upon you with an eye of benignity—that he may pour his blessings from heaven on you—that he may not turn away his face, in his anger, from you, despise or afflict you. But, if we refer this passage, as we ought, to the new dispensation, the meaning will be, *"Seek his face evermore."* Be always ascending in your hearts, in loving and longing for the face of the Lord, until you shall have got to see it in some measure. And, as nobody looks for what he knows nothing of, St. Augustine very properly says that they *"who seek the face of the Lord"* have already found him through faith, while they are still looking for him through hope and desire. Hence we infer that they who have no faith, or do not exercise that faith, do not seek the face of the Lord; and, therefore, that the beginning of the seeking the face of the Lord is to take its rise from the exercise of faith, by thinking and meditating on the excellence of the supreme good, and by firmly persuading themselves, from the Scriptures, that true happiness, such as can completely satisfy our desire, is not to be had but in beholding the infinite beauty of God, to which man can arrive if he seek the face of God as he ought. Now, to do that two things are necessary, viz., to remove all obstacles, and make use of the necessary means, as the Apostle informs Titus, *"Renouncing impiety and worldly desires, we should live soberly, and justly, and piously in this world, waiting for the blessed hope."* The obstacles, then, are bad desires and an attachment to the things of this world; for in proportion to the absence of avarice is the increase of charity. They, then, who desire to be rich, and to amass wealth, administer not to the sufferer in his necessity, and, the slaves of gluttony or luxury, they do not ascend to seek the face of the Lord; but they descend, are farther removed from it, because, instead of removing, they multiply the impediments. True justice, or, in other words, the fulfillment of the law of God, is the means of finding the face of the Lord, as the Lord says, *"Seek first the kingdom of God and his justice,"* the one as the end, the other as the means; and, *"If thou will enter into life, keep the commandments."* The one, then, that always seeks the face of the Lord is he who exercises his faith in reflection and meditation, who mortifies his members in this world, and, having abnegated all secular desires, always lives with a pure heart and good conscience, always longing to behold the face of God.

5. He tells us now for what we are to praise God, and points out a sort of ladder by which we may ascend to the love, and a desire for God, to which two things he invited us in the preceding verses. The subject of God's praise are his wonderful works, that indicate to us his omnipotence, his supreme

wisdom, and his most sweet goodness, which, if faithfully turned in the mind and reflected on, will elevate it to the love of, and a longing for God. *"Remember his marvelous works, which he hath done."* Bring before your memory, and think on all the wonderful things you know to have been done by God; *"His wonders and the judgments of his mouth."* The prodigies he effected through Moses, Josue, Samuel, that could never have been done by natural means; and *"the judgments of his month;"* the dreadful scourges inflicted on Pharao and others, who persecuted his people, being both prodigies and judgments, inasmuch as they were wrought on Pharao for his pride.

6. An explanation of the preceding verse; as if he said, I address you, ye Jews, who are *"the seed of Abraham, and sons of Jacob;"* you who have descended from Abraham, Isaac, and Jacob, and not from Esau or Ismael; for you are *"his servants, his chosen,"* God having chosen you as his own servants, to give you his law, and to teach you how he should be worshipped. St. Augustine observes, that, however applicable this may be to the children in the flesh of Abraham and Jacob, it is more applicable to the children by faith; for the Apostle says, Rom. 4, *"And he (Abraham) received the sign of circumcision, a seal of the justice of the faith, which is in uncircumcision, that he might be the father of all the believers uncircumcised, that to them also it may be reputed to justice, and might be the father of circumcision, not to them only that are of the circumcision, but to them also who follow the steps of the faith that our father Abraham had, being as yet uncircumcised;"* and again, chap. 9, *"For all are not Israelites that are of Israel, neither are all they who are the seed of Abraham children, but in Isaac shall thy seed be called; that is to say, not they who are the children of the flesh are the children of God; but they that are the children of the promise are counted for the seed;"* and again, in Galatians 3, *"Know ye, therefore, that they who are of faith are the children of Abraham, and the Scripture, foreseeing that God justifies the gentiles by faith, told Abraham before: In thee shall all nations be blessed; therefore they who are of the faith shall be blessed with the faithful Abraham;"* and he concludes the chapter thus, *"And if you be of Christ, then you are the seed of Abraham, heirs according to the promise."*

7-8. He now begins to narrate the wonderful works of God, beginning with the fact of God, the ruler of the universe, having chosen Abraham, and having entered into an everlasting compact with him of giving the land of promise forever to his seed, which promise was fulfilled in Christ, whose kingdom will have no end, while the children of Abraham have lost the possession of Palestine. *"He is the Lord our God, his judgments are in all the earth;"* God, whose judgments are all over the world, and who, as supreme King and Monarch, judges all; he, that very same great God, *"hath remembered his covenant forever;"* remembered the covenant he made, and which he intended should last forever, *"the word which he commanded to a thousand generations;"* that is, forever.

9-12. In order to confirm the truth of his assertion, he repeats it, and explains it at greater length, saying, *"Which he made to Abraham;"* he remembered the promise he made to Abraham, and confirmed the same promise *"by his oath to Isaac."* And he appointed *"the same"* sworn promise *"to Jacob for a law;"* a decree, a statute, and as *"an everlasting testament;"* a treaty to hold forever. The words of promise contained in that treaty were, *"I will give thee the land of Chanaan;"* the land of promise, then inhabited by the Chanaanites; *"the lot of your inheritance;"* to be held by your children as their inheritance, usually distributed by lot, which promise was made to Abraham, in Gen. 26, to Isaac, in Gen. 28, and to Jacob, in Gen. 28. These promises were made to the Jews, *"when they were but a small number;"* very few, indeed; *"and sojourners;"* birds of passage, mere strangers in the same land, which leads us the more to admire the counsel, power, and wisdom of God, and his great regard for the patriarchs, in choosing out of the whole world one family, and that a poor one, and promising them, and afterwards fulfilling his promise of giving them a most extensive country, the seat of many kings. Much more wonderful is it that the same God should have chosen the little flock of the elect from out of the whole human race, to give them the kingdom of heaven, of which the land of promise was but a figure, as an eternal inheritance.

13-15. The prophet now records another of God's favors, in having guarded and protected the patriarchs by a singular providence. He alludes to Abraham, who was twice in danger by reason of the beauty of his wife; to Isaac, who also was near suffering in that way; and to Jacob, who was all but ruined, first by Laban, then by Esau, and they all escaped through God's singular care of them. *"And they passed,"* the patriarchs Abraham, Isaac, and Jacob, with their families, *"from nation to nation;"* from one province to another, *"and from one kingdom to another people;"* from the kingdom to the people of the kingdom of Egypt. *"He suffered no man to hurt them;"* nay more, *"he reproved kings for their sake;"* for instance, Pharao, the king of Egypt, and Abimelech, king of Gerara, for he said to those kings, *"Touch ye not my anointed,"* Abraham, Isaac, and Jacob; *"and do no evil to my prophets;"* to the three aforesaid, who are also my prophets, and by virtue thereof, anointed and consecrated to me. Do not molest them, trouble them, or do them any manner of harm. There can be no doubt of the three above named holy patriarchs having been prophets also, for Abraham foresaw the captivity of the people of Israel in Egypt, its duration, and its termination; as we read in Gen. 15. Isaac, shortly before his death, predicted to his son Esau, that he would be subservient to his younger brother Jacob, and that at one time he would shake off his yoke, all which regarded their posterity and not themselves; see Gen. 27. Jacob uttered several prophecies concerning each of his sons, especially Juda, from whose tribe he prophesied the Messias would come. Thus those patriarchs are very properly called prophets, and they are said to be *"anointed,"* not that they were visibly anointed with oil, as were the priests, kings, and sometimes the prophets in after times; but, because they had the internal and spiritual unction of the spirit poured upon them, of which Isaias says, *"The spirit of the Lord is upon one, because the Lord hath anointed me."*

16-23. This is the third favor conferred by God on his people, in which we find a great field for praising the wonderful wisdom of God, who, from such a mass of evil, could bring such an amount of good. He gives an account of the great famine that overshadowed the earth in the time of Jacob, when he and all his family migrated into Egypt; see Gen. 37, etc. *"And he called a famine upon the land."* God, in his providence, caused a dreadful famine, by reason of a dearth of corn, to overspread the earth. He speaks figuratively when he says, *"called a famine,"* as if it were an army he would call from one place to another, to let us see how obedient all things are to God, and how they answered at his nod and bidding; as also to let us see that things we suppose to happen by chance, are so ordained by God, for his own wise purposes. He repeats the same at greater length when he says, *"And he broke in pieces all the support of bread."* That famine was caused by God's having destroyed the bread they had to support them, for during a period of seven years not a grain of corn ripened in the country; as we read in Genesis: *"He sent a man before them, Joseph;"* on the occasion of the approaching famine, God sent into Egypt before the children of Israel, *"a man,"* a great man, *"Joseph,"* for the purpose of delivering Israel and all his family from the famine. History tells us that Joseph, through the envy of his brethren, was sold as a slave to some merchants on their way to Egypt; but David says he was sent there by God, who in his providence suffered him to be sold and transported into Egypt, for the purpose of afterwards introducing Jacob and his sons there in a most wonderful manner. He tells us how Joseph was sent there when he says, *"he was sold for a slave,"* by his brethren, to merchants on their way to Egypt. *"They humbled his feet in fetters."* No sooner had Joseph got into Egypt than he was accused of criminality with his master's wife, was thrown into prison for it, and had his feet bound with fetters of iron. *"The iron pierced his soul until his word came."* His chains being heavy on him, afflicted and weighed him down, until *"his word, that is, his prophecy of the butler's, his fellow captive, being released in a few days, "came,"* was accomplished, and that led to his own liberation; see Genesis. *"The word of the Lord inflamed him."* That word or prophecy of Joseph was not his own; it was the word of the

Lord, inspired and suggested by him. *"The king sent and he released him: the ruler of the people and he set him at liberty."* King Pharao having heard from his butler of Joseph's wisdom, sent to the prison, knocked off his manacles, and let him out free. *"He made him master of his house, and ruler of all his possession."* He not only set him free, but he placed him over his own family and over the entire kingdom, to administer it, *"that he might instruct his princes as himself, and teach his ancients wisdom."* King Pharao placed Joseph over his kingdom, not only for the purpose of administering to the bodily wants of his subjects during the famine, but also for the purpose of instructing his ministers and counselors in that science of government in which he seemed to be such an adept. *"And Israel went into Egypt."* It was on this occasion that the patriarch Jacob came into Egypt; *"and Jacob was a sojourner in the land of Cham;"* and thus, Jacob, or rather those descended from him, began to dwell in Egypt, called the land of Cham, by reason of Mizraim, the son of Cham, the son of Noe, having been the first to dwell therein.

24-27. Next comes the fourth favor, conferred by God on his people, in causing them, through his divine providence, so to increase and multiply in Egypt; and, when they were grievously oppressed by Pharao, in sending Moses and Aaron, with great power, to work signs and prodigies, the consequence of which was the glorious departure of God's people from out of Egypt. He, therefore, says, *"And he increased his people exceedingly; and strengthened them over their enemies."* The meaning of this may be learned from that passage in Exodus, where it is read, *"The children of Israel increased and sprung up into multitudes, and growing exceedingly strong, they filled the land. In the meantime, there arose a new king over Egypt, that knew not Joseph, and he said to his people: Behold, the people of the children of Israel are numerous and stronger than we."* *"He turned their heart,"* of the Egyptians, *"to hate his people; and to deal deceitfully with his servants;"* to oppress them by fraud and cunning. Now, God is said to have *"turned the hearts"* of the Egyptians; not that he implanted any evil designs therein, (for God is not the author of sin) but by pouring down favors on his people, and causing them to multiply in so extraordinary a degree, he more or less gave occasion to the perverted hearts of the Egyptians to envy their neighbors' prosperity, and plot their ruin. And God, when he did so favor his people, fully knew and foresaw the envy and the hatred it would beget among the Egyptians; because he had a right, and he wished it, to turn their perverse thoughts, which he had not created, to good account, in punishing themselves, and delivering his people from captivity. *"He sent Moses his servant, Aaron, the man whom he hath chosen;"* when the people began to be so punished, he sent Moses and Aaron to Pharao. *"He gave them power to show signs, and his wonders in the land of Cham."* When he sent Moses and Aaron to deliver his people, he gave them power to perform miracles in the land of Egypt, that the children of Israel, as well as the Egyptians, might believe that they were sent by him, and that they should obey them as the messengers of the true and Almighty God.

28. He describes, in this and the eight following verses, the prodigies in detail that were performed in Egypt, through which God scourged Pharao and the Egyptians. He does not enumerate all the plagues, nor does he observe the order they are related in Exodus; because he is not writing a history, but chanting a hymn, as we already observed in Psalm 78. He begins, then, with the miraculous darkness that overspread all Egypt for three entire days, it being one of the last recorded in Exodus. *"He sent darkness, and made it obscure."* Covered the whole of Egypt with such darkness that the people did not know each other, and were afraid to move. *"And grieved not his words."* Moses and Aaron did boldly what God desired them, and gave him no reason for being grieved at their noncompliance with his commands.

29-36. All this relating to the plagues of Egypt has been explained in the notes on Psalm 77, which see.

37. Favor the fifth, conferred by God on his people; for he not only delivered them from the captivity of Pharao, but he loaded them with riches on their departure; for he ordered the men among the Jews to borrow from the men among the Egyptians, and the Jewish women to borrow of the Egyptian women their gold and silver vessels, their jewels, precious stones, and robes; and he so lulled the Egyptians asleep that they lent them without any difficulty; and to this the prophet alludes when he says, *"And he brought them out with silver and gold;"* with an immense quantity of gold and silver vessels, and other valuables they had borrowed of the Egyptians. Did they not, then, violate the precept, *"Thou shalt not steal?"* It would have been theft, had not God, the absolute master and owner of all things, transferred the dominion of these valuables from the Egyptians to the Hebrews; and with that, these valuables hardly requited the Jews for the years of toil and labor they had been forced, in their bondage, to yield to the Egyptians; to which Wisdom seems to allude, in chap. 10, when he says, *"And she rendered to the just the wages of their labors, and conducted them in a wonderful way."* Another additional favor was, that while the Egyptians were afflicted with various diseases, and ultimately all their first born were slain, the children of Israel remained unhurt and unharmed by the plague; to which the prophet alludes when he sings, *"And there was not among their tribes one that was feeble."*

38. In addition to the favor just mentioned, there was this, that the Egyptians did not seek to stop the Jews in their departure, nor did they endeavor to get the gold and silver, and other valuables they had lent, back from them;

they rather hurried them away, and rejoiced at their departure, fearing some greater misfortune would come upon them, perhaps the destruction of the whole community, as well as of their first born, were the Jews to remain with them any longer; for thus we read in Exodus, *"And the Egyptians pressed the people to go forth out of the land speedily, saying: We shall all die."*

39. The sixth favor was the pillar of cloud by day, and of fire by night, that God, through the agency of his Angels, set up to guide them when they were going out of the land of Egypt. That cloud was not for their protection from the sun, as the words would seem to imply, but as a guide before them; for we read in Exodus, *"And the Lord went before them to show the way by day in a pillar of cloud, and by night in a pillar of fire, that he might be the guide of their journey at both times."* There never failed the pillar of the cloud by day, nor the pillar of fire by night, before the people. What, then, is the meaning of, *"He spread a cloud for their protection?"* This is explained in Exodus 14. When Pharao and his army pursued the Hebrews, the Angel of the Lord put a cloud between them, so that they could not see each other, nor come near each other, and in that manner the cloud protected them.

40. This is the seventh favor conferred by God on them, the feeding them with bread from heaven, the manna, that daily fell from heaven, and the quails that God supplied them with. It should be remarked that God sent quails to them on two occasions, and that they were severely punished for having asked for them on one occasion, as recorded in Num. 11. That was not the occasion alluded to here, it was the one in Exod. 16, and recorded by the prophet here as one of God's favors.

41. See Exod. 17, and Num. 20.

42. All past and future favors, such as the aforesaid, are justly ascribed to the promise God made to his servant Abraham, for though they were not specifically mentioned in detail, they are all contained in the words he said to Abraham, Gen. 15, *"Know thou beforehand that thy seed shall be a stranger in a land not their own, and they shall bring them under bondage, and afflict them four hundred years. But I will judge the nation which they shall serve; and after this they shall come out with great substance."*

43. Favor the ninth, when, after the destruction of Pharao and his host in the Red Sea, God brought forth his people from bondage, singing with great joy and exaltation, *"Let us sing to the Lord; for he is gloriously magnified,"*

44. The last favor was the introduction of the Jews under Josue, into the lands that belonged to the gentiles, whom they expelled, and got possession of the cities built by, and fields reclaimed by, the labor of those people. We read, in Acts 13, that they were seven in number.

45. All that God requires, in return for so many favors, is the observance of his law; which obedience will prove to be of the greatest value to themselves, for it always leads to fresh favors, of far greater value than the land of promise. By *"justifications"* are meant the ceremonial and judicial law, and by *"law"* is meant the moral law, which is reduced to one precept, charity.

PSALM 105

A confession of the manifold sins and ingratitudes of the Israelites.

1 Give glory to the Lord, for he is good: for his mercy endureth for ever.
2 Who shall declare the powers of the Lord? who shall set forth all his praises?
3 Blessed are they that keep judgment, and do justice at all times.
4 Remember us, O Lord, in the favour of thy people: visit us with thy salvation.
5 That we may see the good of thy chosen, that we may rejoice in the joy of thy nation: that thou mayst be praised with thy inheritance.
6 We have sinned with our fathers: we have acted unjustly, we have wrought iniquity.
7 Our fathers understood not thy wonders in Egypt: they remembered not the multitude of thy mercies: And they provoked to wrath going up to the sea, even the Red Sea.
8 And he saved them for his own name's sake: that he might make his power known.
9 And he rebuked the Red Sea, and it was dried up: and he led them through the depths, as in a wilderness.
10 And he saved them from the hand of them that hated them: and he redeemed them from the hand of the enemy.
11 And the water covered them that afflicted them: there was not one of them left.
12 And they believed his words: and they sang his praises.
13 They had quickly done, they forgot his works: and they waited not for his counsels.
14 And they coveted their desire in the desert: and they tempted God in the place without water.
15 And he gave them their request: and sent fulness into their souls.
16 And they provoked Moses in the camp, Aaron the holy one of the Lord.
17 The earth opened and swallowed up Dathan: and covered the congregation of Abiron.
18 And a fire was kindled in their congregation: the flame burned the wicked.
19 They made also a calf in Horeb: and they adored the graven thing.
20 And they changed their glory into the likeness of a calf that eateth grass.
21 They forgot God, who saved them, who had done great things in Egypt,
22 Wondrous works in the land of Cham: terrible things in the Red Sea.
23 And he said that he would destroy them: had not Moses his chosen stood before him in the breach: To turn away his wrath, lest he should destroy them.
24 And they set at nought the desirable land. They believed not his word,

25 And they murmured in their tents: they hearkened not to the voice of the Lord.
26 And he lifted up his hand over them: to overthrow them in the desert;
27 And to cast down their seed among the nations, and to scatter them in the countries.
28 They also were initiated to Beelphegor: and ate the sacrifices of the dead.
29 And they provoked him with their inventions: and destruction was multiplied among them.
30 Then Phinees stood up, and pacified him: and the slaughter ceased.
31 And it was reputed to him unto justice, to generation and generation for evermore.
32 They provoked him also at the waters of contradiction: and Moses was afflicted for their sakes:
33 Because they exasperated his spirit. And he distinguished with his lips.
34 They did not destroy the nations of which the Lord spoke unto them.
35 And they were mingled among the heathens, and learned their works:
36 And served their idols, and it became a stumblingblock to them.
37 And they sacrificed their sons, and their daughters to devils.
38 And they shed innocent blood: the blood of their sons and of their daughters which they sacrificed to the idols of Chanaan. And the land was polluted with blood,
39 And was defiled with their works: and they went aside after their own inventions.
40 And the Lord was exceedingly angry with his people: and he abhorred his inheritance.
41 And he delivered them into the hands of the nations: and they that hated them had dominion over them.
42 And their enemies afflicted them: and they were humbled under their hands:
43 Many times did he deliver them. But they provoked him with their counsel: and they were brought low by their iniquities.
44 And he saw when they were in tribulation: and he heard their prayer.
45 And he was mindful of his covenant: and repented according to the multitude of his mercies.
46 And he gave them unto mercies, in the sight of all those that had made them captives.
47 Save us, O Lord, our God: and gather us from among nations: That we may give thanks to thy holy name, and may glory in thy praise.
48 Blessed be the Lord the God of Israel, from everlasting to everlasting: and let all the people say: So be it, so be it.

EXPLANATION OF THE PSALM

1. The prophet speaks here in the person of a faithful people sorry for their sins, and returning thanks to God. He invites all to praise God, for his goodness, for his previous direction of man, for the many favors he confers on him and because his mercy in receiving the returning sinner remains ever unchanged; it even exceeds our misery, which we may attribute to our crimes, which even, through God's mercy, speedily disappear, whereas *"his justice continueth forever and ever."*

2. Having invited all to praise God, he now asks where will anyone be found fit to praise him. *"Who shall declare?"* who is equal to the task? *"The power of the Lord;"* the words of his power, or rather, of his omnipotence, which he repeats when he says, *"Who shall set forth all his praises?"* arising from a knowledge of the works of his power. Though the prophet speaks of all the attributes of God as worthy of praise, he speaks principally of his power, to which all his attributes may be reduced. For, of his wisdom it is written, *"She reacheth from end to end mightily, and ordereth all things sweetly;"* and, in fact, God's wisdom is all powerful, and cannot be thwarted, and as such cannot be deceived. By a similar process of reasoning, the works of his mercy may be brought under the head of his power, because God alone is absolutely merciful, for he alone can remove all misery; and thus, he alone is, properly speaking, merciful, and that by reason of his omnipotence. He, then, that could speak of all God's powers, could also cause all his praises to be heard. But where is the man capable of doing that? The just man, in this life, can do it to a certain extent, according to his abilities; but much more fully and satisfactorily will it be done by the blessed in the world to come; and, therefore, the prophet, in answer to his own query, says,

3. As much as to say, they alone are blessed, and, therefore, alone able to declare the power of the Lord, and to set forth his praises, *"who keep judgments, and do justice at all times;"* that is, they who always form a correct judgment on everything they do, by reason of their following the rule of the divine law in all their actions; and thus lead a life of sanctity, in declining from evil, and doing good. This may be applied to the blessed on their pilgrimage, as well as to the blessed in heaven; the former *"keep judgment and do justice,"* to the best of their abilities, as far as human frailty will allow them, and they ask pardon for their daily sins; the latter do it with that amount of perfection that leaves no room for any sin. Thus, both are required to praise God, but in a different way, according to the relative degree of their perfection and happiness.

4-5. Having said that to the just and the blessed belonged the duty of praising God, he wishes that he and his may share in that pleasing duty, and briefly touches on predestination, justification, and glory, the beginning, the means, and the end of human happiness. *"Remember us, O Lord, in the*

favor of thy people." Carry out those benevolent intentions of yours in regard of your people, that of your pure free will you selected before the beginning of the world to be your little flock, and to bestow your everlasting kingdom on them. *"Visit us with thy salvation;"* and, in order to carry that out, visit us through Christ our Savior, cleansing us, through his merits, from our sins, *"that we may see the good of thy chosen."* That, having been predestined, and justified, we may come to see the good of thy chosen, which means that the very face of the Lord may be made conspicuous to us. *"For we shall then be like to him when we shall see him as he is,"* 1 Jn. 3. By the *"good of thy elect"* we are not to understand their own probity or goodness, but the supreme happiness that is their lot. *"That we may rejoice in the joy of thy nation."* That we may partake in that unspeakable joy that arises from the beatific vision, which is the peculiar property of your nation; that is, of your chosen people, of which strangers cannot taste, of which the gospel says, *"Enter into the joy of thy Lord,"*—*"that thou mayest be praised with thy inheritance;"* that all your favors may have the effect of eternal praise being rendered to you and your inheritance; to you for having produced so noble a work, and to the inheritance, as being the work of your own hands; to you, as being a most powerful, wise, superior, and excelling artist, to whom no one can be compared; and to your inheritance, as a most perfect incomparable work, that cannot be equalled. By *"inheritance"* is meant that assembly of the just selected by God as his own possession; for inheritance and possession appear to be synonymous in the Scripture, and are used indiscriminately.

6-12. The prophet, speaking now in the person of those not quite perfect, but still penitent, begins to confess his sins and the sins of their fathers from the time of their departure out of Egypt to the present day, coupling it with praise of God's mercy that never closes its bosom against the penitent. Those verses are easily understood from the book of Exodus and Psalm 77. *"We have sinned with our fathers"* means, we, too, have sinned by imitating them. *"Our fathers understood not thy wonders in Egypt"* refers to the time when they saw Pharao's army in pursuit of them, and got so dispirited that they began to murmur against Moses for having led them out of Egypt; for had they understood the previous miracles that had been performed by the Almighty they would have placed unbounded confidence in his hope and protection. *"And they provoked to wrath"* means, that when they saw the Red Sea before them, and Pharao's army behind them, they provoked God by their diffidence and incredulity. *"Going up to the sea, the Red Sea,"* means, on their journey to the Red Sea. *"He rebuked the Red Sea, and it was dried up,"* is a poetical expression, signifying that the Red Sea retired at God's command, just as a slave would fly from his master's presence on being severely rebuked *"And he led them through the depths;"* that is, through the place that a moment before had been the depths of the sea; an expression similar to *"the blind see, the deaf hear,"* meaning, those who had been so afflicted.

13-15. The prophet goes on with the relation of the ingratitude of the people, and that, after witnessing the astounding miracle performed in the Red Sea, and for which they had thanked God so profoundly; for no sooner did they feel the slightest want of food and drink than they lost all sight of God's providence and omnipotence, and broke out in language of impatience and infidelity. *"They had quickly done,"* without any delay, *"they forgot his works,"* all the miracles they had witnessed; *"and they waited not for his counsel,"* they would not wait for the time appointed by God in his counsel or wisdom; for God, in allowing them to suffer for a while, was only trying their faith, their hope, and their love, while they, in ignorance of God's designs, began to murmur, as if he did not care for them, or could not help them. He now enters into the particulars of their impatience. *"And they coveted their desire in the desert; and they tempted God in the place without water."* They could not have patience even for a short time, or endure for a moment the scarcity of bread and water. *"They coveted their desire"* is not an unusual phrase, meaning, merely, that they longed or wished for. *"And he gave them their request,"* bread and water, that they asked. *"And sent fullness into their hearts,"* by not only giving them food and drink, but giving both in abundance, Exod. 16 and 17, Num. 11 and 20.

16-18. He now alludes to Dathan and Abiron, whose history may be found in Numbers 16. *"They provoked Moses in the camp."* Core, Dathan, and Abiron, provoked him by charging him with having usurped supreme power. *"Aaron, the holy one of the Lord,"* and they provoked Aaron too, who was sanctified by God to be his priest. *"The earth opened,"* etc., and swallowed up the three of them, with all their families and substance, *"and covered the congregation,"* etc. After opening and swallowing them it closed upon the rebels, and covered them and their families. *"And a fire was kindled in the congregation, the flame burned the wicked."* Immediately after the death of those three disaffected, some of the Jews, who were not authorized to offer incense, having presumed to do so, fire from heaven descended and killed two hundred and fifty of them; and when the people began to murmur against Moses, as if he had been the author of it, another fire was sent by God that consumed four thousand seven hundred of them.

19-23. The prophet now gives expression to his detestation of the people's idolatry, in making a calf of gold, and rendering divine worship to it; and, at the same time, praises God's mercy, in having, at the instance of Moses, forgiven so great a sin. Exod. 32. *"They made also a calf in Horeb;"* a calf of gold, to represent an idol they had seen in Egypt, that was made for them by Aaron, who was obliged to comply with their wishes through fear. They did that at Horeb, a mountain quite convenient to mount Sinai. *"And they adored the graven thing;"* the golden heifer; and though it is not a graven thing, but a molten thing, it is called graven, it being a general term for all idols, whether of timber or marble, that are, properly speaking, graven; or of gold or silver, that are usually molten. He alludes to mount Horeb, and to graven things, because it was on mount Horeb that God, when he appeared not long before, said to them, *"Thou shalt not make to thyself any graven thing; thou shalt not adore or worship them;"* and thus a great aggravation in the sin of the Jews was, that they made and set up for adoration this graven or molten thing, on the very spot on which God had forbidden it. *"And they changed their glory into the likeness of a calf that eateth grass."* An aggravation of the folly of the Jews consisted in their setting up an idol in the form of a calf for the true God, thereby changing their glory, the true God, who was their glory, for the image of a brute beast; nor does he say they exchanged God for a beast, but, to render the case worse, for the image of a calf, or, in other words, the most precious thing in existence for the most contemptible. *"They forgot God who saved them, who had done great things in Egypt, wondrous works in the land of Cham, terrible things in the Red Sea."* A further aggravation of the folly of the Jews consisted in their having forgotten or deserted that God who freed them from the captivity of Pharao, for the service of a god who could neither save himself nor anyone else; for Moses smashed the calf, and made powder of it without any resistance, or even consciousness, on the part of the golden calf. They also forgot that God of all power, *"who hath done great things in Egypt,"* which was also called the land of Cham; *"terrible things in the Red Sea;"* by drying it up so as to afford a passage through to the children of Israel, and then letting the waters on so as to suffocate the Egyptians; and, notwithstanding all this, they worshipped an empty, an imbecile god, that is to say, a mute and useless image. *"And he said that he would destroy them, had not Moses his chosen stood before him in the breach."* God, then, determined, and said he would destroy them; and he would have done so, had not Moses, his chosen servant, interfered, and by his intercession succeeded *"in turning away his wrath lest he should destroy them."* He uses a metaphor, taken from a brave soldier who stands in the breach to repel the enemy until his own reinforcements should come up; and from this we can argue in favor of the power of the intercession of the saints.

24-27. The Prophet now records another sin of the Jews, in their despising the land of promise, which God told them was one flowing with milk and honey. *"And they set at naught the desirable land."* They despised and thought little of the land of promise, instead of valuing it highly, as they should have done; for they said, *"The land which we have viewed devoureth its inhabitants."*—*"They believed not his word;"* God's word, that he had spoken so often to them, as to the quality of the land; and *"they murmured in their tents"* against him who had brought them out of Egypt to establish them in the land of promise. *"They hearkened not to the voice of the Lord;"* they did not obey his commands. *"And he lifted up his hand over them; to overthrow them in the desert: And he cast down their seed among the nations, and to scatter them in the countries."* He raised his hand, armed with the sword of justice, over his sinful people, in order to slay the murmurers in the desert, and to scatter their posterity abject and desolate, all over the world, so that they could no longer be called a nation. The former has been already accomplished, for all the murmurers perished in the desert; the latter, at the instance of Moses, was not then and there carried out, but, in consequence of the repeated sins of the people, was fully accomplished, both by the king of Babylon, and by Titus and Vespasian. How incensed, then, must not God feel with those who despise the kingdom of heaven, as announced and promised to us by his Son, when he was so grievously incensed with the Jews for having disregarded the land of promise, that was nothing but earth, and a mere figure of the kingdom of heaven?

28-31. David now alludes to another sin committed by the Jews, the history of which is to be found in Numbers 25. We read there that the children of Israel, seduced by the daughters of Moab, began to commit fornication with them, and to worship an idol of their's, called Beelphegor, which incensed God so much that he ordered all the princes of the people to be hanged on gibbets; but when Phinees, the son of Eleazar, the son of Aaron, in his zeal slew an Israelite in the act of fornication with a Madianite woman, God was so pleased with his zeal, that he forgave the whole people for it. *"They also were initiated to Beelphegor;"* to their other sins the Israelites added that of becoming disciples of Beelphegor, the idol of the Madianites; *"and ate the sacrifice of the dead;"* the sacrifices that were offered to their dead gods, such as Apis and Serapis with the Egyptians, Jupiter and Apollo with the Greeks, instead of sacrificing to the one, true, and living God. *"And they provoked him with their inventions."* They naturally provoked God by the worship of new gods invented by them; not that they were the first to set up Beelphegor, but that they were the first to learn his worship from the Moabites, and introduce it to the Israelites. *"And destruction was multiplied among them,"* in consequence of that sin destruction set in upon them, numbers of them having miserably perished. *"Then Phinees stood up, and pacified him; and the slaughter ceased."* Phinees, full of zeal for the glory of God, stood up courageously against the impious deserters of the old religion, and by his zeal so appeased God, that *"the slaughter ceased."* *"And it was reputed to him unto justice."* God, who searcheth the heart, and well knew the good dispositions of Phinees, did not look upon such slaughter as a sinful act, or one worthy of punishment, but, on the contrary, as a good and a meritorious act, *"and that to generation and generation forevermore;"* in allusion to the promise made by God to Phinees, that in consideration of what he did so nobly, the priesthood should remain in his family as long as the Jewish dynasty should hold.

32-33. He now passes to another sin of the Jews, recorded in Numbers 20. When the people, suffering from want of water, began to wrangle with Moses, who was so frightened that he seemed to have some hesitation, and said, *"Can we bring you forth water from this rock?"* However, on striking the rock twice, water poured forth in the greatest abundance. God, however, half in anger with Moses for his hesitation, in punishment of it did not allow him to introduce the people to the land of promise, and he died on the way to it. *"They provoked him;"* the Jews provoked God *"at the waters of contradiction;"* the place where they upbraided and wrangled with Moses, by reason of their want of water. *"And Moses was quieted, for their sakes,"* troubled and grieved in his mind at the unreasonableness of the people. *"Because they exasperated his spirit."* By their murmurs and reproaches they made Moses, who, at all times was most alive and ready to carry out all God's commands, now truly downcast and disheartened. *"And he distinguished with his lips;"* they so confused him, that when God ordered him to bring the water from the rock, he did not put full faith in God, or give him that implicit obedience he required; for God said to him, *"Speak to the rock before thee, and it shall yield waters,"* instead of doing which he said, *"Can we bring forth water frown this rock?"* and thus, *"he distinguished with his lips."*

34-36. He now records another grievous transgression of the Jews, who, instead of banishing all the idolaters from the land of promise, as they had been ordered by God, began to cohabit with them, and to adopt their superstitions and sacrileges. Herein he alludes to the words of the Angel, who, in the person of God, thus addresses them, Judges 2, *"I made you go out of Egypt, and have brought you into the land for which I swore to your fathers; and I promised that I would not make void any covenant forever, on condition that you should not make a league with the inhabitants of this land, but should throw down their altars; and you would not hear my voice. Why have you done this?"*—*"And they were mingled among the heathens, and learned their works, and served their idols,"* as the whole book of Judges testifies; *"and it became a stumbling block to them;"* proved their ruin; for it caused God to give them up to various idolatrous kings, as we read in the same book; and it was only meet that they who preferred the devil to God, should be handed over to the devil's servants.

37-39. There is no record of all this in the book of Judges, but it must, of necessity be true, as the Holy Ghost inspired the prophet to record it, who possibly had it also by tradition. God once commanded Abraham to slay his son, yet he would not allow him to do it, being satisfied with his readiness to obey; but the false gods, the demons, envying God for such obedience in Abraham, not satisfied with the same readiness on the part of their dupes, actually required of them to sacrifice and spill the blood of their own children. And such was the blindness of man then, that they did rot feel such tyranny on the part of the demons, nor perceive the difference between the sweet yoke of their Maker, and the severe and bitter fetters of the destroyer. *"And they went aside after their own intentions;"* that synagogue of the Jews that was betrothed to God left him, abandoned him, and went in pursuit of idols, to worship them; idols of their own invention, for they learned no such worship from Moses, but rather from the idolaters about them that they thus chose to follow.

40-46. These seven verses are a sort of abridgment of the book of Judges, where we read of God having been so provoked by the sins of the Jews that he frequently allowed them to fall into the hands of their enemies the Moabites, Ammonites, Philistines, and others; but when they would return to penance he was wont to raise up some brave leader, such as Jepthe, Gedeon, Samson, and others, to deliver them. The only verse of those seven requiring an explanation is the last. *"And he gave them unto mercies in the sight of all those that had made them captives."* God so placed them in the bosom of his mercy, to the utter astonishment of those who made them captives, that their very enemies could not deny but that God was fighting for his own people.

47-48. The conclusion of the Psalm, in which the prophet prays to God to gather all his faithful from the nations; that is, to bring back all the strayed ones to the assembly of the pious, that all may together give thanks to God, and praise him, and also glory in praising him. Some think that herein he alludes to the dispersion in the Babylonian captivity, which he foresaw in spirit; but it is more likely that he alludes to the dispersion among the gentiles that were still in the land of promise, and against whom David had waged several wars. He concludes by praising God, saying *"Blessed be the Lord God of Israel"* at all times, or rather forever, and let all the people confirm his prayer by saying, *"So be it, so be it."* And this is the end of the fourth book, according to the Hebrews.

PSALM 106

All are invited to give thanks to God for his perpetual providence over men.

1 Give glory to the Lord, for he is good: for his mercy endureth for ever.
2 Let them say so that have been redeemed by the Lord, whom he hath redeemed from the hand of the enemy: and gathered out of the countries.
3 From the rising and the setting of the sun, from the north and from the sea.
4 They wandered in a wilderness, in a place without water: they found not the way of a city for their habitation.
5 They were hungry and thirsty: their soul fainted in them.
6 And they cried to the Lord in their tribulation: and he delivered them out of their distresses.
7 And he led them into the right way: that they might go to a city of habitation.
8 Let the mercies of the Lord give glory to him: and his wonderful works to the children of men.
9 For he hath satisfied the empty soul, and hath filled the hungry soul with good things.
10 Such as sat in darkness and in the shadow of death: bound in want and in iron.
11 Because they had exasperated the words of God: and provoked the counsel of the most High:
12 And their heart was humbled with labours: they were weakened, and their was none to help them.
13 Then they cried to the Lord in their affliction: and he delivered them out of their distresses.
14 And he brought them out of darkness, and the shadow of death; and broke their bonds in sunder.
15 Let the mercies of the Lord give glory to him, and his wonderful works to the children of men.
16 Because he hath broken gates of brass, and burst the iron bars.
17 He took them out of the way of their iniquity: for they were brought low for their injustices.
18 Their soul abhorred all manner of meat: and they drew nigh even to the gates of death.
19 And they cried to the Lord in their affliction: and he delivered them out of their distresses.
20 He sent his word, and healed them: and delivered them from their destructions.
21 Let the mercies of the Lord give glory to him: and his wonderful works to the children of men.
22 And let them sacrifice the sacrifice of praise: and declare his works with joy.
23 They that go down to the sea in ships, doing business in the great waters:
24 These have seen the works of the Lord, and his wonders in the deep.
25 He said the word, and there arose a storm of wind: and the waves thereof were lifted up.

26 *They mount up to the heavens, and they go down to the depths: their soul pined away with evils.*
27 *They were troubled, and reeled like a drunken man; and all their wisdom was swallowed up.*
28 *And they cried to the Lord in their affliction: and he brought them out of their distresses.*
29 *And he turned the storm into a breeze: and its waves were still.*
30 *And they rejoiced because they were still: and he brought them to the haven which they wished for.*
31 *Let the mercies of the Lord give glory to him, and his wonderful works to the children of men.*
32 *And let them exalt him in the church of the people: and praise him in the chair of the ancients.*
33 *He hath turned rivers into a wilderness: and the sources of water into dry ground:*
34 *A fruitful land into barrenness, for the wickedness of them that dwell therein.*
35 *He hath turned a wilderness into pools of water, and a dry land into water springs.*
36 *And hath placed there the hungry; and they made a city for their habitation.*
37 *And they sowed fields, and planted vineyards: and they yielded fruit of birth.*
38 *And he blessed them, and they were multiplied exceedingly: and their cattle he suffered not to decrease.*
39 *Then they were brought to be few: and they were afflicted through the trouble of evils and sorrow.*
40 *Contempt was poured forth upon their princes: and he caused them to wander where there was no passing, and out of the way.*
41 *And he helped the poor out of poverty: and made him families like a flock of sheep.*
42 *The just shall see, and shall rejoice, and all iniquity shall stop their mouth.*
43 *Who is wise, and will keep these things: and will understand the mercies of the Lord?*

Explanation of the psalm

1-3. This is the preface of the Psalm, in which David exhorts all who have experienced the mercies of the Lord to declare his praise, and especially to give glory to the Lord himself; because he is truly good and merciful, and his mercy never fails. He specially invites the faithful, redeemed by the blood of his only begotten from the bondage of a most powerful enemy, the prince of darkness, who held them in bonds at his own discretion, whom he afterwards collected and gathered together to be one people, one Church, one kingdom, children of his delight, not from Egypt or Babylon, as formerly were the Jews, but *"from the rising and the setting of the sun, from the north and from the sea;"* that is, from the four quarters of the world, as we read in Jn. 10. *"And other sheep I have that are not of the fold; them also I must bring, and they shall hear my voice, and there shall be one fold and one shepherd;"* and in chap. 11, *"For Jesus should die for the nation, and not only for the nation but to gather together into one the children of God that were dispersed."* Though all the faithful, whether Jew or gentile, are specially invited, still the invitation applies in general to all men who may have been at any time, or in any place whatever, delivered by the Lord from any manner of trouble; for redemption is frequently used in the Scripture for any manner of delivery or salvation, without any price having been paid for it. It also applies to those who may have been delivered from the hand—that is, from the power of any enemy; and, finally, to those who may have been delivered from any exile or dispersion in any extremity of the world, and brought back to their country and reunited to their people. The whole world is included in the verse, *"from the rising and from the setting of the sun, from the north and from the sea;"* in other words, from east to west, from north to south.

4-9. This is the first part of the Psalm, containing an explanation of the first affliction. There are four afflictions of the body common to all, and there are also four spiritual afflictions. The corporeal afflictions are hunger and thirst, caused by the infecundity of the earth, or by want of rain; that is to say, from some natural cause extrinsic to the sufferers; secondly, captivity, caused by the violence of others, that is, from some voluntary, extrinsic source; thirdly, disease or sickness, which arises from some intrinsic source, from bad constitution; and fourthly, the danger of shipwreck, caused by an external, natural cause, as also by an internal and voluntary cause, namely, man's curiosity, which, not content with the solidity of the earth, must needs make trial of the liquid deep. There are also four spiritual afflictions, called by theologians natural wounds, wounds left in us through original sin; they are ignorance, concupiscence, bad temper, and malice; to which are opposed prudence, temperance, patience, and justice, which are called the four cardinal virtues. In this first division of the Psalm, then, the prophet sings of God's mercy in delivering us from the first of these afflictions, including both corporal and spiritual; and though he appears to allude barely to the hunger and thirst the Jews suffered in the desert, still, the principles laid down by him are universal, and are applicable to all; and thus, he says, *"They wandered in a wilderness, in a place without water."* Many, in quest of their country, have wandered through a pathless country, and one without water, as occurred to the Jews for forty years. *"They found not the way of a city for their habitation,"* after straying for a long time, and in all directions, they found no way leading to a city where they may safely rest and dwell.

"*They were hungry and thirsty, their soul fainted in them.*" In their wanderings they met with neither meat nor drink, and they in consequence, all but gave up the ghost. "*And they cried to the Lord in their tribulation;*" when all human aid failed them they appealed to God, "*and he delivered them out of their distresses.*" He was not found wanting when they appealed to him, but with that mercy that characterizes him, he delivered them. And he led them into the right way, that they might go to a city of habitation;" the mode he chose for delivering them was to show them the shortest possible way to the city where he dwelt himself. "*Let the mercies of the Lord give glory to him.*" It is, therefore, only right and just that such benefits conferred on man by God in his mercy, should be praised and acknowledged by all, as true favors from God; "*and his wonderful works to the children of men;*" the wonderful things he did for the liberation of mankind should also be duly praised and acknowledged. "*For he hath satisfied the empty soul.*" Because he provided the most extraordinary food, prepared by the hands of the Angels, for a lot of hungry people in the desert, nigh exhausted for want of food. This, as we have already said, is most applicable to the food provided for the Jews; but there can be no doubt but the prophet meant, by this example, to teach all those who have been rescued from ignorance and from the misery of thirst and hunger, that they owe their deliverance to God, and that they should, therefore, thank his mercy. And there can be no doubt but the prophet had specially before his mind that ignorance of the way of salvation, under which so many labor, and who stray about, as it were in a desert, hungering and thirsting for the knowledge of truth, the source of wisdom and of prudence. We naturally look for happiness. There is no one that does not look for it, and, therefore, for the way that leads to it; however, many, preoccupied by the thoughts and the desires of passing good, look for happiness where it is not to be found; nay, even look upon that to be happiness which is anything but happiness; and when they know not in what it consists, naturally know not the way that leads to it. Thus, in their strayings and wanderings, they never find, though they are always hungering and thirsting for the city of their true habitation; because the longings of an immortal soul, capable of appreciating supreme happiness, can never be content with the things of this world, miserable and transitory as they are; while those whom God "*hath redeemed from the hand of the enemy,*" and "*gathered out of the countries,*" beginning to feel their own blindness, through the great gift of God's mercy, "*they cry to the Lord,*" and are heard by him; they are "*led into the right way, that leads to the city;*" they know that the kingdom of God is their ultimate end, and that justice is the means of acquiring it; "*hungering and thirsting,*" then, for justice, they run to the fountain of grace, and, refreshed from that fountain, they arrive at the heavenly city, where they are filled and satisfied with all manner of good things, so that they never hunger or thirst again for all eternity.

10-16. This is the second part of the Psalm, in which he reviews the deliverance from the second affliction, corporal as well as spiritual. The second corporal affliction consists in captivity, through which poor creatures are shut up in dark prisons, bound with chains, and loaded with manacles. He seems to allude to the captivity of the Jews, under various persecutors, in the time of the judges, or perhaps under Pharao; for David does not seem to have taken much trouble in relating matters chronologically; the more so as what he states here is applicable to all captives, to all in chains and fetters, who may at any time have been liberated through the mercy of the Lord. *"Such as sat in darkness and in the shadow of death, bound in want and in iron;"* that is to say, I have known others who were taken by the enemy and were shut up in loathsome prisons and dense darkness, and were loaded with chains and reduced to beggary, *"because they had exasperated the words of God, and provoked the counsel of the Most High."* These were justly afflicted and punished in that manner, because they disregarded God's precepts and despised his advice. *"Exasperating God's words"* means provoking him to anger when he speaks or commands, which is done by those who do not keep his commandments. They, too, may be said to *"exasperate God's words"* who provoke his very commandments to anger; for, as the commandments of God crown those that observe them, so they punish those that transgress them; and in this manner they who transgress the commandments provoke them against themselves. There is a certain amount of figurative language in the whole; for *"God's words"* mean God, in his discourse or his commands; and the word *"exasperating"* means God's punishment being as grievous as if he were capable of being exasperated. A similar figure of speech appears in the following sentence: *"and provoked the counsel of the Most High;"* for the *"counsel of the Most High"* must be understood as applying to God in his goodness, with the best intentions, irritated by those who opposed them; or *"provoked"* may be rendered as condemning or despising, for those who do either provoke, that is, excite to anger. *"And their heart was humbled with labor;"* their pride was brought down by captivity, chains, and fetters. They are just the things to do it. *"They were weakened, and there was none to help them."* They were not able to resist their enemies; and thus, having no one to help them, were led off in captivity. *"Then they cried to the Lord"* etc.; then they began to implore the divine assistance, to free them as well from their dark prisons as from their chains and fetters; and, to show the extent of their obligations to him, he adds, *"he broke gates of brass and burst iron bars,"* to show how firmly secured they bad been, and what power is required to liberate them; and thus, on the whole, they are proved to have been delivered from a most severe and wretched captivity. Now, the second spiritual affliction consists in the concupiscence of this world—such as its goods, its wealth, its pleasure, which, like so many chains and fetters, so tie a man down that, though he is fully aware of true happiness existing in God alone, and that, while he remains here below, he must mortify his members, still he remains a captive, without being able to stir, if the grace of God will not set him free. The beginning of his freedom must have its source in his own humility. He must feel that he is a captive, that he has no strength in him, that his heart has been humbled in his labors, and, satisfied of there being no one able to help him but the one heavenly Father, he must, with a contrite and humble heart, with much interior sorrow, exclaim, Lord, I suffer violence; look on me, and have mercy on me. *"Unhappy man that I am, who shall deliver me from the body of this death?"* The mercy of the Father will most surely be at hand to bring the captive from his prison, to burst his fetters, so that, on gaining his liberty, he can with joy exclaim, *"Lord, thou hast broken my bonds, I will sacrifice to thee the sacrifice of praise."*

17-22. The third part of the Psalm, treating of the third corporeal affliction, which is a most severe disease and languor, such as that of the children of Israel, when God afflicted them with a great plague, through the fiery serpents, so that numbers of them were constantly dying; but no sooner did they cry out to God than they were delivered; and, in like manner, no matter how anyone, or to what extent they may be struck down by sickness or disease, if they will seriously, from the bottom of their heart, in firm faith, and with the other requisites, invoke the Almighty, they will most assuredly be delivered. To enter into particulars, especially as regards expressions not explained before. *"He took them out of the way of their iniquity; for they were brought low for their injustices."* We must, of necessity, supply something here; for instance, God saw some of them lying prostrate, *"and took them,"* that is, raised them up, *"out of the way of their iniquity,"* in which they were miserably plunged; *"for they were brought low for their injustices,"* even to the very earth; *"their soul abhorred all manner of meat; and they drew nigh even to the gates of death."* The disease must have been very severe when they refused the food necessary to support life, so that death must have, in consequence, been actually at their doors. *"He sent his word, and healed them."* And he explains how, by the will or by the command of God alone, without the brazen serpent, or any other created thing; not that things created, such as drugs and medicines, are of no use, but that they have their virtue and efficacy from God, and without his cooperation they are of no value; but God, of himself, without their intervention or application, by his sole word and command, can heal and cure all manner of diseases; in which sense we are to understand that passage in Wisdom, *"For it was neither herb nor mollifying plaster that healed them, but thy word, O Lord, which healeth all things;"* and, in a few verses before, speaking of those who had been bitten by the fiery serpents, and were cured by looking on the brazen one, he says, *"For he that turned to it was not healed by that which he saw, but by the Savior of all."* David speaks figuratively when he says, *"He sent his word, and healed them;"* as if his word were a messenger or an ambassador on the occasion; unless, perhaps, he alludes to the mission of the Word incarnate, through whom many were healed of their corporeal diseases, and without whom nobody could be healed of their spiritual diseases. *"For there is no other name under heaven given to men whereby we must be saved."* The third spiritual affliction consists in the infirmity or weakness and frailty of human nature, corrupted by sin. There are many who understand thoroughly what they ought to do, and are anxious to do it; but they either have no strength, or have not sufficient strength to do it, until they get it from on high. They are also, not infrequently, so affected by a sort of languor or listlessness, that their soul loathes all manner of food; not that they are led into any error, or seduced by any evil concupiscence, but they take no delight in God's word, they know not what it is to feel any heavenly aspirations, and they run the risk of suffering from hunger, not for want of wherewith to satisfy themselves, but from sheer fastidiousness; and such temptations are neither trifling nor uncommon. They have great need of *"crying to the Lord,"* to rectify their bad taste, and bring them to have a desire for the milk of divine consolation; and when they shall have begun to relish the things that are from above, and to taste how sweet is the Lord, let them not take the merit of it to themselves; but *"Let the mercies of the Lord give glory to him; let them sacrifice the sacrifice of praise, and declare his works with joy;"* for it clearly is the work of God, and not of man, to make man, accustomed to nothing but the things of this earth, and to what he sees, to have an ardent desire for and feel a sweet relish in the things of the other world, that are hidden from him.

23-32. This is the fourth part of the Psalm, in which God is praised for his care of those that are in danger at sea. No example of such danger, previous to David's time, occurs in the Scriptures, but subsequent to David, we have that of Jonas, of the Apostles, and of St. Paul. *"They that go down to the sea in ships."* They who cross the deep, and are engaged either in rowing, reefing, or setting the sails, know from experience many wonderful works of God, that many know nothing whatever of, or if they do, have it only from hearsay; for instance, the fury of the storm, the raging and roaring of the waves, the immense extent and depth of the sea, the constant and imminent danger that surrounds them, and the fear that will so lay hold on them betimes, as to make the hearts of the bravest quail. *"He said the word and there arose a storm of wind;"* God spoke, and the storm, in obedience to its Creator, at once arose, sprung up, and, in consequence, *"the waves were lifted up;"* so that they seemed almost to touch the skies; and, ultimately, to expose the lowest depths of the sea; *"their soul pined away with evils;"* fear so laid hold on them, that they became incapable of any manner of exertion; nay more, *"They were troubled and reeled like a drunken man and all their wisdom was swallowed up;"* a most natural description of the state of those in danger from shipwreck; they lose all presence of mind, can adopt no fixed counsel, and, consequently, cannot act upon any; *"and all their wisdom,"* in steering and righting a ship, if ever they had any, seems to have entirely taken leave of them. *"And they cried to the Lord in their affliction."* This verse, occurring now for the fourth time, has been already explained, and the other verses do not seem to need any.—Now, the fourth spiritual affliction is that malice of the will, which principally consists in pride, that is the queen of vice. And, in fact, when the blasts of pride begin to play upon the sea of the human heart then the billows of its desires are raised up even to the very heavens. We are all acquainted with the language of the prince of the sons of pride, *"I will ascend into heaven, I will exalt my throne above the stars of God, I will ascend above the height of the clouds, I will be like the Most High."* It was by him the giants of old were inspired to set about building the tower of Babel, that was to have reached the sky. The descendants of those people are they who seek to add kingdoms to kingdoms, and empires to empires; and to whose ambition there is no bounds; whereas, if they would enter into themselves and carefully consider the fearful storms of reflection, suspicion, fear, desires, presumption and despair, that continually harass them, and must, finally, overwhelm them, they would undoubtedly have cried to God, who would in his pity and mercy have delivered them from such a mass of evils; for he would have infused the spirit of his Son into their hearts, to teach them meekness and humility, that the raging billows of their desires, being thus composed, they may find rest for their souls, and be brought into the harbor of his good will; into that harbor of peace and tranquillity that is naturally coveted by all mankind. And this being the greatest favor of God's mercy, they would naturally chant, *"Let the mercies of the Lord give glory to him, and his wonderful works to the children of men."*

33-34. This is the second part of the Psalm. After having sung of the mercy of God in warding off the four afflictions, he now praises him for the omnipotence and providence through which he sometimes changes the nature of things, proving himself thereby to be their Maker and Ruler. He first says that God sometimes *"turned rivers into a wilderness, and the sources of waters into dry ground,"* that is, that when it pleased him, he dried up entire rivers, and caused the places inundated by them to become perfectly dry; *"a fruitful land into barrenness,"* which is intelligible enough, *"for the wickedness of them that dwell therein,"* as a punishment for the wickedness of its inhabitants; an example of which we have in Genesis, where we read, *"And Lot lifting up his eyes saw all the country about the Jordan, which was watered throughout, before the Lord destroyed Sodom and Gomorrah, as the paradise of the Lord,"* and yet this beautiful and fertile country, a paradise in itself, was dried up by sulphur and fire from heaven, and condemned to everlasting sterility.

35-38. On the other hand, God, when he chose, *"turned a wilderness into pools of waters;"* caused rivers to flow in desert lands, where they were unknown, and made streams of pure water to run where they never ran before. That made the land habitable; men began to build there, to till the land, and to reap its fruits; and thus man and beast began to multiply thereon. It is not easy to determine what land the prophet alludes to; for, though God brought water from the rock for his people, they did not tarry nor settle there, nor build houses there; and when he brought them into the land of promise, there were rivers, cities, houses, and fields all ready for them. I am, therefore, of opinion that the prophet refers to some early colonization subsequent to the deluge; for, as well as he turned the fertile plains of Sodom and Gomorrah into a wilderness, so he also caused rivers to run, and cities to spring up in places that were previously waste and desolate. Isaias seems to have this passage in view when he says, *"I will turn the desert into pools of waters and the impassable land into streams of waters;"* and St. Jerome says that he therein alludes to the condition of the gentiles, who were at one time desert and uncultivated, without faith, without the law, without the prophets or the priesthood; but were afterwards to be highly nourished, through Christ, with the gifts of the Holy Ghost; and, therefore, St. Augustine very properly applies this passage to the synagogue, as contrasted with the Church. The synagogue, that one timed abounded in the waters of the word of God, and like a fertile soil, produced its prophets and priests, had its altars, sacrifices, miracles, and visions, now desert and barren, is turned into dry ground, with not one of those things; while, on the other hand, the Church of the gentiles, from having been dry and barren, is turned into pools of water, is become most fertile, replete with the choicest fruit, and has come to be the people of the Lord, the Church of the living God, a holy nation, a royal priesthood, where alone is to be found the true sacrifice, true priests, true miracles, true holiness, true wisdom, and, finally, all the gifts of the Holy Ghost.

39-43. The prophet now teaches us that there is nothing on earth stable or permanent, for they who have been at one time blessed by God, and multiplied through his blessing, in a little time after have been, by reason of their sins, cut away and reduced to nothing; and they who abound in all the good things of this world have, for the same reason, been driven to the direst extremities; and such has proved to be the case, not only with ordinary mortals, but even with princes whose sins have caused God to bring them to be condemned, by his having deprived them of wisdom and prudence, and thus, in consequence, making many and grievous mistakes in all their affairs. However, at the same time, men of honor and virtue were to be found, raised up by God from poverty, and fed and nourished by him as his own sheep. Hence, ultimately, divine providence caused the just to rejoice, and the wicked to be confounded. What has been said, in general, regarding God's providence towards mankind, applies also to his special providence in regard of the Church, which grew up in a short time; and soon after was lessened, harassed, and afflicted by heresy and schisms; *"her princes,"* that is, her bishops and priests, were held in contempt, for numbers of them fell back from the path of their predecessors, who had set such an example of holiness and piety to the people over whom they had been placed. However, the Church was not abandoned to such an extent altogether as not to leave a considerable number of princes, and bishops, and priests, and holy laics, whom God enriched with spiritual favors, and whom, as being his own sheep, he led to the choicest pastures, and made them increase and multiply. To come now to the text. *"Then they were brought to be few,"* after increasing to such an extent, their numbers began to be reduced *"and they were afflicted with the troubles of evil and sorrow;"* after having had such a flow of prosperity they began to feel sad reverses. *"Contempt was poured forth upon their princes."* One of the greatest misfortunes that could befall any people is to have their rulers, whether secular or ecclesiastical, objects of contempt. *"And he caused them to wander where there was no passing, and out of the way."* The reason why they were despised was, because the princes aforesaid, having been deserted by the light of grace, in consequence of their own sins, as well as those of their people, did not walk in the right way; that is to say they led a bad and immoral life, scandalized the people by their bad example, and made bad laws in favor of the wicked, and against the just. Observe, that when God is said to procure those things, he does not do it directly: he does it indirectly, by withdrawing the light of his grace. *"And he helped the poor out of poverty."* As well as he suffered the proud and haughty princes to fall, and rendered them objects of contempt, so, on the contrary, he raised up the poor and the humble, *"and made him families like a flock of sheep;"* multiplied his posterity, blessed and protected them as a shepherd would his own sheep. *"The just shall see and shall rejoice: and all iniquity shall stop her mouth."* The consequence of this providence of God will be, that the just will rejoice and express their joy in praising and glorifying God; and *"all iniquity,"* all the malicious and the wicked will be struck dumb, and will not presume to offer the slightest opposition. This we sometimes see in partial instances; but it will be fully developed and made apparent only on the day of general judgment.

PSALM 107

The prophet praiseth God for benefits received.

1 My heart is ready, O God, my heart is ready: I will sing, and will give praise, with my glory.

EXPLANATION OF THE PSALM

This Psalm has been explained before; the first five verses of it being identically the same as the last five of Psalm 56, and the last eight verses of it being word for word with the last eight verses of Psalm 59. No reason can be assigned for such repetition, save, perhaps, the making up of 150 Psalms.

PSALM 108

David, in the person of Christ, prayeth against his persecutors; more especially the traitor Judas: foretelling and approving his just punishment for his obstinacy in sin, and final impenitence.

1 God, be not thou silent in my praise: for the mouth of the wicked and the mouth of the deceitful man is opened against me.
2 They have spoken against me with deceitful tongues; and they have compassed me about with words of hatred; and have fought against me without cause.
3 Instead of making me a return of love, they detracted me: but I gave myself to prayer.
4 And they repaid me evil for good: and hatred for my love.
5 Set thou the sinner over him: and may the devil stand at his right hand.
6 When he is judged, may he go out condemned; and may his prayer be turned to sin.
7 May his days be few: and his bishopric let another take.
8 May his children be fatherless, and his wife a widow.
9 Let his children be carried about vagabonds, and beg; and let them be cast out of their dwellings.
10 May the usurer search all his substance: and let strangers plunder his labours.
11 May there be none to help him: nor none to pity his fatherless offspring.
12 May his posterity be cut off; in one generation may his name be blotted out.
13 May the iniquity of his fathers be remembered in the sight of the Lord: and let not the sin of his mother be blotted out.
14 May they be before the Lord continually, and let the memory of them perish from the earth:
15 because he remembered not to shew mercy,
16 But persecuted the poor man and the beggar; and the broken in heart, to put

him to death.

17 And he loved cursing, and it shall come unto him: and he would not have blessing, and it shall be far from him. And he put on cursing, like a garment: and it went in like water into his entrails, and like oil in his bones.

18 May it be unto him like a garment which covereth him; and like a girdle with which he is girded continually.

19 This is the work of them who detract me before the Lord; and who speak evils against my soul.

20 But thou, O Lord, do with me for thy name's sake: because thy mercy is sweet. Do thou deliver me,

21 for I am poor and needy, and my heart is troubled within me.

22 I am taken away like the shadow when it declineth: and I am shaken off as locusts.

23 My knees are weakened through fasting: and my flesh is changed for oil.

24 And I am become a reproach to them: they saw me and they shaked their heads,

25 Help me, O Lord my God; save me according to thy mercy.

26 And let them know that this is thy hand: and that thou, O Lord, hast done it.

27 They will curse and thou will bless: let them that rise up against me be confounded: but thy servant shall rejoice.

28 Let them that detract me be clothed with shame: and let them be covered with the their confusion as with a double cloak.

29 I will give great thanks to the Lord with my mouth: and in the midst of many I will praise him.

30 Because he hath stood at the right hand of the poor, to save my soul from persecutors.

Explanation of the psalm

1. Words extremely like the expressions of Christ when he said, John 17, *"And now glorify thou me, O Father."* Christ, then, as man, asks God, his Father, not to be silent in his praise; that is, as regards his innocence, charity, and other virtues, which was literally accomplished through the Apostles, who, filled with the Holy Ghost, announced the praises of Christ in all languages through the entire world. It was also accomplished through the martyrs, who came after them; through the confessors and doctors, who, with their blood, or by their example, by their preaching, their writings, or their miracles, announced the praises of Christ to all ages and all nations. He then assigns a reason for asking such glory from God, because there are not wanting those who, by their false accusations, will seek to detract from his glory; *"the mouth of the wicked and of the deceitful man,"* of Caiphas and Judas, and, in fact, of all the Jews, *"is opened against me."* He couples the

wicked with the deceitful man, because Christ's persecutors, full as they were of envy and malice, still affected a regard for Christ when they said, *"Master, we know that thou art a true speaker, and teachest the way of God in truth."* Thus they were sinners in hating him. They should have loved; and they were deceitful, because, under the guise of friendship, they sought to entrap him in his discourse. Or some of them were avowed sinners, namely, those who openly blasphemed him, saying, *"he was a seducer, and that it was in Beelzebub he cast out devils;"* while others who were occult sinners and deceitful, put to him questions as if for information, but with a view to lay snares for his character and for his life.

2. He now explains the expression *"the mouth of the wicked and the mouth of the deceitful man is opened against me;"* the mouth of the latter was opened when they praised me as a good master, and, at the same time, were only seeking to take advantage of anything that may slip from me; and the mouth of the former, or of the wicked, was opened, because *"they have compassed me about with words of hatred,"* giving expression to their inward hatred of me when they said, *"This man is not from God. Behold, a man that is a glutton and a wine drinker. Away with him, away with him, crucify him."* But, whether covertly or openly, *"they fought against me without cause;"* for they had no reason whatever in returning evil for good.

3. He explains a phrase in the last verse, *"without cause."* For when they should have returned love for love they only turned to detract me; while I, instead of returning evil for evil, turned to pray for them; which he did openly when he exclaimed on the cross, *"Father, forgive them,"* and which he most likely did also in private as often as he heard their detractions.

4. He repeats that more emphatically, as if he said, for my blessings I got naught but maledictions, hatred for love, numerous wounds for all my cures, death itself for life conferred on them.

5. The prophet now passes on to Judas, who, he foresaw, would be the *"the leader of them that apprehended Jesus;"* and, in the shape of an imprecation, foretells everything that was to happen to him. *"Set thou the sinner over him."* Judas would not have Christ our Lord, the most just and the most meek of men, as a master, and you will, therefore, put the spirit of avarice over him, to which he will be a wretched slave to the day of his death. Judas preferred being a slave to mammon, and, therefore, could not be a servant of Christ; for *"nobody can serve two masters."* Now, the spirit of avarice is one of the greatest injustices; for it gives the honor that is due to God to an idol, as the Apostle calls it, *"the service of idols."*—*"And may the devil stand at his right hand."* The devil will be his guide in all his acts, will constantly stand alongside him, or will rather drag him with the chain of avarice, as he would a dog, and excite him to bite his own master.

6. The prophet now predicts that most unhappy end of Judas; to which prophecy Christ himself seems to refer when he said, *"Those whom thou gavest me I have kept, and none of them have perished except the son of perdition, that the Scripture may be fullfiled."*—*"When he is judged,"* on his departure from this world, *"may he go out;"* meaning, he will go out *"condemned;"* and should he chance to pray to God, his prayer will not only be of no avail, but it will *"be turned into sin."* St. Jerome says that Judas's prayer was turned into sin, by reason of his want of hope when he prayed; and thus it was that in despair he hanged himself. St. Augustine says it was because he did not pray through Christ, as a mediator. Others say it was because Judas, in common with other persecutors, prayed for the extirpation of Christianity. To which may be added, that Judas's prayer was turned to sin because, instead of asking assistance from God, he asked it of the devil, who suggested to him the hanging of himself. We must remark, though, that the prayer of a sinner is not always sinful, but, on the contrary, goes a great way to obtain forgiveness, as did the prayer of the publican; but it becomes sinful when the person praying offers it to those to whom he should not offer it, such as to idols or to the devil; or when he prays for what he should not ask God for, such as for the downfall of his enemies; or when, instead of praying through the one mediator Christ, he presumes on his own merits; or, finally, when he does not pray with faith, hope, and the other necessary accompaniments of prayer. All this applies to the Jews, as well as to Judas, of whom he was the type. The Jews, who depart this life without believing in Christ, will receive eternal punishment: and the prayers they daily use in their synagogues are *"turned to sin to them;"* because they do not pray through the Son; for they know neither him nor the Father, and because they pray for things God does not wish to grant them, such as the destruction of all Christians, and the speedy coming of Antichrist, whom they will acknowledge, as has been foretold in the Scripture.

7. This is the passage quoted by St. Peter, to show the necessity of electing an Apostle in place of Judas, and whereas the Apostles and disciples concurred with Peter in his interpretation of the passage, we are, of necessity, obliged to do the same. *"Men brethren, the Scripture must be fulfilled which the Holy Ghost foretold by the mouth of David, concerning Judas, who was the leader of them that apprehended Jesus."* The prophecy was fulfilled to the letter in Judas; *"his days were few,"* as regards his life, or his Apostleship; *"and another got his bishopric;"* Matthias, who was *"another"* in every sense of the word, being neither a relation, friend, or acquaintance; and like him in nowise either in life or morals. The word *"bishopric,"* in Hebrew, implies inspection, supervision; which a bishop must do frequently, as he has to render an account of his sheep, a thing that cannot be accomplished by those who

reside far from their flocks. This, too, was realized in regard of the Jews; for, after the sin of Judas, short, indeed, were the days of their episcopacy, that is, of their priesthood; and another took it, for the priesthood of Aaron was at once transferred to that of Melchisedech, many of whose priests are this day to be found all over the world, with not one of Aaron.

8. For fear anyone may suppose that Judas was condemned to a certain punishment during his life, which was not shortened though he was deprived of his position as an Apostle, the prophet declares that his days were numbered, for his wife was at once to become a widow, and his children orphans; as actually happened, for he hung himself the same day: and in a very short time after, when Jerusalem was sacked, nearly all the men perished, leaving innumerable widows and orphans to deplore them.

9. Judas's sin was to be visited on his children; they were to be outcasts from their own country, and beggars in another.

10. We are told here how it will come to pass that the children of Judas and the Jews will be in future a lot of paupers and beggars, because their creditors, when they find them unable to pay, will hunt them up and plunder them of everything they can lay hands on; And should anything escape them, the unfortunate people will be robbed of it *"by the strangers,"* by the soldiers of Titus, who even ripped them up in search of the gold and jewels they were suspected of having swallowed.

11. This was literally fulfilled in Judas and the Jews; for when Judas, stung with remorse, came to the Jews and threw up the money, instead of offering him any help or consolation, they only said, *"What is that to us? Look thou to it."* Being thus rejected by the priests, and despairing of pardon from Christ, he went and hanged himself. The Jews, too, when they were besieged by the Romans, had not one that would dare to help them.

12. The prophet now predicts that on the death of Judas's children his name would become quite extinct, for these children were to be the last generation of the family. This is literally true as regards the children of Judas, and is equally true as regards his spiritual children, for he never had any. We know that all the other Apostles had their children in the faith, begotten by them through the preaching of the Gospel; who, in their turn, begot other children in Christ; and thus, their posterity will continue forever; while the spiritual posterity of Judas was and is nil. And though the Jews were not thoroughly extinguished, still their kingdom or constitution expired in one generation; because, after the destruction of Jerusalem, they were scattered among all nations; and then was fulfilled what Osee predicted for them, *"For the children of Israel shall sit many days without king, and without prince, and without sacrifice, and without altar, and without ephod, and without theraphim."*

13. An additional calamity that will fall on Judas and the Jews is, that they will be punished for the sins of their parents, including not only their natural parents, but all the Jews who sinned in the desert and in the land of promise; and the *"sin of his mother"* means, not only his natural mother, but the entire synagogue, or the city of Jerusalem, of which Jeremias says, in Lamentations 1, *"Jerusalem hath grievously sinned."* The Lord himself confirms this prediction of David, when he said, *"That upon you may come all the just blood that hath been shed upon the earth, from the blood of Abel the just, even unto the blood of Zacharias the son of Barachias, whom you killed between the temple and the altar. Amen I say to you, all those things shall come upon this generation."* The cursed Jews even imprecated such vengeance on themselves when they said, *"His blood be upon us, and upon our children."* This in nowise contradicts the expression in Ezechiel, *"The son shall not bear the iniquity of the father"* for Ezechiel speaks of the children who do not imitate the wickedness of the father, while the Psalm alludes to those who do. For God, incensed by the sins of the parents, waits to see would the children come to penance; but if, instead of doing so, they only imitate the parents, and thus fill up the measure of their iniquity, he then exterminates them all, for their past as well as for their present sins; and this is only what God himself promised, when he gave them the law, *"I am the Lord thy God, mighty, jealous, visiting the iniquity of the fathers upon the children, unto the third and fourth generation of them that hate me."*

14-15. He repeats what he said of the sins of the parents, drawing a beautiful contrast between the recollection that would be kept up of their sins, instead of their glory, as much as to say, Let their sins and those of their parents be always remembered, and let not a vestige of the recollection of their glory and happiness remain. He then assigns the cause of the whole, *"Because he remembered not to show mercy;"* for, as St. James writes, *"Judgment without mercy to him that hath not done mercy."* The sin of Judas consisted in seeing the chiefs of the Jews raging against Christ, and, instead of having any pity for his innocent Lord and Master, he most cruelly delivered him up to be slain by them.

16. See the extreme cruelty of Judas and the Jews! in persecuting Christ, *"the poor man and the beggar, and the broken in heart;"* all which terms are most applicable to Christ. He was a poor man; for, as the Apostle says, *"Though being rich, he became poor for your sakes, that, through his poverty, you might be rich;"* he may also be called *"a beggar,"* for he chose to live upon alms, in order that he may devote himself entirely to his ministry and to prayer; and, finally, he was *"broken in heart,"* full of anxiety and solicitude for the safety of the human race; from which we may form a remote idea of the cruelty of his persecutors. They who seek the life of another are usually prompted by revenge for some real or supposed wrongs that have been inflicted on them; or by avarice, through a desire of getting hold of another's wealth; or by envy of another's happiness. Now, Christ, the meek and humble of heart, offered no injury to anyone; no one could court his riches, for he had none; and when his daily business was to deplore the sins of mankind, to exhort them to penance, to despise the things of this world, and to look forward to those of the next, there was no possible cause or reason for anyone's seeking for his death.

17. It is impossible for anyone, looking at curses and blessings in their intrinsic light, to love one and hate the other; but man is said to love one and hate the other when his own wickedness causes him to he cursed instead of being blessed. Thus, Judas, in betraying Christ for a small sum of money, loved cursing, for he caused himself to be cursed by God; in like manner, by forsaking Christ, through whom all nations were to be blessed, *"he would not have blessing,"* inasmuch as himself was the cause of not being blessed by God. That applies to the Jewish people also; for the Son of God came from heaven to bless his people; but they, by putting him to death, were the cause of their being cursed instead of being blessed, and of having the benediction transferred to the gentiles. Now, God's blessing implies an abundance of all good things, as well as his curse implies a heap of all misfortunes. The latter was strikingly exemplified in Judas, who, forthwith, lost not only the money, but the life of this world and of the next; as also in the Jews, who lost their kingdom and their priesthood, and obstinately lived on in blindness and incredulity, until they went down to that exterior darkness to be found only in hell. *"And he put on cursing like a garment; and it went in like water into his entrails, and like oil in his bones."* The prophet, making use of most beautiful similes, declares that the divine malediction is a heap of all internal, as well as external evils; so that no room can be found for any manner of good in one accursed by God. He first compares God's curse to a garment that completely covers the entire body; and as such garment cannot penetrate the interior of man, he compares it to water, which does, not only when man drinks, but when he gets drowned; for then it not only envelopes his exterior, but it gets into his stomach, his breast, and all the interior of his body; then, as water will not penetrate the bones, nor the flesh, nor the nerves, he compares it to oil which insinuates itself into all; and thus the curse of God will fill the body and all its members, the soul and all its affections, the mind and all its faculties of understanding and of will, not only of Judas and of the Jews, but of all who shall come under the sentence, *"Go ye cursed,"* with all manner of evils and misfortunes. If man would seriously reflect on these matters, he would, of necessity, tremble more for his safety.

18. He now adds, that the malediction will not only thoroughly encompass him, but will stick forever to him; that it will be like the clothes he wears to cover his nakedness, of which he can never divest himself; *"and, like a girdle with which he is girded continually,"* the malediction will adhere to him as firmly as if it were tied about him like a cincture, knotted and tied firmly to secure it. Who, then, can form an adequate idea of the firmness or the indissolubility of the knot tied by the unswerving, all powerful will of God?
19. He now concludes his prediction of the miseries of Judas by saying, *"This is the work of them;"* that is to say, this is the reward of their works, for the word work is used in the Scripture to signify the reward of works, as we have in Leviticus, *"The work of him that hath been hired by thee thou shalt not retain until the morning"*—*"Who detract me,"* call me a deceiver, deny that I am the Son of God, *"before the Lord."* Such will be their recompense from the Lord.
20. In this latter part of Psalm 108, Christ prays for himself and for his body, the Church; and, as he predicted all manner of miseries to Judas and the Jews, in the first part of the Psalm, he now, in the shape of a prayer, predicts many blessings for the Church. He first, then, prays to the Lord that he may be always at hand to protect him in the Church, and that for the glory of his own name, *"because thy mercy is sweet,"* or it is kind, and lends itself at once to succor the wretched. He speaks here both for himself and for his body, the Church, and asks for God's assistance against the persecutors of both, for three reasons; first, because God, being supreme Lord of all, can curb those enemies if he likes; secondly, because he asks it with a view to extol the name of God; and, thirdly, because the mercy of God is kind; and, therefore, God can not only show mercy, but he wishes to show it. And, as we said above, this is a prediction in the form of a prayer, or it is both together. We are, therefore, certain that the Church of Christ will be always helped and protected, *"so that the gates of hell will not prevail against it."*
21. The prophet, still speaking in the person of Christ, goes on with his prayer, having, apparently, in view the time when Christ said, *"Now is my soul troubled, and what shall I say? Father, save me from this hour;"* or, perhaps, it refers to the time when he prayed in the garden, and said to his Apostles, *"My soul is sorrowful unto death."*—*"Deliver me"* from this death that stares me in the face, *"for I am poor and needy;"* for I am destitute of all human assistance, having none to fight for me, *"and my heart is troubled within me;"* sorrow and sadness, arising from the consideration of my approaching death, have overwhelmed me. Christ said all this in order to show that he was truly man, and, as such, had a horror of death absolutely considered, and as contrary to nature, while he actually longed for and desired the same death, as being the price settled and decreed by his Father for

the redemption of mankind; and, therefore, when he said in John, *"Save me from this hour,"* he at once added, *"But for this cause I came unto this hour;"* and when, in Matthew, he said, *"Let this chalice pass from me"* he also immediately added, *"Nevertheless, not as I will but as thou wilt."* As regards his body, the Church, he asks that it may be delivered from persecutions and temptation, because its members are poor and needy, depending not on their own strength or merits, but, like a true mendicant, on God alone.

22. This is in allusion to the capture of our Lord after his prayer in the garden. He compares it to a *"shadow when it declineth,"* that flits away insensibly, in profound silence. And thus was the Lord torn away from his disciples, and led captive, brought before various tribunals, even to the very cross, without a murmur, without offering the slightest resistance or defence. *"I am taken away like a shadow when it declineth."* I am hurried away from my disciples before the tribunal of Caiphas, Pilate, and Herod, in silence, as silently as the shadow that fades away; *"and I am shaken off,"* tossed from one tribunal to another, *"as locusts,"* the vilest of all animals, that are scattered by the wind from one place to another.

23. This is in allusion to the weakness Christ suffered from the fast, the watching, and the labor of the night previous to, as well as on, the day of his passion. For though the life of Christ was one continued fast, he must have felt his weakness particularly at that time, and it is in the knees one first feels the debility; *"my flesh is changed for oil;"* my whole person is changed in color and bulk, by reason of the loss of the natural fat or oil necessary to support it.

24. This was the finale of his passion; for immediately after that extreme weakness and debility, the Lord became a reproach to the Jews, when they saw him crucified between two robbers; and while he was yet alive they blasphemed him, wagging their heads and saying, *"Vah, thou that destroyest the temple of God, save thy own self."*

25. The Lord, in his departure from this life, prays to his Father for a speedy resurrection, as we have explained in Psalm 21, 68, and at the same time prays for real salvation of both soul and body, for his mystical body, the Church.

26. Lest it may be supposed that Christ suffered so much, and died so ignominiously, against his will, and lest the Jews should be able to boast that they were an overmatch for him, the prophet, speaking in the person of Christ, says that this was all the work of God; as St. Peter, in Acts 3, says, *"But those things which God hath foretold by the mouth of all the prophets, that his Christ should suffer, he hath so fulfilled."* He, therefore, says, *"And let them know,"* all men, especially the Jews, *"that this is thy hand;"* that this matter, this suffering of mine, this death of mine, has come from your hand, that is, from your

will, pleasure, and power; *"and that thou, O Lord, hast done it."* Neither Jews nor gentiles could prevail over Christ, could persecute or put him to death, had not God so wished it. They are not to be excused, however, of a most grievous sin in putting Christ to death, by reason of their having been the instruments of God's will; for in doing so they did not seek to do God's will, but to indulge their own hatred and malice, and God only took advantage of their malice, of which he was not the author, to redeem the world, through the obedience, love, patience, and humility of his only Son.

27. My persecutors, being quite ignorant of all these prophecies, *"will curse"* me and my Church, and so the Jews do, even to the present day; *"and thou wilt bless"* not only myself, by glorifying and exalting me to your right hand, but you will also, for my sake, bless all nations, by adopting them as children through faith and baptism. Hence will come to pass, that those who persecute and revile me, will ultimately *"be confounded; but thy servant,"* your humble servant and his brethren *"shall rejoice"* forever.

28. He now confirms what he had previously laid down; and in the shape of an imprecation, he predicts that all the adversaries of Christ and of his Church would be, ultimately, as completely covered with shame and confusion as a person is entirely enveloped by a double garment, a thing that will be perfectly accomplished on the day of judgment. Such will be the confusion of the damned on the day of judgment. And what greater confusion can be imagined than to have the ingratitude, the folly, and the other vices of the damned, exposed before the whole world, before men and Angels, from the beginning of creation?

29. What a contrast to the confusion of the wicked! They will be struck dumb with confusion; but Christ and his elect *"will give great thanks to the Lord with their mouth;"* that is, with loud shouts, indicative of great joy, and that *"in the midst of many,"* on this terrestrial theater of ours here; on the day of judgment; and afterwards on the heavenly theater of the celestial Jerusalem for all eternity.

30. They are bound to give all the glory and praise alluded to in the previous verse; *"because he hath stood at the right hand of the poor,"* Christ and his people, *"to save them from persecution;"* to protect Christ from the Jews, who persecuted him, which was accomplished by the speedy resurrection of Christ, and also by the protection of his elect, who obtained life everlasting in spite of the demons and human beings who persecuted them. As regards Christ, his principal persecutors were Caiphas and Pilate, who sentenced him to death; but God's wisdom, the best protection he could enjoy, stood by him, and caused that sentence to be revoked by the resurrection of Christ. As regards the Church, the persecutors consisted of the emperors and kings, and pagan magistrates, who doomed many thousand martyrs to

death; and also of the demons, who acted as God's ministers in carrying out the decree pronounced against the human race; but Christ, in the shape of a most powerful advocate, interfered, by *"blotting out the handwriting of the decree which was against us, which was contrary to us, and the same he took out of the way, fastening it to the cross;"* and thus saved the souls of the poor. We have here to observe that *"God stands at the right hand of the poor;"* that is, of those who acknowledge their poverty, and their want of strength, and, therefore, daily knock at the door of that God who is rich in mercy. *"The poor"* also mean those who have put away all affection for creatures, and, having become poor in spirit, place their riches in God alone.

PSALM 109

Christ's exaltation, and everlasting priesthood.

1 The Lord said to my Lord: Sit thou at my right hand: Until I make thy enemies thy footstool.
2 The Lord will send forth the sceptre of thy power out of Sion: rule thou in the midst of thy enemies.
3 With thee is the principality in the day of thy strength: in the brightness of the saints: from the womb before the day star I begot thee.
4 The Lord hath sworn, and he will not repent: Thou art a priest for ever according to the order of Melchisedech.
5 The Lord at thy right hand hath broken kings in the day of his wrath.
6 He shall judge among nations, he shall fill ruins: he shall crush the heads in the land of the many.
7 He shall drink of the torrent in the way: therefore shall he lift up the head.

EXPLANATION OF THE PSALM

1. David, in spirit, saw the Messias ascending into heaven after his death and resurrection, and tells us the language the Father made use of when he invited him to sit beside him and reign along with him. He makes use of the past tense, *"the Lord said,"* instead of the future; because, in the spirit of prophecy, he looks upon the matter as a thing of the past. *"The Lord said,"* God the Father said, *"to my Lord,"* to Christ, for it cannot apply to Abraham or Ezechias, as some of the Jews will have it, neither of whom sat on the right hand of the Father, nor were they begot from the womb before the day star, nor were they priests according to the order of Melchisedech; and, furthermore, when this passage was quoted by Christ when arguing with the Jews, they did not attempt to question its reference to the Messias. *"Sit thou at my right hand."* Sitting denotes peace and supreme power, which Christ was to enjoy; and sitting *"at my right hand, denotes equality, and an equal share in that supreme power enjoyed by God the Father. Christ, as far* as his divine nature was concerned, had that equality at all times, but he only got it as regards his human nature after his humiliation unto death, even to the death of the cross, as St. Paul says, "Wherefore God also hath exalted him, and hath given him a name which is above every name, that in the name of Jesus every knee should bow of those that are in heaven, on earth, and in hell, and that every tongue should confess that the Lord Jesus Christ is in the glory of God the Father." Sitting on the right hand of God, then, is the same as being in the glory and the majesty of God, and that glory consists in having a name above every name, at which every knee shall bend; for, as the same Apostle has it, *"He must reign until he hath put all enemies under his feet;"* when the Apostle proves that the expression *"sit thou at my right hand"* means nothing more or less than share my sovereign power. The same Apostle, Heb. 1, has, *"For to which of the Angels hath he said at any time, sit on my right hand? Are they not all ministering spirits sent to minister?"* Thus proving the difference between Christ and the Angels, from the fact of the latter being merely ministers and servants, and, therefore, not allowed to sit, but obliged to stand, in readiness for the execution of their Lord's commands; while Christ, as Lord and King, sits with his Father above all creatures. Finally, St. Peter, Acts 2, says, *"Being exalted, therefore, by the right hand of God, he hath poured forth this which you see and hear; for David did not ascend into heaven, but he himself said, The Lord said to any Lord, sit thou at my right hand, until I make thy enemies thy footstool. Therefore, let all the house of Israel know most assuredly that God hath made him Lord and Christ, this same Jesus whom you have crucified."* St. Peter clearly says here that *"sitting at the right hand of God"* means his having ascended into heaven, and ruling and governing in all places as God only can rule and govern. *"Until I make thy enemies thy footstool."* The kingdom of Christ, then, is never to have an end, nor is there any danger of its being subverted by its enemies, God having determined to bring them all under subjection by degrees, that Christ may then reign peaceably forever after. The word, then, *"until,"* does not imply that Christ's reign was only to hold until his enemies should be subjected; but it means that his kingdom would be always extended more and more until as much as one single enemy not bowing the knee to him would not remain; as if he said, in other words, Come on ruling with me, and cease not extending our kingdom so long as one solitary enemy shall remain uunconquered. That extension of Christ's kingdom is daily going on through the conversion of some to faith and obedience, who willingly put themselves under Christ's feet, that he may rest in them as he would on a footstool, and who, after finishing their exile, set out for their country, where they felicitously rest in God: others have either been perverted, or have got hardened in their perversity and are, in the end, hurried away by death to judgment, and, on being condemned, are consigned to hell, where they are, for all eternity, trampled under the feet of Christ. The extension of Christ's kingdom will be completed on the last day, when every knee shall bend of those that are in heaven, on earth, and in hell, to Christ. But why is the assertion *"until I make"* attributed to the Father? does not the Son, too, *"make thy enemies thy footstool?"* Everything done by the Father is also done by the Son, as he himself asserts; but the Father is made to act here, in order, as it were, to reward the obedience of the Son, as the Apostle says, *"Wherefore, God also hath exalted him."* With that, everything implying power is usually attributed to the Father, though the Son has the same power, because the Father shares it with him, though the Son cannot share it with the Father, he having had it from the Father by generation. The Son also, as man, enjoys it but by virtue of the hypostatic union. The part the Son takes in subduing the common enemy will be treated of in the next verse.

2. David having, in spirit, heard the Father saying to the Son, *"Sit thou at my right hand,"* now addresses the Son, and, in the same spirit of prophecy, shows how the propagation of Christ's kingdom on earth was to be commenced. *"The Lord will send forth the scepter of thy power out of Sion;"* that is, God the Father, in order to put your enemies under your feet, will begin to extend the scepter of your royal power out of the city of Jerusalem, and to extend it from Mount Sion, and propagate it to the remotest corners of the earth. This corresponds with the language of our Lord after his resurrection. *"And thus it behoved Christ to suffer, and to rise again from the dead on the third day, and that penance and remission of sins should be preached in his name among all nations, beginning at Jerusalem."* And in the first chapter of the Acts, *"And you shall be witnesses to me in Jerusalem, and in all Judea and Samaria, and even to the uttermost part of the earth."* The scepter of his power was sent out of Sion, as if it grew on that mountain; for it was in Jerusalem that the spiritual kingdom of Christ commenced, as there were the first believers, and there the faith began to be propagated by the Apostles. *"Rule thou in the midst of thy enemies."* All success, triumph, and happiness to you on the way; extend your kingdom to all nations; carry the banner of your cross in the midst of Jews and pagans; plant it where they are thickest and strongest; *"rule everywhere in the midst of them;"* and in spite of them, and in opposition to them, set up your kingdom. That was very soon accomplished; for within a few years, in spite of both Jews and pagans, many Christian churches were established, for the Apostle writes to the Colossians, chap. 1, *"The truth of the Gospel is in the whole world, and bringeth forth fruit and groweth;"* and St. Ireneus, who lived in the century next the Apostles, writes, *"The Church has been planted through the entire world, even to the ends of the earth;"* and he specifies the Churches of Germany, Spain, Lybia, Egypt, France, the East,

and the churches he calls those in the middle of the world, meaning Greece and Italy. The Psalm most appropriately adds, *"in the midst of thy enemies;"* because, however prosperous and triumphant the Church may be, she will always be surrounded by enemies—by pagans, Jews, heretics, and bad Christians—as long as she sojourns here below. But at the end of the world, when the good shall come to be separated from the bad, the kingdom of Christ will be no longer in the midst of her enemies, but will rise above, and be exalted over all her enemies.

3. Having said, *"Rule thou in the midst of thy enemies,"* which meant at the time that Christ's kingdom in this world was besieged by his enemies, he now tells us how matters will be on the last day, when all his enemies shall have been subdued, and made his footstool. *"With thee is the principality in the day of thy strength;"* your power or principality will then be evident to all, and it will be seen that yours is the kingdom. *"In the day of thy strength;"* on the last day, when your strength will move the heavens, darken the sun, shake the earth, raise the dead, and summon all to your tribunal. *"In the brightness of thy saints;"* when you shall be surrounded by your saints, who will shine like the sun. *"From the womb, before the day star, I begot thee;"* you will have such a principality with you, because I, your Almighty Father, *"begot you,"* not as I did all other created things, from nothing, but *"from the womb,"* from my own womb, as my true, natural, and consubstantial Son, and that *"before the day star,"* before I created the stars, before any creature, before all ages. *"From the womb."* The holy fathers very properly use this expression as a proof of the divinity of Christ; for, if he were a creature, he could not be said to be born of the womb, for no one can say that a house, or a seat, or anything manufactured, is born of the womb; nor does God anywhere say that the heavens or the earth were born of the womb. By the womb is meant the secret and intimate essence of the Deity; and, though the womb is to be found in woman only, still it is applied to the Father, to show more clearly the consubstantiality of the Son with him, as also to show that God needed not the cooperation of woman to bring forth and produce. Himself begot and gave birth. As Isaias says, *"Shall not I, that made others to bring forth children, myself bring forth, saith the Lord."*—*"Before the day star."* Here we have a proof of the eternity of Christ; for he was born before the day star, and, consequently, before all created things; but he named the day star, for he himself, as the Son of God, is the increate light. For he is the true light, that enlighteneth every man and Angel.

4. He now passes from the regal to the sacerdotal dignity, and shows that Christ is a priest forever, not by reason of his succeeding to Aaron, but as a priest immediately appointed by God, and of whom Melchisedech was a type. *"The Lord hath sworn,"* hath confirmed his promise by an oath, *"and*

he will not repent;" firmly resolved upon it, a resolution he will never alter; and that is, that though the priesthood of Aaron was to be changed, that of Christ's never would. God is said to be sorry, a thing he cannot be subject to, when he acts as men do who are sorry for anything; thus, God says in Genesis, *"I will destroy man whom I have created from the face of the earth, from man even to the fowls of the air, for it repenteth me that I have made them."* And, again, in 1 Kings 15, the Lord says, *"It repenteth me that I have made Saul king."*—*"Thou art a priest forever."* These are the words of the Father to the Son, and not of David, as St. Paul reasserts in Heb. 5. Now Christ is said to be a priest forever, because the effect of the one sacrifice in which he offered his body on the cross holds forever, as the Apostle, in Heb. 10 has it, *"For by one oblation he hath perfected forever them that are sanctified;"* as also, because he, living forever, daily, through the hands of the priests of his Church, who succeed each other, offers a sacrifice to which the Apostle alludes, when he says, *"And the others indeed were made many priests, because, by reason of death, they were not suffered to continue; but this, for that he continueth forever, hath an everlasting priesthood."*—*"According to the order of Melchisedech;"* that is, the rite, law, or custom of Melchisedech, whose order is distinguished from that of Aaron, and from which it differs in many respects. In the first place, Melchisedech succeeded no priest, nor had he a successor; and, thus, the Apostle says of him, *"without father, without mother, without genealogy, having neither beginning of days, nor end of life."* While in the priesthood of Aaron one succeeded another, the son supplied the father's place. Secondly, Melchisedech was both king and priest; Aaron was simply a priest. Thirdly, Melchisedech's offering consisted of bread and wine, that of Aaron was of sheep and oxen. Fourthly, Melchisedech was the priest of mankind, Aaron's priesthood was confined to the Jews. Fifthly, Melchisedech required neither tent, tabernacle, nor temple for sacrifice, Aaron did; and hence, to the present day, the Jews have no sacrifice, because they have no temple. Christ, then, is a priest according to the order of Melchisedech, by reason of his having succeeded no priest, and by reason of his having had no priest to succeed him in the great dignity of his everlasting priesthood; and he in fact, as to his human nature has really no father, and as to his divine nature has no mother. The same Christ is both King and Priest, and he offered bread and wine at his last supper, that is, his body under the appearance of bread, and his blood under the appearance of wine; and he is the priest, not only of the Jews, but of the gentiles; nor is his priestly office confined to one temple or one tabernacle, but, as Malachy predicted, *"From the rising of the sun, even to the going down, in every place there is sacrifice, and there is offered to my name a clean oblation."*

5. Having asserted that the Son was called a priest forever by the Father, the prophet now addresses the Father, and says that Christ will be really a priest forever; for though many kings of the earth will conspire against him in order to upset his religion and his priesthood, he, however, seated at the right hand of his Father, will break his adversaries down, and, in spite of them all, will perpetuate his priesthood and his sacrifice. *"The Lord at thy right hand;"* Christ, as you spoke to him sitting there, when you said, *"Sit thou at my right hand."* *"Hath broken kings in the day of his wrath;"* when he shall be angry with his enemies, the kings of the earth, for persecuting his Church, he will break them, and, as far as I can foresee, has already broken them; for in the spirit of prophecy, I already see Herod stricken by the Angel. Nero, in his misery, laying violent hands on himself; Domitian, Maximinus and Decius put to death; Valerian taken captive by the barbarians; Diocletian and Maximinus throwing up the reins of government in despair; Julian, Valens, and Honoricus, and nearly all the kings hostile to Christ meeting a miserable end here, and well merited punishment in hell afterwards for all eternity.

6. Having told us how Christ would deal for the present with his enemies, the kings and princes of the earth, he tells us now, in addition, how he will deal, on the day of judgment, with all his enemies, *"He shall judge among nations;"* he who, while here below, beat down the impetuosity of princes, and preserved his Church in time of persecution, will afterwards, at the end of the world, judge all nations; and having condemned all the wicked amongst them, *"he shall fill ruins,"* will utterly exterminate, ruin, and destroy the whole body of the wicked; and thus *"he shall crush the heads in the land of many."* He will humble and confound all the proud, that now, with heads erect, make against him; for he will then trample on their pride, when he shall make their weakness known to the whole world, and thus render them both contemptible and confused; and such is the meaning of crushing their heads: and he adds, *"in the land of many,"* because the truly humble and pious in this world are very few indeed, when compared to the proud and the haughty, who are nearly innumerable.

7. He now assigns a reason for Christ being endowed with such power as to be able to break kings, to judge nations, to fill ruins, and to crush heads, and says, *"He shall drink of the torrent in the way, therefore shall he lift up the head;"* as if he said with the Apostle, *"He humbled himself, becoming obedient unto death, even the death of the cross; wherefore God also hath exalted him, and given him a name, which is above every name."* The torrent means the course of human affairs; for, as a torrent flows with great noise and force, full of mud and confusion, and soon after subsides without leaving even a trace of itself, so it is with the affairs of this mortal life—they all pass away, having,

generally speaking, been much troubled and confused. Great battles and revolutions, such as those in the time of Caesar and Alexander, and others, have been heard of, but they and their posterity have passed away without leaving a trace of their power. The Son of God, through his incarnation, came down this torrent, and *"in the way,"* that is, during his mortal transitory life, drank the muddy water of this torrent in undergoing the calamities consequent on his mortality; nay, even he descended into the very depth of the torrent through his passion, the waters of which, instead of contributing to his ease and refreshment, only increased his pains and sufferings, as he complains in Psalm 68. *"The waters have come in even unto my soul. I stick fast in the mire of the deep, and there is no sure standing. I am come into the depth of the sea, and a tempest hath overwhelmed me."* In consideration, then, of such humiliation, freely undertaken for the glory of the Father and the salvation of mankind, he afterwards *"lifted up his head,"* ascended into heaven, and, sitting at the right hand of the Father, was made Judge of the living and the dead.

PSALM 110

God is to be praised for his graces and benefits to his Church.

1 I will praise thee, O Lord, with my whole heart; in the council of the just: and in the congregation.
2 Great are the works of the Lord: sought out according to all his wills.
3 His work is praise and magnificence: and his justice continueth for ever and ever.
4 He hath made a remembrance of his wonderful works, being a merciful and gracious Lord:
5 He hath given food to them that fear him. He will be mindful for ever of his covenant:
6 He will shew forth to his people the power of his works.
7 That he may give them the inheritance of the Gentiles: the works of his hands are truth and judgment.
8 All his commandments are faithful: confirmed for ever and ever, made in truth and equity.
9 He hath sent redemption to his people: he hath commanded his covenant for ever. Holy and terrible is his name:
10 The fear of the Lord is the beginning of wisdom. A good understanding to all that do it: his praise continueth for ever and ever.

Explanation of the psalm

1. Holy David begins the hymn by an invocation, and tells us at the same time how God should be praised with advantage to ourselves. *"I will praise* thee, O Lord, with my whole heart." Praise, in order to be of any value, must spring from the heart, and not only from the heart, but from the entire heart; that is, with all the affections of the heart, that praises nothing, loves nothing, so much as the thing in question. *"With my whole heart;"* also implies the greatest attention, thinking of nothing else, for it does not become one who is praising that God whom the Cherubim and Seraphim adore in fear, to let his mind down to unworthy matters; *"In the council of the just, and in the congregation,"* that is to say, I will chant thy praises both in the council of the just, who are few in number, and in the congregation of the sinners, who are numerous enough.

2. He praises him first for his works in general, all his works being great, and still so perfect that they carry out God's will in everything. The workman who never makes a small article, an inferior article, but makes all his articles both great and valuable, deserves much praise; and anyone that will study God's works, that we think so little of by reason of their being so constantly before us, cannot fail to behold God's infinite power and wisdom in everyone of them, even though we cannot comprehend them. Truly did Ecclesiastes say, *"All things are hard, man cannot explain them by word,"* chap. 1; and in chap. 8, *"And I understood that man can find no reason of all those works of God that are done under the sun."* And not only are his works great, but *"they are sought out according to all his wills;"* prepared and settled previously, to be applied to any purpose he may choose, according to Psalm 118, *"For all things serve thee;"* for, as St. Augustine most properly observes, nothing seems to be more repugnant to the will of God, than free will, through which sins, forbidden by God, are committed; and yet, God deals as he wills with free will, for he reforms it through grace, or he punishes it in justice; and had he not given free will, there would have been no sin. It is, then, God's peculiar province and his peculiar praise, to be able to produce things that may be adapted and accommodated to all circumstances, and turned to any account.

3. From the work of creation, he now passes to that of government, and he shows him to be worthy of all praise for that too. *"His work is praise and magnificence;"* his direction and government of the world created by him is a subject of praise and thanksgiving, and also a fit subject for declaring his magnificence to all. The wise man speaks similarly when he says, *"The glory of children are their fathers;"* and, *"A father without honor is the disgrace of the son;"* for glory or disgrace is here used for the subject of either; *"and his justice continueth forever and ever;"* that is to say, God, in his government, acts with magnificence in providing most abundantly for all, but he acts with the strictest justice, so that it is always united with his magnificence, and never found without it; for God always keeps his promise, and does no

injury to anyone; and it seems to be specially mentioned here, in order to refute a common complaint of God suffering the wicked to prosper, and the just to suffer and to be oppressed. God's judgments may be severe, but they cannot be unjust, and whatever opinion we may form of them they are always just and worthy of all praise.

4. He now discusses a special work of divine providence, the raining of manna from heaven, which was a work of great mercy, not only to those who were then fed by it in the desert, but also to those who succeeded them, to whom he left an urn full of it as a memorial of the miracles he performed in the desert, see Exod. 16, and Heb. 9. That manna was a type of the Eucharist, that he gave Christians for their spiritual food, and in memory of the wonderful things Christ did while on earth, the most wonderful of which was his glorious passion, that destroyed death itself by death, and triumphed over the prince of this world; and he, therefore, says, *"He hath made a remembrance of his wonderful works, being a merciful and gracious Lord."*

5. The food named here is the manna that God rained from heaven, and gave, *"to them that fear him;"* to the Jews who worship him; for; though there were many sinners among them, still they worshipped the true God, and fearing and worshipping signify the same thing in the Scriptures. And as he wished the people to bear in mind the wonderful things he did when he brought them out of Egypt, and led them through the desert to the land of promise, so he, in turn, promises that he will bear in mind the bargain he made with them; and, therefore, he adds, *"he will be mindful forever of his covenant;"* that is, by his constant providence and protection, he will show that he is mindful of his covenant and his promises.

6-7. The principal point in the treaty that God made with Abraham was, that he should give his posterity the land of the Chanaaneans, which was, consequently, afterwards called the land of promise. He, therefore, shows how *"he is mindful of his covenant,"* when he says, *"he will show forth to his people the power of his works;"* that is to say, bearing his promise in mind, he will display his power to his people, by turning back the waters of the Jordan, by levelling the walls of Jericho with the sound of the trumpet, by stopping the sun and moon at the command of Joshua, by raining down stones from heaven on the enemies of the Jews, and by many other similar miracles. *"That he may give them the inheritance of the gentiles,"* that he may give his faithful the country of Palestine, which the gentiles, the Chanaaneans, held as their inheritance and their property. And, for fear anyone may suspect him of injustice in taking the land of Palestine from the Chanaaneans and giving it to the Jews, he adds, *"the works of his hands are truth and judgment;"* that is, all the works of the Lord, and especially the expulsion of the Chanaaneans from, and the introduction of the Jews into, the land of promise, have been done with great fidelity and justice, for truth here, as it does in many other passages in the Psalms, signifies faithfulness or fidelity. As God promised Abraham, then, that he would give that country to his posterity, he acted in truth or faithfulness; and as he did not expel the Chanaaneans until *"the measure of their sins was filled up,"* for which they deserved to be expelled, he also acted in justice; and, therefore, *"the works of his hands are truth and justice."* That the Chanaaneans deserved to be punished, and to be expelled from the land of promise, the Prophet proves, by reason of their not having observed the natural law, that is common to all, binding all and immutable, for they contain the first principles of justice; for, when God, in Leviticus 18, prohibits incest, adultery, sins against nature, idolatry, and the like, he adds—*"For all these detestable things the inhabitants of the land have done that were before you, and have defiled it. Beware, then, lest in like manner it vomit you also out if you do the like things, as it vomited out the nation that was before you."*

8. All God's precepts, especially those of the natural law, are faithful, for being most right and just they deceive nobody, and thus they cause the good to be rewarded and the wicked to be punished. And they are not only faithful, but they are also immutable, admitting of no dispensation, for in no case can they be found unjust; and, therefore, he adds, *"confirmed forever and ever, made in truth and equity;"* that is, firmly established from eternity, for they are based *"on truth;"* that is, on righteousness *"and equity;"* that is, on justice.

9. Having recorded the favors that were conferred on the fathers of the Old Testament, he now comes to the far superior favors of the new dispensation, consisting, as it does, of real and everlasting redemption. *"He hath sent redemption to his people;"* sent them the Redeemer so often promised and so long expected, of whom Zachary prophesied, *"Blessed be the Lord God of Israel because he hath visited and wrought the redemption of his people."* Now, Christ redeemed his people from the captivity and the slavery of sin and from the powers of darkness, by the price of his blood, and in such manner he really and truly *"hath commanded his covenant forever;"* that is, he ordered and settled it finally, that his covenant or his compact regarding true, real salvation, and the enjoyment of the kingdom of heaven, should be everlasting, and not like that of the possession of Palestine, which was only temporary, as we know from experience; and therefore, Jeremias, chap. 31, has, *"Behold, the days will come, saith the Lord, and I will make a new covenant with the house of Israel, and with the house of Juda. Not according to the covenant which I made with their fathers, in the day that I took them by the hand to bring them out of the land of Egypt: the covenant which they made void, and I had dominion over them, saith the Lord. But this shall be the covenant that I*

will make with the house of Israel, after those days, saith the Lord: I will give my law in their bowels, and I will write it in their heart: and I will be their God, and they shall be my people."—"Holy and terrible is his name." He now tells us, in consequence, how we are to adhere to his covenant, so as to come at what he promises, and he says, *"Holy and terrible is his name;"* that is to say, *"he that commanded his covenant forever"* is holy and terrible, and he, therefore, hates the pollution and uncleanness of sin, by reason of his holiness, and he says, *"Be ye holy, for I the Lord your God am holy;"* and he punishes the polluted and the unclean by reason of his being terrible, and *"It is a terrible thing to fall into the hands of the living God."* Therefore,

10. They really begin to be wise who fear the Lord, and through such fear guard against sin, observe the law, and do good, that so they may by degrees advance from fear to love, and begin to hate evil, more through a love of virtue, than the fear of punishment. *"A good understanding to all that do it."* An explanation of the preceding sentence, as if he said, understanding, which is a part of wisdom, is good, but *"to all that do it;"* that is, those who, influenced by a holy fear, do what their understanding tells them they ought to do; otherwise, it is not only useless but injurious, as St. James says, *"To him, therefore, who knoweth to do good, and doeth it not, to him it is sin."* *"His praise continueth forever and ever;"* he will, in consequence, be one of those who will dwell in the house of the Lord all the days of his life, praising God forever and ever.

PSALM 111

The good man is happy.

1 Blessed is the man that feareth the Lord: he shall delight exceedingly in his commandments.

2 His seed shall be mighty upon earth: the generation of the righteous shall be blessed.

3 Glory and wealth shall be in his house: and his justice remaineth for ever and ever.

4 To the righteous a light is risen up in darkness: he is merciful, and compassionate and just.

5 Acceptable is the man that sheweth mercy and lendeth: he shall order his words with judgment:

6 Because he shall not be moved for ever.

7 The just shall be in everlasting remembrance: he shall not hear the evil hearing. His heart is ready to hope in the Lord:

8 His heart is strengthened, he shall not be moved until he look over his enemies.

9 He hath distributed, he hath given to the poor: his justice remaineth for ever and ever: his horn shall be exalted in glory.

10 The wicked shall see, and shall be angry, he shall gnash with his teeth and pine away: the desire of the wicked shall perish.

EXPLANATION OF THE PSALM

1. In order to induce all to lead a pious life, the prophet proves, by various arguments, the happiness of him who fears the Lord; but as it is not every sort of fear that renders a man happy, he adds, in explanation, *"He shall delight exceedingly in his commandments;"* that is to say, blessed is he who fears the Lord, and through such fear takes the greatest delight in fulfilling his commandments, for *"to delight exceedingly in his commandments,"* means nothing more than to love them exceedingly, to feel an attachment to them, and to find a pleasure in observing them. In a word, happy is he who has a holy interior fear of God, with an exterior readiness to obey his commandments, and is, thus, truly just and pious.

2. A numerous offspring will be the first blessing of him that fears God; *"His seed shall be mighty upon earth;"* his posterity will be most numerous, because *"the generation of the righteous shall be blessed;"* that is, all his posterity will be most numerous and fruitful, by reason of the divine blessing. Blessing, in the Old Testament, implies fecundity. The first blessing will not be perpetual, but it will frequently follow; for we know that Abraham and his son Isaac, and many others, were a long time without being blessed with children. But if the Psalm be understood of good works, springing from the seed of heavenly grace, the blessing will be perpetual, for no truly just and pious person, that constantly sows the seed of good works can be deprived of the great fruit that, in due time, is sure to spring from them.

3. The second blessing or happiness, is an abundance of honor and wealth, which, however, do not lead to sin or lessen one's sanctity. Often it happens that riches and honors either beget pride or become the instruments of gratifying one's carnal pleasures, and then, instead of proving a blessing, they become a positive calamity. He, therefore says, *"Glory and wealth in his house;"* the just man will be blessed not only with a multitude of children, but also with riches and honors to share with them; but he will also (which is the most important point of all) have his mind quite uncorrupted by such blessings, for *"his justice remaineth forever and ever."* This blessing, also, is not constant when there is question of the glory and the riches of this world; but if it be understood of interior glory, and the testimony of a good conscience, and the riches of faith, and that gain of which the Apostle speaks when he says, *"But piety with sufficiency is great gain;"* that is, piety disembarrassed of solicitude about the things of this world when the soul is content with its position in life, then the happiness, or blessing, becomes perpetual; for it is the soul, and not the coffers, that ought to be rich. The soul is rich, indeed, when, satisfied with the necessaries of life, it has no further aspirations, resting quite content, as the Apostle has it, with a sufficiency, which, in another Epistle, he explains when he says, *"For I have learned, in whatever state I am, to be content therewith; I know both how to be brought low and how to abound."*

4. The third blessing enjoyed by those who fear God is the light of prudence and counsel that shines from heaven on them in their difficulties, as also in enabling them to see through the frauds of their false brethren, and, with that, to support them in the trials and troubles of life. *"To the righteous a light is risen up in darkness."* The righteous, then, who fear God, have got the light of counsel and consolation, in the darkness of their troubles and tribulations, that light being God himself, who is *"merciful, compassionate, and just;"* who deals mercifully with the merciful, because it is but just that the merciful should meet with mercy.

5-6. Blessing the fourth consists in that spiritual joy that resides in the heart of those that fear God. They who fear God easily pardon any offense, because they make allowance for, *"and show mercy to,"* human weakness; they also readily lend to those who need it, and thus comply with that precept of the Lord's, *"Forgive, and you shall be forgiven; give, and it shall be given unto you."* Such good works are productive of the greatest joy; while, on the contrary, they who refuse to forgive, or they who will not confer a favor on a neighbor, have their temper always soured by reason of their conscience reproving them, or because they think they are disliked. Blessing the fifth consists in prudence in one's speech, which enables one to steer clear of the greatest troubles in this life, such as enmities, quarrels, detractions, and the like; for he that fears God *"orders his words in judgment;"* makes use of language so matured by his good judgment as to give offence to nobody, and from it derives immense good. And he assigns a reason for his so *"ordering his words in judgment;"* when he says, *"Because he shall not be moved forever;"* because he is constant and steady in what he proposes to himself, prudently looking out for all possible contingencies, so that, happen what may, he *"cannot be moved forever."*

7. The sixth happiness of the person fearing God is, that he will always live in the memory of man, not by reason of his crimes, as do Judas and Cain, Herod and Pilate, Annas and Caiphas; his memory will be a glorious one, *"and all the church of the saints shall declare"* his praises; and not only that, but he will be *"in everlasting remembrance"* among men; and his name, too, will be written in the book of life, never to be blotted out, and thus really and truly he will be *"in everlasting remembrance"* with the Angels in heaven. *"He shall not fear the evil hearing;"* he will not fear the detractions and reproofs of the wicked, nor will he fear that frightful sentence of the eternal

Judge, *"Go ye cursed into everlasting fire."*—*"His heart is ready to hope in the Lord."* This is the seventh blessing of the soul that feareth God; a firm and fixed reliance on the divine protection, through which it fears no evil. *"His heart is ready to hope in the Lord."* That is, in every adversity, in every imminent danger, his heart is ready to take refuge in God, because he is always prepared and ready to hope in God, never loses sight of God's assistance, never distrusts him, never hesitates in putting faith in him.

8. His heart is strengthened in such confidence, so that there is no danger of his failing in it. *"He shall not be moved until he look over his enemies."* He never will have the slightest fear of any impending danger from his enemies, and, of course, much less when he shall look down upon them prostrate and vanquished.

9. Blessing the eighth consists in making good use of riches, for it is through God's grace that God's friends learn the wisdom of transferring their treasures, by means of alms, to heaven, where *"neither the rust nor the moth doth consume, and where thieves do not dig through nor steal."*—*"He hath distributed, he hath given to the poor."* The man who fears God has not shut up his wealth, nor sought to increase it, but scattered it among the poor; that is to say, gave it away abundantly, but with such prudence as to give a little to a great many, rather than a great deal to a few, thus providing the many with necessaries, and avoiding the furnishing of the few with superfluities. We have the like idea in Isaias—*"Break thy bread to the hungry,"* and in Corinthians—*"And if I should distribute all my goods to feed the poor."* We must not deny, however, that it may sometimes be more advisable to give a great deal to one; as, for instance, to give a dowry to a poor virgin, or for the building of a church, or the redemption of a captive. The man who fears God derives two advantages from such generosity; for, if he lessened his money he increased his justice; and *"that justice"*—that is, his good works, *"remain forever and ever,"* to be kept in store for him by God, from whom he will, in the fitting time, receive his full reward, for *"He that hath mercy on the poor lendeth to the Lord."* Then, *"His horn shall be exalted in glory;"* that is, he will have his reward, not only in the world to come, but even in this world he will have an increase of power and glory, signified in the Scriptures by his horn; and one's horn is said to be exalted when he becomes stronger and more powerful; and to be *"exalted in glory"* means for one to become not only strong and powerful, but also full of glory, such as those great men of rank and celebrity to whom all defer. This verse, then, gives us to understand that alms, instead of injuring or lessening anyone in their means, only tends to increase their riches, power, and glory, many examples of which are to be found in the Scriptures, especially in Job and Tobias.

10. The last blessing is, that the person fearing God will overcome all envy. *"The wicked shall see"* the good works of God's servant, and his happiness, while *"the wicked shall see,"* that is to say, shall reflect on the good works of the just, and their happiness, and will be tormented with envy, and *"shall be angry"* at their luck, *"and like a mad dog he shall gnash his teeth and pine away"* in grief; but, meanwhile, *"the desire of the wicked,"* in looking for the destruction of the just, will not be granted, but with the wicked himself shall speedily *"perish."* Blessed and happy, then, is he that feareth the Lord, wretched and miserable is he who does not.

PSALM 112

God is to be praised, for his regard to the poor and humble.

1 Praise the Lord, ye children: praise ye the name of the Lord.
2 Blessed be the name of the Lord, from henceforth now and for ever.
3 From the rising of the sun unto the going down of the same, the name of the Lord is worthy of praise.
4 The Lord is high above all nations; and his glory above the heavens.
5 Who is as the Lord our God, who dwelleth on high:
6 And looketh down on the low things in heaven and in earth?
7 Raising up the needy from the earth, and lifting up the poor out of the dunghill:
8 That he may place him with princes, with the princes of his people.
9 Who maketh a barren woman to dwell in a house, the joyful mother of children.

EXPLANATION OF THE PSALM

1. Children, here, represent the servants of the Lord who worship him in all sincerity. That is clear from the Hebrew for children. Children and servants, however, are so clearly allied that the term may be applied indiscriminately to both, for servants should be as obedient to their masters as children are to their parents. Hence, St. Paul says, *"As long as the heir is a child he differeth nothing from a servant."* We are, therefore, reminded by the term *"children,"* that we should be the pure and simple servants of God, and be directed by his will, without raising any question whatever about it. *"Praise the Lord, ye children; praise ye the name of the Lord."* Let it be your principal study, all you who claim to be servants of God, to reflect with a pure mind on the greatness of your Lord, and with all the affections of your heart to praise his infinite name. A similar exhortation is to be found in Psalm 133, *"Behold now bless ye the Lord, all ye servants of the Lord;"* and in Psalm 134, *"Praise ye the name of the Lord: O you his servants, praise the Lord."*

2. As we, creeping, wretched things, know not how to praise God as we ought, he now tells us how it should be done, and says it should be done at least with affection and desire. Say, therefore, with all the affections of your heart, *"Blessed be the name of the Lord," "from henceforth,"* at the present time, *"and forever,"* to all future generations, so that there shall never be any cessation to his praise.

3. In this and the following verses he explains the subject of God's praise, which he says is to be found everywhere, all his works being so replete with wonders, which, on diligent reflection, redound so much praise on their wonderful Maker. *"From the rising of the sun to the going down of the same;"* throughout the whole world, from one end of it to the other, *"the name of the Lord is worthy of praise,"* by reason of his great works that so abound throughout the world.

4. Matter for God's praise is to be found not only through the length and breadth, but even through the height of the world; for, though there may be many great kings and powerful princes therein, God far out tops them all, and he lords it over, not only *"all the nations,"* but even over all the Angels, for *"his glory is above the heavens,"* and all who dwell therein.

5-6. He now praises God by reason of his wonderful kindness, which, when looked at in conjunction with such sublimity, appears the more extraordinary. *"Who is as the Lord our God who dwelleth on high,"* in the highest heavens, and still *"looketh down on the low things;"* on man who dwells on the earth. The words, *"in heaven,"* according to the Hebrew, should be referred to the first verse. We are here instructed that God, by reason of his excellence, has everything subject to him; and yet, such is his goodness, that he looks after, and attends to the minutest matters, things, and persons, and especially to the meek and humble of heart.

7-8. He explains why God *"looks down"* on the humble, and says it is to exalt them; and though this is most applicable to individuals raised by God from the lowest to the highest position, such as Joseph, Moses, David, and others, it is also most true of the whole human race, that is, of the little flock of the elect, to whom our Savior said, *"Fear not, little flock, for it hath pleased your Father to give you a kingdom."* Now, mankind lay prostrate on the earth, wallowing on the dunghill of original sin, and its consequent evils, and yet God, who is seated in heaven, looked down on the earth, and raised up the needy, that is, the man despoiled by the robbers, who was lying on the dunghill of misery, to *"place him with princes;"* not in the general acceptation of the word; but with *"the princes of his people,"* the possessors of the heavenly Jerusalem, the citizens of the kingdom of heaven. The being raised from the poverty of this world to an abundance of its riches, however great and desirable it may appear in our eyes, is in reality a thing of no value, such things being perishable, given to us merely to make good use of them, and bringing great obligations with them, which, if not properly discharged, will, on the day of judgment, bring down great trouble and affliction of spirit on those who got them. But the elevation from a state of sin and death to that of glory and immortality, to an equality with the Angels, to share in that happiness that forms a part of God's own happiness, that, indeed, is the true, the truly great, and the most to be sought for elevation.

9. With mankind a low and contemptible position is considered a misfortune, while barrenness is looked upon in the same light by womankind; but, as God looks down on the humble man so as to raise him from the lowest to the highest position, he also looks down on the humble woman, thereby changing her barrenness into fertility. This is quite applicable to several females, such as Sara, Rebecca, Rachel, Anne, and others; but it applies, in a higher sense, to the Church gathered from the gentiles, that remained barren a long time, but ultimately begot many children, as the Apostle has it, *"Rejoice thou barren, that bearest not; break forth and cry out, thou that travailest not: for many are the children of the desolate, more than that of her that hath a husband."*

PSALM 113

God hath shown his power in delivering his people; idols are vain. The Hebrews divide this into two psalms.

1 When Israel went out of Egypt, the house of Jacob from a barbarous people:
2 Judea made his sanctuary, Israel his dominion.
3 The sea saw and fled: Jordan was turned back.
4 The mountains skipped like rams, and the hills like the lambs of the flock.
5 What ailed thee, O thou sea, that thou didst flee: and thou, O Jordan, that thou wast turned back?
6 Ye mountains, that ye skipped like rams, and ye hills, like lambs of the flock?
7 At the presence of the Lord the earth was moved, at the presence of the God of Jacob:
8 Who turned the rock into pools of water, and the stony hill into fountains of waters.
9 Not to us, O Lord, not to us; but to thy name give glory.
10 For thy mercy, and for thy truth's sake: lest the gentiles should say: Where is their God?
11 But our God is in heaven: he hath done all things whatsoever he would.
12 The idols of the gentiles are silver and gold, the works of the hands of men.
13 They have mouths and speak not: they have eyes and see not.
14 They have ears and hear not: they have noses and smell not.
15 They have hands and feel not: they have feet and walk not: neither shall they cry out through their throat.
16 Let them that make them become like unto them: and all such as trust in them.

17 *The house of Israel hath hoped in the Lord: he is their helper and their protector.*
18 *The house of Aaron hath hoped in the Lord: he is their helper and their protector.*
19 *They that fear the Lord hath hoped in the Lord: he is their helper and their protector.*
20 *The Lord hath been mindful of us, and hath blessed us. He hath blessed the house of Israel: he hath blessed the house of Aaron.*
21 *He hath blessed all that fear the Lord, both little and great.*
22 *May the Lord add blessings upon you: upon you, and upon your children.*
23 *Blessed be you of the Lord, who made heaven and earth.*
24 *The heaven of heaven is the Lord's: but the earth he has given to the children of men.*
25 *The dead shall not praise thee, O Lord: nor any of them that go down to hell.*
26 *But we that live bless the Lord: from this time now and for ever.*

EXPLANATION OF THE PSALM

1. He begins the Psalm by telling how it was that the Jews, on their departure from Egypt, began to assume the form of a people peculiarly subject to God, and governed by his special providence, as if he were their king alone. Before they went to Egypt, they were a family, not a people, but during their sojourn in Egypt they multiplied greatly, but were still mixed up with the Egyptians, to whose king they were subject; but, on their departure from Egypt, they began to assume the form of a state of their own, Moses, as being God's vicegerent and representative, having supreme authority; and that is what he alludes to when he says, "*When Israel went out of Egypt, the house of Jacob, from a barbarous people.*" Israel means here the people of Israel, who were descended of him, the house of Jacob being only a repetition of the same. The "*barbarous people*" are the Egyptians, who spoke a strange language; and such are called barbarous, according to the Apostle, "*If, then, I know not the power of the voice I shall be to him to whom I speak a barbarian, and he that speaketh a barbarian to me.*" The Egyptians, then, are called a barbarous people by reason of their using a different language from that of the Jews. "*Judea was made his sanctuary.*" It was upon the departure of the Jews from Egypt that God sanctified the Jews, or chose them to be his own people. "*Israel his dominion.*" The same idea in different language; that is, he assumed special care of and dominion over the children of Israel. By Judea we are not to understand the country, but its people; for it is Juda in Hebrew, and it is not unusual in the Scripture to call the Jews sometimes the children of Juda, at other times the children of Israel. Hence the names Jews and Israelites.

2-4. He now recounts the wonderful things that happened on the departure of the children of Israel from Egypt, as also during their stay in the desert, as well as on their entry into the land of promise, in order to prove thereby that their God was the true and all powerful God, whom they should justly fear and worship; and he relates the first miracle, when the sea, at God's word, was divided, in order to let the people pass, as we read in Numbers, but which he relates here in a most beautiful and figurative manner, addressing it as if it had sense, and giving us to understand that it drew back of itself from fear and reverence, on beholding the majesty of the Lord. With it he unites another miracle, though it happened forty years later, as belonging to the same element—the division of the waters of the river Jordan, to admit of the people passing over dry, as we read in Josue 4. He then alludes to the miracles that happened on land when they got the law, when God descended on Mount Sinai; for then the earth was moved, and, struck with terror before God's majesty, seemed, as it were, to dance and to shake, as we read in Exodus, *"All the Mount was terrible;"* the meaning of which is, that such was the tremor in the mountain that it made them all terrible. He finally alludes to another miracle, the production of water in great abundance from the rock. But, to come to particulars, *"The sea saw and fled."* The Red Sea, frightened, as it were, at the sight of the Lord, retired from its natural bed and fled. *"Jordan was turned back."* In the book of Josue it is stated that *"the waters that curve down from above stood in one place, and, swelling up like a mountain, were seen afar off;"* but David gives us to understand that the water was not only raised up but that it was turned back, which is most probable, as the time necessary for many hundred thousand persons to pass over must have been not inconsiderable. If the water, then, did not recede as well as stand up, instead of being like a mountain, it would have been like something much more enormous. It did both, then; it stood up, and it flowed back as David sings, in order to admit a dry passage for the Israelites. *"The mountains skipped like rams, and the hills like lambs of the flock."* The mounds of Sinai, that is, its highest points, and the hills of the same mountains, its lower protuberances, were seen to leap, shake, and tremble, like so many frightened sheep and lambs; and, though the word skipping would seem to imply that it proceeded from joy, yet, here it must be interpreted as from fear, because it was on the same account that the mountains skipped as the sea fled; and, in a few verses after, we have, *"At the presence of the Lord the earth was moved;"* which words imply terror, and go to explain this passage.

5-8. In quite a poetic strain he asks the sea why it fled, the Jordan why it turned back, and the hills and mountains why they trembled; and answers that it was caused by the power of the presence of God, who not only commanded the sea and the river, but, what is much more wonderful, changed one element to another, as he did when he turned the hard and solid rock into purling streams of the purest water. All this was caused *"at the presence of the Lord;"* in other words, because the Lord showed himself, manifested his might and power; and, at once, the whole earth, unable to stand his sight, *"was moved,"* trembled all over. That same Lord, *"who turned the rock into pools of water,' as he did when the people clamored for it, "and the stony hill,"* to show it was no ordinary rock, but a hard, gritty, flinty one that so supplied the water.

9. Having recorded the wonderful things that God did for his people on their departure from Egypt, he now, in the name of the whole people, prays to him not to regard their shortcomings, but his own glory, and to continue to protect his servants. *"Not to us, O Lord, not to us."* We ask not for praise or glory on our own merits, which are none; *"but to thy name give glory;"* protect us for the glory of your name, and not for our own merits.

10. He, in a very short space, assigns three reasons why God ought to seek the glory of his name in preserving his people. First, because he is merciful; secondly, because he is true and faithful in observing his promise; thirdly, that the gentiles, seeing God's people in a state of destitution, may have no cause for blaspheming him and them. He, therefore, says, *"For thy mercy and for thy truth's sake,"* show your glory, or give glory to thy name, for it is then your glory will be exhibited when you show mercy to your people; and then you will have carried out the truth of the promises you made our fathers, *"Lest the gentiles should say: Where is their God?"* lest the incredulous gentiles should get an occasion of detracting from your power, and, perhaps, of ignoring your very existence.

11-15. He now, on account of his having said, *"Lest the gentiles should say: Where is their God?"* gives expression to a most beautiful antithesis between the true and false gods; as much as to say, The gentiles should get no opportunity of reproaching us; but if they should do so, saying, *"Where is their God?"* we will answer, *"Our God is in heaven;"* and the wonderful things he has done bear testimony to it; for *"he hath done all things whatsoever he wished;"* while, on the contrary, their gods are on the earth; and thus hitherto are so unable to do anything that they cannot even make use of the members they appear to be endowed with; for, though they have the shape and figure of man, and appear to have all his members and senses, they neither see, nor hear, nor smell, nor touch, nor walk, nor speak; they do not emit anything in the shape of the voice of man, nor even of beasts.

16. This is a prophecy in the shape of an imprecation, as is usual with the prophets; for the makers of, and the worshippers of idols, will actually become similar to the idols after the resurrection; for, though they will be possessed of feeling and members, the case will be with them as if they had none; they will even desire to have none; for they will see, hear, smell, touch nothing but what will be hateful and disagreeable; and, with their hands and feet tied, they will be cast into exterior darkness, without being able in any way to help themselves. Even in this life they are like idols, because, though they hear and see, it is more in appearance than reality; for they neither see nor hear the things that pertain to salvation, the things that only are worth seeing, so that they may be said more to dream than to see or hear; as St. Mark has it, *"Having eyes ye see not, having ears ye hear not."*

17-19. Having said, Let them that make them become like *"unto them, and all such as trust in them,"* he adds, by way of antithesis, that the children of Israel trusted in the Lord, and that they had him, therefore, as a protector, naming the house of Israel first, which includes the whole Jewish nation; then the house of Aaron, which means the priests and Levites, the elite of God's people, and who should, therefore, have special trust in God; and, finally, all those that fear the Lord; for at all times there were pious souls, however few they may have been, not belonging to the children of Israel who feared and worshipped God in all sincerity; such were Job and his friends, and afterwards Naaman, the Syrian, and others.

20-21. He now confirms what he had asserted, viz., that God would be the helper and the protector of those that trust in him. He ranks himself among the number as having got special help and protection from God. He then, in the same order, confirms his assertions of God having blessed the house of Israel, the house of Aaron, and all who fear him, great or small, without any reference to greatness or littleness, whether of age, power, wisdom, or riches. When God is said to be *"mindful,"* it means that he regards with a singular providence; *"and blessed us,"* by assisting and protecting us—*"us"* meaning the house of Israel, the house of Aaron, and all that fear him.

22-23. *"Out of the abundance of the heart the mouth speaketh,"* as we read in Lk. 6; and as the heart of the holy prophet was burning with desire for the glory of God and the salvation of his neighbor, he turns over the same subject, prophesying at one time, then exhorting, and then by praying all manner of happiness on mankind, in the hope of bringing them to have a holy fear of God, and to repose all their hope in him. Turning, then, to those who fear God, whose blessing he had assured them of, he says to them, *"May the Lord add blessings upon you,"* and not only on you, but *"upon your children."* And thus may you be blessed with a full and entire benediction from the Lord, *"who made heaven and earth;"* that is, by him in whose hand is the dew of heaven and the fatness of the earth. The saints of the Old Testament were very much in the habit of praying to the Lord for the dews of heaven and the fatness of the earth for their people; for all the fruits of the earth depend on them. In a more spiritual meaning, God blesses with the dews of heaven and the fatness of the earth those to whom he gives spiritual and temporal blessings in abundance; as he did to Abraham, Isaac, Joseph, and David, and such others.

24-26. These three verses may be differently interpreted, applying them to the Jews under the Old Testament, or to the Christians in the New. If we apply them to the Jews, the meaning is, Having said, *"Blessed be you of the Lord, who made heaven and earth,"* he now asserts that it is only fair that they who have been blessed by the Lord should, in return, bless him while they live upon this earth, which he gave them for a habitation, leaving to the Angels the duty of blessing him in heaven, that being his habitation and that of his servants who minister unto him. *"The heaven of heavens is the Lord's;"* that is, the supreme heaven belongs peculiarly to God and to the Angels who minister unto him; *"but the earth,"* with the elements that surround it, *"he has given to the children of men"* for their habitation, and for such a splendid portion of the universe man should constantly return thanks to God as long as they live and enjoy the fruits of that earth. Because *"the dead shall not praise thee, O Lord;"* for the dead, being devoid of sense, and no longer in possession of the goods of this world, and being even bereft of life, cannot praise God or return him thanks for his benefits. *"For any of them that go down into hell."* Not only will the dead lying in their sepulchres not praise the Lord, but also *"they that go down to hell;"* the spirits who have gone down to the infernal regions; they, too, will not praise God for temporal blessings they cannot now possibly enjoy. *"But we that live,"* and are in the enjoyment of such blessings, *"bless the Lord from this time now and forever,"* through all succeeding ages. Applying the passage to the Christians under the New Testament, we are to bear in mind that *"the heaven of heaven"* means that supreme part of heaven where the children of God reside; of which the Apostle says, *"For we know that if our earthly house of this habitation be dissolved, that we have a building of God, a house not made with hands, eternal in heaven;"* that house God chose for himself, *"but the earth,"* this visible world, *"he has given to the children of men,"* as distinguished from the children of God; and, therefore, he adds, *"The dead shall not praise thee, O Lord;"* that is, they who, though living bodily, are spiritually dead, they will not praise you; *"nor any of them that go down to hell;"* who have died in their sins, and have gone to eternal punishment; *"but we that live"* the life of grace, adhering to thee through faith and charity, citizens of our heavenly country, though we are detained here for awhile below upon earth, we, I repeat, *"bless the Lord,"* and we *"bless him forever."*

PSALM 114

The prayer of a just man in affliction, with a lively confidence in God.

1 I have loved, because the Lord will hear the voice of my prayer.
2 Because he hath inclined his ear unto me: and in my days I will call upon him.
3 The sorrows of death have encompassed me: and the perils of hell have found me. I met with trouble and sorrow:
4 And I called upon the name of the Lord. O Lord, deliver my soul.
5 The Lord is merciful and just, and our God sheweth mercy.
6 The Lord is the keeper of little ones: I was little and he delivered me.
7 Turn, O my soul, into thy rest: for the Lord hath been bountiful to thee.
8 For he hath delivered my soul from death: my eyes from tears, my feet from falling.
9 I will please the Lord in the land of the living.

Explanation of the Psalm

1. His soul burning with desire for the Lord, also lately says, *"I have loved,"* and does not say whom, taking it for granted that all others are equally in love with one so deserving of love, and, therefore, that they know whom he means. In like manner, when Mary Magdalen, at the sepulchre, was asked, *"Whom seekest thou?"* she answered, *"Sir, if thou hast taken him away, tell me,"* without saying for whom she was looking, or for whom she was weeping, supposing that everyone shared in her love as well as in her sorrow, and knew the object of both. And, in fact, when we all seek for happiness, which, without any sprinkling of evil, we can find in God alone, as St. John intimates, when he says, *"God is light, and in him there is no darkness;"* man should absolutely love God alone, and when they hear the expression, *"I have loved,"* they ought to understand it as applying to the love of the supreme good alone. David, however, from the reasons he assigns, leaves it pretty clear that, when he said, *"I have loved,"* he meant God only; for he adds, *"because the Lord will hear the voice of my prayer;"* that is, I have loved the Lord, because he is kind and merciful, and from his natural kindness will hear the voice of my prayer. What reasons have we not for loving him, when the Supreme Being, who wants nothing from us, is so ready to hear the prayers of his vilest servants, so that we can safely assure ourselves of being heard? This is expressed more clearly in Psalm 85, where he says, *"For thou, O Lord art sweet and mild, and plenteous in mercy to all that call upon thee."* The meaning, then, is, I have loved the Lord, because I am certain that he will hear the voice of my prayer.

2. He now tells us how he learned that God would hear his prayer. I know it thus, because himself inspired me, invited me, when *"he inclined his ear unto me;"* for, why incline his ear unless he were prepared to hear me? Now, God inclines his ear to us when he inspires us with a desire for prayer, for we would not pray at all were not God, by his previous grace, good enough to give us a desire for prayer. David, then, accustomed to such internal calls, and feeling himself internally inspired with a desire for prayer, understood that God's ear was inclined to him, and he, therefore, also adds, *"and in my days I will call upon him;"* that is, while the days of grace are shining on me, while I have light to see God's ear inclined to me, I will not let the opportunity pass, but I will call upon the Lord. He calls the days in which he got the light of previous grace, *"my days;"* for when the light of grace departs, the day is succeeded by the night, that night *"in which no man can work."*

3-4. He now tells us on what his prayers turned; on the dangers and temptations in regard of his eternal salvation, the only subject worth the notice of a soul that truly loves God. In Psalm 17, we find similar expressions, which evidently apply to the temporal difficulties that then surrounded David, so that we are forced here to apply them to his spiritual troubles. When he says, then *"The sorrows of death have compassed me,"* he means, I am tormented with such dreadful temptations that I am compelled to cry out with the Apostle, *"Who shall deliver me from the body of this death?"* He explains it more fully, when he adds, *"The perils of hell have found me,"* for it is through fear of that peril the greatest of all perils, that those near death conceive the greatest fear and alarm. In the Hebrew the expression is, *"The narrow ways of hell,"* giving us the idea of one walking on the edge of a precipice, in danger every moment of falling, and of being dashed to pieces, unless they tread with the greatest care and caution; and such is the way of salvation, difficult and narrow, so that they who walk without extreme caution run every risk of being precipitated into hell. Hence the Apostle warns us, *"See, therefore, brethren, how you walk circumspectly."*—*"I met with trouble and sorrow."* Many persons, engrossed by the prosperity of this world, are compassed by the snares of death, and the perils of hell, without perceiving it; and the more they are compassed by such perils, the less they reflect on them, and thus they are insensible to fear or trouble. David reflected on them, and his reflections brought him to know where he was; and, therefore, in fear and trembling he declares, *"I met with trouble and sorrow,"* while the world, and its pleasures, and enjoyments were smiling on me, I perceived that I was compassed by the chains and sorrows of death, and that I was exposed to the perils of the pit; and, therefore, in my grief and sorrow *"I called upon the name of the Lord;"* and I said, *"O Lord deliver my soul"* from the pains of death, and the dangers of hell.

5. To show what good hope he had in God, he assigns a reason for having had such hope, because *"The Lord is merciful and just, and our God showeth mercy;"* the Lord is merciful, because he goes before sinners, and inspires them with the idea of penance and prayer, *"For he first loved us,"* as the Apostle says. He is also just, for he lets no one go unchastised, as St. Paul

says, *"He scourgeth every son whom he receiveth,"* and he pardons those who do not pardon themselves, and not only forgives their sins, but makes them his heirs.

6. God, as was stated awhile ago, is a God of mercy, but especially to little ones that fear him, which is more clearly expressed in Psalm 102, where he says, *"For according to the height of the heaven above the earth: he hath strengthened his mercy toward them that fear him."* As a father hath compassion on his children, so hath the Lord on them that fear him." We have the same in the canticle of the virgin, *"And his mercy is from generation to generation to them that fear him;"* and as the last words of the previous verse, *"our God showeth mercy,"* which mercy, according to the Hebrew, is that of a father, he now tells us to whom such mercy is extended, and says it is to the little ones, the meek, and the humble, who have a filial fear of God. *"The Lord is the keeper of little ones."* The Lord in his fatherly mercy protects his little ones, as he would so many tender children, for whom he had prepared an everlasting inheritance. And as David, through the inspiration of the Holy Ghost, knew himself to be one of them, he adds, *"I was humbled;"* I endeavored to be a little one, and *"he delivered me,"* or rather, he will deliver me, as it is in the Hebrew.

7. The just man, so delivered, now congratulates himself on the acquirement of such a blessing. *"Turn, O my soul, into thy rest."* Hasten on the wings of desire to the place of true and everlasting rest, to the heavenly Jerusalem, to the real Abraham's bosom, *"for the Lord hath been bountiful to thee."*

8. He now explains the extent of the bounty spoken of in the preceding verse: deliverance from death and life everlasting. *"My eyes from tears,"* a life subject to no trouble, with all blessings in abundance, *"For God wiped away all tears from their eyes;"* and, finally, *"my feet from falling;"* that is, he will give me not only a happy life, but even a secure and everlasting one, from which I can never fall. He will thus deliver me from the sorrows of death, and the perils of the pit, and place me in the security and eternity of a most happy life.

9. He concludes the Psalm by saying, that as he is to enjoy, in security, a life of the best and sweetest sort, a thing that will be very pleasing to him, he will do all in his power to please the Lord *"in the land of the living,"* where all enjoy life to the fullest extent, and thus please the living God in all possible ways and manners; for while we are in this pilgrimage many are dead, and they who live, live, according to the spirit, and not according *"to the body which is dead;"* whence he exclaims, *"Who shall deliver me from the body of this death?"* Rom. 7.

PSALM 115

This in the Hebrew is joined with the foregoing psalm, and continues to express the faith and gratitude of the psalmist.

10 I have believed, therefore have I spoken; but I have been humbled exceedingly.
11 I said in my excess: Every man is a liar.
12 What shall I render to the Lord, for all the things he hath rendered unto me?
13 I will take the chalice of salvation; and I will call upon the name of the Lord.
14 I will pay my vows to the Lord before all his people:
15 Precious in the sight of the Lord is the death of his saints.
16 Lord, for I am thy servant: I am thy servant, and the son of thy handmaid. Thou hast broken my bonds:
17 I will sacrifice to thee the sacrifice of praise, and I will call upon the name of the Lord.
18 I will pay my vows to the Lord in the sight of all his people:
19 In the courts of the house of the Lord, in the midst of thee, O Jerusalem.

Explanation of the psalm

10. He refers to the words, "I will please the Lord in the land of the living;" and, as if a person asked, how do you know of the existence of such a place at all? he replies, that he knows it through faith. *"I have believed"* that such a place exists, though unseen by mortal eye, and, by reason of such faith, I said, *"I will please the Lord in the land of the living."* St. Paul quotes this passage where he says, *"But having the same spirit of faith, as it is written, I have believed; therefore I have spoken. We also believe, and, therefore, we speak, knowing that he who raised up Jesus will raise us up also with Jesus, and place us with you;"* where he teaches that the resurrection of the body, and the true country of the living in which we are to be located with the Lord Jesus, is to be learned in the spirit of faith, and not by any human demonstration. And, as such faith requires a soul truly humble, that it may be subject to the obedience required by faith, he therefore adds, *"but I have been humbled exceedingly."* I have believed, because I have not relied on my own abilities, but I have exhibited the greatest humility and docility to the Holy Spirit, as the Lord says in Mt. 11, *"I give thanks to thee, O Father, Lord of heaven and earth, because thou hast hid these things from the wise and prudent, and hast revealed them to little ones;"* and in another place, Jn. 5, *"How can you believe who receive glory one from another?"*

11. This relates to a vision he had, in which he got such a view of the aforesaid country of the living that he declares that anything that might be said regarding human happiness, when compared to it, is a lie. *"I,"* who humbled myself so much have been, in consequence, so exalted by God as to be favored with a vision, or an excess, and, seeing in that vision how vain and fallacious are the things that seem good and solid to men, I said, *"Every man is a liar;"* that is to say, every man who speaks in the ordinary manner of men concerning happiness, and sets great value on the frail and perishable things of this world is a liar, for true and solid happiness is not to be found but in the country of the living. This explanation solves the sophism proposed by St. Basil. If every man be a liar, then David was a liar; therefore, he lies when he says, every man is a liar—thus contradicting himself, and destroying his own position. This is answered easily; for when David spoke he did so not as man, but from an inspiration of the Holy Ghost. It may be also said, that being a liar, and always telling lies, are different things, as the former may sometimes happen to tell the truth, especially if he be so inspired by God; for man is said to be mendacious by reason of his being naturally subject to error and falsehoods, in which sense we read, *"But God is true, and every man a liar;"* that is to say, lies are impossible to God alone, but all men are liable to them, but it does not, therefore, follow that they are always telling lies.

12. Feeling himself overwhelmed with so many favors, both in having got a knowledge of the country of the living and a foretaste of the joy to be found therein, he asks what he can give the Lord in return for such favors. He made me out of nothing, redeemed me from iniquity, showed me the country of the living, promised me a place in it. What shall I render to him for all these favors?

13. This is universally understood of the sufferings and passion of Christ, concerning which our Savior himself said, *"Can you drink of the chalice that I shall drink?"* and again, *"Let this chalice pass from me;"* and again, John 18, *"The chalice which my Father hath given me shall I not drink it?"* And it is not only in the New Testament that the word chalice is used for a bitter draught of tribulation, but it also occurs in the same sense in many passages in the Old. Thus, in Psalm 74, *"For in the hand of the Lord there is a cup of strong wine, full of mixture;"* and in Isaias 51, *"Stand up, O Jerusalem, which has drunk at the hand of the Lord the cup of his wrath."* In Jeremias 25, *"Take the cup of wine of this fury at my hand."* In Ezechiel 23, *"Thus saith the Lord God: Thou shalt drink thy sister's cup deep and wide: thou shalt be had in derision and scorn, and thou shalt drink it, and drink it up, even to the dregs."* In Habacuc 2, *"Thou art filled with shame instead of glory, drink thou also and fall fast asleep; the cup of the right hand of the Lord shall compass thee, and shameful vomiting shall be on thy glory."* The just man, who loves God, then says, When I have nothing better to offer my Lord in return for all he has conferred on one, *"I will take the chalice of salvation."* I will cheerfully drink the chalice of the Lord, however bitter it may be, whether it consists in tribulations, dangers; or even death itself. For his own honor's sake he will support me; for I know

that this chalice, however bitter, will be wholesome. And, as I do not rely on my own strength, but, with God's help, can do everything, *"I will, therefore, call upon the name of the Lord"* to give me the grace to drink this cup courageously. The Church, in ordering this Psalm to be sung on the feast of a martyr, confirms this explanation.

14-15. Being prepared to drink the chalice of suffering, he says with great confidence, I will offer the sacrifice of praise and thanksgiving to the Lord, not alone in nooks and chambers, but openly and publicly before all the people, enemies included, and even though I may be satisfied of my death being the consequence; for *"Precious in the sight of the Lord is the death of his saints;"* that is, God sets great value on the death of the saints, when suffered for his honor and glory; just as valuable gems, such as those worn in the crowns of monarchs, and which are of great value, are highly prized by mankind. See, says St. Basil, what glory is in store for the martyrs, whose souls are not only crowned in heaven, but even whose relics are highly valued on earth. Formerly, anyone touching a dead body was looked upon as unclean, but at present, anyone touching the bones of the martyrs is supposed to acquire fresh sanctification.

16-17. The holy soul who offers himself entirely in sacrifice to God, has no pride in him; he rather acknowledges his debt of service, and, agreeable to the command of our Lord, says, *"I am an unprofitable servant, I have done that which I ought to do." "O Lord,"* he says, what great thing have I done in paying my vows publicly, in even daring death; in doing so, I only did what I was bound to do; *"for I am thy servant,"* redeemed from the slavery of the devil by the precious blood of your Son. I am thy servant, not only through your having redeemed me, but also through your having created me; and I am *"the son of your handmaid;"* that is, I am not simply a purchased slave, because my mother, too, is a slave of yours, by creation as well as by redemption. He calls himself the son of the female slave, not of the male, because no matter how free the father, when the mother was a slave, the child was one too. Hence Sara said to Abraham, *"Cast out this bondwoman and her son, for the son of the bondwoman shall not be heir with my son Isaac."* Thus Ishmael was a slave by reason of his mother having been one, though Abraham his father was no slave. *"Thou hast broken my bonds."* He tells us he is a servant to the Lord, but that the service is a good one and that he has been rescued from a bad one. As the Lord in the Gospel encourages those who labor, and are heavily laden, to take up his yoke; *"for his yoke is sweet, and his burden is light,"* he does not absolutely free us from the yoke and the burden, but, instead of a rough yoke, he imposes a sweet one, and substitutes a light for a heavy burden. Thus God completely *"broke the bonds"* that Satan had bound about us, the bonds of sin and the burden of concupiscence, that weighed us down to the lower regions; in place of which he binds us down by the sweet yoke of his law, and the light burden of his love, through which we are raised and exalted to heaven. *"Thou hast broken my bonds;"* you have delivered me from a most cruel state of servitude, and wished me to be your servant, your service being, in my mind, a throne. I will, therefore, *"sacrifice to you the sacrifice of praise,"* and no longer invoke false gods; mammon to wit, the appetite, wealth, and honors, to all of which I was heretofore a slave; but I will constantly *"call upon the name of the Lord,"* who alone deserves it.

18-19. This is a repetition of verse 5, with the addition of, *"In the courts of the house of the Lord;"* to give us to understand that the servant of God should offer his vows, his confession, and himself to God, in the Church, indicated by Jerusalem; for they who work outside the Church derive nothing from it.

PSALM 116

All nations are called upon to praise God for his mercy and truth.

1 praise the Lord, all ye nations: praise him, all ye people.
2 For his mercy is confirmed upon us: and the truth of the Lord remaineth for ever.

EXPLANATION OF THE PSALM

1. He addresses the whole Church, and exhorts it to praise God. *"All ye nations"* is directed to the converted gentiles, who are named first by reason of their being in the majority, and the people nearer those of the Jews who had been converted to the faith; and the Apostles themselves, in alluding to a similar expression in the second Psalm, *"Why have the gentiles raged, and the people meditated vain things,"* apply the former to the gentiles, and the latter to the Jews.

2. The reason assigned for praising God is, *"for his mercy is confirmed on us,"* by the arrival of the Messias to Jews and gentiles; *"and the truth of the Lord remaineth forever;"* for the Church was established, *"Against which the gates of hell shall not prevail,"* and his kingdom was established, of which there will be no end.

PSALM 117

The psalmist praises God for his delivery from evils; puts his whole trust in him, and foretells the coming of Christ.

1 Give praise to Lord, for he is good: for his mercy endureth for ever.
2 Let Israel now say that he is good: that his mercy endureth for ever.
3 Let the house of Aaron now say, that his mercy endureth for ever.

4 Let them that fear the Lord now say, that his mercy endureth for ever.
5 In my trouble I called upon the Lord: and the Lord heard me, and enlarged me.
6 The Lord is my helper, I will not fear what man can do unto me.
7 The Lord is my helper: and I will look over my enemies.
8 It is good to confide in the Lord, rather than to have confidence in man.
9 It is good to trust in the Lord, rather than to trust in princes.
10 All nations compassed me about; and in the name of the Lord I have been revenged on them.
11 Surrounding me they compassed me about: and in the name of the Lord I have been revenged on them.
12 They surrounded me like bees, and they burned like fire among thorns: and in the name of the Lord I was revenged on them.
13 Being pushed I was overturned that I might fall: but the Lord supported me.
14 The Lord is my strength and my praise: and he is become my salvation.
15 The voice of rejoicing and of salvation is in the tabernacles of the just.
16 The right hand of the Lord hath wrought strength: the right hand of the Lord hath exulted me: the right hand of the Lord hath wrought strength.
17 I shall not die, but live: and shall declare the works of the Lord.
18 The Lord chastising hath chastised me: but he hath not delivered me over to death.
19 Open ye to me the gates of justice: I will go into them, and give praise to the Lord.
20 This is the gate of the Lord, the just shall enter into it.
21 I will give glory to thee because thou hast heard me: and art become my salvation.
22 The stone which the builders rejected; the same is become the head of the corner.
23 This is the Lord's doing: and it is wonderful in our eyes.
24 This is the day which the Lord hath made: let us be glad and rejoice therein.
25 Lord, save me: O Lord, give good success.
26 Blessed be he that cometh in the name Lord. We have blessed you out of the house of the Lord.
27 The Lord is God, and he hath shone upon us. Appoint a solemn day, with shady boughs, even to the horn of the alter.
28 Thou art my God, and I will praise thee: thou art my God, and I will exalt thee. I will praise thee, because thou hast heard me, and art become my salvation.
29 praise ye the Lord, for he is good: for his mercy endureth for ever.

EXPLANATION OF THE PSALM

1. David invites all to praise God, and assigns a reason for their doing so, "*for he is good;*" nothing more brief, and at the same time more sublime, could be said of him, for God alone can be said to be intrinsically good, and it is such goodness only that deserves to be praised; he adds, *"for his mercy endureth forever;"* to show that God, even in his actions, is good, and as such, is deserving of praise; for the wretched have no better way of coming at a knowledge of God's goodness than through his mercy. For it was his mercy that created, redeemed, protects, and will crown us; and, thus, *"his mercy endureth forever."*

2-4. He tells who he had invited to praise God, namely, the people of Israel first, from whom the Apostles were descended, and who were the first believers in Christ. He names the house of Aaron in the second place, next to the Apostles, *"A great multitude of the priests obeyed the faith,"* Acts 6; and all the gentiles, finally, who believed and united with the rising Church. He thus invites the whole Church, formed of Jews and gentiles, to praise God.

5. He now begins to tell what he is going to praise God for, and it is for his having been in trouble, or, as the Hebrew has it, angustiated, or compassed in a narrow place, and that when he prayed to God he was heard at once, and was enlarged. *"In my trouble I called upon the Lord;"* without boasting of my own merits, or complaining of being unjustly persecuted, I had recourse to God's mercy; *"and the Lord heard me, and enlarged me,"* by delivering me from all the dangers that encompassed me. Anyone reading Psalms 17 and 33, will at once see how applicable all this was to David himself; and it is equally so to the Church, because in its infancy, when Herod threw St. Peter, the chief head and pastor of the Church into prison, *"and when prayer was made without ceasing by the Church to God for him,"* it was heard at once, and by a most wonderful miracle it was enlarged from the depth of tribulation to the fullest extent of peace and consolation; and as often as the same Church was delivered from the persecutions of Nero, Decius, and Diocletian, and such persecutors, it might exclaim with David, *"In my trouble I called upon the Lord; and the Lord heard me, and enlarged me."*

6-7. David, or God's people, if you will, being taught by experience, exults in great confidence, but does not say, the Lord is my helper, and I shall suffer no more, knowing that while he is a pilgrim here below he will have much to suffer from his daily enemies; but be says, *"The Lord is my helper, I will not fear what man can do unto me."* I will not be troubled in regard of any annoyance I may meet with from man, because the Lord will turn all such things to good, for so he reminded us when he said, *"Be not afraid of them that kill the body, and after that have no more that they can do;"* and again, *"A hair from your head shall not perish;"* and the Apostle tells us, *"For our present tribulation, which is momentary and light, worketh for us above measure, exceedingly, an eternal weight of glory."* He, therefore, justly adds, *"and I will look over my enemies;"* for their persecutions only tend to increase my glory.

8-9. He draws a useful admonition from what he has said, on placing all our hope in God, and not in man, however powerful. For God is always both able and willing to help those who put their trust in him; while men are very often unable, or when they are able, being influenced by various passions, are unwilling to offer any help. David knew that by experience, for he confided in Saul his king, at another time in Achis, the Certhean, at another time in Achitophel, his own most prudent minister, besides several others, and they all failed him, but he never confided in God, without feeling the benefit of it. He, therefore, says, strongly advising all, *"It is good to confide in the Lord, rather than to have confidence in men."* Such a comparison is just suited to man's infirmity, as we are well acquainted with the power of man, and especially of princes; while God's power is hidden to many, who neither see it, nor reflect upon it; perhaps, even disbelieve God's greatness, otherwise he should have had to say, it is good to hope in the Lord, and evil to hope in man. So Jeremias says, *"Cursed be the man that trusteth in man."* It is not, however, sinful to put our trust, to a certain extent, in the help of the Angels, or of pious people, because such hope has reference to God, who helps those who trust in him, not only directly through himself; but also indirectly through others.

10-12. From his own example, he shows the advantage of putting one's trust in God; for it was not once, but several times, that he was beset by a most powerful enemy on all sides, and was most miraculously so rescued by God, as to behold them all laid prostrate about him. If we refer the passage to David, everyone knows how often he was overpowered by Saul with a numerous army, and most unexpectedly and miraculously rescued; and it is better known how often God's people have suffered the direst persecutions from powerful kings and innumerable people, and seen God's vengeance wreaked on the instigators of such persecutions. To show it was no ordinary persecution, he adds, *"Surrounding me, they compassed me about,"* so as to leave no chance of escape, *"They surrounded me like bees,"* to show their number and their fury; for bees surrounding a hive can scarcely be numbered; and to show their fury, he says, *"They burned like fire among thorns,"* that can scarcely be checked or extinguished once it gets a hold of them, and destroys them in a minute.

13-14. Having hitherto expatiated on the multitude and the atrocity of his enemies, he now acknowledges his own weakness, as being quite unable to compete with them, that God may thus have greater glory in the matter. I was unable to resist such violence; and thus these attacks of the enemy had nigh accomplished my ruin, had not the Lord, coming in at the proper time, *"supported me."* This may have reference to the various dangers David had from time to time to encounter; and it may also refer to the spiritual dangers of temptation, to which the early Christians were subject when they suffered so much persecution, under which they would have succumbed, had they not been imbued with the spirit of those verses, *"The Lord is my strength and my praise." "The Lord is my strength;"* because it is through him I conquer; *"and my praise,"* because I am always bound to praise him; *"and he is become my salvation;"* has been my Savior.

15. The just who heard of David's liberation rejoiced much thereat; but much more so, on the delivery of the early Christians from persecution, was there the voice of rejoicing and the voice of salvation announcing, in the tabernacles of the just, the joyful news of salvation.

16. The voice of rejoicing and salvation that resounded in the tabernacles of the just is that *"the right hand of the Lord,"* the might and power of the Son of God, *"hath wrought strength;"* has done its work bravely and powerfully; for the Son of God is called in Scripture the arm, or the right hand of the Lord, because it is through the Son that the Father has done, and still does, everything. *"All things were made by him,"* Jn. 1; *"By whom also he made the world,"* Heb. 1; *"Who hath believed our report, and to whom is the arm of the Lord revealed?"* Isaias 53; *"He hath shown might in his arm,"* Lk. 1; *"The right hand of The Lord hath exalted me."* Herein hath the right hand of the Lord wrought strength, inasmuch as it exalted me, and lowered my enemies, which is just as applicable to the Church as to David. The repetition of *"the right hand of the Lord hath wrought strength,"* is for the sake of expressing his joy and gladness.

17-18. The same David, or, if you will, God's people, goes on in recording God's mercy, who permits them to suffer persecution as a father; and not as an enemy, for the purpose, not of destroying, but of purging them. As much as to say, however great the persecutions I have suffered, and am still suffering, *"I shall not die but live."* I will not be utterly exterminated, as my enemies desire; but I will hold out, *"and shall declare the works of the Lord,"* *"who chastising, chastised me"* with the rod of a father; *"but he hath not delivered me to death."*

19-20. The favors he received having inspired him with the courage of aiming at higher ones, he demands an introduction to the heavenly Jerusalem, where no sinners are to be found. *"Open ye to me the gates of justice,"* the gates of the kingdom of heaven which is all justice, for justice is the gate of glory: *"Seek (says our Lord) just the kingdom of God and his justice."*—*"I will go into them, and give praise to the Lord,"* because, according to Psalm 83, *"They that dwell in thy house, O Lord, shall praise thee forever and ever."*—*"This is the gate of the Lord, the just shall enter into it."* This gate of justice is the true gate, the only gate that leads to the Lord, and, therefore, it is only the just shall enter by it.

21. He now explains the expression, *"I will go into them and give praise to the Lord,"* for he says, *"I will give glory to thee,"* when I shall have entered the heavenly Jerusalem, through the gates of justices, *"because thou hast heard me;"* for though the just ask for many and various things in this world, they all tend to one petition, of which Psalm 26, says, *"One thing I have asked of the Lord, this I will seek after; that I may dwell in the house of the Lord all the days of my life."* Concerning this petition, then, he says, *"I will give glory to thee because thou hast heard me,"* which be explains more fully when he adds, *"and art become my salvation;"* you that were my hope have become my salvation; you who fed me on the way are now my reward in heaven.

22-23. Christ having repeatedly quoted this passage in reference to himself, St. Peter having done the same, in which he has been followed by St. Paul, there can be no doubt of its applying solely and exclusively to Christ. David, then, having sung of his own delivery, and of the delivery of God's people from their temporal calamities, and having asked for his own and their admission to eternal happiness, explains now how God opened the way to it; and, undoubtedly, hurried away by an increased light of prophecy, exclaims, *"The stone which the builders rejected the same is become the head of the corner;"* that is to say, God sent a living, precious, chosen stone on earth, but the Jews, who then had the building of the Church, rejected that stones and said of it, *"This man, who observeth not the sabbath is not of God;"* and *"We have no king but Caesar;"* and, *"That seducer said, I will rise after three days;"* and many similar things beside. But this stone, so rejected by the builders as unfit for raising the spiritual edifice, *"Is become the head of the corner;"* has been made by God, the principal architect, the bond to connect the two walls and keep them together, that is to say, has been made the head of the whole Church, composed of Jews and Gentiles; and such a head, that whoever is not under him cannot be saved; and whoever is built under him, the living stone, will certainly be saved. Now all this *"is the Lord's doing,"* done by his election and design, without any intervention on the part of man, and, therefore, it is wonderful in our eyes." For who is there that must not look upon it as a wonderful thing, to find a man crucified, dead and buried, rising, after three days, from the dead, immortal, with unbounded power, and declared Prince of men and Angels, and a way opened through him for mortal man, to the kingdom of heaven, to the society of the Angels, to a happy immortality?

24. *"This day"* on which such a thing was accomplished, is really the day *"which the Lord hath made."* and, therefore, for such a favor *"let us be glad and rejoice therein."* The day of the resurrection, beyond doubt, for, though from his very conception, the Lord Jesus was the Christ, and the head of the Church, hence we find the Angel saying to the shepherds—*"I bring

you tidings of great joy, for this day is born to you a Savior, who is Christ, the Lord, in the city of David;" still, it was necessary for him, first, to be rejected by men, to be humbled, even to the death of the cross; then to be exalted, through his resurrection, then to be declared the chief corner stone, and to have it preached through all nations, *"that there was salvation in none other;"* hence, he said, *"All power is given me in heaven, and on earth, go ye, therefore, and teach all nations, baptizing them in the name of the Father, and of the Son, and of the Holy Ghost."* The day of the resurrection is called *"the day which the Lord hath made,"* either because Christ, by his resurrection, as a Sun of Justice, made that day in a new manner, or because he specially consecrated that day to his service, or because he set it aside, *"that we may be glad and rejoice therein."*

25-26. These are the very praises that the crowd saluted our Savior with on the day of the palms, with the exception of their making use of the word *"Hosanna,"* instead of, *"O Lord, save me,"* as we have it here. Thus, the Lord on that day wished to make a visible exhibition of, and to anticipate the invisible triumph he was about to enjoy on the day of his resurrection. Nor could it be fairly objected to him that he was enjoying a triumph before he obtained the victory, because he was most certain of the victory, and the Prophet, as well as he, foresaw and foretold that Christ would be rejected as the corner stone at the time of his passion, and that he would be afterwards exalted in his resurrection, so as to become the head of the corner, so he also foresaw and foretold the very words the crowd would make use of on the day of Christ's triumph, the day of the palms by which the triumph of the resurrection was signified, and turns to account the fact of both having occurred on the same day, namely, the Lord's day. He, therefore, says, *"Let us be glad, and rejoice on this day,"* saying, *"O Lord, save me, O Lord, give good success"* in the commencement of your reign. *"Blessed be he that cometh in the name of the Lord;"* may the Messias, our King, now become the head of the corner, be blessed by all, *"that cometh in the name of the Lord,"* that does not come of himself, an usurper like Antichrist, but comes, having been sent by his Father, the Lord of heaven and earth, as Christ himself explains, in Jn. 5. *"We have blessed you out of the house of the Lord."* Having explained the whole prophecy regarding the coming of Christ and his triumph, the Prophet now addresses the people, and exhorts them to celebrate a solemn festival in thanksgiving, *"We have blessed you out of the house of the Lord."* We, prophets, have blessed you, a faithful people, by announcing to you those divine mysteries that lead to your salvation.

27. This is, as it were, a summary of all, as much as to say, our Lord is the true God, and he hath shone upon us by showing us the light of his mercies. Therefore, appoint a solemn shady day, by bringing in lots of green

branches to ornament the temple to the very horn of the altar. That is variously interpreted, according to the ceremonies of the Jews, that do not concern us at present.

28-29. These verses are only a repetition of the preceding, in order to express the vehement affections of the prophet.

PSALM 118

Of the excellence of virtue consisting in the love and observance of the commandments of God.

ALEPH
1 Blessed are the undefiled in the way, who walk in the law of the Lord.
2 Blessed are they who search his testimonies: that seek him with their whole heart.
3 For they that work iniquity, have not walked in his ways.
4 Thou hast commanded thy commandments to be kept most diligently.
5 O! that my ways may be directed to keep thy justifications.
6 Then shall I not be confounded, when I shall look into all thy commandments.
7 I will praise thee with uprightness of heart, when I shall have learned the judgments of thy justice.
8 I will keep thy justifications: O! do not thou utterly forsake me.

BETH
9 By what doth a young man correct his way? by observing thy words.
10 With my whole heart have I sought after thee: let me not stray from thy commandments.
11 Thy words have I hidden in my heart, that I may not sin against thee.
12 Blessed art thou, O Lord: teach me thy justifications.
13 With my lips I have pronounced all the judgments of thy mouth.
14 I have been delighted in the way of thy testimonies, as in all riches.
15 I will meditate on thy commandments: and I will consider thy ways.
16 I will think of thy justifications: I will not forget thy words.

GIMEL
17 Give bountifully to thy servant, enliven me: and I shall keep thy words.
18 Open thou my eyes: and I will consider the wondrous things of thy law.
19 I am a sojourner on the earth: hide not thy commandments from me.
20 My soul hath coveted to long for thy justifications, at all times.
21 Thou hast rebuked the proud: they are cursed who decline from thy commandments.
22 Remove from reproach and contempt: because I have sought after thy testimonies.
23 For princes sat, and spoke against me: but thy servant was employed in thy

justifications.

24 For thy testimonies are my meditation: and thy justifications my counsel.

DALETH

25 My soul hath cleaved to the pavement: quicken thou me according to thy word.
26 I have declared my ways, and thou hast heard me: teach me thy justifications.
27 Make me to understand the way of thy justifications: and I shall be exercised in thy wondrous works.
28 My soul hath slumbered through heaviness: strengthen thou me in thy words.
29 Remove from me the way of iniquity: and out of thy law have mercy on me.
30 I have chosen the way of truth: thy judgments I have not forgotten.
31 I have stuck to thy testimonies, O Lord: put me not to shame.
32 I have run the way of thy commandments, when thou didst enlarge my heart.

HE

33 Set before me for a law the way of thy justifications, O Lord: and I will always seek after it.
34 Give me understanding, and I will search thy law; and I will keep it with my whole heart.
35 Lead me into the path of thy commandments; for this same I have desired.
36 Incline my heart into thy testimonies and not to covetousness.
37 Turn away my eyes that they may not behold vanity: quicken me in thy way.
38 Establish thy word to thy servant, in thy fear.
39 Turn away my reproach, which I have apprehended: for thy judgments are delightful.
40 Behold I have longed after thy precepts: quicken me in thy justice.

VAU

41 Let thy mercy also come upon me, O Lord: thy salvation according to thy word.
42 So shall I answer them that reproach me in any thing; that I have trusted in thy words.
43 And take not thou the word of truth utterly out of my mouth: for in thy words have I hoped exceedingly.
44 So shall I always keep thy law, for ever and ever.
45 And I walked at large: because I have sought after thy commandments.
46 And I spoke of thy testimonies before kings: and I was not ashamed.
47 I meditated also on thy commandments, which I loved.
48 And I lifted up my hands to thy commandments, which I loved: and I was exercised in thy justifications.

ZAIN

49 Be thou mindful of thy word to thy servant, in which thou hast given me hope.
50 This hath comforted me in my humiliation: because thy word hath enlivened

me.
51 The proud did iniquitously altogether: but I declined not from thy law.
52 I remembered, O Lord, thy judgments of old: and I was comforted.
53 A fainting hath taken hold of me, because of the wicked that forsake thy law.
54 Thy justifications were the subject of my song, in the place of my pilgrimage.
55 In the night I have remembered thy name, O Lord: and have kept thy law.
56 This happened to me: because I sought after thy justifications.

HETH

57 O Lord, my portion, I have said, I would keep the law.
58 I entreated thy face with all my heart: have mercy on me according to thy word.
59 I have thought on my ways: and turned my feet unto thy testimonies.
60 I am ready, and am not troubled: that I may keep thy commandments.
61 The cords of the wicked have encompassed me: but I have not forgotten thy law.
62 I rose at midnight to give praise to thee; for the judgments of thy justification.
63 I am a partaker with all them that fear thee, and that keep thy commandments.
64 The earth, O Lord, is full of thy mercy: teach me thy justifications.

TETH

65 Thou hast done well with thy servant, O Lord, according to thy word.
66 Teach me goodness and discipline and knowledge; for I have believed thy commandments.
67 Before I was humbled I offended; therefore have I kept thy word.
68 Thou art good; and in thy goodness teach me thy justifications.
69 The iniquity of the proud hath been multiplied over me: but I will seek thy commandments with my whole heart.
70 Their heart is curdled like milk: but I have meditated on thy law.
71 It is good for me that thou hast humbled me, that I may learn thy justifications.
72 The law of thy mouth is good to me, above thousands of gold and silver.

JOD

73 Thy hands have made me and formed me: give me understanding, and I will learn thy commandments.
74 They that fear thee shall see me, and shall be glad: because I have greatly hoped in thy words.
75 I know, O Lord, that thy judgments are equity: and in thy truth thou hast humbled me.
76 O! let thy mercy be for my comfort, according to thy word unto thy servant.
77 Let thy tender mercies come unto me, and I shall live: for thy law is my meditation.
78 Let the proud be ashamed, because they have done unjustly towards me: but I

will be employed in thy commandments.
79 Let them that fear thee turn to me and they that know thy testimonies.
80 Let my heart be undefiled in thy justifications, that I may not be confounded.

CAPH
81 My soul hath fainted after thy salvation: and in thy word I have very much hoped.
82 My eyes have failed for thy word, saying: When wilt thou comfort me?
83 For I am become like a bottle in the frost: I have not forgotten thy justifications.
84 How many are the days of thy servant: when wilt thou execute judgment on them that persecute me?
85 The wicked have told me fables: but not as thy law.
86 All thy statutes are truth: they have persecuted me unjustly, do thou help me.
87 They had almost made an end of me upon earth: but I have not forsaken thy commandments.
88 Quicken thou me according to thy mercy: and I shall keep the testimonies of thy mouth.

LAMED
89 For ever, O Lord, thy word standeth firm in heaven.
90 Thy truth unto all generations: thou hast founded the earth, and it continueth.
91 By thy ordinance the day goeth on: for all things serve thee.
92 Unless thy law had been my meditation, I had then perhaps perished in my abjection.
93 Thy justifications I will never forget: for by them thou hast given me life.
94 I am thine, save thou me: for I have sought thy justifications.
95 The wicked have waited for me to destroy me: but I have understood thy testimonies.
96 I have seen an end to all persecution: thy commandment is exceeding broad.

MEM
97 O how have I loved thy law, O Lord! it is my meditation all the day.
98 Through thy commandment, thou hast made me wiser than my enemies: for it is ever with me.
99 I have understood more than all my teachers: because thy testimonies are my meditation.
100 I have had understanding above ancients: because I have sought thy commandments.
101 I have restrained my feet from every evil way: that I may keep thy words.
102 I have not declined from thy judgments, because thou hast set me a law.
103 How sweet are thy words to my palate! more than honey to my mouth.
104 By thy commandments I have had understanding: therefore have I hated every way of iniquity.

NUN

105 Thy word is a lamp to my feet, and a light to my paths.
106 I have sworn and am determined to keep the judgments of thy justice.
107 I have been humbled, O Lord, exceedingly: quicken thou me according to thy word.
108 The free offerings of my mouth make acceptable, O Lord: and teach me thy judgments.
109 My soul is continually in my hands: and I have not forgotten thy law.
110 Sinners have laid a snare for me: but I have not erred from thy precepts.
111 I have purchased thy testimonies for an inheritance for ever: because they are a joy to my heart.
112 I have inclined my heart to do thy justifications for ever, for the reward.

SAMECH

113 I have hated the unjust: and have loved thy law.
114 Thou art my helper and my protector: and in thy word I have greatly hoped.
115 Depart from me, ye malignant: and I will search the commandments of my God.
116 Uphold me according to thy word, and I shall live: and let me not be confounded in my expectation.
117 Help me, and I shall be saved: and I will meditate always on thy justifications.
118 Thou hast despised all them that fall off from thy judgments; for their thought is unjust.
119 I have accounted all the sinners of the earth prevaricators: therefore have I loved thy testimonies.
120 Pierce thou my flesh with thy fear: for I am afraid of thy judgments.

AIN

121 I have done judgment and justice: give me not up to them that slander me.
122 Uphold thy servant unto good: let not the proud calumniate me.
123 My eyes have fainted after thy salvation: and for the word of thy justice.
124 Deal with thy servant according to thy mercy: and teach me thy justifications.
125 I am thy servant: give me understanding that I may know thy testimonies.
126 It is time, O Lord, to do: they have dissipated thy law.
127 Therefore have I loved thy commandments above gold and the topaz.
128 Therefore was I directed to all thy commandments: I have hated all wicked ways.

PHE

129 Thy testimonies are wonderful: therefore my soul hath sought them.
130 The declaration of thy words giveth light: and giveth understanding to little ones.
131 I opened my mouth and panted: because I longed for thy commandments.

132 Look thou upon me, and have mercy on me, according to the judgment of them that love thy name.
133 Direct my steps according to thy word: and let no iniquity have dominion over me.
134 Redeem me from the calumnies of men: that I may keep thy commandments.
135 Make thy face to shine upon thy servant: and teach me thy justifications.
136 My eyes have sent forth springs of water: because they have not kept thy law.

SADE

137 Thou art just, O Lord: and thy judgment is right.
138 Thou hast commanded justice thy testimonies: and thy truth exceedingly.
139 My zeal hath made me pine away: because my enemies forgot thy words.
140 Thy word is exceedingly refined: and thy servant hath loved it.
141 I am very young and despised; but I forgot not thy justifications.
142 Thy justice is justice for ever: and thy law is the truth.
143 Trouble and anguish have found me: thy commandments are my meditation.
144 Thy testimonies are justice for ever: give me understanding, and I shall live.

COPH

145 I cried with my whole heart, hear me, O Lord: I will seek thy justifications.
146 I cried unto thee, save me: that I may keep thy commandments.
147 I prevented the dawning of the day, and cried: because in thy words I very much hoped.
148 My eyes to thee have prevented the morning: that I might meditate on thy words.
149 Hear thou my voice, O Lord, according to thy mercy: and quicken me according to thy mercy.
150 They that persecute me have drawn nigh to iniquity; but they are gone far off from the law.
151 Thou art near, O Lord: and all thy ways are truth.
152 I have known from the beginning concerning thy testimonies: that thou hast founded them for ever.

RES

153 See my humiliation and deliver me: for I have not forgotten the law.
154 Judge my judgment and redeem me: quicken thou me for thy word's sake.
155 Salvation is far from sinners; because they have not sought thy justifications.
156 Many, O Lord, are thy mercies: quicken me according to thy judgment.
157 Many are they that persecute me, and afflict me; but I have not declined from thy testimonies.
158 I beheld the transgressors, and I pined away; because they kept not thy word.
159 Behold I have loved thy commandments, O Lord; quicken me thou in thy mercy.

160 The beginning of thy words is truth: all the judgments of thy justice are for ever.

SIN

161 Princes have persecuted me without cause: and my heart hath been in awe of thy words.
162 I will rejoice at thy words, as one that hath found great spoil.
163 I have hated and abhorred iniquity; but I have loved thy law.
164 Seven times a day I have given praise to thee, for the judgments of thy justice.
165 Much peace have they that love thy law, and to them there is no stumbling block.
166 I looked to thy salvation, O Lord: and I loved thy commandments.
167 My soul hath kept thy testimonies: and hath loved them exceedingly.
168 I have kept thy commandments and thy testimonies: because all my ways are in thy sight.

TAU

169 Let my supplication, O Lord, come near in thy sight: give me understanding according to thy word.
170 Let my request come in before thee; deliver thou me according to thy word.
171 My lips shall utter a hymn, when thou shalt teach me thy justifications.
172 My tongue shall pronounce thy word: because all thy commandments are justice.
173 Let thy hand be with me to save me; for I have chosen thy precepts.
174 I have longed for thy salvation, O Lord; and thy law is my meditation.
175 My soul shall live and shall praise thee: and thy judgments shall help me.
176 I have gone astray like a sheep that is lost: seek thy servant, because I have not forgotten thy commandments.

Explanation of the psalm

Aleph

1. The prophet, most properly, in praising the excellence and the advantage of the divine law, draws his first argument from happiness, that is, the ultimate end of man; for in the moral order the end holds the same place that first principles do in the order of nature. The meaning of the first verse, then, is, Blessed are they who, in their journey through life, are not soiled by the mud or dirt of sin: and they who escape being thus soiled, and thus blessed, are those *"who walk in the law of the Lord;"* they who abandon every other way, and choose that of the law of the Lord, as being the purest and the clearest. To come to particulars. The word *"blessed"* implies eternal happiness, which alone is complete happiness; and also temporal happiness, as far as such can be had in this world. The meaning, then, is, Blessed are they in eternity; and, even in this life, blessed are they, joyous and content, coveting nothing in this world, are those who live unblemished by sin, by reason of *"their walking in the way of the Lord."* Christ himself informs us that the straight road to eternal happiness is the observance of his law. *"If thou wilt enter into life keep the commandments."* With that, experience, as well as reason, teaches us that, even in this world, none lead a happier life than they who lead an upright and a pious one; for happy must that man be who has all he desires, and wishes for nothing bad; while wicked men wish for many things that are bad, and have not very many of the things that they wish for. On the contrary, the just wish for nothing that is bad, and they have whatever they wish for by reason of their wishing for God alone and the doing of his will. The word *"undefiled"* does not imply the absence of venial sin; if such were the case, we should not have even one to come under such a category. It means the absence of mortal sin, that alone, strictly speaking, leaves a stain on the soul. The metaphor seems to be taken from the spots one picks up in walking through muddy, dusty, or dirty places. *"In the way"* means through life, which is most aptly called a way by reason of the constant changes in it, and, as Job has it, *"must ever continue in the same state,"* from the moment we commence it to the very last stage of our existence. *"In the law of the Lord;"* giving us to understand that God's law is a straight and clear path, because it prohibits all manner of sin. The law of the Lord is here opposed to the law of the flesh, which the Apostle designates as *"the way of concupiscence,"* full of the dust of pride, the mud of luxury, and the dirty water of avarice.

2. He explains the last verse by saying that it is not every observance of the law that will secure happiness. Many observe the law superficially, content with abstaining from murder, theft, adultery, while they do not, in reality, walk as they ought in the way of the Lord, inasmuch as they have a hatred for their neighbor, abound in wealth they have no use for, or indulge in fornication. He, then, that really wishes to be happy must *"search his testimonies,"* must seriously reflect on the meaning of the whole law, called *"his testimonies,"* by reason of its making God's will known to us; for whoever will search the law will find that the precept, *"thou shalt not kill,"* prohibits not only murder, but also hatred and anger, as the Lord himself explained it; nay more, that it even obligates us to love, for *"love is the fulfilling of the law;"* and when God said, *"Thou shalt not kill,"* he said so lest love should be infringed on, which also will be found to apply to the other precepts by anyone *"that will search them."* They may be truly said to search his testimonies who *"seek him with their whole heart;"* for he that seriously seeks for God with his whole heart longs for his grace in this world and a sight of him in the next; such a one most undoubtedly seeks to know God's will in

everything, and to walk according to it. Like travelers on their way to a place they wish to reach as quickly as possible, they earnestly inquire and ask of all they meet the easiest and most direct road to the place they are bound for; while those who travel without any fixed purpose, having no particular place in view, take very little trouble as to what road they may be travelling. The prophet, therefore, says, *"Blessed are they that search his testimonies;"* that is, I called those who walk in the Lord happy, but let it be understood that I mean those only who diligently examine the meaning of the whole law, and of him who gave it; a thing done only by those *"who seek him with their whole heart,"* who neither prefer; not even put, any creature on a level with him, who do not divide their love between him and any creature, but love him solely on his own account, and creatures for him.

3. He proves his assertion, that they only who walk in the way of the Lord are undefiled, inasmuch as not one of those *"that work iniquity,"* and are thus found defiled on the road, have walked *"in the ways,"* that is, in the law of the Lord; a clear proof of which is, that it is the way of the Lord alone that preserves those who walk in it undefiled. His argument, then, stands thus, by reversing the case, *"They that work iniquity,"* and are, consequently, found defiled, have not walked in the way of the Lord; therefore, they who do walk in God's path do not work iniquity, and are, consequently, undefiled. St. Augustine raises what he calls a serious question here. All the saints walk in the way of the Lord, therefore, they work not iniquity, and yet they say, through 1 Jn. 1:8, *"If we say that we have no sin we deceive ourselves, and the truth is not in us, and sin is iniquity."* They who work iniquity certainly do not walk in the way of the Lord, inasmuch as they work iniquity, because they walk in a way directly opposite to God's way, as they do who commit mortal sin; while those who commit venial sin merely walk in a way a little outside of God's way. Now, the saints who have the desire of walking in God's way, and do so habitually, may be said to walk therein; and if they occasionally get off the path, by doing something not directly opposed to God's law, they quickly get on it again through penance and confession.

4. He now draws another argument from the excellence of the legislator, as much as to say, These are not the commands of man, but of God; that God who requires implicit obedience from all his servants. To give greater weight to what he has to say thereon, he addresses God directly, saying, *"Thou hast commanded thy commandments to be kept most diligently."* O Lord, you who can freely command your servants, and punish them severely if they disobey, and who can neither forgive nor forget the transgressor, *"thou hast commanded,"* not by way of advice, but by strict precept, *"thy commandments to be kept,"* not negligently or carelessly, but *"most diligently"* and

studiously. Who, then, will not, at once, give their mind to a thorough observance of them?

5. Looking at the authority, of him that commands, and the strictness of the order, the prophet wishes that God's commands should be most implicitly obeyed, and he expresses such wish himself, to give an example to others of the obedience due by them to God; for, if he, a king, supreme head of his people, so trembles at God's commands, and so ardently desires to comply with them, what should ordinary persons not do? *"O, that my ways,"* all my thoughts, words, and deeds, *"may be directed,"* may be made agreeable to your righteous law, *"to keep thy justifications,"* to observe your law, called *"justifications"* frequently in this Psalm. The law for variety's sake gets different names in the Scripture, such as the precept, the command, the discourse, the speech, the word, sometimes the testimony, by reason of its bearing witness to what God's will is, sometimes the justification, as in this passage, because it is through it we are justified; that is, made more just, according to the Apostle, who says, *"the doers of the law shall be justified;"* observe, though, that I said, they who observe the law shall be made more just, because the first justification, through which we are made just, from being sinners, cannot be ascribed to the law, but to grace, as the same Apostle has it, *"For if justice be by the law, then Christ died in vain."*

6. He draws great fruit from directing his ways to keep the justifications of the Lord. They who regard the greatness of the legislator; and in their actions do not regard the rule of his divine law, and afterwards find their work out of shape, and not in conformity with the direct way of the law of God, they are fearfully confounded and disheartened, they can scarcely lift their eyes to God, saying to themselves, *"Who am I that I should have dared to direct my thoughts, words, or deeds, to anything but what was agreeable to the straight way of the commands of the supreme legislator, who ordered them to be so zealously observed?"* David, then, considering it of great importance, as it really is, to have no reason for being confused on such grounds, says, I always wished to direct my ways to keep God's justifications, because then *"I shall not be confounded,"* I will have no reason for blushing before you, O Lord, *"when I shall look into all thy commandments,"* when I shall have tested all my actions by the rule of your commandments, to see if they are conformable to them. Hence, we learn how far removed from the spirit, and the piety of David, are they who do so many crooked things, anything but conformable to the law of God, and yet are quite unconscious of their deformity, by reason of their not reflecting on the greatness of the legislator.

7. He adds that not only will he not be confounded, but he will even return thanks to God for having, through his grace and assistance, learned how to observe his law. *"I will praise thee,"* and give thee thanks, *"with uprightness of*

heart," with a pure and upright heart, *"when I shall have learned,"* for having the good luck to learn, *"the judgments of thy justice;"* your most just judgments and laws. The word *"learned"* conveys more than simple knowledge; it implies an amount of approbation and persuasion on the part of those who have come at the truth, and, therefore, determine to observe it; in which sense we are to understand it in Jn. 6, where the Lord says, *"Everyone that hath heard of the Father and hath learned, cometh to me."* Now, they learn of the Father, who, by the infusion of the Holy Spirit in their hearts, are firmly persuaded that it is a good thing to believe, to be converted, or to observe the law. Such persuasion springs from uprightness of heart; for God is looked upon as thoroughly good by those who have an upright heart, as Psalm 72 has it, *"How good is God to Israel, to them that are of a right heart."* Now, they who are pleased with God, cannot but be pleased with everything that declares his will, and as it is through the commandments his will is declared, they must take great pleasure in obeying his commandments. By the *"judgments of justice"* we understand the same precepts of the divine law, that are sometimes called judgments, sometimes the *"judgments of justice."* They are called judgments, inasmuch as they are certain opinions judged by God to be most perfect, or certain divine statutes and decrees; they are called justices, as being the rules containing justice; and, finally, they are called the judgments of justice, as being most just judgments and decrees. Thus, the meaning of the verse is, I will praise you with an upright heart, because I am persuaded that your laws are most just, and should be most faithfully observed; all of which I acknowledge proceeds not from me, but from thy grace.

8. This is the conclusion of the first octave, if we may so call the eight verses composing the divisions of the Psalm, and indicated by the letters of the Hebrew alphabet, for which division no satisfactory reason can be assigned; The meaning is, Whereas the observance of your law tends to the happiness of those who keep it, and whereas it has been proposed by you, the supreme legislator, and its observance most strictly ordered, *"I will keep thy justifications;"* I determined and resolved with all my strength to keep them; but do you, on your part, withhold not your grace and your assistance, without which I can do nothing; and if, perchance, in your justice, you shall have to desert me for a while, so that I may feel my own weakness, and learn to fly to thee, and to confide in thee, do not, at all events, *"utterly forsake me,"* that is, altogether and forever.

BETH

9. Having praised the law of God, by reason of its object and of its author, he now praises it by reason of the advantage of it to the person to whom it is given. And as nobody needs the law more than one beginning the world,

such as a young man, he speaks in particular of such. The young man needs the law of God, first, because it is in such persons the law of the members is strongest; secondly, because they have not yet learned prudence by experience; thirdly, as it is of the utmost consequence to a traveler to strike upon the right path in the beginning of his journey, as it may save him the labor of retracing his steps, and beginning it over again; thus, it is of the highest importance to the young man, who means to preserve his innocence, to accustom himself in early life to the observance of the commandments. *"It is good for a man when he hath borne the yoke from his youth,"* says Jeremias. Who are we to understand by *"a young man?"* I don't imagine David means such a young man as the prodigal, for such a one would need the grace of repentance to correct such faults, and a knowledge or observance of the latter would not suffice; nor do I think that he speaks of a young man renovated by grace, as opposed to an old man; for there is question here of the correction of errors, which are not supposed to be found in one renovated. I imagine, then, that David speaks of a young man, in the plain acceptation of the words, who requires a remedy against the natural impulses: of corrupt nature, *"that is prone to evil from his youth."*—*"By what doth a young man correct his way?"* By what means, manner, or art doth a young man correct his way? that is, his actions, or his life, corrupted by natural deprivation through original sin, and prone to evil. He answers, *"by observing thy words;"* for, he that from his youth has been accustomed to fear God, and, under the influence of such holy fear, to observe God's words, that is, his divine laws, will, undoubtedly, avoid many errors. Take, for example, Tobias the younger, whom his father *"taught from his infancy to fear God, and to abstain from all sin."*

10. David, influenced by such advantages, now asks God for grace to observe his commandments, decides firmly on observing them, and teaches us by his example to do the same, and first assigns a reason, the very one assigned in the Gospel, *"Seek, and you shall find."*—*"Everyone that seeketh findeth,"* why he should be heard. *"With my whole heart have I sought after thee."* Such is the reason he assigns for his being heard, for having sought after God with his whole heart, that is, for having asked his grace, for having desired to please him, and to carry out his will; a truly wonderful petition, as if God, who commanded his *"commandments"* to be kept most *"diligently,"* could wish to repel anyone from observing them. This mode of speaking, however, only implies the necessity of grace, a thing known to those only, who are desirous of observing the commandments, while they are conscious of their own weakness.

11-12. Another reason for his being heard, and a fresh petition for grace to keep his law; and the reason is, his great desire to avoid sin, and thus to keep the law. *"Thy words have I hidden in my heart."* I have placed your words, that is, your law, in the inmost recesses of my heart, so that I may never forget them; and my object in doing so was, *"that I may not sin against thee;"* thus, my desire of avoiding sin makes me wish I should never forget God's law; and, for fear I should possibly forget it, I have hidden it in the recesses of my heart, so that nothing can possibly wrest it from me. Having thus premised his reason for being heard, he presents the petition, *"Blessed art thou, O Lord, teach me thy justifications."* The words, *"teach me,"* as we observed on the seventh verse, convey more than the simple imparting of knowledge, for he said before he had such, when he said he hid God's words in his heart; and in verse seven he said he *"had learned the judgments of his justice;"* it includes grace to observe his law. God teaches his justifications when he, through his grace, causes one to delight in his law, and fully persuades one to wish to keep it exactly. The words, *"Blessed art thou,"* contain another argument for his being heard. It means, Do, O Lord, who art blessed by all created things, for you fill all things with your blessing, teach me your justifications. *"For the lawgiver shall give a blessing."* Thus God is blessed, and he in turn blesses; he is blessed when he is praised, and he blesses when he pours down his favors.

13-16. In those four verses he expresses his love for God's law, possibly by reason of his having got that benediction of the lawgiver, that he had just asked for. He says he has the law of God in his mouth, his will, his understanding, and his memory, and thus, in every part of his soul. As to his mouth he says, *"With my lips I have pronounced all the judgments of thy mouth."* I have constantly spoken of, and constantly preached, your commandments to all who may choose to hear them; *"judgments,"* here, mean commandments, and he adds, *"of thy mouth,"* to remind us they are not the precepts of man, but of God, having been declared by his mouth. In regard of his will, he says, *"I have been delighted in the way of thy testimonies, as in all riches."* I have taken a great delight in walking in the way of thy testimonies, as misers take in amassing riches. Great and rare is such affection, when man, in general, for a very trifling lucre, is wont to despise all God's commandments. As to his understanding or reflection he says, *"I will meditate on thy commandments: I will consider thy ways."* I will be constantly occupied in meditation and turning over in my mind all you have commanded or prohibited; and, as regards another affection of the heart, he says, *"I will think of thy justifications."* The Hebrew here implies that he will be delighted in chanting them. Having previously said that *"I have been delighted in the way of thy testimonies, as in all riches."* Where his delight seems to arise from the utility of the subject, he now says that he will be delighted with them by reason of the pleasure to be derived from them, just as the law of the Lord is compared in Psalm 18, to gold and to honey, as being both useful and agreeable. The meaning of the passage, then, is, *"I will think of thy justifications;"* I will occupy myself in chanting the praises of your commandments, in order to delight myself, as I would with sweet and pleasant songs. He now ultimately comes to the memory, saying, *"I will not forget thy words;"* because, by frequent meditation on them, and pleasing chant of them, I cannot possibly forget *"thy words,"* or your law. Hence, we infer that to those who have the benediction of the lawgiver, that is, the spirit of true charity, the law of the Lord is neither heavy nor severe, but that it is, as the Lord himself said, *"a sweet yoke and a light burden."*

Gimel.

17. In the next octave he enumerates the obstacles to the observance of the law, and prays for their removal out of his way. Death of the soul is the first obstacle, for men that are dead cannot observe the commandments of life as they ought, so as to obtain eternal life; and David, even if he could hope to consider himself as one of the living, still, *"as no one knoweth whether he is worthy of love or hatred,"* and, as he assumed the person of the sinner, he, therefore, for himself, or for them, prays and says, *"Give bountifully to thy servant, enliven me; and I shall keep thy words;"* that is to say, Give your servant, should he chance to be dead in sins, spiritual life, and then he will be able *"to keep thy words."*

18. The passions of the soul, such as love, fear, desire, anger, and similar affections form the second obstacle, and often prevent men from coming to right conclusions. Concerning them, he says, *"Open thou my eyes."* Remove, by the infusion of your light, the veil of passion from my intellectual visions with which, when so purified, *"I will consider the wondrous things of thy law,"* the wonderful justice, the wonderful wisdom, the wonderful advantages, and all the other wonderful things that shine forth in thy law.

19. The third obstacle lies in this pilgrimage of ours here below, for while we are here pilgrims, we must needs be earthly and carnal, while *"the law is spiritual."* If God, then, through his grace, will not make us spiritual, we cannot observe a spiritual law. *"I am a sojourner on the earth,"* an earthly animal man, living on the earth, while I am in exile from my country; and, therefore, I ask, *"that thou hide not thy commandments from me;"* that is, that you may, through your grace, make me fit to receive your commandments.

20. The fourth obstacle is imperfection. The perfect, who love God and his law with their whole heart, and do good from the pure love of it, are very rare indeed. Very many have the best intentions, but there they stop. The prophet, then, speaking as if he were one of such, says, *"My soul hath coveted to long for thy justifications at all times."* He dare not say, My soul hath coveted to observe your commandments, but, conscious of his infirmity, he says,

"*It hath coveted to long for,*" and this very acknowledgment of imperfection is a regular petition for that perfection which God grants, when he makes one ardently long to observe his commandments.

21. The fifth and greatest obstacle of all is pride, that prevents man from submitting his neck to the yoke, but which David seems to think has no place in him, or in anyone like him, but solely in God's enemies; thus, without any more ado, he simply execrates it. "*Thou hast rebuked the proud,*" who, from pure contempt, did not observe your commandments. Lucifer, for instance, hurled by God's rebuke to hell, with such violence as to have the Lord himself say of him, "*I saw Satan as lightning falling from heaven.*" Adam, too, whose pride, in wishing to become equal to God, led him to disobey God, was rebuked by him, and bore the sentence of death for himself and for the whole human race. Finally, God will, on the last day administer a dreadful rebuke to all the wicked; and, therefore, the prophet adds, "*They are accursed who decline from thy commandments,*" to wit, those who decline especially through pride and contempt of the legislator, for such will be told specially, "*Go ye cursed into everlasting fire.*"

22-23. The proud not only refuse to obey God, but they even despise and insult those who obey him; but such insolence ultimately reverts on themselves, as David here predicts; for this, like other similar expressions in the Psalms, though in the form of an imprecation, is really a prediction. He, therefore, says, "*Remove from me reproach and contempt;*" the time will come when you will remove both from me, and cast them back on the proud who disobey you; "*because I have sought after thy testimonies,*" which they despised looking after. In the next verse he assigns a reason for this; it is, "*For princes sat and spoke against me; but thy servant was employed in thy justifications.*" Proud princes, sitting on their thrones, presiding at their councils, or luxuriating in their riches and their power, "*spoke against me;*" reproached me with obeying God's commands; "*but thy servant was employed in thy justifications;*" regardless of their threats or their reproaches, I was entirely wrapt up in the consideration, the announcement, and the carrying out of your justifications.

24. An explanation of "*I was employed in thy justifications;*" for he says they were a sweet consolation to him in his troubles, and a faithful counsellor in his doubts.

Daleth

25. In the next eight verses David still assumes the person of one imperfect, who is kept back by the concupiscence of the flesh from the perfect observance of the commandments, and asks for grace and help to observe them. "*My soul hath cleaved to the pavement;*" to the groveling things of this world; "*quicken me according to thy word;*" grant that I may lead a life agreeable to

your law; for, by my love for the things of this world I am become a carnal man; but, if I shall live according to your law, which is a spiritual one, I shall adhere to God, and become one spirit with him. St. Augustine observes that, at present, the soul adheres to the flesh, or to earth, and thus becomes carnal, or earthly, and thus prevented from observing the law to perfection; but, after the resurrection in glory, the flesh will adhere to the soul, and the soul to God; and thus the flesh will then become spiritualized, will, to a certain extent, be deified, will observe the law to the fullest extent, without any trouble; or rather, will need no law, when it will carry out everything ordained by the law to the letter.

26. He makes a further acknowledgment of his own misery, and again asks for grace. *"I have declared my ways;"* I have not been ashamed to acknowledge my bad acts, I have openly avowed them; *"and thou hast heard me,"* and spared me with your usual mercy: *"teach me thy justifications;"* now that I am reconciled, I further beg of you to teach me thy justifications; that is, to make me keep your commandments; for, as we observed before, the word *"teaching,"* in this Psalm, implies more than imparting knowledge; it unites the being persuaded to do the thing so taught.

27. Being very desirous of advancing in the way of the Lord, he becomes more urgent again in praying to God for light. *"Make me to understand the way of thy justifications."* Tell me what your commandments mean, how I should walk in your law; *"and I shall be exercised in thy wondrous works;"* I will be entirely taken up in putting your precepts into practice, precepts so wonderful as to appear nigh impossible of observance; such as, *"Thou shalt love God with thy whole heart;"* and, *"Thou shalt not covet;" "Thou shalt love thy enemy;"* and the like.

28. He comes again to acknowledge the infirmity of his flesh, and to ask for mercy; for, in this our pilgrimage, rarely will anyone be found not to relax at some time or another, and become drowsy and more tepid from the constant struggle between the spirit and the flesh. *"My soul hath slumbered through heaviness;"* while I am tired of the labor I have to undergo in the rebellion of the flesh against the spirit. *"Strengthen thou me in thy words."* Strengthen me while I endeavor to keep your commandments, by the fervor of your grace, through which I may be able to persevere.

29. A copious explanation of the expression, *"strengthen me,"* in the previous verse *"Remove from me the way of iniquity;"* grant, through your grace, that I may keep far away from the way of iniquity, from the path of sin I had just entered on, *"by slumbering, through heaviness;" "and out of thy law have mercy on me;"* in your mercy, cause that I may tread in the path of your law, as the Hebrew clearly indicates.

30. He hitherto acknowledged his own inherent wretchedness; he now, in these verses, tells what the mercy of God may effect, as if he said, Hitherto I have chosen the path of falsehood, but, through that mercy, in which, *"out of thy love, thou hast mercy on me,"* now *"I have chosen the way of truth,"* have seriously proposed to walk in the true way, the way of thy commandments; and, through your mercy, *"I have not forgotten thy judgments;"* that is, thy commandments, however vehemently *"the flesh may lust against the spirit."*

31. Of myself, *"I have cleaved to the pavement,"* but, through your mercy, I have stuck to thy testimonies; and though, in my flesh, I am a slave to the law of sin, in my soul I am a servant to your law, and, therefore, *"put me not to shame,"* to which I must come, if deprived of your help.

32. Of myself, *"I have slumbered through heaviness,"* but, through your mercy, *"I have run the way of thy commandments;"* I have observed them with delight, with readiness, with alacrity, *"when thou didst enlarge my heart"* by the infusion of your love, which makes *"your yoke sweet and your burden light."*

He

33. In the next eight verses he asks, in a certain order, first, for a desire of observing the law; secondly, for light to understand it; thirdly, for grace to observe it; and fourthly, for the removal of all obstacles thereto. In this very long Psalm David, for the purpose of touching the affections, and of guarding against tedium, repeats the same matter frequently, but in different phraseology. The meaning of this verse is, Grant, O Lord, that I may desire to keep no other law than yours. *"Set before me for a law the way of thy justifications, O Lord;"* that is, put a desire for your law alone in my heart. Two questions arise, how can he ask for a law when the law was already given? second, why does the just man ask for a law when the Apostle says, *"The law is not made for the just man?"* The prophet does not absolutely ask for a law, but he asks that the law of sin, or of the world, or of the flesh, may not please him, but the law of God alone; and, through God's grace, he desires that it alone should find a place in his heart, his desires, and his affections, and, therefore, he adds, *"and I will always seek after it;"* which means, if, through your grace, I shall look for it alone, I will never do anything but what is commanded by it.

34. After having asked for a desire or affection for the law, he also asks far understanding; that he may rightly comprehend it, and inquire into its utility, excellence, and other advantages, so that he may *"keep it with my whole heart;"* thereby implying that it was not through curiosity, but for its better observance, that he seeks to understand the law.

35. He now, in the third place, asks for grace to observe the law. *"Lead me in the path of thy commandments;"* make me observe them. They are termed *"the paths,"* because paths are narrow, short, straight, clean passages for people on foot only, and not for horses and carriages; and such is the way of the Lord, as compared with that of the flesh and of the world, all the ways of which are broad, filthy, and crooked, trodden by the brute beasts, the type of carnal, animal man. He assigns a reason for being heard when he says, *"For this same I have desired;"* because, through God's grace, I have chosen this path, and desired to walk in it, and it is only meet that he who gives the will should give the grace to accomplish, as St. Paul says, *"Who worketh in you both to will and to accomplish."*

36. This verse is nearly a repetition of the first of this octave. In that verse he prayed for affection to the law of God, in this he prays for the exclusion of avarice, which is a great obstacle to such affection. *"Incline my heart unto thy testimonies."* Pour an abundant shower of grace into my heart, so as to incline to the observance of thy law, *"and not to covetousness;"* do not incline my heart to avarice. God is said to incline one to evil when, by the withdrawal of his grace, he allows him to incline to evil; and the Scripture, in using such language, merely means to show the power of God's grace; for God, strictly speaking, cannot incline anyone to evil. Similar expressions frequently occur in the Scriptures; thus, in Romans, where it is said, *"God delivereth them unto a reprobate sense,"* and in Isaias; *"Why hast thou caused us to stray from thy way?"*

37. This verse corresponds with the second in this division, for in that he asked for the gift of understanding, to reflect upon the law; here he asks, that his mind's eye may not be averted from the law to vanity. *"Turn away thy eyes that they may not behold vanity,"* that I may not be taken up in reflecting on the things of this world, that are all vanity, but rather make me apply myself entirely to your laws; and so *"quicken me in thy way,"* enliven, refresh, and preserve me, while I walk in thy way, the way of thy commandments.

38. Through a holy fear of you, establish, confirm, and so ground your law in thy servant, that it may remain and persevere most firmly with him. This verse corresponds with the third in this section, in which he asks for grace to observe the law, and here he asks for the grace of perseverance.

39. The not having persevered in the observance of the law of God, when it is not only our own advantage to have done so, but is also sweet and pleasant to observe it, will be a great reproach on the day of judgment, as it is at present in the sight of the Angels; and, therefore, having asked for the grace of perseverance, he assigns a reason for such request; and that is, his fear of the reproach that will follow those who will not persevere. *"Turn away thy reproach which I have apprehended,"* that I feared, should I not persevere in the observance of your law, that is so good in itself.

40. He concludes the petitions of this section by saying, that it is now sufficiently clear that he heartily desires to observe the commandments.

"Behold, I have longed after thy precepts;" behold how evident it is that I have seriously desired to observe them; and, therefore, *"quicken me,"* increase and preserve my spiritual life *"in thy justice,"* in thy commandments; that is, in the observance of them, for the *"just man is still made more just"* so long as he observes them.

Vau

41. In the commencement of the next eight verses the prophet begs for God's mercy; and in the remaining verses of it explains the effect of his mercy, as far as they regard the observance of God's law, which is the whole scope and object of the Psalm. He, therefore, says, *"Let thy mercy come upon me,"* let your grace and mercy descend from on high upon me; and he tells in what that mercy consists, when he adds, *"thy salvation according to thy word;"* that is to say, thy salvation, or thy mercy that saves the soul, *"according to thy word,"* the promise you made of mercy and salvation to those that trust in thee.

42. And when your mercy, according to your promise, shall have come upon me, I will not fear my enemies when they will reproach me with having feared God in vain, for *"so shall I answer them,"* in a manner they will not be able to contradict, *"that I have trusted in thy words,"* because you can keep your promise, by reason of your omnipotence, and you wish to keep it, by reason of your goodness.

43. I pray that you *"take not the word of truth,"* in which I glory over those who reproach me, *"out of my mouth;"* that is to say, that you may not, by depriving me of your grace, so enervate me that I may not have the courage to speak out, that you may not close the mouth of one who has such confidence in you, and so ready to record your promises; or if you choose to withdraw your grace for awhile, in order to prove me, yet do not withdraw it *"utterly,"* altogether, forever, *"for in thy words I have hoped exceedingly,"* for I have had the greatest confidence in your justice and faithfulness.

44. He now tells us the effect of the mercy that so heals the soul, and that is the perpetual observance of God's law.

45-48. In these four verses he explains, in what the observance of the law consists; a thing he promised, when he said, in the fourth verse of this division, that he would observe God's law in his heart, in his words, in his mind, and in his acts; and the prophet seems, all at once, as having been heard, to have changed his mode of speaking, for he says, *"And I walked at large."* When God's mercy visited me, I did not walk in the narrow ways of fear, but in the wide ones of love; that is to say, I observed the law willingly, joyfully, with all the affections of my heart, *"because I have sought after thy commandments"* as a thing of great value, and most important to come at; *"and I spoke"* openly and fearlessly on the justice of your most holy law, even *"before kings, and I was not ashamed;"* and I constantly turned the law in my mind, and made its mysteries the subject of my meditation, *"and I lifted up my hands,"* to carry out his high and sublime commands; that is, his extremely perfect and arduous commands. Finally, in all manner of ways, in heart, mind, word, and deed, *"I was exercised in thy justifications."*

Zain

To the next eight verses the prophet celebrates the eternal reward promised by God to those who observe his law; and says that it induced him to observe the law, that it consoled him in trouble, and made him grieve for the prevarication of the wicked.

49. God is not subject to forgetfulness, nor to fickleness, nor to retracting what he says; but he is, by a figure of speech, said to forget when he defers the execution of a promise, as if he had altogether forgotten it. Now, that he does designedly; and, though determined on carrying out his decrees, he still wishes his faithful servants to ask him to carry them out; and thus, prayer becomes one of the means through which God decreed to fulfill his promises. David, then, in his own person, and of the faithful in general, prays to God, saying, *"Be thou mindful of thy word;"* that is, of thy promise *"in which thou hast given me hope,"* when you said to Abraham, and through him to all his children, *"Walk before me, and be perfect;"* I will be *"thy reward exceedingly great."*

50. The first word in the verse, *"This,"* does not refer to the hope alluded to in the preceding verse; it refers to the concluding portion of this verse, as is evident from the Hebrew; and the meaning of the whole verse is, one thing was a source of great comfort to me in my humiliation, or my affliction, that *"your word,"* meaning your promise, *"hath enlivened me;"* gave me life and spirit, strengthened and fortified me.

51. The life and vigor infused into me by your promise caused me *"not to decline from thy law,"* even though *"the proud did iniquitously altogether;"* doing all in their power, through their jeerings at me, to deter me from its observance.

52. While I was thus humbled and scoffed at, *"I remembered the judgments of old,"* by virtue of which, from time immemorial, you exalted the humble, and depressed the proud; conferring great rewards on those who observed your law, and inflicting signal punishment on those who transgressed it; and from such reflections I derived the greatest consolation in my affliction; *"I was comforted."*

53. The same hope of so great a reward caused me to have the greatest feeling for those sinners, who, by the dereliction of your law, are deprived of so much happiness; and such was the effect of it upon me that it actually induced fits of fainting. Great must have been the love that caused one to faint on beholding the pitiable condition of another.

54. The wicked transgressed the law, deeming it an unpleasant thing to observe it; but to me, aware, as I was, of the rewards in store for those who observe it, *"thy justifications"* were as agreeable as so many sweet and pleasant songs.

55. The happy hope of such promises not only supported me through the day; but even *"in the night I have remembered thy name;"* and, through my affection for it, I persevered, and have thus *"kept thy law."*

56. *"This,"* that is to say, my having reflected on God's promises, and drawn so much hope from them, and the other advantages that followed, *"happened to me, because I sought after thy justifications;"* for the prophet wishes, in this Psalm, which is entirely devoted to praising the law, to attribute everything to a diligent study and love of the law, that he may thus stimulate man to reflect on it, and to observe it.

Heth

57. In the commencement of these eight verses, he lays down the proposition, *"the Lord is my portion;"* and argues from that that he should have the desire of observing his law most faithfully, and that he must constantly pray to God for grace thereto, in spite of all obstacles. *"O Lord, my portion;"* as he says in Psalm 15, *"The Lord is the part of my inheritance;"* and in Psalm 72, *"God that is my portion forever;"* and in Lam. 3, *"The Lord is my portion."* Happy soul that could say from his heart, *"The Lord is my portion,"* or, in other words, I renounce all things created, I seek for no right in them; let who will have them, you, O Lord, suffice for me; I seek for nothing else now, nor will I ever seek for anything else; and, with the view of getting possession of you at one time or other, I have determined to study your will alone; I, therefore, *"have said,"* I resolved, I firmly proposed, *"to keep your law"* because I know you will not stoop to be the portion of those who will not observe it.

58. He said he was determined to observe God's law; but, as man cannot do so without God's assistance, he, therefore, *"entreats the face of the Lord with all his heart,"* and says, *"Have mercy on me according to thy word;"* as you promised it, *"have mercy on me,"* that, through your assistance, I may accomplish what I have decided on through your inspiration.

59. It won't do to pray to God; we must cooperate with his grace; and, therefore, the prophet, having prayed to God, adds, *"I have thought on my ways,"* as to whether they were right or wrong, whether they were agreeable to God's laws or not; and, *"I turned my feet unto thy testimonies;"* I turned my affections from the law of the flesh and of sin to your law, O Lord, it being exclusively the right way.

60. I not only determined to observe your law, but *"I am ready"* to make a beginning in the good work, and *"no trouble"* will retard me in prosecuting it.

61. Many a one, however, sought to keep me back and to confuse me, for *"the cords of the wicked,"* the snares, or the nets of various temptations, usually set by sinners, or by the evil spirits *"have encompassed me;"* but I have not forgotten thy law;" all the temptations could not make me forget your law, or prevent me from obeying it.

62. As you are my portion, O Lord, I devoted myself to the consideration of your law, not only by day, but even by night; nay, even in the very dead of the night, when silence reigns profound; for *"I rose at midnight to give praise to thee;"* to praise you for *"the judgments of thy justification,"* for your most just and wise commandments.

63. This, too, follows from the proposition he laid down originally, *"The Lord is my portion;"* for all who fear God and keep his commandments are united as living members in one body, by a bond of love that cries out, *"the Lord is my portion;"* and thus, each member *"is partaker with all,"* for love makes all things common; and, thus, *"If one member suffer anything, all the members suffer with it; or if one member glory, all the members rejoice with it."* 1 Cor. 12.

64. I am, certainly, *"a partaker with all them that fear thee,"* but, as all the inhabitants of the earth, good and bad, men and beasts, animate and inanimate things, are also partakers of your mercy, have mercy, then, on me, that you may *"teach me thy justifications,"* for the height of misery is the not knowing your law as they do who observe it. May your mercy ward off this misery from me, it being the only thing I covet, the only object of my desire, and that, by reason of your being *"my portion, O Lord."*

TETH

65-66. In these eight verses the prophet asks for three gifts necessary for observing the precepts of the Lord, and proves the necessity of them from their effects; first saying, by way of a preface, *"Thou hast done well with thy servant, O Lord;"* you have shown much sweetness, mildness, and kindness to your servant, *"according to thy word;"* agreeable to your promise. He then asks, *"Teach me goodness, and discipline, and knowledge;"* as well as you have displayed your goodness in my regard, teach me the same goodness or sweetness to my neighbor, that I may not wish to hurt, deceive, or defraud anyone; teach me also *"discipline,"* that is, prudence, to guard against the deceiver and the fraudulent, so that I may have the sweetness and the mildness of the dove, without being devoid of the counsel and the prudence of the serpent. Next to them I ask for *"knowledge,"* that I may know the mysteries of your law; which knowledge, when not accompanied by goodness and discipline, only inflates, but when savored by them, is of the greatest value; *"For I have delivered thy commandments,"* firmly believed in your promises;

or believed your commands to be divine, and therefore deserving of the strictest observance. How many seek for knowledge and for discipline, caring very little for goodness; not so with the prophet, guided by the Holy Spirit, who asks first for goodness, then for the others.

67-68. He explains the necessity of the three gifts aforesaid, stating he had good reason for asking for them, inasmuch as it was through the want of them he transgressed, and for his transgressions was humbled by God in his justice. *"Before I was humbled,"* by being visited with tribulations, *"I offended,"* through ignorance; *"therefore have I kept thy word,"* the promise I made of thenceforward observing your law more attentively; but do *"thou who art good,"* that is, sweet and kind, *"in thy goodness,"* in conformity with your mildness, *"teach me thy justifications,"* that I may sin no more.

69-70. He now explains the necessity of the second gift, discipline, or prudence. *"The iniquity of the proud hath been multiplied;"* proud sinners told me lies without end, to try and make me break your law; hence the necessity for prudence, through which *"I will seek thy commandments with my whole heart." "Their heart is curdled like milk;"* those proud sinners have a heart hard as cheese formed of curdled milk, and I, therefore, dismissed them, and *"have meditated on thy law."*

71-72. From the abundance of the first gift that had been conferred on him, he now declares, *"It is good for me that thou hast humbled me,"* no one but one truly meek and humble of heart, and thus truly good, and who from experience could form an opinion of what is good, could give expression to such a sentiment. For he that is truly good looks upon any humiliation, arising from tribulation, as a great good, inasmuch as it leads to a better observance of God's law, the value of which he expresses, when he says, *"The law of thy mouth is good to me above thousands of gold and silver,"* and so it is, because through the observance of the law we acquire life everlasting, to which no treasures can be compared.

Jod

73. In the next eight verses he assigns many reasons for asking the grace to observe the law; and first, from the fact of his being one of God's creatures, and, therefore, owing him implicit obedience. *"Thy hands have made me and formed me."* Thy power and wisdom, like a pair of hands, *"made me,"* when I had no existence, *"and formed me,"* by working, out of the shapeless mass, my members and my senses, or made me as to my soul, and formed me as to my body. Being thus entirely yours, and owing you the most profound obedience, I ask you *"to give me understanding and I will learn thy commandments,"* that I may not only know them but practice them.

74. The second reason, derived from the edification of the neighbor, *"they that fear thee shall see me"* keeping your commandments, *"and shall be glad,"*

because they shall see that I have *"greatly hoped in thy words,"* in the promises contained in your law.

75. Reason the third, his having confessed his faults. *"I know, O Lord, that thy judgments are equity,"* that your judgments are essentially just, and if *"you have humbled me,"* by depriving me of your grace, I know you have done so *"in truth,"* because I deserved it, I therefore complain not of your justice, but I throw myself on your mercy, saying—

76. The comfort he asks for is grace to observe the law; for he who grieves for his humiliation, by reason of having been deprived of grace, and thus having fallen into sin, will get great consolation, if a profusion of grace will enable him to observe God's laws perfectly and thoroughly.

77. Having asked for the grace of observing the law, that he may draw comfort therefrom, he now tells us in what that comfort he so looks for consists. *"Let thy tender mercies come to me and I shall live."* Have mercy on me, according to the multitude of your tender mercies, that I may get hold of the true life, that which alone is the happy and eternal life. St. Augustine pertinently observes, that he uses the word *"live"* without any addition, because wherever the word of life is thus used, it means eternal life; thus, *"in him was life;"* and again, *"unto the resurrection of life." "If thou wilt enter into life."*—*"For thy law is my meditation;"* here is the reason why he thus ventures to ask for God's mercies, for it is only meet that God should regard one who is constantly occupied in meditating on his law.

78. The fourth reason assigned for getting grace to observe the law, is derived from the confusion it will prove to the wicked, just as the second reason was derived from the satisfaction it would afford to the just. *"Let the proud be ashamed."* Grant me grace to observe your law to the letter, that those proud sinners, who by their persecutions and oppressions seek to make others follow their example, on seeing me, may be thus confounded and ashamed; and while they are thus confounded and ashamed, I will, with increased zeal and vigor, *"be employed in thy commandments,"* in meditating on them and observing them.

79. He now exhorts the pious, if there be any such, who may have been deceived by the sinners, and began to regard them, to return to themselves and unite with him. *"Let those that fear thee and know thy testimonies,"* let all those who fear God, and understand his law, *"turn to me,"* and observe it with me.

80. He concludes by asking again for the grace he had so often asked for, to enable him to observe the commandments of God with a perfect heart,

Caph

81. In the next eight verses David introduces one desirous of observing the commandments, but suffering severely from temptation, and asking in the most pitiable terms for help from heaven. *"My soul hath fainted after thy salvation."* My desire of eternal salvation has been so great, that I have nearly fainted in consequence. *"And in thy word I have very much hoped;"* still your promises held out great hopes to me. Thus, while the delay to one's salvation makes one faint, the hope built on promise strengthens and supports.

82. What an extraordinary expression for the prophet to use, as if the eyes could hear or could speak! But the eyes, the ears, and the tongue of the interior are one and the same, for the intellect hears, sees, and speaks. *"My eyes have failed for thy word,"* my mind, reflecting on the promised help so long deferred, has failed through desire for it, just as the eyes of the body, when fixed for a long time on some one spot, in which they expect something or some person, grow dim and fail, *"saying: When wilt thou comfort me?"* those eyes of my interior, that have so failed from looking out so long, explain the cause of their defect, when they say, When shall we have that perfect consolation that we may no longer fear a relapse, or a violation of your holy law.

83. I had good reason for saying, *"When wilt thou comfort me?"* because I am as arid and as void of the dew of consoling grace, from despair and the pressure of temptation, as a bottle that would be put in the frost when the cold is severest; for then the leathern bottles shrivel up and harden. A similar expression occurs in Psalm 142, *"My soul is as earth without water unto thee."* Yet, however I may labor under such aridity, *"I have not forgotten thy justifications;"* thy commandments.

84. He urges the same petition, praying for consolation, and deliverance from temptation. *"How many are the days of thy servant,"* during which this affliction is to last? when will there be an end to the days of misery and temptation? *"When wilt thou execute judgment on them that persecute me?"* When will you judge and condemn those that persecute and tempt me, that my persecution may cease on their condemnation? He makes no curious inquiries as to the number of the days of his life, or of those of the world, he merely expresses his desire of life everlasting, when all the wicked, consigned to hell, shall cease to harass the just, who, in the enjoyment of supreme and everlasting peace, will serve God in justice and holiness without any fear of their falling from it.

85. The special reason why he desires to be freed from the company of the wicked is, because they always tempt the pious, by relating the pleasures of the world, which are nothing but fables, filthy, fleeting pleasures, more fallacious than real—nothing like the round and solid pleasure that always flows from a pious observance of the law of the Lord.

86. Having said, *"But not as thy law,"* he now says, *"All thy statutes are truth;"* are full of promises, abounding in truth, and, therefore, confer pleasure of the truest sort on those that observe your law. The wicked, therefore, in relating their falsehoods, have *"persecuted me unjustly;"* and, therefore, *"do thou help me"* against their false machinations.

87. So grievously did these sinners, who, with their sweet words, sought to seduce me, press their persecutions, *"that they almost made an end of me on earth;"* still they did not succeed; for *"I have not forgotten thy commandments."*

88. He returns to the first petition, and concludes this division by saying, *"Quicken thou me according to thy mercy,"* in a happy and everlasting life; and then, at length, I will most perfectly *"keep the testimonies of thy mouth;"* thy divine law.

LAMED

89-91. In the next eight verses the prophet argues, from the certainty of God's promises, in exhorting to the observance of his law, which promises so much, both in this and the next life. *"Forever, O Lord, thy word,"* that is, thy promise, *"standeth firm in heaven;"* for, though it may not seem to stand firm on earth, when we see the just depressed, and the wicked exalted, still it stands quite firm in heaven; for God will certainly carry out anything he promised. He will cause the brief tribulation of the just to be turned into everlasting joy; and the short glory of the wicked to be turned into eternal disgrace and punishment. He repeats, or rather explains, the same idea when he adds, *"Thy truth unto all generations;"* it too, stands firm. So does the earth; so do the days; all observe your laws and regulations; and the reason is, *"for all things serve thee;"* and, therefore, in due time it will be seen how you will stand by your promise to the just.

92. Had I not been daily meditating on your law, when I learned the truth of your promises, I, possibly, overcome by temptation, would have *"perished in my abjection."*

93. Strengthened by meditation on the promises that are made in the law, I now confidently assert that *"Thy justifications will I never forget; for by them,"* that is, by having observed them, *"thou hast given me life,"* by an increase of the life of grace and a promise of the life of glory.

94. It is written in Psalm 23, *"The earth is the Lord's and the fullness thereof: the world and all they that dwell therein;"* but I am peculiarly thine, because I avow myself to be thine. I wish to be thine, and having resolved to be a slave to no passion, I wish to have no other Lord; and, therefore, I have a right to ask you to save me, to protect what belongs to you, *"For I have sought thy justifications."* And as I do belong to you, and am your servant alone, I ask for nothing but your commands, that I may obey them. Few, indeed, are they who can say, *"I am thine;"* for few are they whose affections are fixed on God alone.

95. It was not without reason that I said, *"Save thou me,"* because *"the wicked have waited for me"* in a place convenient for laying hold on me, to induce me to yield to temptation, and thus *"destroy me;"* but, through the assistance of your grace, *"I have understood thy testimonies."* I understood what the law commanded, promised, and threatened under such circumstances.

96. *"Having understood thy testimonies,"* that is, thy law, *"I have seen an end of all perfection;"* that is, that the whole perfection of this life consisted *"in thy commandment,"* in that precept of love that *"is exceedingly broad,"* comprehending, as it does, all the commandments, and extending to God, all the Angels, all mankind, not excluding even our enemies.

Mem

97. In the next eight verses he again praises the law, by reason of the various advantages, as well as pleasures, that it brings with it. He first declares the love he entertains for the law, and tells us why, and enumerates its advantages. *"O, how have I loved thy law."* What an ardent love have I not had for it; and, as constant conversation with the beloved is a sign of one's love, *"it is my meditation the whole day."* I think of nothing, speak of nothing, care for nothing but it.

98. The first advantage of the law is, that when a man reflects seriously on it, and observes it faithfully, it directs him what, how, when, and where he ought to speak and to do, or to be silent and take no action; a wisdom that is not enjoyed by the transgressors of the law, who have no regard for a rule, much in keeping with the first principles of rectitude. He, therefore, says, *"through thy commandment thou hast made me wiser than my enemies."* By reflecting daily on thy commandments I have been made much wiser then my enemies; *"for it is ever with me,"* always before my eyes, so that I can never forget it.

99-100. Another advantage of the law is its being productive not only of prudence, but also of wisdom; and thus David, by constant meditation on God's law, became much more learned than those who taught him the law; and got more understanding than those who were much more advanced in years.

101-102. The third advantage of God's law is, that it causes us to avoid many sins. *"I have restrained my feet from every evil way."* I took care not to walk in the paths of the wicked, who have no law but their own desires, the law of sin and of the flesh, and that, in order that *"I may keep thy words,"* or your law, that pointed out a path in the very opposite direction; because *"I have not declined from thy judgments,"* from your commandments, full of justice, *"because thou hast set me a law;"* because you, my God, have given me said holy law.

103. The fourth advantage is, that God's law confers extreme happiness on those that observe it; for *"thy words,"* that is, God's commandments, are sweeter to the palate of the soul than honey is to that of the body. Nothing can be sweeter than a good conscience, and the hope of everlasting happiness, derived from the observance of God's law.

104. He proves that he derived great pleasure from God's law, because it always creates an easy conscience, for *"by thy commandments I have had understanding;"* I have become prudent and wise through the lessons I got from your commandments. *"Therefore have I hated every way of iniquity;"* from the wisdom and prudence I acquired by constant meditation on the law, I not only abstained from sin, but I even got a thorough hatred of all sinful actions. Such hatred is a wonderful preservative of the purity and sanctity of the soul, and generates great confidence in God, which leads to joy unspeakable, to a peace and tranquillity far and away beyond all the treasures and pleasures of this world.

Nun

105. The prophet, in the next eight verses, praises the law of the Lord, by reason of its being of great use to us, and then promises that, no matter what trouble he may be in, he will observe it. A great advantage to us is that the law of the Lord is to us, while here below, like a lamp to one walking in the dark; for the law of sin, our own evil desires, either blinds entirely, or so darkens man's intellect, that he cannot distinguish what is truly good from what is truly bad; and thus, those who follow that law, that is, those who suffer themselves to be led away by their evil desires, tumble down various precipices; now, God's law dispels such darkness, and points out what is truly good, and truly bad; and, therefore, they who follow it stray not, are not moping their way, but proceed on the path that leads direct to their heavenly country. He, therefore, says, *"Thy word is a lamp to my feet;"* thy law is one, *"and a light to my paths,"* to guide me as I go along.

106. The law being a light, and, therefore, a most useful and valuable thing to have, the prophet *"swears and is determined,"* firmly resolved with himself, *"to keep"* the law, which he calls *"the judgment of thy justice;"* that is, his most just judgments.

107. *"I have been humbled;"* persecuted and harassed by reason of my observance of the law; for *"all who live piously in Christ Jesus shall suffer persecution;"* but do you, O Lord, *"quicken me;"* grant me, at last, that true life that will be free from all evils; *"according to thy word;"* according to the promise you made when you said, *"If thou wilt enter into life, keep the commandments."*

108. My having sworn and determined to observe the law, no matter under what amount of persecution, is the free offering of my mouth; I pray, therefore, that this free offering may be acceptable to thee, O Lord and as, of itself, it can have no such merit, *"make it acceptable, O Lord,"* by kindly condescending, in your grace, to approve of it; and that I may offer the sacrifice in due form, *"teach me thy judgments;"* teach me the perfect observance of your law.

109. The fact of my being in daily danger of my life, by reason of my observance of your law, is a proof how serious I was when I swore I would observe it, and how willingly I offered such a sacrifice. *"My soul is continually in my hands;"* I am in constant danger; for what we have in our hands may easily slip out of them, or be snatched out of them, unless one have a firm hold of it. Jephte makes use of a similar expression in Judges 12, *"I put my life in my own hands,"* to show in what a critical position he was placed; the same is said of David, *"And he put his life in his hand, and he slew the Philistine."*

110. I had just reason for saying, *"My soul is continually in my hands,"* because *"sinners have laid a snare for me,"* to take and to slay me; and still, however, *"I have not erred from thy precepts;"* strayed from thy commandments. Such was the case all the time Saul was trying to put David to death, who could have frequently put Saul to death, and thus delivered himself, had he not been afraid of offending God.

111. The reason for my not having *"erred from thy precepts"* was because *"I have purchased thy testimonies for an inheritance forever;"* that is, I have chosen your law as an everlasting inheritance, because it is most sweet and most agreeable to me, and the source of supreme joy and delight.

112. Now, the abundant reward that the observance of the law brings with it is the cause of such delight. *"I have inclined my heart to do thy justifications forever."* When the law of sin would drag me one way, and your law would seek to bring me the other way, *"I have inclined my heart,"* as I would a scale or a balance, to observe your law, and that *"for the reward,"* because I recollected life everlasting to be the reward promised to those who would observe your law.

Samech

113. In the next eight verses the prophet expresses his detestation of those who break the divine law, and proves how much opposed to them he is. St. Augustine observes that the prophet does not say here, *"I have hated iniquity; and loved thy law,"* one being directly opposed to the other; but he says, *"I have hated the unjust,"* to show that he not only hated iniquity, but those who are guilty of it as well; and again, that he does not say, *"I have hated the unjust, and loved the just;"* but *"I have loved thy law;"* to show that he hates the wicked only, inasmuch as they go against the law of God that he so loved. He, therefore, hates the unjust, not by reason of their nature, but by reason of their iniquity; as, on the other hand, he loved his enemies, and therefore, the unjust, not by reason of their iniquity, but by reason of their nature.

114. That I may not fear the wicked whom I hate, and that I may observe the law that I love, *"thou art my helper and protector;"* my helper in observing the law, and my protector in evading the persecution of my enemies. And I, in turn, *"have greatly hoped in thee,"* in the promises you made me.

115. One of the reasons why the prophet so hated the wicked was, because their presence interfered with his meditations, that required quiet and peace of mind. He wishes them, therefore, as he would so many troublesome wasps, to be off with themselves.

116. As well as I wish the malignant to depart, I wish you to approach me, that you may *"uphold me"* in thy bosom; *"according to thy word,"* agreeable to the promises you made me, and then, most truly, *"shall I live,"* when I shall be united to you, who art the life. And as I hope for so much, not through my own merits, but through your goodness, *"let me not be confounded in my expectation."*

117. He repeats the same idea in different language; *"Uphold me, and I shall live,"* and *"Help me, and I shall be saved,"* being the same; and the consequence of his being so helped will be, that he will thenceforward be always able to meditate on God's law without any impediment.

118. He now shows, that if he does hate the wicked and wishes they should keep away from him, he is only following God's example therein, who has a most thorough and most just execration of the wicked. *"Thou hast despised,"* as you would a thing of no value, *"all them that fall off from thy judgments;"* all the wicked who have abandoned the path of God's law; *"for their thought is unjust;"* because they think they ought not be subject to the law of God, and that they should set no value on it, one of the most impious ideas they could possibly entertain, since every creature is strictly bound to obey its Creator. Such were the notions of Lucifer, who instead of being subject to, sought to put himself on an equality with, his Creator. Such was the idea of our first parents, who desired to be like God. Such are the ideas of all proud people, who say in their hearts, *"Who is our Lord?"* It is such as those that God despises, and cares very little if thousands of them perish for all eternity, because the more value they set on themselves, the less will God set on them.

119. St. Augustine raises a serious question on this passage, as to how all sinners can be called prevaricators, whereas the Apostle says, *"For where there is no law, there is no transgression;"* and again, *"For whosoever have sinned without the law, shall perish without the law."* The answer is. The first text is to be understood of law in general, the second text is to be understood of the written law only; and, therefore, that all sinners must be reckoned prevaricators, because they all transgress the natural law that is written on their hearts. But why does the prophet say so? In order to show that sin, the greatest of all evils, arises only from transgression of the law. He adds, *"therefore have I loved thy testimonies."* I have loved your law in order to escape such an amount of misery.

120. He asks, finally, to be confirmed in the fear of God, that, through it, he may persevere in observing his law. *"Pierce thou,"* as if with a nail, *"my flesh with thy fear;"* my carnal desires, so that they cannot make any further commotion, as the Apostle says, *"And they who are of Christ have crucified their flesh with the vices and concupiscences." "For I am afraid of thy judgments;"* for I have begun to fear the dreadful punishments that your judgments threaten; and I, therefore, pray I may be so grounded in your holy fear that I may never be moved from it.

Ain

121. He asks, in the next octave, that he may be delivered from his calumniators, and for help to observe the law to perfection. *"I have done judgment and justice;"* I gave everyone his own, and it is, therefore, only meet that you *"give me not up to them that slander me."*

122. "I have done judgment and justice;" but, that I may always do it, and never fail in doing it, *"uphold thy servant unto good,"* by directing him, so that he may always relish what is good, and then, the consequence will be, that *"the proud will not calumniate me;"* for he that is well established *"unto good,"* and so made up that nothing but what is good and righteous will be agreeable to him, he will so persevere that he will have no reason for fearing *"the proud that calumniate him."*

123. He reasserts his having a most ardent desire for that perfect tendency to good, that will be enjoyed by the elect in eternity. *"My eyes have fainted"* from looking constantly with desire towards your salvation that is to come to us from heaven, *"and for the word of thy justice,"* and towards your most faithful promise. See 1st and 2nd verses of Caph.

124. He goes on with the prayer, begging that God may deal with him not according to his own merits, *"but according to thy mercy,"* which especially consists in teaching him *"thy justifications;"* that is, that he should impress him with a thorough conviction of the observance of God's law being a good thing, and thus teach him not so much the theory as the practice of it. This happens when God gives one a great amount of love, and not when he gives knowledge alone, which, without love, puffs up without edifying.

125. The asking for the same thing repeatedly is a proof of one's great desire for it. *"I am thy servant,"* and thus bound to execute your behests; therefore *"give me understanding,"* make me understand *"thy testimonies,"* that I may learn them perfectly. See first verse of Job.

126. It is time for you, O Lord, to pass judgment on, and punish the wicked, because *"they have dissipated thy law;"* they have not only violated it, but they have altogether dissipated it, by not observing a single particle of it.

127-128. As so many *"have dissipated thy law,"* and I see the most dreadful punishment in store for them in consequence, I am, therefore, on the other hand, the more smitten with a love for thy law, and I value it more than gold or precious stones; and I, therefore, not only loved it, but I did my best to observe it, for; *"therefore was I directed to all thy commandments."* I walked in the direct path of them, turning neither to the right nor to the left; nay, more, *"I have hated,"* and consequently turned away from *"all wicked ways,"* the whole law of the flesh and of sin.

PHE

129. The prophet again returns, in the next eight verses, to praise the law, and to ask for grace for its perfect observance. He, therefore, praises the law by reason of its being wonderful, and having, on that account, studied it diligently. But how does this not contradict the expression of the Lord himself, regarding the commandments in Deuteronomy? *"This commandment, that I command thee this day, is not above thee, nor far off from thee."* The answer is, that God's laws, whether moral, judicial, or ceremonial, are not wonderful, as regards the literal meaning of them, and they are quite clear and easily comprehended, and they who break them cannot plead ignorance, and so Moses affirms in the same chapter. But as regards the mystic meaning, especially of the ceremonial laws, they are wonderful and most obscure, foreshadowing, as they do, all the mysteries of the Christian religion, to which the prophet alludes here. With that, the decalogue that principally contains God's law, is wonderful for being written in such plain and intelligible language, though it contains, in the smallest possible space, all the principles of justice on which all the laws that ever have been, or will be made, are based. All other laws are innumerable, have filled, and are still filling, many large volumes, and yet they are all conclusions or inferences from the laws of the decalogue. Thus; as small seeds are wonderful by reason of their having within them the germs of large trees, so the decalogue is wonderful by reason of its essentially comprising all the laws of the world.

130. As he said that God's commandments were wonderful, he now adds, that if they be explained, either by the infusion of divine light, or by some learned teacher, they wonderfully enlighten the mind. Now, the law is declared or explained, when the mysteries indicated by the figures that are in the ceremonial law, are disclosed to us, when conclusions are drawn from the moral law, and, finally, when the decrees of the judicial law are applied to particular cases.

131. And I, as one of those little ones, *"opened my mouth,"* the mouth of my interior, by asking and praying, *"and panted,"* longed for the spirit of knowledge and piety, that I may understand and observe your commandments, for I longed both to understand and to observe them. The metaphor is taken from our natural respiration, for when we are worked hard, and nearly suffocated in consequence, we open our mouth and pant, on which we draw breath and get better.

132. In opening my mouth to pray, I said, *"Look thou upon me, and have mercy on me."* Look on me with an eye of pity, and have mercy on me, laboring under the load of your commandments, which, through my own strength, I am not able to keep, *"according to the judgment of them that love thy name."* Have the same mercy on me that you have on those friends of yours that truly love you.

133. You will have mercy on me, *"according to the judgment of them that love thy name;"* if you will *"direct my steps according to thy words;"* that is, if you will cause me, through your grace, to walk in the right way in the direction of your law; and thus, *"let no iniquity have dominion over me,"* let me do nothing that may cause me to be held a captive, for, as our Lord says, *"Whosoever committeth sin is the servant of sin."*

134. Direct my steps, then especially, when, confused by calumnies, there may be danger of straying from the right way, for *"Calumny troubleth the wise, and shall destroy the strength of his heart." "Redeem me from the calumnies of men."* Deliver me from their calumnies, that my mind being at rest, *"I may keep thy commandments."*

135. He now repeats, in different words, what he said in verse 132. *"Make thy face to shine upon thy servant."* For, as when the sun's light is obscured by the intervention of the clouds, we are deprived thereby of light and heat, thus, when God does not help us with his grace, he seems either to hide his face or to envelope it in darkness; and, on the contrary, when he illuminates us with the light of his grace, he seems to disperse the envious clouds, and to show the serenity of his face; he, therefore, says, *"Make thy face to shine,"* look upon me with a face of serenity, and by the infusion of your light teach me thy justifications; that is, the knowledge and the observance of your laws.

136. The number of prayers, so oft repeated, for the grace of observing the law, is a proof of the earnest desire David had to keep it; which he now proves from the deep sorrow he feels for having broken it, for he says it was not one or two tears that he shed, but floods of tears (which he calls waters) from his eyes, like so many gushing fountains, *"because they have not kept thy law."* For, though sin, that is, a transgression of the law, is the offspring of the will or the heart, still, the instruments by which it is committed are the eyes, the tongue, the hands. Now, the most grievous sins committed by David, and for which *"he washed his couch every night with his tears,"* were committed through the eyes; for he looked with too much curiosity at a naked female while she was bathing, that led him to concupiscence, and afterwards to adultery and murder.

Sade

137. God's law is praised in this section, for its extreme fairness and justice. He first proves the law to be most just, by reason of its author being most just, one in whom injustice can have no place. He, therefore, says, *"Thou art just, O Lord,"* you are peculiarly just, you are the just one exclusively, you alone have the justice that excludes all manner of injustice, as St. John says, *"God is light, and in him there is no darkness."*—*"And thy judgment is right,"* and, consequently, your judgment, decree, command, is always right and just. Throughout this Psalm the word *"judgment"* always means the law, though taking the word even to mean God's allocation of rewards and punishments, it is then also most just, though we may not see the justice of it.

138. He shows that the law of God is just, not only by reason of its having been imposed by a just God, but also by reason of its containing the very essence of justice, *"Thou hast commanded justice in thy testimonies,"* you have prescribed your testimonies, which are the very essence of truth. St. Thomas infers from this, that the law is one that cannot be dispensed in, inasmuch as it contains the very order of justice; just as if one should order that no one should fall into sin, or do any injustice, then the law would admit of no dispensation; for, in no possible case could it be lawful to commit sin, or do an act of injustice.

139. Your law being thus so extremely just, I could not but grieve, and even languish and pine away, through my zeal, at seeing people, even enemies as they were, *"forget thy words,"* devoid of the slightest regard for your most valuable commandments.

140. He again repeats that the law of God is most just and pure, comparing it to gold tried in the fire; for he says, *"Thy word is exceedingly refined,"* because God's law is like gold in a furnace, that comes out as it went in, by reason of its having no dross, no dirt in it; whence it follows that we should have the greatest esteem for it, and, therefore, he adds, *"and thy servant hath loved it."*

141. David alludes here to his own brothers, saying, *"I am the least among my brethren,"* despised by my father and brothers, and yet I have been raised to the throne, and specially honored by God, because *"I forget not thy justifications."* See 1 Kings, chap. 16.

142. This is a repetition and an explanation of verse 138, for *"the justice of the Lord;"* that is, his most just law *"is justice forever,"* because it is immutable and cannot be dispensed with; and it is also *"the truth,"* for it has nothing false in it, for its promises, as well as its threats, will most certainly be carried out.

143. The aforesaid reflections on God's justice cause me, whenever I am in trouble, to console myself by constant meditation on your law. *"Trouble and anguish have found me."* Whenever they did lay hold of me, *"thy commandments are my meditation;"* my only remedy is to meditate, and revel in meditation on thy commandments.

144. He repeats what he said in verses 138 and 142. Thy commandments, by reason of their extreme justice, *"are justice forever;"* and I, therefore, beg of you to *"give me understanding,"* that I may fairly comprehend them, and, by observing them, *"I shall live;"* for, if I do not observe them, I must, of necessity, die.

Coph

145. In the next eight verses the prophet expresses his love for the law of God by an ardent prayer, expressing his feelings in the first and second verses by the pitch of his voice, and in the third and fourth by the unreasonableness of the hour he selected. *"I cried with my whole heart,"* with all my might, with all my affections; and, therefore, *"hear me, O Lord."* For, as we cannot hear one speaking in a subdued tone, and are sure to hear them when they shout, thus God seems to take no notice, as if he did not hear it at all, of a cold, distracted prayer, but is all attention to an ardent, earnest one, as if he could not avoid hearng it. *"I will seek thy justifications."* Hear me, that I may diligently inquire into and observe your commandments.

146. This may be understood of the salvation that we have through hope in this world, and of the reality, through glory, in the next. *"I cried unto thee,"* prayed to you most earnestly, *"save me,"* through grace, which is the commencement of salvation, *"that I may keep thy commandments,"* as far as human frailty will allow me; and also, *"save me"* in life everlasting, *"that I may keep thy commandments,"* without any fear of breaking them.

147. I anticipated the time of rising, and made great haste to pour forth my prayer before dawn, by reason of the great hope I had in your promises.

148. A repetition of the preceding idea, in which he repeats that he rose long before sunrise, in order, through God's grace, to meditate on his words.

149. He follows up the prayer he commenced in the morning, when the cares of this world having been set aside, and, in profound silence, he prayed with the greatest attention. *"Hear thou my voice,"* not according to my merits, but *"according to thy usual mercy,"*—*"and quicken me,"* by preserving and increasing the spiritual life you already conferred on me, and, by so perfecting and completing it in the world to come, that it will be impossible ever after to move me, *"according to thy judgments"* by virtue of which you always carry out what you promise.

150. It is not without reason that I ask to be quickened; for I am pressed by persecutors, who seek to ruin me by constant temptations; and, be they men or demons, *"they have drawn nigh to iniquity, but they are gone far off from thy law;"* that is, they love iniquity, they cling to it, they seek to persuade others to do the same; as, on the contrary, they hate your law, they eschew it, and seek to make it odious to everyone.

151. Though my persecutors *"have gone far off from thy law,"* they could not go far from you, because *"thou art near"* them, by reason of your justice; *"and all thy ways are truth;"* all your laws, all your judgments are supremely just; thus, they could not possibly escape thy avenging hand. *"Thou art near"* me too, *"O Lord,"* through your assistance; *"and all thy ways are truth;"* you will not allow my persecutors to injure me; for though, perchance, you may give them power over my body, you will give them none over my soul; and all my persecutions will be ultimately turned into a crown of glory.

152. That *"all thy ways are truth,"* nay, even eternal truth, *"I have known from the beginning concerning thy testimonies;"* that is to say, from the first moment that I began to look into your commandments, a careful consideration of them led me to the conclusion, *"that thou hast founded them forever;"* that is, that they are based on eternal truth, and, therefore, clearly immutable, and not to be dispensed in; for it has been already stated that they are immutable, by reason of their having in them the order of justice, and the intention of the legislator.

Res

153-154. The prophet, in the next octave, again puts up his prayer to God, asking to be delivered from his enemies, be they men or demons, who sought to make him break the law by their temptations. *"See my humiliation,"* my affliction and trouble, *"and deliver me; for I have not forgotten thy law;"* that is to say, though I may not observe the law to perfection, still I have not entirely rejected it; nay, I even frequently think and reflect on it, and I am anxious to observe it; and it is, therefore, only right for you to *"deliver me,"* from the enemies that tempt me, and perfect in me what you have begun through your grace. Therefore, *"judge my judgment;"* sit in judgment on my cause, *"and redeem me,"* by your judgment, from the hand of my enemies; *"quicken thou me for thy words' sake,"* by virtue of the promise or the law you made in reference to rewarding the good and the bad; *"quicken me,"* by giving me an additional supply of grace here and glory hereafter.

155. I said, *"Quicken me, for I have not forgotten thy law;"* because I know that *"Salvation is far from sinners, because they have not sought thy justifications."*

For, in the first place, demons, who may, to a certain extent, be called sinners, are very far from salvation, it being a thing they never will see; because, instead of *"seeking for the justifications"* of the Lord, they rather entertained a thorough contempt for them. Other sinners, too, will just be as far from salvation as they were from seeking the law of the Lord, and to them the warning of our Savior, *"If thou wilt enter into life, keep the commandments,"* will prove not to have been an idle one.

156. However severely you may punish those from whom your *"salvation is far,"* still, *"many are thy mercies;"* and I, therefore, pray that *"according to thy judgment,"* through which you mercifully judge those who show mercy and who have a love for your law, that you *"quicken me."*

157. It is not without reason that I ask you to quicken me; for the visible enemies, and the invisible ones who outnumber them, and seek to destroy me, are very numerous, yet, nevertheless, through the help I have had from you, *"I have not declined"* to one side or the other, *"from thy testimonies;"* from thy commandments, the only straight and direct road.

158. Here is real love, indeed! The conduct of the transgressors, his persecutors, grieved and afflicted him; not exactly for the injury inflicted on himself, but for the injury thereby offered to God. This he expressed before, when he said, in this very Psalm, *"A fainting hath taken hold of me because of the wicked that forsake thy law;"* and again, *"My zeal hath made me pine away: because my enemies forgot thy words."*

159. When *"I beheld the transgressors, I pined away;"* and it is, therefore, only just that you, who see that *"I have loved thy commandments"* should *"quicken me in thy mercy."*

160. Your words, whatever you say, spring from truth as their source, their fountain, and, therefore, abound in truth; and *"all the judgments of thy justice,"* through which the just are rewarded and the wicked are punished, *"are forever."*

Sin

161. In the next octave the prophet calls attention to his perseverance in observing God's law, and his desire of guarding against any backsliding therein. *"Princes persecuted me without cause."* Saul persecuted me without any reason whatever, and he returned evil for good; so did his son Isboseth, who, with Abner as his general, waged a most uncalled for war against me; and so did my son Absalom, who sought to dethrone me, and reign in my stead. *"And my heart hath been in awe of thy words."* Still, great as was the temptation, I did not consent to it, and I, therefore, did not injure them; for, I was *"in awe of thy words,"* and, therefore, I more than once spared Saul, avenged the death of Isboseth, and wept for Absalom; thus returning good for evil.

162. I have not only *"been in awe of thy words,"* but I have also loved them; and therefore, *"I will rejoice at thy words"* whenever I shall have occasion to observe them in the same spirit of him that rejoices on meeting with great booty after a signal victory. A most appropriate simile, because David was a warrior, used to battle; and because we have to fight fiercely with the evil spirit when we propose to observe God's commandments; and when we do fight and conquer, we have prepared for us a crown of more value than any amount of spoil left behind by the enemy.

163. He again repeats his love for the law, and his hatred of iniquity, a proof positive of his love of him who gave the law, as the Lord himself says, *"If you love me keep my commandments;"* and further on, in Jn. 14, *"He that hath my commandments, and keepeth them, he it is that loveth me."* Happy soul, who could assert, with the Holy Ghost to bear him out in it, *"I have hated iniquity, and loved thy law."*

164. And a great sign of love is the praising God repeatedly, on account of his judgments being most just, and his laws being the very essence of judgment. And though the number seven is only expressive of a considerable number, just as the text in Proverbs, *"for a just man shall fall seven times;"* that is to say, frequently; still the Church seems to have had some grounds for the institution of the seven canonical hours, partly alluded to in this passage. Being most desirous that her children should imitate this most holy king in his devotions, she decided that seven times in the day they should be required to praise God, which we do in the seven canonical hours, to which, if we add the eighth, indicated by *"At midnight I rose to praise thee,"* we shall have the Holy Trinity praised every third hour by the faithful.

165. The greatest and truest praise that can be conferred on anyone is to say they love God's law; for if they love the law, they love him who gave the law; and if they love him, they love everything belonging to him; and thus, on their part, they have no enemy; but, as far as they are concerned, they are at peace with all. Again, *"To them that love God all things work together unto good;"* and, therefore, he that loves God should be at peace with all; and, therefore, the Apostle, Gal. 5, says, *"The fruit of the spirit is, charity, joy, peace, etc."* By the same process of reasoning, *"there is no stumbling block"* to him *"who loves thy law;"* he runs on smoothly to his country, for he who loves the law cannot give scandal, scandal being a sin, and sin being a breach of the law; but scandal offered by others, either applies to the infirm, who, from their ignorance, look upon as forbidden what is not forbidden at all, and take offense at things they thought were illicit; or it is that of the Pharisees, who put a bad construction on what should have been viewed in quite a different light. But they *"who love thy law"* are neither infirm nor Pharisees, and, therefore, *"to them there is no stumbling block."*

166. He now assumes the person of the perfect, and, therefore, confidently says, *"I looked for thy salvation,"* life everlasting, that is to come from you; and he assigns a reason for it, because *"I loved thy commandments;"* as the Apostle has it, *"I have finished my course, I have kept the faith; for the rest there is laid up for me a crown of justice, which the Lord, the just judge, will render to me at that day."*

167. Speaking still in the person of the same perfect soul, he asserts that he kept the commandments by reason of his great love for them. For, as St. Gregory writes, *"Love, when real, does wonders; and if it do not wonders, it is no love;"* and our Lord himself has, *"He that loveth me not, keepeth not my words."* And the Apostle, Rom. 15, *"The love of the neighbor worketh no evil. Love, therefore, is the fulfillment of the law."*

168. Speaking again in the person of the perfect, he asserts that he kept the *"commandments and the testimonies,"* but from another motive, peculiar to the perfect, viz., because in all his actions he looked upon God to be then and there present, for such is the meaning of the words, *"because all my ways are in thy sight;"* that is to say, whatever I did was done as if your eyes were fixed on me, being fully satisfied of your seeing and knowing everything. Such thoughts have a wonderful effect in controlling men's actions; for, if the presence of a prince of this world has the effect of preventing the subject from transgressing, nay, even more, of making them blush to be found lazy or careless, timid or fearful, what must not the effect be of having constantly before one's eyes the presence of a heavenly and all powerful ruler? Hence the Lord said to Abraham, *"Walk before me, and be perfect."* And Elias and Eliseus said, *"The Lord liveth, in whose sight I stand."*

TAU

169. In this last section, fully aware of the value of perseverance in prayer, as the Lord himself afterwards impressed, he concludes by another prayer to God for the grace and salvation he had so frequently asked for before. *"Let my supplication, O Lord, come near in thy sight;"* that is to say, may my prayer, that does not rely on its own merits, be raised up and ascend, through the aspirations of your grace, and come so near you, that you may deign to take a nearer view of it, and regard it with favor; and that prayer is, *"give me understanding according to thy word,"* agreeable to the promise you made me in Psalm 31, *"I will give thee understanding, and I will instruct thee."* Grant me the grace, therefore, of understanding your commandments, as they are understood by those who observe them, and who, by their observance, have come to life everlasting.

170. A repetition of the same prayer in different language. The words *"deliver me"* indicating his reason for having asked for understanding, for the object of understanding is, the being delivered from sin—*"And you shall know the truth, and the truth shall make you free."*

171. He now promises to return thanks on getting the grace he so often asked. *"When thou shalt teach me thy justifications."* When your grace shall so enlighten and assist me to keep your commandments then, in the fulness of my inward joy, and in acknowledgment of so great a favor, *"my lips shall utter a hymn"* of praise and thanksgiving, because *"from the abundance of the heart the mouth speaketh."*

172. He says that he will not only praise God, but that he will teach mankind, and prove to them how full of justice are the commandments of God. *"My tongue shall pronounce thy word."* I will announce your precepts to man, and I will teach them that *"all thy commandments are justice,"* that they are all based on justice; and it is, therefore, but just that they should be observed by all.

173. He follows up his prayer, asking for the only thing worth asking for, life everlasting, which is the object of the commandments. *"Let thy hand be with me to save me."* Let your wisdom and power be exercised to save me; and as the Apostle teaches, that Christ is the power and wisdom of God, the fathers have very properly explained this prayer to be, *"Let Christ be with me to save me:" "for I have chosen thy precepts."* He could not assign a better reason, Christ himself having said, *"If thou will enter into life keep the commandments."*

174. He assigns a reason for asking so pressingly for salvation; and that is, because he wishes for it above and beyond anything he ever desired, as it is really the only object worthy of such desire, it being the only thing that can effectually satisfy man's desires. And, as it will not suffice to have a desire for salvation without observing the commandments of God, he, therefore, adds, *"And thy law is my meditation,"* I will always, therefore, think on it, and exercise myself in keeping it.

175. "My soul shall live," when it shall have obtained the salvation it so longs for and *"thy hand shall have been with it to save it;"* and then its duty, and its only business, will be to praise you for *"blessed are they who dwell in thy house, O Lord, they shall praise thee forever and ever," "and thy judgments shall help me."* Your commandments, so observed by me, will help me, ultimately, when I shall rise in the resurrection to live forever.

176. Banished from my country, and still an exile, through the sin of my first parent, that extended to the whole human race, *"I have gone astray like a sheep that is lost,"* by seduction, and not like the devil, the roaring lion, who fell through malice. *"Seek thy servant,"* for though you have already partly sought and found him, inasmuch as you justified him from sin, and reconciled him to God; yet the lost sheep is still to be sought for, inasmuch as he expects the redemption of his body, so that he may body and soul be brought to the heavenly mountains, and those most fertile pastures, where the ninety-nine that did not stray had been left; and I confidently ask for this salvation of soul and body, *"because I have not forgotten thy commandments."*

PSALM 119

A prayer in tribulation.

1 In my trouble I cried to the Lord: and he heard me.
2 Lord, deliver my soul from wicked lips, and a deceitful tongue.
3 What shall be given to thee, or what shall be added to thee, to a deceitful tongue?
4 The sharp arrows of the mighty, with coals that lay waste.
5 Woe is me, that my sojourning is prolonged! I have dwelt with the inhabitants of cedar:
6 My soul hath been long a sojourner.
7 With them that hated peace I was peaceable: when I spoke to them they fought against me without cause.

EXPLANATION OF THE PSALM

1. Among the various calamities of this our exile, one is specially to be deplored, and that is the deceitful tongue of those among whom we are obliged to mix; and the prophet, in order to instruct his fellow exiles by his example, sings in this Psalm of his having asked for and obtained deliverance from such an evil. *"In my trouble,"* I did not look for help from man, but *"I cried,"* in prayer, *"to the Lord,"* and he, in his mercy, *"heard me."*

2. He tells what he prayed for when he cried to the Lord. It was, *"O Lord, deliver my soul from wicked lips and a deceitful tongue,"* one of the greatest and most numerous evils of this our pilgrimage. *"Wicked lips"* give expression to detraction, railing, calumny, false testimony, and similar expressions against the law of justice; *"a deceitful tongue"* sends forth words of deceit, flattery, pretence, and fraud. We may meet with *"wicked lips"* without *"the deceitful tongue,"* as when one openly reproaches or calumniates; but when the wicked lips and the deceitful tongue are united, the evil exceeds comprehension, so as scarce to admit of any addition to it, as the next verse will inform us.

3. He assigns a reason for having asked to be delivered from a deceitful tongue, because it is such a calamity as to admit of no addition to it. For what evil can be given to or added to a deceitful tongue?

4. By an elegant metaphor, he explains the enormity of the evil of a deceitful tongue; he says that the words issuing from such a tongue are like arrows that shoot from afar, and with great rapidity, so that they can scarcely be guarded against; and, in order to give greater force and expression to the idea, he adds, that they are not like the arrows shot by an ordinary person, but *"by the mighty;"* that is, by a strong and robust hand; and, furthermore, that they are *"sharp,"* well steeled and pointed by the maker; and, finally, that they are so full of fire that, like the lightnings of heaven that are discharged from the hands of the Almighty, and are truly both sharp and fiery, they can lay everything waste and desolate. Such are words of deceit, especially when used by the devil to ruin souls, and are called by the Apostle *"the fiery darts of the most wicked one."*

5. In consequence of so great and so frequent an evil in this our place of peregrination, he sighs for his country, and thus, truly and from his heart, sings the *"canticle of ascent,"* as these fifteen Psalms are called. *"Woe is me that my sojourning is prolonged;"* for the true pilgrim desires rather to be shut out from his body than from his Lord, and therefore, looks upon the present life as entirely too long, inasmuch as it keeps him the longer away from the Lord. *"I have dwelt with the inhabitants of Cedar."* No wonder I should complain of being detained too long here below, for hitherto *"I have dwelt with the inhabitants of Cedar;"* with wild and barbarous tribes, that live in tents instead of houses, and are black and swarthy. The word Cedar in Hebrew signifies blackness; and hence, in Canticles, we have the *"tents of Cedar"* put in opposition to *"the curtains of Solomon;"* that is, black and rustic tents, to splendid and valuable curtains. And, truly, the cities and palaces of the kings of this world, when compared to the mansions of the heavenly Jerusalem, are but so many rustic tents; and, therefore, the holy pilgrim again mourns, saying—

6. My exile in a foreign land has been entirely too long. Hence we may infer how few are to be found in those days who chant this gradual Psalm from their heart; whereas most people are so attached to the exile and the tents of Cedar that there is nothing they hear with greater pain than any allusion to their leaving it.

7. He concludes by assigning a reason for its being a loss to him to have his exile extended, and at the same time explains the expression, *"the inhabitants of Cedar;"* he there said, *"I have dwelt with the inhabitants of Cedar,"* which he now explains by saying, I have dwelt *"with them that hated peace."* There is nothing I love more than peace; I have dwelt with people of quite different habits, with the wicked, so wicked that they fought equally with friend and foe; and if, perchance, I ever *"spoke to them"* about peace it only caused them the more *"to fight against me without cause."* This Psalm is applicable to all the elect, and especially to Christ, the head of the elect, so far as his human nature is concerned. For he cried to some purpose to his Father, on the night he spent in prayer, and afterwards in the garden, and, finally, on the cross, when God exalted him *"and gave him a name above every name.*

He also truly suffered from "the wicked lips and the deceitful tongue," even to the hour of his death, as can be clearly seen throughout the Gospels. He could say with the greatest truth, *"My sojourning is prolonged,"* whereas, he said in the Gospel, *"O incredulous generation, how long shall I be with you? how long shall I suffer you?"* Truly *"did he dwell with the inhabitants of Cedar,"* for though he was light, and, therefore, did not dwell in Cedar, that is, in darkness, still he was seen by the inhabitants of Cedar, and conversed with them. Finally, *"he was truly peaceable with them that hated peace,"* because *"when he was reviled he reviled not, when he suffered he threatened not,"* "and when he spoke to them" on peace, love, on the kingdom of God, they, on the contrary, *"fought against him without cause,"* as our Savior himself remarked, when he said, *"But that the word may be fulfilled, which is written in their law; They have hated me without cause."*

PSALM 120

God is the keeper of his servants.

1 I have lifted up my eyes to the mountains, from whence help shall come to me.
2 My help is from the Lord, who made heaven and earth.
3 May he not suffer thy foot to be moved: neither let him slumber that keepeth thee.
4 Behold he shall neither slumber nor sleep, that keepeth Israel.
5 The Lord is thy keeper, the Lord is thy protection upon thy right hand.
6 The sun shall not burn thee by day: nor the moon by night.
7 The Lord keepeth thee from all evil: may the Lord keep thy soul.
8 May the Lord keep thy coming in and thy going out; from henceforth now and for ever.

EXPLANATION OF THE PSALM

1. Travelers look at nothing more frequently than the place for which they are bound, and if they cannot see it, they fix their eyes on the point next to it, from which they derive great consolation, so much so that they gather fresh strength and courage to prosecute their journey. The earthly Jerusalem being in the mountains, and the celestial Jerusalem being above all the heavens, this traveler, whether real or imaginary, says, *"I have lifted up my eyes to the mountains,"* where the holy city is situated, *"from whence help shall come to me,"* that of consolation.

2. The traveler declares he expects no help from the mountains to which he raised his eyes, but from him who presides over the holy city that is on the mountains, which he explains more clearly in the beginning of Psalm, 122, where he says, *"To thee have I lifted up my eyes who dwellest in heaven."* He then describes the true God by the creation of heaven and earth, as he did in another Psalm, where he says, *"For all the gods of the gentiles are devils: but the Lord made the heavens."*

3. The prophet, now speaking in his own person, answers the traveler, and says you did well and wisely in raising your eyes to the mountains, in not regarding the vanities you met on the road, and seeking for help and consolation from the founder of your heavenly country; and I, therefore, sincerely hope *"he may not suffer thy foot to be moved,"* that he may not allow you to slip or to fall on the road, but that he may so strengthen your feet that they may continue to be sound during your journey to your country. *"Neither let him slumber that keepeth thee."* I also wish and pray that the Father, who is your guardian, may be always vigilant in guarding you, so as never to suffer your feet to be moved. God is said to slumber, in a figurative sense, when he suffers us, as if he did not advert to it, to fall, as he who slumbers has no cognizance of what is being done. *"Thy foot to be moved,"* is a Hebrew phrase for falling into sin, as in Psalm 17, *"My feet are not weakened,"* and in Psalm 72, *"My feet were almost moved; my steps had well nigh slipt."*

4. The prophet promises the pilgrim the grace he had been asking for, saying, I pray that the Father, who undertook the care of you, may not slumber; and he certainly will not slumber; because he who has charge of his own people, the people of Israel, including all the pilgrims in this world, who hasten to go up to their heavenly country, never sleeps nor slumbers.

5-6. The prophet just assured the pilgrim so confiding in God that he would be protected, that he may not fall on the way; and he now promises another consolation, that he would be protected from the heat of the sun in the daytime, and that of the moon in the night; because God will be like a shade to him, that he can hold in his hand, so as to protect himself on every quarter. The Lord not only protects Israel, his people in general, *"but he is thy protector"* in particular; and his protector, as the Hebrew implies, is like a parasol, held in the hand, and raised over the head, and can be moved so as to give protection on any side.

7. He now adds another consolation, a general one. Not only will the Lord guard you from falling and from fatigue, but he will protect you from every other evil that could possibly befall you on the journey, so that your soul or your life will be preserved whole and intact through the whole journey.

8. The prophet concludes by promising the last and most desirable consolation of all. Not only will the pilgrim, *"who in his heart hath disposed to ascend by steps,"* be so protected in any particular part of his journey; but he will be always protected throughout the journey. Every journey consists of an entrance and exit; for, as we go along, we enter on one road, and when that is finished we leave it; then we enter on another, from which we also depart; so also we come into a city or a house, and we go out of them; we enter another and out we go again, until we finish the journey by arriving at our country. Thus it is that we get along on the road of life, entering on and completing good works; for to begin corresponds with coming into; completing with going out; *"from henceforth now and forever;"* from this day and forever, may the Lord guard thy coming in and thy going out, and protect and save thee.

PSALM 121

The desire and hope of the just for the coming of the kingdom of God, and the peace of his Church.

1 I rejoiced at the things that were said to me: We shall go into the house of the Lord.
2 Our feet were standing in thy courts, O Jerusalem.
3 Jerusalem, which is built as a city, which is compact together.
4 For thither did the tribes go up, the tribes of the Lord: the testimony of Israel, to praise the name of the Lord.
5 Because their seats have sat in judgment, seats upon the house of David.
6 Pray ye for the things that are for the peace of Jerusalem: and abundance for them that love thee.
7 Let peace be in thy strength: and abundance in thy towers.
8 For the sake of my brethren, and of my neighbours, I spoke peace of thee.
9 Because of the house of the Lord our God, I have sought good things for thee.

Explanation of the psalm

1. Such is the language of God's people, expressive of their joy on hearing the welcome news of their return to their country. Jeremias was the person to announce that, after seventy years, there would be an end to the captivity, and that the city and the temple would be rebuilt. Daniel, Aggeus, and Zacharias, who lived at the time the captivity was ended, foretold it more clearly; and they, therefore, created much joy among the people, when, on the completion of the seventy years, they said, *"We shall go into the house of the Lord;"* that is to say, we shall return to our country, where we shall get to see mount Sion and the site of the house of the Lord; and then, when we shall have rebuilt the temple, we will again *"go into the house of the Lord."* Christ, however, was the bearer of a far and away more happy message when he announced, *"Do penance, for the kingdom of heaven is at hand;"* and when he said more clearly, *"In my Father's house there are many mansions. If not, I would have told you; because I go to prepare a place for you. And if I shall go and prepare a place for you I will come again, and will take you to myself, that where I am, you also may be."* Such news fills with unspeakable joy those who have learned the value *"of going into the house of the Lord;"* and to hold in that house, not the position *"of a stranger or a foreigner, but of a fellow citizen with the saints and a domestic of God's."* That must be well known to anyone reflecting seriously on the saying of David, *"They shall be inebriated with the plenty of thy house;"* and in another Psalm, *"We shall be filled with the good things of thy house;"* as also on that saying of the Apostle, *"That you may know what is the hope of his calling, and what are the riches of the glory of his inheritance in the saints."* Such is the man who, from his heart, desires to go into the house of the Lord; and, therefore, from his heart sings, *"I rejoiced at the things that were said to me. We shall go into the house of the Lord."* Now, *"the sensual man perceiveth not the things that are of the spirit of God,"* and, therefore, on the approach of death, or the termination of his exile and pilgrimage, instead of rejoicing, is troubled and laments, and justly, because, as he did not choose during his life time *"to dispose in his heart to ascend by steps,"* he cannot possibly expect to go up to the house of the Lord on high, but rather fears to go down to the prison of the damned, there to be punished forever.

2. He tells us why the Jews were so overjoyed at the idea of their return to their country, and he says it arose from their remembrance of the time previous to the captivity, when they saw Jerusalem in her extent and in her splendor; for many who had been carried off captives in their youth could have remembered Jerusalem as she then was; and in 1 Esdras 3 we read, that many returned from the captivity who had seen the city and the temple. These men, therefore, say, *"Our feet were standing in thy courts, O Jerusalem;"* that is to say, because we recollected the time when we stood in your courts or in your gates, as it is more clearly expressed in the Hebrew. He names the courts or the gates, being, as it were, the vestibules of the city, rather than the public buildings or the streets, because it was at the gates that business was mostly transacted; it was there that the citizens mostly assembled, as we may infer from that verse in Proverbs, *"Her husband is honorable in the gates, when he sitteth among the senators of the land."* It also appears, from 2 Kings 18, that the gates of Jerusalem were not plain, ordinary gates, but that they were double gates, with a considerable space between them, which, perhaps, is here called *"thy courts."* Thus we read in 2 Kings 24, *"And David sat between the two gates."* And again, Jeremias 39, *"And all the princes of the king of Babylon came in and sat in the middle gate;"* and, certainly, no small space was necessary to accommodate all those princes with their retinue. But how can we Christians say, *"Our feet were standing in thy courts, O Jerusalem,"* when we were never in her courts? Well, we have been in her courts, otherwise we would not be now exiles and pilgrims, nor would Christ have redeemed us from captivity had we not been torn from our country and captives in a foreign land. We have been, then, in the

courts of the heavenly Jerusalem, when, through our father Adam, we had possession of paradise, that was the gate of the paradise above; and the state of innocence then and there was the gate and the court to the state of glory; and that, perhaps, was the reason why the Holy Spirit made David write *"in the courts,"* instead of the streets of Jerusalem, that we may understand that the Psalm treats of the celestial, and not the earthly Jerusalem. *"We have (therefore) rejoiced at the things that were said of thee,"* when they said, *"we shall go into the house of the Lord,"* because we remembered the time when *"our feet were standing"* in paradise, and, consequently, in the courts of the paradise above; and, from the idea we got of happiness in the place below, we can guess at the happiness that awaits us above. And though this great place in question is sometimes called the house of the Lord, sometimes the city of Jerusalem, still it is all one and the same place; for our heavenly country is one time called a kingdom, sometimes a city, and at other times a house. It is a kingdom by reason of the multitude and the variety of its inhabitants, as St. John observes, Apoc. 7, *"It is a great multitude which no man could number, of all nations, and tribes, and peoples, and tongues."* It is a city by reason of the friendship and fellowship that exist between the saints and the blessed; for, however great their number may be, they know, recognize, and love each other as so many fellow citizens; and, finally, it is a house by reason of the elect having only one father, one inheritance, in which they are all brethren, under the one Father, God.

3. The prophet now, in the person of the pilgrims hastening to Jerusalem, begins to enumerate its praises, with a view of thereby stirring himself up to make greater haste in his ascent to it. He praises it, first, by reason of the supreme peace enjoyed by all its inhabitants, who were so united in the love of each other that they held all their property in common. *"Our feet were standing in thy courts, O Jerusalem;"* that same Jerusalem whose buildings have so increased, and are daily increasing, that it has now become a city *"which is compact together;"* which is enjoyed and shared in common by all. Referring the passage to a future state it is much more beautiful and more sublime, for the heavenly Jerusalem is truly built up as a city; not that it is, strictly speaking, a city, nor that there were stones used in the building; still, it is built up as a city so long as the living stones, dressed by a consummate workman, and, after being actually squared and fitted, are placed on the building of the celestial habitation; from which it follows, that they who understand it not only bear all manner of persecutions with equanimity, but they even rejoice and glory in their tribulations, being perfectly sensible that it is in such manner they are squared and fitted for being built into and raised upon the heavenly habitation. One of these living stones, St. James, thus admonishes us, *"My brethren, count it great joy when you shall fall into*

diverse temptations." Again, in our heavenly country, we shall have the real community of property; for, in the earthly Jerusalem such community of property was more a matter of fact than a matter of right, and arose from the mutual love of the inhabitants for each other; the same held for a time, in the infancy of the Church, as we read in the Acts, *"Neither did any of them say, that of the things which he possessed, anything was his own, but all things were common to them;"* which still holds among those religious orders that observe the spirit of their institute. But in the heavenly Jerusalem there is complete community of property, the one God being all unto all; that is, the one and the same God being the honor, the riches, and the delight of all those who dwell in his house; and that most happy and most supreme abundance is really always the same, subject to no diminution or alteration whatever.

4. The second subject of praise in Jerusalem is the number of its inhabitants; and this verse has a connection with the second verse, because he now assigns a reason for having said, or rather, for having put in the mouth of God's people, *"Our feet were standing in thy courts, O Jerusalem;"* for, though they were not all citizens of Jerusalem, but inhabitants of different cities, still they all came up to Jerusalem three times in every year. He, therefore, says, *"Our feet were standing in thy courts, O Jerusalem; for thither did the tribes go up, the tribes of the Lord;"* that is, a great many tribes; such repetitions, in the Hebrew, being indicative of multitude; and thus, a great multitude assembled in Jerusalem, *"the testimony of Israel to praise the name of the Lord;"* explaining the cause of such an assemblage in Jerusalem. It was according to *"the testimony,"* that is, the law that obliged all Israel to visit the temple of the Lord at stated times, it being the only temple in the land of promise; and there *"praise the name of the Lord,"* in acts of thanksgiving and praise. From another point of view, which we consider was more intended by the Holy Ghost, the meaning is, A reason is assigned for having said, *"Jerusalem which is built as a city;"* because it was built as a city, by reason of *"the tribes that go up there;"* that is, the holy souls from all tribes and nations, who go up to be built into the spiritual structures, that St. Peter writes of in his first epistle, chap. 2. Now, those blessed souls have gone up to that heavenly Jerusalem, *"to praise the name of the Lord;"* for that is their whole occupation there, to the exclusion of every other business. Hence, in Psalm 83, we have, *"Blessed are they that dwell in thy house, O Lord: they shall praise thee forever and ever;"* and Tobias, speaking of the heavenly Jerusalem, has, *"And Alleluia shall be sung in its streets;"* and such is *"the testimony,"* that is, the command, *"to Israel,"* that is, to the soul enjoying the beatific vision, that it should never desist from praise, inasmuch as it never ceases to love.

5. The third matter for praise in Jerusalem is its being the seat of government, and having a royal palace in it; and the word *"because"* would seem to connect this verse with the preceding; for it looks like assigning a reason why God wished to have a temple, which the people were bound to visit three times a year, in Jerusalem, in consequence of being the residence of royalty, and the metropolis of the kingdom. He, therefore, says, *"Because there,"* in Jerusalem, *"seats have sat in judgment;"* seats of kings in succession, whose business it was to judge the people, *"have sat,"* have been firmly settled and fixed, not like that of Saul's, which was for a while in Gabaa of Benjamin, and made no great stay there either; nor, like that of the judges who preceded the kings, who never had any certain fixed place for *"sitting,"* or delivering judgment, while the kings of the family of David sat permanently in Jerusalem; and he, therefore, adds, *"seats upon the house of David;"* that is, the seat of royalty founded on the family of David, met with rest and stability; for God said to David, 2 Kings 7, *"And thy house shall be faithful, and thy kingdom forever before thy face; and thy throne shall be firm forever."* From the expression, *"seats upon the house of David,"* we are not to infer that they sat in judgment on the family of David alone; for they had authority over the whole family of Jacob, that is, over the twelve tribes of Israel; but they are called seats upon the house of David, because all the kings of God's people sprang from the family of David. All this is much more applicable to Christ and the heavenly Jerusalem. Because, lest the Jews may imagine that the words of the Psalm apply to that earthly Jerusalem, and not to the celestial Jerusalem, of which it was a figure, God permitted the seat of government to be removed from Jerusalem, and, furthermore, Jerusalem itself to be destroyed. The promise, then, applies to the Jerusalem above, and to Christ, according to the prophecy of Isaias, chap. 9; of Daniel, chap. 9; and of the Angel to the Virgin, Lk. 1, *"The Lord God shall give unto him the throne of David his father, and he shall reign in the house of Jacob forever, and of his kingdom there shall be no end."* In the strictest acceptance, then, of the words have *"the seats sat in judgment"* in the heavenly Jerusalem; because Christ's throne and the thrones of those who reign with him have been established most firmly in heaven; and because those very saints who reign and judge with Christ are a throne for God; for *"the soul of the just is the seat of wisdom;"* and those seats really sit in judgment, according to the promise of our Lord, "You that have followed me shall sit upon twelve thrones, judging the twelve tribes of Israel. And those seats are upon the house of David, because all the power of the saints, royal as well as judiciary, is derived from Christ, who is called the son of David in the Gospel, and who got the seat of David his father, and who will reign forever in the house of Jacob, and of whose kingdom there shall be no end.

6. The prophet now exhorts the exiles, on their return from their captivity, to salute, even from afar, the city of Jerusalem, praying for peace and abundance on it, two things that contribute principally to the happiness of cities; for peace, without abundance, is only a firm hold of misery; and abundance, without peace, amounts to doubtful and uncertain happiness; but when both are combined, the city needs nothing necessary for its happiness. He, therefore, says, *"Pray for the things that are for the peace of Jerusalem."* Pray ye to God for true and solid peace for your country, and for *"abundance,"* not only for the city of Jerusalem, but also *"to them that love thee,"* you holy city. *7.* He dictates the very words in which those who pray for peace and abundance to Jerusalem are to salute her. When you salute her say ye, *"Let peace be in thy strength, and abundance in thy towers;"* that is to say, may your walk be always secure and fortified, thereby ensuring perfect peace and quiet to all who dwell within them; *"and abundance in thy towers;"* no lack of meat or drink in your public buildings and private houses. Now, the two last verses, in reference to the heavenly Jerusalem, though they imply prayers for peace and abundance, still they do not mean to insinuate that there can ever possibly be a want of either there, when we read in Psalm 147, *"Who hath placed peace in thy borders; and filleth thee with the fat corn?"* they, therefore, merely express the pious affection we cherish for the blessings of the Jerusalem above, just as we have in the Apocalypse, *"Salvation to our God who sitteth on the throne, and to the Lamb."*

PSALM 122

A prayer in affliction, with confidence in God.

1 To thee have I lifted up my eyes, who dwellest in heaven.
2 Behold as the eyes of the servants are on the hands of their masters, As the eyes of the handmaid are on the hands of her mistress: so are our eyes unto the Lord our God, until he have mercy on us.
3 Have mercy on us, O Lord, have mercy on us: for we are greatly filled with contempt.
4 For our soul is greatly filled: we are a reproach to the rich, and contempt to the proud.

EXPLANATION OF THE PSALM

1. The prophet, speaking at one time in the person of a pilgrim, and at another time in his own, as being a pilgrim indeed, says, that whatever difficulties he was placed in, he had recourse to no one for help but to God alone; because he alone dwells in the highest heavens, whence he beholds and rules all things under him; and because it is from him all our evils come for the purpose of chastising us; and, therefore, that it is idle for us to have recourse to anyone else, for no one can take us out of God's hands.

2. *"Behold, as the eyes of servants are on the hands of their masters, as the eyes of the handmaid are on the hands of her mistress: so are our eyes unto the Lord our God, until he have mercy on us."* He tells us why he raised his eyes to God. It was to look upon God scourging him; in the hope that his wretched appearance may move God to mercy, and cause him to desist from scourging him. He illustrates it by the example of the servants, who, when flogged by their masters, look with a sorrowful countenance on the hand that flogs them, hoping by their looks to move their masters to pity. He applies the simile to maid, as well as to men, servants; for they, too, are pilgrims, and are scourged as they prosecute their pilgrimage. These scourges consist not only of open persecutions and public calamities, but also of secret temptations that daily torment the soul, as also of those fears, sorrows, perplexities, and other troubles, from which no one in this life is exempt; and, therefore, the Psalm does not fix stated times for us to raise our eyes to God, but says it must be done incessantly, *"until he have mercy on us,"* which will not be accomplished until we shall have arrived at our country; for then *"God will crown us with mercy and compassion, when he shall have healed all our diseases, and satisfied our desires with good things,"*

3. Not content with having implored God's mercy, by fixing his eyes on God, the prophet now, with the voice of his heart and his body, cries out, and redoubles the shout, as he prays for himself and fellow pilgrims, saying, *"Have mercy on us, O Lord, have mercy."* And, truly, anyone that attentively considers, and properly reflects on the next sentence, *"for we are greatly filled with contempt,"* will see at once that such is the extent of our misery that we should never cease our cries to that effect. Because man, created to God's image, placed over all created things by him, very often even adopted by him as a son, and predestined to enjoy the kingdom of heaven, is so despised in this our pilgrimage, not only by men and demons, and so constantly annoyed, not only by the aforesaid, but even by animals, even to the minutest of them, and even by the very elements, that the prophet could say with the greatest truth, not only that we are despised, but that we are *"greatly filled with contempt."* For what is there that does not look down upon man, even on the just and the holy, in this valley of tears? However, the contempt principally meant by the prophet here is that which the just suffer from the unjust, and the good from the bad; because most true and universal is that expression of the Apostle, *"And all who live piously in Christ Jesus shall suffer persecution;"* as well as those words of the Lord, *"If you had been of the world, the world would love its own; but because you are not of the world, therefore the world hateth you."* This is easily understood; for good

and evil, being essentially opposed to each other, they cannot possibly be at peace. And, as the just are patient and mild, and have learned of their Master to turn the other cheek to him who strikes on one, and thus to make no resistance to injuries, they are, in consequence, proudly despised, harassed, and ridiculed by the wicked.

4. In this last verse David informs us that the aforesaid scorn and contempt for the poor and humble pilgrims proceeds from the wealthy and the proud. The prophet says, *"Our souls are greatly filled;"* which is but a repetition of a previous sentence. *"For we are greatly filled with contempt."* However, in this passage he says it is the soul that is so filled, contempt being more applicable to the soul; for they who have no soul may be, and are, subject to pain, but not to contempt. The word *"filled"* signifies, in the Hebrew, filled to repletion, which adds great force to the expression; because if they who are filled to repletion, instead of deriving any pleasure from more food, are pained and overburdened by it, however rare and good it may be, how would the case be with those who may chance to be overdosed with bad food, such as contempt and reproaches. The next sentence, *"We are a reproach to the rich, and a contempt for the proud,"* signify the same, reproach and contempt being synonymous, as are the rich and the proud. All proud people are inflated, and are, therefore, rich; but it is in wind, add not in any solid good, that is to say, they abound in high notions and extravagant opinion of themselves. Should they enjoy the riches of this world, they look upon them as their own, never reflecting for a moment that they will have *"to render an account of them."* Should they be in high position and power, they attribute the whole to themselves, never thinking for a moment that they were placed in such positions in order to be useful to and to serve others, that they will have to render a most strict account for such favors; and that when they got them, they got nothing but a load and a burden; in which they are just as absurd as would be the stick in a man's hand that would boast of carrying the person that owned it. Should they excel in talent and learning, they form most exaggerated notions of their abilities, and attribute to themselves what they only got from God. Finally, should they not have those riches, dignities, and honors, and, on the other hand, should they be scourged and punished, they look upon themselves as aggrieved, blaspheme and murmur against God, and all in consequence of their being full, or rather, overcharged with the wind of self conceit and opinion. But the time will come when such reproach and contempt will revert on themselves, when, on the day of judgment, they will cry out, as we read in Wisdom, *"These are they, whom we had sometime in derision, and for a parable of reproach. We fools esteemed their life madness, and their end without honor. Behold, how they are numbered among the children of God, and their lot*

is among the saints. What hath pride profited us? or what advantage hath the boasting of riches brought us? All these things are passed away like a shadow."

PSALM 123

The Church giveth glory to God for her deliverance from the hands of her enemies.

1 If it had not been that the Lord was with us, let Israel now say:
2 If it had not been that the Lord was with us, When men rose up against us,
3 Perhaps they had swallowed us up alive. When their fury was enkindled against us,
4 Perhaps the waters had swallowed us up.
5 Our soul hath passed through a torrent: perhaps our soul had passed through a water insupportable.
6 Blessed be the Lord, who hath not given us to be a prey to their teeth.
7 Our soul hath been delivered as a sparrow out of the snare of the fowlers. The snare is broken, and we are delivered.
8 Our help is in the name of the Lord, who made heaven and earth.

Explanation of the Psalm

1-4. Such abrupt and unfinished expressions in the beginning of the Psalm indicate the great joy and exultation that will not suffer the speaker to finish his sentences. The multitude of the saints, then, delivered from great temptations, exclaim, *"If it had not been that the Lord was with us"* we never could have escaped. Before he finishes the sentence, however, he invites all the people of Israel to unite with him in his tribute of thanks and praise: and again repeats, *"If it had not been that the Lord was with us"*—*"Perhaps they would have swallowed us up alive."* Here is what would have happened to us! had not the Lord been with us and lent us his powerful assistance, *"when men rose up against us, perhaps they had swallowed us up alive."* When our persecutors rose up against us, we were nearly in as much danger of being destroyed by them, as we would of being swallowed up alive by the sea if thrown into it. The persecutors of the just are styled *"men,"* by reason of their being guided by nothing but that reason they have from corrupt nature; for man's reason, since the corruption of nature, has no taste for anything divine, spiritual, or elevated, and has no other object in view beyond the upholding and increasing its own temporal happiness: of such the Apostle says, *"For, whereas there is among you envying and contention, are you not carnal and walk according to man?"* and a little further on, *"Are you not men?"* from which it appears carnal and to be a man to walk according to the flesh, and to walk according to man to be one and the same. The word *"perhaps"* requires some explanation. It would seem to imply that the grace of God had no part in their delivery, or that their destruction was possible. There is no room for fear on that head, for the word *"perhaps"* does not imply that we could resist the enemy in their charge without the aid of his auxiliary grace, but that it was possible we may not be swallowed up alive, because, perhaps, the fury of the enemy did not carry them so far. But as there was danger that the enemy might have carried their cruelty so far, he adds, *"If it had not been that the Lord was with us, perhaps they had swallowed us up alive."* The expressions *"they had swallowed us up alive,"* is taken from a sea or a river that swallows up everything that falls into it, for there are no beasts, no matter how fierce and cruel they may be, that swallow people up alive; they generally tear and mangle them first, and the next sentence, that expresses the same idea in other terms, as often occurs in the Psalms, requires such interpretation for thus it runs, *"when their fury was enkindled against us, perhaps the water had swallowed us up;"* that is to say, as the water would have swallowed us up, so would the rage of our enemies, like a mass of water, have overwhelmed us.

5. He follows up the simile, comparing the persecution of his enemies to a deep and rapid torrent, impassable without very great help. Anyone reflecting on the persecutions of the martyrs by the pagans and heretics, and the temptations of the demons in regard of the holy anchorites and confessors, can compare them to nothing else but to a violent *"torrent;"* and though many holy confessors breasted the torrent with success, still an immense number have been carried away by its fury. The prophet, then, speaking in the person of the beatified, says, *"Our soul hath passed through a torrent"* of persecution, for though the flesh succumbed, and yielded to the rage of the persecutor, still the soul has gloriously *"passed through;"* however, *"if it had not been that the Lord was with us," "perhaps our soul had passed through a water insupportable,"* had got into a torrent too deep to expect getting out of it.

6-7. For the better understanding and the further illustration of God's goodness, the prophet now proposes another simile. He compares persecutions or temptations to the snare of the fowler, and says, we should return thanks to and bless God for not suffering us to become a prey to the teeth of our enemies, that is to say, that he protected us from being taken, killed, and devoured; and he tells us how that was effected when he says, *"Our soul hath been delivered as a sparrow out of the snare of the fowlers."* No doubt, our soul fell into persecution and temptation, as would a sparrow or any other bird, when they are seduced into the snare set by the fowlers; but still it was loosed and delivered from the temptation before the tempter got hold of it to kill it; like a bird caught in a snare but enlarged before the fowler arrived to take it, kill it, and eat it. That was effected by *"the snare being broken and thus we are delivered."* God having by his grace, repressed the temptation before the soul either denied the faith or consented to sin in any other respect, just as the snare that held the bird would be broken, on which the bird flies off, and thus disappoints the fowler of his prey.

8. He concludes by praising God, humbly acknowledging that such a victory and such deliverance from those dangerous temptations should be ascribed not to himself, but to the help he got from Almighty God, a manifest proof of whose omnipotence is, that he made *"the heaven and earth."* Referring to the two verses previous to this one, we can hardly dismiss them or the Psalm without observing on the manner in which God is wont to rescue his servants from grievous temptation, which is barely touched upon in the expression, *"The snare is broken."* The snare usually breaks, when the bird, frightened by some noise, or seeing some more dainty food, makes a violent plunge, and thus breaks the snare. For when the bird is satisfied with the bait in the snare, and has no consciousness of being caught in the snare, it makes no effort to fly away, and thus waits quietly until the fowler comes, catches it, and kills it. So it is with man in temptation; for when God's grace begins to move him, or when he gets alarmed by the noise of hell or of God's judgments, he begins to reflect that the troubles of this world are irksome enough, but that the torments of the next, along with being everlasting, are far and away more irksome and more grievous; or that, sweet as the present life may be, sweet as its pleasures may be, sweet as its riches may be, that they will bear no comparison with the sweet rewards of the life to come, he gets inflamed with the love of such rewards, and with the fear of hell, from which he acquires a great accession of strength, so that, by one vigorous effort of a firm resolution of never offending God again, he breaks the snare of temptation, flies off on being delivered, and joyfully chants, *"Our help is the Lord, who made heaven and earth."* What persecution can subdue, what torments can conquer such reflections?

PSALM 124

The just are always under God's protection.

1 They that trust in the Lord shall be as mount Sion: he shall not be moved for ever that dwelleth

2 In Jerusalem. Mountains are round about it: so the Lord is round about his people from henceforth now and for ever.

3 For the Lord will not leave the rod of sinners upon the lot of the just: that the just may not stretch forth their hands to iniquity.

4 Do good, O Lord, to those that are good, and to the upright of heart.

5 But such as turn aside into bonds, the Lord shall lead out with the workers of iniquity: peace upon Israel.

Explanation of the psalm

1. The prophet commences by laying down a general and most certain promise, and repeats it twice to confirm the truth of it. He says, *"They that trust in the Lord shall be as mount Sion."* All they who truly confide and trust in the Lord will be as unmoved and as secure, no matter how great the storm, as mount Sion, which is immoveable, not only by reason of its being a mountain, but by reason also of its being sacred and most dear to God. He repeats it, and at the same time explains it, when he adds, *"He shall not be moved forever that dwelleth in Jerusalem,"* which last phrase corresponds with the first part of the first sentence, for *"shall be as a mountain"* is but a different mode of expressing what is conveyed, *"He shall not be moved forever,"* and *"he that dwelleth in Jerusalem"* expresses, *"They that trust in the Lord."* Because they who dwell in thought and hope in the heavenly Jerusalem are the very ones that trust in the Lord; for thus such trust and confidence is explained in Psalm 90, *"He that dwelleth in the aid of the Most High shall abide under the protection of the God of heaven."*

2. He proves his assertion as to mount Sion being a strong and secure place, and that those who trust in the Lord are much more so. The reason is, that Sion has *"mountains round about it"* like a wall, but they who trust in the Lord have the Almighty himself round about them; and while the mountains that surround Sion may fall or be leveled, God is round about his people, *"henceforth now and forever."* The meaning, then, of these verses is, that all who trust in the Lord ought to feel quite secure, because he protects them from all evil, for though they may sometimes be temporarily afflicted, it is all for their own good; and if God should at any time deprive them of riches, or health, or the like, he gives them something better in lieu thereof, perhaps patience and consolation, with a view to merit life everlasting. The trust spoken of here is not to be confounded with vain presumption, it is the trust that springs from a sincere faith, a pure heart, a good conscience, and fervent love.

3. He explains a little more clearly how it is that God protects those who confide in his help. For, says he, if God sometimes, for his own just reasons, suffers the wicked to lord it over the just, he will not suffer them to do so for any length of time, for fear the just may despair and turn to the same wickedness; and he, therefore, says, *"For the Lord will not leave the rod of the sinners upon the lot of the just."* God will leave the rod, meaning the scepter, the emblem of power, to the sinners for a while, *"upon the lot of the just,"* on the inheritance, or the portion and lot of the just, but he will not leave them such power long, *"that the just may not stretch forth their hands to iniquity,"* for fear the just, on seeing the happiness of the wicked so continuous, appearing likely to have no termination, may not persevere in justice.

4. Having said there was danger of the just taking scandal at the prolonged power of the wicked, he turns to God, and prays to him *"to do good to those that are good,"* by delivering them as quickly as possible from the power of the wicked; or at least, by giving them a copious supply of interior patience and consolation; and, at the same time, he tells and admonishes us that the truly good are they who are *"upright of heart,"* they who are not scandalized at God's judgments, but take the most favorable view of everything God does, no matter how long he may suffer the wicked to have everything their own way. They are the upright of heart who conform their heart, that is, their judgment and their will, to that most upright rule of the will and judgment of God, even though they understand not why God does this or that, or why he suffers it to be done; and of such people another Psalm says, *"How good is God to Israel, to them that are of a right heart!"* They submit to God in everything; God is pleasing to them, and they are to God, just as a straight rod laid on a straight line agrees and coincides with it accurately; while a crooked rod will not agree or lie fair anywhere but in a crooked place.

5. Having prayed all manner of good on the upright of heart, the prophet now issues a terrible threat against those who *"turn aside"* from such uprightness of heart to a crooked path, who, in persecution or tribulation, lose all patience, or who deny the faith, or complain and murmur against God, and says that they, with the *"workers of iniquity,"* that is, with the persecutors and the wicked, shall *"be led out"* for judgment, because, as St. James has it, *"Now, whosoever shall keep the whole law, but offend in one, is become guilty of all."* And then, ultimately, on the separation of all the bad from the good, there will be everlasting *"peace upon Israel,"* that is, on God's people. The word *"bonds"* has puzzled many, and hence many explanations of it. I look upon it as being put in opposition to the straight path, so much lauded by the prophet; and when he says, *"turn aside into bonds,"* he alludes to those who follow the crooked way indicated by a rope twisted into coils or bonds, which is the only interpretation that harmonizes with the rest of the Psalm.

PSALM 125

The people of God rejoice at their delivery from captivity.

1 When the lord brought back the captivity of Sion, we became like men comforted.
2 Then was our mouth filled with gladness; and our tongue with joy. Then shall they say among the Gentiles: The Lord hath done great things for them.
3 The Lord hath done great things for us: we are become joyful.
4 Turn again our captivity, O Lord, as a stream in the south.
5 They that sow in tears shall reap in joy.

6 Going they went and wept, casting their seeds.
7 But coming they shall come with joyfulness, carrying their sheaves.

Explanation of the psalm

1. When we first heard of the decree of our emancipation, and of our return to our country, we could, through joy, hardly believe it; and we were like those who, when in great affliction and trouble, get some comforting news, becoming, all at once blithe and merry, from being grave and sad. And this self same unspeakable consolation is always felt by those who are seriously converted to God, and, despising the hopes of this world, and abandoning all desire for the goods of this world, *"direct their steps in the path of peace."* They know the value of being rescued from the captivity of the devil, from the depths of the pit, and the being prepared for the enjoyment of true liberty and everlasting peace, through the call and the guidance of the Almighty. Interior joy will not fail to show itself externally, which it does by the expression of joy on the countenance and gladness on the tongue. *"Then,"* when we got the good news of our delivery, *"was our mouth filled with gladness,"* our face appeared blithe and merry, and *"our tongue, with joy,"* burst out into expressions of joy and gladness. *"Then shall they say among the gentiles."* The news of said emancipation not only gladdened the hearts of the emancipated, but it even astonished the gentiles when they heard it, and they could not help exclaiming, *"The Lord hath done great things for them;"* the Lord has behaved most magnificently to his people; for though it was Cyrus that liberated the Jews after so long a captivity, we can easily understand that he was prompted thereto by God, for he did it at the very time Jeremias prophesied it would be done, after seventy years; and Cyrus himself avowed that he got his power and command from heaven, and that he got an order from heaven to let the people go, and to build the temple in Jerusalem; and, finally, it could not be expected that any king would let so many thousand captives go free without the smallest ransom, and not only so dismiss them, but load them with presents on their departure, had he not felt himself constrained thereto from above. The gentiles, then, could not help attributing the whole to divine interposition.

2–3. The emancipated, quite pleased with the gentiles' notions on the matter being only in accordance with the facts, thus reply. It is the fact that the Lord dealt nobly with us, beyond our merits and our expectations, when he brought us from a miserable captivity to this our sweetest native land; and thus *"we are become joyful;"* we who had hitherto been groaning in sorrow, captives as we were.

4. As all the captives did not come home together—for some came, in the first instance, with Esdras, and then another party with Nehemias—the first party, then, pray to God for the return of all the captives, and they take up the simile of a torrent that is wont to run with great force and violence in a southerly gale; hence they say, *"Turn again, O Lord, our captivity."* Bring back our captives, the majority of whom are still in the land of the stranger; and bring them back at once, as quickly *"as a stream in the south;"* for when the wind blows from the south, the rain falls, the streams and the rivers rise, and the great flood rolls rapidly on to the ocean, and that without delay or obstruction. If the exiles, on their return, prayed to God so earnestly, what amount of earnestness will not be required of us, still exiles as we are? For though some have got home, have come to their country, yet many are still in exile, on the road, nay more, many are quite reconciled to the captivity, and have become so attached to the things of this world that they don't bestow even a thought on their country; it was, then, absolutely necessary that the Lord, with all the violence of a torrent, when the south wind blows, should force them and compel them to ascend. In conclusion, then, the former, as well as the latter, are, to a certain extent, captives; for *"all expect that every creature shall be delivered from the servitude of corruption;"* and even the blessed in heaven included. It is for this perfect liberty of the children of God, of which St. Paul treats in Rome, chap. 8, that we most properly pray when we say, *"Turn again our captivity as a stream in the south."* The south means the south wind that usually preceded rain, and caused the streams and rivers to fill and run with rapidity; most expressive of the tide of captives returning back again in crowds and in haste to their beloved country.

5. Having asked God to bring back all the captives to their country, he now addresses the captives themselves, and exhorts them not to be deterred by the labor of the journey, or to be detained by regard for any property they may have acquired in a foreign land, as they were sure to have much more and more valuable property in their own; and most happily compares them to the sower and the reaper; the one ordinarily does his work in grief and sorrow, being obliged to put his corn into the ground without having any certainty of ever getting the smallest return from it; and, therefore, seems to labor and to tire himself in order to lose what he has; but when the harvest comes, he reaps with great joy when he sees the corn that, to all appearance, was lost, is now, instead of being lost, returned to him with an enormous increase. This applies peculiarly to us, pilgrims as we are; for those who are content with their captivity, and are so engaged by the love of this world as never to think on their country, heaven; they look upon the road adopted by the just to be nothing better than a positive loss and an injury. While the true exiles make all the haste they can to their country above; they freely give to the poor, who will never return what is given; they labor, without fee or reward, in teaching their brethren, as did the Apostles; they

freely renounce all manner of pleasure; all which seems the height of folly to those who know not what is to come of it, while, in reality, it is *"sowing in tears,"* that they may afterwards, in due time, *"reap in joy."* And if they who are still so attached to their captivity, would seriously reflect on this, they certainly would change their mind, would begin to go up, and, no matter what it may cost them, they would sow the seed, that they may soon after reap it in joy in the kingdom of heaven.

6-7. He now describes, at greater length, the process of sowing and reaping. *"Going they went;"* the laborers and farmers went from their house to the field; *"and wept, casting their seeds;"* had much pain and trouble while shaking the seed, from the uncertainty of their ever having any return. But, in harvest time, when coming home, *"they shall come with joyfulness, carrying their sheaves;"* bringing back whole armsfull in return for a few grains. This so peculiarly applies to the virtue of almsgiving that it cannot but be of use to consider in what respect the seed may be compared with alms, in the hope that they *"who have in their heart disposed to ascend by steps"* may be more encouraged to divide freely with the poor. The grain that is sown is very small, and yet produces such a number of grains as to seem almost incredible; thus it is with alms, a small thing, a poor thing as being a human act; but when properly sown, produces, not money, nor food, nor clothes, but an eternal kingdom; Just as if the grain of wheat that we sow should produce an ear of gold instead of an ear of wheat, studded with precious stones instead of grains of wheat. Then, the grain put into the ground must corrupt and die or else it will not sprout, as our Lord has it in the Gospel, *"Unless the grain of wheat fall into the ground and die, itself remaineth alone;"* thus alms must be freely bestowed as a right, and not as a loan, and to those only who cannot return it; and it must be given to corrupt and perish, that is, without the slightest hope of getting it back in this world; for when thus lost and corrupted, it will not fail to shoot out again, and produce much fruit in life everlasting. Again, the grain put into the ground needs both sun and rain to germinate; and so with alms, which, as well as all other good works, needs the sun of divine grace, and the showers of the blood of the Mediator; that is, in order to become meritorious, they must spring from the grace of God, that has its source in the blood of Christ; for then a matter of the greatest insignificance becomes one of the greatest value, by reason of the stamp impressed upon it by grace; and thus merits, not only as a favor, but as a right, the grace of life everlasting. There is this difference between the sowing of the seed and the distribution of alms, that many things may occur to the former that may prevent the reaping in gladness, though they may have sowed in tears; because the seed may not sprout for want of rain; or it may be cut down, after sprouting, by slugs and worms; or, even after ripening, it may he stolen or burned. But alms, when given with a proper intention, is always safe; for it is stored up in heaven, where neither moths, nor flies, nor thieves can come near it. They, then, who sow such spiritual seed in tears, will unquestionably reap fruit in great joy.

PSALM 126

Nothing can be done without God's grace and blessing.

1 Unless the Lord build the house, they labour in vain that build it. Unless the Lord keep the city, he watcheth in vain that keepeth it.
2 It is vain for you to rise before light, rise ye after you have sitten, you that eat the bread of sorrow. When he shall give sleep to his beloved,
3 Behold the inheritance of the Lord are children: the reward, the fruit of the womb.
4 As arrows in the hand of the mighty, so the children of them that have been shaken.
5 Blessed is the man that hath filled the desire with them; he shall not be confounded when he shall speak to his enemies in the gate.

Explanation of the Psalm

1. These words were addressed to the Jews when they were building the house of God, that is, the temple, at a time that the work was progressing but slowly, by reason of the obstructions offered by the surrounding nations, as we read in 1 Esdras. They are admonished to bear in mind that the work of man is of no value, unless God, the principal builder, be there to help them; and, therefore, that they should work not only with their hands, but also with their hearts and their lips, in invoking God, and confiding mainly in his help. *"Unless the Lord build the house;"* unless God, on being invoked with confidence, assists the workmen, *"they labor in vain that build it;"* all their labor is gone for nothing, and will be so. This is also addressed to the heads of the Church who, by the preaching of God's word, seek to bring souls to him, and of them, to build up a temple, (the Church,) to the Lord, as we read in Corinthians, *"You are God's building;"* and further on, *"As a wise architect I have laid the foundation, and another buildeth thereon."* But unless the primary architect be there, he who said, *"On this rock I will build my church,"* in vain will men build, and doctors preach, because, as the Lord himself said, *"Without me you can do nothing."* The same applies to everyone of us, for we are bound, through acts of faith, hope, and love, to build up a house in heaven; for, as St. Augustine has it, *"Such a house is founded on faith, built up on hope, and finished off by charity; nor is anyone who has not previously prepared such a house ever admitted as a citizen in the heavenly country."* Such a house is constructed rather by prayer and lamentation, than by manual labor, because, *"we are not sufficient to think anything of ourselves, as of ourselves."*—*"Unless the Lord keep the city, he watcheth in vain that keepeth it."* When the city was being built after the captivity, they had to build it and guard it at the same time, as we read in 2 Esdras. The nations round about them not only sought to prevent them from building, but they demolished everything that was built if they could; and thus the children of Israel had to proceed with the sword in one hand, and the tools in the other, and many had to stand guard continually. Yet all this guarding would have been of no avail, had not the Lord chosen to guard the city. This, too, applies to the heads of the Church, whose duty it is both to build it up, and to guard it. Because we are surrounded by enemies, who hate nothing more than the extension of the Church, and though bishops get a very high position in the Church to look out as if from a watch tower, from which they can see everything, and thus guard the people; still, as they cannot penetrate men's hearts, nor be everywhere with everyone, they cannot but feel that, *"Unless the Lord keep the city, he watcheth in vain that keepeth it."* The same is very apt to occur to ourselves, when we, through good works, begin to build up a house, for enemies will not be wanting to seek to destroy the work so begun, by various temptations; and, hence, the Apostle arms us when he says, *"Wherefore take unto you the armor of God, that you may be able to resist in the evil day;"* and a little further on, *"In all things taking the shield of faith, wherewith you may be able to extinguish all the fiery darts of the most wicked one."* But unless God be with us, to guard us who slumber so often, and fight for us, all our labor will be in vain.

2. It is vain for you to rise before light: rise ye after you have sitten, you that eat the bread of sorrow. When he shall give sleep to his beloved:

3. The children of Israel, in their anxiety, while so harassed, were wont to rise before day, in order to expedite the building; and, therefore, the Holy Ghost admonishes them that their turning to work before day would be of no advantage to them, unless the Lord would assist them; but with him as a helper, with their hope firmly reposed in him, that the work would go on prosperously, even though they may not go to work until after the rising of the sun. *"It is vain for you to rise before light;"* you have no business whatever in beginning to work before day, unless the Lord shall build with you; and, therefore, trust in him, put up your prayers constantly to him. *"Rise ye after you have sitten;"* after the necessary rest of the night, rise to your work, *"you that eat the bread of sorrow,"* you who now lead a miserable and a sorrowful life by reason of the continual harassing of your enemies. In the meaning more in the mind of the Holy Ghost the prelates of the Church, and the faithful, individually, are admonished, that in the building of a house, whether for themselves or for a community, they should not confide

more in working than in praying, and should seek to imitate our Lord, who watched all night in prayer, as we read in Luke, *"And he passed the whole night in the prayer of God,"* while by day he addressed people, and confirmed what he said by miracles; as also the Apostle, who says in the Acts, *"But we will give ourselves continually to prayer, and to the ministry of the word."*—*"It is vain for you to rise before light,"* to waste all your time in building and watching it. *"Rise ye after you have sitten,"* go to your work after you shall have rested in prayer and contemplation. *"You that eat the bread of sorrow;"* you who, in your longings for your heavenly country, daily groan and exclaim, *"My tears have been my bread day and night, whilst it is said to me daily, where is thy God?"* For ardent lovers, when they cannot behold the thing they love, are supported by sighing and groaning for it, and thus their tears become bread to them day and night; that is, a dinner by day and a supper by night. *"When he shall give sleep to his beloved."* He now consoles them after his exhortations and admonitions, prophesying that it would come to pass, that after the present tribulations God would give peace to his people, and that the children of Israel would be manifestly *"God's inheritance,"* would become so powerful and so brave that they would never again have to suffer anything from the enemy, a prophecy that concerns the new people; that is, the Church of Christ, of which the temple and the city were a type. For as St. Augustine proves, after the restoration of the city and the temple, matters were every day getting worse with the Jews, until the city was laid in ruins, and the temple burned, under Titus and Vespasian. He, therefore, says, *"When he shall give sleep to his beloved,"* when he shall have given peace and rest to his people, by sending them the true Solomon, to build up the real temple, the Church which he will establish and propagate, and to which he will subject all the rulers of the world. *"Behold, the inheritance of the Lord are children, the reward the fruit of the womb;"* that is to say, then, it will appear that many children are the inheritance of the Lord, as he says in Psalm 2, *"Ask of me, and I will give thee the gentiles for thy inheritance, and the utmost parts of the earth for thy possession,"* and the *"reward"* of the same Christ our Lord will be the fruit of the womb; that is, many children, according to Isaias, *"If he shall lay down his life for sin, he shall see a long lived seed;"* for, as we have frequently remarked, repetitions are of most common occurrence in the Scripture, and thus *"the inheritance of the Lord are children,"* is one and the same with *"the reward the fruit of the womb;"* that is to say, the inheritance and the reward of Christ, our Lord, will be many children, who are nothing else than the fruit of the womb. If we look for a more sublime meaning in these words, we must make them foretell the happiness of the Jerusalem above; that is, which awaits those, who, in the resurrection, after the sleep of a temporary death, hastened, as they ought, to get up to their country on the wings of faith and love; and he, therefore, says, *"When he shall give sleep to his beloved;"* when, after various labors and contests, God shall give all his beloved, the pastors of his Church, who were its builders, as well as the faithful, in particular, who built up their own house by good works, the sleep and repose of a happy death. *"Behold, the inheritance of the Lord are children; the reward, the fruit of the womb."* It will appear on the day of judgment, that God's children are God's inheritance, because they will then obtain life everlasting, and will pass over to the everlasting possession and inheritance of God; and they will also be the reward of Christ, who is the fruit of the womb, because the salvation of the elect is Christ's reward, inasmuch as it was he, who, by his sufferings and death, got grace and glory for them.

4. The prophet now relates the strength of the children of Christ, who are his inheritance and his reward, and says, they will have great strength and power, as great as the arrows that are shot from the bow of a strong and powerful archer, which pierce everything; and this is only in reference to their spiritual strength, which is as remarkable in its action as it is in its power of endurance; for when they confound like thunder and lightning, when they bring infidels to the faith, or sinners to penance, by the fire of their preaching, by the brightness of their sanctity, and the power of their miracles; and when, in their struggles for the faith and for piety, they endure, even unto death, all manner of torments with the most incredible patience and fortitude, what else are they but arrows in the hand of the mighty? But why are those brave children called *"the children of them that have been shaken?"* Because they are the children of the outcasts and the wretched, the children of the prophets and the Apostles; and of the former, the Apostle writes, Heb. 11, *"Others had trial of mockeries and stripes, moreover also of bonds and prisons; they were stoned, they were cut asunder, they were tempted, they were put to death by the sword, they wandered about in sheep skins, in goat skins, being in want, distressed, afflicted; of whom the world was not worthy;"* and, speaking of the Apostles, the same Apostle says, 1 Cor. 4, *"For I think that God hath set forth us, Apostles, the last, as it were, men destined to death; because we are made a spectacle to the world, and to Angels, and to men. Even unto this hour, we both hunger and thirst, and are naked, and are buffeted, and have no fixed abode; and we labor, working with our own hands; we are reviled and we bless; we are persecuted, and we suffer it; we are ill spoken of, and we entreat: we are made as the refuse of this world; the off scouring of all even till now."* And yet, they, so shaken off and rejected, turned out to be the bravest of the brave, and had a most extraordinary triumph over the world and the demons. All the elect are the children of the aforesaid, who, *"like arrows in the hand of the mighty,"* have wounded and conquered their enemies.

5. He now concludes the Psalm by long and loud congratulations to Christ our Lord. *"Blessed is the man that hath filled his desire with them."* Truly happy is he, Christ to wit, *"that hath filled his desire with them;"* his children, because he got the full extent of his desire, the salvation and glory of his children, for whom he did and suffered so much; and therefore, *"he shall not be confounded when he shall speak to his enemies in the gates;"* that is to say, in the last judgment, that will be held in a tolerably extensive gate; for it will be in the assemblage of the whole world. *"He shall not be confounded when he shall speak to his enemies,"* be they demons or sinners; but he will rather confound them, and bring them in guilty of injustice and imbecility; for the whole contention between Christ and the devil and his ministers, from the beginning to the end of the world, turned upon the salvation of mankind, on whose ruin the evil spirit was always bent, and in order to effect which he raised up, in so many succeeding ages, so many persecutions of Jews, pagans, heretics, and bad members of all classes against the Church. But when, on the day of judgment, the countless thousands of the elect reigning in glory with Christ, crowned in triumph, and in great rejoicing shall appear; and, on the other hand, the wicked shall appear deprived of all power, and having been justly condemned to eternal punishment, shall have no hope of getting up the war again, then Christ, instead of being confounded, will confound all his enemies.

PSALM 127

The fear of God is the way to happiness.

1 Blessed are all they that fear the Lord: that walk in his ways.
2 For thou shalt eat the labours of thy hands: blessed art thou, and it shall be well with thee.
3 Thy wife as a fruitful vine, on the sides of thy house.
4 Behold, thus shall the man be blessed that feareth the Lord.
5 May the Lord bless thee out of Sion: and mayest thou see the good things of Jerusalem all the days of thy life.
6 And mayest thou see thy children's children, peace upon Israel.

EXPLANATION OF THE PSALM

1. The prophet teaches the exiles, on their return to their country, how they should conduct themselves, if they wish to avoid being made captives again, and to enjoy the blessings of Jerusalem forever. A very suitable instruction for the captives of this world, who long to get back to their country; as well as for those who are on their pilgrimage to the country above, and are in haste to get there. He then says, *"Blessed are all they,"* be they men or women, great or small, nobles or plebeians, learned or unlearned, in one word, all without exception; then alone will they be truly happy, that is, fortunate, contented, joyful, in the very best possible temper, a thing so much coveted by all, when they really fear God; that is, when they dread offending him, and, under the influence of such fear, never fall from God's grace, which is the fountain of all good. Now, a sign of such fear is *"to walk in his ways;"* because such holy fear springs from love; and the Lord says, *"If you love me, keep my commandments;"* and again, *"He that has my commandments, and keepeth them, he it is that loveth me;"* and again, *"He that loveth me not keepeth not my commandments."*

2. Addressing the man who so fears God, he begins to enumerate his blessings. Your first blessing will be, *"For thou shalt eat the labors of thy hands;"* you will enjoy all the property you have acquired by your industry, by the labor of your hands. Here we should reflect that the prophet does not make happiness to consist in great riches, but in such as have been acquired by the labor of one's hands, and they are, generally speaking, moderate. Great riches either come by inheritance, or from plunder or usury, or some other bad source. St. Jerome quotes an old saying, and a true one, *"The rich man is either a rogue or the heir of a rogue;"* and in Psalm 36, we have, *"Better is a little to the just than the great riches of the wicked;"* and again, in Psalm 143, *"Their storehouses are full, flowing out of this into that. Their sheep fruitful in young, abounding in their goings forth. Their oxen fat. There is no breach of wall or passage, nor crying out in their streets. They have called the people happy that hath these things, happy is that people whose God is the Lord."* Holy David then addresses not only the Jews, but all Christians, when he makes happiness to consist not in great riches, but in a sufficiency; the having wherewithal to live by one's just labor; and he censures two extremes—one, that of those who live on the others entirely; and the other, that of those who will not touch the labor of their hands, but, in a spirit of avarice, put it aside to increase their riches. They alone, then, are truly happy *"who eat the labors of their hands."* It may happen, however, that some *"who fear God,"* and *"walk in his ways,"* may not be able to eat of the *"labors of their hands,"* and have to endure hunger and thirst, by reason of their having been despoiled, or defrauded of their labor; but that will not bar the promise made in this passage; for if God sometimes lets his friends down so low that they would be glad to satisfy the cravings of their hunger with the fragments that fall from the table of the rich, as was the case with Lazarus, he will certainly give them something better, far better, instead; and that is joy from tribulation, as the Apostle has it, *"You received with joy the plundering of your goods;"* and again, *"I exceedingly abound with joy in all our tribulations;"* and the meaning of this verse will be, *"For thou shalt eat the labors of thy hands; blessed art thou, and it shall be well with thee;"* that is to say, you shall now eat of the

labor, you shall be refreshed by the joy consequent on labor and tribulation, but afterwards you shall be fattened by the fruit of said labor, by the reward in store for your good works; and *"blessed art thou"* now in hope, *"and it shall be well with thee"* hereafter in the reality. This is peculiarly applicable to the pilgrims, who *"rejoice in the tribulation"* of want and difficulties; *"for they know tribulation worketh patience, and patience trial, and trial hope, and hope confoundeth not, because the charity of God is poured out into our hearts."*

3. The second blessing enjoyed by the man *"that fears God and walks in his ways"* consists in his having only one wife, should he ever marry; and, in marrying, that he will be influenced more by a desire of propagating the human race than by any sinful or unworthy desires, as the Angel admonished Tobias when he said, *"Thou shalt take the virgin with the fear of the Lord, moved rather for love of children than for lust;"* and Tobias himself truly said, *"And now, Lord, thou knowest that not for fleshly lust do I take my sister to wife, but only for the love of posterity."* He, therefore, says, *"thy wife,"* not thy wives nor thy concubines, *"as a fruitful vine,"* with a large family, like a fruitful vine that sends out a number of branches, *"on the sides of the house;"* a domestic wife, that stays at home, looking after the business indoors, while her husband cares the business outside. This, to be sure, is a blessing to a certain extent; but, to give us to understand that it is not so very great a blessing, God was pleased to withhold it from many of his most faithful and devoted friends in the married state, such as Abraham and Sara, Isaac and Rebecca, Zachary and Elizabeth; and he also inspired many with a resolution of observing holy virginity, such as it is credibly believed of the holy prophets Elias and Jeremias, and is well known of the Blessed Virgin, St. John Baptist, St. Joseph, and hosts besides, who certainly would not have been deprived of the happiness had not virginity been a much superior gift. With that, those saints who never married, or had no offspring, if they had no family in one sense they had in another, far and away beyond it. Christ, for instance, who is the head of all the saints, was never married, had no children in the flesh, yet he had the Church for his spouse, and children in the spirit, nearly innumerable. So with Abraham, who had only one child by Sara, and yet, by faith, was made the father of many nations; for all the faithful are called *"children of Abraham"* by the Apostle. And what is more wonderful, these holy men are not only the fathers, but they are even the mothers of those whom they have brought to the faith, or to penance; for they are their fathers by reason of their preaching to them by word and example, and they are their mothers by reason of their praying and sighing for them. The same Apostle calls himself father when he says, *"I write not these things to shame you, but I admonish you as my dearest children; for, if you have ten thousand instructors in Christ, yet not many fathers. For in Christ Jesus I have begotten you through the*

Gospel;" and he calls himself their mother in another place, where he says, *"My little children, of whom I am in labor again."*—*"Thy children as olive plants round about thy table."* The third blessing, the education of the children, is now introduced. They who fear God and walk in his ways, will not only have many children, but they will be well brought up and educated, because they will be taught, from their earliest infancy, to fear God and to walk in his ways. He, therefore, says, *"Thy children as olive plants, round about thy table."* They will be like the choicest shrubs, the olive plants, that are evergreens, and bear most valuable fruit, and not like briars, or brambles, or shrubs that bear no fruit, and they will be *"round about thy table,"* that, by beholding them all together, eating with them, and living with them, you may have the greater pleasure and enjoyment with them. This, too, applies to the children in the Spirit, whom the father feeds with the word of God; and when he sees how they progress is wonderfully delighted, and, with the Apostle, says, *"My joy and my crown; so stand fast in the Lord, my most dearly beloved."*

4-6. Blessing the fourth, through which the man who fears God will be joyful for the blessings conferred on himself in particular, and also for those conferred on the community in general; and he, therefore, adds, that he will be so blessed by the Lord who dwells in Sion, that during his lifetime he will see all manner of good things abounding in Jerusalem, and will see his children's children therein equally happy; and, finally, a lasting peace, that guards and protects everything, enjoyed by the people of Israel. In a spiritual sense, and in one more intended by the Holy Ghost, a happiness as far above the three last named, as the heavens are above the earth, and God above his creatures, is described; and the prophet therefore, does not describe it by way of narration, but rather preaches and announces it to us. *"Behold,"* he says, in addition to all I have said, *"thus shall the man be blessed that feareth the Lord,"* for to him will be said, *"May the Lord bless thee out of Sion;"* may he bless you not only on earth, by bestowing all earthly blessings on you, but may he, furthermore, bless you from his holy mountain, from his highest dwelling place, and grant you *"that thou mayest see the good things of Jerusalem all the days of thy life;"* that you may see God, in whom are all the good things of Jerusalem, *"all the days of thy life,"* forever, unto ages of ages; for as the soul is immortal, as is the body, too, after the short sleep of death, when it will rise immortal, unquestionably the good things we see here are not seen all the days of our life, on the contrary they are only seen during a small portion of the days of our life, so that we may truly say, *"The days of our life are few, and full of evil;"* while we shall really see the good things of the heavenly Jerusalem all the days of our life, which will have no end, as will the wicked see the evil things of Babylon all the days of their everlasting death. We are not to be surprised at the prophets having said, *"mayest thou see,"* instead of mayest thou possess the good things of Jerusalem, because the good things of the Jerusalem above are possossed by seeing them, as perfect happiness consists purely of the beatific vision as St. John, in his first Epistle says, *"We shall be like to him,"* most blessed and happy, and almost gods, *"because we shall see him as he is."* Another addition to the happiness of the blessed in their country above, will consist in their beholding there *"the children of their children;"* that is, not only those who, through them, were born to God, but also the children of those children who, to the end of the world, shall have been brought to God, and will thus have cause of rejoicing for them all as if they belonged to themselves. To crown their happiness, they will see *"peace upon Israel,"* firm, lasting, and solid peace, inspiring the greatest confidence and security in all the inhabitants of the heavenly Jerusalem for all eternity; for they will see all their enemies laid perfectly prostrate under Christ's footstool; that is, hurled down to the lowest depths, and bound there in chains for eternity, for *"the earth is God's footstool;"* and all the wicked will lie shut up under it through everlasting ages.

PSALM 128

The Church of God is invincible; her persecutors come to nothing.

1 Often have they fought against me from my youth, let Israel now say.
2 Often have they fought against me from my youth: but they could not prevail over me.
3 The wicked have wrought upon my back: they have lengthened their iniquity.
4 The Lord who is just will cut the necks of sinners:
5 Let them all be confounded and turned back that hate Sion.
6 Let them be as grass on the tops of houses: which withered before it be plucked up:
7 Wherewith the mower filleth not his hand: nor he that gathereth sheaves his bosom.
8 And they that have passed by have not said: The blessing of the Lord be upon you: we have blessed you in the name of the Lord.

EXPLANATION OF THE PSALM

1. God's people, in trouble, console themselves by the reflection that troubles and difficulties are nothing new to them, and that, through God's assistance, they have always got through them. This applies to the Jews, and the repeated attacks of the neighboring nations, while the temple and the city were being rebuilt; and it also applies to the Church of Christ, that scarcely ever had a moment's respite from the assaults of pagans, heretics, or bad Christians. He, therefore, says, *"Often have they fought against me from my youth, let Israel now say."* Let not Israel, God's people, be surprised if her enemies assail her; for it is no new story with her; because, from her very infancy, at the first dawn of the Church, she suffered persecution from Cain, and similar persecutions have been going on to the present day.

2. He assigns a reason for the enemies having come so often to the charge, and says it was because *"they could not prevail over him;"* for, had they prevailed over and destroyed God's people, they would have had no occasion to renew the fight. The history of the Church bears testimony to this.

3. He now repeats and confirms by similes and metaphors what he had just expressed in plain language. *"The wicked have wrought upon my back."* They used my back for an anvil that the smith so repeatedly hammers; for their persecutions were so fierce and so numerous, that they could be compared to nothing else. *"They have lengthened their iniquity."* It was not once or twice they so hammered me, but they repeated it, kept it up and continued it.

4-5. The prophet now consoles God's people by predicting that the divine vengeance was not far off from the wicked persecutors of the just; as if he said, Cheer up, you just, for your persecutors, to be sure, wrought upon your back, or your necks; but, in a very short time, God, in his justice, instead of working on their necks, will cut them off with his sword, so that they will never again have the power of harming you; and then, finally, all those who had been so puffed up in their pride *"shall be confounded,"* and all they *"that hate Sion,"* and persecuted God's people, shall fly, and fall, and *"be turned back."* We must remark that the expression, *"will cut the necks of sinners,"* applies only to the impenitent sinners; for God, instead of cutting the necks of those who humbly confess their sins with a fixed purpose of amendment, *"heals all their diseases."* The words, *"Let them all be confounded and turned back that hate Sion,"* is not to be read in the sense of an imprecation, but of a prophecy; as we have frequently remarked.

6-7. Another imprecation, which, too, is to be read as a prediction, for it conveys to us the briefness of the happiness of the wicked, and, by a very happy idea, compares it to grass, a vile and fragile substance, and, as is said of it, *"which is to day, and tomorrow will be cast into the fire;"* and, not content with comparing it to grass, he adds, that it is like the grass that grows on the top of a house, a thing of no value, so much so that nobody ever thinks of cutting it, saving it, or making it into bundles, but leaves it where it grows to wither and to rot. At present, we don't see the full extent of this comparison, though we know of nothing, perhaps, more worthless, or of less value than such grass; but when we shall all come to be judged we shall see that such a comparison, instead of being over the mark, is considerably under it. What will be, then, to see those who abounded in the riches and power of this world, and who imagined they had, through such riches, established themselves and their families in their kingdoms and empires, shoved out ignominiously, and hurled into the lowest pit? and, furthermore, to see those who had reveled in pleasures and enjoyments, who knew not how to put up with the slightest inconvenience, consigned to everlasting torments, without the slightest hope of the smallest relief for all eternity?

8. As he said that the grass on the house top was not usually cut or gathered, he adds, that neither will the mowers of such grass be saluted or blessed by the passers by, as they are wont to salute the reapers or mowers of the hay or corn that grows in the fields; which will be another ingredient in the confusion of the wicked, who are compared to the grass on the house top. He, therefore, says, it never occurred, nor will it occur, that the passers by should salute or bless them that mow you, for you were never mowed, but when there was occasion to clean the roof you were pulled up and thrown into the fire or the sewer; and though the blessing of the passers by is given to the mowers, still it has its own effect on what is being mowed, for it includes the abundance and the ripeness of the crop and thus, the absence of any benediction on the wicked will have its effect on them too, because, in the last judgment, nobody will bless or salute them, nobody will have pity on them; they will be despised and condemned by all, which will tend very much to their further disgrace. No one will say to them, *"The blessing of the Lord be upon you,"* nor *"We have blessed you in the name of the Lord;"* but, on the contrary, they will be told by Christ, the judge, and by all his saints, *"Go, ye cursed, into everlasting fire."*

PSALM 129

A prayer of a sinner, trusting in the mercies of God. The sixth penitential psalm.

1 Out of the depths I have cried to thee, O Lord:
2 Lord, hear my voice. Let thy ears be attentive to the voice of my supplication.
3 If thou, O Lord, wilt mark iniquities: Lord, who shall stand it.
4 For with thee there is merciful forgiveness: and by reason of thy law, I have waited for thee, O Lord. My soul hath relied on his word:
5 My soul hath hoped in the Lord.
6 From the morning watch even until night, let Israel hope in the Lord.
7 Because with the Lord there is mercy: and with him plentiful redemption.
8 And he shall redeem Israel from all his iniquities.

Explanation of the psalm

1-2. The prophet being about to pray to God, first demands an audience, and then explains what he wants. He begins by comparing himself to one in a low valley, or a very deep well, who, unless he calls with a very loud voice, cannot be heard by one who is on a very high mountain, and thus, in fact, matters stand with us. For though God, by reason of his essence and power, be everywhere, still the sinner, by reason of his dissimilitude to God, is removed very far from God. God is always just and happy, and *"dwelleth on high."* The sinner is always bad and miserable, and like Jonas the prophet, who, for his disobedience to God, was thrown not only into the depths of the sea, but even into the depths of the belly of the whale; and, nevertheless, when be cried from thence he was heard, for a fervent prayer breaks through and penetrates everything. David then says, *"From the depths,"* not from the depth, because a true penitent has need to cry from two depths, the depth of misery and the depth of his heart; from the former, as if from the valley of tears, or as another Psalm expresses it, *"Out of the pit of misery and the mire of dregs,"* and from the latter, the depth of his heart; that is, from a thorough consideration and deep reflection on his own misery; for he that is not aware of, and that does not reflect on the depth in which he lies, has no wish to rise out of it, and, therefore, despises it, and thus sinks deeper again, as the Proverbs say, *"The wicked man when he is come into the depth of sins contemneth."* But whoever will, on profound reflection, feel that he is an exile, a pilgrim, and in great danger of never arriving at his country; and what is infinitely worse, that though he is not just now in the lowest depths of hell, he deserves to be there by reason of his sins, it is impossible for such a one not to be thoroughly frightened and horrified, or to avoid calling out with all his might to him who alone can rescue him from such a dreadful depth, and extend a hand to him to get up. *"Lord, hear my prayer."* However deep I may be, and however high you may be, as I cry with a very fond voice, you can hear me, and therefore, I beg of you to *"hear my voice."*—*"Let thy ears be attentive to the voice of my supplication."* However loud one may cry, he will not be heard, unless the person to whom he cries attend to him. People are often so absorbed in other matters, that they pay no heed to one talking to them, and then one talks to them in vain. Now, God always sees and hears everything, but when he does not grant what we ask, he is like one that does not attend to us, as if he were thinking of something else, and, therefore, David, being most anxious for a hearing, and not content with having called out with a loud voice, asks, furthermore, that God may deign to attend to him; that is, to receive his prayer, and grant what it asked.

3. Having got an audience, he now tells what he wants, and that is, that God should not deal with him in his justice, but in his mercy; that he should not require an exact account of the debt, but mercifully wipe it out; and, as he cannot summon sufficient courage to make such a request openly, he lays down a proposition with wonderful tact, and which must have been specially suggested by the Holy Ghost, from which he hopes to move God to grant his prayer. He, therefore, says as follows, *"If thou, O Lord, wilt mark*

iniquities," you will condemn the whole world; and, as it would not be consistent with your goodness to do that, I should not be looked upon as too forward in asking you to pardon my sins, and to rescue me from those depths into which my sins alone have plunged me. As regards the words, iniquity means all sorts of sin that break the law; as we read in 1 Jn. 3, *"All sin is iniquity;"* for all sins, strictly speaking, are not iniquity; that is, sins against justice; because there are sins of pride, of luxury, of the flesh, and many others. The word *"observe"* does not mean simply to look at; it means to note down, to record, to make an entry, as a creditor would against a debtor. The expression, *"who shall stand it?"* means, that should God choose to judge us, save in his mercy, nobody could pass his judgment; because any offence offered to God is infinite, and we, without his grace, are not only unable to offer condign satisfaction, but we are even incapable of seeing the enormity of the offence, or of having a perfect sorrow for it, or even of the manner in which we should set about doing penance for it; besides, we know not the number nor the heinousness of our sins; for, *"Who can understand sins?"* Now, God knows exactly the number of our sins; and he has them all written in his book; for, as Job says, *"Thou indeed hast numbered my steps."* He, too, knows, and is the only one that knows, the infinite enormity of mortal sin, and how, then, can weak, ignorant men render an account to so exact a calculator, and so powerful an exactor? Thus, like one who is able to throw himself into a well without being able to get out of it, is the sinner who can transgress, but cannot make satisfaction for the transgression, unless he be mercifully helped thereto.

4-5. To be truly penitent, (the subject of the prophet's instruction in this penitential Psalm,) we need two things; to reflect on our own wretched condition, and to know the extent of God's mercy; because he that is ignorant of the state he is in, seeks for no medicine, does no penance; and he that has no idea of God's mercy, falls into despair, and looks upon penance as of no value. The prophet, then, having clearly shown, in the preceding verses, that he was fully aware of his nothingness, because he cried from the depths, and because he said that his sins were so grievous, that if God were to be influenced by his judgment alone, no one could stand the ordeal; he now shows that he has an idea of God's mercy, and, therefore, however great and numerous his sins may be, that he still hopes for pardon of them, and for salvation; and, in consequence, he says, *"For with thee there is merciful forgiveness and by reason of thy law I have waited for thee, O Lord;"* as much as to say, though no one can stand before you if you choose to mark our iniquities, still, knowing you, as I do, to be naturally merciful, and knowing that *"with thee there is merciful forgiveness,"* and that, *"by reason of the law"* you imposed on yourself, to show no mercy to the impenitent, but to receive the penitent, it is *"by reason of such law that I have waited for thee, O Lord,"* in the hope and expectation of pardon for my sins. *"My soul hath relied on his word."* He now begins to exhort others, whom he encourages by his own example, to put their hope in God, saying, I have been in the lowest depths of misery, but I never despaired of God's mercy; for *"my soul,"* wounded, as it was, with the gores of sin, *"relied,"* looked for a cure, *"in his word,"* on his promise; for God frequently, through Moses, in Deuteronomy, and in various other parts of the Scripture, promised pardon to those who do penance. *"And when thou shalt seek the Lord thy God, thou shalt find him; yet if thou seek him with all thy heart, and all the affliction of thy soul."* Hence David himself previously said, in Psalm 118, *"Be thou mindful of thy word to thy servant, in which thou hast given me hope."* And he then repeats more clearly what he had just expressed rather obscurely, when he adds, *"My soul hath hoped in the Lord,"* that he would get the pardon he looked for. David's example ought to be of great value to us; for he was in the depth of misery, whether we regard his sins or what he suffered for them. His sins were most grievous; he had been guilty of adultery, took the life of a most faithful soldier; offended that God who had bestowed a kingdom on him, the gift of prophecy, strength, beauty, prudence, riches on him. He was also in the depths of misery when he was constantly persecuted by Saul, and in daily danger of his life; and yet, as he did not despair; but rather clung to hope, he was delivered.

6. Let all Israel, that is, all God's people, do what I do; let them, in whatever depth they may be, hope in the Lord: be they oppressed by sin or by the punishment of sin, let them trust in God's help. *"From the morning watch even until night.;"* the whole day, from day break to the end of the night, let them not, for as much as one moment, cease to trust in God. We are bound to hope in God during the whole day, and during the whole night, for two reasons: first, because we are always in danger; nor is there one moment in which we do not need God's help and assistance; secondly, because we are at liberty to hope at all times in God; and our conversion or penance is always acceptable, be it in the morning; that is, in our youth; or at midday, in the prime of life; or in the evening, in our old age; or be it in the day time of our prosperity; or in the night of our adversity.

7. He assigns a reason why we should always confide in God; and at the same time predicts the redemption of man, through Jesus Christ our Lord. We can justly hope in God all day and night, *"Because with the Lord there is mercy."* There are works of mercy that are not in God; hence we read, *"the earth is full of the mercy of the Lord;"* and in another place, 'Thy mercy is to the heavens;" pious souls, too, have a certain share of mercy; but mercy, properly speaking, is found with God alone, rests in his bosom alone;

mercy it is that removes misery; for, who can remove misery but one that cannot be subject to it? who can cure all defects but the one that is free from them, who is Almighty? To God only can be applied what the same prophet says, *"For thou, O Lord, art sweet and mild, and plenteous in mercy to all that call upon thee;"* and, therefore, it is that our holy mother, the Church, when appealing to God in her prayers, most commonly commences with, *"O Almighty and merciful God."* Nor should we hope in God by reason of his being merciful only, but with that, because *"there is plentiful redemption with him;"* because, when God in his mercy determined to spare the human race, in order that he may satisfy his justice, he offered a ransom of infinite value, the blood of his only begotten, sufficient to redeem any number of captives in the most plentiful manner, to any amount. Man could have sold himself as a captive for his sins, or he could have been given up to the devil, to whose temptations he had yielded, to torture him for his sins, but he never could have redeemed himself, nor have rescued himself from the power of the devil. What man was unable to do, therefore, God's mercy did for him, and that through the blood of the only begotten. Now, when this Psalm was being written, the said mercy was with God, in his counsel and resolve, but at present *"the earth is full of the mercy of the Lord,"* because the price that was paid for the redemption of the captives is being daily expended, and hence the Apostle says, *"For you are bought with a great price, glorify and bear God in your body,"* which is more clearly expressed by St. Peter, when he says, *"You were not redeemed with corruptible gold or silver, but with the precious blood of Christ, as of a lamb unspotted and undefiled."* Such redemption is called *"plentiful,"* because *"he is the propitiation for our sins; and not for ours only, but also for those of the whole world,"* not only because such a ransom redeems us from captivity, but, besides, raises us to share in the inheritance, and the kingdom, whereby we become *"heirs of God and coheirs of Christ."*

8. The *"plentiful redemption"* will be clearly manifested to all, when *"Israel"*— that is, God's people—shall be redeemed; not as the carnal Jews idly expect, from the sovereign powers now in possession of it, but *"from all his iniquities;"* a thing the Angel promised would be accomplished by our Savior, when he said to St. Joseph, *"And thou shalt call his name Jesus, for he shall save his people from their sins."* This redemption has begun, and is going on, and will be completely accomplished on the last day, when we shall be delivered not only from our sins, but even from the punishment due to them, and from any danger of relapse, as is conveyed to us by David in Psalm 102, when he says, *"As far as the east is from the west, so far hath he removed our iniquities from us;"* and, again, in the same Psalm, *"Who forgiveth all thy iniquities, who healeth all thy diseases, who redeemeth thy life from destruction, who satisfieth thy desire with good things;"* and most clearly in Daniel, *"That*

transgression may be finished, and sin may have an end, and iniquity may be abolished, and everlasting justice may be brought."

PSALM 130

The prophet's humility.

1 Lord, my heart is not exalted: nor are my eyes lofty. Neither have I walked in great matters, nor in wonderful things above me.
2 If I was not humbly minded, but exalted my soul: As a child that is weaned is towards his mother, so reward in my soul.
3 Let Israel hope in the Lord, from henceforth now and for ever.

Explanation of the Psalm

1. The prophet, being quite certain of saying nothing but the truth, directly addresses God, whom no one can deceive, and asserts that he was never subject to pride, either in his interior or his bearing. Many, with a semblance of humility, are full of interior pride and self importance; and many look down upon their neighbors without the slightest effort at concealing their pride and impudence; while David's *"heart was not exalted, nor were his eyes lofty;"* he was humble in his heart, and he expressed it in his looks. *"Neither have I walked in great matters, nor in wonderful things above me."* Having thus disposed of interior and exterior pride, he now comes to the pride arising from our words and our actions. Some are fond of boasting of being able to do, or of having done, or of being about to do greater or more wonderful things than they could possibly do; and thus, *"they walk in things above them,"* as to their speech; and others undertake to do what they are quite unequal to, and *"they walk in things above them,"* in their actions or in their works; but David, grounded in true humility, knew his own place; neither in word nor deed *"walked above himself in great and wonderful things;"* that is to say, never boasted of having done great and wonderful things beyond his strength, nor attempted to do what he felt himself unequal to.

2. Not satisfied with having declared to God, the searcher of hearts, that he always had the greatest abhorrence of all manner of pride, he confirms it by an oath or imprecation, in order to make it more thoroughly believed by all; and therefore, says, *"If I was not humbly minded"* about myself, *"but exalted in my soul;"* and thus, looking down upon others; *"as a child that is weaned is towards his mother;"* as a child recently weaned, lies crying and moaning on its mother's lap or breast, by reason of being deprived of that usual nourishment that was so sweet and agreeable to it; *"so reward in my soul;"* so may my soul be deprived of the sweetness of divine consolation, my especial, and nearly my only delight. They alone who have been filled with the same spirit, and have tasted how sweet God is, can form an idea of the amount of punishment the holy prophet thus imprecates on himself; for the Psalms that were composed, like so many amatory ditties, testify to his disregard for the wealth of this world or the glory of a throne, as compared with his love for God. Take a few of the numberless proofs of it. *"O! how great is the multitude of thy sweetness, O Lord, which thou hast hidden for them that fear thee."* *"O taste and see, that the Lord is sweet."* *"My heart hath said to thee, my face hath sought thee; thy face, O Lord, will I still seek. Turn not away thy face from me."* *"My soul refused to be comforted, I remembered God, and was delighted."* *"Give joy to the soul of thy servant, for to thee, O Lord, I have lifted up my soul, for thou, O Lord, art sweet and mild."* *"But I will take delight in the Lord."* *"And I will rejoice under the cover of thy wings; my soul hath stuck close to thee."* *"For what have I in heaven? and besides thee what do I desire upon earth? Thou art the God of my heart, and the God that is my portion forever; but it is good for me to adhere to my God;"* as much as to say, let others run after ideal happiness, whether in air or on earth, *"My good is to adhere to my God;"* he is my supreme happiness, he is *"the God of my heart;"* my share, my inheritance, my portion, my all; with him alone I am, and ever will be, content. When David, then, in his humility and his simplicity, like a child just weaned, placed all his happiness in the milk of divine love, he could not have wished himself a greater evil than to be in the position of a child prematurely weaned, who refuses all manner of consolation on being debarred from its mother's breast.

3. The conclusion of the Psalm explains the object of the great praise so conferred on humility; for the holy soul did not mean or intend to hold himself up as an example of it, but he wanted to admonish the people how little they ought to confide in themselves, and how much in God; and he, therefore, says, *"Let Israel hope in the Lord."* If I, a king and a prophet, dare not take a shine out of myself by reason of my power and my wisdom, and, instead of relying on myself, cast all my hope on God, it certainly is only right that Israel, my people, and who are also God's people, should not *"imagine that they are something when they are nothing,"* nor confide in their own strength, but hope in the Lord—they will hope in him, not only today and tomorrow, but forever and ever.

PSALM 131

A prayer for the fulfilling of the promise made to David.

1 Lord, remember David, and all his meekness.
2 How he swore to the Lord, he vowed a vow to the God of Jacob:
3 If I shall enter into the tabernacle of my house: if I shall go up into the bed wherein I lie:
4 If I shall give sleep to my eyes, or slumber to my eyelids,

5 Or rest to my temples: until I find out a place for the Lord, a tabernacle for the God of Jacob.
6 Behold we have heard of it in Ephrata: we have found it in the fields of the wood.
7 We will go into his tabernacle: We will adore in the place where his feet stood.
8 Arise, O Lord, into thy resting place: thou and the ark, which thou hast sanctified.
9 Let thy priests be clothed with justice: and let thy saints rejoice.
10 For thy servant David's sake, turn not away the face of thy anointed.
11 The Lord hath sworn truth to David, and he will not make it void: of the fruit of thy womb I will set upon thy throne.
12 If thy children will keep thy covenant, and these my testimonies which I shall teach them: Their children also for evermore shall sit upon thy throne.
13 For the Lord hath chosen Sion: he hath chosen it for his dwelling.
14 This is my rest for ever and ever: here will I dwell, for I have chosen it.
15 Blessing, I will bless her widow: I will satisfy her poor with bread.
16 I will clothe her priests with salvation: and her saints shall rejoice with exceeding great joy.
17 There will I bring forth a horn to David: I have prepared a lamp for my anointed.
18 His enemies I will clothe with confusion: but upon him will my sanctification flourish.

EXPLANATION OF THE PSALM

1. Such is the language of Solomon, who is supposed to be the author of this Psalm, in which he prays to God through the merits of his father, David, *"Lord, remember David,"* your friend, and all his good qualities, the principal of which was *"his meekness."* The word *"remember"* does not imply that God is subject to forgetfulness; it means that when he does not regard the just he seems to act as if he did not remember their merits. The meaning, then, of such expression is, that he wishes we should pray for many things which, without our prayers, he would not have granted. An instance of it occurs in 3 Kings, where God, through the prophet, speaks to Jeroboam, and says he is highly incensed at the sins of Solomon; still, that he would preserve the kingdom for him during his life, *"on account of David, his servant, who observed his precepts and commandments;"* from which it appears that this prayer of Solomon was heard. Solomon alludes to David's mildness, without taking any notice of his other virtues; because David was most remarkable for mildness, as was evident from his refusing to take Saul's life, though he might have done so, and he knew Saul was seeking to take his, and that without cause; as, also, because mildness is of great value in the sight of

God, being the constant companion of humility and charity, and because it makes man like to God, who is *"sweet, and mild, and plenteous in mercy to all that call upon him."* Thus, previous to David, Moses was God's greatest friend, *"because Moses was a man exceeding meek, above all men that dwelt upon earth;"* and Christ our Lord, who was full of grace and truth, held up no other virtue more for our imitation. *"Learn of me, for I am meek and humble heart."* Nor is it inconsistent with the meekness of David or Moses to have taken the lives of so many, nor with that of Christ to have turned the buyers and sellers out of the temple, and to upset their tables; for meekness is not inconsistent with justice, it is rather sister to zeal for the honor of God; and they who readily put up with a personal offence, which is the office of meekness, are the more fit to punish one offered to God or to the neighbor, because it is evident to all that they are not influenced by any private pique or selfish motive, but by a pure love of justice; as, also, because they seem to forget themselves altogether, and to be entirely absorbed in seeking and extending God's honor and glory.

2-5. Solomon now tells the consequence of the meekness and the humility of his father David. Being meek and humble in heart, he looked upon it as a reproach, that he should have a house wherein to dwell, and a bed whereon to lie, while the Ark of the Testament had no fixed place of residence, no temple where it may be worshipped with the reverence due to it; but was constantly shifted from one place to another; and, therefore, he swore that he would not enter his house, nor lie on his bed; nay, more, that he would not close his eyes anywhere, or take any manner of rest, so long as the Ark had no resting place. We have no exact account of David's having made such a vow, unless we can infer it from 2 Kings 8, where David tells Nathan the prophet that he had determined to build a temple to the Lord, because he was ashamed of living in *"a house of cedar,"* while the Ark of God was under a tent. On that very night God ordered Nathan to tell David that it was not his wish that he should build the temple, but that he should leave it to his son to build it; and he repeated the same to David, in Par. 22, and 28. If David, then, bound himself by oath to build the temple, why did not he build it? Why did not he even make the attempt? He was forbidden by God; and besides, the words of the oath contain an exaggeration not unusual in the Scriptures; and they mean no more here than the expression of David's great anxiety to build the temple. Thus, in Psalm 1, the words, *"And on his law he shall meditate day and night,"* contain a similar exaggeration; and again, *"I will bless the Lord at all times, his praise shall be ever in my mouth;"* and a more striking one in Isaias, *"Upon thy walls I have appointed watchmen, all the day and all the night they shall never hold their peace;"* and Solomon prescribes the same anxiety to perform a promise that he here attributes to his father, when he says, *"Run about, make haste, stir up thy friend, give not sleep to thy eyes, neither let thy eyelids slumber."* Similar expressions occur in the New Testament, *"We ought always to pray, and not to faint;"* and, further on, *"Watch ye, therefore, praying at all times."* Such expressions do not imply that we must be praying at every given moment, but that we must pray often, and in matters of importance, and that we must not suffer the cares of the world, however urgent, to interfere with our ordinary prayers. The oath, then, may be thus explained, *"If I shall enter into the tabernacle of my house,"* so as to forget the obligation of building God's house, which I swear never to forget—*"If I shall go up into the bed where I lie,"* I swear I will never go into it without thinking on the bed, the site of the temple, where the Ark of the Lord may rest in dignity. *"If I shall give sleep to my eyes, or slumber to my eyelids;"* I swear that I will not sleep or rest, without waking to consider on the necessity of building up a temple to the Lord, which oath and vow he most faithfully fulfilled, as can be seen in Par. 29, *"And I, with all my ability, have prepared the expenses for the house of my God. Gold for vessels of gold, and silver for vessels of silver, brass for things of brass, iron for things of iron, wood for things of wood: and onyx stones, and stones like alabaster, and of diverse colors, and all manner of precious stones, and marbles of Paros in great abundance. Now, over and above the things which I have offered into the house of my God, I give of my own proper goods, gold and silver for the temple of my God, besides what things I have prepared for the holy house. Three thousand talents of gold of the gold of Ophir: and seven thousand talents of refined silver to overlay the walls of the temple."* Besides this large amount of property, he drew up a most elaborate specification of all parts of the temple, of its halls, porches, supper rooms, chapter rooms, and the like, as well as of all the ornamentation of it. Now, these were all types and figures of Christ, the true David, who, in his desire of raising a living temple, and an everlasting tabernacle to God, spent whole nights in prayer, and, truly, neither entered his house, nor went up into his bed, nor gave slumber to his eyelids nor rest to his temples, and presented to himself *"a glorious Church, not having spot nor wrinkle, nor any such thing,"* nor built *"with corruptible gold or silver,"* but with his own precious sweat and more precious blood; it was with them he built that city in heaven that was seen by St. John in the Apocalypse, and *"was ornamented with all manner of precious stones."* Hence, we can all understand the amount of care, cost, and labor we need to erect a becoming temple in our hearts to God.

6. He tells the reason why David was so anxious to build a temple, and it was because the Ark of the Lord had no fixed or certain residence. *"Behold, we have heard of it in Ephrata,"* of the Ark being in Ephrata, in the land of Ephraim, that was when it was in Silo, in Samuel's time; then *"we found it*

in the fields of the woods," when it was sent off by the Philistines, and found in the field of Joshua the Bethsamite, which must have been a woody place, as it was taken from thence to the neighboring town Cariathiarim, which means the city of woods.

7. Having expressed the wishes and desires of his father David, Solomon being now about to bring the Ark into the temple he had built, says, *"We will go into his tabernacle;"* in other words, hitherto, the Lord has been a stranger in various places, but now he shall have a fixed residence, and, therefore, *"we will go into his tabernacle,"* now erected, and built on Sion, and *"we will adore in the place where his feet stood,"* we will turn towards the holy Ark which is his footstool, where his feet stood, and are wont to stand, and adore there. The sanctuary in the interior of the tabernacle was so constructed that the Ark was the footstool, and the propitiatory was the seat of the Lord, and was supported by two Cherubim.

8. Solomon, now about to introduce the Ark to a temple built in a most magnificent style, most poetically addresses it, inviting it to come in and take its habitation there. *"Arise, O Lord,"* from the place in which you have been hitherto but as a guest, and enter your own house, to stay there, and no longer to wander about from place to place, as you have done hitherto. And he lets us see that, when he speaks thus to the Lord, he does not address him, as he essentially exists, for, as such, *"the heaven of heavens do not contain him,"* but as he is peculiarly in the Ark of the Testament, because it was from it he gave his answers, and he, therefore, adds, *"Thou and the ark which thou hast sanctified;"* that is, you and your throne, and the footstool of your feet, which footstool is *"the ark which thou hast sanctified,"* and through which you will be sanctified and honored by all who know it. In the Hebrew it is the *"Ark of thy strength,"* because it was through it God displayed his strength. When the priests brought it to the Jordan, the river at once turned back; when it was carried seven times round the city of Jericho, down came the walls; when it was taken by the Philistines, and lodged in the temple of Dagon, the idol was found in the morning stretched on the ground before the Ark; and wherever it was carried about by them, innumerable were killed, so that the Philistines were at length forced to say, *"The Ark of the God of Israel shall not stay with us; for his hand is heavy upon us, and upon Dagon our god."* When the Bethsamites inspected the Ark with too much curiosity, over forty thousand of them were slain; and Oza, for merely touching it, was at once slain by God.

9. The Ark having been brought into the temple, Solomon puts up a prayer, first for the priests, then for the king, that is, for himself; for on them depend the whole safety of the people, the priests being the rulers in spiritual matters, as are the kings in temporal. He asks for the priests, that they may

be just and holy, as they ought to be, in order to discharge their duty properly, and that they should be alive in praising God, that being their peculiar province because they are bound to give God the tribute of praise and thanksgiving, both on their own part, and on that of the people, for the favors we are constantly receiving from him; and so to praise and thank our benefactor is to stir up his kindness to continue and increase his blessings. He, therefore, says, I beg of you, O Lord, that *"thy priests be clothed with justice,"* interior and exterior, within and without; that justice may appear in their lives, words, and actions, and that nothing disgraceful should turn up in those who are to minister to you and to teach your people. The metaphor of a robe is used here to give us to understand, that as such an article not only covers the deformities, but also adds to the appearance of those who wear it, and distinguishes them too; so should priests, through their virtues, and their extreme sanctity, not only rise above the imputation of anything mean or disgraceful, but should hold themselves up as a bright model and example to the flocks they have in charge, so that it may not be said of them, that *"the people are as bad as the priest." "And let thy saints rejoice."* Let the same priests, who, strictly speaking, are your saints, at least they ought to be, as being consecrated and segregated to you, let them exult and rejoice in praising you, and thus properly discharge their duty. If such was the justice, holiness, and promptness required of the priests who sacrificed but sheep and oxen, what amount of those virtues will be required of the priests who sacrifice the Lamb? Woe to us wretched, who have been called to so sublime a ministry, and are so far short of the fervor that Solomon required in the priests who were but foreshadows of the priests of the new law!

10. He now prays for the kings that is, for himself; and in order to get what he wants more easily, he draws upon the merits of his father David, and his prayer consists in asking that he may be heard whenever he may pray. *"For thy servant David's sake."* In consideration of the faithful services of David my father, *"turn not away the face of thy anointed."* Do not cause me who have been anointed king in his place, to retire in confusion from you at the rejection of my prayer, and thus cause me to turn my face away from you. To turn away the face of the supplicant means, to refuse his prayer, to dismiss him in confusion, as when Solomon's mother said to him, *"I desire one small thing of thee, do not put me to confusion. And the king said to her: My mother, ask, for I must not turn away thy face."* However true all this may be, there is still a more spiritual meaning in this verse. Every good act of ours has a reference to God and to ourselves; to God, in order that he may look upon us with the love of a father, and that we should look upon him with the affection of a child; for such reciprocal love is the source and origin of all our good, but God's love or regard precedes, and causes our regard for him. As

St. John says, *"In this is charity, not as if we have loved God, but because he first loved us."* Thus, when God loves us, he causes us to love him, and when he regards us as children he makes us regard him as a father; and though we, of our own free will, turn our face away from God by the commission of sin, still, should God deign to look upon us, and to look upon us in his mercy, he will mercifully cause us to take no further pleasure in sin, and not to turn away our face from him, or should we chance to do so, that we will at once turn to him again, just as when the Lord looked on Peter, who had turned his face from him, and thereby converted him so effectually, that, *"he went out at once and wept bitterly."* David put up the same prayer, when he said, *"Look thou upon me, and have mercy on me;"* and thus, Solomon prays here, *"turn not away the face of thy anointed;"* let not my face be turned away from you, which will be caused by your not turning your face away from me.

11. He now begins to refer to the promise that were made by God to David his father, in the hope of more easily obtaining what he asks for through such reference, as he seems to demand it as a debt fairly due. *"The Lord hath sworn truth to David;"* as much as to say, David, having sworn to the Lord, that he would build a temple to his glory, and the Lord swore, in return, that he would establish the sovereign power in David's family for all eternity; for God will not be outdone in liberality, and rewards not only our actions, but even our words and our thoughts, with the most unheard of generosity. The oath here implies the fixed determination on the subject, intimating that God, not satisfied with a promise he was sure not to break, went further, and confirmed it by an oath. He then reconfirms the matter, by adding, *"and he will not make it void;"* his oath will not be left unaccomplished, as he expresses it in another Psalm, *"The Lord hath sworn, and he will not repent."* He next proceeds to tell us what the truth was that he promised and confirmed by an oath, and says, *"Of the fruit of thy womb I will set upon thy throne;"* in other words, I will make your son your successor on the throne; words that should be literally applied to Christ, and not to Solomon, unless we look upon him as the type of Christ, for in Psalm 88, that refers to the same oath, we read, *"Once have I sworn by my holiness I will not lie unto David; his seed shall endure forever; and his throne as the sun before me; and as the moon perfect forever, and a faithful witness in heaven."* The phrase, then, *"I will set,"* does not mean I will put there, but I will establish, and put there forever, which does not apply to Solomon. Furthermore, St. Peter, speaking of David, says, Acts 2, *"Whereas, therefore, he was a prophet, and knew that God had sworn to him with an oath, that of the fruit of his loins one should sit upon his throne; foreseeing he spoke of the resurrection of Christ; for neither was he left in hell, neither did his flesh see corruption;"* in which passage St. Peter explains an expression in Psalm 30, by another in Psalm 131, now before us, and this

is also alluded to by the Angel in saluting the Virgin, when he said, *"And the Lord shall give unto him the throne of David his father, and he shall reign in the house of Jacob forever."*

12. The oath and the promise in reference to his only son Christ, of whose kingdom there will be no end, was given and made unconditionally; but not so to others—it was on condition, *"if they will keep my covenant;"* the treaty I entered into with them of having no strange gods, and of their observing *"my testimonies,"* my commandments, in which case *"they shall sit upon thy throne,"* and if not, they will be cast out. David expressed this idea much more clearly to Solomon, when he said, *"If thou seek him thou shalt find him; At if thou forsake him, he will cast thee off forever;"* and God himself, speaking of Solomon, a short time before, says, *"And I will establish his kingdom forever, if he continue to keep my commandments, and my judgments, as at this day;"* and in Psalm 88, where we read, *"And if his children forsake my law, I will visit their iniquities with a rod;"* and he does not add, but my mercy I will not take away from them, *"but from him,"* that is, from David, whose throne was everlasting, by reason of his being the type of Christ, even though the temporal sovereignty of Solomon, Roboam, and their successors may have an end.

13-14. These verses apply, to a certain extent, to the city of Jerusalem, inasmuch as it was a type of the Church militant, and afterwards triumphant; because God chose that city for a time as the seat of royalty and of the priesthood, and in it were to be found the throne and the temple. But, as that city was soon to be laid in ruins, and the kingdom upset, and the temple itself to be burned, we are constrained to say that these verses apply to the Church, the kingdom of Christ, and that the Sion, or Jerusalem, alluded to here is that of which he speaks in the second Psalm, when he says, *"But I am appointed king by him over Sion, his holy mountain,"* a continuation of which we have in verse 11 of this Psalm. *"The Lord hath sworn truth to David, and he will not make it void, of the fruit of thy womb I will set upon thy throne;"* that is to say, he swore to David that he would place and establish his Son, Christ, on his throne, which is Sion, and which is, consequently, called the city of David, because *"the Lord hath chosen Sion,"* that is, the Church, *"as his dwelling forever,"* and said in regard of it, *"This is my rest forever and ever;"* that is to say, I will never desert this Church, but I will rest forever in her, because I will remove her to a perfect certainty in heaven; and there *"I will dwell"* in her forever, *"because I have chosen it,"* by a firm and everlasting decree.

15. This and the following verses promise many blessings to Sion, the city of David, which are, to a certain extent, applicable to that city, inasmuch as she was a type of the Church, but they are much more applicable to the Church itself. He, first, promises such an abundance of the good things of this world

that even the widows, who are generally destitute, and all the poor in general, will enjoy an abundance. Now, this abundance, as applied to the Church, means an abundance of spiritual food, of the food of the word of God and of the sacraments, an abundance of which is enjoyed by the children of the Church, especially by those who are poor in spirit.

16. The second blessing conferred on the holy city will consist in its priests being conspicuous for their justice and their holiness, because, as iniquity is the disease of the soul, so is justice its salvation; and, as Solomon previously prayed that *"her priests be clothed with justice,"* God now says, that *"he will clothe those priests with salvation,"* which is the same as justice when there is question of our spiritual salvation.

17. The third and the greatest blessing to be conferred on holy Sion will be, that there will the kingdom of David have its rise. The horn metaphorically means the power and the dignity of the king, and that by reason of its preeminence and durability. But, in a literal sense, the horn of David means the kingdom of the Messiah, that was to have its rise in Sion, and to be propagated from thence throughout the entire world. Zacharias announced it when he said, Lk. 1, *"And he hath raised up a horn of salvation to u in the house of David, his servant."* The prophet, too, foretold it; for Isaias says, chap. 9, *"He shall sit upon the throne of David and upon his kingdom, to establish it and strengthen it forever."* Jeremias has the following: *"Behold, the days come, saith the Lord, and I will raise up to David a just branch, and a king shall reign and shall be wise, and shall execute judgment and justice."* Ezechiel not only foretells the kingdom of Christ, but even describes his triumphal chariot, drawn by four animals, a man, a lion, a calf, and an eagle, meaning the four Evangelists. In Daniel 2, we have, *"But in the days of those kings the God of heaven will set up a kingdom that shall never be destroyed;"* and Zach. 9, *"Rejoice greatly, O daughter of Sion, shout for joy, O daughter of Jerusalem, behold, thy king will come to thee, the just and Savior; he is poor and riding upon an ass, and upon a colt, the foal of an ass."* From all of which prophecies it is clear that this verse cannot possibly apply to Solomon or to his kingdom, for he was then alive and on his throne, whereas some future king is evidently intended. The expression, *"will I bring forth,"* means, I will make David's horn, or power, spring up, as it were, and germinate, wherein he evidently foretells the destruction of Jerusalem, and the establishment of the everlasting kingdom of the Messias in place of the temporal power enjoyed hitherto by its kings. *"I have prepared a lamp for my anointed."* St. Augustine says, the lamp alludes to St. John Baptist; for, as the Messias was to come without any show, pomp, or retinue, it was likely that the carnal Jews, who expected quite a different Messias, would hardly receive him had not John preceded him, who, by his singular sanctity and austerities, *"like a*

light shining in a dark place," brought the eyes of all upon him. *"There will I bring forth a horn to David;"* this means, I have established the eternal kingdom of the Messias; *"I have prepared a lamp,"* the precursor, who will be as a lamp, *"for my anointed,"* for the Messias; and Christ himself seems to allude to this verse when he said of St. John, *"He was a burning and a shining lamp."*
18. He prophesies that Christ will have many enemies, as, in truth, he had amongst the Jews, who said, *"We will not have this man to reign over us;"* and when they said to Pilate, *"We have no king but Caesar;"* but he also prophesies the punishment in store for them. *"His enemies I will clothe with confusion."* I will brand them with infamy, as we see all over the world. Soon after the death of Christ, the Romans sacked and destroyed the city, slew immense numbers of them, sold many of them as slaves, and exposed a great many of them to wild beasts in the public games; and from thence to the present day, the Jewish race are everywhere in a state of slavery, and are everywhere despised; but on the last day, then not only will Jews, but all pagans, heretics, and all false brethren, who, through his brethren, have been enemies to Christ, will be *"clothed with confusion."* While they shall be *"clothed with confusion,"* Christ will be clothed with glory, because the seed that had been buried in the earth will then flower forth into glory, by budding forth the flowers of sanctification; and not only will Christ be clothed with glory, but so will all his members too, because such sanctification will then produce flowers of incredible beauty, when grace shall be turned into glory.

PSALM 132

The happiness of brotherly love and concord.

1 Behold how good and how pleasant it is for brethren to dwell in unity.
2 Like the precious ointment on the head, that ran down upon the beard, the beard of Aaron, Which ran down to the skirt of his garment:
3 As the dew of Hermon, which descendeth upon mount Sion. For there the Lord hath commandeth blessing, and life for evermore.

EXPLANATION OF THE PSALM

1. Such is the language of those who begin to feel the sweetness as well as the advantage of perfect charity. He calls it *"good"* by reason of its advantages, and *"pleasant"* by reason of its sweetness; for though some things are good without being pleasant, such as penance; and pleasant without being good, such as sin; still, both are found combined in the peace and harmony of *"brethren dwelling together."* For virtue so combined is greater and stronger, and is easier and better preserved, which thus tends to their mutual advantage; and where many are so united by charity as to form *"one heart and one soul,"* everyone rejoices in the happiness of the others as well as he does in his own, and thus tends to increase the mutual pleasure of all.

2-3. He explains the pleasure and the advantages of living together by two similes; first, comparing the pleasure to the precious ointment used for anointing the head of the high priest, which was most highly perfumed, as appears from Exodus 30, and which dropped from his head on his beard, and from thence on the upper fringe of his robe; not on the lower, as the word skirt would seem to imply, which is quite plain in the Greek and Hebrew, and which common sense seems to indicate. We have to observe here, that the ointment on the head could be communicated to the parts only in connection with the head; for if the beard had not been united to the head, it would have received none of the ointment as it fell; and so with the garment, if that had not been in connection with the head, it too would have caught none of the ointment; and thus the ointment was communicated to all through their union with each other; and thus it becomes necessary for *"brethren to dwell together,"* and to be united by the bond of love, in order to get the supernatural graces that flow from Christ, as the head, and from him on the prelates of the Church, who are indicated by the beard, and through them on the faithful in general, indicated by the fringe of his garment. He then compares such union of brethren to the dew that falls on the mountain, which confers no pleasure thereon, but certainly great benefits; for the dew causes the grass to spring up, and clothes the mountain with verdure. He names two mountains, Hermon and Sion, considerably distant from each other; one of them a very high mountain, Hermon, and the other a very low one, Sion, as if the Holy Ghost would have us infer therefrom, that the union, most pleasing to God, is that of the heart and not of the body, as we read in the Acts, of the first Christians, of whom it is said, *"And the multitude of the believers had but one heart and one soul."* He, therefore, says, that the advantage of brethren living together is like *"the dew of Hermon which descendeth upon mount Sion;"* but how the dew of Hermon can descend upon Sion, at such a distance, cannot be easily explained, though attempted by many. I imagine that Hermon, being a lofty and extensive mountain, and Sion a low and small one, that Hermon, to a certain extent, shared its dew with Sion, inasmuch us the dew falling on Sion would seem to have come from Hermon; and such precisely should be the system of brethren living together, one sharing with the other, for brethren in such harmony may be well compared to the hill of Sion, on whom a heavenly dew falls from Hermon; that is, from Christ, who is so elevated, and so abounds in such heavenly dew; and, therefore, St. John said, *"And of his fulness we have all received."* Christ, however, does not share his grace and glory with us to the extent in which he enjoys it himself, but in a similar, though inferior manner. *"For there the Lord hath commanded blessing and life for evermore."* He now assigns a reason why an assembly of brethren, living together in peace and concord, should enjoy so many blessings. *"For there the Lord hath commanded blessings,"* because the Lord sends his blessing to such; and that is, the source of all blessings, and numberless favors always flow from the Lord's blessing. As nothing, then, is more gratifying to God than to see brethren living together, united in peace and harmony, he pours down all manner of favors on them; and those not temporary or transient favors, but eternal; and it was for such reason that to the blessing he adds, *"And life for evermore,"* all of which blessings we enjoy here in hope; and when we get to our country, we shall enjoy in the reality. We, therefore, had good reason to say, in the beginning of this Psalm, how appropriate it is to us, pilgrims, here below, on our journey to our country above, for it is there we are to look for perfect harmony; there the ointment of perfect love constantly flows from Christ, the head on all the members, and the dew of the light of glory from mount Hermon on all the hills of Sion. Hermon means a light on an elevated place, and Sion means a watch tower, a lookout; and, therefore, most justly, does a share in that divine light, or in other words, the Lord's blessing, which means an abundance of all imaginable goods, descend on those who are worthy to *"look out"* on God, face to face. And there, in conclusion, is *"life for evermore,"* never to have an end.

PSALM 133

An exhortation to praise God continually.

1 Behold now bless ye the Lord, all ye servants of the Lord: Who stand in the house of the Lord, in the courts of the house of our God.
2 In the nights lift up your hands to the holy places, and bless ye the Lord.
3 May the Lord out of Sion bless thee, he that made heaven and earth.

Explanation of the psalm

1. Now that you have been delivered from all temptations and persecutions, it is time for you to give your whole thoughts to praising God; and, therefore, *"bless ye the Lord, all ye servants of the Lord,"* who now have nothing else to do, but to render him the tribute of everlasting praise and thanks. *"Who stand in the house of the Lord, in the courts of the house of our God;"* you, who have now a permanent house, and no longer, like pilgrims, have to dwell in tents. And, in addition to the house you have, is *"a court,"* so that you cannot but be supremely happy, having a house within, in which to behold God, and a court without, in which to behold his creatures.

2. The night, when silence prevails everywhere, is the fittest time for prayer, and for praising God. Hence David, in another Psalm, says, *"I rose at* midnight to give praise to thee;" and, Isaias says, "*My soul hath desired thee in the night;*" and in Lamentations, "*Arise and give praise in the night, in the beginning of the watches.*" Our Lord constantly spent the night in prayer; and, in Acts 16, we read, "*And at midnight, Paul and Silas, praying, praised God.*" It is, therefore, with great justice that the prophet reminds God's servants that it is at night especially that they should raise their hands towards the Holy of Holies, where the Ark and the Propitiatory lie, and bless God. In a moral sense, the verse means that we should bless God in the daylight of prosperity, as well as in the night and gloom of adversity. However, in the sense that was principally intended, we are given to understand here, that, as when there is question of light or darkness, it is always day in the country above, so it is always night there when there is question of labor or rest; for, the moment they enter into said rest, "*the Spirit tells them they may rest from their labors; for their works follow them,*" Apoc. 14. That is, the night alluded to in Psalm 138, "*And night shall be my light in my pleasures;*" and of which the Lord says, "*The night cometh in which no one can work;*" and, therefore, should be specially devoted to praising God. In those most quiet, but still most brilliant nights, therefore, "*lift up your hands,*" you happy servants of God; and turned towards the true sanctuary where God himself resides, "*Bless ye the Lord.*"

3. Having exhorted the holy servants of God to bless him, he now calls down a blessing from God on them, in the singular number, knowing them to be so united in charity as if they consisted of one person only; to which unity of persons he says, "*May the Lord out of Sion bless thee, he that made heaven and earth.*"

PSALM 134

An exhortation to praise God: the vanity of idols.

1 Praise ye the name of the Lord: O you his servants, praise the Lord:
2 You that stand in the house of the Lord, in the courts of the house of our God.
3 Praise ye the Lord, for the Lord is good: sing ye to his name, for it is sweet.
4 For the Lord hath chosen Jacob unto himself: Israel for his own possession.
5 For I have known that the Lord is great, and our God is above all gods.
6 Whatsoever the Lord hath pleased he hath done, in heaven, in earth, in the sea, and in all the deeps.
7 He bringeth up clouds from the end of the earth: he hath made lightnings for the rain. He bringeth forth winds out of his stores:
8 He slew the firstborn of Egypt from man even unto beast.
9 He sent forth signs and wonders in the midst of thee, O Egypt: upon Pharao, and upon all his servants.
10 He smote many nations, and slew mighty kings:

11 Sehon king of the Amorrhites, and Og king of Basan, and all the kingdoms of Chanaan.
12 And gave their land for an inheritance, for an inheritance to his people Israel.
13 Thy name, O Lord, is for ever: thy memorial, O Lord, unto all generations.
14 For the Lord will judge his people, and will be entreated in favour of his servants.
15 The idols of the Gentiles are silver and gold, the works of men's hands.
16 They have a mouth, but they speak not: they have eyes, but they see not.
17 They have ears, but they hear not: neither is there any breath in their mouths.
18 Let them that make them be like to them: and every one that trusteth in them.
19 Bless the Lord, O house of Israel: bless the Lord, O house of Aaron.
20 Bless the Lord, O house of Levi: you that fear the Lord, bless the Lord.
21 Blessed be the Lord out of Sion, who dwelleth in Jerusalem.

EXPLANATION OF THE PSALM

1-2. Those two verses are word for word with the first verse of the last Psalm, and are now repeated, with a view of keeping up the praise then and there commenced. The prophet, then, addressing the servants of the Lord, exhorts them to praise his name and himself. And he tells what servants he means when he adds, *"You that stand in the house of the Lord, in the courts of the house of our God;"* you that are not now exiles, nor on the road, nor pilgrims, who need prayer more than praise; but you who have come home, and who now stand in the house; of whom another Psalm says, *"Blessed are they who dwell in thy house, O Lord, they will praise thee forever and ever."* The Psalm, then, seems specially adapted to those who have arrived at their home above, and have entered that house not made by the hands of man, but that everlasting one in heaven. It may be also applied to those who, in hope and desire, have begun to dwell in that house above; such as those who, with the Apostle, can say, *"But our conversation is an heaven;"* and it is peculiarly applicable to the clergy, whose duty it is to stand in the houses consecrated to God, and to minister to him with zeal and propriety. All God's servants are bound to that, but the clergy especially are bound by virtue of their peculiar obligations.

3-4. Having exhorted God's people to praise him, he now assigns a reason why they should do so. First, because he deserves it highly. Secondly, because it will turn to our own benefit and pleasure. Thirdly, because we are specially bound thereto, more so than others, by reason of the many favors he conferred on us. *"Praise ye the Lord, for the Lord is good;"* for a good thing is worthy of praise—a bad thing, of censure. Now, God is so good, that he alone is absolutely good, and so good in every respect, because he does not derive his goodness from anyone or thing but himself, and nothing can be good but by his gift and favor. Other things are good to a certain extent, such as a good man, house, or clothes; but God is goodness itself, having in him all the essence of goodness. *"Sing ye to his name, for his name is sweet."* Reason the second, because it is neither troublesome nor laborious, but sweet, pleasant, and agreeable. The saints in heaven know how sweet it is to sing to the Lord, and thus, they never desist a moment from his praise, and that by reason of their constantly tasting of his sweetness at the very source of it; we find it sometimes sweet enough, and at other times irksome enough, because it is not always that we taste of God's sweetness; it is only, when through the grace of God, and previous meditation, we come to know him, and burn to love him, *"For the Lord hath chosen Jacob unto himself: Israel for his own possession."* Here is the third reason derived from justice and obligation. As God, by a special gift of his grace, chose the children of Jacob to be his own people, it is only just, and due to that people, that they should be the foremost in praising him. We must here remark, that God, the founder of the universe, directs all nations by his providence, that he gave to them all the light of reason, and the natural law inscribed on their hearts, with Angels guardian, not only to each individual, but also to every kingdom and province; and that such favors are enjoyed by all nations in common with the people of Israel; that he adopted Abraham, with his posterity, through Isaac and Jacob, to be, as it were, his own inheritance, portion, and possession, and gave them a written law and ceremonies for his worship; and the prophets, as so many messengers, through whom he would instruct them. Secondly, that this was a wonderful gift from God; because he selected that people as his possession, for the purpose of heaping favors upon them, and cultivating them as he would his chosen vineyard; and all this was his own gratuitous gift. He chose them not on account of their merits, but because it so pleased himself; as is clear from the predestination for eternity, alluded to by Malachy, chap. 1; and St. Paul, Rom. 9, *"For when the children were not yet born, (Jacob and Esau,) nor had done any good or evil, that the purpose of God, according to election, might stand, it was said to her: The elder shall serve the younger, as it is written, Jacob I have loved, but Esau I have hated."* Thirdly, all that has been said, and a great deal more, applies to the Christian people collected from the gentiles; for, as St. Paul teaches, the gentiles were the wild olives, in reference to the Jews, who were the natural branches of the olive; and when most of them got broken off by their incredulity God adopted the wild olives, and engrafted them on the good olive; that is to say, he built up the gentiles *"on the foundation of the Apostles and prophets,"* by calling them through faith to his people, and making them *"fellow citizens with the saints, and the domestics of God."* We, then, ought, nay, even we are bound, in justice, to praise God; but it is Jacob and Israel, the elect, now in possession, the Jerusalem above, the assembly, to wit, of the saints, to whom is specially directed the order, *"Praise the Lord, Jerusalem, praise your God, Sion,"* who are specially bound.

5-6. He now answers a question that may be put to him, viz., why he invited God's people in so pressing a manner to praise him? *"For I have known that the Lord is great,"* and that, not only over men, but even *"above all gods;"* and, therefore, I cannot be silent; therefore I cry out, I chant, I sing, and I invite all to join me therein. He then proves both assertions of God's being great, and of his being greater than any other gods. His greatness is shown in his omnipotence, because, *"whatsoever the Lord pleased he hath done,"* throughout the universe, *"in heaven, earth, sea, and in all the deeps,"* which deeps may mean the lower regions, for such they are called in the Gospel, Lk. 8, where *"the devils besought him, that he would not command them to go into the deep,"* and thus all parts of the world are included, the heavens above, hell below, and earth and sea between them. Compare then, for a moment, our infirmity with God's power. *"Whatsoever the Lord pleaseth he hath done,"* for *"nothing is impossible to him."* We wish to do many things but cannot do them. God did those things because he wished it; of his own free will, and not through any necessity, for he needs nothing. We generally work because we need, and if necessity did not compel us we would lie idle. Finally, God did everything he wished, by reason of his being Lord of all things; and when we cannot carry out even our own wishes, how can we do anything else? It is, therefore, but just, that instead of praising ourselves, we should constantly praise the Lord our God.

7-9. He now adduces some examples of God's action on the air, the earth, and the waters, when it so pleases him; for God does wonderful things, both among his Angels above, and in the abyss below. As we know nothing, however, of what happens in either of those places, he gives us an example of what he does in the places we are acquainted with, the sky, the earth, and the waters, though we cannot account for those wonderful things. First, as regards the clouds; they rise from the earth, are formed in the sky, and return to the earth again, after being turned into rain. *"He bringeth up clouds from the end of the earth."* In speaking thus, he accommodates himself to the general notions then about the earth, which was that of an extensive plain, from the four quarters of which, as the wind varied, the clouds were supposed to ascend; and though the familiarity of the matter makes us regard the thing with very little surprise, it is a matter of great wonder and surprise, how the vapor ascending so imperceptibly from the earth and the sea, should all at once become so condensed as to veil the whole heavens with clouds, and that in a moment; the only thing that makes it cease to be wonderful is, its being the work of the Almighty. The next is more wonderful.

"He hath made lightnings for the rain." He mixed them both together, a most wonderful thing! for one would suppose the lightning would dry up the rain, or the rain would extinguish the lightning. He, possibly, alludes to that passage in Exodus, where it is said, *"And the hail and fire mixed with it, drove on together."*—*"He bringeth forth winds out of his stores."* The third example of the greatness of God is taken from his production of the winds. We are well acquainted with them, we sometimes feel them acutely, and still nothing is more obscure than the mode of their production, and, therefore, the Lord himself said, *"The spirit breatheth where he will; and thou hearest his voice, but thou knowest not whence he cometh, nor whither he goeth;"* as much as to say, you hear the noise, and that's all you know about it. The expression, *"out of his stores,"* is quite figurative, for God has no such stores, but when he sends gales of wind, it looks as if they had been locked up for some time, and let suddenly loose. To this third example of God's power, he now adds the fourth, which consisted in the slaughter of all the first born of Egypt, men as well as beasts, as related in Exodus 12, and he couples it with the generation of the winds, because, just as the winds are a sort of corporeal spirits, who, by reason of the minuteness of their composition are all but invisible, and still cause a wonderful havoc among the trees in the country, the houses in the cities, and the ships at sea; thus the celestial spirits, who were invisible to human eyes, in a twinkling, at God's beck, slew all the first born of Egypt, beasts as well as men; a thing that could not be ascribed to pestilence or to any other natural cause, whereas, none but the first born suffered, and of the Hebrews, not one at all. He finally alludes to all the miracles that God wrought in Egypt, through Moses, as may be read in Exodus.

10-12. To the miracles wrought in Egypt against Pharaoh he now adds the miracles that were wrought on the journey, against two most powerful kings, Sehon and Og, who were conquered by the Israelites in a most miraculous manner, see Num. 21. And he finally alludes to the miracles that God did in the very land of promise against thirty-one kings who were in possession of it. Many were the miracles performed there: for instance, that of the walls of Jericho tumbling to the ground at the sound of the trumpets by the priests; and of the sun and moon standing still at the command of Josue. God, then, gave all that country to his people of Israel, to be held by them as their own inheritance, just as he wishes the kingdom of heaven, of which it was a type, to be had by fighting and laboring for it. However, if he did not go before, accompany, and follow up all our labors with his grace, we could do nothing whatever. He it is, then, that saves us, frees us from captivity, and bestows on us an everlasting inheritance.

13-14. He now concludes the first proposition he undertook to prove, namely, God's greatness, and having proved it satisfactorily, he says, *"Thy name, O*

Lord, is forever." These wonderful acts of yours will keep your memory alive forever, which, as usual, he reiterates, when he says, *"Thy memorial,"* you name, will be remembered *"unto all generations." "For the Lord will judge his people,"* as he always did, by severely punishing all her enemies; *"and will be intreated in favor of his servants,"* will always leave himself open to attend to their prayers.

16-17. He now goes on to prove that God is greater than any other god, that being the second proposition he laid down in verse 5. And, though it is not saying much for God's being superior to idols of gold and silver, excelling, as he does, all kings, demons, and Angels, still the prophet thought right to compare them with God, to show their weakness and infirmity the more clearly; as also, because, though many of the idols of the gentiles were really demons, still the gentiles did not know that, and looked upon them as so many gods, as is evident from the history of Dagon. And, finally, because from it may be inferred the weakness and infirmity of those demons, who could give neither life nor feeling to those images, as the true God did to his image, man, to whom he gave the spirit of life, feeling, and motion, and what is of much more value, liberty and free will. David, then, justly proves that God is greater than any other of those gods, who, though they may have mouth, eyes, and ears, have them to no purpose, because the breath of life has not been infused into them, the prophet evidently alluding to the expression in Genesis, *"And breathed into his face the breath of life."* See Psalm 113, for further explanation.

18-20. Having compared the true with the false gods, he now institutes a comparison between their relative worshippers, and, by way of imprecation, predicts that the votaries of the former would be like their idols, dumb, blind, and deaf, as regards the seeking for, and finding, and praising, what is truly good; and he invites the servants of the true God to bless the Lord, for they, as being images of the living God, see, hear, and speak, and are, therefore, bound to exercise their tongue in praising that God, from whom they have the senses of feeling, life, and understanding. He invites, in the first place, the house of Israel in general, and then, severally, the house of Aaron, in the order of precedence, as being the priestly family; then the house of Levi, as the Levites who attended the priests; and, finally, *"all that fear the Lord;"* that is, all the laity. Now, though the contrast drawn here between the worshippers of the true God and the worshippers of idols applies specially to the pagans, as distinguished from Christians, still it applies also to the avaricious; for avarice is a worship of idols, and to those whose god is their belly, and to all who, while they acknowledge that they know God, deny him by their acts, as contradistinguished from the pious, *"whose conversation is in heaven."* For the former, like idols, do not see what is truly good or truly bad, though they have eyes, as it would appear; nor do they hear God's voice, nor chant his praises, though they appear to have ears and a tongue: on the other hand, the truly pious, whose heart is in heaven, have eyes for the interior; and they see the ears of their heart erect, and they understand; their tongue free and unrestrained, *"to bless God at all times, and to have his praise always in their mouth."* See Psalm 113.

21. He concludes by praying that out of Sion may come the blessing of the Lord, *"who dwelleth,"* as in his seat of governments *"in Jerusalem;"* or, in other words, that all the citizens of Sion and Jerusalem should never cease to bless God, who is a great king, and who selected Jerusalem as his seat of royalty; all which is most applicable to the Church militant, but much more so to the Church triumphant, which, free from all trouble, and devoid of all care, has no one thing else to do *"but to be still, and see that the Lord is God."*

PSALM 135

God is to be praised for his wonderful works.

1 Praise the Lord, for he is good: for his mercy endureth for ever.
2 Praise ye the God of gods: for his mercy endureth for ever.
3 Praise ye the Lord of lords: for his mercy endureth for ever.
4 Who alone doth great wonders: for his mercy endureth for ever.
5 Who made the heavens in understanding: for his mercy endureth for ever.
6 Who established the earth above the waters: for his mercy endureth for ever.
7 Who made the great lights: for his mercy endureth for ever.
8 The sun to rule over the day: for his mercy endureth for ever.
9 The moon and the stars to rule the night: for his mercy endureth for ever.
10 Who smote Egypt with their firstborn: for his mercy endureth for ever.
11 Who brought Israel from among them: for his mercy endureth for ever.
12 With a mighty hand and a stretched out arm: for his mercy endureth for ever.
13 Who divided the Red Sea into parts: for his mercy endureth for ever.
14 And brought out Israel through the midst thereof: for his mercy endureth for ever.
15 And overthrew Pharao and his host in the Red Sea: for his mercy endureth for ever.
16 Who led his people through the desert: for his mercy endureth for ever.
17 Who smote great kings: for his mercy endureth for ever.
18 And slew strong kings: for his mercy endureth for ever.
19 Sehon king of the Amorrhites: for his mercy endureth for ever.
20 And Og king of Basan: for his mercy endureth for ever.
21 And he gave their land for an inheritance: for his mercy endureth for ever.
22 For an inheritance to his servant Israel: for his mercy endureth for ever.
23 For he was mindful of us in our affliction: for his mercy endureth for ever.

24 And he redeemed us from our enemies: for his mercy endureth for ever.
25 Who giveth food to all flesh: for his mercy endureth for ever.
26 Give glory to the God of heaven: for his mercy endureth for ever.
27 Give glory to the Lord of lords: for his mercy endureth for ever.

EXPLANATION OF THE PSALM

1-3. In these three first verses the Trinity is praised, by reason of its essence; and in the remaining verses, by reason of the works that have been wrought by it. In the first verse, we find that name consisting of four letters in the Hebrew, that belongs to God alone, and is never applied to any created being, the meaning of which is, that he exists, as God himself explained in Exodus, when he said, *"I am who am."* And since existence and perfection are convertible and synonymous terms, and everything that exists of itself is perfect, and everything that is supreme is supremely perfect; perfection is, therefore, here united absolutely to one already absolute. *"Praise the Lord."* Render your tribute of praise to him who independently exists, *"for he is good,"* absolutely so; and he is not only absolutely good, but *"his mercy endureth forever and ever;"* for he that is so essentially good has no mixture of evil or of misery in him; and he alone, therefore, can remove the miseries and misfortunes of others, and actually does remove them, and will forever. Nonexistence is a great misery; and while God upholds the existence of certain things for eternity, he is merciful to them forever; and when he renders the holy Angels and men happy for eternity, he displays eternal mercy to them, not by removing the misery of unhappiness that was, but which would have been, had he not conferred eternal happiness on them. Now, this first need of praise may be applied to the Father, he being the source of existence, which he communicates to the Son by generation, and to the Holy Ghost by procession, in which the Son is united with him. The second tribute of praise is given to the Son, in the second verse, for he is called *"the God of gods."* Angels and men are called gods, but they are created gods; thus, in Psalm 81, *"I have said you are gods, and all of you the sons of the Most High;"* but the only begotten Son of God is God of gods, being the natural Son of God, while all others are only adopted sons, and, therefore, as much inferior to God the Son as any thing created is to its maker. And though the gods alluded to deserve the name to some extent, in respect of those beneath them, still, in respect of the only begotten Son of God, they are mere creatures. Praise ye, therefore the God of gods, that is to say, the only begotten Son of God, through whose mercy you are allowed to share in the name. *"For his mercy endureth forever."* For in union with the Father, he removes all miseries from his creatures. The third tribute of praise may be applied to the Holy Ghost. Lordship implies free will, and they who do as they please are called Lords, while they who must needs submit to the will of another are called servants. Now, the liberty of the Holy Ghost is boundless, as we read, 2 Cor. 3, *"Where the spirit of the Lord is, there is liberty;"* and in Jn. 3, *"The Spirit breatheth where he will;"* and in 1 Cor. 12, *"But all these things, one and the same Spirit worketh, dividing to everyone according as he will."* David, therefore, says, *"Praise ye the Lord of Lords;"* praise ye the Holy Ghost, the increate and omnipotent love, *"for his mercy endureth forever."*

4. The expression, *"praise ye the Lord,"* is to be prefixed to this verse, as well as to all the remaining verses of the Psalm. He now begins to praise God, by reason of his great and wonderful works; works that no one else could produce, such as the creation, for in other matters God has employed the Angels, and even other creatures. His mercy is praised especially in these works, because, as we have already stated, God did nothing from necessity, as if he needed creatures; all was done through his great and unspeakable mercy.

5. The heavens, as all know, was God's first work; and he made them *"in understanding,"* that is to say, in or by his wisdom, *"for his mercy endureth forever;"* because it was his will to bring the heavens out of nothing, and at the same time to prepare an everlasting home for men and Angels.

6. Another principal work of God was the earth. For, *"in the beginning God made the heavens and the earth."* The heavens were made as a palace for immortals, the earth as a mansion for mortals. The air and the water are intermediate elements for the use of man. Now, he says *"the earth was established above the water,"* not that the water was below, in the bottom of the globe, but that the surface of the earth was, to a great extent, higher than the surface of the water, so as to enable man and other animals to live on its surface. Of the earth's being in the depths of the world David writes in another Psalm, 103, *"Who hath founded the earth upon its own bases; it shall not be moved forever and ever."* The earth, therefore, so held the water in its caverns and depths as to lie beneath the water in some places, and to rise above it in others. God's mercy is seen here in three different ways—first, in regard of the earth, which he brought out of nothing; secondly, in respect to the water, for which he provided a fixed and permanent place; and, thirdly, in respect to man, on whom he bestowed the earth so denuded of water, and still sufficiently irrigated by it, as to render it habitable, fit for cultivation, and fruitful.

7-9. His third great and wonderful work was the creation of the sun, moon, and stars, that belong to both heaven and earth, inasmuch as they adorn the heavens and benefit the earth. He calls them *"great lights,"* as, in fact, they are greater than we can well imagine, whereas the stars, that, by reason of their distance, seem so diminutive to us, are much larger than our globe.

The sun is said to rule the day and the moon and stars the night, because they afford light both by day and by night to man, to follow his avocations, as is recorded in Genesis. Mention is made in Genesis of two great lights only, the sun and moon, because the two shed more light on the earth than all the stars together; still David calls even the stars great lights, because, in fact, they are; and, if we believe astronomers, even larger than the moon.

10-22. God is praised in these verses for his works of Providence, all of which are recorded in Exodus and in the previous Psalm. Question may be raised, though, how such acts as the destruction of the Egyptians, the slaying of the first born, and of the kings, can be called *"works of mercy?"* when they appear to be acts of justice rather than of mercy. They were, certainly, acts of justice, in regard of the wicked, who were stricken and slain; but in respect to God's people, they were acts of mercy; and, as the delivery of the people was the principal object intended by God, all those acts are in consequence attributed to his mercy. God sometimes shows his mercy even to the wicked, by shortening their time in this world, thus preventing them of an accumulation of sin, and the treasuring up, in consequence, of a greater amount of punishment *"on the day of anger and the just judgment of God."*

23-24. These verses may refer to the delivery of the Jews from the slavery of Pharao, the Philistines, and Nabuchodonosor; as also to the delivery of the Church from the persecutions of tyrants and heretics; and, finally, with the greatest propriety, to the delivery of the elect from the captivity of the devil, and all the dangers of this world.

25. The prophet now includes those who suffer no persecution, for fear they may imagine they were exempt from the obligation of praising the Lord. He, therefore, says, *"Praise the Lord"* everyone of you, without exception, because it is he who supports and preserves every living creature, especially man, and that because *"his mercy endureth forever."*

26-27. He concludes by repeating the two last verses of the first three, for by the *"God of heaven"* he evidently intends the *"God of gods,"* for he is called the God of heaven, as being the only true God, as Psalm 95 has it, *"For all the gods of the gentiles are devils, but the Lord made the heavens;"* and as also because, seated as he is in the highest heavens, as on his throne, he proves from this fact that he is the God of gods.

PSALM 136

The lamentation of the people of God in their captivity in Babylon.

1 Upon the rivers of Babylon, there we sat and wept: when we remembered Sion:
2 On the willows in the midst thereof we hung up our instruments.
3 For there they that led us into captivity required of us the words of songs. And they that carried us away, said: Sing ye to us a hymn of the songs of Sion.

4 How shall we sing the song of the Lord in a strange land?
5 If I forget thee, O Jerusalem, let my right hand be forgotten.
6 Let my tongue cleave to my jaws, if I do not remember thee: If I make not Jerusalem the beginning of my joy.
7 Remember, O Lord, the children of Edom, in the day of Jerusalem: Who say: Rase it, rase it, even to the foundation thereof.
8 daughter of Babylon, miserable: blessed shall he be who shall repay thee thy payment which thou hast paid us.
9 Blessed be he that shall take and dash thy little ones against the rock.

EXPLANATION OF THE PSALM

1. Such was the language of the captives who were brought away from Jerusalem to Babylon, and who were not detained in the city, but were employed in various laborious tasks through the country, along the banks of the rivers, in which the province abounded, on which they would seat themselves betimes, and burst into tears, at the recollection of, and through longing for their country. When he says, "*The rivers of Babylon,*" we are not to understand that all these rivers ran through the city; for it is well known that the Euphrates was the only river that ran through it, and the expression, therefore, includes the country about Babylon; or, perhaps, by Babylon, he means the province of that name, as Samaria, the city, gave its name to the country about it. In a spiritual sense, such is the language of God's elect, who are held here below in captivity, are inwardly detached from the world, and know themselves to be citizens of the Jerusalem above, for such holy exiles sit on the banks of the rivers, instead of being hurried away by their waters, and rolled along to the sea. The rivers of Babylon mean the temporal things of this world; and when one gets attached to them by his desires, such as the avaricious, the ambitious, the voluptuary, they are carried away by the rapids, and hurled headlong into the sea, into the great abyss, to be punished there for eternity. Here, then, is the position of the citizens of the country above, and the first distinctive mark to tell anyone to which people he belongs, for they who are in a high position in this world, and still have their hearts in heaven, and long for the things of this world, these are they who belong to Jerusalem, and not to Babylon. Again: the aforesaid *"fellow citizens with the saints" "sit on the banks of the rivers,"* on a very low spot; they seek not an elevated one, they have no desire for place or power, they pride themselves not on their wisdom; and should they chance to be raised to rule over a Babylon, as was the case with David, and many Christian kings, however high their position may be, their ideas do not go up with it, nor do they look upon their elevation as an honor, but as a burden, under which to groan; and, instead of glorying in it, as far as they are personally concerned, they will seek to sit in the lowest place, if they have the true spirit of him *"who was meek and humble of heart."* Thirdly, they will not only seat themselves lowly down, but they will lament and deplore, not the loss of the things of this world, but their own captivity, when they bring their sweetest country to their recollection, that of mount Sion. They who forget it fraternize with the children of Babylon; but they who long for it, and whose longings cause them to remember their country, however prosperous they may be, they don't feel satisfied, but still sigh for their country, and the severest test we can apply to ourselves, as to whether we belong to Babylon or to Jerusalem, is to reflect on what pleases us, or what delights us, for *"where our treasure is, there our heart will be also."*

2. The Jews, in their captivity, hung up their musical instruments *"on the willows in the midst thereof"* of Babylon, that all its inhabitants may see how they threw away those instruments of joy, in order to show that they were more inclined to weep than to sing. Pious souls are fond of doing the same; for when they come to understand fully their exile and banishment, they say with the same prophet, *"My soul refused to be comforted; I remembered God and was delighted;"* for though the citizens of the celestial Jerusalem cannot rejoice and sing with the Babylonians, nor of their success and prosperity, still they sing, in their hearts, to God, and rejoice in the hope of future happiness. *"We hung up our instruments"* means the consigning those instruments of joy and pleasure to the votaries thereof, who, like so many unproductive trees, are daily watered by the rivers of Babylon, and produce no fruit. Let such people for whom eternal wailing is in store hereafter, strike the harp, and burst forth in song here.

3. The captive Jews hung up their harps on the branches of the trees, not only through grief and sadness, but also that they may not oblige the Babylonians, who were anxious to hear and to mock the sacred hymns they were wont to sing on their holy festivals. St. John Chrysostom observes the improvement such tribulation effected in the Jews, who previously derided, nay, even put to death, some of the prophets; but now that they were captives in a foreign land, they would not attempt to expose their sacred hymns to the ridicule of the gentiles.

4. Such was their answer when asked, *"Sing ye to us a hymn of the songs of Sion."* They say that such is their longing and grief for their country, that they cannot possibly sing while so removed from it, fearing to give offense to their masters, by telling them the principal reason, which was, for fear of their sacred hymns being turned into ridicule. In a spiritual view, holy souls, citizens of the Jerusalem above, feeling that rejoicing is suited to their country, and lamentation to their exile and captivity, exclaim, How can we sing amidst so many dangers and temptations! *"Laughter I counted error; and to*

mirth I said: *Why art thou vainly deceived?"* They, too, sing the song of the Lord in a strange land, who sing sacred hymns and chants in such a manner as to please the ear, seeking only to catch it by various inflections and variations, never considering that sacred music was intended to raise the soul to God rather than please the senses. There are to be found too, some who will bring the songs of Babylon into the house of God and into holy Sion, who so adapt sacred words to profane tunes as to cause the audience to attend exclusively to the air, and overlook the meaning of such hymns,

5-6. They who said, *"How shall we sing the song of the Lord in a strange land?"* the whole people, as if they formed only one person, are introduced, swearing unanimously, and resolving firmly, that they will never forget their country; and, as the striking the harp or chanting of a hymn, may be construed into a sign of their forgetting their country, they pray to God with a solemn imprecation, that the hand that strikes the harp may wither, and the tongue that sings the song may be paralyzed. *"If I forget thee, O Jerusalem,"* as I certainly will, when I strike the harp in a foreign land, *"let my right hand be forgotten."* May it rot and perish, and be of no use, in which case it will be forgotten, *"let my tongue cleave to my jaws,"* so that it will not be able to move, if I not only forget thee, but if I do not even go further, and *"make Jerusalem, the beginning of my joy."* make the holy city of Jerusalem the beginning and the sum total of my joy. Such, in fact, is the peculiarity and the distinguishing mark of the elect, if they neither in prosperity nor adversity lose sight of their future country, and would hesitate in losing hand or tongue, should God's glory, and their own eternal salvation require it, and if they take no real pleasure in anything but in longing and hoping for that celestial home that is not made by the hand of man, where is to be found that joy of which the Lord speaks in the Gospel, when he says, *"Enter into the joy of thy Lord."*

7-9. In the end of the Psalm, David predicts the destruction of the children of Edom, and the Babylonians who thus persecuted the children of Israel. The Babylonians, under king Nabuchodonosor, sacked Jerusalem, and brought its inhabitants away captives to Babylon. The Idumeans, the descendants of Esau, who was also called Edom, had encouraged them to it; that is clearly related by Abdias the prophet, and David prophesies it here long before it happened; and David therefore takes up the Idumeans first, either because they were the originators of so much misery to the Jews, or because he chose to take up first those who had been guilty of the lesser injury. *"Remember, O Lord, the children of Edom in the day of Jerusalem,"* in the days when Jerusalem was sacked and demolished, and he then tells what they did. *"Who say: Raze it, raze it, even to the foundation thereof,"* for such was their language to the Babylonians when they were marching against it. When he says, *"remember,"* it means remember to punish, as God is said to forget when he forgives; thus, in Ezechiel, *"I will not remember all his iniquities which he hath done;"* and in Tobias, *"Neither remember my offences, nor those of my parents."* He then turns to Babylon, and by way of imprecation, foretells its destruction. *"O daughter of Babylon, miserable"* as I foresee you will be, however happy you may seem to be now. *"Blessed shall he be who shall repay thee thy payment which thou hast paid us,"* blessed will be the king of the Medes and Persians, for he will succeed in conquering you, and will indict all the hardships on you, that you have indicted on us, as eventually happened. And he further prophesies that such will be the cruelty of the Medes and Persians, that they *"will take and dash thy little ones against the rock,"* and thus show them not the slightest mercy. All this has a spiritual meaning. First, in an allegorical sense, looking upon the Idumeans as the Jews, and the Babylonians as the pagans; for, in point of fact, it was the pagans that principally sought to tear up the Church of Christ from its very foundations, and that on the suggestion, counsel, and exhortation of the Jews; for it was upon the charges made by the Jews, that the pagans passed sentence of death on Christ. Herod put St. James to death, and bound St. Peter with chains, *"seeing it was agreeable to the Jews;"* and the same Jews did all in them lay to get the Romans to put St. Paul to death. In various other places, and at various other times, the same Jews *"stirred up and incensed the minds of the gentiles against the brethren,"* as we read in the Acts; but God *"remembered"* both Jews and gentiles, to punish the one and the other. He razed their chief city, upset their kingdom, and scattered themselves all over the world; and he so swept away the pagan empire and kingdoms, who then held the whole world in sway, as not to leave scarce a pagan power now in existence. And, as idolatry and pagan rule have been supplanted, not by violence or force of arms, but by the preaching of God's word, the prophet addresses God, saying, *"Blessed shall he be who shall repay thee thy payment which thou hast paid us,"* for the pagans most unsuccessfully persecuted the Christians, who, in return, most successfully persecuted them. It would have been of the highest advantage to them, if, on the extinction of idolatry, they had died to sin and began to live to justice, as occurred to their children, who had not been so deeply rooted in the errors and vices of paganism. For it is a well known fact, that an immense number of the youth and other simple minded persons were easily converted to the Christian religion, and held out even unto death for it against the idolatry of their fathers, allusion to which is made in the words, *"Blessed he that shall take and dash thy little ones against the rock;"* that is to say, who shall bring the little ones to the rock, Christ, to get a fortunate dash against it, and die the death of the old man, to rise a new man. Secondly, to take this passage in a moral point of view, we may look upon the Idumeans as representing the carnal, and the Babylonians as the evil spirits, and it is more in the spirit of the Psalm; for, as we set out with it, the captivity of Babylon was a type of the captivity of mankind, a captivity still to some extent in existence, and will, *"as long as the flesh lusteth against the spirit,"* and the elect exclaim, *"Who will deliver me from the body of this death?"* and the Apostle says, *"Even we ourselves groan within ourselves, waiting for the adoption of the sons of God, the redemption of our body;"* and, finally, we are but *"pilgrims and strangers"* in a foreign land; and though not belonging to it, we are in the midst of a wretched world. God, then, will repay to Babylon what Babylon imposed upon us; for, as the evil spirit, the king of Babylon, bound us with a chain that still hangs on the neck of all the children of Adam, so, on the day of judgment, will Christ, the King of Jerusalem, lead the evil spirit captive, and will so tie him down with the chains of eternal punishment, that he will never rise again to do any harm; of which St. Jude speaks when he says, *"And the Angels who kept not their principality, but forsook their own habitation, he hath reserved in everlasting chains, unto the judgment of the great day."* And it is not only the devil that Christ will tie down in everlasting chains, he will also bind down the worldlings, who persecuted the pious, and kept them in captivity; for the Angels will bind them up *"in bundles to be burned."* And, as the same king of Babylon makes the little ones of Christ, they who have not grown up nor advanced in Christ, and always need milk, the principal objects of his snares, in order to bring them away captives; so, on the contrary, blessed is he, who, by a happy dash on the rock, kills sin, those who have not been too deeply stained with it, that they may live to justice.

PSALM 137

Thanksgiving to God for his benefits.

1 I will praise thee, O lord, with my whole heart: for thou hast heard the words of my mouth. I will sing praise to thee in the sight of his angels:
2 I will worship towards thy holy temple, and I will give glory to thy name. For thy mercy, and for thy truth: for thou hast magnified thy holy name above all.
3 In what day soever I shall call upon thee, hear me: thou shall multiply strength in my soul.
4 May all the kings of the earth give glory to thee: for they have heard all the words of thy mouth.
5 And let them sing in the ways of the Lord: for great is the glory of the Lord.
6 For the Lord is high, and looketh on the low: and the high he knoweth afar off.
7 If I shall walk in the midst of tribulation, thou wilt quicken me: and thou hast stretched forth thy hand against the wrath of my enemies: and thy right hand hath saved me.
8 The Lord will repay for me: thy mercy, O Lord, endureth for ever: O despise not the work of thy hands.

Explanation of the psalm

1-2. The prophet commences by promising a sacrifice of praise, and that with his whole heart, inasmuch as he was about to return thanks for his own everlasting, and that of the whole people's, salvation. *"I will praise thee, O Lord;"* I will give you a tribute of praise and thanksgiving; no lip one; but from the deepest recesses of my heart; quite alive to it, with my affections engaged on it; *"for thou hast heard, the words of my mouth;"* in other words, the prayer I put before you. *"I will sing praise to thee in the sight of thy Angels."* He declares that his praise will be commensurate to the dignity of the audience. As he is to sing before the Angels who attend on the Almighty, he will be more careful of what he will sing, as he knows before whom he has to sing. Undoubtedly, if we, when we recite the same Psalms, would consider or reflect that we are seen and heard by the holy Angels, who praise our attention and devotion, or who note our carelessness and our distractions, we would recite them much better than we usually get through them. *"I will worship towards thy holy temple,"* in thy material temple, while singing to your name; I will turn in spirit to your temple aloft, and, fixed therein by prayer and contemplation, *"I will give glory to thy name. For thy mercy and for thy truth: for thou hast magnified thy holy name above all."* Here will be the subject of my song. I will praise you with my whole heart, for your great mercy, and your truth in adhering to what you promised our fathers, by virtue of which you took pity on the human race, and thus magnified Christ, who is your holy word and name, inasmuch as you gave him a name that is above every name. For, by such an act you showed your unspeakable mercy—mercy we should never cease to laud—when you exalted mankind, that had been degraded even to hell by sin, above all the heavens and all created things, through Christ, and you thus more than carried out the truth that always marks your promise.

3. From the fact of your having so magnified thy holy name, I ask you to hear me whenever I shall put my wants before you; for your Holy One has said, *"Whatever you ask of the Father in my name he will give you." "Thou shalt multiply strength in my soul."* What I earnestly beg of you is to multiply, which means to increase, not the number of my years, nor my wealth, nor my children, nor anything else of the sort; *"but strength in my soul,"* so as to enable me to resist my evil desires, to bear all crosses with patience, to tread in the path of justice without fatigue, to offer violence to the kingdom of heaven, that thus I may ultimately come to him, *"whom thou hast magnified."*

4. As he said previously, *"Thou hast magnified thy holy name above all,"* making use of the past, instead of the future tense, inasmuch as, by the spirit of prophecy, he looked at the future as if it were actually gone by, so he now predicts the conversion of the gentiles, in the imperative mood. Your Holy

One having been magnified by his resurrection and ascension, may all the kings of the earth, (as they will,) *"give glory to thee;"* because, through the preaching of the Apostles, *"they have heard all the words of thy mouth;"* that is, all you chose to reveal to the world through the prophets and Apostles, words which were at first confined to Judea; *"because the words of God were committed to them,"* but were afterwards heard by all the kings and people of the world, through the Apostles; *"for their sound went all over the earth."*

5. He goes on with the explanation of the mystery of the calling of the gentiles, *"And let them sing in the ways of the Lord;"* that is, the kings and people aforesaid will tread in the ways of the Lord, which are mercy and truth; for it is by them that God comes down to man, and man gets up to God; his mercy being exercised by mercifully forgiving the penitent, and justly punishing the impenitent; and our mercy being exercised by freely forgiving those who injure us, by dealing justly with all, and by giving to God and the neighbor what we owe to both. Such people will set about their work in no lazy, grudging manner, but in joy and good spirits; for they will sing, *"great is the glory of the Lord."* For they will every other day have a better knowledge of, and will more admire the great things God will have accomplished, and how wonderfully he will have glorified his Christ, who is our head, and the extent of the riches of the glory of the inheritance to the saints.

6. The great glory of the Lord consists in this, that high as he is, nay, even the very highest, by reason of his nature, dignity, power, wisdom, and authority; still, *"he looketh on the low,"* for he came down from heaven to them, for *"he was seen upon earth, and conversed with men;" "and the high he knoweth afar off,"* because he draws far away from the proud, or casts them far away from him as he cast the devil, the prince of the proud, from heaven into hell. This doctrine of holy humility is most necessary to all, especially to all in any responsible position, for such people run a great risk of being carried away by their pride. But why does God, the High One, love the lowly instead of the high, whereas all love what is similar to themselves? God loves those who are truly raised on high, and not those who place themselves on a false elevation; for the former are very like, the latter most unlike him. And thus, the humble, conscious that they have nothing from themselves, are replenished with all manner of good, and are raised by God to the highest dignity; while the proud, *"who thought they were something when they were nothing,"* remain empty, and being filled and distended with vanity alone, are utterly discarded.

7. As God, who is on high, regards the low with the greatest kindness, David, fully cognizant of his own low position, confidently promises himself God's assistance in every trouble. *"If I shall walk in the midst of tribulation,"* so as to be surrounded on all sides by it, still *"thou wilt quicken me;"*

you will preserve me alive, unhurt, unharmed. *"And thou hast stretched forth thy hand against the wrath of my enemies;"* when my enemies surrounded me, and sought to devour me, you interposed and protected me, *"and thy right hand hath saved me;"* your strength and power, Christ, hath saved me.
8. He explains how God's *"right hand saves us,"* because *"the Lord,"* who is your right hand, *"will repay for me;"* will satisfy you, the Father, for my sins; as he says in another place, *"then did I pay that which I took not away;"* he will also repay my enemies, as I am not able to repay them by punishing them. *"Thy mercy, O Lord, endureth forever;"* has no end, and, therefore, I ask you, *"do not despise the work of thy hands."* Don't give up the work you have commenced in your mercy, through the inspiration of faith, hope, and charity, but complete it by preserving, by increasing, by perfecting it. With great propriety he says, *"the works of thy hands,"* not of our hands, because whatever good we have we have it from God's bounty, without whom we are not only unable to do anything, but even *"we are not sufficient to think anything of ourselves, as of ourselves."* 2 Cor. 3:5.

PSALM 138

God's special providence over his servants.

1 Lord, thou hast proved me, and known me:
2 Thou hast know my sitting down, and my rising up.
3 Thou hast understood my thoughts afar off: my path and my line thou hast searched out.
4 And thou hast foreseen all my ways: for there is no speech in my tongue.
5 Behold, O Lord, thou hast known all things, the last and those of old: thou hast formed me, and hast laid thy hand upon me.
6 Thy knowledge is become wonderful to me: it is high, and I cannot reach to it.
7 Whither shall I go from thy spirit? or whither shall I flee from thy face?
8 If I ascend into heaven, thou art there: if I descend into hell, thou art present.
9 If I take my wings early in the morning, and dwell in the uttermost parts of the sea:
10 Even there also shall thy hand lead me: and thy right hand shall hold me.
11 And I said: Perhaps darkness shall cover me: and night shall be my light in my pleasures.
12 But darkness shall not be dark to thee, and night shall be light as day: the darkness thereof, and the light thereof are alike to thee.
13 For thou hast possessed my reins: thou hast protected me from my mother's womb.
14 I will praise thee, for thou art fearfully magnified: wonderful are thy works, and my soul knoweth right well.
15 My bone is not hidden from thee, which thou hast made in secret: and my

substance in the lower parts of the earth.
16 Thy eyes did see my imperfect being, and in thy book all shall be written: days shall be formed, and no one in them.
17 But to me thy friends, O God, are made exceedingly honourable: their principality is exceedingly strengthened.
18 I will number them, and they shall be multiplied above the sand: I rose up and am still with thee.
19 If thou wilt kill the wicked, O God: ye men of blood, depart from me:
20 Because you say in thought: They shall receive thy cities in vain.
21 Have I not hated them, O Lord, that hated thee: and pine away because of thy enemies?
22 I have hated them with a perfect hatred: and they are become enemies to me.
23 Prove me, O God, and know my heart: examine me, and know my paths.
24 And see if there be in me the way of iniquity: and lead me in the eternal way.

Explanation of the psalm

1-2. David, speaking not only for himself but for all mankind, asserts that God has a most intimate knowledge of us, and of everything connected with us. *"Lord, thou hast proved me;"* you have searched and examined me, for such is the meaning of the word in the Hebrew. Now, God is said to search and examine, in a metaphorical sense, because he wishes to have the most perfect and exact knowledge of everything, as he really has; and because they who wish for such perfect and complete knowledge of a matter, examine and inquire into it with the greatest diligence; and David, therefore, expresses himself in such manner, without, for a moment, supposing that God needs such inquiry or examination. The meaning, then, is, you are not content, O Lord, with a superficial knowledge of our affairs, but you would have as intimate a knowledge of them as they who search and examine; and, in point of fact, you have a most accurate knowledge of me. *"Thou hast known my sitting down, and my rising up."* He now enters into details of his general assertion, saying, you have known from eternity, when, where, and why I should sit and I should rise; and not only as regards the motions of my body, but also of my soul, when, where, and why I should be humbled or exalted. If God has such an intimate knowledge, then, of man in general, how much more so must not have been his knowledge of Christ, the head of men and Angels; and it is, therefore, with great propriety that the Church uses these words in the Liturgy, on the feast of the Resurrection. *"Thou hast known my sitting down, and any rising up."*
3. He now tells us that God not only knows every downfall and every uprise connected with our whole life, but that he also knows in detail all our thoughts, all our counsels, everything that is to happen us; or, perhaps, after

having informed us that God knows everything connected with our exterior, our rise, or downfall, to wit, he now tells us that he is equally acquainted with our interior, meaning our thoughts and desires. *"Thou hast understood my thoughts afar off;"* you knew what my thoughts would turn upon long before I began to think. *"My path;"* my progress and path through life, not only as far as my body is concerned, but also in regard of my soul which has strayed, and that through various doubts and difficulties; *"and my line,"* to what end I was likely to come, what inheritance I was to fall in for, what rest to secure, thou *"hast searched out,"* have been in full possession of. Briefly, you had, from eternity, a thorough knowledge of the motives, means, and end of all my actions.

4. Having stated that God foresaw our thoughts, counsels, and actions, he now adds, that he also foresees all our other acts, however indifferent, such as our idle words; *"for there is no speech in my tongue"* that you have not foreseen. Hence the Lord assures us in the Gospel, that men will have to render account, on the day of judgment, of every idle word that falls from them; and it was in terror thereat that holy Job exclaimed, *"Thou, indeed, hast numbered my steps, but spare my sins."* For God observes everything, weighs everything, that he may, in his own time, bring everything to judgment.

5. He proves, by two arguments, that God knows everything that appertains to man: first, because he knows everything past and future; and it, therefore, should not be surprising if he had an intimate knowledge of everything connected with man, whose actions are not the least important among the daily events of life. Secondly, having created man, and being his sovereign Lord, there can be no doubt that he has a knowledge of everything connected with him. *"Behold, O Lord, thou hast known all things, the last and those of old"*—everything past and future. With that, *"thou hast formed me,"* created me in human shape; and when you did so make me you did not, like other workmen, lose sight of me, but thou *"hast laid thy hand upon me,"* to guide, support, and protect me; for, otherwise, I should have at once returned to the dust, from whence I sprang, or, rather, to my original nothingness.

6. Having proved, by the two aforesaid arguments, that God's knowledge extends to everything connected with man, lest anyone should suppose that we have, in consequence, come to complete and just notions of God's knowledge, he adds the present verse, that we may understand that, however satisfied we may be of God's knowledge being supreme, and extending to all things, still, that we are quite in the dark—that, in fact, we know nothing at all about it in detail; that is to say, that it is perfectly incomprehensible how God can foresee what is to happen, especially human acts, which man may do or not do as it pleases or suits him, such as all our thoughts, desires, words, and all our actions. The same applies to the essence and attributes of

God. We know that he exists, that he is powerful, wise, good, just, and merciful; but who knows or who can explain his essence, or how, with so many attributes, he can be essentially one? He, therefore, says, *"Thy knowledge is become wonderful to me,"* more wonderful than I can comprehend; such is the meaning of the phrase in the Hebrew; *"It is high, and I cannot reach to it;"* far beyond my capacity.

7-10. He now adduces another argument to prove that no one can escape God's ken, inasmuch as God is everywhere, penetrating everything. *"Whither shall I go from thy spirit?"* to hide myself from you, to escape from your mind or intelligence, *"or whither shall I fly from your face?"* from your eyes. *"If I ascend into heaven,"* to the very highest—*"if I descend into hell,"* to the depth of the abyss, the greatest possible distance from heaven—there, too, you are present. *"If I take my wings early in the morning,"* could I assume the wings of a bird, and fly all the day with the greatest rapidity, *"and dwell in the uttermost part of the sea,"* so as to reach the other extremity of the world, I could not, even thus, escape from you; *"for thy hand shall lead me and hold me;"* because without God's help we cannot stir, nor can we go along but as he carries us, for *"in him we live, move, and have our being."*

11-12. He raises an objection to himself, saying it is possible to hide one's self from God in the dark; and he answers it by saying such is not possible, because darkness ceases to be darkness with God, *"for God is light,"* as St. John asserts in his epistle; and he also asserts, *"The light shineth in darkness, and the darkness did not comprehend it."* For as the sun's light cannot be obscured by darkness, because it dissipates all darkness by its presence—and wherever the sun is, there day is—so it is with the spiritual and increate light, God, that cannot be obstructed by any darkness, because its presence dissipates all darkness; and, thus, there is no hiding place left for man in which to hide himself from God's all seeing eye. *"And I said, perhaps, darkness shall cover me;"* perhaps dense darkness may envelope me, and I may thus escape God's eye, *"and night shall be my light in my pleasures;"* darkness will not cover you, because the very night will be turned into light, that they may be visible. The literal meaning, then, of the two verses is, the night, so naturally dark, will cease to be such with God; instead of being dark, it will *"be my light in my pleasures,"* will throw a light on and expose me, indulging in my sinful pleasures; for those who are devoted to impurity always seek the darkness of the night, when they think they can be seen by none, and thus commit sin with greater security; and hence the Apostle says, *"For they who sleep, sleep in the night; and they who are drunk, are drunk in the night, and he might have added, and they who abandon themselves* "to chambering and impurities," do so mostly in the night. But to no purpose, for the all seeing eye of God, brighter than the sun itself, penetrates all darkness, and there is nothing hidden from it. He repeats it, by way of confirmation. *"But darkness shall not be darkness to thee, and night shall be light as the day."* The night, instead of being dark to you, will be as bright as the day.

13. That God sees in the dark, and that nothing, however secret, is hidden from him, the prophet now proves, from the formation of our interior members, while still in the mother's womb, where they are doubly hid; first, by reason of their being interior parts of the infant itself; secondly, by reason of that very infant being hidden in the mother's womb. For thou *"hast possessed my reins;"* that day or night, light or darkness, is all the same to you, is evident from the fact of your having formed my reins, the most secret part of my body, and that even when my whole body lay concealed and covered in my mother's womb.

14. He now interrupts his narration of the formation of man, by an address to God, in admiration of the wisdom and knowledge displayed in the formation of man by God. *"I will praise thee"* when I reflect on these your works; I will render to you my tribute of praise, for *"thou art fearfully magnified."* I am filled with terror through admiration and reverence for you—and he explains in what respect, when he says, *"Wonderful are thy works, and my soul knoweth right well."* Your creating man in his mother's womb, in a place so hidden and obscure, is truly a most wonderful work, and I am fully alive to the greatness of such a work. We are not to infer that the latter part of this sentence implies a thorough knowledge of God's works, it merely means that we know them to be great and wonderful. Thus, we neither see nor know the extent of the sea, yet we know it to be very extensive; and that from the mere fact of our not being able to take the whole of it in at a glance, from any one given point. In like manner, though we cannot look directly on the sun, we know from that very fact that its light is intense.

15. He returns to the knowledge and wisdom displayed by God in the formation of man. *"My bone is not hidden from thee;"* you know the use, object, arrangement, and structure of every bone in my body; no wonder you should, because thou *"hast made"* them all, and that *"in secret,"* enveloped in my own skin and flesh; and in addition to it, by my mother's womb. *"And my substance in the lower part of the earth;"* a repetition of the former idea, with this addition, that my astonishing formation took place *"in the lower parts of the earth,"* where one would suppose I was so far removed from God's handiwork. Anyone acquainted with the anatomy of the human frames cannot fail to be struck with astonishment at the wisdom of God, in the fabrication of so many bones, large ones, middling ones, small and minute ones, so marvelous by being connected with each other; and the whole thing accomplished in the smallest and obscurest possible place, without either tools or machinery.

16. He goes further in showing the wisdom of God as displayed in the structure of the human frame. *"My imperfect being,"* means the embryo in the mother's womb, before the formation of the bones, so as to be distinguished. *"Thy eyes did see my imperfect being,"* and they not only saw it, but they knew what was to come from it, what it was to turn into; and he tells why, when he says, *"and in thy book all shall be written;"* because you have, as it were, a book, as would a painter or a sculptor, containing copies or designs of all the works you may want to produce; *"days shall be formed;"* all these embryos will be formed from time to time, and brought to perfection, *"and no one in them"* will fail, or fall short of the object of its creation; ordinarily speaking, no human being, conceived in the womb, will fail in coming to perfection, or will be found deficient in any of his natural members; and, when abortions occur, such as the being born blind, or with any other such defect, such does not happen through any deficiency in the first cause, it generally arises from secondary causes. All this may apply also to the perfection of man in respect to his soul, that is, in regard of his wisdom, prudence, moral virtues, grace, and glory. For the Lord knows our imperfect state, that, of ourselves, we are nothing but an unformed mass, but by reason of our being written in the book of life we are every other day formed and made more perfect, until we become *"conformable to the image of the Son of God,"* and *"be made like to the body of his glory."* And it is on looking at such extraordinary perfection of body and soul, to which the favored of God are brought, out of so much imperfection, that makes the prophet exclaim in the following verse,

17. On reflecting from what a depth of imperfection God brings his friends to the very highest and most exalted perfection, thereby displaying his own providence in the management of human affairs, as if they were his own, in highly rewarding the good, and severely punishing the wicked, the prophet now exclaims, in great surprise and admiration, *"But to me,"* with me, or in my opinion, *"thy friends, O God, are made exceedingly honorable;"* they have been honored beyond my comprehension, for *"their principality is exceedingly strengthened;"* for they have been rescued from a mass of corruption, and from the bondage of the evil one, and translated to an everlasting kingdom, put on a level with the Angels, children and heirs of God, and brethren and coheirs of the only begotten, *"whom he hath appointed heir of all things."*

18. He now explains how *"their principality is exceedingly strengthened,"* and says it arises from the wonderful propagation of it in so very short a time. And such was the fact because these principalities became so numerous, that St. John had to declare, *"I saw a great crowd that no one could count, from all nations, tribes, and tongues;"* as also, because after the last judgment all created things, the very demons as well as the reprobate, will be laid prostrate under the feet of the saints, and will be subject to them. He, therefore, says, *"I will number them;"* I will endeavor to number them, I mean God's friends, or if you will, the subjects of the principalities of those friends, and such will be the number of them that I will fail in it; *"for they shall be multiplied above the sand,"* will be more numerous than the grains of sand on the sea shore. This, to be sure, is an exaggeration, but not unusual in the Scriptures; thus, the Lord said to Abraham, *"I will make thy seed as the dust of the earth;"* and again, *"I will multiply thy seed as the stars of heaven, and as the sand that is by the sea shore."* Having said so much, the prophet now reverts to himself, and says that from having come to know the great glory of the saints and friends of God, he, too, was greatly moved to love him affectionately, and got the greatest desire of sharing in the same glory. *"I rose up"*—or rather as the Hebrew implies—I waked up to this new light, and rose up through love and desire of you, *"and am still,"* to the present moment, *"with thee,"* adhering to you, depending on you, with an earnest desire of final perseverance.

19-20. Having said that the just, the friends of God, were exceedingly honored by God, and that he wished for a place among them, he now, on the contrary, asserts that the wicked, the enemies of God would be slain by his just judgment; and he repudiates any friendship or companionship with such people. *"If thou wilt kill the wicked, O God."* If you, in justice, honor and exalt the virtuous, you will, with equal justice, reprobate the wicked, and condemn them to eternal punishment; and I, therefore, want to have nothing to say to them; and I, therefore, tell them, *"Ye men of blood depart from me;"* which expression includes not only homicides, who shed human blood, but all other wicked and evil doers, who injure, or seek to injure others, or who slay their own souls by sin, or the souls of others by scandal; all of whom may be truly called homicides; for hatred may be called the mainspring of homicide; and thus St. John says, *"Who hateth his brother is a homicide."*—*"Because you say in thoughts;"* you think with yourselves, and say in your hearts, *"They shall receive thy cities in vain."* The just shall receive the cities of God in vain, because they will shortly be deprived of them. This has reference to *"their principality is exceedingly strengthened;"* that is, widely propagated by the conversion of the gentiles to the faith, and of sinners to justice; and as, in consequence thereof, many cities, that is, congregations, were rescued from the slavery of the demons, and the worship of idols, the wicked remnants of idolatry, envying the propagation of Christ's kingdom, said in their hearts, *"They shall receive thy cities in vain,"* foolishly hoping that they would return to idolatry.

21-22. It is no wonder that he who has his eyes fixed on God, and who cleaves to him with his whole heart, should avow that he hated them who hated him, and that he should pine away with grief and sadness on beholding him so insulted by the wicked. And his hatred of them was intense; for it was *"a perfect hatred,"* consummate and irreconcilable, but applying to the sin, and not to the sinner; and he, therefore, observes, *"And they are become enemies to me."* I was no enemy of theirs—for I merely sought to correct and reform them—but they became enemies to me, by reason of my having so reproved and sought to reform them.

23-24. He now implores of God to do what he said, in the beginning of the Psalm, God had already done; that is, to go on in the search of his heart and his ways, that is, of his thoughts, desires, progress, and conduct, with the view that if God *"see if there be any of the way of iniquity in him,"* he may take him at once out of such way, *"and lead him in the eternal way;"* that is, to reflect on, to desire, and to do everything that tends to eternal happiness.

PSALM 139

A prayer to be delivered from the wicked.

1 Deliver me, O Lord, from the evil man: rescue me from the unjust man.
2 Who have devised iniquities in their hearts: all the day long they designed battles.
3 They have sharpened their tongues like a serpent: the venom of saps is under their lips.
4 Keep me, O Lord, from the hand of the wicked: and from unjust men deliver me. Who have proposed to supplant my steps.
5 The proud have hidden a net for me. And they have stretched out cords for a snare: they have laid for me a stumblingblock by the wayside.
6 I said to the Lord: Thou art my God: hear, O Lord, the voice of my supplication.
7 Lord, Lord, the strength of my salvation: thou hast overshadowed my head in the day of battle.
8 Give me not up, O Lord, from my desire to the wicked: they have plotted against me; do not thou forsake me, lest they should triumph.
9 The head of them compassing me about: the labour of their lips shall overwhelm them.
10 Burning coals shall fall upon them; thou wilt cast them down into the fire: in miseries they shall not be able to stand.
11 A man full of tongue shall not be established in the earth: evil shall catch the unjust man unto destruction.
12 I know that the Lord will do justice to the needy, and will revenge the poor.
13 But as for the just, they shall give glory to thy name: and the upright shall dwell with thy countenance.

Explanation of the Psalm

1. The prayer of the faithful in general. By the evil man, St. Augustine says he means the devil, who is called in the Gospel *"the enemy."* Others will have it that it means evil men in general, who are excited and governed by the devil. Both interpretations are true, and, therefore, may be united; and thus, the meaning will be, *"Deliver me from the evil man,"* be he the evil spirit, who directly, or through servants of his, harasses me. And as the word *"me"* does not apply to one individual in particular, but to the faithful in general, in like manner the expression, *"the evil man,"* is not confined to one individual persecutor, but to persecutors in general, or to every persecutor. The next sentence, *"Rescue me from the unjust man,"* is no more than a repetition; for, though some sinners may not be looked upon as being unjust, still, to a certain extent, every sinner is an unjust man, because he is, at all events, unjust to himself, and to others, if he injures them by his example, as St. John says, *"Whosoever committeth sin, committeth also iniquity, and sin is iniquity."*

2. He assigns a reason for having said, *"Deliver me,"* and the reason is because he was assailed through thought, word, and deed; and so repeatedly, that they might be called daily, without intermission or truce; and the Apostle, therefore, justly exhorts us *"to put on the armor of God,"* or, as the Greek has it, all sorts of armor, to wit, the helmet, coat of mail, shield, and sword, to enable us to offer the necessary resistance, and to stand perfect in every respect. First, then, in regard to our engagement, in respect of thought. *"Who have devised iniquity in their hearts."* This proves that the expression, *"the evil man,"* in the first verse, is not intended for an individual, such as Saul, but for a lot of evil men, be they demons or men; *"to devise iniquity in their hearts,"* means their having recourse to all manner of deception, scheming, and intrigue. *"All the day long they devised battles."* They never ceased arranging the plans of battle they had previously decided on. All this may, possibly, refer to the interior struggle within us, in respect of bad thoughts the prince of darkness turns up to us; such as unchaste thoughts, temptations, infidelities to grace, scruples, and mental perplexities; all the source of much annoyance and trouble.

3. The second persecution of our enemies is that of the tongue, which consists in calumny, detraction, abuse, deception, and the like, resorted to by our fellow creatures, either through selfishness or through revenge, and by the evil spirit, with a view of provoking man to impatience or anger, or hatred of his neighbor, and to the sins consequent thereon. The aforesaid wicked, then, *"have sharpened their tongue like a serpent,"* the more easily to pierce the ears and the heart; *"the venom of asps,"* the most deadly of all poison, *"is under their lips;"* in store, ready to shoot it with their tongues on their hearers.

4. Next in order is persecution the third, or personal persecution, in reference to which the just ask for protection, to *"keep off the hand of the wicked"* from harming them. By the *"wicked,"* he seems to have the prince of darkness in view; and then he, furthermore, asks, *"And from unjust men deliver me,"* they being members of the prince of darkness; and, for fear they, too, may have got the power of doing harm. The harm he dreads, and from which he seeks to be delivered, is explained as follows: *"Who have proposed to supplant my steps."* The object of the prince of darkness is to keep us out of the path of salvation, from which he irreparably fell. He and his Angels, therefore, have the one object in view, at all times, and that is, *"to supplant our steps,"* so that we may no longer walk in the path of the Lord, that we may fall therein, or turn back, or, at least, make slow progress in it. They accomplish that by laying snares for, and by concealing them in the way as we move along, as we are told in the following verse.

5. The demons could not be called by a more appropriate name than *"proud,"* because their fall was not owing to the concupiscence of the flesh, nor to the concupiscence of the eyes, but to *"the pride of life;"* they would be equal to the supreme being; hence we have in Tobias, *"Never suffer pride to reign in thy mind or in thy words: for from it all perdition took its beginning;"* and in the book of Job the devil is styled, *"king over all the children of pride."* Now, the devil *"hides his net"* when he displays the advantage of any human act, and hides the evil of it; that is, when he causes man to look upon the utility or the pleasure of anything, without reflecting on the consequent sorrow and suffering sure to follow from it. Thus, he causes the adulterer to revel in the beauty of the object of his desire, and hides the heinousness of the sin from him. He makes the thief gloat over the stolen property, and keeps from his view his having lost the kingdom of heaven for it. He puts before the eyes of the ambitious the advantages of their preeminence, and conceals the danger of a fall from such a height. Finally, he never fails in bringing under our notice the pleasure of the transgression, while he studiously conceals the bitterness of the consequent punishment. *"And they have stretched out cords for a snare;"* set additional snares; for no sooner has one snare taken its victim, than the evil spirits set another; thus, he who has fallen into the snare of adultery will at once fall into that of murder, in the hope of concealing it, and they soon lead him to perjury, in order to conceal both, and thereby escape a well deserved sentence. Finally, *"they have laid for me a stumbling block by the wayside;"* for in the way of the Lord there can be no stumbling block; as we read in Psalm 118, *"Much peace have they that love thy law; and to them there is no stumbling block."* The moment we turn out of that way we fall into all manner of snares, and knock against all manner of stumbling

blocks. The only remedy, then, is that of the Apostle, *"to walk with caution,"* and never to let our foot outside the path of the Lord.

6-7. He now invokes the divine assistance, without which we can do nothing against so many dangers. *"I said to the Lord thou art my God,"* and I am, therefore, your people. *"Thou art my Lord,"* and I am, in consequence, your servant; and, therefore, as I belong to you, *"hear the voice of my supplication."* In order, then, to show that the dangers were present and pressing, he again appeals to the Lord, saying, *"O Lord, the strength of my salvation,"* I appeal to you with such confidence, because you are my strength, on whom I depend for salvation; you are the only power to save and protect me from my enemies. *"Thou hast overshadowed my head in the day of battle."* It is not the first time you have protected me; you did so in the day of battle, when I was hemmed in on all aides by my enemies, when *"you overshadowed my head,"* as if with a helmet, and saved me from the death that stared me in the face, and that now emboldens me to appeal to you with so much confidence. This may also apply to a spiritual overshadowing of not only the head, but of the whole person; *"in the day of battle,"* the interior battle, in which man has to fight against his own concupiscences, because poor man, tired and feverish through temptation and bad desires, would wither and succumb altogether if not overshadowed by God Almighty.

8. In consequence of the foregoing, he now asks for constant overshadowing, or protection, from the fire of his evil desires, because, if concupiscence had not got a hold of us, vain would be the temptation of the evil one or the rage of man. *"Give me not up, O Lord;"* that is, do not suffer me to be given up *"from my desire to the wicked,"* be he man or demon that tempts me. *"We are given up from our desires to the wicked"* when concupiscence holds us captive, and gives us up to the power of Satan; for instance, when you look on another with an eye of concupiscence you become guilty at once, and subject to temptation; when death, in the time of persecution, is threatened, nothing can be offered to the evil one by the persecutor but the desire of life; when the tempter puts an opportunity for committing fraud in the way of man he can offer him nothing but the desire of lucre, and so of other sins. *"They have plotted against me, do not thou forsake me."* The reason why I am so desirous of the overshadowing of your grace is, because my enemies *"hath plotted against me,"* have laid snares for me, and, if they chance to take me, will *"triumph,"* and glory, and rejoice, for not only having conquered me, but you along with me.

9. He now begins to predict the punishment sure to overtake the wicked, who so persecuted the just. There is a degree of obscurity as to the nature of that punishment here that is so clearly expressed in Psalm 7, where he says, *"He is fallen into the hole he made, his sorrow shall be turned on his own head;"*

the persecutions they prepared for the just will recoil on themselves, and will *"overwhelm them."* The wicked feel that at their death, and, on the day of judgment, the whole world will see it; for on that day all the sufferings of the just will be turned into glory, and all the sins of the wicked into eternal misery. *"The head of their compassing me about;"* the sum total of their snares, which the wicked sought to lay by going round and round about me, just like the devil, who *"goes about like a roaring lion,"* will all recoil on themselves, *"and overwhelm them;"* and he repeats it when he adds, *"the labor of their lips shall overwhelm them;"* that is to say, the labor of affliction or trouble inflicted on the just by their lips, by their bad or vicious language, will also overwhelm them.

10. A further relation of the punishments of the wicked: *"coals"* imply they will be punishments of the severest description; and the expression, *"shall fall,"* conveys that they will come from above, from the supreme and sovereign Judge. Lest we should imagine they will be few in number, he adds, *"thou wilt cast them down into the fire;"* for such will be the quantity of fire rained down upon them that it will completely cover and overwhelm them, as if they had been cast into the fire; and, in order to explain it more fully, he adds, *"in miseries, they shall not be able to stand;"* they will be stretched so prostrate by all the misery that will accumulate on them that they will not be able to rise or to stand erect.

11. Having predicted the future punishment of the wicked, he now turns to the punishments in store for them here below. *"A man full of tongue."* The man, too, given to talk, the liar, the flatterer, the detractor, the scold, the brawler, *"shall not be established in the earth,"* for such people are hated by the wicked, even as well as by the good, and, therefore, St. James desires, *"And let every man be swift to hear, but slow to speak, and slow to anger."* *"Evils shall catch the unjust man unto destruction."* Not only will the man full of tongue, and, therefore, an unjust man, neither thrive nor prosper, *"But the evils that will catch him,"* which would have gone to reward his patience, as they do to the just, will tend to his everlasting *"destruction."* The expression *"catch"* implies a sudden unexpected catch, like that of a hunter; and such is the mode in which the wicked are generally surprised, while they are bent on the capture and spoliation of the just; they apprehend no danger from the devil, who is as intent on them as would a hunter on a wild beast. And it is not alone by the devil that they are led away captives; for they are captives to much misery, anxiety, troubles, fears, and bad passions, with this difference, however, between them and the virtuous who, too, have to contend against the like, that with them all such things *"cooperate unto good,"* while, with the wicked, they only tend to their eternal condemnation.

12-13. He now comes to the conclusion, that the delivery and the happiness of the just are certain, as are also the miserable state and the punishment of the wicked. *"I knew that the Lord will do justice to the needy."* I am convinced, both from my own experience, from the records of my ancestors, as well as from a knowledge of God's promises and of his justice, that he regards the humble and the poor; which include those abounding in the wealth of the world, yet, by reason of their not looking upon such wealth as their own, but as so much entrusted to them by God to dispense, as being but so many stewards, are still really poor in spirit. *"I know that the Lord will,"* beyond any manner of doubt, *"do justice to the needy;"* and he will also *"revenge the poor,"* by punishing those that persecuted them, with the greatest severity. *"But as for the just, they shall give glory to thy name,"* giving themselves credit for nothing, but attributing all to God, *"and the upright shall dwell with thy countenance,"* will see him, and know him, as he is. One is known from their countenance. Look at anyone's person, you will never recognize him; look at his face alone, and you need no more!

PSALM 140

A prayer against sinful words and deceitful flatterers.

1 I have cried to the, O Lord, hear me: hearken to my voice, when I cry to thee.
2 Let my prayer be directed as incense in thy sight; the lifting up of my hands, as evening sacrifice.
3 Set a watch, O Lord, before my mouth: and a door round about my lips.
4 Incline not my heart to evil words; to make excuses in sins. With men that work iniquity: and I will not communicate with the choicest of them.
5 The just shall correct me in mercy, and shall reprove me: but let not the oil of the sinner fatten my head. For my prayer also shall still be against the things with which they are well pleased:
6 Their judges falling upon the rock have been swallowed up. They shall hear my words, for they have prevailed:
7 As when the thickness of the earth is broken up upon the ground: Our bones are scattered by the side of hell.
8 But o to thee, O Lord, Lord, are my eyes: in thee have I put my trust, take not away my soul.
9 Keep me from the snare, which they have laid for me, and from the stumblingblocks of them that work iniquity.
10 The wicked shall fall in his net: I am alone until I pass.

EXPLANATION OF THE PSALM

1. Such is the language of Christ's body, or the body of the faithful, from the midst of the enemy. *"I have cried to thee, O Lord,"* to help me, surrounded as I am by so many dangers; and as *"I have cried"* with all the powers of my interior, and with great affection, *"hear me."* In the Hebrew it is, hasten to help me, and thus prove that you hear me. And hear me not only on this occasion, but *"hearken to my voice, when I cry to thee;"* as much as to say, be sure to attend to my prayers, whenever I put them up to thee.

2. He now tells what he wants, and in what respect he wishes God should hear him. He first, and most properly, begs of God to assist him in praying well; for, as the Apostle has it, *"For we know not what we should pray for;"* and we are equally ignorant of the manner in which we should pray for anything, unless the Spirit help our infirmity. He, therefore, begs of God to afford him the assistance of his grace to enable him to pray well. He then declared the conditions of prayer by comparing it to the incense that was daily, morning and evening, by God's command, offered up in the temple. *"Let my prayer be directed as incense in thy sight."* My first request is, that my prayer, through your grace, may ascend like incense. Now, incense suggests the following remarks: First, it was composed of four gums that were highly fragrant and aromatic, frankincense, gum, alkanet, and myrrh, which emitted a most exquisite fragrance. Secondly, it was offered up in the inmost recess, in the most noble part of the temple, called the Holy of Holies, where the tables of the law and the altar of gold were kept. Thirdly, it was offered by the high priest. Fourthly, it was put on the fire, from which it ascended in the form of smoke, mounting up in a direct straight line. The four aromatic substances represent the four virtues, Faith, Hope, Love, Humility, and the most grateful prayer that can be put up to God is composed of them. Man is the temple of God, for the Apostle says, *"Your members are the temple of the Holy Ghost,"* the inmost part of which is the soul, in which is the law, written there by the finger of God; there, also, is the will, representing the altar of gold, namely, a pure heart, adorned by the grace of God. Christ is the high priest, for it is through him, as being our advocate, that we must always pray; and it is for that reason that we conclude every prayer with *"through our Lord Jesus Christ."* Finally, the fire that produced the fragrant smoke, that rose up and ascended so directly, is fervor of desire, but in order that it should ascend in a straight and direct line, there must be a pure intention and constant attention; for they who pray with a view to attract notice have their incense aside by the draught of the world, and it will not ascend in a direct line; while they who allow the cares of this world, and its distractions, to interfere with them when they pray, they do not give proper direction to their prayer, and such distractions, like so many currents, blow away, and dissipate the incense of their prayer, and will not suffer it to soar aloft, as it ought; and it was a consciousness of this that makes the prophet pray, *"Let my prayer be directed as incense in thy sight."* The lifting up

of my hands as evening sacrifice." A repetition of the preceding: *"lifting up the hands"* signifies prayer, for the Jews, as well as ourselves, were wont to raise up their hands in prayer; thus, in Psalm 133, *"In the nights lift up your hands to the holy places"* and the Apostle, *"Lifting up pure hands, without anger and strife."* The *"evening sacrifice"* means the sacrifice of incense, that was offered up every evening. The meaning, then, is, *"the lifting up of my hands,"* the prayer I offer with uplifted hands, may it be like the sacrifice of incense offered up every evening. The prophet wishes that his prayer should be like the evening, rather than the morning sacrifice; perhaps, because it was in the evening he composed the Psalm, as it is in the evening the Church sings it too; or, perhaps, because the evening sacrifice was of more value as being a figure of the sacrifice on the cross, that occurred in the evening.

3. The second petition he lays before God, is to give him the grace of knowing when he ought to speak, and when to be silent; for as St. James says, *"If any man offend not in word, the same is a perfect man;"* and according to Ecclesiastes, there is *"a time to speak and a time to be silent;"* and in order to explain it, the prophet uses a figure, taken from the guard put on the gates of a house or a city. Two things are necessary to ensure freedom of exit to those entitled to it, and detention to those not entitled to it; and the two things are, gates, and a porter to stand by the gates; for a gate without a porter will not suffice, for it must, of necessity, in such case, be always shut or always open; nor will a porter without a gate do the business, unless he keep guard at all hours and be strong enough to prevent any forcible ingress or egress; but with a gate and a porter all is right and safe; and he, therefore, says, *"Set a watch, O Lord, before my mouth;"* my mouth being the gates through which pass the language that causes so much mischief and harm, I pray you to set a porter or a watchman on it, to guard it with the greatest diligence; *"and a door round about my lips."* As a porter would hardly suffice to restrain my words, or to keep sufficient guard, I further beg of you to put *"a door round my lips;"* that is to say, a strong, secure one, that cannot easily be stormed. The porter and the gate signify two gifts of the Holy Ghost, one pertaining to the understanding, that man may know when, how, and what to say, or to do; and the other having reference to the will; that is to say, that one should have the courage to speak when they ought to speak, and fear to speak when they should be silent; these are the gifts which Isaias calls *"the spirit of counsel and fortitude,"* which are nearly identical with prudence and charity. Now, we are not to ask these gifts of God without doing all in us lies to cooperate with his grace, at the same time that we are also to bear in mind that such cooperation is also a gift from God; and, therefore, that we should glory in nothing, when, in point of fact, we have nothing.

4. His third petition is, that as, in spite of all his diligence, yet, such is human frailty, that even the *"just man falls seven times,"* and *"we all offend in many things;"* that God may give us the grace to make a free confession of our sins, for fear, by representing ourselves in a state of perfect health, we may prevent our heavenly physician from curing us. *"Incline not my heart to evil words."* Do not allow us, when we shall have fallen into sin, to let our heart incline" to lies and excuses. *"To make excuses in sins;"* instead of acknowledging our guilt, to excuse ourselves in all possible forms. *"With men that work iniquity; and I will not communicate with the choicest of them."* Here is the fourth petition, for God to guard us, and keep us from the company, and from making too free with the wicked. Many and many a one would have preserved their innocence only for the company they fell into! To understand this latter part of the verse we must connect it with the first part, and then the meaning will be, Do not incline my heart to evil words, to make excuses for sinners, as their fellows do, for fear, by doing so, I may become one too; and thus, *"I will not communicate with the choicest of them;"* your grace will enable me to avoid and shun the very choicest of them.

5. The fifth petition is, that, through God's grace, we may fall in with friends, who will correct us in charity, instead of fawning flatterers, who deceive by their false praise. And one of the greatest blessings from God is to meet faithful friends, to tell us the truth in regard of ourselves, and also to give us the grace to heal them willingly, and to be thankful to them. For with those who belong to the world, and have not got such grace from God, *"flattery creates friends, and truth hatred."* *"The just man shall correct me in mercy;"* he will reprove me with a view to my correction, in order to heal me, and not as the sinner would, to destroy me; because he will do it *"in mercy,"* that is to say, in charity, from a feeling for my wretched state; and not in anger or bitterness, from a desire of revenge. Such a man *"shall reprove me"* with pleasure; but *"let not the oil of the sinner fatten my heart;"* that sweet unction the sinner will seek to lay on the soul of another poor sinner, in extenuation of, or frequently in defense of, nay, more, in praise of, their sins. *"For my prayer also shall still be against the things with which they are well pleased."* All allow this to be a most obscure passage. St. Chrysostom explains it thus, I will not only shut off all communication with the wicked, but, furthermore, *"my prayer shall be against the things with which they are well pleased;"* against the crimes and the vices in which they revel, which will be very transitory; because

6. The career of the wicked will be short; because *"their judges,"* the great ones amongst them, will fall upon the rock, as if they were battling with a seething sea, that dashes them unmercifully on a rock, and shivers them to pieces. *"They shall hear my words, for they have prevailed."* An allusion to *"My prayer also shall still be against the things with which they are well pleased;"* by which he gives us to understand that many unfortunate souls, who prided themselves on their sins, would hear his words, and be converted to God through them; for as the hardest soil is entered by the plough, so the heart of man, however hardened it may be, will be entered and stirred up by the power and the efficacy of the word of God.

7. Those poor souls, already alluded to, will hear my words; for these words were most effectual in moving them; as effectual as a spade or a plough, to enter into and turn up the thick, sluggish clay. *"Our bones are scattered by the side of hell."* Such and so numerous are the temptations that surround us, that *"our bones,"* which represent our strength and courage, are so scattered, weakened, and debilitated as to be brought almost nigh to the gates of hell, to the last extremities.

8. This is the last petition, similar to the first, in which he asked to deliver us from all the dangers of temptation; and he now repeats it, on consideration of the miserable state alluded to in the preceding verse. *"To thee, O Lord, are my eyes"* looking out for help from you; *"in thee have I put my trust;"* and I, therefore, pray that you *"take not away my soul."* Do not suffer my life to be taken, myself to be lost.

9. He tells from what quarter he apprehends death, and says it is from the snares and stumbling blocks, that is, from the temptation of the devil and from bad example. *"Keep me from the snare which they have laid before me"*— be it the concupiscence of the flesh, the concupiscence of the eyes, or the pride of life, *"and from the stumbling blocks of them that work iniquity,"* from the examples set by the carnal, the covetous, and the proud.

10. He finally tells us, that all those attached to sin will fall into the net of the evil spirit; while he, and all who, like him, have a hatred of sin, will escape it; an admonition that proves man to be endowed with free will, and one that must prove a great consolation to those who fear God. *"The wicked,"* all those who take pleasure in sin, that is, who are at present, and wish to remain, sinners, *"shall fall in his net,"* in the net of the archhunter, the devil; *"I am alone until I pass,"* I will keep aloof from the whole world, until I should have passed all snares and stumbling blocks. Though I may be kept an exile for a time in this world, I will not belong to it. *"I am alone,"* until I shall have passed to my country, where I shall have no shares or stumbling blocks to encounter.

PSALM 141

A prayer of David in extremity of danger.

1 I cried to the Lord with my voice: with my voice I made supplication to the Lord.

2 In his sight I pour out my prayer, and before him I declare my trouble:
3 When my spirit failed me, then thou newest my paths. In this way wherein I walked, they have hidden a snare for me.
4 I looked on my right hand, and beheld, and there was no one that would know me. Flight hath failed me: and there is no one that hath regard to my soul.
5 I cried to thee, O Lord: I said: Thou art my hope, my portion in the land of the living.
6 Attend to my supplication: for I am brought very low. Deliver me from my persecutors; for they are stronger than I.
7 Bring my soul out of prison, that I may praise thy name: the just wait for me, until thou reward me.

Explanation of the psalm

1-2. We learn nothing more from these two verses, but that David put up a certain prayer to God, but the several expressions in them are worth attention. *"With my voice,"* intimating that David did not pray with his lips alone, as they do who do not attend to, or understand what they are about; but he prayed *"with his voice,"* that was formed in his heart, and sent forth through the organs he got for the purpose. *"I cried."* We have already explained, that such expression implies, crying with earnestness. *"I made supplication,"* is an explanation of the nature of his cry, viz., that he cried not by way of reproach or blasphemy, but in prayer and invocation. *"In his sight I pour out my prayer,"* implying his prayer was put up from the cave when he was flying from Saul, where God alone beheld him, and as if he foresaw the monition of Christ, who advises us to pray in our closed chamber; and with that, as is principally intended here, to signify that the cry was principally in the interior, where God alone can hear or see it. *"And before him I declare my trouble,"* is no more than an explanation of *"in his sight I pour out my prayer."*

3. He now tells why and when he declared his trouble before God. It was when he was at death's door, *"when my spirit failed me,"* when he was lurking in the cave, and in great danger for his life. This is more applicable to Christ in the garden, or on the cross. *"Then thou knewest my paths."* When my spirit failed me, I prayed to you, who well *"knew my paths,"* my thoughts, actions, and desires, and how unjustly I was suffering so much persecution. *"In this way wherein I walked, they have hidden a snare for me."* He tells us that such persecution commenced by his enemies privately plotting against him, and then, that they had recourse to open violence. Saul frequently sought David's death privately by sending him to fight where he expected he would be slain; but when he did not succeed in that, he openly attacked him. And so with the Pharisees, who frequently sought to take advantage of our Lord in his language; but when his wisdom proved superior to their malice, they openly charged him and demanded his crucifixion. *"In this way wherein I walked"* in the way of justice and of God's commandments, in the very path you know so well. *"They have hidden a snare for me."* To give an example. Saul promised his daughter in marriage to David, on condition of his killing two hundred Philistines, with whom God's people were then, justly, at war; and he did so, in the hope of David being killed in the battle. David, however, through God's assistance, in obedience to the king, set out to battle, and killed the two hundred Philistines. Thus, the Pharisees watched Christ, to see would he heal on the sabbath, that they may afterwards be able to say, *"This man is not of God who keepeth not the sabbath,"* and thus they, too, *"hid snares in the way"* of the commandments of God. Christ, however, did work in curing on the sabbath, and showed that he did not violate the sabbath thereby, inasmuch as it was only servile works, and not works of charity, that were forbidden on the sabbath. They also *"hid snares in his way,"* when they brought the adulteress before him saying, *"Moses ordered such one to be stoned, what say you?"*

4. This refers to the violence offered him; for his enemies, on seeing that their private plots against him did not succeed, had recourse to open violence. Under such persecution, he says, *"I looked to the right,"* for help from my friends, *"and beheld,"* to see was any friend or companion coming to my aid, *"and there was no one that would know me,"* not one that would dare to acknowledge his having the slightest knowledge of me. This applies to David, who, when persecuted by Saul, flew for protection, to King Achis, who refused to receive him, whereon he had to hide himself in a cave. It applies much more forcibly to Christ, who, in his passion, saw many on his left hand, his enemies and accusers, and not one on his right hand, his friends and acquaintances. For, as the Gospel has it, *"And all his acquaintance stood afar off,"* and Peter himself the principal one among them, swore with an oath, *"I know not the man;"* and with just reason, therefore, might the Lord say, *"There was no one that would know me." "Flight hath failed me."* He was now reduced to such extremities that, so far from having any hope of external aid, he was even unable to run away, and thus save himself by flight. *"Flight hath failed me,"* and I, therefore, have no means of escape, *"and there is no one that hath regard to any soul,"* not one having the least concern for me, or caring to save me from utter destruction. David complained of his being unable to fly away by reason of his inability; but Christ was unable to do so because be would not do so, and because both he and his Father had interdicted it. Flight fails the one who will not fly as effectually as the one who cannot fly. And, in fact, not one appeared: *"to have regard"* to Christ's life in order to save it, though he said, *"I lay down my life;"* and again, *"The

good shepherd layeth down his life for his sheep;" and though he said to his Father, *"My Father, why hast thou forsaken me?"*

5. Having now no hope whatever of any aid from man, he has recourse to God, to whom *"nothing is difficult;"* and being a spiritual man, fully aware that God sometimes afflicts his friends in their pilgrimage, with a view to crown them with additional glory in their country, he says, *"I cried to thee O Lord; I said: Thou art my hope,"* down here in my pilgrimage; *"my portion"*— in other words, my inheritance *"in the land of the living."*

6. He now uses two arguments to move God to deliver him because he is brought very low, and his enemies are made very strong. *"Attend to my supplication,"* and hear me at last, *"for I am brought very low,"* grievously depressed and afflicted. *"Deliver me from my persecutors, for they are stronger than I."* They have become so much stronger and more powerful than I that they must easily overcome me. However true this may have been of David lurking in a cave while his enemy, Saul, was at the head of a powerful army, it is more literally true of Christ, who could truly say, *"I am brought very low,"* because *"he humbled himself, becoming obedient unto death, even to the death of the cross."* He was also *"brought very low,"* when he, that had the right of sitting on the cherubim, hung between two robbers. Truly, also, were his enemies *"stronger than him"* when *"their hour came,"* and *"power was given to darkness,"* so as to appear, for a while, to eclipse the sun of justice itself.

7. As regards David, St. John Chrysostom says, *"the prison"* means the troubles and afflictions that caused him to hide himself in the cave, so that the meaning would be, Bring me clear of those afflictions, so that I may be able to leave this cave, and, upon being set at liberty, that I may praise thy name. *"The just wait for me;"* for they all expect you, in your providence, will free me, innocent as I am. Still, perhaps, David, holy as he was, and devoured with great lights from God, had loftier aspirations, and, in his desire to be freed from his mortality, as he would from a prison, said, with the Apostle, *"Who shall deliver me from the body of this death?"* for they who thus ascend to the dwelling of those who praise the Lord forever and ever are those who really praise his name, which is confirmed by the subsequent sentence, *"the just wait for me until thou reward me;"* for the souls of the holy prophets in Limbo were waiting for the just Prophet, to see him rewarded; and so were the holy Angels in heaven, who were looking out for the true and eternal happiness to be secured by his merits. As regards Christ, he prays *"to be brought out of the prison"* of the flesh, and, through his resurrection, to put on his spiritual body, to praise the name of the Lord; so that he, who had had so much labor in preaching to the people, may thenceforth be at rest in praising his Father. A number of the holy fathers agree in saying that the words, *"the just wait for me until thou reward me,"* are most applicable to

Christ, because all the just, including all from the very beginning of the world, as well as the Apostles and the other faithful then alive, waited most ardently for the resurrection and the glorification of Christ, because they were all to receive from *"the fullness of his glory;"* for, as St. John says, *"For as yet the Spirit was not given, because Jesus was not yet glorified,"* so we, too, can say, the souls of the saints had not ascended from the prison of Limbo to the kingdom of heaven, because Christ, the King of Glory, had not yet entered into his glory.

PSALM 142

The psalmist in tribulation calleth upon God for his delivery. The seventh penitential psalm.

1 Hear, O Lord, my prayer: give ear to my supplication in thy truth: hear me in thy justice.
2 And enter not into judgment with thy servant: for in thy sight no man living shall be justified.
3 For the enemy hath persecuted my soul: he hath brought down my life to the earth. He hath made me to dwell in darkness as those that have been dead of old:
4 And my spirit is in anguish within me: my heart within me is troubled.
5 I remembered the days of old, I meditated on all thy works: I meditated upon the works of thy hands.
6 I stretched forth my hands to thee: my soul is as earth without water unto thee.
7 Hear me speedily, O Lord: my spirit hath fainted away. Turn not away thy face from me, lest I be like unto them that go down into the pit.
8 Cause me to hear thy mercy in the morning; for in thee have I hoped. Make the way known to me, wherein I should walk: for I have lifted up my soul to thee.
9 Deliver me from my enemies, O Lord, to thee have I fled:
10 Teach me to do thy will, for thou art my God. Thy good spirit shall lead me into the right land:
11 For thy name's sake, O Lord, thou wilt quicken me in thy justice. Thou wilt bring my soul out of trouble:
12 And in thy mercy thou wilt destroy my enemies. And thou wilt cut off all them that afflict my soul: for I am thy servant.

EXPLANATION OF THE PSALM

1. The Psalmist commences by asking for an audience in truth and justice, and tells us what he wants, because he takes it for granted that God knows full well what he wants, namely, forgiveness of the sin that he was now paying the penalty of. Now, God knew full well why he asked for it, and wished his prayer should be heard, because he saw the desires of his heart, as also, perhaps, understood them from his groans and sighs, arising from perfect contrition. Thus, we read of Mary Magdalen, who made no expression when she sought for forgiveness, but let the tears, with which she washed the Savior's feet, convey to the Savior what she sought; and, hence, the immediate reply, *"Thy sins are forgiven thee."* David, then, full of contrition, and groaning internally, in asking pardon for his sin says, *"Hear, O Lord, my prayer,"* the purport of which you are well acquainted with; and repeats it, saying, *"Give ear to my supplication in thy truth;"* that is to say, in accordance with the faithful observance of the promise you made of forgiveness to the truly penitent. And he repeats it again when he adds, *"Hear me in thy justice,"* justice meaning here a strict adherence to, and observance of, his promise. St. John Chrysostom interprets justice to mean the kindness with which God receives the penitent; and he says that David studiously says, *"hear me in thy justice,"* instead of hear me in justice, became the justice God exhibits towards the penitent deserves rather the name of inexpressible kindness. The moment God sees anyone truly penitent, and acknowledging their faults, he at once forgives them, as he says, through Isaias 43, *"Tell if thou hast anything to justify thyself."* Judges here below seek a confession from the accused, in order to condemn him; God seeks for it in order to absolve him. Finally, the father of the prodigal son, that is, God, the moment he beheld the son on his return, exclaiming, *"Father, I have sinned against heaven, and against thee,"* threw himself on his neck, kissed and embraced him, ordered the best robe and ring to clothe him, and the fatted calf to be killed to celebrate his return.

2. Having asked for pardon on the ground of God's promises, to which he faithfully adheres, he asks for pardon again, on the ground of the frailty and infirmity of human nature. *"And enter not into judgment with thy servant."* Don't dispute the matter with me, I will make no defense, I will avow my guilt instead of pleading my innocence, *"for in thy sight no man living shall be justified;"* because not only one like me, but any human being whatever will be cast when they come to stand in judgment before you. Human beings may be divided into sinners, the just here below, and the just in heaven. Sinners, such as homicides, adulterers, and the like, may justify themselves in the eyes of man, their crimes being of the occult, or incapable of proof; but they will not be justified before God, who knows their hearts and sees their conscience, and will bring them in guilty on its testimony. The just, in this place of trial, will not be justified before God, because they will not dare to justify themselves, but will rather say with the Apostle, *"For I am not conscious to myself of anything; yet in this I am not justified but he that judgeth me is the Lord;"* for, perhaps, he sees something in me that I do not see; and with Job, then, I should rather say, *"I, who although I should have any just thing, would not answer, but would make supplication to my judge."* Another

reason why they *"will not be justified"* is, because they feel that their justice has not been acquired by themselves, but is a free gift of God; and thus, they will not justify themselves before God, as if the justification proceeded from themselves, but they will rather return thanks to him who justifies them. Finally, *"they will not be justified"* in the sight of the Lord, because, however just they may be, and free from sin, they still feel themselves to be sinners, inasmuch as they are subject to sin every day, and need to say with the rest of the saints, *"Forgive us our trespasses;"* and with St. John, *"If we say that we have no sin we deceive ourselves."* The just in heaven, who are not only free from crime and sin, but are even beyond the reach of either, *"are not justified in thy sight,"* because they do not attribute their justice to themselves, but to the God who conferred it on them, and compared with whose justice all others may be looked upon as pure injustice, for *"the stars are not pure in his sight."*

Lutherans and Calvinists seek to prove from this passage, that there is no real justice in the justified soul, it being merely imputed to it; and that all the acts of the just are so many mortal sins, deserving eternal punishment, if God chose to impute them so. In reply, we must observe, that David did not say that there was no just person to be found; on the contrary, in Psalm 17, he says, *"And the Lord will reward me according to my justice, and will repay me according to the cleanness of my hands, because I have kept the ways of the Lord, and have not done wickedly against my God, and I shall be spotless with him,"* etc.; and in Psalm 118, *"Blessed are the undefiled in the way, who walk in the law of the Lord."* Observe, also, that David does not say no one will be justified, but he says no one *"will be justified in thy sight,"* either because the justice anyone may come to is not from themselves, but from God; or, because, however just anyone may get to be, they still are not free from venial sins and imperfections; or, finally, because no matter how just and perfect anyone may become, they can be called anything but just, when compared to the infinite and increate justice of God; just as all light, however brilliant, dwindles into insignificance, when compared to that of the sun, to which Job alludes, when he says, chap. 4, *"Shall man be justified in comparison of God? and, again, in chap. 9, "Indeed I know it is so, and that man cannot be justified compared with God."*

3. He now puts forward a third reason for obtaining pardon, derived from the grievousness of the temptation under which he fell; for it was not spontaneously, or without being under the influence of temptation, as did the reprobate angels, who, consequently, were not forgiven, that he fell, but it was under a most grievous temptation of the devil, our enemy, *"who goes about like a roaring lion, seeking whom he may devour,"* that he was laid prostrate and hurled from the height of innocence to the lowest depths of

mortal sin. The word *"for,"* then, is to be read with *"hear me in thy justice;"* as much as to say, hear me, because you are just, because you adhere to your promise, because *"in thy sight no man living shall be justified;"* because *"the enemy hath persecuted my soul,"* by exciting me to adultery, and tempting me to murder, and thus *"brought down my life to the earth,"* made me vile and contemptible in thy sight, and that of the holy Angels. *"He hath made me to dwell in darkness,"* etc. He goes on to detail the calamities in which he got involved through sin, into which he fell through the persecution of the devil. Having *"brought down his life to the earth."* he next made him *"dwell in darkness,"* in spiritual darkness; and that by blinding the eyes of the interior, so as to be taken up with false for true happiness, not to advert to the depths and precipices, and to lose sight entirely of the way that leads to life; and finally, to cause him to dwell in darkness, as completely as those who have been dead and buried for many years, speaking of which darkness the Apostle, says, Ephes. 4, *"Having the understanding obscured with darkness, alienated from the life of God, through the ignorance which is in them, because of the blindness of their heart;"* and in chap. 6, *"For our wrestling is not against flesh and blood, but against principalities and powers, against the rulers of this world of darkness."*

4. He now explains how, by the light of divine grace, he began to see the darkness in which he had been enveloped, and how he had fallen in his love for the things of this world, and how therefrom arose great anxiety and fear of God's judgments, and of the wretched state into which he had fallen through sin. Such is the first stage of penance. He was in such a state of anxiety as nigh caused his death, had he not been consoled with the hope of mercy. *"My heart within me is troubled."* When I began to reflect on my miserable state I was troubled not lightly, nor superficially but in the inmost recesses of my heart, as should all those who seek to imitate the repentance of David.

5. He now tells how he began to get his breathing in such anxiety, and by his example shows the way to recovery after a relapse. *"I remembered the days of old."* I began to remember the mercy with which you dealt with our fathers from time immemorial, when you bore their infirmities, healed their sores, and spared their iniquities And it was not a passing thought I bestowed on them, but *"I meditated on all thy works."* I studied all your works, whether of nature or of grace, with the greatest care; and I saw that mercy predominated in everyone of them, which he repeats, when he adds, *"I meditated upon the works of thy hands"*—was quite absorbed in reflection on all your works.

6. The consideration of God's mercy having inspired him with hope, he began to sigh and to look up to him. *"I stretched forth my hands to thee"* in prayer; for my soul thirsts as much for your grace, as the parched earth

does for the rain. A most appropriate comparison; for as the earth, when devoid of moisture, does not adhere together, is not clothed with herbage, nor adorned with flowers, produces no fruit, and is altogether idle and unproductive; so the soul, without God's grace, offers no resistance to temptation; but like the dust, that is carried about by the wind, has neither the clothing of justice, nor the ornaments of wisdom, nor the fruit of good works, of all which the penitent had practical experience, and was therefore the more thirsty.

7. The turpitude of the sin he acknowledged and the desire of grace now so presses on the penitent, that he can brook no further delay; and the fact of the penitent not deferring his confession, and the other remedies suggested, from day to day, but running at once to his spiritual physician, just as one taken suddenly ill would urgently send for the doctor, or one suffering from thirst would run to the water, is a sign of true contrition. *"Hear me speedily;"* I cannot bear my wretched state any longer; wash me quickly from my iniquities; heal, at once, my disease; because *"my spirit hath fainted away;"* I am in the last extremities, can scarce draw my breath. *"Turn not away thy face from me"*—the same petition in different language—as much as to say, do not refuse to be reconciled, be not inexorable; look upon me with a face of benignity and mercy, *"lest I become like those that go down into the pit;"* the lowest pit of hell; for such is the fate of those whom God refuses to pardon, and from whom he withholds his grace.

8. He again reverts to the same subject, in another manner, however. *"Cause me to hear thy mercy in the morning;"* that is, at once, in the very beginning of the day; or the morning may mean that dawn of grace that succeeded the dark night of sin in which he had so long lain; as if he were to say, The night of sin, in which I have been enveloped, has been long enough; through your mercy, let the day of grace and reconciliation now commence, and let me hear your voice, saying, *"I am thy salvation, for in thee have I hoped;"* that is to say, may the grace of hope already given me, merit the grace of forgiveness; for though the sinner can merit nothing with God, still, grace itself merits an increase of it, that by its increase it may merit the being perfected; and, as St. Augustine observes, that as justification is obtained through faith, the same may also be said of hope. *"Make the way known to me wherein I should walk; for I have lifted up my soul to thee."* The penitent having now succeeded in securing his justification, and fearful of a relapse, earnestly arks for the grace of knowing the path of justice, and of walking in it, and the desire of forming such rule of life as becomes a friend and child of God, after being reconciled to him, is also a mark of a true penitent. *"Make the way known to me wherein I should walk;"* so illuminate my mind as to know the path of justice, through the aid of which I may be able to come to you; because *"I*

have lifted up my soul to thee;" because it is to you I have directed my course; for you I have renounced the desires of the world; thee alone I desire; and I, therefore, ask for the light of wisdom, for fear of straying from thee.

9-11. He follows up the same petition, begging to be delivered from the temptations of the devil, who frequently seeks to blind up the mind, so that it may not see the path of justice. These concupiscences so raised up by the devil, make things appear in a very different light from what they really are; and hence arises an error of judgment. *"Deliver me from my enemies;"* from his temptations; for I have renounced him, and fled to thee. *"Teach me to do thy will."* Assist me by your light to repel his temptations, and find out the true path, and so understand your good will and your thorough good pleasure; *"for thou art my God;"* I desire and wish to serve you alone; because you are my God, the source and the end of all the goods I enjoy, from whom I have got existence and all the goods of soul and body, and from whom I expect happiness and everlasting glory. *"Thy good spirit shall lead me into the right land."* Having previously asked for wisdom, which appertains to the understanding—for we, then, in reality, tread the paths of justice when we understand, and we intend to do what is right. *"Thy good Spirit;"* not my spirit, but yours, which is essentially good and of which the Savior says, *"How much more will your Father from heaven give the good Spirit to them that ask him?"* That good Spirit is the Holy Ghost, who is essentially good, and through whom *"the charity of God is poured out into our hearts;"* and this it is that makes us wish to work and carry out our wishes; and it is of it Ezechiel speaks when he says, *"And I will put my Spirit in the midst of you, and I will cause you to walk in my commandments."* This good Spirit *"shall lead me into the right land;"* in that plain and direct road, the Lord's law, which is most plain and direct. The *"right land"* may also mean our country above, where all is right and straight, and nothing distorted or crooked. *"For thy name's sake thou wilt quicken me in thy justice."* To show us that justification, which is a sort of spiritual resuscitation, is not to be had from our own merits, but from the gratuitous gift of God, he adds, *"For thy name's sake,"* for the glory that will accrue to you by the gift of so much grace, *"thou wilt quicken me in thy justice."*

12. He concludes, by predicting his own salvation and deliverance, and the ruin of all his enemies, which will certainly be accomplished on the last day. And what the prophet says of himself is equally applicable to all the true servants of God, who have preserved their innocence, or who, by true penance, have returned to the paths of justice.

PSALM 143

The prophet praiseth God, and prayeth to be delivered from his enemies. No worldly happiness is to be compared with that of serving God.

1 Blessed be the Lord my God, who teacheth my hands to fight, and my fingers to war.

2 My mercy, and my refuge: my support, and my deliverer: My protector, and I have hoped in him: who subdueth my people under me.

3 Lord, what is man, that thou art made known to him? or the son of man, that thou makest account of him?

4 Man is like to vanity: his days pass away like a shadow.

5 Lord, bow down thy heavens and descend: touch the mountains and they shall smoke.

6 Send forth lightning, and thou shalt scatter them: shoot out thy arrows, and thou shalt trouble them.

7 Put forth thy hand from on high, take me out, and deliver me from many waters: from the hand of strange children:

8 Whose mouth hath spoken vanity: and their right hand is the right hand of iniquity.

9 To thee, O God, I will sing a new canticle: on the psaltery and an instrument of ten strings I will sing praises to thee.

10 Who givest salvation to kings: who hast redeemed thy servant David from the malicious sword:

11 Deliver me, And rescue me out of the hand of strange children; whose mouth hath spoken vanity: and their right hand is the right hand of iniquity:

12 Whose sons are as new plants in their youth: Their daughters decked out, adorned round about after the similitude of a temple:

13 Their storehouses full, flowing out of this into that. Their sheep fruitful in young, abounding in their goings forth:

14 Their oxen fat. There is no breach of wall, nor passage, nor crying out in their streets.

15 They have called the people happy, that hath these things: but happy is that people whose God is the Lord.

Explanation of the psalm

1. The prophet praises God, and returns him thanks for the singular favor conferred on him, in enabling him to conquer the giant Goliath, the source of all his glory. *"Who teacheth my hands to fight."* He uses the word *"teacheth,"* instead of strengtheneth, because the victory was owing more to skill than to strength; for, as we read in 1 Kings 17, *"David prevailed over the Philistine with a sling and a stone."* It certainly required no small amount of skill to let a stone fly from a sling so as to hit an adversary in one particular vital spot, on such an occasion; which, however, the prophet, in his wisdom, does not attribute to his own science, skill, or coolness, but entirely to the gift of God. In like manner, we need art rather than strength in the spiritual contests we have daily to maintain with the devil; and Christ himself, of whom David was the type, conquered the devil more by his wisdom than by his power. It was by his patience and his humility that he laid his proud and cruel enemy prostrate; and, therefore, the prophet, instead of saying, *"Who armeth my hands,"* says, *"Who teacheth my hands,"* which he repeats when he says, *"and my fingers to war."*

2. In five expressions the prophet tells the order in which God helped him to the victory, and in which he will help us too, if we put our entire confidence in him. First, God in his mercy looked upon David; for God's mercy is the primary source of all our blessings, and precedes all merit whatsoever; and he, therefore, places *"my mercy"* first. Having been thus called and taken by the hand through God's mercy, he looked towards him, and through hope and prayer fled to him, and thus God became *"my refuge."* Thirdly, God did not despise him, when he thus made him his refuge, hut reached out his hand to him to protect and assist him, and he, therefore, adds, *"my support."* Fourthly, he delivered him, after having thus supported him, from captivity and from the imminent danger of death, and thus, he became *"his deliverer."* Finally, after having so delivered him, he protected, and continued to protect him as long as the fight lasted, lest he may be wounded or made captive, and he therefore styles him *"my protector,"* and he adds, *"and I have hoped in him who subdueth my people under me,"* as much as to say, God surely is my mercy, my refuge, my support, my deliverer, my protector, having done more for me than I could have ever hoped for or dreamed of, and I therefore, will put my whole hope and confidence in him, inasmuch as he not only saved me from the hand of Goliath, but he also set me as a prince over his people; for, immediately after his victory over Goliath, Saul gave him the command of a thousand soldiers, which soon extended to the whole kingdom, as we read in Kings, *"All Israel and Juda loved David, for he came in and went out before them."*

3. From the consideration of such favors David bursts forth into great admiration, that such a God, than whom nothing greater can be imagined, should condescend to make so much of man, a thing of nothing, as to deign to wish to be known and to be loved by him! And if such was the language of David, and expressed with so much piety, what should we not feel, say, and do, to whom God not only made himself known, but even assumed the form of a servant, and in such form, *"humbled himself, becoming obedient unto death, even the death of the cross,"* and thereby obtained a victory for us, *"not against flesh and blood, but against principalities and powers, against*

rulers of the world of this darkness, against the sphirits of wickedness in the high places," and who brought *"many people under subjection to us,"* and after raising us to a share in his kingdom, placed us with Christ, *"over all his goods."* But to come to the text. *"Lord, what is man, that thou art made known to him?"* What did you see in man when you condescended to let yourself so down, and reveal so much about your wonderful mysteries and attributes to him?—*"or the Son of Man that thou makest account of him?"*—a repetition of the preceding sentence, in which he again expresses his astonishment at the wonderful regard of God for man, with whom he desires so to commune, and to establish such relations of familiarity and friendship.

4. He now tells why he is so wrapt in admiration; it is because man is so insignificant a thing, and his very insignificance of such short duration, thus drawing the greatest possible contrast between the nothingness of man, and the greatness of God. God is the fullness of all good, and is so at all times, and never subject to change or diminution. While man, though he is not, exactly, vanity, *"he is like to vanity,"* because there is some little trifle in him that is capable of being turned to great account, should God take him in hands; but until he does, man is like a vain and empty thing; which he further elucidates by comparing man to *"the shadows that pass;"* for, as the shadows of the mountains are constantly shifting their position during the day, and ultimately disappear altogether on the approach of night; so with man, who is everyday advancing to the moment of his final departure from this world. All this applies to man in regard of his temporal life alone, as contrasted with that of God, because, in other respects, man is a being of great consequence and importance, inasmuch as he is created to the image and likeness of God, in order to know and to love him; and a being for whom the only begotten Son of God did not hesitate to spill his blood; and, in fine, a being destined to rank with the Angels in a state of eternal happiness, should he persevere in this his pilgrimage; in faith, hope, and charity. Though man should therefore, when compared to God, avow himself to be no more than dust and ashes, yet, whenever the devil would tempt him by the suggestion of the evil desires that reduce him to the level of the beast, he should reflect on his own dignity, and seek rather to aspire to the place intended for him among the Angels.

5-6. The holy prophet from having been lost in admiration at the extent of God's goodness to man, and then at his mercy in regarding a thing so miserable as man; now, rejecting on the other hand, on the pride and blindness of many, who, in contempt of God, are entirely devoted to the oppression of the poor and the accumulation of riches, prays to God to display his power in regard of such people, who, as they will not be influenced by the love of justice or reverence for their Creator, may, at all events, be deterred from crime, through the fear of punishment. *"Lord, bow down thy heavens, and descend."* Since all your favors have not had the effect of reducing the pride of man, to acknowledge or to fear you, make yourself known to them by your dark and gloomy clouds, by your fire from heaven, by your lightnings and thunder that cause mankind so to fear and tremble. God is said to *"bow down the heavens"* when he visits them with dark, heavy, and gloomy clouds, that look as if they were a part of the firmament; and he is said to *"descend"* by them, inasmuch as they demonstrate his interference by their effects, which are usually thunder and lightning. Thus, in Exodus, God is said to have descended on mount Sinai, when he enveloped the whole mountain with a thick cloud and dense darkness, and heated the whole mountain so that it began to smoke, which he alludes to here, when he adds, *"touch the mountains and they shall smoke."* God, however, principally displays his presence and his power, through the astounding roar of his thunder and the coruscations of his lightning, than which nothing more subtle, more fleet, more efficacious, or more horrible can be imagined; and he, therefore, adds, *"Send forth lightning and thou shalt scatter them,"* meaning the proud, aforesaid; *"shoot out thy arrows,"* those celestial arrows, *"and thou shalt trouble them,"* for even the most hardened and fierce will quail before that thunder of yours, that no human power can resist; hence, we read, in 1 Kings 2, *"The adversaries of the Lord shall fear him; and upon them shall he thunder in the heavens."*

7. It would appear, from this verse, that the Psalm was not written after David's accession to the throne, and that the subject is not the same as that of Psalm 17; because, in that Psalm, he returns thanks for his delivery from Saul, and from all his enemies; while it would appear, from the present Psalm, that he is still at war with his *"strange children,"* the Philistines, and prays for victory over them. Having, then, prayed to God against the proud and the wicked in general, he now prays for himself in particular, saying, *"Put forth thy hand from on high."* Display your power from heaven; *"take me out, and deliver me from many waters;"* from the multitude of my enemies, the infidels, who daily harass me; and he explains the metaphor when he adds, *"from the hand of strange children;"* from the Philistines, with whom he was then at war.

8. He gives a description of the strange children by saying they were sinners in word and deed. *"Whose mouth hath spoken vanity,"* instead of your truth, or your law, or anything good; *"and their right hand"* does nothing but plunder, oppression of the poor, homicide, adultery, etc.

9-11. After a parenthesis of two verses, expressive of his affection for God, he returns to a description of the *"strange children."*—*"To thee, O Lord, I will sing a new canticle."* Though I do not forget the favors I have received, I am about to ask for more, and I will, therefore, *"sing a new canticle,"* a beautiful one, one never heard before; and while singing it I will play upon the psaltery, too, on one of ten strings, and that because *"you give salvation to kings,"* as when you saved king Saul through my interference; and thou *"hast redeemed thy servant David from the malicious sword;"* from the sword of Goliath the giant; and as you have hitherto so regarded me, *"deliver me."* Rescue me, I say, from *"the strange children,"* who are full of wickedness in words, as well as in deeds.

12. He now tells us what he means by the *"strange children,"* by informing us of their ideas and their affections; they are the persons who neither know nor care for anything but the pleasures of this world, the fecundity and the prosperity of their sons and daughters, the abundance of their corn, wine, and oil, their flocks and herds, and their produce, and the enjoyment of all those things in peace. Such is the first source of happiness with the *"strange children."* A second source of happiness with them is handsome, beautiful daughters, likely to meet, at once, with good husbands. *"Their daughters decked out, adorned round about after the similitude of a temple;"* with a beautiful shape, and finely turned limbs. *"After the similitude of a temple,"* as beautiful as the temple that was studded with gold, silver, precious stones, silks, and fine linen.

13. The third source of happiness to *"the strange children"* consists in the fullness of their granaries, which are so replete with all the necessaries of life that they must needs remove them from one store to another. Happiness from this source is well described in the Gospel, where the rich man said, *"What shall I do because I have not where to lay up together my fruits? This will I do, I will pull down my barns, and will build greater."* A thing that usually happens when the harvest is being brought in, and the surplus of the preceding crop is stowed away, to make room for the new. *"Their sheep fruitful in young abounding in their goings forth. Their oxen fat."* Such is the fourth source of temporal happiness; numerous and fruitful flocks of sheep, *"abounding in their goings forth,"* which seem nigh countless, as they go out to pasture; and with them herds of fat oxen, too.

14. The last of the temporal blessings enjoyed by them consists not only in their houses and palaces being in perfect repair, but even their wall and their streets, in which there is neither noise nor confusion, but all is tranquil and peaceful.

15. Such is the conclusion of the holy prophet, who, while he states that though *"the strange child"* may look on all those who enjoy the above named blessings to be happy, yet, in his opinion, it is not the people who have such things, but the people who have the Lord for their God, that can be accounted happy. It must be remarked here that the abundance or the want of

the things of this world makes no difference whatever between the children of God and the aforesaid *"strange children."* Many children of God abound in the things of this world, and the Lord himself even promised a hundred fold for anything we may give up, with life everlasting in the next; and, on the other hand, many of the children of this world have had a wretched end, in want, in exile, in chains, or on the scaffold. The whole difference between the sons of the kingdom and the sons of hell, the children of this world and the children of light, consists in the affections; for they who look upon the things of this world as of immense value, and have such an affection for them as to despise their eternal happiness for them; and, on the other hand, who look upon the crosses of this life as the greatest of misfortunes, and so dread them as not to hesitate in offending God, and running the risk of losing their eternal salvation in order to escape them, they are *"the children of the darkness of this world and of the pit,"* and they are the parties the prophet has in view when he says, *"They have called the people happy that hath these things."* While they who look upon the goods of this world to be things of nothing, as they really are, and the loss of them as a matter of no moment; and, on the other hand, they who reckon the grace of God and the country above among the greatest blessings, and the offending God, or the loss of eternal life, as the greatest of all misfortunes, they are truly the children of light, the children of God, the children of the kingdom, who have not turned a deaf ear to *"Seek ye, therefore, first the kingdom of God, and his justice, and all these things shall be added unto you;"* and that is what is conveyed in the words, *"happy is that people whose God is the Lord;"* that is to say, the good things of this world may be good in their way, but happiness does not consist in them. What constitutes a man supremely happy is the possession of the supreme good, which consists in the beatific vision.

PSALM 144

A psalm of praise, to the infinite majesty of God.

1 I will extol thee, O God my king: and I will bless thy name for ever; yea, for ever and ever.
2 Every day I will bless thee: and I will praise thy name for ever; yea, for ever and ever.
3 Great is the Lord, and greatly to be praised: and of his greatness there is no end.
4 Generation and generation shall praise thy works: and they shall declare thy power.
5 They shall speak of the magnificence of the glory of thy holiness: and shall tell thy wondrous works.
6 And they shall speak of the might of thy terrible acts: and shall declare thy greatness.

7 They shall publish the memory of the abundance of thy sweetness: and shall rejoice in thy justice.
8 The Lord is gracious and merciful: patient and plenteous in mercy.
9 The Lord is sweet to all: and his tender mercies are over all his works.
10 Let all thy works, O lord, praise thee: and let thy saints bless thee.
11 They shall speak of the glory of thy kingdom: and shall tell of thy power:
12 To make thy might known to the sons of men: and the glory of the magnificence of thy kingdom.
13 Thy kingdom is a kingdom of all ages: and thy dominion endureth throughout all generations. The Lord is faithful in all his words: and holy in all his works.
14 The Lord lifteth up all that fall: and setteth up all that are cast down.
15 The eyes of all hope in thee, O Lord: and thou givest them meat in due season.
16 Thou openest thy hand, and fillest with blessing every living creature.
17 The Lord is just in all his ways: and holy in all his works.
18 The Lord is nigh unto all them that call upon him: to all that call upon him in truth.
19 He will do the will of them that fear him: and he will hear their prayer, and save them.
20 The Lord keepeth all them that love him; but all the wicked he will destroy.
21 My mouth shall speak the praise of the Lord: and let all flesh bless thy holy name for ever; yea, for ever and ever.

EXPLANATION OF THE PSALM

1. The two first verses contain a preface, in which the prophet tells us what he proposes singing of in this Psalm, and he does so in a poetical manner by addressing himself directly to God. *"I will extol thee;"* I will celebrate thee in these my verses, in order that, supreme as you are, you may be looked upon and considered as the most supreme by men. He styles God *"his King,"* either to show that, king as he was himself, he still had God as a King, who rules all, and is ruled by none over him, or because he was about to praise God for the works and attributes that pertained to him as King and Governor of mankind and of all created things. *"And I will bless thy name,"* which is no more than a repetition of the previous sentence; and he adds, *"forever, yea, forever and ever,"* to give us to understand that his praise would be everlasting, commencing with himself and continued by the succeeding generations, who were to chant his Psalms to the end of the world, and after that without end in the country above, as he says in Psalm 83, *"Blessed are they that dwell in thy house, O Lord; they shall praise thee forever and ever."* This is more clearly repeated and explained in verse 2, where he says, *"Every day will I bless thee;"* I will praise thee forever, whether in prosperity or in adversity, while I am here below, and hereafter in heaven. *"I will praise thy name forever and ever."*

2. Greatness consists in breadth, length, height, and depth, which, to a certain extent, exist in God, according to the Apostle, *"That you may be able to comprehend with all the saints, what is the breadth, and height, and depth,"* etc. The prophet then commences by praising God by reason of his greatness, and if we apply it to his divine essence, he is great therein in breadth, because it is immense; in length, because it is everlasting; in height, because it is most sublime; and in depth, because it is incomprehensible. Or if you will have the prophet call him great by reason of his sovereign power, he is great as to breadth or extent, inasmuch as all created things, from the highest Angel to the crawling insect, are subject to him; as to length, because his kingdom is to last forever; as to height, because he rules everything with supreme and absolute power; and as to depth, because he not only rules our bodies, but also our hearts with its most intimate and secret thoughts and affections; and, finally, there is nothing so secret or so hidden, that the scepter of his kingdom does not reach. Therefore, *"great is the Lord,"* and on that account, *"greatly to be praised,"*—*"and of his greatness there is no end."* Whether as to length, breadth, height, or depth. God's greatness, then, is infinite, and therefore, quite incapable of being investigated by us, who are finite beings; which does not imply that we are thoroughly ignorant of God's greatness, for we know him to be great, and that there is no end of his greatness, though we cannot take it in or comprehend it. This infinite greatness of God admonishes us, that as well as his greatness has no end, so our praises should have no end. It also reminds us that we should not be satisfied with moving in the narrow limits in which we are placed here below, but that we should daily endeavor to increase in that real greatness that arises from virtue, as Psalm 83, has it. *"In his heart he hath disposed to ascend by steps in the vale of tears; they shall go from virtue to virtue,"* for they who seek to increase in riches and in power, that they may get above others, they, instead of being great, are only swollen; instead of being full of juice, they are only distended with wind, for pride and magnanimity are two very different things.

3-4. He passes now from the essence of the great king, which is inscrutable, to his wonderful works, that convey some idea of his power; and he does not say, I will praise thy works, but, *"generation and generation shall praise thy works."* I, of myself, am inadequate to praise your works, but generations unborn will praise them, for there never will be wanting souls to reflect on them, admire them, and praise them, *"and they shall declare thy power."* The unborn generations who shall study your works, will constantly proclaim the power that shines forth in them.

5. Having spoken, in general, of the wonderful works of God, he now distinguishes three sorts of his works, some of them glorious and beautiful, and therefore, wonderful, by reason of their surpassing beauty and splendor; some of them terrible, and therefore, very wonderful, by reason of the great terror inspired by them; and some of them most lovely, and from their being the channels of conveying God's kindness to us, no less wonderful than the others. In this verse, then, the works that are wonderful, by reason of their splendor and beauty, are praised, such as the heavens, than which nothing more beautiful can be imagined, and speaking of which he says in another Psalm, *"The heavens show forth the glory of God,"* as also the sun, moon, and the other heavenly bodies, whose number, variety, splendor, and perpetual motion, without fatigue or labor, are truly wonderful. *"They shall speak of the magnificence of the glory of thy holiness."* All future generations shall speak in praise of the excellence of the glorious works of your magnificence, and in thus praising them, *"shall tell thy wondrous works,"* that appear so numerous and so conspicuous therein.

6. This is the second sort of God's works, in which the fear of the divine majesty, in punishing the wicked, is shown, *"And they shall speak of the might of thy terrible acts,"* they shall be talking of the dreadful and severe scourges with which you chastised the wicked, such as the deluge, the destruction of whole cities by fire from heaven, the plagues of Egypt and of Pharao, the opening of the earth to swallow Dathan and Abiron alive; and finally, the earthquakes, plagues, thunderbolts, inundations, and storms, which frequently express God's anger to man.

7. Here is the third sort of God's works that appertain to mercy, which is expressed at greater length, and more redolent of gratitude, as all God's faithful servants should be. *"They shall publish the memory of the abundance of thy sweetness;"* that is to say, all generations having been filled with the abundance of the sweetness and the kindness of thy mercy, for *"the earth is full of God's mercy,"* such abundance will cause them to publish the memory of the sweetness that so abounds, or in other words, they will hand down to posterity the record of so many and so great favors conferred on them; and they will not confine themselves to so publishing the memory of these favors, but they will, themselves, *"rejoice in thy justice,"* by reason of your having so faithfully carried out what you promised. To this class of favors belong the innumerable gifts of providence bestowed so bountifully on man, such as the alternations of night and day, the rains of heaven, the fruitfulness of the earth, the countless multitude of cattle, birds, and fish, designed for the use and behoof of man, the verdant groves and beautiful gardens, the seas and the rivers, that serve for transport, and many other blessings beside. And all those, nothing, positively nothing, as compared with the gifts of grace;

for instance, the Incarnation of the Divine Word, the passion, resurrection, and ascension of Christ, the sending of the Holy Ghost, the calling of the gentiles, the preaching, the promise, and the publication of the kingdom of heaven. Let anyone devoutly meditate on these points, and it will be truly wonderful, if in his fullness he will not *"publish the memory of the abundance of the sweetness"* of God.

8-9. Not content with having said that such was the abundance of God's sweetness that all generations would publish the memory of it, he comes out the first to publish and to proclaim it, saying, *"The Lord is gracious and merciful, patient, and plenteous in mercy."* He is the Lord because he removes all troubles, by forgiveness, by justification, by glorification; and he is not only *"gracious,"* but he is *"merciful,"* as merciful as a father; and, furthermore, he is *"patient,"* which means that his mercy is continuous; for no matter how often we may provoke him, he will not turn to anger at once, but rather waits to see would we do penance; and finally, such mercy is not small, confined, or illiberal, but on the contrary, *"most plenteous."* That is most fully explained in the next verse, where he says, *"The Lord is sweet to all;"* and so he is to those who can appreciate his sweetness; and he is not only sweet and kind to all, and merciful too, but *"his tender mercies, are over all his works;"* for there is no one of his works, however insignificant, to which he does not extend his mercy. The expression, *"The Lord is sweet to all,"* is absolutely true, because God *"maketh his sun to rise upon the good and the bad, and raineth upon the just and the unjust;"* and in Psalm 85, we read, *"For thou, O Lord, art sweet and mild, and plenteous in mercy, to all that call upon thee;"* and again, in Psalm 102, *"For according to the height of the heaven above the earth, he hath strengthened his mercy to those that fear him. As a father hath compassion on his children, so hath the Lord compassion on them that fear him. But the mercy of the Lord is from eternity and unto eternity upon them that fear him;"* which the blessed Virgin also expressed, when she said, *"And his mercy is from generation to generation to them that fear him."*

10-13. Having hitherto sung of the glorious, terrible, and lovely works of God, he now comes to describe his kingdom, and then the virtues peculiar to the King himself. *"Let all thy works, O Lord, praise thee."* Let all the works for which I have been hitherto praising you, now unite with me in praising you; for the productions of an artist, when they are beautiful, redound to his praise and glory, and God's works are such as to admit of no improvement, either by adding or taking from them. *"And God saw all the things that he had made, and they were very good;"* and in Psalm 110, *"Great are the works of the Lord sought out according to all his wills."* These words may be considered as a conclusion to the first part of the chapter, as he now enters on a different subject with the words, *"and let thy saints bless thee;"* that is to say, generations unborn will praise thee by reason of the works that are visible to all, but it is the saints alone, through the revelation of the Holy Ghost, that are aware of the nature of your kingdom I am now about to speak of; and, therefore, *"let thy saints,"* to whom it has been revealed by the Holy Ghost, *"bless thee,"* which means praise thee; and he tells for what, when he adds, *"They shall speak of the glory of thy kingdom, and shall tell of thy power."* The glory of a kingdom is synonymous with its power. The power of a kingdom consists in the number of its subjects, and the sufficiency of its revenue, to maintain them. Now, the glory, or the power of God's kingdom, may be inferred from the difference between it and that of man. There are four points of difference. First, the kings of this world have but few subjects, without much wealth; not more than the population and wealth of one kingdom, or one province, while God reigns over all Angels, all men, all demons, and all the wealth on land, in the sea, or in the air, belong to him. There is another difference, that while the kings of this world rule their subjects, they are still ruled by them, they are dependent on them, can do nothing without them; and, however, abundant their revenues may be, they are generally in want, nay even in debt, and, consequently, always calling for fresh tributes and taxes; but God, while he governs all, is subject to none, because he needs nobody's help or assistance; instead of being in want, he abounds in everything, because he could, in one moment, bring from nothing much more than he now beholds or enjoys. The third difference is a consequence of the second, while the kings of this world seem so to enjoy their honors and dignities, they are, at the same time, suffering acutely from interior fears, doubts, and cares, which have sometimes been so burdensome, as to cause them to abdicate altogether. God never suffers such pressure, is subject to no fear, no misgivings, but reigns absolutely in perfect tranquillity. The fourth difference, an essential one, is, that the kings of this world reign but for a time; but God reigneth forever. Now, the first difference is touched upon in the verse, *"They shall speak of the glory of thy kingdom, and shall tell of thy power;"* your saints will proclaim the power and the glory of your kingdom, which consists in the number of your subjects, and the inexhaustible abundance of your wealth. The second and third are included in the words, *"To make thy might known to the sons of men, and the glory of the magnificence of thy kingdom,"* which indicate an immense difference between the kingdom of God and any human kingdom, for he says, *"To make known to the sons of men,"* to make them understand that their kingdoms are a mere nothing as compared with that of God, and not content with having said, *"To make thy might known,"* he adds, *"and thy glory;"* and not content with that even, he adds again, *"of the magnificence of thy kingdom,"* or the glory of your most magnificent kingdom. The fourth difference is apparent in the verse, *"thy kingdom,"* etc. *"The Lord is faithful in all his words, and holy in all his works."* He now enters on the virtues that belong to a king, that are so conspicuous in God, and in Christ, as man, and which all kings, and all in power, should constantly look to and seek to imitate. The first virtue that should distinguish a king is uprightness, with a strict adherence to truth, for the king's example is all powerful, and of Christ, the King, we read, *"Who did no sin, neither was guilt found in his mouth,"* nearly word for word with what the prophet says here, *"The Lord is faithful in all his words;"* that is to say, truthful, no liar, no deceiver, observing all his promises most faithfully; *"and holy in all his works;"* or in other words, *"Innocent, undefiled, separated from sinners,"* and immaculate in all his actions.

14. Here is the second virtue that should adorn a king and a pastor, for both should rule in such a manner that their subjects may not fall; and if they chance to fall, that they should be prompt in raising them. That virtue is called mercy, and one essential to all in power. The expression *"lifteth up,"* in the Hebrew, conveys the idea not only of lifting up, but enabling the person so lifted to keep up, as we read in another Psalm, *"Being pushed I was overturned, that I might fall, but the Lord supported me."* But is it true that God lifts up all that fall, when we daily see many falling without being lifted, either as regards soul or body? God is said to lift up all that fall, inasmuch as those who fall not when tempted, keep up, through God's grace; and they who rise after falling, are set up by God's grace; while they who fall, or do not rise after falling, must blame themselves for it, and not God, which Osee expresses in different language, when he says, *"Destruction is thy own, O Israel, thy help is only in me."* That David did not mean to say absolutely that all, without any exception, that may chance to fall would be raised, is clear from the following expression, where he says, *"And setteth up all that are cast down."* For if God were to support all that were about to fall, he would have no occasion to set up anyone, or nobody would fall; how, then, is it true that he *"setteth up all that are cast down"*? These words are to be taken in a spiritual sense. As to the actual falling of anyone, it remains to be said that God is naturally inclined to raise and to set up all; and if he does not do so by all, nay, more, if he sometimes precipitates and brings them down, he does so either with a view to prove them and to crown them, as he does to the just, in which case it proves a raising up rather than a taking down, or he does so in order to punish and chastise, and that when the sins of the parties themselves call for it, and thus the very first root of the evil springs from ourselves, and thus what Osee said, *"Destruction is thy own, O Israel, thy help is only in me,"* will always be true.

15-16. Liberality is the third virtue that should adorn a king. Kings should not fleece their subjects, and seek to squeeze money out of them under various pretences, and thus, perhaps, reduce them to poverty; on the contrary, they should deal liberally with them, supporting them, as if they were their own children; but, yet, taking care not to allow them to eat to excess, or spend whole days in feasting. *"The eyes of all hope in thee, O Lord."* The eyes of all living things look to thee, expecting food from thee, that they may be supported by it, and keep up their life, *"and thou givest them meat;"* and you, through the agency of the creatures subject to you, the earth, the sun, and the rain, produce fruits in abundance, as meat for all living creatures, and that *"in due season,"* when they have need of it, for they should not be always eating; and thus, they who eat to excess, have not their meat from God, but from their own gluttony. *"In due season"* also implies when hunger calls for it, when it is useful or necessary; and therefore, they who accumulate and hoard up their superfluities, steal so much from the community; and it cannot be a matter of surprise to find so many in dire necessity. He also gives it *"in due season,"* when it is right to give it, because sometimes it is better to withhold it, because man's sins deserve it, as the physician will sometimes prescribe total abstinence from food and strong drink; and hence God, not infrequently, visits sinners with dearth and famine, in punishment of their sins. *"In due season"* also expresses the variety of food that God provides for us in the various seasons. That we may carry with us the fact of God's liberality, being the primary source of all our blessings, he next adds, *"Thou openest thy hand, and fillest with blessing every living creature,"* every word of which is expressive of profuse liberality. *"Thou openest thy hand."* It is not with a closed but an open hand that you give to your creatures; it is with extreme liberality; *"and fillest,"* satisfy to the fullest extent of their desires, *"every living creature,"* not only man, but all living things; *"with blessing,"* in the most abundant manner; such is the sense in which St. Paul uses the word blessing, when he writes to the Corinthians to have the alms collected, *"to be ready, so as a blessing, not as covetousness;"* that is, that their alms should be liberal. But if God fills every living thing so abundantly, whence have we so many beggars, so many poor, hungry, thirsty? We have already observed that a good deal of it arises from the injustice of the rich, who either hoard up, or sinfully squander, what they should share with the poor; and we added, that such often arises from the just punishment of God, that is called for by the sins of the parties themselves; and finally, we may add, that the very poor in question are often themselves the cause of it, either because they depend more on their scheming than they do on God, or because they cannot content themselves with the food and raiment befitting their station in life, or because they will often spend in one day's debauch what they may have been earning for an entire week.

17. Justice is the fourth virtue befitting a sovereign, and one of absolute necessity, in order to ensure peace and tranquillity among the people. *"The Lord is just in all his ways."* The Lord displays extreme justice in his external acts, by which alone we can form an idea of his justice; for he renders to all what is due to them, and he repeats the same in the next sentence when he says, *"and holy in all his works."*

18. The fifth virtue becoming a king consists in his being easy of access to all who come to him looking for assistance. This God does to a wonderful extent, for *"he is nigh unto all them that call upon him;"* no matter how high above the heavens he may be, he comes nigh at once to all that call upon him, never refusing an audience to anyone. Hence, Moses boasts in Deuteronomy, *"Neither is there any other nation so great, that hath gods so nigh them, as our God is present to all our petitions;"* and he tells us how we are to understand the expression, *"to all that call upon him,"* when he repeats it with the addition of *"in truth,"* for that expression comprehends all the conditions that are necessary for prayer. He that prays without faith does not pray *"in truth,"* because, instead of calling on God, he calls on the idol of his own brain. He that prays without hope does not pray *"in truth,"* because, he cannot be serious in praying to anyone by whom he does not hope to be heard. And he who prays without charity, or, at least, without inchoate love, does not invoke God *"in truth,"* because nobody will seriously pray to one whom he hates, and who, he has reason to think, hates him. They, too, who pray without affection and desire, such as those who recite the Psalms or any other prayers, without any desire of obtaining what they ask, though they appear to do so, *"do not invoke God in truth."* They also who pray without attention, without knowing what they are saying, pray merely with their lips, and they also *"do not call upon him in truth,"* because, instead of calling on him, they only show an empty appearance of calling on him.

19. Benignity, or kindness, is the sixth royal attribute, by virtue of which the king not only admits his subjects to an audience, but graciously grants all their petitions, provided it be right for him to grant them. *"He will do the will of them that fear him;"* on having heard their prayer, he will do what they want, but he qualifies it by adding, *"of them that fear him,"* for it is but fair that God should do the will of those only that do his will; and those who have a holy horror of offending God, and would lose the whole world rather than his grace, are the people that do his will. That, as usual, he repeats, when he says, *"and he will hear their prayer."* He finally adds, *"and save them,"* to give us to understand how God always hears the prayers of those that fear him. God frequently appears not to hear the prayers of such people, as when he would not deliver St. Paul from *"the sting of his flesh,"* though he had prayed three times to be delivered from it; and still he really hears the principal desire of such people, which consists in a desire of eternal salvation. For, as the Lord ordered to *"seek first the kingdom of God and his justice,"* or in other words, his glory and his grace; thus all they who fear God with the holy fear becoming him, will first and principally, in every prayer of theirs, ask for inchoate salvation or grace; and then for perfect salvation which is glory. God, then, always hears those that fear him, for *"he will save them;"* that is to say, he hears them in the time and the mode most conducive to their salvation.

20. The last but most necessary virtue for a king is that of providence, by virtue of which he protects the just from oppression on the part of the wicked, and prevents the wicked, if not from injuring the just, at least from injuring them to the extent of their wishes. For though he sometimes allows the just to suffer much from sinners, still he so protects them, that such suffering cannot harm them; nay more, that it turns to their advantage. God suffered the holy martyrs to be flogged and to be slain, but he *"kept them,"* by the gift of constancy, in their faith, and patience in their sufferings, with a view to securing glory to their souls, and a glorious and immortal body, and thereby realizing the truth of the promise, *"A hair from your head shall not be lost."* As to the sentence, *"but all the wicked he will destroy;"* the truth of that will appear either because the wicked will be converted, and will then not be there, as wicked, for destruction; or because they persevere in final wickedness, and will then be scattered by being consigned to hell, so that they can never again come near the just.

21. He now concludes the Psalm by uniting the first and last verses, as if he said, In consequence of all I have stated regarding the greatness of God, of his works, of the perpetuity of his kingdom, of his royal qualities that are so numerous and so perfect in him, *"My mouth shall speak the praise of the Lord"* forever. And I not only mean to do so myself, but I earnestly desire that *"all flesh,"* that every human being, everything that lives and breathes, should praise the name of the Lord forever.

PSALM 145

We are not to trust in men, but in God alone.

1 Praise the Lord, O my soul, in my life I will praise the Lord: I will sing to my God as long as I shall be. Put not your trust in princes:
2 In the children of men, in whom there is no salvation.
3 His spirit shall go forth, and he shall return into his earth: in that day all their thoughts shall perish.
4 Blessed is he who hath the God of Jacob for his helper, whose hope is in the Lord his God:
5 Who made heaven and earth, the sea, and all things that are in them.

6 Who keepeth truth for ever: who executeth judgment for them that suffer wrong: who giveth food to the hungry. The Lord looseth them that are fettered:
7 The Lord enlighteneth the blind. The Lord lifteth up them that are cast down: the Lord loveth the just.
8 The Lord keepeth the strangers, he will support the fatherless and the widow: and the ways of sinners he will destroy.
9 The Lord shall reign for ever: thy God, O Sion, unto generation and generation.

EXPLANATION OF THE PSALM

1-2. This Psalm commences in the shape of a dialogue. The exile finding his flesh beginning to groan in the hardships of his exile, exhorts his soul, just beginning to taste of happiness in hope, to praise God, and thereby to refresh the entire man. Addressing his soul; then, he says, *"praise the Lord, O my soul."* The soul answers, *"In my life I will praise the Lord."* I will praise him when I come to enjoy the true life, because here below, instead of singing and praising him, we must rather weep and pray to him; for though we do praise him, even at present, to some extent, it is not praise properly so called, or full praise, but is mingled with prayers and with tears; but when we come to the true life, then, indeed, will our praise deserve the name of praise, for it will be pure, everlasting, and most delightful. He repeats the same when he adds, *"I will sing to my Lord as long as I shall be,"* when I shall have come to eternal life I will sing unceasingly to my God. At present I cannot sing while I have so many things to interrupt me, but when I shall have been disengaged and free from all care, *"I will sing to my God as long as I shall be,"* or during the whole space of that true life; and as I shall never have any fear of dying, I shall sing forever without failing. *"Put not your trust in princes,"* seeing that many are retarded on the road to salvation by their admiration of place and power. As if such things could confer happiness on those who enjoy such positions, in pity for their blindness, he exclaims, *"Put not your trust in princes,"* which he explains, by calling them *"the sons of men,"* mere mortals like yourselves, there being only one true prince, the Creator of mankind, in whom we should put our trust: and he assigns a reason why we should place no trust in them when he adds, *"in whom there is no salvation,"* because the princes of this world, when they cannot save others, have no salvation in themselves, nor are they saved themselves, but must be saved like all others, if they deserve it. If such be the case, how did Christ, who was man, and the *"Son of Man,"* as he was wont to style himself, save the whole human race? He saved them through his divinity.

3. The prophet might have adduced many arguments to prove that *"there is no salvation in the children of men,"* inasmuch as they are infirm, variable, deceitful, often aiming at what they are unable to accomplish, and as often refusing to accomplish what they are equal to; but he puts forward one simple reason alone, one that no one can contradict, one taken from death that is common to us all, for how can he save others who cannot save himself? for, beyond aye or nay let him shut himself in a fortified tower, let him surround it with a powerful army for protection, were he even monarch of the universe, *"his spirit shall go forth"* from his body, and then his body shall *"return into his earth,"* of which it was composed, and then, *"in that day all their thoughts shall perish,"* the thoughts of all those who put their hope in him, depended on him, expected riches, places, appointments from him; but the moment God takes away the spirit, that is, the life of him on whom they so depended, all their castle building tumbles to the ground, and thus, *"all their thoughts shall perish."*

4-5. The prophet now tells us that the person who will sincerely desire to arrive at true and everlasting salvation will have to place no confidence whatever in the princes of this world, but in the only true God alone. *"Blessed is he,"* at least in hope, and in the safe and direct road to actual happiness, *"who hath the God of Jacob for his helper,"* who has the one true God to assist and to protect him in this world. He calls the true God *"the God of Jacob,"* by reason of Jacob's people adhering to God, while the Moabites, Ammonites, Philistines, and the other surrounding nations, worshipped false gods. And he tells at once whom God will help, when he says, *"whose hope is in the Lord his God,"* or, God will help all who hope in him, of which there is abundant testimony in the Scriptures, *"No one hath hoped in the Lord, and hath been confounded,"* Eccli. 2; and in Psalm 113, *"The house of Israel hath hoped in the Lord, he is their helper and their protector."* He then proves the advantage of hoping in the Lord, because it was he *"who made heaven and earth, the sea, and all things that are in them."* Whence it follows that there are no bounds to his power, that he is Lord of all things, and that all things are subject to him, and therefore, that anyone protected by him has no reason for fear from any quarter.

6. As the exile might have said, in reply, I know God is all powerful, and that he can, if he choose, protect and assist me, but how do I know that he will? the prophet takes him up, and proves that God will do it, by reason of his justice, and of his mercy. By reason of his justice, *"he keepeth truth forever;"* that is to say, he always stands to what he has promised, and he has promised help to those who put their trust in them. In like manner, in consequence of his being supremely just, *"he executes judgment for them that suffer wrong;"* that is to say, he gives just judgment in favor of the just against the wicked, by punishing the latter, and rewarding the former; and inasmuch as he is merciful, *"he gives food to the hungry,"* providing for the temporal as well as the spiritual wants of those who trust in him, in a most extraordinary and wonderful manner.

7. As it would not be enough for the exiles, on their return to their country, to be ensured safe conduct from robbers, and wherewithal to support them on the journey, if their feet were not at liberty, and themselves wide awake, besides being in rude health, he therefore, in order to show how determined God is to assist those who put their trust in him, adds, *"The Lord looseth them that are in fetters,"* the fetters of concupiscence, which he does gradually, by destroying all their evil desires; and as concupiscence always blinds us, *"the Lord enlighteneth the blind,"* by giving them the light of wisdom and of interior prudence; and as sin was the cause, not only of concupiscence and blindness, but also of human infirmity, man having been brought, by means of sin, to the condition of him, who going down from Jericho, fell in with robbers who despoiled him, and left him more dead than alive, the prophet therefore adds, *"he lifteth up them that are cast down,"* and finally, he adds, *"the Lord loveth the just,"* in order, that man, after having been healed, set free, and enlightened through grace, may look forward to perseverance through the goodness of God.

8. He now repeats that God will both help and protect the pilgrims who move along *"the narrow way"* to their country. *"The Lord keepeth the strangers,"* they who do not belong to Babylon, nor to this world, but the true pilgrims in a strange land. *"He will support the fatherless and the widow."* The fatherless are the just who have no one to protect them, who have no father in this world, and who put their hope in nothing in this world. The widow is the Church, who is truly a widow, so long as she is separated from her spouse, and subject to all the trials and troubles daily pouring in upon her. These orphans and this widow will be all taken into God's house at the fitting time, and then *"he will destroy the ways of sinners,"* the prosperous ways in which they walk being so many broad ways that lead to destruction, all of which God will, in the end of the world, thoroughly upset and destroy.

9. Finally, on the termination of the exile, and on the ways of the wicked, as well as the wicked themselves having been exterminated, Christ's eternal kingdom shall commence, for *"the Lord shall reign"* with his saints, *"forever."* Your God, I repeat, O holy Sion, will reign with his children forever and ever. Amen.

PSALM 146

An exhortation to praise God for his benefits.

1 Praise ye the Lord, because psalm is good: to our God be joyful and comely praise.

2 The Lord buildeth up Jerusalem: he will gather together the dispersed of Israel.

3 Who healeth the broken of heart, and bindeth up their bruises.
4 Who telleth the number of the stars: and calleth them all by their names.
5 Great is our Lord, and great is his power: and of his wisdom there is no number.
6 The Lord lifteth up the meek, and bringeth the wicked down even to the ground.
7 Sing ye to the Lord with praise: sing to our God upon the harp.
8 Who covereth the heaven with clouds, and prepareth rain for the earth. Who maketh grass to grow on the mountains, and herbs for the service of men.
9 Who giveth to beasts their food: and to the young ravens that call upon him.
10 He shall not delight in the strength of the horse: nor take pleasure in the legs of a man.
11 The Lord taketh pleasure in them that fear him: and in them that hope in his mercy.

Explanation of the psalm

1. The prophet exhorts all to praise God; because it is most agreeable to him, and of the greatest advantage to us. *"To our God be joyful and comely praise."* See that the praise be in a joyful strain, and *"comely,"* yet still in a becoming, decent manner, befitting the majesty of that God to whom it is offered. There can be no doubt of the benefits the chanting of God's praise confers on us; because, if he who prays to God derives much benefit therefrom, why should he not, too, who praises him. Secondly, such praise tends to raise the soul from the things of this world to those of the world above; Thirdly, it becomes a sort of foretaste of the bliss of heaven, and unites us with the Angels and saints. Fourthly, it is most agreeable by reason of its proceeding from love; for nothing is sweeter to the lover than to praise his beloved. Fifthly, it is of much benefit to us; because we thereby pay the tribute that is due of us; for it is only but just that we should praise the source of all good, and return thanks to our supreme benefactor. Hence, in the holy Sacrifice, when the priest says, *"Let us return thanks to the Lord our God,"* he is answered, *"It is meet and just;"* and then the priest says, in addition, *"It is truly meet, just, right, and conducive to salvation that we always and in all places give thanks to the Lord."* Of the fact of our praise being agreeable and pleasing to God there can be no doubt, from the fact of his having created men and Angels for no other purpose, but that they may know, serve, and praise him; hence we read in Isaias 43, *"And everyone that calleth upon my name, I have created him for my own glory;"* and that cannot be called ambition, being purely justice. Now *"God is just, and hath loved justice; his countenance hath beheld righteousness."* With that, God is delighted with sacrifice as with a most sweet and agreeable odor; and the sacrifice of praise is the most excellent of all, according to Psalm 69. *"The sacrifice of praise shall glorify me."* Finally, becoming praise is most pleasing to God; because he is delighted with our blessings, especially with those of much value, such as our virtues, all of which, such as faith, hope, charity, religion, devotion, humility, are brought into play when we offer him our tribute of praise.

2. He now commences pointing out the matter for which we are to praise God, and says God should be praised, in the first place, for his kindness towards his people; as if he were to say, Praise the Lord, because he built Jerusalem; and *"he will gather together the dispersed of Israel;"* meaning the children of Israel, scattered through the world. This may apply to the rebuilding of the temple, which had been destroyed by Nabuchodonosor, and which the Jews, upon regaining their liberty from Cyrus and Darius, set at once about rebuilding, and which David then, in the spirit of prophecy, foresaw. Or it may be understood of the building of the Church, through the Apostles, and the gathering the dispersed children of God together; as we read in Jn. 11, *"That Jesus should die for the nation, and not only for the nation, but to gather together in one the children of God that were dispersed."* Finally, it may be understood of the heavenly Jerusalem, that is daily being built up like a city, by the accession of living stones, to which all the pilgrims, who are now scattered through the plains of Babylon, will be gathered.

3. He now tells how the dispersed of Israel will be gathered together. As regards the Babylonian captivity, it means that God would heal the Jews, now nigh brokenhearted, overwhelmed and depressed by innumerable calamities, and would *"bind up their bruises,"* by inspiring Cyrus to harass them no longer, but to restore them to their country. In a more spiritual view of it, God collects the dispersed of Israel when he heals those who are contrite of heart; that is, when despising not the humble and contrite, he heals them from the disease of sin; as David himself explains in Psalm 102, *"Who forgiveth all thy iniquities, who healeth all thy diseases."* The expression, *"And bindeth up all their bruises,"* explains the mode in which God deals with such bruises, by binding them up, as the surgeons do. Now, the sacraments are the visible ligatures that God makes use of to bind up our wounds; and as such ligatures are removed when the cure is effected, so, on the resurrection, when all our diseases shall have been cured, there will be no further need for sacraments.

4. He asserts, secondly, that God should be praised by reason of his wisdom. This appears in the infinite number of the stars created by him, that appear countless to us, but of which he has such intimate knowledge that he can call them individually by name, a proof of his great wisdom; and if it did not require great wisdom, God would not have said to Abraham, *"Number the stars if thou canst;"* nor would he have compared the number of the stars to the sand on the sea shore, of which Ecclesiasticus says, *"Who hath numbered the sand of the sea."* With that he adds, *"And calleth them all by their names,"*

to let us see what a distinct, separate, and intimate knowledge he has of the nature and properties of everyone of them. It also implies their obedience, when from nonexistence they started into existence, at a call. For God, by a call, endows with existence things that previously had no existence; as, in Baruch, *"The stars were called, and they said: Here we are; and with cheerfulness they have shined forth to him who made them."* Finally, it implies that the stars are like a body of soldiers, who, on being called upon to advance, do so as quickly as possible; as in Isaias 40, *"Lift up your eyes on high, and see who hath created these things; who bringeth out their hast by number, and calleth them all by their names."* With great justice, then, does the prophet add,

5. Here we have not only God's wisdom, but also his power, praised, by reason of his not only knowing the number, nature, and properties of the stars, but also by his naming them, and giving them the existence and the power of motion. The expression, *"Of his wisdom there is no number,"* means that the things God, in his wisdom knows, are countless. For God's wisdom knows all things past, present, future, and possible; all our words, our thoughts, our desires, past, present, future, even to eternity.

6. The third source of God's praise is taken from his justice and his mercy; for the Lord being both pious and merciful, protects the humble and the meek, and exalts them to the very heavens; and, on the contrary, in his justice, humbles and lays low the proud sinners, who would, in imitation of their king, Satan, raise themselves above the stars, leaving them to grovel on the ground in wretchedness and misery.

7. Previous to his praising God for his providence, he again exhorts them to praise and to sing to him, *"Sing ye to the Lord with praise;"* begin your praise by singing a hymn, and then *"sing on the harp;"* follow it up by playing on the harp. In a spiritual point of view it means, that, after praising God with our lips, we should follow it up by our good works, so that there should be no discordance between the tongue and the hands, and that it may not be said of us, as of the Pharisees, *"They say and do not."*

8. He tells that the subject of his praise now will be God's providence, that sometimes obscures the whole firmament with clouds, not for the purpose of shutting out the light of the sun from us, but in order to prepare the rain necessary for the earth, without which the earth would yield no fruit. In a spiritual sense, God *"covers the heavens with clouds"* when he shortens the days of our prosperity, in order that the rain of the grace of God may descend upon us in our trouble, through patience and humility. *"Who maketh grass to grow on the mountains, and herbs for the service of man."* He now explains the use of such rain, it making the grass to grow on the mountains, and the herbs that man uses for food. The expression, *"who maketh to grow,"* implies that both earth and rain would be of no use without God's cooperation;

nay more, that, as the rain could not be had but from the clouds, and that through God, so the rain itself would not produce the herbs but through God. The expression, *"on the mountains,"* means the necessity they are under of having much rain, for the plains and the valleys may be irrigated, while the mountains cannot.

9. He proceeds in recording God's providence in regard of the beasts and of the birds, with a view to let man see that he will never be forsaken by God in his providence. The same argument is made use of in the Gospel; thus giving us to understand that the God who so bounteously feeds the wild beasts and the young ravens will never desert those made to his own image and likeness.

10-11. Having said that God provides for the young ravens that call on him, he concludes the Psalm by telling God that it is not the proud, who confide in their own strength, that are grateful to him, but the humble, who fear him and confide in him; who may be compared to the young ravens, who, conscious of their own infirmity, seek, by croaking, to get help from others. *"He shall not delight in the strength of the horse."* God has no regard for, takes no delight in, the pleasure of the horse, when men take so much pride in it. *"Nor take pleasure in the legs of a man;"* nor does it please him to look at the handsome legs of a robust man, when men seem to confide in them to the extent of excluding God's providence from having any share in protecting them; but *"the Lord taketh pleasure in them that fear him;"* with the humble, who tremble at his commands, and put their entire hope, not in their own strength, but in God's mercy.

PSALM 147

The Church is called upon to praise God for his peculiar graces and favors to his people. In the Hebrew this psalm is joined to the foregoing.

12 Praise the Lord, O Jerusalem: praise thy God, O Sion.
13 Because he hath strengthened the bolts of thy gates, he hath blessed thy children within thee.
14 Who hath placed peace in thy borders: and filleth thee with the fat of corn.
15 Who sendeth forth his speech to the earth: his word runneth swiftly.
16 Who giveth snow like wool: scattereth mists like ashes.
17 He sendeth his crystal like morsels: who shall stand before the face of his cold?
18 He shall send out his word, and shall melt them: his wind shall blow, and the waters shall run.
19 Who declareth his word to Jacob: his justices and his judgments to Israel.
20 He hath not done in like manner to every nation: and his judgments he hath not made manifest to them. Alleluia.

Explanation of the psalm

12. Jerusalem is a holy city, the more noble part of which is mount Sion, where the temple of the Lord was built, and is often used to express the city itself; and, therefore, *"praise the Lord, O Jerusalem,"* and *"praise thy God, Sion,"* signify one and the same thing. If it be referred to the Jerusalem above, nothing more appropriate could be applied to it; for in that heavenly city no one need be occupied in it providing for their personal wants, or those of their neighbors, there being no poor, no needy, to be found therein, and can, therefore, devote their whole time, as they really do, in praising God. Most justly, then, does he address the city, saying, *"Praise the Lord,"* for you have nothing else to do; for you are specially bound thereto by reason of the signal favors he has conferred on you; and, finally, because it has been your great good fortune to get so close a view of the beauty and the excellence of the Lord. The Church, in her exile, should also praise the Lord; but the whole Church cannot, nor can the Church at all times do it, in the midst of the cares and troubles that frequently disturb her. And if the Church cannot accomplish it, much less can the synagogue.

13. The reason why Jerusalem should bless the Lord arises from the fact of his having conferred on her that abundance and security of which human happiness consists. Security, without abundance, is no better than poverty, and abundance, without security, is replete with fear and danger. God, therefore, so strengthened the bolts of the gates of Jerusalem that they could not possibly be stormed, and those inside are quite safe, inasmuch as no enemy can enter, no friend will be excluded; nothing bad can come in, nothing good will go out; and the divine blessing brought an abundance of all good things into this highly fortified city; for it was not a particular blessing that God gave the holy city, but a general, an absolute one, to use the expression of the Apostle, *"Who hath blessed us with all spiritual blessings in heavenly places."* These two things perfectly apply to the Jerusalem above, where the security is eternal, and the blessing consists in the enjoyment of the supreme good. They also apply, to a certain extent, to the Church in her exile, though not so entirely; *"for the gates of hell will not prevail against her,"* and she has many blessings within her; but, meanwhile, many wicked enter into her, and good revolt from her; she has the chaff mixed with the grain, the good with the bad fish, the kids with the lambs. There are other points of agreement also with the earthly Jerusalem, inasmuch as by reason of her being situated in the mountains, she appeared to be well fortified, and abounded, at one time, with inhabitants and with wealth; but, as she was more than once sacked and destroyed, it does not appear that the expression, *"he hath strengthened the bolts of thy gates,"* is quite applicable to her. One would rather say the expression in Lament. 2 was, *"Her gates are *sunk into the ground: he hath destroyed and broken her bars; and the bulwark hath moved; and the wall hath been destroyed together.*" Nor was there such an abundance in the city at the same time, when we read, "*They said to their mothers, where is corn and wine? when they fainted away as the wounded in the streets of the city, when they breathed out their souls in the bosoms of their mothers.*"

14. Not only is the holy city of Jerusalem highly fortified, but it is even exempt from the dangers of war, hence its name, Jerusalem, which signifies "*The vision of peace,*" and the first that attempted to disturb that peace was expelled with such violence as to cause the Lord to say, "*I saw Satan as lightning falling from heaven.*" "*Who hath placed peace in thy borders;*" who hath established universal peace through the length and breadth of Jerusalem. And further, not only does this city enjoy abundance, but even the most exquisite dainties, as conveyed in the expression, "*the fat of corn;*" and these without limit, as we can infer from the expression, "*who filleth.*" All this applies to our heavenly country in the strict sense of the words, for there alone will our inferior be in strict peace with our superior parts, and our superior parts with God; and there, too, will be strict peace between the citizens of all grades, high and low; for there will be one heart, one soul, and as the Lord expresses it, Jn. 7, "*Made perfect in one.*" There, too, "*will all be filled with the fat of corn,*" for truth and wisdom being the food of the soul, they will have actual truth as it is in itself, and not in figures or enigmas, and they will taste of the sweetness of the Word Eternal without being enveloped by the sacraments or the Scriptures; they will drink of the fountain of wisdom, instead of applying to the streams that flow from it, or to the "*showers falling gently upon the earth.*" They will be so filled that they will never again hunger nor thirst for all eternity. In the Church militant also, which, to a certain extent, is the Jerusalem, we have peace with God, though we, at the same time, suffer pressure from the world. We do what we can to keep in peace with all; but we are in the midst of those who hate peace, and, therefore, "*Combats without, fears within,*" are never wanting, and though we may feed on "*the fat of corn,*" it is enveloped by too many coverings. We have the Word of God, but in the flesh; and though we eat of the flesh it is covered by the sacrament. We drink of the waters of wisdom, but it is from the shower of the Scriptures, and we are, therefore, never so satiated with those blessings as to make our happiness consist in hungering and thirsting for more. Much less applicable is all this to the earthly Jerusalem, the old synagogue of the Jews, to which it was applicable in a figurative sense only.

15. Having exhorted the holy city to thank God for the favors conferred on itself, he now exhorts it to praise God for the favors conferred on other nations, from which they may learn how much more liberal he has been in

their regard. He, therefore, exhorts them to praise that God, *"who sendeth forth his speech to the earth,"* who issues the precepts and decrees of his providence to the whole world; and *"his word runneth quickly;"* such precepts and decrees are borne with the greatest expedition to all created beings, penetrate all things, and are put into immediate execution. These words explain the order of divine providence that extends itself to everything, and that with the greatest velocity because God is everywhere, *"upholding all things by the word of his power,"* Heb. 1; and *"reaches from end to end mightily, and ordereth all things sweetly,"*—Wisdom 8. Hence, David says, in Psalm 118, *"All things serve thee."*

16-17. From God's universal providence he now takes up one particular effect of it, in which the admirable power and wisdom of God are most conspicuous, and for which he deserves merited praise, even from the citizens above, exempt as they are from such changes. The wonderful effects of God's power and wisdom, which, however, are most familiar and visible to us all, are to be found in his creation of heat and cold in the air. In certain countries, snow, frost, and ice will so abound, at certain times, that lakes, rivers, and even seas will become so congealed, that wagons, heavily laden, will be carried over them, as they would through so many roads or fields. The ice becomes so hard that bars of iron will hardly break it; and yet, God, when it pleaseth him, by a simple change in the wind, in one instant causes all to melt, and streams of water flow down from the housetops, from the hills, and the mountains. Thus, God, in one moment, converts the extreme cold into a most agreeable warmth. To enter into particulars. *"Who giveth snow like wool;"* who rains down snow in such abundance, that every flake of it looks like flocks of wool, not only by reason of its whiteness, but also of its size. *"Scattereth mists like ashes;"* raises mists so dense, that they seem more like a cloud of ashes than of vapor. *"He sendeth his crystal like morsels;"* who congeals the water when forming it into hail, so as to appear in small crystals like crumbs of bread. *"Who shall stand before the face of his cold?"* An apostrophe of the prophet in admiration of God's great power in producing so much cold; as much as to say, who can stand or bear so much cold?

18. Having described the extreme cold caused by the snow, frost, and ice, he now shows with what ease and celerity God causes them all to disappear. *"He shall send out his word,"* his simple command, *"and shall melt them,"* the snow, frost, and ice, and, at once, the cold disappears; and he explains how simply God effects that, when he adds, *"His wind shall blow, and the waters shall run;"* at his command the wind shifts to the south, causing the snow and the ice to thaw, and thus converting them into water.

19-20. He concludes by showing how differently God, in his providence, deals with his own people, and with other nations, because he instructed other nations, merely by natural causes and effects, so as to know their Creator through the things created by him; but he taught his own people through the prophets. *"Who declareth his word to Jacob;"* that is to say, Jerusalem praise that Lord, *"who declared his word to his people Jacob,"* by speaking to them through Moses, and the prophets, and who pointed out *"his justices and his judgments to Israel,"* through the same Moses, to whom he gave the law, in order to hand it over to his people of Israel, and from it you will be able to understand *"that he hath not done in like manner to every nation,"* because to you alone, and to none others, *"hath he made manifest his judgments,"* meaning his laws. All this applies literally to the Jerusalem on earth, to whom God sent his prophets to announce his words, and explain his laws; but it is much more applicable to the spiritual Jerusalem, the Church, that received the incarnate word of God himself, through the preaching of the Apostles, and learned a much more sublime law, judgments and justifications. It is more applicable, again, to the Jerusalem above, to which God openly announces his word; and in his word all its inhabitants behold the judgments of God, the order, disposition, and secrets of his divine providence, that to us are a great abyss.

PSALM 148

All creatures are invited to praise their creator.

1 Praise ye the Lord from the heavens: praise ye him in the high places.
2 Praise ye him, all his angels: praise ye him, all his hosts.
3 Praise ye him, O sun and moon: praise him, all ye stars and light.
4 Praise him, ye heavens of heavens: and let all the waters that are above the heavens
5 Praise the name of the Lord. For he spoke, and they were made: he commanded, and they were created.
6 He hath established them for ever, and for ages of ages: he hath made a decree, and it shall not pass away.
7 Praise the Lord from the earth, ye dragons, and all ye deeps:
8 Fire, hail, snow, ice, stormy winds which fulfill his word:
9 Mountains and all hills, fruitful trees and all cedars:
10 Beasts and all cattle: serpents and feathered fowls:
11 Kings of the earth and all people: princes and all judges of the earth:
12 Young men and maidens: let the old with the younger, praise the name of the Lord:
13 For his name alone is exalted.
14 The praise of him is above heaven and earth: and he hath exalted the horn of his people. A hymn to all his saints: to the children of Israel, a people approaching to him. Alleluia.

Explanation of the psalm

1-2. The Angels, as residing in the supreme heavens, as it were, in the very palace of the eternal King, get the first invitation. The words *"praise ye"* are not used in a spirit of command or exhortation, as if the Angels were deficient in their duty, and needed such; it is spoken in a spirit of invitation and strong affection by the prophet, who is highly excited and inflamed with the love of God, as if he said, Oh that all created things would praise their Creator! and you, ye Angels, who hold the first place in creation, follow up the praise you daily offer him; *"from the heavens,"* indicates where the Angels reside, which he repeats when he adds, *"praise ye him in the high places."* This he explains more clearly when he adds who they are that dwell there, saying, *"praise ye him, all his hosts,"* meaning the heavenly powers, and not the sun, moon, and stars, as some will have it; first, because nothing is more usual than such repetitions with David; secondly, the holy fathers are unanimous that these words refer to the Cherubim, Seraphim, and the other Angels; thirdly, from Lk. 2, where the Angels are called *"The multitude of the heavenly host;"* and fourthly, from Psalm 102, where the Angels are more clearly indicated, when he says, *"Bless the Lord, all ye his hosts; you ministers of his, that do his will."*

3-4. From the Angels, who, as being endowed with reason and intelligence, praise God in the strict sense of the word, he descends to the heavenly bodies who do not offer that intellectual praise they are incapable of, but still praise him by reason of their greatness, grandeur, size, speed, efficacy, splendor, and beauty, just as every beautiful work redounds to the credit of its maker. He names the sun first, it being universally allowed to be the principal body in nature; next, the moon, it being apparently next in size to the sun; then he calls upon the stars, concluding with *"the light,"* by which he means the light derived from the sun, moon, and stars. Having enumerated the heavenly bodies, he then calls upon *"the heaven of heavens,"* that is, the superior heavens, beneath which lie the inferior heavens in which the clouds and the birds move about; whence we read in the Scriptures, *"the birds of heaven, the clouds of heaven."* To those upper heavens he adds the waters that lie above the heavens, thus leaving no one thing in the superior part of the world without an invitation. In regard of those waters men are at liberty to argue to a certain extent, but in other respects they are not. First, it is certain that the waters named here are material, not spiritual waters, an error into which Origen fell, and which was exposed by the holy fathers. Secondly, that these waters are above, and not in, the heavens, as some erroneously imagine, for the prophet indicates it clearly here, by calling on the *"heaven of heavens"* to praise him, and at once adds, *"all the waters that are above the heavens,"* those heavens, surely, that he had just quoted; and in Psalm 103, when speaking of the same heavens, he says, *"Who stretchest out the heavens like a pavilion, who coverest the higher rooms thereof with water;"* and Moses, in the first chapter of Genesis, clearly places water over the firmament, in which firmament he shortly after places the stars; and more clearly in Daniel 3, where all the works of the Lord are enumerated, in order; first are placed the Angels, then the heavens, then the waters that are over the heavens, then the sun, moon, stars, and other inferior beings. Thirdly, these waters are incorruptible and eternal, for to them, as well as to the other things hereinbefore enumerated, applies what he subsequently adds, *"He hath established them forever, and for ages of ages."*

5-6. The reason why all those things aforesaid should praise God is, because they were all made by him, and will remain forever incorrupt; and what is much more wonderful, they were made without any labor, without any loss of time, by one word or command brought from nonexistence to existence, and that for eternity. He merely said, *"Let there be light, and there was light."* He commanded a thing that had no existence to start into existence, and at once it, in obedience to his command, appeared. *"He hath established them forever, and for ages of ages."* He endowed them with immortality, in order that, like the inferior bodies, they may not rise up and die again. *"He hath made a decree,"* passed a decree on this matter; *"and it shall not pass away,"* a decree that will not evaporate or become a dead letter, but will remain, and by remaining will preserve the very things it has reference to, so that they shall not pass away.

7. He now passes to the perishable elements and to the world below, which consists of the earth, the air, the water, the beasts, fishes, fowl, as also the thunder, lightning, hail, winds, and other such matters. And as he first said, *"Praise ye the Lord from the heavens,"* he now says, *"Praise the Lord from the earth;"* and as he classified all the superior beings under the head of the things belonging to heaven which is the seat of the Angels, so he deems it right now to bring all the inferior things under the head of those belonging to the earth, it being the seat of man. Hence, his reason for not naming fire, or air, or water; in the first place, because the earth constitutes the second part of the world, and all other things, whether fire, air, or water, are subject to man, who inhabits it. *"Praise the Lord from the earth,"* all you who live on the earth, or belong to it, and he mentions first the waters and the fishes who dive in the depths of the earth; for the dragons mean the sea monsters; and the deeps, the deep seas in which they reside; as we read in Psalm 103, *"The sea dragon which thou hast formed to play therein,"* that is, the sea; and in Psalm 73, *"Thou didst crush the heads of the dragons in the waters."*

8. From the waters he passes to the air, where the fires exist; viz., lightning, thunderbolts, coruscations, as also hail, snow, ice, and the stormy winds,

those furious winds that cause the storms and bring so much rain with them, all of which *"fulfil his word;"* that is, obey his commands, which last expression he adds with a view to let us see that all those accidents, that are looked upon by man as so many calamities, come from the hand of God, who makes use of them as so many instruments of his justice or of his mercy to punish the wicked or to deter the just from sin; and, therefore, that they do not come from chance, nor should they be called calamities but blessings, being the instruments of a good and gracious God.

9. From the air he now reverts to the earth, and first alludes to the more striking parts of it, the *"mountains and hills,"* which, of course, include the plains and the valleys, for you cannot have one without the other. He then passes to the products of the earth, naming the trees first that produce fruit, and then those that do not, such as the cedar, which however, serves for house and shipbuilding. He then touches on the animals that are to be found on the earth, briefly enumerating the principal ones, the wild, the domestic, and the beasts of burden; and finally, the serpents that crawl along the ground, and the birds that fly aloft in the air. He calls upon and challenges them all to praise God, not that they are capable of any such thing, but that man, by reflecting on their use and benefit to him, may praise God, and return him due thanks for them. But what benefit do the wild beasts, the lions, serpents, even the gnats and the wasps confer on man? A great deal, for, whether they inspire us with terror, or annoy and torment us, they are calculated to remind us of our weakness and infirmity, and to what we have come through the disobedience of our first parents, by which we lost a great part of the dominion we previously had over all animals.

10-13. He finally invites all mankind to praise God, and, in order to comprehend all manner of people, he mentions three different classes of people in respect of power, sex, and age. *"Kings and people,"* they who command and they who obey; and, as all those who do command are not equal in authority, he adds, *"princes,"* having supreme power, *"and all judges of the earth,"* having subordinate authority; and here is the difference of power. *"Young men and maidens,"* which includes the sexes, *"the old with the younger,"* to comprehend all ages. All, then, be they princes or subjects, men or women, old or young, are summoned to praise the Lord. *"For his name alone is exalted;"* for there is no other name truly sublime, and worthy of all praise, but the name of God. Created things, however great, when compared with God's greatness, sink into insignificance; and whatever greatness or excellence they may be possessed of they have entirely from him, who alone is called, and justly is, the Most High.

14. He assigns a reason for having said, *"For his name alone is exalted,"* because, says he, *"The praise of him is above heaven and earth;"* that is, everything in heaven and on earth declare his praise so full of everything of his glory, or, as Habacuc has it, *"His glory covered the heavens, and the earth is full of his praise;"* therefore *"his name alone is exalted."* And *"he hath exalted the horn of his people;"* he, of himself, alone exalted and sublime, has exalted the power and glory of his people Israel, because he selected them as his own people, gave them divine laws, written with his own finger, and cared them with a special providence. *"A hymn to all his saints; to the children of Israel, a people approaching to him, Alleluia."* This is the conclusion of the Psalm, as it were to say, The hymn, then, to be sung to God should be specially sung by all his saints; that is, by all those dedicated and consecrated to him, the children of Israel especially, inasmuch as they come nearer to God than any other people, through true knowledge and faith, true worship and adoration, true filial confidence and love. This, however, as St. Augustine properly observes, applies not to the children of Israel according to the flesh, but according to the spirit; for the former being stiff necked never made any approach to God, as St. Stephen reproached them. *"You always resist the Holy Ghost; as your fathers did so do you also. Which of the prophets have not your fathers persecuted? and they have slain those who foretold of the coming of the Just One, of whom you have been the betrayers and murderers;"* and the Apostle, Rom. 9, points out who are the true children of Israel when he says, *"For all are not Israelites that are of Israel; neither are all they who are the seed of Abraham's children;"* that is to say, not they who are the children of the flesh are the children of God, but they that are the children of the promise are counted for *"the seed."* And in the same epistle, chap. 4, he tells them that they were the children of Abraham *"who follow the steps of the faith that our father Abraham had,"* be they circumcised or not circumcised. Nor should we exclude all the children of Israel according to the flesh, for in such case we would exclude the prophets and the Apostles; we exclude those only who are Israelites according to the flesh alone, of whom St. Stephen speaks as above, and to whom the Precursor said, *"Ye offspring of vipers, who hath shown you to flee from the wrath to come? do not begin to say, We have Abraham for our father,"* and to whom the Lord himself said, *"If you be the children of Abraham do the works of Abraham—you are of your father the devil."* Finally, such are they, who, after having renounced the Lord, are scattered all over the world, without a king, a priesthood, and even without a God.

PSALM 149

The Church is particularly bound to praise God.

1 Sing ye to the Lord a new canticle: let his praise be in the church of the saints.
2 Let Israel rejoice in him that made him: and let the children of Sion be joyful in their king.

3 Let them praise his name in choir: let them sing to him with the timbrel and the psaltery.
4 For the Lord is well pleased with his people: and he will exalt the meek unto salvation.
5 The saints shall rejoice in glory: they shall be joyful in their beds.
6 The high praise of God shall be in their mouth: and two-edged swords in their hands:
7 To execute vengeance upon the nations, chastisements among the people:
8 To bind their kings with fetters, and their nobles with manacles of iron.
9 To execute upon them the judgment that is written: this glory is to all his saints. Alleluia.

EXPLANATION OF THE PSALM

1. This first verse is directed to those he addressed in the last verse of the preceding Psalm, when he said, *"A hymn to all his saints, to a people approaching to him;"* for these three last Psalms are so connected, and one appears to be such a continuation of the other, that they appear to form one Psalm, which, perhaps, is the reason that the three are read under one antiphon in the end of lauds. He, therefore, says, O you saints, the people approaching to God, *"Sing to the Lord a new canticle;"* let other creatures sing a canticle for their creation, which is an old canticle, but sing you a canticle for your regeneration, justification, glorification, which is *"a new canticle,"* on a new subject, and to be chanted by new men. *"Let his praise be in the church of the saints;"* a reason assigned for having asked them to sing in such manner, being as much as to say, You saints, *"sing ye to the Lord a new canticle,"* because it is but meet that God's praise should be heard, especially in the congregation of the saints.

2. The new canticle is calculated to inspire great joy; for it announces the favor of perfect happiness, and springs from most ardent love. Israel, the chosen people of God, therefore, that sings this new canticle, rejoice in singing *"in him that made him;"* in their Creator, who not only called them into existence, but endowed them with grace, thus giving them not only existence, but to be Israel. *"And let the children of Sion be joyful in their king,"* which is no more than a repetition of the above.

3. Not content with singing this new canticle with joy and gladness, they will blend instrumental with vocal music, so that their hands, as well as their tongues, or in other words, their actions, as well as their words, shall be directed to God's praise and glory. The following Psalm would seem to indicate that the 'choir" named here is a musical instrument as well as the timbrel and the psaltery; but it may also signify a number of voices in concert, and in such sense it has been understood by the fathers

4. The reason for singing this new canticle is because the Lord hath been well pleased with his people, that is to say, loved them from eternity, from his own pure kindness, which good will of God is the foundation and primary source of all our blessings; for predestination, vocation, justification, glorification, all are owing to God's having been *"well pleased with his people;"* and, touching on this, the Lord himself said, *"Fear not, little flock; for it hath pleased your Father to give you a kingdom."* This good pleasure of God is frequently alluded to by St. Paul, and it justly forms the subject of the new canticle; *"and he will exalt the meek unto salvation;"* God not only resolved in his mind to deal thus kindly with his people, but he will carry it into immediate effect, because *"he will exalt the meek unto salvation,"* he will exalt to the highest degree possible, to eternal happiness, his meek and humble people, as being true members of him who said, *"I am meek and humble of heart."*

5. He now describes the future glory of the elect, for which they are with all their hearts to sing this new canticle. *"The saints shall rejoice in glory,"* to which none but the truly just arrive, and at the same time *"shall be joyful in their beds,"* in that place of supreme rest, *"from henceforth now, saith the spirit, that they may rest from their labors,"* Apoc. 14. Thus, *"the saints in glory"* shall rest from their labors, but not from their praise; they will *"be in their beds,"* to rest there, but not to sleep.

6. The saints in their supreme felicity will not be altogether idle, for they will find occupation in chanting God's praise and brandishing their swords, and the latter refers to the judiciary power with which they will be invested on the last day, to strike down all their persecutors, according to Deut. 32, *"If I shall whet my sword as the lightning, and my hand take hold on judgment."*

7. The use the saints will make of the two edged swords will be to wreak vengeance on their enemies on the day of judgment, to chastise them and to reproach them with their iniquities, for *"Then shall the just stand with great constancy against those that have afflicted them."*

8. Having said that *"the two edged swords"* represent the judiciary power entrusted to the saints on the last day, it will not appear strange they should use such power *"to execute vengeance,"* and *"to bind kings in fetters,"* for such power includes the one as well as the other, and both will be fully exercised on the last day, when, in union with Christ, they will pass sentence on the Antiochuses, the Herods, the Neros, the Diocletians, and the other infidel princes, and will say, *"Having bound their hands and feet, cast them into the exterior darkness."*

9. The prophet now explains clearly why he said *"to execute vengeance,"* and *"to bind kings in fetters."* That the saints, who on earth have suffered unjust persecution, may now *"execute the judgment"* that was long since *"written"* like a decree or a resolution, deeply engraved on a pillar, one that could not be changed or erased. *"This glory is to all his saints,"* the glory of sitting with Christ on the clouds, and judging the world; and its ruler will be the peculiar privilege of the saints, as St. Paul has it, *"Know you not that the saints shall judge this world? And if the world shall be judged by you, are you unworthy to judge the smallest matters?"* Truly, therefore, *"is this glory to all his saints."*

PSALM 150

An exhortation to praise God with all sorts of instruments.

1 Praise ye the Lord in his holy places: praise ye him in the firmament of his power.
2 Praise ye him for his mighty acts: praise ye him according to the multitude of his greatness.
3 Praise him with sound of trumpet: praise him with psaltery and harp.
4 Praise him with timbrel and choir: praise him with strings and organs.
5 Praise him on high sounding cymbals: praise him on cymbals of joy: let every spirit praise the Lord. Alleluia.

EXPLANATION OF THE PSALM

1. You saints and elect, praise the Lord who dwell in the heavenly sanctuary, *"praise him in the firmament of his power,"* a repetition of the first part of the verse, Praise him who resides in the heavens as he would in a highly fortified palace or on a splendid throne, for the Lord says, in Mt. 5, *"Swear not by heaven for it is God's throne."*

2. He now teaches that God is to be praised, not because he simply resides in heaven, but because he resides there as the all powerful Ruler and Lord of all things. Praise him for his mighty acts, for his great strength and power, *"Praise ye him according to the multitude of his greatness,"* praise him beyond measure, for such is his greatness, being simply and absolutely great.

3. Praise him with all manner of instruments, wind instruments such as the trumpet, and stringed such as the psaltery and harp.

4. All sorts of instruments are now enumerated, for though there is no certainty what sort of instrument their organ was, the probability is, that it was an instrument composed of a number of pipes joined together, such as our organ of the present day.

5. Cymbals are musical instruments, whose music is elicited by shaking them; and they are called *"cymbals of joy,"* as being used on festive occasions, as peals of bells are with Christians. *"Let every spirit praise the Lord."* Various are the interpretations offered of this sentence; but in my mind, the most satisfactory is to take the words, *"every spirit,"* as comprehending everything that has life, be it spiritual, such as that of the Angels, or animal, such as that of animals, or both united, such as that of man; or even a figurative life, such as that of material objects, which, inanimate as they may be, are still said *"to live"* in reference to God; because they serve and obey him, as if they had sense and feeling, and understood the commands of the Creator. Hence the invitatory, *"The king to whom all things live;"* and in Baruch, *"The stars were called, and they said: Here we are."* Such is also the expression in the Gospel, *"He commanded the fever, and it left her;"* and, in Mk. 4, *"And he rebuked the wind, and said to the sea: Peace, be still. And the wind ceased; and there was made a great calm."* The prophet, then, after having summoned a number of persons and things to praise God, and finding that he could not severally enumerate and invite every person and thing in one general invitation, he comprehends all, and calls upon them to praise the Lord. *"Let every spirit praise the Lord."* But, then, if he wanted to include everything, why not say, Let everything, instead of every spirit, praise the Lord? The reason is, because it is only the living that are able to praise, and it would appear absurd to invite dead things or souls to join in choir, especially when the same prophet said, in Psalm 113, *"The dead will not praise thee, O Lord;"* and Ezechias exclaims, *"The living, the living, he shall give praise to thee."* David, then, preferred the expression, Every spirit or living thing, to everything existing, to show that he invited everything that has life in any respect to unite in praising God. Here, then, is the end of this Commentary. I pray Almighty God, that, as he enabled us to explain those divine Psalms somehow, so he may grant us, in his mercy, after this our pilgrimage here below, to arrive at our true country, where, face to face, we may love him with our whole heart, and praise him without end. Amen. Praise be to God. *"But piety with sufficiency is great gain."* (1 Tim. 6.)

ABOUT THE TRANSLATOR

Father John O'Sullivan, Archdeacon of Aghadoe, Parish Priest of Kenmare, and Vicar-General of the Diocese of Kerry, Latin scholar, was a fierce defender and advocate of the poor, especially during the Irish Potato Famine, making trips to England to move those with power and money to rectify the human devastation, for which the exploitation and mismanagement by English colonization was partly responsible. A Kerry historian at the time of O'Sullivan's death (1874), wrote this of him: "Archdeacon O'Sullivan was on the whole an excellent specimen of a type of Irish priest, with something of the virtues and faults of a Columba in him, now it is to be feared nearly stamped out in Ireland... throughout his long life he has been most deservedly respected by men of all creeds and classes... His exertions for his flock in the disastrous famine years were immense, and saved innumerable lives." O'Sullivans's Bishop, Moriarty, delivered a eulogy praising O'Sullivan's efforts and achievements in having founded several schools, a convent, building Holy Cross Church, as well as helping the poor. Fr. John O'Sullivan's remains were buried in Holy Cross Church, beneath an altar inscribed in his memory.

Bringing you spiritual riches
of the Holy Roman Catholic Tradition
at the most affordable prices possible.
CaritasPublishing.com

www.ingramcontent.com/pod-product-compliance
Lightning Source LLC
Chambersburg PA
CBHW070711160426
43192CB00009B/1150